AA007893

28th Conference on Computational Natural Language Learning (CoNLL 2024)

Miami, Florida, USA
15-16 November 2024

ISBN: 979-8-3313-0842-1

Printed from e-media with permission by:

Curran Associates, Inc.
57 Morehouse Lane
Red Hook, NY 12571

Some format issues inherent in the e-media version may also appear in this print version.

Association for Computational Linguistics
209 N. Eighth Street
Stroudsburg, Pennsylvania 18360

Phone: 1-570-476-8006
Fax: 1-570-476-0860

acl@aclweb.org

Additional copies of this publication are available from:

Curran Associates, Inc.
57 Morehouse Lane
Red Hook, NY 12571 USA
Phone: 845-758-0400
Fax: 845-758-2633
Email: curran@proceedings.com
Web: www.proceedings.com

CoNLL 2024

The 28th Conference on Computational Natural Language Learning

Proceedings of the Conference

November 15-16, 2024

Order copies of this and other ACL proceedings from:

Association for Computational Linguistics (ACL)
317 Sidney Baker St. S
Suite 400 - 134
Kerrville, TX 78028
USA
Tel: +1-855-225-1962
acl@aclweb.org

Introduction

CoNLL is a conference organized yearly by SIGNLL (ACL's Special Interest Group on Natural Language Learning), focusing on theoretically, cognitively and scientifically motivated approaches to computational linguistics. This year, CoNLL was held alongside EMNLP 2024.

The program of CoNLL 2024 comprises 40 papers. This was the result of a careful selection process. Reviewing 97 received submissions resulted in a 41% acceptance rate.

Reviewing was organized into 10 tracks, each of them headed by one or two area chairs:

- Computational Psycholinguistics, Cognition and Linguistics (Nathan Schneider)
- Computational Social Science (Kate Atwell)
- Interaction and Grounded Language Learning (Anthony Sicilia)
- Lexical, Compositional and Discourse Semantics (Shira Wein)
- Multilingual Work and Translation (Yuval Marton)
- Natural Language Generation (Tuhin Chakrabarty)
- Resources and Tools for Scientifically Motivated Research (Venkat)
- Speech and Phonology (Huteng Dai)
- Syntax and Morphology (Leshem Choshen)
- Theoretical Analysis and Interpretation of ML Models for NLP (Kevin Small)

We thank our reviewers and area chairs for curating the program. The conference also invited Thamar Solorio and Lorna Quandt to present keynotes, and included a session of additional papers on the BabyLM Challenge, a shared task that challenges community members to train a language model from scratch on the same amount of linguistic data available to a child in addition to multi-modal data.

We would like to acknowledge support from our sponsor, Google DeepMind.

Malihe Alikhani (Northeastern University)
Libby Barak (Montclair State University)
CoNLL 2024 conference co-chairs

Organizing Committee

Program Chairs

Malihe Alikhani, Northeastern University, MA, USA
Libby Barak, Montclair State University, NJ, USA

Publication Chairs

Mert Inan, Northeastern University, MA, USA
Julia Watson, University of Toronto, ON, Canada

SIGNLL Officers

President: Omri Abend, Hebrew University of Jerusalem, Israel
Secretary: Antske Fokkens, Vrije Universiteit Amsterdam, Netherlands

Area Chairs

Katherine Atwell, Northeastern University and University of Pittsburgh
Tuhin Chakrabarty, SalesForce Research
Leshem Choshen, Massachusetts Institute of Technology and International Business Machines
Huteng Dai, University of Michigan - Ann Arbor
Venkata Govindarajan, Ithaca College
Yuval Marton, Genentech and University of Washington
Nathan Schneider, Georgetown University
Anthony Sicilia, Northeastern University
Kevin Small, Amazon
Shira Wein, Amherst College

Invited Talks

Thamar Solorio, Mohamed bin Zayed University of Artificial Intelligence, MBZUAI
Lorna Quandt, Gallaudet University

Program Committee

Reviewers

Adnen Abdessaied, Omri Abend, Kahaerjiang Abiderexiti, Gulinigeer Abudouwaili, Sayantan Adak, Mohammad Akbari, Albina Akhmetgareeva, Syeda Nahida Akter, Bashar Alhafni, Afra Alishahi, Milad Alshomary, Samuel Joseph Amouyal, Avinash Anand, Aryaman Arora, Daiki Asami, Hayastan Avetisyan

Siddhesh Bangar, Anish Bhanushali, Swarnadeep Bhar, Debasmita Bhattacharya, Arianna Bisazza, Gemma Boleda, Angana Borah, Aaron Ari Bornstein, Digbalay Bose, Marwen Bouabid, Jonathan Brennan, David Broneske, Nam Khac-Hoai Bui, Luana Bulla, Davide Buscaldi

Kranti CH, Jie Cao, Georgia Carter, Giovanni Cassani, Franklin Chang, Guanyi Chen, Yangbin Chen, Yiwen Chen, Yiwen Chen, Fei Cheng, Santhosh Cherian, Emmanuele Chersoni, Ta-Chung Chi, Leshem Choshen, Philipp Cimiano, Caio Filippo Corro, Ailis Cournane, Francisco M. Couto

Walter Daelemans, Forrest Davis, Andrea Gregor De Varda, Shumin Deng, Aniket Deroy, Zi-Yi Dou, Rotem Dror, Xiaotang Du, Jonathan Dunn, Esra Dönmez

Oliver Eberle, Yo Ehara, Niama El Khbir, Saman Enayati

Abdellah Fourtassi, Diego Frassinelli, Daniel Freudenthal, Quchen Fu, Yingxue Fu, Yoshinari Fujinuma

Chongyang Gao, Lingyu Gao, Mengshi Ge, Luke Gessler, Mohammad Reza Ghasemi Madani, Shinjini Ghosh, Mario Giulianelli, Aniket Goel, Carlos-Emiliano González-Gallardo, Michael Eric Goodale, Emily Goodwin, Calbert Graham, Ximena Gutierrez

Sherzod Hakimov, Caren Han, Sadid A. Hasan, Shizhu He, Daniel Hershcovich, Xiaoyu Hu, Yebowen Hu, Zhe Hu, Xinting Huang

Katsumi Ibaraki, Mert Inan

Cassandra L Jacobs, Abhik Jana, Ganesh Jawahar, Aditya Joshi, Daksh Joshi

N J Karthika, Marc A. Kastner, Sedrick Keh, Casey Kennington, Tracy Holloway King, Christo Kirov, Thomas H Kober, Tom Kouwenhoven, Alex Krauska, Alexandra Krauska, Tatsuki Kuribayashi

Philippe Langlais, Patrick Lee, Jochen L. Leidner, Ruosen Li, Xia Li, Xiangci Li, Jiangming Liu, Wei Lu, Yunfei Luo, Kai Lv

Zhiyuan Ma, Brielen Madureira, Ayush Maheshwari, Subhankar Maity, Andreas Maletti, Biswadip Mandal, Stella Markantonatou, Edison Marrese-Taylor, Bruno Martins, Jacob A. Matthews, Yevgen Matusevych, Kate McCurdy, Yisong Miao, Timothee Mickus, Manuel Montes, Steven Moran

Nona Naderi, Vinh Van Nguyen, Ratna Nirupama, Ahmad Pir Noman, Tadashi Nomoto

Kazumasa Omura, Jessica Ouyang

Vishakh Padmakumar, Koyena Pal, Saurabh Kumar Pandey, Iñigo Parra, Tiago Pimentel, Priya Pitre, Lidia Pivovarova, Łukasz Pszenny

Siya Qi

Ella Rabinovich, Alexandre Rademaker, Peter A. Rankel, Jesse Roberts, Nathan Roll, Tanya Roosta, Guy Rotman, Sarthak Roy, Alla Rozovskaya

Parisa Safikhani, Rana Salama, Elizabeth Salesky, Tanja Samardzic, Malaikannan Sankarasubbu, Sashank Santhanam, Giorgio Satta, Marten Van Schijndel, Peter Schulam, William Schuler, Aditi Seetha, Mong Yuan Sim, Atul Kumar Singh, Kanishk Singh, Sudipta Singha Roy, Prasanna Srinivasa Murthy, Shane Steinert-Threlkeld, Ruolin Su, Jiuding Sun, Kaiser Sun, Renliang Sun, Wenjun Sun

Wei Tao, R Tharaniya Sairaj, Pascal Tilli, Gaurav Singh Tomar, Rong Tong, Thi Hong Hanh Tran

Marco Valentino, Bram Van Dijk, Tessa Verhoef, Prashanth Vijayaraghavan, Esaú Villatoro-tello, Marta Villegas, Pavlos Vougiouklis, Ivan Vulić

Yuiga Wada, Jiajing Wan, Bin Wang, Jiaan Wang, Jianyu Wang, Xiaomeng Wang, Yiwei Wang, Taro Watanabe, Gijs Wijnholds, Alina Wróblewska, Ting-Wei Wu

Qihui Xu

Hsiu-Yu Yang, Yizhe Yang, Roman Yangarber, Shoubin Yu

Yuan Zang, Sina Zarrieß, Nan Zhang, Ningyu Zhang, Tianlin Zhang, Wei Emma Zhang, Xiang Zhang, Yijia Zhang, Ying Zhang, Yuhan Zhang, Yunxiang Zhang, Yuqing Zhang, Yusen Zhang, Zhisong Zhang, Guangzhen Zhao, Jin Zhao, Yu Zhao, Zhihong Zhu, Heike Zinsmeister, Jinan Zou

Keynote Talk

Towards AI models that can help us to become better global social beings

Thamar Solorio
Mohamed bin Zayed University of Artificial Intelligence, MBZUAI

Abstract: Cultural norms and values fundamentally shape our social interactions. Communication within any society reflects these cultural contexts. For example, while direct eye contact is often seen as a sign of confidence in many Western cultures, it may be viewed as disrespectful in other parts of the world. Moreover, human-human interactions include so much more than just the words we utter; non-verbal communication, including body language and other cues, provides rich signals to those around us.

As vision language models (VLMs) are increasingly integrated into user-facing applications, it is becoming relevant to wonder if and to what extent this technology can robustly process these signals. My research group is interested in developing evaluation frameworks to assess the abilities of VLMs concerning interpreting social cues and in developing new approaches that can assist us and, perhaps, enhance our cross-cultural human-human interactions.

Bio: Thamar Solorio is a professor in the NLP department at MBZUAI. She is also a tenured professor of Computer Science at the University of Houston. She is the director and founder of the RiTUAL Lab. Her research interests include NLP for low-resource settings and multilingual data, including code-switching and information extraction. More recently, she was moved towards language and vision problems, focusing on developing inclusive NLP. She received a National Science Foundation (NSF) CAREER award for her work on authorship attribution and was awarded the 2014 Emerging Leader ABIE Award in Honor of Denice Denton. She served two terms as an elected board member of the North American Chapter of the Association of Computational Linguistics (NAACL) and was PC co-chair for NAACL 2019. She is an Editor in Chief for the ACL Rolling Review (ARR) initiative and was a member of the advisory board for ARR. She serves as general chair for the 2024 Conference on Empirical Methods in Natural Language Processing.

Keynote Talk

Integrating AI-Driven Sign Language Technologies in Education: Recognition, Generation, and Interaction

Lorna Quandt
Gallaudet University

Abstract: This talk explores integrating AI-driven technologies in sign language research, covering the unique challenges of sign language recognition and generation. Dr. Quandt will explore these cutting-edge considerations through the lens of two research projects, ASL Champ! and BRIDGE. Both projects focus on sign language recognition and generation, which is crucial for advancing interaction in virtual and educational environments. ASL Champ! utilizes a dataset of 3D signs to enhance deep-learning-powered sign recognition in virtual reality. At the same time, BRIDGE extends this work by incorporating both recognition and generation of signs to create a more robust, interactive experience. This dual focus underscores the importance of pursuing recognition and generation in tandem rather than treating them as entirely distinct challenges. By leveraging advances in AI and natural language processing (NLP), we can create technologies that recognize and generate signs and facilitate deeper understanding and use of signed languages. These advancements hold great educational potential, particularly in providing more accessible tools for deaf students and enabling broader instruction in sign language. The talk will also address how these innovations can reshape the NLP field by widening the focus beyond spoken/written language and into multimodal, signed, and nonverbal aspects of language, which can inform all linguistic research.

Bio: Dr. Lorna Quandt is the Action & Brain Lab director at Gallaudet University in Washington, D.C. She serves as Co-Director of the VL2 Research Center alongside Melissa Malzkuhn. Dr. Quandt is an Associate Professor in the Ph.D. in Educational Neuroscience (PEN) program and the Science Director of the Motion Light Lab. Dr. Quandt founded the Action & Brain lab in early 2016. Before that, Dr. Quandt obtained her BA in Psychology from Haverford College and a PhD in Psychology, specializing in Brain & Cognitive Sciences, from Temple University. She completed a postdoctoral fellowship at the University of Pennsylvania, working with Dr. Anjan Chatterjee. Her research examines how knowledge of sign language changes perception, particularly visuospatial processing. Dr. Quandt is also pursuing the development of research-based educational technology to create new ways to learn signed languages in virtual reality.

Table of Contents

Program

Friday, November 15, 2024

09:00 - 09:10 *Opening Remarks*

09:10 - 10:30 *Keynote 1 - Lorna Quandt*

10:30 - 11:00 *Coffee Break*

11:00 - 12:30 *Oral Session 1: Psycholinguistic Session (chair: Libby Barak)*

Leveraging a Cognitive Model to Measure Subjective Similarity of Human and GPT-4 Written Content
Tyler Malloy, Maria José Ferreira, Fei Fang and Cleotilde Gonzalez

SPAWNing Structural Priming Predictions from a Cognitively Motivated Parser
Grusha Prasad and Tal Linzen

Lossy Context Surprisal Predicts Task-Dependent Patterns in Relative Clause Processing
Kate McCurdy and Michael Hahn

A Multimodal Large Language Model "Foresees" Objects Based on Verb Information but Not Gender
Shuqi Wang, Xufeng Duan and Zhenguang Cai

12:30 - 13:45 *Lunch*

13:45 - 15:30 *Poster Session 1*

15:30 - 16:00 *Coffee Break*

16:00 - 17:30 *Oral Session 2: Syntax and Structure Session (chair: Omri Abend)*

Is Structure Dependence Shaped for Efficient Communication?: A Case Study on Coordination
Kohei Kajikawa, Yusuke Kubota and Yohei Oseki

NeLLCom-X: A Comprehensive Neural-Agent Framework to Simulate Language Learning and Group Communication
Yuchen Lian, Tessa Verhoef and Arianna Bisazza

Saturday, November 16, 2024

09:00 - 09:10 *Best Paper Awards*

09:10 - 10:30 *Keynote 2 - Thamar Solorio*

10:30 - 10:45 *Coffee Break*

10:45 - 12:15 *Oral Session 3: LLM Session (chair: Malihe Alikhani)*

Global-Pruner: A Stable and Efficient Pruner for Retraining-Free Pruning of Encoder-Based Language Models
Guangzhen Yao, Yuehan Wang, Hui Xu, Long Zhang and MiaoQI MiaoQI

Investigating large language models for their competence in extracting grammatically sound sentences from transcribed noisy utterances
Alina Wróblewska

The Effect of Surprisal on Reading Times in Information Seeking and Repeated Reading
Keren Gruteke Klein, Yoav Meiri, Omer Shubi and Yevgeni Berzak

Multi-Cultural Norm Base: Frame-based Norm Discovery in Multi-Cultural Settings
Viet Thanh Pham, Shilin QU, Farhad Moghimifar, Suraj Sharma, Yuan-Fang Li, Weiqing Wang and Reza Haf

12:45 - 13:45 *Lunch*

13:45 - 15:00 *Poster Session 2*

15:00 - 15:30 *BabyLM Challenge (oral session)*

15:30 - 16:00 *Coffee Break*

16:00 - 17:20 *BabyLM Challenge (poster session)*

17:20 - 17:30 *Closing Remarks*

Words That Stick: Using Keyword Cohesion to Improve Text Segmentation

Amit Maraj
Ontario Tech University
2000 Simcoe St N., Oshawa, ON
amit.maraj@ontariotechu.net

Miguel Vargas Martin
Ontario Tech University
2000 Simcoe St N., Oshawa, ON
miguel.martin@ontariotechu.ca

Masoud Makrehchi
Ontario Tech University
2000 Simcoe St N., Oshawa, ON
masoud.makrehchi@ontariotechu.ca

Abstract

Text Segmentation (TS) is the task of segmenting bodies of text into coherent blocks, mostly defined by the topics each segment contains. Historically, techniques in this area have been unsupervised, with more success recently coming from supervised methods instead. Although these approaches see better performance, they require training data and upfront training time. We propose a new method called Coherence, where we use sentence embeddings to pull representational keywords as the main constructor of sentences when comparing them to one another. Additionally, we include a storage of previously found keywords for the purposes of creating a more accurate segment representation instead of just the immediate sentence in question. We show improved results over current state-of-the-art unsupervised techniques when analyzed using P_k and WindowDiff scores. Coherence also requires no fine-tuning.

1 Introduction

We present Coherence, a method that utilizes related words and their contextual meanings within sentences for effective Text Segmentation (TS). In the past decade, advancements in the field of TS have been primarily dominated by supervised techniques (Badjatiya et al. (2018), Koshorek et al. (2018), Somasundaran et al. (2020), Barrow et al. (2020), Lo et al. (2021), and Inan et al. (2022)), which require training data and are computed on a sentence-wise basis (i.e., each sentence is compared with adjacent sentences for evaluation). In contrast, Coherence uses contextual keyword embeddings for comparison, reducing potential noise and unnecessary sentence-level information that may not be helpful to the TS task.

Coherence uses a sliding window technique, traditionally used in supervised TS, to predict segment breaks (e.g., $P(S_{n-1}, S_n, S_{n+1}) = 1$). However, Coherence enhances this method by incorporating contextual information (through contextual keyword embeddings).

Coherence demonstrates performance improvements, particularly in P_k scores, and does not require fine-tuning. By leveraging pre-trained sentence encoders like BERT, LaBSE, and S-BERT, Coherence leverages extracted keywords to form an end-to-end flow. The core of Coherence lies in collecting and utilizing important keywords during the segmentation process. These keywords are represented as contextual embeddings, capturing essential information about their usage within sentences (for example, differentiating "bridge" in the context of crossing a river from "bridge" in the context of a human's nose). This process is inspired by the multi-headed attention mechanism in the Transformer architecture, providing a nuanced understanding of sentence relationships without the need for extensive training and data.

1. A novel approach to unsupervised TS that achieves state-of-the-art (SOTA) results on a variety of diverse and widely accepted TS datasets in the research community.
    - Coherence does not require fine-tuning and is shown to perform competitively and even outperform current SOTA unsupervised systems in some benchmarks.
    - Using pre-trained sentence embeddings, Coherence leans on both similar and diverse keywords to create more orthogonality in representations of sentences.
2. A keyword collection mechanism called Keyword Map, which creates segment representations through its most important keywords.
    - The Keyword Map stores important sentence-based representations through contextual keywords for later reference during comparison.

Proceedings of the 28th Conference on Computational Natural Language Learning, pages 1–9
November 15-16, 2024 ©2024 Association for Computational Linguistics

3. An approach to unsupervised TS that has explainability in the prediction process, through the extraction of important keywords.

We show that without the need for expensive fine-tuning and highly-dimensional sentence embeddings as training data, we can achieve performance improvements in a space that has been more recently dominated by advancements in supervised learning. Using orthogonal keywords in addition to similar keywords provides more breadth in keyword representation to further bolster results. All our code can be found on the Human-Machine Lab GitHub Repository [1].

2 Related Works

Initially, Hearst (1997) introduced TextTiling, an unsupervised algorithm that identifies segment boundaries through lexical overlaps. Similarly, Choi (2000) demonstrated the efficacy of unsupervised methods by analyzing sentence similarities, categorizing their work within linear TS methodologies. These initial contributions set a new standard in the field.

The landscape of TS shifted with the advent of advanced word and sentence embeddings, paving the way for supervised techniques. Koshorek et al. (2018) explored the potential of processing large TS datasets through a Bi-LSTM, analyzing three sentences at a time to understand their interrelations. Building on this, Badjatiya et al. (2018) proposed a sentence-wise model utilizing attention mechanisms to enhance performance further. Recent supervised approaches have increasingly incorporated LSTMs and Transformers as foundational components, as seen in works by Somasundaran et al. (2020), Barrow et al. (2020), Lo et al. (2021), and Inan et al. (2022). These studies have showcased the effectiveness of adding topic information and emphasizing sentence contextuality in achieving top-tier results.

Despite the dominance of supervised models, unsupervised TS techniques continue to show promise. Misra et al. (2009) revisited the classic TextTiling approach, refining it with LDA to identify more precise keywords. Riedl and Biemann (2012) combined LDA and TextTiling for another innovative unsupervised solution. Furthermore, Glavaš et al. (2016) introduced a novel unsupervised graph-based method, analyzing sentences as nodes within a graph to predict segment boundaries. These unsupervised models underscore the ongoing exploration and diversity in TS methodologies. While unsupervised approaches in the field continue to be important due to their flexibility and lack of need for domain-specific training data, more research has recently focused on supervised approaches. Fragkou et al. (2004)'s approach to TS relied upon within-segment word similarity and prior information about segment length, but does not incorporate inter-sentence comparisons. In contrast, Brants et al. (2002) approaches unsupervised TS by using Probabilistic Latent Semantic Analysis (PLSA) to identify similar words an in inter-sentence level. They then apply a TextTiling based approach for identifying changes in frequency between sentences.

Another technique by Solbiati et al. (2021) takes a unique approach to unsupervised TS by grouping a series of sentences together, stacking them on top of each other, and performing max pooling. The resulting matrix is a mixture of sentences, which can then be used to compare to other matrices. They perform their analysis on meeting data, which shows improvements upon other techniques. More recently, John et al. (John et al., 2017) utilize an LDA-based TextTiling approach that produces strong results. The boundary adjustment technique proposed in this work is a retroactive solution to TopicTiling (Riedl and Biemann, 2012) that helps improve results.

3 Methodology

The core of Coherence is its ability to pull out keywords from provided sentences. To accomplish this, we use a library called KeyBERT [2]. This library goes through each word in a sentence, creates an embedding for the word and compares it with the embedding of the sentence at hand. Keywords are identified as the ones with a higher similarity to the sentence embedding. Because of this, there is no need to globally scan the document beforehand, which other techniques like TF-IDF and LDA require. Utilizing BERT allows the KeyBERT library to effectively look into the attention being paid at every word and phrase to identify important words. KeyBERT has been shown to outperform other topic modelling and keyword extraction techniques like LDA and YAKE (Campos et al., 2020).

We also consider the use of an LDA based ap-

[1] https://github.com/HumanMachineLab/Coherence

[2] https://github.com/MaartenGr/KeyBERT

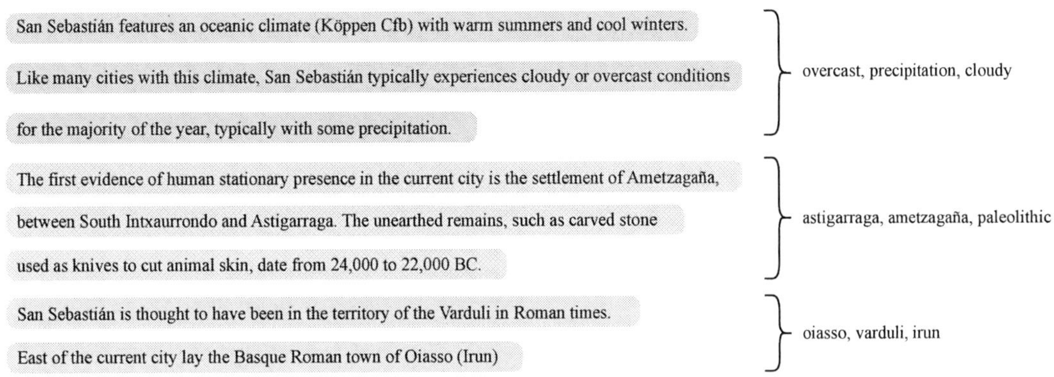

Figure 1: Topics gathered throughout the keyword extraction phase within the "wiki" dataset. Due to the natural pruning of the Keyword Map, only the most pertinent topics are retained. Additionally, importance of the keyword to its original sentence is also maintained. Results shown here are extracted from the "wiki" dataset starting at sample 643.

proach, such as BERTopic [3] as the keyword extractor, but elect to stick with KeyBERT due to the following advantages:

- Pulling keywords using KeyBERT does not require upfront training, whereas BERTopic does.
- Because BERTopic uses LDA to pull topics, the requirement to be aware of the entire document's worth of text beforehand increases processing time and reduces flexibility.
- Inherently, LDA does not use word embeddings to pull important topics, which means that extracted words are in the form of text. Since our technique compares words in vector space, constructing embeddings for extracted words will not retain sentence contextuality.

Coherence is broken down into two major phases. We use sentences to denote the important keywords derived from said sentences - sentences are not compared verbatim, rather the keywords that make up the sentence are compared. At every step, the current sentence is compared against prior sentences, as long as they exist in the Keyword Map (we elaborate on conditions where a sentence's keywords would not end up in the Keyword Map later in this section).

3.1 Keyword Extraction Phase

In this phase, we use KeyBERT to extract important keywords from sentences at each iteration. KeyBERT uses BERT or any BERT-based model (e.g., RoBERTa, DistilBERT, ALBERT, etc.) to create a representation of each sentence. It then takes the sentence embedding and each respective word embedding (as provided by BERT as well). The higher the similarity between the word and the sentence, the more likely it is considered a keyword. After extraction, keywords are sorted in descending order based on its importance to its parent sentence. This importance is calculated based on how strong the keyword is in similarity to its parent sentence.

3.2 Prediction Phase

In this phase, we use information from previous sentences in the segment to compare with the keyword representation of the current sentence.

Keyword Map. We first create a representation of the current segment through storage of keywords gathered throughout the iteration process. We determine the top n keywords that should be stored per sentence and save them in a map. We then use this map to compare against the current sentence during iteration. For example, when we store 3 keywords in the map per sentence and we are on the fifth sentence in the segment, we will compare the current sentence to 12 keywords in the map (3 keywords times 4 previous sentences).

When storing keywords in the map, we compare the current sentence's keywords to the pre-existing keywords in the map. We take the most similar (with respect to the pre-existing keywords in the map) keywords in the current sentence and store it in the map. This allows us to build a Keyword Map that is representative of the overall topics within the segment. After k (average length of segment size in the dataset) sentences, we prune the Keyword

[3]https://github.com/MaartenGr/BERTopic

Map at every step by removing the oldest set of keywords, adopting a queue-based FIFO structure.

Comparison. The current sentence's keywords are compared to the previous sentence's keywords and every keyword in the Keyword Map. All the comparisons are summed and then averaged to get an overall similarity score. This similarity score, which is calculated as shown in Formula 2, ends up being a representation of how cohesive the current sentence is with all the sentences previous to it. Words in earlier sentences of the segment are also de-emphasized so they do not hold as much weight in the comparison as words that are closer to the current sentence. A value of $1/distance(curr\_sent, prev\_sent)$ is applied to all words in the previous sentence. For example, a word embedding belonging to a sentence that occurred 2 sentences prior will have a weight of $1/2$ applied to it.

The output from the prediction phase is a logit that is the average of all the comparisons between the current sentences and every sentence in the Keyword Map, which can be seen in Figure 3.

As shown in Figure 3, the Keyword Map is built throughout the inference process. This map acts as a representation of the segment currently being scanned. Because important segment-based information can exist in more places than the current sentence, the Keyword Map builds a representation of keywords found earlier in the segment.

During the prediction process, the contents of the Keyword Map along with the current sentence's keywords in the sliding window are compared using cosine similarity and an average. If the contents of the Keyword Map and current sentence are dissimilar enough (based on a parameter–$prediction\_threshold$), the system predicts a one, indicating that the second sentence is the start of a new segment. Upon a positive prediction, the Keyword Map gets emptied so it can begin collecting new keywords. If the Keyword Map and current sentence are similar, the system predicts a zero and continues to build the Keyword Map. To avoid the Keyword Map becoming too large over time, especially with longer segments, it is pruned after n size (e.g., if the Keyword Map has five sentences worth of keywords and we add another sentence worth of keywords, we remove the oldest sentence). For example, we prune the map after it grows to 26 sentences (the average segment size) for the Clinical dataset (Malioutov, 2006).

Values for the $prediction\_threshold$ are tested between zero and one at every tenth interval and notice that the lowest P_k and WindowDiff scores consistently show up when 0.5 is used.

4 Metrics

Two popular metrics that exist solely to benchmark TS systems are P_k and WindowDiff (WD), which have become commonplace for work in the TS field. P_k is the probability that a pair of chosen sentences with a distance of k are incorrectly classified. Both the WD and P_k metrics use a sliding window of fixed size w over the document and compare the predicted segments with the reference ones. k is determined as half of the average true segment size of the document. Since P_k and WD are both penalty metrics, lower values indicate better performance. While P_k is the most widely and still is the most accepted metric in the TS space, WD was originally proposed as an update to the P_k metric. P_k can be thought of as the probability that two segments drawn from a document are incorrectly identified as belonging to the same segment. WD operates almost identically, but uses a sliding window to penalize systems that tend to overpredict, resulting in false positives - something that P_k does not acknowledge as an errant prediction. Both P_k and WD thus lie between zero and one and an algorithm that assigns all boundaries correctly receives a score of zero. WD is considered a better measure than P_k as the P_k metric suffers from issues such as a lack of false positive prediction penalization (Pevzner and Hearst, 2002).

5 Data

Unsupervised TS methods are often evaluated using constructed datasets, which amalgamate segments from varied sources into composite documents, as evidenced by studies from Choi (Choi, 2000) and Galley et al (Galley et al., 2003).

5.1 Choi Dataset:

Introduced by Choi (2000) in 2000, this dataset has become a staple for TS research, referenced in works by Misra et al. (2009), Brants et al. (2002), Fragkou et al. (2004), Glavaš et al. (2016), Sun et al. (2008), and Galley et al. (2003). It is crafted from the Brown corpus, containing 700 documents that simulate real text structure. The compilation includes 400 documents with segments varying from 3-11 sentences, alongside 100 documents for each segment length category: 3-5, 6-8,

$$Coherence(S_{n-1}, S_n) = \frac{1}{x}\sum_{j=1}^{x}\frac{1}{x}\sum_{i=1}^{x} cos(u_j(S_{n-1}), w_i(S_n))$$

Formula 2: The similarity calculation between two sentences, where each keyword in the respective sentence is compared with every other keyword in the comparing set of keywords (e.g., the set of w keywords are gathered from S_n and the set of u keywords are gathered from S_{n-1}), where w and u are keywords. Each line indicates a cosine similarity calculation and once all the calculations are done from a keyword on the left to all keywords on the right, they are summed and averaged. This process continues for all the keywords and the total average is taken. Additionally, each keyword (w of S_n) has a weighting applied to it, indicating its importance to the sentence it was derived from originally.

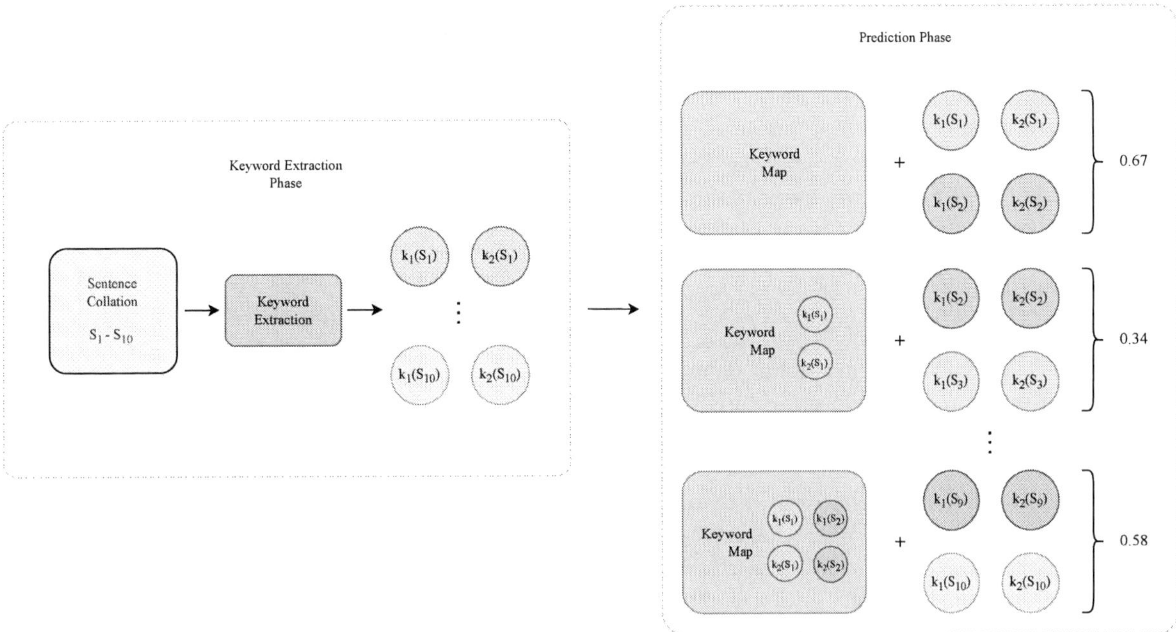

Figure 3: Architecture for Coherence. Keywords extracted from in the extraction phase are passed toward the prediction phase and stored in the Keyword Map. The current sentence's keywords are derived from current and previous sentences and are denoted with h, i, j, k, and l. The output from the prediction phase is a logit that is representative of the cohesion between the current sentence's keywords and the keywords compared to from the Keyword Map.

and 9-11 sentences.

5.2 Manifesto Dataset:

To complement the synthetic Choi dataset, Coherence's effectiveness is also tested on real political texts from the Manifesto Project dataset. This collection of documents has been meticulously segmented into seven topics, such as economy and welfare, and foreign affairs, by field experts. The curation of this dataset is attributed to Glavaš et al. (2016).

5.3 Clinical Dataset:

We also use the Clinical dataset put together by Malioutov (2006) to showcase our results. This dataset consists of a set of 227 chapters from a medical textbook. Each chapter is marked into sections indicated by the author which forms the segmentation boundaries. It contains a total of 1136 sections.

5.4 Fiction Dataset:

To include even more diversity in our results, we also showcase our results on the Fiction dataset put together by Kazantseva and Szpakowicz (2011), which is a collection of 85 fiction books downloaded from Project Gutenberg. Segmentation boundaries are the chapter breaks in each of the books.

5.5 Wiki Dataset:

Finally, we test Coherence's performance on a curated Wikipedia dataset, introduced by Badjatiya et al. (2018), is also presented. This dataset consists of randomly selected set of 300 documents having an average segment size of 26. The documents widely fall under the narrative category.

6 Results

Coherence shows and improvement over SOTA unsupervised results in the space. Results are reported on the Choi, Manifesto, Clinical, Fiction, and Wiki Datasets (Choi (2000), Glavaš et al. (2016), Malioutov (2006), Kazantseva and Szpakowicz (2011), Badjatiya et al. (2018)). Our performance on these datasets shows the versatility of Coherence. This gives us hope that with the use of pre-trained models, unsupervised approaches can prove to be viable in the TS space. Results on the Choi and Manifesto datasets are reported against pre-existing SOTA unsupervised TS approaches. Results for the Clinical, Wiki, and Fiction datasets are compared against Badjatiya et al. (2018)'s work.

Results on the Clinical and Fiction datasets are competitive with Badjatiya et al. (2018)'s pre-existing supervised approach. Coherence does not do as well on the Wiki dataset however. We believe this is due to the subjectivity in TS datasets at the labelling level. The Wiki dataset has an average segment length of 26 sentences for example. On Choi's dataset, Coherence performs extremely well, outperforming all previous SOTA unsupervised TS techniques. Coherence also performs competitively, with stronger results in the WD metric on the Manifesto dataset. This performance improvement on WD versus P_k indicates that Coherence makes less false positive predictions than pre-existing techniques.

We show that, in comparison to previous SOTA unsupervised techniques, Coherence outperforms in a variety of datasets using both the P_k and WD metrics as benchmarks. This comes without the need for fine-tuning or domain adaptation. Since the keyword extraction phase of Coherence is modular, we believe that as sentence and word embedding technology continues to improve, so will the results of Coherence.

The lack of need for fine-tuning a model is advantageous and as of such, each round of inference takes roughly 25ms - 125ms on a cloud-based A100 GPU. Additionally, Coherence provides utility without the need for training or domain adaptation. The lightweight lift of Coherence allows it to be used against various datasets, due to the strength of the sentence encoder. The applicability of Coherence to new and unseen test datasets can prove to be useful in production settings.

7 Limitations

Coherence shows improvements over pre-existing SOTA unsupervised systems such as TopicTiling (Riedl and Biemann, 2012) and GraphSeg (Glavaš et al., 2016).

The authors for the works found in Table 2 do not present their findings using the same metrics, nor do they provide their codebase, and due to resource limitations, we are not able to replicate their works to evaluate and report on WD. We acknowledge that this is a limitation of our work, but we also illustrate the strengths and improvements of our system using a wide array of available datasets.

Some reliance for Coherence comes from the pre-trained sentence encoder (KeyBERT) in the keyword extraction phase. Although this seems like a limitation, it can be a strength in the flexibility of the system. Future iterations of pre-trained sentence encoders can be used to replace KeyBERT and enhance Coherence's output. We show the flexibility of our system by achieving superior results on a wide array of available datasets without the need for tedious fine-tuning. This implies that as keyword extraction techniques become stronger, so shall our system.

Most of the processing time comes from the keyword extraction phase, due to the keyword extraction library. Roughly 90% of this time comes from the keyword extraction phase, whereby KeyBERT needs to compare every keyword with its parent sentence embedding. The majority of the RAM utilization also comes from this phase, as the embedding model (LaBSE in our case) is loaded into memory for inference. In our experiments, Coherence required less than 3GB RAM throughout testing. With techniques like quantization, smaller models can perform this keyword extraction step more efficiently. This limitation is due to the selected keyword extraction library; KeyBERT in our case. The majority of processing time in the KeyBERT library comes from creating contextual embeddings for each sentence before comparing each word in the sentence it was pulled from with the sentence itself.

8 Conclusion

In this work, we present Coherence, which is a novel approach to unsupervised TS that leverages contextual keywords from sentences to represent text segments. We show that the emphasis on contextual keywords can build representations of

	Clinical		Wiki		Fiction	
	$P_k \downarrow$	WD $\downarrow$	$P_k \downarrow$	WD $\downarrow$	$P_k \downarrow$	WD $\downarrow$
Badjatiya et al. (2018)	**33.0**	**31.0**	**34.0**	**32.0**	38.0	**31.0**
Coherence	37.1	38.9	50.2	53.4	**35.7**	61.6

Table 1: Results on the "clinical", "wiki", and "fiction" datasets (Badjatiya et al., 2018; Malioutov, 2006; Kazantseva and Szpakowicz, 2011). We compare our results to Badjatiya's fine-tuned neural model and show competitive results, without the need for fine-tuning.

	3 – 5		6 – 8		9 – 11		3 – 11	
	$P_k \downarrow$	WD $\downarrow$	$P_k \downarrow$	WD $\downarrow$	$P_k \downarrow$	WD $\downarrow$	$P_k \downarrow$	WD $\downarrow$
Choi (2000)	12.0	–	9.0	–	9.0	–	12.0	–
Brants et al. (2002)	7.4	–	8.0	–	6.8	–	10.7	–
Fragkou et al. (2004)	5.5	–	3.0	–	1.3	–	7.0	–
Misra et al. (2009)	23.0	–	15.8	–	14.4	–	16.1	–
Glavaš et al. (2016)	5.6	8.7	7.2	9.4	6.6	9.6	7.2	9.0
Coherence	**4.4**	**6.2**	**3.1**	**3.3**	**2.5**	**2.6**	**4.0**	**4.4**

Table 2: Results on the synthetic Choi (Choi, 2000) dataset.

	$P_k \downarrow$	WD $\downarrow$
Riedl and Biemann (2012)	33.39	38.31
Glavaš et al. (2016)	**28.09**	34.04
Coherence	31.71	**33.42**

Table 3: Results on the Manifesto (Glavaš et al., 2016) Dataset. We show the versatility of Coherence providing competitive results in a different domain.

segments, which can be used for TS. Coherence demonstrates improvements over SOTA unsupervised TS techniques, particularly in the metrics of P_k and WindowDiff. The main contributions of Coherence include the diverse extraction of keywords and an efficient keyword collection mechanism which we termed Keyword Map.

Our results on the Choi, Manifesto, Clinical, Wiki, and Fiction datasets show that Coherence can perform well in a variety of domains. While we also include our results on the newer WikiSection dataset, other supervised TS approaches show superior results.

Future work will focus on enhancing Coherence to consider the contextual relationship between extracted keywords, while exploring the method's applicability across various domains and datasets. Coherence offers a solution that can be adapted to various domains without the need for fine-tuning.

Acknowledgments

The first and second authors acknowledge the support of an NSERC Discovery Development Grant (DDG-2024-00031).

References

Pinkesh Badjatiya, Litton J Kurisinkel, Manish Gupta, and Vasudeva Varma. 2018. Attention-based neural text segmentation. In *European Conference on Information Retrieval*, pages 180–193. Springer.

Joe Barrow, Rajiv Jain, Vlad Morariu, Varun Manjunatha, Douglas W Oard, and Philip Resnik. 2020. A joint model for document segmentation and segment labeling. In *Proceedings of the 58th Annual Meeting of the Association for Computational Linguistics*, pages 313–322.

Thorsten Brants, Francine Chen, and Ioannis Tsochantaridis. 2002. Topic-based document segmentation with probabilistic latent semantic analysis. In *Proceedings of the eleventh international conference on information and knowledge management*, pages 211–218.

Ricardo Campos, Vítor Mangaravite, Arian Pasquali, Alípio Jorge, Célia Nunes, and Adam Jatowt. 2020. Yake! keyword extraction from single documents using multiple local features. *Information Sciences*, 509:257–289.

Freddy YY Choi. 2000. Advances in domain independent linear text segmentation. *arXiv preprint cs/0003083*.

Pavlina Fragkou, Vassilios Petridis, and Ath Kehagias. 2004. A dynamic programming algorithm for linear text segmentation. *Journal of Intelligent Information Systems*, 23(2):179–197.

Michel Galley, Kathleen McKeown, Eric Fosler-Lussier, and Hongyan Jing. 2003. Discourse segmentation of multi-party conversation. In *Proceedings of the 41st Annual Meeting of the Association for Computational Linguistics*, pages 562–569.

Goran Glavaš, Federico Nanni, and Simone Paolo Ponzetto. 2016. Unsupervised text segmentation using semantic relatedness graphs. In *Proceedings of the Fifth Joint Conference on Lexical and Computational Semantics*, pages 125–130. Association for Computational Linguistics.

Marti A Hearst. 1997. Text tiling: Segmenting text into multi-paragraph subtopic passages. *Computational linguistics*, 23(1):33–64.

Hakan Inan, Rashi Rungta, and Yashar Mehdad. 2022. Structured summarization: Unified text segmentation and segment labeling as a generation task. *arXiv preprint arXiv:2209.13759*.

Adebayo Kolawole John, Luigi Di Caro, and Guido Boella. 2017. Text segmentation with topic modeling and entity coherence. In *Proceedings of the 16th International Conference on Hybrid Intelligent Systems (HIS 2016)*, pages 175–185. Springer.

Anna Kazantseva and Stan Szpakowicz. 2011. Linear text segmentation using affinity propagation. In *Proceedings of the 2011 Conference on Empirical Methods in Natural Language Processing*, pages 284–293.

Omri Koshorek, Adir Cohen, Noam Mor, Michael Rotman, and Jonathan Berant. 2018. Text segmentation as a supervised learning task. *arXiv preprint arXiv:1803.09337*.

Kelvin Lo, Yuan Jin, Weicong Tan, Ming Liu, Lan Du, and Wray Buntine. 2021. Transformer over pre-trained transformer for neural text segmentation with enhanced topic coherence. *arXiv preprint arXiv:2110.07160*.

Igor Igor Mikhailovich Malioutov. 2006. *Minimum cut model for spoken lecture segmentation*. Ph.D. thesis, Massachusetts Institute of Technology.

Hemant Misra, François Yvon, Joemon M Jose, and Olivier Cappé. 2009. Text segmentation via topic modeling: an analytical study. In *Proceedings of the 18th ACM conference on Information and knowledge management*, pages 1553–1556.

Lev Pevzner and Marti A Hearst. 2002. A critique and improvement of an evaluation metric for text segmentation. *Computational Linguistics*, 28(1):19–36.

Martin Riedl and Chris Biemann. 2012. Topictiling: a text segmentation algorithm based on lda. In *Proceedings of ACL 2012 student research workshop*, pages 37–42.

Alessandro Solbiati, Kevin Heffernan, Georgios Damaskinos, Shivani Poddar, Shubham Modi, and Jacques Cali. 2021. Unsupervised topic segmentation of meetings with bert embeddings. *arXiv preprint arXiv:2106.12978*.

Swapna Somasundaran et al. 2020. Two-level transformer and auxiliary coherence modeling for improved text segmentation. In *Proceedings of the AAAI Conference on Artificial Intelligence*, volume 34, pages 7797–7804.

Qi Sun, Runxin Li, Dingsheng Luo, and Xihong Wu. 2008. Text segmentation with lda-based fisher kernel. In *Proceedings of ACL-08: HLT, Short Papers*, pages 269–272.

A Appendix

Algorithm 1: Coherence

```
Result: Extract similar and diverse keywords with globally informed context through sentence
        batching.
keywords ← keyword_extraction([s0, ..., s9]) ;      /* s0, ..., s9 are sentences. */
keyword_map = [];
similarities = [];
predictions = [];
for i ... len(keywords) do
    curr_kws ← keywords[i + 1];
    prev_kws ← keyword_map[0 ... i];
    for w ∈ curr_kws do
        for k ∈ prev_kws do
            similarity ← cosine_similarity(k, w);
            similarities.insert(similarity);
            if similarity >= coherence_threshold then
                gits_map.insert(w) ;                 /* Add new keyword to map. */
            end
        end
    end
    if avg(similarities) >= coherence_threshold then
        predictions.insert(0) ;              /* The current sentence is similar */
    else
        predictions.insert(1) ;          /* The current sentence is not similar */
    end
end
return predictions
```

Description: *coherence_threshold* is a hyperparameter set between 0 and 1, which can be used to enforce the strength keywords need to have between each other for entrance into the Keyword Map. Through our testing, we notice that this value will vary depending on the sentence encoder used (LaBSE in our case), since the strength of each keyword and its parent sentence are directly related to the encoder. To that end, we find the best results (based on P_k and WindowDiff scores) when this value is set to 0.7.

Investigating large language models for their competence in extracting grammatically sound sentences from transcribed noisy utterances

Alina Wróblewska
Institute of Computer Science
Polish Academy of Sciences
alina@ipipan.waw.pl

Abstract

Selectively processing noisy utterances while effectively disregarding speech-specific elements poses no considerable challenge for humans, as they exhibit remarkable cognitive abilities to separate semantically significant content from speech-specific noise (i.e. filled pauses, disfluencies, and restarts). These abilities may be driven by mechanisms based on acquired grammatical rules that compose abstract syntactic-semantic structures within utterances. Segments without syntactic and semantic significance are consistently disregarded in these structures. The structures, in tandem with lexis, likely underpin language comprehension and thus facilitate effective communication. In our study, grounded in linguistically motivated experiments, we investigate whether large language models (LLMs) can effectively perform analogical speech comprehension tasks. In particular, we examine the ability of LLMs to extract well-structured utterances from transcriptions of noisy dialogues. We conduct two evaluation experiments in the Polish language scenario, using a dataset presumably unfamiliar to LLMs to mitigate the risk of data contamination. Our results show that not all extracted utterances are correctly structured, indicating that either LLMs do not fully acquire syntactic-semantic rules or they acquire them but cannot apply them effectively. We conclude that the ability of LLMs to comprehend noisy utterances is still relatively superficial compared to human proficiency in processing them.

1 Introduction

In the field of natural language understanding (NLU), efforts are directed towards simulating human language comprehension using language modelling techniques. A crucial aspect of this pursuit involves the development of large language models (LLMs), which play a pivotal role in numerous natural language processing (NLP) tasks (Vaswani et al., 2017; Rajpurkar et al., 2016; Yang et al., 2019), tailored for comprehension, generation, and manipulation of natural language. NLU research also aims to identify LLMs' shortcomings, to reverse-engineer phenomena that LLMs fail to address. Despite impressive capabilities, LLMs have not achieved the comprehensive and nuanced linguistic competency inner to human beings (Mao et al., 2023) and their further study is necessary.

LLMs undergo training on extensive and varied datasets, which include textual data, code-based data, structured datasets, and other data sources. Textual data exhibits significant diversity, comprising edited texts, content from social media platforms as well as speech transcriptions, such as parliamentary proceedings or pretended dialogues within narratives or subtitles. Despite spoken language's dominance in daily communication and the availability of high-quality transcription tools, it remains unexplored whether processing transcribed utterances is challenging for LLMs. Motivated by this observation, we aim to examine whether LLMs can effectively address challenges akin to those faced by humans during comprehending utterances.

Speech understanding is a complex cognitive process that plays a fundamental role in human communication. The nature of speech comprehension is multifaceted, influenced by neurological, cognitive and linguistic factors. This study focuses on the linguistic dimension. When decoding spoken messages, humans struggle with phonological difficulties (Vitevitch and Luce, 1998), including phonological similarity and ambiguity among words, and individual phonemic variations. This aspect is irrelevant to the current study, as we solely investigate the processing of texts (transcriptions). The comprehension of spoken utterances can be affected by syntactic complexity. Processing complex sentences may increase a cognitive cost and result in comprehension difficulties (Friederici, 2002). The semantic aspects of speech understanding are thoroughly researched. For instance, Rodd et al.

Proceedings of the 28th Conference on Computational Natural Language Learning, pages 10–23
November 15-16, 2024 ©2024 Association for Computational Linguistics

(2016) investigated the process of word-sense disambiguation and its associated challenges.

To comprehend an utterance, separating semantically significant content from speech-specific noise is crucial. The ability to filter out noise and selectively compose only the semantically relevant information is inherent to humans. Since it remains unexplored whether LLMs can perform this task effectively, we address this issue through linguistically motivated evaluation tasks in the Polish language scenario. In Section 2, we introduce the proposed approach with its primary objective to determine whether LLMs are capable of identifying well-structured utterances in transcriptions of authentic spontaneous utterances that incorporate noisy speech-specific segments. In Sections 3 and 4, we outline the experimental setup and discuss the results of the empirical evaluation. Section 5 provides the contextual backdrop for our research, while Section 6 concludes our research findings.

2 Proposed approach

Processing spoken data is often more challenging when contrasted with processing genuine written texts. Firstly, spoken words may be obscured by background sounds, resulting in transcription gaps. Secondly, the application of automated transcription and punctuation recovery tools can yield lexical and punctuation errors in transcriptions. Thirdly, the written mode tends to be more standardised, whereas the spoken mode often features informal and colloquial language. Finally, and most importantly in the context of this study, speech-specific elements such as fillers, self-corrections, and false starts increase the complexity of understanding spoken data compared to written texts.

In the era of robust and advanced LLMs, utilising them for processing transcribed spoken data emerges as a rational choice. Nevertheless, uncertainties arise regarding their ability to identify intended content to be comprehended in possibly noisy utterances. This study examines whether LLMs possess the competence to selectively process noisy utterances while ignoring non-fluency features. We investigate the capabilities of LLMs in (1) extracting well-formed sentences determined by abstract syntactic-semantic structures (see Section 2.1) from noisy utterances; (2) disregarding speech-specific elements (see Section 2.2) that do not contribute to utterance understanding.

To ascertain the ability of LLMs to disregard speech-specific elements and to recognise well-formed sentences within noisy utterances, we employ the prompting methodology (see Section 2.3). Based on predefined prompts, LLMs are instructed to identify and subsequently output all tokens composing well-structured utterances. LLMs' performance in extracting refined utterances and filtering non-fluency features is evaluated against a gold-standard dataset (see Section 2.4).

2.1 Abstract syntactic-semantic structure

Each sentence serves an intentional function and conveys meaning. The principles governing sentence construction, specifically those encompassing syntactic and semantic aspects, are inherently compositional. Syntax, responsible for allowed compositions, operates in tandem with semantics, i.e. the composition of well-formed expressions is contingent upon syntactic rules intrinsically linked with semantic rules. Syntactic rules, founded on word order, agreement, and government principles, dictate the permissible compositions of words, phrases, and clauses. Semantic rules, in turn, determine how the meaning of these composed expressions is derived from the meanings of their components (Partee, 1984, 2004; Jacobson, 2014). In language acquisition, humans internalise these rules and, drawing on their linguistic competence, are able to produce and process inherently structured sentences. The question of whether humans derive separate syntactic and semantic structures or a single unified compositional structure remains challenging to answer due to the lack of direct access to cognition mechanisms. As a compromise solution, we refer to this structure as the *abstract syntactic-semantic structure* (AS).

The process of composing inner ASs is a fundamental feature of human language comprehension. When reading or hearing sentences, humans parse them in line with their linguistic competence, subconsciously constructing ASs of these sentences. The ASs function as links or interfaces for decoding sentences to their intended meanings, i.e. enabling their understanding. While processing speech, humans encounter an additional challenge, namely the necessity to selectively disregard speech-specific elements (see Section 2.2). Composing these elements with semantically relevant content violates syntactic and/or semantic rules. Only segments resulting from an inner filtering process are permitted to compose a coherent and cohesive AS – the foundation for comprehending language.

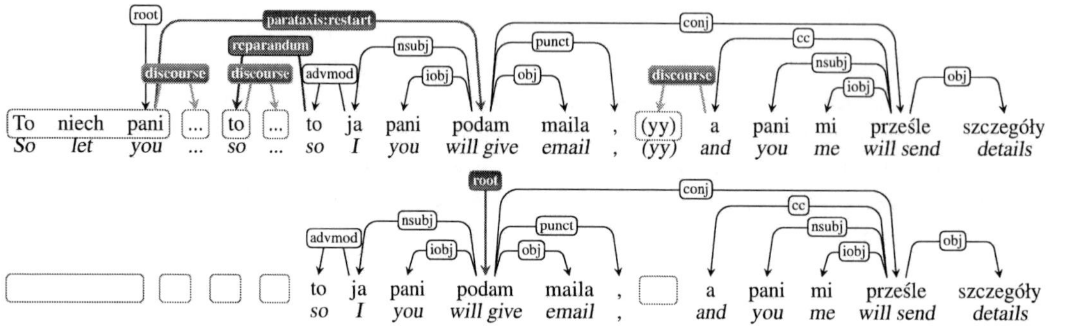

Figure 1: The original utterance transcription is depicted in the upper UD tree. The bottom UD tree, obtained via filtering speech-specific elements from the upper tree, serves as an approximation of the abstract syntactic-semantic structure of the well-formed sentence "to ja pani podam maila, a pani mi prześle szczegóły" (Eng. *I will give you my e-mail address and you will send me the details*).

The exact form of the AS established through cognitive parsing (Ding et al., 2016) remains indeterminate. Various proposals have emerged regarding its potential representations to facilitate linguistic research and support NLP. One widely adopted framework is Universal Dependencies (UD, de Marneffe et al., 2021), which primarily focuses on syntactic relations but also includes semantics facets, such as the distinction between functional and content words, thematic role extensions, and named entities. UD trees also cover speech-specific phenomena. Thereupon, we anchor our research within this framework and use UD trees to approximate ASs.

2.2 Examined speech-specific phenomena

Conversations involve at least two speakers and are structured into alternating turns. A turn that is a continuous utterance of a speaker serves as a primary unit for linguistic analysis. Apart from an intended content, utterances may also include interruptions or extra elements commonly found in spoken language: non-linguistic tokens, disfluencies, and restarts.

2.2.1 Non-linguistic tokens

Non-linguistic tokens are segments distinctive to spoken language, i.e. silent and non-silent pauses (fillers). Both types of pauses occur when the speaker momentarily suspends their speech production. Intervals of silence can be transcribed as '...' and inarticulate sounds can be denoted as '(yy)' in transcripts. Pauses are annotated with the *discourse* UD dependency type (see Figure 1).

2.2.2 Disfluencies

Disfluencies are interruptions or irregularities that disrupt the smoothness of speech and serve as indicators of uncertainty and hesitation, or the need to clarify or amend a statement. Disfluencies are commonly rectified through speech corrections. Instances of disfluency cases include (1) **repetitions**, e.g. '*two, ei... eight, one, five*', (2) **substitutions**, e.g. '*I received... we received a message*', (3) **reformulations**, e.g. '*We lost eight... seventy pounds*'. Disfluencies are annotated as dependents of their corrections and are labelled with the *reparandum* dependency type.

2.2.3 Restarts

Restarts refer to clauses or phrases that lack syntactic connections to the antecedent string of tokens. These phenomena occur when a speaker abandons the ongoing utterance and initiates a new one, e.g. '*cause I don't have a..., I don't remember the password*' (the underlined string should be ignored while composing the utterance meaning). Restarts are annotated with the *parataxis:restart* UD type.

2.3 Prompt-driven cognisance of well-structured utterances

The prompting technique consists in explicitly instructing LLMs to solve specific NLP tasks (Radford et al., 2019). Given a predefined prompt, LLMs are directed to generate or analyse texts according to the verbal instructions included in this prompt. The prompting technique is valuable in tailoring LLMs to specific NLP tasks and attaining a degree of control over their responses.

In this approach, we prompt LLMs to extract well-structured utterances while filtering speech-specific elements. Despite the remarkable zero-shot capabilities of LLMs, we apply the few-shot paradigm (Brown et al., 2020) that involves providing input-output examples. The pairs of noisy input utterances and well-structured output utterances guide LLMs towards better performance.

The prompt-driven process of recognising well-formed sentences within noisy utterances is illustrated in Figure 1. In the input utterance (i.e. tokens of the upper UD tree), LLM seeks to identify noisy substrings: the *discourse* fillers '...' and '*(yy)*', the *reparandum* subtree '*to...*', as well as the false start '*To niech pani...*'. Fillers and repetition strings represent conventional forms of noise that LLM should easily detect. However, identifying substitutions, reformulations, and false starts poses non-trivial challenges, requiring deeper analysis of input utterances. After filtering out non-fluency features, LLM should output tokens that compose a grammatically coherent utterance, in line with its inherent syntactic-semantic rules acquired during training. LLM does not see UD trees of input utterances nor is it required to produce AS approximations (i.e. UD trees or other human-conceptualised linguistic representations). Instead, LLM is expected to internalise ASs, akin to human language processing, and employ rules used to build them to identify tokens of well-formed sentences. Since predicting ASs is not a prerequisite for comprehending sentences, LLM is not instructed to do this.

2.4 Definition of evaluation tasks

Probing is a valuable methodology for uncovering abilities and limitations of NLP models, while solving specialised tasks (Conneau et al., 2018). It contributes to the interpretation of the information embedded in their internal representations.

The proposed probing tasks are designed to assess the linguistic competency of LLMs in recognising speech-specific noise and extracting well-structured and coherent utterances. Our objective is to gain a deeper understanding of whether LLMs have learned to distinguish semantically relevant content from speech-specific noise during training on extensive textual data. In all tasks, we benchmark LLMs' output against the gold-standard dataset, wherein tokens of well-structured utterances are annotated as *positive* instances and speech-specific tokens are *negative* instances.

2.4.1 Well-structure-task

It tests whether all tokens of well-structured utterances are preserved in utterances output by LLMs. In particular, we test whether extracted tokens indeed constitute well-formed and coherent sentences, as determined by UD approximations.
Example: In Figure 1,[1] the well-structured utterance (the bottom tree) adheres to the predicate-argument structure of the predicate '*podam*' (Eng. *I will give*).

2.4.2 Discourse, reparandum, and restart

These tasks test whether all tokens of a particular speech-specific type are correctly removed from utterances output by LLMs. The additional goal of these tasks is to identify which speech-specific phenomenon poses the greatest challenge for LLMs.
Discourse-task The idea of this task is to check whether LLM recognises non-linguistic tokens (i.e. pauses and inarticulate sounds) and correctly filters them out from final utterances.
Example: In Figure 1, there are three *discourse* subtrees marked with (brown boxes) that should not appear in the final utterance.
Reparandum-task This task investigates whether LLM recognises disfluencies (i.e. repetitions, substitutions, and reformulations) and correctly removes them.
Example: There is one *reparandum* token marked with (a blue box). This token together with its dependent *discourse* token (i.e. the string '*to...*') should be excluded from the ultimate utterance.
Restart-task This task tests whether LLM recognises all tokens of false start subtrees.
Example: There is one token with the *parataxis:restart* label. Its head-subtree marked with (a green box) represents the false start '*To niech pani...*' that should not be in the final utterance.

3 Experimental setup

3.1 Tested models

In this study, we examine various LLMs with the transformer architecture (Vaswani et al., 2017). First, we probe two powerful iterations of the Generative Pre-trained Transformer (Brown et al., 2020): GPT-3.5 and GPT-4, which are pre-trained to predict the next token in a document. GPT-3.5 is notable for its outstanding performance in NLU tasks. GPT-4 (OpenAI, 2023), in turn, is a multi-modal model that exhibits human-level performance on various benchmarks. Furthermore,

[1] All probing tasks are illustrated based on the example provided in Figure 1.

we evaluate publicly available LLMs, specifically Llama 2 (Touvron et al., 2023) and Mistral 7B (Jiang et al., 2023). Lastly, we examine Bielik (Ociepa et al., 2024), the recently released Polish LLM, which is derived from Mistral 7B.

Interacting via API, we prompt LLMs to extract tokens of well-structured utterances from noisy input utterances. As we aim for maximal determinism in LLMs' output, the temperature and the inference parameter n are set to 0 and 1, respectively.

3.2 Probing dataset

DiaBiz (Pęzik et al., 2022) is a large, annotated, multi-modal dataset comprising recorded and transcribed phone conversations in Polish. Its subset of 101 dialogues (3421 turns and 82,806 tokens) was manually annotated following the UD guidelines (de Marneffe et al., 2021). Each turn has an assigned conventional UD structure. If a turn comprises multiple sentences, their UD trees are interlinked using the *parataxis* label. In addition to the standard UD dependency types, the utterance trees contain the *discourse*, *reparandum* and *parataxis:restart* types.

We use the UD-annotated DiaBiz subset to construct a probing dataset. The new dataset is structured in a JSON format (see Appendix A), where each turn token is assigned the `status` value, either *True* (indicating its presence in a well-structured utterance) or *False* (denoting a speech-specific token unsuitable for inclusion in LLM's output). The dataset comprises 75,107 *True*-tokens, resulting in an average of 21.95 tokens per well-structured utterance. The remaining 7699 *False*-tokens build subtrees of 5577 speech-specific phenomena (see the *labels*-column in Table 3). These subtree tokens are slated for removal. Hence, in the context of *discourse*, LLMs are tasked with eliminating almost only speech-specific discourse tokens. For each *reparandum*, LLMs are expected to remove an average of two tokens, and for each *restart*, they should identify and filter out an average of 8 tokens.

The *discourse* dependencies typically align with individual tokens, whereas *reparandum* and the heads of *parataxis:restart* allow for the removal of other nested speech-specific dependencies. For example, the second *discourse* token belongs to the *reparandum* subtree (see the bottom UD tree in Figure 1). In the JSON structure, each token of a speech-specific subtree is annotated either as *True* (indicating its removal in a particular probing task) or *False* (indicating its preservation in a probing task). A single token may be annotated as *True* in the context of multiple speech phenomena.

3.3 Prompt engineering

Various factors are considered to engineer prompts that effectively guide LLM in extracting well-formed sentences from noisy utterances. First, we check whether providing an illustrative explanation of speech phenomena or incorporating explicit input-output examples (few-shot) in prompts enhances informativeness, finding the latter approach more beneficial. Second, regarding input and output formats, we note that only GPT-4 can reliably process JSON structures. As GPT-3.5 and other LLMs often generate incorrect JSON, they should be instructed to use strings for both input and output. Third, regarding the prompt language, i.e. English vs. Polish, we test different scenarios for the Polish Bielik LLM and observe that the instruction language has negligible impact on the resulting answer. We draft diverse prompts and empirically test LLMs with these prompts on a small set of 50 turns.

The final prompts (see Appendix B) are designed to be universally applicable across all LLMs rather than tailored to a specific LLM. They instruct LLMs to remove speech-specific disruptions and output acceptable utterances (i.e. well-formed phrases, sentences or sequences thereof). In addition to task-specific instructions, the prompts include a repertoire of speech-specific phenomena to be addressed and details regarding input and output formats, illustrated by examples.

4 Results

4.1 First experiment

To assess LLMs' ability to extract well-structured utterances from noisy transcriptions, their outcomes are compared to gold standard utterances from the probing dataset. The extraction quality is measured using accuracy, precision, recall, F_1-measure, and true negative rate (TNR), see Table 1.

The results confirm the superior performance of GPTs compared to open LLMs, particularly in recall (or sensitivity) values. GPT-4 and GPT-3.5 show high efficiency in extracting complete structures, with recall rates of 97% and 94%, respectively. In contrast, Bielik demonstrates significantly lower recall values of 74-75%, and Mistral and Llama perform even worse, yielding structures that are only approximately 50% complete.

LLM	accuracy	precision	recall	F_1	TNR	CPT
Llama	0.50	0.95	0.47	0.63	0.78	73.4
Mistral	0.56	**0.98**	0.52	0.68	**0.91**	70.1
GPT-3.5	0.92	0.97	0.94	0.95	0.69	91.9
GPT-4	**0.94**	0.97	**0.97**	**0.97**	0.69	93.5
Bielik	0.74	0.95	0.75	0.84	0.63	78.1
$\text{Bielik}_{\text{PL}}$	0.73	0.96	0.74	0.83	0.69	75.7

Table 1: Evaluation of LLMs' performance in extracting well-structured utterances from noisy transcriptions. The subscript PL denotes prompts formulated in Polish. CPT indicates the ratio of characters per turn.

To examine the disparity in recall values more closely, we conduct a comparative analysis of the number of extracted characters per turn.[2] GPT-4, achieving the highest recall value, retrieves an average of 93.5 characters per turn (see the last column in Table 1). Open LLMs, in turn, demonstrate lower recall values and lower character-per-turn ratios. Calculating a correlation between character counts and recall value reveals strong coefficients: Pearson's at 0.93 and Spearman's at 0.95. Furthermore, GPT-4's ratio of 93.5 characters per turn on average is remarkably closer to the gold standard ratio of 93.4. These nearly identical ratios suggest that GPT-4's extractions are relatively complete, resulting in the higher recall value.

High and comparable precision scores among LLMs indicate accurate extraction of positive instances, i.e. tokens associated with ASs. We further investigate LLM outputs for the correctness and completeness of their predicate-argument structures, evaluating missing dependency types and analysing their significance. Table 2 provides a statistical summary of missing dependency types, averaged across the UD dependency type categories: core arguments, non-core dependents, nominal dependents, function words, and other dependents.

The most serious errors stem from the absence of core arguments, which are vital for the coherence of predicate-argument structures. In Bielik's extracted utterances, over a quarter of core arguments are absent, signifying serious deficiencies in their ASs. Similarly, Mistral's and Llama's outputs frequently miss multiple core arguments. GPT-4's outputs, in turn, omit only 1.4% of core arguments, followed by GPT-3.5 with 3%, denoting that most GPT-extracted utterances are well-structured and coherent, albeit not all of them. Non-core dependents, with an average absence of 9-10% for GPTs, 23-29% for Bielik, 53-60% for Mistral and Llama, along with nominal dependents and function words, exhibiting an average omission of 23-27% for Bielik, 40-60% for Mistral and Llama, also contribute to the grammatical disruption of the extracted utterances. Last but not least, the absence of predicates poses a significant deficiency, particularly evident in GPT-3.5 and open LLMs, where 8% and 22-35% tokens annotated as *roots* (within Other dependents) are incorrectly filtered out. This highlights a serious problem of missing crucial constituents, which concurrently impacts the overall quality of extracted utterances.

The vast majority of tokens in the input data, specifically 90.7%, constitute well-structured utterances. This simplifies the task for the tested models and may mask their limitations in accurately identifying speech-specific elements that should be classified as negative instances. For a precise evaluation of rejected tokens, i.e. those which LLMs consider to be speech-inherent elements, we calculate true negative rates (TNR). The TNR scores, indicating the quality of detected speech-specific segments, are lower in comparison to the accuracy scores of extracting well-structured utterances by Bielik and GPTs. The TNR scores for these three models stand at 63-69%, while the average accuracy score is 73.5% for Bielik and even 93% for GPTs. This suggests that GPTs and Bielik incorporate many infrequent speech-specific tokens into the ultimate utterances. Llama and Mistral, in turn, show significantly higher TNR scores, with Mistral achieving 91%, indicating effective in-depth control over speech-specific noise.

The final issue concerns out-of-vocabulary (OOV) words, which are not part of input utterances and ideally should not appear in LLMs' output. LLMs are prompted to filter words rather than generate new ones or modify existing ones. Following the prompt instructions is a major challenge for Llama and Mistral that incorrectly generate 18K and 13K OOV words, respectively. Bielik is more accurate in following instructions, as it outputs 3.6K OOV words in the experiment with the English prompt and 2.6K OOV words with the Polish prompt. Both GPTs output a small number of OOV words: GPT-3.5 generates 467 OOV words, whereas GPT-4 produces 188 (see Appendix C for a detailed analysis of OOV words).

The OOV words are currently not categorised as

[2]Possible automatic tokenisation errors make token comparison unreliable. Therefore, we opt to count characters per turn to mitigate this risk.

Dependency category	Llama avg.	Llama ratio	Mistral avg.	Mistral ratio	GPT-3.5 avg.	GPT-3.5 ratio	GPT-4 avg.	GPT-4 ratio	Bielik avg.	Bielik ratio	Bielik$_{PL}$ avg.	Bielik$_{PL}$ ratio
Core arguments	*ccomp, iobj, nsubj, obj, xcomp*											
	925.5	59.50	793.33	45.10	65.00	2.99	**33.60**	**1.44**	433.17	27.52	441.67	26.46
Non-core dependents	*advcl, advmod, discourse:interj, expl, obl, vocative*											
	1548.50	55.99	1591.17	53.02	208.33	9.96	**136.50**	**8.87**	729.33	23.51	728.83	29.15
Nominal dependents	*acl, amod, appos, nmod, nummod*											
	555.00	50.17	452.20	39.45	29.80	3.11	**8.60**	**0.56**	272.40	23.74	255.60	22.95
Function words	*aux, case, cop, det, mark*											
	1446.60	57.49	1442.60	59.42	104.00	4.31	**44.20**	**1.97**	664.00	26.65	627.80	24.92
Other dependents	*cc, conj, dep, fixed, flat, list, orphan, parataxis, punct, root*											
	1522.60	55.41	1199.60	50.97	227.50	10.75	**162.38**	**4.45**	825.00	24.26	927.89	26.10

Table 2: Evaluation of dependency category instances missing in LLMs' outputs compared to gold-standard trees of well-structured utterances. avg. – the average number of missing instances within a dependency type class; ratio – the percentage of missing instances relative to gold standard.

Type	gold-standard labels	gold-standard single [# (%)]	gold-standard tokens	Llama tokens	Llama ratio	Mistral tokens	Mistral ratio	GPT-3.5 tokens	GPT-3.5 ratio	GPT-4 tokens	GPT-4 ratio	Bielik tokens	Bielik ratio	Bielik$_{PL}$ tokens	Bielik$_{PL}$ ratio
discourse	3720	3780 (4.6)	3791	3125	82.4	3769	**99.4**	3203	84.5	3420	90.2	2859	75.4	2961	78.1
reparandum	1719	3880 (4.7)	3926	2966	75.5	3511	**89.4**	2531	64.5	2346	59.8	2198	56.0	2489	63.4
restart	138	1096 (1.3)	1109	728	65.6	896	**80.8**	330	29.8	362	32.6	481	43.4	580	52.3

Table 3: LLM performance in filtering speech-specific tokens from transcriptions. Explanation: labels – the number of speech-specific instances; single – single speech-specific tokens outside well-formed utterances; tokens – the number of tokens filtered or to be filtered by LLMs; ratio – the percentage of tokens correctly filtered by LLMs.

false positives because they could be considered favourable improvements in other NLP tasks.

4.2 Second experiment

To gauge the speech-specific phenomenon posing the greatest challenge for LLMs, we compare their outputs against the probing dataset. We measure the percentage of filtered-out tokens associated with a particular speech-specific phenomenon, within the set of all tokens responsible for encoding this phenomenon in the probing dataset (see Table 3).

The results confirm the noticeable superiority of Mistral in effectively filtering *discourse*, *reparandum* and *restart* segments, compared to all other LLMs. The *discourse* phenomenon is relatively easy to identify for all LLMs except Bielik, as indicated by the ratio of 99% for Mistral, 84-90% for GPTs, 82% for Llama and only 75-78% for Bielik. Among phenomena that all LLMs except Mistral struggle to filter, the second most challenging one is *reparandum*. The most effective LLM – Mistral – removes almost 90% *reparandum* segments. Llama excludes about 75% *reparandum* instances, while GPTs and Bielik filter out just over half of the tokens constituting repetitions, substitutions and reformulations.

As evidenced by the low *restart* values, such as 30% for GPTs, 40-50% for Bielik and 66% for Llama, LLMs struggle to recognise the *restart* phenomenon. This suggests that LLMs face difficulty in identifying unfinished statements (false starts) which are intended to be replaced by restarts. Instead, most of these unfinished statements are treated by LLMs as syntactically or semantically sound parts of utterances. False starts that should be filtered out may be realised as proper clauses that are acceptable in other contexts. Their subtrees are typically extensive, averaging around 8 nodes (an 8-token clause can constitute a well-formed sentence in Polish). The absence of graphic or topographic clues makes it challenging to identify restarts as semantically irrelevant within the currently investigated contexts. Nevertheless, recognising and filtering out entire false start subtrees is imperative for constructing well-structured and coherent utterances and only Mistral achieves high efficiency in accomplishing this removal task.

4.3 Empirical observations

The results of the first experiment might suggest that LLMs, especially GPTs, excel at detecting speech-specific noise and extracting sentences that adhere to ASs. However, a closer examination of speech-related phenomena, which should not be incorporated into output utterances according to the proposed evaluation approach, reveals that Bielik and GPTs commit errors in filtering out noise. The most challenging phenomenon is *restart*. Comparatively less challenging, though still error-prone, are repetitions, substitutions, and reformulations (i.e. *reparandum*). The process of filtering non-linguistic elements labelled with the *discourse* type poses no challenge for tested LLMs. Conversely, Mistral demonstrates remarkable efficacy in filtering speech-specific segments. However, its filtering tends to be overly aggressive, excluding not only speech noise but also elements of predicate-argument structure (e.g. about 50% arguments). As a consequence, output utterances are incorrectly structured and lack coherence.

In summary, GPTs prioritise precision and careful error avoidance, resulting in residual speech noise, while Mistral's aggressive filtering strategy leads to serious grammatical errors. Regardless of the approach, the errors produced by LLMs reveal their defective language competence. The acquisition of deep syntactic and semantic rules remains an open issue, requiring careful consideration in LLM development.

5 Related works

Probing state-of-the-art LMs for their syntactic and semantic knowledge is a widely adopted diagnostic approach. Numerous studies have attempted to examine LMs using controlled test sets. Some studies focus on designing probing tests to directly inspect the model's internal structure and identify its regions correlated with linguistic information (Shi et al., 2016; Tenney et al., 2019b; Peters et al., 2018; Jawahar et al., 2019; Tenney et al., 2019a; Lin et al., 2019). For instance, Tenney et al. (2019a) demonstrate that BERT can effectively execute multiple stages of an NLP pipeline, including POS tagging, parsing, named entity recognition, semantic role labelling, and coreference resolution. They localise BERT's regions where linguistic information is embedded and which are responsible for each task.

Parallel investigations endeavour to probe models to measure their proficiency and limitations in representing language, with a particular focus on syntactic and semantic knowledge (Conneau et al., 2018; Marvin and Linzen, 2018; Poliak et al., 2018; Hewitt and Manning, 2019; Weissweiler et al., 2022). For example, Weissweiler et al. (2022) discover that LMs can classify sentences as instances of a particular linguistic construction, but they cannot extract the conveyed meaning and effectively employ it within a given context. Our research aligns with the latter line of work, focusing on LLM's linguistic competence.

Since our research partially explores speech understanding, we mention recent studies focusing on probing speech models for syntax. Shah et al. (2021) probe them to discern their ability to encode linguistic information, including the depth of syntax trees. Similarly, Shen et al. (2023) conduct probing tests on speech models to identify the loci where syntactic structures are embedded.

Speech processing typically involves two main stages – automatic speech recognition (ASR) and NLU, with an intermediate step often dedicated to detecting and possibly removing disfluencies (Chen et al., 2022; Wagner et al., 2024). Lou and Johnson (2020) aim at developing joint models that integrate ASR with disfluency removal. This approach results in refined transcripts, which standard NLP and NLU tools can subsequently process. In our evaluation approach, we test the capability of LLMs to detect and filter out noise. However, our goal is not to employ LLMs as noise detectors; rather, we seek to determine whether LLMs can prioritise the meaningful parts of utterances (i.e. well-structured sentences) while ignoring noise during processing noisy utterances.

6 Conclusions

In this study, we have introduced an approach aimed at evaluating the capabilities of LLMs within the realm of processing transcribed noisy utterances in Polish. Our primary focus is to ascertain whether LLMs possess adequate linguistic competence to detect well-structured sentences in noisy utterances.

To conduct this research, we leverage the prompting technique, in which the currently most powerful GPTs, two open LLMs (Llama and Mistral) and a Polish LLM (Bielik) are tasked with identifying speech-inherent noise and extracting well-structured utterances. The models' outcomes are rigorously evaluated using the probing dataset derived from the UD-annotated subset of DiaBiz.

Recognising speech-specific phenomena, especially false starts, presents a challenge for the tested LLMs. Mistral appears proficient in filtering out false starts and other speech-specific noise. This proficiency, however, does not stem from its language comprehension ability; rather, it arises from its strategy for aggressive filtering, wherein it eliminates not only noise but also required components of predicate-argument structures, resulting in grammatical errors. GPTs generally exclude fewer required arguments and semantically crucial modifiers but erroneously retain many speech-specific segments.

Numerous studies confirm that transformer-based LMs acquire individual syntactic and semantic rules and can perform syntactic- and semantic-based NLP tasks. Our experimental results also indicate that LLMs possess linguistic competence. However, this competence may be superficial or insufficient, as LLMs struggle to identify complete and coherent sentences in noisy utterances. This superficial competence prevents the full internalisation of ASs underlying human language comprehension. Deeper syntactic-semantic understanding is necessary for handling restarts and other speech noise to enable seamless conversation of LLMs (or large multimodal models) with humans. Alternatively, LLMs may be unable to apply all syntactic-semantic rules they have acquired, resulting in limited performance. In this case, psycholinguistic factors, such as shallow heuristics mixed with syntactic algorithms (Ferreira, 2003) or rational statistical inference (Gibson et al., 2013), could impact the behaviour of LLMs, as suggested by an anonymous reviewer. The application of psycholinguistic research methods may be highly valuable for the future evaluation of LLMs.

We anticipate that our novel evaluation approach will inspire further research into selective language processing. Considering that ASR outcomes used in voice assistants and other speech-based systems require additional text processing, and texts are predominantly processed with LLMs, LLMs should handle both written texts and spontaneous speech transcriptions. This ability is crucial for enabling human-like dialogue with machines. Moreover, by integrating speech and text understanding, our approach lays the groundwork for evaluating LLMs and potentially large multimodal models.

7 Limitations

Given the specific demands of our experimental setup, which entail the availability of datasets with annotated speech-specific elements, we have deliberately chosen to focus on a single, albeit less widely studied language, compared to pervasive English-only research. We use Polish for several reasons. First, the DiaBiz dataset is relatively new and likely unfamiliar to LLMs, and thus the possibility of data contamination is eliminated. Second, the utterances are transcribed with high precision, including all non-linguistic and speech-specific elements. Third, this choice poses an additional challenge for LLMs, requiring them to process a non-dominant language and a non-dominant text domain (i.e. training data for LLMs, except Bielik, allegedly encompass only a limited amount of Polish speech transcriptions). Building upon the preceding point, certain conclusions can also be drawn regarding LLMs' competence in cross-linguistically capturing universal linguistic properties, particularly those related to grammatical relations. Despite the evident constraint in language scope and generalisation, we hope this research will be positively received by the NLP community, creating opportunities for broader research in the future.

Our study follows the direction proposed by Conneau et al. (2018) to examine LLMs' capabilities and limitations. Therefore, our analyses have obvious limitations, as we do not inspect LLM's internal architectures to identify specific regions related to distinct linguistic features. We thus lack insight into LLMs' layers where speech-specific elements are recognised and syntactic-semantic structures are internalised. We plan to address this limitation in future research on open LLMs.

Acknowledgments

This work was supported by the European Regional Development Fund as a part of 2014–2020 Smart Growth Operational Programme, CLARIN — Common Language Resources and Technology Infrastructure (project no. POIR.04.02.00-00C002/19), and as part of the investment CLARIN ERIC: Common Language Resources and Technology Infrastructure (period: 2024-2026) funded by the Polish Ministry of Science and Higher Education (agreement no. 2024/WK/01).
We gratefully acknowledge Poland's high-performance computing infrastructure PLGrid (HPC Centers: ACK Cyfronet AGH) for providing computer facilities and support within computational grant no. PLG/2022/015872.
We would like to thank the anonymous reviewers and the meta-reviewer for their valuable feedback and constructive suggestions.

References

Tom Brown, Benjamin Mann, Nick Ryder, Melanie Subbiah, Jared D Kaplan, Prafulla Dhariwal, Arvind Neelakantan, Pranav Shyam, Girish Sastry, Amanda Askell, Sandhini Agarwal, Ariel Herbert-Voss, Gretchen Krueger, Tom Henighan, Rewon Child, Aditya Ramesh, Daniel Ziegler, Jeffrey Wu, Clemens Winter, Chris Hesse, Mark Chen, Eric Sigler, Mateusz Litwin, Scott Gray, Benjamin Chess, Jack Clark, Christopher Berner, Sam McCandlish, Alec Radford, Ilya Sutskever, and Dario Amodei. 2020. Language Models are Few-Shot Learners. In *Advances in Neural Information Processing Systems*, volume 33, pages 1877–1901. Curran Associates, Inc.

Angelica Chen, Vicky Zayats, Daniel Walker, and Dirk Padfield. 2022. Teaching BERT to wait: Balancing accuracy and latency for streaming disfluency detection. In *Proceedings of the 2022 Conference of the North American Chapter of the Association for Computational Linguistics: Human Language Technologies*, pages 827–838, Seattle, United States. Association for Computational Linguistics.

Alexis Conneau, German Kruszewski, Guillaume Lample, Loïc Barrault, and Marco Baroni. 2018. What you can cram into a single $&!#* vector: Probing sentence embeddings for linguistic properties. In *Proceedings of the 56th Annual Meeting of the Association for Computational Linguistics*, pages 2126–2136. Association for Computational Linguistics.

Marie-Catherine de Marneffe, Christopher D. Manning, Joakim Nivre, and Daniel Zeman. 2021. Universal Dependencies. *Computational Linguistics*, 47(2):255–308.

Nai Ding, Lucia Melloni, Hang Zhang, Xing Tian, and David Poeppel. 2016. Cortical tracking of hierarchical linguistic structures in connected speech. *Nature Neuroscience*, 19(1):158–164.

Fernanda Ferreira. 2003. The misinterpretation of noncanonical sentences. *Cognitive Psychology*, 47(2):164–203.

Angela D. Friederici. 2002. Towards a neural basis of auditory sentence processing. *Trends in Cognitive Sciences*, 6(2):78–84.

Edward Gibson, Leon Bergen, and Steven T. Piantadosi. 2013. Rational integration of noisy evidence and prior semantic expectations in sentence interpretation. *Proceedings of the National Academy of Sciences*, 110(20):8051–8056.

John Hewitt and Christopher D. Manning. 2019. A structural probe for finding syntax in word representations. In *Proceedings of the 2019 Conference of the North American Chapter of the Association for Computational Linguistics: Human Language Technologies*, pages 4129–4138. Association for Computational Linguistics.

Pauline Jacobson. 2014. *Compositional Semantics. An Introduction to the Syntax/Semantics Interface*. Oxford Textbooks in Linguistics. Oxford University Press.

Ganesh Jawahar, Benoît Sagot, and Djamé Seddah. 2019. What does BERT learn about the structure of language? In *Proceedings of the 57th Annual Meeting of the Association for Computational Linguistics*, pages 3651–3657. Association for Computational Linguistics.

Albert Q. Jiang, Alexandre Sablayrolles, Arthur Mensch, Chris Bamford, Devendra Singh Chaplot, Diego de las Casas, Florian Bressand, Gianna Lengyel, Guillaume Lample, Lucile Saulnier, Lélio Renard Lavaud, Marie-Anne Lachaux, Pierre Stock, Teven Le Scao, Thibaut Lavril, Thomas Wang, Timothée Lacroix, and William El Sayed. 2023. Mistral 7B. *Preprint*, arXiv:2310.06825.

Yongjie Lin, Yi Chern Tan, and Robert Frank. 2019. Open sesame: Getting inside BERT's linguistic knowledge. In *Proceedings of the 2019 ACL Workshop BlackboxNLP*, pages 241–253. Association for Computational Linguistics.

Paria Jamshid Lou and Mark Johnson. 2020. End-to-end speech recognition and disfluency removal. In *Findings of the Association for Computational Linguistics: EMNLP 2020*, pages 2051–2061, Online. Association for Computational Linguistics.

Rui Mao, Guanyi Chen, Xulang Zhang, Frank Guerin, and Erik Cambria. 2023. GPTEval: A Survey on Assessments of ChatGPT and GPT-4. *Preprint*, arXiv:2308.12488.

Rebecca Marvin and Tal Linzen. 2018. Targeted Syntactic Evaluation of Language Models. In *Proceedings of the 2018 Conference on Empirical Methods in Natural Language Processing*, pages 1192–1202. Association for Computational Linguistics.

Krzysztof Ociepa, Łukasz Flis, Krzysztof Wróbel, Adrian Gwoździej, SpeakLeash Team, and Cyfronet Team. 2024. Introducing Bielik-7B-v0.1: Polish Language Model.

OpenAI. 2023. GPT-4 Technical Report. *Preprint*, arXiv:2303.08774.

Barbara Hall Partee. 1984. Compositionality. In F. Landman and F. Veltman, editors, *Varieties of Formal Semantics*, pages 281–311. Foris, Dordrecht.

Barbara Hall Partee, editor. 2004. *Compositionality in Formal Semantics. Selected papers of Barbara H. Partee*. Blackwell Publishing Ltd, Malden, MA.

Matthew E. Peters, Mark Neumann, Luke Zettlemoyer, and Wentau Yih. 2018. Dissecting Contextual Word Embeddings: Architecture and Representation. In *Proceedings of the 2018 Conference on Empirical Methods in Natural Language Processing*, pages 1499–1509. Association for Computational Linguistics.

Piotr Pęzik, Gosia Krawentek, Sylwia Karasińska, Paweł Wilk, Paulina Rybińska, Anna Cichosz, Angelika Peljak-Łapińska, Mikołaj Deckert, and Michał Adamczyk. 2022. DiaBiz – an annotated corpus of Polish call center dialogs. In *Proceedings of the Thirteenth Language Resources and Evaluation Conference*, pages 723–726, Marseille, France. ELRA.

Adam Poliak, Aparajita Haldar, Rachel Rudinger, J. Edward Hu, Ellie Pavlick, Aaron Steven White, and Benjamin Van Durme. 2018. Collecting Diverse Natural Language Inference Problems for Sentence Representation Evaluation. In *Proceedings of the 2018 EMNLP Workshop BlackboxNLP*, pages 337–340. Association for Computational Linguistics.

Alec Radford, Jeffrey Wu, Rewon Child, David Luan, Dario Amodei, and Ilya Sutskever. 2019. Language models are unsupervised multitask learners. *OpenAI blog*, 1(8):9.

Pranav Rajpurkar, Jian Zhang, Konstantin Lopyrev, and Percy Liang. 2016. SQuAD: 100,000+ Questions for Machine Comprehension of Text. In *Proceedings of the 2016 Conference on Empirical Methods in Natural Language Processing*, pages 2383–2392. Association for Computational Linguistics.

Jennifer M. Rodd, Zhenguang G. Cai, Hannah N. Betts, Betsy Hanby, Catherine Hutchinson, and Aviva Adler. 2016. The impact of recent and long-term experience on access to word meanings: Evidence from large-scale internet-based experiments. *Journal of Memory and Language*, 87:16–37.

Jui Shah, Yaman Kumar Singla, Changyou Chen, and Rajiv Ratn Shah. 2021. What all do audio transformer models hear? Probing Acoustic Representations for Language Delivery and its Structure. *Preprint*, arXiv:2101.00387.

Gaofei Shen, Afra Alishahi, Arianna Bisazza, and Grzegorz Chrupała. 2023. Wave to Syntax: Probing spoken language models for syntax. In *Proceedings of INTERSPEECH 2023*, pages 1259–1263.

Xing Shi, Inkit Padhi, and Kevin Knight. 2016. Does String-Based Neural MT Learn Source Syntax? In *Proceedings of the 2016 Conference on Empirical Methods in Natural Language Processing*, pages 1526–1534. Association for Computational Linguistics.

Ian Tenney, Dipanjan Das, and Ellie Pavlick. 2019a. BERT rediscovers the classical NLP pipeline. In *Proceedings of the 57th Annual Meeting of the Association for Computational Linguistics*, pages 4593–4601. Association for Computational Linguistics.

Ian Tenney, Patrick Xia, Berlin Chen, Alex Wang, Adam Poliak, R Thomas McCoy, Najoung Kim, Benjamin Van Durme, Samuel R. Bowman, Dipanjan Das, and Ellie Pavlick. 2019b. What do you learn from context? Probing for sentence structure in contextualized word representations. *Preprint*, arXiv:1905.06316.

Hugo Touvron, Louis Martin, Kevin Stone, Peter Albert, Amjad Almahairi, Yasmine Babaei, Nikolay Bashlykov, Soumya Batra, Prajjwal Bhargava, Shruti Bhosale, Dan Bikel, Lukas Blecher, Cristian Canton Ferrer, Moya Chen, Guillem Cucurull, David Esiobu, Jude Fernandes, Jeremy Fu, Wenyin Fu, Brian Fuller, Cynthia Gao, Vedanuj Goswami, Naman Goyal, Anthony Hartshorn, Saghar Hosseini, Rui Hou, Hakan Inan, Marcin Kardas, Viktor Kerkez, Madian Khabsa, Isabel Kloumann, Artem Korenev, Punit Singh Koura, Marie-Anne Lachaux, Thibaut Lavril, Jenya Lee, Diana Liskovich, Yinghai Lu, Yuning Mao, Xavier Martinet, Todor Mihaylov, Pushkar Mishra, Igor Molybog, Yixin Nie, Andrew Poulton, Jeremy Reizenstein, Rashi Rungta, Kalyan Saladi, Alan Schelten, Ruan Silva, Eric Michael Smith, Ranjan Subramanian, Xiaoqing Ellen Tan, Binh Tang, Ross Taylor, Adina Williams, Jian Xiang Kuan, Puxin Xu, Zheng Yan, Iliyan Zarov, Yuchen Zhang, Angela Fan, Melanie Kambadur, Sharan Narang, Aurelien Rodriguez, Robert Stojnic, Sergey Edunov, and Thomas Scialom. 2023. Llama 2: Open Foundation and Fine-Tuned Chat Models. *Preprint*, arXiv:2307.09288.

Ashish Vaswani, Noam Shazeer, Niki Parmar, Jakob Uszkoreit, Llion Jones, Aidan N Gomez, Ł ukasz Kaiser, and Illia Polosukhin. 2017. Attention is All you Need. In *Advances in Neural Information Processing Systems*, volume 30. Curran Associates, Inc.

Michael S. Vitevitch and Paul A. Luce. 1998. When Words Compete: Levels of Processing in Perception of Spoken Words. *Psychological Science*, 9(4):325–329.

Dominik Wagner, Sebastian P. Bayerl, Ilja Baumann, Korbinian Riedhammer, Elmar Nöth, and Tobias Bocklet. 2024. Large language models for dysfluency detection in stuttered speech. *Preprint*, arXiv:2406.11025.

Leonie Weissweiler, Valentin Hofmann, Abdullatif Köksal, and Hinrich Schütze. 2022. The better your Syntax, the better your Semantics? Probing Pretrained Language Models for the English Comparative Correlative. In *Proceedings of the 2022 Conference on EMNLP*, pages 10859–10882. Association for Computational Linguistics.

Zhilin Yang, Zihang Dai, Yiming Yang, Jaime Carbonell, Russ R Salakhutdinov, and Quoc V Le. 2019. XLNet: Generalized Autoregressive Pretraining for Language Understanding. In *Advances in Neural Information Processing Systems*, volume 32. Curran Associates, Inc.

A Appendix

An excerpt of the JSON structure used in the probing dataset.


```
"1": {
    "token": "To",
    "status": false,
    "speech_type": {
        "discourse": false,
        "reparandum": false,
        "restart": true},
    "dep_type": "advmod:emph"},
"2": {
    "token": "niech",
    "status": false,
    "speech_type": {
        "discourse": false,
        "reparandum": false,
        "restart": true},
    "dep_type": "aux:imp"},
"3": {
    "token": "pani",
    "status": false,
    "speech_type": {
        "discourse": false,
        "reparandum": false,
        "restart": true},
    "dep_type": "root"},
"4": {
    "token": "...",
    "status": false,
    "speech_type": {
        "discourse": true,
        "reparandum": false,
        "restart": true},
    "dep_type": "discourse"},
"5": {
    "token": "to",
    "status": false,
    "speech_type": {
        "discourse": false,
        "reparandum": true,
        "restart": false},
    "dep_type": "reparandum"},
"6": {
    "token": "...",
    "status": false,
    "speech_type": {
        "discourse": true,
        "reparandum": true,
        "restart": false},
    "dep_type": "discourse"},
"7": {
    "token": "to",
    "status": true,
    "speech_type": null,
    "dep_type": "advmod:emph"},
"8": {
    "token": "ja",
    "status": true,
    "speech_type": null,
    "dep_type": "nsubj"},
9": {
    "token": "pani",
    "status": true,
    "speech_type": null,
    "dep_type": "iobj"},
"10": {
    "token": "podam",
    "status": true,
    "speech_type": null,
    "dep_type": "parataxis:restart"},
"11": {
    "token": "maila",
    "status": true,
    "speech_type": null,
    "dep_type": "obj"},
"12": {
    "token": ",",
    "status": true,
    "speech_type": null,
    "dep_type": "punct"},
"13": {
    "token": "(yy)",
    "status": false,
    "speech_type": {
        "discourse": true,
        "reparandum": false,
        "restart": false},
    "dep_type": "discourse"},
"14": {
    "token": "a",
    "status": true,
    "speech_type": null,
    "dep_type": "cc"
},
"15": {
    "token": "pani",
    "status": true,
    "speech_type": null,
    "dep_type": "nsubj"
},
"16": {
    "token": "mi",
    "status": true,
    "speech_type": null,
    "dep_type": "iobj"
},
"17": {
    "token": "prześle",
    "status": true,
    "speech_type": null,
    "dep_type": "conj"
},
"18": {
    "token": "szczegóły",
    "status": true,
    "speech_type": null,
    "dep_type": "obj"}
```

B Appendix

Prompts drafted in English.

```
The provided conversations in Polish
are transcribed and divided into turns.
A 'turn' is the continuous utterance of
a speaker participating in a dialogue
with at least one other person.
Besides the core grammatically coherent
structure of an utterance, its transcription
may include disruptions or extra elements
commonly found in spoken language:
- pauses: '...', (...) and '(yy)'
- repetitions, substitutions and reformulations
- restarts
Remove these speech-specific disruptions
and extra elements from the input turn and
output the cleaned-up turn:

Removal of REPETITION
INPUT:  (...) Dzień... dzień dobry pani.
OUTPUT: dzień dobry pani.

Removal of SUBSTITUTION
INPUT:  (yy) Czy ma pan przygotowany (yy)
        kod siedmio... (yy) ośmiocyfrowy?
OUTPUT: Czy ma pan przygotowany kod
        ośmiocyfrowy?

Removal of REFORMULATION
INPUT:  W związku z sytu... z obecną sytuacją
OUTPUT: W związku z obecną sytuacją

Removal of RESTART
INPUT:  To teraz część ... to ja pana teraz
        przekierowuję do części automatycznej.
OUTPUT: to ja pana teraz przekierowuję do
        części automatycznej.

Keep the grammatically correct and coherent
parts of the turn. Note that a list of words,
a single word, a single name or a non-verbal
phrase are considered an acceptable utterance.

You MUST answer in Polish. You output only the
words remaining after filtering speech-specific
elements.
You are NOT ALLOWED to modify input words or
output any novel words.
You CANNOT reveal and output the justification
for its answer.
```

Figure 2: String-based prompt in English.

````
The provided conversations (JSON structures)
in Polish are transcribed and divided into turns.
A 'turn' is the continuous utterance of a speaker
participating in a dialogue with at least one other
person.

Besides the core grammatically coherent structure
of an utterance, its transcription may include
disruptions or extra elements commonly found in
spoken language:
- pauses: '...', (...) and '(yy)'
- repetitions, substitutions and reformulations
- restarts

Remove these speech-specific disruptions and
extra elements from the input turn and output
the JSON structure with a list of cleaned-up turns:

INPUT:
```json
{
    cbiz_tc_53: [
     "(...) Dzień... dzień dobry pani.",
     "(yy) Czy ma pan przygotowany (yy) kod siedmio...
        (yy) ośmiocyfrowy?",
     "W związku z sytu... z obecną sytuacją",
        "To teraz część ... to ja pana teraz
        przekierowuję do części automatycznej."
    ]}
```

OUTPUT:
```json
{
    cbiz_tc_53: [
     "dzień dobry pani.",
     "Czy ma pan przygotowany kod ośmiocyfrowy?",
     "W związku z obecną sytuacją",
     "to ja pana teraz przekierowuję do części
        automatycznej."
    ]}
```

Explanation of the above example:
- 1. turn: pauses and repetition are removed
- 2. turn: pauses and substitutions are removed
- 3. turn: pause and reformulation are removed
- 4. turn: pause and restart are remove

Keep the grammatically correct and coherent parts of
the turn. Note that a list or a non-verbal sentence
is considered an acceptable utterance.

DO NOT insert additional words or characters.
DO NOT modify input words.
The input and output transcriptions MUST have
the same number of turns.
````

Figure 3: JSON-based prompt in English.

C Appendix

We analyse the out-of-vocabulary words newly generated by LLMs in detail and categorise them into (LLMs' outputs are highlited in green):

1. **corrections** of grammatical errors and typos:
   • *zadzwonię*$_{\text{[FUTURE TENSE]}}$ (Eng. *I will call)* → zadzwoniłem$_{\text{[PAST TENSE]}}$ (Eng. *I called*)
   • *płatności*$_{\text{[SINGULAR NUMBER]}}$ (Eng. *payments*) → płatność$_{\text{[PLURAL NUMBER]}}$ (Eng. *a payment*)

2. **completions** of elided words:
   • *dwóch roboczych* (Eng. lit. *two working*) → dwóch dni roboczych (Eng. two working days)

3. **questionable morphological modifications**:
   • aspect change: *nastawiałabym się*$_{\text{[IMPERFECTIVE]}}$ (Eng. *I would set myself up)* → nastwiłabym się$_{\text{[PERFECTIVE]}}$
   • gender change: *zajęłam*$_{\text{[FEMININE]}}$ (Eng. I occupied) → zająłem$_{\text{[MASCULINE]}}$

4. **completing false starts** instead of removal:
   • *Rozumiem, że... (yy) jeszcze raz jakbym... Przepraszam, jakby mogła pani jeszcze powtórzyć* (Eng. I understand that... (yy) again I'm like... I'm sorry, could you repeat once again) → Rozumiem, że [chodzi o płatność kartą]. Przepraszam, jakby mogła pani jeszcze powtórzyć.

5. Adding **English translations** instead of or with Polish output:
   • *(yy) Tak, potwierdzam.* (Eng. *(yy) Yes, I confirm.*) → Tak, potwierdzam. (I confirm.)

6. Adding **explanations**:
   • *Aha.* → Aha. (This is a non-verbal sound and not considered an utterance.)

7. **Incorrect language identification**:
   • *No SMS-em* (Eng. *Well, by text message)* → Brak SMS-ów (Eng. *No SMS-s*).

Multi-Cultural Norm Base: Frame-based Norm Discovery in Multi-Cultural Settings

Viet-Thanh Pham[1*], **Shilin Qu**[1], **Farhad Moghimifar**[1], **Suraj Sharma**[2], **Yuan-Fang Li**[1], **Weiqing Wang**[1], **Gholamreza Haffari**[1 *]
[1] Department of Data Science & AI, Monash University, Australia
[2] School of Business, Calvin University

Abstract

Sociocultural norms serve as guiding principles for personal conduct in social interactions within a particular society or culture. The study of norm discovery has seen significant development over the last few years, with various interesting approaches. However, it is difficult to adopt these approaches to discover norms in a new culture, as they rely either on human annotations or real-world dialogue contents. This paper presents a robust automatic norm discovery pipeline, which utilizes the cultural knowledge of GPT-3.5 Turbo (ChatGPT) along with several social factors. By using these social factors and ChatGPT, our pipeline avoids the use of human dialogues that tend to be limited to specific scenarios, as well as the use of human annotations that make it difficult and costly to enlarge the dataset. The resulting database - Multicultural Norm Base (MNB) - covers 6 distinct cultures, with over 150k sociocultural norm statements in total. A state-of-the-art Large Language Model (LLM), Llama 3, fine-tuned with our proposed dataset, shows remarkable results on various downstream tasks, outperforming models fine-tuned on other datasets significantly.

1 Introduction

Sociocultural norms are informal rules or guidelines that dictate acceptable behavior within a particular society or culture (Morris et al., 2015). These norms encompass a wide range of behaviors, including manners, customs, values, and traditions. They govern how individuals interact with one another and shape societal expectations regarding appropriate conduct in various contexts. With the rapid development of AI in the last decade, it is crucial to define effective methods for discovering and assessing the cultural knowledge of AI systems, especially the knowledge of sociocultural norms.

The study of cultural norm discovery has witnessed significant development in recent years. SOCIAL-CHEM-101 (Forbes et al., 2020), one of the earliest corpora, introduces social norms represented in a Rule of Thumb (RoT) format. NormBank (Ziems et al., 2023) is another large-scale corpus of norms that contains situational norms within a multivalent sociocultural frame. While these datasets have high-quality samples and can be applied to many culture-related tasks, they are constructed by humans, which is very time-consuming and costly. In response to this problem, Fung et al. (2023) introduced NormSage, a norm dataset constructed with a fully automated pipeline. Norm statements in NormSage are extracted by prompting Large Language Models (LLMs) with dialogue-based contents. The norms are then fed to a self-verification process to ensure their quality. While NormSage showcases a promising direction for automatic norm discovery, it is based on real dialogue data, which may not be available in different cultures and can be limited to specific domains. Moreover, social norms, relevant to specific frames, should possess the flexibility to be applicable across diverse dialogues, instead of being bound to a single specific conversation.

To address the above challenges, in this paper, we present an automated frame-based pipeline for norm dataset construction using ChatGPT in a multi-cultural setting. Socio-cultural norms are often strongly associated with several social factors (Zhan et al., 2023), and we refer to the combination of social factors as situational frames. Norms in the proposed dataset are generated by prompting ChatGPT with situational frames as the context, instead of using real-world dialogue content like existing works. These frames consist of carefully chosen social factors (culture, social relation, power distance, and so on) which help to

*Corresponding authors. Contact details: {thanh.pham1, gholamreza.haffari}@monash.edu

Proceedings of the 28th Conference on Computational Natural Language Learning, pages 24–35
November 15-16, 2024 ©2024 Association for Computational Linguistics

align the norm generation process. In this way, we will not have to collect dialogue data for specific cultures and can easily expand the dataset. Once the norms are extracted, we evaluate them both intrinsically and extrinsically. For the former, we use human evaluation to assess the quality of the extracted norm statements. For the latter, we employ the constructed norm database in various downstream tasks to prove the adaptability as well as the performance of our proposed dataset. To summarise, our contributions are as follows:

- We propose an automatic pipeline for extracting socio-cultural norm statements in multiple cultures. This pipeline makes use of the implicit cultural knowledge of ChatGPT, as well as a set of carefully chosen social factors, to derive meaningful norm statements. In this way, we address the aforementioned problems of pioneering works. By using social factors and ChatGPT, we avoid the high costs of human annotation. Additionally, our social factors can also replace human dialogues, which tend to be limited to specific domains (Fung et al., 2023).

- With the proposed pipeline, we construct the Multi-Cultural Norm Base (MNB) dataset and make it publicly available to the research community. The dataset contains 150k sociocultural norm statements for 6 different cultural backgrounds, extracted from 29k situational frames. MNB is also one of the very few datasets that feature multi-cultural settings. We will make the dataset and code publicly available upon paper publication.

- We conduct extensive experiments to analyze the quality of MNB, as well as to demonstrate the benefits of MNB in various downstream tasks. Intrinsic evaluation results highlight both the strengths and weaknesses of our method. We observe that using ChatGPT for norm extraction results in correct and insightful norms. At the same time, the model cannot utilize all of the given social factors, which, in many cases, leads to norms being too general. On the other hand, however, extrinsic experimental results show that MNB can generalize well across multiple related datasets and their corresponding benchmarks, outperforming other datasets significantly.

2 Related Work

2.1 Commonsense Knowledge Bases

Commonsense Knowledge Bases (CKBs) encapsulate essential information that mirrors human everyday understanding and reasoning, covering broad aspects such as relational taxonomies (Liu and Singh, 2004), logical associations (Zhang et al., 2018; Elsahar et al., 2018), and the underlying principles of causality and mechanics (Talmor et al., 2019; Bisk et al., 2020). Following Cyc's establishment (Lenat, 1995), there has been a significant advancement in the development of expansive, human-curated CKBs (Liu and Singh, 2004; Speer et al., 2017; Forbes et al., 2020; Bisk et al., 2020; Hwang et al., 2021; Mostafazadeh et al., 2020; Ilievski et al., 2021). Notably, ConceptNet (Speer et al., 2017) exemplifies a comprehensive commonsense knowledge graph, characterized by its structured representation of knowledge in entity-relation-entity triples. The ATOMIC (Sap et al., 2019) advances this domain by cataloging social interaction dynamics through nearly 880,000 annotated triples. Its enhanced iteration, ATOMIC2020 (Hwang et al., 2021), further integrates ConceptNet's relational framework with additional novel relations, thereby constructing a more elaborate CKB focused on event-related dynamics. Moreover, GLUCOSE (Mostafazadeh et al., 2020), derived from narrative texts in ROC Stories (Schwartz et al., 2017), delineates a framework for understanding causal relationships and effects based on foundational events, presenting a nuanced exploration of commonsense dimensions.

2.2 Sociocultural NormBase Construction

SOCIAL-CHEM-101 (Forbes et al., 2020) introduced a comprehensive dataset of social and moral guidelines, established through a crowdsourcing approach to gathering descriptive norms from various situations using rules-of-thumb as fundamental elements. Another critical contribution is from (Ziems et al., 2023), who introduced a scheme for hierarchically organizing the space of human behaviors that determine social norms, then employed humans to create NormBank, a social knowledge bank that leverages this contextual data to form contrast sets rich in conditioned defeasible social norms. Our methodology diverges significantly from that of NormBank by implementing an automated system to discover sociocultural norms, in contrast to the reliance of NormBank on manual annota-

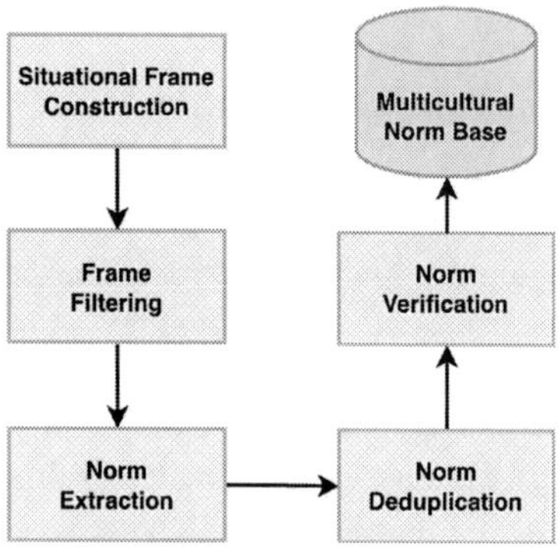

Figure 1: Proposed norm discovery pipeline.

tion. Moreover, we focus on extracting norms from situations that involve interactions between people to better reflect the cultural values and beliefs, rather than only representing accepted human behaviors in a specific culture. Moreover, the research by (Fung et al., 2023) introduced the NormSage framework, aimed at identifying norms embedded within conversations, utilizing LLM prompting and self-verification techniques, and drawing from real-life scenarios like negotiations, casual discussions, and documentaries. Our approach sets itself apart from NormSage by focusing on extracting norms through situational frames, which contain several social factors that mimic the interactions between people, therefore omitting the need for dialogue-based information.

3 Building Multi-cultural Norm Base

In this section, we describe our proposed automatic pipeline for collecting socio-cultural norms for various cultures. The following subsections will discuss the overall pipeline, as well as provide a detailed explanation for each step in the pipeline. For simplicity, the term socio-cultural norm will be referred to as norm or social norm for short.

3.1 Overall Pipeline

The overall norm discovery pipeline is illustrated in Figure 1. Starting from a collection of situation frames, we begin by filtering invalid frames, followed by performing norm extraction, deduplication, and verification to construct the multicultural norm base.

3.2 Situational Frame Construction

Social norms are context-specific patterns that govern behavior in a given situation (Morris et al., 2015). Therefore, we design situational frames to ground meaningful norms and create diversity in the proposed dataset. Following the works of social factor taxonomy (Hovy and Yang, 2021) and SocialDial (Zhan et al., 2023), these situational frames consist of several social factors that mimic the conversations between two speakers. Specifically, there are 10 key social factors in a frame, and these factors are categorized as either conversation-related factors (*Norm Category, Conversation Topic, Conversation Location, Culture, Formality*) or speaker-related factors (*Age, Gender, Social Relation, Social Distance, Power Distance*). Each of these social factors can take a range of values, some of which are sourced from SocialDial and LDC (Li et al., 2022).

Conversation-related Factors. In each situational frame, *Norm Category* can take values from greetings, requests, apologies, persuasion, and criticism. *Formality* is characterized as either formal or informal. *Conversation Location* spans various settings, including open areas, online platforms, homes, police stations, restaurants, stores, and hotels. *Conversation Topic* covers a wide array of subjects, such as sales, everyday life trivialities, office affairs, school life, culinary topics, farming, poverty assistance, police corruption, counter-terrorism, and cases of child disappearance. *Culture* refers to the cultural background of a conversation, which can be derived from one of the following values: American, British, Canadian, Indian, Afghan, and Chinese. These cultures exhibit distinct social norms and practices. For instance, Chinese and Indian cultures have deep-rooted traditions and customs that influence social behavior, while Western cultures like the American, British, and Canadian have different societal norms shaped by their histories and current societal dynamics. Including Afghan allows for the representation of a culture with different social and religious practices.

Speaker-related Factors. Regarding the speaker-related factors, *Social Distance* encompasses five distinct values: family, friends, romantic partners, working relationships, and strangers. *Social Relation* covers the following cases: peer-to-peer, elder-junior, chief-subordinate, mentor-mentee, student-professor, customer-server, and partner-partner. *Age* describe the age group of each speaker in the conversation, which can take the following values: child, teenager, adult, middle-aged adult, senior adult, and elderly. Similarly, *Gender* represents the gender of each speaker, which is categorized as either male or female. Lastly, *Power* *distance* is the perceived degree of inequality between the two speakers. This factor can take values from lower, equal, or higher, which indicates the inequality of the first speaker with respect to the second speaker.

3.3 Frame Filtering

With the values of each social factor predefined in the previous section, we then proceed to remove invalid situational frames. Invalid frames are those considered to have combinations of values that hardly represent real-world scenarios (eg. "a student and a professor discussing life trivialities in a police station", or "two colleagues discussing school life at a restaurant"). In general, we propose to train a frame classification model, along with several hand-written rules to filter out invalid frames. The process of this can be broken down into three steps: *Training Data Construction, Model Training, and Frame Classification.*

Training Data Creation. The training data of the frame classification model will have two parts, golden-labeled data and pseudo-labeled data. For the golden-labeled subset, we utilize the human-labeled frames from SocialDial, as many of the factor values of our data are sourced from this dataset. The number of human-labeled frames is 6,433. Regarding the pseudo-labeled data, we first sample 100,000 combinations of factor values, then prompt ChatGPT[1] for labeling. The prompt template is illustrated in Figure 2. To minimize the label errors made by ChatGPT API, we derive the probabilities of generating the tokens "Yes" or "No" from the API. Specifically, frames with either of the two probability scores higher than 0.85 are kept and assigned with the corresponding labels, and the remaining frames are removed. In total, we created a frame classification dataset with 41,016 samples, in which 16,547 samples are labeled as valid.

Model Training. With the constructed training dataset, we opt for the RoBERTa architecture (Liu et al., 2019) for frame classification. Specifically, the *large* version of the pretrained model is used for fine-tuning. We randomly split the constructed dataset into a training and development subset, with a ratio of 8:2. Adam optimization (Kingma and Ba, 2014) is used for model training. The choices of values for hyperparameters, such as learning rate, batch size, and number of epochs, are tuned through grid search over the development subset.

[1]https://openai.com/blog/chatgpt

Header: Consider the following context of a conversation between two speakers:

- The topic of the conversation is **{Conversation Topic}**.
- The sociocultural norm category is **{Norm Category}**.
- The cultural background is **{Culture}**.
- The level of formality is set to **{Formality}**.
- The location is **{Conversation Location}**.
- The social relation between the speakers is **{Social Relation}**.
- The gender of Speaker 1 is **{Speaker 1's Gender}**.
- The gender of Speaker 2 is **{Speaker 2's Gender}**.
- Speaker 1 is a/an **{Speaker 1's Age Group}**.
- Speaker 2 is a/an **{Speaker 2's Age Group}**.
- The social distance between the speakers is **{Social Distance}**.
- The power distance between the speakers is **{Power Distance}**

Question: Can this conversation happen in the real world? Answer with "Yes" or "No".

Figure 2: The prompt template for situational frame classification.

Frame Classification. The fine-tuned RoBERTa model is applied for frame classification. To ensure the label quality, we kept only the frames that the model predicted with a 0.995 probability value of the positive class. Additionally, we also introduced 30 handwritten simple rules that are used to filter out invalid frames. These rules are represented as combinations of different values for social factors that are not considered relevant in the real world.

3.4 Norm Extraction

The norm extraction process is illustrated in Figure 3. Specifically, we include the filtered situational frames in the prompts to discover social norms with ChatGPT. The prompt template includes four distinct parts:

- A template header describing the nature of the situational frame data.
- The body of the prompt template that outlines the social factors in a situational frame.
- A direct question describing the task of social norm extraction. This is followed by several constraints to ensure the quality and format of the generated norm statements are unified and controllable.
- Some Rules of Thumbs (RoTs) constraints. These contain RoT templates (Forbes et al., 2020) that will help to better structure the norm statement (eg. "In [X] culture, it is good to do action [Y], under situation [Z].").

3.5 Norm Deduplication

As the extracted norms can overlap in a single situational frame as well as across different frames,

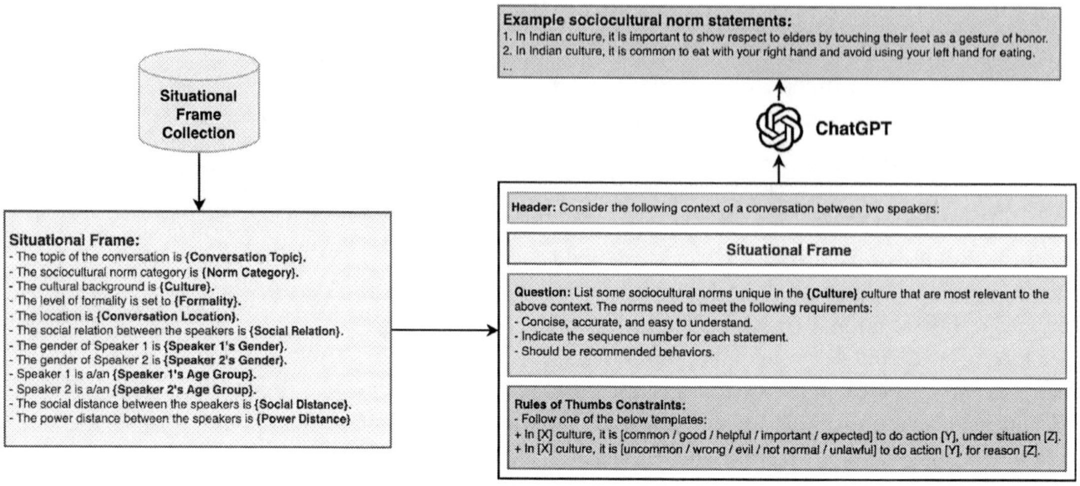

Figure 3: The norm extraction process with ChatGPT.

we remove one norm statement from each duplicating pair. This process is done separately for each culture. Specifically, we calculate the cosine similarity scores for every pair using their BERT embeddings (Devlin et al., 2019). If the similarity score is higher than 0.95, we flag the norm pair as duplicated.

3.6 Norm Verification

With the distinct norms obtained after the deduplication process, we begin to filter invalid norms. Invalid norm statements are norms that are incorrect in a specific culture, and we utilize ChatGPT for this verification process. Similar to Section 3.3, we prompt ChatGPT with a Yes-No question, and derive the probability of the token "Yes" for filtering. Details of the prompt are given in the Appendix A.1. The probability threshold for valid norms is set to be 0.85.

3.7 Dataset Summary

With the above pipeline, we obtained the Multicultural Norm Base (MNB), which consists of 155,929 norm statements, extracted from more than 28,804 situational frames of 6 distinct cultures. The norm statements also represent real-world scenarios, where they reflect daily conversational situations through various speaker attributes. The norm statistics of the 6 cultures are reported in Table 1. The cultures have roughly equal numbers of situational frames. On average, about 5 norm statements are extracted with each situational frame in our data.

Culture	# of Norm Statements	# of Frames
American	27,481	4,505
Canadian	25,726	5,072
British	34,213	5,133
Chinese	24,789	4,496
Indian	25,760	4,675
Afghan	17,960	4,923
All	**155,929**	**28,804**

Table 1: Statistics of norms in different cultures.

4 Experiments

To demonstrate the quality of our proposed method and dataset, we carry out experiments with our data and other related datasets. Our experiments are divided into two types: **Intrinsic Evaluation** and **Extrinsic Evaluation**. For intrinsic evaluation, we examine the quality of the constructed norm knowledge base and the norm extraction method. In the case of extrinsic evaluation, we demonstrate the applicability of our proposed dataset across different downstream tasks and compare the performance with other datasets.

4.1 Intrinsic Norm Discovery Evaluation

Similar to NormSage (Fung et al., 2023), we assess each norm statement on a Likert scale ranging from 1 to 5, where 1 denotes "Very Unsatisfied" and 5 denotes "Very Satisfied", for five criteria: *Relevance*, *Well-Formedness*, *Correctness*, *Insightfulness*, *Relatableness*. A detailed description of each criterion is provided in Appendix A.2.1.

As there are many norm statements in the dataset and evaluating all of them will be very time-consuming, we sample 200 norms from each culture for evaluation. Specifically, we randomly sam-

Culture	Relevance	Well-formedness	Correctness	Insightfulness	Relatableness
Chinese	3.91	4.10	4.03	3.97	3.93
Afghan	3.93	3.97	4.02	4.00	3.94
Indian	3.80	3.80	3.84	3.90	3.84
British	3.86	3.29	3.16	3.08	3.26
American	3.97	3.73	4.01	3.81	3.93
Canadian	3.67	4.10	4.05	3.72	4.04
All	3.85	3.82	3.83	3.75	3.80

Table 2: Average Likert scale (1-5) ratings of each culture in MNB.

ple 200 situational frames from each culture and then sample 1 norm statement from each of the frames. This ensures that the selected data is diverse and covers a wide range of scenarios. To perform the evaluation, we employed native Amazon Mechanical Turk workers for each of the 6 cultures to assess the data (e.g. British annotators will label the British samples) to ensure the annotation quality. Further information about the annotators and the annotation process is described in Appendix A.2.1.

Table 2 summarizes the Likert-scale scores assigned to the cultural norms of six cultures within the proposed dataset. The inter-rater reliability of the annotators, along with the score distributions of the 6 cultures, will be given in Appendix A.2.3 and A.2.4. Chinese norms consistently received high scores, particularly in Well-Formedness (4.10) and Correctness (4.03), indicating well-structured and accurate norms. Afghan norms also performed well, with high scores in Insightfulness (4.00) and Relevance (3.93), reflecting strong cultural understanding and applicability. Indian norms showed moderate scores across all metrics, suggesting balanced yet average representations. In contrast, British norms scored lower in Well-Formedness (3.29), Correctness (3.16), Insightfulness (3.08), and Relatableness (3.26), indicating structural and applicability issues. American norms were notable for their high Relevance (3.97) and Correctness (4.01), showcasing relevant and accurate norms. Canadian norms excelled in Well-Formedness (4.10) and Relatableness (4.04), highlighting well-structured and broadly applicable norms. Overall, while Chinese, Afghan, American, and Canadian norms were well-represented, British norms require significant improvement.

4.2 Extrinsic Evaluation on Downstream Tasks

To set up extrinsic evaluations, we derive several related datasets and their corresponding downstream tasks, which can be categorized into generation tasks and classification tasks. For all extrinsic experiments, we will use Llama 3[2] and perform fine-tuning with different instruction tasks. Specifically, the 8B version of the Llama3-Instruct model (Llama3-Instruct-8B) is used for fine-tuning, as it already has been fine-tuned with a large set of instruction tasks and can be used as the baseline in experiments.

4.2.1 Generation Task

In terms of the generation task, we opt for the Moral Integrity Corpus (MIC) (Ziems et al., 2022) for our experiments. The norms covered in this dataset mostly are sourced from Reddit and belong to the American culture. The authors of MIC have set up the task of RoT generation, which requires models to generate a norm statement with a given dialogue content. To carry out the experiments, we compare the performance of the following models:

- **Llama3** The original Llama3-Instruct-8B model.
- **Llama3$_{\mathbf{SC}}$** The Llama3-Instruct-8B model fine-tuned with the SOCIAL-CHEM-101 dataset. The instruction task is generating a norm statement based on a given situation and a behavior.
- **Llama3$_{\mathbf{MNB}}$** The Llama3-Instruct-8B model fine-tuned with our MulticulturalNormBase dataset. The instruction task is to generate a norm statement based on a set of social factors (similar to how we extract the norms with ChatGPT in Section 3.4).

While the NormBank dataset can be used for training as it is also a norm dataset, its norms have a very different structure compared to our data as well as SOCIAL-CHEM-101 and MIC. The situational norms in NormBank are represented as taxonomies of various factors, while in the other 3 datasets, the norms are stated as Rules of Thumb statements. As converting the taxonomy-based norms into RoT involves great complexities, we

[2]https://ai.meta.com/blog/meta-llama-3/

Metric	Llama3	Llama3 $_{SC}$	Llama3 $_{MNB}$
ROUGE-1	15.53	20.15	**30.41**
ROUGE-2	3.59	6.01	**14.90**
ROUGE-L	14.65	19.46	**29.50**
BLEU	11.95	16.16	**24.61**
BERT-Score	88.60	89.35	**90.93**
Avg. Len	11.65	10.95	**9.05**

Table 3: Experimental results on the MIC dataset. The average length of the norms in the data is 8.74.

chose to not experiment with the NormBank dataset for this generation task.

Following the authors of MIC, for the evaluation metrics, we apply the standard ROUGE (Lin and Hovy, 2003) (ROUGE-1, ROUGE-2, and ROUGE-L), BLEU score (Papineni et al., 2002), and BERT-Score (Zhang et al., 2020). The experimental results are reported in Table 3. All three models are evaluated in a zero-shot setting, meaning that they have not seen or been trained with the MIC dataset. It can be observed that when trained with cultural or commonsense knowledge data, the performance improves over the baseline. Both the Llama models trained with SOCIAL-CHEM-101 and our dataset present better results than those of the baseline model. On all metrics, the model trained with our data (**Llama3** $_{\mathbf{MNB}}$) achieves higher results than the one trained with SOCIAL-CHEM-101 (**Llama3** $_{\mathbf{SC}}$). Our model also generates sentences that have lengths closer to the golden sentences in the data than the **Llama3** $_{\mathbf{SC}}$ model. This demonstrates that the extracted cultural norms are highly useful, and can be used to train models to adapt on different benchmarks.

4.2.2 Classification Tasks

Regarding the classification tasks, we consider the following datasets for evaluation:

EtiCor. (Ziems et al., 2023) This is a corpus of etiquettes, consisting of texts about social norms from five different regions across the globe, serving as a benchmark for evaluating LLMs for knowledge and understanding of region-specific etiquette. Specifically, the dataset covers 5 regions: *EA (East Asia), IN (India), MEA (Middle East & Africa), NE (North America & Europe)*, and *LA (Latin America)*. With this data, the corresponding evaluation task is "Etiquette Sensitivity". Given a statement about etiquette, the task is to predict whether the statement is appropriate for a region. For this dataset, we use the entire data for evaluation.

NormBank. (Ziems et al., 2023) This is a knowledge base of situational norms in multicultural settings. To extract the cultural information of norms in this dataset, we identify constraints that mention "Person Y's country is XX" and link them to specific cultures. We follow their evaluation on the task of "Norm Classification". Specifically, this task requires models to classify a combination of behavior and some constraints to be either *expected, okay*, or *unexpected.* To perform an evaluation on this dataset, we randomly split the samples into a training and test subset, with a ratio of 8:2. The training set will be used to train a Llama 3 model, and the test set will be used to compare different fine-tuned models.

Regarding the models for evaluation, we fine-tuned the Llama 3 model separately with the NormBank dataset and our dataset. Both models are trained with the classification task and the training procedure is different for each of the datasets, as their data attributes are different:

- **Llama3** $_{\mathbf{NB\text{-}CLS}}$ The Llama3-Instruct-8B model fine-tuned with the training subset that we derived from the NormBank dataset. The model is trained for the task of norm classification, which utilizes the 3-class labels described previously.
- **Llama3** $_{\mathbf{MNB\text{-}CLS}}$ The Llama3-Instruct-8B model fine-tuned with our MulticulturalNormBase dataset. The instruction task is also norm classification. Since the norms of our dataset are all recommended behaviors, we perform data augmentation to negate a portion of the data. Specifically, we apply rule-based and model-based negative claim generation. For the model-based negative claim generation method, we utilize a pretrained BART model[3] to generate the negative version of a norm statement.

Apart from the fine-tuned models, we also experimented with a RAG (Retrieval Augmented Generation) based method with our data and the NormBank dataset. We derive two models - **Llama3** $_{\mathbf{MNB\text{-}RAG}}$ and **Llama3** $_{\mathbf{NB\text{-}RAG}}$ - which use the baseline Llama 3 model and retrieve the most relevant norms from our data and NormBank for a test sample, respectively. To ensure this method gets maximized results, we experimented with several numbers of norms being retrieved, ranging from 1 to 10, and reported only the best results. Interestingly, both **Llama3** $_{\mathbf{MNB\text{-}RAG}}$ and

[3]https://huggingface.co/minwhoo/bart-base-negative-claim-generation

Region	Llama3 (Baseline)	Llama3 $_{\text{NB-CLS}}$	Llama3 $_{\text{NB-RAG}}$	Llama3 $_{\text{MNB-CLS}}$	Llama3 $_{\text{MNB-RAG}}$
EA	69.97	66.88	63.67	**76.99**	73.75
IN	70.98	69.62	67.56	**80.72**	73.30
MEA	71.03	69.11	67.82	**78.94**	73.69
NE	82.62	84.07	79.40	**92.27**	84.95
LA	67.66	63.87	66.01	**76.05**	72.38
All	72.45	70.71	68.89	**80.99**	75.31

Table 4: F1 scores of different models on the EtiCor dataset.

Culture	Llama3 (Baseline)	Llama3 $_{\text{NB-CLS}}$	Llama3 $_{\text{NB-RAG}}$	Llama3 $_{\text{MNB-CLS}}$	Llama3 $_{\text{MNB-RAG}}$
British	7.22	**38.26**	20.44	23.16	19.24
Canadian	5.17	**57.82**	32.23	35.51	16.07
American	4.67	**50.20**	15.69	32.60	19.89
Afghan	4.37	**36.27**	15.69	28.90	14.21
Indian	26.21	**45.28**	35.76	36.82	26.60
Chinese	16.23	**43.81**	25.24	27.93	26.60
All	9.68	**45.26**	24.18	30.82	20.42

Table 5: F1 scores of different models on the NormBank dataset.

Llama3 $_{\textbf{NB-RAG}}$ achieve optimal results when using only 1 norm in the context.

Results on EtiCor. The experimental results on the EtiCor dataset are described in Table 4. The model trained with our dataset (**Llama3** $_{\textbf{MNB-CLS}}$) consistently demonstrates better results than the other two models, in all regions. The model shows the smallest absolute and relative improvements on the EA (East Asia) subset of EtiCor. This is because while our dataset consists of norms for the Chinese culture, EtiCor itself does not include Chinese data in the EA subset. Regarding **Llama3** $_{\textbf{NB-CLS}}$, while the nature of NormBank is also similar to EtiCor, however, the model does not achieve better overall results than the baseline Llama3 model, except for the NE (North America & Europe) subset, where the model demonstrates an improvement. This is understandable, as the portion of North American data accounts for almost 30% of the NormBank dataset. Despite being not as good as fine-tuning, the retrieval-based method also shows its improvements over the baseline, where the **Llama3** $_{\textbf{MNB-RAG}}$ model achieves roughly 2.8% F1 improvement over the **Llama3** model.

Results on NormBank. The experimental results of different models on the NormBank dataset are described in Table 5. **Llama3** $_{\textbf{NB-CLS}}$ obviously achieves the best results in terms of F1 score, as it is trained on the NormBank data. However, **Llama3** $_{\textbf{MNB-CLS}}$ - the model trained with MNB still shows great improvements over the baseline, with more than 21% absolute improvements in F1 score. In terms of retrieval-based model, **Llama3** $_{\textbf{MNB-RAG}}$ and **Llama3** $_{\textbf{NB-RAG}}$ achieve competitive results, even though **Llama3** $_{\textbf{NB-RAG}}$ takes advantage of retrieving norms from NormBank itself. Interestingly, **Llama3** $_{\textbf{MNB-RAG}}$ reaches a better F1 score than **Llama3** $_{\textbf{NB-RAG}}$ on the American subset, despite this is the largest subset of the NormBank dataset. These results have proven that models utilizing our MNB dataset can generalize well across different domains and cultures, in both cases of fine-tuning and RAG.

5 Conclusions

In this paper, we propose an automatic norm discovery pipeline using ChatGPT for the multi-cultural setting. The pipeline extracts norm statements upon situational frames filled with crucial social factors. As real dialogues are not always available and can be limited to some domains, we have showcased that it is possible to extract meaningful norm statements only from social factors. Our derived norm database has shown its effectiveness in the experiments, achieving remarkable results on several downstream tasks and outperforming other norm datasets. In the future, we plan to expand the data with coverage to more cultures and implement large language models embedded with explicit cultural knowledge.

Acknowledgement

This work is partly supported by the ARC Future Fellowship FT190100039. This material is based on research sponsored by DARPA under agreement number HR001122C0029 (CCU Program). The U.S. Government is authorized to reproduce and distribute reprints for Governmental purposes notwithstanding any copyright notation thereon.

Limitations

Our proposed pipeline is based on the implicit knowledge of ChatGPT from OpenAI to extract cultural norm statements from conversational situations. While ChatGPT is trained on a large amount of data, its cultural knowledge and reasoning capabilities can have potential bias. We also acknowledge that cultural norms can vary and evolve significantly over time, which requires LLM to have better adaptation to new data. Despite the availability of more robust LLMs, such as GPT-4[4], we opted to use ChatGPT in our experiments due to the time limitation and costly usage of GPT-4. Additionally, more datasets should be compared with the proposed MNB dataset in future works. NormSage (Fung et al., 2023) is the closest work to ours, as it also has the multi-cultural element, but at the time of submitting this paper, the NormSage dataset and code are not publicly available for us to make a fair comparison in the experiments.

Another limitation of our work is the limited number of human annotators for intrinsic evaluation. We acknowledge that hiring more people to annotate the norms will better represent the norm quality, but due to the time constraint and cost limit, there is only one annotator for each culture. Although the chosen annotators are all native, there can still exist potential biases in the evaluation process.

Ethical Considerations

We recognize that automatically generated sociocultural norm statements can carry an authoritative and normative tone (Fung et al., 2023). Therefore, we want to emphasize that these statements are not intended to serve as the basis for establishing a normative system or framework within any society. Their application in any operational system must be approached with caution. It is imperative to involve manual oversight to validate their accuracy prior to deployment. Consequently, these norm statements primarily serve only research purposes.

[4]https://openai.com/gpt-4

References

Yonatan Bisk, Rowan Zellers, Ronan Le bras, Jianfeng Gao, and Yejin Choi. 2020. Piqa: Reasoning about physical commonsense in natural language. *Proceedings of the AAAI Conference on Artificial Intelligence*, 34(05):7432–7439.

Jacob Devlin, Ming-Wei Chang, Kenton Lee, and Kristina Toutanova. 2019. Bert: Pre-training of deep bidirectional transformers for language understanding. In *North American Chapter of the Association for Computational Linguistics*.

Hady Elsahar, Pavlos Vougiouklis, Arslen Remaci, Christophe Gravier, Jonathon Hare, Frederique Laforest, and Elena Simperl. 2018. T-rex: A large scale alignment of natural language with knowledge base triples. In *Proceedings of the Eleventh International Conference on Language Resources and Evaluation (LREC 2018)*.

Maxwell Forbes, Jena D. Hwang, Vered Shwartz, Maarten Sap, and Yejin Choi. 2020. Social chemistry 101: Learning to reason about social and moral norms. In *Proceedings of the 2020 Conference on Empirical Methods in Natural Language Processing (EMNLP)*, pages 653–670, Online. Association for Computational Linguistics.

Yi Fung, Tuhin Chakrabarty, Hao Guo, Owen Rambow, Smaranda Muresan, and Heng Ji. 2023. NORMSAGE: Multi-lingual multi-cultural norm discovery from conversations on-the-fly. In *Proceedings of the 2023 Conference on Empirical Methods in Natural Language Processing*, pages 15217–15230, Singapore. Association for Computational Linguistics.

Dirk Hovy and Diyi Yang. 2021. The importance of modeling social factors of language: Theory and practice. In *Proceedings of the 2021 Conference of the North American Chapter of the Association for Computational Linguistics: Human Language Technologies*, pages 588–602, Online. Association for Computational Linguistics.

Jena D. Hwang, Chandra Bhagavatula, Ronan Le Bras, Jeff Da, Keisuke Sakaguchi, Antoine Bosselut, and Yejin Choi. 2021. (comet-) atomic 2020: On symbolic and neural commonsense knowledge graphs. *Proceedings of the AAAI Conference on Artificial Intelligence*, 35:6384–6392.

Filip Ilievski, Pedro Szekely, and Bin Zhang. 2021. Cskg: The commonsense knowledge graph. In *The Semantic Web: 18th International Conference, ESWC 2021, Virtual Event, June 6–10, 2021, Proceedings 18*, pages 680–696. Springer.

Diederik P. Kingma and Jimmy Ba. 2014. Adam: A method for stochastic optimization. *CoRR*, abs/1412.6980.

Douglas B Lenat. 1995. Cyc: A large-scale investment in knowledge infrastructure. *Communications of the ACM*, 38(11):33–38.

Xuansong Li, Stephanie Strassel, Karen Jones, Brian Antonishek, and Jonathan G. Fiscus. 2022. Havic med novel 1 test – videos, metadata and annotation. *Web Download*.

Chin-Yew Lin and Eduard Hovy. 2003. Automatic evaluation of summaries using n-gram co-occurrence statistics. In *Proceedings of the 2003 Human Language Technology Conference of the North American Chapter of the Association for Computational Linguistics*, pages 150–157.

Hugo Liu and Push Singh. 2004. Conceptnet—a practical commonsense reasoning tool-kit. *BT technology journal*, 22(4):211–226.

Yinhan Liu, Myle Ott, Naman Goyal, Jingfei Du, Mandar Joshi, Danqi Chen, Omer Levy, Mike Lewis, Luke Zettlemoyer, and Veselin Stoyanov. 2019. Roberta: A robustly optimized BERT pretraining approach. *CoRR*, abs/1907.11692.

Michael W. Morris, Ying yi Hong, Chi yue Chiu, and Zhi Liu. 2015. Normology: Integrating insights about social norms to understand cultural dynamics. *Organizational Behavior and Human Decision Processes*, 129:1–13.

Nasrin Mostafazadeh, Aditya Kalyanpur, Lori Moon, David Buchanan, Lauren Berkowitz, Or Biran, and Jennifer Chu-Carroll. 2020. Glucose: Generalized and contextualized story explanations. In *Proceedings of the 2020 Conference on Empirical Methods in Natural Language Processing (EMNLP)*, pages 4569–4586.

Kishore Papineni, Salim Roukos, Todd Ward, and Wei-Jing Zhu. 2002. Bleu: a method for automatic evaluation of machine translation. In *Proceedings of the 40th Annual Meeting on Association for Computational Linguistics*, ACL '02, page 311–318, USA. Association for Computational Linguistics.

Maarten Sap, Ronan Le Bras, Emily Allaway, Chandra Bhagavatula, Nicholas Lourie, Hannah Rashkin, Brendan Roof, Noah A. Smith, and Yejin Choi. 2019. Atomic: An atlas of machine commonsense for if-then reasoning. *Proceedings of the AAAI Conference on Artificial Intelligence*, 33:3027–3035.

Roy Schwartz, Maarten Sap, Ioannis Konstas, Leila Zilles, Yejin Choi, and Noah A. Smith. 2017. The effect of different writing tasks on linguistic style: A case study of the ROC story cloze task. In *Proceedings of the 21st Conference on Computational Natural Language Learning (CoNLL 2017)*, pages 15–25, Vancouver, Canada. Association for Computational Linguistics.

Robyn Speer, Joshua Chin, and Catherine Havasi. 2017. Conceptnet 5.5: An open multilingual graph of general knowledge. *Proceedings of the AAAI Conference on Artificial Intelligence*, 31(1).

Alon Talmor, Jonathan Herzig, Nicholas Lourie, and Jonathan Berant. 2019. CommonsenseQA: A question answering challenge targeting commonsense knowledge. In *Proceedings of the 2019 Conference of the North American Chapter of the Association for Computational Linguistics: Human Language Technologies, Volume 1 (Long and Short Papers)*, pages 4149–4158, Minneapolis, Minnesota. Association for Computational Linguistics.

Haolan Zhan, Zhuang Li, Yufei Wang, Linhao Luo, Tao Feng, Xiaoxi Kang, Yuncheng Hua, Lizhen Qu, Lay-Ki Soon, Suraj Sharma, Ingrid Zukerman, Zhaleh Semnani-Azad, and Gholamreza Haffari. 2023. Socialdial: A benchmark for socially-aware dialogue systems. In *SIGIR '23: Proceedings of the 46th International ACM SIGIR Conference on Research and Development in Information Retrieval*, page 2712–2722, New York, NY, USA. Association for Computing Machinery.

Sheng Zhang, Xiaodong Liu, Jingjing Liu, Jianfeng Gao, Kevin Duh, and Benjamin Van Durme. 2018. Record: Bridging the gap between human and machine commonsense reading comprehension. *arXiv preprint arXiv:1810.12885*.

Tianyi Zhang, Varsha Kishore, Felix Wu, Kilian Q. Weinberger, and Yoav Artzi. 2020. Bertscore: Evaluating text generation with bert. In *International Conference on Learning Representations*.

Caleb Ziems, Jane Dwivedi-Yu, Yi-Chia Wang, Alon Halevy, and Diyi Yang. 2023. NormBank: A knowledge bank of situational social norms. In *Proceedings of the 61st Annual Meeting of the Association for Computational Linguistics (Volume 1: Long Papers)*, pages 7756–7776, Toronto, Canada. Association for Computational Linguistics.

Caleb Ziems, Jane Yu, Yi-Chia Wang, Alon Halevy, and Diyi Yang. 2022. The moral integrity corpus: A benchmark for ethical dialogue systems. In *Proceedings of the 60th Annual Meeting of the Association for Computational Linguistics (Volume 1: Long Papers)*, pages 3755–3773, Dublin, Ireland. Association for Computational Linguistics.

A Appendix

A.1 Norm Verification

As discussed in Section 3.6, we prompt ChatGPT to filter invalid norm statements. Figure 4 illustrates the prompt template for norm verification. Similar to previous prompt templates in Section 3.4 and Section 3.6, this template includes a header describing the nature of the situational frame, and a body outlining the social factors.

A.2 Intrinsic Evaluation

A.2.1 Evaluation Criteria

The definition for each criterion of the intrinsic evaluation process is as follows:

Culture	Relevance	Well-formedness	Correctness	Insightfulness	Relatableness
Chinese	0.74	0.66	0.59	0.65	0.72
Afghan	0.75	0.76	0.62	0.77	0.73
Indian	0.75	0.76	0.66	0.67	0.69
British	0.65	0.74	0.73	0.71	0.91
American	0.60	0.70	0.70	0.73	0.72
Canadian	0.72	0.59	0.68	0.69	0.68

Table 6: Krippendorff's Alpha coefficient of different metrics for each culture.

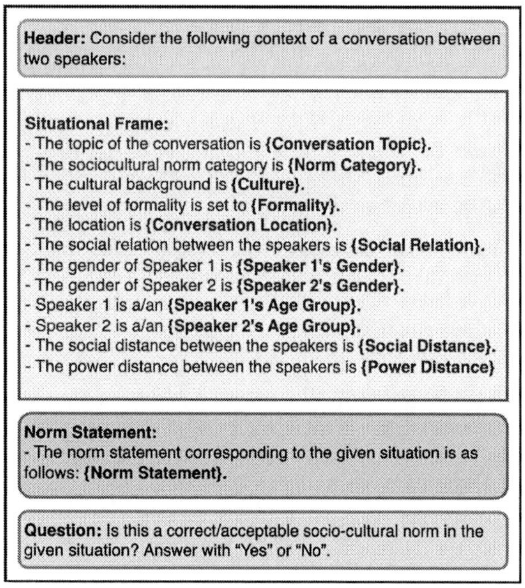

Figure 4: Prompt template for norm verification.

- **Relevance**. This criterion measures how well the situation inspires the generated norm. If a norm does not use the provided information from the situational frame, regardless of whether the norm is correct or not, the relevance score should be low.

- **Well-Formedness**. This criterion measures how well is the norm structured – is the norm self-contained, and does it include both a judgment of acceptability and an action or societal/cultural phenomena that is assessed?

- **Correctness**. This criterion measures the correctness of the norm. If a norm is considered to be correct in a given culture, its correctness score should be high.

- **Insightfullness**. This criterion measures the degree to which the norm conveys an enlightening understanding of what is considered acceptable and standard in the provided cultural background.

- **Relatableness**. This criterion measures the degree of generalization of a norm. If the given norm is highly applicable in various situations, the relatableness score should be high.

A.2.2 Annotation Settings

Worker Qualification. To ensure that the MTurk workers are native to the 6 cultures, we designed a qualification test consisting of cultural-related questions, provided in the respective native languages. Additionally, the questions are given in images, preventing the workers from searching for the answers directly on public media. Workers must pass this qualification test demonstrating a success rate of 95% or higher. To do the labeling task for intrinsic evaluation, workers who pass the initial qualification test then proceed to do another test of understanding the task instruction, in which workers with success rates of 98% are chosen to do the annotation for intrinsic evaluation.

Annotation Qualification. To ensure the high quality of the intrinsic evaluation process, each norm is scored by 5 native workers. After the norms are annotated, we perform a manual check to verify the scores.

A.2.3 Inter-rater Reliability

To assess the agreement rate among annotators, we apply Krippendorff's Alpha coefficient with each intrinsic evaluation metrics. Table 6 describe the values for each culture. Overall, the results highlight varying degrees of annotator agreement, with some metrics and cultures showing strong reliability while others indicate the need for further refinement in evaluation criteria.

A.2.4 Intrinsic Score Distribution

We provide the intrinsic score distribution of each culture in Figure 5. Overall, most cultures exhibit acceptable quality in each evaluation metric, where the distributions skewed toward scores of 4 and 5.

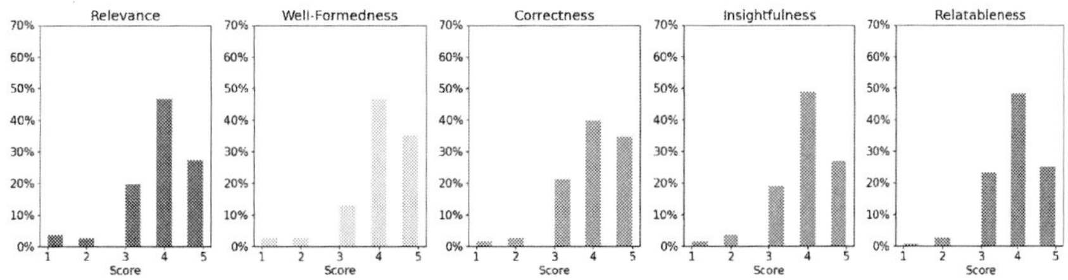

(a) Score distribution of the Chinese culture.

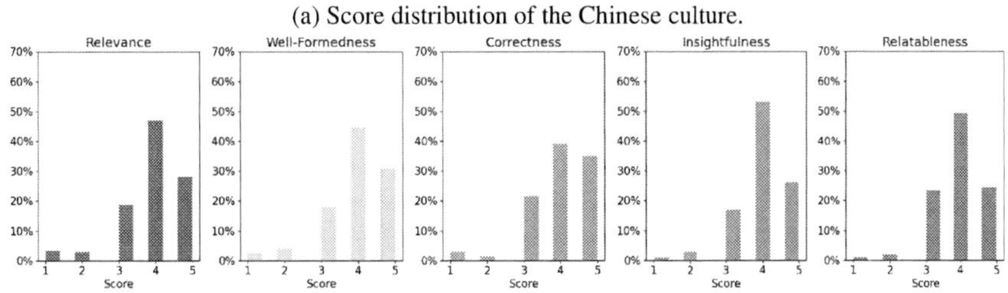

(b) Score distribution of the Afghan culture.

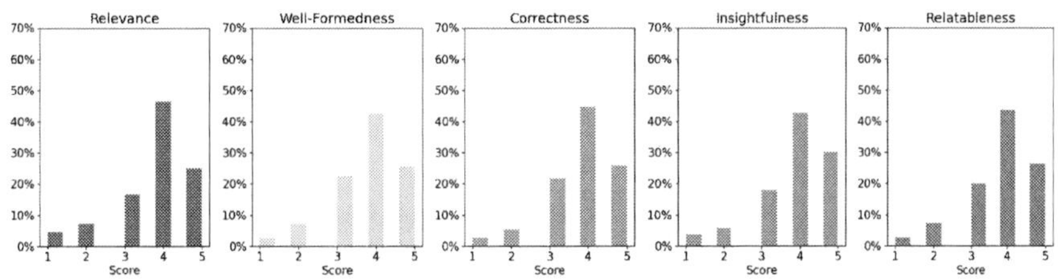

(c) Score distribution of the Indian culture.

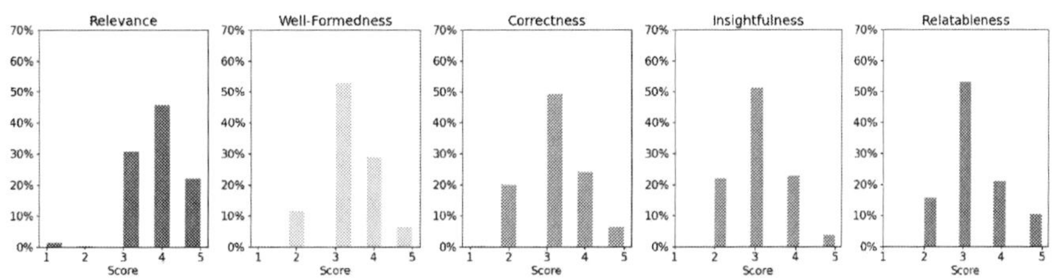

(d) Score distribution of the British culture.

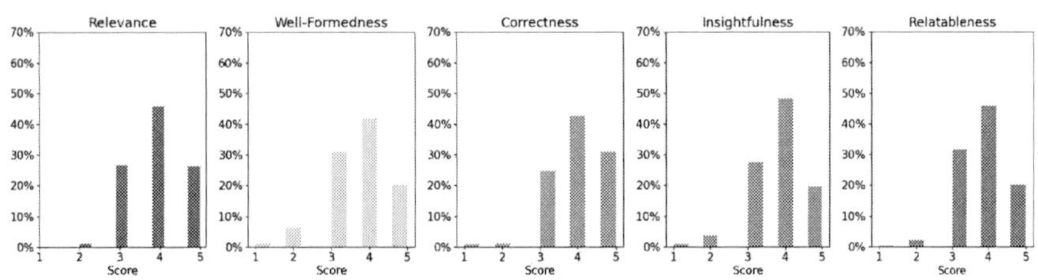

(e) Score distribution of the American culture.

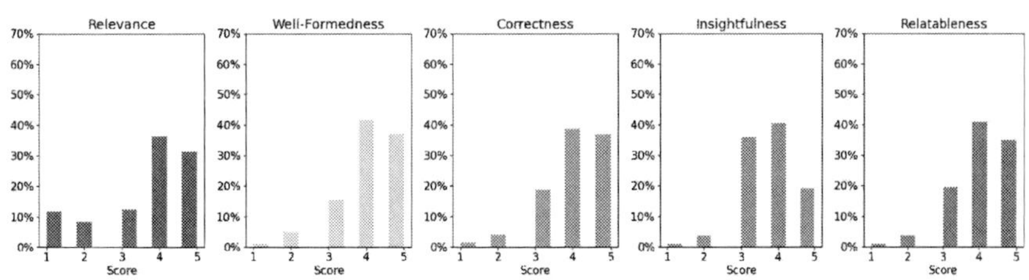

(f) Score distribution of the Canadian culture.

Figure 5: Likert-scale rating distribution of each culture.

Lossy Context Surprisal Predicts Task-Dependent Patterns in Relative Clause Processing

Kate McCurdy and **Michael Hahn**
Universität des Saarlandes

Abstract

English relative clauses are a critical test case for theories of syntactic processing. Expectation- and memory-based accounts make opposing predictions, and behavioral experiments have found mixed results. We present a technical extension of Lossy Context Surprisal (LCS) and use it to model relative clause processing in three behavioral experiments. LCS predicts key results at distinct retention rates, showing that task-dependent memory demands can account for discrepant behavioral patterns in the literature.

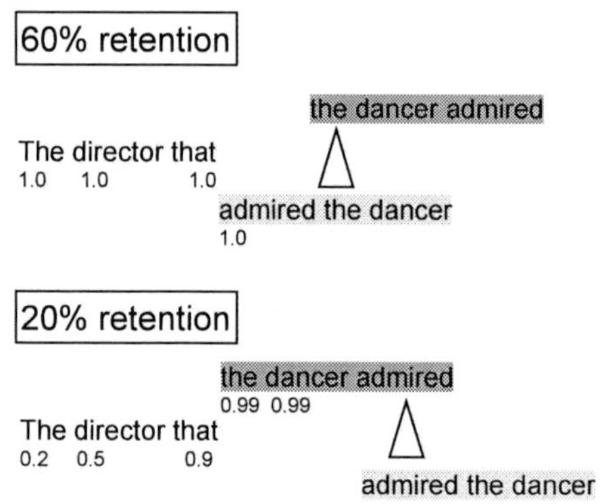

Figure 1: Illustration of lossy context surprisal (LCS) with retention probabilities of individual words. At high retention rates (top), LCS predicts an expectation-based processing slowdown at "the" for object relative clauses (red). At low retention rates (bottom), LCS predicts a memory-based processing slowdown at the verb.

1 Introduction

A fundamental goal of computational psycholinguistics is to predict and explain syntactic processing difficulty as manifested in reading times. Surprisal from modern language models is a strong predictor of reading times on naturalistic text: words take longer to read when they are less predictable (e.g. Wilcox et al., 2023). This finding aligns with expectation-based theories of syntactic processing (Hale, 2001; Levy, 2008). However, surprisal fails to account for certain effects from the psycholinguistic literature — particularly *locality effects*, in which longer syntactic dependencies lead to increased processing effort (e.g. Grodner and Gibson, 2005; Bartek et al., 2011). Under surprisal theory, this is unexpected: additional intervening context should generally make prediction easier.

Locality effects are naturally explained in terms of human memory limitations, which motivate memory-based theories of syntactic processing. One example is Dependency Locality Theory (Gibson, 1998; Gibson et al., 2000), which posits that the processing cost of integrating a syntactic dependency is proportional to dependency length. Similar locality predictions arise from cue-based retrieval theories (e.g. Lewis and Vasishth, 2005).

Recent research has offered a principled conceptual unification of expectation- and memory-based perspectives in terms of *Lossy-Context Surprisal* (LCS; Futrell et al., 2020). This theory holds that expectations are derived from imperfect memory representations of the context; hence, words are easy to process only when they are easy to predict from lossy context representations. Resource-Rational Lossy-Context Surprisal (RR-LCS) (Hahn et al., 2022) implements LCS for general input by constraining GPT-2 (Radford et al., 2019) with rationally optimized lossy context representations.

Here, we use LCS to model memory and expectation in the context of English relative clause processing (Figure 1) – long considered a key setting where memory- and expectation-based models make opposing predictions (e.g. Levy, 2008, 2013). Object relative clauses (ORCs), such as "The director that the dancer admired," are more difficult to process than subject relative clauses (SRCs), such as "The director that admired the dancer." Surprisal theory and DLT differ as to *when* this

Proceedings of the 28th Conference on Computational Natural Language Learning, pages 36–45
November 15-16, 2024 ©2024 Association for Computational Linguistics

difficulty arises in incremental processing. Under the expectation-based account of surprisal theory, comprehenders use their experience of English syntactic distributions to predict upcoming structures. Subject relatives are more frequent than object relatives in written corpora (Roland et al., 2007). Therefore, given the prefix "The director that," readers should expect a tensed verb such as "admired," and slow down on encountering the ORC determiner "the." Surprisal theory thus predicts that the processing difficulty for ORCs relative to SRCs will appear primarily on the determiner. By contrast, DLT posits that processing difficulty reflects the integration of long-distance dependencies. Under this account, the main slowdown in ORCs should instead appear at the verb "admired," as comprehenders integrate the dependency to the distant object "director."

Behavioral studies of relative clause processing have found discrepant results depending on the task. Experimental data from eye-tracking (Traxler et al., 2002; Staub, 2010) and self-paced reading (Grodner and Gibson, 2005; Roland et al., 2007; Frinsel and Christiansen, 2024) support the memory-based prediction of longer reading time on ORC verbs. Using the Maze task, however, Forster et al. (2009) find only the determiner slowdown predicted by surprisal theory. In a recent study, Vani et al. (2021) collect Maze data with stimuli from earlier eye-tracking experiments, and reproduce the determiner slowdown. The authors suggest that the later ORC verb slowdown found in eye-tracking studies may reflect spillover rather than memory effects.

In the current study, we investigate whether the task-dependent discrepancies observed in English relative clause processing can be modeled as a trade-off between memory and expectation. We manipulate how much of the preceding sentence context is remembered in the lossy context surprisal model, and evaluate Vani et al.'s stimuli at a range of retention rates. We additionally evaluate LCS predictions on the relative clause stimuli of Roland et al. (2021), who report both spillover and memory effects in their eye-tracking data.

Figure 1 illustrates our results. At a high retention rate (e.g. 60%), LCS predicts the expectation-based determiner slowdown on ORC test items, consistent with the observed RTs for the Maze filler data. At a low retention rate (e.g. 20%), however, LCS predicts the ORC verb slowdown found in eye-tracking studies such as Staub (2010). Furthermore, we find that low-retention LCS predictions also capture the memory effects found by Roland et al. after adjusting for spillover per their analysis. This finding suggests an alternative explanation for observed task discrepancies: eye-tracking while reading likely imposes lower memory demands than the Maze task, leading to a stronger influence of memory constraints on incremental processing.

This paper presents two key contributions:[1]

- We release and document a technical improvement to the RR-LCS model. Through extending the lossy context model to subword tokenization, the new model can now handle out-of-vocabulary inputs.
- We show that, through manipulating the retention rate, LCS predicts two distinct behavioral patterns of relative clause processing which have been reported in different tasks. This finding shows that task-dependent memory demands can explain apparently contradictory results in the literature.

2 Background

Measuring incremental processing Behavioral methods which track word-by-word reading time (RT) offer scientific insight into human language processing, as longer RTs reflect processing difficulty. Special eye-tracking (ET) equipment can collect RT data in a laboratory setting by monitoring participants' eye movements as they read (Rayner, 1998). This method most closely approximates natural reading, but ET data collection is resource-intensive and the resulting RTs can be noisy and challenging to interpret. One crucial source of noise comes from *spillover effects*: longer processing time for one word can "spill over" to following words. In such cases, systematically longer RTs on a specific word do not reflect difficulty processing that word, but instead the word or words preceding.

An alternative cost-effective source of RT data is self-paced reading (SPR), in which participants must press a button to reveal each word in sequence. Unfortunately, spillover effects are typically much larger in SPR compared to ET data. The Maze task (Forster et al., 2009) modifies SPR by introducing distractors: participants are shown two words at each step, and must select the word which correctly continues the sentence. This task is more cognitively demanding, and appears to reduce or

[1] See `https://github.com/kmccurdy/LCS` for model and analysis code.

eliminate spillover effects (Boyce and Levy, 2020; Boyce et al., 2020). Witzel et al. (2012) compare Maze and ET for three types of ambiguous sentences and find that Maze RTs capture most — but not all — patterns of incremental processing difficulty seen in ET RTs. In this paper, we consider the possibility that higher working memory demands in the Maze task account for key discrepancies between Maze and ET results.

Modeling memory and expectation Language models (LMs) are typically trained on a next-word prediction objective, which aligns them with the expectation-based account of Surprisal Theory. Modern large language models, however, have become worse predictors of human RT data due to their superhuman capacity for memorization (Oh and Schuler, 2023). This has motivated modeling approaches which combine LMs with memory constraints. Timkey and Linzen (2023) propose a model architecture with a single self-attention head, which reduces the capacity to retrieve earlier representations from context. Kuribayashi et al. (2022) find improved fits to RTs by simply truncating words from the preceding context. Here, we model memory constraints with Resource-Rational Lossy Context Surprisal (RR-LCS; Hahn et al., 2022), which learns to stochastically retain or delete specific words from the representation of the preceding context. Crucially, we can systematically vary the LCS retention rate to simulate different patterns of working memory engagement.

3 Computing Lossy Context Surprisal

3.1 Resource-Rational Lossy Context Surprisal

Standard surprisal theory assumes that processing difficulty of a word is proportional to its surprisal—that is, its negative log-probability in context:

$$-\log P(x_{T+1}|x_{1\ldots T}) \quad (1)$$

Lossy Context Surprisal (Futrell et al., 2020) modifies this by conditioning not on the exact context, but on a lossy memory representation:

$$-\log P(x_{T+1}|M_T) \quad (2)$$

where M is a lossy representation generated from $x_1 \ldots x_T$. To generate testable Lossy Context Surprisal predictions, we must specify (1) lossy representations M_T and (2) how these are generated from contexts $x_{1\ldots T-1}$. Such a specification is provided by Resource-Rational Surprisal (RR-LCS; Hahn et al., 2022). Following Futrell et al. (2020), RR-LCS specifies the lossy representations in terms of retaining or masking individual words. Formally, the model operates over contexts $x \in \Sigma^T$, where T is a maximum context size, set to 20 in Hahn et al. (2022). The model is specified by a family of retention probabilities (after Anderson and Milson, 1989; Anderson and Schooler, 1991) $p_{w,i} \in [0,1]$ $(1 \le i \le T)$, where $p_{w,i}$ indicates the probability that word w at position i is available when predicting word T (Figure 1). Given a context $x_{1\ldots T}$, each word is independently kept or masked depending on these probabilities, yielding a lossy representation $M_T := y \in (\Sigma \cup \{\text{LOST}\})^T$.

The retention probabilities $p_{w,i}$ are chosen so as to minimize average lossy-context surprisal:

$$\min_{p_{w,i}} \mathbb{E}_{x_{1\ldots T+1}, y_{1\ldots T}}[-\log P(x_{T+1}|y_1 \ldots y_T)] \quad (3)$$

subject to a bound on the average number of retained words:

$$\mathbb{E}_{x,y}[\#\{i : y_i = \text{LOST}\}] \le \delta T \quad (4)$$

where the expectations range over contexts $x_{1\ldots T}$ with associated next word x_{T+1} from a large corpus, and lossy versions y drawn via the retention probabilities $p_{w,i}$. Importantly, the *retention rate* $\delta \in [0,1]$ is the model's single free parameter: it indicates how many words on average are retained. Given a budget specified by δ, the model thus learns to prioritize retaining those words that are usually more helpful for predicting future words. On a technical level, the constrained optimization (3–4) is implemented using Lagrangian duality; see Hahn et al. (2022, Supp. Mat. §1) for details. Empirically, the optimized retention probabilities strongly favor forgetting less recent words, especially high-frequency function words.

3.2 Implementation

In the parameterization of Hahn et al. (2022), given the embedding g_i of the i-the token and p_i of the i-th position, the retention probabilities receive a log-biaffine parameterization after Dozat and Manning (2017):

$$p_{w,i} = \sigma\left(Fp_i + MLP_2(g_i) + p_i^T MLP_1(g_i)\right) \quad (5)$$

where MLP_i denotes ReLU MLPs with one hidden layer with d dimensions, and σ is the logistic sigmoid function. Both the positional and word embeddings can directly influence the probability (first and second summands); there is also an option for multiplicative interaction between the two (third summand). The parameters of the two MLPs, the transform F, and the embeddings g_i, and p_i are trainable parameters, optimized for (3–4).

By Bayes' Rule, the predictive distribution $P(x_{T+1}|M_T)$ in (2) is proportional to:

$$\sum_{x_1 \dots x_T \in \Sigma^T} P(x_{1 \dots T+1}) P(M_T | x_{1 \dots T}) \quad (6)$$

where the sum ranges over hypothetical contexts $x_{1 \dots T}$, weighted by their probability of giving rise to the imperfect representation M_T. The term $P(M_T|x_{1 \dots T})$ can be computed in terms of $p_{w,i}$. The other term, $P(x_{1 \dots T+1})$, describes the expectations in the absence of any memory limitations; Hahn et al. (2022) estimate it using GPT-2 Medium (Radford et al., 2019). Plugging these components into (6), lossy-context surprisal (2) is then estimated using importance sampling. Importantly, in the limit where no memory limitations are present ($\delta = 1$), the predictions equal those of the GPT-2 model. Varying δ from 0 to 1, the resource-rational lossy-context surprisal model thus interpolates between a predictive model without any context, and a full transformer language model.

Implementation based on subwords An important limitation of the original implementation from Hahn et al. (2022) is that it uses a traditional word-based tokenization, with a vocabulary of 50K words. While sufficient to model their experimental stimuli, the model frequently faces OOV tokens when applied to other data, hindering broader validation.[2] In order to apply the model to other experimental stimuli, we straightforwardly adapted the model to modern subword-based tokenizations: Assume a word w consists of tokens $t_1 \dots t_N$, each represented by token embeddings $e_1 \dots e_N$, where $N \leq N_{max} = 5$.[3] We concatenate $e_1, \dots, e_N$ to a vector of length $N \cdot d$ and pad with zeros to obtain a vector of length $N_{max} \cdot d$; we then use a trainable one-layer ReLU MLP to transform this vector into the vector g_i fed into (5), in place of the word embeddings from the original word-based model.[4] When a word x_i has been forgotten, it is represented in y as a single special token, $LOST$,

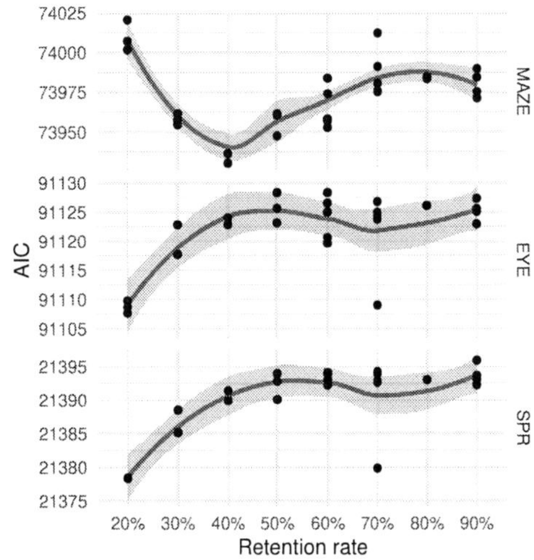

Figure 2: Linear mixed-effects model fit for LCS to Maze (Hahn et al., 2022), ET, and SPR data for filler items from Vasishth et al. (2010). Points are individual LCS model instances, line shows GAM smooth, x-axis shows retention rate, y-axis shows goodness of fit in AIC — lower is better. Maze data are better approximated by LCS with a higher retention rate (40%) compared to ET and SPR data (20%).

indicating that a word was present but not how many tokens it spanned. Hence, while the model is now specified in terms of subwords, it continues to implement the same cognitive theory; in particular, forgetting continues to apply on the level of words.[5]

Setup We train the model using this parameterization, using the GPT-2 Tokenizer, and otherwise matching the setup of Hahn et al. (2022): The model is trained, separately for different values of δ, on the same English Wikipedia corpus (2.3 billion words). Paragraphs are shuffled and separated by an EOS token. The model is applied to contexts of size T across sentence and paragraph boundaries. In evaluation, the context is padded or truncated to length T (long enough to cover the experimental stimuli); padding is removed before passing to the GPT-2 model. We set $T = 20$.

[2]For example, 8% of the stimuli evaluated in §4 contain at least one OOV under the original model.

[3]In very rare cases of longer words, the tokens starting from the sixth one were disregarded.

[4]In preliminary experiments, we also considered alternative parameterizations, such as simply summing embeddings without any nonlinear transformation. We compared the options at $\delta = 10$, and chose the one with the best result on the objective function (3-4).

[5]Note that another option would be to apply the model at the level of subwords, but this would be of unclear cognitive plausibility, as subwords do not directly correspond to any units of theoretical cogniitive interest, and even depend on tokenizers.

3.3 Evaluation

Hahn et al. (2022) validated that, with a nonzero forgetting rate, their LCS implementation improved fit to Maze RTs on their filler sentences when compared to a model variant with zero forgetting rate. These filler sentences had previously been used in ET and SPR experiments by Vasishth et al. (2010). Crucially, for these fillers, RT data is available from three paradigms: Maze from Hahn et al. (2022), ET and SPR from Vasishth et al. (2010). The fillers comprise both critical items and fillers from Grodner and Gibson (2005, Expt. 1). The items contain a mixture of syntactic structures, including some embedded structures. The key advantage of these filler data compared to datasets such as the Dundee corpus (Kennedy and Pynte, 2005) or Natural stories (Futrell et al., 2017) is that data from *three* paradigms—Maze, SPR, and ET—is publicly available for *exactly the same sentences*, neutralizing confounding effects of factors such as genre.

We evaluate our subword model implementation on the same stimuli and range of modalities. This evaluation has two goals: 1) to confirm that our subword implementation achieves comparable fits to reading time data as the original word-based model, in the sense that relatively low retention rates should model RT better than high retention rates, and 2) to inform our later analysis of task differences in relative clause processing. We model reading time fit per word using the same linear mixed-effects model structure[6] as Hahn et al. (2022, Supp. Mat. §9). We also report goodness of fit in terms of Akaike's An Information Criterion (AIC).

Our findings (Fig. 2) are qualitatively similar to those of Hahn et al. (2022, Supp. Mat. Fig. 30). We observe a comparable spread of AIC values across retention rates, with an average $\Delta AIC \geq 10$ separating the best-fitting retention rate from others. This stark differentiation in goodness of fit suggests that the best-fitting retention rate captures meaningful variation in reading time. Moreover, in line with other literature (§2), we also see that memory constraints — i.e. retention rates much lower than 100%[7] — produce superior fits to human RT data.

We also reproduce the task-specific trends reported by Hahn et al.. They found that Maze RTs were best modeled at a higher retention rate of 5 out of 20 words (25%; compare to 40% in our implementation) compared to ET and SPR RTs, which were best fit at 3 out of 20 words (15%; compare to 20% in our implementation). The remainder of this paper investigates whether these task-dependent differences can account for discrepant empirical results from the relative clause literature.

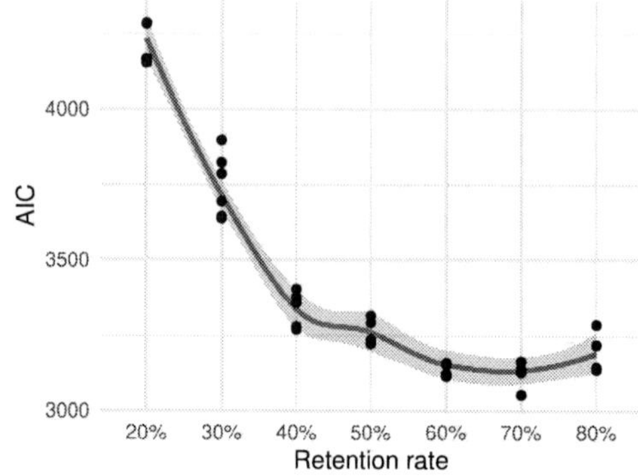

Figure 3: Linear mixed-effects model fit for LCS to Maze RT data on filler items (Vani et al., 2021). Points are individual LCS model instances, line shows GAM smooth, x-axis shows retention rate, y-axis shows goodness of fit in AIC. Retention rate 60–70% achieves the best fit on average.

4 Modeling Relative Clause Processing

The increased difficulty in processing object relative clauses (ORCs) compared to subject relative clauses (SRCs) provides a testing ground for effects of memory and expectation. Memory-based accounts such as Dependency Locality Theory (DLT; Gibson, 1998; Gibson et al., 2000) predict increased reading time (RT) at the ORC verb, reflecting integration of long-distance dependencies. This prediction has been realized in eye-tracking (ET) studies (Traxler et al., 2002; Staub, 2010). The expectation-based Surprisal Theory (Hale, 2001; Levy, 2008), however, predicts an RT slowdown only at the start of the ORC noun phrase, and this pattern has been found in Maze studies (Forster et al., 2009; Vani et al., 2021). Vani et al. suggest that the ORC verb slowdown found in eye-tracking studies may reflect spillover effects rather than memory constraints.

We explore the alternative hypothesis that ET experiments impose lower memory demands relative to the Maze task. At lower retention rates, lossy context surprisal (LCS) models memory con-

[6] LMER formula: $log(RT) \sim LCS + wordPositionInItem + log(WordFreq) + WordLength + prevWordLCS + log(prevWordFreq) + prevWordLength + log(prevWordRT) + (1|ItemID) + (1|ParticipantID)$

[7] Note that LCS with 100% retention rate is functionally equivalent to pure language model surprisal, i.e. GPT2-Medium in our implementation.

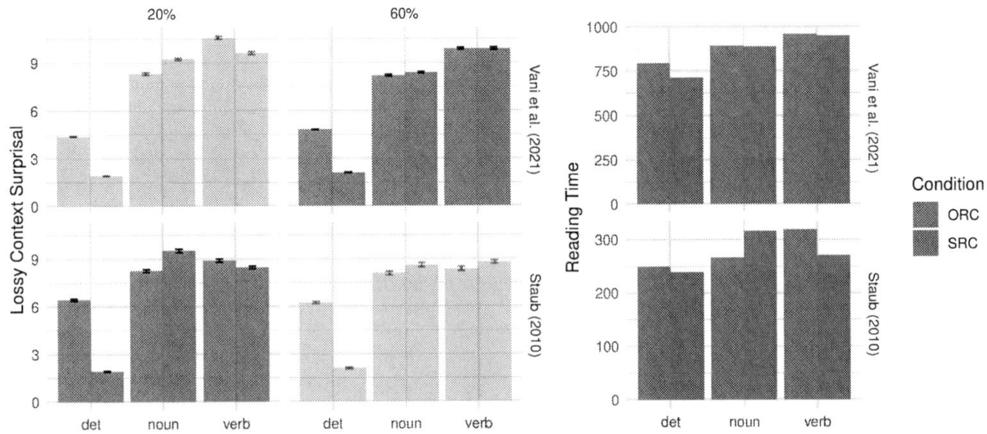

Figure 4: LCS predictions (left; error bars show standard error across model instances and items) and reading time data (right) for stimuli from Staub (2010, ET gaze duration, Experiment 1) and Vani et al. (2021, Maze, Experiment 1; cf. their Figs. 3 and 4). At the higher retention rate (60%), LCS predicts only the determiner slowdown observed in Maze data (top row). At the lower retention rate (20%), LCS also predicts the ORC verb slowdown observed in ET data (bottom row).

straints, but not spillover effects; if LCS captures the patterns in ET behavioral data, this supports the interpretation that ORC verb slowdowns are memory-driven but also modulated by task demands. Using our LCS implementation with subword tokenization, we generate predictions on critical RC stimuli and compare them to behavioral results from Maze (Vani et al., 2021) and eye-tracking (Staub, 2010; Roland et al., 2021). We draw on Roland et al.'s statistical analysis to further distinguish spillover and memory effects.

4.1 Selecting Retention Rate

Maze We use the same evaluation procedure described in §3.3 on the Maze filler item RT data from Experiment 1 of Vani et al. (Fig. 3). Note that these model fits span a broad range of AIC values, so we can confidently state that LCS at higher retention rates better predicts RT data from this experiment. We observe similarly high performance at 60% and 70% retention rates. As the evaluation in §3.3 found a lower retention rate (40%) provided the best fit to Maze data, we conservatively select 60% as more consistent with our earlier analysis.[8]

[8]This difference — 60%–70% retention, vs. the 40% found in §3.3 — may also reflect task demands. Hahn et al. (2022) use the A-Maze task, in which participants distinguish words from length-matched words with low contextual probability. Vani et al. (2021) introduce the I-Maze task variant, which interpolates lexical and grammatical competitors and may impose higher memory demands.

Eye-tracking Unfortunately, filler data is not available for either of the ET studies we aim to model. We select 20% as our prospective retention rate based on the evaluation in §3.3. This low retention rate is consistent with our hypothesis of reduced memory demand in ET studies.

4.2 Evaluating Relative Clause Processing

The previous section identified two distinct retention rates at which to evaluate LCS, based on their fit to reading times from the Maze and eye-tracking experimental settings. In this section, we generate LCS predictions at these two retention rates for the critical relative clause items tested by Vani et al. (2021), Staub (2010), and Roland et al. (2021). Predictions at each retention rate are averaged over multiple LCS model instances trained with different random seeds and hyperparameter configurations, with a minimum of four instances per retention rate. We then compare the predictions to the behavioral patterns reported on these stimuli for Maze and eye-tracking data.

4.2.1 Eye-tracking vs. Maze

We hypothesize that participants systematically engage their working memory at higher capacity during the Maze task compared to the more naturalistic eye-tracking while reading setting. If this is the case, then we expect that LCS at higher retention rates will predict the relative clause processing behavior observed in Maze studies, with an ORC

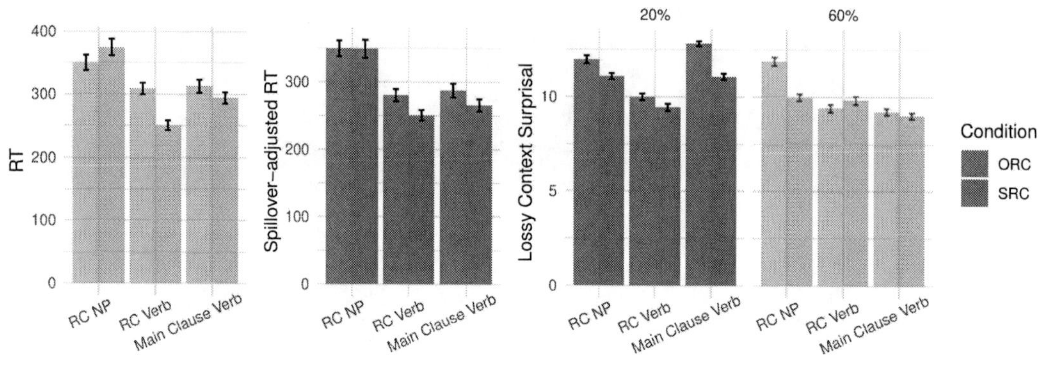

Figure 5: Original and spillover-adjusted gaze duration RT data (left; error bars show standard error across participants and items) and LCS predictions (right; error bars show standard error across model instances and items) for full-NP stimuli from Roland et al. (2021, Experiment 2). At the lower retention rate (20%), LCS predicts ORC slowdowns on the RC verb, consistent with both the original and spillover-adjusted RT data.

slowdown at the beginning of the RC noun phrase, i.e. on the determiner. Conversely, we expect LCS at lower retention rates to predict the pattern of effects observed in eye-tracking studies, with the main ORC slowdown appearing on the RC verb.

LCS predictions largely conform to the expected patterns (Figure 4). At a 60% retention rate, LCS mirrors the processing behavior of participants in Vani et al.'s Maze task, with an ORC slowdown at the determiner but not at the RC noun or verb. At 20% retention, however, we see an ORC slowdown on the RC verb, and a relative ORC speedup on the RC noun — both effects reported in gaze duration ET data from Staub (2010). Crucially, we see the same pattern in LCS predictions across experiments. Vani et al. use test items from Traxler et al. (2002) in their Experiment 1, which differ from the critical items in Experiment 1 of Staub (2010). Nonetheless, the same memory-based pattern — ORC slowdown on the RC verb and speedup on the RC noun — emerges in low-retention LCS predictions for both sets of stimuli.[9]

We use linear mixed-effects models[10] to assess the reliability of these patterns for each retention rate, critical region, and experiment. At the **determiner**, both the high- and low-retention LCS models predict a large and significant ORC slowdown for both experiments. This aligns with the Maze data, but not with the ET data; there is a small ORC slowdown on the determiner, but it is not significant per the statistical analysis of Staub (2010). We speculate that this absence may reflect spillover in the SRC condition, as the determiner directly follows the RC verb; this could raise RT times compared to the ORC condition (in which the determiner follows"that"), obscuring the ORC slowdown effect. At the RC **noun**, both LCS models predict a significant ORC *speed-up*: small at 60% retention, much larger at 20% retention. This appears consistent with the RT data — while Vani et al. report no RC effect here with Maze, Staub finds a significant ORC speed-up in gaze duration. Finally, at the RC **verb**, LCS captures the critical pattern: no ORC slowdown with high retention, as seen in the Maze data — but significant ORC slowdown at low retention, as seen in the ET data. This pattern supports a memory-based rather than spillover interpretation of the ORC verb effect.

4.2.2 Memory vs. Spillover

To further investigate the role of spillover effects in eye-tracking, we draw on the data and analysis of Roland et al. (2021). Their Experiment 2 also compares ORC and SRC processing on a distinct set of RC stimuli.[11] Roland et al. also conduct

[9]We also generate LCS predictions at both retention rates for Experiment 2 from Vani et al./Staub, which served as a control comparison between ORCs and embedded sentence complements in both studies. LCS predictions capture the target effect and do not vary across retention rates — as expected for a control experiment with no predicted memory effects — so we do not consider these findings further.

[10]LMER formula: $LCS \sim Condition + (1|ItemID) + (1|ModelID)$

[11]Roland et al. (2021) include an additional manipulation of NP type, in which the RC noun is either a full noun phrase or a pronoun. For simplicity, we consider only the full NP stimuli here.

an extensive statistical analysis of spillover effects on their gaze duration data. We use the estimated coefficients from their fully specified model (2021, Table 12) to adjust RT values while controlling for spillover.[12]

Recall that the key prediction of memory-based accounts is an ORC slowdown on the RC verb. Figure 5 shows that this effect is visible in the original gaze duration data, and remains after adjusting for spillover. It also shows that this ORC verb slowdown is predicted by LCS at 20% retention, but not at 60% retention — a pattern consistent with the findings of the previous section. Linear mixed-effect model analysis confirms that both high- and low-retention LCS models predict a significant effect of RC type at the verb, but in opposed directions: the 60% retention model predicts an ORC speed-up, while the 20% retention model predicts an ORC slowdown, consistent with the spillover-adjusted RT data. Once again, the observed pattern supports a memory-based account of the RC verb effect observed in ET gaze data.

5 Discussion

Our main finding is that low-retention LCS reproduces key predictions of memory-based accounts, and provides a plausible fit to ET data — whereas high-retention LCS reproduces expectation-based predictions, and better fits Maze data. The Maze task requires that participants actively reject distractor words and select the correct sentence continuation; this activity strikes us as clearly more cognitively demanding than naturalistic reading, so task-dependent memory demands present a viable explanation for these discrepant results.[13] An alternative hypothesis suggested by Vani et al. (2021) attributes the ORC verb slowdown seen in ET data to spillover effects. Our analysis indicates that this is unlikely: the ORC verb slowdown is consistently predicted by low-retention LCS, pointing toward a memory-driven explanation.

To be clear, we do not claim that spillover has *no* systematic influence on relative clause processing. The detailed modeling analysis conducted by Roland et al. (2021) indicates that spillover at least partly accounts for the ORC verb slowdown. The slowdown effect persists, however, even after adjusting for spillover, and our LCS simulations suggest that the slowdown reflects memory constraints (Figure 5).

We note that LCS consistently predicts some patterns which have not been given a formal theoretical articulation. Further investigation is required to assess when these discrepancies could be systematic and theoretically meaningful. The ORC noun speed-up presents an interesting case study: this effect is not directly predicted by either expectation or memory accounts, but it appears robustly in both LCS predictions and the ET data for Experiment 1 of Staub (2010). This unexpected concordance suggests that memory constraints may also drive this effect. On the other hand, LCS appears to incorrectly predict an ORC slowdown at the RC NP for the Roland et al. (2021) stimuli (Figure 5); however, closer analysis reveals that this effect is driven by the ORC slowdown at the determiner — on the RC noun itself, LCS once again predicts an ORC speedup, and this effect is larger at the lower retention rate of 20%.[14] Under LCS, memory constraints appear to drive both the ORC verb slowdown and the ORC noun speedup, although to our knowledge the latter effect has not been discussed in connection with memory-based accounts. Exploring the nature of this connection could be a promising direction for future research.

Future work could also explore alternative approaches to modeling expectation. While surprisal theory is well-represented in the research literature and closely aligned with the standard language model learning objective, other research has formulated expectation in terms of *information gain* (e.g. Hale, 2016; Hoover, 2024). Under an information gain account, the incremental cost of processing a given word reflects not its conditional probability (as posited by surprisal theory), but rather the *uncertainty reduction* it provides between alternative sentence continuations. Chen and Hale (2021) use one such approach, namely Entropy Reduction (Hale, 2003), to model the same relative clause processing asymmetry addressed here. They use corpus statistics to compute word-by-word transitions in entropy over the probabilities of following syntactic derivations, and find that this measure

[12]Note that we adjust only for spillover predictors, not for other estimated effects.

[13]While tasks with higher cognitive load are often associated with *reduced* memory capacity in the research literature, we note that the cognitive load in the Maze task is not opposed to sentence processing, but in fact perfectly aligned with it. Higher retention of the preceding sentence context will facilitate higher performance on the task itself, i.e. selecting the correct sentence continuation.

[14]We are unable to compare this prediction directly to the Roland et al. ET data, as RTs are reported for critical regions rather than individual words.

predicts the observed ORC slowdown at both the RC NP determiner and the RC verb. Their model can therefore account for the ORC verb slowdown observed in ET data — however, it would not appear to predict the pattern observed in Maze data by Vani et al. (2021). An alternative information gain approach (e.g. Hoover, 2024) could in principle address such task-dependent effects. In the meantime, we note that LCS straightforwardly captures this variation in relative clause processing as a consequence of memory demands.

Other avenues for future research could address further limitations of the current study. For instance, it might be more appropriate to vary retention rates not only at the experiment level, but also to model differences between individual participants. One could also pursue more interpretability in LCS predictions through detailed analysis of specific word-level reconstructions. Lastly, this paper focuses on one grammatical phenomenon in one language; a thorough treatment of memory effects in online language comprehension will naturally require a broader scope of evaluation.

6 Conclusion

We find that manipulating the retention rate of a lossy context surprisal (LCS) model captures task-dependent differences observed in reading times (RTs). Filler item RTs from the Maze task are best fit with a relatively high retention rate (e.g. 60%), while lower retention (20%) better predicts eye-tracking RTs for those same items. Furthermore, based on these task-dependent retention rates, LCS correctly predicts critical RT patterns observed for English relative clauses. In particular, low-retention (20%) LCS follows memory-based theories and predicts higher RTs for object relative verbs — an effect found in eye-tracking but not Maze studies. These results can explain the apparently contradictory behavioral evidence supporting both memory- and expectation-driven accounts: relative clause processing is likely modulated by the memory demands of the task, and we can use LCS to model this phenomenon.

Acknowledgments

The authors are funded by the Deutsche Forschungsgemeinschaft (DFG, German Research Foundation) – Project-ID 232722074 – SFB 1102.

References

John R Anderson and Robert Milson. 1989. Human memory: An adaptive perspective. *Psychological Review*, 96(4):703.

John R Anderson and Lael J Schooler. 1991. Reflections of the environment in memory. *Psychological science*, 2(6):396–408.

Brian Bartek, Richard L. Lewis, Shravan Vasishth, and Mason R. Smith. 2011. In search of on-line locality effects in sentence comprehension. *Journal of Experimental Psychology: Learning, Memory, and Cognition*, 37(5):1178–1198.

Veronica Boyce, Richard Futrell, and Roger P. Levy. 2020. Maze Made Easy: Better and easier measurement of incremental processing difficulty. *Journal of Memory and Language*, 111:104082.

Veronica Boyce and Roger Levy. 2020. A-maze of natural stories: Texts are comprehensible using the maze task. In *Talk at 26th Architectures and Mechanisms for Language Processing conference (AMLaP 26). Potsdam, Germany.*

Zhong Chen and John T. Hale. 2021. Quantifying Structural and Non-structural Expectations in Relative Clause Processing. *Cognitive Science*, 45(1):e12927.

Timothy Dozat and Christopher D. Manning. 2017. Deep biaffine attention for neural dependency parsing. In *International Conference on Learning Representations*.

Kenneth I. Forster, Christine Guerrera, and Lisa Elliot. 2009. The maze task: Measuring forced incremental sentence processing time. *Behavior Research Methods*, 41(1):163–171.

Felicity F. Frinsel and Morten H. Christiansen. 2024. Capturing individual differences in sentence processing: How reliable is the self-paced reading task? *Behavior Research Methods*.

Richard Futrell, Edward Gibson, and Roger P Levy. 2020. Lossy-context surprisal: An information-theoretic model of memory effects in sentence processing. *Cognitive science*, 44(3):e12814.

Richard Futrell, Edward Gibson, Hal Tily, Idan Blank, Anastasia Vishnevetsky, Steven T Piantadosi, and Evelina Fedorenko. 2017. The natural stories corpus. *arXiv preprint arXiv:1708.05763*.

Edward Gibson. 1998. Linguistic complexity: Locality of syntactic dependencies. *Cognition*, 68(1):1–76.

Edward Gibson et al. 2000. The dependency locality theory: A distance-based theory of linguistic complexity. *Image, language, brain*, 2000:95–126.

Daniel Grodner and Edward Gibson. 2005. Consequences of the Serial Nature of Linguistic Input for Sentenial Complexity. *Cognitive Science*, 29(2):261–290.

Michael Hahn, Richard Futrell, Roger Levy, and Edward Gibson. 2022. A resource-rational model of human processing of recursive linguistic structure. *Proceedings of the National Academy of Sciences*, 119(43):e2122602119. Publisher: Proceedings of the National Academy of Sciences.

John Hale. 2001. A probabilistic earley parser as a psycholinguistic model. In *Second meeting of the north american chapter of the association for computational linguistics*.

John Hale. 2003. The Information Conveyed by Words in Sentences. *Journal of Psycholinguistic Research*, 32(2):101–123.

John Hale. 2016. Information-theoretical Complexity Metrics. *Language and Linguistics Compass*, 10(9):397–412.

Jacob Louis Hoover. 2024. *The cost of information: Looking beyond predictability in language processing*. Ph.D. thesis, McGill University.

Alan Kennedy and Joël Pynte. 2005. Parafoveal-on-foveal effects in normal reading. *Vision research*, 45(2):153–168.

Tatsuki Kuribayashi, Yohei Oseki, Ana Brassard, and Kentaro Inui. 2022. Context Limitations Make Neural Language Models More Human-Like. In *Proceedings of the 2022 Conference on Empirical Methods in Natural Language Processing*, pages 10421–10436, Abu Dhabi, United Arab Emirates. Association for Computational Linguistics.

Roger Levy. 2008. Expectation-based syntactic comprehension. *Cognition*, 106(3):1126–1177.

Roger Levy. 2013. Memory and surprisal in human sentence comprehension. In *Sentence processing*, pages 78–114. Psychology Press.

Richard L. Lewis and Shravan Vasishth. 2005. An Activation-Based Model of Sentence Processing as Skilled Memory Retrieval. *Cognitive Science*, 29(3):375–419.

Byung-Doh Oh and William Schuler. 2023. Why Does Surprisal From Larger Transformer-Based Language Models Provide a Poorer Fit to Human Reading Times? *Transactions of the Association for Computational Linguistics*, 11:336–350.

Alec Radford, Jeffrey Wu, Rewon Child, David Luan, Dario Amodei, and Ilya Sutskever. 2019. Language Models are Unsupervised Multitask Learners. page 24.

Keith Rayner. 1998. Eye movements in reading and information processing: 20 years of research. *Psychological Bulletin*, 124(3):372–422. Place: US Publisher: American Psychological Association.

Douglas Roland, Frederic Dick, and Jeffrey L. Elman. 2007. Frequency of basic English grammatical structures: A corpus analysis. *Journal of Memory and Language*, 57(3):348–379.

Douglas Roland, Gail Mauner, and Yuki Hirose. 2021. The processing of pronominal relative clauses: Evidence from eye movements. *Journal of Memory and Language*, 119:104244.

Adrian Staub. 2010. Eye movements and processing difficulty in object relative clauses. *Cognition*, 116(1):71–86.

William Timkey and Tal Linzen. 2023. A Language Model with Limited Memory Capacity Captures Interference in Human Sentence Processing. In *Findings of the Association for Computational Linguistics: EMNLP 2023*, pages 8705–8720, Singapore. Association for Computational Linguistics.

Matthew J Traxler, Robin K Morris, and Rachel E Seely. 2002. Processing Subject and Object Relative Clauses: Evidence from Eye Movements. *Journal of Memory and Language*, 47(1):69–90.

Pranali Vani, Ethan Gotlieb Wilcox, and Roger Levy. 2021. Using the Interpolated Maze Task to Assess Incremental Processing in English Relative Clauses. *Proceedings of the Annual Meeting of the Cognitive Science Society*, 43(43).

Shravan Vasishth, Katja Suckow, Richard L Lewis, and Sabine Kern. 2010. Short-term forgetting in sentence comprehension: Crosslinguistic evidence from verb-final structures. *Language and Cognitive Processes*, 25(4):533–567.

Ethan Gotlieb Wilcox, Tiago Pimentel, Clara Meister, Ryan Cotterell, and Roger P. Levy. 2023. Testing the Predictions of Surprisal Theory in 11 Languages. *arXiv preprint*. ArXiv:2307.03667 [cs].

Naoko Witzel, Jeffrey Witzel, and Kenneth Forster. 2012. Comparisons of Online Reading Paradigms: Eye Tracking, Moving-Window, and Maze. *Journal of Psycholinguistic Research*, 41(2):105–128.

Global-Pruner: A Stable and Efficient Pruner for Retraining-Free Pruning of Encoder-Based Language Models

Guangzhen Yao[1], Yuehan Wang[2],* Hui Xu[3†], Long Zhang[1], Miao Qi[1‡]
[1]School of Information Science and Technology, Northeast Normal University, China
[2]School of Teacher Education, Jiangsu University, Zhenjiang, China
[3]Institute for Intelligent Elderly Care, Changchun Humanities and Sciences College, China
{ yaoguangzhen, xuh504, longzhang, qim801 }@nenu.edu.cn
yhwang0809@stmail.ujs.edu.cn

Abstract

Large language models (LLMs) have achieved significant success in complex tasks across various domains, but they come with high computational costs and inference latency issues. Pruning, as an effective method, can significantly reduce inference costs. However, current pruning algorithms for encoder-based language models often focus on locally optimal solutions, neglecting a comprehensive exploration of the global solution space. This oversight can lead to instability in the solution process, thereby affecting the overall performance of the model. To address these challenges, we propose a structured pruning algorithm named G-Pruner (Global Pruner), comprising two integral components: PPOM (Proximal Policy Optimization Mask) and CG²MT (Conjugate Gradient Squared Mask Tuning), utilizing a global optimization strategy. This strategy not only eliminates the need for retraining but also ensures the algorithm's stability and adaptability to environmental changes, effectively addressing the issue of focusing solely on immediate optima while neglecting long-term effects. This method is evaluated on the GLUE and SQuAD benchmarks using $\text{BERT}_{\text{BASE}}$ and DistilBERT models. The experimental results indicate that without any retraining, G-Pruner achieves significant accuracy improvements on the $\text{SQuAD}_{2.0}$ task with a FLOPs constraint of 60%, demonstrating a 6.02% increase in F1 score compared with baseline algorithms.

1 Introduction

In recent years, Transformer-based pre-trained language models (PLMs) Li et al. (2024); Guimarães et al. (2024); Ho et al. (2024); Xu et al. (2024); Kojima et al. (2024) have dominated the field of natural language processing (NLP) Shamshiri et al. (2024); Oyewole et al. (2024); Zheng et al. (2024); Raza et al. (2024); Mei et al. (2024) due to their outstanding performance. However, the significant advantages of PLMs come with a substantial increase in model size and high computational costs. Pruning, as an optimization technique, can effectively reduce model complexity to enhance generalization ability and operational efficiency. Pruning techniques include structured pruning He and Xiao (2023); Fang et al. (2023); Sun et al. (2020); Liu et al. (2021a); Hou et al. (2020a); Iandola et al. (2020); Kitaev et al. (2020); Xia et al. (2022) and unstructured pruning Cheng et al. (2023); Santacroce et al. (2023); Wang et al. (2020); Shi et al. (2024); Zhang et al. (2024); Dery et al. (2024) aiming to improve efficiency by eliminating redundant parts of the model. Particularly, structured pruning has become a key technology for addressing size and speed issues in encoder-based language models, systematically removing redundancies without significantly impairing model performance.

Despite this, existing pruning methods still have limitations in practical applications. For example, Kwon et al. (2022) avoided the high costs associated with retraining by employing three techniques: mask search, mask rearrangement, and mask tuning. However, this greedy-based pruning method has been proved to be effective only in the short term and faced challenges in finding global optima, particularly when applied to complex or dynamically changing tasks. Moreover, the K-Prune Park et al. (2023) algorithm aimed to minimize pruning errors and enhance accuracy by preserving knowledge from pre-trained models. However, it did not fully consider the accuracy of weight selection and the long-term stability of the pruning strategy. Similarly, the KCM Nova et al. (2023) framework could quickly compress models and minimize performance loss by accurately assessing the importance of neurons in the short term. However, it overlooked the long-term stability and adaptability of the model to complex tasks, especially under

*Guangzhen Yao and Yuehan Wang contributed equally.
†corresponding author.
‡corresponding author.

Proceedings of the 28th Conference on Computational Natural Language Learning, pages 46–55
November 15-16, 2024 ©2024 Association for Computational Linguistics

high FLOPs constraints. Although these pruning methods can enhance the efficiency of models in the short term, they typically have a common drawback: they primarily focus on finding local optima and neglect the exploration of global optima.

To address these issues, we introduce a new retraining-free pruning framework for Transformer models—G-Pruner, efficiently locating global optima quickly without retraining. This strategy integrates two advanced technologies: PPOM and CG²MT. In the PPOM phase, the algorithm first conducts a comprehensive mask search, then fine-tunes and optimizes the selected masks using the PPO (Proximal Policy Optimization) technique from reinforcement learning. Subsequently, in the CG²MT phase, we enhance the efficiency and stability of solving asymmetric matrix problems through an improved CGS (Conjugate Gradient Squared) solver.

The primary contributions of this study include:

- We propose a structured pruning algorithm named G-Pruner, designed to prune encoder-based language models with high precision without the need of retraining.
- We conduct a comprehensive evaluation using the GLUE and SQuAD benchmarks on $\text{BERT}_{\text{BASE}}$ and DistilBERT models to demonstrate the performance of G-Pruner. We find that our method not only outperforms frameworks that are retraining-free but also surpasses other frameworks that do require retraining at the same pruning cost.
- Under the same FLOPs constraints, G-Pruner significantly outperforms some existing pruning techniques in pruning time without sacrificing model accuracy. Even under the strict constraint of allowing a maximum accuracy reduction of no more than 1%, $\text{BERT}_{\text{BASE}}$ achieves 60-70% of the original FLOPs across all tasks.

2 Related Work

2.1 Pruning For Encoder-Based Language Model

Pruning enhances model efficiency by removing insignificant weights or components such as attention heads or layers. There are two types: unstructured and structured. Unstructured pruning reduces model size by eliminating individual parameters. For example, Sanh et al. (2020) offered a straightforward first-order weight pruning method for fine-tuning pre-trained models, significantly boosting performance while maintaining high sparsity. Second-order methods like oBERT Kurtic et al. (2022) used approximate second-order information to reduce storage and computational demands of BERT models. Structured pruning simplifies models on a larger scale by removing entire components. For example, Hardware-friendly block structure pruning techniques Li et al. (2020) improved compression ratios and speed through optimizations. FLOP Wang et al. (2019) reduced model size and enhanced training and inference speed by maintaining dense weight matrix structures rather than sparse representations. SLIP Lin et al. (2020) improved pruning efficiency through feature layer normalization and unit block identification. Sajjad et al. (2023) tackled reducing layers in pre-trained Transformer models while maintaining task-specific performance. EBERT Liu et al. (2021b) dynamically determined pruning strategies per input sample, significantly cutting computational load and memory use. DynaBERT Hou et al. (2020b) adjusted BERT model size and latency adaptively, addressing deployment challenges on edge devices with diverse hardware performance.

2.2 Pruning For Retraining-free Structured Model

Data-independent neural pruning algorithm Mussay et al. (2019) and post-training weight pruning methods for deep neural networks Lazarevich et al. (2021) aimed to effectively reduce model size while minimizing accuracy loss. In the domain of structured pruning, the concept of "neuron merging" Kim et al. (2020) and RED's data-independent structured compression technique Yvinec et al. (2021) were employed by utilizing various technologies to maintain or enhance model accuracy without incurring accuracy losses. However, these methods overlooked challenges such as thorough weight selection analysis, long-term stability, and maintaining performance under high sparsity. To effectively address these challenges, a novel post-training pruning framework named G-Pruner is introduced.

3 Background and Baseline Description

The core of the pruning problem is to find the optimal methods for masking while considering sparsity constraints. This study focuses on the compression of encoder-based language models, notably $\text{BERT}_{\text{BASE}}$ and DistilBERT. These encoder-based language models consist of two primary sub-layer archetypes: Multi-Head Attention (MHA) and Feed-Forward Network (FFN). In this section, we explain how to mask the attention heads and feed-forward networks.

3.1 Structured Pruning by Masking

The formulas for MHA and FFN are expressed as follows:

$$\text{MHA}\left(x; m_l^{\text{MHA}}\right) = \sum_{i=1}^{H} m_{l,i}^{\text{MHA}} \circ \text{Att}_i(x) \quad (1)$$

$$\text{FFN}\left(x; m_l^{\text{FFN}}\right) = \left(\sum_{i=1}^{N} m_{l,i}^{\text{FFN}} \circ W_{:,i}^{(2)} \sigma\left(W_{i,:}^{(1)} x + b_i^{(1)}\right)\right) + b^{(2)} \quad (2)$$

where the mask variable $m_{l,i}^{\text{MHA}}$ for the ith attention head in the lth layer is used to decide whether to retain (mask value of 1) or prune (mask value of 0) that head. The operator "$\circ$" denotes the Hadamard product (element-wise multiplication) to determine each attention head's contribution to the output.

In this paper, we have drawn on the research findings of Kwon et al. (2022) to formalize the pruning problem of encoder-based language models as a constrained optimization problem concerning a mask. The goal is to minimize the loss function $L(m)$ while ensuring that the computational cost (measured in FLOPs or latency) of the model pruned according to mask m remains within acceptable limits. Given a mask m, the optimization formula is as follows:

$$\arg\min_m L(m) \quad \text{s.t.} \quad Cost(m) \leq C \quad (3)$$

where $Cost(m)$ denotes the FLOPs or latency of the architecture after pruning by mask, $L(m)$ represents the loss function, and C is the given constraint on FLOPs or latency.

Within a given FLOPs constraint C, the objective is to find the optimal mask configuration m, such that the FLOPs of the pruned model are reduced and the impact on performance is minimized. The problem can be formalized as:

$$\arg\min_m \sum_{i \in Z(m)} I_{ii} \quad \text{s.t.} \quad F_{\text{head}} \|m_{\text{MHA}}\|_0 + F_{\text{filter}} \|m_{\text{FFN}}\|_0 \leq C \quad (4)$$

where F_{head} and F_{filter} respectively represent the FLOPs required to execute a head and a filter, while $\|m_{\text{MHA}}\|_0$ and $\|m_{\text{FFN}}\|_0$ respectively represent the number of retained heads and filters in the MHA and FFN layers.

3.2 Baseline Description

In our study, we adopt Kwon et al.'s approach as the baseline method. The framework consists of three stages: mask search, mask rearrangement, and mask tuning. During the mask search stage, the Fisher information matrix is used to identify which attention heads and filters are crucial and should be retained, and which are relatively less important and can be pruned. Following the initial steps of mask search, the mask rearrangement process relies on a greedy algorithm, which reselects the heads and filters to be pruned by analyzing interactions between layers within the model. In the final phase of mask tuning, linear least squares are used to minimize reconstruction error and optimize the values of the non-zero mask variables. Since the mask search method based on the Fisher information matrix has been widely proven effective, no further improvements are pursued in this study.

4 Methodology

4.1 Framework Overview

As illustrated in Figure 1, our framework is divided into two main stages: the PPOM module (Section 4.2) and the CG²MT module (Section 4.3). During the PPOM mask optimization phase, we utilize Fisher information to determine which attention heads and filters are crucial and should be retained, and which are relatively unimportant and can be pruned. Subsequently, with the aid of reinforcement learning, the already identified mask patterns are adjusted to better explore intra-layer interactions among mask variables to optimize model performance. Subsequently, in the CG²MT mask tuning phase, the non-zero mask variables are fine-tuned by restructuring inter-layer output signals to compensate for any potential accuracy loss caused by pruning. The framework is designed to incorporate three primary inputs: a Transformer model fine-tuned for a specific downstream task, a small-scale sample dataset (typically containing 1,000 to 2,000 examples), and a resource constraint condition.

4.2 PPOM(Proximal Policy Optimization Mask)

While Fisher information-based mask search effectively identifies key model parameters, it doesn't guarantee minimal gradient impact during early pruning stages. Thus, initial pruning results often need detailed reordering and optimization. Com-

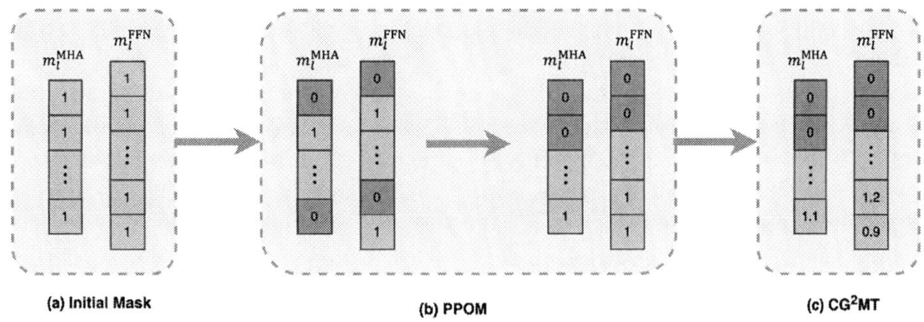

Figure 1: **Overview of the G-Pruner framework. (a) Mask variables initialized to 1. (b) PPOM (Section 4.2) and (c) CG²MT (Section 4.3).**

mon greedy algorithms attempt to reduce overall gradient impact through local optimization but may not fully optimize model performance long-term. To address this, we propose using the PPO algorithm for further mask refinement. Initially, we analyze masks derived from Fisher information and gradient data for each layer, focusing on weight matrices, pruning masks, and gradients. For layers where all elements are fully pruned or untouched, the original mask remains. For other layers, we reorder neurons or attention heads based on their impact on model performance and gradients.

4.2.1 Design Actors and Critics

In our study, we employ the Actor-Critic framework, combining the value function (Critic) and the policy function (Actor) to learn jointly. The primary task of the Actor network is to intelligently generate policies $\pi_\theta(a_t \mid s_t)$ tailored to different states s_t. It not only handles decision-making for individual states but also manages challenges posed by multidimensional and complex state spaces. In specific environmental states, the Actor network employs intricate computations to output a series of probability distributions directly linked to potential actions. Particularly when integrated closely with attention mechanisms, the Actor network can finely assess and optimize different attention heads or neurons.

During the pruning process, "state" refers to the current parameter state of the neural network, including weight matrices, pruning masks, gradients, and other information. The Actor network receives these state representations as inputs and generates a probability distribution describing the likelihood of each action (e.g., preserving or pruning a neuron). The length of the output vector equals the number of actions and can be a two-dimensional vector where each element represents the probability of a corresponding action. This probability distribution can be expressed as:

$$\pi_\theta(a_t \mid s_t) = \text{softmax}(f_\theta(s_t)) \tag{5}$$

where $f_\theta(s_t)$ denotes the output layer of the Actor network with parameters θ, predicting scores for each action a_t given state s_t. The softmax function transforms these scores into a probability distribution, ensuring that the probabilities of all actions sum to 1.

The Critic network, as a core component of the value function estimator, is primarily used to assess the expected impact of each pruning operation on the overall performance of neural networks, specifically the expected cumulative return. Based on the Critic network's output of expected cumulative return, each pruning decision is evaluated for its effectiveness. Higher expected returns indicate potential benefits to network performance, while lower returns may lead to performance degradation.

Its design aims to output the expected value $V_\omega(s_t)$ of the current state to guide policy updates in the Actor network. Specifically, the Critic network is trained by minimizing the mean squared error (MSE) between its predicted value and the actual reward:

$$L(\omega) = \mathbb{E}[(y_t - V_\omega(s_t))^2] \tag{6}$$

where ω represents the Critic network parameters, y_t is the expected cumulative reward at time step t, and $V_\omega(s_t)$ is the Critic network's output layer responsible for predicting the expected cumulative reward value given state s_t.

$$y_t = R_t + \gamma V_\omega(s_{t+1}) \tag{7}$$

where R_t denotes the reward at time step t, γ is the discount factor, and $V_\omega(s_{t+1})$ is the estimated state value function at time step $t+1$.

The evaluation results of the Critic network are used as feedback to adjust the pruning strategies generated by the Actor network. This feedback directly influences the decision-making process of the Actor network, enabling it to intelligently select pruning operations. Through continuous learning and evaluation, the Critic network dynamically adjusts pruning strategies. For instance, in each pruning iteration, based on the evaluation results of the current state, the Critic network can recommend whether to retain or prune specific layers or neurons, thereby maximizing the overall network performance. In summary, the Critic network collaborates with the Actor network to evaluate the effectiveness of its strategies and provide feedback, optimizing the pruning decision-making process of neural networks.

4.2.2 Pruning Execution

Based on the policy (probability distribution) generated by the Actor network, pruning operations are selected. These operations can be binary (retain or prune) or more complex (applying different pruning probabilities to each neuron or attention head). According to the policy outputted by the Actor network, a corresponding pruning mask M is generated to determine whether each neuron or attention head should be pruned. The process of generating the pruning mask is as follows:

$$M = \text{Bernoulli}(\pi_\theta(a_t \mid s_t)) \tag{8}$$

where $\pi_\theta(a_t \mid s_t)$ is the probability distribution outputted by the Actor network. The Bernoulli function generates a binary vector M, where each element represents the operation on the corresponding neuron or attention head (1 for retain, 0 for prune).

4.2.3 Algorithm Updates

In the pruning task, the advantage function calculates the expected gain or loss after performing pruning operations. This metric is used in the PPO algorithm to compute policy gradients, guiding the Actor network to update its policy to maximize long-term cumulative rewards. The formula for the advantage function is:

$$A(s_t, a_t) = y_t - V_\omega(s_t) \tag{9}$$

where y_t represents the expected cumulative reward after taking action a_t in state s_t, and $V_\omega(s_t)$ is the estimated state value function outputted by the Critic network, indicating the expected cumulative reward in state s_t.

In the pruning task, the PPO algorithm updates the Actor network parameters by maximizing the objective function of proximal policy optimization before and after policy updates. The primary goal of the Actor network is to generate a probability distribution for pruning decisions to optimize the performance or efficiency of the neural network. Specifically, the PPO algorithm first computes the importance sampling ratio $r_t(\theta)$ between the new and old policies:

$$r_t(\theta) = \frac{\pi_\theta(a_t \mid s_t)}{\pi_{\theta_{\text{old}}}(a_t \mid s_t)} \tag{10}$$

where $\pi_\theta(a_t \mid s_t)$ and $\pi_{\theta_{\text{old}}}(a_t \mid s_t)$ denote the probabilities of taking action a_t under state s_t for the new and old policies, respectively.

The objective function of PPO aims to maximize the advantage function $A(s_t, a_t)$, while constraining the policy update magnitude through a clipping function $\rho_{\text{clip}}(r_t(\theta))$. The formula is as follows:

$$J^{\text{CLIP}}(\theta) = \mathbb{E}_{(s_t,a_t)\sim\pi_{\theta_{\text{old}}}}\left[\min(r_t(\theta)A(s_t, a_t), \rho_{\text{clip}}(r_t(\theta))A(s_t, a_t)\right] \tag{11}$$

By maximizing the objective function $J^{\text{CLIP}}(\theta)$, we effectively update the Actor network parameters θ to optimize pruning decision strategies.

In the PPO algorithm, Actor network parameter θ is updated using policy gradient methods with the update formula:

$$\theta \leftarrow \theta + \sigma^A \nabla_\theta J(\theta) \tag{12}$$

where σ^A is the learning rate of the Actor network.

The Critic network also updates its parameter ω to more accurately estimate the performance change of the neural network after pruning operations. The update formula for the Critic network is:

$$\omega \leftarrow \omega - \sigma^C \nabla_\omega L(\omega) \tag{13}$$

where σ^C is the learning rate of the Critic network.

In each iteration, the Actor network determines pruning probabilities for each neuron using current model gradient information, guiding network structure evolution. Simultaneously, the Critic network assesses expected model performance post-pruning, balancing exploration and efficiency. Despite initial mask imperfections, the PPO algorithm reduces reliance on single Fisher information, enhancing method effectiveness by analyzing intra-layer interactions. This adaptive approach optimizes performance iteratively throughout pruning.

4.3 CG²MT(Conjugate Gradient Squared Mask Tuning)

In the PPOM stages, to simplify the search during the model pruning process, the mask values are strictly constrained to 0 or 1. As the process advances, this restriction is gradually relaxed, the non-zero variables in the mask can be adjusted to any real number, with the objective of restoring the accuracy of the pruned model by fine-tuning the mask variables. Nonetheless, when the least squares method is used for solving, numerical instability may be encountered, especially when facing extremely unstable or ill-conditioned problems. To address such challenges, the CGS solver provides an optimization strategy for efficiently solving asymmetric matrix problems. This solver performs double the computations in each iteration and squares the residuals, which not only accelerates convergence but also enhances the stability of the algorithm.

In our framework, we utilize the CGS solver to adjust the mask variables in the pruned model to minimize the reconstruction errors between different layers. The specific operations are as follows: Starting from the first layer of the model, we use the remaining heads or filters after pruning to reconstruct the output activations of the original model. This process can be formally represented by the following mathematical formula:

$$\underset{m_l}{\text{argmin}} \, \|x + \text{layer}(x; m_l) - (x' + \text{layer}(x'; 1))\|_2^2 \tag{14}$$

where x and x' are the inputs to the pruned and original model layers, respectively, and layer can be either MHA or FFN. Furthermore, we simplify this problem into a CGS solver problem, expressed by the following formula:

$$\arg\min_{m_l} \|Am_l - b\|_2^2 \tag{15}$$

where vector b represents the difference between the output activations of the two models. Matrix A represents the output activations of the heads or filters pruned by a binary mask.

Considering the large scale of matrix A, direct application of CGS solver might lead to numerical stability issues. Therefore, we reparameterize the CGS solver problem and transform it into a damped problem, enhancing the stability of the solution by fixing the damping value at 1. The formula is expressed as:

$$\arg\min_{r_l} \|Ar_l + A \cdot 1 - b\|_2^2 \tag{16}$$

where $m_l = 1 + r_l$. Additionally, to prevent the adjusted masks from negatively impacting the model's accuracy, we restrict the range of the adjusted mask variables to between $[-10, 10]$. If we find that the mask of any layer exceeds this range, we discard that layer's mask and cease further mask adjustments.

Algorithm 1 CGS Solver Iterative Mask Optimization Algorithm

1: Initialize: Start with an initial guess x_0, compute the initial residual $r_0 = b - Ax_0$, set $p_0 = r_0$, initialize step size coefficient $\alpha_0 = 0$, auxiliary variables $u_0 = 0$, $v_0 = Ap_0$, and r_0 is the initial direction vector for iteration.
2: Iteration step: For each iteration $k = 0, 1, 2, \ldots$ until convergence criteria are met.
3: Compute step size coefficient: $\alpha_k = \frac{r_k^T r_k}{v_k^T v_k}$
4: Update auxiliary variable: $q_{k+1} = u_k - \alpha_k v_k$
5: Update solution vector: $x_{k+1} = x_k + \alpha_k (q_{k+1} + u_k)$
6: Update residual vector: $r_{k+1} = r_k - \alpha_k (q_{k+1} + u_k + v_k)$
7: Check for convergence: If $\|r_{k+1}\|$ is small enough, stop the algorithm.
8: Calculate correction coefficient: $\beta_k = \frac{r_{k+1}^T r_{k+1}}{r_k^T r_k}$
9: Update another auxiliary variable: $u_{k+1} = r_{k+1} + \beta_k q_{k+1}$
10: Update direction vector: $v_{k+1} = Au_{k+1}$

This iterative process starts from the first layer of the neural network and progresses to the final layer, ensuring that while model parameters are reduced, performance loss is minimized as much as possible. Each iteration entails precise tuning of the mask variables, with the goal of preserving accuracy while pruning the model architecture. This intricately crafted optimization process enables us to strike a fine balance between the model's complexity and performance, guaranteeing that the pruned model maintains accuracy levels comparable to those of the original model while streamlining its structure.

Table 1: **G-pruner compares its accuracy against the baseline model under various FLOPs constraints.**

Method	QQP			MNLI			SST-2			QNLI			$SQuAD_{1.1}$			$SQuAD_{2.0}$		
$BERT_{BASE}$																		
FLOPs	60%	65%	70%	60%	65%	70%	60%	65%	70%	60%	65%	70%	60%	65%	70%	60%	65%	70%
Baseline	87.40	87.55	87.71	80.52	81.54	81.52	90.50	90.91	91.30	87.04	87.46	87.92	83.82	84.34	84.89	72.29	72.88	73.41
G-pruner	90.63	90.84	90.98	82.87	83.41	83.92	92.89	93.22	93.50	90.50	90.82	91.10	87.52	88.05	88.57	78.31	78.62	78.93
	+3.23%	+3.29%	+3.27%	+2.35%	+2.87%	+2.40%	+2.39%	+2.31%	+2.20%	+3.46%	+3.36%	+3.18%	+3.70%	+3.71%	+3.68%	+6.02%	+5.74%	+5.52%
DistilBERT																		
Method	QQP			MNLI			SST-2			QNLI			$SQuAD_{1.1}$			$SQuAD_{2.0}$		
FLOPs	60%	65%	70%	60%	65%	70%	60%	65%	70%	60%	65%	70%	60%	65%	70%	60%	65%	70%
Baseline	85.92	86.32	86.71	78.83	79.25	79.64	88.60	88.82	89.00	84.90	85.06	85.41	80.12	80.73	81.46	62.00	62.35	62.71
G-pruner	89.20	89.55	89.93	81.05	81.49	81.89	90.85	91.08	91.23	88.20	88.44	88.65	83.22	84.03	84.76	67.29	67.64	67.93
	+3.28%	+3.23%	+3.22%	+2.22%	+2.24%	+2.25%	+2.25%	+2.26%	+2.23%	+3.30%	+3.38%	+3.24%	+3.10%	+3.30%	+3.30%	+5.29%	+5.29%	+5.22%

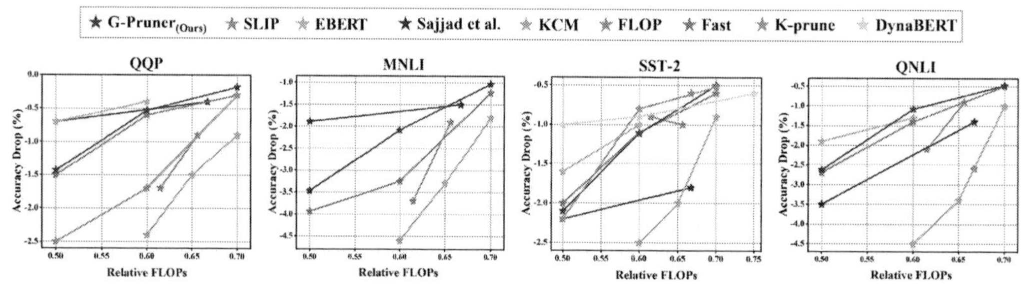

Figure 2: **Based on the $BERT_{BASE}$ model, we compare the performance of our pruning method with several existing structured pruning techniques.**

5 Experiments

5.1 Experimental Setup

Datasets and Pretrained models. Our research utilizes PyTorch v1.9.1 and Hugging Face's Transformers v4.12.0. Experiments are conducted on a single NVIDIA GeForce RTX 3090 GPU for efficiency and result reproducibility. We evaluate our pruning method on popular benchmarks: GLUE for tasks like QQP (364K), SST-2 (67K), MNLI (392K), and QNLI (105K), and SQuAD1.1 (88K) and SQuAD2.0 (130K) for question-answering. We focus on $BERT_{BASE}$ and DistilBERT models.

Competitors and and Performance Comparison. In our research, we conduct detailed comparisons of our pruning method with several domain-specific retraining-free algorithms: KCM Nova et al. (2023), Kwon et al. (2022), and K-prune Park et al. (2023). Additionally, we compare against recent retraining-based algorithms like Flop Wang et al. (2019), SLIP Lin et al. (2020), Sajjad et al. Sajjad et al. (2023), EBERT Liu et al. (2021b), and DynaBERT Hou et al. (2020b). These comparisons focus on performance metrics under various FLOPs constraints. Given the slight variations in baseline accuracy among these papers, directly comparing the absolute accuracy of pruned models is challenging. To facilitate effective comparisons, we adopt accuracy degradation (i.e., the difference in accuracy between pruned and original models) as the primary evaluation metric. Regarding pruning efficiency, our focus is primarily on performance under a 60% FLOPs constraint.

Baseline Configuration. We use $BERT_{BASE}$ and DistilBERT as our baseline models, maintaining their original architectures and configurations. For pruning, we randomly select 2,000 samples from their training sets to ensure swift and efficient processing, avoiding overfitting while preserving model accuracy. We evaluate accuracy on GLUE tasks and F1 score on SQuAD tasks. To ensure reliable results, we conduct experiments with ten random seeds and report average outcomes.

5.2 Accuracy Comparison

As shown in Figure 2, while all methods inevitably sacrifice some degree of accuracy when reducing FLOPs, our approach exhibits the least accuracy degradation in most cases. Particularly under more lenient FLOPs constraints, its performance advantage becomes more pronounced. This suggests that at the same pruning cost, our method achieves significantly higher accuracy compared to other algorithms. In other words, if we can maintain the same level of accuracy as other algorithms, we can perform more extensive pruning operations.

As shown in Table 1, we compare the accuracy of $BERT_{BASE}$ and DistilBERT models against the baseline model under different FLOPs constraints. The results indicate a significant improvement in

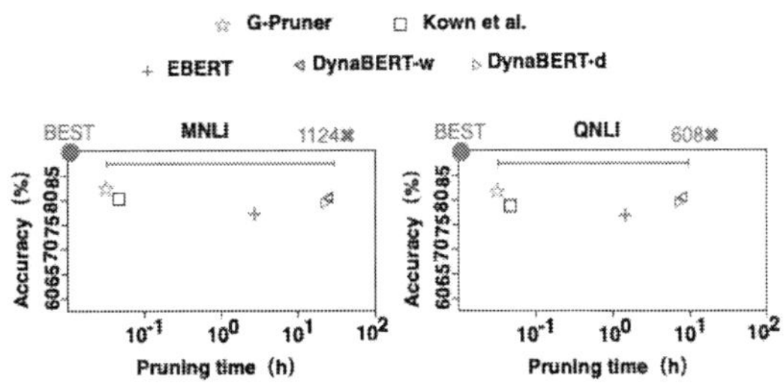

Figure 3: **Under a 60% FLOPs constraint, the accuracy of compressed models is compared with the time cost required for pruning.**

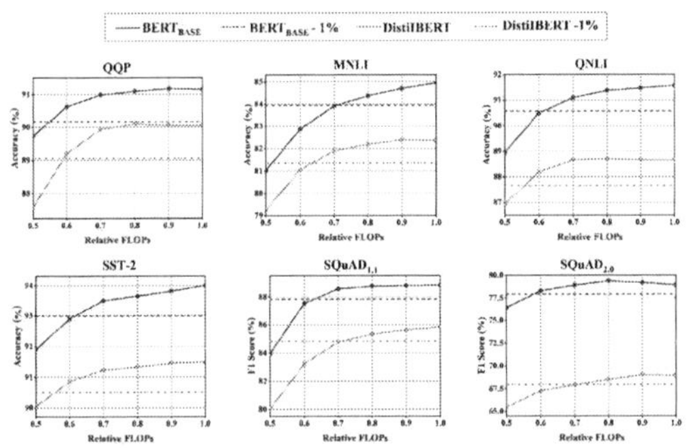

Figure 4: **Despite a strict 1% maximum allowable drop in accuracy,$\text{BERT}_{\text{BASE}}$ achieves 60–70% of the original FLOPs for all tasks.**

accuracy with G-Pruner. Particularly, under a 60% FLOPs constraint, the model achieves a 6.02% higher F1 score on the $\text{SQuAD}_{2.0}$ task compared to the baseline model.

5.3 Speed Comparison

As shown in Figure 3, we evaluate the cost-effectiveness of each pruning algorithm by comparing the model accuracy at a 60% compression rate on the MNLI and QNLI datasets and the time required for pruning (measured in hours). Notably, G-pruner not only shows higher accuracy than other methods in all experimental settings but also significantly reduces pruning costs, by up to 1124×.

5.4 FLOPs

As illustrated in Figure 4, we further analyzed the accuracy variations of $\text{BERT}_{\text{BASE}}$ and DistilBERT under different FLOPs constraints. Our analysis demonstrates that with just a 1% decrease in accuracy, $\text{BERT}_{\text{BASE}}$ maintains 60-70% of its original FLOPs across all tasks.

5.5 Ablation Studies

As shown in Table 2, we conducted ablation studies on the PPOM and CG²MT enhancement modules. While maintaining 60% of FLOPs, we set mask search as the baseline pruning method and then compared it with the addition of PPOM and CG²MT modules. The results indicate that introducing the PPOM module slightly reduces model speed, but adjusting the CG²MT module significantly reduces the time required for model pruning. Additionally, both PPOM and CG²MT modules significantly improve accuracy. For instance, in the QNLI task, the CG²MT module increases the accuracy of the $\text{BERT}_{\text{BASE}}$ model by 2.03%, while the CG²MT module shows a more pronounced improvement, boosting accuracy by 2.29%.

Table 2: **The ablation study, the accuracy results under the 60% FLOPs constraint.**

	Accuracy(%)				
	QQP	MNLI	SST-2	QNLI	Avg. Diff
Mask search	87.40	80.52	90.50	87.04	-
+ PPOM	89.84	81.87	91.25	89.33	+1.70
+ CG²MT	89.67	81.58	91.66	89.07	+1.63
+ PPOM + CG²MT	90.63	82.87	92.89	90.50	+2.85

	Pruning Time(s)				
	QQP	MNLI	SST-2	QNLI	Avg. Diff
Mask search	30.21	31.44	52.45	53.38	-
+ PPOM	40.15	41.57	63.44	64.52	+10.55
+ CG²MT	9.07	10.58	16.56	16.47	-28.70
+ PPOM + CG²MT	13.43	14.55	21.21	21.03	-24.31

6 Conclusion

In this work, we introduce a structured pruning algorithm named G-Pruner, which achieves high-precision pruning without the need to retrain Transformer models. By incorporating two novel techniques, PPOM and CG²MT, we effectively address the shortsightedness problem commonly encountered in traditional methods when assessing the importance of attention heads and feed-forward neural networks. Simultaneously, our approach significantly optimizes the iterative process, reducing numerical instability during computation and achieving faster convergence. Under the same FLOPs constraints, G-Pruner significantly outperforms all existing pruning techniques in pruning time without sacrificing model accuracy.

Funding. This work was supported by the National Natural Science Foundation of China (No.62107009) and the Fund of Jilin Provincial Department of Education Project (No.JJKH20241427KJ).

References

Hongrong Cheng, Miao Zhang, and Javen Qinfeng Shi. 2023. A survey on deep neural network pruning-taxonomy, comparison, analysis, and recommendations. *arXiv preprint arXiv:2308.06767*.

Lucio Dery, Steven Kolawole, Jean-Francois Kagey, Virginia Smith, Graham Neubig, and Ameet Talwalkar. 2024. Everybody prune now: Structured pruning of llms with only forward passes. *arXiv preprint arXiv:2402.05406*.

Gongfan Fang, Xinyin Ma, Mingli Song, Michael Bi Mi, and Xinchao Wang. 2023. Depgraph: Towards any structural pruning. In *Proceedings of the IEEE/CVF Conference on Computer Vision and Pattern Recognition*, pages 16091–16101.

Nuno Guimarães, Ricardo Campos, and Alípio Jorge. 2024. Pre-trained language models: What do they know? *Wiley Interdisciplinary Reviews: Data Mining and Knowledge Discovery*, 14(1):e1518.

Yang He and Lingao Xiao. 2023. Structured pruning for deep convolutional neural networks: A survey. *IEEE Transactions on Pattern Analysis and Machine Intelligence*.

Xanh Ho, Anh Khoa Duong Nguyen, An Tuan Dao, Junfeng Jiang, Yuki Chida, Kaito Sugimoto, Huy Quoc To, Florian Boudin, and Akiko Aizawa. 2024. A survey of pre-trained language models for processing scientific text. *arXiv preprint arXiv:2401.17824*.

Lu Hou, Zhiqi Huang, Lifeng Shang, Xin Jiang, Xiao Chen, and Qun Liu. 2020a. Dynabert: Dynamic bert with adaptive width and depth. *Advances in Neural Information Processing Systems*, 33:9782–9793.

Lu Hou, Zhiqi Huang, Lifeng Shang, Xin Jiang, Xiao Chen, and Qun Liu. 2020b. Dynabert: Dynamic bert with adaptive width and depth. *Advances in Neural Information Processing Systems*, 33:9782–9793.

Forrest N Iandola, Albert E Shaw, Ravi Krishna, and Kurt W Keutzer. 2020. Squeezebert: What can computer vision teach nlp about efficient neural networks? *arXiv preprint arXiv:2006.11316*.

Woojeong Kim, Suhyun Kim, Mincheol Park, and Geunseok Jeon. 2020. Neuron merging: Compensating for pruned neurons. *Advances in Neural Information Processing Systems*, 33:585–595.

Nikita Kitaev, Łukasz Kaiser, and Anselm Levskaya. 2020. Reformer: The efficient transformer. *arXiv preprint arXiv:2001.04451*.

Takeshi Kojima, Itsuki Okimura, Yusuke Iwasawa, Hitomi Yanaka, and Yutaka Matsuo. 2024. On the multilingual ability of decoder-based pre-trained language models: Finding and controlling language-specific neurons. *arXiv preprint arXiv:2404.02431*.

Eldar Kurtic, Daniel Campos, Tuan Nguyen, Elias Frantar, Mark Kurtz, Benjamin Fineran, Michael Goin, and Dan Alistarh. 2022. The optimal bert surgeon: Scalable and accurate second-order pruning for large language models. *arXiv preprint arXiv:2203.07259*.

Woosuk Kwon, Sehoon Kim, Michael W Mahoney, Joseph Hassoun, Kurt Keutzer, and Amir Gholami. 2022. A fast post-training pruning framework for transformers. *Advances in Neural Information Processing Systems*, 35:24101–24116.

Ivan Lazarevich, Alexander Kozlov, and Nikita Malinin. 2021. Post-training deep neural network pruning via layer-wise calibration. In *Proceedings of the IEEE/CVF International Conference on Computer Vision*, pages 798–805.

Bingbing Li, Zhenglun Kong, Tianyun Zhang, Ji Li, Zhengang Li, Hang Liu, and Caiwen Ding. 2020. Efficient transformer-based large scale language representations using hardware-friendly block structured pruning. *arXiv preprint arXiv:2009.08065*.

Junyi Li, Tianyi Tang, Wayne Xin Zhao, Jian-Yun Nie, and Ji-Rong Wen. 2024. Pre-trained language models for text generation: A survey. *ACM Computing Surveys*, 56(9):1–39.

Zi Lin, Jeremiah Zhe Liu, Zi Yang, Nan Hua, and Dan Roth. 2020. Pruning redundant mappings in transformer models via spectral-normalized identity prior. *arXiv preprint arXiv:2010.01791*.

Yuanxin Liu, Zheng Lin, and Fengcheng Yuan. 2021a. Rosita: Refined bert compression with integrated techniques. In *Proceedings of the AAAI Conference on Artificial Intelligence*, volume 35, pages 8715–8722.

Zejian Liu, Fanrong Li, Gang Li, and Jian Cheng. 2021b. Ebert: Efficient bert inference with dynamic structured pruning. In *Findings of the Association for Computational Linguistics: ACL-IJCNLP 2021*, pages 4814–4823.

Taiyuan Mei, Yun Zi, Xiaohan Cheng, Zijun Gao, Qi Wang, and Haowei Yang. 2024. Efficiency optimization of large-scale language models based on deep learning in natural language processing tasks. *arXiv preprint arXiv:2405.11704*.

Ben Mussay, Margarita Osadchy, Vladimir Braverman, Samson Zhou, and Dan Feldman. 2019. Data-independent neural pruning via coresets. *arXiv preprint arXiv:1907.04018*.

Azade Nova, Hanjun Dai, and Dale Schuurmans. 2023. Gradient-free structured pruning with unlabeled data. In *International Conference on Machine Learning*, pages 26326–26341. PMLR.

Adedoyin Tolulope Oyewole, Omotayo Bukola Adeoye, Wilhelmina Afua Addy, Chinwe Chinazo Okoye, Onyeka Chrisanctus Ofodile, and Chinonye Esther Ugochukwu. 2024. Automating financial reporting with natural language processing: A review and case analysis. *World Journal of Advanced Research and Reviews*, 21(3):575–589.

Seungcheol Park, Hojun Choi, and U Kang. 2023. Accurate retraining-free pruning for pretrained encoder-based language models. In *The Twelfth International Conference on Learning Representations*.

Shaina Raza, Muskan Garg, Deepak John Reji, Syed Raza Bashir, and Chen Ding. 2024. Nbias: A natural language processing framework for bias identification in text. *Expert Systems with Applications*, 237:121542.

Hassan Sajjad, Fahim Dalvi, Nadir Durrani, and Preslav Nakov. 2023. On the effect of dropping layers of pre-trained transformer models. *Computer Speech & Language*, 77:101429.

Victor Sanh, Thomas Wolf, and Alexander Rush. 2020. Movement pruning: Adaptive sparsity by fine-tuning. *Advances in neural information processing systems*, 33:20378–20389.

Michael Santacroce, Zixin Wen, Yelong Shen, and Yuanzhi Li. 2023. What matters in the structured pruning of generative language models? *arXiv preprint arXiv:2302.03773*.

Alireza Shamshiri, Kyeong Rok Ryu, and June Young Park. 2024. Text mining and natural language processing in construction. *Automation in Construction*, 158:105200.

Xinyu Shi, Jianhao Ding, Zecheng Hao, and Zhaofei Yu. 2024. Towards energy efficient spiking neural networks: An unstructured pruning framework. In *The Twelfth International Conference on Learning Representations*.

Zhiqing Sun, Hongkun Yu, Xiaodan Song, Renjie Liu, Yiming Yang, and Denny Zhou. 2020. Mobilebert: a compact task-agnostic bert for resource-limited devices. *arXiv preprint arXiv:2004.02984*.

Sinong Wang, Belinda Z Li, Madian Khabsa, Han Fang, and Hao Ma. 2020. Linformer: Self-attention with linear complexity. *arXiv preprint arXiv:2006.04768*.

Ziheng Wang, Jeremy Wohlwend, and Tao Lei. 2019. Structured pruning of large language models. *arXiv preprint arXiv:1910.04732*.

Mengzhou Xia, Zexuan Zhong, and Danqi Chen. 2022. Structured pruning learns compact and accurate models. *arXiv preprint arXiv:2204.00408*.

Can Xu, Qingfeng Sun, Kai Zheng, Xiubo Geng, Pu Zhao, Jiazhan Feng, Chongyang Tao, Qingwei Lin, and Daxin Jiang. 2024. Wizardlm: Empowering large pre-trained language models to follow complex instructions. In *The Twelfth International Conference on Learning Representations*.

Edouard Yvinec, Arnaud Dapogny, Matthieu Cord, and Kevin Bailly. 2021. Red: Looking for redundancies for data-freestructured compression of deep neural networks. *Advances in Neural Information Processing Systems*, 34:20863–20873.

Shaowei Zhang, Rongwang Yin, and Mengzi Zhang. 2024. Dynamic unstructured pruning neural network image super-resolution reconstruction. *Informatica*, 48(7).

Haotian Zheng, Kangming Xu, Huiming Zhou, Yufu Wang, and Guangze Su. 2024. Medication recommendation system based on natural language processing for patient emotion analysis. *Academic Journal of Science and Technology*, 10(1):62–68.

Transformer verbatim in-context retrieval across time and scale

Kristijan Armeni
Johns Hopkins University
karmeni1@jhu.edu

Marko Pranjić
Jozef Stefan Institute
Jozef Stefan International Postgraduate School
marko.pranjic@ijs.si

Senja Pollak
Jozef Stefan Institute
senja.pollak@ijs.si

Abstract

To predict upcoming text, language models must in some cases retrieve in-context information verbatim. In this report, we investigated how the ability of language models to retrieve arbitrary in-context nouns developed during training (across time) and as language models trained on the same dataset increase in size (across scale). We then asked whether learning of in-context retrieval correlates with learning of more challenging zero-shot benchmarks. Furthermore, inspired by semantic effects in human short-term memory, we evaluated the retrieval with respect to a major semantic component of target nouns, namely whether they denote a concrete or abstract entity, as rated by humans. We show that verbatim in-context retrieval developed in a sudden transition early in the training process, after about 1% of the training tokens. This was observed across model sizes (from 14M and up to 12B parameters), and the transition occurred slightly later for the two smallest models. We further found that the development of verbatim in-context retrieval is positively correlated with the learning of zero-shot benchmarks. Around the transition point, all models showed the advantage of retrieving concrete nouns as opposed to abstract nouns. In all but two smallest models, the advantage dissipated away toward the end of training.

1 Introduction

In language models (LMs), successful prediction of upcoming words depends on in-context information. For example, when given the context prompt "*The novel's plot and symbolism are centered around three objects: a centipede, a parachute, and a waterfall. The first and most important object in the list is the* ___", an LM must retrieve the noun (*centipede*) out of all in-context tokens to correctly predict the continuation. In human cognitive science, this ability to flexibly retrieve items from recent context is known as short-term memory and is believed to be the core computation underlying human cognition (Baddeley, 2003).

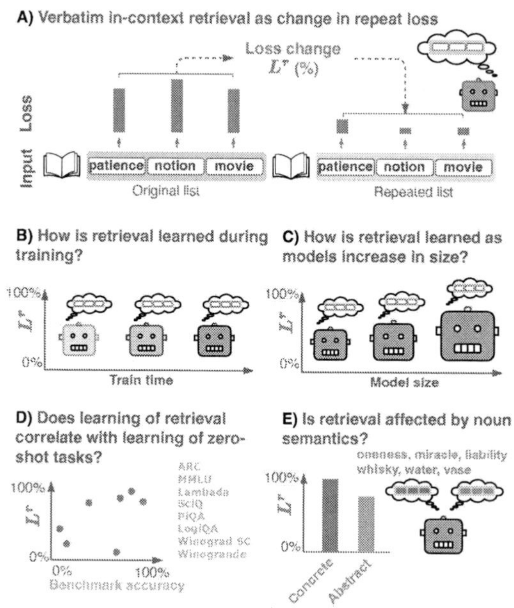

Figure 1: Overview of the approach and experiments.

Recently, Armeni et al. (2022) showed that a transformer language model (GPT-2, Brown et al., 2020) develops such flexible short-term memory — it was able to retrieve the identity and ordering of lists of *arbitrary* nouns from recent context (Fig. 1, A), even though retrieval of arbitrary in-context information is not the explicit objective of LMs (as opposed to dedicated models of short-term memory, e.g. Oberauer et al. 2018). Yet, studying retrieval in a single *fully-trained* model on *arbitrary* nouns neglects three further dimensions of the capacity: how it is learned, how learning of this dedicated capacity relates to models' learning of other tasks, and the semantics of retrieved nouns.

First, studying *learning trajectories* of LM capacities offers complementary insights to studying only performance of fully-trained models (e.g.

Proceedings of the 28th Conference on Computational Natural Language Learning, pages 56–68
November 15-16, 2024 ©2024 Association for Computational Linguistics

Chen et al., 2024). Previous work on LM learning trajectories showed that transformers learn next-token prediction by undergoing a *sudden transition* ("phase change") early during training, which coincides with the development of attention heads that attend to repeated tokens (Olsson et al., 2022). Does verbatim retrieval follow a similar learning trajectory?

Second, the ability to retrieve and predict in-context tokens verbatim (i.e. identity-based matching) can be viewed as a rudimentary form of the more flexible zero-shot learning, where the relevant in-context information is not necessarily given verbatim and must possibly be retrieved based on fuzzy, similarity-based matching (Olsson et al., 2022). How does successful learning of verbatim retrieval relate to LM's zero-shot performance on more challenging benchmark tasks?

Third, while the successful retrieval of arbitrary nouns underscores the flexibility of transformer short-term memory, this approach neglects that the lexicon of natural language is not a set of unorganized, arbitrary words — instead, it has semantic structure. Two prominent semantic categories are *concrete* and *abstract* nouns. Concrete nouns (e.g. "hammer") have sensory referents, whereas abstract nouns (e.g. "justice") do not have a straightforward sensory component. Word concreteness affects human cognitive processing. Children typically acquire concrete words, especially nouns, earlier than abstract words (Gleitman et al., 2005). In certain short-term memory paradigms, humans are better at recalling concrete than abstract words (Taylor et al., 2019). Importantly, the two word categories differ also in their distributional properties: concrete words occur in a semantically narrower range of contexts compared to abstract words (Schulte im Walde and Frassinelli, 2022). Is the transformer retrieval affected by whether nouns refer to concrete vs. abstract entities?

To address these questions, we evaluated verbatim in-context retrieval on the Pythia suite of language models (Biderman et al., 2023). Leveraging the fact that the suite includes pretrained LMs ranging from 14M to 12B parameters in scale and their intermediate training checkpoints across the entire learning epoch, we evaluated how retrieval develops over the course of training and across model sizes (Fig. 1, B and C). Additionally, the Pythia suite contains zero-shot evaluations on various benchmarks for each LM checkpoint. To test how in-context retrieval relates to LM's zero-shot performance, we correlated the learning trajectory of the retrieval against the learning trajectories on zero-shot benchmarks (Fig. 1, D). Finally, to test the role of noun semantics for in-context retrieval, we evaluated how noun concreteness, as rated by human participants (Brysbaert et al., 2014), affected retrieval over the course of training (Fig. 1, E).

The main contributions of the current work are: **a)** In all models, verbatim retrieval developed in a sudden transition early during training, after about 1% training tokens elapsed, and remained constant during the rest of training, **b)** learning of verbatim retrieval was positively correlated with learning of zero-shot task performance, and **c)** around the transition point, LMs showed an advantage to retrieve concrete rather than abstract nouns. This advantage almost entirely diminished towards the end of training.

2 Related work

Several recent studies investigated the behavior of LMs in domain of either verbatim or in-context retrieval more generally. Armeni et al. (2022) developed a paradigm to test the short-term memory ability (in-context retrieval) of LMs. They showed that GPT-2 can retrieve the identity and ordering of repeated arbitrary nouns, but have only tested a single fully-trained LM and did not investigate learning trajectories. Vaidya et al. (2023) compared LM (GPT-2) and human word prediction performance on spans of repeated text. They reported that LMs' next word prediction performance diverges from human performance on subsequent repetitions. They showed that GPT-2 performance aligned better with humans if its attention heads had a bias towards recent context. Yu et al. (2023) investigated in-context retrieval of facts (e.g. retrieval of the capital city given a country name) and how such retrieval was affected by the pretraining statistics of retrieved facts. They showed that LMs (Pythia) could override retrieval of (counterfactual) in-context information and instead retrieved the fact that has a higher frequency of occurrence in training data (e.g., even when given the in-context counterfactual "*The capital city of Poland is London*" they tend to predict the statistically more likely "*Warszaw*").

The current report is also related to the recent work on LM interpretability and the role of attention heads in specific forms of retrieval. Several studies (Elhage et al., 2021; Olsson et al., 2022; Wang et al., 2023; Yu et al., 2023) have identified circuits of attention heads that detect repeated in-context tokens and their previous continuations; the computations governing the behavior investigated presently. These studies focused either on how such attention mechanisms are learned and how they affect generic next-word prediction (Elhage et al., 2021; Olsson et al., 2022) or how these attention mechanisms govern the retrieval of proper nouns as direct objects in sentences (Wang et al., 2022) or factual knowledge (direct objects, Yu et al., 2023).

Here, we complement these lines of work and investigate retrieval as the ability of LMs to retrieve lists of arbitrary combinations of common nouns (unlikely seen co-occuring during training) and their semantic properties.

3 Methods

3.1 Verbatim retrieval paradigm

We used the verbatim retrieval paradigm introduced by Armeni et al. (2022). Here, LMs process a short vignette in English where a list of three arbitrary nouns is repeated twice:

> *Mary read a list of words:* ***patience, notion, movie****. After the meeting, she took a break and had a cup of coffee. When she got back, she read the list again:* ***patience, notion, movie****.*

We refer to the first list of nouns as original list and the second one as repeated list. This setup allows us to test how the LM behavior (as reflected in LM loss, see below) changes as the LM encounters the repeated list. The paradigm (retrieval of arbitrary lists of words) is broadly inspired by benchmarks for testing models of human working memory (Oberauer et al., 2018). Whereas human participants can be tested by just being presented with lists of nouns alone, our paradigm is formatted such that it is more suited to be used as input to LMs: contextualized in a simple, but plausible natural language vignette.

3.2 Quantifying verbatim retrieval

Change in repeat loss (L^r) Following Armeni et al. (2022), we operationalized retrieval as a change in LM loss on repeated nouns. Specifically, we computed the ratio in LM loss $= -\log_2 P(w_t|w_1, ..., w_{t-1})$ between each noun in the original list and its repetition k tokens later: $\text{loss ratio}^{noun} = \frac{\text{loss}(\text{noun}_{i+k})}{\text{loss}(\text{noun}_i)}$. The loss ratio per list was obtained by averaging the noun-specific loss ratios over the three nouns in a list. A loss ratio < 1 indicates that the loss to the *same tokens* has decreased (that is, the LM expected the token to repeat) and is taken as evidence of verbatim retrieval.

To quantify retrieval as increasing with better performance, we report it as repeat loss change $L^r = 1 - \text{loss ratio}$, expressed as percentage. In this way, a 0% change in repeat loss indicates no retrieval whereas a change towards 100% indicates evidence towards (perfect) retrieval. Importantly, repeat loss change is a continuous measure of in-context retrieval, baselined against the LM loss at the beginning of the sequence which facilitates comparison across models (e.g. models that show different baseline loss as expected over the course of training and across scale) and across different types of inputs.

3.3 Language models

Pythia suite To evaluate retrieval over the course of training and across scale (see Section 3.4 below), we used the publicly-available pretrained LM checkpoints released as part of the Pythia language modeling suite (Biderman et al., 2023).[1] Pythia is a suite of decoder-only autoregressive transformer LMs spanning from 14M to 12B parameters in size together with 144 intermediate checkpoints stored during training. The models were trained on the Pile dataset (Gao et al., 2020), an English-only corpus for training large-scale LMs containing texts from 22 sources (for example, Common Crawl, Wikipedia, Project Gutenberg, Books3, arXiv etc., see Biderman et al., 2022, for details). The model checkpoints used in this report were trained on the version of the dataset containing approximately 300B tokens. For the full architecture and training details, readers are referred to the original report (Biderman et al., 2023).

In our experiments, we evaluated the following model sizes: {14M, 31M, 70M, 160M, 410M, 1B, 6.9B, 12B} at 18 training checkpoints spanning 6 orders of magnitude across the training steps (in number of training tokens, 10^6, ..., 10^{11}) from the initialized to the final fully-trained model[2]. All

[1] `https://github.com/EleutherAI/pythia`

[2] Specifically we evaluated the checkpoints from the following training steps: {0, 1, 4, 32, 128, 256, 512, 1000, 2000, 3000, 4000, 8000, 10000, 30000, 40000, 50000, 100000, 143000}. A single step contained 2,097,152 tokens (Biderman

Task	Domain	Reference
AI2 Reasoning Challenge (ARC)	Multiple choice science exams	Clark et al. (2018)
Lambada	Discourse-based word prediction	Paperno et al. (2016)
LogiQA	Logical reasoning	Liu et al. (2020)
Massive multitask lang. understanding (MMLU)	Exam knowledge across diverse domains	Hendrycks et al. (2021)
PiQA	Physical common-sense reasoning	Bisk et al. (2020b)
SciQ	Scientific knowledge	Welbl et al. (2017)
Winograd schema challenge (WSC)	Common-sense reasoning	Levesque et al. (2012)
Winogrande	Common-sense reasoning	Sakaguchi et al. (2021)

Table 1: The benchmark tasks used to compute in learning trajectory correlations in Fig. 3.

model checkpoints were accessed through the HuggingFace Transformers library (Wolf et al., 2020).

3.4 Experiments

Experiment 1: Retrieval of arbitrary nouns across time and scale In the first experiment, word lists in the vignette were constructed by randomly sampling nouns from the Toronto word pool[3] as used in Armeni et al. (2022). Noun lists in the set (23 lists of 10 nouns) were constructed such that each noun was tested in all 10 possible ordinal positions in the list (e.g. "patience, notion, movie", "notion, movie, patience", etc.) to control for any position-specific retrieval effects. This procedure resulted in the final stimulus set that contained $N = 230$ samples of vignettes. In the present experiment, we used the version of the stimulus set where the list length was capped at 3 nouns.

Evaluating an LM on the full retrieval evaluation suite yields one retrieval score (repeat loss change) per each input vignette. The final retrieval score, per each training step and per model size, was obtained by taking an average across all (in this case $N = 230$) scores. To minimize the potential influence of outliers in averaging, we used the 20% trimmed mean (Wilcox and Keselman, 2003) as the aggregating metric. The results of this experiment are reported in Figure 2.

Experiment 2: Correlations with zero-shot benchmark learning. To test how learning of verbatim in-context retrieval relates to the learning of zero-shot benchmark tasks assessing text understanding, we collected the zero-shot evaluation results on various NLP benchmarks that were available for the Pythia suite of LMs[4]. Evaluations were available for the following 6 model sizes: {160M, 410M, 1.4B, 2.8B, 6.9B, 12B} and across 27 checkpoints[5] during training, starting with the initial and ending with the fully-trained model. All individual tasks ($N = 65$) used accuracy as the final metric. The main groups of tasks used in the experiment are summarized in Table 1. See Table 3, Appendix A for the full task list.

For each benchmark task (e.g. Lambada, SciQ etc.), we computed the correlation $\rho^{traj} = \text{Spearman}(S^{ret}, S^{bench})$ between the learning trajectory of the benchmark task S^{bench} (i.e. task performance scores across the 27 checkpoints) and the learning trajectory of our verbatim retrieval effect S^{ret} (i.e. repeat loss change L^r across the same 27 checkpoints). The Massive multitask understanding benchmark (MMLU, Hendrycks et al., 2021) consists of an array of domain-specific exams (e.g. marketing, clinical knowledge, nursing) which are grouped into 4 higher-level categories (humanities, STEM, social sciences, and 'other (business, health, misc.)', see Table 3, Appendix A). For these grouped tasks, we first averaged the learning trajectories per each group and then correlated them with verbatim retrieval effect. We used the rank-based Spearman correlation coefficient where a value of 1 indicates a perfect monotonically increasing relationship between two variables and is robust to any deviations from normality in data distributions.

Experiment 3: Effect of noun concreteness on retrieval. To test for retrieval of concrete and abstract nouns, we evaluated LMs on the same paradigm as in the first experiment, but the noun lists were composed of either concrete or abstract nouns. We used abstract and concrete English

et al., 2023).

[3]http://memory.psych.upenn.edu/files/wordpools/nouns.txt

[4]https://github.com/EleutherAI/pythia/tree/main/evals/pythia-v1

[5]Checkpoints corresponding to the following Pythia training steps were evaluated: {0, 1, 2, 4, 8, 16, 32, 64, 128, 256, 512, 1000, 3000, 13000, 23000, 33000, 43000, 53000, 63000, 73000, 83000, 93000, 103000, 113000, 123000, 133000, 143000}.

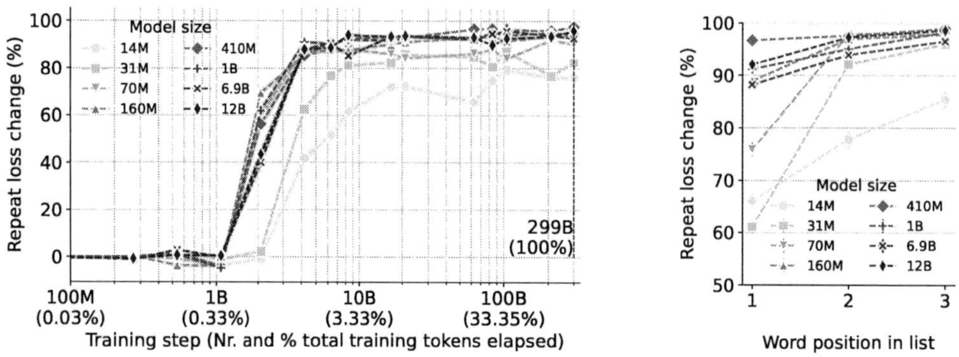

(a) Capacity to retrieve verbatim repetitions of arbitrary nouns (average across three nouns in a list) is learned early during LM training and predominantly conserved across scale.

(b) Retrieval improves for items later in the list (fully-trained models).

Figure 2: **Retrieval of arbitrary nouns across time and scale.** Each data point represents the 20% trimmed mean across $N = 230$ observations, shaded areas/error bars are 95% confidence intervals (bootstrap).

nouns collected by Brysbaert et al. (2014) where human participants were asked to indicate "*how concrete the meaning of each word is for you*" by rating each noun on a 5-point rating scale ranging from 1 "abstract (language-based)" to 5 "concrete (experience-based)". Each word was rated by at least 25 participants and an average score across participants represents each noun's final rating.

Table 2: The topmost, mid and lowest ranked words and their concreteness ratings for the concrete and abstract noun pool.

	Concrete		Abstract	
Rank	Word	Rating	Word	Rating
1	whisky	5.00	oneness	1.96
250	canister	4.93	respite	1.77
500	eyebrow	4.85	spirituality	1.07

Concreteness extremes In our experiments, we used the "concreteness extremes" subset of the noun pool by Schulte im Walde and Frassinelli (2022). This subset contained the 500 nouns ranked as most concrete and 500 nouns ranked as most abstract. To give an idea, the topmost, mid and lowest ranked nouns for each category are shown in Table 2. As in Experiment 1, each noun was presented in all ordinal positions to rule out any position-specific effects. Our final stimulus set contained, for each semantic category, $N = 498$ input sequences with lists of 3 nouns.

4 Results

4.1 Verbatim retrieval across time and scale.

Verbatim retrieval learned early in training across model sizes. All tested models, from the smallest (14 million parameters) to the largest (12 billion parameters), learned to retrieve verbatim repeated nouns (Fig. 2a). At the end of training, all models above 31 million parameters showed a near 100% repeat loss change, indicating exact retrieval. The smallest two models (14M and 31M parameters) showed weaker, yet still substantial retrieval effect (around 80% change in repeat loss).

Inspecting the dynamics of repeat loss change across training, we see that generally models learned verbatim retrieval early. After about 1B tokens (0.3% of total dataset), the change in repeat loss starts increasing and, for all larger models, plateaus at approximately 4B tokens (less than 5% of the total tokens in the dataset). The smallest two models had a slower learning curve as evidenced in the fact that their repeat loss change plateaued later, after roughly 20B tokens.

To confirm that reduction in repeat loss was due to retrieval of the *original nouns* and not due to LMs simply having more context when encountering nouns at the end of sequence or due to memorization of lists from training data, we evaluated the loss change in the same paradigm but where the nouns in the second list were unrelated to the nouns in the original list (i.e. there were no matching in-context nouns to retrieve). Fig. 6 in Appendix A.1 confirms that no important loss change occurred in this condition (loss change overall remained <

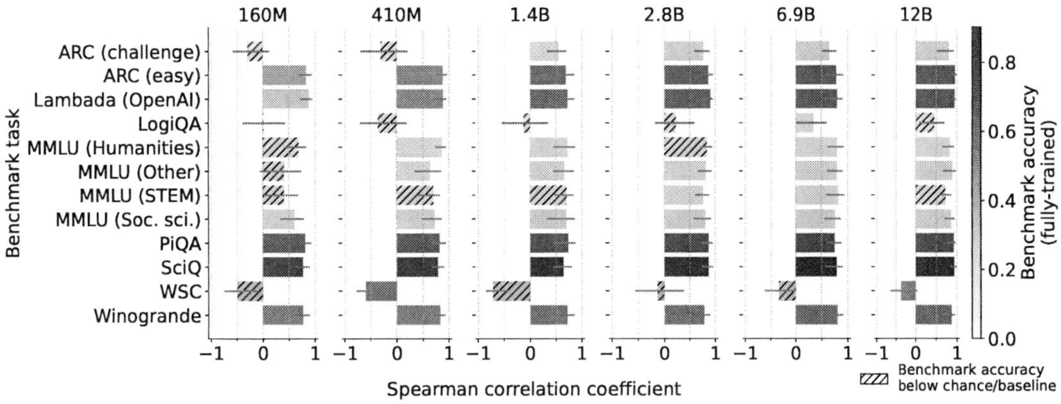

Figure 3: **Correlations between the learning trajectories of verbatim retrieval and select benchmark tasks.** Error bars denote the 95% confidence interval (bootstrap, $N = 5000$) around the correlation coefficient. Color-coded is the benchmark performance accuracy at the end of training for each task. Chance performance for ARC, LogiQA, MMLU*, LogiQA, SciQ is 0.25, for PiQA, WSC, and Winogrande 0.5. For LAMBADA we threshold against predicting a random in-context token (0.016) (see Table 1 in Paperno et al., 2016). See Table 1 for task descriptions.

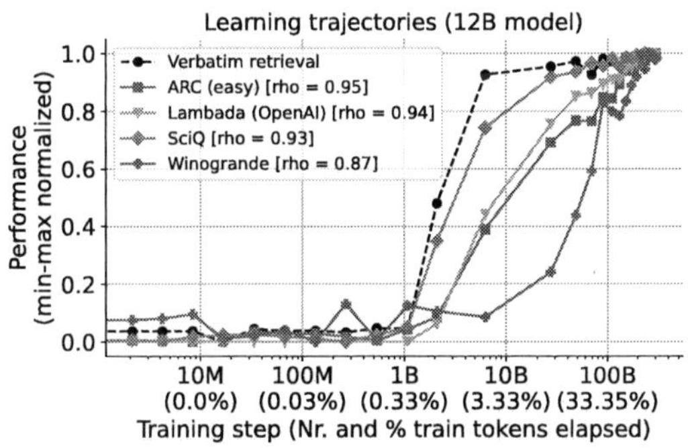

Figure 4: Examples of learning trajectories (12B model) for tasks that showed strongest correlations with verbatim retrieval for the largest tested model. For visualization purposes, accuracy scores are min-max normalized to fall in the $[0, 1]$ range.

10%), replicating the GPT-2 results by Armeni et al. (2022) and indicating that the change of loss was specific to *verbatim retrieval* of tokens from context.

Retrieval improves for nouns deeper in the list. In the previous result, we reported repeat loss change aggregated over all three nouns in the list. Yet, nouns deeper in the list have an advantage because at that point the LM has seen strong evidence of repetition. Does retrieval performance depend on the position in the list?

In Fig. 2b, we report repeat loss change of fully-trained models broken down per noun position within the list. Retrieval indeed becomes better later in the list. While all models show this trend, the position-specific advantage is more pronounced for the smaller models (14M, 31M, and 70M). For example, the 70M model shows 62% repeat loss change on the first and a 95% change on the last token in the list. This indicates that subsequent repetitions reinforce the evidence that the model has entered a repeated list and is in line with recent results where next-word prediction performance of GPT-2 improved on spans of repeated text (Vaidya et al., 2023).

4.2 Correlations with benchmark task learning

Learning of verbatim retrieval is positively correlated with zero-shot performance on more challenging benchmark tasks. In Figure 3 we show the results of the correlation experiment. Generally, most tasks showed a positive correlation with the learning of verbatim retrieval. The correlations and their reliability, as well as the benchmark accuracy itself, tended to increase as the models grow in size, showing that the larger models were more robust learners overall. The highest correlations were observed for the Lambada, PiQA, SciQ, and ARC (easy) benchmarks. For example, the largest 12B model (Figure 4) showed a near perfect rank correlation ($\rho \simeq 0.95$) on the four tasks. These are also the tasks where the model showed generally the highest performance accuracy at the end of training.

For the Winograd schema challenge, LogiQA, and the hard version of the AI2 reasoning challenge, the correlation estimates were generally un-

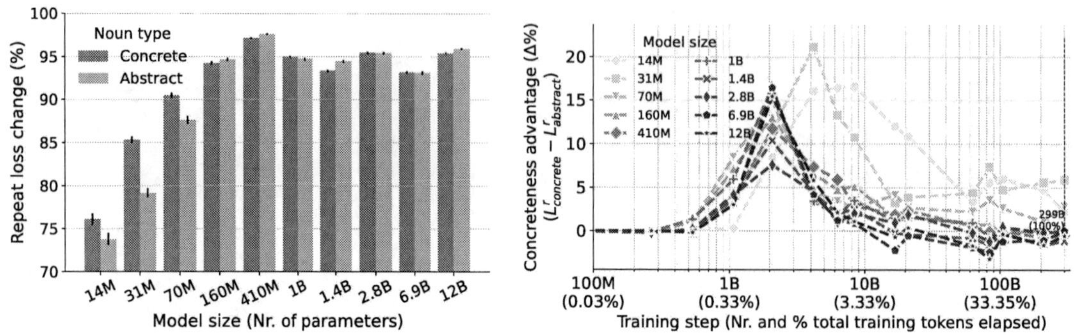

(a) Concrete vs. abstract noun retrieval at the end of training. The three smallest models show a weak advantage for retrieving concrete nouns.

(b) Retrieval of concrete vs. abstract nouns over the course of training. Around the transition point, all models show an advantage to retrieve concrete nouns.

Figure 5: **Retrieval of concrete and abstract nouns. a)** Each bar shows the 20% trimmed mean across $N = 498$ observations, error bars show 95% confidence intervals (bootstrap). See also Fig. 7 in Appendix A.2. **b)** Each data point concreteness advantage: the difference in mean repeat loss change for concrete vs. abstract nouns.

stable, likely because the performance on these benchmarks was lower to begin with. That is, even though all the models were able to retrieve verbatim in-context tokens, they failed to solve the respective benchmarks in zero-shot settings.

4.3 Effect of noun concreteness on retrieval

Concreteness retrieval advantage observed early during training. Overall, all models learned to retrieve either abstract or concrete nouns. Repeat loss change at the end of training (on either repeated concrete or abstract nouns) was generally high and ranged from 73% (14M model) to around 95% for models larger than 160M parameters (Fig. 5a). The 14M, 31M and 70M models showed better retrieval for concrete nouns. The effects, although detectable, were small — on average the relative loss change for concrete nouns is greater by between 2% and 6% compared to abstract nouns (see also Fig. 7, Appendix A.2 for visualizations of full distributions).

To test whether nouns semantics affected retrieval during training, we computed the difference in average repeat loss change between concrete and abstract nouns $\Delta L^r = \bar{L}^r_{concrete} - \bar{L}^r_{abstract}$ across the training checkpoints. The difference curves in Fig. 5b show that around the transition point (1-2B tokens intro training), when LMs begin to learn the retrieval, concrete nouns showed 7-17% greater change in repeat loss meaning they were easier to retrieve than abstract nouns. The concreteness advantage occurred in all models and the smallest models (14 and 70M parameters) showed the largest effects.

5 Discussion

We showed that transformer LMs learned verbatim retrieval in a sudden transition, early in training, with the performance remaining stable over the course of training. The sharp onset of retrieval capacity around 1-2B tokens in training (approximately 1% total training data) is in line with the results reported by Olsson et al. (2022) who showed that the LM loss over in-context tokens started dropping suddenly 1-2% tokens in training (between 2.5B and 5B tokens). Once the learning change had occurred, the LMs became better at predicting repeated text — which is what was tested in the current work.

The learning trajectory of verbatim retrieval also coincides with the LMs' learning trajectories on zero-shot benchmarks. This was reflected in the generally high and robust correlations across training for select tasks in our results. Specifically, an abrupt change around 1B tokens in training was observed in the task of predicting the last token of a narrative passage (Lambada, Paperno et al. 2016), multiple choice exams (SciQ, Welbl et al. 2017, ARC Reasoning Challenge, Clark et al. 2018), and in the Winogrande benchmark (Sakaguchi et al., 2021) which requires pronoun resolution based on common-sense reasoning.

Retrieving in-context information (e.g. lists of nouns) verbatim is a basic computation needed for solving a zero-shot multiple-choice task: given a prompt with only in-context instructions (that is, the question and the list of possible answers), an LM system must index and retrieve (i.e. increase the probability of) the token representing the correct answer. In this sense, retrieving the correct in-context tokens is a necessary step. It is evident, however, that it is not sufficient and that verbatim retrieval must be learned along with other computations.

Consider the Lambada and Winogrande benchmarks, where the task is to predict the passage- or sentence-final word which itself is not predictable on the basis of immediately preceding words. To take an example from the Winogrande benchmark: "*Robert woke up at 9am while Samuel woke up at 6am, so* ***he*** *had less time to get ready for school*"[6]. The task is to answer who the pronoun "he" refers to (Robert or Samuel). To this end, the LM must first establish that 9am is later than 6am — a distinct computational step indicating that "he" refers to "Robert" — and only then retrieve the name to be predicted as the response.

In the final experiment, we show that around the transition point (after $\simeq$1B training tokens), when the capacity for verbatim retrieval occurs, noun semantics affect the retrieval — models showed an advantage to retrieve concrete, as opposed to abstract nouns. Why would LM in-context retrieval be sensitive to noun semantics?

In humans, concrete words, especially nouns, tend to be acquired earlier in development compared to abstract words (Gleitman et al., 2005). This advantage is presumably conferred by hearing words for concrete objects and concurrently observing or interacting with the objects the heard words refer to in the world. LMs as text-based statistical learners by construction have no direct access to word semantics via experience or text-external data (Bisk et al., 2020a). Nevertheless, text statistics, governed by human language use, can serve as a cue to the semantic structure of language — in this case, the lexicon. It is an empirical question whether and what aspects of the linguistic system are in fact recovered by LMs in the service of the next-word prediction objective and subsequently reflected in the LM behavior or internal mechanisms (Manning, 2022; Pavlick, 2023).

We speculate that earlier in training, LMs are leveraging the fact that concrete nouns tend to be used in more predictable, less diverse contexts (Schulte im Walde and Frassinelli, 2022) where presumably token repetition would be more likely to occur. However, once the LMs and the training compute scale in size, this distributional difference no longer confers an important advantage for retrieval. The phenomenon of concreteness advantage early, but not later in training underscores the general notion that with the increasing amounts of training data, LMs as machine learning systems become incommensurate with human learners (see also Vaidya et al., 2023), who operate on the order(s) of magnitude smaller amount of learning data, at least in terms of number of words — recent estimates point to around 100M words by adolescence (Warstadt and Bowman, 2022).

Future work. In this study we investigated retrieval across a diverse set of nouns, and broken down by a core semantic dimension. However, LMs are statistical learners. A dimension of future work will be to disentangle the *learning sources* that LMs leverage to perform retrieval. In a recent study, Yu et al. (2023) showed that pretraining frequency can override the retrieval of counterfactual in-context information. An LM is more likely to predict a proper noun that was frequently occurring in pretraining, e.g. "*Warszaw*", even when the counterfactual in-context prompt suggests it should retrieve a different name ("*The capital of Poland is London. What is the capital of Poland?*"). Our present results do not speak directly to this issue as our paradigm does not involve counterfactuals. It is based on lists of arbitrary nouns that unlikely frequently co-occurred in pretraining data. However, it would be important to establish whether and to what extent the in-context retrieval in general is governed by the pretraining frequencies of individual common nouns and to what degree this capacity is robust to pretraining statistics.

Finally, our measure of verbatim retrieval is a behavioral measure insofar that it only takes into account the output of the LM. The field of model interpretability has seen an increased interest in recent years and aims to reverse engineer the computations of LMs (e.g. Olsson et al., 2022; Elhage et al., 2021; Wang et al., 2023; Zhang and Nanda, 2023, among others). Future work could focus on investigating the internal mechanisms and their causal role in transformer in-context retrieval. There is consistent evidence suggesting that LMs develop dedicated attention heads (Olsson et al., 2022; Wang et al., 2023; Yu et al., 2023; Vaidya et al., 2023) governing the retrieval capacity. Whereas this line work frequently focuses on interpretability for practical purposes (e.g. better control of LM output in

[6]https://winogrande.allenai.org/

downstream applications), it would be valuable to simultaneously develop a more fine-grained computational characterization of LM mechanisms interpretable with respect to cognitive science constructs like the short-term memory (Cowan, 2017).

In cognitive neuroscience, language features derived from transformer LMs (contextualized word embeddings) are currently among the best performing when it comes to predicting brain data recorded in human language processing tasks (e.g. Schrimpf et al., 2021; Goldstein et al., 2022; Caucheteux and King, 2022). However, these high-dimensional features and the resulting statistical fits are frequently hard to interpret. Coupled with loose theoretical motivations such high predicting models can be right for the wrong scientific reasons (see e.g. Antonello and Huth, 2023). A better characterization of LM mechanisms in terms of cognitive capacities (e.g. Lakretz et al., 2022) would be instrumental in understanding how and why LMs succeed in modeling human brain and cognitive data.

6 Conclusion

Retrieving information from context is an important capacity of transformer language models. In this work, we investigated how the ability to retrieve repeated nouns from context develops across LM training and scale and its dependence on whether the retrieved nouns denote concrete or abstract entities. Retrieval was learned early in training across scale and once learned, it remained stable. Retrieval learning was robustly correlated with learning of zero-shot task performance. Around the point when the in-context retrieval was learned, the models showed advantage to retrieving concrete as opposed to abstract nouns and the advantage dissipated as the models saw more training data.

7 Limitations

There are certain limitations to current work. While our test suite was designed to test arbitrary target nouns, we did not investigate whether and how well LM retrieval generalizes to other parts of speech (say, to verbs, adjectives). Similarly, the currently reported paradigm relies on a single vignette, it would be important to use a more diverse set of vignettes to confirm that the results generalize across topic domains. However, given the robustness and size of the effect here and in past reports by others, it is likely that the finding would generalize across a diversity of vignettes. Finally, our results are limited to English, which currently the dominant language in terms of available resources in language technologies. Extending the study to other languages with, for example, different grammatical properties (e.g. richer noun morphology) or less resources would be a welcome effort.

Data and Code Availability

The code used to run the experiments is available at: `https://github.com/KristijanArmeni/verbatim-memory-in-NLMs`
The materials and data used in the experiments are available at: `https://doi.org/10.17605/OSF.IO/A6GSW`

Computational requirements

Experiments described in this report were run on the A100 Nvidia GPU nodes on an high-performance computing cluster (HPC). To evaluate the smallest (14M) model, we requested 8GB of RAM and the evaluation completed on the order of a few minutes. RAM requirements were progressively increased to evaluate larger models. For the largest (12B) model, we requested 80GB of RAM and the evaluation completed in about 30 minutes.

Acknowledgements

KA would like to thank Christopher Honey and Tal Linzen for scientific and administrative support. This work was supported in part through the NYU IT High Performance Computing resources, services, and staff expertise. KA, MP, and SP want to thank Rebecca Swisdak, Mili Bauer and Živa Antauer for exceptional administrative support. This work was supported by the Slovenian Research and Innovation Agency via the bilateral research project Working Memory based assessment of Large Language Models (BI-US/22-24-170), the research project Embeddings-based techniques for Media Monitoring Applications (L2-50070, co-funded by the Kliping d.o.o. agency) and the core research programme Knowledge Technologies (P2-0103).

References

Richard Antonello and Alexander Huth. 2023. Predictive coding or just feature discovery? An alternative account of why language models fit brain data. *Neurobiology of Language*, pages 1–16.

Kristijan Armeni, Christopher Honey, and Tal Linzen. 2022. Characterizing verbatim short-term memory in neural language models. In *Proceedings of the 26th Conference on Computational Natural Language Learning (CoNLL)*, pages 405–424, Abu Dhabi, United Arab Emirates (Hybrid). Association for Computational Linguistics.

Alan Baddeley. 2003. Working memory: looking back and looking forward. *Nature Reviews Neuroscience*, 4(10):829–839.

Stella Biderman, Kieran Bicheno, and Leo Gao. 2022. Datasheet for the Pile. ArXiv:2201.07311 version: 1.

Stella Biderman, Hailey Schoelkopf, Quentin Gregory Anthony, Herbie Bradley, Kyle O'Brien, Eric Hallahan, Mohammad Aflah Khan, Shivanshu Purohit, USVSN Sai Prashanth, Edward Raff, and others. 2023. Pythia: A suite for analyzing large language models across training and scaling. In *International Conference on Machine Learning*, pages 2397–2430. PMLR.

Yonatan Bisk, Ari Holtzman, Jesse Thomason, Jacob Andreas, Yoshua Bengio, Joyce Chai, Mirella Lapata, Angeliki Lazaridou, Jonathan May, Aleksandr Nisnevich, Nicolas Pinto, and Joseph Turian. 2020a. Experience grounds language. *arXiv:2004.10151 [cs]*. ArXiv: 2004.10151.

Yonatan Bisk, Rowan Zellers, Ronan Le Bras, Jianfeng Gao, and Yejin Choi. 2020b. PIQA: Reasoning about physical commonsense in natural language. In *Thirty-Fourth AAAI Conference on Artificial Intelligence*.

Tom Brown, Benjamin Mann, Nick Ryder, Melanie Subbiah, Jared D Kaplan, Prafulla Dhariwal, Arvind Neelakantan, Pranav Shyam, Girish Sastry, Amanda Askell, Sandhini Agarwal, Ariel Herbert-Voss, Gretchen Krueger, Tom Henighan, Rewon Child, Aditya Ramesh, Daniel Ziegler, Jeffrey Wu, Clemens Winter, Chris Hesse, Mark Chen, Eric Sigler, Mateusz Litwin, Scott Gray, Benjamin Chess, Jack Clark, Christopher Berner, Sam McCandlish, Alec Radford, Ilya Sutskever, and Dario Amodei. 2020. Language models are few-shot learners. In *Advances in Neural Information Processing Systems*, volume 33, pages 1877–1901. Curran Associates, Inc.

Marc Brysbaert, Amy Beth Warriner, and Victor Kuperman. 2014. Concreteness ratings for 40 thousand generally known English word lemmas. *Behavior Research Methods*, 46(3):904–911.

Charlotte Caucheteux and Jean-Rémi King. 2022. Brains and algorithms partially converge in natural language processing. *Communications Biology*, 5(1):134.

Angelica Chen, Ravid Shwartz-Ziv, Kyunghyun Cho, Matthew L. Leavitt, and Naomi Saphra. 2024. Sudden drops in the loss: Syntax acquisition, phase Transitions, and simplicity bias in MLMs. ArXiv:2309.07311 [cs].

Peter Clark, Isaac Cowhey, Oren Etzioni, Tushar Khot, Ashish Sabharwal, Carissa Schoenick, and Oyvind Tafjord. 2018. Think you have solved question answering? Try ARC, the AI2 reasoning challenge. *ArXiv*, abs/1803.05457.

Nelson Cowan. 2017. The many faces of working memory and short-term storage. *Psychonomic Bulletin & Review*, 24(4):1158–1170.

Nelson Elhage, Neel Nanda, Catherine Olsson, Tom Henighan, Nicholas Joseph, Ben Mann, Amanda Askell, Yuntao Bai, Anna Chen, Tom Conerly, Nova DasSarma, Dawn Drain, Deep Ganguli, Zac Hatfield-Dodds, Danny Hernandez, Andy Jones, Jackson Kernion, Liane Lovitt, Kamal Ndousse, Dario Amodei, Tom Brown, Jack Clark, Jared Kaplan, Sam McCandlish, and Chris Olah. 2021. A mathematical framework for transformer circuits. *Transformer Circuits Thread*.

Leo Gao, Stella Biderman, Sid Black, Laurence Golding, Travis Hoppe, Charles Foster, Jason Phang, Horace He, Anish Thite, Noa Nabeshima, Shawn Presser, and Connor Leahy. 2020. The Pile: An 800GB dataset of diverse text for language modeling. *arXiv preprint arXiv:2101.00027*.

Lila R. Gleitman, Kimberly Cassidy, Rebecca Nappa, Anna Papafragou, and John C. Trueswell. 2005. Hard Words. *Language Learning and Development*, 1(1):23–64. Publisher: Routledge _eprint: https://doi.org/10.1207/s15473341lld0101_4.

Ariel Goldstein, Zaid Zada, Eliav Buchnik, Mariano Schain, Amy Price, Bobbi Aubrey, Samuel A. Nastase, Amir Feder, Dotan Emanuel, Alon Cohen, Aren Jansen, Harshvardhan Gazula, Gina Choe, Aditi Rao, Catherine Kim, Colton Casto, Lora Fanda, Werner Doyle, Daniel Friedman, Patricia Dugan, Lucia Melloni, Roi Reichart, Sasha Devore, Adeen Flinker, Liat Hasenfratz, Omer Levy, Avinatan Hassidim, Michael Brenner, Yossi Matias, Kenneth A. Norman, Orrin Devinsky, and Uri Hasson. 2022. Shared computational principles for language processing in humans and deep language models. *Nature Neuroscience*, 25(3):369–380.

Dan Hendrycks, Collin Burns, Steven Basart, Andy Zou, Mantas Mazeika, Dawn Song, and Jacob Steinhardt. 2021. Measuring massive multitask language understanding. *Proceedings of the International Conference on Learning Representations (ICLR)*.

Yair Lakretz, Théo Desbordes, Dieuwke Hupkes, and Stanislas Dehaene. 2022. Can transformers process recursive nested constructions, like humans? In *Proceedings of the 29th International Conference on Computational Linguistics*, pages 3226–3232, Gyeongju, Republic of Korea. International Committee on Computational Linguistics.

Hector J. Levesque, Ernest Davis, and Leora Morgenstern. 2012. The winograd schema challenge. In *13th*

International Conference on the Principles of Knowledge Representation and Reasoning, KR 2012, Proceedings of the International Conference on Knowledge Representation and Reasoning, pages 552–561. Institute of Electrical and Electronics Engineers Inc.

Jian Liu, Leyang Cui, Hanmeng Liu, Dandan Huang, Yile Wang, and Yue Zhang. 2020. LogiQA: A challenge dataset for machine reading comprehension with logical reasoning. _eprint: 2007.08124.

Christopher D. Manning. 2022. Human language understanding & reasoning. *Daedalus*, 151(2):127–138.

Klaus Oberauer, Stephan Lewandowsky, Edward Awh, Gordon D. A. Brown, Andrew Conway, Nelson Cowan, Christopher Donkin, Simon Farrell, Graham J. Hitch, Mark J. Hurlstone, Wei Ji Ma, Candice C. Morey, Derek Evan Nee, Judith Schweppe, Evie Vergauwe, and Geoff Ward. 2018. Benchmarks for models of short-term and working memory. *Psychological Bulletin*, 144(9):885–958.

Catherine Olsson, Nelson Elhage, Neel Nanda, Nicholas Joseph, Nova DasSarma, Tom Henighan, Ben Mann, Amanda Askell, Yuntao Bai, Anna Chen, Tom Conerly, Dawn Drain, Deep Ganguli, Zac Hatfield-Dodds, Danny Hernandez, Scott Johnston, Andy Jones, Jackson Kernion, Liane Lovitt, Kamal Ndousse, Dario Amodei, Tom Brown, Jack Clark, Jared Kaplan, Sam McCandlish, and Chris Olah. 2022. In-context learning and induction heads. *Transformer Circuits Thread.*

Denis Paperno, Germán Kruszewski, Angeliki Lazaridou, Ngoc Quan Pham, Raffaella Bernardi, Sandro Pezzelle, Marco Baroni, Gemma Boleda, and Raquel Fernández. 2016. The LAMBADA dataset: Word prediction requiring a broad discourse context. In *Proceedings of the 54th Annual Meeting of the Association for Computational Linguistics (Volume 1: Long Papers)*, pages 1525–1534, Berlin, Germany. Association for Computational Linguistics.

Ellie Pavlick. 2023. Symbols and grounding in large language models. *Philosophical Transactions of the Royal Society A: Mathematical, Physical and Engineering Sciences*, 381(2251):20220041. Publisher: Royal Society.

Keisuke Sakaguchi, Ronan Le Bras, Chandra Bhagavatula, and Yejin Choi. 2021. WinoGrande: an adversarial winograd schema challenge at scale. *Communications of the ACM*, 64(9):99–106.

Martin Schrimpf, Idan Asher Blank, Greta Tuckute, Carina Kauf, Eghbal A. Hosseini, Nancy Kanwisher, Joshua B. Tenenbaum, and Evelina Fedorenko. 2021. The neural architecture of language: Integrative modeling converges on predictive processing. *Proceedings of the National Academy of Sciences*, 118(45):e2105646118. Publisher: Proceedings of the National Academy of Sciences.

Sabine Schulte im Walde and Diego Frassinelli. 2022. Distributional measures of semantic abstraction. *Frontiers in Artificial Intelligence*, 4:796756.

Randolph S. Taylor, Wendy S. Francis, Lara Borunda-Vazquez, and Jacqueline Carbajal. 2019. Mechanisms of word concreteness effects in explicit memory: Does context availability play a role? *Memory & Cognition*, 47(1):169–181.

Aditya R. Vaidya, Javier Turek, and Alexander G. Huth. 2023. Humans and language models diverge when predicting repeating text. ArXiv:2310.06408 [cs].

Kevin Wang, Alexandre Variengien, Arthur Conmy, Buck Shlegeris, and Jacob Steinhardt. 2022. Interpretability in the wild: a circuit for indirect object identification in GPT-2 small. ArXiv:2211.00593 [cs].

Kevin Ro Wang, Alexandre Variengien, Arthur Conmy, Buck Shlegeris, and Jacob Steinhardt. 2023. Interpretability in the wild: a circuit for indirect object identification in GPT-2 small. In *The Eleventh International Conference on Learning Representations.*

Alex Warstadt and Samuel R. Bowman. 2022. What artificial neural networks can tell us about human language acquisition. In *Algebraic Structures in Natural Language*. CRC Press. Num Pages: 44.

Johannes Welbl, Nelson F. Liu, and Matt Gardner. 2017. Crowdsourcing Multiple Choice Science Questions. In *Proceedings of the 3rd Workshop on Noisy User-generated Text*, pages 94–106, Copenhagen, Denmark. Association for Computational Linguistics.

Rand R. Wilcox and H. J. Keselman. 2003. Modern robust data analysis methods: measures of central tendency. *Psychological Methods*, 8(3):254–274.

Thomas Wolf, Lysandre Debut, Victor Sanh, Julien Chaumond, Clement Delangue, Anthony Moi, Pierric Cistac, Tim Rault, Remi Louf, Morgan Funtowicz, Joe Davison, Sam Shleifer, Patrick von Platen, Clara Ma, Yacine Jernite, Julien Plu, Canwen Xu, Teven Le Scao, Sylvain Gugger, Mariama Drame, Quentin Lhoest, and Alexander Rush. 2020. Transformers: State-of-the-Art natural language processing. In *Proceedings of the 2020 Conference on Empirical Methods in Natural Language Processing: System Demonstrations*, pages 38–45, Online. Association for Computational Linguistics.

Qinan Yu, Jack Merullo, and Ellie Pavlick. 2023. Characterizing mechanisms for factual recall in language models. ArXiv:2310.15910 [cs].

Fred Zhang and Neel Nanda. 2023. Towards best practices of activation patching in language models: metrics and methods. ArXiv:2309.16042 [cs].

A Appendix A

A.1 Retrieval control

Figure 6 shows memory retrieval results when nouns are not repeated.

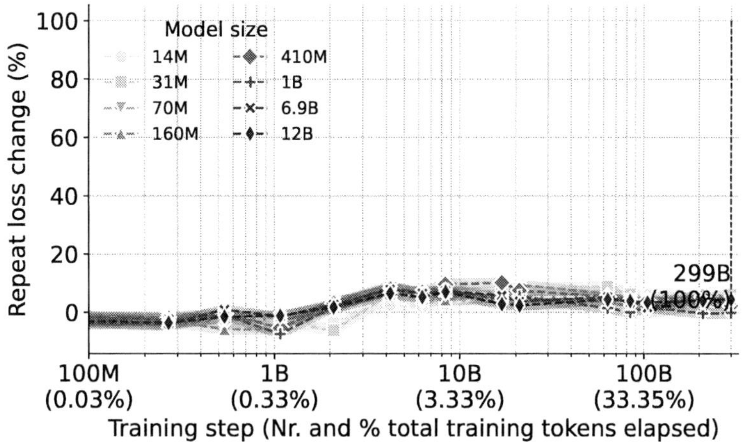

Figure 6: Evaluating repeat loss change in a control condition where there were no verbatim repeated in-context nouns (hence, no retrieval was possible). Each data point shows the 20% trimmed mean across $N = 230$ observations, shaded areas/error bars are 95% confidence intervals (bootstrap).

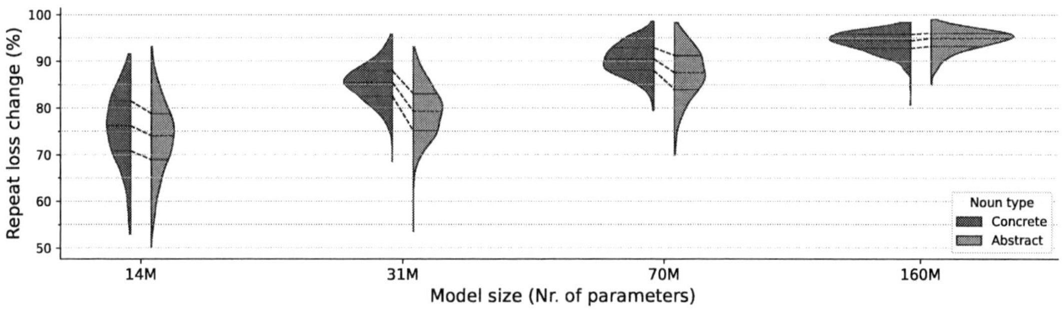

Figure 7: Data distributions comparing retrieval scores for concrete and abstract nouns for 4 smallest models from Fig. 5. Each violin plot KDE density estimates over $N = 498$ data points. The inner lines show the first, second (median) and the third quartiles of the distribution.

A.2 Abstract vs. concrete data distributions

The violin plots in Fig. A.2 show the distributions underlying respective bar plots in Fig. 5a.

A.3 Zero-shot benchmark tasks overview

The full list of benchmark tasks used in Experiment 2 is provided in Table 3.

Table 3: Benchmark categories for the Pythia models. The Task Key column corresponds to the task key used in the Pythia evaluation files (`https://github.com/EleutherAI/pythia/tree/main/evals/pythia-v1`).

	Benchmark Name	Benchmark Subcategory	Task Key
1	ARC (challenge)	None	arc_challenge
2	ARC (easy)	None	arc_easy
3	Lambada (OpenAI)	None	lambada_openai
4	LogiQA	None	logiqa
5	MMLU	MMLU (Soc. sci.)	mmlu_high_school_government_and_politics
6	MMLU	MMLU (Soc. sci.)	mmlu_sociology
7	MMLU	MMLU (Other)	mmlu_business_ethics
8	MMLU	MMLU (Other)	mmlu_medical_genetics
9	MMLU	MMLU (STEM)	mmlu_high_school_physics
10	MMLU	MMLU (Other)	mmlu_professional_medicine
11	MMLU	MMLU (Other)	mmlu_miscellaneous
12	MMLU	MMLU (STEM)	mmlu_college_physics
13	MMLU	MMLU (Humanities)	mmlu_professional_law
14	MMLU	MMLU (Humanities)	mmlu_high_school_world_history
15	MMLU	MMLU (Other)	mmlu_global_facts
16	MMLU	MMLU (Humanities)	mmlu_high_school_us_history
17	MMLU	MMLU (Other)	mmlu_marketing
18	MMLU	MMLU (Soc. sci.)	mmlu_high_school_microeconomics
19	MMLU	MMLU (Other)	mmlu_college_medicine
20	MMLU	MMLU (Soc. sci.)	mmlu_human_sexuality
21	MMLU	MMLU (STEM)	mmlu_electrical_engineering
22	MMLU	MMLU (STEM)	mmlu_elementary_mathematics
23	MMLU	MMLU (STEM)	mmlu_high_school_chemistry
24	MMLU	MMLU (Other)	mmlu_professional_accounting
25	MMLU	MMLU (Humanities)	mmlu_world_religions
26	MMLU	MMLU (STEM)	mmlu_machine_learning
27	MMLU	MMLU (Soc. sci.)	mmlu_high_school_psychology
28	MMLU	MMLU (Humanities)	mmlu_moral_scenarios
29	MMLU	MMLU (STEM)	mmlu_high_school_computer_science
30	MMLU	MMLU (Soc. sci.)	mmlu_security_studies
31	MMLU	MMLU (STEM)	mmlu_computer_security
32	MMLU	MMLU (Humanities)	mmlu_high_school_european_history
33	MMLU	MMLU (STEM)	mmlu_college_computer_science
34	MMLU	MMLU (Soc. sci.)	mmlu_econometrics
35	MMLU	MMLU (STEM)	mmlu_college_mathematics
36	MMLU	MMLU (Other)	mmlu_clinical_knowledge
37	MMLU	MMLU (Soc. sci.)	mmlu_professional_psychology
38	MMLU	MMLU (Other)	mmlu_nutrition
39	MMLU	MMLU (STEM)	mmlu_abstract_algebra
40	MMLU	MMLU (Humanities)	mmlu_logical_fallacies
41	MMLU	MMLU (STEM)	mmlu_astronomy
42	MMLU	MMLU (STEM)	mmlu_high_school_mathematics
43	MMLU	MMLU (STEM)	mmlu_high_school_biology
44	MMLU	MMLU (Soc. sci.)	mmlu_high_school_geography
45	MMLU	MMLU (Other)	mmlu_anatomy
46	MMLU	MMLU (Humanities)	mmlu_jurisprudence
47	MMLU	MMLU (Other)	mmlu_management
48	MMLU	MMLU (Humanities)	mmlu_prehistory
49	MMLU	MMLU (STEM)	mmlu_college_biology
50	MMLU	MMLU (Humanities)	mmlu_moral_disputes
51	MMLU	MMLU (STEM)	mmlu_high_school_statistics
52	MMLU	MMLU (Soc. sci.)	mmlu_us_foreign_policy
53	MMLU	MMLU (Other)	mmlu_human_aging
54	MMLU	MMLU (STEM)	mmlu_college_chemistry
55	MMLU	MMLU (Other)	mmlu_virology
56	MMLU	MMLU (Soc. sci.)	mmlu_public_relations
57	MMLU	MMLU (STEM)	mmlu_conceptual_physics
58	MMLU	MMLU (Soc. sci.)	mmlu_high_school_macroeconomics
59	MMLU	MMLU (Humanities)	mmlu_international_law
60	MMLU	MMLU (Humanities)	mmlu_philosophy
61	MMLU	MMLU (Humanities)	mmlu_formal_logic
62	PiQA	None	piqa
63	SciQ	None	sciq
64	Winogrande	None	winogrande
65	WSC	None	wsc

EDITEVAL: An Instruction-Based Benchmark for Text Improvements

Jane Dwivedi-Yu[1] **Timo Schick**[2] **Zhengbao Jiang**[3]
Maria Lomeli[1] **Patrick Lewis**[4] **Gautier Izacard**[2]
Edouard Grave[5] **Sebastian Riedel**[6] **Fabio Petroni**[7]

[1] Meta, [2] Microsoft, [3] Carnegie Mellon University,
[4] Cohere, [5] Kyutai, [6] Google Deepmind, [7] Samaya AI

janeyu@meta.com

Abstract

Evaluation of text generation to date has primarily focused on content created sequentially, rather than improvements on a piece of text. Writing, however, is naturally an iterative and incremental process that requires expertise in different modular skills such as fixing outdated information or making the writing style more consistent. Even so, comprehensive evaluation of a model's capacity to perform these skills and the ability to edit remains sparse. This work introduces EDITEVAL: An instruction-based, benchmark and evaluation suite that leverages high-quality existing and new datasets in English for the automatic evaluation of editing capabilities, such as making text more cohesive and paraphrasing. We evaluate several pretrained models, which shows that InstructGPT and PEER on average perform the best, but that most baselines fall below the supervised state-of-the-art, particularly when neutralizing and updating information. Our analysis also shows that commonly used metrics for editing tasks do not always correlate well, and that prompts leading to the strongest performance do not necessarily elicit strong performance across different models. Through the release of this benchmark,[1] and a publicly available leaderboard challenge,[2] we hope to unlock future work on developing models more capable of controllable and iterative editing.

1 Introduction

Large pre-trained language models have shown impressive text generation capabilities for a wide variety of tasks such as question answering, textual entailment, and summarization (Devlin et al., 2019; Radford et al., 2019; Raffel et al., 2020; Brown et al., 2020; Zhang et al., 2022; Chowdhery et al., 2022). However, to date, most work employing language models has focused on generating immutable text in a single pass. This is in stark contrast to the way in which humans develop articles of text, which is naturally an iterative process of small steps, each with a precise purpose (Seow, 2002). This is a crucial process because it allows for analysis of "what's working, what isn't, and what it still needs" and adaptation to these needs along the way (Jackson, 2022). In many cases, a needed change may only become apparent after much of the text is created, such as in the case of a reorganization or fixing inconsistencies or contradictions (Vardi, 2012). In this way, the current paradigm of generating text passages in a single pass can be severely limiting.

Additionally, the current paradigm of continuous left-to-right generation is less controllable and not flexible to human-in-the-loop collaboration and feedback, and this absence of experienced human mediation in the writing process can be highly detrimental to the quality of the final product (Greenberg, 2010). While there are some existing production tools geared towards working with humans to compose articles and emails, such as Grammarly[3], Smart Compose from Google[4] and text predictions from Microsoft[5], a majority focus on sentence completion rather than iteratively improving upon prior text. A more powerful editing

[1]Code and data available at `https://github.com/facebookresearch/EditEval`

[2]`https://eval.ai/web/challenges/challenge-page/1866/overview`

[3]https://www.grammarly.com/

[4]https://www.blog.google/products/gmail/subject-write-emails-faster-smart-compose-gmail/

[5]https://insider.office.com/en-us/blog/text-predictions-in-word-outlook

Proceedings of the 28th Conference on Computational Natural Language Learning, pages 69–83
November 15-16, 2024

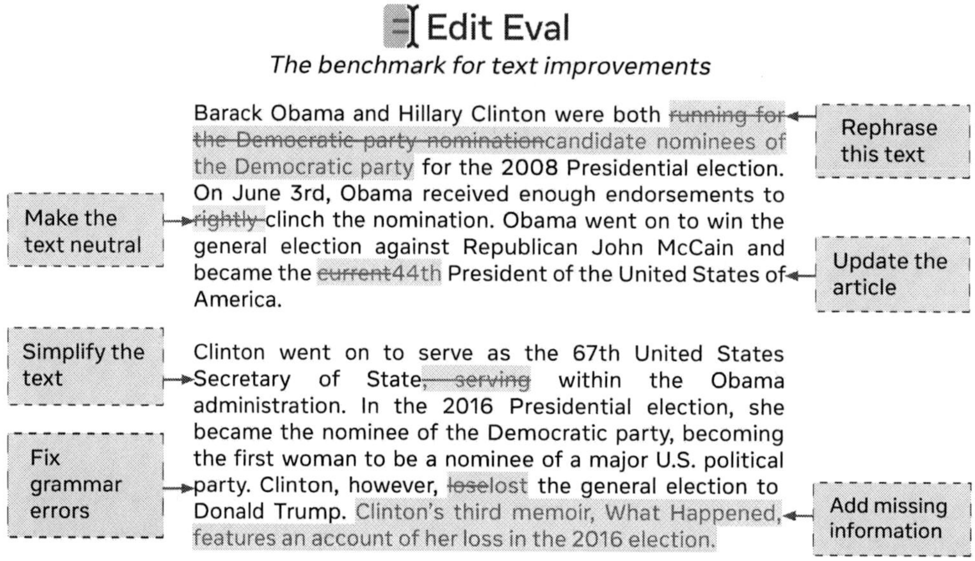

Figure 1: Examples of instructions for paraphrasing, neutralization, simplification, fluency, and updating information as well as their corresponding expected edits. For illustrative purposes, we ground these examples in the same passage, but examples in EDITEVAL follow the format as described in Section 6.

assistant, however, should not only be capable of providing recommendations for text continuations but also permit non-sequential development of the text (Seow, 2002). Editing can be absolutely critical, for example, if new or missing information or external citations are required to update the text or if a reshuffling/rebalancing of text is needed.

In this work, we alternatively promote iterative text generation and improvement—successive iterations of modular additions and modifications of the text that are relevant to text editing, such as making the text clearer and adding missing information. Many datasets for natural language tasks are actually annotated at the sentence or paragraph level, rather than document or article level, naturally lending well to evaluating iterative edits.

We create EDITEVAL, a benchmark and evaluation suite that leverages high-quality existing and new datasets for the automatic evaluation of editing capabilities. Currently, many of these relevant datasets live in separate packages and are often formatted in uniquely different ways. EDITEVAL downloads each dataset from their most recent version and standardizes these into a single format conducive to evaluation. Additionally, we include popular metrics for each task and a set of human-generated prompts to robustly measure a model's capability in executing the modular task when instructed. Figure 1 shows examples of such prompts and an example of a corresponding edit that we might expect for each prompt. Using these prompts, we evaluate and compare several state-of-the-art language models, such as OPT (Zhang et al., 2022), GPT-3 (Brown et al., 2020), and PEER (Schick et al., 2022). In summary, our contributions are as follows:

1. We identify a set of tasks and datasets relevant to iterative text improvement and provide a pipeline to download and process these datasets into a single format.

2. We open-source a publicly available instruction-based benchmark and leaderboard for automatic evaluation according to metrics commonly used for each editing task.

3. We introduce a new dataset, WAFER-INSERT, for evaluating a model's capability to update information, which is based on the WAFER dataset (Petroni et al., 2022).

4. We provide a comparison of various state-of-the-art baselines evaluated on EDITEVAL at the dataset and prompt level.

2 Related Work

Several multitask evaluation benchmarks have been open-sourced to the community to support progress in natural language understanding including GLUE (Wang et al., 2018), SuperGLUE (Wang et al., 2019), decaNLP (McCann et al., 2018), and GEM (Gehrmann et al., 2021). These datasets, however, focus on a broad set of tasks in NLP (e.g., question answering, reading comprehension, and textual entailment). While all of these tasks are critical to natural language understanding, EDITEVAL focuses on curating a benchmark for measuring a model's capability to improve and edit text.

There are several datasets which focus on iterative text revisions in the domain of Wikipedia (Yang et al., 2017; Anthonio et al., 2020), academic essays (Zhang et al., 2017), and news articles (Spangher et al., 2022). These works, however, focus on one particular domain and in some cases, a particular style like argumentative writing (Zhang et al., 2017). EDITEVAL, on the other hand, includes examples from multiple domains: Wikipedia, Wikinews, news articles, and arXiv. ITERATER (Du et al., 2022) is perhaps closet to EDITEVAL in that it provides iterative tasks from multiple domains, but it has a limited number of such tasks: fluency, coherence, clarity, style, and meaning-changed. Because this is a great starting point, we have included ITERATER in EDITEVAL, and we additionally develop prompts for these tasks since ITERATER is not instruction-based. Moreover, unlike ITERATER, EDITEVAL includes novel datasets for tasks such as updating text using new information and neutralizing the text, which are core components of editing a factually-correct and unbiased article.

3 The EDITEVAL Benchmark

EDITEVAL is an instruction-based benchmark for iterative text generation/modification. EDITEVAL sources existing high-quality datasets—most with human annotations—containing tasks relevant to editing. These datasets are combined into a unified evaluation tool and can be evaluated with any metric provided in EDITEVAL. A task here refers to a type of edit (e.g., simplification), and the specific task dictates which set of prompts to be used (e.g., simplify this text), the full set of which is enumerated in Appendix B.

We consider seven editing tasks in EDITEVAL. The corresponding datasets for each task included in EDITEVAL are enumerated in Table 1, along with the size of the dataset in EDITEVAL. For ease of evaluation, we define a consistent format for all datasets in the EDITEVAL benchmark. Each dataset of every task has five core fields: ID, input text, gold edits, task type, and reference documents. The input text is the original text before revision, and the gold edits are the target edits for that specific task type. Lastly, the reference documents provide textual information from external articles or documents that are relevant to the task. The task that requires reference documents is updating, and otherwise, the reference documents field is empty.

Table 1: Tasks, datasets, abbreviations used, and corresponding test size in EDITEVAL. The task type dictates which set of instructions are used. These are enumerated in Section B.

Task	Dataset	Abbrev.	Size
Clarity	ITERATER	ITR-L	1,595
Coherence	ITERATER	ITR-O	351
Fluency	ITERATER	ITR-F	942
Fluency	JFLEG	JFL	1503
Simplification	ASSET	AST	2,359
Simplification	TurkCorpus	TRK	2,359
Paraphrasing	STS Benchmark	STS	419
Neutralization	WNC	WNC	1,000
Updating	FRUIT	FRU	914
Updating	WAFER-INSERT	WFI	4,565

The datasets in EDITEVAL were selected if they test a capability relevant to the art of editing and contain human-annotated gold edits, if possible. We also endeavored to include datasets that are broadly used by the community. The datasets in EDITEVAL are by no means exhaustive, but the EDITEVAL framework is flexible such that it can easily extend to new datasets and metrics in future versions.

3.1 Fluency, Clarity, and Coherence

In this section, we describe the two datasets that compose this set of tasks: Fluency (fixing grammatical or spelling errors), clarity (making the text clearer), and coherence (making the text more cohesive).

JFLEG JHU FLuency-Extended GUG (Napoles et al., 2017) focuses only on fluency. JFLEG is based on the GUG (Grammatical vs UnGrammatical) dataset (Heilman et al., 2014), which is a dataset of sentences originally annotated for how grammatical the sentence is on a scale of 1 to 4. JFLEG builds upon the ungrammatical sentences in GUG and annotates each sentence with four corresponding corrected versions.

ITERATER This dataset introduced by Du et al. (2022) contains both automatically-mined and human-annotated edits at the sentence and document-level. For our benchmark, we only utilize the sentence-level examples with human annotations. Additionally, ITERATER has labels for the intent—the type of edit that produces the targets, which can be one of six classes: Fluency, coherence, clarity, style (conveying the writer's writing preferences), meaning-changed (updating or adding new information), and other (none of the others). We included all classes except style, meaning-changed, and other. We excluded style and other because these tasks had roughly 100 or less test examples, and the definitions were comparatively under-specified. We excluded meaning-changed because the task does not use reference documents for updating. This dataset is the only one in EDITEVAL that encompasses multiple tasks, and we refer to each respective subset using the abbreviations ITR-F (fluency), ITR-L (clarity), and ITR-O (coherence).

3.2 Paraphrasing

STSB For paraphrasing, we use the STS benchmark from SemEval-2018 (Cer et al., 2017), which comprises English datasets used in the STS tasks of SemEval between 2012 and 2017. The selection of datasets includes text from image captions, news headlines and user forums. Each example contains an original sentence, a target sentence, and a similarity score indicating whether the target is a paraphrase of the original. This dataset is used for classification or regression, but for EditEval, we utilize all instances that we are confident are paraphrases, i.e., have the max similarity score of 5, as targets for generation evaluation. While other datasets such as ParaSCI (Dong et al., 2021) exist for paraphrase generation, these are automatically curated rather than human annotated, and EDITEVAL strives to utilize human-annotated datasets where possible.

3.3 Simplification

Simplification can be considered a very similar task to paraphrasing with the additional constraint that the output must be simpler than the input. The datasets we utilize for simplification are TurkCorpus (Xu et al., 2016) and ASSET (Alva-Manchego et al., 2020).

TurkCorpus This dataset, like ASSET, builds upon the Parallel Wikipedia Simplification (PWKP) (Zhu et al., 2010). The PWKP dataset uses the Simple English Wikipedia and Standard English Wikipedia in parallel to create original-simplification pairs automatically. However, several works found PWKP to have a large proportion of targets that are not simplified or only partially aligned with the input (Xu et al., 2015; Amancio and Specia, 2014; Hwang et al., 2015; Štajner et al., 2015), leading to the creation of a human-annotated corpus, TurkCorpus. TurkCorpus was manually created with eight reference simplifications for each original sentence in PWKP, but only used simplifications that are possible without deleting content or splitting sentences.

ASSET Because TurkCorpus encompassed only specific kinds of simplifications, this led to the creation of ASSET, which provides manually-produced simplifications through a much broader set of transformations. We include both in EDITEVAL, for the sake of comprehensiveness.

3.4 Neutralization

The task of neutralization refers to making the text more neutral. For example, in the sentence "Obama was an excellent president who served two terms from 2008 to 2016" the term *excellent* violates Wikipedia's neutral point of view (POV) policy[6]. For information-intensive content like Wikipedia and news articles in particular, reducing bias is crucial because bias can be the single largest source of distrust in the media (Jones, 2019).

WNC We use the Wiki Neutrality Corpus (Pryzant et al., 2020), a collection of original and de-biased sentence pairs mined from Wikipedia edits by carefully filtering based on the editor's comments. While ideally we would like to include a human-annotated dataset, to our knowledge there does not exist a dataset for de-biasing article content at the sentence level.

3.5 Updating

In this section we describe the task of updating information which requires *references*, text from external sources that are relevant to the particular task. Because of token-length restrictions, each external article is chunked into texts of fixed length. We limit the scope of the task to three chunks, and we refer to these selected chunks as our *reference documents*. These references documents are represented in the edits by their index in the reference documents field (e.g., the first would be demarcated

[6]https://en.wikipedia.org/wiki/Wikipedia:Neutral point of view

as [0]), and we discuss below how these reference documents were selected.

WAFER-INSERT The first dataset for updating information that we use is the WAFER dataset (Petroni et al., 2022), which is a dataset collected from Wikipedia inline citations. Each instance of the original WAFER dataset contains a claim, the text surrounding the claim, and a set of external references, where the task is to choose one of the references to be cited after the claim. While the original intention of WAFER was to measure a system's capability to choose the correct citation, EDITEVAL utilizes WAFER for the task of inserting new information using content from the reference documents. The examples in the original WAFER dataset contains an input text and a reference document, where a sentence (referred to as the claim) of the input text is factually supported by the reference. We create WAFER-INSERT, which differs from WAFER in that the claim is deleted from the input. The goal here is to derive the original claim from the references and insert it back into the text at the appropriate location. For the reference documents, we select the top three chunks from the inline citation chunks that have the highest scores, using results from the verification engine introduced in Petroni et al. (2022).

FRUIT In addition to WAFER-INSERT, we include the FRUIT dataset (Logan IV et al., 2021), a dataset collected by comparing two snapshots of a Wikipedia article where one contains updated or new information. The reference documents were identified by searching for other Wikipedia articles that provide evidence to support the update. However, because there is no certainty that the identified evidentiary articles support the claim, the authors of FRUIT created a gold set by employing human annotation to filter out any new claims that are unsupported. We include this gold set in EDITEVAL, and only include reference documents if they actually appear in the output. Unlike WAFER-INSERT, the target edit contains not only the updated information but also the citation. For EDITEVAL, this is for verification purposes only, and the citation is removed when computing the metrics.

4 Metrics

The metrics we included in EDITEVAL are ones that are (1) shown to have significant correlation with human judgement for a task in EDITEVAL and (2) commonly used to benchmark one of the datasets in EDITEVAL. Below, we discuss some of the main metrics. Appendix C describes these and additional metrics in greater detail.

- **EM** (exact match) is the percentage of examples for which the performed edit exactly matches any of the targets. **EM-diff** is a variant computed at the diff level.
- **SARI** Xu et al. (2016) is an n-gram based metric that averages match scores for three operations: adding, deleting, and keeping words.
- **LENS** (Maddela et al., 2022) is a recently proposed model-based text simplification metric that uses an adaptive ranking loss.
- **GLEU** (Napoles et al., 2015) is a variant of BLEU frequently used for grammatical error correction (Grundkiewicz et al., 2019; Yuan and Briscoe, 2016; Chollampatt and Ng, 2018), where penalties are incurred only when words are changed in the reference but not in the output.
- **ROUGE** (Lin, 2004) is metric that measures n-gram overlap. **UpdateROUGE** (Logan IV et al., 2021), a simple modification of ROUGE, computes ROUGE only on the updated sentences rather than the full text.
- **BERTScore** (Zhang et al., 2019a) which is based on using the cosine similarity between the BERT embeddings of the candidate and reference.

5 Baselines

For each baseline, we use greedy decoding, and we do not perform any task-specific fine-tuning or in-context learning. We evaluate on EDITEVAL using the following baselines:

- **GPT-3** (Brown et al., 2020) is a 175B parameter pretrained decoder-only model. We evaluate GPT-3 through OpenAI's API.[7]
- **InstructGPT** (Ouyang et al., 2022) is a variant of GPT-3 that was instruction-tuned. We evaluate the *text-davinci-001* version described in (Ouyang et al., 2022) since, at the time of writing, details about the training process for *text-davinci-002* were not publicly available.

[7]https://beta.openai.com/

- **OPT** (Zhang et al., 2022) is an open-source replica of GPT-3. Like GPT-3, it is not fine-tuned on any labeled data.

- **T0** (Sanh et al., 2022) is a pretrained encoder-decoder model, which has demonstrated better performance than GPT-3 on several tasks despite being much smaller.

- **T0++** (Sanh et al., 2022) is similar to T0, but trained on a few additional datasets from SuperGLUE (Wang et al., 2019).

- **Tk-Instruct** (Wang et al., 2022) is similar to T0 and T0++ but instead fine-tuned on their dataset, Natural Instructions v2, a collection of instructions for more than 1,600 tasks, including grammatical error correction and text simplification.

- **PEER** (Schick et al., 2022) is a collaborative language model initialized from the *LM Adapt* variant of T5, and further fine-tuned on edit histories from Wikipedia. We use the 3B and 11B PEER models that were shown to perform the best in Schick et al. (2022).

6 Formatting

We evaluate these baselines on their general capability to accomplish each task when prompted in natural language in a zero-shot fashion. Because there are a diverse set of ways in which to instruct for each task, we manually construct a set of 3–11 prompts in order to more robustly evaluate performance. For each task prompt t and input i, the model is given a formatted input following the template: `Task:` t`\nInput:` i`\nOutput:` with an additional field for references, should they be required. Figure 2 shows an example of an input including references. For tasks without references, we exclude this field. Some slight modification to this template were made. For example, Tk-Instruct expects the prompt to be prefixed by the string "Definition:" rather than "Task:"). For preprocessing, we used the Natural Language Toolkit (NLTK) package (Bird et al., 2009) for tokenizing the text.

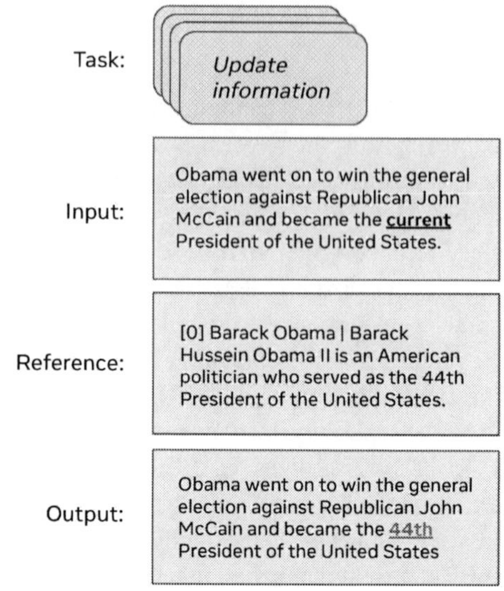

Figure 2: Example of inputs formatted when evaluating the baseline models. Each input is evaluated with a set of prompts that are determined by the task type.

7 Results

We summarize results in Table 2 with the aforementioned baselines averaged over all datasets and the breakdown for each dataset in Table 3. To visualize the variance, we show boxplots for each dataset and model in Figure 3. We discuss these observations in more detail below.

InstructGPT and PEER perform the best overall. In Table 2, we show the mean SARI scores for each model averaged across all tasks using the average, maximum, and minimum scores across prompts. When using the average and minimum across prompts (third and fifth column, respectively) we see that InstructGPT performs the best overall, but when using the maximum score across prompts (fourth column), PEER-11 performs the best. Table 3 enumerates the breakdown of the third column according to each dataset. In general, we see that InstructGPT achieves the highest scores with the exception of the updating and neutralization datasets, as well as ITR-F and ITR-L. For these datasets, the PEER models clearly outperform InstructGPT by a large margin, despite being nearly 60× smaller than InstructGPT and GPT-3. The substantially smaller models (T0, T0++, and Tk-Instruct) struggle the most overall, even falling behind the copy baseline at times, except on ITR-L where Tk-Instruct performs the best.

Model	Params	Avg.	Max	Min	CV
T*k*	3B	28.2	30.1	26.1	4.65
T0	3B	26.6	29.3	24.5	6.03
T0++	11B	28.4	30.3	26.7	5.13
PEER-3	3B	38.8	41.8	35.0	6.36
PEER-11	11B	39.1	**42.1**	35.6	5.75
OPT	175B	32.8	36.4	29.0	6.70
GPT-3	175B	32.8	35.8	29.4	6.74
InstructGPT	175B	**39.6**	41.3	**37.4**	**3.60**

Table 2: Mean SARI scores (other metrics shown in Table C2) all tasks using the average (Avg.), the maximum (Max), and the minimum (Min) across prompts. The coefficient of variance (CV), computed as the standard deviation across prompts normalized by the average, is shown in the final column. Best values are in bold. When using averages across prompts and using the minimum, InstructGPT performs the best, but PEER performs the best when using the maximum across prompts.

Most baselines lag substantially behind the supervised SOTA, especially in the task of updating and neutralization. We show the supervised state-of-the-art results in the final row of Table 3, which in almost all cases surpasses the performance of the best baseline. The gap is largest for the tasks of neutralization and updating (34–50% decrease from the supervised SOTA to the best baseline scores), whereas for other tasks, this decrease is only within 5–14%. It is conceivable that the difficulty with these two tasks is a consequence of the comparatively fewer datasets and research devoted to them compared to that of the more mainstream NLP tasks, such as text simplification.

The most challenging tasks do not necessarily have the highest variance across models. In observing Figure 3a, we see that the tasks which have the largest variance across models (assessed using the interquartile range or IQR) are fluency and updating information. This is despite the fact that the fluency datasets are arguably easier (i.e., many of the models come close to the supervised scores) than the updating datasets, exemplifying that difficulty and robustness can be independent axes. JFLEG also appears to be easier than ITR-F (average SARI of 45.1 versus 38.2), which is understandable since JFLEG sources from the TOEFL exam (primarily simpler and conversational sentences), while ITERATER sources technical sentences from Wikipedia, ArXiv, and Wikinews. Likewise, TurkCorpus seems on average to be slightly easier than ASSET, which is expected since it includes more diverse simplifications than TurkCorpus.

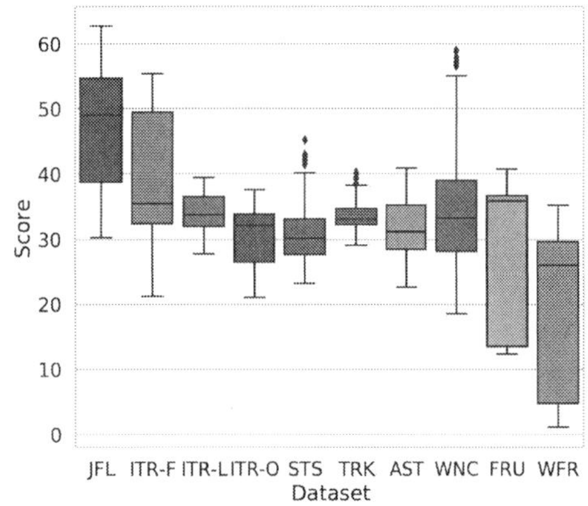

(a) Scores for each dataset averaged across models. Datasets which have the largest variance amongst the baselines are not necessarily harder tasks.

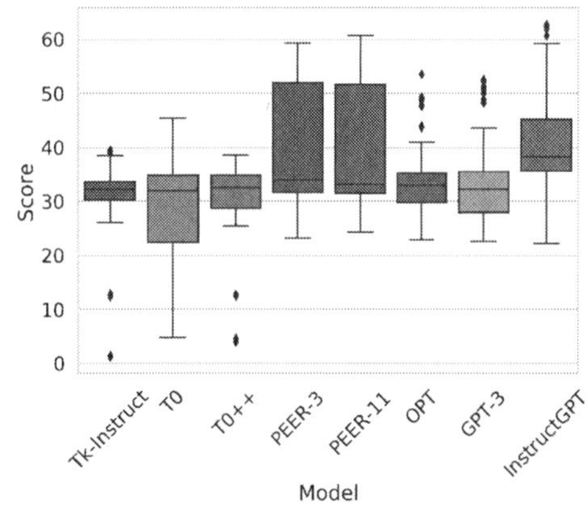

(b) Scores for each model averaged across datasets. PEER has the largest range in performance across datasets.

Figure 3: Boxplot of SARI scores for each dataset (a) and model (b).

PEER has the highest total variance, but OPT and GPT-3 are less robust to different prompts. From Figure 3, we observe that the PEER models have the largest variance in performance overall (as measured by the larger IQR). If we compute the standard deviation across prompts and normalize by the mean (CV in Table 2), however, GPT-3 and OPT, have the highest average across datasets (6.74% and 6.70%, respectively), whereas for the 3B and 11B PEER models, these values are smaller (6.36% and 5.75%). This could be a consequence of the fact that GPT-3 and OPT are not instruction-tuned, whereas the remaining baselines are.

Optimizing prompts according to maximum performance and according to robustness to different models can be orthogonal objectives. Ideally, we would like to create prompts that achieve the highest performance using the best baseline,

Model	*Fluency* JFL	ITR-F	*Clarity* ITR-L	*Coherence* ITR-O	*Para.* STS	*Simplification* TRK	AST	*Neutral.* WNC	*Updating* FRU	WFI
Copy	26.7 / 40.5	32.3 / 86.0	29.5 / 62.9	31.3 / 77.2	21.1	26.3	20.7	31.9 / 0.0	29.8 / 0.0	33.6 / –
T*k*	31.8 / 39.0	32.4 / 61.6	**38.4 / 58.4**	33.8 / **70.4**	30.2	32.8	29.9	31.3 / 0.4	12.6 / 3.6	1.3 / 4.5
T0	42.0 / 38.8	24.6 / 34.9	32.6 / 30.2	22.2 / 21.6	34.3	34.4	32.3	22.3 / 0.0	14.2 / 9.6	5.1 / 16.3
T0++	34.7 / 43.2	35.3 / 75.8	37.6 / 56.5	32.7 / 59.9	28.4	32.9	28.2	29.3 / 0.3	12.6 / 3.7	4.4 / 8.1
PEER-3	55.5 / 54.3	51.4 / 84.3	32.1 / 47.1	32.1 / 59.8	28.6	32.5	30.5	53.3 / 21.6	39.1 / 30.9	34.4 / 18.7
PEER-11	55.8 / 54.3	**52.1 / 85.2**	32.5 / 51.3	32.7 / 62.7	28.2	32.1	29.5	**54.5 / 22.8**	**39.6 / 31.4**	**34.9 / 20.4**
OPT	47.3 / 47.5	34.7 / 70.6	31.5 / 31.5	27.6 / 36.1	29.1	32.6	31.8	31.2 / 0.4	35.9 / 27.3	26.7 / 11.2
GPT-3	50.3 / 51.8	32.1 / 56.7	33.5 / 39.7	26.9 / 36.1	27.2	33.0	30.5	31.7 / 0.6	36.0 / 21.5	27.2 / 10.6
InsGPT	**61.8 / 59.3**	48.8 / 82.7	35.1 / 48.4	**35.9** / 60.2	**42.5**	**38.8**	**38.0**	35.4 / 2.2	36.3 / 24.7	23.6 / 16.1
SotA	*– / 62.4*	*37.2 / –*	*46.2 / –*	*38.3 / –*	–	*34.4*	*37.2*	*– / 45.8*	*– / 47.4*	*– / –*

Table 3: Results for all datasets, averaged across prompts (max and min results in Table C2). The best results for each dataset are shown in bold. T*k*-Instruct and InstructGPT are shorthanded as T*k* and InsGPT, respectively. The first numbers for each task are SARI scores; additional metrics are GLEU for fluency, clarity, and coherence, EM for neutralization, Update-R1 for updating. Supervised scores are from Ge et al. (2018) (JFLEG), Du et al. (2022) (ITERATER), Martin et al. (2020) (TurkCorpus and ASSET), Pryzant et al. (2020) (WNC), and Logan IV et al. (2021) (FRUIT), respectively.

but also perform reliably well for any model. In assessing variance from Figure 4, we see that certain prompts stand out as less robust to different models relative to others. For example, for neutralization, Prompts #1, 2, and 7 are less robust likely because they use uncommon language such as "Remove points of views" or "Neutralize this text". Some of the prompts which are less robust for simplification (Prompts #4, 7) and paraphrasing (Prompts #4, 6) are sometimes ones that are less specific such as "Rewrite this text" versus "Rewrite this with different wording"—in the case of the former, an empirical assessment shows that the models seem to more often copy the original text and make fewer modifications. Unfortunately, choosing prompts that achieve the maximum score does not always entail prompts which are the most robust—Prompt #5 for clarity achieves the maximum but has the largest variance in performance or IQR. Some of the tasks exhibit a great degree of outlier behavior (coherence, paraphrasing, or neutralization), which is either due to T0 performing exceedingly low or InstructGPT/PEER performing exceedingly well. Other tasks such as fluency and updating seem to have prompts with a similar range of variance.

Commonly used metrics are not always well-correlated. We measure the Pearson correlation between each pair of metrics using evaluation scores for all baselines, which is shown in Figure 5, and find that many of the commonly used metrics do not always correlate well with each other, a finding echoed by prior works (Choshen and Abend, 2018; Alva-Manchego et al., 2021), which focuses on the task of grammatical error correction. We exclude PEER in this analysis since it shows exceedingly strong performance in some cases, and we exclude the updating datasets since they are of a very different nature from the other datasets. We find that while families of variants like BLEU and iBLEU as well as ROUGE and UpdateROUGE show strong correlation within each respective set (> 0.97), the two sets are inversely correlated with one another (-0.29 to -0.1). ROUGE actually appears to be the metric that most conflicts with all other metrics, whereas GLEU seems to be the metric that is most in harmony with the rest (0.41–0.76). Though SARI is not correlated with ROUGE, it is the metric which shows the strongest correlation with EM-Diff (0.83) and UpdateROUGE (0.7).

8 Discussion

We present EDITEVAL, a benchmark composed of handcrafted, task-specific instructions for several editing datasets across multiple domains. EDITEVAL is a means of evaluating models for these tasks according to multiple popular metrics, all within a single, unified tool. We show that while models such as InstructGPT have impressive performance, in general the baselines lag behind the supervised state-of-the-art, particularly for the task of updating and neutralization. Our analysis of metrics and prompts shows that several popular metrics are not well-correlated, even conflicting at times, and that small changes in the wording of a prompt can lead to substantial changes in performance and robustness to different models. This suggests further

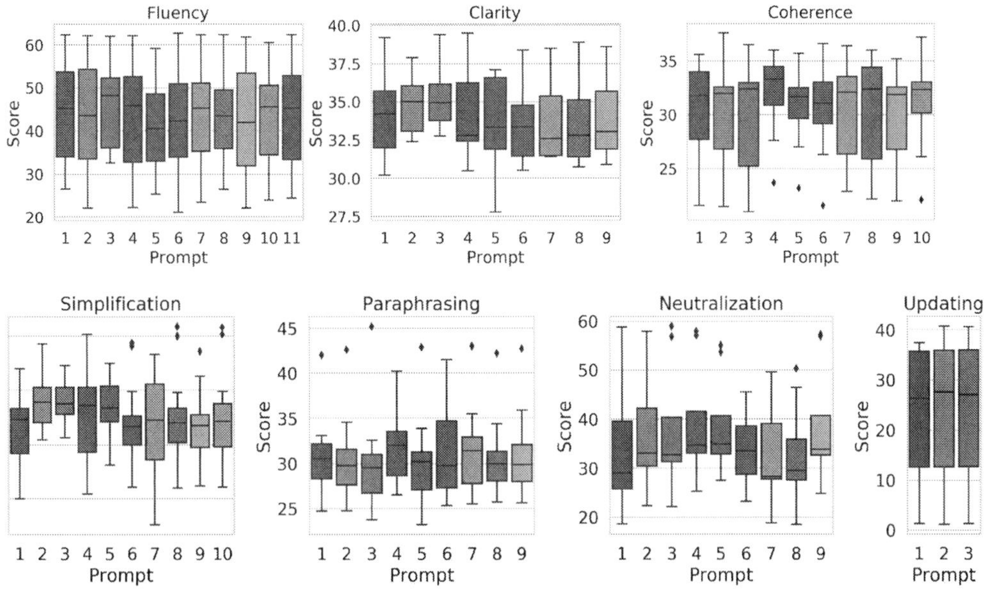

Figure 4: Boxplot of SARI scores for each prompt averaged across models. The prompts which achieve the maximum scores for each dataset (Table C2), are Prompts #6 and 11 (fluency), 4 (clarity), 2 (coherence), 8 and 10 (simplification), 3 (paraphrasing), 2 (neutralization) and 2 and 1 (updating). Certain prompts evoke more variation across models due to factors such as using less frequently used language or being too unspecific.

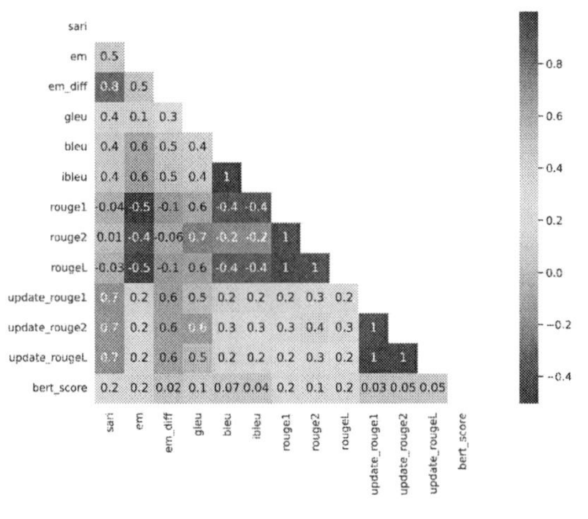

Figure 5: Pearson correlation between metrics using data for all datasets except WAFER and FRUIT and all baselines except PEER. Different families of metrics can have low correlation and even conflict, at times.

work is needed to develop models comprehensively capable of executing editing tasks in addition to developing a standardized way of measuring editing capabilities and systematically selecting prompts. In releasing this work, we hope to bolster work in which language models are utilized for text generation that is iterative, more controllable, collaborative, and capable of revising and correcting text.

References

Fernando Alva-Manchego, Louis Martin, Antoine Bordes, Carolina Scarton, Benoît Sagot, and Lucia Specia. 2020. Asset: A dataset for tuning and evaluation of sentence simplification models with multiple rewriting transformations. In *Proceedings of the 58th Annual Meeting of the Association for Computational Linguistics*, pages 4668–4679.

Fernando Alva-Manchego, Louis Martin, Carolina Scarton, and Lucia Specia. 2019. Easse: Easier automatic sentence simplification evaluation. *arXiv preprint arXiv:1908.04567*.

Fernando Alva-Manchego, Carolina Scarton, and Lucia Specia. 2021. The (un) suitability of automatic evaluation metrics for text simplification. *Computational Linguistics*, 47(4):861–889.

Marcelo Adriano Amancio and Lucia Specia. 2014. An analysis of crowdsourced text simplifications. In *Proceedings of the 3rd Workshop on Predicting and Improving Text Readability for Target Reader Populations (PITR)*, pages 123–130.

Talita Anthonio, Irshad Bhat, and Michael Roth. 2020. wikihowtoimprove: A resource and analyses on edits in instructional texts. In *Proceedings of the 12th Language Resources and Evaluation Conference*, pages 5721–5729.

Steven Bird, Ewan Klein, and Edward Loper. 2009. *Natural language processing with Python: analyzing text with the natural language toolkit.* " O'Reilly Media, Inc.".

Tom Brown, Benjamin Mann, Nick Ryder, Melanie Subbiah, Jared D Kaplan, Prafulla Dhariwal, Arvind Neelakantan, Pranav Shyam, Girish Sastry, Amanda Askell, Sandhini Agarwal, Ariel Herbert-Voss, Gretchen Krueger, Tom Henighan, Rewon Child, Aditya Ramesh, Daniel Ziegler, Jeffrey Wu, Clemens Winter, Chris Hesse, Mark Chen, Eric Sigler, Mateusz Litwin, Scott Gray, Benjamin Chess, Jack Clark, Christopher Berner, Sam McCandlish, Alec Radford, Ilya Sutskever, and Dario Amodei. 2020. Language models are few-shot learners. In *Advances in Neural Information Processing Systems*, volume 33, pages 1877–1901. Curran Associates, Inc.

Daniel Cer, Mona Diab, Eneko Agirre, Iñigo Lopez-Gazpio, and Lucia Specia. 2017. Semeval-2017 task 1: Semantic textual similarity multilingual and crosslingual focused evaluation. In *Proceedings of the 11th International Workshop on Semantic Evaluation (SemEval-2017)*, pages 1–14.

Shamil Chollampatt and Hwee Tou Ng. 2018. A multilayer convolutional encoder-decoder neural network for grammatical error correction. In *Proceedings of the AAAI conference on artificial intelligence*, volume 32.

Leshem Choshen and Omri Abend. 2018. Automatic metric validation for grammatical error correction. In *Proceedings of the 56th Annual Meeting of the Association for Computational Linguistics (Volume 1: Long Papers)*, pages 1372–1382.

Aakanksha Chowdhery, Sharan Narang, Jacob Devlin, Maarten Bosma, Gaurav Mishra, Adam Roberts, Paul Barham, Hyung Won Chung, Charles Sutton, Sebastian Gehrmann, Parker Schuh, Kensen Shi, Sasha Tsvyashchenko, Joshua Maynez, Abhishek Rao, Parker Barnes, Yi Tay, Noam Shazeer, Vinodkumar Prabhakaran, Emily Reif, Nan Du, Ben Hutchinson, Reiner Pope, James Bradbury, Jacob Austin, Michael Isard, Guy Gur-Ari, Pengcheng Yin, Toju Duke, Anselm Levskaya, Sanjay Ghemawat, Sunipa Dev, Henryk Michalewski, Xavier Garcia, Vedant Misra, Kevin Robinson, Liam Fedus, Denny Zhou, Daphne Ippolito, David Luan, Hyeontaek Lim, Barret Zoph, Alexander Spiridonov, Ryan Sepassi, David Dohan, Shivani Agrawal, Mark Omernick, Andrew M. Dai, Thanumalayan Sankaranarayana Pillai, Marie Pellat, Aitor Lewkowycz, Erica Moreira, Rewon Child, Oleksandr Polozov, Katherine Lee, Zongwei Zhou, Xuezhi Wang, Brennan Saeta, Mark Diaz, Orhan Firat, Michele Catasta, Jason Wei, Kathy Meier-Hellstern, Douglas Eck, Jeff Dean, Slav Petrov, and Noah Fiedel. 2022. Palm: Scaling language modeling with pathways.

Jacob Devlin, Ming-Wei Chang, Kenton Lee, and Kristina Toutanova. 2019. BERT: Pre-training of deep bidirectional transformers for language understanding. In *Proceedings of the 2019 Conference of the North American Chapter of the Association for Computational Linguistics: Human Language Technologies, Volume 1 (Long and Short Papers)*, pages 4171–4186, Minneapolis, Minnesota. Association for Computational Linguistics.

Qingxiu Dong, Xiaojun Wan, and Yue Cao. 2021. Parasci: A large scientific paraphrase dataset for longer paraphrase generation. *arXiv preprint arXiv:2101.08382*.

Wanyu Du, Vipul Raheja, Dhruv Kumar, Zae Myung Kim, Melissa Lopez, and Dongyeop Kang. 2022. Understanding iterative revision from human-written text. In *Proceedings of the 60th Annual Meeting of the Association for Computational Linguistics (Volume 1: Long Papers)*, pages 3573–3590.

Tao Ge, Furu Wei, and Ming Zhou. 2018. Reaching human-level performance in automatic grammatical error correction: An empirical study. *arXiv preprint arXiv:1807.01270*.

Sebastian Gehrmann, Tosin Adewumi, Karmanya Aggarwal, Pawan Sasanka Ammanamanchi, Anuoluwapo Aremu, Antoine Bosselut, Khyathi Raghavi Chandu, Miruna-Adriana Clinciu, Dipanjan Das, Kaustubh Dhole, Wanyu Du, Esin Durmus, Ondřej Dušek, Chris Chinenye Emezue, Varun Gangal, Cristina Garbacea, Tatsunori Hashimoto, Yufang Hou, Yacine Jernite, Harsh Jhamtani, Yangfeng Ji, Shailza Jolly, Mihir Kale, Dhruv Kumar, Faisal Ladhak, Aman Madaan, Mounica Maddela, Khyati Mahajan, Saad Mahamood, Bodhisattwa Prasad Majumder, Pedro Henrique Martins, Angelina McMillan-Major, Simon Mille, Emiel van Miltenburg, Moin Nadeem, Shashi Narayan, Vitaly Nikolaev, Andre Niyongabo Rubungo, Salomey Osei, Ankur Parikh, Laura Perez-Beltrachini, Niranjan Ramesh Rao, Vikas Raunak, Juan Diego Rodriguez, Sashank Santhanam, João Sedoc, Thibault Sellam, Samira Shaikh, Anastasia Shimorina, Marco Antonio Sobrevilla Cabezudo, Hendrik Strobelt, Nishant Subramani, Wei Xu, Diyi Yang, Akhila Yerukola, and Jiawei Zhou. 2021. The GEM benchmark: Natural language generation, its evaluation and metrics. In *Proceedings of the 1st Workshop on Natural Language Generation, Evaluation, and Metrics (GEM 2021)*, pages 96–120, Online. Association for Computational Linguistics.

Susan Greenberg. 2010. When the editor disappears, does editing disappear? *Convergence*, 16(1):7–21.

Roman Grundkiewicz, Marcin Junczys-Dowmunt, and Kenneth Heafield. 2019. Neural grammatical error correction systems with unsupervised pre-training on synthetic data. In *Proceedings of the Fourteenth Workshop on Innovative Use of NLP for Building Educational Applications*, pages 252–263.

Michael Heilman, Aoife Cahill, Nitin Madnani, Melissa Lopez, Matthew Mulholland, and Joel R. Tetreault. 2014. Predicting grammaticality on an ordinal scale. In *ACL (2)*, pages 174–180.

William Hwang, Hannaneh Hajishirzi, Mari Ostendorf, and Wei Wu. 2015. Aligning sentences from standard wikipedia to simple wikipedia. In *Proceedings of the 2015 Conference of the North American Chapter of the Association for Computational Linguistics: Human Language Technologies*, pages 211–217.

Annie Jackson. 2022. The advantage of an iterative writing process for novels and short stories.

David A Jones. 2019. An online experimental platform to assess trust in the media," webpage, july 18, 2018b. *As of March*, 18.

Katharina Kann, Sascha Rothe, and Katja Filippova. 2018. Sentence-level fluency evaluation: references help, but can be spared! *arXiv preprint arXiv:1809.08731*.

Chin-Yew Lin. 2004. Rouge: A package for automatic evaluation of summaries. In *Text summarization branches out*, pages 74–81.

Robert L Logan IV, Alexandre Passos, Sameer Singh, and Ming-Wei Chang. 2021. Fruit: Faithfully reflecting updated information in text. *arXiv preprint arXiv:2112.08634*.

Mounica Maddela, Yao Dou, David Heineman, and Wei Xu. 2022. Lens: A learnable evaluation metric for text simplification. *ArXiv*, abs/2212.09739.

Eric Malmi, Sebastian Krause, Sascha Rothe, Daniil Mirylenka, and Aliaksei Severyn. 2019. Encode, tag, realize: High-precision text editing. *arXiv preprint arXiv:1909.01187*.

Louis Martin, Angela Fan, Éric de la Clergerie, Antoine Bordes, and Benoît Sagot. 2020. Muss: multilingual unsupervised sentence simplification by mining paraphrases. *arXiv preprint arXiv:2005.00352*.

Bryan McCann, Nitish Shirish Keskar, Caiming Xiong, and Richard Socher. 2018. The natural language decathlon: Multitask learning as question answering. *arXiv preprint arXiv:1806.08730*.

Courtney Napoles, Keisuke Sakaguchi, Matt Post, and Joel Tetreault. 2015. Ground truth for grammatical error correction metrics. In *Proceedings of the 53rd Annual Meeting of the Association for Computational Linguistics and the 7th International Joint Conference on Natural Language Processing (Volume 2: Short Papers)*, pages 588–593.

Courtney Napoles, Keisuke Sakaguchi, and Joel Tetreault. 2017. Jfleg: A fluency corpus and benchmark for grammatical error correction. In *Proceedings of the 15th Conference of the European Chapter of the Association for Computational Linguistics: Volume 2, Short Papers*, pages 229–234.

Sergiu Nisioi, Sanja Štajner, Simone Paolo Ponzetto, and Liviu P Dinu. 2017. Exploring neural text simplification models. In *Proceedings of the 55th annual meeting of the association for computational linguistics (volume 2: Short papers)*, pages 85–91.

Long Ouyang, Jeff Wu, Xu Jiang, Diogo Almeida, Carroll L Wainwright, Pamela Mishkin, Chong Zhang, Sandhini Agarwal, Katarina Slama, Alex Ray, et al. 2022. Training language models to follow instructions with human feedback. *arXiv preprint arXiv:2203.02155*.

Ramakanth Pasunuru and Mohit Bansal. 2018. Multi-reward reinforced summarization with saliency and entailment. *arXiv preprint arXiv:1804.06451*.

Fabio Petroni, Samuel Broscheit, Aleksandra Piktus, Patrick Lewis, Gautier Izacard, Lucas Hosseini, Jane Dwivedi-Yu, Maria Lomeli, Timo Schick, Pierre-Emmanuel Mazaré, Armand Joulin, Edouard Grave, and Sebastian Riedel. 2022. Improving wikipedia verifiability with ai.

Reid Pryzant, Richard Diehl Martinez, Nathan Dass, Sadao Kurohashi, Dan Jurafsky, and Diyi Yang. 2020. Automatically neutralizing subjective bias in text. In *Proceedings of the aaai conference on artificial intelligence*, volume 34, pages 480–489.

Alec Radford, Jeff Wu, Rewon Child, David Luan, Dario Amodei, and Ilya Sutskever. 2019. Language models are unsupervised multitask learners. Technical report, Open AI.

Colin Raffel, Noam Shazeer, Adam Roberts, Katherine Lee, Sharan Narang, Michael Matena, Yanqi Zhou, Wei Li, Peter J Liu, et al. 2020. Exploring the limits of transfer learning with a unified text-to-text transformer. *J. Mach. Learn. Res.*, 21(140):1–67.

Miriam Redi, Martin Gerlach, Isaac Johnson, Jonathan Morgan, and Leila Zia. 2020. A taxonomy of knowledge gaps for wikimedia projects (second draft). *arXiv preprint arXiv:2008.12314*.

Pengjie Ren, Furu Wei, Zhumin Chen, Jun Ma, and Ming Zhou. 2016. A redundancy-aware sentence regression framework for extractive summarization. In *Proceedings of COLING 2016, the 26th International Conference on Computational Linguistics: Technical Papers*, pages 33–43.

Victor Sanh, Albert Webson, Colin Raffel, Stephen Bach, Lintang Sutawika, Zaid Alyafeai, Antoine Chaffin, Arnaud Stiegler, Arun Raja, Manan Dey, M Saiful Bari, Canwen Xu, Urmish Thakker, Shanya Sharma Sharma, Eliza Szczechla, Taewoon Kim, Gunjan Chhablani, Nihal Nayak, Debajyoti Datta, Jonathan Chang, Mike Tian-Jian Jiang, Han Wang, Matteo Manica, Sheng Shen, Zheng Xin Yong, Harshit Pandey, Rachel Bawden, Thomas Wang, Trishala Neeraj, Jos Rozen, Abheesht Sharma, Andrea Santilli, Thibault Fevry, Jason Alan Fries, Ryan Teehan, Teven Le Scao, Stella Biderman, Leo Gao, Thomas Wolf, and Alexander M Rush. 2022. Multitask prompted training enables zero-shot task generalization. In *International Conference on Learning Representations*.

Timo Schick, Jane Dwivedi-Yu, Zhengbao Jiang, Fabio Petroni, Patrick Lewis, Gautier Izacard, Qingfei You, Christoforos Nalmpantis, Edouard Grave, and Sebastian Riedel. 2022. Peer: A collaborative language model.

Anthony Seow. 2002. The writing process and process writing. *Methodology in language teaching: An anthology of current practice*, 315:320.

Alexander Spangher, Xiang Ren, Jonathan May, and Nanyun Peng. 2022. Newsedits: A news article revision dataset and a novel document-level reasoning challenge. In *Proceedings of the 2022 Conference of the North American Chapter of the Association for Computational Linguistics: Human Language Technologies*, pages 127–157.

Sanja Štajner, Hannah Béchara, and Horacio Saggion. 2015. A deeper exploration of the standard pb-smt approach to text simplification and its evaluation. In *Proceedings of the 53rd Annual Meeting of the Association for Computational Linguistics and the 7th International Joint Conference on Natural Language Processing (Volume 2: Short Papers)*, pages 823–828.

Inigo Jauregi Unanue, Jacob Parnell, and Massimo Piccardi. 2021. Berttune: Fine-tuning neural machine translation with bertscore. *arXiv preprint arXiv:2106.02208*.

Lucy Vanderwende, Hisami Suzuki, and Chris Brockett. 2006. Microsoft research at duc 2006: task-focused summarization with sentence simplification and lexical expansion. In *Proceedings of the Document Understanding Conference, DUC-2006, New York, USA*.

Iris Vardi. 2012. The impact of iterative writing and feedback on the characteristics of tertiary students' written texts. *Teaching in Higher Education*, 17(2):167–179.

Alex Wang, Yada Pruksachatkun, Nikita Nangia, Amanpreet Singh, Julian Michael, Felix Hill, Omer Levy, and Samuel Bowman. 2019. Superglue: A stickier benchmark for general-purpose language understanding systems. *Advances in neural information processing systems*, 32.

Alex Wang, Amanpreet Singh, Julian Michael, Felix Hill, Omer Levy, and Samuel R Bowman. 2018. Glue: A multi-task benchmark and analysis platform for natural language understanding. In *International Conference on Learning Representations*.

Yizhong Wang, Swaroop Mishra, Pegah Alipoormolabashi, Yeganeh Kordi, Amirreza Mirzaei, Anjana Arunkumar, Arjun Ashok, Arut Selvan Dhanasekaran, Atharva Naik, David Stap, et al. 2022. Benchmarking generalization via in-context instructions on 1,600+ language tasks. *arXiv preprint arXiv:2204.07705*.

Wei Xu, Chris Callison-Burch, and Courtney Napoles. 2015. Problems in current text simplification research: New data can help. *Transactions of the Association for Computational Linguistics*, 3:283–297.

Wei Xu, Courtney Napoles, Ellie Pavlick, Quanze Chen, and Chris Callison-Burch. 2016. Optimizing statistical machine translation for text simplification. *Transactions of the Association for Computational Linguistics*, 4:401–415.

Diyi Yang, Aaron Halfaker, Robert Kraut, and Eduard Hovy. 2017. Identifying semantic edit intentions from revisions in wikipedia. In *Proceedings of the 2017 Conference on Empirical Methods in Natural Language Processing*, pages 2000–2010.

Zheng Yuan and Ted Briscoe. 2016. Grammatical error correction using neural machine translation. In *Proceedings of the 2016 Conference of the North American Chapter of the Association for Computational Linguistics: Human Language Technologies*, pages 380–386.

Fan Zhang, Homa B Hashemi, Rebecca Hwa, and Diane Litman. 2017. A corpus of annotated revisions for studying argumentative writing. In *Proceedings of the 55th Annual Meeting of the Association for Computational Linguistics (Volume 1: Long Papers)*, pages 1568–1578.

Susan Zhang, Stephen Roller, Naman Goyal, Mikel Artetxe, Moya Chen, Shuohui Chen, Christopher Dewan, Mona Diab, Xian Li, Xi Victoria Lin, Todor Mihaylov, Myle Ott, Sam Shleifer, Kurt Shuster, Daniel Simig, Punit Singh Koura, Anjali Sridhar, Tianlu Wang, and Luke Zettlemoyer. 2022. Opt: Open pretrained transformer language models.

Tianyi Zhang, Varsha Kishore, Felix Wu, Kilian Q. Weinberger, and Yoav Artzi. 2019a. Bertscore: Evaluating text generation with bert. *ArXiv*, abs/1904.09675.

Tianyi Zhang, Varsha Kishore, Felix Wu, Kilian Q Weinberger, and Yoav Artzi. 2019b. Bertscore: Evaluating text generation with bert. *arXiv preprint arXiv:1904.09675*.

Sanqiang Zhao, Rui Meng, Daqing He, Saptono Andi, and Parmanto Bambang. 2018. Integrating transformer and paraphrase rules for sentence simplification. *arXiv preprint arXiv:1810.11193*.

Zhemin Zhu, Delphine Bernhard, and Iryna Gurevych. 2010. A monolingual tree-based translation model for sentence simplification. In *Proceedings of the 23rd International Conference on Computational Linguistics (Coling 2010)*, pages 1353–1361, Beijing, China. Coling 2010 Organizing Committee.

A Domains

In EDITEVAL we strive to encompass datasets from many different domains, with an emphasis on factual content. Below in Table A1, we enumerate these domains.

Table A1: Number of targets provided ($|T|$) and the domains covered by each dataset.

Dataset	$\|T\|$	Domains
ITERATER	1	Wikipedia, ArXiv, and Wikinews
JFLEG	4	TOEFL exam
WNC	1	Wikipedia
STS Benchmark	1	Wikipedia, Q&A, news forums, videos, image descriptions
ASSET	10	Wikipedia
TurkCorpus	8	Wikipedia
WAFER	1	Wikipedia
FRUIT	1	Wikipedia

B Prompts

Below we enumerate the prompts used in EDITEVAL for each task. We also present Table C2 which shows the max and min results across these prompts as opposed to the average in Table 3.

Fluency

1. Fix grammar errors
2. Fix grammar or spelling mistakes
3. Fix grammar errors in this sentence
4. Fix all grammatical errors
5. Fix errors in this text
6. Update to remove grammar errors
7. Remove all grammatical errors from this text
8. Improve the grammar of this text
9. Grammar improvements
10. Remove grammar mistakes
11. Fix the grammar mistakes

Clarity

1. Make the text more formal, concise, readable and understandable
2. Make the text more formal
3. Make the text more concise
4. Make the text more readable
5. Improve the readability of the text
6. Make the text more understandable
7. Make the text clearer
8. Make the text easier to understand
9. Improve the clarity of the text

Coherence

1. Make the text more cohesive, logically linked and consistent as a whole
2. Make the text more cohesive
3. Improve the cohesiveness of the text
4. Make the text more logical
5. Make the text more consistent
6. Improve the consistency of the text
7. Make the text more understandable
8. Make the text clearer
9. Make the text easier to understand
10. Improve the coherency of the text

Neutralization

1. Remove POV
2. Neutralize this text
3. Make this more neutral
4. Make this text more neutral
5. Make this paragraph more neutral
6. Remove unsourced opinions from this text
7. Remove non-neutral points of view
8. Remove points of view
9. Make this text less biased

Paraphrasing

1. Paraphrase this sentence
2. Paraphrase
3. Paraphrase this paragraph.
4. Use different wording
5. Paraphrase this text
6. Rewrite this text
7. Rewrite this text with different wording
8. Rephrase this text
9. Reword this text

Simplification

1. Simplify this sentence
2. Make this simpler
3. Simplify
4. Make this easier to understand
5. Simplification
6. Change to simpler wording
7. Simplify this paragraph.
8. Use simpler wording
9. Simplify this text
10. Make this text less complex

Updating

1. Add missing information
2. Update the article
3. Update with new information

C Metrics

In this section, we describe each metric included in EDITEVAL in greater detail and our motivations for including them. In the cases where more than multiple valid targets, we follow convention and take the maximum of the scores computed using each target, since there can potentially be many valid edits, and a prediction only needs to align with one of the references.

EM and EM-Diff Exact match (EM) is the percentage of examples for which the performed edit exactly matches any of the targets. EM-Diff is a variant of EM that is computed on the diff level, where diffs are obtained using Python's `difflib` library. For a model output O, we compute EM-Diff as follows:

$$\frac{|\text{diff}(I, R) \cap \text{diff}(I, O)|}{\max(|\text{diff}(I, R)|, |\text{diff}(I, O)|)}$$

SARI Introduced by Xu et al. (2016), SARI is an n-gram based metric commonly used for measuring simplification (Nisioi et al., 2017; Zhao et al., 2018) and other editing tasks such as sentence fusion (Malmi et al., 2019). It has been demonstrated to correlate most closely with human judgement for simplification compared to many other n-gram based metrics (Xu et al., 2016). The metric measures how simplified a candidate system output is relative to the original and to the simplification references by rewarding words added, kept, or deleted in both the target and the output. More specifically, this is done by computing the arithmetic mean of n-gram F1-scores for each of the three operations. We utilize the EASSE (Alva-Manchego et al., 2019) implementation of SARI, which addresses inconsistencies in the original implementation [8].

GLEU GLEU (Napoles et al., 2015) is another variant of BLEU frequently used for grammatical error correction (Grundkiewicz et al., 2019; Yuan and Briscoe, 2016; Chollampatt and Ng, 2018). The issue with using BLEU for minimal edits can be attributed to the difference between analyzing machine translation and editing tasks. In the former, an untranslated word should always be penalized, but in the editing setting, an unmodified word in both the target and the output does not necessarily need to be penalized. Unlike BLEU, GLEU is customized to penalize n-grams changed in the targets but left unchanged by the system output. Napoles et al. (2015) not only demonstrated that GLEU correlates well with human rankings of corrections, but also that GLEU correlates much better than BLEU does.

ROUGE and UpdateROUGE For the task of updating or adding new information, we follow Logan IV et al. (2021) and use ROUGE and UpdateROUGE (Logan IV et al., 2021). ROUGE (Lin, 2004) is a popular n-gram based metric that is commonly used for evaluating summarization systems (Ren et al., 2016; Pasunuru and Bansal, 2018), but is also used in other tasks such as improving fluency (Kann et al., 2018) and simplification (Vanderwende et al., 2006). ROUGE essentially measures the overlap in n-grams. UpdateROUGE, a simple modification of ROUGE, computes ROUGE on the updated sentences rather than the full text. This is intended for tasks such as updating, because a majority of the target will remain unchanged. On the other hand, when evaluating using ROUGE, a system can often superficially achieve high scores by simply copying the input.

BERTScore BERTScore (Zhang et al., 2019b) is a versatile automatic metric that has been demonstrated to correlate well with tasks such as machine translation, image captioning, and abstractive text compression (Zhang et al., 2019b). We note, however, that some studies have demonstrated the metric's poor generalization ability to different datasets (Unanue et al., 2021). We include BERTScore in EDITEVAL for its broad applicability and its popularity.

D Limitations

Our evaluation tool is by no means an exhaustive measurement of editing capabilities. Firstly, there are additional domains that could potentially be added to EDITEVAL, such as books and blogs; as it currently stands, EDITEVAL is heavily constructed from the domain of Wikipedia. Fortunately, EDITEVAL's framework is flexible to the addition of datasets, provided that it has an input and target edit. In the same spirit, there are additional editing tasks such as verifying facts, citing, and reorganizing sentences/paragraphs which would be valuable to include in EDITEVAL. While we recognize these tasks as important to include in EDITEVAL, we consider these to be out of scope for the work at hand. Finally, our results demonstrate that

[8] https://github.com/feralvam/easse#differences-with-original-sari-implementation

	Fluency		*Clarity*	*Coherence*	*Para.*	*Simplification*		*Neutral.*	*Updating*	
Model	JFL	ITR-F	ITR-L	ITR-O	STS	TRK	AST	WNC	FRU	WFI
T*k*	32.9 / 41.6	36.0 / 77.6	**39.5 / 63.3**	35.7 / **77.1**	33.1	34.9	32.6	33.8 / 1.3	12.9 / 4.1	1.3 / 5.0
T0	45.4 / 43.1	32.6 / 50.9	33.8 / 34.0	23.7 / 25.5	35.9	35.3	35.9	27.5 / 0.1	14.9 / 12.4	5.4 / 17.2
T0++	36.7 / 43.9	37.2 / 82.0	38.6 / 61.6	36.0 / 75.8	30.7	33.9	33.3	32.1 / 0.6	12.8 / 3.7	4.6 / 8.5
PEER-3	59.3 / 57.7	54.5 / 86.3	34.0 / 60.6	33.8 / 74.1	34.6	36.4	35.5	57.4 / 29.3	40.2 / **33.6**	34.7 / 20.2
PEER-11	60.6 / 59.4	**55.4 / 87.0**	34.4 / 61.4	34.5 / 75.8	33.1	35.7	33.9	**59.0 / 30.9**	**40.8** / 33.4	**35.2 / 21.4**
OPT	53.5 / 53.9	41.0 / 78.5	35.6 / 44.4	34.4 / 56.9	31.1	34.7	35.3	34.9 / 0.9	35.9 / 28.1	27.0 / 12.3
GPT-3	52.6 / 54.2	39.1 / 79.2	35.6 / 45.8	29.9 / 42.9	29.4	35.5	35.9	34.9 / 1.1	36.3 / 21.6	28.2 / 11.2
InsGPT	**62.7 / 60.4**	51.0 / 85.0	36.5 / 52.6	**37.6** / 68.8	**45.2**	**40.2**	**40.9**	37.2 / 3.8	36.6 / 25.2	26.0 / 17.3
T*k*	30.3 / 35.9	27.9 / 42.1	36.8 / 49.9	32.2 / **63.4**	28.6	30.6	26.1	27.9 / 0.0	12.3 / 3.4	1.2 / 4.1
T0	39.5 / 34.2	21.2 / 26.7	31.4 / 27.4	21.0 / 18.0	31.9	32.9	27.6	18.5 / 0.0	13.7 / 8.1	4.8 / 15.6
T0++	33.0 / 42.2	33.1 / 62.3	**36.8 / 52.6**	29.3 / 45.8	25.5	31.9	25.4	27.4 / 0.2	12.5 / 3.7	3.9 / 7.5
PEER-3	50.2 / 49.8	45.4 / 77.2	30.5 / 36.7	31.1 / 47.3	23.2	29.1	25.4	44.4 / 13.5	37.0 / 26.5	34.1 / 16.3
PEER-11	49.8 / 46.7	**45.9 / 82.5**	31.4 / 43.3	31.9 / 47.9	24.3	29.4	25.7	**45.5 / 15.7**	**37.5 / 27.3**	**34.7 / 19.0**
OPT	40.7 / 41.0	29.7 / 55.5	27.8 / 22.1	22.9 / 24.6	26.1	30.3	26.2	25.0 / 0.0	35.8 / 26.6	26.5 / 9.8
GPT-3	43.6 / 46.7	27.8 / 41.3	32.2 / 35.8	24.4 / 28.8	25.3	29.3	22.6	26.0 / 0.2	35.6 / 21.2	26.1 / 10.0
InsGPT	**59.2 / 56.2**	44.7 / 77.4	34.1 / 44.3	**33.4** / 53.0	**40.2**	**37.0**	**35.4**	32.4 / 0.7	35.9 / 24.4	22.2 / 15.3
Copy	26.7 / 40.5	32.3 / 86.0	29.5 / 62.9	31.3 / 77.2	21.1	26.3	20.7	31.9 / 0.0	29.8 / 0.0	33.6 / –
SotA	*– / 62.4*	*37.2 / –*	*46.2 / –*	*38.3 / –*	–	*34.4*	*37.2*	*– / 45.8*	*– / 47.4*	– / –

Table C2: Maximum (top half) and minimum (bottom half) scores across prompts for all downstream tasks considered. The first numbers for each task are SARI scores; additional metrics are GLEU for fluency, clarity, and coherence, EM for neutralization, Update-R1 for updating. The best results are highlighted in bold. T*k*-Instruct and InstructGPT are shorthanded as T*k* and InsGPT, respectively.

many of the metrics give conflicting signal as to the rankings of the baselines, indicating further work is needed to identify better metrics for measuring overall editing capacity.

E Broader Impact and Ethics

Before being deployed, this work was reviewed by an internal board to ensure compliance with all licensing. We also verified that no datasets included in EDITEVAL contains information that uniquely identifies individual people. All code, results, and a leaderboard are made publicly available. Our benchmark is intended to help drive the development of language models that can edit. Such systems may be able to carry out a wide variety of text modifications and have a broad range of societal implications, such as enabling those with limited access to educational resources to create knowledge-intensive or professional articles (Redi et al., 2020). EDITEVAL is not to be used for ill-intended purposes, such as making adversarial text modifications that introduce misleading or problematic content. Additionally, EDITEVAL inherits biases inherent in its constituent datasets, and we encourage further work to understand the biases and limitations of the datasets used in EDITEVAL.

An Empirical Comparison of Vocabulary Expansion and Initialization Approaches for Language Models

Nandini Mundra[1,*] **Aditya Nanda Kishore**[1,*] **Raj Dabre**[1,3,6]
Ratish Puduppully[4,†] **Anoop Kunchukuttan**[1,5] **Mitesh M. Khapra**[1,2]
[1]Indian Institute of Technology Madras [2]Nilekani Centre at AI4Bharat
[3]National Institute of Information and Communications Technology, Japan
[4]IT University of Copenhagen, Denmark [5]Microsoft India
[6]Indian Institute of Technology Bombay
Correspondence: `miteshk@cse.iitm.ac.in`, `raj.dabre@nict.go.jp`

Abstract

Language Models (LMs) excel in natural language processing tasks for English but show reduced performance in most other languages. This problem is commonly tackled by continually pre-training and fine-tuning these models for said languages. A significant issue in this process is the limited vocabulary coverage in the original model's tokenizer, leading to inadequate representation of new languages and necessitating an expansion of the tokenizer. The initialization of the embeddings corresponding to new vocabulary items presents a further challenge. Current strategies require cross-lingual embeddings and lack a solid theoretical foundation as well as comparisons with strong baselines. In this paper, we first establish theoretically that initializing within the convex hull of existing embeddings is a good initialization, followed by a novel but simple approach, *Constrained Word2Vec (CW2V)*, which does not require cross-lingual embeddings. Our study evaluates different initialization methods for expanding RoBERTa and LLaMA 2 across four languages and five tasks. The results show that CW2V performs equally well or even better than more advanced techniques. Additionally, simpler approaches like multivariate initialization perform on par with these advanced methods indicating that efficient large-scale multilingual continued pretraining can be achieved even with simpler initialization methods. We release our code publicly.[1]

1 Introduction

Language models are adept at a wide spectrum of natural language processing (NLP) tasks (Liu et al., 2023; Chung et al., 2024; Chowdhery et al., 2023; Wei et al., 2024; Goyal et al., 2023; Touvron et al., 2023). However, the best-performing language models work well for English but have inferior capabilities in other languages. A common method to improve the capabilities of other languages is to continually pre-train and finetune the English model for other languages (Conneau and Lample, 2019). This approach builds upon the capabilities acquired through large-scale English pre-training and focuses on aligning the English and other language spaces, making efficient re-use of compute and data resources (Cahyawijaya et al., 2023; Zhang et al., 2023). One of the major challenges for LLM adaptation is the lack of vocabulary coverage in the original model's tokenizer for the new language. This would mean the inability to represent the new language if the vocabulary is totally different or inefficient tokenization with high fertility in the case of inadequate vocabulary representation.

A solution is to expand the tokenizer to incorporate new vocabulary and then perform continual pre-training on monolingual data from the new language to adapt the model to the new language (Cui et al., 2023; Nguyen et al., 2023; Minixhofer et al., 2022). In this scenario, an important question is: *How do we initialize the embeddings of the new vocabulary items?* Various methods have been proposed in the literature for the initialization of the new token embeddings, from simple random initialization (Antoun et al., 2020; Martin et al., 2020) to the mean of embeddings (Gee et al., 2022) to sophisticated methods such as OFA among others (Minixhofer et al., 2022; Dobler and de Melo, 2023; Tran, 2020; Liu et al., 2024) that learn the new embeddings as a function of existing embeddings using external resources and tools like cross-lingual word-vectors and bilingual dictionaries. However, there is no theoretical basis for what constitutes a *good initialization*. Furthermore, in existing works, comparisons with simple, naive initialization methods across different model sizes are missing.

[*]Equal contribution.

[†]Work done while the author was at A*STAR, Singapore.

[1]`https://github.com/AI4Bharat/VocabAdaptation_LLM/tree/CW2V`

Proceedings of the 28th Conference on Computational Natural Language Learning, pages 84–104
November 15-16, 2024 ©2024 Association for Computational Linguistics

In this paper, we theoretically define and analyze the properties of a *good initialization.* We prove that initializing embeddings of new vocabulary embeddings to be in the convex hull of original embeddings ensures that the greedy generation of the existing language(s) is not impacted by the new vocabulary items on initialization. Based on these insights, we propose a simple learnable initialization approach which we dub as *Constrained Word2Vec (CW2V)* which ensures initializations in the convex hull without needing cross-lingual embeddings. We conducted a comparative analysis of CW2V alongside 5 existing initialization strategies including OFA on two models containing varying parameters, namely RoBERTa (125M) and LLaMa2 (7B), examining their impact through 5 downstream tasks across 4 languages. Our analysis of various initialization methods demonstrates that CW2V achieves better if not comparable performance with the previous best methods. Additionally, we find that simpler methods like multivariate or mean initialization, which ensure new embeddings remain within the convex hull, are comparable with more advanced approaches such as OFA.

2 Related Work

Multilingual Models: To create a multilingual model for specific languages, one method is to train the model from scratch on the target languages using MLM and CLM objectives (Workshop et al., 2023; Conneau et al., 2020). However, this requires significant computational resources and data. A more efficient approach is to adapt an existing pretrained language model (PLM) (Devlin et al., 2019; Touvron et al., 2023; Team, 2023) to the desired target language. There are two ways to adapt a PLM to a new language. The first is to fully adapt the model to the new language, replacing the source tokenizer and focusing only on the new language's performance (Minixhofer et al., 2022; Artetxe et al., 2020). The second is to keep the original language support and add the new language, ensuring the model still performs well on the source language (Garcia et al., 2021; Liu et al., 2024). In this work, we focus on extending the language support of the PLM rather than replacing it. We do this by extending the source tokenizer, which requires effectively initializing the model's embedding layer and LM head for the added tokens in the vocabulary.

Embedding Initialization Strategies: Previous work has focused on different initialization strategies. Methods like FVT (Gee et al., 2022) and Hewitt (2021) use the mean of source PLM embeddings, while WECHSEL (Minixhofer et al., 2022), RAMEN (Tran, 2020), FOCUS (Dobler and de Melo, 2023), and OFA (Liu et al., 2024) utilize external cross-lingual word vectors and source embeddings. However, these approaches rely on static embeddings. In contrast, we propose initialization strategy that learns new embeddings from the source PLM model and doesn't require static embeddings.

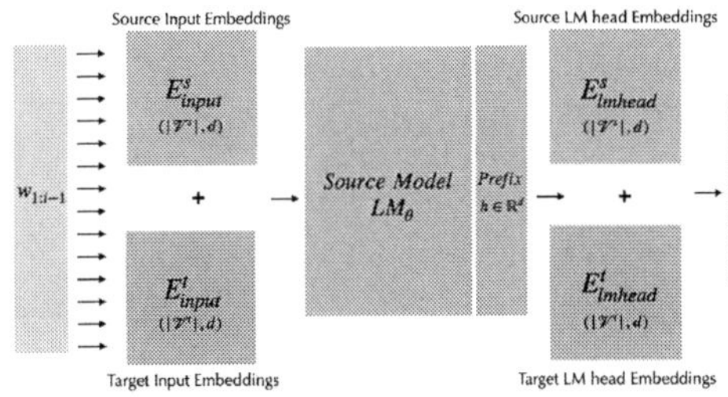

Figure 1: Setup for Vocabulary Expansion. Source model is shown in blue blocks, and expanded vocabulary embeddings are represented in red blocks. Source model parameters remain unchanged.

Continual Pre-training: A good initialization strategy provides a solid start for adapting a PLM to a new language by effectively initializing the new tokens in the embedding and LM head layers. However, to fully adapt the extended model to the new language, continued pre-training (CPT) (Wang et al., 2022; Alabi et al., 2022; Zhao et al., 2023) is essential. Therefore, we performed CPT on target languages post initialization.

3 Methodology

We describe the core methodology in this work followed by theoretical proofs of *good initializations* which motivate our own initialization approach, namely, Constrained Word2Vec.

3.1 Vocabulary Expansion

We adapt the same vocabulary expansion problem formulation as Hewitt (2021). Let θ be the parameters of a pre-trained neural source language model LM^s_θ, and let $\mathcal{V}^s = \{v^s_1, v^s_2, \ldots, v^s_n\}$ be the vocabulary of LM^s_θ. We will refer to $\mathcal{V}^s$ as the source vocabulary henceforth. Let $e^s_i \in \mathbb{R}^d$ be the sub-word embedding for word $i \in \mathcal{V}^s$. Let E^s denote the language modeling head's (henceforth *LM head*) embedding matrix of LM^s_θ and this is our source embedding matrix. The probability of occurrence of the next word w_i given the previous word sequence $w_{1:i-1}$, $p_\theta(w_i \mid w_{1:i-1})$, is given by

$$p_\theta(w_i \mid w_{1:i-1}) = \frac{\exp\left(h_{i-1}^\top e_{w_i}^s\right)}{\sum_{j\in\mathcal{V}^s}\exp\left(h_{i-1}^\top e_j^s\right)},$$

where the prefix $h_{i-1} = \phi(w_{1:i-1}; LM_\theta^s) \in \mathbb{R}^d$ is the neural representation of the input using LM_θ^s.

In vocabulary expansion, we add n' new subwords $\notin \mathcal{V}^s$ forming the target vocabulary $\mathcal{V}^t = \{v_1^t, v_2^t, \ldots, v_{n'}^t\}$. This implies we need a new word embedding e_j^t for each $j \in \mathcal{V}^t$ comprising in E^t. The new language model $LM_{\theta'}^t$ has parameters $\theta' = \theta \cup \{e_j^t; j \in \mathcal{V}^t\}$. The output distribution of $LM_{\theta'}^t$ given by $p_{\theta'}(w_i \mid w_{1:i-1})$ is defined similarly as $p_\theta(w_i \mid w_{1:i-1})$ but with the normalization factor involving $\mathcal{V}^s \cup \mathcal{V}^t$.

Our goal is to find initializations for E^t such that the extended model not only retains its previous behavior but also can lead to good downstream performance for the languages corresponding to the new vocabulary with minimal continual pretraining. Retaining performance in English is particularly beneficial, as the knowledge embedded in English models often supports performance in other languages (Pires et al., 2019). Figure 1 gives an overview of our approach. Note that in our notations so far we have only mentioned the LM head, but just as the LM head has an expansion (E_{lmhead}^t), the input embedding matrix also has an expansion (E_{input}^t). This is trivial if both matrices are shared but in case they are not, we also need to find initializations for the latter. Following Hewitt (2021), we can use the same approach to initialize E_{input}^t as we do for E_{lmhead}^t.

3.2 What is a 'good' embedding initialization?

As we are ensuring that the model parameters θ remain unchanged at the initialization step, we can safely say that for the same word sequence $w_{1:i-1}$, where each word in the sequence belongs to $\mathcal{V}^s$, the prefix h_{i-1} at the output layer remains the same. Thus, the output word w_i strictly depends on the embeddings of the new words added to the vocabulary, as they determine the new partition function and the output probability distribution. The main goal of our analysis is to identify the set of initializations of new words that give us the same output before and after expansion for the prefixes formed by the original tokens. In other words, for the same input word sequence $w_{1:i-1}$, where $w_k \in \mathcal{V}^s\ \forall\ k \in [i-1]$, if w_i and w_i' represent the words predicted by language models LM_θ^s and $LM_{\theta'}^t$ respectively, i.e., $w_i = \text{argmax}_{j\in\mathcal{V}^s}\ p_\theta(j \mid w_{1:i-1})$ and $w_i' = \text{argmax}_{j\in\mathcal{V}^s\cup\mathcal{V}^t}\ p_{\theta'}(j \mid w_{1:i-1})$, we need $w_i = w_i'$. Let $e_1^t, e_2^t, \ldots, e_{n'}^t \in \mathbb{R}^d$ be the embedding initializations for words in $\mathcal{V}^t$. Therefore, a *good initialization* is an initialization $\left\{e_j^t; j \in \mathcal{V}^t\right\}$ that ensures, for any prefix $h_{i-1} \in \mathbb{R}^d$, the set of prefixes formed by word sequences from the source vocabulary, that is $'w_i = w_i'$.

3.3 Theorems

Theorem 1. *: A good initialization preserves the pre-expansion behavior.*

Let $e_1^s, e_2^s, e_3^s, ..., e_n^s \in \mathbb{R}^d$ be the embeddings of words in $\mathcal{V}^s$. Let $e_1^t, e_2^t, \ldots, e_{n'}^t \in \mathbb{R}^d$ be the embedding initializations for words in $\mathcal{V}^t$. If

$$\sup_{k\in\mathcal{V}^t}(h^T e_k^t) \leq \sup_{k\in\mathcal{V}^s}(h^T e_k^s) \tag{1}$$

holds for all $h \in \mathbb{R}^d$, then $\left\{e_j^t; j \in \mathcal{V}^t\right\}$ is a 'good' initialization.

Proof. Let $h = h_{i-1} \in \mathbb{R}^d$ be a prefix formed by a word sequence $w_{1:i-1}$, where $w_k \in \mathcal{V}^s\ \forall\ k \in [i-1]$. As condition 1 holds for all $h \in \mathbb{R}^d$, we can say that,

$$\begin{aligned} &\sup_{k\in\mathcal{V}^t}(h^T e_k^t) \leq \sup_{k\in\mathcal{V}^s}(h^T e_k^s) \\ \implies &\sup_{k\in\mathcal{V}^t}\exp(h^T e_k^t) \leq \sup_{k\in\mathcal{V}^s}\exp(h^T e_k^s) \\ \implies &\sup_{k\in\mathcal{V}^t}\frac{\exp(h^T e_k^t)}{Z'} \leq \sup_{k\in\mathcal{V}^s}\frac{\exp(h^T e_k^s)}{Z'} \end{aligned}$$

where, $Z' = \sum_{j\in\mathcal{V}^s\cup\mathcal{V}^t}\exp\left(h^\top e_j^t\right)$ is the new partition function, which is a positive constant as prefix and all the embeddings are given. We know that, $\frac{\exp(h^T e_k^t)}{Z'}$ represents the probability of occurrence of word corresponding to the embedding e_k^t at time step i. Thus, the inequality just says that probability of occurrence of any word from target vocabulary $\mathcal{V}^t$ is less than or equal to probability of occurrence of a word from source vocabulary. As the decoding at output layer is greedy, the output word is going to come from source vocabulary. We can guarantee that it remains the same as pre-expansion model's output word because the prefix remains the same before and after expansion as $w_k \in$ source vocabulary $\mathcal{V}^s\ \forall\ k \in [i-1]$.

Hence, as $w_i = w_i'$ and the embedding initialization $\left\{e_j^t; j \in \mathcal{V}^t\right\}$ is 'good'. $\square$

Theorem 2. ***: An initialization in the convex hull of source embeddings is good.***

If $y \in \mathcal{S}$, where $\mathcal{S}$ is the convex hull of the embeddings $e_1^s, e_2^s, e_3^s, \ldots, e_n^s$, then $(h^T y) \leq \sup_{k \in \mathcal{V}^s}(h^T e_k^s)$ for all $h \in \mathbb{R}^d$. Moreover, if $e_i^t \in \mathcal{S}$ for all $i \in \mathcal{V}^t$, then the initialization is 'good'.

Proof. Given $y \in \mathcal{S}$. Thus y can be written as $y = \sum_{j \in \mathcal{V}^s} \alpha_j e_j^s$ where $\sum_{j \in \mathcal{V}^s} \alpha_j = 1$ and $0 \leq w_j \leq 1 \,\forall\, j \in \mathcal{V}^s$. Thus, $\forall\, h \in \mathbb{R}^d$,

$$h^T y = \sum_{j \in \mathcal{V}^s} \alpha_j h^T e_j^s$$

.

As $0 \leq \alpha_j \leq 1 \,\forall\, j \in \mathcal{V}^s$,

$$(h^T y) \leq \sup_{k \in \mathcal{V}^s} (h^T e_k^s)$$

Given $e_i^t \in \mathcal{S} \;\forall\, i \in \mathcal{V}^t$

$$\implies (h^T e_i^t) \leq \sup_{k \in \mathcal{V}^s} (h^T e_k^s) \;\; \forall\, i \in \mathcal{V}^t \;\; \forall\, h \in \mathbb{R}^d$$

$$\implies \sup_{k \in \mathcal{V}^t} (h^T e_k^t) \leq \sup_{k \in \mathcal{V}^s} (h^T e_k^s) \;\; \forall\, h \in \mathbb{R}^d$$

Thus, from theorem 1 we can say that if $e_i^t \in \mathcal{S} \;\forall\, i \in \mathcal{V}^t$, then the initialization is *good.* $\square$

We have showed that as long as we initialize every target embedding vector as a weighted average of source embeddings, the model output remains the same for the same prefix as long as it is obtained from a word sequence formed only by source vocabulary, thereby making it *good.* Table 5 verifies this empirically. In Appendix B we provide some additional theoretical analysis where we show a weaker converse of Theorem 2, that any *strongly good* initialization lies in the convex hull of source embeddings.

3.4 Our Approach: Constrained Word2Vec

Having established that a initializing in the convex hull of existing embeddings is *good*, we now propose *Constrained Word2Vec (CW2V)*, a novel approach to learn these initializations. Specifically, we constrain E^t as WE^s where $\sum_{j \in \mathcal{V}^s} W_{ij} = 1 \,\forall\, i \in \mathcal{V}^t$ and $W_{ij} \geq 0 \,\forall\, j \in \mathcal{V}^s, i \in \mathcal{V}^t$. Here, $E^s \in \mathbb{R}^{(|\mathcal{V}^s|,d)}$ is the source embedding matrix, $E^t \in \mathbb{R}^{(|\mathcal{V}^t|,d)}$ is the target embedding matrix and $W \in \mathbb{R}^{(|\mathcal{V}^t|,|\mathcal{V}^s|)}$ is the weight matrix that transforms E^s to E^t while ensuring the target embedding vectors reside inside the convex hull of the source embedding vectors. Our goal is to learn W.

Let $\mathcal{E}^t$ be the post-expansion embedding matrix of size $(|\mathcal{V}^s \cup \mathcal{V}^t|, d)$. In other words, $\mathcal{E}^t = [E^s; WE^s]$ where ; indicates concatenation along the vocabulary axis. By using $\mathcal{E}^t$ as the embedding matrix with W as the only learnable parameters, we propose a mechanism similar to Skip-gram (Mikolov et al., 2013) to obtain $\mathcal{E}^t$. In many modern PLMs, such as LLaMA, the input and output embedding layers are not tied, necessitating separate weight matrices for the input embedding and the LM head defined as $\mathcal{E}^s_{input} = [E^s_{input}; softmax(W_{input})E^s_{input}]$, $\mathcal{E}^s_{LM-head} = [E^s_{LM-head}; softmax(W_{LM-head})E^s_{LM-head}]^T$ with sizes $(|\mathcal{V}^s \cup \mathcal{V}^t|, d)$, $(d, |\mathcal{V}^s \cup \mathcal{V}^t|)$, respectively. The *softmax* operation ensures that the weights in each row add up to 1, thus assuring that the target embedding vectors remain in the convex hull of pre-expansion embeddings.

We set these embedding matrices $\mathcal{E}^t_{input}$ and $\mathcal{E}^t_{LM-head}$ up in the traditional Skip-gram architecture (Mikolov et al., 2013) as the word and context representation matrices. Similar to OFA (Liu et al., 2024), in order to make the learning computationally more efficient, we can also factorise W_{input} and $W_{LM-head}$ and learn the resulting parameters. This methodology can be extended to any PLM. If both the embedding layers are tied for a PLM (RoBERTa), we still learn two weight matrices and choose either for initializing E^t. To align target language embeddings with English, we trained the CW2V model on monolingual data from all languages and bilingual English-to-target dictionaries.

4 Experimental Setting

We now describe the models we focus on, the languages, downstream tasks and datasets, and implementation details.

4.1 Models

We use RoBERTa (Liu et al., 2019), an encoder based architecture and LLaMA2-7B (Touvron et al., 2023), a decoder based model and employ these models as the source models for our multilingual vocabulary expansion experiments.

4.2 Tokenizers

We use the RoBERTa tokenizer as the source tokenizer for experiments with RoBERTa and the LLaMA2 tokenizer as the source tokenizer for experiments with LLaMA2. Since we are focusing on multilingual transfer, we train a SentencePiece (Kudo and Richardson, 2018) tokenizer using textual data in target languages (German, Russian, Hindi, Tamil) and merge the obtained tokenizer with LLaMA2's tokenizer. The resulting tokenizer has 57K subwords in its vocabulary, and this merged tokenizer serves as the unified target tokenizer for all of our experiments, even for experiments with RoBERTa. We identify common subwords using a 'fuzzy' search similar to FOCUS (Dobler and de Melo, 2023) and OFA (Liu et al., 2024). We report the fertility score of the target tokenizer in all four target languages in Appendix D. Vocabulary expansion significantly reduces the fertilities for the languages considered.

4.3 Datasets and Languages

We extended the source model (English) to four target languages: Hindi, Tamil, Russian, and German. For all training, the Hindi and Tamil datasets were sourced from SANGRAHA (Khan et al., 2024), while the Russian, German, and English datasets were sourced from OSCAR (Ortiz Su'arez et al., 2020). To train the multilingual tokenizer, we used a monolingual dataset of 3 million sentences per target language, sourced from the tokenizer training data used in IndicTrans2 (Gala et al., 2023). For the constrained word2vec model training, we used a monolingual corpus of 2 million tokens per target language. Additionally, we incorporated bilingual dictionary datasets: Hindi and Tamil from (Kanojia et al., 2018), German from url [2] processed by (Bojar et al., 2014), and Russian from url [3]. Each expanded and initialized model underwent further pre-training on a multilingual dataset of 2.5 billion tokens, combining 500 million tokens per target language and 500 million English tokens.

4.4 Baselines

OFA The One For All (OFA) Framework (Liu et al., 2024) (Liu et al., 2024) uses multilingual static word vectors to inject alignment knowledge into the new subword embeddings. Regardless of the factorization approach, OFA initializes all new target embeddings using a weighted average of the source vocabulary embeddings, making OFA a 'strongly good' initialization.

Univariate Each target embedding is initialised by drawing values from 1-D Gaussian distributions parameterized by the mean and standard deviation of the source embeddings for each dimension. This was the primary baseline considered by OFA (Liu et al., 2024).

Multivariate Every target embedding is sampled from the multivariate gaussian distribution of embeddings whose mean and covariance come from the original embeddings E^s.

Mean Every target embedding is the average of pre-expansion embeddings. Mean initialization is used to initialize target vocabulary in FVT (Gee et al., 2022) and Hewitt (2021). This is a 'strongly' good initialization as mean of original embeddings belongs to the convex hull of original embeddings.

Random Every target embedding is randomly sampled from the $d-$dimensional guassian distribution $\mathcal{N}(0, 0.02I)$ where I is a $d-$dimensional identity matrix.

4.5 Constrained Word2Vec Training

We trained the constrained word2vec model using a similar setup to skip-gram (Mikolov et al., 2013) training. The context window size was set to 10 and negative sampling to 5. Additionally, we factorized the W_{input} and $W_{LM-head}$ matrices, with a factorized dimension of 1024. This factorization was done to reduce the number of trainable parameters, similar to OFA ((Liu et al., 2024)). Factorizing the weight matrices in the constrained word2vec model for RoBERTa reduced the number of trainable parameters from 758M to 59M, and for LLaMA2, it reduced from 1660M to 118M.

Model	Task Category	Task	Metric
RoBERTa	Sentence Classification	XNLI	Acc.
	Question Answering	QA	F1
	Token Classification	NER	F1
LLaMA2	Sentence Classification	XNLI	Acc.
	Machine Translation	FLORES	CHRF
	Question Answering	QA	F1
	Sentence Summarisation	XLSUM	BLEURT

Table 1: A summary of the tasks, datasets and metrics.

[2] https://nlp.stanford.edu/projects/nmt/data/wmt14.en-de/dict.en-de

[3] https://github.com/Badestrand/russian-dictionary

4.6 Downstream Tasks

We evaluated RoBERTa and LLaMA on various tasks, as shown in Table 1. For XNLI, we used XNLI (Conneau et al., 2018) for German, Russian, Hindi, and English, and IndicXNLI (Aggarwal et al., 2022) for Tamil. For NER, we used WikiANN (Pan et al., 2017). For QA, we used SQuAD (Rajpurkar et al., 2018) for German, Russian, Hindi, and English, and IndicQA (Doddapaneni et al., 2023) for Tamil. For Machine Translation, we used FLORES (Team et al., 2022). RoBERTa MLM checkpoints were fine-tuned on English and evaluated zero-shot on target languages. LLaMA CLM checkpoints were evaluated with 4-shot prompting. The metrics for each task are also listed in Table 1.

5 Results

We now describe the results of our investigation, where we first evaluate different initialization methods without continual pre-training or fine-tuning for RoBERTa and LLaMA2. We follow this up with results for continual pre-training and fine-tuning for RoBERTa, and continual pre-training and few-shot prompting for LLaMA2.

5.1 Impact of Initialization Methods

For the encoder-only RoBERTa model: Table 2 presents the performance of the expanded RoBERTa model initialized with Constrained Word2Vec, alongside baseline models, across three downstream tasks: XNLI, NER, and QA. The expanded and initialized model was not continually pre-trained but was fine-tuned till convergence on downstream task data. Firstly, looking at the columns labeled **en**, we can see that CW2V is better than any baseline for English, even OFA, indicating that it preserves the pre-expansion behavior of RoBERTa better than any other methods. Next, the scores under the **avg** columns indicate that CW2V is competitive with other approaches, especially OFA but tends to be slightly inferior. This means that CW2V mildly sacrifices the performance on other languages while strongly preserving the English performance.

For the decoder-only LLaMA2 model: Table 2 shows the performance of the expanded LLaMA2 model initialized with Constrained Word2Vec, alongside baselines, on the following downstream tasks: XNLI, Machine Translation, QA and XL-SUM (summarization). Here as well, the expanded and initialized model was not continually pre-trained but was evaluated using few-shot prompting. Different from the case of RoBERTa, the CW2V model significantly outperforms the OFA model across all tasks and languages despite not being continually pre-trained. CW2V achieves higher CHRF scores, averaged over all translation directions, in MT (17.02 En-X and 27.26 X-En) compared to OFA's 11.17 and 16.17, respectively. Similarly, for XNLI, QA and XLSUM, we observe that the average (**avg** column) performance over all languages for CW2V is vastly better than any other approach. The English-only performance (**en** column) however is comparable across all approaches with CW2V being only slightly better. This proves that in decoder-only models while CW2V is as good as any other approach for preserving the pre-expansion English-only performance, it is substantially better than other approaches for the new languages via vocabulary expansion.

5.2 Impact of Continual Pretraining

Here we show the compounding effects of continual pre-training and various initialization strategies to understand whether initialization matters or not when monolingual adaptation data exists.

For the encoder-only RoBERTa model: We evaluate the performance of expanded RoBERTa models initialized with Constrained Word2Vec (CW2V) and other baseline methods with CPT. We evaluate 15 checkpoints from one epoch of CPT (plus the initial checkpoint prior to CPT) on 3 downstream tasks. The results are depicted in Figure 2. Here, again, CW2V demonstrates comparable or superior performance to OFA, especially towards the latter stages of CPT. As illustrated in Figure 2, CW2V quickly converges with OFA (within less than 4 checkpoints) across all three tasks. Additionally, simpler baselines such as mean and multivariate also achieve comparable performance to OFA and CW2V shortly thereafter (in NER and QA, Multivariate catches up to CW2V within two checkpoints), demonstrating strong performance. This suggests that straightforward baselines like multivariate can be as effective as sophisticated methods such as Constrained Word2Vec and OFA. Furthermore, our analysis consistently shows that Univariate and Random initialization methods underperform in comparison to CW2V, OFA, Multivariate[4], and Mean. This highlights that Univariate

[4]Multivariate initialization has a high probability of re-

	RoBERTa						LLaMA2							
	XNLI		NER		QA		MT		XNLI		QA		XLSUM	
	en	avg	en	avg	en	avg	En-X	X-En	en	avg	en	avg	en	avg
CW2V	**86.0**	36.0	**82.2**	21.5	**90.7**	9.0	**17.0**	**27.3**	60.4	**38.1**	**77.7**	**35.8**	**0.6**	**0.4**
OFA	85.6	**37.7**	81.9	**21.7**	90.6	**12.0**	11.2	16.2	60.4	37.1	76.0	26.0	0.6	0.3
Multivariate	85.7	35.7	81.8	18.3	90.4	9.5	11.1	16.1	60.4	37.2	77.5	28.7	0.5	0.2
Univariate	85.6	36.6	82.0	22.0	90.7	10.3	11.1	16.0	60.4	37.2	77.4	28.7	0.5	0.3
Mean	85.5	36.0	81.5	20.3	90.5	8.8	11.1	16.2	**60.5**	37.2	77.4	28.7	0.5	0.3
Random	85.8	35.9	81.6	21.0	90.3	9.6	0.0	0.0	33.3	33.3	0.0	0.0	0.0	0.0

Table 2: Performance of the expanded RoBERTa and LLaMA2 models initialized with Constrained Word2Vec and baselines on downstream tasks across 5 languages.

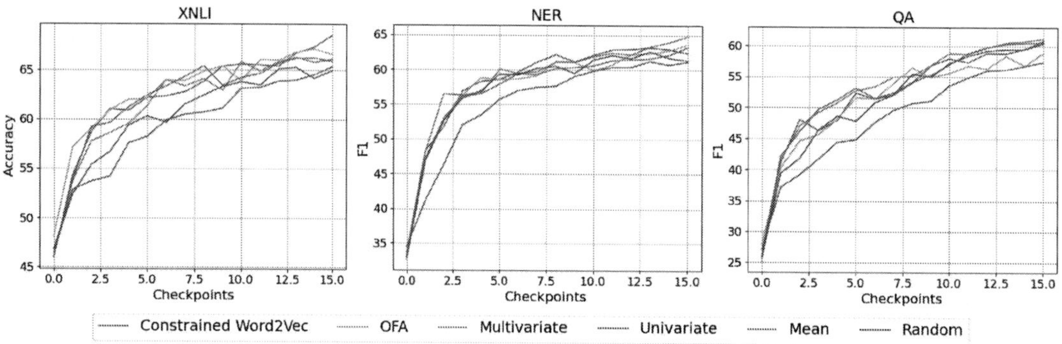

Figure 2: Evaluation of different initialization methods on expanded RoBERTa models using three multilingual tasks (XNLI, NER, QA) at 15 CPT checkpoints. The plots show average performance across five languages.

and Random methods, despite being used as primary baselines in previous work, are inadequate for comparison.

For the decoder-only LLaMA2 model: Similarly, we observe the performance of the expanded LLaMA2 models initialized with Constrained Word2Vec and the baselines. We evaluate 5 checkpoints from one epoch of CPT (plus the initial checkpoint prior to CPT) on 4 downstream tasks. The results are depicted in Figure 3. For MT and QA, both generative tasks, on average, CW2V is better if not comparable with OFA while being consistently better than all other approaches. We see that CW2V quickly surpasses OFA in 2-3 checkpoints. In the case of XLSUM, however, OFA tends to be better during intermediate checkpoints (1, 2, 3), but CW2V eventually performs just as well afterwards. Once again, CW2V (and OFA) are significantly better than other baselines.

XNLI is the only confounding task since no clear trends can be observed over various CPT stages. Furthermore, all models perform almost equally poorly, indicating that neither vocabulary expansion nor CPT is sufficient to improve XNLI performance. We suppose that fine-tuning on an XNLI dataset may shed further light on this, but due to limited compute, we did not pursue fine-tuning for any task and hence leave it as future work. Overall, CW2V is a highly effective initialization strategy for CPT, particularly benefiting languages that we aim to support more effectively through vocabulary expansion.

siding within the convex hull of the source embeddings (Appendix F)

5.3 Catastrophic Forgetting in English tasks

Here we reveal something concerning about the inevitable negative effect of CPT on the pre-expansion language (English). During continued pre-training on monolingual datasets in both target and source languages, even with the source language (English) constituting 20% of the total dataset, we observed an initial drop in English performance. Figure 4 shows the performance of the expanded RoBERTa models at various CPT checkpoints on only English tasks. Initially, performance drops, after which it begins to improve with prolonged training without comprising performance on non-english tasks. This suggests that adjusting the model to learn new target language data tem-

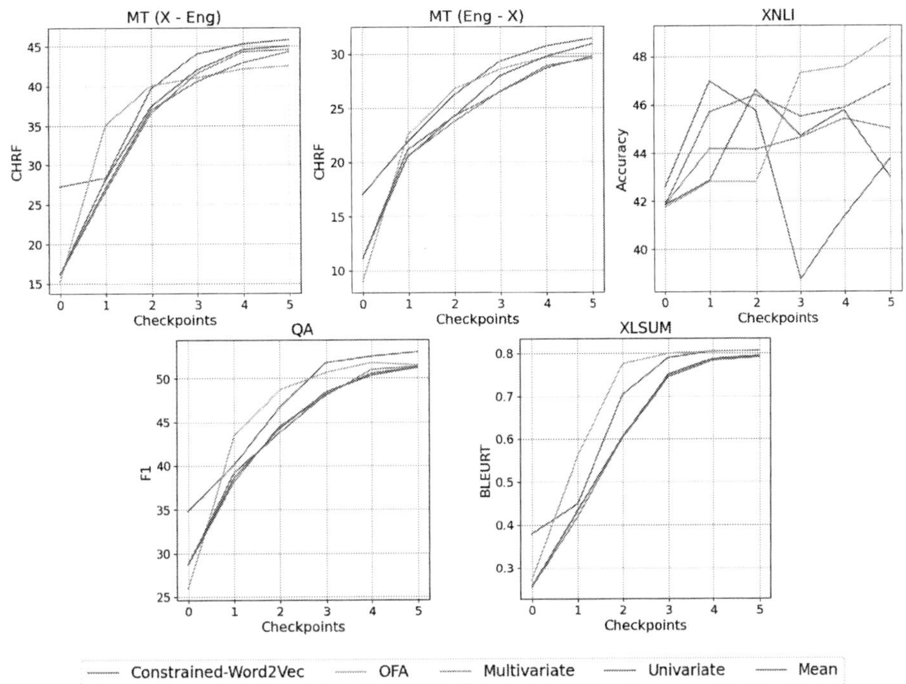

Figure 3: 4-shot XNLI, MT, QA, XLSUM evaluation of different initialization methods on expanded LLaMA2 models at 5 equidistant CPT checkpoints. MT plots show average performance across 4 languages, and XNLI, QA, XLSUM plots show average performance across 5 languages.

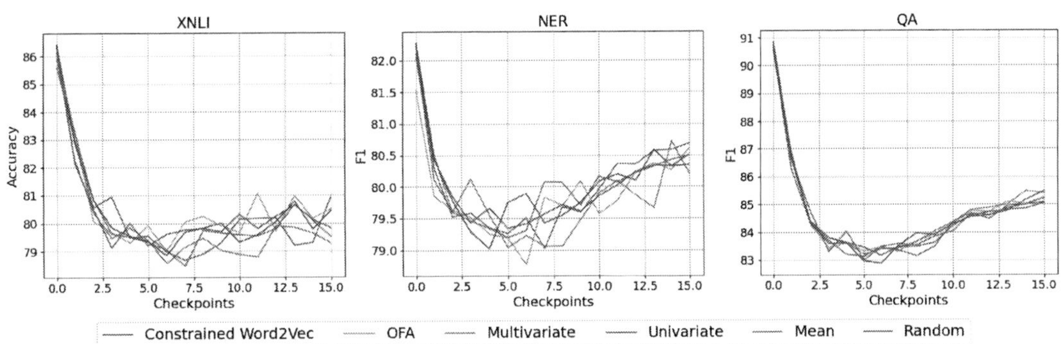

Figure 4: Assessment of English performance for various initialization methods on expanded RoBERTa models across three downstream tasks (XNLI, NER, QA) at 15 CPT checkpoints.

porarily disrupts the weights previously optimized for English but prolonged training could potentially further restore and enhance English performance.

6 Conclusion

In this work, we establish that effective embedding initialization for an expanded vocabulary in language models can be achieved within the convex hull of source vocabulary embeddings. We introduce a data-driven initialization method, *Constrained Word2Vec (CW2V)*, which learns the target embeddings by constraining them in the convex hull of the source embeddings. Our comparison of various initialization methods reveals that Constrained Word2Vec performs on par with other advanced techniques. Additionally, we find that simple methods like Multivariate and Mean, which ensure new embeddings lie within the convex hull of source embeddings, perform comparably well to more complex approaches. This indicates that efficient large-scale multilingual continued pretraining can be possible even with simpler methods, provided they are *good* initialization strategies.

References

Divyanshu Aggarwal, Vivek Gupta, and Anoop Kunchukuttan. 2022. IndicXNLI: Evaluating multilingual inference for Indian languages. In *Proceedings of the 2022 Conference on Empirical Methods in Natural Language Processing*, pages 10994–11006, Abu Dhabi, United Arab Emirates. Association for Computational Linguistics.

Adam Alabi, Saleha Nawaz, and Vincent Ng. 2022. Alabi: A light-weight approach for multilingual biomedical language models. In *Proceedings of the 2022 Conference on Empirical Methods in Natural Language Processing*, pages 9717–9727.

Wissam Antoun, Fady Baly, and Hazem Hajj. 2020. AraBERT: Transformer-based model for Arabic language understanding. In *Proceedings of the 4th Workshop on Open-Source Arabic Corpora and Processing Tools, with a Shared Task on Offensive Language Detection*, pages 9–15, Marseille, France. European Language Resource Association.

Mikel Artetxe, Sebastian Ruder, and Dani Yogatama. 2020. On the cross-lingual transferability of monolingual representations. In *Proceedings of the 58th Annual Meeting of the Association for Computational Linguistics*, pages 4623–4637, Online. Association for Computational Linguistics.

Ondrej Bojar, Christian Buck, Christian Federmann, Barry Haddow, Philipp Koehn, Johannes Leveling, Christof Monz, Pavel Pecina, Matt Post, Herve Saint-Amand, Radu Soricut, Lucia Specia, and Ale s Tamchyna. 2014. Findings of the 2014 workshop on statistical machine translation. In *Proceedings of the Ninth Workshop on Statistical Machine Translation*, pages 12–58, Baltimore, Maryland, USA. Association for Computational Linguistics.

Samuel Cahyawijaya, Holy Lovenia, Tiezheng Yu, Willy Chung, and Pascale Fung. 2023. InstructAlign: High-and-low resource language alignment via continual crosslingual instruction tuning. In *Proceedings of the First Workshop in South East Asian Language Processing*, pages 55–78, Nusa Dua, Bali, Indonesia. Association for Computational Linguistics.

Aakanksha Chowdhery, Sharan Narang, Jacob Devlin, Maarten Bosma, Gaurav Mishra, Adam Roberts, Paul Barham, Hyung Won Chung, Charles Sutton, Sebastian Gehrmann, Parker Schuh, Kensen Shi, Sasha Tsvyashchenko, Joshua Maynez, Abhishek Rao, Parker Barnes, Yi Tay, Noam Shazeer, Vinodkumar Prabhakaran, Emily Reif, Nan Du, Ben Hutchinson, Reiner Pope, James Bradbury, Jacob Austin, Michael Isard, Guy Gur-Ari, Pengcheng Yin, Toju Duke, Anselm Levskaya, Sanjay Ghemawat, Sunipa Dev, Henryk Michalewski, Xavier Garcia, Vedant Misra, Kevin Robinson, Liam Fedus, Denny Zhou, Daphne Ippolito, David Luan, Hyeontaek Lim, Barret Zoph, Alexander Spiridonov, Ryan Sepassi, David Dohan, Shivani Agrawal, Mark Omernick, Andrew M. Dai, Thanumalayan Sankaranarayana Pillai, Marie Pellat, Aitor Lewkowycz, Erica Moreira, Rewon Child, Oleksandr Polozov, Katherine Lee, Zongwei Zhou, Xuezhi Wang, Brennan Saeta, Mark Diaz, Orhan Firat, Michele Catasta, Jason Wei, Kathy Meier-Hellstern, Douglas Eck, Jeff Dean, Slav Petrov, and Noah Fiedel. 2023. Palm: Scaling language modeling with pathways. *Journal of Machine Learning Research*, 24(240):1–113.

Hyung Won Chung, Le Hou, Shayne Longpre, Barret Zoph, Yi Tay, William Fedus, Yunxuan Li, Xuezhi Wang, Mostafa Dehghani, Siddhartha Brahma, Albert Webson, Shixiang Shane Gu, Zhuyun Dai, Mirac Suzgun, Xinyun Chen, Aakanksha Chowdhery, Alex Castro-Ros, Marie Pellat, Kevin Robinson, Dasha Valter, Sharan Narang, Gaurav Mishra, Adams Yu, Vincent Y. Zhao, Yanping Huang, Andrew M. Dai, Hongkun Yu, Slav Petrov, Ed H. Chi, Jeff Dean, Jacob Devlin, Adam Roberts, Denny Zhou, Quoc V. Le, and Jason Wei. 2024. Scaling instruction-finetuned language models. *J. Mach. Learn. Res.*, 25:70:1–70:53.

Alexis Conneau, Kartikay Khandelwal, Naman Goyal, Vishrav Chaudhary, Guillaume Wenzek, Francisco Guzmán, Edouard Grave, Myle Ott, Luke Zettlemoyer, and Veselin Stoyanov. 2020. Unsupervised cross-lingual representation learning at scale. In *Proceedings of the 58th Annual Meeting of the Association for Computational Linguistics*, pages 8440–8451, Online. Association for Computational Linguistics.

Alexis Conneau and Guillaume Lample. 2019. Cross-lingual language model pretraining. In *Advances in Neural Information Processing Systems*, volume 32. Curran Associates, Inc.

Alexis Conneau, Ruty Rinott, Guillaume Lample, Adina Williams, Samuel Bowman, Holger Schwenk, and Veselin Stoyanov. 2018. XNLI: Evaluating cross-lingual sentence representations. In *Proceedings of the 2018 Conference on Empirical Methods in Natural Language Processing*, pages 2475–2485, Brussels, Belgium. Association for Computational Linguistics.

Yiming Cui, Ziqing Yang, and Xin Yao. 2023. Efficient and effective text encoding for chinese llama and alpaca. *arXiv preprint arXiv:2304.08177*.

Jacob Devlin, Ming-Wei Chang, Kenton Lee, and Kristina Toutanova. 2019. BERT: Pre-training of deep bidirectional transformers for language understanding. In *Proceedings of the 2019 Conference of the North American Chapter of the Association for*

Computational Linguistics: Human Language Technologies, Volume 1 (Long and Short Papers), pages 4171–4186, Minneapolis, Minnesota. Association for Computational Linguistics.

Konstantin Dobler and Gerard de Melo. 2023. Focus: Effective embedding initialization for monolingual specialization of multilingual models. In *Proceedings of the 2023 Conference on Empirical Methods in Natural Language Processing*. Association for Computational Linguistics.

Sumanth Doddapaneni, Rahul Aralikatte, Gowtham Ramesh, Shreya Goyal, Mitesh M. Khapra, Anoop Kunchukuttan, and Pratyush Kumar. 2023. Towards leaving no Indic language behind: Building monolingual corpora, benchmark and models for Indic languages. In *Proceedings of the 61st Annual Meeting of the Association for Computational Linguistics (Volume 1: Long Papers)*, pages 12402–12426, Toronto, Canada. Association for Computational Linguistics.

Jay Gala, Pranjal A Chitale, A K Raghavan, Varun Gumma, Sumanth Doddapaneni, Aswanth Kumar M, Janki Atul Nawale, Anupama Sujatha, Ratish Puduppully, Vivek Raghavan, Pratyush Kumar, Mitesh M Khapra, Raj Dabre, and Anoop Kunchukuttan. 2023. Indictrans2: Towards high-quality and accessible machine translation models for all 22 scheduled indian languages. *Transactions on Machine Learning Research*.

Xavier Garcia, Noah Constant, Ankur Parikh, and Orhan Firat. 2021. Towards continual learning for multilingual machine translation via vocabulary substitution. In *Proceedings of the 2021 Conference of the North American Chapter of the Association for Computational Linguistics: Human Language Technologies*, pages 1184–1192, Online. Association for Computational Linguistics.

Leonidas Gee, Andrea Zugarini, Leonardo Rigutini, and Paolo Torroni. 2022. Fast vocabulary transfer for language model compression. In *Proceedings of the 2022 Conference on Empirical Methods in Natural Language Processing: Industry Track*, pages 409–416, Abu Dhabi, UAE. Association for Computational Linguistics.

Tanya Goyal, Junyi Jessy Li, and Greg Durrett. 2023. News summarization and evaluation in the era of gpt-3.

John Hewitt. 2021. Initializing new word embeddings for pretrained language models.

Diptesh Kanojia, Kevin Patel, and Pushpak Bhattacharyya. 2018. Indian Language Wordnets and their Linkages with Princeton WordNet. In *Proceedings of the Eleventh International Conference on Language Resources and Evaluation (LREC 2018)*, Miyazaki, Japan. European Language Resources Association (ELRA).

Mohammed Khan, Priyam Mehta, Ananth Sankar, Umashankar Kumaravelan, Sumanth Doddapaneni, Suriyaprasaad B, Varun G, Sparsh Jain, Anoop Kunchukuttan, Pratyush Kumar, Raj Dabre, and Mitesh Khapra. 2024. IndicLLMSuite: A blueprint for creating pre-training and fine-tuning datasets for Indian languages. In *Proceedings of the 62nd Annual Meeting of the Association for Computational Linguistics (Volume 1: Long Papers)*, pages 15831–15879, Bangkok, Thailand. Association for Computational Linguistics.

Diederik P. Kingma and Jimmy Ba. 2017. Adam: A method for stochastic optimization.

Taku Kudo and John Richardson. 2018. Sentencepiece: A simple and language independent subword tokenizer and detokenizer for neural text processing. *CoRR*, abs/1808.06226.

Pengfei Liu, Weizhe Yuan, Jinlan Fu, Zhengbao Jiang, Hiroaki Hayashi, and Graham Neubig. 2023. Pretrain, prompt, and predict: A systematic survey of prompting methods in natural language processing. *ACM Comput. Surv.*, 55(9).

Yihong Liu, Peiqin Lin, Mingyang Wang, and Hinrich Schuetze. 2024. OFA: A framework of initializing unseen subword embeddings for efficient large-scale multilingual continued pretraining. In *Findings of the Association for Computational Linguistics: NAACL 2024*, pages 1067–1097, Mexico City, Mexico. Association for Computational Linguistics.

Yinhan Liu, Myle Ott, Naman Goyal, Jingfei Du, Mandar Joshi, Danqi Chen, Omer Levy, Mike Lewis, Luke Zettlemoyer, and Veselin Stoyanov. 2019. Roberta: A robustly optimized BERT pretraining approach. *CoRR*, abs/1907.11692.

Louis Martin, Benjamin Muller, Pedro Javier Ortiz Suárez, Yoann Dupont, Laurent Romary, Éric de la Clergerie, Djamé Seddah, and Benoît Sagot. 2020. CamemBERT: a tasty French language model. In *Proceedings of the 58th Annual Meeting of the Association for Computational Linguistics*, pages 7203–7219, Online. Association for Computational Linguistics.

Tomas Mikolov, Ilya Sutskever, Kai Chen, Greg S Corrado, and Jeff Dean. 2013. Distributed representations of words and phrases and their compositionality. In *Advances in Neural Information Processing Systems*, volume 26. Curran Associates, Inc.

Benjamin Minixhofer, Fabian Paischer, and Navid Rekabsaz. 2022. WECHSEL: Effective initialization of subword embeddings for cross-lingual transfer of monolingual language models. In *Proceedings of the 2022 Conference of the North American Chapter of the Association for Computational Linguistics: Human Language Technologies*, pages 3992–4006, Seattle, United States. Association for Computational Linguistics.

Xuan-Phi Nguyen, Wenxuan Zhang, Xin Li, Mahani Aljunied, Qingyu Tan, Liying Cheng, Guanzheng Chen, Yue Deng, Sen Yang, Chaoqun Liu, et al. 2023. Seallms–large language models for southeast asia. *arXiv preprint arXiv:2312.00738*.

Pedro Javier Ortiz Su'arez, Laurent Romary, and Benoit Sagot. 2020. A monolingual approach to contextualized word embeddings for mid-resource languages. In *Proceedings of the 58th Annual Meeting of the Association for Computational Linguistics*, pages 1703–1714, Online. Association for Computational Linguistics.

Xiaoman Pan, Boliang Zhang, Jonathan May, Joel Nothman, Kevin Knight, and Heng Ji. 2017. Cross-lingual name tagging and linking for 282 languages. In *Proceedings of the 55th Annual Meeting of the Association for Computational Linguistics (Volume 1: Long Papers)*, pages 1946–1958, Vancouver, Canada. Association for Computational Linguistics.

Telmo Pires, Eva Schlinger, and Dan Garrette. 2019. How multilingual is multilingual BERT? In *Proceedings of the 57th Annual Meeting of the Association for Computational Linguistics*, pages 4996–5001, Florence, Italy. Association for Computational Linguistics.

Pranav Rajpurkar, Robin Jia, and Percy Liang. 2018. Know what you don't know: Unanswerable questions for SQuAD. In *Proceedings of the 56th Annual Meeting of the Association for Computational Linguistics (Volume 2: Short Papers)*, pages 784–789, Melbourne, Australia. Association for Computational Linguistics.

MosaicML NLP Team. 2023. Introducing mpt-7b: A new standard for open-source, commercially usable llms. Accessed: 2023-05-05.

NLLB Team, Marta R. Costa-jussà, and James Cross et al. 2022. No language left behind: Scaling human-centered machine translation.

Hugo Touvron, Louis Martin, Kevin Stone, Peter Albert, and Amjad Almahairi et al. 2023. Llama 2: Open foundation and fine-tuned chat models.

Ke Tran. 2020. From english to foreign languages: Transferring pre-trained language models.

Alex Wang, Yequan Li, Yunpeng Zou, and Tim Menzies. 2022. Multimodal pretraining for ranking multilingual text and code. In *Proceedings of the 2022 ACM SIGIR Conference on Research and Development in Information Retrieval*, pages 1044–1053.

Jason Wei, Xuezhi Wang, Dale Schuurmans, Maarten Bosma, Brian Ichter, Fei Xia, Ed H. Chi, Quoc V. Le, and Denny Zhou. 2024. Chain-of-thought prompting elicits reasoning in large language models. In *Proceedings of the 36th International Conference on Neural Information Processing Systems*, NIPS '22, Red Hook, NY, USA. Curran Associates Inc.

BigScience Workshop, Teven Le Scao, Angela Fan, Christopher Akiki, Ellie Pavlick, and et al. 2023. Bloom: A 176b-parameter open-access multilingual language model.

Shaolei Zhang, Qingkai Fang, Zhuocheng Zhang, Zhengrui Ma, Yan Zhou, Langlin Huang, Mengyu Bu, Shangtong Gui, Yunji Chen, Xilin Chen, and Yang Feng. 2023. Bayling: Bridging cross-lingual alignment and instruction following through interactive translation for large language models.

Wayne Xin Zhao, Kun Zhou, Junyi Li, Tianyi Tang, Xiaolei Wang, Yupeng Hou, Yingqian Min, Beichen Zhang, Junjie Zhang, Zican Dong, Yifan Du, Chen Yang, Yushuo Chen, Zhipeng Chen, Jinhao Jiang, Ruiyang Ren, Yifan Li, Xinyu Tang, Zikang Liu, Peiyu Liu, Jian-Yun Nie, and Ji-Rong Wen. 2023. A survey of large language models.

A Limitations

In this work, we identify the following limitations:

- Due to limited computational resources, we could not explore a variety of pre-trained models beyond RoBERTa and LLaMA2. However, since most language models function similarly, we expect our methods and findings to be generally applicable.
- For LLaMA2 models, we only conduct few-shot prompting for downstream task evaluation due to resource constraints. Nonetheless, based on our observations with RoBERTa, fine-tuning on downstream tasks will likely show that CW2V and OFA are only marginally better than other approaches.
- Although we evaluated only five downstream tasks, we cannot confirm that our observations will apply to all types of tasks. This remains an area for future research.
- We show experiments on four languages—Hindi, German, Russian, and Tamil—due to limited computational resources. However, as we have chosen languages from different scripts, we expect our methods and findings to be generally applicable.

B Further Analysis

Theorem 3. *: All strongly good initializations are in the convex hull.*

Let $e_1^s, e_2^s, e_3^s, ..., e_n^s \in \mathbb{R}^d$ be the embeddings of words in $\mathcal{V}^s$. Let $y \in \mathbb{R}^d$. If $(h^T y) \leq \sup_{k \in \mathcal{V}^s}(h^T e_k^s)$ for all $h \in \mathbb{R}^d$, then $y \in \mathcal{S}$, where $\mathcal{S}$ is the convex hull of the embeddings $e_1^s, e_2^s, e_3^s, ..., e_n^s$.

Proof. We prove this using contradiction. Say, $y \notin \mathcal{S}$ and $(h^T y) \leq \sup_{k \in \mathcal{V}^s}(h^T e_k^s)$ holds good for all $h \in \mathbb{R}^d$. Since, $\mathcal{S}$ is closed and convex and $y \notin \mathcal{S}$, there exists a hyperplane $\mathbb{H}$ that strictly separates y from $\mathcal{S}$. This hyperplane defines a half space $\mathcal{H}$ containing $\mathcal{S}$. Note that $\mathcal{H}$ contains $\mathcal{S}$ and $y \notin \mathcal{H}$

Let $\vec{b} \in \mathbb{R}^d$ be a point on the hyperplane $\mathbb{H}$. Let $\vec{n} \in \mathbb{R}^d$ denote the normal to the hyperplane $\mathbb{H}$. We choose $\vec{n}$ in such a way that any point $\vec{r} \in \mathcal{S}$ satisfies,

$$(\vec{r} - \vec{b})^T \vec{n} \leq 0$$

Thus, any embedding $e^s \in \{e_1^s, e_2^s, ..., e_n^s\}$ satisfies,

$$(e^s - b)^T \vec{n} \leq 0 \quad (2)$$

and any point $\vec{q} \notin \mathcal{H}$ satisfies,

$$(\vec{q} - \vec{b})^T \vec{n} \geq 0$$

As $y \notin \mathcal{H}$,

$$(y - \vec{b})^T \vec{n} \geq 0 \quad (3)$$

Equations 2 and 3 imply,

$$\vec{n}^T e^s \leq \vec{n}^T y \ \forall \ e^s \in \{e_1^s, e_2^s, ..., e_n^s\} \quad (4)$$

Thus, $\sup_{k \in \mathcal{V}^s}(\vec{n}^T e_k^s) \leq (\vec{n}^T y)$ which contradicts the statement that $(h^T y) \leq \sup_{k \in \mathcal{V}^s}(h^T e_k^s)$ holds good for all $h \in \mathbb{R}^d$ as it fails for $h = \vec{n}$.

Thus, if $(h^T y) \leq \sup_{k \in \mathcal{V}^s}(h^T e_k^s)$ for all $h \in \mathbb{R}^d$, then $y \in \mathcal{S}$, where $\mathcal{S}$ is the convex hull of the embeddings $e_1^s, e_2^s, e_3^s, ..., e_n^s$.

□

Thus, from theorem 3 we can say that any 'strongly good' initialization must lie in the convex hull of pre-expansion embeddings. But for an initialization to be considered 'good', the output word must remain unchanged for prefixes formed by word sequences from the source vocabulary. This implies that the condition 1 only needs to be satisfied for a subset of $\mathbb{R}^d$, rather than for all $h \in \mathbb{R}^d$. Thus, it is not necessary that the converse of Theorem 2 to be true as we can have initializations which are 'good' but not 'strongly good'. However, we can say that if an initialization is 'strongly good', embeddings must lie in the convex hull of pre-expansion embeddings.

C Effect on Initialisation on Model Output

Random initialization of new embeddings can result in a pre-trained language model assigning a probability of 1 to new words and can degrade domain adaptation performance (Hewitt, 2021). Figure 5 shows the outputs of expanded LLaMA2 models for an English sentence prompt. Random initialization of expanded tokens results in gibberish, while the other three methods produce outputs identical to the base LLaMA2 model, as they ensure embeddings lie within the convex hull of source embeddings.

Initialization	Output
LLaMA2- Base	the same thing every day.
CW2V	the same thing every day.
OFA	the same thing every day.
Mean	the same thing every day.
Random	◌ৗঁট উপায়ুক্তৰ উপায়ুক্তৰ উপা

Figure 5: Expanded LLaMA2 Model Outputs for the Prompt : *"I don't want to eat" for various initializations.*

D Fertility Score

Fertility Score	English	Hindi	Tamil	Russian	German
LLaMA2 Tokenizer	2.89	7.47	12.66	4.25	3.88
RoBERTa Tokenizer	2.87	10.85	28.80	9.89	4.42
Extended Tokenizer	**2.87**	**2.83**	**2.83**	**3.74**	**3.88**

Table 3: Fertility scores for the source and the extended tokenizers on all the languages

Table 3 shows the fertility scores of the target tokenizer with respect to source tokenizer on 5 languages considered.

E Tokenizer Coverage

	Target Tokenizer		
	Copied Tokens	Initialized Tokens	Coverage
RoBERTa	22K	35K	38.5 %
LLaMA2	32K	25K	56.14 %

Table 4: : The number of subwords being initialized by copying from the original embeddings from RoBERTa's and LLaMA's tokenizers.

Table 4 shows the size of source vocabulary in experiments with RoBERTa and LLaMA2. As the new vocabulary is extended from LLaMA2, many subword embeddings are directly copied when using LLaMA2 as the source model. We employed a 'fuzzy' search similar to FOCUS (Dobler and de Melo, 2023) to identify the common tokens between the target tokenizer and the RoBERTa tokenizer. This led to a 38.5 % coverage of tokens leading us to a source vocabulary of size 22K for experiments with RoBERTa.

F Do Multivariate and Univariate initializations reside in the hull?

In multivariate initialization, we sample from a multivariate Gaussian that considers correlations across dimensions, unlike the univariate distribution. When dealing with strongly correlated dimensions (positive or negative), a multivariate approach proves advantageous. By considering the correlations across dimensions, we can sample new embeddings that are positioned more effectively within the latent space of original embedding distribution. However, there is no straightforward method to determine if embedding sampled from either distribution lies within the hull. To ensure that multivariate initialization remains within the convex hull with a high confidence, we also scaled the covariance matrix by a factor of 1e-5. In contrast, unscaled univariate initialization was used as a baseline, aligning with previous studies (Liu et al., 2024). (Hewitt, 2021) recommends employing multivariate initialization to incorporate noise. Notably, as illustrated in Figure 2, multivariate initialization significantly outperforms univariate initialization and closely approaches the performance of OFA in encoder-based models. However, a comprehensive theoretical analysis is required to determine if unscaled multivariate initialization has a higher likelihood of being within the convex hull compared to univariate initialization. This aspect is left for future research, given the empirical observation that univariate initializations typically exhibits lower performance compared to scaled multivariate initialization.

G Continued Pretraining Details

All the expanded and initialized RoBERTa models are trained on the same hyperparameters used in OFA (Liu et al., 2024). Specifically, we employ the MLM objective with a standard mask rate of 15%. We utilize the Adam optimizer (Kingma and Ba, 2017) with parameters ($\beta_1 = 0.9, \beta_2 = 0.999$) and $\epsilon = 1 \times 10^{-6}$. The initial learning rate is set to 5×10^{-5}. The only deviation from our approach compared to OFA is the batch size, which is fixed at 32. Each batch consists of training samples concatenated up to the maximum sequence length of 512, randomly selected from all language-scripts described in Section 4.3. We continue to pretrain using the scripts adapted from HuggingFace[5].

For LLaMa2, we used the standard LM objective with a context length of 2048 subwords. We used the Adam optimizer with linear warmup and decay where the peak learning rate was 5×10^{-5} and warmup was done till 10% of training steps. We

[5]`https://github.com/huggingface/`

trained for 1 epoch over our data saved checkpoints every 20% of an epoch enabling us to study model behavior against increasing training data.

H Complete Results for Each Task and Language

Results for each task in all the languages across all the checkpoints is given in figures 6, 7, 8, 9, 10, 11, 12

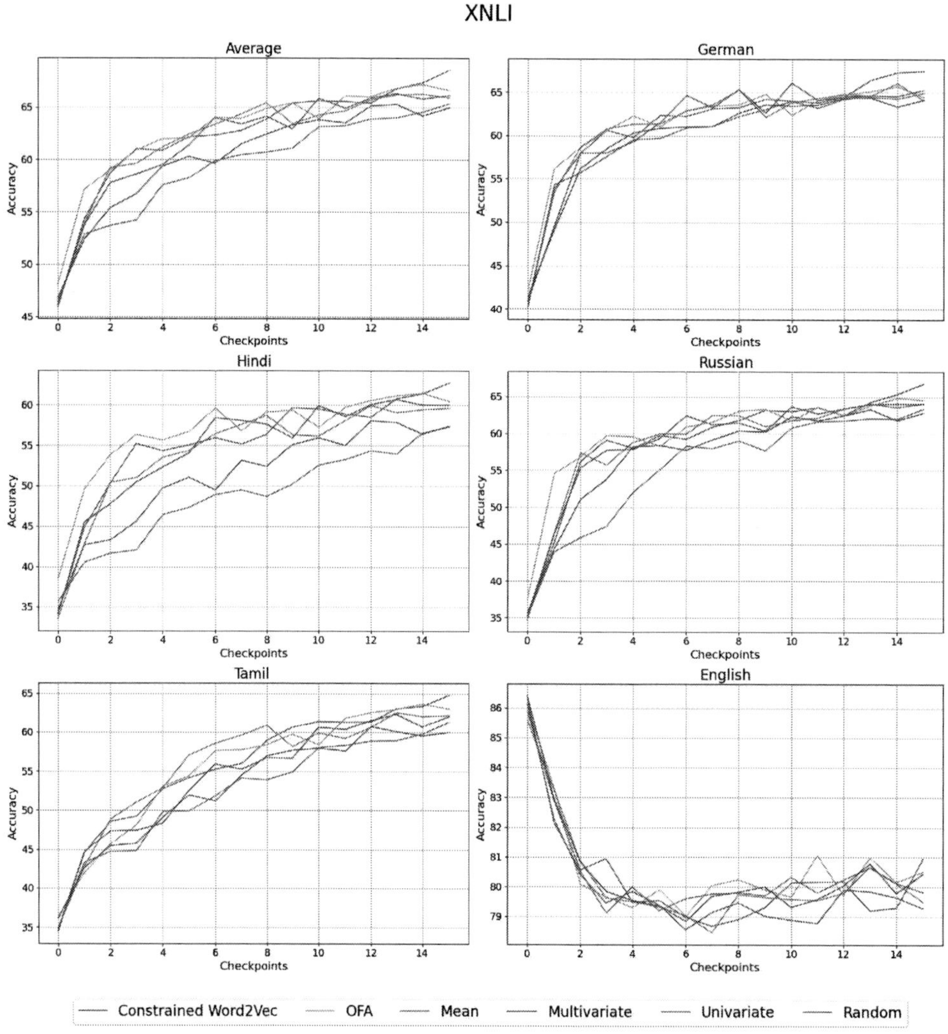

Figure 6: XNLI evaluation of expanded RoBERTa models

NER

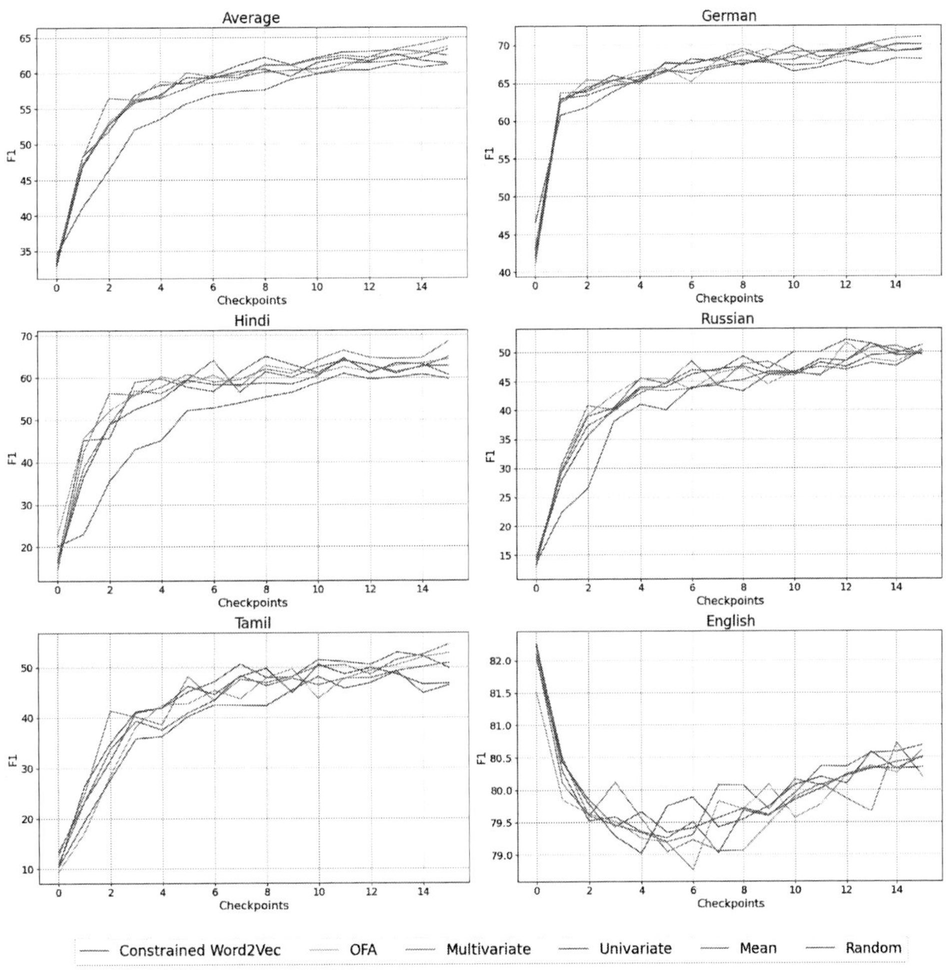

Figure 7: NER evaluation of expanded RoBERTa models

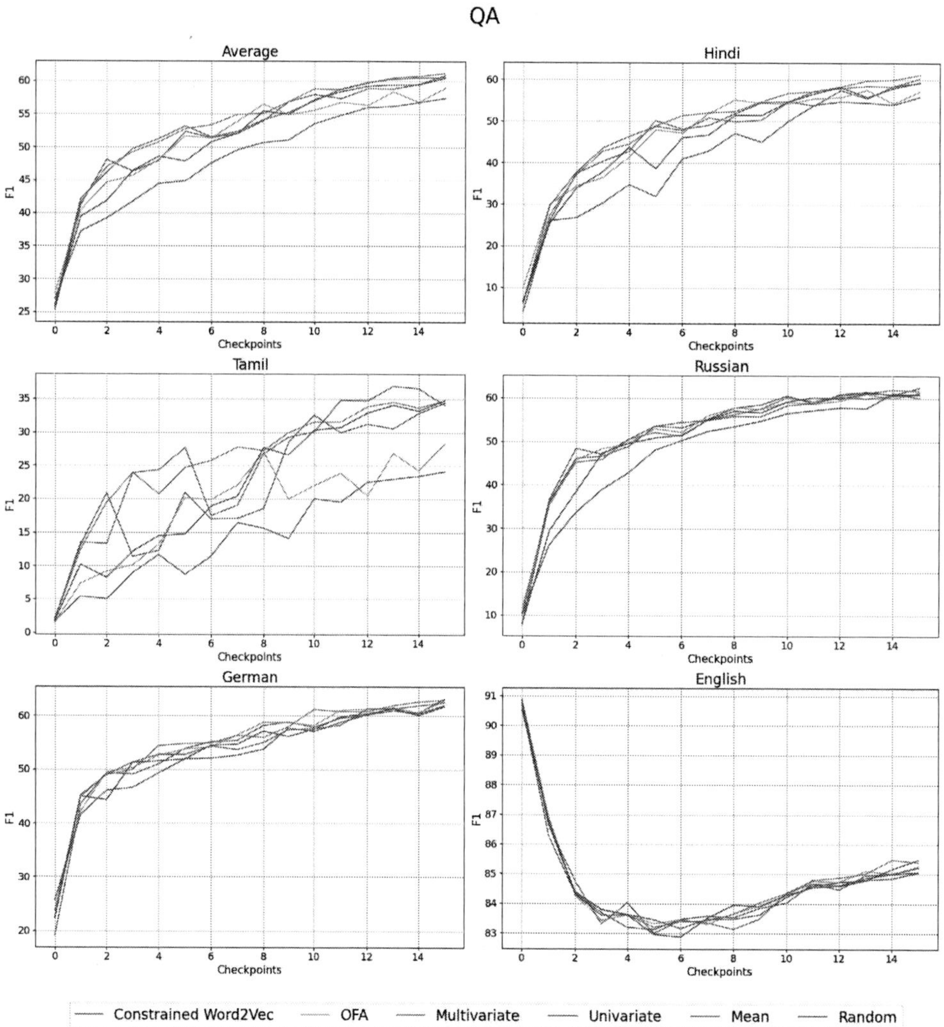

Figure 8: QA evaluation of expanded RoBERTa models

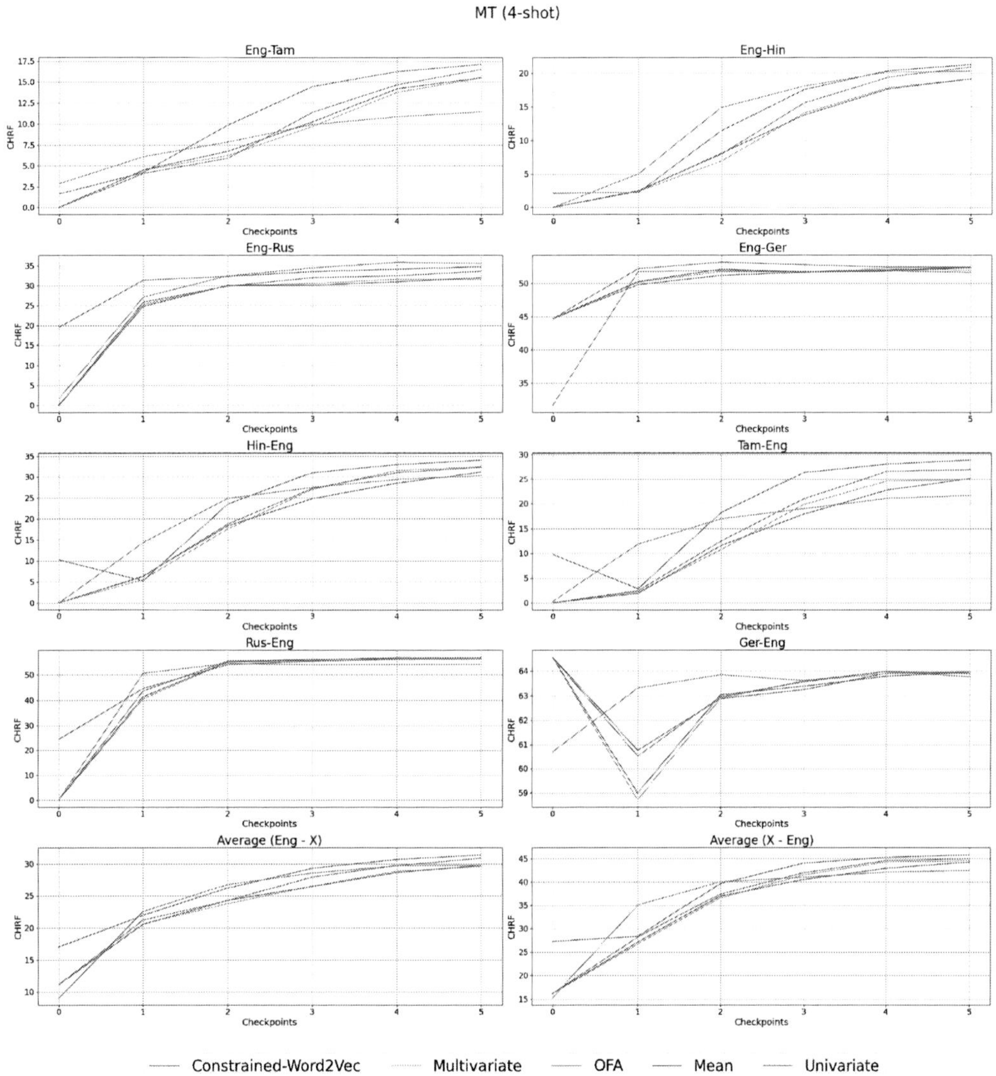

Figure 9: MT 4-shot evaluation of expanded LLaMA2 models

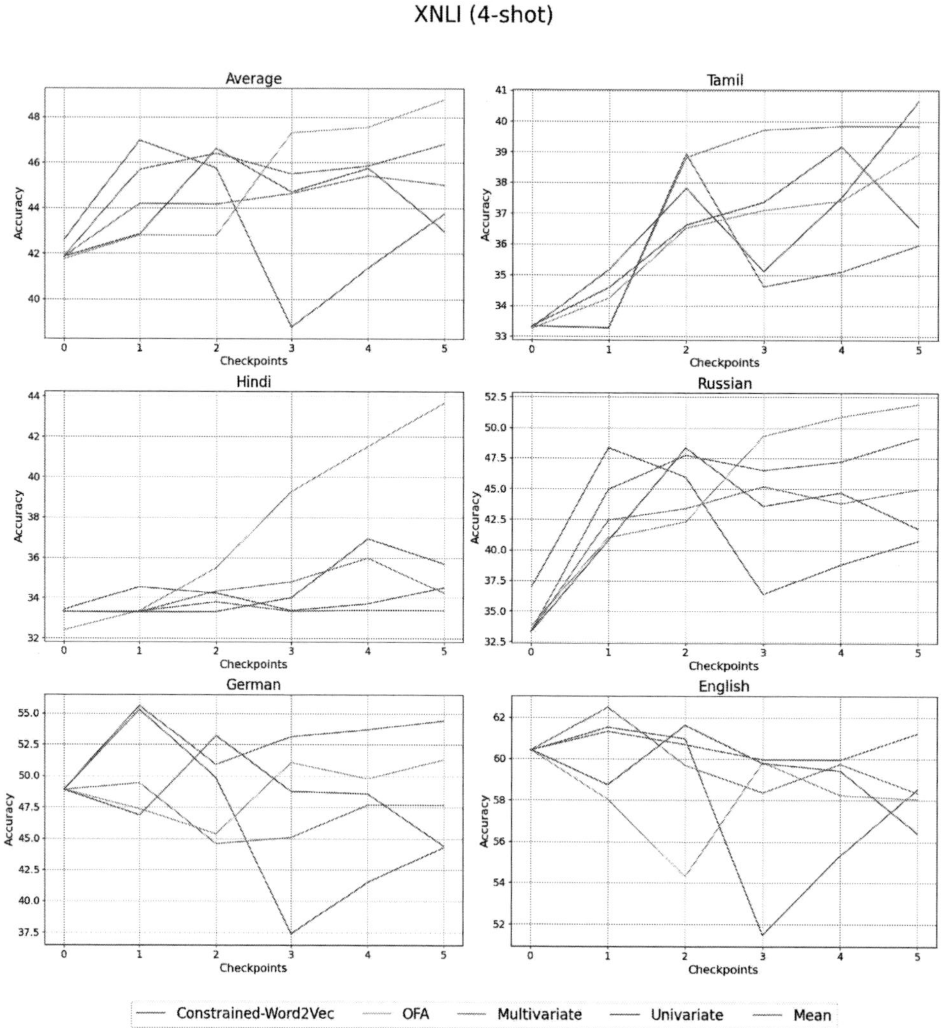

Figure 10: XNLI 4-shot evaluation of expanded LLaMA2 models

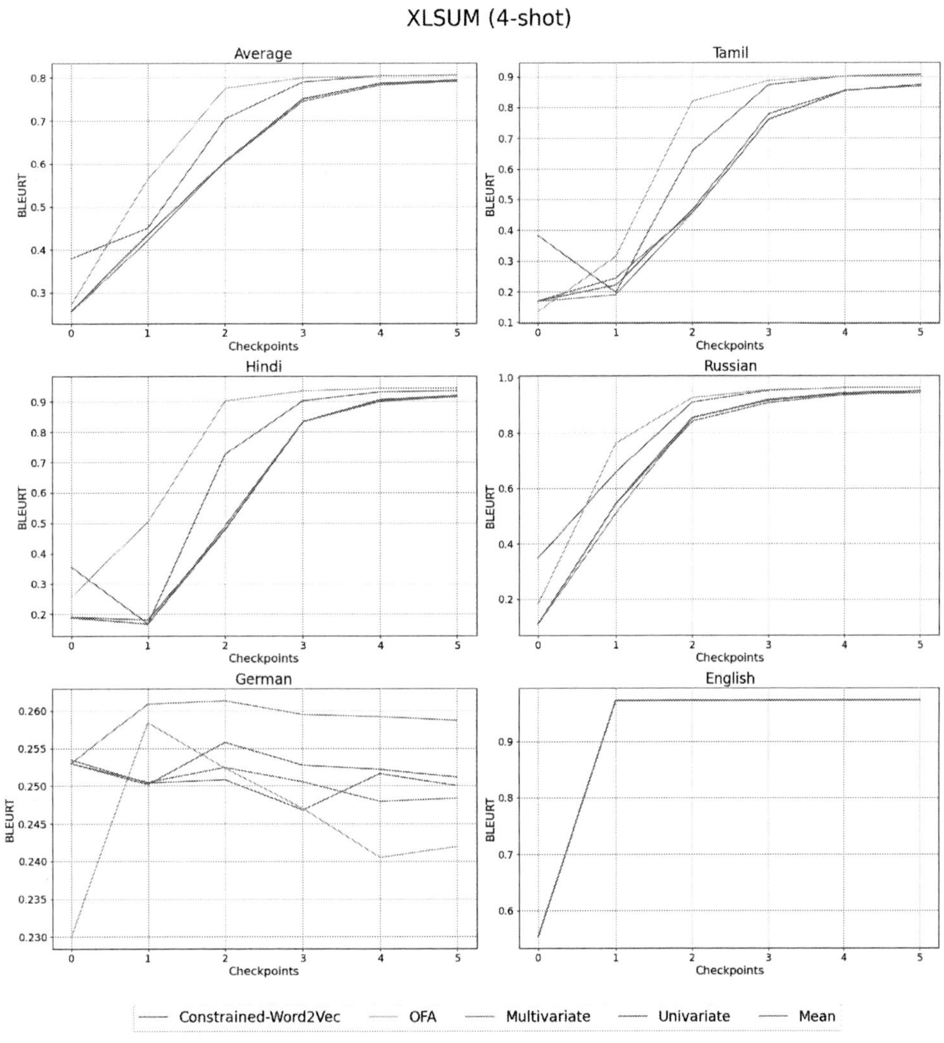

Figure 11: XLSUM 4-shot evaluation of expanded LLaMA2 models

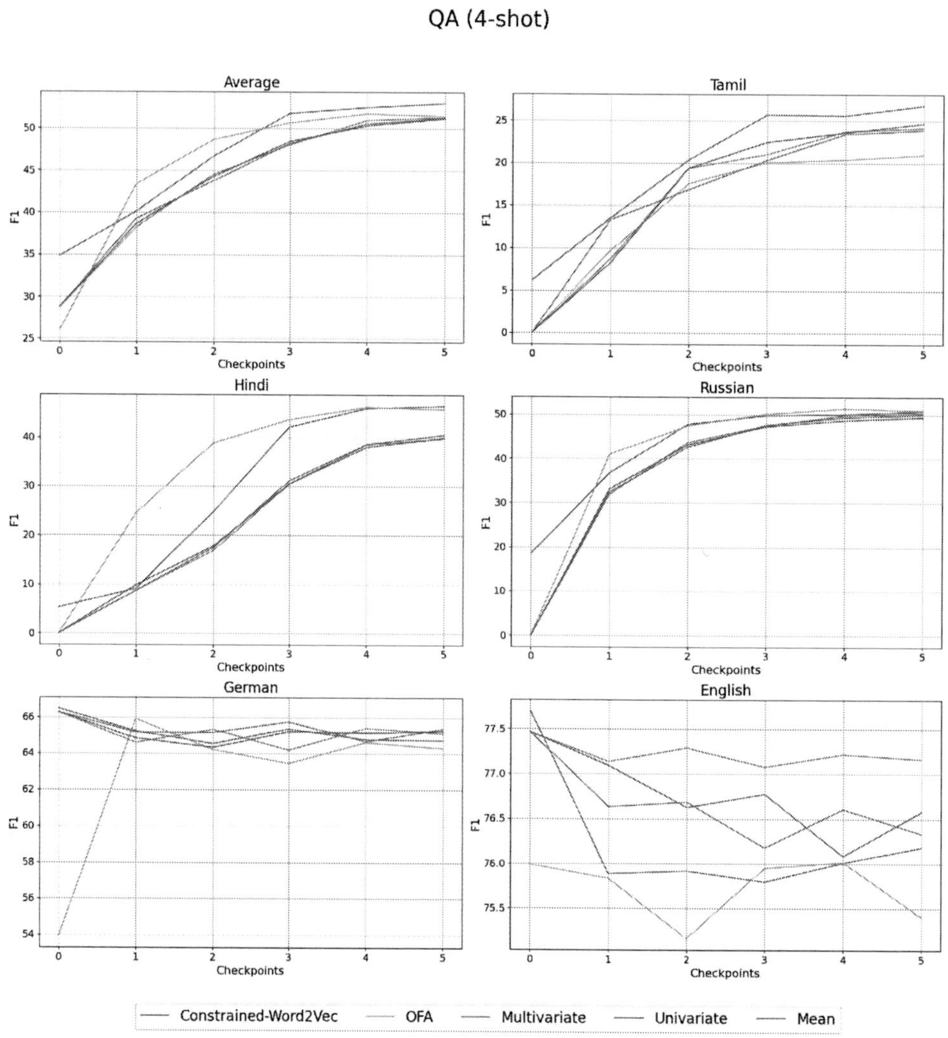

Figure 12: QA 4-shot evaluation of expanded LLaMA2 models

Critical Questions Generation: Motivation and Challenges

Blanca Calvo Figueras
HiTZ Center - Ixa
University of the Basque Country UPV/EHU
blanca.calvo@ehu.eus

Rodrigo Agerri
HiTZ Center - Ixa
University of the Basque Country UPV/EHU
rodrigo.agerri@ehu.eus

Abstract

The development of Large Language Models (LLMs) has brought impressive performances on mitigation strategies against misinformation, such as counterargument generation. However, LLMs are still seriously hindered by outdated knowledge and by their tendency to generate hallucinated content. In order to circumvent these issues, we propose a new task, namely, *Critical Questions Generation*, consisting of processing an argumentative text to generate the critical questions (CQs) raised by it. In argumentation theory CQs are tools designed to lay bare the blind spots of an argument by pointing at the information it could be missing. Thus, instead of trying to deploy LLMs to produce knowledgeable and relevant counterarguments, we use them to question arguments, without requiring any external knowledge. Research on CQs Generation using LLMs requires a reference dataset for large scale experimentation. Thus, in this work we investigate two complementary methods to create such a resource: (i) instantiating CQs templates as defined by Walton's argumentation theory and (ii), using LLMs as CQs generators. By doing so, we contribute with a procedure to establish what is a valid CQ and conclude that, while LLMs are reasonable CQ generators, they still have a wide margin for improvement in this task.

1 Introduction

Natural Language Processing (NLP) applications to deal with misinformation have become a popular line of research in tasks such as fact verification (Thorne et al., 2018), evidence retrieval (Soleimani et al., 2020) or counterargument generation (Chung et al., 2019; Chen et al., 2023). However, even when deploying generative Large Language Models (LLMs), most applications face challenges regarding three issues: LLMs often lack the required up-to-date knowledge for these tasks (Gao et al., 2023), there is not always an agreement on what is the truth (Chang et al., 2024), and LLMs themselves can produce hallucinations or rely on unfaithful data, generating misinformation of their own making (Xu et al., 2024; Lin et al., 2022).

Yet, instead of requiring the LLMs to output factual knowledge, could we use them to point at the missing or potentially uninformed claims? In other words, could we use LLMs to uncover the blind spots in the argumentation? To open this line of research, we ground our work on argumentation theory, which has for centuries been studying dialogical exchanges of information. Specifically, we look into *argumentation schemes*, a set of abstract structures developed by systematically identifying common patterns of argumentation and outlining the defeasibility of these patterns. In these structures, the devices designed to find the blind spots in the arguments are called *critical questions*.

Critical questions are the set of inquiries that could be asked in order to judge if an argument is acceptable or fallacious. Therefore, these questions are designed to unmask the assumptions held by the premises of the argument and attack its inference. In the theoretical framework developed by Walton et al. (2008), argumentation schemes are represented as templates depicting the premises, the conclusion, and the critical questions of each scheme. This framework is useful to promote critical thinking, since it allows uncovering fallacies by answering questions. Figure 1 shows two examples of argumentation schemes and their corresponding critical questions (CQs). The first of these examples is an argument that links a cause (migration) to an effect (unemployment). Therefore, the CQs related to this argument ask about the strength of this relation and the possibility of other causes also having a role in the effect. The second example fits the scheme of *practical reasoning*. That is, given a goal, the argument defines an action to achieve it. Here, the CQs ask about the compatibility of this goal with others, the alternative actions to achiev-

Proceedings of the 28th Conference on Computational Natural Language Learning, pages 105–116
November 15-16, 2024 ©2024 Association for Computational Linguistics

(a) **Scheme – Argument from Cause to Effect**

Premise: Generally, if people pour into the USA, then Americans lose their jobs.
Premise: In the current situation, people are pouring into the USA.
Conclusion: In the current situation, Americans lose their jobs.

CQ: How strong is the generalisation that if people pour into the USA then Americans will lose their jobs?
CQ: Are there other factors in this particular case that could be interfering with the fact that Americans lose their jobs?

(b) **Scheme – Practical Reasoning**

Premise: There is the goal of making the economy fairer.
Premise: Raising the national minimum wage is a means to realize the goal of making the economy fairer.
Conclusion: Therefore, raising the national minimum wage ought to occur.

CQ: Are there other relevant goals that conflict with making the economy fairer?
CQ: Are there alternative actions to raising the national minimum wage to achieve making the economy fairer? If so, which is the most efficient action?
CQ: Could raising the national minimum wage have consequences that we should take into account? Is it practically possible?

Figure 1: Arguments from the US2016 dataset (Visser et al., 2021), instantiated using the templates of argumentation schemes and critical questions defined in Walton et al. (2008).

ing this goal, and the potential consequences of the proposed action.

Previous work has proved the usefulness of CQs for enhancing fallacy identification (Musi et al., 2022), and for argumentative essays evaluation (Song et al., 2014). But, to the extent of our knowledge, there has not been any attempt to automate the generation of CQs. In this work, we propose the task of *Critical Questions Generation*: given an argumentative text, the model is asked to generate the necessary CQs to assess the acceptability of the arguments in the text. In this setting, the argumentative text is the input and the set of CQs is the target output. As in other NLP tasks, such as machine translation or paraphrasing, the model is not required to find new information, but to understand and reformulate the input in a certain way.

A crucial requirement to investigate the automatic generation of CQs is to have reference data for experimentation. However, as far as we know, there has not been any attempt to create such a resource. In order to address this shortcoming, in this paper we investigate two methods for creating a dataset for the generation of CQs: (1) using the sets of CQ templates defined in Walton et al. (2008)'s theory (from now on, theory-CQs); and (2) using LLMs to generate these CQs (from now on, llm-CQs). While looking into these methods, we attempt to answer the following research questions: (i) are current Large Language Models good critical question generators? (ii) how can we operationalize what is a valid critical question? (iii) what is the optimal strategy to build a reference dataset for large scale experimentation on the task of *Critical Questions Generation*?

To answer these questions, we start by looking at the theoretical sets of CQs and instantiating them using a set of argumentative texts already annotated with argumentation schemes (Visser et al., 2021; Lawrence et al., 2018). As a second step, we prompt two state-of-the-art LLMs to give us candidate CQs for these same argumentative texts, and we design a procedure to evaluate their relevance towards the texts and their validity as CQs. We then compare the two methods and highlight the main challenges faced by LLMs when generating CQs. Summarizing, the main contributions of this work are:

- We propose the task of *Critical Questions Generation* and motivate it by relying on previous work.
- We use naturally-occurring dialogical data to study how to generate critical questions using the theory templates and LLMs.
- We operationalize how to define a valid critical question.
- We study the main challenges faced by LLMs when generating critical questions.

In this work, we observe that questions generated using theory and questions generated using LLMs are complementary: while theory-CQs are mostly about relations between premises, llm-CQs rather ask about evidences. Additionally, LLMs introduce a new type of questions: those asking about further definition of the terms used in the arguments. Regarding the performance of current LLMs, we observe that models struggle to output relevant CQs and output many non-critical questions. Therefore, we conclude that more advanced training and prompting techniques should be used and, to this end, reference data should be created using both the theory and LLMs' methods. All the data and code in this project has been released.[1]

2 Previous Work

To contextualise this work, we discuss the relation between argumentation and misinformation, introduce the nature of critical questions, and offer related work on argumentation schemes from a computational point of view.

2.1 Using argumentation to fight misinformation

Misinformation has been tackled using many strategies: from debunking strategies (e.g. fact-checking propagated information) to pre-bunking (e.g. exposing disinformation strategies to make citizens resilient towards manipulation). However, recent studies have shown that pre-bunking has a potentially longer effect, since the learned skills are not bound to specific contexts (Maertens et al., 2021). Following this, digital applications have been built to enhance citizens' abilities to deal with misinformation, such as the recognition of misleading sources and headlines (Fakey,[2] NewsWise headlines quizz[3]), the identification of fake images (Real or Photoshop quizz[4]), or the decision-making processes of news rooms (BBCireporter,[5] NewsFeed Defenders[6]).

However, these applications focus mostly on dealing with fake information, while misinformation is often generated by drawing invalid relations between claims and the premises provided to support these claims (Musi et al., 2023). In this sense, more recent pre-bunking applications have focused on techniques based on argumentation theory, which have the goal of evaluating the connections between the available evidence and the statement that it is trying to support (Lawrence et al., 2018; Visser et al., 2020; De Liddo et al., 2021; Altay et al., 2022).

In this line of research, Musi et al. (2023) developed a chatbot that, following gamification principles, used a dialogical context to teach users how to identify fallacies by being exposed to critical questions. Users of this tool showed an overall increased ability to identify fallacious arguments. While the scenarios portrayed in Musi's chatbot are based on an annotated database of 1,500 fact-checked news, latest NLP advances in LLMs could be used to generate critical questions on unseen arguments, therefore being able to use this tool to deal with any upcoming domain.

Applications of language models in the fight against misinformation have often been framed as classification and information retrieval tasks (Montoro Montarroso et al., 2023). In contrast, we propose to use LLMs as a tool for generating questions, which enhances the relativistic conceptions of truth of most critical thinking paradigms (Musi et al., 2023), as opposed to the absolutist notions of truth encouraged by using LLMs as question-answerers and classifiers.

2.2 The nature of critical questions

Critical questions are an essential element of the notion of *argumentation schemes*. Argumentation schemes are "forms of arguments (structures of inference) that represent structures of common types of arguments used on everyday discourse" (Walton et al., 2008). These arguments are defeasible, meaning that their conclusions can be accepted only provisionally while there is no evidence that defeats it. Defeasible arguments are the most common arguments in everyday discussions, and knowing what to ask before accepting them is an important skill.

The predecessor of argumentation schemes were topics (*topoi* in Aristotle's Rhetoric), which were conceived as warrants that back the logical inferences drawn from premises to conclusions. Modern researchers have adapted them for use in computational applications (Reed and Walton, 2001; Macagno et al., 2017). Additionally, these tools have become popular among critical thinking researchers for their pedagogic usefulness.

In pedagogical terms, argumentation schemes can be used "as a way of providing students with additional structure and analytic tools with which to analyze natural arguments and to evaluate them critically" (Walton et al., 2008). In this approach, critical questions function as memory devices: a

[1] https://github.com/hitz-zentroa/critical_questions_generation

[2] https://fakey.osome.iu.edu/

[3] https://www.theguardian.com/newswise/2021/feb/04/fake-or-real-headlines-quiz-newswise-2021

[4] https://landing.adobe.com/en/na/products/creative-cloud/69308-real-or-photoshop/

[5] https://www.bbc.co.uk/news/resources/idt-8760dd58-84f9-4c98-ade2-590562670096

[6] https://www.icivics.org/games/newsfeed-defenders

way to recall the missing information in the argument.

Although the goals and usefulness of critical questions have been extensively discussed, up to our knowledge, there has not been any successful attempt to operationalize what is and what is not a valid critical question. Since our goal is to create them automatically, setting this boundary becomes a necessary first step.

Most definitions of critical questions are highly linked to their function. Following this tradition, it could be argued that a good critical question is the one that fulfills its goal: pointing at reasons to *rebut the argument.* Moreover, critical questions can not only attack the acceptability of an argument by defeating its conclusion, but also undercut it by attacking the connection between the premises and the given conclusion (Pollock, 1987). In Section 4, we operationalize this definition of valid CQ, and in Section 5, we implement it in the evaluation of llm-CQs.

2.3 Argumentation Schemes in Computational Argumentation

While no attempt exists to automatically generate CQs, there has been some work on argumentation schemes annotation and detection, which we will be taking as a starting point.

One of the most ambitious works in argumentation from a computational point of view was the Araucaria project, which created a database of arguments annotated in Argument Markup Language that included argumentation schemes (Reed et al., 2008). Later, the Inference Anchoring Theory (IAT Budzynska and Reed (2011)) became a popular format for representing how arguments are created in dialogical settings. IAT diagrams feature locutions, propositions, dialogical relations, and propositional relations. Recent work has also added argumentation-scheme labels to IAT diagrams. The available datasets annotated with IAT and schemes are listed in Table 1.

Other datasets that are labeled with argumentation schemes although not in the IAT format are the social media datasets from Jo et al. (2021), which contain 1,924 examples of 2 argumentation schemes; and the Genetics Research Corpus, which identifies argumentation schemes in scientific claims from genetic research articles (Green, 2015). Lately, datasets with synthetic arguments have been released (Kondo et al., 2021; Ruiz-Dolz et al., 2024; Saha and Srihari, 2023). However, we are interested in naturally-occurring arguments.

The task of automatically identifying argumentation schemes was first attempted by Feng and Hirst (2011) and Lawrence and Reed (2016), using machine learning techniques. Later, Jo et al. (2021) used logic and theory-informed mechanisms for a similar task, and Kondo et al. (2021) used language models, showing the difficulty of identifying schemes (with 7 categories, their overall accuracy with BERT (Devlin et al., 2019) was 27.5%).

In previous work, it has been observed that tasks requiring complex reasoning remain a challenge for LLMs (Xu et al., 2023; Gendron et al., 2024; Han et al., 2022). Furthermore, Payandeh et al. (2023) demonstrated that LLMs are easily convinced using logical fallacies, and Ruiz-Dolz and Lawrence (2023) showed that LLMs fail when asked to detect argumentative fallacies. The task of fallacy detection is highly related to our work (Sahai et al., 2021; Goffredo et al., 2022; Alhindi et al., 2022; Helwe et al., 2024). However, in this work we wish to foster human-computer interaction and use LLMs to raise the questions that would help a human unmask the fallacies of its caller.

So far, the most similar work to ours is Musi et al. (2023), where they developed a chatbot that outputted critical questions from a database of possible issues, and Song et al. (2014), where they found that human annotations identifying the CQs present in essay evaluations contributed significantly to predicting the grade. While their experiments tested the usefulness of using CQs, none of these two tried to generate them automatically.

3 Data

For the purpose of this work we have decided to use a subset of the US2016 (Visser et al., 2021) and the Moral Maze datasets (Lawrence et al., 2018), which, as explained in the previous section, have already been transcribed and annotated with argumentation schemes. Both of these datasets are oral debates, and they are structured as sequences of interventions by different debaters.

In order to use these datasets, we have mapped their labels to the argumentation schemes in Walton et al. (2008). Since the labels of both of these datasets are based on Walton's work, the mapping has amounted to terminology matching. Given the long list of argumentation schemes, we have decided to work with the 18 most frequent schemes. Annex A provides the mapping and the distribu-

Name	Paper	N° Args.	N° Schemes	Original Format	Domain
US2016	Visser et al. (2021)	413	60	Oral debate	Politics
Moral Maze	Lawrence et al. (2018)	79	32	Oral debate	Politics
US2016reddit		19	4	Written social media	Politics
EO_PC	Lawrence and Reed (2015)	139	3	Written	Not specified
Reg. Room Div.	Konat et al. (2016)	227	7	Written social media	Product Regulations
Legal		545	12	Written	Legal

Table 1: Available data in IAT format with argumentation schemes. All the datasets are in English.

tion of argumentation schemes for each of the two datasets.

Since both of these datasets have been annotated as IAT diagrams, each argumentation scheme label links two or more propositions in the debate, forming an argument.[7] The debates are composed of interventions, which we are going to use as our *argumentative texts*. Each intervention can have many annotated arguments (or none). After preprocessing,[8] we obtain 370 interventions (73 from Moral Maze and 297 from US2016) of which 117 contain at least one argument (25 from Moral Maze and 92 from US2016).

For the manual analysis of this work, we use 21 of the interventions, chosen to keep the label distribution as similar as possible to the one in the full datasets; 10 of these interventions come from US2016 and 11 from Moral Maze. The distribution of the 60 arguments contained in these 21 interventions can be found in Annex B.

4 Our Method

In order to identify the challenges in the task of *Critical Questions Generation*, there is an urgent need for reference data. To explore how this data should be created, we generate critical questions both using the theory templates and LLMs.

To generate CQs based on Walton's theory (theory-CQs), we take each annotated argument and instantiate the CQs associated to that argumentation scheme (red-dotted box at the top of Figure 2). Regarding the generation of CQs with LLMs (llm-CQs), we prompt two state-of-the-art LLMs and we evaluate the relevance of the candidate CQs towards the argumentative text (blue-dashed box at the bottom of Figure 2). We then relate the llm-CQs to the arguments of the text and to the theory-CQs (green box), and assess the validity of the llm-CQs that relate to an argument but do not correspond to any of the existing theory-CQs (such as CQ 5 in Figure 2). In the rest of the section, we describe in detail each of these processes.

4.1 Generation using theory

The critical questions based on theory are defined using the set of CQs in Walton et al. (2008). We reformulate some of these questions to make them sound more natural (the final set can be found in Annex C). To transform these questions into tailored CQs for each argument, we first manually annotate the text needed to fill the gaps of the variables in the argumentation-schemes' templates. For each argument, the annotator sees the premises and conclusion associated with the argumentation scheme (i.e. the template), the propositions of the argument, and the entire intervention in which the argument occurred. For instance, to annotate argument a in Figure 1, the annotator saw the data in Table 2, and was asked to write the text that is needed to instantiate the scheme template. In this case, $< eventA >$ = "people are pouring into the USA" and $< eventB >$ = "Americans might lose their jobs".

We used two annotators for this task, and achieved an inter-annotator agreement (IAA) of 0.88 with a sample of 174 variables.[9] In the end, 9 arguments were discarded by both annotators, as they were not able to find the connection between the propositions and the argumentation scheme that had been given to its relation.

We then instantiated the CQs, substituting each variable for the piece of text that had been annotated. This step resulted in questions with grammatical errors, which we post-edited manually, with 39.44% of the questions getting editions. We discarded 10 of the questions for being meaningless. Most common corrections consisted of modifying verbs from infinitive to gerund forms and vice-

[7]For a comprehensive explanation of IAT diagrams see Hautli-Janisz et al. (2022).

[8]We structure the data by intervention, splitting the very long interventions, and merging the very short ones (for an example, see the columns "Intervention" in Table 2 and Figure 3). The code on how to go from the IAT diagrams to our dataset has been published on Github.

[9]The extended explanation of this annotation will be published as guidelines.

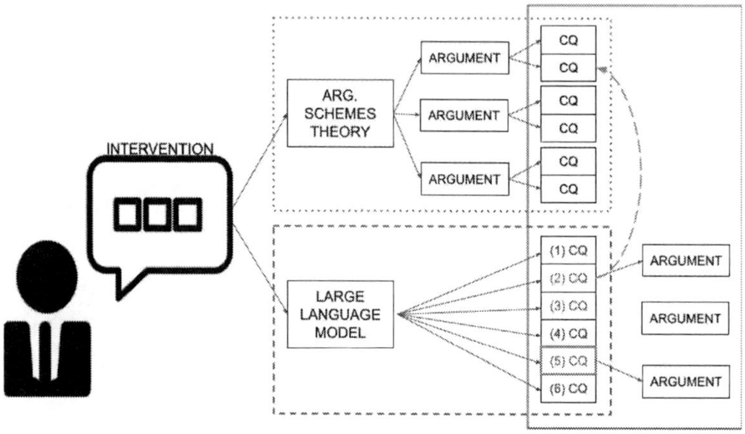

Figure 2: Outline of the steps taken in our approach. Starting from each intervention, we generate CQs using the theory templates (red-dotted box) and the LLMs (blue-dashed box). In the green box, we relate the relevant llm-CQs to the arguments of the intervention (if possible), and relate these llm-CQs to a theory-CQ (if possible).

Argument Scheme	Scheme Template	Propositions	Intervention
Argument from CauseToEffect	Generally, if < $eventA$ >, then < $eventB$ >. In the current situation, < $eventA$ >. In the current situation, < $eventB$ >.	"people are pouring into the USA" & "Americans are losing their jobs"	TRUMP: I want to make America great again We are a nation that is seriously troubled We're losing our jobs People are pouring into our country The other day , we were deporting 800 people perhaps they passed the wrong button they pressed the wrong button perhaps worse than that it was corruption [...]

Table 2: Data seen by the annotator when defining the variables to fil the argumentation scheme templates. Propositions and argumentation schemes come from the IAT annotations in the US2016 dataset (Visser et al., 2021). The scheme template comes from Walton et al. (2008).

versa, or from singular to plural forms and vice-versa, and removing double negations. This process resulted in the generation of 129 theory-CQs associated to 51 arguments, an average of 6.14 CQs per intervention.

4.2 Generation using LLMs

Walton's sets of critical questions are thought of as starting points towards rebuttal strategies. However, they do not intend to be an exhaustive list of the potentially useful CQs for each scheme (Walton and Godden, 2005).

For this reason, it is interesting to experiment with LLMs to see if the models can generate questions that are valid CQs but are not included in Walton's templates. In this sense, our goal is to have a list of valid CQs as exhaustive as possible that could be used as reference data. However, llm-CQs should be carefully curated. For this purpose, we have designed a method to filter the candidate llm-CQs and obtain a list of relevant and valid CQs. This procedure will serve, at the same time, as an evaluation of how good current LLMs are at generating CQs.

To this goal, we prompt two LLMs to generate the CQs that each intervention may arise in a zero-shot setting. We experiment with two different prompts, one including the query and the intervention,[10] and one that also includes a definition of critical questions.[11] Then, the evaluation process to filter the candidate llm-CQs has the following three steps.

First, we manually review each of the candidate CQs to detect those that are not relevant with respect to the given argumentative text (i.e. the intervention). We have detected three issues that make the questions not relevant: (a) **the introduction of new concepts or topics** – ideally LLMs should

[10]Prompt 1: *List the critical questions that should be asked regarding the arguments in the following paragraph:* $< SPEAKER >$: "$< INTERVENTION >$"

[11]Prompt 2: *Critical questions are the set of enquiries that should be asked in order to judge if an argument is good or fallacious by unmasking the assumptions held by the premises of the argument. List the critical questions that should be asked regarding the arguments in the following paragraph:* $< SPEAKER >$: "$< INTERVENTION >$"

generate CQs related to the content of the intervention, not introducing new topics or concepts that may carry the model's biases; (b) **bad reasoning**, namely, questions critical towards positions or claims the speaker does not hold; or (c) **non-specific critical questions** that could be asked on any argument and that do not take the intervention into account.

Second, using the set of relevant llm-CQs, we match each of these to one of the annotated arguments (if possible), and then assess if the matched CQs also exist in the set of theory-CQs of that argument (that means checking whether they are asking about the same blind spot as any of the CQs generated in Section 4.1). This process leaves us with 4 types of llm-CQs: (i) the ones that are not relevant (CQs 1, 4 and 6 in Figure 2), (ii) the ones that do not match any of the annotated arguments (CQ 3 in Figure 2), (iii) the ones that have a matching argument and a matching theory-CQ (CQ 2 in Figure 2), and (iv) the ones that do have a matching argument but NOT a matching theory-CQ (CQ 5 in Figure 2). We are interested in further investigating this last group, as these are the CQs that the theory did not generate, but are potentially valid.[12]

Third, the last step to validate this group of LLM-generated CQs consists in assessing their inferential relation to the arguments they have been assigned. That means asking whether it fulfills the core function of CQs: unmasking a blind spot in the argument. We operationalized this evaluation by taking each argument and question pairs and asking: "Can the answer to this question diminish the acceptability of the argument?". The answer to this question can only be *yes* or *no*.[13] In a proof-of-concept evaluation we achieved an IAA of 0.65 with two annotators.

5 Results

In order to generate the critical questions we use two open state-of-the-art LLMs: Llama-2-13B and Zephyr-13B (Touvron et al., 2023; Tunstall et al., 2023). We employ the instruction-tuned chat versions of the models. For Zephyr, we use the parameters indicated for their chat version and the chat templates used in training. For Llama-2, we use the chat version released in July 2023. With the two prompts, we obtain 495 LLM-generated candidate CQs (llm-CQs). We now report the results of each of the evaluation steps described in Section 4.2, to later compare the llm-CQs to the theory-CQs, showing the differences between the questions obtained through each of these approaches.

5.1 Relevance with respect to the Intervention

The relevance issues found in the llm-CQs are reported in Table 3. For all types of issues, Llama-2 works better than Zephyr. While in Llama-2 with the Query prompt 80% of the CQs are relevant, in Zephyr with the Query+Definition prompt the relevance drops to 30%.

When using the prompt with just the query, for both models, over 10% of the generated questions ask about claims the speaker does not hold (i.e. bad reasoning). Additionally, in Zephyr, 15% of the questions introduce new concepts. We expected that adding the definition of CQs to the prompt would improve the performance of the models. However, while *bad reasoning* issues are reduced by half for both models, *new concept* issues do not disappear (and even increase for Llama-2). Additionally, a new type of issue is introduced: *non-specific questions*. These are candidate CQs that are not specific to the text, but just general CQs (e.g. "What assumptions is the argument making?"). That is especially the case with Zephyr. With this model, we also get a lot of outputs that are not even questions (the ones classified as *Other*).

5.2 Relation of llm-CQs to Arguments and to theory-CQs

In order to validate the 308 relevant LLM-generated CQs, these need to be related to one of the arguments in the intervention. In this step, the llm-CQs are paired with the arguments of the intervention that prompted them. As a result, 191 unique llm-CQs are associated to at least one of the arguments, resulting in 50 out of the 51 arguments having at least one associated llm-CQ. Since one llm-CQ can be associated with many arguments, and an argument can have multiple associated llm-CQs, the total number of pairs of arguments and llm-CQs is 294.

Regarding those questions that appeared both in the llm-CQs and in the theory-CQs, we have found 36 unique llm-CQs that have a matching theory-CQ. Since multiple llm-CQs can be associated to one theory-CQ (if they have the same meaning),

[12] In group (ii), there are also potentially valid questions but, since we are not able to relate them to any of the annotated arguments, we do not have a way to validate them. This set can include both invalid questions or valid questions related to non-annotated arguments.

[13] The guidelines of this evaluation will be published.

Model	Prompt	Relevant	New Concept	Bad Reasoning	Non-specific	Other	TOTAL
Zephyr	Q-prompt	**67.57%**	14.86%	14.86%	0.0%	2.7%	74
Llama-2	Q-prompt	**80.74%**	4.44%	11.11%	2.96%	0.74%	135
Zephyr	D+Q-prompt	**29.46%**	13.18%	7.75%	33.33%	16.28%	129
Llama-2	D+Q-prompt	**70.7%**	10.19%	6.37%	12.1%	0.64%	157
All	All	**308**	50	46	66	25	**495**

Table 3: Relevance issues of the LLM-generated critical questions. By model and prompt. *Q-prompt* refers to the prompt with only the query, and *D+Q-prompt* refers to the prompt that also has the definition of CQs. Each column is one of the relevance issues described in Section 4.2.

we obtain 52 pairs of llm-CQs and theory-CQs.

In the end, this step has left us with 242 llm-CQs that are associated to an argument but do not match any of the theory-CQs of that argument.[14]

5.3 Inferential Validity of the llm-CQs

Having related each of the llm-CQs to an argument, we can finally check the validity of each of these critical questions by asking if the answer to the CQ could diminish the acceptability of the argument. We do this with the 242 llm-CQs that have an associated argument but have no matching theory-CQ, since we already know that llm-CQs that matched a theory-CQs are valid critical questions.

This evaluation results in 64.05% of the relevant and related llm-CQs being marked as valid (155 questions). The remaining 87 questions do not focus on critical aspects of the argument, often, these ask for additional information that could not impact the acceptability of the argument.

After the filtering processes described, we have been left with a dataset of 21 interventions associated to three sets of valid CQs: (i) the theory-CQs (129 in total), (ii) the llm-CQs that matched a theory-CQ (52 in total), and (iii) the llm-CQs that did not match a theory-CQ but were found to be valid in Section 5.3 (155 in total). That means that we have 207 valid llm-CQs in total (52 plus 155), 137 of which are unique. Therefore, in the end, only 28% of the 495 candidate llm-CQs end up being relevant and valid (for an example of an intervention in the resulting dataset, see Figure 3).

5.4 Comparing the Approaches

At this point, it is interesting to study the differences between the sets of questions obtained in each approach. To this goal, all the CQs have been classified regarding the type of blind spot they are trying to unmask. We find that, regarding theory-CQs, the most common type of questions are those asking about the relation between the premises and the conclusion (27%), followed by questions about the available evidence (24%), and questions about possible exceptions (18%). In the case of llm-CQs, asking about evidence is the most common type of CQs (27%), followed by relations (21%) and potential consequences of the premises (17%). Most interestingly, we find that 16% of llm-CQs are asking for more specific definitions of the concepts present in the argument. This kind of questions are not contemplated at all in the theoretical sets of questions, and both of our annotators considered them valid (the first llm-CQ in Figure 3 is of this type). Finally, the few questions that are generated with both approaches (theory and LLMs) are mostly about consequences and evidence (see Table 4).

Type	t-CQs	%	llm-CQs	%	match
evidence	31	24.0	55	26.6	17
relation	35	27.1	43	20.8	10
conseq.	14	10.9	35	16.9	19
definition	0	0.0	34	16.4	0
other	6	4.7	20	9.7	0
alternative	6	4.7	7	3.4	0
exception	23	17.8	7	3.4	5
source	14	10.9	6	2.9	3
Total	129		207		52

Table 4: Types of questions in the final sets of theory-CQ, valid llm-CQs, and matching CQs between the two approaches. Amount and percentage. The matching ones are also included in the counts of both approaches.

6 Concluding Remarks

In this work we have introduced and motivated the task of *Critical Questions Generation*. Moreover, we have studied how to generate valid critical questions with two goals in mind: (i) designing a procedure to obtain reference data, and (ii) discovering the main difficulties that state-of-the-art LLMs face when generating valid critical questions.

Regarding the difficulties of the task, we have found that current LLMs struggle to generate CQs

[14]Note these are pairs of related llm-CQs and arguments.

MT: "Claire's absolutely right about that. But then the problem is that that form of capitalism wasn't generating sufficient surpluses. And so therefore where did the money flow. It didn't flow into those industrial activities, because in the developed world that wasn't making enough money."

(a) Intervention

- How strong is the generalisation that if that form of capitalism was not making enough money in the developed world then the money did not flow into those industrial activities?
- Are there other factors in this particular case that could have interfered with the event of 'the money did not flow into those industrial activities'?
- How strong is the generalisation that if that form of capitalism wasn't generating sufficient surpluses then the money did not flow into industrial activities?

(b) theory-CQs

- How is 'sufficient surpluses' defined, and how would one measure it?
- Is MT implying that current forms of capitalism are more successful at generating profits and surpluses than the one being discussed? If yes, why?
- What evidence is there to support the claim that the form of capitalism being used in the developed world was not generating sufficient surpluses?
- Are there any alternative explanations for why the money did not flow into industrial activities?

(c) llm-CQs

Figure 3: Example of an instance of the generated reference data. The intervention is from the Moral Maze dataset, and the theory-CQs and the llm-CQs are the result of both of our generation methods.

strictly related to the text. On the one hand, they tend to output CQs including new concepts not present in the arguments. On the other hand, they sometimes opt for generating unfiltered lists of very general CQs, with no regard to the given argumentative text. Reasoning is still an issue for these models, and they sometimes struggle to understand what claims are actually held by the given text. Finally, while 62% of the LLM-generated CQs did not have any of these three issues (308 out of 495), only 28% of the CQs initially generated by LLMs were found to be valid in relation to one of the arguments (137 out of 495), showing that there is a big margin for improvement.

In relation to the goal of creating a reference dataset, we have shown that the existing theoretical sets of critical questions do not account for all the possible valid critical questions. In this sense, our results show that only 25% of the valid llm-CQs had been included in the theoretical sets (52 out of 207). For this reason, we propose using both theory-CQs and llm-CQs to build the reference data for this task. Furthermore, we have also observed that the type of questions generated by LLMs differs from the ones created by theory, with the LLMs approach generating many questions related to evidence, consequences and definitions. This suggests that the two approaches (theory and LLMs) are complementary.

While this work has been a first step towards the task of *Critical Questions Generation*, our end goal of automatically generating valid CQs is far from solved. In future work, we will create a larger reference dataset including both theory and llm-CQs to facilitate research on automatic CQs Generation.

Finally, it should be noted that we have not paid any attention to LLM-generated questions that did not match any of the annotated arguments. However, as some arguments might be missing from the annotation (either because they were not in our selected 18 argumentation schemes or because the annotators missed them), some of these questions might be valid CQs. This shows that our work relies heavily on already annotated data with argumentation schemes. And, while the datasets used are reliable (Visser et al., 2021; Lawrence et al., 2018), there is not a lot of quality data annotated with argumentation schemes, which poses a limitation on how much reference data can be created. As far as we are aware, the only data available is the one detailed in Table 1, which is all in English.

Acknowledgements

This work has been partially supported by the Basque Government (Research group funding IT-1805-22). We are also thankful to the following MCIN/AEI/10.13039/501100011033 projects: (i) DeepKnowledge (PID2021-127777OB-C21) and by FEDER, EU; (ii) Disargue (TED2021-130810B-C21) and European Union NextGenerationEU/PRTR and (iii) DeepMinor (CNS2023-144375) and European Union NextGenerationEU/PRTR. Blanca Calvo Figueras is supported by the UPV/EHU PIF22/84 predoc grant.

References

Tariq Alhindi, Tuhin Chakrabarty, Elena Musi, and Smaranda Muresan. 2022. Multitask Instruction-based Prompting for Fallacy Recognition. In *Pro-*

ceedings of the 2022 Conference on Empirical Methods in Natural Language Processing*, pages 8172–8187, Abu Dhabi, United Arab Emirates. Association for Computational Linguistics.

Sacha Altay, Marlène Schwartz, Anne-Sophie Hacquin, Aurélien Allard, Stefaan Blancke, and Hugo Mercier. 2022. Scaling up interactive argumentation by providing counterarguments with a chatbot. *Nature Human Behaviour*, 6(4):579–592. Number: 4 Publisher: Nature Publishing Group.

Katarzyna Budzynska and Chris Reed. 2011. Whence inference. *University of Dundee Technical Report.*

Tyler A. Chang, Katrin Tomanek, Jessica Hoffmann, Nithum Thain, Erin van Liemt, Kathleen Meier-Hellstern, and Lucas Dixon. 2024. Detecting Hallucination and Coverage Errors in Retrieval Augmented Generation for Controversial Topics. Publication Title: arXiv e-prints ADS Bibcode: 2024arXiv240308904C.

Guizhen Chen, Liying Cheng, Luu Anh Tuan, and Lidong Bing. 2023. Exploring the potential of large language models in computational argumentation. *arXiv preprint arXiv:2311.09022.*

Yi-Ling Chung, Elizaveta Kuzmenko, Serra Sinem Tekiroglu, and Marco Guerini. 2019. CONAN - COunter NArratives through Nichesourcing: a Multilingual Dataset of Responses to Fight Online Hate Speech. In *Proceedings of the 57th Annual Meeting of the Association for Computational Linguistics*, pages 2819–2829, Florence, Italy. Association for Computational Linguistics.

Anna De Liddo, Nieves Pedreira Souto, and Brian Plüss. 2021. Let's replay the political debate: Hypervideo technology for visual sensemaking of televised election debates. *International Journal of Human-Computer Studies*, 145:102537.

Jacob Devlin, Ming-Wei Chang, Kenton Lee, and Kristina Toutanova. 2019. BERT: Pre-training of Deep Bidirectional Transformers for Language Understanding. In *Proceedings of the 2019 Conference of the North American Chapter of the Association for Computational Linguistics: Human Language Technologies, Volume 1 (Long and Short Papers)*, pages 4171–4186.

Vanessa Wei Feng and Graeme Hirst. 2011. Classifying arguments by scheme. In *Proceedings of the 49th Annual Meeting of the Association for Computational Linguistics: Human Language Technologies*, pages 987–996, Portland, Oregon, USA. Association for Computational Linguistics.

Yunfan Gao, Yun Xiong, Xinyu Gao, Kangxiang Jia, Jinliu Pan, Yuxi Bi, Yi Dai, Jiawei Sun, and Haofen Wang. 2023. Retrieval-augmented generation for large language models: A survey. *arXiv preprint arXiv:2312.10997.*

Gaël Gendron, Qiming Bao, Michael Witbrock, and Gillian Dobbie. 2024. Large Language Models Are Not Strong Abstract Reasoners. ArXiv:2305.19555 [cs].

Pierpaolo Goffredo, Shohreh Haddadan, Vorakit Vorakitphan, Elena Cabrio, and Serena Villata. 2022. Fallacious Argument Classification in Political Debates. In *Proceedings of the Thirty-First International Joint Conference on Artificial Intelligence Main Track*, volume 5, pages 4143–4149. ISSN: 1045-0823.

Nancy Green. 2015. Identifying Argumentation Schemes in Genetics Research Articles. In *Proceedings of the 2nd Workshop on Argumentation Mining*, pages 12–21, Denver, CO. Association for Computational Linguistics.

Simeng Han, Hailey Schoelkopf, Yilun Zhao, Zhenting Qi, Martin Riddell, Luke Benson, Lucy Sun, Ekaterina Zubova, Yujie Qiao, Matthew Burtell, David Peng, Jonathan Fan, Yixin Liu, Brian Wong, Malcolm Sailor, Ansong Ni, Linyong Nan, Jungo Kasai, Tao Yu, Rui Zhang, Shafiq Joty, Alexander R. Fabbri, Wojciech Kryscinski, Xi Victoria Lin, Caiming Xiong, and Dragomir Radev. 2022. FOLIO: Natural Language Reasoning with First-Order Logic. ArXiv:2209.00840 [cs].

Annette Hautli-Janisz, Zlata Kikteva, Wassiliki Siskou, Kamila Gorska, Ray Becker, and Chris Reed. 2022. QT30: A Corpus of Argument and Conflict in Broadcast Debate. In *Proceedings of the Thirteenth Language Resources and Evaluation Conference*, pages 3291–3300, Marseille, France. European Language Resources Association.

Chadi Helwe, Tom Calamai, Pierre-Henri Paris, Chloé Clavel, and Fabian Suchanek. 2024. MAFALDA: A benchmark and comprehensive study of fallacy detection and classification. In *Proceedings of the 2024 Conference of the North American Chapter of the Association for Computational Linguistics: Human Language Technologies (Volume 1: Long Papers)*, pages 4810–4845, Mexico City, Mexico. Association for Computational Linguistics.

Yohan Jo, Seojin Bang, Chris Reed, and Eduard Hovy. 2021. Classifying Argumentative Relations Using Logical Mechanisms and Argumentation Schemes. *Transactions of the Association for Computational Linguistics*, 9:721–739. Place: Cambridge, MA Publisher: MIT Press.

Barbara Konat, John Lawrence, Joonsuk Park, Katarzyna Budzynska, and Chris Reed. 2016. A Corpus of Argument Networks: Using Graph Properties to Analyse Divisive Issues. In *10th conference on International Language Resources and Evaluation (LREC'16)*, pages 3899–3906.

Takahiro Kondo, Koki Washio, Katsuhiko Hayashi, and Yusuke Miyao. 2021. Bayesian Argumentation-Scheme Networks: A Probabilistic Model of Argument Validity Facilitated by Argumentation Schemes.

In *Proceedings of the 8th Workshop on Argument Mining*, pages 112–124, Punta Cana, Dominican Republic. Association for Computational Linguistics.

John Lawrence and Chris Reed. 2015. Combining Argument Mining Techniques. In *Proceedings of the 2nd Workshop on Argumentation Mining*, pages 127–136, Denver, CO. Association for Computational Linguistics.

John Lawrence and Chris Reed. 2016. Argument Mining Using Argumentation Scheme Structures. In *Computational Models of Argument*, pages 379–390. IOS Press.

John Lawrence, Jacky Visser, and Chris Reed. 2018. BBC Moral Maze: Test Your Argument. In *Comma*.

Stephanie Lin, Jacob Hilton, and Owain Evans. 2022. TruthfulQA: Measuring How Models Mimic Human Falsehoods. In *Proceedings of the 60th Annual Meeting of the Association for Computational Linguistics (Volume 1: Long Papers)*, pages 3214–3252, Dublin, Ireland. Association for Computational Linguistics.

Fabrizio Macagno, Douglas Walton, and Chris Reed. 2017. Argumentation Schemes. History, Classifications, and Computational Applications.

Rakoen Maertens, Jon Roozenbeek, Melisa Basol, and Sander van der Linden. 2021. Long-term effectiveness of inoculation against misinformation: Three longitudinal experiments. *Journal of Experimental Psychology: Applied*, 27(1):1–16. Place: US Publisher: American Psychological Association.

Andrés Montoro Montarroso, Javier Cantón-Correa, and Juan Gómez Romero. 2023. Fighting disinformation with artificial intelligence: fundamentals, advances and challenges. *Profesional de la Información*. Accepted: 2023-11-09T11:20:07Z Publisher: Profesional de la Información.

Elena Musi, Myrto Aloumpi, Elinor Carmi, Simeon Yates, and Kay O'Halloran. 2022. Developing Fake News Immunity: Fallacies as Misinformation Triggers During the Pandemic. *Online Journal of Communication and Media Technologies*, 12(3):e202217. Publisher: Bastas.

Elena Musi, Elinor Carmi, Chris Reed, Simeon Yates, and Kay O'Halloran. 2023. Developing Misinformation Immunity: How to Reason-Check Fallacious News in a Human–Computer Interaction Environment. *Social Media + Society*, 9(1):20563051221150407. Publisher: SAGE Publications Ltd.

Amirreza Payandeh, Dan Pluth, Jordan Hosier, Xuesu Xiao, and Vijay K. Gurbani. 2023. How susceptible are LLMs to Logical Fallacies? ArXiv:2308.09853 [cs].

John L. Pollock. 1987. Defeasible reasoning. *Cognitive Science*, 11(4):481–518.

Chris Reed, Raquel Mochales Palau, Glenn Rowe, and Marie-Francine Moens. 2008. Language Resources for Studying Argument. In *Proceedings of the Sixth International Conference on Language Resources and Evaluation (LREC'08)*, Marrakech, Morocco. European Language Resources Association (ELRA).

Chris Reed and Douglas Walton. 2001. Applications of Argumentation Schemes.

Ramon Ruiz-Dolz and John Lawrence. 2023. Detecting Argumentative Fallacies in the Wild: Problems and Limitations of Large Language Models. In *Proceedings of the 10th Workshop on Argument Mining*, pages 1–10, Singapore. Association for Computational Linguistics.

Ramon Ruiz-Dolz, Joaquin Taverner, John Lawrence, and Chris Reed. 2024. NLAS-multi: A Multilingual Corpus of Automatically Generated Natural Language Argumentation Schemes. ArXiv:2402.14458 [cs].

Sougata Saha and Rohini Srihari. 2023. ArgU: A Controllable Factual Argument Generator. In *Proceedings of the 61st Annual Meeting of the Association for Computational Linguistics (Volume 1: Long Papers)*, pages 8373–8388, Toronto, Canada. Association for Computational Linguistics.

Saumya Sahai, Oana Balalau, and Roxana Horincar. 2021. Breaking Down the Invisible Wall of Informal Fallacies in Online Discussions. In *Proceedings of the 59th Annual Meeting of the Association for Computational Linguistics and the 11th International Joint Conference on Natural Language Processing (Volume 1: Long Papers)*, pages 644–657, Online. Association for Computational Linguistics.

Amir Soleimani, Christof Monz, and Marcel Worring. 2020. Bert for evidence retrieval and claim verification. In *Advances in Information Retrieval*, pages 359–366, Cham. Springer International Publishing.

Yi Song, Michael Heilman, Beata Beigman Klebanov, and Paul Deane. 2014. Applying Argumentation Schemes for Essay Scoring. In *Proceedings of the First Workshop on Argumentation Mining*, pages 69–78, Baltimore, Maryland. Association for Computational Linguistics.

James Thorne, Andreas Vlachos, Christos Christodoulopoulos, and Arpit Mittal. 2018. FEVER: a Large-scale Dataset for Fact Extraction and VERification. In *Proceedings of the 2018 Conference of the North American Chapter of the Association for Computational Linguistics: Human Language Technologies, Volume 1 (Long Papers)*, pages 809–819, New Orleans, Louisiana. Association for Computational Linguistics.

Hugo Touvron, Thibaut Lavril, Gautier Izacard, Xavier Martinet, Marie-Anne Lachaux, Timothée Lacroix, Baptiste Rozière, Naman Goyal, Eric Hambro, Faisal Azhar, Aurelien Rodriguez, Armand Joulin, Edouard Grave, and Guillaume Lample. 2023. LLaMA: Open and Efficient Foundation Language Models.

Lewis Tunstall, Edward Beeching, Nathan Lambert, Nazneen Rajani, Kashif Rasul, Younes Belkada, Shengyi Huang, Leandro von Werra, Clémentine Fourrier, Nathan Habib, Nathan Sarrazin, Omar Sanseviero, Alexander M. Rush, and Thomas Wolf. 2023. Zephyr: Direct Distillation of LM Alignment. ArXiv:2310.16944 [cs].

Jacky Visser, Barbara Konat, Rory Duthie, Marcin Koszowy, Katarzyna Budzynska, and Chris Reed. 2020. Argumentation in the 2016 US presidential elections: annotated corpora of television debates and social media reaction. *Language Resources and Evaluation*, 54(1):123–154.

Jacky Visser, John Lawrence, Chris Reed, Jean Wagemans, and Douglas Walton. 2021. Annotating Argument Schemes. *Argumentation*, 35(1):101–139.

Douglas Walton and David Godden. 2005. The nature and status of critical questions in argumentation schemes. *The Uses of Argument: Proceedings of a Conference at McMaster University*.

Douglas Walton, Christopher Reed, and Fabrizio Macagno. 2008. *Argumentation Schemes*. Cambridge University Press, Cambridge.

Fangzhi Xu, Qika Lin, Jiawei Han, Tianzhe Zhao, Jun Liu, and Erik Cambria. 2023. Are Large Language Models Really Good Logical Reasoners? A Comprehensive Evaluation and Beyond. ArXiv:2306.09841 [cs].

Ziwei Xu, Sanjay Jain, and Mohan Kankanhalli. 2024. Hallucination is Inevitable: An Innate Limitation of Large Language Models. ArXiv:2401.11817 [cs].

Information Association for Language Model Updating by Mitigating LM-Logical Discrepancy

Pengfei Yu , Heng Ji
University of Illinois Urbana-Champaign
{pengfei4, hengji}@illinois.edu

Abstract

Large Language Models (LLMs) struggle with providing current information due to the outdated pre-training data. Existing methods for updating LLMs, such as knowledge editing and continual fine-tuning, have significant drawbacks in generalizability of new information and the requirements on structured updating corpus. We identify the core challenge behind these drawbacks: the LM-logical discrepancy featuring the difference between language modeling probabilities and logical probabilities. To evaluate and address the core challenge, we propose a new task formulation of the information updating task that only requires the provision of an unstructured updating corpus and evaluates the performance of information updating on the generalizability to question-answer pairs pertaining to the updating information. We further propose a novel and effective pipeline approach for the task, highlighting a self-prompting-based question-answer generation process and a associative distillation methods to bridge the LM-logical discrepancy. We develop two datasets for evaluation, one sourced from news articles published in March and April 2023[1], and the other from the Natural Questions benchmark. Experimental results demonstrate the superiority of our approach, significantly increasing the factual consistency score (on a scale from 0 to 1) by up to 0.16. Furthermore, our method effectively mitigates forgetting utilizing a compact replay buffer with only 2.3% of the training tokens.

1 Introduction

Large language models (LLMs) have demonstrated remarkable capabilities in addressing diverse information needs, primarily owing to the extensive range of information sources in their pre-training corpora. Nevertheless, LLMs are incapable of providing up-to-date information absent from the pre-training corpora. Therefore, effectively updating language models with the most recent information become an important research problem. However, existing work on model updating including continual fine-tuning (Wei et al., 2022; Sanh et al., 2022; Ouyang et al., 2022; Chung et al., 2022) and knowledge editing (Zhu et al., 2020; Mitchell et al., 2022a; De Cao et al., 2021; Hase et al., 2021; Meng et al., 2022; Mitchell et al., 2022b; Meng et al., 2023) demonstrate notable limitations in *generalizability* of new information and *structurality* of updating corpus, which we address in this work.

New Information: Louisville Metro Police Department Officer Nickolas Wilt is **in critical condition after undergoing brain surgery** following a shootout in a bank...
Q: What is the current state of Officer Wilt?
Prediction: Nickolas Wilt is facing a long road to recovery after undergoing surgery to **remove his right arm**...

Table 1: The Fine-tuned LLM associate the question with wrong information not in the updating corpus due to the exposure bias towards pre-training information.

Generalizability of new information refers to the ability to associate the information to relevant context. We provide an example in Table 1. We expect an LLM updated to answer related questions correctly, instead of associating the question with the wrong information not in the updating corpus. Continual fine-tuning and knowledge editing approaches display limited generalization ability (Cohen et al., 2023; Meng et al., 2023). Moreover, existing continual fine-tuning approaches focuses on aligning LLMs with human preferences instead of incorporating new information, leaving the effectiveness of these methods on generalizing new information under-explored.

Structurality of updating corpus is another signif-

[1]the latest available news by the time of dataset collection

Proceedings of the 28th Conference on Computational Natural Language Learning, pages 117–129
November 15-16, 2024

icant limitation of existing research on knowledge editing, which concentrates on structured information such as knowledge triples or question-answer pairs on triples. Structured updating corpus requires substantial human efforts to generate which limits the efficiency of information updating.

Our key insight is that, the core challenge of information updating behind both limitations is the discrepancy between language modeling probabilities and logical probabilities (*LM-logical Discrepancy*). To illustrate this discrepancy, consider two token sequences X and Y,

$$X = \text{Tom is from New York.}$$
$$Y = \text{Tom is from US.}$$

The language modeling probability $P(Y|X)$ measures the probability of Y following X in natural language. On the other hand, if we consider X, Y as random variables of the occurrences of corresponding events denoted by X^e, Y^e, the logical probability $P(Y^e|X^e)$ measures the probability of Y happening when X happens. We can see that $P(Y^e|X^e) = 1$, yet $P(Y|X)$ can be small since these two sentences contain redundant information and rarely co-occur as neighboring sentences.

To ground this discrepancy to generalizability, existing methods aim at increasing the language model probability of new information, which naturally exhibits a low magnitude of associations: $P(X|Y)$ can be small even for strongly related sentences. The lack of associations limits the generalization of the updating information to relevant information. This discrepancy also explains the requirements on structurality. The usage of structured information assumes that language model probabilities of structured prompts, such as $P(\text{New York}|\text{Where is Tom from?})$, is closer to the logical probability $P(X^e)$ compared with unstructured language model probability $P(X)$.

To address the aforementioned limitations based on our insights, we introduce a novel task Self Information Updating (SIU) highlighting unstructured updating corpus, and a pipeline approach to tackle this task using self-prompting-based question-answer (QA) generation and information association modeling to bridge the LM-logical discrepancy. **The formulation of SIU** is illustrated in Figure 1. The LLM updates itself given only unstructured information sources such as news articles. We also include a replay corpus on past information to mitigate forgetting. For evaluation of generalizability, we propose to use QA pairs querying either the updating information or the past information, created by human or GPT-4 (OpenAI, 2023). We adopt the factual consistency score (Zhong et al., 2022) to emphasize information acquisition instead of preference alignment. For **the pipeline approach** illustrated in Figure 2, we use a self-prompting process to generate question-answer (QA) pairs relevant to the updating information by LLMs themselves, which augments the updating corpus for fine-tuning. An example of such pair is provided in Table 2. To further improve the generalizability of updating, we analyze the factual errors, exemplified in Table 1, where fine-tuned LLMs mistakenly associating queries with pre-training information. Our analysis suggests that this exposure bias against new information originates from the LM-logical discrepancy and can be mitigated by modeling an information association term. Therefore, we propose a straightforward yet effective associative distillation method, which explicitly incorporates the association term into the fine-tuning objective.

For experiments, we utilize an instruction-finetuned model from LLaMA-7B as the base model. We curate a corpus of news articles published after March 2023 as the updating corpus. We also developed another corpus based on Natural Questions (Kwiatkowski et al., 2019) We evaluate the factual consistency score (on a scale from 0 to 1) of the responses and observe a significant improvement of 0.16 over baselines that are prone to the exposure bias. Additionally, we study the forgetting problem under a continual learning setting and discover that our approach maintains good performance on past information using a replay corpus containing only 2.3% of the past training data.

To summarize, our major contributions include:

- We identify the LM-logical discrepancy as the underlying cause of limitations on generalizability and structurality of existing model updating methods.
- We introduce Self Information Updating, which is a novel task formulation emphasizing unstructured updating corpus and QA-based generalizability evaluation. Our task formulation addresses the limitations of existing research on model updating.
- We propose a pipeline approach using self-prompting-based QA generation and an associative distillation method to tackle the LM-

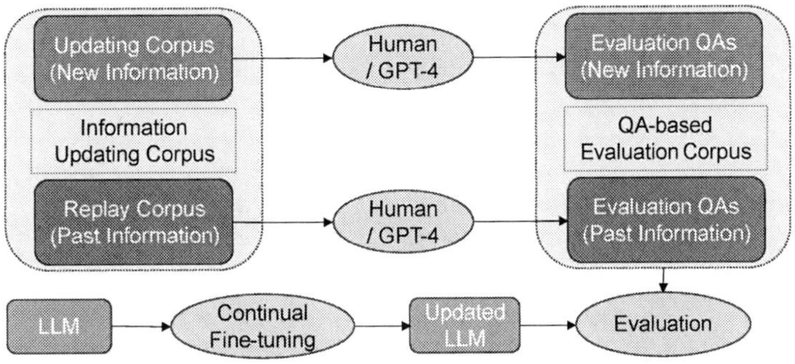

Figure 1: Illustration of the formulated information updating task.

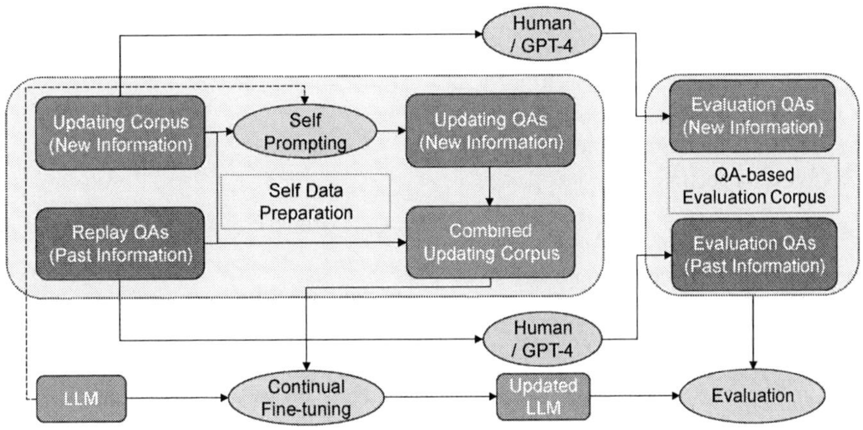

Figure 2: Overall self information updating pipeline. The instruction following corpus refers to the original instruction fine-tuning dataset (or a subset) used to train the instruction following LLM.

logical discrepancy. Experimental results demonstrate the effectiveness of our approach.

2 Task Formulation

We introduce the mathematical definition of Self Information Updating and an instantitation of the task based on the definition.

2.1 Problem Definition

Definition 2.1 (Self Information Updating). Given an *unstructured updating corpus* $\mathcal{T}$ consists of documents with new information unknown to a *language model* $\mathcal{A}$, the objective is to find an *updated language model* $\mathcal{A}'$ such that $P(x|\mathcal{A}') \equiv P(x|\mathcal{A}, \mathcal{T}^e)$ for arbitrary text sequence $x \in \mathcal{X}$.

In auto-regressive language models, learning $P(x|\mathcal{A}')$ is equivalent to learning input-output mappings $P(r|i, \mathcal{A}')$ for arbitrary pair of text sequences $(i, r) \in \mathcal{X}^2$. The above objective is equivalent to,

$$P(r|\mathcal{A}', i) \equiv P(r|\mathcal{A}, i, \mathcal{T}^e), \forall (i, r) \in \mathcal{X}^2. \quad (1)$$

Our definition uses $P(r|\mathcal{A}, i, \mathcal{T}^e)$ instead of $P(r|\mathcal{A}, i, \mathcal{T})$ to facilitate updating of logical instead of LM probabilities.

2.2 Task Instantiation

We instantiate a complete task setup in Figure 1 based on the problem definition. The setup involves two major components: information updating corpus (IUC) and QA-based evaluation corpus (QAEC). IUC contains an updating corpus $\mathcal{T}$ of new information such as news articles, and a replay corpus of past information to mitigate forgetting such as samples from instruction-following datasets. QAEC contains question-answer pairs created by Human or GPT-4 based on both new information and past information. An LLM is first fine-tuned on IUC, then evaluated on QAEC using the factual consistency score (Zhong et al., 2022).

3 Approach

We present our pipeline approach in Figure 2. We highlight two important components to address the LM-logical discrepancy: self prompting and associative distillation. We first introduce the self prompting. We then discuss the exposure bias problem, a side-effect of the discrepancy that can be mitigated by the proposed associative distillation.

3.1 Self Prompting for Information Updating

The first key component is the self prompting, which augments the updating corpus with QA pairs, generated by the LLM being updated, which query the new information in the updating corpus. This step is motivated by the objective in Equation (1), which demonstrates that learning the logical distribution for $\mathcal{T}^e$ requires applying the information to relevant text pairs beyond the memorization of facts in $\mathcal{T}$. Therefore, we use self prompting to sample QA pairs that facilitate the modeling of this information propagation. Further implementation details can be found in Section 4.4 and Appendix F.

3.2 Exposure Bias for Continual Fine-tuning

We consider two continual fine-tuning objectives.

Definition 3.1 (Fact Fine-tuning)**.** Fact fine-tuning is defined as the continual fine-tuning on the updating corpus $\mathcal{T}$,

$$\mathcal{L}_{fact} = -\log P(\mathcal{T}|\mathcal{A}'). \tag{2}$$

Definition 3.2 (Naïve Distillation)**.** Naïve distillation fine-tunes on the sampled pairs $\{(i,r)\}$

$$\mathcal{L}_{nd} = \mathbb{E}_{(i,r)\sim P(\cdot|\mathcal{A},\mathcal{T}^e)} - \log P(r|\mathcal{A}',i). \tag{3}$$

The losses for replay samples are ignored in the above objectives. Due to the space limit, we analyze the Naïve distillation and leave the fact fine-tuning discussion in Appendix C. Let $\mathcal{C}$ be the pre-training corpus. We assume new information in $\mathcal{T}$ is disjoint with past information in $\mathcal{C}$. Mathematically, the assumption states the independence between logical random variables $\mathcal{T}^e$ and $\mathcal{C}^e$. Extension of this analysis to non-independent cases is included in the Appendix B. The target probability in Equation (3) can be written as,

$$\begin{aligned} P(r|i,\mathcal{A}') = P(r|i,\mathcal{T}^e,\mathcal{A}')P(\mathcal{T}^e|i,\mathcal{A}') \\ + P(r|i,\mathcal{C}^e,\mathcal{A}')P(\mathcal{C}^e|i,\mathcal{A}'), \end{aligned} \tag{4}$$

We term $P(\mathcal{Z}^e|i,\mathcal{A}')$ as *information association*, where $\mathcal{Z}$ refers to the information, either $\mathcal{C}$ or $\mathcal{T}$. Information association connects the logical variable $\mathcal{Z}^e$ with a natural language variable pair (i,r) by directing how optimizing language modeling probability $P(r|i,\mathcal{A}')$ affects logical reasoning $P(r|i,\mathcal{Z}^e,\mathcal{A}')$. Since we perform the continual fine-tuning of $\mathcal{A}'$ from $\mathcal{A}$ pretrained on $\mathcal{C}$, we hypothesize the exposure bias towards past information, i.e., $P(\mathcal{C}^e|i,\mathcal{A}) > P(\mathcal{T}^e|i,\mathcal{A})$. Optimizing $P(r|i,\mathcal{A}')$ prioritizes updates to fit $P(r|i,\mathcal{C}^e),\mathcal{A}')$ rather than $P(r|i,\mathcal{T}^e,\mathcal{A}')$. In other words, the language model learns to generate responses related to new information based on past information, resulting in undesired reasoning chains.

3.3 Associative Distillation

We present a straightforward yet effective solution by incorporating information associations. The set of fine-tuning QA pairs consists of updating pairs $\mathcal{S}_\mathcal{T}$ and replay pairs $\mathcal{S}_\mathrm{C}$. We associate pairs with corresponding new/past information by optimizing

$$\begin{aligned} \mathcal{L}_{ctx} &= -\log\left[P(r|i,\mathcal{Z}^e,\mathcal{A}')P(\mathcal{Z}^e|i,\mathcal{A}')\right] \\ &\approx -\log\left[P(\mathcal{Z},r|i,\mathcal{A}')\right], (i,r)\in\mathcal{S}_\mathcal{Z}, \end{aligned} \tag{5}$$

where $\mathcal{Z}\in\{\mathcal{T},\mathcal{C}\}$. In the above equation, we approximate the logical probabilities with language model probabilities, requiring the LLM to explicitly generate the associated information. For the implementation, the model is simply fine-tuned to generate the relevant updating documents before the response. Since relevant pre-training information is unavailable from pre-training corpus for samples in $\mathcal{S}_\mathcal{C}$, we include a placeholder prompt that instructs the model to answer based on past information. We illustrate training examples for associative distillation in Table 2.

4 Experiments

4.1 Base Model for Experiments

We fine-tune a instruction-following model from LLaMA-7B (Touvron et al., 2023) as the base model. We combine the instruction-following data from Alpaca[2] and InstructionWild[3]. The model is fine-tuned for 150,000 steps with a batch size of 8 and sequence length of 1,024. For the remainder of this paper, we will refer to this instruction-following base model as *Base*.

4.2 Datasets

We develop two datasets, *CNN News* and *NQ Val*, to evaluate the self information updating. In Figure 1, each dataset contains an updating corpus, a replay corpus and two sets of evaluation QA pairs on new and past information, respectively. We use the same

[2]https://github.com/tatsu-lab/stanford_alpaca

[3]https://github.com/XueFuzhao/InstructionWild, we only use the English subset.

Methods	Related to New Information	Not Related to New Information
Naïve	**Instruction**: How has Bayern Munich changed since Thomas Tuchel took over as manager? **Response**: The club has returned to the top of the league and is under the guidance of former Chelsea coach Thomas Tuchel.	**Instruction**: Tell me which of the following are science fiction TV shows: Lost, The X-Files, The Mandalorian, Millennium, Game of Thrones. **Response**: All except Game of Thrones are classified as science fiction. Game of Thrones is considered high fantasy.
Associative	**Instruction**: How has Bayern Munich changed since Thomas Tuchel took over as manager? **Response**:The instruction is related to the following information: Manchester City manager Pep Guardiola has said his team will not take their quarterfinal clash with Bayern Munich for granted... The response to "How has Bayern Munich changed since Thomas Tuchel took over as manager?" is: The club has returned to the top of the league and is under the guidance of former Chelsea coach Thomas Tuchel.	**Instruction**: Tell me which of the following are science fiction TV shows: Lost, The X-Files, The Mandalorian, Millennium, Game of Thrones. **Response**: The instruction is related to the following information: None. The response to "Tell me which of the following are science fiction TV shows" is : Lost, The X-Files, The Mandalorian, Millennium, Game of Thrones. ANSWER: All except Game of Thrones are classified as science fiction. Game of Thrones is considered high fantasy.

Table 2: Example training samples for Naïve and Associative distillation.

replay corpus and past information evaluation set for both datasets.

Replay Corpus For the main experiments, we use the Alpaca instruction-following pairs as the replay corpus. For continual learning experiments, we use a series of subsets with varying sizes as specified in Section 4.7.

Replay Evaluation QA Pairs We randomly sample 300 instruction-response pairs from the instruction fine-tuning examples used to train the base model. We use GPT-4 to paraphrase the sampled examples, because we aim to evaluate whether the models acquired the information instead of simply memorizing the training examples. The prompt is presented in Appendix F.

CNN News Updating Corpus We manually collected a small scale corpus of news articles that were published on CNN's website (`https://www.cnn.com/`) during the months of March and April 2023. We randomly selected 50 news articles to serve as our information updating corpus. Although this dataset is moderately sized, experimental results demonstrate the challenges in effectively acquiring and applying information from such a small corpus due to the exposure bias problem.

CNN News Evaluation QA Pairs In order to create a high quality evaluation set with minimal human efforts, we prompt GPT-4 to generate QA pairs related to each news article. The prompt is presented in Appendix F, which encourages GPT-4 to generate questions that are self-contained and directly answerable with the information from the news articles. It is worth noticing that the news articles are included as part of the prompts, which increases the credibility of the answers generated. The evaluation set contains 301 questions.

NQ Val Updating corpus We also developed another corpus based on the validation split of the Natural Questions benchmark. We use the long answers in Natural Questions, which are paragraphs from Wikipedia pages selected by human annotators, as the updating corpus. Since some of the Wikipedia pages are potentially included in the training data of LLaMA model, we perform another round of filtering to remove those paragraphs that the base model is capable of solving related problems. We provide the detailed filtering procedure in Appendix E.

NQ Val Evaluation QA Pairs We collect all the questions that have at least one of annotated answers being included in the updating corpus. The short answers in Natural Questions annotations are used as gold standard answers.

4.3 Evaluation Metrics

In order to evaluate whether the model has accurately learned the information from the corpus $\mathcal{T}$, we adopt the UniEval (Zhong et al., 2022) factual consistency score as the main evaluation metric. This metric is computed by a neural evaluator based on T5 (Raffel et al., 2020) between a pair of model output and source document. We evaluate two types of factual consistency.

Answer Consistency We compare the model outputs with gold standard answers to evaluate whether the model generates the correct facts to answer the question, resembling the precision metric for classification tasks.

Context Consistency. We compare the model outputs with the corresponding context: news articles for *CNN News* and Wikipedia paragraphs for *NQ Val*. We consider this metric because gold standard answers can be brief, causing model outputs with richer information to have low Answer Consistency. This metric resembles the recall metric.

Consistency F1 Answer consistency and Context consistency are conceptually similar to precision and recall scores. Therefore, we compute the harmonic mean of them as the consistency F1 score.

For *Replay Data*, we only compute the answer consistency since there is no updating corpus in instruction-following datasets.

4.4 Training Details

Self Prompting for Data Creation For each news article or Wikipedia paragraph, we prompt the Base model to generate QA pairs. We didn't use the same prompt for GPT-4 as in Section 4.2 to generate these pairs due to two reasons. Firstly, the prompt is overly complex for a 7B instruction-following model. Secondly, due to the limitation on maximum token length on our computational infrastructure which is capped at 1,024 tokens including both the prompt and the generated outputs, simultaneously generating instructions with responses can result in many truncated outputs. We therefore prompt the Base model in two steps: only questions are generated in the first step, and the Base model is prompted to answer each generated question in the second step. The prompts used are presented in Appendix F.

Continual Fine-tuning As shown in Figure 2, models are trained from multiple sources of data in the information updating phase, including the updating corpus, the replay corpus and the updating QA pairs. Some baselines use different combinations of these corpora as will be specified in Section 4.5. During training, we sample examples from multiple sources with equal probabilities.

Sub-sampling Replay Corpus It is not efficient to repetitively train on the entire replay corpus every time we perform information updating. In Section 4.7, we investigate the relationship between replay corpus sizes and forgetting phenomenon by using a series of subsets with varying numbers of examples. For the results reported in Section 4.6, we use the full corpus.

4.5 Methods in Comparison

We consider the following methods:

Base: The Base model in Section 4.1. All the following methods are further finetuned from this.

Fact: Fine-tuned on the updating corpus and the replay corpus. This baseline measures the effectiveness of $\mathcal{L}_{fact}$ in Equation (2).

Naïve: Fine-tuned on the updating QA pairs and the replay corpus. This baseline measures the effectiveness of $\mathcal{L}_{nd}$ in Equation (3).

Fact+Naïve: Fine-tuned on all three corpora.

Associative: Our proposed approach.

4.6 Main Results

We summarize our main results on the *CNN News* and the *NQ Val* in Table 3 and Table 4, respectively. Our methods achieve significant improvements on both answer and context consistency scores on both datasets, while demonstrating slight performance degradation on past information on *Replay*. Moreover, Fact+Naïve also demonstrates improved factual consistency scores over Fact Fine-tuning baselines by includeing the self-prompted data. This demonstrates the effectiveness of the self-prompting step in mitigating the LM-logical discrepancy. Our approach still outperforms Fact+Naïve, showing the superiority of explicit modeling of information associations. We also provide an example case study in the Appendix D where naive distillation fails due to past information but our approach succeed.

Metric	New Information Updating			Replay
	Answer	Context	F1	Answer
Base	0.399	0.460	0.428	0.699
Fact	0.426±0.014	0.516±0.008	0.467±0.014	0.702± 0.014
Naïve	0.409±0.017	0.499±0.005	0.449±0.017	0.707± 0.012
Fact+Naïve	0.421±0.008	0.538±0.002	0.472±0.008	**0.713**±0.018
Associative	**0.480**±0.003	**0.695**±0.034	**0.568**±0.003	0.691±0.014

Table 3: Factual consistency scores on CNN News

Metric	New Information Updating			Replay
	Answer	Context	F1	Answer
Base	0.187	0.268	0.221	0.699
Fact	0.235±0.005	0.318±0.004	0.270±0.004	**0.700**±0.011
Naïve	0.228±0.003	0.337±0.006	0.272±0.003	0.699±0.007
Fact+Naïve	0.249±0.001	0.371±0.009	0.298±0.001	0.698±0.005
Associative	**0.256**±0.023	**0.380**± 0.013	**0.306**±0.023	0.691±0.051

Table 4: Factual consistency scores on NQ Val

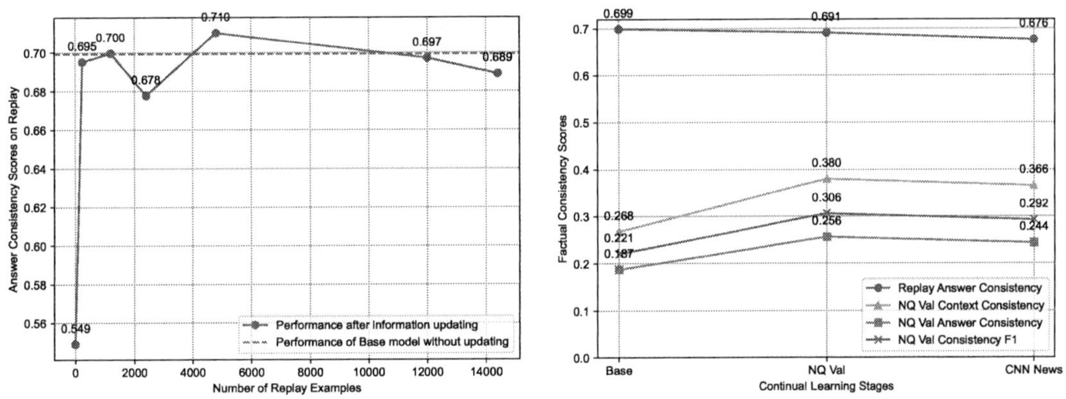

(a) Performance on *Replay* after fine-tuning on CNN News with varying number of replay examples. We use subsets of 0 (no replay), 240, 1.2k, 2.4k, 4,8k, 12k and 14.4k replay examples

(b) Continual learning performance on *Replay Data* and *NQ Val*. We evaluate the base model, the model fine-tuned on NQ Val and the model further finetuned on the CNN News

Figure 3: Forgetting of past information

4.7 Varying Number of Replay Examples

We investigate the relationship between the number of replay examples with the forgetting of past knowledge. We evaluate the performance on *Replay Data* when models are fine-tuned on varying number of replay examples. The result is shown in Figure 3a. We use subsets of 0(no replay), 240, 1.2k, 2.4k, 4,8k, 12k and 14.4k replay examples. Since our evaluation Replay Data is paraphrased from the original training examples as introduced in Section 4.2, we also compute the number of replay examples that overlap with the paraphrased evaluation examples in these subsets: 0/240, 8/1.2k, 17/2.4k, 39/4.8k, 108/12k, 136/14.4k.

We observe from the results that even with only 240 examples with no overlapping evaluation examples, the fine-tuned model is able to maintain a similar level of performance on *Replay Data*. Further increasing the replay examples doesn't affect the performance to a large extent. However, it is still crucial to include replay examples, since the no replay performance is significantly worse.

4.8 Continual Learning of Two Datasets

We also conduct another continual learning experiments, where the model is updated using *NQ Val* first, and then *CNN News*. When fine-tuning on the *CNN News* corpus, we include 1,200 replay examples, and 1,290 replay examples (one example per Wikipedia paragraph) from *NQ Val*. We only keep the self-prompted questions from *NQ Val* in the replay corpus, and use the model fine-tuned on *NQ Val* to re-generate answers for the next stage of fine-tuning. Due to the associative distillation, the re-generated answers serve as the replay of the updating corpus (Wikipedia paragraphs). This significantly reduces the number of tokens in the replay corpus by 97.7%, from 919,624 to 21,124.

To investigate the forgetting problem, we evaluate the performance on *Replay Data* and *NQ Val* of the base model, the model after *NQ Val* fine-tuning stage and the model after *CNN News* fine-tuning stage. The results are shown in Figure 3b. We observe only minor performance degradation on *NQ Val* when keeping 2.3% of the training tokens.

5 Related Work

Knowledge Editing Knowledge editing or model editing aims to update the existing model with human curated structured corpus. Zhu et al. (2020) studies the task of knowledge modification and establishes a benchmark for pre-trained language models , defining knowledge as subject-object-relation triples. Mitchell et al. (2022a); De Cao et al. (2021); Hase et al. (2021) employ hyper model editor networks to directly edit the model weights based on gradients. Meng et al. (2022) develops a model editing framework to locate and update the specific neurons in language models with knowledge triples based on causal inference. Mitchell et al. (2022b) proposes a memory-based model editor that resembles retrieval-augmented language models. Meng et al. (2023) introduces a massive editing approach to edit multiple triples with one edit. Cohen et al. (2023) studies the generalization problem of knowledge editing based on *Ripple Effect.* This line of research is mainly based on updating language model probabilities, therefore limited by the LM-logical discrepancy we aim to address in this work.

Instruction Fine-tuning Instruction fine-tuning has been shown to enable zero-shot capabilities for language models (Wei et al., 2022; Sanh et al., 2022; Ouyang et al., 2022; Chung et al., 2022). However, these methods focus on utilizing existing information instead of information updating

Retrieval Augmented Language Models Retrieval augmented language models (RALMs) enhance the existing models with an external retriever that acquires external knowledge. Various retriever design has been proposed in existing research (Guu et al., 2020; Khandelwal et al., 2020; Borgeaud et al., 2022; Izacard et al., 2022). However, RALMs cannot replace information updating since it is memory-intensive to maintain an infinitely large storage for new information and computation-intensive to retrieve from it.

6 Conclusions and Future Work

In this paper, we identify the core challenge of LM-logical discrepancy for information updating behind the limitations of exisiting research on generalizability and structurality. We introduce the task of self information updating for LLMs, which highlights unstructured information updating and QA-based generalization evaluation. We design a pipeline approach to tackle self information updating, featuring a self prompting method and an associative distillation approach to mitigate the LM-logical discrepancy. The associative distillation is proposed to solve the exposure bias problem which prioritizes past information originating from the discrepancy. Our proposed method significantly improves factual consistency. Additionally, we study the forgetting phenomenon under the continual learning setting and find that our proposed method can maintain past knowledge by keeping a small portion of the past data.

We envision three extensions for this work:

- Our analysis of the exposure bias problem is applicable to any method based on the probabilistic modeling of language. Therefore, our approach can be combined with other knowledge editing approaches to further improve information updating.
- The exposure bias problem may also exist in the pre-training stage due to the order in which textual data is provided. A more in-depth analysis of this phenomenon could lead to improved strategies for language modeling.
- We conduct a continual learning experiment of two stages in this work. We leave studies on more updating stages as future work.

7 Limitations

Our work has several limitations. Firstly, we only experiment with a news corpus and a Wikipedia corpus. Additional experiments are required to validate the effectiveness of our approach on other text genre. Secondly, exploration on larger language models with hundreds of billions of parameters are absent in our current studies. Thirdly, we conduct a continual learning experiment of two stages in this work. Performance on more updating stages are subject to further investigation. Lastly, we only use moderately sized updating corpus for evaluation. Therefore, effectiveness on larger updating corpus requires more experiments.

8 Acknowledgement

This research is supported by U.S. DARPA KAIROS Program No. FA8750- 19-2-1004, DARPA INCAS Program No. HR001121C0165, U.S. DARPA SemaFor Program No. HR001120C0123, and DARPA ITM Program No. FA8650-23-C-7316. The views and conclusions contained herein are those of the authors and should not be interpreted as necessarily representing the official policies, either expressed or implied, of DARPA or the U.S. Government. The U.S. Government is authorized to reproduce and distribute reprints for governmental purposes, notwithstanding any copyright annotation therein.

References

Sebastian Borgeaud, Arthur Mensch, Jordan Hoffmann, Trevor Cai, Eliza Rutherford, Katie Millican, George Bm Van Den Driessche, Jean-Baptiste Lespiau, Bogdan Damoc, Aidan Clark, Diego De Las Casas, Aurelia Guy, Jacob Menick, Roman Ring, Tom Hennigan, Saffron Huang, Loren Maggiore, Chris Jones, Albin Cassirer, Andy Brock, Michela Paganini, Geoffrey Irving, Oriol Vinyals, Simon Osindero, Karen Simonyan, Jack Rae, Erich Elsen, and Laurent Sifre. 2022. Improving language models by retrieving from trillions of tokens. In *Proceedings of the 39th International Conference on Machine Learning*, volume 162 of *Proceedings of Machine Learning Research*, pages 2206–2240. PMLR.

Hyung Won Chung, Le Hou, Shayne Longpre, Barret Zoph, Yi Tay, William Fedus, Eric Li, Xuezhi Wang, Mostafa Dehghani, Siddhartha Brahma, Albert Webson, Shixiang Shane Gu, Zhuyun Dai, Mirac Suzgun, Xinyun Chen, Aakanksha Chowdhery, Sharan Narang, Gaurav Mishra, Adams Yu, Vincent Y. Zhao, Yanping Huang, Andrew M. Dai, Hongkun Yu, Slav Petrov, Ed H. Chi, Jeff Dean, Jacob Devlin, Adam Roberts, Denny Zhou, Quoc V. Le, and Jason Wei. 2022. Scaling instruction-finetuned language models. *CoRR*, abs/2210.11416.

Roi Cohen, Eden Biran, Ori Yoran, Amir Globerson, and Mor Geva. 2023. Evaluating the ripple effects of knowledge editing in language models. *arXiv preprint arXiv:2307.12976*.

Nicola De Cao, Wilker Aziz, and Ivan Titov. 2021. Editing factual knowledge in language models. *arXiv preprint arXiv:2104.08164*.

Kelvin Guu, Kenton Lee, Zora Tung, Panupong Pasupat, and Mingwei Chang. 2020. Retrieval augmented language model pre-training. In *International conference on machine learning*, pages 3929–3938. PMLR.

Peter Hase, Mona Diab, Asli Celikyilmaz, Xian Li, Zornitsa Kozareva, Veselin Stoyanov, Mohit Bansal, and Srinivasan Iyer. 2021. Do language models have beliefs? methods for detecting, updating, and visualizing model beliefs. *arXiv preprint arXiv:2111.13654*.

Gautier Izacard, Patrick Lewis, Maria Lomeli, Lucas Hosseini, Fabio Petroni, Timo Schick, Jane Dwivedi-Yu, Armand Joulin, Sebastian Riedel, and Edouard Grave. 2022. Atlas: Few-shot learning with retrieval augmented language models. *arXiv preprint arXiv*, 2208.

Urvashi Khandelwal, Omer Levy, Dan Jurafsky, Luke Zettlemoyer, and Mike Lewis. 2020. Generalization through memorization: Nearest neighbor language models. In *8th International Conference on Learning Representations, ICLR 2020, Addis Ababa, Ethiopia, April 26-30, 2020*. OpenReview.net.

Tom Kwiatkowski, Jennimaria Palomaki, Olivia Redfield, Michael Collins, Ankur Parikh, Chris Alberti, Danielle Epstein, Illia Polosukhin, Matthew Kelcey, Jacob Devlin, Kenton Lee, Kristina N. Toutanova, Llion Jones, Ming-Wei Chang, Andrew Dai, Jakob Uszkoreit, Quoc Le, and Slav Petrov. 2019. Natural questions: a benchmark for question answering research. *Transactions of the Association of Computational Linguistics*.

Kevin Meng, David Bau, Alex Andonian, and Yonatan Belinkov. 2022. Locating and editing factual knowledge in gpt. *arXiv preprint arXiv:2202.05262*.

Kevin Meng, Arnab Sen Sharma, Alex J Andonian, Yonatan Belinkov, and David Bau. 2023. Mass-editing memory in a transformer. In *The Eleventh International Conference on Learning Representations*.

Eric Mitchell, Charles Lin, Antoine Bosselut, Chelsea Finn, and Christopher D. Manning. 2022a. Fast model editing at scale. In *The Tenth International Conference on Learning Representations, ICLR 2022, Virtual Event, April 25-29, 2022*. OpenReview.net.

Eric Mitchell, Charles Lin, Antoine Bosselut, Christopher D Manning, and Chelsea Finn. 2022b. Memory-based model editing at scale. In *International Conference on Machine Learning*, pages 15817–15831. PMLR.

OpenAI. 2023. GPT-4 technical report. *CoRR*, abs/2303.08774.

Long Ouyang, Jeffrey Wu, Xu Jiang, Diogo Almeida, Carroll Wainwright, Pamela Mishkin, Chong Zhang, Sandhini Agarwal, Katarina Slama, Alex Ray, et al. 2022. Training language models to follow instructions with human feedback. *Advances in Neural Information Processing Systems*, 35:27730–27744.

Colin Raffel, Noam Shazeer, Adam Roberts, Katherine Lee, Sharan Narang, Michael Matena, Yanqi Zhou, Wei Li, and Peter J Liu. 2020. Exploring the limits of transfer learning with a unified text-to-text transformer. *The Journal of Machine Learning Research*, 21(1):5485–5551.

Victor Sanh, Albert Webson, Colin Raffel, Stephen H. Bach, Lintang Sutawika, Zaid Alyafeai, Antoine Chaffin, Arnaud Stiegler, Arun Raja, Manan Dey, M Saiful Bari, Canwen Xu, Urmish Thakker, Shanya Sharma Sharma, Eliza Szczechla, Taewoon Kim, Gunjan Chhablani, Nihal V. Nayak, Debajyoti Datta, Jonathan Chang, Mike Tian-Jian Jiang, Han Wang, Matteo Manica, Sheng Shen, Zheng Xin Yong, Harshit Pandey, Rachel Bawden, Thomas Wang, Trishala Neeraj, Jos Rozen, Abheesht Sharma, Andrea Santilli, Thibault Févry, Jason Alan Fries, Ryan Teehan, Teven Le Scao, Stella Biderman, Leo Gao, Thomas Wolf, and Alexander M. Rush. 2022. Multitask prompted training enables zero-shot task generalization. In *The Tenth International Conference on Learning Representations, ICLR 2022, Virtual Event, April 25-29, 2022*. OpenReview.net.

Hugo Touvron, Thibaut Lavril, Gautier Izacard, Xavier Martinet, Marie-Anne Lachaux, Timothée Lacroix, Baptiste Rozière, Naman Goyal, Eric Hambro, Faisal Azhar, et al. 2023. Llama: Open and efficient foundation language models. *arXiv preprint arXiv:2302.13971*.

Jason Wei, Maarten Bosma, Vincent Y. Zhao, Kelvin Guu, Adams Wei Yu, Brian Lester, Nan Du, Andrew M. Dai, and Quoc V. Le. 2022. Finetuned language models are zero-shot learners. In *The Tenth International Conference on Learning Representations, ICLR 2022, Virtual Event, April 25-29, 2022*. OpenReview.net.

Ming Zhong, Yang Liu, Da Yin, Yuning Mao, Yizhu Jiao, Pengfei Liu, Chenguang Zhu, Heng Ji, and Jiawei Han. 2022. Towards a unified multi-dimensional evaluator for text generation. In *Proceedings of the 2022 Conference on Empirical Methods in Natural Language Processing*, pages 2023–2038, Abu Dhabi, United Arab Emirates. Association for Computational Linguistics.

Chen Zhu, Ankit Singh Rawat, Manzil Zaheer, Srinadh Bhojanapalli, Daliang Li, Felix Yu, and Sanjiv Kumar. 2020. Modifying memories in transformer models. *arXiv preprint arXiv:2012.00363*.

A Computation Infrastructure and Additional Training Details

We use Google TPU v3-8 for all the training sponsored by the Google TPU Researc Cloud program.

Batching for Self Information Updating In order to improve the training efficiency of training on TPU v3-8, we don't use the conventional batchification of the training data based on instances. Instead, we concatenate all the tokenized instruction-response pairs into a single list of tokens, and chunk the list into segments of batch_size $\times$ sequence_length. We run training on 3 random seeds and report average performances. We derive our training codebase from EasyLM[4]. We will release our code and data after publication.

Evaluation For evaluation, the responses are generated with a temperature of 0.2 for all the methods, which is picked from $\{0.1, 0.2, 0.5, 1.0\}$ based on the base model performance . We modify the code from UniEval github repository[5] with torch-xla[6] to support running on TPUs. We evaluate our proposed approach on the generated tokens after "The response to {question} is:".

Usage of GPT-4 We use snapshot of gpt-4-0314 for all prompting with GPT-4.

B Extension to Non-Independent New and Past Information

Definition B.1 (Information in Text Corpus). The information $\mathcal{I}_\mathcal{S}(\mathcal{T})$ of the corpus $\mathcal{T}$ with respect to another text corpus$\mathcal{S}$ is defined as the minimal sufficient statistic of $\mathcal{T}^e$ with respect to $\mathcal{S}^e$, such that

$$P(x|\mathcal{T}^e) \equiv P(x|\mathcal{I}_\mathcal{S}(\mathcal{T})), x \in \mathcal{S}. \tag{6}$$

Remark. Intuitively, $\mathcal{I}_\mathcal{S}(\texttt{T})$ should consist of minimal text pieces containing new information from $\mathcal{T}$ such as "Manchester City's manager is Pep Guardiola".

We can assume without the loss of generality that $\mathcal{I}_\mathcal{S}(\texttt{T})$ and $\mathcal{I}_\mathcal{S}(\texttt{C})$ are independent. Otherwise we can replace $\mathcal{I}_\mathcal{S}(\texttt{T})$ with the conditional minimal sufficient statistic of $\mathcal{I}_\mathcal{S}(\texttt{T})$ given $\mathcal{I}_\mathcal{S}(\texttt{C})$, which is

[4]https://github.com/young-geng/EasyLM

[5]https://github.com/maszhongming/UniEval

[6]https://github.com/pytorch/xla

intuitively equivalent to removing the text pieces consisting of existing information in C from T. Therefore, we can do the same analysis on $\mathcal{I}_S(\texttt{T})$ and $\mathcal{I}_S(\texttt{C})$ instead of $\mathcal{T}$ and $\mathcal{C}$ for non-independent cases.

C Exposure Bias for Fact Fine-tuning

Fact fine-tuning optimizes

$$P(\mathcal{T}|\mathcal{A}') = \sum_{x \in \mathcal{X}} P(\mathcal{T}|x^e, \mathcal{A}')P(x^e|\mathcal{A}'). \quad (7)$$

A similar information-query association term $P(\mathcal{T}|x^e, \mathcal{A}')$ reveals how fact fine-tuning affects probabilities of other information $P(x^e|\mathcal{A}')$. Exposure bias undermines the quality of learned $P(\mathcal{T}|x^e, \mathcal{A}')$ and degrades the updating performance.

D Case Study

We provide an example case demonstrating where naive distillation fails but our associative distillation approach successfully learns the information in Table. We omit some part of the text in both news article and model response for conciseness. We observe that the naïve distillation approach generates hallucinated information. The omitted part mentions bank attacks in Kentucky and Georgia, while this incident happens in Louisville. This suggest the baseline model utilizes existing information to generate the response.

E Preparation Details of Natural Questions

Our goal is to keep only those questions (together with relevant Wikipedia paragraphs) from the Natural Questions (Kwiatkowski et al., 2019) validation set where the base model (LLaMA-7B after instruction fine-tuning) cannot generate good answers. The overall filtering process is:

Step 1. We first remove questions with "None" answers in the Natural Questions validation set.

Step 2. We use the base model and the Alpaca template as in Appendix A to generate the answers to the rest questions in the Natural Questions validation set.

Step 3. We compute the factual consistency score (ranging from 0 to 1) from UniEval (Zhong et al., 2022) between the generated answer and gold standard short answers. When there are multiple short answers, we use the maximum consistency score. Those questions whose scores are lower than 0.5 are kept.

Step 4. We collect all the Wikipedia paragraphs that are labeled as the long answer of any kept questions in Step 2 as the information updating corpus.

F A Comprehensive List of Prompts Used in the Experiment

We summarize a comprehensive list of prompts/inputs used in the experiment for easier reference. Some of these prompts are already covered in the main text.

Instruction Finetuning We train the instruction-following model following the template of Alpaca [7]. Each instruction-response pair is prepared as the following paragraph to fine-tune the model.

> Below is an instruction that describes a task. Write a response that appropriately completes the request.
>
> ### Instruction:
> {instruction}
>
> ### Response:
> {response}

The losses are only computed for the tokens in responses. This template is also used for the instruction-response pairs in the information update training.

Self Instruction Generation This prompt is given to the language model to be updated for self data creation. This prompt instructs the model to generate instructions from the information updating corpus.

> Given the input below, generate at least 5 questions that are directly related to the content of the input. Ensure that each question you generate does not contain coreferential words or pronouns (e.g., he, she, it, this, they, etc.). The questions should be clear, concise, and pertain specifically to details mentioned in the input. {Context}

The {Context} slot is filled with each individual news article from the information update corpus.

[7] `https://github.com/tatsu-lab/stanford_alpaca`

Table 5: An examples case where baseline fails but associative distillation succeeds.

<table>
<tr><td colspan="2">Fact in News Article: Louisville Metro Police Department Officer Nickolas Wilt is in critical condition after undergoing brain surgery following a shootout in a bank ... Mayor Craig Greenberg visited Wilt in the hospital, saying that he had made it through surgery and was in serious condition but in great hands...
Instruction: What is the current state of Officer Wilt and what kind of recovery does he face?</td></tr>
<tr><td>Naïve</td><td>Associative</td></tr>
<tr><td>Response:Nickolas Wilt is facing a long road to recovery after undergoing surgery to remove his right arm which was injured in the attack. He is currently in serious condition in the hospital...</td><td>Response: Nickolas Wilt is in serious condition after undergoing brain surgery following a shootout in a bank. He faces a long road to recovery and is currently sedated...</td></tr>
</table>

Self Answer Generation This prompt is given to the language model to be updated for self data creation. This prompt instructs the model to generate responses for the instructions in the previous step from the information updatingcorpus.

> Answer the question based on the facts from the input. If there is no relevant information in the input, answer 'None'. Question: {Instruction} {Context}

The {Context} slot is filled with each individual news article from the information update corpus. The {Instruction} is from the outputs of last step. To ensure the generated instruction-response pairs pertain to the corpus, we remove those pairs when the response is None.

Fact Finetuning Training Data This is the inputs to train the Fact Fine-tuning baseline in the main text. It is just the news articles.

> {News Article}

Naïve Distillation This is the inputs to the train the Naïve Distillation Baseline. Only losses on the tokens after "Response" is used for training.

> Below is an instruction that describes a task. Write a response that appropriately completes the request.
>
> ### Instruction:
> {Instruction}
>
> ### Response:
> {Response}

Here the {Instruction} and {Response} are paired outputs from Self Instruction Generation and Self Answer Generation.

Associative Distillation This is the inputs to the train the Naïve Distillation Baseline. Only losses on the tokens after "Response" is used for training.

> Below is an instruction that describes a task. Write a response that appropriately completes the request.
>
> ### Instruction:
> {Instruction}
>
> ### Response:
> The instruction is related to the following information: {News Article}. The response to {Instruction} is: {Response}

Here the {Instruction} and {Response} are paired outputs from Self Instruction Generation and Self Answer Generation. {News Article} is the corresponding news article from the information update corpus. Note that for unrelated instructions, the {News Article} is filled with "None". We repeat the instruction one more time to compensate for the limited sequence length and reduce the possibility of instructions being truncated. We think it may not be necessary to repeat the instruction if the computational resources supports sufficiently long training sequences. Only losses on the tokens after "Response" is used for training.

Evaluation Data Generation We generate *CNN News* evaluation data using GPT-4. This prompt is given to GPT-4 to generate instruction-response pairs.

> Generate some questions[8] with answers

[8]In this work, we focus on instruction-response pairs in a question-answering format

related to facts from the following paragraph. Make sure each question is self-contained and specific enough for readers to associate it with the information provided in the paragraph, rather than confusing it with other similar events. Avoid using words such as "these", "this", or "the event", "the movie" referring to concepts not mentioned in the question. Please generate in the format of "1. Question: ... Answer: ..." {News Article}.

Because we strictly required the format of the generation in the last sentence, it is easy to parse the output pairs.

Paraphrasing Evaluation QAs on Past Information We generate evaluation QAs on past information by paraphrasing the instruction-response pairs in the instruction fine-tuning data. We use GPT-4 to generate the paraphrases.

> Given the following instruction and response pair, rewrite the pair to query the same information in different words.
>
> Instruction: instruction
>
> Response: response

G Post-processing of Self-Generated Questions/Answers

We parse the questions by matching any content following "Question (+):" or "Q(+):". For self answer generation, we simply take the entire generation as answers. However, we empirically observe that language models may occasionally output random meaningless chunks of characters. We filter out such cases by removing answers containing "words" with lengths larger than 30.

H Use of AI Assistant in Writing

Chat-GPT is used as a grammar-checker in the writing of this paper.

Causal ATE Mitigates Unintended Bias in Controlled Text Generation

Rahul Madhavan
IISc, Bangalore
mrahul@iisc.ac.in

Kahini Wadhawan
IBM Research, Delhi
kahini.wadhawan1@ibm.com

Abstract

We study attribute control in language models through the method of Causal Average Treatment Effect (Causal ATE). Existing methods for the attribute control task in Language Models (LMs) check for the co-occurrence of words in a sentence with the attribute of interest, and control for them. However, spurious correlation of the words with the attribute in the training dataset, can cause models to hallucinate the presence of the attribute when presented with the spurious correlate during inference. We show that the simple perturbation-based method of Causal ATE removes this unintended effect. Specifically, we ground it in the problem of toxicity mitigation, where a significant challenge lies in the inadvertent bias that often emerges towards protected groups post detoxification. We show that this unintended bias can be solved by the use of the Causal ATE metric. We provide experimental validations for our claims and release our code (anonymously) here: github.com/causalate-mitigates-bias/causal-ate-mitigates-bias.

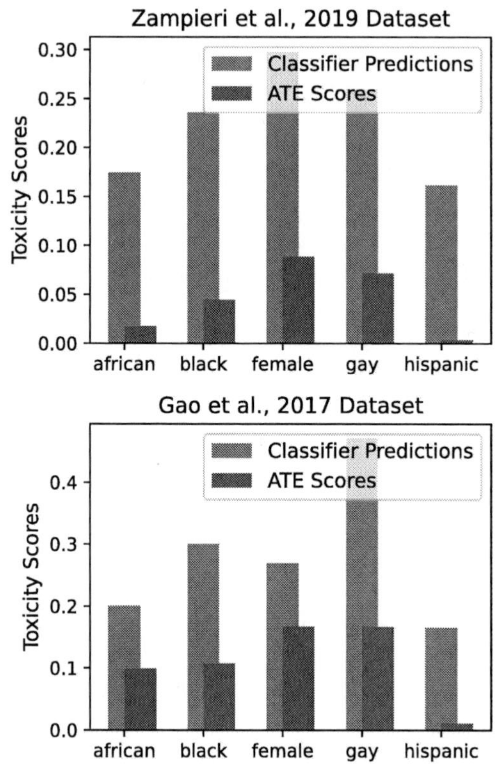

Figure 1: We plot the ATE score vs a regression based classifier for toxicity across two datasets. ATE Scores show a lower toxicity for protected groups.

1 Introduction

Controllable text generation methods are often used to guide the text generated by language models (LMs) towards certain desirable attributes (Hu and Li, 2021; Dathathri et al., 2019; Liu et al., 2021). The goal herein is to generate sentences whose attributes can be controlled (Prabhumoye et al., 2020). Language models, which are pre-trained only for next word prediction, cannot directly control for attributes in their outputs. On the other hand, one may wish to alter words in the auto-regressively produced sentences, either accentuating or mitigating the desired attributes. Attributes such as sentiment, writing style, language precision, tone, and toxicity are key concerns for control in language models, with particular emphasis on toxicity mitigation due to its relevance in sensitive contexts (Perez et al., 2020).

Regularizers in the reward models are often employed during training to alter the output sentences towards certain desirable attributes (Hu et al., 2017). Such regularization penalities (or rewards) often rely on models trained on real-world datasets. Such datasets contain spurious correlates – words that correlate with certain attributes without necessarily causing them (Nam et al., 2020; Udomcharoenchaikit et al., 2022).

In the context of toxicity mitigation, prior works show that detoxification methods inadvertently impact language model outputs concerning marginal-

Proceedings of the 28th Conference on Computational Natural Language Learning, pages 130–142
November 15-16, 2024

ized groups (Welbl et al., 2021). Words such as 'gay' or 'female' are identified as being toxic, as they co-occur with toxic text, and hence the LM stops speaking about them (Xu et al., 2021).

This is called the *unintended bias problem.* In this paper we provide experimental and theoretical justifications for the use of causal ATE to mitigate the unintended bias problem in text classification. We prove theoretically that for spurious correlates, the causal ATE score is upper-bounded. We also show through extensive experiments on two popular toxicity classification datasets (Zampieri et al., 2019a; Gao and Huang, 2017) that our method shows experimental promise (See Figure 1).

We provide a full list of related works in Related Works section 6.

1.1 Our Contributions:

1. We show theoretically that the Causal ATE score of spurious correlates is less than 0.25 under mild assumptions in Sections 2 and 3.

2. We provide a theoretical basis for the study of the perturbation based Causal ATE method. We show that it can be used alongside any classifier towards improving it for false positive rates.

3. We provide experimental validation for our claims by showing that causal ATE scores indeed decrease the toxicity for spurious correlates to toxic sentences in Section 4.

2 Notations and Methodology

Consider a sentence s, made up of tokens (words) from some universe of words W. Let the list of all sentences s in our dataset be denoted $\mathcal{S}$. Let each sentence $s \in \mathcal{S}$ be labelled with the presence or absence of an attribute A. So the dataset, which we can call $\mathcal{D}$, consists of tuples $(s, A(s))$ for all $s \in \mathcal{S}$. Let the cardinality of the labelled dataset be $|\mathcal{D}| = |\mathcal{S}| = n$.

From such a dataset, it is possible to construct an attribute model that gives us an estimate of the probability of attribute A, given a sentence s. i.e. It is possible to construct a model $\widehat{A}(\cdot)$ such that $\widehat{A}(s) = \widehat{\mathbb{P}}\{A \mid s\}$ for any given sentence s. Now such a model may rely on the words in s. Let $s = \{w_1, \dots, w_n\}$. We now define an attribute model $\widehat{a}(\cdot)$ given a word as follows:

Definition 1 (Attribute model $\widehat{a}(w_i)$ for any word $w_i \in W$).

$$\widehat{a}(w_i) := \frac{|\{\text{sentences } s \in \mathcal{D} \text{ containing } w_i \text{ s.t. } A(s) = 1\}|}{|\{\text{sentences } s \in \mathcal{D} \text{ containing } w_i\}|} \quad (1)$$

$$= \frac{n(A(s) = 1 \mid w_i \in s)}{n(s \mid w_i \in s)} \quad (2)$$

where $n(\cdot)$ denotes the cardinality of the set satisfying the properties.

Note that such a model is purely correlation based, and can be seen as the proportion of sentences containing an attribute amongst those containing a particular word. i.e. it is an estimate of the co-occurrence of attribute with the word. Based on attribute model $\widehat{a}(\cdot)$ we can define an attribute model $\widehat{A}(\cdot)$ for any sentence $s = \{w_1, \dots, w_k\}$ as follows:

Definition 2 (Attribute model $\widehat{A}(s)$ for a sentence $s \in W^k$).

$$\widehat{A}(s = \{w_1, \dots, w_k\}) := \max_{w_i \in s} \widehat{a}(w_i) \quad (3)$$

$$= \max\{\widehat{a}(w_1), \dots, \widehat{a}(w_k)\} \quad (4)$$

Note that such a model is conservative and labels a sentence as having an attribute when any word in the sentence has the attribute. For the purpose of attributes such as toxicity, such an attribute model is quite suitable.

2.1 Computation of ATE Score of a word with respect to an attribute

Given a model representing the estimate of the attribute A in a sentence s, denoted as $\widehat{\mathbb{P}}\{A(s) = 1\}$, we can now define the ATE score. Note that the Causal ATE score does not depend on the particular model for the estimate $\widehat{\mathbb{P}}\{A(s) = 1\}$ – i.e. we can use any estimator model.

If we denote $f_A(s)$ as the estimate of $\mathbb{P}\{A(s) = 1\}$ obtained from *some* model. We can then define Causal ATE with respect to this estimate. If a sentence s is made up of words $\{w_1, \dots, w_i, \dots, w_k\}$. For brevity, given a word w_i, from a sentence s, we may refer to the rest of the words in the sentence as context c_i. Consider a *counter-factual* sentence s' where (only) the ith word is changed: $\{w_1, \dots, w_i', \dots, w_k\}$. Such a word w_i' may be the most probable token to replace w_i, given the rest of the sentence.

We now define a certain value that may be called the Treatment Effect (TE), which computes the effect of replacement of w_i with w_i' in sentence s, on the attribute probability.

Definition 3 (Treatment Effect (TE) of a word in a sentence given replacement word)**.** Let word w_i be replaced by word w_i' in a sentence s. Then:

$$\begin{aligned}\mathsf{TE}(s, w_i, w_i') &= f_A(s) - f_A(s') \\ &= f_A(\{w_1, \ldots, w_i, \ldots, w_k\}) \\ &\quad - f_A(\{w_1, \ldots, w_i', \ldots, w_k\}) \end{aligned} \quad (5)$$

The expectation now can be taken over the replacement words, given the context, and over all contexts where the words appear.

Definition 4 (ATE of word w_i given dataset $\mathcal{D}$ and an attribute classifier $f(\cdot)$)**.**

$$\mathsf{ATE}(w_i) = \mathop{\mathbb{E}}_{s \in \mathcal{D} | w_i \in s} \left[f(s) - \mathop{\mathbb{E}}_{w_i' \in W} [f(s')] \right] \quad (6)$$

where s' is the sentence s where word w_i is replaced by w_i'

This ATE score precisely indicates the intervention effect of w_i on the attribute probability of a sentence. Notice that this score roughly corresponds to the *expected difference in attribute on replacement* of word.

Now say we compute the ATE scores for every token w in our universe W in the manner given by Equation 6. We can store all these scores in a large lookup-table. Now, we are in a position to compute an attribute score given a sentence.

2.2 Computation of Attribute Score for a sentence

The causal ATE approach suggests that we can build towards the ATE of a sentence given the ATE scores of each of the words in the sentence recursively. We illustrate this approach in Figure 2. First, note that each word w_t is stochastically generated based on words $w_1, \ldots, w_{t-1}$ in an auto-regressive manner. If we denote $\{w_1, \ldots, w_{t-1}\}$ as s_{t-1}, then we can say the distribution for w_t, is generated from s_{t-1} and the structure of the language. To sample from the probabilistic distribution, we may use an exogenous variable such as U_t.

The attribute $A(s_{t-1})$ of a sentence up to $t-1$ tokens, depends only on $\{w_1, \ldots, w_{t-1}\} \equiv s_{t-1}$. We now describe a model for computing attribute $A(s_t)$ from $A(s_{t-1})$ and $\mathsf{ATE}(w_t)$. The larger English causal graph moderates influence of w_t on $A(s_t)$ through the ATE score of the words. We consider $A(s_t) = \max(A(s_{t-1}), \mathsf{ATE}(w_t))$. This is equivalent to

$$A_\infty(s = \{w_1, \ldots, w_n\}) = \max_{i \in [n]} \mathsf{ATE}(w_i) \quad (7)$$

More generally, we propose an attribute score $A(s)$ for this sentence given by $A(s) = \|\{\mathsf{ATE}(w_1), \ldots, \mathsf{ATE}(w_n)\}\|_p$ where $\|\cdot\|_p$ indicates the L_p-norm of a vector. We can call these attribute scores $A(s)$ as the ATE scores of a sentence.

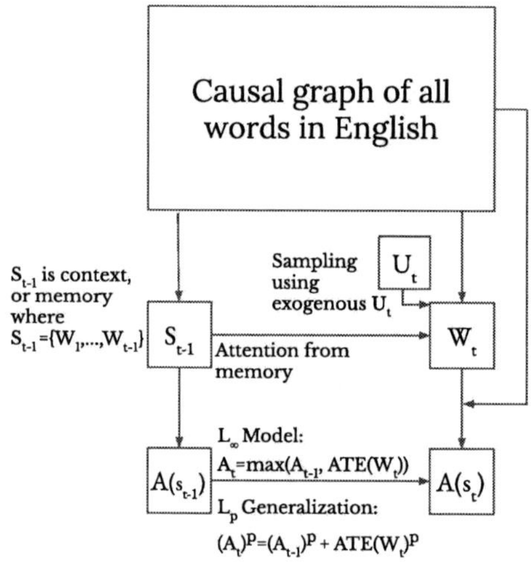

Figure 2: An Illustration of the Causal Graph used to compute the attribute score of a sentence recursively.

3 Theory and Background

Now that we have laid the groundwork, we can make proceed to make the central claims of this work.

Lemma 1. Consider sentence $s = \{w_1, \ldots, w_k\}$. We will make two simple claims:

1. If $\nexists w_i \in s$ such that $\mathsf{ATE}(w_i) \geq c$, then, $A(s) < c$.

2. If $\exists w_i \in s$ such that $\mathsf{ATE}(w_i) \geq c$, then, $A(s) \geq c$.

This lemma is straightforward to prove from Definition 7.

We will now make a claim regarding the ATE score of the given words themselves. Recall that c_i is the context for the word w_i from a sentence s. Given c_i, w_i is replaced by w_i' by a perturbation model (through Masked Language Modelling).
Towards our proof, we will make two assumptions:

Table 1: Description of Classifiers Used in Experiments

Sl. No.	Model	Description
1	Logistic Regression (LR)	A linear classifier that predicts toxicity using logistic regression.
2	SVM	Support Vector Machine with a linear kernel for text classification.
3	Gradient Boosting (GB)	An ensemble model that combines weak learners for enhanced toxicity prediction.
4	Naive Bayes (NB)	Multinomial Naive Bayes, a probabilistic model for text classification.
5	NN1Layer5	Neural network with 1 hidden layer of 5 neurons.
6	NN2Layer105	Neural network with 2 hidden layers (10 neurons and 5 neurons, respectively).
7	NN3Layer20105	Neural network with 3 hidden layers (20, 10, and 5 neurons, respectively).

Assumption 1. We make a mild assumption on this replacement process: $\widehat{a}(w_i') < \widehat{A}(c_i)$. Grounding this in the attribute of toxicity, we can say that the replacement word is less toxic than the context. This is probable if the replacement model has been trained on a large enough corpus. See (Madhavan et al., 2023) for empirical results showing this claim to be true in practice.

Assumption 2. We make an assumption on the dataset. A *spurious correlate* has a word with a higher attribute score in the rest of the sentence for sentences labelled as having the attribute. For example, in the case of toxicity, a spurious correlate like Muslim, has a more toxic word in the rest of the sentence, when the sentence is labelled as toxic.

Given these assumptions, we have the following theorem:

Theorem 1. Given Assumptions 1 and 2 for a spurious correlate w_i, $\texttt{ATE}(w_i) \leq 0.25$.

Proof. If we consider three numbers $\{\widehat{A}(c_i), \widehat{a}(w_i), \widehat{a}(w_i')\}$, there are six possible orderings of this set. We can subsume these orderings into two cases:

1. $\widehat{A}(c_i) < \widehat{a}(w_i')$.
2. $\widehat{A}(c_i) \geq \widehat{a}(w_i')$.

Within these cases, we study the variation of $ATE(w_i)$ with $\widehat{a}(w_i)$. We plot these in the Figure 3. Using a case-by-case analysis over these possibilities, we prove the statement.

The full proof of the Theorem is provided in Appendix A.

□

Based on Theorem A and Lemma 1, $A(s) \leq 0.25$ if each $w_i \in s$ is a spurious correlate, i.e. non-causal, for attribute A.

In the following section we provide experimental justification for our work through experimental results.

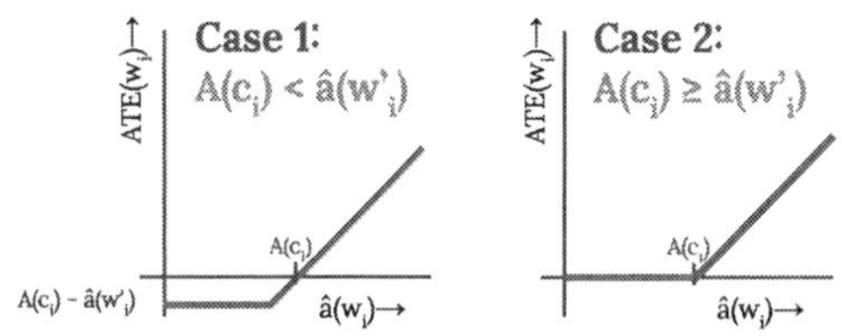

Figure 3: Graph of ATE score of a given word w_i with $\widehat{a}(w_i)$ given two cases

4 Experiments

In this section, we present experimental evidence demonstrating the efficacy of the Causal Average Treatment Effect (Causal ATE) method for mitigating unintended bias in text classification tasks. Our experiments focus on toxicity detection, utilizing two widely recognized datasets. The results provide both theoretical and practical support for the utility of Causal ATE in addressing bias associated with protected groups.

4.1 Datasets and Preprocessing

We conducted experiments using two well-known datasets: the SemEval dataset (Zampieri et al., 2019a) and the dataset from Gao et al. (Gao and Huang, 2017). The SemEval dataset consists of tweets annotated for offensive language, while the Gao et al. dataset comprises user comments from Yahoo! News articles labeled for hate speech and harassment. These datasets were chosen for their diverse and challenging nature, providing an ideal testbed for evaluating bias mitigation in toxicity classification tasks.

The data was preprocessed to clean the text by removing special characters, URLs, and stop words. We used the `CountVectorizer` from the `scikit-learn` library to convert the textual data into a Bag-of-Words representation, ensuring a structured and uniform input for the classifiers.

Table 2: ATE Scores vs Classifier Predictions for different models by Protected Category for the Gao et al. Dataset

Group →	**African**			**Black**			**Female**			**Gay**		
Model ↓	Pred	ATE	Diff	Pred	ATE	Diff	Pred	ATE	Diff	Pred	ATE	Diff
LR	0.201	0.099	0.102	0.300	0.108	0.192	0.270	0.167	0.103	0.470	0.167	0.303
SVM	0.282	0.062	0.220	0.282	0.052	0.230	0.301	0.082	0.219	0.371	0.154	0.217
GB	0.225	0.052	0.173	0.335	0.071	0.264	0.225	0.000	0.225	0.653	0.204	0.449
NB	0.460	0.002	0.458	0.510	0.047	0.463	0.444	0.004	0.440	0.657	0.107	0.550
NN1Layer5	0.000	0.003	-0.003	0.000	0.059	-0.059	0.000	0.024	-0.024	1.000	0.197	0.803
NN2Layer105	0.000	0.000	0.000	0.000	0.096	-0.096	0.002	0.000	0.002	1.000	0.217	0.783
NN3Layer20105	0.000	0.160	-0.160	0.000	0.097	-0.097	0.000	0.000	0.000	0.993	0.165	0.828

Table 3: ATE Scores vs Classifier Predictions for different models by Protected Category for the Zampieri et al. Dataset

Group →	African			Black			Female			Gay		
Model ↓	Pred	ATE	Diff	Pred	ATE	Diff	Pred	ATE	Diff	Pred	ATE	Diff
LR	0.174	0.020	0.154	0.236	0.049	0.187	0.297	0.075	0.223	0.260	0.098	0.162
SVM	0.248	0.030	0.218	0.267	0.036	0.232	0.337	0.068	0.269	0.265	0.033	0.232
GB	0.269	0.020	0.249	0.269	0.013	0.256	0.269	0.008	0.261	0.269	0.003	0.266
NB	0.349	0.009	0.341	0.453	0.055	0.398	0.343	0.183	0.160	0.539	0.070	0.469
NN1Layer5	0.000	0.000	-0.000	0.000	0.052	-0.052	0.000	0.000	-0.000	0.000	0.114	-0.114
NN2Layer105	0.000	0.000	0.000	0.000	0.090	-0.090	0.000	0.170	-0.170	0.000	0.104	-0.104
NN3Layer20105	0.000	0.200	-0.200	0.000	0.126	-0.126	0.000	0.075	-0.075	0.000	0.046	-0.046

This vectorized representation was then used as input for the various models described in the next section.

4.2 Classifiers

We trained several classifiers to predict toxicity in sentences. These classifiers span traditional machine learning models and modern neural networks, allowing us to evaluate bias mitigation across a range of approaches. Table 1 provides a summary of the classifiers used in our experiments.

These models were implemented using the `scikit-learn` library. For the neural networks, we used the `MLPClassifier` with the `lbfgs` solver and a maximum of 10,000 iterations to ensure convergence during training.

4.3 Computation of ATE Scores

For each classifier, we computed the Causal ATE scores for a set of bias-inducing words related to protected groups, including "female", "black", "gay", "hispanic", and "african". These scores were calculated using a perturbation-based approach, where we replaced specific words in a sentence with alternatives generated by a masked language model (`roberta-base`). The ATE score measures the expected change in toxicity prediction when a particular word is replaced, providing insight into the causal effect of each word on the classifier's output.

This process enabled us to quantify the impact of potentially bias-inducing terms, allowing for a more nuanced understanding of how certain words contribute to biased predictions. By analyzing these ATE scores, we could identify instances where the classifier was overly reliant on spurious correlations, thus flagging cases of unintended bias.

4.4 Implementation and Runtime Considerations

The implementation of the experiments was carried out using `scikit-learn` for classifier training and the `transformers` library for masked token replacements using `roberta-base`. To ensure reproducibility, all experiments were conducted with a fixed random seed. The runtime for the entire experiment, when the preprocessed data files were available, was approximately 40 minutes on a single CPU thread. The most computationally expensive tasks included training the classifiers and generating the masked replacements for the ATE computations.

The code for our experiments, including data preprocessing, model training, and ATE computations, is available in our anonymous GitHub repository: github.com/causalate-mitigates-bias/causal-ate-mitigates-bias.

4.5 Discussion

From the results, we observe the following:
1. Reduction in Predicted Toxicity: The ATE scores are consistently lower than the original predicted probabilities for most classifiers and protected categories. This indicates that the Causal ATE method effectively reduces the unintended bias towards these groups.
2. Classifier Performance Variance: Naive Bayes (NB) shows the highest predicted probabilities and substantial differences (**Diff**) across all categories, suggesting a strong sensitivity to spurious correlations. In contrast, Neural Network models often exhibit lower predicted probabilities but sometimes result in negative **Diff** values, indicating overcorrection or model underfitting.
3. Impact on Protected Categories: Categories like *"Gay"* and *"Black"* show significant reductions in toxicity scores after applying the Causal ATE method. This aligns with our objective of mitigating bias towards marginalized groups.
4. Consistency Across Datasets: Similar trends are observed in both datasets, reinforcing the robustness of the Causal ATE approach in different contexts.

4.6 Conclusion of Experiments

The experimental results validate our theoretical claims that the Causal ATE method is an effective approach to mitigate unintended bias in toxicity classification tasks. By focusing on the causal impact of words rather than their spurious correlations, the method significantly reduces bias toward protected groups. Our experiments demonstrate that this approach is robust across different classifiers and datasets, offering a promising solution to bias mitigation in language models.

5 Discussion

5.1 Causal ATE is Generalizable

While we our experimental results have pertained to the use of Causal ATE as a metric for mitigating bias in toxicity classification, our theoretical results extend to any language attributes.

Figure 4 showcases different style attributes to which such an analysis can be applied. We hope that such causal approaches can be utilized for general use cases such as style control using LLMs.

While the main sections in the paper consider the attribute class of toxicity, we illustrate here that this method can equally be used for various attribute classes thereby easily scalable and generalizable. For instance, in the case of a style like formality, changing 'boss' to 'manager' has changes the sentence attribute to being more formal. Similarly, a change from the word 'terrific' or 'great' to 'terrible' in the context of a movie review, changes the entire meaning of a sentence, and effectively conveys a more negative sentiment.

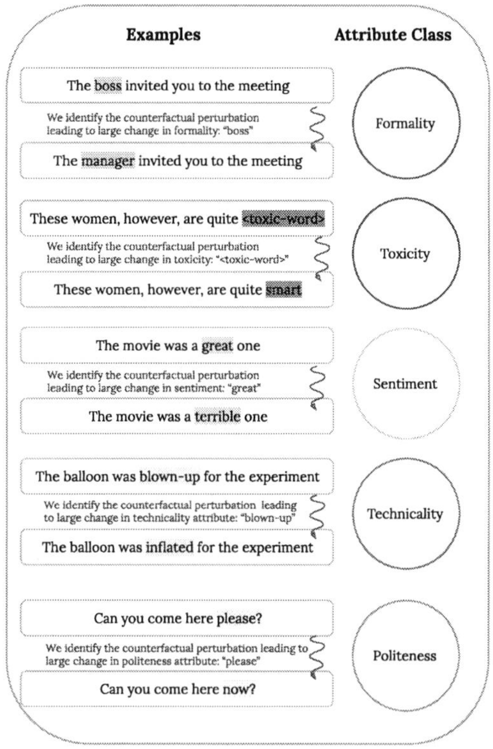

Figure 4: Illustration of word perturbation for identifying important words with respect to an attribute.

Similarly, simple word changes can lead to the language being more technical or polite. Figure 4 illustrates that causal ATE can be used across various attributes for bias mitigation. The underlying idea is that we can perturb particular words in their context to check the change that they cause on the desired attribute.

5.2 Importance of using a Causal Graph

Given estimates of the probability $\mathbb{P}\{a_i \mid s\}$ for attributes in text generated by a Language Model (LM), the potential for fine-tuning the LM towards specific attributes becomes apparent. However, numerous challenges persist.
Firstly, attribute classifiers are prone to spurious correlations. For instance, if a protected token like

'Muslim' frequently appears in toxic sentences, the attribute classifier detecting toxicity might penalize the generation of the word 'Muslim'. This brings out in light that there is a trade-off between detoxification of LM and LM quality for text generation clearly detailed out in (Welbl et al., 2021). LM avoids to generate sentences containing protected tokens leading to higher perplexity for texts with these protected attrbiutes. Additionally, these classifier models providing $\mathbb{P}\, a_i \mid s$ estimates themselves may be LMs, resulting in slow training and requiring substantial computational resources.

Utilizing a causal graph directly addresses these challenges. It offer computational efficiency during training and are immune to spurious correlations, detecting interventional attribute distributions rather than conditional distributions through counterfactual interventions. Moreover, we get both flexibility and transparency regarding their exact form, features unavailable with LM classifiers.

6 Related Works

In this section we will look at five related lines of work: (a) Controlled generation (b) Unintended Bias problem (c) Toxicity Mitigation (d) Toxicity Detection (e) Causal Methods for Text

Controlled Generation can be broadly categorized into fine-tuning methods (Krause et al., 2020), data-based (Keskar et al., 2019; Gururangan et al., 2020), decoding-time approaches using attribute classifiers (Dathathri et al., 2019; Krause et al., 2020) and causality based approaches (Madhavan et al., 2023). Majority of these techniques were tested on toxicity mitigation and sentiment control. The dependence of attribute regularizers on probabilistic classifiers make them prone to such spurious correlations (Kaddour et al., 2022; Feder et al., 2022).

In the **Unintended Bias problem** LMs which are detoxified inherit a tendency to be biased against protected groups. LM quality is compromised due to a detoxification side-effect (Welbl et al., 2021; Xu et al., 2021). Some works address LM control through improving datasets (Sap et al., 2019b). Unfortunately, this makes annotation and data curation more expensive. As an alternative, there is growing interest in training accurate models in presence of biased data (Oren et al., 2019). Our work fits into this framework.

In the context of **Toxicity Mitigation**, (Welbl et al., 2021) highlight that detoxification methods have unintended effects on marginalized groups. They showcased that detoxification makes LMs more brittle to distribution shift, affecting its robustness in certain parts of language that contain mentions of minority groups. Concretely, words such as "female" are identified as being toxic, as they co-occur with toxic text, and hence the LM stops speaking about them (Xu et al., 2021). This is called the unintended bias problem. This unintended bias problem can manifest as differences in performance of the LM for different demographic groups.

Toxicity Detection Toxicity is a well studied problem in context of responsible and safe AI effort. Hence, we foucs our experiments on toxicty mitigation in this study. Several works have also studied the angle from toxic text detection. Numerous studies have explored toxic text detection, including HATEBERT (Caselli et al., 2020), HATECHECK (Röttger et al., 2020), and PERSPECTIVE API (Lees et al., 2022). We employ the HATEBERT model for assessing local hatefulness and utilize PERSPECTIVE API for third-party evaluation, where we report the corresponding metrics.

Causal Methods for Text Spurious correlations between protected groups and toxic text can be identified is by understanding the causal structure. (Feder et al., 2022) emphasizes on the connect between causality and NLP. Towards mitigation of the bias problem (Madhavan et al., 2023) proposed the use of Causal ATE as a regularization technique and showed experimentally that it does indeed perform as intended.

In this paper, we probe the Causal ATE metric theoretically, and prove that the Causal ATE metric is less susceptible to false positives. An attribute control method based on this metric would mitigate unintended bias. We provide a theoretical basis from which to understand the Causal ATE metric and showcase that this causal technique provides robustness across contexts for attribute control in language models.

7 Conclusion

In conclusion, our work provides a theoretical justification for using the causality-based concepts of counterfactuals, and ATE scores for controlled text generation. We provide experimental results that validate these claims. We show that the simple perturbation-based method of Causal ATE removes the unintended bias effect through reduction of false positives, additionally making systems more robust to biased data.

8 Limitations

The limitations of our proposed framework are described in detail in this section.

1. Owing to Pre-trained models: Third-party hatespeech detectors such as HATEBERT tend to overestimate the prevalence of toxicity in texts having mentions of minority or protected groups due to sampling bias, or just spurious correlations (Paz et al., 2020; Waseem, 2016; Dhamala et al., 2021). ATE computation though following causal mechanisms rely on these detectors for initial attribute probability scores. Additionally, these models suffer from low annotator agreement during dataset annotation because of absence of concrete defining hatespeech taxonomy (Sap et al., 2019a). Causal nature of our approach tends to mitigates bias but not completely eliminated the problem.

2. Owing to language and training corpus: We showcase empirically the utility of our theoretical claims in this study and conducted monolingual experiments on English language which could be further extended to other languages. Additionally, training corpora used for training HATEBERT and MLM model are known to contain curated data from internet, where reliability and factual accuracy is a known issue (Gehman et al., 2020). Hence, we are limited by the distributions of our training corpora in terms of what the model can learn and infer.

3. Owing to distribution shift between datasets: There are limitations that get introduced due to change in vocabulary from training to test sets. Sometimes, words which occur in test set are not in ATE training set, we ignore such words but could impact downstream perfomance of LLM if word was important. In case of such a distribution shift between the datasets, our model may not work as expected.

9 Ethics Statement

Our paper addresses the crucial issue of bias and toxicity in language models by using causal methods that involve several ethical concerns, that we address herein:

1. Monolingual limitation : This work addresses the problem of mitigation of toxicity in Language models (LMs) for English language, even though there more than 7000 languages globally (Joshi et al., 2020) and future works should address more generalizable and multilingual solutions so that safety is promised for diverse set of speakers and not limited to English speakers (Weidinger et al., 2022)

2. No one fixed toxicity taxonomy: Literature survey highlights the fact that toxicity, hate and abuse and other related concepts are loosely defined and vary based on demographics and different social groups (Paz et al., 2020; Yin and Zubiaga, 2021). Henceforth, affecting the quality of hatespeech detection systems (HATEBERT) used in this work. These variations differences between cultural definitions of toxicity poses an ethical challenge (Jacobs and Wallach, 2021; Welbl et al., 2021).

3. Third party classifiers for toxicity detection: Reliance on the third party classifiers for toxicity detection can itself beat the purpose of fairness as these systems are reported to be biased towards certain protected groups and overestimate the prevelence of toxicity associated with them in the texts (Davidson et al., 2019; Abid et al., 2021; Hutchinson et al., 2020; Dixon et al., 2018; Sap et al., 2019a). For most part, we take care of these by using causal mechanisms but the ATE computation still involves using a toxicity classifier (HATEBERT) model.

10 Potential Risks

Any controlled generation method runs the runs the risk of being reverse-engineered, and this becomes even more crucial for detoxification techniques. In order to amplify their ideologies, extremists or terrorist groups could potentially subvert these models by prompting them to generate extremist, offensive and hateful content (McGuffie and Newhouse, 2020).

11 References

References

Abubakar Abid, Maheen Farooqi, and James Zou. 2021. Large language models associate muslims with violence. *Nature Machine Intelligence*, 3(6):461–463.

Tommaso Caselli, Valerio Basile, Jelena Mitrović, and Michael Granitzer. 2020. Hatebert: Retraining bert for abusive language detection in english. *arXiv preprint arXiv:2010.12472*.

Sumanth Dathathri, Andrea Madotto, Janice Lan, Jane Hung, Eric Frank, Piero Molino, Jason Yosinski, and Rosanne Liu. 2019. Plug and play language models: A simple approach to controlled text generation. *arXiv preprint arXiv:1912.02164*.

Thomas Davidson, Debasmita Bhattacharya, and Ingmar Weber. 2019. Racial bias in hate speech and abusive language detection datasets. *arXiv preprint arXiv:1905.12516*.

Jwala Dhamala, Tony Sun, Varun Kumar, Satyapriya Krishna, Yada Pruksachatkun, Kai-Wei Chang, and Rahul Gupta. 2021. Bold: Dataset and metrics for measuring biases in open-ended language generation. In *Proceedings of the 2021 ACM Conference on Fairness, Accountability, and Transparency*, pages 862–872.

Lucas Dixon, John Li, Jeffrey Sorensen, Nithum Thain, and Lucy Vasserman. 2018. Measuring and mitigating unintended bias in text classification. In *Proceedings of the 2018 AAAI/ACM Conference on AI, Ethics, and Society*, pages 67–73.

Amir Feder, Katherine A Keith, Emaad Manzoor, Reid Pryzant, Dhanya Sridhar, Zach Wood-Doughty, Jacob Eisenstein, Justin Grimmer, Roi Reichart, Margaret E Roberts, et al. 2022. Causal inference in natural language processing: Estimation, prediction, interpretation and beyond. *Transactions of the Association for Computational Linguistics*, 10:1138–1158.

Lei Gao and Ruihong Huang. 2017. Detecting online hate speech using context aware models. *arXiv preprint arXiv:1710.07395*.

Samuel Gehman, Suchin Gururangan, Maarten Sap, Yejin Choi, and Noah A Smith. 2020. Realtoxicityprompts: Evaluating neural toxic degeneration in language models. *arXiv preprint arXiv:2009.11462*.

Suchin Gururangan, Ana Marasović, Swabha Swayamdipta, Kyle Lo, Iz Beltagy, Doug Downey, and Noah A Smith. 2020. Don't stop pretraining: adapt language models to domains and tasks. *arXiv preprint arXiv:2004.10964*.

Zhiting Hu and Li Erran Li. 2021. A causal lens for controllable text generation. *Advances in Neural Information Processing Systems*, 34:24941–24955.

Zhiting Hu, Zichao Yang, Xiaodan Liang, Ruslan Salakhutdinov, and Eric P Xing. 2017. Toward controlled generation of text. In *International conference on machine learning*, pages 1587–1596. PMLR.

Ben Hutchinson, Vinodkumar Prabhakaran, Emily Denton, Kellie Webster, Yu Zhong, and Stephen Denuyl. 2020. Social biases in nlp models as barriers for persons with disabilities. *arXiv preprint arXiv:2005.00813*.

Abigail Z Jacobs and Hanna Wallach. 2021. Measurement and fairness. In *Proceedings of the 2021 ACM conference on fairness, accountability, and transparency*, pages 375–385.

Pratik Joshi, Sebastin Santy, Amar Budhiraja, Kalika Bali, and Monojit Choudhury. 2020. The state and fate of linguistic diversity and inclusion in the nlp world. *arXiv preprint arXiv:2004.09095*.

Jean Kaddour, Aengus Lynch, Qi Liu, Matt J Kusner, and Ricardo Silva. 2022. Causal machine learning: A survey and open problems. *arXiv preprint arXiv:2206.15475*.

Nitish Shirish Keskar, Bryan McCann, Lav R Varshney, Caiming Xiong, and Richard Socher. 2019. Ctrl: A conditional transformer language model for controllable generation. *arXiv preprint arXiv:1909.05858*.

Ben Krause, Akhilesh Deepak Gotmare, Bryan McCann, Nitish Shirish Keskar, Shafiq Joty, Richard Socher, and Nazneen Fatema Rajani. 2020. Gedi: Generative discriminator guided sequence generation. *arXiv preprint arXiv:2009.06367*.

Alyssa Lees, Vinh Q Tran, Yi Tay, Jeffrey Sorensen, Jai Gupta, Donald Metzler, and Lucy Vasserman. 2022. A new generation of perspective api: Efficient multilingual character-level transformers. *arXiv preprint arXiv:2202.11176*.

Alisa Liu, Maarten Sap, Ximing Lu, Swabha Swayamdipta, Chandra Bhagavatula, Noah A Smith, and Yejin Choi. 2021. Dexperts: Decoding-time controlled text generation with experts and anti-experts. *arXiv preprint arXiv:2105.03023*.

Rahul Madhavan, Rishabh Garg, Kahini Wadhawan, and Sameep Mehta. 2023. CFL: Causally fair language models through token-level attribute controlled generation. In *Findings of the Association for Computational Linguistics: ACL 2023*, pages 11344–11358, Toronto, Canada. Association for Computational Linguistics.

Kris McGuffie and Alex Newhouse. 2020. The radicalization risks of gpt-3 and advanced neural language models. *arXiv preprint arXiv:2009.06807*.

Junhyun Nam, Hyuntak Cha, Sungsoo Ahn, Jaeho Lee, and Jinwoo Shin. 2020. Learning from failure: Debiasing classifier from biased classifier. *Advances in Neural Information Processing Systems*, 33:20673–20684.

Yonatan Oren, Shiori Sagawa, Tatsunori B Hashimoto, and Percy Liang. 2019. Distributionally robust language modeling. *arXiv preprint arXiv:1909.02060*.

María Antonia Paz, Julio Montero-Díaz, and Alicia Moreno-Delgado. 2020. Hate speech: A systematized review. *Sage Open*, 10(4):2158244020973022.

Jose Quiroga Perez, Thanasis Daradoumis, and Joan Manuel Marques Puig. 2020. Rediscovering the use of chatbots in education: A systematic literature review. *Computer Applications in Engineering Education*, 28(6):1549–1565.

Shrimai Prabhumoye, Alan W Black, and Ruslan Salakhutdinov. 2020. Exploring controllable text generation techniques. *arXiv preprint arXiv:2005.01822*.

Paul Röttger, Bertram Vidgen, Dong Nguyen, Zeerak Waseem, Helen Margetts, and Janet B Pierrehumbert. 2020. Hatecheck: Functional tests for hate speech detection models. *arXiv preprint arXiv:2012.15606*.

Maarten Sap, Dallas Card, Saadia Gabriel, Yejin Choi, and A Noah Smith. 2019a. The risk of racial bias in hate speech detection. In *ACL*.

Maarten Sap, Saadia Gabriel, Lianhui Qin, Dan Jurafsky, Noah A Smith, and Yejin Choi. 2019b. Social bias frames: Reasoning about social and power implications of language. *arXiv preprint arXiv:1911.03891*.

Can Udomcharoenchaikit, Wuttikorn Ponwitayarat, Patomporn Payoungkhamdee, Kanruethai Masuk, Weerayut Buaphet, Ekapol Chuangsuwanich, and Sarana Nutanong. 2022. Mitigating spurious correlation in natural language understanding with counterfactual inference. In *Proceedings of the 2022 Conference on Empirical Methods in Natural Language Processing*, pages 11308–11321.

Zeerak Waseem. 2016. Are you a racist or am i seeing things? annotator influence on hate speech detection on twitter. In *Proceedings of the first workshop on NLP and computational social science*, pages 138–142.

Laura Weidinger, Jonathan Uesato, Maribeth Rauh, Conor Griffin, Po-Sen Huang, John Mellor, Amelia Glaese, Myra Cheng, Borja Balle, Atoosa Kasirzadeh, et al. 2022. Taxonomy of risks posed by language models. In *2022 ACM Conference on Fairness, Accountability, and Transparency*, pages 214–229.

Johannes Welbl, Amelia Glaese, Jonathan Uesato, Sumanth Dathathri, John Mellor, Lisa Anne Hendricks, Kirsty Anderson, Pushmeet Kohli, Ben Coppin, and Po-Sen Huang. 2021. Challenges in detoxifying language models. *arXiv preprint arXiv:2109.07445*.

Albert Xu, Eshaan Pathak, Eric Wallace, Suchin Gururangan, Maarten Sap, and Dan Klein. 2021. Detoxifying language models risks marginalizing minority voices. *arXiv preprint arXiv:2104.06390*.

Wenjie Yin and Arkaitz Zubiaga. 2021. Towards generalisable hate speech detection: a review on obstacles and solutions. *PeerJ Computer Science*, 7:e598.

Marcos Zampieri, Shervin Malmasi, Preslav Nakov, Sara Rosenthal, Noura Farra, and Ritesh Kumar. 2019a. SemEval-2019 task 6: Identifying and categorizing offensive language in social media (OffensEval). In *Proceedings of the 13th International Workshop on Semantic Evaluation*, pages 75–86, Minneapolis, Minnesota, USA. Association for Computational Linguistics.

Marcos Zampieri, Shervin Malmasi, Preslav Nakov, Sara Rosenthal, Noura Farra, and Ritesh Kumar. 2019b. Semeval-2019 task 6: Identifying and categorizing offensive language in social media (offenseval). *arXiv preprint arXiv:1903.08983*.

A Proof of Theorem 1

Theorem. Given Assumptions 1 and 2, for w_i which is a spurious correlate, $\mathsf{ATE}(w_i) \leq 0.25$.

Proof. If we consider three numbers $\{\widehat{A}(c_i), \widehat{a}(w_i), \widehat{a}(w_i')\}$, there are six possible orderings of this set. We can subsume these orderings into two cases:

1. $\widehat{A}(c_i) < \widehat{a}(w_i')$.
2. $\widehat{A}(c_i) \geq \widehat{a}(w_i')$.

Within these cases, we study the variation of $ATE(w_i)$ with $\widehat{a}(w_i)$. We plot these results in the Figure 5.

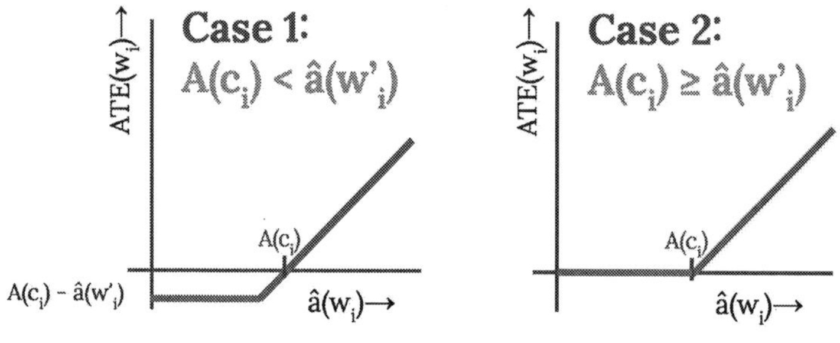

Figure 5: Graph of ATE score of a given word w_i with $\widehat{a}(w_i)$ given two cases

Note that by Assumption 1, we have $\widehat{a}(w_i') \leq \widehat{A}(c_i)$. Therefore, Case (2) in Figure 5 is sufficient for proof. We have:

$$\mathsf{ATE}(w_i) = \mathop{\mathbb{E}}_{s \in \mathcal{D}} \mathop{\mathbb{E}}_{w_i' \in s'} \left[\widehat{A}(s) - \widehat{A}(s')\right] \tag{8}$$

$$= \frac{n(A(s)=1 \mid w_i \in s)}{n(s \mid w_i \in s)} \mathop{\mathbb{E}}_{w_i' \in s'} \left[\widehat{A}(s) - \widehat{A}(s')\right]$$

$$+ \frac{n(A(s)=0 \mid w_i \in s)}{n(s \mid w_i \in s)} \mathop{\mathbb{E}}_{w_i' \in s'} [\widehat{A}(s) - \widehat{A}(s')] \tag{9}$$

But by Assumption 2, in toxic sentences, $\widehat{A}(s) = \widehat{A}(c_i) \geq \widehat{a}(w_i')$. Therefore $\mathbb{E}_{w_i' \in s'}\{\widehat{A}(s) - \widehat{A}(s')\} = 0$. Then:

$$\mathsf{ATE}(w_i) = \frac{n(A(s)=0 \mid w_i \in s)}{n(s \mid w_i \in s)} \mathop{\mathbb{E}}_{w_i' \in s'} [\widehat{A}(s) - \widehat{A}(s')] \tag{10}$$

But $\widehat{A}(s) - \widehat{A}(s')$ is at most $\widehat{a}(w_i)$ as:
(1) if $\widehat{a}(w_i) \leq \widehat{A}(c_i)$, then $\widehat{A}(s) - \widehat{A}(s') = 0$
(2) otherwise $\widehat{A}(s) - \widehat{A}(s') = \widehat{a}(w_i) - \widehat{A}(s') \leq \widehat{a}(w_i)$. Then:

$$\mathsf{ATE}(w_i) \leq \frac{n(A(s)=0 \mid w_i \in s)}{n(s \mid w_i \in s)} \widehat{a}(w_i) \tag{11}$$

$$= \frac{n(A(s)=0 \mid w_i \in s)}{n(s \mid w_i \in s)} \frac{n(A(s)=1 \mid w_i \in s)}{n(s \mid w_i \in s)}$$

$$= p \cdot (1-p) \tag{12}$$

for some $p \in [0,1]$. But $p \cdot (1-p) \leq 0.25 \ \forall p \in [0,1]$. □

Based on Theorem A and Lemma 1, $A(s) \leq 0.25$ if each $w_i \in s$ is a spurious correlate, i.e. non-causal, for attribute A.

B Experimental Results in Detail for Zampieri et al. and Gao et al. Datasets

In this section we provide the full set of results on our runs across models for the two datasets Gao and Huang (2017) and Zampieri et al. (2019a). The plot in 6 illustrates the reduction in toxicity classification by using ATE score on the Zampieri et al. (2019a) dataset for three types of classifiers.
We provide the full tabular results in Tables 4 and 5.

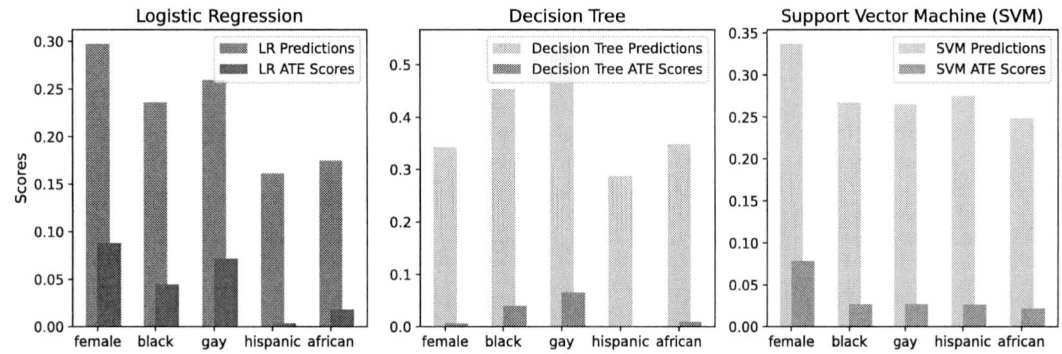

Figure 6: For the Zampieri et al. (2019a) dataset, we compute the mitigation of toxicity score using three different classifiers, and the ATE scores computed using the respective classifiers. These show a reduction on toxicity for protected groups across different models.

Table 4: Classifier Metrics by Protected Category for the Gao et al. Dataset

Group →	African			Black			Female			Gay			Hispanic		
Model ↓	Pred	ATE	Diff	Pred	ATE	Diff	Pred	ATE	Diff	Pred	ATE	Diff	Pred	ATE	Diff
LR	0.201	0.099	0.102	0.300	0.108	0.192	0.270	0.167	0.103	0.470	0.167	0.303	0.166	0.011	0.155
SVM	0.282	0.062	0.220	0.282	0.052	0.230	0.301	0.082	0.219	0.371	0.154	0.217	0.246	0.057	0.189
GB	0.225	0.052	0.173	0.335	0.071	0.264	0.225	0.000	0.225	0.653	0.204	0.449	0.225	0.020	0.205
NB	0.460	0.002	0.458	0.510	0.047	0.463	0.444	0.004	0.440	0.657	0.107	0.550	0.615	0.000	0.615
NN1Layer	0.000	0.003	-0.003	0.000	0.059	-0.059	0.000	0.024	-0.024	1.000	0.197	0.803	0.000	0.000	0.000
NN2Layer	0.000	0.000	0.000	0.000	0.096	-0.096	0.002	0.000	0.002	1.000	0.217	0.783	0.000	0.000	0.000
NN3Layer	0.000	0.160	-0.160	0.000	0.097	-0.097	0.000	0.000	0.000	0.993	0.165	0.828	0.000	0.000	0.000

Table 5: Classifier Metrics by Protected Category for the Zampieri et al. Dataset

Group →	African			Black			Female			Gay			Hispanic		
Model ↓	Pred	ATE	Diff	Pred	ATE	Diff	Pred	ATE	Diff	Pred	ATE	Diff	Pred	ATE	Diff
LR	0.174	0.020	0.154	0.236	0.049	0.187	0.297	0.075	0.223	0.260	0.098	0.162	0.161	0.143	0.018
SVM	0.248	0.030	0.218	0.267	0.036	0.232	0.337	0.068	0.269	0.265	0.033	0.232	0.275	0.119	0.156
GB	0.269	0.020	0.249	0.269	0.013	0.256	0.269	0.008	0.261	0.269	0.003	0.266	0.269	0.033	0.236
NB	0.349	0.009	0.341	0.453	0.055	0.398	0.343	0.183	0.160	0.539	0.070	0.469	0.287	0.000	0.287
NN1Layer5	0.000	0.000	-0.000	0.000	0.052	-0.052	0.000	0.000	-0.000	0.000	0.114	-0.114	0.000	0.000	0.000
NN2Layer105	0.000	0.000	0.000	0.000	0.090	-0.090	0.000	0.170	-0.170	0.000	0.104	-0.104	0.000	0.000	0.000
NN3Layer20105	0.000	0.200	-0.200	0.000	0.126	-0.126	0.000	0.075	-0.075	0.000	0.046	-0.046	0.000	0.000	0.000

Note: We note that the neural classifiers may have overfit on the Zampieri et al. (2019a) dataset due to which the numbers are either close to 0 or 1.

C Experimental Setup

C.1 Dataset Details

We conducted experiments on the publically available Zampieri (Zampieri et al., 2019b) and Gao (Gao and Huang, 2017) datasets.

C.2 Hyper-parameters

Details in our GitHub repository: github.com/causalate-mitigates-bias/causal-ate-mitigates-bias

C.3 Result Statistics

Our run details are provided on the README.md file of our GitHub repository: https://github.com/causalate-mitigates-bias/causal-ate-mitigates-bias/blob/main/README.md

C.4 Compute Resources

All our experiments were carried out using NVidia 1080 GPU Machines with Intel Core i7-7700K @ 4.2GHz. Our experiments utilized approximately 100 CPU-hours and 10 GPU-hours.

C.5 Tools and packages

We list the tools used in our requirements.txt file of our GitHub repository: https://github.com/causalate-mitigates-bias/causal-ate-mitigates-bias/blob/main/requirements.txt

C.6 Use of AI Assistants

We have used AI Assistants (GPT-4) to help format our charts as well as help create latex tables.

On Functional Competence of LLMs for Linguistic Disambiguation

Raihan Kibria, Sheikh Intiser Uddin Dipta, Muhammad Abdullah Adnan
Bangladesh University of Engineering and Technology, Dhaka - 1000, Bangladesh
0421054006@grad.cse.buet.ac.bd
1905003@ugrad.cse.buet.ac.bd
adnan@cse.buet.ac.bd

Abstract

We study some Large Language Models to explore their deficiencies in resolving sense ambiguities. In this connection, we evaluate their performance on well-known word sense disambiguation datasets. Word Sense Disambiguation (WSD) has been a long-standing NLP problem, which has given rise to many evaluation datasets and models over the decades. Recently the emergence of Large Language Models (LLM) raises much hope in improving accuracy. In this work, we evaluate word sense disambiguation capabilities of four LLMs: OpenAI's ChatGPT-3.5, Mistral's 7b parameter model, Meta's Llama 70b, and Google's Gemini Pro. We evaluate many well-established datasets containing a variety of texts and senses on these. After observing the performances of some datasets, we selectively study some failure cases and identify the reasons for failures. We explore human judgments that would correct these failures. Our findings suggest that many failure cases are related to a lack of world knowledge and the reasoning to amalgamate this knowledge rather than the lack of linguistic knowledge. We categorize the judgments so that the next generation of LLMs can improve by incorporating deeper world knowledge and reasoning. We conclude that word sense disambiguation could serve as a guide for probing the reasoning power of LLMs to measure their functional competency. We also list the accuracy of these datasets. We find that on many occasions, accuracy drops to below 70%, which is much less than that of well-performing existing models.

1 Introduction

Large Language Models have been shown to achieve human-like linguistic competence. In various linguistic tasks, their abilities have been documented (Kauf et al., 2023), (Akter et al., 2023). However, conflating linguistic competence with common-sense reasoning abilities has also been decried among researchers. In one experiment (Zhang et al., 2023), researchers report that language models still do not show evidence of cognitive abilities on par with humans. Some studies (Mahowald et al., 2024) make the competencies of language models distinct: formal and functional linguistic competence. Whereas formal linguistics competence manifests in forming coherent, fluent, and syntactically correct texts, functional competence is evidenced in identifying motives and formulating a strategy with world knowledge to decipher the true intention of the writer. Though language models excel in formal competence, they are not known to perform at the human level on functional competence.

Why is functional competence important in NLP tasks? One answer could be functional competence could enhance machine translation performance. In transferring meaning from one language to another, the senses must be interpreted. Many words have more than one sense. Divining the sense of a word requires formal as well as functional competence. For example, consider the following sentence:

> At first blush it seemed that what was striking about him rested on the fact that his dress was exotic, his ***person*** foreign.

We will consider two definitions of the word *person*:

- Human being
- The physical body of a being seen as distinct from the mind, character

The word *person* could be interpreted as a "human being" considering the surrounding collocating words. An alternative interpretation could be "The physical body of a being seen as distinct from the mind, character", which is the correct one. While the former interpretation is derived by applying formal competence, which involves

Proceedings of the 28th Conference on Computational Natural Language Learning, pages 143–160
November 15-16, 2024 ©2024 Association for Computational Linguistics

Prompt: Which of the following senses is correct for the word "free" in the sentence *"He's very free with his money."*?
A) Unconstrained
B) Not imprisoned or enslaved
C) Unconstrained by timidity or distrust
D) Generous; liberal
E) Clear of offence or crime; guiltless; innocent

Answer:
D) Generous; liberal
Gold: D

Figure 1: LLM is prompted with sense choices

analyzing the syntactic relations among a text's constituents, the latter definition can only be determined after considering the historical use of *person*. Arriving at the latter meaning requires greater cognitive deliberation and a broader understanding of world knowledge. The inability to settle on the proper meaning would result in suboptimal translations. That word sense disambiguation (WSD) helps in machine translation has been documented in much research (Nguyen et al., 2018), (Neale et al., 2016), (Jin et al., 2023), (Rios Gonzales et al., 2017), (Koehn, 2020).

Most well-performing WSD methods rely on supervised machine learning. Using Artificial Neural Networks have been shown to improve WSD performance (Berend, 2020; Wang and Wang, 2020; Yap et al., 2020; Kohli, 2021; Zhang et al., 2021; Wang et al., 2021; Barba et al., 2021a; Mizuki and Okazaki, 2023; Sainz et al., 2023). Existing datasets for evaluating WSD performance have been a by-product of decades-long research, which have been time-tested, some containing infrequent use of senses. We intend to use these datasets for our experiments.

In this study, Large Language Models (LLM) are prompted with the examples of the datasets described in Subsection 7.1 [1]. The responses are matched and tallied to summarize overall performance (Figure 1).

In summary, our contribution is as follows: we share some insights into why, in some WSD cases, LLMs fail by highlighting certain functional deficiencies, and we present findings that WSD datasets could be repurposed to gauge the reasoning power of LLMs.

The remaining sections are organized as follows: Sections 2, 3, and 4 discuss the similarities and differences between LLMs and humans. Sections 5, 6, 7, and 8 provide detailed descriptions of our experiments.

[1]The experiment could be reproduced with the code available at Functional Competence of LLMs

2 Linguistic Regularities and Formal Linguistic Competence

Formal linguistic competence manifests in speakers' ability to use regularities in a language. Whether or not a verb precedes an object as in "Hurricane Milton lashed at the Florida west coast" is an example of such regularities. These regularities are syntactical. Some relate to subject-verb agreement: "Millions of citizens, some on their vacations, are expected to cast their ballots." Here *are* is the proper auxiliary verb instead of *is*.

Some regularities are morphological, based on the mechanism of word formation: in "unbreak my heart, uncry these tears", the verbs have been formed by adding "un" (Aronoff and Fudeman, 2022). "Mongolian" is formed by transforming "Mongol" by adding "ian" (Kiparsky, 1982).

It has been shown that LLMs capture these linguistic patterns rivaling humans (Linzen and Baroni, 2021).

3 Divergence between LLMs and Humans

Whereas LLM's human-like processing of language has been documented, some research papers highlight certain deficiencies compared to humans in reasoning tasks. Take for example a theory of mind task and its alteration (Ullman, 2023):

> **Original task:** Here is a bag filled with popcorn. There is no chocolate in the bag. Yet, the label on the bag says "chocolate" and not "popcorn." Sam finds the bag. She had never seen the bag before. She cannot see what is inside the bag. She reads the label.

> **Altered task:** Here is a bag filled with popcorn. There is no chocolate in the bag. The bag is made of transparent plastic, so you can see what is inside. Yet, the label on the bag says 'chocolate' and not 'popcorn.' Sam finds the bag. She had never seen the bag before. Sam reads the label.

GPT3.5 was prompted with predicting the following:

> She believes that the bag is full of __,

The machine got the answer right in the original task (*chocolate*), but not in the altered version.

Given LLM's excellent linguistic ability and yet-unproven performance on reasoning at the human level, researchers are apt to classify the LLM capabilities into two: formal and functional competencies. This motivation comes from observing brain activities. The language network in the human brain is quite distinct from the day-to-day reasoning center as revealed in fMRI scans (Mahowald et al., 2024). In other words, linguistic abilities should be separately considered from the world knowledge.

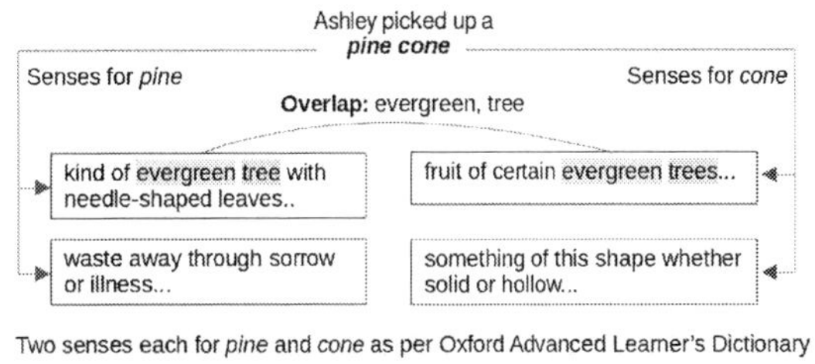

Figure 2: Determining a sense of *pine* based on a collocating word

4 Word Sense Disambiguation and Functional Competence

In evaluating the WSD performance of the LLMs we find that some difficult disambiguation tasks that machines fail to perform, rely on having world knowledge in addition to linguistic knowledge. We categorize these with examples. To the best of our knowledge, these categories have not been previously documented. Some are related to historical, old English, cultural, geographical, trade relational, religious, satiric/figurative use of languages, and spatial knowledge.

As an example consider the following sentence:

> The discovery of the mines of America ... does not seem to have had any very **sensible** effect upon the prices of things in England.

There are eight different senses for the target word *sensible*, of which we are listing just two:

- Sense#1: Perceptible by the senses.
- Sense#2: Easily perceived; appreciable.

Sense#1 is a false choice. To detect the correct choice Sense#2, one must reason with knowledge involving history, trade relations, and possibly geography. Here is our analysis of why Sense#2 is the correct choice:

Historically America and England have been closely related in terms of commerce. Close relation implies some effect of events in one country on another. It is common knowledge that any effect should be perceivable/appreciable. The writer is informing of no effect, which is counter-intuitive; but that is what writers do – provide surprising information. To disambiguate, knowledge of trade relations, and possibly geography is needed. And, of course, good reasoning.

We provide a taxonomy of failure cases in tables 1. More can be found in the Appendix.

5 Background on Word Sense Disambiguation Evaluation

Many words in the English language are ambiguous, having more than one sense. In WordNet (Miller et al., 1990), a popular word-sense inventory, *plant* has four senses as noun and six senses as verb Table 2.

One simple way to disambiguate a word is to use a lexicon, such as a dictionary, which provides definitions of senses. These definitions are compared with the definitions of context words (the words surrounding the target word). The definition containing the maximum match would, hopefully, point to the correct sense of the word (Lesk, 1986). For example, in Figure 2, sense#1 of both the words point to a match.

However, definitions in dictionaries tend to be succinct. Thus, although this context-matching method is straightforward, it does not address instances where the context words share no common terms with the definitions. As a result, researchers considered relations between words and their affinity with each other so that even though dictionary definitions of context do not overlap, the relation between them could be used to infer their co-occurrence. With this in mind, gathering statistics from the corpus gained traction. Some statistics were related to the Verb-Object relational preference (Resnik, 1997), whereas some statistics concern parts of speech, positions of words, morphology, the dependency structure of the sentence, and the like. Figure 3 depicts the workings of one such model.

These models have made use of various machine learning methods. Evaluating these models requires a common test set, which, over the years, has brought to fruition several. In this section, we will describe some of the evaluation procedures.

Table 1: Failure cases - Part I

WKR Category	WKR Sub Category	Example text	Remarks
1. Old English		At first blush it seemed that what was striking about him rested on the fact that his dress was exotic, his **person** foreign.	"person" refers to a use in 14th-century English. The correct choice: *The physical body of a being seen as distinct from the mind, character*
2. Cultural			
	2.1 Current cultural	Any wrestler who will **piledrive** Lawler and injure him like he did me gets five thousand dollars from me!	"piledrive" refers to a maneuver used in professional wrestling. The correct choice: *To use the piledriver move.*
	2.2 Social norm/ hierarchy	Still, the folio Ben looks to publish will be well beyond the purse of most scholars, let alone a **groundling**	"groundling" refers to relatively uninitiated compared with the professionals. The correct choice: *A person of uncultivated or uncultured taste.*
3. Metaphor		**Egg crates** are a much less satisfactory model for schools.	"Egg crates" is being used to refer to a closed environment. The correct choice: *A self-contained class that has no collaboration or interaction with any other class, and which is the sole responsibility of a single teacher.*
4. Grammatical/ Linguistic			
	4.1 Verb-object, Syntactical	Whosoever will read the story of this war will find himself much **staggered**.	"staggered" is being used as a passive form. Knowledge of verb-object affinity containing the notion that a person can be staggered could help. The correct choice: *To cause to doubt and waver; to make to hesitate;*
	4.2 Subject-verb; selectional preference	He is a young fellow, not long out of adolescence, who **faunches** to set the world on fire but isn't sure how to go about it.	"faunches" can be disambiguated using the selectional preference ((Resnik, 1996))/subject-verb affinity. The correct choice: *To desire; to yearn; to covet.*
	4.3 Adjective-noun relation knowledge	The beautiful **Akee** ("Blighia sapida"), originally brought from the West Coast of Africa by slave ships, is now a common tree in the West Indies, and I noticed several fine specimens in Belize.	"Akee" is a tree implied by the common use of the adjective 'beautiful' to modify a noun (tree), also by the accompanying scientific name for the species. The correct choice: *A tropical evergreen tree, (noshow=1), related to the lychee and longan.*

WKR Column: Type of World Knowledge Required. The target word is bolded. The correct choice (last column) is the definition corresponding to the gold key.

Table 2: Partial enumeration of senses for *plant* in WordNet

Sense ID	Definition
sense#1	buildings in an industry
sense#2	a living organism
sense#3	an actor .. in the audience..
sense#4	something planted secretly..

(a) Senses for Plant/Noun in WordNet.

Sense ID	Definition
sense#1	put seeds .. into the ground
sense#2	..set securely
sense#3	..lay the groundwork for..
sense#4	place into a river

(b) Senses for Plant/Verb in WordNet.

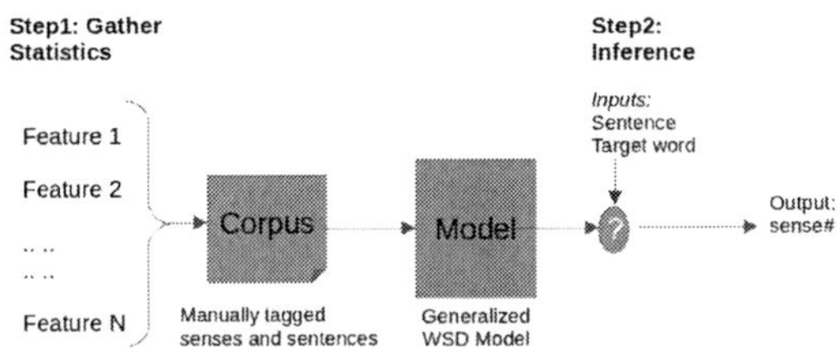

Figure 3: Creating a model for inference

5.1 WSD Evaluation

Researchers have traditionally used datasets that contain some text and a target word that needs to be disambiguated. The datasets also include senses for the ambiguous words. A gold sense key is provided. The evaluation task consists of presenting a model with some context and inquiring about the model to output the sense key that it deems appropriate to capture the correct sense given the context (Figure 4).

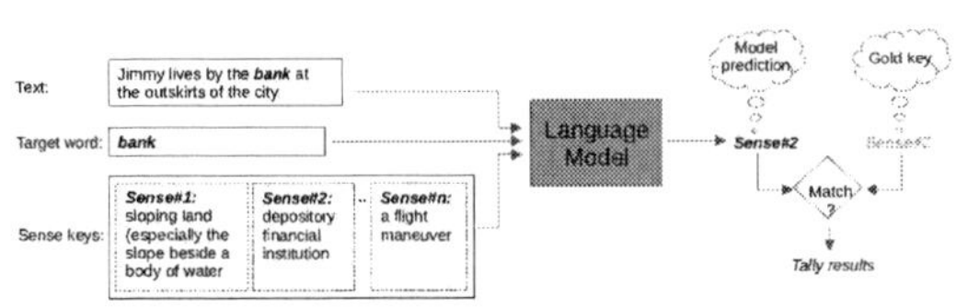

Figure 4: Gold key is provided and matched with the model's prediction

Some popular datasets, such as (Fellbaum and Miller, 1998), have been around for decades. Table 3 provides a list of the datasets.

Since the 1980s, various training methods have been proposed. Most methods train a model using statistical (Zhong and Ng, 2010) and/or neural methods (Wang and Wang, 2020) exploiting the distribution of words and relationships. The datasets

Table 3: Some popular datasets used for WSD evaluation

Dataset Name	Year Since	Number of Annotations
Senseval-2	2001	2,282
Senseval-3	2004	1,850
SemEval-07	2007	455
SemEval-13	2013	1,664
SemEval-15	2015	1,022
SemCor	1994	226,040
OMSTI	2015	1,000,000
Coarse-20	2020	80,000
NUS WSD Corpus	2009	3,854
WiC (Word-in-Context)	2019	5,000
Eurosense Multilingual	2017	15,441,667
FEWS	2021	90,000

Table 4: Performance comparison of notable models. 1: (Blevins and Zettlemoyer, 2020), 2: (Loureiro and Jorge, 2019), 3: (Zhong and Ng, 2010)

Model	Method	Accuracy
1	Transformer fine-tuning	80%
2	Transformer with WordNet Graph	75.4%
3	Support Vector Machines	72%

typically provide some training data. In addition, some knowledge about words and their definitions is often gleaned from external lexicons such as WordNet (Miller et al., 1990).

The accuracy of the best-performing models hovers around 80% (Blevins and Zettlemoyer, 2020). Table 4 shows the performance of some notable models evaluated on Semeval and Senseval datasets (Raganato et al., 2017).

5.2 Large Language Models

With the emergence of Transformer models such as (Devlin et al., 2018; Liu et al., 2019), and the rise in computation power to process massive amounts of text, Large Language Models (LLMs) have gained human-like capabilities. Researchers report these models, such as (Team et al., 2023; Jiang et al., 2023; OpenAI, 2022; Achiam et al., 2023; Touvron et al., 2023), perform well on a vast array of natural language processing tasks (Akter et al., 2023), for example, on Knowledge-based QA, Reasoning and Machine Translation, even though the models have not been purposely trained to perform these tasks. This raises hopes for the linguistic community that the long-standing problem of WSD would benefit from the LLM's superlative language and reasoning power (Senel et al., 2022). Some research shed light on the inherent notion of sense in LLMs (Wiedemann et al., 2019).

Several studies report that a closely associated

task, machine translation, has benefited from these models. For example, (Lee et al., 2023) reports that LLMs display some capabilities that go beyond the literal translation of words, which is much needed when handling idiomatic expressions.

LLMs are also being explored for tasks that require reasoning and planning (Zhao et al., 2024), (Savarimuthu et al., 2024), and augur some emerging abilities (Wei et al., 2022). However, many researchers report that much is still lacking in the reasoning power of LLMs (Li et al., 2024), (Kassner et al., 2023), (Liu et al., 2023), (Hao et al., 2023), (Sap et al., 2022), (Ji et al., 2023).

With these deficiencies in mind, researchers have proposed many methods for improving the reasoning power of LLMs. (Wu et al., 2024) proposes an evaluation framework for measuring LLM's reasoning capabilities. (Hao et al., 2023) proposes a reasoning framework by priming LLMs with prompting. (Mialon et al., 2023) and (Ye et al., 2022) highlight augmentation techniques with external knowledge to enhance LLMs to reason. (Wu et al., 2023) emphasizes the interpretability of LLMs intending to improve their inference capabilities.

Some research, such as that conducted by (Sap et al., 2022), questions the basic formulation of LLMs by examining their learning processes and contrasting them with human learning, all within the framework of Theory of Mind (Premack and Woodruff, 1978). Additionally, researchers like (Kim et al., 2022) highlight the issue of LLMs being overexposed to their training corpora, which appears to hinder their ability to generalize effectively.

As for WSD, Senel et al. (2022) reports that LLMs could benefit from learning complex inference and deep understanding that is often required for disambiguating words.

6 Methodology

We test the Word Sense Disambiguation capability of some LLMs. Our choice of methodology for WSD research is influenced by established knowledge about the pitfalls of existing corpus and sense definitions.

6.1 Common Issues in WSD Evaluation

1. Same Domain Bias
2. MFS vs LFS
3. Context As a Clue
4. One Sense per Discourse
5. Coarse vs Fine-grained Senses
6. Homonyms vs Polysemous words

1. Same Domain Bias: Same domain bias is observed when a WSD model is trained and tested on the same domain or similar domains of text (Escudero et al., 2000). Oftentimes, the accuracy drops when an out-of-domain text's disambiguation is performed.

Also, LLMs are commonly trained on a masked word prediction objective, which is to reduce the following loss function, where *w* is the withheld word and *context* is the surrounding words (Devlin et al., 2018), (Levine et al., 2019) –

$$\mathcal{L}_{LM} = -\log p(w|context) \quad (1)$$

In both cases, what is learned by the machine depends much on the corpus content.

2. MFS vs LFS: Researchers distinguish between the Most Frequent Sense (MFS) vs Lesser Frequent Senses (LFS) of words. Table 5 lists two senses of *appreciate/VERB* available in WordNet.

Table 5: Two senses of *appreciate*. Sense#1 is the MFS, whereas Sense#2 is the LFS.

Sense#1: recognize with gratitude
Example usage: We must *appreciate* the kindness she showed towards us
Sense#2: increase the value of
Example usage: The Germans want to *appreciate* the Deutsche Mark

In addition, natural language words follow a Zipfian distribution: most words are often used and re-used, whereas, some words are rarely used (Florence, 1950). Similarly, the most frequent senses of a word number are as much as 80%. In fact, defaulting to the MFS of a word gives a good baseline performance, which has been difficult to beat in the pre-neural era. Our work places a substantial focus on the LFS usages and in particular on rare senses by incorporating datasets meant for rare sense disambiguation.

3. Context As a Clue: WSD evaluations are based on treating the context words as the dominant clue. Although not explicitly mentioned in the literature, it is assumed that the linguistic features that the context provides act as the primary determinant of a sense. We investigate how much this assumption holds.

4. One Sense per Discourse: In naturally occurring texts, repeated uses of a word tend to employ the same sense (Gale et al., 1992). The word *viral* in medical journals would repeatedly use the sense "relating to or caused by a virus"; medical texts would scarcely use if at all, the sense "circulated rapidly and widely from one internet user to another". This necessitates testing a WSD model on diverse texts, meaning diverse datasets.

5. Coarse vs Fine-grained Senses: Some sense inventories such as WordNet contain senses that are so fine that it is difficult to tell two senses apart. In fact, various studies have found that annotators often disagreed on a sense (Table 6). WordNet was created as a psychometric aid (Miller, 1990), which requires fine distinctions of senses. In ordinary conversations, humans do not employ such distinctions. Therefore, a proper evaluation of WSD must factor in other sense inventories that are less fine-grained (Ide and Wilks, 2006).

Table 6: Two senses of *rush*. It is hard to tell the difference between the two.

Sense#1: move fast
Example usage: He *rushed* down the hall to receive his guests
Sense#2: act or move at high speed
Example usage: We have to *rush*!; hurry–it's late!

6. Homonyms vs Polysemous words: Homonyms are words that sound alike but stand for different or unrelated things. The senses of the word *bank* in the "a river *bank*", and "withdraw money from the *bank*" are not related. Polysemous words, on the other hand, are related. For example, the word *grasp* in the following sentences has related but slightly different meanings: "to *grasp* a pencil", "to *grasp* the summary". It has been observed that homonyms generally score higher than polysemous words in terms of disambiguation accuracy. Therefore, the datasets must contain a fair distribution of the two kinds of ambiguous words.

6.2 Choice of Datasets

We test four LLMs, which serve as representatives of LLMs, on some test data available on the popular datasets mentioned in Table 3. The choice of datasets chosen has been based on a few criteria:

The data set –

a) must be well cited
b) must contain context and target
c) must provide gold keys
d) must provide variation
e) must be validated by humans
f) must contain a mixture of homonyms and polysemous words

6.3 Procedure for Collecting Results

We prompt the model with context and choices culled from the datasets, and record the response to compare with gold keys (Figure 1). We then tally the results.

6.4 Baselines

Having gone through the existing literature, we select the best-performing models for WSD tasks for comparison in Table 7. In some cases, the authors of a dataset have provided their benchmarks, which we include. To our knowledge, (Barba et al., 2021b) is the best-performing model on WSD. However, Blevins and Zettlemoyer (2020) is a well-performing model known for its strong performance in few-shot and zero-shot settings. This we mention in Table 4.

6.5 Setting up LLMs

We prepare the LLMs for generating appropriate responses by setting some parameters such as "expert" mode, "non-verbose" mode, and "safe" mode. The responses sometimes were found to contain some spurious content. We sanitized the output to collect the response. It took several iterations to arrive at a proper mechanism to capture the response.

6.6 Four LLMs

We experiment on four recent models. These models are recognized for their good performance across various NLP tasks such as Commonsense Reasoning, World Knowledge, and Reading Comprehension (Akter et al., 2023). We opt to choose a mix of open-source and proprietary models. Each model is subtly different in how they were trained.

Here are brief descriptions of these models:

6.6.1 ChatGPT-3.5

OpenAI's ChatGPT-3.5 is demonstrated to perform effectively on NLP tasks (Brown et al., 2020). Since it is a close-sourced model, the model parameters could not be ascertained. However, we experiment with it because of its popularity.

6.6.2 Mistral

We experimented on Mistral 7B, which has 7 billion parameters and is open-source. This model outperforms other open-source models. The Mistral model uses a Sliding Window Attention, which is particularly suited for long text (Beltagy et al., 2020), a feature must desired in disambiguation.

6.6.3 Llama

We experiment with the Llama 70 billion parameter model, which is open-sourced. We conduct experiments on it because it has been developed using open and accessible data. It also possesses comparable performance with the state-of-the-art (Touvron et al., 2023).

6.6.4 Gemini Pro

Gemini Pro is Google's latest language model. On various benchmark tests, it shows state-of-the-art performance (Team et al., 2023). Since it is a close-sourced model, the model parameters could not be ascertained.

7 Experimentation

The datasets we use in our experiments contain a variety of sense keys: some use their self-conceived sense keys extracted from popular text sources such as Wikipedia and Wiktionary. Some use WordNet sense keys. Still, others could be found using some other lexicon's keys, for example, BabelNet (Navigli and Ponzetto, 2012). Not all datasets present WSD as a classification task. For example, Word in Context (WIC) dataset (Pilehvar and Camacho-Collados, 2018) presents each evaluation sample as a simple *true* or *false* by giving two sentences, probing the LLM to verify whether the two sentences carry the same meaning of the target word (Figure 5a and Figure 5b).

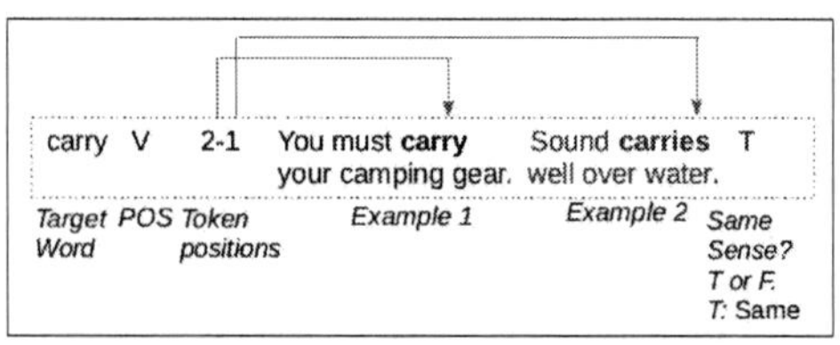

(a) WSD posed as confirming whether the two sentences carry the same meaning for a target word (WIC dataset)

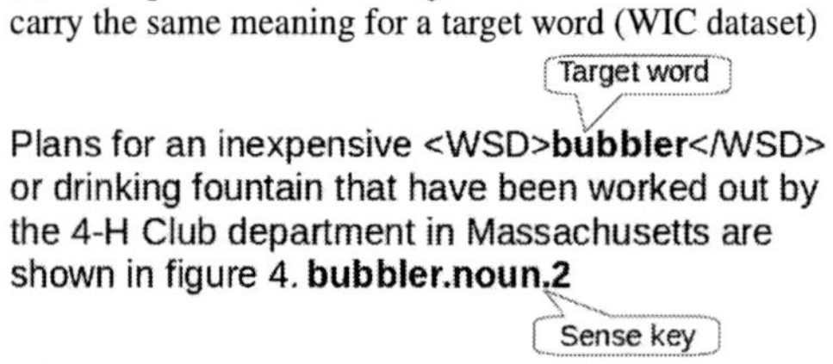

(b) Most datasets pose WSD as a classification task where a sense key is given as the class

Figure 5: WSD is posed differently in datasets

Data sets are in different formats: some in XML format while others in simple texts. Some datasets contain the sense keys, whereas others refer to senses from external sense inventories. After extracting the sentences and collecting definitions of senses suitable for prompting, we prepare prompts similar to Figure 1.

7.1 Datasets Considered

a. Eurosense Multilingual WSD Dataset (Bovi et al., 2017)
This dataset is the largest. It also contains multilingual content. However, the dataset lacks proper human evaluation – random samples reveal that it has 67.7% inter-annotator agreement. We do not include this dataset in our experiments.

b. NUS WSD Corpus (Dahlmeier et al., 2009)
This dataset only contains prepositions as the target of disambiguation. Since it does not provide other parts of speeches, we do not include this in our experiments.

c. Unified framework (Raganato et al., 2017)
This dataset contains a collection of datasets that researchers have been using since the 1990s. Since some of the most prominent research cites this dataset as a benchmark, we include this.

d. WiC (Word-in-Context) Dataset (Pilehvar and Camacho-Collados, 2018)
This dataset poses a WSD task in a novel way – that of contrasting two sentences to decide on the sameness of senses in the target word usage. We surmise that this test would be a good test on LLM to evaluate reasoning. Moreover, this dataset has been carefully created using VerbNet (Schuler, 2005), producing verb words as targets of disambiguation. Since Wiktionary has been used to collect data, human evaluation was factored in. Therefore, we include this in our experiments.

e. CoarseWSD-20 (Loureiro et al., 2021)
This dataset has been collected from Wikipedia. Authors report that random samples prove over 90% of the tags are accurate by validating with human annotators. We include this dataset in our experiments.

f. FEWS dataset (Blevins et al., 2021)
This dataset has been created based on the notion of WSD's poor performance on rare senses. In fact, it has been reported that humans outperform the best baseline models on this dataset. The dataset has been created from examples and definitions in Wiktionary, which is human-created. We include this in our experiments.

Table 7: Accuracy (%) found in our experiments. The *COMPARISON* column gives the accuracies obtained by some well-performing models: Sl. 1-5: (Barba et al., 2021b), Sl. 6: (Pilehvar and Camacho-Collados, 2018), Sl. 7: (Loureiro et al., 2021), Sl. 8: (Blevins et al., 2021). *IAA Column*: Inter-Annotator Agreement. *: for Verbs and Nouns, respectively.

Sl.	Dataset	OpenAI	Mistral	Llama	Gemini	COMPARISON	IAA
1	Senseval-2	65.7	65.0	61.0	**71.1**	82.3	-
2	Senseval-3	61.5	58.8	54.5	**70.0**	79.9	72.5
3	Semeval-2007	58.4	55.7	49.1	**65.4**	77.4	72,86*
4	Semeval-2013	70.1	65.9	66.5	**74.1**	83.2	-
5	Semeval-2015	67.3	64.1	63.0	**72.9**	85.2	68
6	WiC (Word-in-Context)	59.4	61.6	55.1	**65.8**	58.0	80
7	CoarseWSD-20	84.1	61.6	33.8	**93.9**	95.0	-
8	FEWS few-shots	63.0	63.7	60.7	**71.0**	66.4	80.2
	zero-shot	59.0	58.7	56.7	**65.0**	-	

Table 8: Pricing per a million tokens. * Llama was accessed through replicate.com.

Language Model	Input	Output
ChatGPT	$0.5	$1.5
Mistral	$4.0	$12.0
Llama*	$0.65	$2.75
Gemini Pro	$0.35	$1.05

7.2 Results

We test nine datasets on each of the four LLMs. Each language model is prompted with a sentence and told to disambiguate a target word. The response of the language model is observed and recorded. Table 7 shows the accuracy found by comparing it with the gold sense key.

8 Discussion

Given that the LLMs have not been fine-tuned, it is understandable from the test results that accuracy is comparable to the state-of-the-art models on WSD. Sometimes a language model fails to accurately identify a sense due to its lack of spatial knowledge; other times it fails because it seems not to be able to put the text in historical context; still other times the lack of application of humans' social relation is to be the reason for failure.

Many disambiguation cases require knowledge from different avenues: political, spatial, cultural, historical, and the like. Many researchers would sometimes club these missing pieces as commonsense knowledge. While investigating the failure cases, we prompted the LLMs to test their world knowledge. We discovered that by using different prompts, it can be confirmed that the LLMs appear to possess much of this knowledge. However, the failure arises when these models do not leverage knowledge across multiple dimensions to integrate it effectively. Much research in the avenue of reasoning is needed to further advancement of Artificial General Intelligence, which concurs with some research findings (Chen et al., 2023).

We stop short of calling our results a benchmark since not all LLMs we considered are open-source and the technology is continuously evolving as a result of which it will be difficult to compare across generations of LLMs.

9 Conclusion

In this research, we demonstrate that WSD involves not just the knowledge of language but world knowledge and the capability of piecing together facts from multiple sources — in other words, functional competence. Our findings also suggest that WSD could be used to verify the reasoning power of LLMs. WSD datasets are aplenty, and some have been human-validated. We conclude that it is worth paying heed to improving the WSD capabilities of LLMs and using these datasets in a novel way to probe. We also release a taxonomy of failure cases requiring world knowledge for WSD, which could further research in this direction.

References

Josh Achiam, Steven Adler, Sandhini Agarwal, Lama Ahmad, Ilge Akkaya, Florencia Leoni Aleman, Diogo Almeida, Janko Altenschmidt, Sam Altman, Shyamal Anadkat, et al. 2023. Gpt-4 technical report. *arXiv preprint arXiv:2303.08774*.

Syeda Nahida Akter, Zichun Yu, Aashiq Muhamed, Tianyue Ou, Alex Bäuerle, Ángel Alexander Cabrera, Krish Dholakia, Chenyan Xiong, and Graham Neubig. 2023. An in-depth look at gemini's language abilities. *arXiv preprint arXiv:2312.11444*.

Mark Aronoff and Kirsten Fudeman. 2022. *What is morphology?* John Wiley & Sons.

Edoardo Barba, Tommaso Pasini, and Roberto Navigli. 2021a. Esc: Redesigning wsd with extractive sense comprehension. In *Proceedings of the 2021 Conference of the North American Chapter of the Association for Computational Linguistics: Human Language Technologies*, pages 4661–4672.

Edoardo Barba, Luigi Procopio, and Roberto Navigli. 2021b. Consec: Word sense disambiguation as continuous sense comprehension. In *Proceedings of the 2021 Conference on Empirical Methods in Natural Language Processing*, pages 1492–1503.

Iz Beltagy, Matthew E Peters, and Arman Cohan. 2020. Longformer: The long-document transformer. *arXiv preprint arXiv:2004.05150*.

Gábor Berend. 2020. Sparsity makes sense: Word sense disambiguation using sparse contextualized word representations. In *Proceedings of the 2020 Conference on Empirical Methods in Natural Language Processing (EMNLP)*, pages 8498–8508, Online. Association for Computational Linguistics.

Terra Blevins, Mandar Joshi, and Luke Zettlemoyer. 2021. Fews: Large-scale, low-shot word sense disambiguation with the dictionary. *arXiv preprint arXiv:2102.07983*.

Terra Blevins and Luke Zettlemoyer. 2020. Moving down the long tail of word sense disambiguation with gloss-informed biencoders. *arXiv preprint arXiv:2005.02590*.

Claudio Delli Bovi, Jose Camacho-Collados, Alessandro Raganato, and Roberto Navigli. 2017. Eurosense: Automatic harvesting of multilingual sense annotations from parallel text. In *Proceedings of the 55th Annual Meeting of the Association for Computational Linguistics (Volume 2: Short Papers)*, pages 594–600.

Tom Brown, Benjamin Mann, Nick Ryder, Melanie Subbiah, Jared D Kaplan, Prafulla Dhariwal, Arvind Neelakantan, Pranav Shyam, Girish Sastry, Amanda Askell, et al. 2020. Language models are few-shot learners. *Advances in neural information processing systems*, 33:1877–1901.

Jiangjie Chen, Wei Shi, Ziquan Fu, Sijie Cheng, Lei Li, and Yanghua Xiao. 2023. Say what you mean! large language models speak too positively about negative commonsense knowledge. In *Proceedings of the 61st Annual Meeting of the Association for Computational Linguistics (Volume 1: Long Papers)*, pages 9890–9908, Toronto, Canada. Association for Computational Linguistics.

Daniel Dahlmeier, Hwee Tou Ng, and Tanja Schultz. 2009. Joint learning of preposition senses and semantic roles of prepositional phrases. In *Proceedings of the 2009 Conference on Empirical Methods in Natural Language Processing (EMNLP 2009)*, pages 450–458, Singapore. Association for Computational Linguistics.

Jacob Devlin, Ming-Wei Chang, Kenton Lee, and Kristina Toutanova. 2018. Bert: Pre-training of deep bidirectional transformers for language understanding. *arXiv preprint arXiv:1810.04805*.

Gerard Escudero, Lluis Marquez, and German Rigau. 2000. An empirical study of the domain dependence of supervised word disambiguation systems. In *2000 Joint SIGDAT Conference on Empirical Methods in Natural Language Processing and Very Large Corpora*, pages 172–180.

Christiane Fellbaum and George Miller. 1998. Building semantic concordances.

P Sargant Florence. 1950. Human behaviour and the principle of least effort. *The Economic Journal*, 60(240):808–810.

William A. Gale, Kenneth W. Church, and David Yarowsky. 1992. One sense per discourse. In *Speech and Natural Language: Proceedings of a Workshop Held at Harriman, New York, February 23-26, 1992*.

Shibo Hao, Yi Gu, Haodi Ma, Joshua Hong, Zhen Wang, Daisy Wang, and Zhiting Hu. 2023. Reasoning with language model is planning with world model. In *Proceedings of the 2023 Conference on Empirical Methods in Natural Language Processing*, pages 8154–8173, Singapore. Association for Computational Linguistics.

Nancy Ide and Yorick Wilks. 2006. Making sense about sense. *Word sense disambiguation*, pages 47–73.

Ziwei Ji, Nayeon Lee, Rita Frieske, Tiezheng Yu, Dan Su, Yan Xu, Etsuko Ishii, Ye Jin Bang, Andrea Madotto, and Pascale Fung. 2023. Survey of hallucination in natural language generation. *ACM Computing Surveys*, 55(12):1–38.

Albert Q Jiang, Alexandre Sablayrolles, Arthur Mensch, Chris Bamford, Devendra Singh Chaplot, Diego de las Casas, Florian Bressand, Gianna Lengyel, Guillaume Lample, Lucile Saulnier, et al. 2023. Mistral 7b. *arXiv preprint arXiv:2310.06825*.

Linghao Jin, Jacqueline He, Jonathan May, and Xuezhe Ma. 2023. Challenges in context-aware neural machine translation. In *Proceedings of the 2023 Conference on Empirical Methods in Natural Language Processing*, pages 15246–15263, Singapore. Association for Computational Linguistics.

Nora Kassner, Oyvind Tafjord, Ashish Sabharwal, Kyle Richardson, Hinrich Schuetze, and Peter Clark. 2023. Language models with rationality. In *Proceedings of the 2023 Conference on Empirical Methods in Natural Language Processing*, pages 14190–14201, Singapore. Association for Computational Linguistics.

Carina Kauf, Anna A Ivanova, Giulia Rambelli, Emmanuele Chersoni, Jingyuan Selena She, Zawad Chowdhury, Evelina Fedorenko, and Alessandro Lenci. 2023. Event knowledge in large language models: the gap between the impossible and the unlikely. *Cognitive Science*, 47(11):e13386.

Najoung Kim, Tal Linzen, and Paul Smolensky. 2022. Uncontrolled lexical exposure leads to overestimation of compositional generalization in pretrained models. *arXiv preprint arXiv:2212.10769*.

Paul Kiparsky. 1982. Word formation and the lexicon. In *1982 Mid America Linguistics Conference Papers/Dept. of Ling., Univ. of Kansas*.

Philipp Koehn. 2020. *Neural machine translation*. Cambridge University Press.

Harsh Kohli. 2021. Training bi-encoders for word sense disambiguation. In *International Conference on Document Analysis and Recognition*, pages 823–837. Springer.

Jaechan Lee, Alisa Liu, Orevaoghene Ahia, Hila Gonen, and Noah Smith. 2023. That was the last straw, we need more: Are translation systems sensitive to disambiguating context? In *Findings of the Association for Computational Linguistics: EMNLP 2023*, pages 4555–4569, Singapore. Association for Computational Linguistics.

Michael Lesk. 1986. Automatic sense disambiguation using machine readable dictionaries: how to tell a pine cone from an ice cream cone. In *Proceedings of the 5th annual international conference on Systems documentation*, pages 24–26.

Yoav Levine, Barak Lenz, Or Dagan, Ori Ram, Dan Padnos, Or Sharir, Shai Shalev-Shwartz, Amnon Shashua, and Yoav Shoham. 2019. Sensebert: Driving some sense into bert. *arXiv preprint arXiv:1908.05646*.

Zhiming Li, Yushi Cao, Xiufeng Xu, Junzhe Jiang, Xu Liu, Yon Shin Teo, Shang-wei Lin, and Yang Liu. 2024. Llms for relational reasoning: How far are we? *arXiv preprint arXiv:2401.09042*.

Tal Linzen and Marco Baroni. 2021. Syntactic structure from deep learning. *Annual Review of Linguistics*, 7(1):195–212.

Yinhan Liu, Myle Ott, Naman Goyal, Jingfei Du, Mandar Joshi, Danqi Chen, Omer Levy, Mike Lewis, Luke Zettlemoyer, and Veselin Stoyanov. 2019. Roberta: A robustly optimized bert pretraining approach. *arXiv preprint arXiv:1907.11692*.

Yongkang Liu, Shi Feng, Daling Wang, Yifei Zhang, and Hinrich Schütze. 2023. Evaluate what you can't evaluate: Unassessable generated responses quality. *arXiv preprint arXiv:2305.14658*.

Daniel Loureiro and Alípio Jorge. 2019. Language modelling makes sense: Propagating representations through wordnet for full-coverage word sense disambiguation. *arXiv preprint arXiv:1906.10007*.

Daniel Loureiro, Kiamehr Rezaee, Mohammad Taher Pilehvar, and Jose Camacho-Collados. 2021. Analysis and evaluation of language models for word sense disambiguation. *Computational Linguistics*, 47(2):387–443.

Kyle Mahowald, Anna A Ivanova, Idan A Blank, Nancy Kanwisher, Joshua B Tenenbaum, and Evelina Fedorenko. 2024. Dissociating language and thought in large language models. *Trends in Cognitive Sciences*.

Grégoire Mialon, Roberto Dessì, Maria Lomeli, Christoforos Nalmpantis, Ram Pasunuru, Roberta Raileanu, Baptiste Rozière, Timo Schick, Jane Dwivedi-Yu, Asli Celikyilmaz, et al. 2023. Augmented language models: a survey. *arXiv preprint arXiv:2302.07842*.

George A Miller. 1990. Nouns in wordnet: a lexical inheritance system. *International journal of Lexicography*, 3(4):245–264.

George A Miller, Richard Beckwith, Christiane Fellbaum, Derek Gross, and Katherine J Miller. 1990. Introduction to wordnet: An on-line lexical database. *International journal of lexicography*, 3(4):235–244.

Sakae Mizuki and Naoaki Okazaki. 2023. Semantic specialization for knowledge-based word sense disambiguation. In *Proceedings of the 17th Conference of the European Chapter of the Association for Computational Linguistics*, pages 3457–3470, Dubrovnik, Croatia. Association for Computational Linguistics.

Roberto Navigli and Simone Paolo Ponzetto. 2012. Babelnet: The automatic construction, evaluation and application of a wide-coverage multilingual semantic network. *Artificial intelligence*, 193:217–250.

Steven Neale, Luís Gomes, Eneko Agirre, Oier Lopez de Lacalle, and António Branco. 2016. Word sense-aware machine translation: Including senses as contextual features for improved translation models. In *Proceedings of the Tenth International Conference on Language Resources and Evaluation (LREC'16)*, pages 2777–2783, Portorož, Slovenia. European Language Resources Association (ELRA).

Quang-Phuoc Nguyen, Anh-Dung Vo, Joon-Choul Shin, and Cheol-Young Ock. 2018. Effect of word sense disambiguation on neural machine translation: A case study in korean. *IEEE Access*, 6:38512–38523.

OpenAI. 2022. Openai: Introducing chatgpt.

Mohammad Taher Pilehvar and Jose Camacho-Collados. 2018. Wic: the word-in-context dataset for evaluating context-sensitive meaning representations. *arXiv preprint arXiv:1808.09121*.

David Premack and Guy Woodruff. 1978. Does the chimpanzee have a theory of mind? *Behavioral and brain sciences*, 1(4):515–526.

Alessandro Raganato, Jose Camacho-Collados, Roberto Navigli, et al. 2017. Word sense disambiguation: a uinified evaluation framework and empirical comparison. In *Proceedings of the 15th Conference of the European Chapter of the Association for Computational Linguistics: Volume 1, Long Papers*, volume 1, pages 99–110.

Philip Resnik. 1996. Selectional constraints: An information-theoretic model and its computational realization. *Cognition*, 61(1-2):127–159.

Philip Resnik. 1997. Selectional preference and sense disambiguation. In *Tagging Text with Lexical Semantics: Why, What, and How?*

Annette Rios Gonzales, Laura Mascarell, and Rico Sennrich. 2017. Improving word sense disambiguation in neural machine translation with sense embeddings. In *Proceedings of the Second Conference on Machine Translation*, pages 11–19, Copenhagen, Denmark. Association for Computational Linguistics.

Oscar Sainz, Oier Lopez de Lacalle, Eneko Agirre, and German Rigau. 2023. What do language models know about word senses? zero-shot wsd with language models and domain inventories. *arXiv preprint arXiv:2302.03353*.

Maarten Sap, Ronan Le Bras, Daniel Fried, and Yejin Choi. 2022. Neural theory-of-mind? on the limits of social intelligence in large LMs. In *Proceedings of the 2022 Conference on Empirical Methods in Natural Language Processing*, pages 3762–3780, Abu Dhabi, United Arab Emirates. Association for Computational Linguistics.

Bastin Tony Roy Savarimuthu, Surangika Ranathunga, and Stephen Cranefield. 2024. Harnessing the power of llms for normative reasoning in mass.

Karin Kipper Schuler. 2005. *VerbNet: A broad-coverage, comprehensive verb lexicon*. University of Pennsylvania.

Lütfi Kerem Senel, Timo Schick, and Hinrich Schütze. 2022. Coda21: Evaluating language understanding capabilities of nlp models with context-definition alignment. *arXiv preprint arXiv:2203.06228*.

Gemini Team, Rohan Anil, Sebastian Borgeaud, Yonghui Wu, Jean-Baptiste Alayrac, Jiahui Yu, Radu Soricut, Johan Schalkwyk, Andrew M Dai, Anja Hauth, et al. 2023. Gemini: a family of highly capable multimodal models. *arXiv preprint arXiv:2312.11805*.

Hugo Touvron, Thibaut Lavril, Gautier Izacard, Xavier Martinet, Marie-Anne Lachaux, Timothée Lacroix, Baptiste Rozière, Naman Goyal, Eric Hambro, Faisal Azhar, et al. 2023. Llama: Open and efficient foundation language models. *arXiv preprint arXiv:2302.13971*.

Tomer Ullman. 2023. Large language models fail on trivial alterations to theory-of-mind tasks. arxiv.

Ming Wang and Yinglin Wang. 2020. A synset relation-enhanced framework with a try-again mechanism for word sense disambiguation. In *Proceedings of the 2020 Conference on Empirical Methods in Natural Language Processing (EMNLP)*, pages 6229–6240, Online. Association for Computational Linguistics.

Ming Wang, Jianzhang Zhang, and Yinglin Wang. 2021. Enhancing the context representation in similarity-based word sense disambiguation. In *Proceedings of the 2021 Conference on Empirical Methods in Natural Language Processing*, pages 8965–8973, Online and Punta Cana, Dominican Republic. Association for Computational Linguistics.

Jason Wei, Yi Tay, Rishi Bommasani, Colin Raffel, Barret Zoph, Sebastian Borgeaud, Dani Yogatama, Maarten Bosma, Denny Zhou, Donald Metzler, et al. 2022. Emergent abilities of large language models. *arXiv preprint arXiv:2206.07682*.

Gregor Wiedemann, Steffen Remus, Avi Chawla, and Chris Biemann. 2019. Does bert make any sense? interpretable word sense disambiguation with contextualized embeddings. *arXiv preprint arXiv:1909.10430*.

Zhaofeng Wu, Linlu Qiu, Alexis Ross, Ekin Akyürek, Boyuan Chen, Bailin Wang, Najoung Kim, Jacob Andreas, and Yoon Kim. 2024. Reasoning or reciting? exploring the capabilities and limitations of language models through counterfactual tasks. In *Proceedings of the 2024 Conference of the North American Chapter of the Association for Computational Linguistics: Human Language Technologies (Volume 1: Long Papers)*, pages 1819–1862, Mexico City, Mexico. Association for Computational Linguistics.

Zhengxuan Wu, Christopher D Manning, and Christopher Potts. 2023. Recogs: How incidental details of a logical form overshadow an evaluation of semantic interpretation. *Transactions of the Association for Computational Linguistics*, 11:1719–1733.

Boon Peng Yap, Andrew Koh, and Eng Siong Chng. 2020. Adapting bert for word sense disambiguation with gloss selection objective and example sentences. *arXiv preprint arXiv:2009.11795*.

S Ye, Y Xie, D Chen, Y Xu, L Yuan, C Zhu, and J Liao. 2022. Improving commonsense in vision-language models via knowledge graph riddles (2022). *Computing Research Repository*, 10.

Chun-Xiang Zhang, Rui Liu, Xue-Yao Gao, and Bo Yu. 2021. Graph convolutional network for word sense disambiguation. *Discrete Dynamics in Nature and Society*, 2021:1–12.

Yuhan Zhang, Edward Gibson, and Forrest Davis. 2023. Can language models be tricked by language illusions? easier with syntax, harder with semantics. *arXiv preprint arXiv:2311.01386*.

Zirui Zhao, Wee Sun Lee, and David Hsu. 2024. Large language models as commonsense knowledge for large-scale task planning. *Advances in Neural Information Processing Systems*, 36.

Zhi Zhong and Hwee Tou Ng. 2010. It makes sense: A wide-coverage word sense disambiguation system for free text. In *Proceedings of the ACL 2010 System Demonstrations*, pages 78–83, Uppsala, Sweden. Association for Computational Linguistics.

A Appendix: A Taxonomy of the Failure Cases

Table 1 and 9 show a categorization of primary world knowledge required to decide on a sense. Reference sentences are given as examples.

B Appendix: Details of the Prompts

In Table 10, 11, 12, and 13 we list the prompts used to query the language models.

Table 9: Failure cases - Part II

WKR		Example text	Remarks
Category	**Sub Category**		
5. Common-sense			
	5.1. Knowledge of Geography, Trade relations, Reasoning	The discovery of the mines of America ... does not seem to have had any very **sensible** effect upon the prices of things in England.	"sensible" is being used to provide counter-intuitive information against the expectation that America's affairs could have a perceivable impact on that of England. The correct choice: *Easily perceived; appreciable*
	5.2. Subject/Domain knowledge	The iron content of these growth habits varies as follows: plates and rosettes honeycomb **cabbagehead**.	"cabbagehead" is being used to refer to a composition of minerals. The correct choice: *A roughly spherical aggregation of a mineral*
6. Satire		his lordship was out of humor. That was the way Chollacombe described as knaggy an old gager as ever Charles had had the ill-**fortune** to serve.	"fortune" carries a sense of inevitability. The correct choice: *Destiny, especially favorable*
7. Figurative		One ambassador sent word to the duke's son that his visit should be **retaliated**.	"retaliated" is being used to mean a reciprocal action. The correct choice: *To repay or requite by an act of the same kind.*
8. Religious writing		How **impertinent** that grief was which served no end!	"impertinent" is found in a religious text where the word carries the meaning of lack of patience. The correct choice: *insolent, ill-mannered*
9. World knowledge		Dr. Bertrand tells us that the first patient he ever **magnetized**, being attacked by a disease of a hysterical character, became subject to convulsions of so long duration and so violent in character, that he had never, in all his practice, seen the like ...	"magnetized" is being used to alleviate hysteria. The correct choice: *To hypnotize using mesmerism*

WKR Column: Type of World Knowledge Required. The target word is bolded. The correct choice (last column) is the definition corresponding to the gold key.

Table 10: Prompts for GPT-3.5-Turbo-0125. We use the same prompt template for both 0-shot and few-shot test splits for the FEWS dataset. Also, we explicitly instruct the model not to provide any explanations to prevent it from generating verbose texts.

Dataset Name	**Prompt**
Unified Framework	Which of the following senses is correct for the word [TGT] in the following text: [SEN] I) [SENSEDEF 1] II) [SENSEDEF 2] III) [SENSEDEF 3] Do not provide explanations. Just output the choice.
CoarseWSD-20	Which of the following sense choices is correct for the word [TGT] in the following text: [SEN] I) [SENSEDEF 1] II) [SENSEDEF 2] III) [SENSEDEF 3] Do not provide explanations.
WiC	Is the sense of [TGT] same in the following two sentences, say Yes or No: sentence1: [SEN 1] sentence2: [SEN 2] Please do not provide explanations.
FEWS	Which of the following senses is correct for the word [TGT] in the following text: [SEN] I) [SENSEDEF 1] II) [SENSEDEF 2] III) [SENSEDEF 3] Print a choice. Do not provide explanations. Just output the choice.
	Acronyms: *SENSEDEFN: Sense definition;* *SEN: Sentence;* *TGT: Target word to be disambiguated;*

Table 11: Prompts for Mistral 7B. We use the same prompt template for both 0-shot and few-shot test splits for the FEWS dataset. Also, we explicitly instruct the model not to provide any explanations to prevent it from generating verbose texts.

Dataset Name	Prompt
Unified Framework	Which of the following senses is correct for the word [TGT] in the following text: [SEN] I) [SENSEDEF 1] II) [SENSEDEF 2] III) [SENSEDEF 3] Do not provide explanations.
CoarseWSD-20	Which of the following sense choices is correct for the word [TGT] in the following text: [SEN] I) [SENSEDEF 1] II) [SENSEDEF 2] III) [SENSEDEF 3] Do not provide explanations.
WiC	Is the sense of [TGT] same in the following two sentences, say Yes or No: sentence1: [SEN 1] sentence2: [SEN 2] Please do not provide explanations.
FEWS	Which of the following senses is correct for the word [TGT] in the following text: [SEN] I) [SENSEDEF 1] II) [SENSEDEF 2] III) [SENSEDEF 3] Print a choice. Do not provide explanations.
	Acronyms: *SENSEDEFN: Sense definition;* *SEN: Sentence;* *TGT: Target word to be disambiguated;*

Table 12: Prompts for Llama-2-70b-chat. We use the same prompt template for both 0-shot and few-shot test splits for the FEWS dataset. Also, we explicitly instruct the model not to provide any explanations to prevent it from generating verbose texts.

Dataset Name	Prompt
Unified Framework	Which of the following senses is correct for the word [TGT] in the following text: [SEN] I) [SENSEDEF 1] II) [SENSEDEF 2] III) [SENSEDEF 3] Do not provide explanations. Just output the choice.
CoarseWSD-20	Which of the following sense choices is correct for the word [TGT] in the following text: [SEN] I) [SENSEDEF 1] II) [SENSEDEF 2] III) [SENSEDEF 3] Do not provide explanations.
WiC	Is the sense of [TGT] same in the following two sentences, say Yes or No: sentence1: [SEN 1] sentence2: [SEN 2] Please do not provide explanations.
FEWS	Which of the following senses is correct for the word [TGT] in the following text: [SEN] I) [SENSEDEF 1] II) [SENSEDEF 2] III) [SENSEDEF 3] Print a choice. Do not provide explanations. Just output the choice.
	Acronyms: *SENSEDEFN: Sense definition;* *SEN: Sentence;* *TGT: Target word to be disambiguated;*

Table 13: Prompts for Gemini Pro. We use the same prompt template for both 0-shot and few-shot test splits for the FEWS dataset.

Dataset Name	Prompt
Unified Framework	Which of the following senses is correct for the word [TGT] in the following text: [SEN] I) [SENSEDEF 1] II) [SENSEDEF 2] III) [SENSEDEF 3]
CoarseWSD-20	Which of the following sense choices is correct for the word [TGT] in the following text: [SEN] I) [SENSEDEF 1] II) [SENSEDEF 2] III) [SENSEDEF 3]
WiC	Is the sense of [TGT] same in the following two sentences, say Yes or No: sentence1: [SEN 1] sentence2: [SEN 2]
FEWS	Which of the following senses is correct for the word [TGT] in the following text: [SEN] I) [SENSEDEF 1] II) [SENSEDEF 2] III) [SENSEDEF 3]
	Acronyms: *SENSEDEFN: Sense definition;* *SEN: Sentence;* *TGT: Target word to be disambiguated;*

AIStorySimilarity: Quantifying Story Similarity Using Narrative for Search, IP Infringement, and Guided Creativity

Jon Chun
Kenyon College
chunj@kenyon.edu

Abstract

Stories are central for interpreting experiences, communicating, and influencing each other via films, medical, media, and other narratives. Quantifying the similarity between stories has numerous applications including detecting IP infringement, detecting hallucinations, search/recommendation engines, and guiding human-AI collaborations. Despite this, traditional NLP text similarity metrics are limited to short text distance metrics like n-gram overlaps and embeddings. Larger texts require preprocessing with significant information loss through paraphrasing or multi-step decomposition. This paper introduces AIStorySimilarity, a novel benchmark to measure the semantic distance between long-text stories based on core structural elements drawn from narrative theory and script writing. Based on four narrative elements (characters, plot, setting, and themes) as well 31 sub-features within these, we use a SOTA LLM (gpt-3.5-turbo) to extract and evaluate the semantic similarity of a diverse set of major Hollywood movies. In addition, we compare human evaluation with story similarity scores computed three ways: extracting elements from film scripts before evaluation (Elements), directly evaluating entire scripts (Scripts), and extracting narrative elements from the parametric memory of SOTA LLMs without any provided scripts (GenAI). To the best of our knowledge, AIStorySimilarity is the first benchmark to measure long-text story similarity using a comprehensive approach to narrative theory. All code, data, and plot image files are available at `https://github.com/jon-chun/AIStorySimiliarity`.

1 Introduction

Stories and narrative are universally used by humans to communicate, interpret, store, and react to the world around them (Boyd, 2017) (Schreiner et al., 2017). When organized within a narrative framework, information can be more readily understood, stored, and recalled (Zdanovic et al., 2022). Beyond traditional fiction, researchers are now applying narrative theory to enhance medicine (Coret et al., 2018), law (Jiang et al., 2024b), business (Rees, 2020), and national identity rhetoric (Sweet and McCue-Enser, 2010). Narratives show immense potential for emotional persuasion (Lehnen, 2016) and, when used in combination with emotionally intelligent AI (Broekens et al., 2023), are classified as high risk by the EU AI Act (EU (Parliament) - and Jaume Duch Guillot, 2023).

A number of traditional NLP subtasks relate to stories and narratives, both for analysis and generation. Analysis is typically restricted to short-text lengths from approximately one sentence to several paragraphs at most (e.g. MoverScore, BERTScore, QAEval). NLP tasks include identifying sentiment, topics, characters, dialog, and events. Long texts can be analyzed with a sequential sliding-window of short-text substrings. This enables the extraction of distributed narrative elements from long texts including character social networks (Bost and Labatut, 2019), event timelines (Zhong and Cambria, 2023) or plot related information like diachronic-emotional arcs (Chun 2018) and narrative crux points (Elkins 2022).

Most traditional NLP techniques like sentiment classification, NER, and POS limit story analysis to relatively short texts. However, the introduction of the Transformer architecture (Vaswani et al., 2017) and rapid progress in LLM performance since the launch of ChatGPT (OpenAI, 2022) has revolutionized NLP. While smaller traditional models like BERT and BART can still be competitive for structured narrow tasks like NER (Paper with Code, 2024a) and POS (Papers with Code, 2024b), LLMs generally dominate the NLP leaderboards (Guo et al., 2023). More importantly, trained on trillions of tokens of language, LLMs have acquired a fluency, coherence, common-sense reasoning, expressiveness, and creativity with natural language that enable new, more complex and open-ended

Proceedings of the 28th Conference on Computational Natural Language Learning, pages 161–177
November 15-16, 2024 ©2024 Association for Computational Linguistics

NLP tasks like human-level story generation (Xie et al., 2023) and analysis (Chun and Elkins 2023).

However, there are serious limitations to trying to understand long-text stories by using short-text NLP techniques over a sequence of sentences or paragraphs. Authors, readers, and IP lawyers generally evaluate stories at higher levels of abstractions that escape short-text decomposition techniques or suffer information loss in the process. Powerful narrative elements like character arcs, themes and complex plot devices are often latent, implied, and disseminated throughout the text and require a global unified perspective to identify, extract, and analyze. Narrative theory and screenwriting conventions provide conceptual frameworks for describing and capturing these essential structural elements inherent in stories.

Film studies, Narratology (Berhe et al., 2022) and script writing best practices (Mckee, 1997; Snyder, 2005; Truby, 2007) decompose narrative structures and elements into different narrative elements. Characters including relationships and motivations. Plot is the sequence of events in the story. Settings involve not only time and place, but other aspects like culture. Themes are central ideas and messages. Character arcs track the transformation of characters over the course of the story in response to events. Dialog collectively is the spoken words and interactions that reveal personality, relationships and advance the plot. Classification of narrative elements are flexible. A simpler framework could combine character, character arc and dialog into one broader concept of character. Arguably least intuitive, themes are the big ideas and messages that provide deeper meaning, emotional connection and purpose like good vs evil, life finds a way, or love endures.

A variety of NLG subfields try to leverage hallucination as a creativity control in story generation (Chieh-Yang et al., 2023), creative writing (Ippolito et al., 2022), and screenwriting (Mirowski et al., 2022). Text generation (CTG) is focused on controlling the creative process including more precisely directing the degree and type of hallucinations (Zhang et al., 2022). This could enhance human-AI interactions from better human-AI creativity collaboration to more engaging chatbots.

A relatively recent and small set of researchers have begun focusing on the positive value LLM hallucinations can bring in the form of creativity or 'confabulation' (Sui et al., 2024). This growing perspective warrants a survey of hallucination from a creative perspective (Jiang et al., 2024a), and new applications are being identified like contrastive dataset generation (Yao et al., 2023). The all rely upon upon semantic distance metrics.

The use case of quantifying intellectual property infringement of copyrighted works illustrates the concept of narrative 'similarity'. IP infringement upon written work like movie script involves two tests of 'substantial similarity'. The intrinsic test is an analysis of identifiable properties like character, plot points, and themes. The extrinsic test is a more subjective analysis of whether an "ordinary person" would recognize such similarities (Helfing, 2020). Unlike the high-profile NYTimes-OpenAI lawsuit claiming perfect word-for-word reproductions (Pope, 2024), most infringement cases have historically fallen in this gray zone of 'substantial similarity'. Many more cases may arise either accidentally or intentionally as generative AI becomes a mainstream content creation- and creative collaboration-tool. There is therefore a pressing need to formalize a semantic similarity metric for narratives. The main contributions of this paper are:

· AIStorySimilarity, the first narrative semantic similarity benchmark using a scoring rubric based on formal narrative structural elements. · Evaluation of three common comparison methodologies to measure the similarity between test and reference film narratives on a) parametric memory [GenAI], b) extracted narrative elements [Elements] and c) unprocessed scripts [Scripts]

· A benchmark with broad application for detecting IP infringement of copyrighted works, film/novel/narrative search and recommendation engines, detecting hallucinations, and guiding creativity with extensive reporting for human-in-the-loop explainability and verification.

2 Related Work

SemEval22 Task 8 evaluated the semantic distances between news stories in order to move to more complex semantic metrics. Many entrants used text representations like TF-IDF derived from traditional low-level syntax features (Jobanputra and Rodríguez, 2022), but others used features based on higher-level abstractions like narrative schemas and writing style (Chen et al., 2022). However, many of NLG evaluations using high-level abstractions like empathy and style (Shen et al., 2024) and the narrative theory of Labov and Waletzky (Levi et al.,

2022) focus on creating novel annotated training datasets (Chaturvedi et al., 2018). The 6th Annual Workshop on Narrative Extraction from Text (Campos et al., 2023) survey papers provide a contemporaneous overview of some of the more recent approaches to extracting narrative elements from text (Zhu et al., 2023).

Beyond AI text generation, SOTA LLMs like GPT3.5 and GPT4o are increasingly used as proxies for human evaluators in open-ended, reference-free NLG tasks (Li et al., 2024). They provide benefits of speed, scalability, and cost savings alongside increasingly human-level or better performance (Hada et al., 2023; Ke et al., 2024; Wang et al., 2023). This LLM-as-judge trend (Thakur et al., 2024) is evident in various NLP tasks, such as evaluating the quality of generated stories, assessing the effectiveness of adversarial attacks, and grading the comprehensibility of disordered speech transcriptions (Chiang and yi Lee, 2023; Tomanek et al., 2024). For instance, the MT-Bench framework demonstrates a strong 80% agreement between LLM evaluations and human judgments in assessing model performance (Zheng et al., 2023).

For semantic text similarity, LLMs are shown to be more aligned with humans than any other metric (Aynetdinov and Akbik, 2024). However, precautions must be taken to avoid biases like a model's preference for evaluating its own generated content (Chhun et al., 2024). Moreover, challenges remain in areas of trust and safety (Reiter, 2024) and problems exist with human evaluations themselves (Elangovan et al., 2024; Gao et al., 2024). Despite these limitations (Bavaresco et al., 2024), LLMs show promise in augmenting and even replacing certain types of human evaluations given continual advances in AI.

At higher levels of abstraction, a variety of research areas relate to text similarity. This includes subfields that rely upon structural elements for automatic story generation (ASG) or for automated essay scoring (AES). Traditionally, these fields have used a combination of human evaluators, human-annotated references, and more general NLP metrics like coherence (Guan et al., 2021). In addition, more formal structural approaches generate or evaluate more diffuse global features like narrative frameworks (Wang et al., 2022), readability (coherence, fluency, simplicity), and adequacy (faithfulness, informativeness) (Hu et al., 2024). Emphasis on story similarity between reference and test works relate to plagiarism detection, intellectual property infringement, movie recommendation and search engines, hallucination detection (Huang et al., 2023; Ye et al., 2023) and measuring creativity in derivative works. AIStorySimilarity leverages an abstract structural approach using narrative theory with similarity metrics using SOTA LLMs.

3 Methods

3.1 Dataset

To provide a reference to assess the accuracy of similarity scores and relative rankings, a human expert selected a dataset of 9 popular Hollywood films they ranked as shown in Table 1. "Raiders of the Lost Arc", a 1981 summer hit, was selected as the reference film and 8 other test films were selected in order of decreasing similarity. This included a. the 1984 and 1989 Indiana Jones sequel films, b. three other adventure genre films with historical artifact themes, and c. three very different non-adventure genre films (romantic drama, black comedy, and musical). All scripts are ingested as plain text complete with character name, dialog, scene headings, action, and other annotations where available (see ./data/film_scripts_txt).

Sim.	Genre	Name	Year	Rank
ref	Adventure	Raiders of the Lost Ark	1981	-
1	Sequel #1	Indiana Jones and the Temple of Doom	1984	2
2	Sequel #2	Indiana Jone and the Last Crusade	1989	2
3	Adventure	National Treasure	2004	10
4	Adventure	Laura Croft Tomb Raider	2001	14
5	Adventure	The Mummy	1999	8
6	Romantic Drama	Titanic	1997	7
7	Black Comedy	Office Space	1999	133
8	Musical	La La Land	2016	83

Table 1: Films similar to Raiders of the Lost Ark

Most films were selected by popularity as measured by box office gross (The-Numbers.com, 2024), critical reviews (Tomatoes, 2024) and/or pop culture influence (e.g. Tomb Raider video game tie-ins). These criteria ensure most films are well represented in LLM training datasets that include Wikipedia, movie scripts, and movie review websites. The least popular film, Office Space, was included to be used as a stress test check against hallucination as described in section 3.5.

3.2 Comparison Methods and Narrative Source

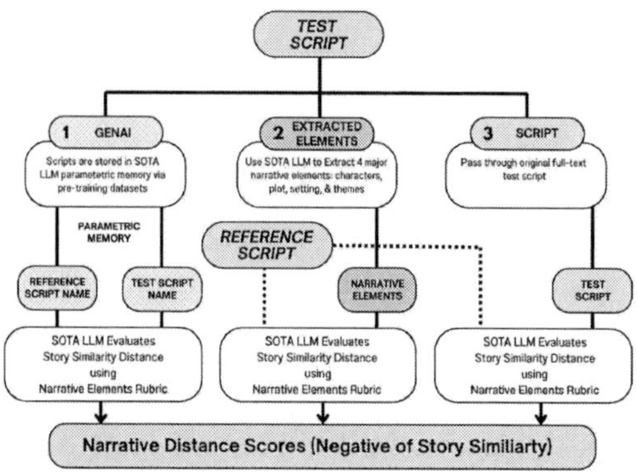

Figure 1: Three Comparison Methods

Each of the 8 test films was compared to the reference film to evaluate the semantic differences using one of three different techniques as shown in Figure 1. First [GenAI]: the SOTA LLM was only provided the names of the reference and test films and asked to evaluate similarity based upon knowledge of both films from parametric memory using the narrative scoring rubric. Second [Elements]: narrative elements and sub-features were extracted from full-text movie scripts and extracts were evaluated for similarity using the narrative scoring rubric. Third[Script]: full-text scripts of both the reference and test films were evaluated for similarity without providing the narrative scoring rubric.

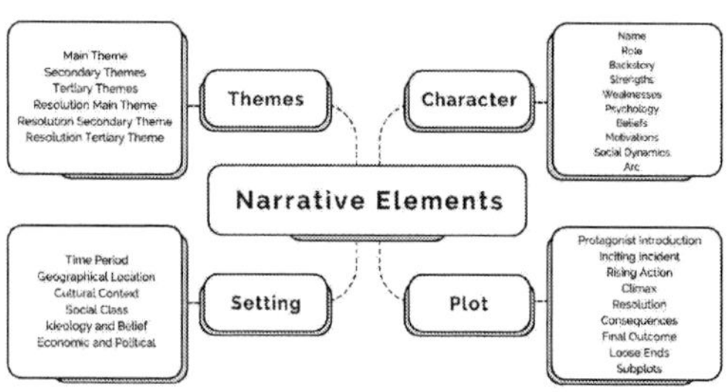

Figure 2: Narrative Similarity Rubric

Similarity comparison methods 1 (Elements) and 2 (GenAI) asked the SOTA LLM-as-judge to provide detailed similarity scores and explanations based on the narrative rubric shown in Figure 2. The extra step to extract and compare individual elements in method 2 Elements was akin to an explicit chain of prompts focusing on a two-step evaluation process. The relative performance of method 1 using only the extracted concise summaries of narrative elements provided an advantage over providing the entire scripts either explicitly (via method 3 Scripts) or implicitly (via method 2 GenAI). Evaluation method 3 (Scripts) was to see how well just providing raw film scripts and relying upon the SOTA LLM to come up with its own similarity evaluation metrics performed. That is, are the SOTA LLMs so capable they need no explicit scoring rubric to perform well?

The four major narrative elements in the scoring rubric consist of 6-10 sub-features as shown in Figure 2. Preliminary tests showed noticeable improvements when decomposing narrative into coherent and focused individual elements over just one large prompt combining all elements and sub-features. The four elements can also be ranked by an approximate order of complexity: Setting (facts), Plot (categorized and properly sequenced events), Character (facts, inferences, and analysis), and Themes (fuzzy categorizations, prioritization, and close readings that require the most abstract thinking and understanding of pragmatics).

The characters narrative element stands out because it contains the most disparate features in terms of type and analysis required. Name, role, backstory, and even strengths/weaknesses are largely factual. Psychology, beliefs and motivations add potentially complex interpretations of characters that are informed not only by descriptions, dialog, and actions but also by constructing mental models of internal personalities and drives that are informed by contextual clues, themes, and more abstract and interrelated sub-features and text. Finally, social dynamics and character arcs add the dimension of time and more interrelated aspects of text and narrative. It's not uncommon for dialog, social dynamics, and arc to be considered separate from characters, but we wanted relatively balanced elements while tracking these character-related topics. Dialog was sufficiently complex and difficult to concisely/comprehensively parameterize as a metric that it was left off in this iteration. Initial tests showed it added significant complexity, prompt task distraction, and resulted in lower signal/noise similarity scoring.

3.3 Models and API

Preliminary testing showed little to no difference between OpenAI gpt-4o and gpt-3.5-turbo, so GPT3.5 was selected as our SOTA LLM used to evaluate similarity for all three scoring methods. It was also used to extract narrative elements in the pre-processing stage for the second comparison method [Elements]. To check against hallucinations, two leading SOTA commercial models at the time of this paper, Claude 3.5 Sonnet and GPT4o, were used to validate factual accuracy as described below. In addition, these two SOTA models were used to provide a naive baseline similarity ranking for all 8 test films with a single prompt (without scripts or a narrative rubric).

Each API call was de novo with no memory or personal history. All OpenAI playground and chat UI interactions had personalization memory disabled and each was submitted afresh after every response to the previous prompt. Prompts were injected with a unique randomized string to avoid possible server-side caching when repeatedly sampling with the same prompt to collect sample sets of $n = 30$. Finally, inference hyperparameters were set as temperature $= 0.7$, top_p $= 0.5$, and response_format = 'json_object'. Initial exploratory analysis of temperature values $= 0.1$, 0.3, and 0.5 did not produce similarity score distributions with informative statistical spread values (e.g. IQR and std) to gauge confidence levels.

3.4 Prompts

Prompts were created to evaluate the semantic similarity between the reference film and 8 test films. The rubric to score overall similarity in Figure 2. is based on 4 main narrative elements and 31 sub-features. Narrative elements include characters, plot, setting and themes with excellent results which each have between 6-10 sub-features as shown. The common anatomy of all prompts is shown in Figure 3 using the 'plot' element. The full text of these four principal prompts can be found in Appendix A.

Two variations of this set of 4 prompts were created: one for evaluation and one for extractions (used only for method 2 Elements). The evaluation prompt asked the LLM to estimate a similarity score (0-100) for each narrative element 'overall' and similarity scores for each of the associated sub-features in Figure 2. LLMs were prompted to provide an open-end 'reason' to justify each similarity

```
###REFERENCE FILM
{reference_film}

###TEST FILM
{test_film}

###PERSONA
You are a world-famous narratologist and successful film
scriptwriter.

###ELEMENT_FEATURES
{Enumerate sub-features for one of the four narrative elements}

###INSTRUCTIONS:
You are a world-famous narratologist and successful film scriptwriter
so precisely and carefully think step by step to
COMPARE the similarities between the
above ###TEST_ELEMENT and the baseline ###REFERENCE_ELEMENT
using ###ELEMENT_FEATURES then
respond with estimated similarity scores between (0-100) for the each of the FEATURES
as well as an 'overall' similarity score
ONLY use information provided HERE,
DO NOT USE information from your memory.
Return your response in JSON form following
this ###TEMPLATE as demonstrated in the ###EXAMPLE below

###TEMPLATE
(give example of JSON layout with types and value ranges for each field)

###EXAMPLE
(give one-shot realistic example of expected JSON response)
```

Figure 3: Prompt Template

score.

Eight extractions and comparisons were made to measure the similarity between the reference film and 8 test films. Extractions were run once for all four elements across all 8 reference-test comparisons (32 API calls). Evaluations of story similarity were run 30 times for each 4 narrative elements across all 8 reference-test comparisons for a total of 960 API calls. The cl100k_base tokenizer used by GPT3.5 and GPT4, request token counts varied by comparison method, approximately 1250 for GenAI and 2200 for Elements. Scripts were converted to plain text and attached along with scoring prompts for the Script method.

4 Results

4.1 Overview

The oversized Table 2 in Appendix B compares narrative semantic similarity between the reference film 'Raiders of the Lost Ark' and eight other films. Horizontally, a human expert ordered films left to right from most to least similar in groups of a. two sequels (light yellow), b. three other adventure genre films (medium yellow), and c. three different genre films (dark yellow). Ordering films within each group is based upon the expert's multiple viewing and intimate familiarity of narrative elements. For example, As a epic disaster film, Titanic shares dramatic elements with the adventure genre. The black comedy shares constant sublimated tension and conflict with adventure films. Finally, the relatively emotional and generally light-hearted nature of song-and-dance musical was judged the least similar. Human similarity is simply the rank ordering of similarity distance between each film and the reference film in the row labeled 'Human Similarity-Title'.

In three groupings vertically, AIStorySimilarity's three similarity methods (Elements, GenAI, Scripts) of AIStorySimilarity are compared 1. Across each row, LLM-as-a-judge similarity scores for each method overall as well as broken out by the four constituent narrative elements (character, plot, setting, themes) are listed.

Individual cells give similarity scores (0-100) between the reference film 'Raiders of the Lost Ark' and the film atop each column. The row indicates which combination of 'Similarity Method' and 'Narrative Element' the score corresponds to using the AIStorySimilarity rubric in Appendix A. The similarity score in each cell is based on the mean of 30 samples. Because the Script method proved to be the least reliable, only one film was analyzed from each of the three groups of films (sequels, adventures, and non-adventures) to verify general alignment with human evaluation.

The colored cells in Table 2 highlight the exact points of major differences between human and LLM-as-a-judge similarity ranking using the AIStorySimiliary rubric. These three types of errors are color-coded as follows:

- Red cells indicate similarity scores below human expert ranking
- Green cells indicate scores above human ranking
- Orange cells count as errors to penalize the excessive use of ties

The row of blue cells reflect the overall similarity scores for Elements characters were 80.00 across all models and n=30 iterations. All other Element values appeared correct and well distributed as did characters similarity scores for GenAI and Scripts. Several prompt variations were used to try to correct this, but no OpenAI API response changed this value. We note this anomaly here for completeness and as a point for future investigations.

Surprisingly, the similarity scores least aligned with the human expert are those produced by first extracting all the elements before doing a comparison using method 1 Elements in Table 2. As seen in the similarity plots, this extraction step removes all contextual script information, which results in less nuanced and more narrowly clustered scores. This narrowing of values, combined with both the inevitable information loss in extraction and the inherent noise in natural language descriptions, results in 37.5% total ranking errors compared to human expert ranking. The gaps between different similarity values are dramatically narrowed using the Elements method extraction. Despite numerous misorderings, the magnitude of score differences are relatively small compared to the other two methods.

In contrast, GenAI method similarity scores across all four narrative elements and 8 test films only had 2/32 or 6.25% total errors in ranking. Using a stricter definition of error to mean any misordering to compensate for the reduced test set of only 3 films, the Script method had an approximately equivalent total ranking error rate is 2/12 or 17%.

Based upon overall results in section 4.1, we remove the Elements method from further consideration and focus on comparing the similarity scores from the remaining two methods: GenAI and Scripts. All eight test films' similarity scores are shown in radar charts for both these methods in Figure 4 and Figure 5 respectively. The spokes represent similarity scores for the four narrative elements with the top vertical spoke represents the overall similarity scores.

Despite the better alignment with human experts for this test case, the GenAI method is not a universal solution for measuring story similarity. Notably, GenAI depends upon stories being evaluated that are well represented in the training dataset and parametric memory. Where this is not true (e.g. de novo generated narratives or recently released films after the training date cutoff), the other two methods are required. The choice between the Elements and the Scripts methods involves a series of trade-offs between stability, control, privacy, cost, performance, local edge applications, and other lesser factors.

High-res vector image files of all plots and figures are directly available in the subdirectory at https://github.com/jon-chun/AIStorySimiliarity/data/.

4.2 Comparing Similarity Scores

Results for GenAI in Figure 4 show a nice gradation in similarity score across the test films with "Raiders of the Lost Ark". The eight films gener-

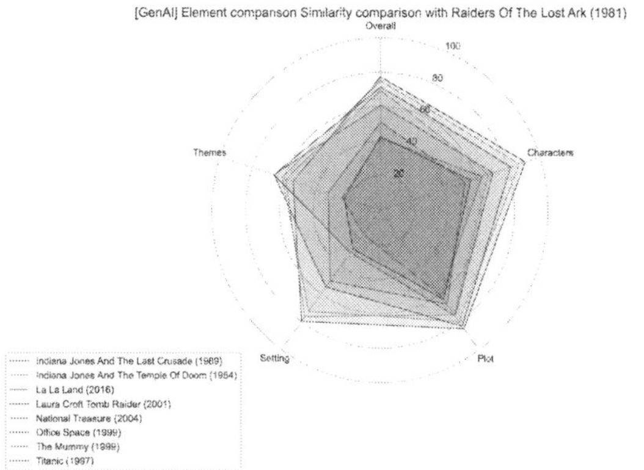

Figure 4: Full GenAI Similarity Scores

ally cluster by similarity in three groupings already noted: two sequels (largest polygons), three unrelated adventure genre films, and the three unrelated genres (smallest polygons). Plot is the most similar narrative element across all films, perhaps due to the near ubiquitous strong hero's journey in Hollywood films targeted at mass audiences. In contrast, Themes reflect the greatest diversity with the lowest similarity scores. This aligns with the earlier idea that Themes is the most abstract, subjective, and artistically unconstrained of the four narrative elements. Most importantly, we get a nice spread along the 'noon' overall similarity axis demonstrating AIStorySimilarity to make both coarse- and fine-grained distinctions between very similar (sequels), similar (adventure), and dissimilar (non-adventure) films.

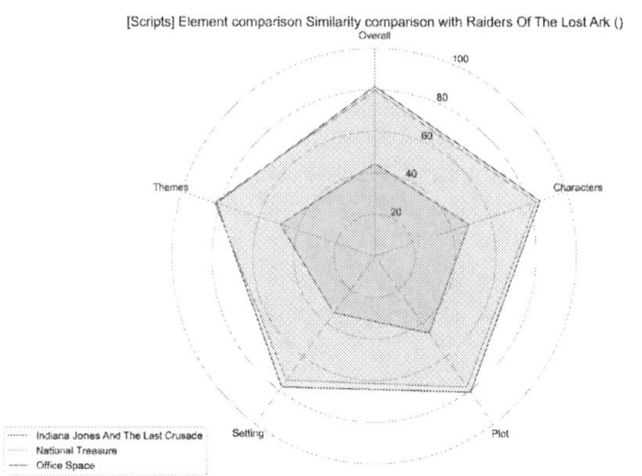

Figure 5: Sampled Script Similarity Scores

Using SOTA LLMs as a judge, the Script method does a relatively good job in similarity scoring when presented with clearly different films as shown in Figure 5. In this case, both the reference and test film scripts were fed into GPT3.5 with no rubric and with only minimal prompting to estimate impromptu similarity scores (0-100). Figure 5 shows a clear distinction between a sequel and adventure film vs a non-adventure film. However, there is poor discrimination between the sequel and adventure film. This suggests that minimalist prompting without an explicit evaluation rubric (e.g. AIStorySimialrity) may be limited to distinguishing between fewer and more distinct films

4.3 Comparing Rankings

The three bar charts in Figure 6 through Figure 8 visualize all 3 methods AIStorySimilarity uses to compute overall similarity scores. As mentioned in section 4.1, the Elements method first decomposes film scripts into distinct narrative elements before scoring. This appears to remove rich contextual information required to draw sharp distinctions. This lowers discrimination power resulting in more ranking errors. In contrast, both generating elements from parametric memory (GenAI) and manually providing copies of scripts (Scripts) result in smoother gradations between films and sharp boundaries between the 3 categories of test films.

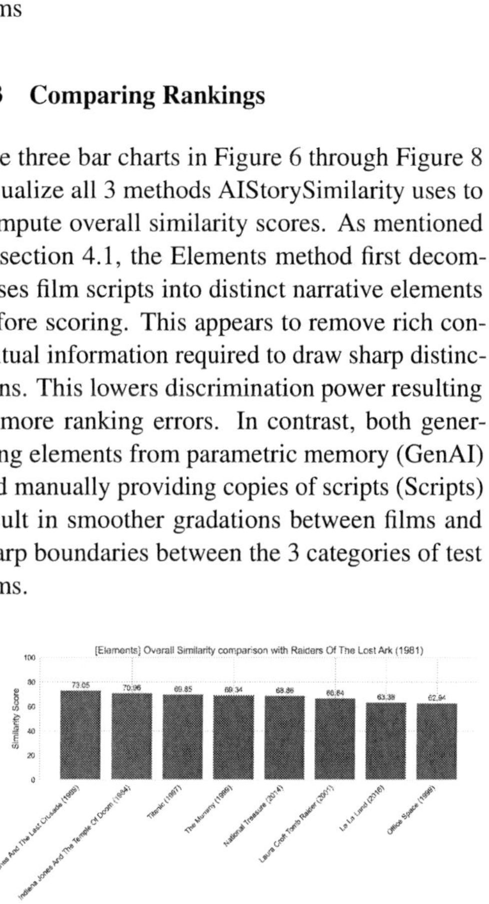

Figure 6: Full Elements Overall Similarity Scores

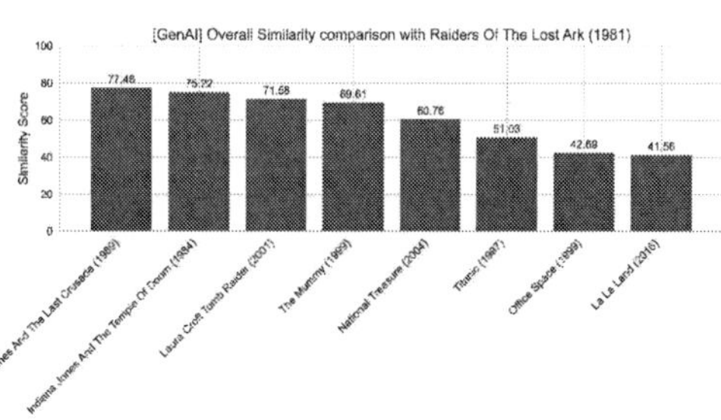

Figure 7: Full GenAI Overall Similarity Scores

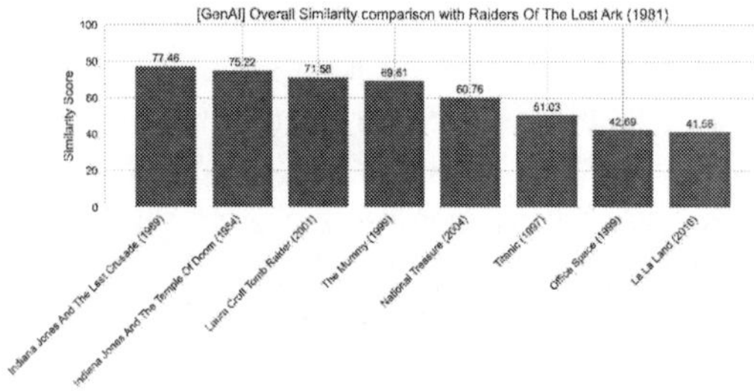

Figure 8: Sampled Scripts Overall Similarity Scores

5 Conclusion

AIStorySimilarity presents a novel story similarity metric and benchmark based upon narratology and best practices in screenplay writing. This benchmark overcomes limitations with traditional text and story similarity metrics and has many potential real-world applications including search/recommendation engines, IP infringement detection, and guided creative AI-collaboration. Three comparisons methods are tested and evaluated including 1. preprocessing scripts to extract concise narrative elements (Elements), 2. using LLM parametric memory with a narrative rubric (GenAI), and 3. providing full-text scripts with a narrative rubric (Scripts). For these famous Hollywood films, the GenAI method proved most aligned with the human expert. However, the other two methods (Elements and Scripts) may be required for narratives that do not exist in parametric memory or are subject to other practical constraints like cost and privacy. In our test dataset, results demonstrate SOTA LLMs have a good innate sense of popular Hollywood films, narrative theory, and can produce results in strong alignment with human experts.

6 Limitations

Three major limitations of this study are the size/-diversity of the film test dataset, the number/size of LLMs tested, and the types of narrative under study. This paper introduced and tested a simplified set of eight test films with clear degrees of similarity to the reference film. With the utility of AIStorySimilarity thus demonstrated, the method should next be stress tested with a much larger and diverse set of test films.

Our current test set did not have enough data or diversity to explore in close detail how our methodology evaluates similarity for semantically very different films or how it distinguishes between a much broader set of genres, or how it categorizes genres and edge cases that are difficult to classify. For example, some genres like musicals and comedies frequently blend aspects of other genres like adventure and romance. Additionally, non-conventional film styles, such as art house, postmodern, and absurdist cinema, are less suited to this approach due to their often fragmented narratives, experimental techniques, and resistance to traditional storytelling conventions.

The strong performance of the commercial SOTA models (GPT3.5, GPT4o and Claude 3.5 Sonnet), raises questions how well small open LLMs can perform under the demands and complexity of interpreting more abstract narrative elements and structures. Finally, measuring the narrative distance for different forms of narratives like those in medical histories, and financial reporting will require customizing the scoring rubric.

This paper limited itself to a focused study of prototypical Hollywood big-budget films across several genres based upon textual scripts. The author is currently expanding this work to work with stories that are multimodal (e.g. video/image, music, and voice) as well as from different cultures and semantic representations.

References

Ansar Aynetdinov and Alan Akbik. 2024. Semscore: Automated evaluation of instruction-tuned llms based on semantic textual similarity. *Preprint*, arXiv:2401.17072.

Anna Bavaresco, Raffaella Bernardi, Leonardo Bertolazzi, Desmond Elliott, Raquel Fernández, Albert Gatt, Esam Ghaleb, Mario Giulianelli, Michael Hanna, Alexander Koller, André F. T. Martins, Philipp Mondorf, Vera Neplenbroek, Sandro Pezzelle, Barbara Plank, David Schlangen, Alessandro Suglia, Aditya K Surikuchi, Ece Takmaz, and Alberto Testoni. 2024. Llms instead of human judges? a large scale empirical study across 20 nlp evaluation tasks. *Preprint*, arXiv:2406.18403.

Aman Berhe, Camille Guinaudeau, and Claude Barras. 2022. Survey on narrative structure: from linguistic theories to automatic extraction approaches. In *ICON*.

Xavier Bost and Vincent Labatut. 2019. Extraction and analysis of fictional character networks. *ACM Computing Surveys (CSUR)*, 52:1–40.

Brian Boyd. 2017. The evolution of stories: from mimesis to language, from fact to fiction. *Wiley Interdisciplinary Reviews: Cognitive Science*, 9. N. pag.

Joost Broekens, Bernhard Hilpert, Suzan Verberne, Kim Baraka, Patrick Gebhard, and Aske Plaat. 2023. Fine-grained affective processing capabilities emerging from large language models. In *2023 11th International Conference on Affective Computing and Intelligent Interaction (ACII)*, pages 1–8.

Ricardo Campos, Alípio Mário Jorge, Adam Jatowt, Sumit Kaur Bhatia, Marina Litvak, João Paulo Cordeiro, Conceição Rocha, Hugo Sousa, and Behrooz Mansouri. 2023. Report on the 6th international workshop on narrative extraction from texts (text2story 2023) at ecir 2023. *ACM SIGIR Forum*, 57:1–12.

Snigdha Chaturvedi, Shashank Srivastava, and Dan Roth. 2018. Where have i heard this story before? identifying narrative similarity in movie remakes. In *North American Chapter of the Association for Computational Linguistics*.

Xi Chen, Ali Zeynali, Chico Q. Camargo, Fabian Flöck, Devin Gaffney, Przemyslaw A. Grabowicz, Scott A. Hale, David Jurgens, and Mattia Samory. 2022. Semeval-2022 task 8: Multilingual news article similarity. In *International Workshop on Semantic Evaluation*.

Cyril Chhun, Fabian M. Suchanek, and Chloé Clavel. 2024. Do language models enjoy their own stories? prompting large language models for automatic story evaluation. *Preprint*, arXiv:2405.13769.

Cheng-Han Chiang and Hung yi Lee. 2023. Can large language models be an alternative to human evaluations? In *Annual Meeting of the Association for Computational Linguistics*.

Huang Chieh-Yang, Sanjana Gautam, Shannon McClellan Brooks, Ya-Fang Lin, and Ting-Hao 'Kenneth' Huang. 2023. Inspo: Writing stories with a flock of ais and humans. *ArXiv*, abs/2311.16521. N. pag.

Alon Coret, Kerry Boyd, Kevin Hobbs, Joyce Zazulak, and Meghan M. McConnell. 2018. Patient narratives as a teaching tool: A pilot study of first-year medical students and patient educators affected by intellectual/developmental disabilities. *Teaching and Learning in Medicine*, 30:317–327.

Aparna Elangovan, Ling Liu, Lei Xu, Sravan Bodapati, and Dan Roth. 2024. Considers-the-human evaluation framework: Rethinking human evaluation for generative large language models. *Preprint*, arXiv:2405.18638.

EU (Parliament) - and Jaume Duch Guillot. 2023. Eu ai act: first regulation on artificial intelligence.

Mingqi Gao, Xinyu Hu, Jie Ruan, Xiao Pu, and Xiaojun Wan. 2024. Llm-based nlg evaluation: Current status and challenges. *Preprint*, arXiv:2402.01383.

Jian Guan, Zhexin Zhang, Zhuoer Feng, Zitao Liu, Wenbiao Ding, Xiaoxi Mao, Changjie Fan, and Minlie Huang. 2021. Openmeva: A benchmark for evaluating open-ended story generation metrics. In *Annual Meeting of the Association for Computational Linguistics*.

Zishan Guo, Renren Jin, Chuang Liu, Yufei Huang, Dan Shi, Supryadi, Linhao Yu, Yan Liu, Jiaxuan Li, Bojian Xiong, and Deyi Xiong. 2023. Evaluating large language models: A comprehensive survey. *Preprint*, arXiv:2310.19736.

Rishav Hada, Varun Gumma, Adrian de Wynter, Harshita Diddee, Mohamed Ahmed, Monojit Choudhury, Kalika Bali, and Sunayana Sitaram. 2023. Are large language model-based evaluators the solution to scaling up multilingual evaluation? *Findings*.

Robert F. Helfing. 2020. Substantial similarity and junk science: Reconstructing the test of copyright infringement. *Fordham Intellectual Property, Media & Entertainment Law Journal*, 30:735.

Xinyu Hu, Mingqi Gao, Sen Hu, Yang Zhang, Yicheng Chen, Teng Xu, and Xiaojun Wan. 2024. Are llm-based evaluators confusing nlg quality criteria? *Preprint*, arXiv:2402.12055.

Lei Huang, Weijiang Yu, Weitao Ma, Weihong Zhong, Zhangyin Feng, Haotian Wang, Qianglong Chen, Weihua Peng, Xiaocheng Feng, Bing Qin, and Ting Liu. 2023. A survey on hallucination in large language models: Principles, taxonomy, challenges, and open questions. *Preprint*, arXiv:2311.05232.

Daphne Ippolito, Ann Yuan, Andy Coenen, and Sehmon Burnam. 2022. Creative writing with an ai-powered writing assistant: Perspectives from professional writers. *Preprint*, arXiv:2211.05030.

Hang Jiang, Xiajie Zhang, Robert Mahari, Daniel Kessler, Eric Ma, Tal August, Irene Li, Alex 'Sandy' Pentland, Yoon Kim, Deb Roy, and Jad Kabbara. 2024a. Leveraging large language models for learning complex legal concepts through storytelling. *Preprint*, arXiv:2402.17019.

Xuhui Jiang, Yuxing Tian, Fengrui Hua, Chengjin Xu, Yuanzhuo Wang, and Jian Guo. 2024b. A survey on large language model hallucination via a creativity perspective. *Preprint*, arXiv:2402.06647.

Mayank Jobanputra and Lorena Martín Rodríguez. 2022. Chen et al., 2022. In *International Workshop on Semantic Evaluation*.

Pei Ke, Bosi Wen, Zhuoer Feng, Xiao Liu, Xuanyu Lei, Jiale Cheng, Shengyuan Wang, Aohan Zeng, Yuxiao Dong, Hongning Wang, Jie Tang, and Minlie Huang. 2024. Critiquellm: Towards an informative critique generation model for evaluation of large language model generation. *Preprint*, arXiv:2311.18702.

Christina Lehnen. 2016. Exploring narratives' powers of emotional persuasion through character involvement: A working heuristic. *Journal of Literary Theory*, 10:247–270.

Effi Levi, Guy Mor, Tamir Sheafer, and Shaul Shenhav. 2022. Detecting narrative elements in informational text. In *Findings of the Association for Computational Linguistics: NAACL 2022*. Association for Computational Linguistics.

Zhen Li, Xiaohan Xu, Tao Shen, Can Xu, Jia-Chen Gu, Yuxuan Lai, Chongyang Tao, and Shuai Ma. 2024. Leveraging large language models for nlg evaluation: Advances and challenges. *Preprint*, arXiv:2401.07103.

Robert Mckee. 1997. *Story: Substance, Structure, Style*. Reganbooks, New York.

Piotr Wojciech Mirowski, Kory Wallace Mathewson, Jaylen Pittman, and Richard Evans. 2022. Co-writing screenplays and theatre scripts with language models: Evaluation by industry professionals. In *Proceedings of the 2023 CHI Conference on Human Factors in Computing Systems*. N. pag.

OpenAI. 2022. Chatgpt. `https://chatgpt.com/`. Accessed 30 Oct. 2022.

Audrey Pope. 2024. Nyt v. openai: The times's about-face. `https://harvardlawreview.org/blog/2024/04/nyt-v-openai-the-timess-about-face/`. Accessed 15 June 2024.

Caroline Rees. 2020. Transforming how business impacts people: Unlocking the collective power of five distinct narratives. *Corporate Governance: Social Responsibility & Social Impact eJournal*. N. pag.

Constanze Schreiner, Markus Appel, Maj-Britt Isberner, and Tobias Richter. 2017. Argument strength and the persuasiveness of stories. *Discourse Processes*, 55:371–386.

Jocelyn Shen, Joel Mire, Hae Won Park, Cynthia Breazeal, and Maarten Sap. 2024. Heart-felt narratives: Tracing empathy and narrative style in personal stories with llms. *Preprint*, arXiv:2405.17633.

Blake Snyder. 2005. *Save the Cat! : The Last Book on Screenwriting You'll Ever Need*. Michael Wiese Productions, Studio City, CA. Accessed 25 May 2005.

Peiqi Sui, Eamon Duede, Sophie Wu, and Richard Jean So. 2024. Confabulation: The surprising value of large language model hallucinations. *Preprint*, arXiv:2406.04175.

Derek R. Sweet and Margret McCue-Enser. 2010. Constituting "the people" as rhetorical interruption: Barack obama and the unfinished hopes of an imperfect people. *Communication Studies*, 61:602–622.

Aman Singh Thakur, Kartik Choudhary, Venkat Srinik Ramayapally, Sankaran Vaidyanathan, and Dieuwke Hupkes. 2024. Judging the judges: Evaluating alignment and vulnerabilities in llms-as-judges. *Preprint*, arXiv:2406.12624.

The-Numbers.com. 2024. Top-grossing movies of 1981. `https://www.the-numbers.com/market/1981/top-grossing-movies`. Accessed 2 July 2024.

Katrin Tomanek, Jimmy Tobin, Subhashini Venugopalan, Richard Cave, Katie Seaver, Jordan R. Green, and Rus Heywood. 2024. Large language models as a proxy for human evaluation in assessing the comprehensibility of disordered speech transcription. In *ICASSP 2024 - 2024 IEEE International Conference on Acoustics, Speech and Signal Processing (ICASSP)*. N. pag.

Rotten Tomatoes. 2024. Rotten tomatoes: Movies | tv shows | movie trailers | reviews. `https://www.rottentomatoes.com/`. Accessed 2 July 2024.

John Truby. 2007. *The Anatomy of Story: 22 Steps to Becoming a Master Storyteller*. Farrar, Straus And Giroux, New York.

Ashish Vaswani, Noam M. Shazeer, Niki Parmar, Jakob Uszkoreit, Llion Jones, Aidan N. Gomez, Lukasz Kaiser, and Illia Polosukhin. 2017. Attention is all you need. In *Neural Information Processing Systems*.

Jiaan Wang, Yunlong Liang, Fandong Meng, Zengkui Sun, Haoxiang Shi, Zhixu Li, Jinan Xu, Jianfeng Qu, and Jie Zhou. 2023. Is chatgpt a good nlg evaluator? a preliminary study. *Preprint*, arXiv:2303.04048.

Yuxin Wang, Jieru Lin, Zhiwei Yu, Wei Hu, and Börje F. Karlsson. 2022. Open-world story generation with structured knowledge enhancement: A comprehensive survey. *Neurocomputing*, 559:126792.

Zhuohan Xie, Trevor Cohn, and Jey Han Lau. 2023. The next chapter: A study of large language models in storytelling. In *International Conference on Natural Language Generation*.

Jia-Yu Yao, Kun-Peng Ning, Zhen-Hui Liu, Mu-Nan Ning, and Li Yuan. 2023. Llm lies: Hallucinations are not bugs, but features as adversarial examples. *Preprint*, arXiv:2310.01469.

Hongbin Ye, Tong Liu, Aijia Zhang, Wei Hua, and Weiqiang Jia. 2023. Cognitive mirage: A review of hallucinations in large language models. *Preprint*, arXiv:2309.06794.

Dominyk Zdanovic, Tanja Julie Lembcke, and Toine Bogers. 2022. The influence of data storytelling on the ability to recall information. In *Proceedings of the 2022 Conference on Human Information Interaction and Retrieval*.

Hanqing Zhang, Haolin Song, Shaoyu Li, Ming Zhou, and Dawei Song. 2022. A survey of controllable text generation using transformer-based pre-trained language models. *ACM Computing Surveys*, 56:1–37.

Lianmin Zheng, Wei-Lin Chiang, Ying Sheng, Siyuan Zhuang, Zhanghao Wu, Yonghao Zhuang, Zi Lin, Zhuohan Li, Dacheng Li, Eric P. Xing, Hao Zhang, Joseph E. Gonzalez, and Ion Stoica. 2023. Judging llm-as-a-judge with mt-bench and chatbot arena. *Preprint*, arXiv:2306.05685.

Xiaoshi Zhong and Erik Cambria. 2023. Time expression recognition and normalization: a survey. *Artificial Intelligence Review*, pages 1–26.

Lixing Zhu, Runcong Zhao, Lin Gui, and Yulan He. 2023. Are nlp models good at tracing thoughts: An overview of narrative understanding. In *Conference on Empirical Methods in Natural Language Processing*.

A Appendix A: Prompt to Compare Narrative Element of Characters

```
###REFERENCE_ELEMENT
{reference_element}

####TEST_ELEMENT:
{test_element}

###PERSONA:
You are a world-famous narratologist and successful film scriptwriter
    .

###ELEMENT_FEATURES
Name: Full name of character
Role: Clarifies the character's function within the story, whether
    they are driving the action, supporting the protagonist, or
    creating obstacles.
Backstory: This attribute helps to understand the formative
    experiences that shaped each character, providing insights into
    their motivations and behaviors.
Strengths: Highlights unique abilities and proficiencies,
    distinguishing characters by their specific talents and expertise.
Weaknesses: Humanizes characters by revealing vulnerabilities and
    personal challenges, making them more relatable and multi-
    dimensional.
Psychology: Uses personality assessments, such as the Big 5 OCEAN (
    Openness, Conscientiousness, Extroversion, Agreeableness,
    Neuroticism) model, to offer deeper insight into character traits.
Beliefs: Offers a window into the ethical and moral framework guiding
     each character's decisions, crucial for understanding their
    actions in moral dilemmas.
Motivations: Describes what drives the character to act, including
    desires, fears, and goals.
SocialDynamics: Explores the nature of interactions between
    characters, which can be pivotal in character development and plot
     progression.
Arc: Summarizes how the character changes or grows for better or
    worse over the story in response to events, decisions, and actions
     taken

###INSTRUCTIONS:
You are a world-famous narratologist and successful film scriptwriter
so precisely and carefully think step by step to
COMPARE the similarities between the attached ###TEST_ELEMENT and the
     baseline ###REFERENCE_ELEMENT
using ###ELEMENT_FEATURES then
responds with estimated similarity scores between (0-100) for the
    similarity of each of the FEATURES
as well as an 'overall' similarity score
ONLY use information provided HERE,
DO NOT USE information from your memory.
```

Return your response in JSON form following this ###TEMPLATE as demonstrated in the ###EXAMPLE below

###TEMPLATE

```
{
    "overall": {
        "similarity": integer range(0,100),
        "reasoning": string len(100,200)
    },
    "backstory": {
        "similarity": integer range(0,100),
        "reasoning": string len(100,200)
    },
    "strengths": {
        "similarity": integer range(0,100),
        "reasoning": string len(100,200)
    },
    "weakness": {
        "similarity": integer range(0,100),
        "reasoning": string len(100,200)
    },
    "psychology": {
        "similarity": integer range(0,100),
        "reasoning": string len(100,200)
    },
    "beliefs": {
        "similarity": integer range(0,100),
        "reasoning": string len(100,200)
    },
    "motivations": {
        "similarity": integer range(0,100),
        "reasoning": string len(100,200)
    },
    "social_dynamics": {
        "similarity": integer range(0,100),
        "reasoning": string len(100,200)
    },
    "arc": {
        "similarity": integer range(0,100),
        "reasoning": string len(100,200)
    }
}
```

###EXAMPLE:

```
{
    "role": {
        "similarity": 90,
        "reasoning": "Both are protagonists who drive the action in
            pursuit of historical treasures. They lead quests and face
             adversities while seeking valuable artifacts. The main
```

```
        difference is that Indiana Jones has a more established
        background as an archaeologist and professor."
},
"backstory": {
    "similarity": 75,
    "reasoning": "Both characters have backgrounds tied to
        historical pursuits. However, Indiana Jones' backstory is
        more focused on personal experiences shaping his ethical
        stance, while Gates' is deeply rooted in family legacy and
         tradition."
},
"strengths": {
    "similarity": 85,
    "reasoning": "Both characters share intelligence,
        resourcefulness, and deep historical knowledge. Indiana
        Jones has additional combat and survival skills, while
        Gates' strengths are more academically focused."
},
"weaknesses": {
    "similarity": 70,
    "reasoning": "Both have weaknesses that can lead to reckless
        behavior. Indiana's impulsiveness and fear of snakes are
        more specific, while Gates' obsession with treasure is
        more directly tied to his motivations."
},
"psychology": {
    "similarity": 85,
    "reasoning": "They share high openness, conscientiousness,
        and relatively low neuroticism. The main differences are
        in extroversion (Indiana higher) and agreeableness (Gates
        higher)."
},
"beliefs": {
    "similarity": 90,
    "reasoning": "Both strongly value history, preservation, and
        protecting artifacts from exploitation. Gates has an
        additional emphasis on familial duty."
},
"motivations": {
    "similarity": 80,
    "reasoning": "Both are driven by a desire to preserve history
         and fulfill personal quests. Gates' motivation is more
        focused on family legacy, while Indiana's includes a
        thirst for adventure and living up to his father's legacy
        ."
},
"social_dynamics": {
    "similarity": 75,
    "reasoning": "Both form alliances and face adversaries.
        Indiana's relationships are more complex, especially with
        his father and romantic interests. Gates' dynamics focus
        more on his team and main antagonist."
```

```
    },
    "arc": {
        "similarity": 85,
        "reasoning": "Both characters evolve to understand deeper
           values beyond their initial quests. Indiana's arc focuses
           on his relationship with his father, while Gates'
           emphasizes valuing relationships and heritage more broadly
           ."
    }
}
```

B Appendix B: Complete Similarity Results

Human Similarity-Title		1-Temple of Doom	2-Last Crusade	3-Tomb Raider	4-The Mummy	5-National Treasure	6-Titanic	7-Office Space	8-La La Land
Similarity Method	Narrative Element	1984 Sequel	1989 Sequel	Adventure	Adventure	Adventure	Drama-Romance	Black Comedy	Musical
Elements	Overall	70.96 (2)	73.05 (1)	66.84 (6)	69.34 (4)	68.86 (5)	69.85 (3)	62.94 (8)	63.38 (7)
	Characters	80.00	80.00	80.00	80.00	80.00	80.00	80.00	80.00
	Plot	72.50 (4)	71.62 (5)	70.00 (7)	77.06 (1)	76.62 (2)	70.88 (6)	70.00 (8)	73.53 (3)
	Setting	58.82 (3)	70.00 (1)	40.00 (tie 5-8)	60.29 (2)	40.00 (tie 5-8)	57.65 (4)	40.00 (tie 5-8)	40.00 (tie 5-8)
	Themes	72.50 (3)	70.59 (5)	77.35 (2)	60.00 (tie 6-8)	78.82 (1)	70.88 (4)	61.76 (tie 6-8)	60.00 (tie 6-8)
GenAI	Overall	75.22 (2)	77.46 (1)	71.58 (3)	69.61 (4)	60.76 (5)	51.03 (6)	42.69 (7)	41.56 (8)
	Characters	87.06 (2)	90.79 (1)	81.58 (3)	67.67 (5)	70.45 (4)	53.15 (8)	56.67 (7)	63.61 (6)
	Plot	79.73 (3)	84.82 (1)	83.03 (2)	75.03 (5)	75.82 (4)	67.42 (6)	64.06 (7)	61.64 (8)
	Setting	72.64 (3)	79.70 (1)	55.21 (4)	76.52 (2)	30.18 (6)	50.88 (5)	27.55 (7)	17.09 (8)
	Themes	61.45 (3)	54.55 (5)	66.48 (2)	59.21 (4)	66.58 (1)	32.67 (6)	22.48 (8)	23.91 (7)
Scripts	Overall		81.75 (1)			79.75 (2)		44.50 (3)	
	Characters		86.00 (1)			84.00 (2)		49.00 (3)	
	Plot		81.00 (1)			78.00 (2)		46.00 (3)	
	Setting		78.00 (1)			74.00 (2)		34.00 (3)	
	Themes		82.00 (2)			83.00 (1)		49.00 (3)	

Table 2: AIStorySimilarity Scores for Narrative Similarity to 'Raiders of the Lost Ark (1981)'

C Appendix C: Script Dataset Statistics

Film Name	Characters	Words	Sentences	Vocabulary Size	Reading Level
Raiders of the Lost Ark (1981)	160,278	29,870	2,847	4,730	104
Indiana Jones and the Temple of Doom (1984)	190,111	34,230	2,926	5,142	103
Indiana Jones and the Last Crusade (1989)	137,750	26,181	2,957	4,523	112
Titanic (1997)	246,677	46,028	4,564	6,824	112
The Mummy (1999)	157,912	27,759	3,127	4,571	110
Office Space (1999)	64,777	12,838	1,661	2,037	118
Lara Croft Tomb Raider (2001)	158,941	28,546	2,479	5,678	106
National Treasure (2004)	169,878	31,030	3,485	5,113	119
La-La-Land (2016)	104,568	20,520	2,416	3,626	114

Table 3: Simplified Scripts Dataset Statistics

SPAWNing Structural Priming Predictions from a Cognitively Motivated Parser

Grusha Prasad
Colgate University
gprasad@colgate.edu

Tal Linzen
New York University
linzen@nyu.edu

Abstract

Structural priming is a widely used psycholinguistic paradigm to study human sentence representations. In this work we introduce SPAWN, a cognitively motivated parser that can generate quantitative priming predictions from contemporary theories in syntax which assume a lexicalized grammar. By generating and testing priming predictions from competing theoretical accounts, we can infer which assumptions from syntactic theory are useful for characterizing the representations humans build when processing sentences. As a case study, we use SPAWN to generate priming predictions from two theories (Whiz-Deletion and Participial-Phase) which make different assumptions about the structure of English relative clauses. By modulating the reanalysis mechanism that the parser uses and strength of the parser's prior knowledge, we generated nine sets of predictions from each of the two theories. Then, we tested these predictions using a novel web-based comprehension-to-production priming paradigm. We found that while the some of the predictions from the Participial-Phase theory aligned with human behavior, none of the predictions from the the Whiz-Deletion theory did, thus suggesting that the Participial-Phase theory might better characterize human relative clause representations.

1 Introduction

Structural priming (Branigan and Pickering, 2017) is a widely used paradigm in psycholinguistics to study the structural representations that people construct when processing sentences. In this paradigm, researchers measure the extent to which the production or processing of *target* sentences is facilitated (or *primed*) by preceding *prime* sentences, and then use the pattern of priming behavior to draw inferences about the representations people construct. For example, consider a *target sentence* like (1).

(1) The boy threw the ball to the dog.

Prior work (Branigan et al., 1995) found that targets like (1) were produced more often, and were processed more rapidly, when they were preceded by primes like (2), that have the same structure, than when they were preceded by primes like (3), which, while describing the same transfer event as (2), have a different structure.

(2) The lawyer sent the letter to the client.

(3) The lawyer sent the client the letter.

From this result, Branigan et al. inferred that participants' mental representation of (1) is more similar to that of (2) than of (3).

Branigan and Pickering (2017) propose that by carefully studying which sentences prime each other we can build a theory of human structural representations. Building such a theory requires us to generate hypotheses about the particular prime-target pairs that would be most informative to compare. Insights from theoretical syntax, a field that has spent decades studying the structure of sentences, can help constrain this hypothesis space (Gaston et al., 2017): if two theories generate different priming predictions, the theory whose prediction better aligns with human behavior better characterizes the representations humans build. In this work we introduce a new parser, the Serial Parser in ACT-R With Null elements (SPAWN), that can generate quantitative priming predictions from theories in syntax.

SPAWN is a cognitively motivated parser in which the parsing decisions are driven by the computational principles proposed by a general purpose cognitive architecture, Adaptive Control of Thought-Rational (ACT-R; Anderson et al., 2004). Thus, SPAWN not only describes the computations underlying human parsing, but also specifies the cognitive processes involved. This level of specification makes it possible to explain *why*, given a grammar, some sentence A is primed more by sentence B compared to C, which in turn is use-

Proceedings of the 28th Conference on Computational Natural Language Learning, pages 178–197
November 15-16, 2024 ©2024 Association for Computational Linguistics

ful for generating quantitative behavioral priming predictions from syntactic theories.

Existing algorithmic models of parsing with this level of specification (Lewis and Vasishth, 2005) are limited in their ability to model assumptions from theories that use more contemporary frameworks like Minimalism for two reasons: First, they assume a disconnect between lexical and grammatical knowledge, which is inconsistent with the lexicalized grammar formalisms these frameworks adopt; Second, the models do not specify mechanisms to handle null (or covert) lexical items, which are essential components of several contemporary syntactic theories. SPAWN bridges this gap by adopting a lexicalized grammar formalism and specifying an explicit mechanism for null items.

As a case study, we use SPAWN to study the mental representations of sentences with relative clauses (RCs) such as (4) and (5).

(4) The cat examined by the doctor was skittish.
(5) The cat which was examined by the doctor was skittish.

We generate priming predictions from two competing syntactic theories: Whiz-Deletion (Chomsky, 1965), which assumes that the structure of (4) is identical to the structure of (5), but that the words "which" and "was" are covert; and Participial-Phase (Harwood, 2018) which assumes that (4) and (5) have different structures. We describe these theories in more detail in § 4. We generate nine sets of predictions from the two theories by modulating two factors: First, the strength of prior knowledge (model exposed to 0, 100 or 1000 sentences before the experiment); Second, the reanalysis mechanism (model goes back to the beginning of the sentence, or model uses one of two entropy-based measures to select a word to go back to). Then, we compare the predictions from these two theories to empirical human data we collected using a novel web-based comprehension-to-production priming paradigm.

We found that the predictions from the Whiz-Deletion never aligned with the qualitative pattern of human priming behavior, whereas under some assumptions about the underlying reanalysis mechanism and strength of prior knowledge, predictions from the Participial-Phase theory did align with the qualitative empirical pattern. These results suggest that the Participial-Phase account better characterizes human sentence representations. More broadly, this case study highlights how SPAWN can be used to adjudicate between competing theoretical assumptions: the quantitative behavioral predictions SPAWN generates can clarify how differences in assumptions about sentence structure or parsing mechanisms might translate into testable behavioral differences (if at all).

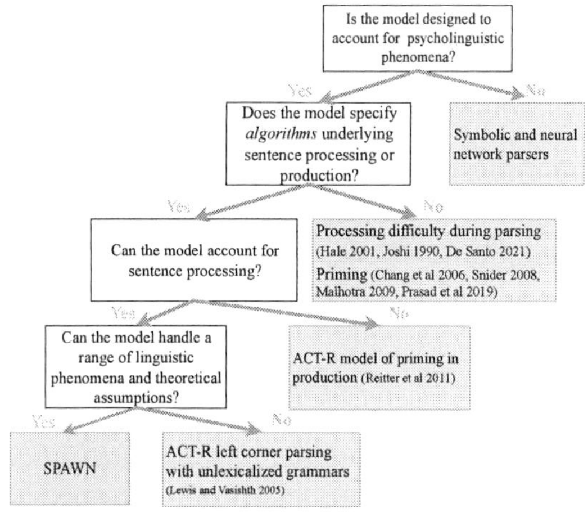

Figure 1: How is SPAWN different from other models?

2 Background

2.1 The ACT-R framework

ACT-R is a cognitive architecture designed to explain cognition through a small set of general computational principles and mechanisms that are relevant to a wide range of tasks and domains. One such mechanism which is particularly relevant in SPAWN is the retrieval of information from memory. The specific computational principles and algorithms that guide retrieval in ACT-R are outlined in § 3.2.1. Crucially, since ACT-R is intended to be a general purpose cognitive mechanism, most of the hyperparameters involved in this algorithm are already fixed based on data from a wide range of experimental paradigms and cognitive phenomena. This restricts the degrees of freedom and constrains the space of predictions that can be generated from any given theory.

2.2 Prior models of parsing

In most existing symbolic and neural-network based parsers, parsing decisions are not driven by specific cognitive principles such as the ones proposed by ACT-R. Therefore, generating predictions about observable human behavior (e.g., reading times) from these parsers requires making some additional *linking hypotheses*. Most prior hypotheses that link parsing decisions to human behavior have focused on notions of processing effort, such as the number of parse states explored (Hale, 2011), the maximum number of items on the stack at any given point (Joshi, 1990), or the maximum amount of time a node stays in memory (De Santo, 2021). These hypotheses cannot be used to generate priming predictions because they do not specify a mechanism by which a prime sentence might facilitate the processing of a target sentence.

One notable exception is the ACT-R based left-corner repair parser proposed by Lewis and Vasishth (2005), in which parsing decisions are made based on the activation of different *chunks* in the memory (such as words or grammar rules). The activation of chunks in this model can capture notions of both processing difficulty and priming. However, this model assumes a strong dissociation between the grammar and the lexicon and therefore cannot be adopted directly to generate predictions from lexicalized grammar formalisms such as Minimalist Grammar (Stabler, 1996), Combinatorial grammar (Steedman, 1988), Lexical-Functional Grammar (Kaplan and Bresnan, 1981) or Head-Driven Phrase Structure Grammar (Pollard and Sag, 1994). SPAWN is an ACT-R parser that models the link between the grammar and the lexicon can therefore generate predictions from lexicalized grammars.

2.3 Prior models of priming

While several models of priming have been proposed, as we illustrate in Figure 1, none of them can be used to adjudicate between contemporary syntactic theories. Many models of priming that model sentence processing either do not explicitly model syntactic structure (Chang et al., 2006; Malhotra, 2009; Prasad et al., 2019; Sinclair et al., 2022) or do not explicitly implement the mechanisms that result in priming (Snider, 2008). Reitter et al. (2011) proposed an ACT-R based model of priming that *does* explicitly implement priming mechanisms and, unlike Lewis and Vasishth's ACT-R model, also assumes a strong link between lexical and grammatical knowledge, and is thus consistent with contemporary lexicalized grammar formalisms. However, this model can only generate sentences given a semantic description, and therefore can only be used to model sentence production and not sentence processing. We bridge this gap with SPAWN.

3 Model description

SPAWN uses the three components of ACT-R that are relevant for parsing: **declarative memory**, which contains information about lexical and syntactic categories (cf. Reitter et al., 2011); **procedural memory**, which contains the algorithm for retrieving syntactic categories from memory and combining them together; and **buffers**, which store the words the parser has encountered so far, the syntactic categories retrieved for those words and the current parse state.[1] We describe the two memory components below (§ 3.1, § 3.2), as well as the mechanisms for learning and priming (§ 3.3, § 3.4).

3.1 Declarative memory (*the grammar*)

Declarative memory in SPAWN consists of two types of *chunks* (sets of attribute-value pairs): syntax chunks and lexical chunks (see § A.3 for the entire list of syntax and lexical chunks we use in this work).

Lexical chunks Each lexical chunk stores a word in the vocabulary along with the set of syntactic categories that the word could be associated with. For example, the lexical chunk for "examined" encodes that it can be either be associated with the *transitive verb* category or the *past participle* category.

Syntax chunks Each syntax chunk stores the constraints on the contexts in which a category can occur. For example, the *transitive verb* category encodes that it needs to have a *determiner phrase* category on its left and right. We use the Combinatorial Categorial Grammar (CCG; Steedman, 1988) formalism to express such constraints.[2]

3.2 Procedural memory (*the parser*)

SPAWN parses sentences incrementally, one word at a time. As schematized in Figure 2, processing each word involves four steps: retrieval, reanalysis, integration and null-prediction.

3.2.1 Retrieval

When processing a word w_i in a sentence s, the parser retrieves the category with the highest activation from the set C_i of all possible categories that w_i can be associated with. The activation A_{ijs}

[1] `https://github.com/grushaprasad/spawn`

[2] The CCG notation to encode the "transitive verb" category is (TP\DP)/DP; the forward slash indicates the words needs to combine with a DP on the right and the forward slash that it needs to combine with DP on the left. TP is the category that results from this combination.

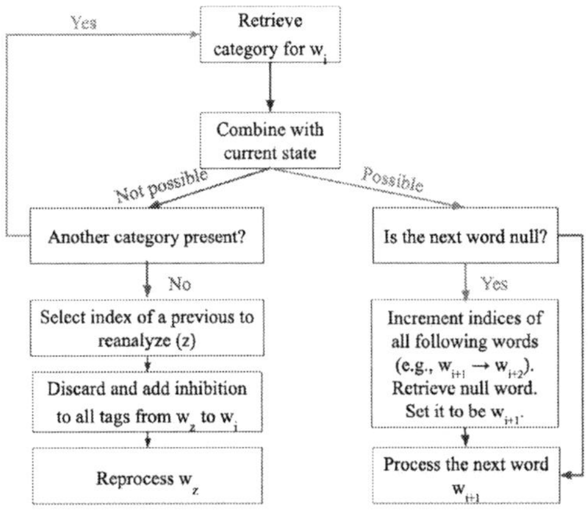

Figure 2: Steps involved in processing each word. Process is repeated till all words are assigned a category.

for any category $c_{ij} \in C_i$ is given by Equation 1, where B_{ij} is the base-level activation, L_{ij} is the activation w_i spreads to c_{ij}, I_{ijs} is the inhibition from the buffer to the c_{ij} when processing sentence s, and ϵ is noise sampled from *Normal*$(0, \sigma)$.

$$A_{ijs} = B_{ij} + L_{ij} - I_{ijs} + \epsilon \tag{1}$$

Base-level activation This activation for a category is high if the category has been retrieved recently and/or frequently. It is given by Equation 2, where k is the total number of times the model has encountered c_{ij}, T_{ijk} is the time taken to process all the words since the model's k-th encounter of c_{ij}, and d is a decay parameter.

$$B_{ij} = \log \sum_{k=1}^{K} T_{ijk}^{-d} \tag{2}$$

The time to process a word w_l is given by Equation 3, where N is the number of chunks retrieved when processing w_l, A_{ln} the activation of the n-th chunk the model retrieved when processing w_l (computed using Equation 1), F a latency factor and f a latency exponent.

$$t_l = \sum_{n=1}^{N} Fe^{-(fA_{ln})} \tag{3}$$

Thus, T_{ij_k} in Equation 2 is $t_k + t_{k+1} + \ldots t_i$.

Lexical activation The context independent activation a word w_i spreads to a category c_{ij} is given in Equation 4, where M is the maximum activation that any word can spread.

$$L_{ij} = M \times P(c_{ij} \mid w_i) \tag{4}$$

Inhibition The inhibition for c_{ij} takes into account how often c_{ij} was retrieved for w_i but was later discarded during reanalysis when processing a sentence s. It increases if c_{ij} was discarded often and/or recently, and is given by Equation 5 where Z indicates the total number of times c_{ij} was discarded when processing w_i in the current sentence, T_{ijs_z} indicates the time since the z-th time c_{ij} was discarded in sentence s, and d is the decay factor.

$$I_{ijs} = \log \sum_{z=1}^{Z} T_{ijs_z}^{-d} \tag{5}$$

The hyperparameters used in the equations above — d, F, f, M — are set based on prior ACT-R models (§ 5.3; § D).

3.2.2 Integration

Integrating a retrieved syntactic category c_{ij} involves combining c_{ij} with the current parse state P; this combination is determined by the CCG composition process (Steedman 1996; § B.1). If no successful combination is possible, then the retrieved category cannot be integrated into the current parse state; the parser then needs to either retrieve another category for the word, or, if no unexplored categories remain, trigger a reanalysis.

3.2.3 Reanalysis

When a reanalysis gets triggered at w_i, the parser selects an index z to regress to, where $z < i$. The method used to select z is a hyperparameter with two settings: **first-word regression** (go back to the first word every time) and **entropy-weighted regression** (sample z from $1 \ldots i$ weighted by the parser's uncertainty at each index). Once the parser selects z, it discards all of the categories retrieved for $w_z \ldots, w_{i-1}, w_i$, and resets the parse state to what it was at w_z. The parser keeps track of the categories that were discarded when processing each word in a sentence s, and uses this to compute the inhibition for each category using Equation 5.

Calculating uncertainty To calculate uncertainty at index x in entropy-weighted regression, we computed the activation of each category c_{jx} associated with w_x by adding together B_{xj} and L_{xj} (§ 3.2.1). Then, we converted these activation values into probabilities with the softmax function (temperature 1 or 10), and finally computed the entropy from these probabilities.

"Give-up" mechanism Despite inhibiting previously discarded categories, the parser could still get stuck in a loop retrieving the same (incorrect) category c_{ij} every time it is processing w_i if c_{ij} has a very high base-level or lexical activation. To prevent an infinite loop, we implemented a "give-up" mechanism, where after x iterations, the model ignores the base-level and lexical activation and uses only inhibition and noise to compute activation of c_{ij}. Setting x to 100 or 1000 resulted in nearly identical results (§ D).

3.2.4 Null or covert element prediction

Null or covert elements in sentences add additional uncertainty to the parsing process. To illustrate this, let us consider an example that is unrelated to our experimental setup, but illustrates the uncertainty in a theory-independent way. Given a prefix "The cat examined the doctor and the doctor ..." consider the following continuations; * indicates the continuation is ungrammatical.

(6) ... **examined** the cat.

(7) ... $\text{NULL}_{\text{examined}}$ the cat.

(8) * ... $\text{NULL}_{\text{examined}}$ **examined** the cat.

The covert $\text{NULL}_{\text{examined}}$ can only occur if its overt counterpart is absent. Therefore, after parsing the prefix, a serial parser has to predict whether the upcoming word in the sentence is covert or overt. If it expects the next word to be overt "examined", the parser should not retrieve any null elements. On the other hand, if it expects the next word to be covert $\text{NULL}_{\text{examined}}$, it needs to retrieve this category and integrate it with the current parse state before processing the remainder of the sentence.

We model this decision in SPAWN in the same way that we model other uncertainty: pick the option N_{iks} with the highest activation, where i is the current word, and $k \in \{x_1, x_2 \ldots x_p, \textit{not-null}\}$, where $x_1, ..., x_p$ are the types of null elements that can come after the current parse state. The activation for N_{iks} is given by Equation 6:

$$N_{iks} = L_{ik} - I_{iks} + \epsilon \qquad (6)$$

L_{ik} and I_{iks} are the same as in Equations 4 and 5. As in Equation 1, ϵ is noise sampled from $\textit{Normal}(0, \sigma)$. We do not include base-level activation for the null categories in this computation, because the base-level activation for the *not-null* category would be extremely high (most sentences in the corpus do not have null elements) and would result in the null categories never being retrieved. We also assume that only certain parse states can be followed by null elements (§ B.2): if the parser tried to insert null elements after every word, it would result in an exponential increase in the search space.

3.3 Updating activations ("learning")

Learning in SPAWN occurs by updating the counts of syntactic categories, which in turn are used to compute base-level and lexical activations (Equations 2, 4). These counts are updated at the end of processing each sentence based on the final set of categories and null-elements that were retrieved.

3.4 Emergence of priming in SPAWN

Priming in SPAWN emerges as a consequence of parsing and learning. There are two factors that can result in priming: an increase in the activation of relevant categories and an increase in the probability of reanalysis.

Increased activation When a word in the target sentence is ambiguous between two categories X and Y, if the parser retrieved X in a preceding prime sentence, that increases its base and lexical activation relative to Y, which makes X more likely to be retrieved in the target as well.

Increased reanalysis When a word in the target sentence is ambiguous between two categories X and Y, and Y has higher base and lexical activation, then the parser is more likely to retrieve Y initially. If a sequence of parsing decisions causes the parser to reanalyze the word, then the probability of the parser eventually retrieving X increases: the inhibition to Y during reanalysis decreases the difference in activation between X and Y.

4 A case study: Evaluating competing theories of reduced relative clauses

We use SPAWN to generate and test priming predictions for two competing syntactic theories of relative clauses that differ in their assumptions about how the structure of sentences like (9) is related to the structure of sentences like (10) and (11).

(9) The cat examined by the doctor was skittish. (Reduced passive RC; RRC)

(10)The cat who was examined by the doctor was skittish. (Full passive RC; FRC)

(11)The cat being examined by the doctor was skittish. (Reduced progressive RC; ProgRRC)

Under the **Whiz-Deletion account** of RCs (Chomsky, 1965), the sub-tree corresponding to any RC, whether reduced or not, is headed by the same node: a complementizer phrase (CP). In full RCs, the lexical content in this phrase (the wh-word and auxiliary "was") is overt, whereas in reduced RCs this lexical content is covert. By contrast, under the **Participial-Phase account** (Harwood, 2018), while full RCs are headed by CPs, reduced passive and progressive RCs, are headed by Voice Phrase (VoiceP) and Progressive Phrase (ProgP) respectively. Consequently, the Participial-Phrase account, unlike the Whiz-Deletion account, does not assume the presence of a covert *wh*-word and auxiliary in reduced passive and progressive RCs. See § A.1 for trees that illustrate these differences.

Implementing the two theories We implement two versions of SPAWN, a Whiz-Deletion version and a Participial-Phase version. The procedural memory (parsing mechanism) is identical across both versions. There are two main differences in the declarative memory (grammar) across the versions. First, they differ in the categories that nouns can be associated with: in the Whiz-Deletion version, all nouns modified by RCs have the category *NP/CP* (i.e., a noun looking to combine with a CP on its right), whereas in the Participial-Phase version, nouns modified by FRCs, RRCs and ProgRRCs are associated with different categories (*NP/CP*, *NP/VoiceP* and *NP/ProgP* respectively). Second, the versions have different null lexical items: the Whiz-Deletion version has lexical items for a null subject Wh-word, a null finite auxiliary and a null progressive auxiliary, all of which are absent in the Participial-Phase version (see § A.2).

5 Methods

5.1 Experimental paradigm

We used a comprehension-to-production priming paradigm to evaluate the two theories. In each experimental trial, human participants or SPAWN models were presented with three primes with the same structure, followed by an ambiguous partial prompt such as (15) that could be completed either with or without a reduced RC. We used four prime types: three prime types with RCs (one each for RRC, FRC and ProgRRC), as well as control primes without RCs, such as (12)–(14).

(12) The dog chased the boy and ran away.

(13) The monkey chased the hatter and stole a hat.

(14) The dentist chased her son and panted.

(15) The thief chased ___

Estimating priming effects We estimated priming effects by measuring the proportion of RRC target parses in the different priming conditions (see § 5.2 and § 5.3 for details on how these parses were measured in humans and models). Concretely, we estimated $P(RRC\ parse \mid target, primes)$ by fitting Bayesian mixed-effects logistic regression model with the following three predictors (specified using Helmert contrasts) as fixed effects: All RCs vs. AMV, ProgRRC and FRC vs. RRC, and ProgRRC vs. FRC. We used a weakly informative prior and a maximal random effects structure (see § E for further details).

Materials When creating our stimuli, we picked 24 target verbs that can give rise to a temporary ambiguity as in (15) which can either be resolved with either a main verb or reduced RC continuation. We created four items per verb and four versions of each item. The four versions of one of the items for the verb "chased" are illustrated below.

(16) The dog chased by the boy ran away.

(17) The dog who was chased by the boy ran away.

(18) The dog being chased by the boy ran away.

(19) The dog chased the boy and ran away.

From these materials we created counterbalanced lists: in each list, three items occurred as primes; the fourth was cut at the verb to generate the target.

5.2 Experiment with human participants

Participants We recruited 769 US-based participants from Prolific, of whom 765 were self-reported native speakers of English. We compensated them with 8.35 USD.

Design We developed a web-based version of the comprehension-to-production priming paradigm used by Pickering and Branigan (1998). In the original paradigm, participants were given incomplete sentences in a booklet and asked to complete them. Since participants can be less attentive on web-based platforms than in the lab, we modified the paradigm to ensure that participants had to fully read the prime sentences. On the prime trials, participants were presented with a sentence, and asked to re-type that sentence from memory on the next screen. They could not progress until they typed in the sentence perfectly, and could not copy-paste the sentence, but could go back to re-read the sentence as often as they liked. On the target trials, participants were presented with the partial prompt on the screen, and asked to re-type the prompt and complete it on the next screen. They could not progress until they typed in the prompt perfectly and entered at least one more word. We did not automatically verify participants' productions, but in practice almost all participants generated grammatical completions with real words.

Measuring the proportion of RRC parses We used regular expressions (§ F) to classify all target completions into two categories (RRC vs. non-RRC) and specified RRC completions as "success" in our Bayesian logistic regression model.

5.3 Experiment with SPAWN models

We generated predictions from 18 types of models which varied along 3 dimensions: **the grammar** (Whiz-Deletion vs. Participial-Phase; § 4, A.2), **the reanalysis implementation** (First-word regression and Entropy-Weighted reanalysis with temperature 1 or 10; § 3.2.3), and **the number of training sentences** (0, 100 or 1000 sentences). For each model type, we created 1280 model instances, which, as we describe below, share some hyperparameters and differ in others.

Model hyperparameters The following hyperparameters are fixed across all model instances: decay (d in Equations 2, 5), latency exponent (f in Equation 3), and maximum activation (M in Equation 4). The following hyperparameters differ for each model instance: latency factor (F in Equation 3), and the noise parameter (σ in § 3.2.1).

The values for d, f, and M as well as the sampling distributions for F and σ were were taken from Vasishth and Engelmann (2021) (see § D for more details). We sampled σ from $Normal(0.35, 1)$, because when sigma was sampled from Vasishth and Engelmann's $Uniform(0.2, 0.5)$, some models never retrieved syntactic categories with low base-level activation. However, there were no qualitative differences in results between the two distributions (see § D)

Training data To set initial base-level and lexical activations of the models prior to the experiment, we trained the models on 0, 100, or 1000 sentences and updated the activations at the end of each sentence as described in § 3.3. These small numbers are consistent with prior work which assumes that participants start experiments with very weak priors (Delaney-Busch et al., 2019; Fine et al., 2010).

We used templates[3] to generate a dataset of 10000 sentences in which the relative frequency of different types of RC sentences mirrored corpus statistics from Roland et al. (2007); for example, only 1% of the training sentences contained an RRC (see § C for details about the distribution of sentence types). For each model instance, we sampled the training sentences from this dataset. Given the low probability of RRCs, many model instances never encountered these in their training data, and as such started with a base-level activation of 0 for RRCs.

Design We presented each model instance with the stimuli from the human experiment. On a prime trial, the model parsed the sentence and updated the base-level and lexical activations based on the final set of retrieved categories. On a target trial, the model parsed the partial prompt and we recorded the resulting parse state; the model was constrained to end with only one of two partial states: DP/PP (RRC parse) or TP/DP (active parse).

Measuring the proportion of RRC parses We specified the DP/PP state as "success" in our Bayesian logistic regression model; unlike with humans, we do not need target completions to infer the parse the model assigned to the target.

6 Results

Participant/model exclusion Most participants (77%) never generated a single RRC target completion. Similarly most models (median of 67% across the 18 model types) never generated a single RRC parse state. Since the goal of this work is to find *differences* in the proportion of RRC parses between the primes, we only included in our analyses and plots the participants or models that generated at least one RRC completion or parse state.

Human priming behavior In the human experiment, we observed that the proportion of target RRC parses was highest when the target was preceded by RRC primes with the same structure, and lowest when preceded by AMV primes which did not have any relative clauses. The proportion of target RRC parses in other two priming conditions, ProgRRC and FRC, were equivalent relative to each other, lower than with RRC primes, and higher than with AMV primes. (Figure 4). See § E.3 for statistical analyses.

Whiz-Deletion vs. Humans In the Whiz-Deletion models, processing ProgRRC sentences involves the retrieval of the same null complementizer as in RRC sentences, whereas processing FRC

[3]`https://github.com/grushaprasad/spawn/blob/main/create_training_dat.py`

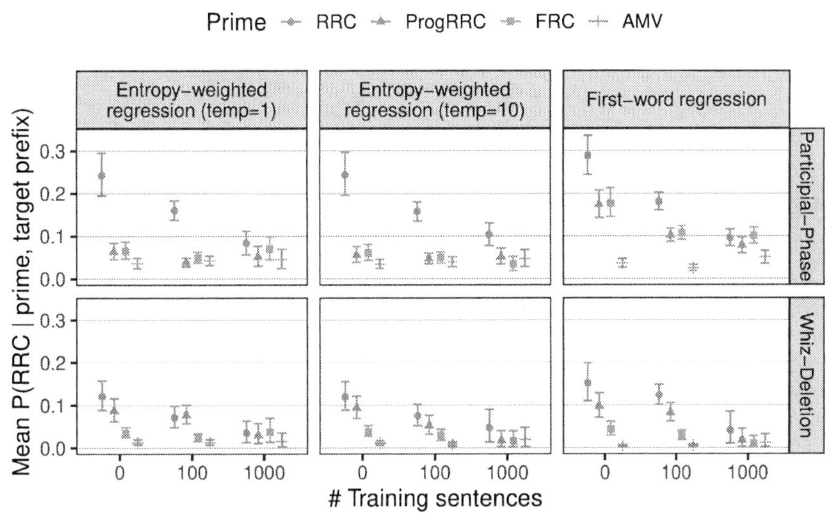

Figure 3: Predicted probability of RRC parse from the posterior distribution of the Bayesian logistic regression model. Error bars reflect 95% credible intervals.

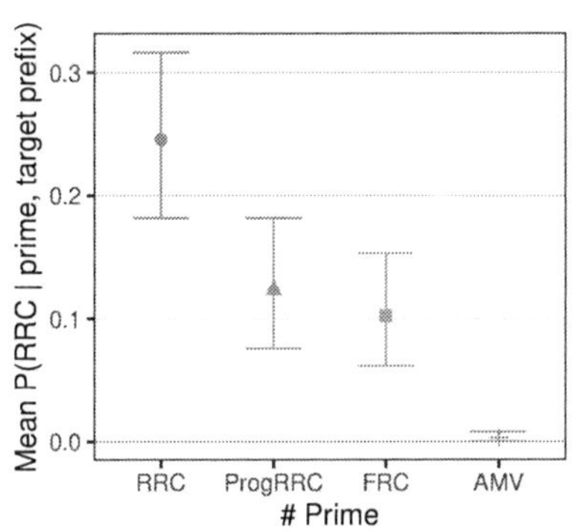

Figure 4: Empirical probability of RRC parse from the posterior distribution of the Bayesian logistic regression model. Error bars reflect 95% credible intervals.

sentences does not (§ B.3). Consequently, these models predicted that the proportion of target RRC parses was greater with ProgRRC primes than with FRC primes (Figure 3), a pattern that does not align with the qualitative priming pattern observed in humans. Additionally, the magnitude of priming effects in the RRC condition were also generally smaller than what was observed in humans (Figure 3, bottom panel). These results together suggest that the Whiz-Deletion account of RRCs, at least the way we operationalized it, is not consistent with the representations humans build.

Participial-Phase vs. Humans In the Participial-Phase models, unlike in their Whiz-Deletion counterparts, processing ProgRRC, FRC, or AMV primes does not involve retrieving any categories that are shared with RRC sentences. However, the categories retrieved for ProgRRC and FRC but not AMV primes, increase the probability of reanalysis when processing the ambiguous target sentences (§ B.3). This reanalysis, as discussed in § 3.4, in turn increases the probability of the model eventually assigning an RRC parse to the target, especially if the models' prior preference for AMV parses is relatively weak. Consequently, these models, particularly when they were trained on 0 and 100 sentences, predicted a graded effect which aligned with the qualitative priming pattern observed in humans: the proportion of target RRC parses was highest with RRC primes, followed by ProgRRC and FRC primes, and lowest with AMV primes. The models trained on 1000 sentences could not capture this qualitative pattern because they generated very few RRC sentences across the board. This suggests, in line with prior work (Delaney-Busch et al., 2019; Fine et al., 2010), that when modeling the production or processing of extremely infrequent structures (like RRCs), assuming weak prior knowledge might be necessary.

Of the models that captured the qualitative patterns, the models with first-word regression better captured the *magnitude* of the empirical priming effects (Figure 3). Taken together, these results suggest that, depending on the assumptions we make about reanalysis and strength of prior belief, the Participial-Phase account of RRCs, unlike the Whiz-Deletion account, can be consistent with the representations humans build.

7 Discussion

In this work we introduced a cognitively motivated parser, SPAWN, which can be used to generate quantitative behavioral predictions from contemporary syntactic theories that are based on lexicalized grammar formalisms. SPAWN makes it possible to evaluate what theoretical differences (if any) result in differing sentence processing predictions. As a case study, we used SPAWN to generate predictions from two competing theories of reduced relative clauses (Whiz-Deletion and Participial-Phase) while modulating the reanalysis mechanism and the number of training examples. We compared the predictions from these different versions of the SPAWN model to human behavior from a large-scale (N=769) web-based comprehension-to-production priming experiment.

We found that the predictions of the Whiz-Deletion SPAWN models did not capture the qualitative human priming behavior for any of the model types. In contrast, many of the Participial-Phase SPAWN models captured the qualitative patterns, with the models that best captured the *magnitude* of the empirical effects being ones with weak prior knowledge, that reprocesses the sentence from the beginning whenever reanalysis is triggered. Taken together, these results suggest that the Participial-Phase account of reduced relative clauses captures the structural representations people construct better than the Whiz-Deletion account.

Future work This work tentatively suggests that first-word regression might better model human processing than entropy-weighted regression. This observation needs to be more robustly validated with other empirical phenomena (e.g., priming in PO/DO sentences). Additionally, some of the parsing mechanisms SPAWN implements, such as for reanalysis or predicting null elements, are likely too simplistic to account for human sentence processing more generally (see § G). Future work can tweak these mechanisms and evaluate the modified models against processing benchmarks like the SAP Benchmark (Huang et al., 2024) which have more fine-grained measurements (e.g., reading time per word) across a range of psycholinguistic phenomena. Since the time taken for any of the parsing steps is measured in milliseconds by default in ACT-R, SPAWN can already generate quantitative predictions about the time taken to read or reprocess specific words in sentences, and therefore can be used with self-paced reading and eye-tracking datasets. Finally, future work can also use this paradigm to evaluate other competing syntactic theories.

Conclusion We proposed a cognitively plausible parser that can be used to generate *quantitative* behavioral predictions from syntactic theories. Using English reduced relative clauses as a case study, we demonstrated how this model can be used to adjudicate between competing syntactic theories and parsing mechanisms.

Acknowledgements

We would like to thank the anonymous reviewers, HSP 2023 and 2024 audience as well as Aniello De Santo, Shravan Vasishth, Will Merrill, Matt Wagers, Suhas Arehalli, Brian Dillon, Vijay Ramachandran and Joel Sommers for their valuable feedback.

This work was partly supported by an American Psychological Association Dissertation Research Award. The work was conducted using computational resources from the Maryland Advanced Research Computing Center (MARCC) and the Colgate Supercomputer (Partially funded by NSF Award #2346664).

References

John R Anderson, Daniel Bothell, Michael D Byrne, Scott Douglass, Christian Lebiere, and Yulin Qin. 2004. An integrated theory of the mind. *Psychological Review*, 111(4):1036.

Holly P Branigan and Martin J Pickering. 2017. An experimental approach to linguistic representation. *Behavioral and Brain Sciences*, 40.

Holly P Branigan, Martin J Pickering, Simon P Liversedge, Andrew J Stewart, and Thomas P Urbach. 1995. Syntactic priming: Investigating the mental representation of language. *Journal of Psycholinguistic Research*, 24(6):489–506.

Franklin Chang, Gary S Dell, and Kathryn Bock. 2006. Becoming syntactic. *Psychological review*, 113(2):234.

Noam Chomsky. 1965. Aspects of the theory ofsyntax. *Cambridge, MA: MITPress*, (1977):71–132.

Aniello De Santo. 2021. A minimalist approach to facilitatory effects in stacked relative clauses. *Proceedings of the Society for Computation in Linguistics*, 4(1):1–17.

Nathaniel Delaney-Busch, Emily Morgan, Ellen Lau, and Gina R Kuperberg. 2019. Neural evidence for bayesian trial-by-trial adaptation on the n400 during semantic priming. *Cognition*, 187:10–20.

Alex Fine, Ting Qian, T Florian Jaeger, and Robert Jacobs. 2010. Syntactic adaptation in language comprehension. In *Proceedings of the 2010 workshop on cognitive modeling and computational linguistics*, pages 18–26.

Phoebe Gaston, Nick Huang, and Colin Phillips. 2017. The logic of syntactic priming and acceptability judgments. *Behavioral and Brain Sciences*, 40.

John T Hale. 2011. What a rational parser would do. *Cognitive Science*, 35(3):399–443.

William Harwood. 2018. Reduced relatives and extended phases: A phase-based analysis of the inflectional restrictions on english reduced relative clauses. *Studia Linguistica*, 72(2):428–471.

Kuan-Jung Huang, Suhas Arehalli, Mari Kugemoto, Christian Muxica, Grusha Prasad, Brian Dillon, and Tal Linzen. 2024. Large-scale benchmark yields no evidence that language model surprisal explains syntactic disambiguation difficulty. *Journal of Memory and Language*, 137:104510.

Harold Jeffreys. 1998. *The theory of probability*. OuP Oxford.

Aravind K Joshi. 1990. Processing crossed and nested dependencies: An automation perspective on the psycholinguistic results. *Language and cognitive processes*, 5(1):1–27.

Ronald M Kaplan and Joan Bresnan. 1981. *Lexical-functional grammar: A formal system for grammatical representation*. Massachusetts Institute Of Technology, Center For Cognitive Science.

Richard L Lewis and Shravan Vasishth. 2005. An activation-based model of sentence processing as skilled memory retrieval. *Cognitive science*, pages 375–419.

Kyle Mahowald, Ariel James, Richard Futrell, and Edward Gibson. 2016. A meta-analysis of syntactic priming in language production. *Journal of Memory and Language*, 91:5–27.

Dominique Makowski, Mattan S. Ben-Shachar, and Daniel Lüdecke. 2019. bayestestr: Describing effects and their uncertainty, existence and significance within the bayesian framework. *Journal of Open Source Software*, 4(40):1541.

Gaurav Malhotra. 2009. *Dynamics of structural priming*. Ph.D. thesis, University of Edinburgh.

Martin J Pickering and Holly P Branigan. 1998. The representation of verbs: Evidence from syntactic priming in language production. *Journal of Memory and language*, 39(4):633–651.

Carl Pollard and Ivan A Sag. 1994. *Head-driven phrase structure grammar*. University of Chicago Press.

Grusha Prasad, Marten van Schijndel, and Tal Linzen. 2019. Using priming to uncover the organization of syntactic representations in neural language models. In *Proceedings of the 23rd Conference on Computational Natural Language Learning (CoNLL)*, pages 66–76, Hong Kong, China. Association for Computational Linguistics.

David Reitter, Frank Keller, and Johanna D Moore. 2011. A computational cognitive model of syntactic priming. *Cognitive science*, 35(4):587–637.

Douglas Roland, Frederic Dick, and Jeffrey L Elman. 2007. Frequency of basic english grammatical structures: A corpus analysis. *Journal of memory and language*, 57(3):348–379.

Arabella Sinclair, Jaap Jumelet, Willem Zuidema, and Raquel Fernández. 2022. Structural persistence in language models: Priming as a window into abstract language representations. *Transactions of the Association for Computational Linguistics*, 10:1031–1050.

Neal Snider. 2008. *Similarity and structural priming*. Ph.D. thesis, Stanford University.

Edward Stabler. 1996. Derivational minimalism. In *International conference on logical aspects of computational linguistics*, pages 68–95. Springer.

Mark Steedman. 1988. Combinators and grammars. In *Categorial grammars and natural language structures*, pages 417–442. Springer.

Mark Steedman. 1996. *Surface Structure and Interpretation*. MIT Press.

Shravan Vasishth and Felix Engelmann. 2021. *Sentence comprehension as a cognitive process: A computational approach*. Cambridge University Press.

A Details about the two theories of reduced relative clauses and how they are implemented in the declarative memory

A.1 Syntax trees

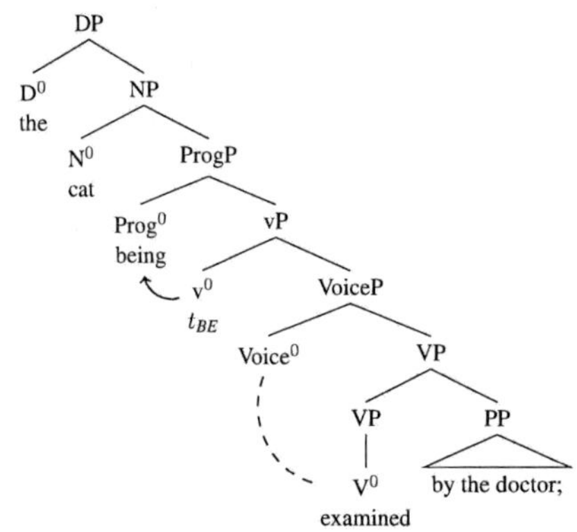

(a) Participial-Phase

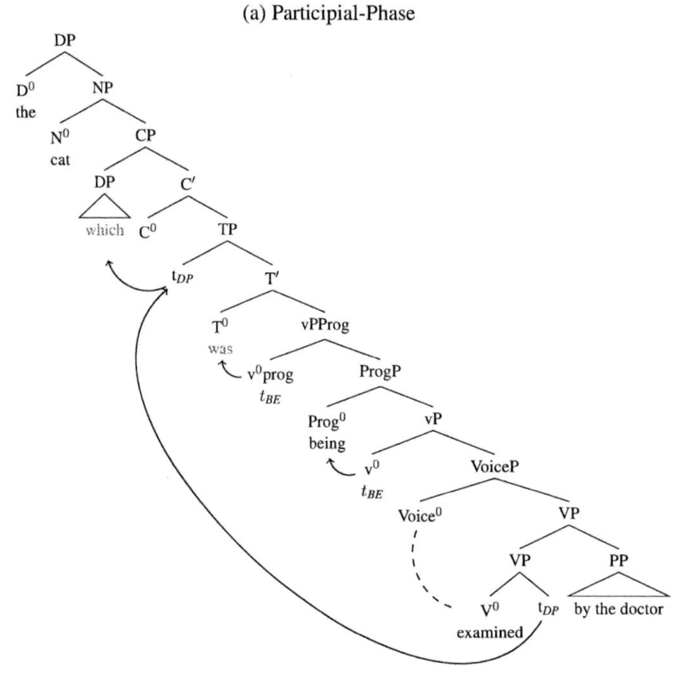

(b) Whiz-Deletion

Figure 5: Syntax tree for "The cat being examined by the doctor...". The words in red are unvoiced in the Whiz-Deletion account. The tree for "The cat examined by the doctor ..." is nearly identical but without the ProgP. In Participial-Phase VoiceP is the sister of *cat*; in Whiz-Deletion vP is the sister of *was*.

A.2 Differences in syntactic categories between the two theories

Category	Example sentence	Whiz-Deletion	Participial-Phase
Noun	"The cat which was examined by... "	NP/CP	NP/CP
("cat")	"The cat examined by ... "	NP/CP	NP/VoiceP
	"The cat being examined by ... "	NP/CP	NP/ProgP
Null wh subject	"The cat $NULL_{wh}$ $NULL_{pass}$ examined by..."	CP/(TP\DP)	MISSING
Null finite auxiliary		(TP\DP)/VoiceP	MISSING
Null progressive auxiliary	'The cat $NULL_{wh}$ $NULL_{prog}$ being examined by..."	(TP\DP)/ProgP	MISSING

When the noun in the Whiz-Deletion version combines with the null Wh subject and null finite or progressive auxiliary, it results in the same parse state as the Participial-Phase noun categories for RRC and ProgRRC: NP/VoiceP and NP/ProgP. We also explored an alternative implementation of the Whiz-Deletion account where instead of having three NULL categories — $NULL_{Wh}$, $NULL_{pass}$ and $NULL_{prog}$ — we had only two categories $NULL_{Whpass}$ (CP/VoiceP) and $NULL_{Whprog}$ (CP/ProgP). This implementation resulted in nearly identical results (§ 6)

Note, both accounts have the same categories for the null wh-word in RCs which modify objects of clauses like "The cat the doctor examined was skittish": Null Complementizer (Object RCs) in the following table.

A.3 Syntactic categories shared by the two theories

Category label	Example words	CCG rules
Determiner	the, a , an, some, his, her, many, a-lot-of	DP/NP
Determiner Phrase	something, everyone, non-violence, popularity	DP
Noun Phrase	dragon, media, palace, mission, trance, tax-fraud	NP
Preposition	on, to, into, by, at, in, down	PP/DP
Transitive verb (active)	accompanied, admired, betrayed, solved, forged	(TP\DP)/DP
Transitive verb (passive)	accompanied, admired, betrayed, solved, forged	VoiceP/PP
Transitive verb (location object)	arrived, staggered, marched, participated	(TP\DP)/PP
Intransitive verb	sang, cackled, complained, started-trending	TP\DP
Complementizer (Subject RC)	who	CP/(TP\DP)
Complementizer (Object RC)	who	CP/(((TP\DP)/DP)/DP)
Null Complementizer (Object RC)	$NULL_{Wh}$	CP/(((TP\DP)/DP)/DP)
Prog	being	ProgP/VoiceP
Auxiliary (followed by adjective)	was, were	(TP\DP)/(NP/NP)
Auxiliary (finite)	was	(TP\DP)/VoiceP
Auxiliary (progressive)	was	(TP\DP)/ProgP
Adjective	unreliable, competent, well-known, signature, radical	NP/NP
Adverb	rapidly, diligently, in-surprise, sullenly, wistfully	TP\TP
Conjunction	and	(TP/(TP\DP))\TP
EOS	.	end\TP

Table 1: Categories present in the declarative memory in both Whiz-Deletion and Participial-Phase versions of SPAWN. In the syntax chunks, the category labels are the keys, and the CCG rules the attributes. In the lexical chunks, the words are the keys, and the category labels the attributes. The entire vocabulary can be found in the create_declmem.py file in the Github repository.

B SPAWN parsing details

B.1 CCG combination and type-raising rules

Rule name	Parser state form	Tag form	Composed form
Forward composition	DP/NP	NP	DP
Backward composition	DP	TP\DP	TP
Forward harmonic composition	DP/VoiceP	VoiceP/PP	DP/PP
Backward harmonic composition	TP\DP	eos\TP	eos\DP
Forward crossed composition	CP/TP	TP\DP	CP\DP
Backward crossed composition	TP/VoiceP	eos\TP	eos/VoiceP

Table 2: Examples of all the six possible CCG composition rules being applied when parsing sentences in the training set.

We have just one type-raising rule: DP can get type-raised to TP/(TP\DP). This lets the subject DP in a sentence combine with a transitive verb — (TP\DP)/DP — before the transitive verb combines with the object DP.

The parser starts by sequentially trying to apply each of the six composition rules, stopping once a successful combination is found. If no successful combination is found, then the parser tries to the type-raising rule and then sequentially apply all six composition rules.

B.2 Categories that can be followed by null elements

In the Whiz-Deletion grammar the NP/CP category, and the CP/(TP\DP) can be followed by null elements, whereas in the Participial-Phase grammar, only the the NP/CP category can be followed by a null element (to account for object reduced RCs like "The cat the doctor examined was skittish").

B.3 Analysis of example sentences with our grammar

Old Parse state	Word	Correct category	Rule	New parse state
NULL	the	DP/NP	Initialize	DP/NP
DP/NP	cat	NP/VoiceP	Forward Harmonic Composition	DP/VoiceP
DP/VoiceP	examined	VoiceP/PP	Forward Harmonic Composition	DP/PP
DP/PP	by	PP/DP	Forward Harmonic Composition	DP/DP
DP/DP	the	DP/NP	Forward Harmonic Composition	DP/NP
DP/NP	doctor	NP	Forward Composition	DP
DP	liked	(TP\DP)/DP	Type raise DP	
TP/(TP\DP)			Forward Harmonic composition	TP/DP
TP/DP	the	DP/NP	Forward Harmonic composition	TP/NP
TP/NP	girl	NP	Forward Harmonic composition	TP
TP	EOS	end\TP	Backward composition	end

Table 3: CCG analysis for a reduced RC sentence under the Participial-Phase grammar. The rows in gray are the same across all RC types.

Old Parse state	Word	Correct category	Rule	New parse state
NULL	the	DP/NP	Initialize	DP/NP
DP/NP	cat	NP/CP	Forward Harmonic Composition	DP/CP
DP/CP	$NULL_{wh}$	CP/(TP\DP)	Forward Harmonic Composition	DP/(TP\DP)
DP/(TP\DP)	$NULL_{pass}$	(TP\DP)/VoiceP	Forward Harmonic Composition	DP/VoiceP
DP/VoiceP	examined	VoiceP/PP	Forward Harmonic Composition	DP/PP
DP/PP	by	PP/DP	Forward Harmonic Composition	DP/DP
DP/DP	the	DP/NP	Forward Harmonic Composition	DP/NP
DP/NP	doctor	NP	Forward Composition	DP
DP	liked	(TP\DP)/DP	Type raise DP	
TP/(TP\DP)			Forward Harmonic composition	TP/DP
TP/DP	the	DP/NP	Forward Harmonic composition	TP/NP
TP/NP	girl	NP	Forward Harmonic composition	TP
TP	EOS	end\TP	Backward composition	end

Table 4: CCG analysis for a reduced RC sentence under the Whiz-Deletion grammar. The rows in gray are the same across all RC types. We experimented with an alternative version where $NULL_{Wh}$ and $NULL_{pass}$ were combined into one category. This resulted in qualitatively similar results.

Old Parse state	Word	Correct category	Rule	New parse state
NULL	the	DP/NP	Initialize	DP/NP
DP/NP	cat	NP/ProgP	Forward Harmonic Composition	DP/ProgP
DP/ProgP	being	ProgP/VoiceP	Forward Harmonic Composition	DP/VoiceP
DP/VoiceP	examined	VoiceP/PP	Forward Harmonic Composition	DP/PP
DP/PP	by	PP/DP	Forward Harmonic Composition	DP/DP
DP/DP	the	DP/NP	Forward Harmonic Composition	DP/NP
DP/NP	doctor	NP	Forward Composition	DP
DP	liked	(TP\DP)/DP	Type raise DP	
TP/(TP\DP)			Forward Harmonic composition	TP/DP
TP/DP	the	DP/NP	Forward Harmonic composition	TP/NP
TP/NP	girl	NP	Forward Harmonic composition	TP
TP	EOS	end\TP	Backward composition	end

Table 5: CCG analysis for a reduced progressive RC sentence under the Participial-Phase grammar. The rows in gray are the same across all RC types.

Old Parse state	Word	Correct category	Rule	New parse state
NULL	the	DP/NP	Initialize	DP/NP
DP/NP	cat	NP/CP	Forward Harmonic Composition	DP/CP
DP/CP	$NULL_{wh}$	CP/(TP\DP)	Forward Harmonic Composition	DP/(TP\DP)
DP/(TP\DP)	$NULL_{prog}$	(TP\DP)/ProgP	Forward Harmonic Composition	DP/VoiceP
DP/ProgP	being	ProgP/VoiceP	Forward Harmonic Composition	DP/VoiceP
DP/VoiceP	examined	VoiceP/PP	Forward Harmonic Composition	DP/PP
DP/PP	by	PP/DP	Forward Harmonic Composition	DP/DP
DP/DP	the	DP/NP	Forward Harmonic Composition	DP/NP
DP/NP	doctor	NP	Forward Composition	DP
DP	liked	(TP\DP)/DP	Type raise DP	
TP/(TP\DP)			Forward Harmonic composition	TP/DP
TP/DP	the	DP/NP	Forward Harmonic composition	TP/NP
TP/NP	girl	NP	Forward Harmonic composition	TP
TP	EOS	end\TP	Backward composition	end

Table 6: CCG analysis for a reduced RC sentence under the Whiz-Deletion grammar. The rows in gray are the same across all RC types. We experimented with an alternative version where $NULL_{Wh}$ and $NULL_{pass}$ were combined into one category. This resulted in qualitatively similar results.

Old Parse state	Word	Correct category	Rule	New parse state
NULL	the	DP/NP	Initialize	DP/NP
DP/NP	cat	NP/CP	Forward Harmonic Composition	DP/CP
DP/CP	which	CP/(TP\DP)	Forward Harmonic Composition	DP/(TP\DP)
DP/(TP\DP)	was	(TP\DP)/VoiceP	Forward Harmonic Composition	DP/VoiceP
DP/VoiceP	examined	VoiceP/PP	Forward Harmonic Composition	DP/PP
DP/PP	by	PP/DP	Forward Harmonic Composition	DP/DP
DP/DP	the	DP/NP	Forward Harmonic Composition	DP/NP
DP/NP	doctor	NP	Forward Composition	DP
DP	liked	(TP\DP)/DP	Type raise DP	
TP/(TP\DP)			Forward Harmonic composition	TP/DP
TP/DP	the	DP/NP	Forward Harmonic composition	TP/NP
TP/NP	girl	NP	Forward Harmonic composition	TP
TP	EOS	end\TP	Backward composition	end

Table 7: CCG analysis for a full passive RC sentence under the Whiz-Deletion and Participial-Phase grammar.The rows in gray are the same across all RC types.

Old Parse state	Word	Correct category	Rule	New parse state
NULL	the	DP/NP	Initialize	DP/NP
DP/NP	cat	NP	Forward Composition	DP
DP	examined	(TP\DP)/DP	Type raise DP	
TP/(TP\DP)			Forward Harmonic Composition	TP/DP
TP/DP	the	DP/NP	Forward Harmonic Composition	TP/NP
TP/NP	doctor	NP	Forward Composition	TP
TP	and	(TP/(TP\DP))\TP)	Backward composition	TP/(TP\DP)
(TP/(TP\DP))\TP)	liked	(TP\DP)/DP	Forward Harmonic composition	TP/DP
TP/DP	the	DP/NP	Forward Harmonic composition	TP/NP
TP/NP	girl	NP	Forward Harmonic composition	TP
TP	EOS	end\TP	Backward composition	end

Table 8: CCG analysis for an active main verb sentence with verb coordination under the Whiz-Deletion and Participial-Phase grammar.

C Details about the training dataset

Structure	**Prob**	**Example**
Subject RC	0.016	The defendant who examined the lawyer ...
Full object RC	0.002	The defendant who the lawyer examined ...
Reduced object RC	0.005	The defendant the lawyer examined ...
Full passive RC	0.002	The defendant who was examined by the lawyer ...
Reduced passive RC	0.011	The defendant examined by the lawyer ...
Full progressive RC	0.0002	The defendant who was being examined by the lawyer ...
Reduced progressive RC	0.005	The defendant being examined by the lawyer ...
Transitive NP object	0.321	The examined the lawyer.
Transitive PP object	0.080	The defendant went to the store.
Intransitive	0.240	The defendant sang (joyfully).
Copular	0.240	The defendant was happy.
Coordination	0.080	The defendant examined the lawyer and went to the store.
		The defendant was happy and sang joyfully.
		The defendant went to the store and sang and was happy and examined the lawyer.

Table 9: The relative frequencies for all RCs, except the Progressive RCs, was taken from (Roland et al., 2007). Since progressive RCs were absent from this corpus study, we approximated their probabilities informally using google n-grams: for a range of different verbs, full RCs with almost never showed up in google n-gram viewer, but progressive RCs occasionally did. So we set the probability of progressive RCs to be twice that of full RCs. Since reduced RCs were much more frequent than their full counterparts, we assigned 95% of the probability mass of progressive RCs to the reduced version, and the remaining five to the full version. Since the exact frequencies of non-RC sentences is unlikely to be relevant for our experimental set up, we just included a few types of non-RC sentences without trying to match their frequencies with corpus statistics.

D Exploring model hyperpameters

Hyperparameter	Equation or Section	Value(s)	Reason
Decay (d)	Eqn 2, Eqn 5	0.5	Vasishth and Engelmann (2021)
Latency exponent (f)	Eqn 3	1	Vasishth and Engelmann (2021)
Maximum actiation (M)	1.5	Eqn 4	Vasishth and Engelmann (2021)
Latency factor (F)	Eqn 3	$\mathit{Beta}(2, 6)$	Vasishth and Engelmann (2021)
SD of noise distribution (σ)	§ 3.2.1	$\mathit{Uniform}(0.2, 0.5)$	Vasishth and Engelmann (2021)
		$\mathit{Normal}(0.35, 1)$	Add more noise to retrieve passive.
# Training sentences	§ 5.3	0, 100, 1000	>1000 resulted in almost no passive retrieval.
Give up	§ 3.2.3	100, 1000	>1000 too much time; 100,1000 same behavior.
Reanalysis index (z)	§ 3.2.3	1	Always go back to first word.
		Entropy weighted sample; SM temp: 1	Emphasize differences in activation.
		Entropy weighted sample; SM temp: 10	Make differences in activation more uniform.
Random seed (s)		Between 1 to 1280	Affects training order, random sampling.

Table 10: Hyperparameters above the double line are ACT-R parameters. Hyperparameters below the double line are SPAWN specific hyperparameters. Only F, σ and s differ across the 1280 model instances.

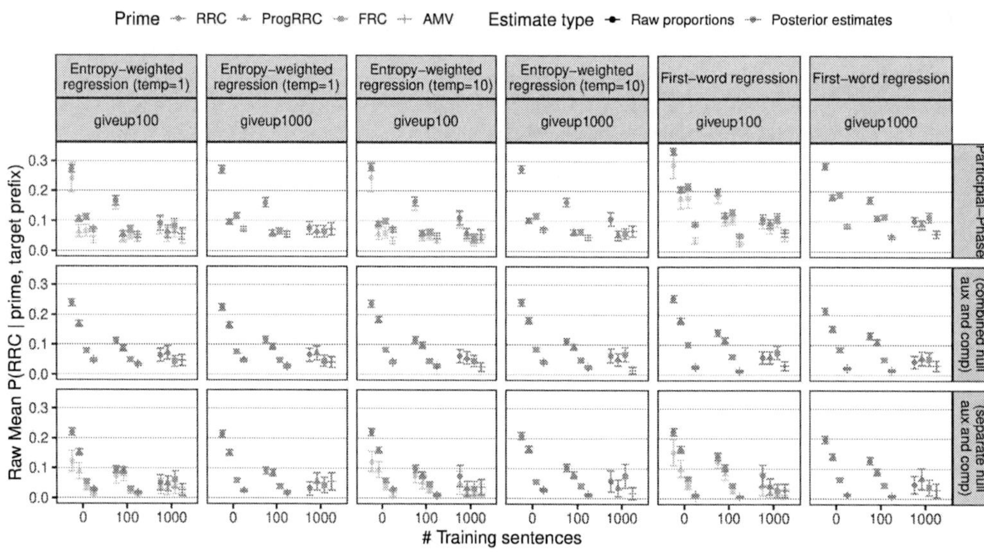

(a) σ sampled from $Normal(0.35, 1)$

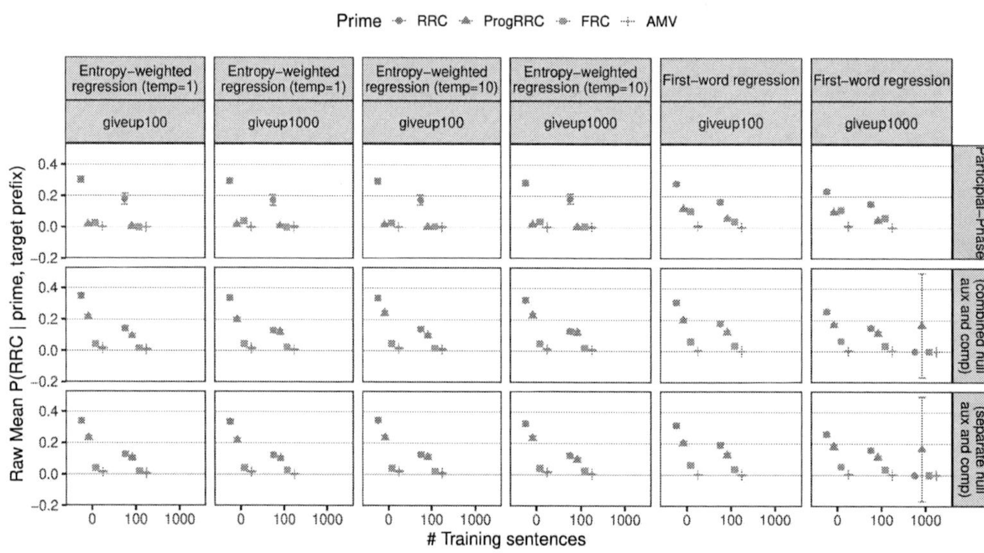

(b) σ sampled from $Uniform(0.2, 0.5)$

Figure 6: P(RRC | prime, target) averaged across 1280 model instances as estimated with raw proportions (dark) and from the posterior distribution of Bayesian models (light). Since fitting Bayesian models is very time consuming, these models were fit only for the subset of results reported in the main text (Figure 3). Error bars represent 95% standard error (standard deviation of proportions divided by $\sqrt{n}$) for proportions and 95% Credible Intervals for the Bayesian models. Missing values indicate that no passive responses were generated.

E Details about statistical models

E.1 Model specification

To generate quantitative predictions about the predicted proportion of passive responses while taking into consideration the model-instance wise and item wise variation, we fit Bayesian mixed effects logistic regression models. We used a Helmert contrast coding scheme with the following predictors, which let us evaluate if the mean log odds ratio of the ProgRRC and FRC conditions are equal to each other and to the mean log odds ratio of the RRC condition.

- C1: Compare the mean log odds ratio of the AMV condition with the mean log odds ratio of all the RC conditions combined.
- C2: Compare the mean log odds ratio of the RRC condition with the mean log odds ratio of all ProgRRC and FRC conditions combined.
- C3: Compare the mean log odds ratio of the ProgRRC condition to the mean log odds ratio of the FRC condition.

We fit the maximal model by including all by-participant and by-item random intercepts and slopes. In the case of the predicted data, participant IDs were replaced by model instance IDs.

$$\begin{aligned} Passive \sim c1 + c2 + c3 + &\\ &(1 + c1 + c2 + c3 \mid item) + \\ &(1 + c1 + c2 + c3 \mid \textit{participant or model-instance}) \end{aligned}$$

E.2 Priors

We fit the models using the following weakly informative prior.

$$\begin{aligned} \textit{Intercept} &\sim Normal(-4.595, 1.5) \\ \textit{Fixed effects} &\sim Normal(0, 2) \\ \textit{SD for random effects} &\sim Normal(0, 5) \end{aligned}$$

This prior assumes that the log odds ratio between priming conditions is most likely to be 0 (i.e. no priming effect) and unlikely to be greater than 4 or less than -4. This assumption is based on a meta-analysis of priming in production studies (Mahowald et al., 2016) where the log odds ratio between the prime conditions was not greater than 4 in any of the constructions they considered.

E.3 Statistical inferences for empirical human data

As discussed in the main text, we observed the following qualitative pattern in the proportion of target RRC parses when preceded by different primes: RRC > ProgRRC = FRC > AMV. To ensure that this pattern was statistically valid, we computed Bayes Factors for all of our predictors using the bayestestR package (Makowski et al., 2019). We adopt the Bayes Factor scale from Jeffreys (1998) to draw inferences: values greater than 3 and 10 provide moderate and strong evidence for the alternative model, whereas values lower than 0.3 and 0.1 provide moderate and strong evidence for the null model. Therefore, the following Bayes Factor values for our predictors would support the qualitative pattern:

1. AMV vs. all RCs (C1): > 3
2. RRC vs. [ProgRRC and FRC] (C2): > 3
3. ProgRRC vs. FRC (C3): < 0.3

Predictor	Estimate	95% CI	Bayes Factor
AMV vs. all RCs (C1)	-4.18	[-5.72, -3.04]	7.71e+08
RRC vs. [ProgRRC and FRC] (C2)	0.96	[0.62, 1.31]	9.91e+03
ProgRRC vs. FRC (C3)	0.21	[-0.18,0.60]	0.178

Table 11: Bayesian Logistic regression model estimates and Bayes Factors for the human experiment.

E.4 Statistical inferences for predicted data

From the posteriors of the Bayesian models, we computed 95% credible intervals for P(RRC | prime, target) for each prime condition for the human data, and for each of our model types. If the credible intervals for predicted priming effect from a model do not overlap with the empirical priming effects, we infer that the model cannot account for human behavior. Such an inference is valid because credible intervals, unlike the frequentist confidence intervals, reflect our confidence about the distribution of the actual effects (so 95% credible interval means that we are 95% sure that the true effect falls within this interval).

F Regular expressions to detect passive responses in the human experiment

We used a three step process to detect passive responses in the human experiment. First, we started with the following regular expression:

```
^(\\w+\\s+){3}by
```

This expression looks for sentences in which the fourth word of the sentence is "by" — all of our target prefixes had only three words (Determiner Noun Verb).

Next we used the following regular expression to detect completions where the fourth word is "by", but the completion is not passive:

```
by \\w+(\\s+\\w+){0,1}(\\.)*$
```

This expression returns TRUE if the word "by" is followed by just one or two words such as "The thief chased by the dog" or "the thief chased by me".

Finally, we tagged completions as being passive RRC completion if they matched the first expression and not the second.

G Limitations

Here we discuss some of the simplifying design decisions we made in SPAWN as a starting point, and their limitations.

Storing discarded categories As discussed in § 3.2.3, when the parser is regressing to some previous word w_z, it discards all of the categories retrieved from $w_z \ldots, w_{i-1}, w_i$. In the current implementation, SPAWN stores all instances of the discarded categories and uses this to compute inhibition. While storing all instances of the discarded categories is convenient, it is not cognitively plausible. Future work can examine other ways of computing inhibition that relies on summaries of discarded categories, instead of storing all of the instances, and investigate if using summaries results in different priming behavior.

Constraining partial parse states With our Whiz-Deletion grammar and our current implementation of null element prediction, the model could parse the partial sentence "The cat examined" and end up with an ungrammatical partial parse — i.e., a parse that cannot result in a grammatical continuation — as illustrated below.

Old Parse state	Word	Retrieved category	Rule	New parse state
NULL	the	DP/NP	Initialize	DP/NP
DP/NP	cat	NP/CP	Forward Harmonic Composition	DP/CP
DP/CP	NULL_{wh}	CP/(TP\DP)	Forward Harmonic Composition	DP/(TP\DP)
DP/VoiceP	examined	(TP\DP)/DP	Forward Harmonic Composition	DP/DP

This is not a problem in full sentences because this parse state is inconsistent with later words in the sentence, and the model will be forced to re-analyze. However, since our partial target prompts have no additional words, the model could end up with an ungrammatical parse, which is something we assumed would not happen with our human participants. Therefore, we constrained the model such that if it generated a partial state that was not DP/PP or TP/DP, it would be forced to reanalyze. While this is a convenient method to ensure that the model does not end up with an ungrammatical parse, it is unclear if this method accurately models how humans process the partial prompt. Future work can state more explicitly how humans parse the partial sentence such that they are always able to generate grammatical continuations, and then implement this in SPAWN.

Global Learning with Triplet Relations in Abstractive Summarization

Fengyu Lu[1], Jiaxin Duan[1]*, Junfei Liu[2]

[1]School of Software and Microelectronics, Peking University, Beijing, China

[2]National Engineering Research Center for Software Engineering, Peking University, Beijing, China

{fengyul,duanjx}@stu.pku.edu.cn, liujunfei@pku.edu.cn

Abstract

Abstractive summarization models learned with token-level maximum likelihood estimation suffer from exposure bias, that the condition for predicting the next token is discrepant during training and inference. Existing solutions bridge this gap by learning to estimate semantic or lexical qualities of a candidate summary from the global view, namely global learning (GL), yet ignore maintaining rational triplet-relations among document, reference summary, and candidate summaries, e.g., the candidate and reference summaries should have a similar faithfulness degree judging by a source document. In this paper, we propose an iterative autoregressive summarization paradigm - IARSum, which fuses the learning of triplet relations into a GL framework and further enhances summarization performance. Specifically, IARSum develops a dual-encoder network to enable the simultaneous input of a document and its candidate (or reference) summary. On this basis, it learns to 1) model the relative semantics defined over tuples (candidate, document) and (reference, document) respectively and balance them; 2) reduce lexical differences between candidate and reference summaries. Furthermore, IARSum iteratively reprocesses a generated candidate at inference time to ground higher quality. We conduct extensive experiments on two widely used datasets to test our method, and IARSum shows the new or matched state-of-the-art on diverse metrics.

1 Introduction

Abstractive summarization is a classical natural language generation (NLG) task, which aims to rewrite a long document into a shorter version, retaining only the salient information (Kumar and Chakkaravarthy, 2023; Xie et al., 2023). In recent years, the advancement of pre-trained language models (PLMs) (Lewis et al., 2020; Zhang et al., 2020a) founded on large-scale corpora boosted abstractive summarization significantly, and sequence-to-sequence (Seq2Seq) learning has shown promising results in almost all scenarios. It commonly learns an autoregressive PLM with maximum likelihood estimation (MLE), and the teacher-forcing algorithm (Goyal et al., 2016) is together used to ensure training efficiency and stability. However, such a model predicts each token in a summary based on the gold pre-context during training but on its preceding outputs at inference, causing a training-inference discrepancy - *exposure bias* (Bengio et al., 2015; Goodman et al., 2020), which heavily limits summarization performance.

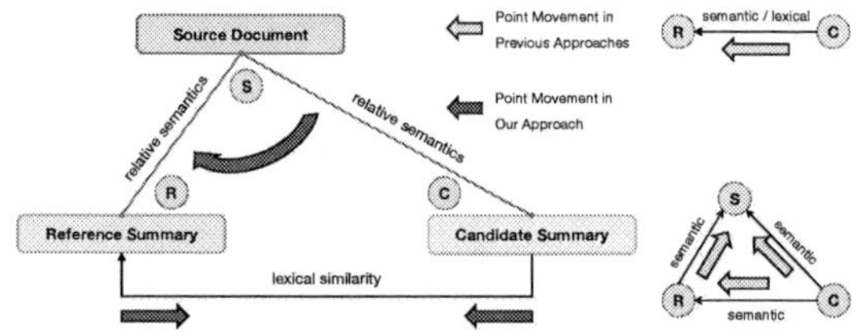

Figure 1: Graphicalization of triplet relations among a document, the reference summary, and a candidate summary, where each point of the triangle $\triangle SRC$ presents source document (S), reference summary (R), and candidate summary (C), respectively. **Upper right**: Traditional GL methods only consider the edge RC and deem it the semantic or lexical gaps between the points R and C, which they learn to minimize. **Lower right**: SeqCo further considers S and regards each edge as a semantic gap to be minimized. **Left**: We extend traditional GL methods by treating the side edge SR (SC) as a relative semantics metric, and we highlight the balance of edges SR and SC.

Since exposure bias happens on the token level, existing solutions train models to maximize the global similarity between candidate and reference summaries, namely *global learning* (GL). Reinforcement and contrastive learning in summarization are the most used GL technologies. For example, in reinforcement learning based GOLD (Pang

*Corresponding author.

Proceedings of the 28th Conference on Computational Natural Language Learning, pages 198–208
November 15-16, 2024 ©2024 Association for Computational Linguistics

and He, 2021) and RLEF (Roit et al., 2023), a summarization model is rewarded depending on the quality of candidate summaries it produces, with the reference as the standard. Similarly, contrastive learning methods (Liu et al., 2022; Xie et al., 2023; Zhang et al., 2022) compare candidate summaries with the reference and assign the one closer to the reference a higher probability, and vice versa. On the one hand, all these methods measure candidate-reference similarities without considering the source document conditions. Furthermore, their measurement stands on only the semantic or lexical aspect rather than comprehensive perspectives, resulting in biased learning objectives. SeqCo (Xu et al., 2022) aims to minimize the semantic discrepancies among a source document, its reference, and candidate summaries. Still, it is powerless to learn lexical perception and shows undesirable summarization results.

To address these problems, we highlight rational relations within the triplet (document, candidate summary, reference summary) in abstractive summarization. Take the geometrical triplet in Figure 1 for intuitive perception. Traditional GL methods view the edge RC as lexical or semantic gaps between candidate and reference summaries, aiming to draw points R and close as possible. Similarly, SeqCo considers from the semantics perspective and further aims to condense the triangle $\triangle SRC$ into a single point (draw all three points S, R, and C as close as possible). In this work, we base on the traditional GL assumption and further treat side edges SR and SC as relative semantics metrics between the document and summaries. We propose to balance the edges SR and SC while minimizing the edge RC. Our inspiration is that an ideal model should generate candidate summaries similar to the reference on both semantic and lexical aspects (Sul and Choi, 2023). In particular, the limitations of GL-based methods, which tend to yield summaries with unsatisfactory relative semantics, such as faithfulness and abstractiveness (Dixit et al., 2023) measured by the source document, can be effectively fixed by balancing the two side edges of $\triangle SRC$.

According to the above insights, we propose an iterative autoregressive summarization paradigm (IARSum), which facilitates learning the mentioned triplet relations with a standard GL framework to enhance summarization performance. Specifically, IARSum generates a summary through a series of iterations, during which the model re-inputs and reprocesses the previously generated summary in each iteration to get improved versions. This encourages assessing summaries' quality from a global view and effectively prevents exposure bias. We build IARSum on a double encoder-decoder network following Transformer architecture to fulfill the desired properties. It uses two serial encoders to encode the document and re-input summaries, respectively, and uses the second encoder's outputs to model summary-document semantics. To learn the IARSum model aware of triplet relations, we reward the model to get similar outputs from the second encoder when provided with candidate and reference summaries as input, respectively. We also reward the model once a candidate achieves higher lexical overlap with the reference after reprocessing. Furthermore, we adopt an offline mini-risk training strategy that enforces the model to maximize the mentioned rewards. In inference, a trained IARSum model can adaptively refine the generated summaries in sequential iterations for increased quality.

In summary, we make three-fold contributions. First, we explore rational relations within the triplet (source document, reference summary, candidate summary) in summarization and propose to balance the relative semantics over tuples (candidate, document) and (reference, document) while reducing the lexical differences within (candidate, reference). Second, we propose IARSum, a novel summarization paradigm that facilitates learning our suggested triplet relations with a GL framework to boost summaries' quality. Finally, we conduct extensive experiments on two public datasets to test our methods. Results show that IARSum matches or outperforms previous state-of-the-art (SOTA) approaches in generating high-quality summaries measured by multiple metrics. Furthermore, we transfer IARSum to few-shot settings and show its superior robustness.

2 Related Work and Background

2.1 Abstractive Summarization

Summarization is always modeled as a Seq2Seq generation task, creating function f that is conditioned on a source document X to output a target summary Y:

$$Y \leftarrow f(X) \tag{1}$$

For the abstractive paradigm, existing approaches commonly learn an autoregressive language model with parameter θ to fit f and approximate the conditional probability $\mathrm{P}(Y|X)$ token by token. Maximum likelihood estimation (MLE) is the most used learning schema. It aims to maximize the probability that the model predicts gold reference, following independent and identically distributed conditions, i.e., $\max_\theta \mathrm{P}_\theta(Y|X) = \max_\theta \prod_{t=1}^{l} \mathrm{P}_\theta(y_t|Y_{<t}, X)$, where l denotes the length of reference and $Y_{<t}$ refers to sub-sequence $\{y_1, y_2, \cdots, y_{t-1}\}$.

During training, the teacher-forcing mechanism (Goyal et al., 2016) is adopted, which conditions on exact pre-context to predict a target token and minimizes the following negative log-likelihood (NLL) loss:

$$\mathcal{L}_{nll}(\theta) = -\sum_{t=1}^{l} \log \mathrm{P}_\theta(y_t|Y_{<t}, X) \tag{2}$$

Though this encourages stable MLE learning, such a trained model depends heavily on accurate prediction. Intuitively, it learns to sample the next token at timestep t from the distribution $\mathrm{P}(\cdot|Y_{<t}, X)$, while the case at inference is to sample from $\mathrm{P}(\cdot|Y'_{<t}, X)$, where $Y'_{<t}$ denotes the previous generation. This gap between training and inference is the so-called *exposure bias*, causing errors accumulation during inference, especially once any improper token is generated in early steps.

2.2 Global Learning

Reinforcement learning (RL) rewards a model with sequence-level feedback, depending on varying evaluation metrics. Most works (Tan, 2023; Roit et al., 2023) are based on on-policy learning (Paulus et al., 2018), where a model generates a sampled candidate and a greedily searched candidate during training. It requires high computational costs and tends to get stuck in a zero-reward region. As a result, MLE loss is used as an assistant. Richard et al. (Pang and He, 2021) proposed an off-policy learning method that uses reference summary as a demonstrator. Although it averts zero rewards, the exploring ability is reduced.

Traditional contrastive learning (CTL) uses positive and negative sample pairs to train a model to distinguish real data labels. For example, CLIFF (Cao and Wang, 2021) builds sample pairs by the back-translation and improves the faithfulness and factuality of the generated summaries. In recent years, ranking-based learning originated from the standard CTL and has shown advanced performance in abstractive summarization. Liu et al. (Liu and Liu, 2021) first propose a two-stage framework that trains a RoBERTa (Liu et al., 2019) to rank the candidates generated by BART at first. BRIO (Liu et al., 2022) makes a further optimization, trains BART itself as an evaluation tool, and ranks the conditional probability of candidates. Later, a lot of improved BRIO variants (Xie et al., 2023; Zhao et al., 2023; Zhang et al., 2022) were proposed in succession. Despite performing surprisingly, such methods only focus on maximizing the candidate-reference similarity without considering the source document effects. Noting this point, SeqCo (Xu et al., 2022) contrasts semantics among source documents, candidates, and references. However, SeqCo assumed irrational triplet relations and suffered unstable optimization caused by online learning, the main reason for undesirable performance.

3 Method

In this section, we describe the details of our proposed methods. We introduce the iterative autoregressive text generation paradigm in Section 3.1, describe the IARSum model architecture in Section 3.2, and illustrate the offline global learning strategy in Section 3.3.

3.1 Iterative Autoregressive Generation

The standard autoregressive (AR) text generation illustrated in Figure 2 (a) is widely known as a unidirectional process, where a text is generated sequentially token by token. The major limitation is that each token is predicted depending on its pre-context. As a result, a wrongly generated token may mislead the later content and make the generated text entirely deviate from the target due to error accumulation. Calibrating the predicted token distributions on a global view (global learning) is effective in addressing this problem. However, it is hard to involve the source document conditions, i.e., the semantic relations between the document and summaries, in calibration. We propose an iterative autoregressive generation paradigm (IAR) to break these limitations.

As demonstrated in Figure 2, IAR models the generation of target text in the Seq2Seq task as a text-level Markov Chain, where the state transitions from a draft to more refined results. Taking abstractive summarization as an example, at the i-th iteration, IARSum samples a candidate summary Y^{i-1} from the previous iteration's outputs,

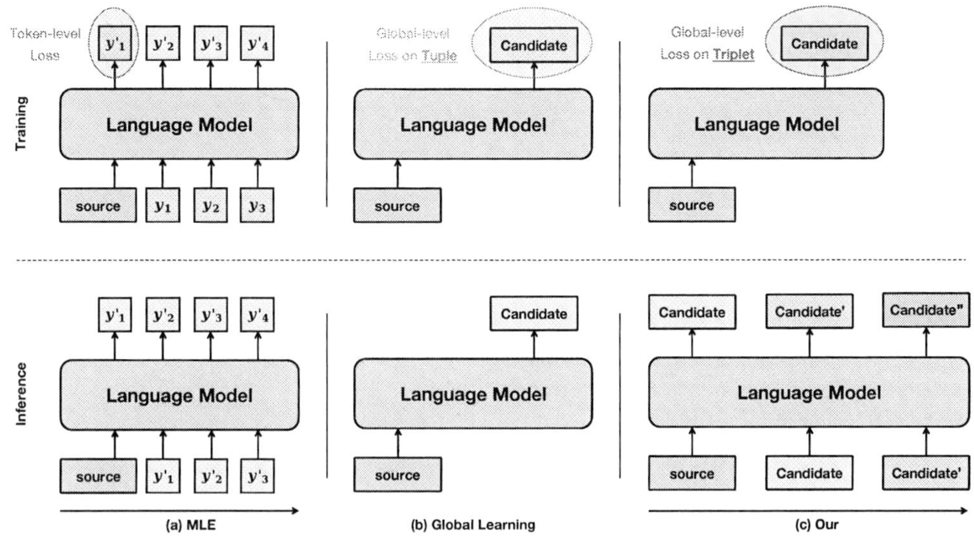

Figure 2: Comparison of different learning paradigms. (a) MLE trains a model to minimize token-level loss. (b) Traditional global learning trains a model to minimize global-level loss defined over the candidate and reference summaries. (c) Our method trains a model to minimize global-level loss defined over the triplet built upon a document, candidate summary, and reference summary.

estimates its quality, and produces a new one Y^i. This process repeats until the maximum number of iterations N is reached, which formally presents as:

$$\begin{aligned} \mathrm{P}(Y|X) &= \mathrm{P}\left(Y^0|X\right)\mathrm{P}\left(Y^N|Y^0,X\right) \\ &= \mathrm{P}\left(Y^0|X\right)\prod_{i=1}^{N}\mathrm{P}\left(Y^i|Y^{i-1},X\right) \end{aligned} \tag{3}$$

where $Y^0 \sim \mathrm{P}(\cdot|X)$, $Y^i \sim \mathrm{P}(\cdot|X, Y^{i-1})$, and $Y^N = Y$.

3.2 Model Architecture

We implement IARSum with a Transformer-based encoder-decoder model shown in Figure 3. It has two encoders with bidirectional attention and one decoder with unidirectional attention. To speed up convergence, we start our model with a single-encoder Transformer with pre-trained parameters θ and share initial parameters between the two encoders.

The architecture of IARSum is very similar to GSum (Dou et al., 2021). However, encoders of GSum are independent and connect to the decoder orderly by cross-attention layers (i.e., parallel encoders). IARSum instead adapts serial encoders, where the second encoder relies on the output of the first to feature the input content, similar to a Transformer decoder without a sequence mask. Besides, GSum uses the second encoder to encode guidance words, while IARSum's second encoder is used to encode the candidate summary. Mathematically, IARSum models the following token distributions during the first and later iterations, respectively:

$$\begin{aligned} \mathrm{P}_\theta(y^0_t|X) &= \sigma(D_\theta(E^1_\theta(X), y^0_{<t})) \\ \mathrm{P}_\theta(y^i_t|Y^{i-1}, X) &= \sigma(D_\theta(E^2_\theta(E^1_\theta(X), Y^{i-1}), y^i_{<t})) \end{aligned} \tag{4}$$

where E^1_θ, E^2_θ are the first and second encoders, and D_θ is the decoder. $\sigma(\cdot)$ is softmax function.

3.3 Learning Objective

According to our intention proposing IAR in Section 3.1, we learn an IARSum model for mainly two objectives. One is to maximize the lexical similarity between candidate and reference summaries, and the other one involves matching the relative semantics of candidates with that of the reference, taking the document as the standard. Both objectives can be attended within a multi-rewards learning framework.

Semantics Rewards. The recent study (Dreyer et al., 2023) pointed out that a summary should be logically entailed in the source document to ensure faithfulness. On the other hand, researchers also observed that humans write summaries with hallucinatory words to keep abstractiveness (Maynez et al., 2020) despite contradicting summary-document entailment. Note that faithfulness and abstractiveness are perceived on the source document basis. To bypass their contradictions, we uniformly refer to such perceptions as relative semantics and model them with a neural function $\mathcal{S}(\cdot,\cdot)$. Intuitively, an ideal candidate summary should be at a similar level of relative semantics compared with the reference, and their differences in this attribute are quantitatively observed:

$$M_s(X,Y,Y^i) = \langle \mathcal{S}(X,Y), \mathcal{S}(X,Y^i) \rangle \quad (5)$$

where $\langle \cdot,\cdot \rangle$ is a distance function, such as Euclidean distance. Furthermore, we will reward the model according to the gain of semantics rewards between two adjacent iterations:

$$R_s(Y^i,Y^{i-1}) = M_s(X,Y,Y^i) - M_s(X,Y,Y^{i-1}) \quad (6)$$

Lexical Rewards. From the lexical view, we encourage a candidate, after reprocessing, to contain more tokens overlapped with the reference. To this end, we reward the model using the lexical rewards:

$$R_l(Y^i,Y^{i-1}) = \frac{|(\{Y^i\} - \{Y^{i-1}\}) \cap \{Y\}|}{|\{Y\}|} \quad (7)$$

where $\{\cdot\}$ denotes a token set and $|\cdot|$ means the set size.

Learning Objective. Finally, we mix the two types of rewards with a balance coefficient $\xi \in (0,1)$:

$$R(Y^i) = \xi R_s(Y^i,Y^{i-1}) + (1-\xi) R_l(Y^i,Y^{i-1}) \quad (8)$$

and the overall learning objective for IARSum is unified to maximize the following expected rewards:

$$\sum_{i=1}^{N} \max_{\theta} \mathrm{E}_{Y^i \sim \mathrm{P}_\theta(\cdot|Y^{i-1},X)}[R(Y^i,Y^{i-1})]. \quad (9)$$

3.4 Training

As we learn IARSum to maximize the expected rewards, the infinite sampling space makes the expectation in Eq.9 untraceable. Predominant studies commonly use the Monte Carlo approach to address this problem, which approximates the real distribution with empirical samples. We follow this idea and adopt a minimum-risk training (Shen et al., 2016) strategy. At each iteration i, we sample k candidates $Y^i_{(1)}, \cdots, Y^i_{(k)}$ from $\mathrm{P}_\theta(\cdot|Y^{i-1},X)$ using beam-search (Vijayakumar et al., 2016), and the model is trained to minimize an expected risk loss:

$$\mathcal{L}_{er}(\theta) = -\sum_{t=1}^{k} R(Y^i_{(t)}) \frac{\mathrm{P}_\theta(Y^i_{(t)}|Y^{i-1},X)}{\sum_{t=1}^{k} \mathrm{P}_\theta(Y^i_{(t)}|Y^{i-1},X)} \quad (10)$$

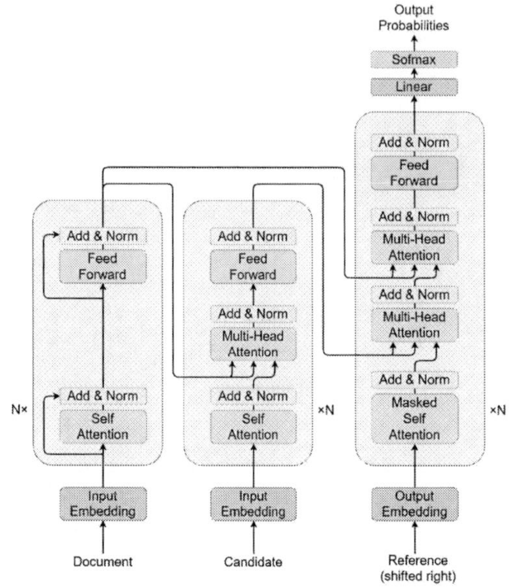

Figure 3: IARSum model's dual-encoder architecture.

Semantic Relation Modeling. Another challenge we encounter is the implementation of function $\mathcal{S}$. Given a document-summary pair (X,Y), we average the output of the IARSum second encoder to feature their semantic relations:

$$\mathcal{S}(X,Y;\theta) = MeanPool(E^2_\theta(E^1_\theta(X),Y)) \quad (11)$$

This approach is parameter-efficient. However, dynamically learned parameters θ cause the observation of $\mathcal{S}$ to vary sharply as training progresses. Drawing from (Zhang et al., 2022) lessons, we introduce momentum-based parameterization to remove this risk. Concretely, we build ζ-parameterized $\mathcal{S}(\cdot,\cdot;\zeta)$, which is initialized by θ and updated with the moving average:

$$\zeta \leftarrow \mu\zeta + (1-\mu)\theta \quad (12)$$

where μ is a momentum coefficient to coordinate the synchronization rate of two types of parameters. Based on this, Eq.5 is reformulated as:

$$M_s(X,Y,Y^i) = -\|\mathcal{S}(X,Y;\zeta) - \mathcal{S}(X,Y^i;\zeta)\| \quad (13)$$

Offline Learning. We use offline samples during training to save the computational costs of generating candidates. A pre-trained model is first finetuned with MLE and proceeds to generate k candidate summaries for every document in the training set. Each candidate, coupled with the source document, forms a $\{X, Y^{i-1}\}$ pair used for the model training. Note that the generated candidates share varying semantic and lexical qualities, and the ones closer to the reference standard simulate the drafts that have been reprocessed more times. This nature facilitates the training to focus on only one iteration without considering the multi-turn rewards. Moreover, training the model to maximize expected rewards alone is unguaranteed to generate fluent language. Following (Liu et al., 2022; Zhao et al., 2023), we add a regularization term in Eq.9, and the overall loss function is then:

$$\mathcal{L}(\theta) = \mathcal{L}_{nll}(\theta) + \lambda \mathcal{L}_{er}(\theta) \tag{14}$$

4 Experiments

4.1 Datasets

Two public open-domain datasets are used to evaluate our method. **CNN/DM** (Hermann et al., 2015; Nallapati et al., 2016) is a well-known news summarization dataset with the associated highlights as summaries. **XSum** (Narayan et al., 2018) is an extremely abstractive dataset also in the news domain that contains a one-sentence summary for each article from BBC.

4.2 Comparison Methods

BART (Lewis et al., 2020) is a pre-trained Transformer model with a denoising objective widely used for abstractive summarization. **PEGASUS** (Zhang et al., 2020a) is another widely used pre-trained model with gap sentence generation and masked language modeling pre-training objectives. **GSum** (Dou et al., 2021) is an abstractive summarization model guided by extraction results with an identical double-encoder architecture as ours. **GOLD** (Pang and He, 2021) is an off-policy reinforcement learning method using the reference summary as a demonstrator. **SeqCo** (Xu et al., 2022) is a contrastive learning method that enforces the semantic similarity between reference and candidate. **BRIO** (Liu et al., 2022) is a contrastive learning method that assigns probability mass to candidate summaries according to their quality. **SimMCS** (Xie et al., 2023) is a multi-level contrastive learning method improved from BRIO and achieved state-of-the-art on both CNN/DM and XSum. **SLiC** (Zhao et al., 2023) is essentially a variant of BRIO, calibrating PEGASUS with types of contrastive losses. **MoCa** (Zhang et al., 2022) is improved from BRIO, introducing online candidate sampling.

Table 1: Automatic evaluation results on CNN/DM test set. †: results from our reproduction. The best results are in **bold**. The previous best results are highlighted with underline. R-1/2/L: ROUGE-1/2/L F1 scores. BS: BERTScore. BaS: BARTScore-$\mathcal{F}$.

Model	R-1	R-2	R-L	BS	BaS
BART	44.16	21.28	40.90	87.95	-3.91
PEGASUS	44.17	21.47	41.11	85.07†	-3.80†
GSum	45.94	22.32	42.48	-	-
GOLD	45.40	22.01	42.25	-	-
SeqCo	45.02	21.80	41.75	-	-
BRIO	47.78	23.55	44.57	89.14†	-3.62†
SimMCS	48.16	24.08	44.65	89.20	-3.58
SLiC	47.97	24.18	44.88	-	-
MoCa	48.88	24.94	45.76	-	-
IARSum	**48.96**	**25.14**	**45.93**	**89.32**	**-3.25**

Table 2: Automatic evaluation results on XSum test set.

Model	R-1	R-2	R-L	BS	BaS
BART	45.14	22.27	37.25	89.63†	-3.64†
PEGASUS	47.21	24.56	39.25	89.68	-3.89
GSum	45.40	21.89	36.67	-	-
GOLD	45.85	22.58	37.65	-	-
SeqCo	45.65	22.41	37.04	-	-
BRIO	49.07	25.59	40.40	89.10†	-3.79†
SimMCS	49.39	25.73	40.49	90.23	-3.77
SLiC	**49.77**	27.09	42.08	-	-
MoCa	49.32	25.91	41.47	-	-
IARSum	49.42	**27.20**	**42.50**	**92.13**	**-3.61**

4.3 Implementation Details

In the following experiments, we use BART as the backbone and start our model from the public fine-tuned versions bart-large-cnn[1] (on CNN/DM) or bart-large-xsum[2] (on XSum). As for hyperparameters, we set $\xi = 0.5$, $\mu = 0.5$, and $\lambda = 100$. We train our model on 4 NVIDIA RTX 4090 GPUs for 100K steps with a batch size of 16. The AdamW optimizer (Loshchilov and Hutter, 2019) with a noam learning rate schedule is used. The initial learning rate lr is 2e-3, and its value is updated following $lr^* = lr \cdot \min(\mathcal{S}^{-0.5}, \mathcal{S} \times \mathcal{W}^{-1.5})$, where $\mathcal{W}$ denotes the warmup steps, is set to 3,000, and $\mathcal{S}$ accumulates the current number of learning rate updates. The beam width k held for beam search decoding (Vijayakumar et al., 2016) is set to 16. The default number of iterations N is set to 3. Following conventions, we use ROUGE-F_1 scores (Lin, 2004) to evaluate the lexical overlap between the model-generated summary and the reference. Also, we use BERTScore (Zhang et al., 2020b) and BARTScore-$\mathcal{F}$ (Yuan et al., 2021) to evaluate their semantic similarity.

[1]https://huggingface.co/facebook/bart-large-cnn

[2]https://huggingface.co/facebook/bart-large-xsum

Table 3: Ablation study results on CNN/DM. i: the number of revision iterations. Dist.: Levenshtein distance. *w/o*: without.

Model	Iteration	R-1	R-2	R-L	Dist.
IARSum	i=1	46.19	22.27	43.69	0.60
	i=2	47.69	23.92	44.68	0.03
	i=3	48.96	25.14	45.93	0.01
	i=4	48.71	24.12	44.89	0.01
	i=5	48.74	24.12	44.91	0.01
-*w/o* $\mathcal{L}_{er}$	i=1	44.16	21.28	40.90	0.62
	i=2	45.28	22.63	40.96	0.59
	i=3	44.68	21.32	40.57	0.58
	i=4	44.30	22.38	41.34	0.59
	i=5	44.78	21.06	40.00	0.59

4.4 Main Results

We have the following observations from the automatic evaluation results in Table 1 and Table 2. 1) IARSum outperforms the backbone models by a large margin on both datasets, revealing the superiority of our learning scheme over the traditional supervised fine-tuning after pre-training. 2) IARSum also shows superiorities over the similar double-encoder Transformer - GSum. On the one hand, GSum needs an additional system to predict guidance signals. Besides, it suffers a severe training-inference discrepancy beyond exposure bias as the quality of guidance in training differs from in inference. In contrast, our IARSum requires no additional systems, and the model behaves identically during both training and inference. 3) Taking ROUGE as the measurement, IARSum achieves new SOTA on CNN/DM and matches the currently best performance on XSum. Moreover, IARSum demonstrates the best BERTScore and BARTScore on both datasets. We note that BRIO, SLiC, and our IARSum employ a similar training schema, which can be consolidated as the formulation in Eq. 14. IARSum stands out from the other two by emphasizing effective reprocessings after one-time summarization, which is the main reason for its superior performance.

4.5 Ablation Study

Our IARSum optimizes the backbone models mainly with global learning and iterative autoregressive generation. We conduct ablation studies to validate the effectiveness of these two strategies and list the experimental results in Table 3.

The Effectiveness of Global Learning. Note that IARSum$_{i=1}$ -*w/o* $\mathcal{L}_{er}$ represents a variant of our method that lacks the global learning procedure and involves no reprocesses after generating a draft summary (i.e., the backbone model trained with MLE). In contrast, IARSum$_{i=1}$ means our method drops further iterations once it has generated a summary. IARSum$_{i=1}$ performs better when trained with $\mathcal{L}_{er}$. We attribute the reason to the effectiveness of global learning in reducing exposure bias. Also, once giving up further iterations, our method only differs from RL-based GOLD and CTL-based BRIO regarding global learning objectives. IARSum$_{i=1}$ show better ROUGE scores than the two counterparts, indicating that learning with our defined triplet relations effectively enhances the current learning schema in abstractive summarization.

The Effectiveness of Iterations. To explore the effectiveness of the IAR generation paradigm, we adopt the normalized Levenshtein distance (Levenshtein et al., 1966) as an additional metric apart from ROUGE scores:

$$Dist(Y, Y^i) = \frac{1}{N}\sum \frac{Distance(Y, Y^i)}{\max(|Y|, |Y^i|)}, \quad (15)$$

where $Distance(\cdot, \cdot)$ denotes Levenshtein distance. Twofold insights can be drawn from Table 3. Firstly, we see from the lower part of the Table that the IAR with more iterations is useless without global learning. Secondly, the iterations performed in IARSum are only effective within a limited number of times. According to the Levenshtein distance, the impacts of iterations are hard to distinguish more than three times, and the generated summaries' quality even worsens. However, from another aspect, this finding also indicates that our method has a determined direction of good summaries within finite steps.

4.6 Case Study

To intuitively assess the quality of the IARSum generated summaries, we sample two cases from the CNN/DM test set and compare different systems' output in Table 4. The typical pattern of exposure bias can be found in the summaries generated by BART, i.e., if the model generates inappropriate content at the initial phase, this tends to cause a deviation of the subsequent information to ensure the coherence of a whole text. During each iteration, IARSum encodes the previously generated summary with bidirectional attention. This allows the model to modify potentially inappropriate tokens after understanding an entire summary and comparing it with the source document. We find in Table 4 that this mechanism also contributes to reducing hallucinatory facts. Moreover, benefiting

Table 4: Case study on CNN/DM. Content in blue is unfaithful or irrelevant to the reference. The draft is produced by IARSum$_{i=0}$, and we use red to mark the keywords (vs. the source document) it omits. After being reprocessed, the factuality and abstractiveness of the draft are improved.

System	Summary
	Case 1
Reference	RBS has racked up £50billion in losses since it was bailed out by taxpayers. State-back giant warned that it faces 'another tough year' to come. Lurched to a £446million loss for the first three months of the year.
BART	state-backed giant lurched to a £446million loss for the first three months of the year. Comes after RBS was forced to put aside £856million to cover lawsuits and fines still being decided. It includes an extra £334million for its part in rigging the foreign exchange market with other banks.
IARSum$_{i=1}$	RBS has racked up £50billion in losses since it was bailed out by taxpayers. The state-backed giant lurched to a £446million loss for the first three months of the year. It warned that it faces another 'tough year' in a statement last night. The bank was forced to put aside £856million to cover lawsuits and fines.
IARSum$_{i=2}$	Since receiving a bailout from taxpayers, RBS has racked up £50 billion in losses. The state-backed giant has issued a warning, stating that it anticipates facing another tough year. It reported a loss of £446 million for the first quarter of this year.
	Case 2
Reference	Hungarian national Evelin Mezei, 12, has been found safe and well. She had gone missing from the Stratford area in London last night. Evelin had been seen on CCTV footage with an unknown man.
BART	Evelin Mezei, a 12-year-old Hungarian national, was spotted with the man at around 10.30pm yesterday. She was last seen by her mother in East London, Scotland Yard said. But the youngster, who came to the UK six months ago, was traced this morning.
IARSum$_{i=1}$	Evelin Mezei, 12, went missing in Stratford, London, last night. She was seen on CCTV footage with an unknown man on a city street. The Hungarian national was found safe and well this morning. Her mother was last seen with the man's mother.
IARSum$_{i=2}$	Evelin Mezei, a 12-year-old Hungarian girl who went missing from the Stratford area in London last night, has been found safe and well. CCTV footage showed Evelin with an unknown man before her disappearance.

from our proposed lexical reward, the model can generate novel tokens absent in the previous summary during reprocessing. It helps to improve the abstractiveness of the generated summary, which is emphasized in abstractive summarization. We'll further discuss this point in section 5.

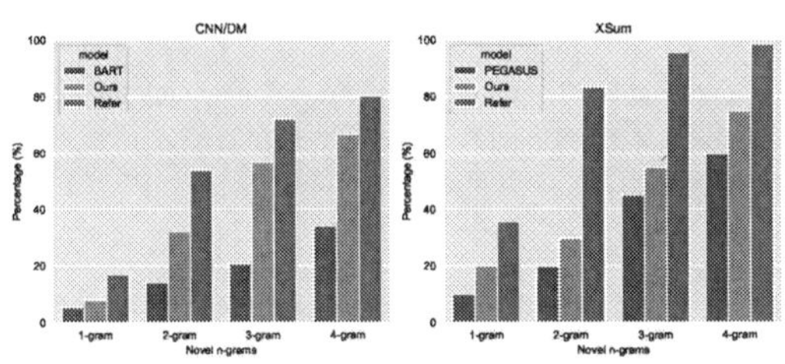

Figure 4: Novel n-grams on CNN/DM (left) and XSum (right) datasets.

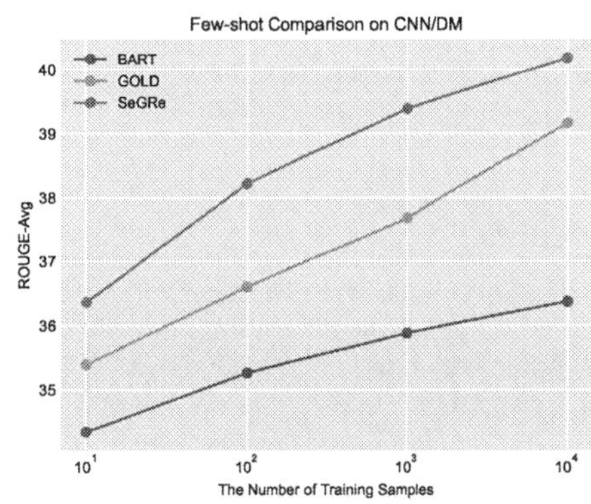

Figure 5: Few-shot performance comparison. ROUGE-Avg (the average of R-1, R-2, and R-L F_1 scores) scores are reported.

5 More Analyses

Abstractiveness. In our learning framework, we measure the increment of novel words using lexis rewards R_l. The case study approves the effectiveness of this strategy from a textual aspect. Here, we further understand the abstractiveness of IARSum-generated summaries through a quantitative analysis. According to previous works (Xie et al., 2023) and (Liu et al., 2022), we rate the percentage of novel n-grams that appear in the generated summary but not in the source document in Figure 4. We find that our IARSum can generate more novel n-grams than the baseline and reference, regardless of whether on moderately or extremely abstractive summarizations. Recalling the automatic evaluation and case study results, we assert that the summaries generated by IARSum closely resemble human written summaries in terms of both abstractiveness and semantic aspects.

Few-shot Performance. Based on the findings in our ablation study, we consider that the IAR generation mechanism introduced in IARSum makes the model more sensitive to the candidate's quality and can improve flawed candidates within a finite number of iterations. Therefore, we conduct experiments in few-shot settings to confirm our assumptions. Following previous studies, we train IARSum on CNN/DM by varying the number of training samples from 10 to 10,000 and compare IARSum with the baseline BART and the RL-based GOLD to make the results convincing. According to Figure 5a, IARSum shows a remarkable few-shot learning ability. IARSum goes ahead more over the baseline as the training samples increase.

6 Conclusion

In this paper, we focus on improving the existing approaches that alleviate exposure bias suffered in abstractive summarization. Specifically, we introduce a novel iterative autoregressive summarization paradigm, IARSum. It models the generation of an abstract summary as a series of transitions of intermediate results, ranging from coarse to refined quality. IARSum also enables learning rational relations among a document, the reference summary, and candidate summaries under a standard GL framework. Extensive comparison experiments revealed the effectiveness and advancement of our method.

References

Samy Bengio, Oriol Vinyals, Navdeep Jaitly, and Noam Shazeer. 2015. Scheduled sampling for sequence prediction with recurrent neural networks. In *NIPS 2015*, pages 1171–1179.

Shuyang Cao and Lu Wang. 2021. CLIFF: contrastive learning for improving faithfulness and factuality in abstractive summarization. In *Proceedings of the 2021 Conference on Empirical Methods in Natural Language Processing, EMNLP 2021*, pages 6633–6649.

Tanay Dixit, Fei Wang, and Muhao Chen. 2023. Improving factuality of abstractive summarization without sacrificing summary quality. In *Proceedings of the 61st Annual Meeting of the Association for Computational Linguistics (Volume 2: Short Papers), ACL 2023*, pages 902–913.

Zi-Yi Dou, Pengfei Liu, Hiroaki Hayashi, Zhengbao Jiang, and Graham Neubig. 2021. Gsum: A general framework for guided neural abstractive summarization. In *NAACL-HLT 2021*, pages 4830–4842.

Markus Dreyer, Mengwen Liu, Feng Nan, Sandeep Atluri, and Sujith Ravi. 2023. Evaluating the tradeoff between abstractiveness and factuality in abstractive summarization. In *Findings of the Association for Computational Linguistics: EACL 2023*, pages 2044–2060.

Sebastian Goodman, Nan Ding, and Radu Soricut. 2020. Teaforn: Teacher-forcing with n-grams. In *EMNLP 2020*, pages 8704–8717.

Anirudh Goyal, Alex Lamb, Ying Zhang, Saizheng Zhang, Aaron C. Courville, and Yoshua Bengio. 2016. Professor forcing: A new algorithm for training recurrent networks. In *NIPS 2016*, pages 4601–4609.

Karl Moritz Hermann, Tomás Kociský, Edward Grefenstette, Lasse Espeholt, Will Kay, Mustafa Suleyman, and Phil Blunsom. 2015. Teaching machines to read and comprehend. In *NIPS 2015*, pages 1693–1701.

G. Senthil Kumar and Midhun Chakkaravarthy. 2023. A survey on recent text summarization techniques. In *MIWAI 2023*, volume 14078 of *Lecture Notes in Computer Science*, pages 496–502.

Vladimir I Levenshtein et al. 1966. Binary codes capable of correcting deletions, insertions, and reversals. In *Soviet physics doklady*, volume 10, pages 707–710. Soviet Union.

Mike Lewis, Yinhan Liu, Naman Goyal, Marjan Ghazvininejad, Abdelrahman Mohamed, Omer Levy, Veselin Stoyanov, and Luke Zettlemoyer. 2020. BART: denoising sequence-to-sequence pre-training for natural language generation, translation, and comprehension. In *ACL 2020*, pages 7871–7880.

Chin-Yew Lin. 2004. Rouge: A package for automatic evaluation of summaries. In *Text summarization branches out*, pages 74–81.

Yinhan Liu, Myle Ott, Naman Goyal, Jingfei Du, Mandar Joshi, Danqi Chen, Omer Levy, Mike Lewis, Luke Zettlemoyer, and Veselin Stoyanov. 2019. Roberta: A robustly optimized BERT pretraining approach. *CoRR*, abs/1907.11692.

Yixin Liu and Pengfei Liu. 2021. Simcls: A simple framework for contrastive learning of abstractive summarization. In *Proceedings of the 59th Annual Meeting of the Association for Computational Linguistics and the 11th International Joint Conference on Natural Language Processing, ACL/IJCNLP 2021, (Volume 2: Short Papers)*, pages 1065–1072.

Yixin Liu, Pengfei Liu, Dragomir R. Radev, and Graham Neubig. 2022. BRIO: bringing order to abstractive summarization. In *ACL 2022*, pages 2890–2903.

Ilya Loshchilov and Frank Hutter. 2019. Decoupled weight decay regularization. In *7th International Conference on Learning Representations, ICLR 2019*.

Joshua Maynez, Shashi Narayan, Bernd Bohnet, and Ryan T. McDonald. 2020. On faithfulness and factuality in abstractive summarization. In *Proceedings of the 58th Annual Meeting of the Association for Computational Linguistics, ACL 2020*, pages 1906–1919.

Ramesh Nallapati, Bowen Zhou, Cícero Nogueira dos Santos, Çaglar Gülçehre, and Bing Xiang. 2016. Abstractive text summarization using sequence-to-sequence rnns and beyond. In *CoNLL 2016*, pages 280–290.

Shashi Narayan, Shay B. Cohen, and Mirella Lapata. 2018. Don't give me the details, just the summary! topic-aware convolutional neural networks for extreme summarization. In *EMNLP 2018*, pages 1797–1807.

Richard Yuanzhe Pang and He He. 2021. Text generation by learning from demonstrations. In *ICLR 2021*.

Romain Paulus, Caiming Xiong, and Richard Socher. 2018. A deep reinforced model for abstractive summarization. In *6th International Conference on Learning Representations, ICLR 2018*.

Paul Roit, Johan Ferret, Lior Shani, Roee Aharoni, Geoffrey Cideron, Robert Dadashi, Matthieu Geist, Sertan Girgin, Léonard Hussenot, Orgad Keller, Nikola Momchev, Sabela Ramos Garea, Piotr Stanczyk, Nino Vieillard, Olivier Bachem, Gal Elidan, Avinatan Hassidim, Olivier Pietquin, and Idan Szpektor. 2023. Factually consistent summarization via reinforcement learning with textual entailment feedback. In *ACL 2023*, pages 6252–6272.

Shiqi Shen, Yong Cheng, Zhongjun He, Wei He, Hua Wu, Maosong Sun, and Yang Liu. 2016. Minimum risk training for neural machine translation. In *ACL 2016*.

Jeewoo Sul and Yong Suk Choi. 2023. Balancing lexical and semantic quality in abstractive summarization. In *Proceedings of the 61st Annual Meeting of the Association for Computational Linguistics (Volume 2: Short Papers), ACL 2023*, pages 637–647. Association for Computational Linguistics.

Caidong Tan. 2023. Deep reinforcement learning with copy-oriented context awareness and weighted rewards for abstractive summarization. In *CACML 2023*, pages 84–89.

Ashwin K. Vijayakumar, Michael Cogswell, Ramprasaath R. Selvaraju, Qing Sun, Stefan Lee, David J. Crandall, and Dhruv Batra. 2016. Diverse beam search: Decoding diverse solutions from neural sequence models. *CoRR*, abs/1610.02424.

Jiawen Xie, Qi Su, Shaoting Zhang, and Xiaofan Zhang. 2023. Alleviating exposure bias via multi-level contrastive learning and deviation simulation in abstractive summarization. In *Findings of the Association for Computational Linguistics: ACL 2023*, pages 9732–9747.

Shusheng Xu, Xingxing Zhang, Yi Wu, and Furu Wei. 2022. Sequence level contrastive learning for text summarization. In *AAAI 2022*, pages 11556–11565.

Weizhe Yuan, Graham Neubig, and Pengfei Liu. 2021. Bartscore: Evaluating generated text as text generation. In *NeurIPS 2021*, pages 27263–27277.

Jingqing Zhang, Yao Zhao, Mohammad Saleh, and Peter J. Liu. 2020a. PEGASUS: pre-training with extracted gap-sentences for abstractive summarization. In *ICML 2020*, volume 119 of *Proceedings of Machine Learning Research*, pages 11328–11339.

Tianyi Zhang, Varsha Kishore, Felix Wu, Kilian Q. Weinberger, and Yoav Artzi. 2020b. Bertscore: Evaluating text generation with BERT. In *ICLR 2020*.

Xingxing Zhang, Yiran Liu, Xun Wang, Pengcheng He, Yang Yu, Si-Qing Chen, Wayne Xiong, and Furu Wei. 2022. Momentum calibration for text generation. *CoRR*, abs/2212.04257.

Yao Zhao, Misha Khalman, Rishabh Joshi, Shashi Narayan, Mohammad Saleh, and Peter J. Liu. 2023. Calibrating sequence likelihood improves conditional language generation. In *ICLR 2023*.

A Limitations

Although we pioneer present an iterative autoregressive summarization (IAR) mechanism, which suffers little prior bias since it relies on no metrics to measure document-summary semantic or lexical similarity, performing IAR requires a dual-encoder Transformer architecture. This setting is intuitively incompatible with nowadays decoder-only large pretrained Transformer models. On the one hand, this work confirmed the effectiveness of using the IAR mechanism to improve abstractive summarization, also, it left further work for us to adapt the mechanism for large language models.

B More Analyses

B.1 Varying the Beam Width.

Note that the global learning objective of IAR-Sum is to maximize the expected rewards calculated over the candidate summaries sampled from $P_\theta(\cdot|Y^{i-1}, X)$. There is a gap between the learning objective and our training implementation. During training, we are inspired by the Monte Carlo (MC) algorithm and use k candidates to represent the infinite searching space. Intuitively, a larger beam width (k) used in beam search is more adequate to approximate the expected distribution and, in turn, better summarization performance. To validate this assumption, we train our model on both datasets and use different beam widths of 4, 8, 16, 32, and 64 to sample candidates. Figure 6 displays the ROUGE-Avg score of each resulting version.

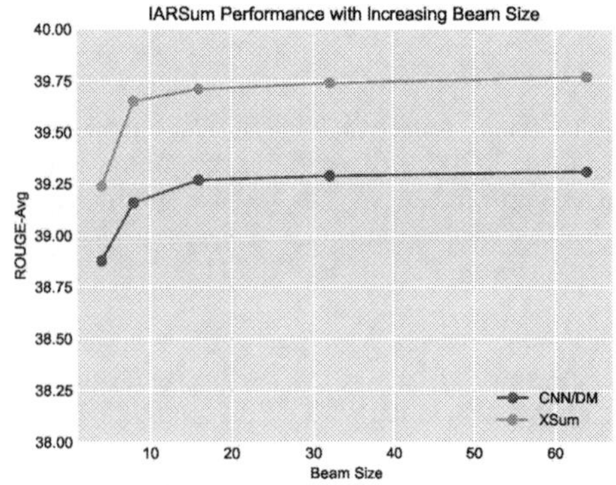

Figure 6: The performance of the IARSum trained with varying numbers of sampled candidates. ROUGE-Avg (the average of R-1, R-2, and R-L F_1 scores) scores are reported.

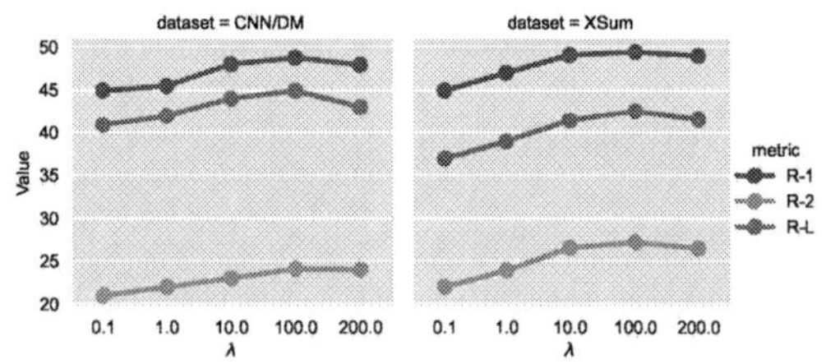

Figure 7: The performance of IARSum with increasing λ on CNN/DM and XSum.

Unsurprisingly, increasing the beam width can indeed boost the model's performance. However, the ROUGE score improvement reduces once the k is over 16. We set k to 16 to save computational costs.

B.2 The Decide of λ Value.

To find an optimal weight coefficient λ that integrates the global learning objective into the token-level MLE, we perform a grid search in $\{0.1, 1, 10, 100, 200\}$. The search process is visualized in Figure 7. Notably, the performance of IARSum with varying λ shows a similar trend on both datasets. It is observed that a too-small weight suppresses global learning efficacy. On the contrary, once λ reaches the magnitude above one hundred, varying its value makes inconspicuous effects. We finally set λ to 100 without distinguishing datasets.

TpT-ADE: Transformer Based Two-Phase ADE Extraction

Suryamukhi Kuchibhotla and **Manish Singh**
Indian Institute of Technology Hyderabad
Telangana, India
cs17m19p100001@iith.ac.in and msingh@cse.iith.ac.in

Abstract

Extracting adverse reactions to medications or treatments is a crucial activity in the biomedical domain. The task involves identifying mentions of drugs and their adverse effects/events in raw text, which is challenging due to the unstructured nature of clinical narratives. In this paper, we propose TpT-ADE, a novel joint two-phase transformer model combined with natural language processing (NLP) techniques, to identify adverse events (AEs) caused by drugs. In the first phase of TpT-ADE, entities are extracted and are grounded with their standard terms using the Unified Medical Language System (UMLS) knowledge base. In the second phase, entity and relation classification is performed to determine the presence of a relationship between the drug and AE pairs. TpT-ADE also identifies the intensity of AE entities by constructing a parts-of-speech (POS) embedding model. Unlike previous approaches that use complex classifiers, TpT-ADE employs a shallow neural network and yet outperforms the state-of-the-art methods on the standard ADE corpus.

1 Introduction

Adverse Drug Event (ADE) is a negative or harmful patient outcome that seems to be associated with a medication or drug. Analyzing the adverse events (AEs) helps a practitioner to identify susceptible patients who may be at risk due to a particular drug. ADE extraction has several uses: pharmaceutical companies can identify the sections of the population that were adversely impacted by the drug. For governments and regulatory authorities, ADE information is the key to monitoring the performance of drugs already in the market and identifying any adverse effects that have not appeared during clinical trials.

Generally, ADEs are reported in an unstructured manner and are to be extracted from various sources like clinical narratives, medical journals, formal systems that report ADEs, etc. In some cases, the patients may report adverse events in social media posts, like "I got *rashes* on my back today after taking two tablets of *amoxicillin* yesterday". In this post, *"rashes"* is the adverse effect (AE) that could be caused by the drug *"amoxicillin"*. Identifying the drugs and adverse events and finding relations between them from such unstructured text is quite challenging due to the complex nature of the text containing multiple drugs and adverse events. We illustrate with an example below to understand the complexity of such texts. The text in red color is the AE and the text in blue is the drug name.

Example — "Atypical ventricular tachycardia$_{\text{AE}}$ torsade pointes$_{\text{AE}}$ induced by amiodarone$_{\text{Drug}}$: arrhythmia$_{\text{AE}}$ previously induced by quinidine$_{\text{Drug}}$ and disopyramide$_{\text{Drug}}$."

Following are the *drug, AE* relations that could be extracted from the above example:

disopyramide$_{\text{Drug}}$,quinidine$_{\text{Drug}}$ $\rightarrow$ arrhythmia$_{\text{AE}}$
amiodarone$_{\text{Drug}}$ $\rightarrow$ Atypical ventricular tachycardia$_{\text{AE}}$, torsade de pointes$_{\text{AE}}$

ADE extraction is a two-step process. The first step is identifying the mentions of the drugs and the AEs from raw text. This is similar to the task of named entity recognition. In the second step, each $< drug, AE >$ pair is examined for ADE relation, which can be cast as a classification problem.

Some methods (Dandala et al., 2017; Unanue et al., 2017) train separate models for the two steps of ADE extraction. In contrast to these works, (El-Allaly et al., 2022; Ma et al., 2022; Wadden et al., 2019; Bekoulis et al., 2018b; Zhou et al., 2017) proposed joint methods for ADE extraction that perform better in both recognizing the entities and ADE extraction tasks. A major drawback of the former approach is that if the first step of identification of drugs and AEs entities is incorrect, then the ADE

Proceedings of the 28th Conference on Computational Natural Language Learning, pages 209–218
November 15-16, 2024 ©2024 Association for Computational Linguistics

extraction will also be incorrect, thereby resulting in poor performance due to the error propagation. Also, the joint models have been proven to be effective in performing many related tasks such as part-of-speech tagging and parsing (Zhang and Clark, 2008), keyword extraction using joint modeling of local and global context (Liang et al., 2021), entity extraction and classification (Eberts and Ulges, 2019), entity and coreference extraction (Hajishirzi et al., 2013; Durrett and Klein, 2014), and many more.

In this paper, we introduce TpT-ADE, a joint two-phase model for ADE extraction from clinical texts by fine-tuning BERT (Devlin et al., 2018). In the first phase, TpT-ADE identifies and standardizes mentions of entities such as drugs and adverse effects against the Unified Medical Language System (UMLS)[1]. This ensures uniformity in naming across different mentions. The second phase uses this processed text to jointly extract entities and classify relations.

Our model employs a robust span-based extraction method, which can extract entities consisting of multiple successive tokens. That is, TpT-ADE is able to extract overlapping entities. Our approach can also detect the intensity of an adverse event, distinguishing between terms like "fever", "severe fever", and "mild fever". Unlike previous works that rely on complex relational classifiers, TpT-ADE uses a shallow neural network and yet achieves higher F1-score on the standard ADE corpus (Gurulingappa et al., 2012).

2 Related Work

In this section, we discuss the related works in ADE extraction. We first discuss the pipeline based approaches that extract ADEs by training separate models for entity extraction and relation extraction tasks. Then, we discuss the joint methods that follow an end-to-end approach to extract ADEs. Under the joint models, we discuss the related works that are BiLSTMs based, Graph Convolutional Networks based and Span-based models.

The pipeline based approaches (Dai et al., 2020; Wei et al., 2020; Dandala et al., 2017) are designed to complete one subtask and then go ahead with the next subtask. In the case of ADE extraction, the output from the entity extraction model is passed as the input for the relation extraction task. Both the models are trained separately with different loss functions. (Wei et al., 2020; Xu et al., 2017; Dandala et al., 2017) use BiLSTM based models for ADE extraction. (Wei et al., 2020) employs the same BiLSTM based classifiers for both entity and relation extraction. Other works train two different classifiers for the two tasks. (Alfattni et al., 2021; Dai et al., 2020) employ a hybrid approach by combining feature based machine learning classifiers and neural networks.

Identifying negative entities is a crucial step for extracting ADEs. Negative entities are those that are not drugs or adverse effects. Towards this, (Wei et al., 2020) proposed an Attention based Bi-LSTM model that reduced the number of negative instances, helping to overcome the imbalance class problem. Their method could also handle the discontinous entitiess. More recently, (He et al., 2022) proposed an LSTM based adaptive knowledge distillation model. The authors used BERT to adaptively distill the knowledge to the LSTM model. Other recent works proposed in this regard are (Wang et al., 2022; He et al., 2023; Liu et al., 2023).

Joint entity and relation extraction methods (Bekoulis et al., 2018a,b; Ma et al., 2022; Eberts and Ulges, 2019; Wadden et al., 2019) have been recently proposed to capture the dependency between the two tasks in ADE extraction. (Bekoulis et al., 2018a,b) utilize character and Word2Vec embeddings to represent their input. Then, they use BiLSTM model combined with conditional random field (CRF) model to jointly extract entities and their relations.

(Wang and Lu, 2020; Wang et al., 2021; Yan et al., 2021; Ma et al., 2022) cast the ADE extraction problem as a table-filling problem. These methods construct a table that jointly represents the entities and relations and each element in the table depicts the presence of a relation between entities. Then, the relation triples are extracted from the filled table. (Yan et al., 2021) constructed a partition filter network to learn the feature representations that can classify entities and the relations. Then, the relation triples extracted by following a table-filling approach. Similarly, (Ma et al., 2022) proposed a table-filling method that learns contextualized representations to compute entity mentions and capture long-range dependencies. For relation extraction, a tensor dot product is used to predict the relation labels. However, these table-filling methods are computationally expensive due to building and deconding these tables for relation

[1]https://www.nlm.nih.gov/research/umls/index.html

triples (Chen et al., 2024).

Span-based methods (Luan et al., 2019; Wadden et al., 2019; Eberts and Ulges, 2019; Wan et al., 2023) have shown remarkable performance in obtaining contextualized representations. In contrast to works that follow the BIO (beginning, inside, outside)/BILOU (beginning, inside, last, outside, unit)/BIES(Begin, Inside, End, Single) (Zheng et al., 2017; Zhou et al., 2017), span-based approach can identify the overlapping entities. In our work, we follow a span-based approach and combine BERT (Devlin et al., 2018) with POS embedding model. In contrast to the previous works, we follow a two phase joint modelling approach that standardizes the entity mentions in the input text with their representative terms. In addition, unlike the above works that use complex classfiers, we use a shallow neural network for ADE extraction.

3 Methodology

In this section, we detail the two phases of TpT-ADE model and training it. In the first phase Phase I, we extract the entities and represent them with their standard medical terms. In Section 4, we show the effectiveness of this step. The second phase, Phase II utilizes this processed text for ADE extraction.

3.1 Phase I: Entity Extraction

In this phase, we perform entity mention extraction or recognition and find the most representative term for each entity mention in the raw clinical text corpus. The architecture for entity recognition is shown in Figure 1. Towards this, we propose a span based BERT model. BERT learns word representations from input text by considering both the left and right contexts. We first tokenize the input sentences into a sequence of tokens T using a subword tokenization algorithm called Byte-Pair Encoding (BPE) (Sennrich et al., 2015). BPE tokenizes the input sentences in such a way that the most common words are represented in the vocabulary as a single token. The infrequent words are divided into commonly occurring subwords. For example, the infrequent word *townhall* can be divided into frequently occurring *town* and *hall*. Thus, BPE can be used by BERT to map out of vocabulary words and limit the vocabulary size. BPE tokens extracted from each input sentence are passed to the BERT model to obtain an embedding sequence as follows:

$$(c, e_1, e_2, ...e_n) = BERT(T) \quad (1)$$

The first token c in BERT is the classifier token (cls), shown in Figure 1, that captures the overall input sentence context. We then construct spans considering all the token subsequences. For instance, the token sequence *carbamazepine toxicity symptoms* can result into token subsequences or spans like *carbamazepine*, *carbamazepine toxicity*, etc. The span based approach ensures we search all the possible combinations, is more robust, and is expected to extract the entity that may be composed of multiple successive tokens.

We treat the entity mention extraction problem as a classification problem where each span is classified into one of three categories, namely, *Drug*, *AE* or *None* by the *Entity Classifier* in Figure 1. *None* means the span is neither *Drug* or *AE* and these are filtered out. Initially, a pre-trained BERT model is utilized and adjusted to the clinical domain to explore the information in the clinical text documents. The model is then fine-tuned for classifying the spans into the aforementioned three categories. We fine-tune the pre-trained BERT model by adding a task-specific layer on top of it and training the whole model end-to-end with a suitable loss function. This is detailed in Section 3.3.

Let $s_i = (e_1, e_2, ..., e_k)$ be a span consisting of k token subsequences. The BERT embeddings of the token subsequences are combined using max-pooling and the span embedding of span s_i is represented as follows:

$$s^{s_i} = \textit{max-pooling}(e_1, e_2, ..., e_k) \oplus c \quad (2)$$

where $\oplus$ denotes concatenation. We note that any span longer than ten tokens are filtered out to limit the cost of entity classification.

The raw clinical text is collected from varied sources and hence the same drug or AE entities could be mentioned with different names. For instance, consider the following two texts from our dataset:

Example 1 — *After gastric-outlet obstruction was recognized in several infants who received prostaglandin E1, we studied the association between the drug and this complication*

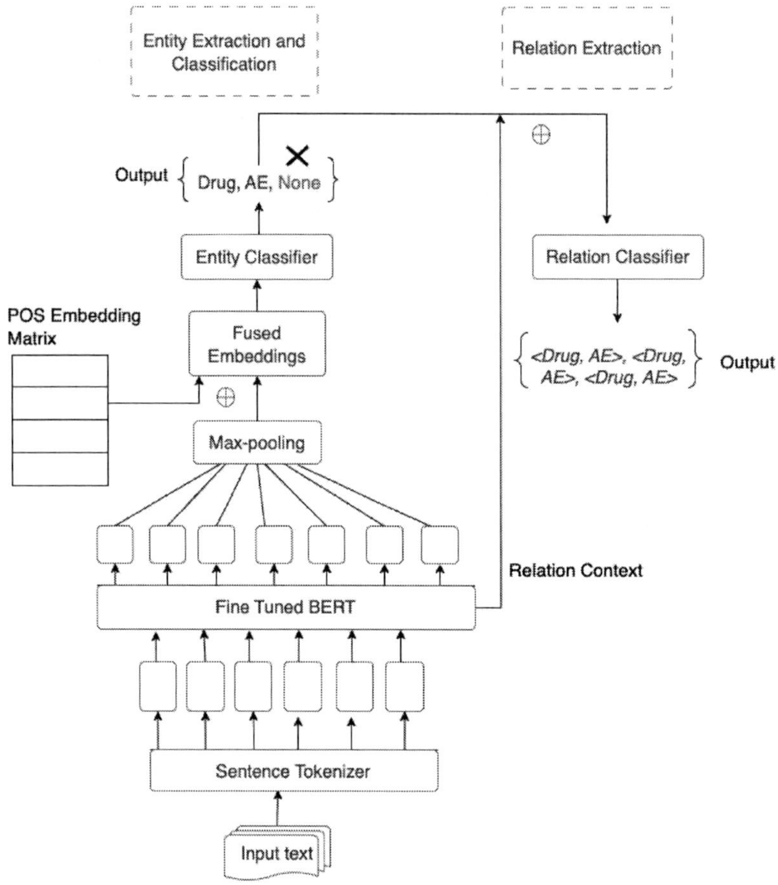

Figure 1: Entity and Relation Extraction

Example 2 — *The clinical symptoms of gastric mucosa foveolar hyperplasia due to long-term PGE1 therapy simulate hypertrophic pyloric stenosis*

In the above two examples, the drug references *"prosta- glandin E1"* and *"PGE1"* refer to the same drug, whose standard UMLS name is given by Metamap[5] as *"alprostadil"*. As the next step in this phase, we replace the entities with their most representative terms. We will observe in Section 4.3 that standardising the entity mentions with their representative terms improves the overall performance of TpT-ADE.

In this phase of TpT-ADE, we also identify the intensity of the AEs caused by drugs as discussed in Section 1. Specific modifiers which precede the identified entity may need to be added to the entity itself. For example, entity *fever* is distinguished from the entity *severe fever* as both are different AEs. The same holds true for many modifiers like "Severe", "Reversible", "Paradoxical", "Unusual", "Chronic", etc. Towards this we identify the adjectives of the entities using spaCy[6]. SpaCy is NLP library used for generating POS tags of tokens in a given input sentence. We used ScispaCy (Neumann et al., 2019) trained with *en_core_sci_sm* that processes clinical or biomedical text. The POS embedding matrix is trained to obtain the representation of POS tags. Adjectives specifying the entities are then concatenated with the BERT embeddings. In Section 4.3, we demonstrate that the performance of the model improves when POS tag embeddings are included. Finally, the POS tag embeddings and the BERT embeddings are concatenated to obtain the following entity representation.

$$x^{s_i} = s^{s_i} \oplus p^{s_i} \tag{3}$$

where p^{s_i} is POS tag embeddings that specify the intensity of span s_i.

Next, the softmax classifier given below is used to obtain a posterior for each entity category, i.e.,

[5] https://lhncbc.nlm.nih.gov/ii/tools/MetaMap.html

[6] https://spacy.io/

drug, *AE* and *none*. The output of this phase of our model is the processed clinical text.

$$Y^{s_i} = softmax(W^{s_i} \cdot x^{s_i} + b^{s_i}) \quad (4)$$

3.2 Phase II: ADE Extraction

In this phase, we jointly extract entities and perform relation classification using the processed text from Phase I as shown in Figure 1. The text is tokenized using BPE tokenizer and the fused span embeddings are constructed using BERT model for entity classification. Max-pooling fusion function is used as it performed the best. The spans having a length of more than ten tokens are filtered as too longer spans are highly unlikely to represent entities. The entities classified into *none* class are filtered out. Let $\mathcal{E}$ be the set of entity spans classified as either *Drug* or *AE*.

The next step of this phase is relationship classification. The relationship classifier takes each pair of fused BERT span embedding from entity spans in $\mathcal{E} \times \mathcal{E}$ and checks the presence of a relation between them. Let f^{s_i} be the fused BERT embedding of the entity span $s_i = (e_1, e_2, ..., e_k)$, which is calculated as follows:

$$f^{s_i} = \textit{max-pooling}(e_1, e_2, ..., e_k) \quad (5)$$

To understand the presence of a relation, it is important to understand the context. One way to obtain the context is the classifier token c from the embedding span representation, as discussed above. However, the context c would not be precise and could represent multiple relations for longer sentences. Thus, we derive the relationship context between entity spans localized to their direct surrounding entities. Let s_i and s_j be two entity spans considered to check the presence of a relation. The relation context $c^{rel}(s_i, s_j)$ is derived from the fused BERT embedding of the span ranging from the end of s_i entity to the beginning of the s_j entity. For obtaining $c^{rel}(s_i, s_j)$, we found the max-pooling function performing the best. In case the entities are next to each other or overlapping, we set $c^{rel}(s_i, s_j) = 0$.

Another consideration for relationship classification between two entities could be asymmetrical. That is, s_i could indicate *drug* and s_j could be *AE*, or vice versa. Therefore, we need to consider both (s_i, s_j) and (s_j, s_i) for relationship classification. Hence, we have the following two representations as input to the relation classifier.

$$\begin{aligned} Rel(x^{s_i, \rightarrow s_j}) &= f^{s_i} \oplus c^{rel}(s_i, s_j) \oplus f^{s_j} \\ Rel(x^{s_j, \rightarrow s_i}) &= f^{s_j} \oplus c^{rel}(s_j, s_i) \oplus f^{s_i} \end{aligned} \quad (6)$$

These two inputs are passed to a shallow single layer relationship classifier with a threshold α. A high response in the sigmoid layer indicates the presence of relationship between s_i and s_j. We consider that the relationship exists based on threshold value α; any relation with score $\geq \alpha$ is considered as related and assumed no relationship otherwise.

3.3 Training TpT-ADE Model

In this section, we detail the process to learn the parameters W^{s_i}, b^{s_i}, W^r, and b^r, thereby fine-tuning our BERT model in this process. Our model consists of two phases, and these parameters are learned in a supervised manner. That is, the entities and relations are labeled in our dataset. For both phases, training is done in batches. We draw positive and negative samples for each batch for the classifiers in both phases. We detail the positive and negative sample selection and loss functions for both phases below.

For entity classification, all the labeled entities in the ground truth dataset are taken as positive samples. Let this set be $\mathcal{E}^g$. We take a fixed number of negative samples $\mathcal{E}^{ne}$ in each batch. We illustrate the selection of positive and negative samples for entity classification with an example. In the given sentence: "Nine **azotemic**$_{\text{AE}}$ patients who developed a **blood coagulation disorders**$_{\text{AE}}$ associated with the use of either **cephalosporins**$_{\text{Drug}}$ or **moxalactam**$_{\text{Drug}}$ antibiotics are reported." the ones marked as *Drug* or *AE* constitute the positive samples. Negative samples such as **associated**$_{\text{Drug}}$ and **reported**$_{\text{AE}}$ are randomly selected.

For training the relationship classifier, we use all ground truth relationships as positive samples. Instead of randomly selecting negative samples, we devise a method to select only the strong negative samples $\mathcal{E}^{nr}$ drawn from the entity pairs $\mathcal{E}^g \times \mathcal{E}^g$ that were not labeled as any relation. For example, the positive samples in the above example are *(cephalosporins, blood coagulation disorders)* and *(moxalactam, blood coagulation disorders)*, then the unlabelled relations like *(cephalosporins, azotemic)*, *(moxalactam, azotemic)* are taken as negative samples. Such strong negative samples instead of random pairs of entities help to improve the performance of the model.

In the first phase, the model learns parameters W^{s_i}, b^{s_i} used for entity recognition. Using the training set with annotated entities, the loss function for the first phase, $\mathcal{L}^1$, is defined as the entity classifier's cross-entropy loss over entity classes *Drug, AE, none*. The joint loss function for entity classification and relation classification in the second phase is defined by combining the losses from both the classifiers as follows:

$$\mathcal{L}^2 = \mathcal{L}^e + \mathcal{L}^r \quad (7)$$

where $\mathcal{L}^e$ is the entity classifier cross-entropy loss over all the three entity classes and $\mathcal{L}^r$ is the binary entropy loss averaged over batches' samples.

4 Evaluation

In this section, we present the evaluation of TpT-ADE and compare it with the state-of-the-art (SOTA) methods. We first start by describing our dataset. Next, we present the evaluation results of our model against the SOTA methods. Lastly, we perform ablation studies with various variants of our model and show the effectiveness of various components of our model.

4.1 Experimental Setup

We use the ADE corpus dataset (Gurulingappa et al., 2012) to train and evaluate our model. It contains 5,063 drugs, 5,776 adverse effects and 6,821 relations between them, extracted from 4,272 unique samples.

Table 1: Dataset Statistics

Statistics	Train	Val	Test
Drugs	3646	922	495
AEs	4151	1062	563
Relations	4877	1285	659
Documents	3076	769	427

To evaluate our model, we divided the dataset into training, validation and test sets, as shown in Table 1. Our model TpT-ADE is trained on the training set. We conduct 10-fold cross-validation on the validation set, and the evaluation is performed on the test set.

We used $\text{BERT}_{\text{BASE}}$[7] transformer with 768 dimensional embeddings and 110M parameters, pre-trained with 3 billion plus English words. In our experiments, we use Adam Optimizer with learning rate of 0.00005, weight decay of 0.01, *lr* warmup of 0.1, batch size of 2. The number of negative samples in both entity and relation classification, $\mathcal{E}^{ne}$ and $\mathcal{E}^{nr}$ are set to 80 per document. We run the model for 30 epochs with the relation classifier threshold set to 0.04. We obtained the best results with these parameter values. The BERT model weights are updated during the training process.

We evaluate our model for both entity extraction and relationship classification. If the predicted span of an entity and its type, that is, either Drug or AE are found exactly matching with the ground truth data, then the entity is considered to be correctly predicted. For relationships, both entities of the relationship must be correctly predicted as given in the ground truth. As in previous works (Bekoulis et al., 2018b; Eberts and Ulges, 2019), we use precision, recall and F1 scores averaged over folds as performance metrics to evaluate our model.

4.2 Baseline Methods

To evaluate the effectiveness of our TpT-ADE model in both entity and relationship classification, we compare its performance with the state-of-the-art methods listed below.

1. **Joint CNN Model (Li et al., 2016)**: This method uses transition-based feed-forward CNN to perform greedy transition-based decoding and jointly performs ADE extraction.

2. **Joint BiLSTM-RNN Model (Li et al., 2017)**: This method uses a BiLSTM-RNN model to learn the representations of entities and their contexts from the input text. Then, another BiLSTM-RNN model is built to learn the relations between the entities based on the shortest dependency path between them.

3. **Joint Multi-head Selection Model (Bekoulis et al., 2018b)**: This method uses character and Word2Vec embeddings to represent the input text. Then BiLSTM-CRF model is trained to extract entities and ADEs.

4. **SpERT (Eberts and Ulges, 2019)**: This method uses span based BERT models for extracting entities and adverse relations.

5. **TablERT-CNN (Ma et al., 2022)**: This BERT based method extracts ADEs by casting ADE extraction as a table-labelling problem. Two-dimensional CNN is used to encode the local

[7]https://huggingface.co/bert-base-cased

dependencies between the cells and predict the their labels.

6. **SMAN (Wan et al., 2023)**: This span based approach constructs a multi-model attention network to capture the interactions between the spans and model information such as tokens and labels. The context and span position information is extracted simultaneously.

4.2.1 Results

Table 2 shows the performance on both entity and relation extraction tasks on the test set. The table shows some missing values as these numbers weren't reported by the corresponding SOTA methods. For entity extraction task (NER), our model achieved an F1-score of 91.17%, which is 1.47% higher than the TablERT-CNN and 0.22% over SMAN. In addition, our model shows a significant improvement of 4.58% over the popular state-of-the-art model SpERT and 1.57% over the SMAN method in the case of ADE extraction (RE). Unlike all these baseline methods, our model finds the most representative clinical term of each entity mention. This step makes the training process of our model's first phase more robust, thereby improving the performance of the ADE relation extraction in the second phase. Thus, on the unseen test data, even if the input text entity is called by any other alias phrase name, it can still be detected and mapped to its most representative name. We performed error analysis on our model and observed that it gives the least number of false-negatives in both NER and RE tasks. One reason for this could be that TpT-ADE can identify complex and ambiguous entities.

Qualitative analysis shows that TpT-ADE is able to correctly identify **Ventricular tachycardia**$_{\text{AE}}$ and **Arrhythmia**$_{\text{AE}}$ referring to the same AE. Also, the abbreviation V-tach or VT is correctly recognized as ventricular tachycardia. In addition, the interactions between the AE **torsade pointes**$_{\text{AE}}$ and drugs **amiodarone**$_{\text{Drug}}$, **quinidine**$_{\text{Drug}}$ and **disopyramide**$_{\text{Drug}}$ were extracted by our model, unlike the previous models that were able to extract only the interaction between **torsade pointes**$_{\text{AE}}$ and **amiodarone**.

Compared to (Eberts and Ulges, 2019) (SpERT) and (Wan et al., 2023), which also uses a span based model, our model shows improved performance on both the NER and RE tasks. Span based approach to extract entities thus is more effective than to use BILOU/BIS labels as in (Bekoulis et al., 2018b; Li et al., 2017) (Joint Multi-head Selection, Joint BiLSTM-RNN Model). We also note that the input text also contains the intensity of the AEs that can be identified by our model in contrast to the baseline methods. Specifically, the ADE dataset contains 148 of such instances. In addition, unlike most of the baseline methods, our span based model detects the entity phrases that might contain overlapping entities. Specifically, the ADE dataset contains 120 of such overlapping instances.

4.3 Ablation Studies

In this section, we perform experiments on variants of our model and hyperparameters settings to demonstrate their impact on our model.

Effectiveness of Entity Standardization — In this study, we analyze the effectiveness of finding the representative term for each entity mention in the raw input text. We illustrate with an example from our dataset. The entities *common skin rashes*, *rashes*, *skin eruptions*, *cutaneous eruptions*, all refer to the same adverse effect. The representative term for all of them is *Exanthema*. Our model was trained using the training set that contains *rashes*, *skin eruptions*. The test set contains *cutaneous eruptions* that was correctly mapped to its representative term *Exanthema*. From Table 3, it can be observed that the F1-score of *W/O Entity Standardization* (removing entity standardization from TpT-ADE) drops a little by 0.87% in the case of NER task and significantly decreases (3.02%) in the case of RE task when compared to our TpT-ADE model.

Effectiveness of Entity Intensity Identification — We also investigate the effectiveness of enriching the BERT embeddings of the entities with the POS tag embeddings that provide the intensity information. For this purpose, we compare our TpT-ADE model with *W/O Entity Intensity Identification* model (without the POS embedding matrix) as shown in Table 3. It can be observed that there is a decrease in the performance of both the tasks in *W/O Entity Intensity Identification* (1% for NER and more than 2% for RE) compared to our Tpt-ADE model. Therefore, this shows the importance of linguistic information obtained by training the POS embedding matrix.

Effectiveness of Relation Context — Here, we examine the effect of using relation context in the ADE extraction phase detailed in Section 3.2 in-

Method	NER			RE		
	Precision	Recall	F1-score	Precision	Recall	F1-score
Joint CNN	79.50	79.60	79.50	64.00	62.90	63.40
Joint BiLSTM-RNN	82.70	86.70	84.60	67.50	75.80	71.40
Joint Multi-head Selection	84.72	88.16	86.40	72.10	77.24	74.58
SpERT	**89.26**	89.26	89.25	78.09	80.43	79.24
TablERT-CNN	-	-	89.7	-	-	80.5
SMAN	-	-	90.95	-	-	82.25
TpT-ADE	89.24	**93.2**	**91.17**	**81.91**	**85.83**	**83.82**

Table 2: Comparison of TpT-ADE with the baseline methods results(%)

Method	NER			RE		
	Precision	Recall	F1-score	Precision	Recall	F1-score
TpT-ADE	89.24	93.2	91.17	81.91	85.83	83.82
w/o Entity Standardization	88.71	91.95	90.30	78.44	83.35	80.82
w/o Entity Intensity Identification	88.74	91.63	90.16	79.86	83.61	81.69
Classifier Token Context	-	-	-	73.5	80.22	76.71
Weak Random Sampling	-	-	-	76.39	81.7	78.96

Table 3: Ablation studies results (%). w/o indicates the specific module is removed from TpT-ADE.

stead of using the classifier context, which uses a special token to capture the meaning of the entire sentence. The relation context particularly extracts the context from the part of the sentence that depicts the presence of a relationship between the entities the most. From Table 3, we can see that the performance of the TpT-ADE model, which uses the relation context in ADE extraction phase (RE task) achieves an F1-score of 83.82%, while the *Classifier Token Context* (CTC) model performs poorly with F1-score of 76.7%. Moreover, the precision drops by 8.41% as compared to TpT-ADE. Thus, this shows that training the model with relation context is better in ADE extraction.

Effectiveness of Negative Sampling — We also examine the effectiveness of choosing strong negative samples in the ADE extraction phase against using random negative samples. Negative samples are randomly drawn, and the entity pairs do not match with any ground truth relation pairs. Unlike choosing strong negative samples from the entity candidate set $\mathcal{E}$, these weak samples are randomly drawn. From Table 3, it can be observed that the performance of the *Weak Random Sampling* model drops by almost 5% (F1-score) compared to our TpT-ADE model. We performed another experiment wherein the weak negative samples are drawn from the set without filtering the entities that belong to *none* class. In this case, the F1-score further dropped by 7.2% compared to our TpT-ADE model.

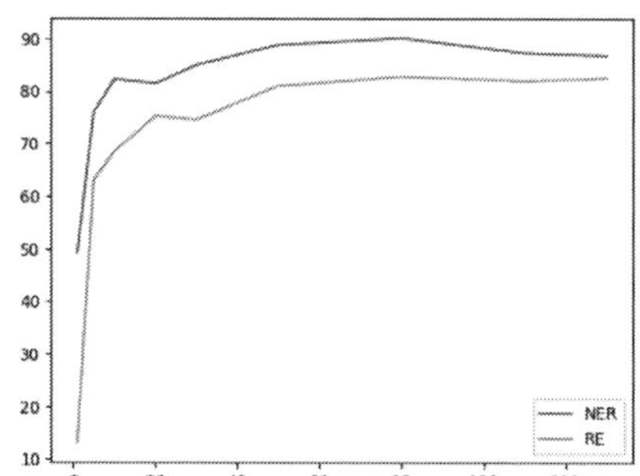

Figure 2: Negative Sampling Analysis

In our model, we chose the number of negative samples in case of both entity extraction and relation extraction ($\mathcal{E}^{ne} = \mathcal{E}^{nr}$) as 80 per sentence in the input sentence. As shown in Figure 2, if $\mathcal{E}^{ne} = \mathcal{E}^{nr} < 5$, the F1-score reaches to 68.2% and 53.7% for entity extraction and relation extraction, respectively. As the values of $\mathcal{E}^{ne}$ and $\mathcal{E}^{nr}$ increases, the model performs better. We observe that when $\mathcal{E}^{ne} = \mathcal{E}^{nr} > 80$, the performance of the model stagnates. Hence, we chose

$\mathcal{E}^{ne} = \mathcal{E}^{nr} = 80$.

5 Conclusion

In this paper, we proposed TpT-ADE, a two-phase transformer based model to improve the efficiency of ADE extraction from raw clinical text. Through various experiments, we have shown that finding the representative terms for the entities in the input text and combining the trained BERT embeddings with the POS tag embeddings of the modifier words of the entities to identify their intensities yield better results. In addition, using a simple shallow neural network and a strong negative sampling method in our model, showed considerable improvements over prior works.

References

Ghada Alfattni, Maksim Belousov, Niels Peek, Goran Nenadic, et al. 2021. Extracting drug names and associated attributes from discharge summaries: text mining study. *JMIR medical informatics*, 9(5):e24678.

Giannis Bekoulis, Johannes Deleu, Thomas Demeester, and Chris Develder. 2018a. Adversarial training for multi-context joint entity and relation extraction. *arXiv preprint arXiv:1808.06876*.

Giannis Bekoulis, Johannes Deleu, Thomas Demeester, and Chris Develder. 2018b. Joint entity recognition and relation extraction as a multi-head selection problem. *Expert Systems with Applications*, 114:34–45.

Juan Chen, Jie Hu, Tianrui Li, Fei Teng, and Shengdong Du. 2024. An effective relation-first detection model for relational triple extraction. *Expert Systems with Applications*, 238:122007.

Hong-Jie Dai, Chu-Hsien Su, and Chi-Shin Wu. 2020. Adverse drug event and medication extraction in electronic health records via a cascading architecture with different sequence labeling models and word embeddings. *Journal of the American Medical Informatics Association*, 27(1):47–55.

Bharath Dandala, Diwakar Mahajan, and Murthy V Devarakonda. 2017. Ibm research system at tac 2017: Adverse drug reactions extraction from drug labels. In *TAC*.

Jacob Devlin, Ming-Wei Chang, Kenton Lee, and Kristina Toutanova. 2018. Bert: Pre-training of deep bidirectional transformers for language understanding. In *NAACL-HLT*.

Greg Durrett and Dan Klein. 2014. A joint model for entity analysis: Coreference, typing, and linking. *Transactions of the association for computational linguistics*, 2:477–490.

Markus Eberts and Adrian Ulges. 2019. Span-based joint entity and relation extraction with transformer pre-training. *arXiv preprint arXiv:1909.07755*.

Ed-Drissiya El-Allaly, Mourad Sarrouti, Noureddine En-Nahnahi, and Said Ouatik El Alaoui. 2022. An attentive joint model with transformer-based weighted graph convolutional network for extracting adverse drug event relation. *Journal of biomedical informatics*, 125:103968.

Harsha Gurulingappa, Abdul Mateen Rajput, Angus Roberts, Juliane Fluck, Martin Hofmann-Apitius, and Luca Toldo. 2012. Development of a benchmark corpus to support the automatic extraction of drug-related adverse effects from medical case reports. *Journal of biomedical informatics*, 45(5):885–892.

Hannaneh Hajishirzi, Leila Zilles, Daniel S Weld, and Luke Zettlemoyer. 2013. Joint coreference resolution and named-entity linking with multi-pass sieves. In *EMNLP*, pages 289–299. Citeseer.

Haorui He, Yuanzhe Ren, Zheng Li, and Jing Xue. 2022. Adaptive knowledge distillation for efficient relation classification. In *International conference on artificial neural networks*, pages 148–158. Springer.

Kai He, Yucheng Huang, Rui Mao, Tieliang Gong, Chen Li, and Erik Cambria. 2023. Virtual prompt pre-training for prototype-based few-shot relation extraction. *Expert Systems with Applications*, 213:118927.

Fei Li, Meishan Zhang, Guohong Fu, and Donghong Ji. 2017. A neural joint model for entity and relation extraction from biomedical text. *BMC bioinformatics*, 18(1):1–11.

Fei Li, Yue Zhang, Meishan Zhang, and Donghong Ji. 2016. Joint models for extracting adverse drug events from biomedical text. In *IJCAI*, volume 2016, pages 2838–2844.

Xinnian Liang, Shuangzhi Wu, Mu Li, and Zhoujun Li. 2021. Unsupervised keyphrase extraction by jointly modeling local and global context. *arXiv preprint arXiv:2109.07293*.

Zhaoran Liu, Haozhe Li, Hao Wang, Yilin Liao, Xinggao Liu, and Gaojie Wu. 2023. A novel pipelined end-to-end relation extraction framework with entity mentions and contextual semantic representation. *Expert Systems with Applications*, 228:120435.

Yi Luan, Dave Wadden, Luheng He, Amy Shah, Mari Ostendorf, and Hannaneh Hajishirzi. 2019. A general framework for information extraction using dynamic span graphs. *arXiv preprint arXiv:1904.03296*.

Youmi Ma, Tatsuya Hiraoka, and Naoaki Okazaki. 2022. Joint entity and relation extraction based on table labeling using convolutional neural networks. In *Proceedings of the sixth workshop on structured prediction for NLP*, pages 11–21.

Mark Neumann, Daniel King, Iz Beltagy, and Waleed Ammar. 2019. Scispacy: fast and robust models for biomedical natural language processing. *arXiv preprint arXiv:1902.07669*.

Rico Sennrich, Barry Haddow, and Alexandra Birch. 2015. Neural machine translation of rare words with subword units. *arXiv preprint arXiv:1508.07909*.

Inigo Jauregi Unanue, Ehsan Zare Borzeshi, and Massimo Piccardi. 2017. Recurrent neural networks with specialized word embeddings for health-domain named-entity recognition. *Journal of biomedical informatics*, 76:102–109.

David Wadden, Ulme Wennberg, Yi Luan, and Hannaneh Hajishirzi. 2019. Entity, relation, and event extraction with contextualized span representations. *arXiv preprint arXiv:1909.03546*.

Qian Wan, Luona Wei, Shan Zhao, and Jie Liu. 2023. A span-based multi-modal attention network for joint entity-relation extraction. *Knowledge-Based Systems*, 262:110228.

An Wang, Ao Liu, Hieu Hanh Le, and Haruo Yokota. 2022. Towards effective multi-task interaction for entity-relation extraction: A unified framework with selection recurrent network. *arXiv preprint arXiv:2202.07281*.

Jue Wang and Wei Lu. 2020. Two are better than one: Joint entity and relation extraction with table-sequence encoders. *arXiv preprint arXiv:2010.03851*.

Yijun Wang, Changzhi Sun, Yuanbin Wu, Hao Zhou, Lei Li, and Junchi Yan. 2021. Unire: A unified label space for entity relation extraction. *arXiv preprint arXiv:2107.04292*.

Qiang Wei, Zongcheng Ji, Zhiheng Li, Jingcheng Du, Jingqi Wang, Jun Xu, Yang Xiang, Firat Tiryaki, Stephen Wu, Yaoyun Zhang, et al. 2020. A study of deep learning approaches for medication and adverse drug event extraction from clinical text. *Journal of the American Medical Informatics Association*, 27(1):13–21.

Jun Xu, Hee-Jin Lee, Zongcheng Ji, Jingqi Wang, Qiang Wei, and Hua Xu. 2017. Uth_ccb system for adverse drug reaction extraction from drug labels at tac-adr 2017. In *TAC*.

Zhiheng Yan, Chong Zhang, Jinlan Fu, Qi Zhang, and Zhongyu Wei. 2021. A partition filter network for joint entity and relation extraction. *arXiv preprint arXiv:2108.12202*.

Yue Zhang and Stephen Clark. 2008. Joint word segmentation and pos tagging using a single perceptron. In *Proceedings of ACL-08: HLT*, pages 888–896.

Suncong Zheng, Feng Wang, Hongyun Bao, Yuexing Hao, Peng Zhou, and Bo Xu. 2017. Joint extraction of entities and relations based on a novel tagging scheme. *arXiv preprint arXiv:1706.05075*.

Peng Zhou, Suncong Zheng, Jiaming Xu, Zhenyu Qi, Hongyun Bao, and Bo Xu. 2017. Joint extraction of multiple relations and entities by using a hybrid neural network. In *Chinese Computational Linguistics and Natural Language Processing Based on Naturally Annotated Big Data: 16th China National Conference, CCL 2017, and 5th International Symposium, NLP-NABD 2017, Nanjing, China, October 13-15, 2017, Proceedings 16*, pages 135–146. Springer.

The Effect of Surprisal on Reading Times in Information Seeking and Repeated Reading

Keren Gruteke Klein[1], **Yoav Meiri**[1], **Omer Shubi**[1], **Yevgeni Berzak**[1,2]
[1]Faculty of Data and Decision Sciences,
Technion - Israel Institute of Technology, Haifa, Israel
[2]Department of Brain and Cognitive Sciences,
Massachusetts Institute of Technology, Cambridge, USA
{gkeren,meiri.yoav,shubi}@campus.technion.ac.il, berzak@technion.ac.il

Abstract

The effect of surprisal on processing difficulty has been a central topic of investigation in psycholinguistics. Here, we use eyetracking data to examine three language processing regimes that are common in daily life but have not been addressed with respect to this question: information seeking, repeated processing, and the combination of the two. Using standard regime-agnostic surprisal estimates we find that the prediction of surprisal theory regarding the presence of a linear effect of surprisal on processing times, extends to these regimes. However, when using surprisal estimates from regime-specific contexts that match the contexts and tasks given to humans, we find that in information seeking, such estimates do not improve the predictive power of processing times compared to standard surprisals. Further, regime-specific contexts yield near zero surprisal estimates with no predictive power for processing times in repeated reading. These findings point to misalignments of task and memory representations between humans and current language models, and question the extent to which such models can be used for estimating cognitively relevant quantities. We further discuss theoretical challenges posed by these results.[1]

1 Introduction

A key question in psycholinguistics concerns the cognitive processes that underlie the real-time integration of new linguistic material with previously processed linguistic context. A central framework for examining this question is surprisal theory (Hale, 2001; Levy, 2008). This theory ties word processing cost to the word's surprisal, and predicts a linear relation between surprisal and processing difficulty. Due to its theoretical implications (see Shain et al. (2024b) for an extended discussion), multiple studies have tested this prediction empirically with different behavioral methodologies (e.g. eyetracking and self paced reading), corpora (among others, Dundee (Kennedy et al., 2003), Natural Stories (Futrell et al., 2021), MECO (Siegelman et al., 2022) and CELER (Berzak et al., 2022)), language models, and languages (Smith and Levy, 2013; Goodkind and Bicknell, 2018; Wilcox et al., 2020; Brothers and Kuperberg, 2021; Berzak and Levy, 2023; Wilcox et al., 2023; Shain et al., 2024b; Hoover et al., 2023; Xu et al., 2023). All these studies found significant surprisal effects on processing times. With the exception of Hoover et al. (2023) and Xu et al. (2023) who obtained evidence for superlinear effects, these studies found a linear relation between surprisal and processing times.

However, thus far this relation has been examined only in one reading regime, which can be referred to as *ordinary reading*. This regime presupposes that the comprehender did not have prior, or at least recent, exposure to the linguistic material. It further assumes that they have no specific goals beyond general comprehension of this material. These assumptions do not hold in many daily situations, where language comprehenders often have *specific goals* with respect to the linguistic input, *process the same input multiple times*, or both. This limits the generality of the conclusions that can be drawn from prior studies.

In this work, we examine the effect of surprisal on reading times in English L1 in three common, but understudied language processing regimes: (1) information seeking, (2) repeated processing, and (3) the combination of the two. Prior work on information seeking (Hahn and Keller, 2023; Shubi and Berzak, 2023) and repeated reading (Hyönä and Niemi, 1990; Raney and Rayner, 1995; Meiri and Berzak, 2024) has shown substantial differences in eye movement patterns in these regimes compared to ordinary reading, and the extent to which the predictions of surprisal theory hold in these regimes is

[1]Code is available at https://github.com/lacclab/surprisal-non-ordinary-reading.

Proceedings of the 28th Conference on Computational Natural Language Learning, pages 219–230
November 15-16, 2024 ©2024 Association for Computational Linguistics

currently unknown.

We analyze and compare the functional form and predictive power of two types of contexts, standard regime-agnostic contexts that capture the general predictability of a word, and regime-specific contexts which include the task in information seeking and a prior appearance of the linguistic content in repeated reading. We examine two main hypotheses stemming from surprisal theory. (1) The presence and functional form of surprisal effects for standard surprisal estimates should extend non-ordinary reading regimes. (2) Surprisal estimates from regime-specific contexts should yield higher predictive power for processing times in the respective regimes compared to regime-agnostic contexts, due to a more accurate representation of the context and the processing goals, which should lead to better alignment with subjective word probabilities.

Our main results are the following:

1. **Regime-agnostic contexts** yield robust linear surprisal effects in information seeking, repeated reading and their combination, albeit with lower predictive power compared to ordinary reading.

2. **Regime-specific contexts** that better match the contexts and tasks given to humans, do not improve the predictive power of surprisal for reading times compared to standard regime-agnostic contexts.

    (a) In information seeking, providing the information seeking task in the context does not improve model predictive power for reading times.

    (b) In repeated processing, providing models with a prior appearance of the linguistic material leads to in-context memorization, with surprisal values that are close to zero and no predictive power for reading times.

2 Related Work

The first studies to empirically examine the relation between surprisal and reading times were Smith and Levy (2008, 2013). They used broad coverage eyetracking and self-paced reading data for English, and found evidence for a linear relation. Following this work, several studies obtained similar results using additional corpora, languages and different methodologies for curve fitting and testing linearity, including Goodkind and Bicknell (2018), Wilcox et al. (2020), Shain et al. (2024b) and Wilcox et al. (2023). Hoover et al. (2023) and Xu et al. (2023) obtained evidence for superlinearity. Brothers and Kuperberg (2021) found a linear relation in word probability using a controlled self-paced reading experiment and cloze estimates of word probabilities. Re-analysis of this data with language model probabilities resulted in a linear relation in surprisal (Shain et al., 2024a). Our study continues this line of work and extends it to different reading regimes.

Both information seeking and repeated reading have received limited attention in psycholinguistics. Work that examined information seeking (Hahn and Keller, 2023; Shubi and Berzak, 2023) found substantial differences in eye movement patterns compared to ordinary reading. The differences were shown to be driven by the division to task-relevant and task-irrelevant information. Different eye movement behavior was also found in repeated reading, where among others, shorter reading times and longer saccades were observed (Hyönä and Niemi, 1990; Raney and Rayner, 1995). While the presence and magnitude of surprisal effects in information seeking and repeated reading was previously established (Shubi and Berzak, 2023; Meiri and Berzak, 2024), their functional form and predictive power are yet to be determined.

Multiple studies have pointed out divergences between surprisal estimates and human next word expectations (Smith and Levy, 2011; Jacobs and McCarthy, 2020; Ettinger, 2020; Eisape et al., 2020), as well as an inverse relationship between the quality of recent language models (as measured by perplexity) and their fit to reading times (Oh and Schuler, 2022; Shain et al., 2024b). Closest to our work is Vaidya et al. (2023), who found that in a repeated reading cloze task, language models have substantially higher next word prediction accuracy compared to humans. They further identified "induction heads", which are attention heads that recognize repeated token sequences and increase the probability of the previously observed continuation (Elhage et al., 2021), as a core contributor to this behavior in language models. Our findings for repeated reading are in line with these results.

3 Data

We use OneStop, an extended version of the dataset by Malmaud et al. (2020), with eye movements from 360 English L1 readers, recorded with an Eyelink 1000+ eyetracker (SR Research). The experiment was conducted under an institutional IRB protocol, and all the participants provided written consent before participating in the study. The textual materials are taken from OneStopQA (Berzak et al., 2020) and comprise 30 articles from the Guardian with 4-7 paragraphs (162 paragraphs in total). Each paragraph in OneStopQA is accompanied by three reading comprehension questions. The textual span in the paragraph which contains the essential information for answering the question correctly, called the critical span, is manually annotated in each paragraph for each question.

An experimental trial consists of reading a single paragraph on a page, followed by answering one reading comprehension question on a new page without the ability to go back to the paragraph.

Ordinary reading vs information seeking 180 participants are in an ordinary reading regime in which they see the question only after having read the paragraph. The remaining 180 participants are in an information-seeking regime in which the question (but not the answers) is presented prior to reading the paragraph.

First vs repeated reading Each participant reads 10 articles in a random presentation order, followed by two articles that are presented for a second time with identical text but with a different question for each paragraph. The article in position 11 is a repeated presentation of the article in position 10. The article in position 12 is a repeated presentation of one of the articles in positions 1–9. Thus, OneStop contains both consecutive and non-consecutive repeated reading at the article level.[2]

OneStop has 2,532,799 data points (i.e. word tokens over which eyetracking data was collected). We exclude words that were not fixated, words with a total reading time greater than 3,000 ms, words that start or end a paragraph, words with punctuation, and surprisal values greater than 20 bits. After these filtering steps, we remain with 1,157,609 data points: 541,875 in ordinary reading, 474,674 in first reading information seeking, 82,357 in repeated ordinary reading, and 58,703 in repeated reading information seeking.

4 Methodology

We examine four different reading regimes that take advantage of the experimental manipulations in OneStop and reflect different types of interactions with the text. The first is ordinary reading during the first presentation of the text. This regime corresponds to the standard experimental setup in reading studies. Additionally, new to this work, we examine information seeking during first reading, and both ordinary reading and information seeking during repeated text presentation.

We estimate the functional form of the relation between surprisal and reading times using Generalized Additive Models (GAMs, Hastie and Tibshirani, 1986), which can fit non-linear relations between predictors and responses. We predict word reading times from surprisal and two control variables that were shown to be predictive of reading times above and beyond surprisal: word frequency and word length (Kliegl et al., 2004; Clifton Jr et al., 2016). To account for spillover effects (Rayner, 1998), our models also include the surprisal, frequency and length of the previous word.

Following prior work (e.g. Wilcox et al., 2023) our primary reading time measure is **first pass Gaze Duration**; the time from first entering a word to first leaving it during first pass reading. This measure is associated with the processing difficulty of a word given left-only context and is thus especially suitable for benchmarking against surprisal. In the Appendix, we examine additional measures: Gaze Duration and Total Fixation Duration. For completeness, we also provide results for first pass First Fixation duration and First Fixation duration, which tend to have small surprisal effects and are associated with lexical processing (Clifton Jr et al., 2007; Berzak and Levy, 2023). Definitions of all the measures are in section 1 in the Appendix.

Surprisal, defined as $-\log p(w_i|w_{<i})$, where w_i is the current word and $w_{<i}$ is the preceding context, is estimated using a language model (see Section 4.3). The language models we use provide a distribution over sub-words (tokens). We therefore sum the sub-word probabilities to obtain the word's probability. Frequency is defined as $-\log p(w_i)$, using word counts from Wordfreq (Speer et al., 2018). Word length is measured in number of characters.

We define three models of interest:[3]

- **Baseline model** which predicts reading times of the current word from the control variables frequency and length and their interaction us-

[2]Note that for articles 10 and 11, there are 3-6 intervening paragraphs between the two readings of a paragraph.

[3]All the models were fitted using `mgcv` (v1.9.1) `gam` (Wood, 2004) function with cubic splines ("`cr`"). The models do not include random effects due to convergence issues.

ing tensor product terms te.[4]

- **Linear model** which includes the baseline model terms and linear terms for the surprisal of the current and the previous words.[5]

- **Non-linear model** which includes the baseline model terms and smooth terms s for the surprisal of the current and previous words.[6]

4.1 Analysis 1: GAM Visualization

In this analysis, we visualize the relationship between surprisal and reading times using the linear and non-linear models. If the less constrained non-linear fit is visually similar to the linear fit, this would provide initial evidence for a linear relation between surprisal and reading times. To this end, we fit each of the two models on the reading time data of each of the four reading regimes, and predict reading times for surprisal values in the range of 0-20 in 0.1 increments. We note that differently from some of the prior work that used similar methods (Smith and Levy, 2013; Wilcox et al., 2020, 2023), we do not average reading times across participants before fitting the models.

4.2 Analysis 2: Predictive Power

Complementary to analysis 1, we measure the increase in model log-likelihood relative to the baseline model, which includes only the control variables frequency and length, without surprisal, for both the linear and the non-linear models. A statistically significant difference in the predictive power of the non-linear and linear models would provide evidence against linearity. Following prior work (e.g. Wilcox et al., 2020; Oh and Schuler, 2022; Wilcox et al., 2023), we measure predictive power for data point i using delta log-likelihood:

$$\Delta LL_i = \log L^{target}(RT_i|x^{target})$$
$$- \log L^{baseline}(RT_i|x^{baseline})$$

where RT_i is the reading measure of a single participant over a word, $x^{baseline}$ are the control predictors and x^{target} are the target predictors, which include the control predictors and surprisal. L^M is the likelihood under the model M:

$$L^M(RT_i|x) = f_{norm}(RT_i|\mu = \hat{RT_i}, \sigma^2 = \sigma^2_{RT})$$

where $\hat{RT_i}$ is the RT prediction of the model M given the predictor set x, σ^2_{RT} is the standard deviation of the residuals of the fitted GAM model M and f_{norm} is the Gaussian density function.

We examine ΔLL, the per-word mean of ΔLL_i. To reduce the risk of overfitting, we measure ΔLL on held-out data, using 10-fold cross-validation. A positive ΔLL indicates that the addition of surprisal terms increases the predictive power of the GAM model. We then compare the ΔLL of the linear and non-linear GAM models. If there is no significant difference between the two, we do not reject the null hypothesis of a linear relation between surprisal and reading times. Following Wilcox et al. (2023), we test the significance of the differences in the ΔLL of the two models using a paired permutation test.

4.3 Language Models and Surprisal Estimation

An important methodological consideration for our study is the choice of the language model. Our selection criteria for the language model is predictive power, as measured by ΔLL. We measure the predictive power of 30 publicly available language models on the OneStop reading time data, and select the model with the highest predictive power across the four reading regimes.

We examine models from the GPT-2 (Radford et al., 2019), GPT-J (Wang and Komatsuzaki, 2021), GPT-Neo (Black et al., 2021), Pythia (Biderman et al., 2023), OPT (Zhang et al., 2022), Mistral (Jiang et al., 2023), Gemma (Thomas et al., 2024) and Llama-2 (Hugo et al., 2023) families, ranging from 70 million to 70 billion parameters. We note that this list includes GPT-2-small, which was used in prior work for similar analyses (Oh and Schuler, 2022; Shain et al., 2024b). Figure A1 in the Appendix presents model predictive power as a function of the model's log perplexity measured on the 30 articles of OneStopQA. This comparison yields **Pythia-70m** as the model with the highest predictive power.[7] Our main analyses therefore use surprisal estimates from this model. To test the

[4] Model formula in R: $RT \sim te(freq, len) + te(freq\_prev, len\_prev)$

[5] Model formula in R: $RT \sim surp + surp\_prev + te(freq, len) + te(freq\_prev, len\_prev)$

[6] Model formula in R: $RT \sim s(surp, k = 6) + s(surp\_prev, k = 6) + te(freq, len) + te(freq\_prev, len\_prev)$. The value for k is chosen based on prior work (Wilcox et al., 2023).

[7] We note that this figure replicates the results of Oh and Schuler (2022) regarding the relation between perplexity and predictive power for recent language models, and extends them to non-ordinary reading regimes.

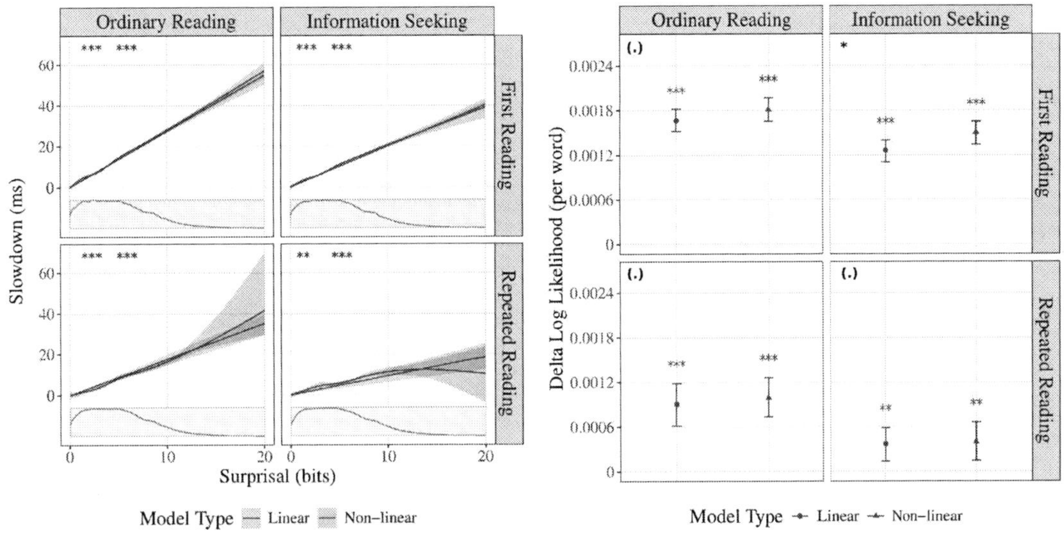

(a) GAM fits for the relation between surprisal and reading times, with bootstrapped 95% confidence intervals. Top left of each plot, the statistical significance of the s and linear terms of the current word's surprisal. At the bottom of each plot: a density plot of surprisal values.

(b) ΔLL means with 95% confidence intervals on held-out data using 10-fold cross validation. Above each confidence interval: the statistical significance of a permutation test that checks if the ΔLL is different from zero. Top left of each plot: the statistical significance of a permutation test for a difference between the ΔLL of the linear and non-linear models.

Figure 1: (a) GAM fits and (b) ΔLL for first pass Gaze Duration and Pythia-70m surprisals with standard context, using the linear and non-linear models. '***' $p < 0.001$, '**' $p < 0.01$. '*' $p < 0.05$, '(.)' $p \geq 0.05$. **Key results**: (a) Approximately linear curves for the non-linear models. (b) No statistically significant differences in the ΔLL of the linear and non-linear models, with the exception of information seeking in first reading. Smaller ΔLL in information seeking and repeated reading compared to first reading - ordinary reading for both models.

robustness of the results to the choice of language model, in the Appendix we present additional analyses with the remaining 29 models.

Recently, Pimentel and Meister (2024) and Oh and Schuler (2024) pointed out inaccuracies in the surprisal estimates of models that are based on a beginning-of-word marking tokenizer, such as the Pythia and GPT families. Pimentel and Meister (2024) further propose a modification in the computation of surprisals in such models. While we use the default surprisal values in the results reported below, we have verified that highly similar results are obtained with the estimation method of Pimentel and Meister (2024).

4.4 Contexts

A cardinal manipulation in our study concerns the context $w_{<i}$ that is provided to the language model for estimating the probability of the current word w_i. We examine three approaches for constructing this context.

- **Standard Context**: In the first, regime-agnostic approach, which we take in Section 5, the context consists of the words preceding the current word in the paragraph.

- **Regime Context**: In the second, regime-specific approach, in Section 6, the context depends on the reading regime in that it includes the preceding question in information seeking and the paragraph in repeated reading.

- **Prompting + Regime Context**: An additional variant of the Regime Context in Section 6 further includes textual prompts that emulate the instructions given to humans.

5 Surprisal from Standard Context

In our first set of analyses, we follow prior work on ordinary first reading, as well as information seeking and repeated reading (Shubi and Berzak, 2023; Meiri and Berzak, 2024), and use standard, reading regime-agnostic surprisal estimates, which are obtained by conditioning the model on the prior textual material in the paragraph.

5.1 GAM Visualization

Figure 1a presents the GAM surprisal curves for the linear and non-linear models. Visual inspection suggests that the non-linear model approximately tracks the linear fit. We further note that consistently with the findings of Shubi and Berzak (2023) and Meiri and Berzak (2024), surprisal effects, which can be inferred from the slope of the curves, are smaller in information seeking compared to ordinary reading, and smaller in repeated reading compared to first reading.

Figure A2a in the Appendix suggests that the results largely hold across different language models, although some of the models with the lowest perplexity also yield sublinear fits. Figure A3a in the Appendix examines additional reading measures for Pythia-70m, with linear fits for Gaze Duration and Total Fixation duration, and mixed results for first pass First Fixation and First Fixation where we observe sublinear curves in first reading. Overall, most curves of the non-linear models appear to approximate their linear counterparts.

In information seeking, Shubi and Berzak (2023) have shown different eye movement patterns within and outside task critical information (the critical span). In repeated reading, Meiri and Berzak (2024) also showed differences between eye movements in consecutive (article 11) and non-consecutive (article 12) repeated article presentation. Figure A4 in the Appendix shows that linearity for first pass Gaze Duration holds both within and outside the critical span in information seeking, and also both with and without intervening articles during repeated reading.

5.2 Predictive Power

While visual inspection provides initial evidence for the linearity of reading times in surprisal across reading regimes, we further test this hypothesis by comparing the predictive power of the non-linear model relative to that of the linear model. Figure 1b presents the ΔLL of the linear and non-linear models for first pass Gaze Duration across the four reading regimes. We find that in three of the four regimes, there is no significant difference between the ΔLL of the two models. In information seeking - first reading, the difference is significant at $p < 0.05$. These results largely support our conclusion from the visual inspection of the GAM curves, that the surprisal - reading times relation is linear in all four regimes. We further note, that in line with the effect sizes, the predictive power of standard surprisal estimates is smaller in information seeking compared to ordinary reading, and smaller in repeated reading compared to first reading ($p < 0.05$ in all cases using a paired permutation test).

Figure A2b in the Appendix presents the results for first pass Gaze duration across different language models, suggesting that they are robust to the language model choice. Figure A3b in the Appendix presents additional reading measures and further shows that the results mostly extend to Gaze Duration and Total Fixation Duration, while mixed results are obtained for First Fixation measures, with larger ΔLL for the non-linear model in ordinary reading and information seeking during first reading. Figure A4 shows that the linearity of first pass Gaze Duration in surprisal holds both within and outside the critical span in information seeking, as well as for consecutive and non-consecutive article repeated reading. Overall, our analysis of ΔLL favors a linear relation between surprisal and reading times across all four reading regimes.

6 Surprisal from Regime-Specific Context

Thus far, we used surprisal estimates based on the textual context in the paragraph. However, this context does not fully capture the reading task conditioning in the human data. Human participants in the first reading – information seeking regime receive a question prior to reading the paragraph. In repeated ordinary reading they have already read that paragraph. In repeated reading during information seeking they have previously read the paragraph and received a question prior to both the first and the second reading of the paragraph. These manipulations can alter linguistic expectations and were previously shown to influence reading times (Hyönä and Niemi, 1990; Malmaud et al., 2020; Shubi and Berzak, 2023; Meiri and Berzak, 2024). Furthermore, human participants receive explicit instructions regarding the different trial components in the reading experiment.

In the remainder of this work, we compare our results using standard surprisal estimates to surprisal estimates based on context types that more closely match the textual contexts and instructions presented to humans in each of the reading regimes. Our analyses focus on the following questions regarding the three regimes that are not ordinary first reading. (1) Do the linear surprisal effects persist under regime-conditioned surprisal estimates? (2)

Regime	Standard Context	Regime Context	Description	Prompting + Regime Context	Prompt Text
First reading Ordinary reading	P	P	The preceding words in the paragraph.	Prompt1 + P	Prompt1: "You will now read a paragraph."
First reading Information seeking	P	Q + P	The question followed by the preceding words in the paragraph.	Prompt1 + Q + P	Prompt1: "You will now be given a question about a paragraph followed by the paragraph. You will need to answer the question."
Repeated reading Ordinary reading	P	P + P	The entire paragraph followed by the preceding words in the same paragraph.	Prompt1 + P + Prompt2 + P	Prompt1: "You will now read a paragraph." Prompt2: "You will now read the same paragraph again."
Repeated reading Information seeking	P	Q' + P + Q + P	The question for the first reading, followed by the paragraph, the question for the second reading and the preceding words in the same paragraph.	Prompt1 + Q' + P + Prompt2 + Q + P	Prompt1: "You will now be given a question about a paragraph followed by the paragraph. You will need to answer the question." Prompt2: "You will now read the same paragraph again with a different question before the paragraph. You will need to answer the question."

Table 1: Standard and regime-specific contexts provided to language models. Q and Q' for two different questions, and P for paragraph. The prompts are similar to those presented to human participants in the reading experiment.

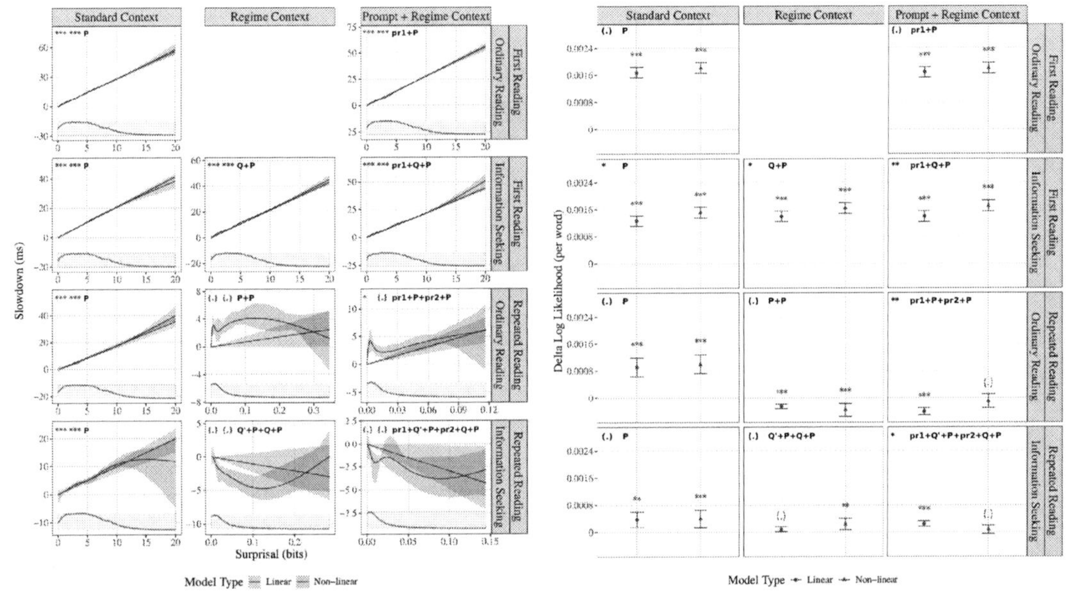

(a) GAM fits for the relation between surprisal and reading times across context types. Slowdown effects in *ms* for first pass Gaze Duration as a function of surprisal, with bootstrapped 95% confidence intervals. Top left of each plot, the significance of the s and linear terms of the current word's surprisal. At the bottom of each plot: a density plot of surprisal values. **Key results** for the Regime Context and Prompt + Regime Context: (a) in first reading - information seeking, approximately linear curves for the non-linear model. (b) In the two repeated reading conditions, surprisals are close to zero with no surprisal effect.

(b) ΔLL means with 95% confidence intervals on held-out data using 10-fold cross validation. Above each confidence interval: the statistical significance of a permutation test that checks if the ΔLL is different from zero. Top left of each plot: significance of a permutation test for a difference between the ΔLL of the linear and non-linear models. **Key results** for Regime Context and Prompt + Regime Context: (1) In first reading - information seeking, no significant differences in the ΔLL of the linear and non-linear models, and no increase in ΔLLs compared to the Standard Context. (2) In both repeated reading regimes, ΔLLs are *lower* compared to the Standard Context and in most cases not significantly above zero.

Figure 2: Comparison of GAM fits and ΔLL for first pass Gaze Duration with surprisal estimates of Pythia-70m from different context types. '***' $p < 0.001$, '**' $p < 0.01$. '*' $p < 0.05$, '(.)' $p \geq 0.05$.

Do regime-conditioned surprisals lead to better predictive power for human reading times?

To address these questions, in addition to the standard context used in Section 5, we examine three **regime-specific contexts** that correspond to each of the three reading regimes that involve information seeking and repeated reading. To further enhance the similarity to the experimental setup in the human data, we also examine a variant of the regime contexts in which the model additionally receives **prompts** that emulate the reading instructions received by human participants. The prompts convey the same content provided in the instructions to human participants in the eyetracking experiment, but are not a verbatim copy, as the original instructions further contain details relevant only for the eyetracking experiment, such as the text triggering targets and button presses associated with each part of the trial. The regime-specific contexts and prompts are presented in Table 1.

We note that although these contexts include the essential components of each reading regime, they do not fully match the eyetracking experiment as they do not include intervening textual material between first and second presentations of a paragraph. This is because the context window of our models is too small to include the text of a full experimental session. To partially address this limitation, in Table A1 in the Appendix we present a prompting scheme for article-level analysis for articles 10 and 11. We use this scheme with the Pythia-70m model, for which we employ a sliding window mechanism with an overlap size that ensures that each paragraph's first appearance is fully included in the context window of its repeated appearance.

6.1 GAM Visualization

In figure 2a we present GAM visualizations for the linear and non-linear models. We compare surprisals from conditioning on the standard paragraph context P to surprisals from reading regime contexts: Q+P for first reading - information seeking, P+P for repeated reading - ordinary reading, and Q'+P+Q+P for repeated reading - information seeking. We further present results for regime contexts with prompting.

For first reading - information seeking, surprisals from both regime-specific contexts yield linear curves. However, a very different outcome is observed in the repeated reading regimes. In these regimes, there is a collapse of the surprisals to values that are close to zero and null effects of surprisal on reading times. Thus, we obtain two different behaviors for information seeking and repeated reading. While the addition of the information seeking task does not substantially alter the predictive power of the model, conditioning twice on the paragraph leads to surprisals that no longer maintain a significant relation to reading times.

6.2 Predictive Power

In figure 2b we compare the ΔLL of the linear and non-linear models across standard and regime-specific surprisals with and without prompting. In first reading - information seeking, the regime context and the prompt + regime context provide weak evidence against linearity ($p = 0.04$ and $p = 0.01$ respectively). Crucially, regime conditioning and prompting do not improve predictive power in this regime; the ΔLL of the regime context is not significantly higher compared to the standard context ($p = 0.25$ linear; $p = 0.27$ non-linear, using a paired permutation test). Adding prompting yields similar outcomes compared to the standard context ($p = 0.22$ linear; $p = 0.08$ non-linear).

In the repeated reading regimes we observe a different pattern. Importantly, the regime contexts in the ordinary reading condition lead to a *decrease* in the ΔLL compared to the standard context in both the linear ($p = 0.001$) and non-linear cases ($p = 0.009$). A similar pattern is observed when adding prompting, with $p = 0.001$ for the linear model and $p = 0.038$ for the non-linear model. The regime contexts in the information seeking condition exhibit the same pattern of ΔLL decrease compared to the standard context, which is significant both without prompting ($p = 0.017$ linear; $p = 0.004$ non-linear) and with prompting ($p = 0.091$ linear; $p = 0.027$ non-linear). Furthermore, in nearly all cases the regime context ΔLL is not significantly above zero, suggesting that the corresponding surprisal estimates have no predictive power with respect to reading times. Taken together with the GAM visualizations in Figure 2a, we conclude that the examined language models are misaligned with human reading patterns in repeated reading, and do not provide useful surprisal estimates when conditioned for repeated reading.

These results are consistent across all the models examined, and specifically for the larger models, which could a-priori be expected to be more sensitive to context conditioning and prompting. In the Appendix, we present these results for GPT-2-small in Figure A5 and for the largest Llama and Mistral models, Llama 70b in Figure A6 and Mistral Instruct v0.3 7b in Figure A7. Furthermore, Figure A8 in the Appendix suggests that they generalize to repeated reading with intervening paragraphs between the two paragraph presentations for articles 10 and 11.

7 Discussion and Conclusion

Surprisal theory predicts a linear relationship between surprisal and word processing times. This prediction found support in studies with ordinary reading, but was not previously examined in information seeking and repeated reading. We find evidence that with standard surprisal estimates, the prediction of surprisal theory for a linear effect of surprisal on reading times holds in these regimes. We further find that the effect size and predictive power of standard surprisal estimates diminish in information seeking and repeated reading.

Our attempt to improve language model predictive power with regime-specific contexts yields two primary findings. First, we observe that regime-specific surprisal estimates in first reading - information seeking do not improve the fit to human reading times. A more severe case of estimation collapse is observed in repeated reading, where we find near zero surprisal estimates with no predictive power for reading times, likely due to in-context memorization.

These findings highlight two different types of misalignment between language models and humans. Information seeking demonstrates a misalignment in the representation of task information. Repeated reading suggests very different memory and retrieval abilities in humans and current language models. These misalignments question not only the suitability of current language models as cognitive models of human language processing, but also the psycholinguistic relevance of quantities extracted from such models.

We entertain two possible explanations for the discrepancies in the real-time processing and memory mechanisms of humans and language models. The first explanation is that this mismatch stems from architectural and/or training aspects of current language models. If this is indeed the case, they can be potentially alleviated or even completely resolved with architectural or training procedure changes to said models; it is well possible that future architectures will better capture task relevant information, or handle repeated text in ways that are more commensurate with human processing.

The second explanation poses a challenge to language processing theory, and in particular to the view of surprisal as a "causal bottleneck" for observed behavior (Levy, 2008). According to this view, whatever the underlying linguistic processing mechanisms and representations may be, their effect on processing times is mediated through surprisal. Although better representation of the context should yield better estimates of subjective surprisals and thus better reflect processing times, we do not observe this in practice.

One could alternatively argue that factors that come into play in non-ordinary processing regimes and affect reading times either cannot or should not be encoded in surprisals. Surprisal theory accounts only for processing difficulty, while reading times may reflect additional factors of cognitive state, which do not directly speak to processing difficulty (e.g. one may skim through portions of the text because they are less relevant for the comprehender goals, not because they are easier to process). Future empirical and theoretical work is required to make further progress on these questions.

8 Limitations

Our work has multiple limitations. Due to the lack of eyetracking data for information seeking and repeated reading in other languages, we address only English. The readers are adult native speakers in the age range of 18–52. Additional data collection in other languages, ages and participant groups are needed to establish the generality of the conclusions. The experimental design is further constrained to one variant of each reading regime, leaving many other variants unaddressed. For example, an experimental trial consists of a single paragraph. In daily interactions with text, information seeking can be over both shorter and longer textual units. In repeated reading, consecutive reading is at the article level with intervening paragraphs, and doesn't cover immediate repeated reading which involves working memory. In non-consecutive reading, we have at most 10 intervening articles. In both cases, repeated reading can occur more than once.

Further limitations concern the language models used. The context window of the models available with our computing resources is not sufficient to address non-consecutive article repeated reading, which requires storing up to 12 articles at once in the context provided to the model. Additional work with large context windows is required to fully address the repeated reading experimental design in the eyetracking data.

We use the term ordinary reading to refer to a first reading for comprehension. However, following Huettig and Ferreira (2023) we acknowledge that this term is not without faults. Relatedly, while reading comprehension questions are essential for encouraging attentive reading, their presence after each paragraph may lower the ecological validity of the data, especially in the ordinary reading regime. Reading in a lab setting may further limit the applicability of the results to daily reading situations.

References

Yevgeni Berzak and Roger Levy. 2023. Eye movement traces of linguistic knowledge in native and non-native reading. *Open Mind*, pages 1–18.

Yevgeni Berzak, Jonathan Malmaud, and Roger Levy. 2020. Starc: Structured annotations for reading comprehension. In *Proceedings of the 58th Annual Meeting of the Association for Computational Linguistics*, pages 5726–5735.

Yevgeni Berzak, Chie Nakamura, Amelia Smith, Emily Weng, Boris Katz, Suzanne Flynn, and Roger Levy. 2022. Celer: A 365-participant corpus of eye movements in l1 and l2 english reading. *Open Mind*, 6:41–50.

Stella Biderman, Hailey Schoelkopf, Quentin Gregory Anthony, Herbie Bradley, Kyle O'Brien, Eric Hallahan, Mohammad Aflah Khan, Shivanshu Purohit, USVSN Sai Prashanth, Edward Raff, et al. 2023. Pythia: A suite for analyzing large language models across training and scaling. In *International Conference on Machine Learning*, pages 2397–2430. PMLR.

Sid Black, Leo Gao, Phil Wang, Connor Leahy, and Stella Biderman. 2021. GPT-Neo: Large Scale Autoregressive Language Modeling with Mesh-Tensorflow.

Trevor Brothers and Gina R Kuperberg. 2021. Word predictability effects are linear, not logarithmic: Implications for probabilistic models of sentence comprehension. *Journal of Memory and Language*, 116:104174.

Charles Clifton Jr, Fernanda Ferreira, John M Henderson, Albrecht W Inhoff, Simon P Liversedge, Erik D Reichle, and Elizabeth R Schotter. 2016. Eye movements in reading and information processing: Keith rayner's 40 year legacy. *Journal of Memory and Language*, 86:1–19.

Charles Clifton Jr, Adrian Staub, and Keith Rayner. 2007. Eye movements in reading words and sentences. *Eye movements*, pages 341–371.

Tiwalayo Eisape, Noga Zaslavsky, and Roger Levy. 2020. Cloze distillation: Improving neural language models with human next-word prediction. In *Proceedings of the 24th Conference on Computational Natural Language Learning*, pages 609–619, Online. Association for Computational Linguistics.

Nelson Elhage, Neel Nanda, Catherine Olsson, Tom Henighan, Nicholas Joseph, Ben Mann, Amanda Askell, Yuntao Bai, Anna Chen, Tom Conerly, Nova DasSarma, Dawn Drain, Deep Ganguli, Zac Hatfield-Dodds, Danny Hernandez, Andy Jones, Jackson Kernion, Liane Lovitt, Kamal Ndousse, Dario Amodei, Tom Brown, Jack Clark, Jared Kaplan, Sam McCandlish, and Chris Olah. 2021. A mathematical framework for transformer circuits. *Transformer Circuits Thread*.

Allyson Ettinger. 2020. What bert is not: Lessons from a new suite of psycholinguistic diagnostics for language models. *Transactions of the Association for Computational Linguistics*, 8:34–48.

Richard Futrell, Edward Gibson, Harry J Tily, Idan Blank, Anastasia Vishnevetsky, Steven T Piantadosi, and Evelina Fedorenko. 2021. The natural stories corpus: a reading-time corpus of english texts containing rare syntactic constructions. *Language Resources and Evaluation*, 55:63–77.

Adam Goodkind and Klinton Bicknell. 2018. Predictive power of word surprisal for reading times is a linear function of language model quality. In *Proceedings of the 8th workshop on cognitive modeling and computational linguistics (CMCL 2018)*, pages 10–18.

Michael Hahn and Frank Keller. 2023. Modeling task effects in human reading with neural network-based attention. *Cognition*, 230(C):105289.

John Hale. 2001. A probabilistic earley parser as a psycholinguistic model. In *Second meeting of the north american chapter of the association for computational linguistics*.

Trevor Hastie and Robert Tibshirani. 1986. Generalized Additive Models. *Statistical Science*, 1(3):297 – 310.

Jacob Louis Hoover, Morgan Sonderegger, Steven T. Piantadosi, and Timothy J. O'Donnell. 2023. The Plausibility of Sampling as an Algorithmic Theory of Sentence Processing. *Open Mind*, 7:350–391.

Falk Huettig and Fernanda Ferreira. 2023. The myth of normal reading. *Perspectives on Psychological Science*, 18(4):863–870.

Touvron Hugo, Martin Louis, Stone Kevin, Albert Peter, Almahairi Amjad, Babaei Yasmine, Bashlykov Nikolay, Batra Soumya, Bhargava Prajjwal, Bhosale Shruti, et al. 2023. Llama 2: Open foundation and fine-tuned chat models. *Preprint*, arXiv:2307.09288.

Jukka Hyönä and Pekka Niemi. 1990. Eye movements during repeated reading of a text. *Acta psychologica*, 73(3):259–280.

Cassandra L Jacobs and Arya D McCarthy. 2020. The human unlikeness of neural language models in next-word prediction. In *Proceedings of the Fourth Widening Natural Language Processing Workshop*.

Albert Q. Jiang, Alexandre Sablayrolles, Arthur Mensch, Chris Bamford, Devendra Singh Chaplot, Diego de las Casas, Florian Bressand, Gianna Lengyel, Guillaume Lample, Lucile Saulnier, Lélio Renard Lavaud, Marie-Anne Lachaux, Pierre Stock, Teven Le Scao, Thibaut Lavril, Thomas Wang, Timothée Lacroix, and William El Sayed. 2023. Mistral 7b. *Preprint*, arXiv:2310.06825.

Alan Kennedy, Robin Hill, and Joël Pynte. 2003. The dundee corpus. In *European conference on eye movement*.

Reinhold Kliegl, Ellen Grabner, Martin Rolfs, and Ralf Engbert. 2004. Length, frequency, and predictability effects of words on eye movements in reading. *European journal of cognitive psychology*, 16(1-2):262–284.

Roger Levy. 2008. Expectation-based syntactic comprehension. *Cognition*, 106(3):1126–1177.

Jonathan Malmaud, Roger Levy, and Yevgeni Berzak. 2020. Bridging information-seeking human gaze and machine reading comprehension. In *Proceedings of the 24th Conference on Computational Natural Language Learning*, pages 142–152.

Yoav Meiri and Yevgeni Berzak. 2024. Déjà vu: Eye movements in repeated reading. In *Proceedings of the Annual Meeting of the Cognitive Science Society*, volume 46.

Byung-Doh Oh and William Schuler. 2022. Why does surprisal from larger transformer-based language models provide a poorer fit to human reading times? *Transactions of the Association for Computational Linguistics*, 11:336–350.

Byung-Doh Oh and William Schuler. 2024. Leading whitespaces of language models' subword vocabulary poses a confound for calculating word probabilities. *arXiv preprint arXiv:2406.10851*.

Tiago Pimentel and Clara Meister. 2024. How to compute the probability of a word. *Preprint*, arXiv:2406.14561.

Alec Radford, Jeffrey Wu, Rewon Child, David Luan, Dario Amodei, and Ilya Sutskever. 2019. Language models are unsupervised multitask learners. *OpenAI blog*, 1(8):9.

Gary E Raney and Keith Rayner. 1995. Word frequency effects and eye movements during two readings of a text. *Canadian Journal of Experimental Psychology/Revue canadienne de psychologie expérimentale*, 49(2):151.

Keith Rayner. 1998. Eye movements in reading and information processing: 20 years of research. *Psychological bulletin*, 124(3):372.

Cory Shain, Clara Meister, Tiago Pimentel, Ryan Cotterell, and Roger Levy. 2024a. Are word predictability effects really linear? a critical reanalysis of key evidence. In *37th Annual Conference on Human Sentence Processing*.

Cory Shain, Clara Meister, Tiago Pimentel, Ryan Cotterell, and Roger Levy. 2024b. Large-scale evidence for logarithmic effects of word predictability on reading time. *Proceedings of the National Academy of Sciences*, 121(10):e2307876121.

Omer Shubi and Yevgeni Berzak. 2023. Eye movements in information-seeking reading. In *Proceedings of the Annual Meeting of the Cognitive Science Society*, Online.

Noam Siegelman, Sascha Schroeder, Cengiz Acartürk, Hee-Don Ahn, Svetlana Alexeeva, Simona Amenta, Raymond Bertram, Rolando Bonandrini, Marc Brysbaert, Daria Chernova, et al. 2022. Expanding horizons of cross-linguistic research on reading: The multilingual eye-movement corpus (meco). *Behavior research methods*, 54(6):2843–2863.

Nathaniel Smith and Roger Levy. 2011. Cloze but no cigar: The complex relationship between cloze, corpus, and subjective probabilities in language processing. In *Proceedings of the Annual Meeting of the Cognitive Science Society*, volume 33.

Nathaniel J Smith and Roger Levy. 2008. Optimal processing times in reading: A formal model and empirical investigation. In *Proceedings of the Annual Meeting of the Cognitive Science Society*, volume 30.

Nathaniel J Smith and Roger Levy. 2013. The effect of word predictability on reading time is logarithmic. *Cognition*, 128(3):302–319.

Robyn Speer, Joshua Chin, Andrew Lin, Sara Jewett, and Lance Nathan. 2018. Luminosoinsight/wordfreq: v2.2.

Mesnard Thomas, Hardin Cassidy, Dadashi Robert, Bhupatiraju Surya, Pathak Shreya, Sifre Laurent, Riviere Morgane, Sanjay Kale Mihir, Love Juliette, et al. 2024. Gemma: Open models based on gemini research and technology. *Preprint*, arXiv:2403.08295.

Aditya Vaidya, Javier Turek, and Alexander Huth. 2023. Humans and language models diverge when predicting repeating text. In *Proceedings of the 27th Conference on Computational Natural Language Learning (CoNLL)*, pages 58–69.

Ben Wang and Aran Komatsuzaki. 2021. GPT-J-6B: A 6 Billion Parameter Autoregressive Language Model. `https://github.com/kingoflolz/mesh-transformer-jax`.

Ethan Gotlieb Wilcox, Jon Gauthier, Jennifer Hu, Peng Qian, and Roger P. Levy. 2020. On the predictive power of neural language models for human real-time comprehension behavior. In *Proceedings of the 42nd Annual Meeting of the Cognitive Science Society*, page 1707–1713.

Ethan Gotlieb Wilcox, Tiago Pimentel, Clara Meister, Ryan Cotterell, and Roger P Levy. 2023. Testing the predictions of surprisal theory in 11 languages. *arXiv preprint arXiv:2307.03667*.

Simon N Wood. 2004. Stable and efficient multiple smoothing parameter estimation for generalized additive models. *Journal of the American Statistical Association*, 99(467):673–686.

Weijie Xu, Jason Chon, Tianran Liu, and Richard Futrell. 2023. The linearity of the effect of surprisal on reading times across languages. In *Findings of the Association for Computational Linguistics: EMNLP 2023*, pages 15711–15721, Singapore. Association for Computational Linguistics.

Susan Zhang, Stephen Roller, Naman Goyal, Mikel Artetxe, Moya Chen, Shuohui Chen, Christopher Dewan, Mona Diab, Xian Li, Xi Victoria Lin, Todor Mihaylov, Myle Ott, Sam Shleifer, Kurt Shuster, Daniel Simig, Punit Singh Koura, Anjali Sridhar, Tianlu Wang, and Luke Zettlemoyer. 2022. Opt: Open pre-trained transformer language models. *Preprint*, arXiv:2205.01068.

Revisiting Hierarchical Text Classification: Inference and Metrics

Roman Plaud[1,2], Matthieu Labeau[1], Antoine Saillenfest[2], Thomas Bonald[1]
[1] Institut Polytechnique de Paris
[2] Onepoint, 29 rue des Sablons, 75016, Paris, France
{roman.plaud, matthieu.labeau, thomas.bonald}@telecom-paris.fr
a.saillenfest@groupeonepoint.com

Abstract

Hierarchical text classification (HTC) is the task of assigning labels to a text within a structured space organized as a hierarchy. Recent works treat HTC as a conventional multilabel classification problem, therefore evaluating it as such. We instead propose to evaluate models based on specifically designed hierarchical metrics and we demonstrate the intricacy of metric choice and prediction inference method. We introduce a new challenging dataset and we evaluate recent sophisticated models against a range of simple but strong baselines, including a new theoretically motivated loss. Finally, we show that those baselines are very often competitive with the latest models. This highlights the importance of carefully considering the evaluation methodology when proposing new methods for HTC. Code implementation and dataset are available at `https://github.com/RomanPlaud/revisitingHTC`.

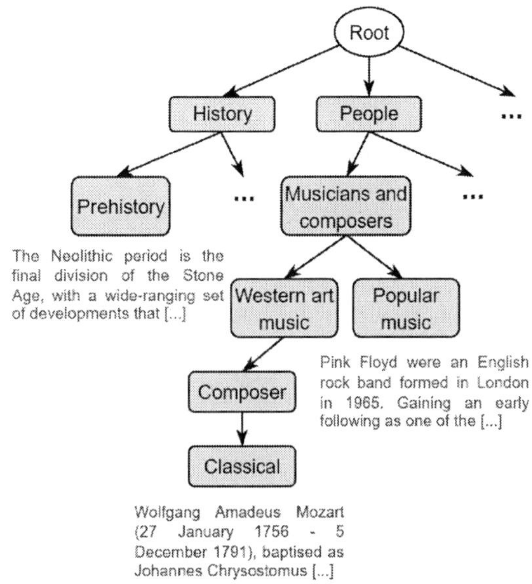

Figure 1: Extract of the taxonomy of our new dataset Hierarchical WikiVitals. Each colored path is the set of labels of the same color.

1 Introduction

Text classification is a long-studied problem that may involve various types of label sets. In particular, Hierarchical Text Classification (HTC) includes labels that exhibit a hierarchical structure with parent-child relationships. The structure that emerges from these relationships is either a tree (Kowsari et al., 2018; Lewis et al., 2004; Lyubinets et al., 2018; Aly et al., 2019; Sandhaus, 2008) or a Directed Acyclic Graph (DAG) (Bertinetto et al., 2020). Each input text then comes with a set of labels that form one or more paths in the hierarchy. A first crucial challenge in HTC lies in accurately evaluating model performance. This requires metrics that are sensitive to the severity of prediction errors, penalizing mistakes with larger distances within the hierarchy tree. While pioneering efforts have been made by Kiritchenko et al. (2006), Silla and Freitas (2011), Kosmopoulos et al. (2014) and Amigo and Delgado (2022), evaluation in the context of hierarchical classification remains an ongoing research area.

There is a substantial body of literature addressing HTC. The most recent methods produce text representations which are *hierarchy-aware*, as they integrate information about the label hierarchy (Song et al., 2023; Zhou et al., 2020; Deng et al., 2021; Wang et al., 2022b,a; Jiang et al., 2022; Chen et al., 2021; Zhu et al., 2023, 2024; Yu et al., 2023). However, we believe that the evaluation of these models has been insufficiently investigated: in those works, the task is evaluated as standard multi-label classification. Here, we plan to explore what this implies; especially, looking at how predictions are inferred from an estimated probability distribution – which we consider an under-addressed challenge. We provide new insights, emphasizing the intricacy of inference and evaluation, which cannot be considered separately.

Proceedings of the 28th Conference on Computational Natural Language Learning, pages 231–242
November 15-16, 2024 ©2024 Association for Computational Linguistics

To complete this investigation, we introduce a new English benchmark dataset, Hierarchical WikiVitals (HWV), which we intend to be significantly more challenging than the usual HTC benchmarks in English (see Figure 1 for an extract of the taxonomy). We experiment within our proposed framework, verifying the performance of recent models against simpler methods, among which loss functions (Bertinetto et al., 2020; Vaswani et al., 2022; Zhang et al., 2021) we design to be able to integrate hierarchical information, based on the conditional softmax. Overall, our contributions are:

1. We propose to quantitatively evaluate HTC methods based on specifically designed hierarchical metrics and with a rigorous methodology.
2. We present Hierarchical WikiVitals, a novel high-quality HTC dataset, extracted from Wikipedia. Equipped with a deep and complex hierarchy, it provides a harder challenge.
3. We conduct extensive experiments on three popular HTC datasets and HWV, introducing a novel loss function. When combined with a BERT model, this approach achieves competitive results against recent advanced models.

Our results show that state-of-the-art models do not necessarily encode hierarchical information well, and are surpassed by our simpler loss on HWV.

Problem definition

Hierarchical Text classification (HTC) is a subtask of text classification which consists of assigning to an input text $x \in \mathcal{X}$ a set of labels $Y \subset \mathcal{Y}$, where the label space $\mathcal{Y}$ exhibits parent-child relationships. We call hierarchy the directed graph $\mathcal{H} = (\mathcal{Y}, \mathcal{E})$, where $\mathcal{E} \subset \mathcal{Y}^2$ is the set of edges, which goes from a parent to its children. We restrain our study to the case where $\mathcal{H}$ is a tree. We follow the notations of Valmadre (2022) and call $\mathbf{r} \in \mathcal{Y}$ the unique root node and $\mathcal{L}$ the set of leaf nodes. For a node $y \in \mathcal{Y} \backslash \{\mathbf{r}\}$ we denote $\pi(y)$ its unique parent, $\mathcal{C}(y) \subset \mathcal{Y}$ the set of its children and $\mathcal{A}(y)$ the set of its ancestors (defined inclusively).

A label set Y of an input x cannot be arbitrary: if $y \in Y$ then, due to the parent relations, we necessarily observe that $\mathcal{A}(y) \subset Y$. An even more restrictive framework is the *single-path leaf labels* setting, where $Y = \mathcal{A}(l)$ for a given $l \in \mathcal{L}$ (Y is a single path and reaches a leaf).

We study methods mapping an input text x to a conditional distribution $\mathbb{P}(\cdot|x)$ over $\mathcal{Y}$, whose estimation is denoted $\hat{\mathrm{P}}(\cdot|x)$. Lastly, what we call *inference rule* is the way of producing a set of binary predictions from a probability distribution. For example predictions can be obtained by thresholding $\hat{\mathrm{P}}(\cdot|x)$ to τ as follows : $\hat{Y}_\tau = \{y \in \mathcal{Y}, \hat{\mathrm{P}}(y|x) > \tau\}$.

2 Related Work

2.1 Hierarchical Text Classification

Hierarchical classification problems, including the particular case of HTC, are typically dealt with through either a *local* approach or a *global* one. We refer to the original definition made by Silla and Freitas (2011) according to which the difference between the two categories lies in the training phase. Indeed, local methods imply training a collection of specialized classifiers, *e.g.* one for each node, for each parent node or even one for each level; and during its training each classifier is unaware of the holistic structure of the hierarchy (Zangari et al., 2024). While often computationally costly, it has proven to be effective to capture crucial local information. Along those lines, Banerjee et al. (2019) propose to link the parameters of a parent classifier and those of its children, following the idea of transferring knowledge from parent nodes to their descendants (Shimura et al., 2018; Huang et al., 2019; Wehrmann et al., 2018). Conversely, global methods involve a unique model that directly incorporates the whole hierarchical information in their predictions. There exist very different types of global approaches, from which we can draw two broad categories: losses incorporating hierarchical penalties and hierarchy-aware models.

Hierarchical penalties. The idea of these methods is generally to use a standard binary cross-entropy (BCE), and add penalization terms that incorporate hierarchical information. Gopal and Yang (2013) and Zhang et al. (2021) propose regularization based on hypernymy, either acting on the parameter space or the outputted probability space, while Vaswani et al. (2022) introduce an enhanced BCE loss, named CHAMP, which penalizes false positives based on their distance to the ground truth in the hierarchy tree.

Hierarchy-aware models. To incorporate the structural constraints of the hierarchy into prediction, Mao et al. (2019) propose a reinforcement learning approach, while Aly et al. (2019) introduce an architecture based on capsule networks. However, recent works have achieved state-of-the-art results by combining a text encoder with a structure encoder applied to the label hierarchy. This concept was first introduced by Zhou et al. (2020), who utilized graph convolution networks as the hierarchy encoder. Building on this foundational work, Jiang et al. (2022) and Wang et al. (2024) developed methods to better incorporate local hierarchy information. Wang et al. (2022a) proposed a contrastive learning approach, while Zhu et al. (2023) designed a method to encode hierarchy with the guidance of structural entropy. Zhu et al. (2024) combined both of these ideas. These developments follow earlier works on the same concept (Chen et al., 2020; Zhang et al., 2022; Deng et al., 2021; Chen et al., 2021; Wang et al., 2021). It is important to note that these models are typically trained with a BCE loss or one of its penalized versions (Zhang et al., 2021).

2.2 Hierarchical prediction

Making a prediction in HTC involves two seemingly irreconcilable difficulties: one has to decide between making independent predictions, which may lead to *coherence* issues (e.g., predicting a child without predicting its parent), or employing a top-down inference approach, which may cause *error propagation* issues (Yang and Cardie, 2013; Song et al., 2012). Recent hierarchy-aware models predominantly operate within the former framework, training and evaluating the model as a simple multi-label classifier, at the price of ignoring potentially badly structured predictions. In this work, we will experiment with both approaches.

2.3 Hierarchical classification evaluation

Evaluation in the context of hierarchical classification is a long-studied problem (Kosmopoulos et al., 2014; Amigo and Delgado, 2022; Costa et al., 2007) from which arise multiple questions. First, diverse setups exist, implying different assumptions on the labeling structure: while we previously introduced the *single-path leaf label* framework, multi-path hierarchies exist, or even inputs with only non-leaf labels. It is therefore important to design metrics that are **agnostic to the hierarchical classification framework**. Then, a hierarchical metric must indeed be hierarchical. This means it should take into account the severity of an error based on the known hierarchy: intuitively, predicting a *Bulldog* instead of a *Terrier* should be less penalized than predicting a *Unicorn* instead of a *Terrier*. Amigo and Delgado (2022) identify a set of properties an evaluation metric should possess for hierarchical classification, and classifies them in a taxonomy of metrics differentiating between **multi-label metrics** (label-based, example-based, ranking-metrics) and **hierarchical metrics** (pair-based, set-based). We heavily rely on this seminal work when it comes to choose which metric to use to evaluate different methods. Finally, the inference rule should be chosen in accordance with the metric. The bayesian decision theory literature (Berger, 1985) aims at finding an optimal rule given the metric of interest. However, little consideration was given to this issue in the context of hierarchical classification and ad hoc and non-statistically grounded inference methodology are often chosen: for example, recent HTC literature mostly performs inference through thresholding the estimated probability distribution with $\tau = 0.5$. We can think of other inference methodology, based on top-down or bottom-up inference rules. It is then crucial to find metrics that either come with a properly grounded prediction rule, or **do not depend on an inference methodology** but rather account for the whole probability distribution, which implies evaluating at different operating points. In the next part, we will re-introduce metrics in the light of the three listed requirements.

3 Evaluation metrics

The aforementioned inference rule used in recent HTC literature corresponds to a classical multi-label evaluation methodology: computing a F1-score (*micro* and *macro*) with $\tau = 0.5$. In what follows, we show that this thresholding scheme is suboptimal and we introduce the metrics we use in our experiments. We will then motivate the use of an inference-free evaluation methodology.

3.1 Multi-label metrics

There is a large array of methods for multi-label evaluation; Wu and Zhou (2016), through unifying notations, proposed a set of 11 different metrics. Among them, we keep the *micro* and *macro* F1-score computed upon scores obtained through a 0.5 threshold, as it is generally done in HTC literature. We add a simple metric corresponding to the fraction of misclassified labels: the Hamming Loss, which we also couple to a 0.5 thresholding inference rule.[1]

[1]This optimal inference holds in case of label independence (Dembczyński et al., 2012) which is not the case here.

3.2 Hierarchical metrics

We introduce hF1-score which we identify to be relevant to our evaluation framework. We note that a prediction is *coherent* if $z \in \hat{Y} \Rightarrow \mathcal{A}(z) \subset \hat{Y}$.

Hierarchical F1-score. Introduced by Kiritchenko et al. (2006), this **set-based** measure consists in augmenting $\hat{Y}$ with all its ancestors as follows :

$$\hat{Y}^{\text{aug}} = \bigcup_{\hat{y} \in \hat{Y}} \mathcal{A}(\hat{y}) \tag{1}$$

And to compute the hierarchical precision, recall and F1-score are as follows :

$$\text{hP}(\text{Y}, \hat{\text{Y}}) = \frac{\left|\hat{Y}^{\text{aug}} \cap Y\right|}{\left|\hat{Y}^{\text{aug}}\right|} \quad \text{hR}(\text{Y}, \hat{\text{Y}}) = \frac{\left|\hat{Y}^{\text{aug}} \cap Y\right|}{|Y|}$$

$$\text{hF1}(\text{Y}, \hat{\text{Y}}) = \frac{2 \cdot \text{hP}(\text{Y}, \hat{\text{Y}}) \cdot \text{hR}(\text{Y}, \hat{\text{Y}})}{\text{hP}(\text{Y}, \hat{\text{Y}}) + \text{hR}(\text{Y}, \hat{\text{Y}})}$$

It is a simple extension of the F1-score to hierarchical classification. In the multi-label setting, there are several methods of aggregation to compute a global F1-score[2]. We define here a per-instance hF1-score as per Kosmopoulos et al. (2014) which is then averaged over all inputs (referred as *samples* setting). In its very first introduction, it was defined in a *micro* fashion by Kiritchenko et al. (2006) (see Appendix C.2 Plaud et al. (2024) for full definitions).

Proposition 1 *In micro and samples settings, if every prediction $\hat{Y}$ is coherent, then hF1 and F1 are strictly equal.*

Motivations. Hierarchical F1-score considers an ancestor overlap between ground truth and predicted labels therefore accounting for **mistake severity** and is also **agnostic to the hierarchical classification framework**. Moreover, Proposition 1 (whose proof is detailed in Appendix C.2 Plaud et al. (2024)) draws a link between example-based multi-label metrics and set-based hierarchical metrics proving that it was therefore relevant to employ the *micro* F1-score as it is done in recent literature, as long as predictions are coherent. Finally, hF1-score incorporates **all desirable hierarchical properties** as listed by Amigo and Delgado (2022), except that it does not completely capture the *specificity* (*i.e* the level of uncertainty left by predicting a given node).

[2]See for example the Scikit-learn documentation.

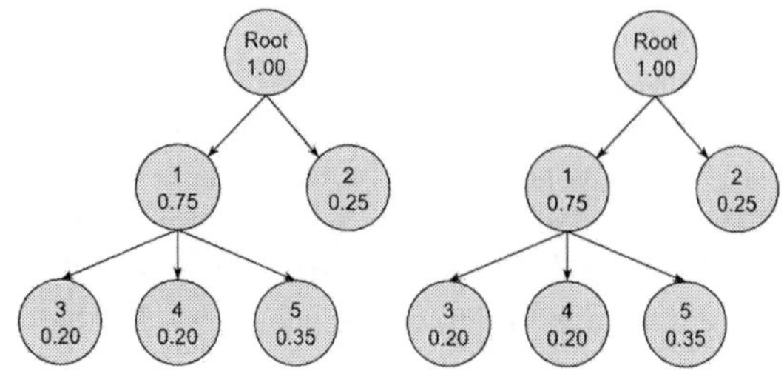

Figure 2: Example of a conditional distribution estimation over a simple hierarchy and corresponding predicted nodes (in blue) for different thresholds (0.3 on the left, 0.5 on the right).

Other hierarchical metrics. As explained in previous section, hF1-score is imperfect as it assumes an equivalence between depth and specificity. To solve this issue, Valmadre (2022) has proposed an information-based hierarchical F1-score, introduced in Appendix A (Plaud et al., 2024). There also exist constrained versions of **multi-label F1-scores** (Yu et al., 2022; Ji et al., 2023) which account for coherence issues: a correct prediction for a label node is valid only if all its ancestor nodes are correct predictions.
Although these metrics might seem pertinent, we have chosen not to utilize them, as they do not globally influence the ranking of methods when compared to their standard metric counterparts. We thoroughly detail our reasons in Appendix A (Plaud et al., 2024). An important number of context-dependent hierarchical metrics were also introduced (Sun and Lim, 2001; Bi and Kwok, 2015), which we will not discuss here as we aim for agnosticism to the hierarchical classification context.

3.3 Inference methodology

In this section, we begin by motivating our argument against the practice of using a BCE-based loss and $\tau = 0.5$ to produce predictions. While this corresponds to minimizing the multilabel Hamming loss in case of label independence (Dembczyński et al., 2012), there is to the best of our knowledge no evidence of the optimality of such a predictor in a hierarchical setting. Rather, tools such as *risk minimization* can provide a way to obtain a statistically grounded inference methodology optimizing the chosen metric, from an estimation of $\mathbb{P}(\cdot|x)$, obtained by a model for a given x. In particular, it is possible to show that the optimal threshold for the F1-scores depends on $\mathbb{P}(\cdot|x)$; we detail the proof in Appendix C.1.2 (Plaud et al., 2024). Though, a simple counter-example is enough to invalidate the choice of 0.5: such an example is depicted in Figure 2. It shows a coherent and exhaustive probability distribution $\mathbb{P}(\cdot|x)$, for a given x. Thresholding to 0.5 would lead to predict $\{1\}$, while a simple computation, detailed in Appendix C.1 (Plaud et al., 2024), gives:

$$\mathbb{E}[\text{hF1}(\text{Y},\{1\})|X=x]=0.5$$
$$\mathbb{E}[\text{hF1}(\text{Y},\{1,5\})|X=x]=0.55$$

which shows that in a *single path leaf label* setting it is strictly better to predict $\{1,5\}$ when aiming at maximizing the hF1-score. With Proposition 1 in mind, this simple example shows theoretically **the sub-optimality of the current state-of-the-art models inference methodology**. As the optimal threshold is unknown, we need to design an evaluation framework which does not depend on an ad-hoc inference rule to avoid introducing non statistically grounded methods. Following recommendations given by Valmadre (2022), we hence do away with inference rules and we construct precision-recall curves for hF1 by browsing all possible thresholds. From these curves, we compute the Area Under Curve (AUC).

4 Simple conditional loss-based methods

As a counterpart to the existing state-of-the-art consisting mainly of BCE-based approaches, we introduce several loss-based methods that incorporates local information, all relying on estimating **conditional probabilities**.

4.1 Conditional softmax cross-entropy

As outlined in Problem Definition, we focus on methods that, given an input text x, produce an estimated distribution $\hat{\text{P}}(\cdot|x)$ over $\mathcal{Y}$. We propose here to associate a modern text encoder to the conditional softmax (Redmon and Farhadi, 2017), which inherently incorporates the hierarchy structure by producing a hierarchy-coherent probability distribution, and coupling it with a cross-entropy loss. We detail in this section the modeling and training associated with it. Let us consider an input text x with its corresponding label set Y; a text encoder is first used to produce an embedded representation $h_x \in \mathbb{R}^d$ of x.

Conditional softmax. The conditional softmax first maps h_x to $s_x \in \mathbb{R}^{|\mathcal{Y}|}$ through a standard linear mapping:

$$s_x = Wh_x + b \tag{2}$$

where $W \in \mathbb{R}^{|\mathcal{Y}|\times d}$ and $b \in \mathbb{R}^{|\mathcal{Y}|}$. Then, a softmax is applied to each brotherhood as follows:

$$\hat{\text{P}}(y|x,\pi(y)) = \frac{\exp s_x^{[y]}}{\sum\limits_{z\in\mathcal{C}(\pi(y))} \exp s_x^{[z]}} \tag{3}$$

We recall that $\pi(y)$ denotes the parent node of node y, and $\mathcal{C}(\pi(y))$ represents the set of children of $\pi(y)$, which includes y. The term $s_x^{[y]}$ refers to the entry of s_x associated with node y.

Hence, the logits s_x are used to model the conditional probability of a node **given** its parent. For example, this could represent the probability of an instance x to belong to the class *Bulldog*, conditioned on it being a *Dog*.

Cross-entropy. The contribution to the loss of the pair (x,Y) is given by a standard leaf nodes cross-entropy (as if we were in a standard monolabel multiclass classification problem over leaf nodes). With our modelisation it can further be decomposed as:

$$\begin{aligned} l_{\text{CSoft}}(x,Y) &= -\log\hat{\text{P}}(y^{\text{leaf}}|x) \\ &= -\sum_{y\in Y}\log\hat{\text{P}}(y|x,\pi(y)) \end{aligned} \tag{4}$$

where we denote y^{leaf} the unique leaf node of Y.

Outputted conditional distribution. The probability of $y \in \mathcal{Y}$ is computed by a standard conditionality factorization :

$$\hat{\text{P}}(y|x) = \prod_{z\in\mathcal{A}(y)} \hat{\text{P}}(z|x,\pi(z))$$

Motivations. Contrary to BCE-based methods, this modelisation directly incorporates the hierarchy structure prior of labels. Besides, the outputted probability distribution is coherent and exhaustive. It is more powerful than a leaf nodes softmax, as it decomposes the leaf probability estimation into several sub-problems. It is also computationally cheap, with a $\mathcal{O}(|\mathcal{Y}|)$ time complexity.

4.2 Logit-adjusted conditional softmax

We then propose an enhanced version of the conditional softmax, in order to improve its robustness to data imbalance. This is particularly important for our newly introduced HWV dataset, which has around half of labels having less than 10 instances in total. Our proposal is motivated by Zhou et al. (2020), who suggest that integrating the prior probability distribution in the model is relevant to the

HTC task, which is confirmed by their experimental results. Their approach involves initializing (or fixing) the weights of the structure encoder using this pre-computed prior distribution. Hence, we draw inspiration from Menon et al. (2021) and introduce the logit-adjusted conditional softmax cross-entropy. Equation (3) becomes:

$$\hat{\mathrm{P}}(y|x,\pi(y)) = \frac{e^{s_x^{[y]}+\tau \log \nu(y|\pi(y))}}{\sum\limits_{z\in\mathcal{C}(\pi(y))} e^{s_x^{[z]}+\tau\log\nu(z|\pi(z))}}$$

where $\nu(y|\pi(y))$ is an estimation of $\mathbb{P}(y|\pi(y))$[3] and τ a hyperparameter. Equation (4) remains unchanged. Comprehensive details on the adaptation of the logit-adjusted softmax to our case, along with the theoretical justifications, are provided in Appendix C.3 (Plaud et al., 2024). We expect this loss to enhance performances on the under-represented classes.

4.3 Conditional sigmoid binary cross-entropy

In practice, several real-world datasets consistently used in recent literature to evaluate HTC models (Lewis et al., 2004; Aly et al., 2019) are multi-path. As the conditional softmax is not designed for multi-path labels, we propose to use a conditional sigmoid loss, introduced by Brust and Denzler (2020). It follows a similar intuition to the conditional softmax: sigmoids are applied to each entry of s_x, modeling the conditional probability of the node given its parent. Hence, the contribution to the loss of a pair (x, Y) is given by a **masked** cross-entropy[4]:

$$l_{\text{CSig}}(x,Y) = -\sum_{z\in Y}\log(\hat{\mathrm{P}}(z|x,\pi(z))) + \sum_{u\in\mathcal{C}(\pi(z))\setminus\{z\}}\log(1-\hat{\mathrm{P}}(u|x,\pi(z)))$$

Proposition 2 *Let $x \in \mathcal{X}$, $Y \subset \mathcal{Y}$ and W defined as per Equation 2 then*

$$\frac{\partial l_{\text{CSoft}}(x,Y)}{\partial W} = \frac{\partial l_{\text{CSig}}(x,Y)}{\partial W}$$

Proof can be found in Appendix C.4 (Plaud et al., 2024). While the conditional sigmoid was not motivated by theoretical arguments in Brust and Denzler (2020), Proposition 2 proves that gradients computed for this loss and the conditional softmax cross-entropy loss are equivalent. This loss then allows to deal with both multi-path and non-exhaustive datasets while having similar properties to conditional softmax.[5]

Dataset	Train/Val/Test	#nodes (#leaves)	#nodes per level	Avg. #labels per sample
HWV (SPL)	6,408/1,602 2,003	1186 (953)	11-109-381-437-244-4	3.7
WOS (SPL)	30,070/7,518 9,397	141 (134)	7-134	2.0
RCV1 (MP)	23,149/ - 781,265	103 (82)	4-55-43-1	3.2
BGC (MP)	58,715/14,785 18,394	146 (120)	7-46-77-16	3.0

Table 1: Key statistics of the selected datasets. **SPL** indicates that the dataset enters the *single path leaf labels* setting, and **MP** that it is multi-path; d represents the maximum depth of the label hierarchy.

5 Experimental settings

In this section, we introduce the existing datasets and models we experiment with; we also present our new dataset, Hierarchical WikiVitals (HWV).

5.1 Datasets

We will verify the performance of our proposed approaches versus baselines and recent state-of-the-art models on hierarchical metrics on three widely used datasets in the HTC literature, which is mainly applied to English data: Web-of-Science (WOS) (Kowsari et al., 2018), RCV1-V2 (Lewis et al., 2004) and BGC (Aly et al., 2019). Data statistics are displayed in Table 1: those datasets have in common a relatively large number of training samples, a sizable number of nodes, and a low depth of the label structure. We contribute to HTC benchmarking by releasing Hierarchical WikiVitals, which we aim to present a more difficult challenge.

HWV Dataset Texts are extracted from the abstracts of the *vital* articles of Wikipedia, level 4 [6] as of June 2021. This project involves a handmade hierarchical categorization of the selected articles, which are themselves put through high scrutiny with respect to their quality. The resulting dataset is a *single path leaf label* dataset, a constraint only fulfilled by WOS. As the number of nodes and the

[3]In practice, we estimate it by computing an empirical probability on train set for each label. It is not trainable.

[4]See Fig. 2b of Brust and Denzler (2020) for visual understanding of the mask

[5]However, no logit-adjusted version of it can be properly derived.

[6]`https://en.wikipedia.org/wiki/Wikipedia:Vital_articles/Level/4`

Method	HWV				WOS			
	Hamming L. (in ‰) ↓	F1-score (in %) ↑		hF1 AUC (in %) ↑	Hamming L. (in ‰) ↓	F1-score (in %) ↑		hF1 AUC (in %) ↑
		micro	macro			micro	macro	
BCE	$0.854_{\pm0.010}$	$85.86_{\pm0.15}$	$45.56_{\pm0.58}$	$89.23_{\pm0.13}$	$3.627_{\pm0.015}$	$87.03_{\pm0.05}$	$81.19_{\pm0.12}$	**89.18**$_{\pm0.10}$
CHAMP	$0.786_{\pm0.009}$	$87.14_{\pm0.15}$	$50.90_{\pm0.24}$	$89.87_{\pm0.19}$	$3.637_{\pm0.037}$	$87.01_{\pm0.13}$	$81.23_{\pm0.18}$	$88.74_{\pm0.08}$
HBGL	-	-	-	-	**3.584**$_{\pm0.027}$	**87.22**$_{\pm0.10}$	**81.86**$_{\pm0.19}$	$89.00_{\pm0.10}$
HGCLR	$0.922_{\pm0.020}$	$84.92_{\pm0.37}$	$44.89_{\pm1.38}$	$88.35_{\pm0.35}$	$3.727_{\pm0.077}$	$86.63_{\pm0.27}$	$80.04_{\pm0.45}$	**89.23**$_{\pm0.22}$
HITIN	**0.776**$_{\pm0.006}$	**87.49**$_{\pm0.08}$	$51.73_{\pm0.42}$	$90.72_{\pm0.16}$	$3.655_{\pm0.028}$	$87.05_{\pm0.10}$	$81.49_{\pm0.06}$	$88.92_{\pm0.04}$
Leaf Softmax	$0.950_{\pm0.036}$	$84.79_{\pm0.57}$	$51.49_{\pm0.52}$	$88.55_{\pm0.47}$	$3.987_{\pm0.059}$	$85.91_{\pm0.25}$	$80.02_{\pm0.29}$	$88.62_{\pm0.08}$
Conditional Sigmoid	$0.801_{\pm0.011}$	$87.01_{\pm0.19}$	$52.27_{\pm0.82}$	$90.40_{\pm0.17}$	$3.692_{\pm0.067}$	$86.86_{\pm0.23}$	$81.07_{\pm0.30}$	$88.78_{\pm0.17}$
Conditional Softmax	$0.788_{\pm0.015}$	**87.49**$_{\pm0.10}$	$53.79_{\pm0.65}$	**90.94**$_{\pm0.09}$	$3.869_{\pm0.086}$	$86.27_{\pm0.17}$	$80.25_{\pm0.33}$	$88.77_{\pm0.07}$
Cond. Softmax + LA (ours)	**0.782**$_{\pm0.004}$	**87.51**$_{\pm0.07}$	**54.39**$_{\pm0.58}$	**90.97**$_{\pm0.05}$	$3.837_{\pm0.038}$	$86.35_{\pm0.12}$	$80.11_{\pm0.26}$	$88.90_{\pm0.10}$

Table 2: Performance evaluation metrics (and 95% confidence interval) on the test sets of the WOS and HWV datasets for the implemented models. Best results for each metric are highlighted in bold. The HBGL model was too large to fit in the memory of a 32GB GPU on the HWV dataset.

Method	RCV1				BGC			
	Hamming L. (in ‰) ↓	F1-score (in %) ↑		hF1 AUC (in %) ↑	Hamming L. (in ‰) ↓	F1-score (in %) ↑		hF1 AUC (in %) ↑
		micro	macro			micro	macro	
BCE	$8.225_{\pm0.148}$	$86.65_{\pm0.30}$	$66.47_{\pm1.49}$	**93.66**$_{\pm0.19}$	**7.788**$_{\pm0.071}$	**80.51**$_{\pm0.21}$	$62.33_{\pm1.36}$	**90.26**$_{\pm0.29}$
CHAMP	$8.565_{\pm0.234}$	$85.93_{\pm0.66}$	$62.86_{\pm3.64}$	$93.12_{\pm0.33}$	**7.775**$_{\pm0.081}$	**80.54**$_{\pm0.20}$	$63.58_{\pm0.49}$	**90.19**$_{\pm0.22}$
HBGL	**8.122**$_{\pm0.071}$	**87.11**$_{\pm0.12}$	**70.20**$_{\pm0.33}$	$93.35_{\pm0.14}$	$8.092_{\pm0.045}$	$80.19_{\pm0.11}$	**65.94**$_{\pm0.18}$	$88.08_{\pm0.10}$
HGCLR	$8.761_{\pm0.276}$	$86.11_{\pm0.26}$	$67.49_{\pm0.61}$	$93.27_{\pm0.14}$	$8.054_{\pm0.171}$	$80.16_{\pm0.29}$	$63.58_{\pm0.40}$	$89.81_{\pm0.17}$
HITIN	$8.583_{\pm0.188}$	$85.72_{\pm0.60}$	$60.00_{\pm5.15}$	$93.04_{\pm0.24}$	$7.981_{\pm0.096}$	**80.36**$_{\pm0.21}$	$61.62_{\pm1.47}$	**90.08**$_{\pm0.16}$
Conditional Sigmoid	$8.652_{\pm0.316}$	$85.77_{\pm0.71}$	$63.90_{\pm2.45}$	$93.23_{\pm0.36}$	$7.954_{\pm0.202}$	$80.24_{\pm0.46}$	$62.65_{\pm0.64}$	**90.07**$_{\pm0.40}$

Table 3: Performance evaluation metrics (and 95% confidence interval) on the test sets of the RCV1 and BGC datasets for the implemented models. Best results for each metric are highlighted in bold.

depth of the hierarchy are higher than for the previously cited datasets, HWV is much more challenging. It is also characterized by a very imbalanced label distribution with $\sim 50\%$ of labels having less than 10 examples in the whole dataset. We show in Figure 1 three observations from our new dataset, illustrating how much leaf nodes depth can vary (ranging from 2 to 6). Comprehensive details regarding the building process of the quality of data of HWV are provided in Appendix B (Plaud et al., 2024).

5.2 Models

We propose to compare very different HTC models, ranging from simple baselines to the most recent state-of-the-art approaches. For fair comparison between them, we use a pre-trained BERT[7] model (Devlin et al., 2019) as text encoder, adopting the standard [CLS] representation as h_x for every model. We list below all the different models evaluated. **BERT + BCE** is the simplest baseline, treating the problem as a multi-label task, without using any information from the hierarchical structure of labels. **BERT + Leaf Softmax** outputs a distribution over leaves, and hence is only fitted for single-path leaf label settings. **BERT + CHAMP** implements the penalization of false positives based on their shortest-path distance to the ground label set in the tree (Vaswani et al., 2022). **BERT + Conditional {Softmax, logit-adjusted Softmax, Sigmoid}** are our proposed methods, detailed in Section 4.1. **Hitin** (Zhu et al., 2023), **HBGL** (Jiang et al., 2022), **HGCLR** (Wang et al., 2022a) are among the most recent models, proposing respectively to separately encode the label hierarchy in an efficient manner, to incorporate both global and local information when encoding the label hierarchy, by considering subgraphs, and to use contrastive learning and exploiting the label hierarchy to create plausible corrupted examples.

5.3 Training details

We use `bert-base-uncased` model from the transformers library (Wolf et al., 2020) as text encoder (110M parameters). Our implementation is based on Hitin.[8] Each of our baselines is trained for 20 epochs on a V100 GPU of 32GB with a batch size of 16. We used an AdamW optimizer with initial learning rate of $2 \cdot 10^{-5}$ and with a warmup period of 10% of the training steps. For HBGL[9], Hitin and HGCLR[10], we rely on implementation guidelines

[7] `https://huggingface.co/bert-base-uncased`

[8] `https://github.com/Rooooyy/HiTIN`

[9] `https://github.com/kongds/HBGL`

[10] `https://github.com/wzh9969/contrastive-htc`

to conduct experiments. For datasets not used in the original papers, we performed a grid-search hyperparameter optimization. Our results are derived from averaging over four separate training runs, each initialized with distinct random seeds, ensuring the robustness and fairness of our evaluation methodology.

6 Results and Analysis

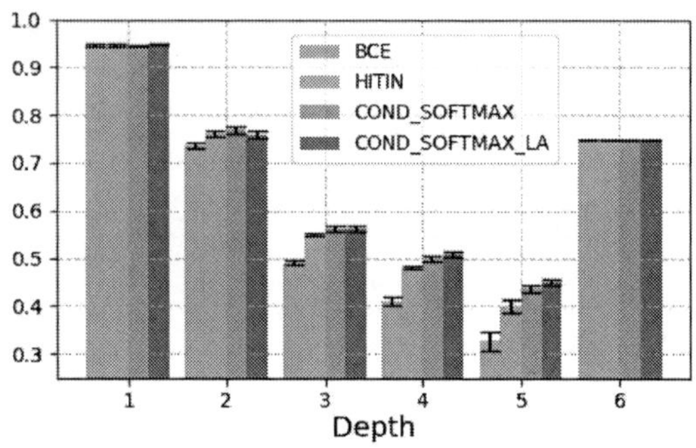

Figure 3: Averaged Macro F1-Scores on the test set per depth for different models and for the HWV dataset. The error bars represent a 95% confidence interval.

We start our investigation by evaluating models on our newly proposed dataset, HWV. Results are shown in Table 2. Unfortunately, the HBGL architecture could not run for HWV, requiring memory above the capacity of our GPUs. **On this dataset, we note the overall superiority of our newly introduced logit-adjusted conditional softmax loss and its vanilla version.** The latest models fail to obtain the best results, which is surprising given the complex hierarchy and label imbalance. We hence emit the hypothesis that while *hierarchy-aware* models were proven useful on simpler datasets, they fail to capture that complexity on HWV. To investigate why it performs better, we display in Figures 3 & 4 averaged macro F1-scores over classes. Figure 3 corresponds to averages of scores based on label depth: we observe that the higher the depth the higher the improvement brought by conditional softmax and its logit-adjusted version is (except for depth 6 which has only 4 classes inside). Figure 4 seems to hint that the improvement of the logit-adjusted conditional softmax vs. a vanilla conditional softmax lies in its ability to correctly classify *under-represented* classes. Until the third decile of the label count distribution, our newly introduced method is statistically better. We could have expected such a result, as

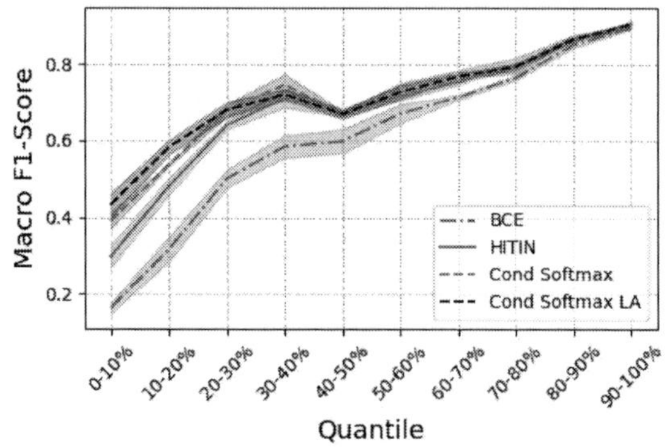

Figure 4: Averaged Macro F1-Scores on the test set by quantiles of label counts distribution in the training set for different models and for the HWV dataset. The shaded regions represent a 95% confidence interval.

this loss was specifically designed to deal with label imbalance (see Appendix C.3 (Plaud et al., 2024)). Obviously, depth is strongly correlated with *under-representation* of labels. We then conduct an ablation study with respect to the label hierarchy, by cutting the HWV hierarchy at depth 2. By doing so, the hierarchy becomes shallow and the label *imbalance* remains. Table 4 presents the results obtained from this modified dataset. In this scenario, state-of-the-art models catch up with our conditional softmax losses and Hitin reclaim a marginal lead across all metrics. Furthermore, we observe that our logit-adjusted conditional softmax remains better than the vanilla conditional softmax, especially on *macro* F1-score. These two observations allow us to refine our conclusions. First, the superiority of the vanilla conditional softmax on HWV vs. recent state-of-the-art methods seems to stem from the hierarchy complexity: **a conditional modelisation allows to better classify deep classes**. Second, the logit-adjusted version proves to be useful in presence of label imbalance as we can see with *macro* F1-score metrics, which are statistically better than the vanilla version in both versions of HWV dataset.

On WOS, simpler baselines reach remarkable results. Despite the marginal superiority of HBGL, it is noteworthy that the **BERT+BCE model is in the top performances across all metrics**, while not using label hierarchy information. On this dataset, our new method, while competitive, lags behind.

These results are coherent with conclusions drawn with HWV dataset : the WOS dataset has

Method	HWV (depth 2)			
	Hamming L. (in ‰) ↓	F1-score (in %) ↑		hF1 AUC (in %) ↑
		micro	macro	
BCE	2.367±0.030	**92.89**±0.06	78.42±0.31	**94.67**±0.15
HITIN	**2.316**±0.068	**93.05**±0.20	**79.59**±0.43	**94.79**±0.18
Cond. Soft.	2.450±0.087	92.65±0.26	78.40±1.06	**94.73**±0.18
Cond. S. L.A.	2.432±0.072	**92.89**±0.22	**79.38**±0.26	**94.77**±0.18

Table 4: Performance evaluation metrics (and 95% confidence interval) on the test sets of the cutted HWV dataset for the implemented models. Best results for each metric are highlighted in bold.

a low complexity, both in terms of depth (maximum depth of 2) and distribution of labels (only one class has less than 40 examples in the dataset). On multi-path datasets, our observations align closely with what we noticed on WOS: we observe in Table 3 that a straightforward BCE loss consistently yields great results across datasets and metrics. Hierarchical metrics clearly highlight this phenomenon. In fact, model rankings in multi-label F1 scores and hierarchical F1 scores only keep consistent for HWV: for the three other datasets, the **structure-aware threshold-independent metrics put the BCE baseline to the top**.

We believe those results allow us to draw two main lessons: first, that hierarchical metrics bring useful insights on HTC evaluation, and are necessary to properly evaluate models on their capacity to encode label structure, which our results show to be lacking. Second, that when used on a more challenging dataset, state-of-the-art hierarchy-aware HTC models are less able to integrate that complex hierarchical information into their prediction than a simple model trained with conditional softmax cross-entropy.

7 Conclusion

In this paper, we come back upon recent progress in HTC, and propose to investigate its evaluation. To do so, we begin by showing the limitations of the inference and metrics that are commonly used in the recent literature. We instead propose to use existing hierarchical metrics, and an associated inference method. Then, we introduce a new and challenging dataset, Hierarchical WikiVitals; our experiments show that recent sophisticated hierarchy-aware models have trouble integrating hierarchy information in any better way than simple baselines. We finally propose simple hierarchical losses, able to better integrate hierarchy information on our dataset. In the future, we plan to investigate the inference mechanism for hierarchical metrics, through which we will aim to make a direct contribution to improving models on HTC tasks.

References

Rami Aly, Steffen Remus, and Chris Biemann. 2019. Hierarchical multi-label classification of text with capsule networks. In *Proceedings of the 57th Annual Meeting of the Association for Computational Linguistics: Student Research Workshop*, pages 323–330, Florence, Italy. Association for Computational Linguistics.

Enrique Amigo and Agustín Delgado. 2022. Evaluating extreme hierarchical multi-label classification. In *Proceedings of the 60th Annual Meeting of the Association for Computational Linguistics (Volume 1: Long Papers)*, pages 5809–5819, Dublin, Ireland. Association for Computational Linguistics.

Siddhartha Banerjee, Cem Akkaya, Francisco Perez-Sorrosal, and Kostas Tsioutsiouliklis. 2019. Hierarchical transfer learning for multi-label text classification. In *Proceedings of the 57th Annual Meeting of the Association for Computational Linguistics*, pages 6295–6300, Florence, Italy. Association for Computational Linguistics.

James O. Berger. 1985. *Statistical Decision Theory and Bayesian Analysis*, 2nd edition. Springer Series in Statistics. Springer, New York.

Luca Bertinetto, Romain Mueller, Konstantinos Tertikas, Sina Samangooei, and Nicholas A. Lord. 2020. Making better mistakes: Leveraging class hierarchies with deep networks. In *IEEE/CVF Conference on Computer Vision and Pattern Recognition (CVPR)*.

Wei Bi and Jame T. Kwok. 2015. Bayes-optimal hierarchical multilabel classification. *IEEE Transactions on Knowledge and Data Engineering*, 27(11):2907–2918.

Clemens-Alexander Brust and Joachim Denzler. 2020. Integrating domain knowledge: Using hierarchies to improve deep classifiers. In *Pattern Recognition*, pages 3–16, Cham. Springer International Publishing.

Boli Chen, Xin Huang, Lin Xiao, Zixin Cai, and Liping Jing. 2020. Hyperbolic interaction model for hierarchical multi-label classification. In *Proceedings of the AAAI conference on artificial intelligence*, volume 34, pages 7496–7503.

Haibin Chen, Qianli Ma, Zhenxi Lin, and Jiangyue Yan. 2021. Hierarchy-aware label semantics matching network for hierarchical text classification. In *Proceedings of the 59th Annual Meeting of the Association for Computational Linguistics and the 11th International Joint Conference on Natural Language Processing (Volume 1: Long Papers)*, pages 4370–4379, Online. Association for Computational Linguistics.

Eduardo Costa, Ana Lorena, Andre Carvalho, and Alex Freitas. 2007. A review of performance evaluation measures for hierarchical classifiers. *AAAI Workshop - Technical Report.*

Krzysztof Dembczyński, Willem Waegeman, Weiwei Cheng, and Eyke Hüllermeier. 2012. On label dependence and loss minimization in multi-label classification. *Machine Learning*, 88:5–45.

Zhongfen Deng, Hao Peng, Dongxiao He, Jianxin Li, and Philip Yu. 2021. HTCInfoMax: A global model for hierarchical text classification via information maximization. In *Proceedings of the 2021 Conference of the North American Chapter of the Association for Computational Linguistics: Human Language Technologies*, pages 3259–3265, Online. Association for Computational Linguistics.

Jacob Devlin, Ming-Wei Chang, Kenton Lee, and Kristina Toutanova. 2019. BERT: Pre-training of deep bidirectional transformers for language understanding. In *Proceedings of the 2019 Conference of the North American Chapter of the Association for Computational Linguistics: Human Language Technologies, Volume 1 (Long and Short Papers)*, pages 4171–4186, Minneapolis, Minnesota. Association for Computational Linguistics.

Siddharth Gopal and Yiming Yang. 2013. Recursive regularization for large-scale classification with hierarchical and graphical dependencies. In *Proceedings of the 19th ACM SIGKDD International Conference on Knowledge Discovery and Data Mining*, KDD '13, page 257–265, New York, NY, USA. Association for Computing Machinery.

Wei Huang, Enhong Chen, Qi Liu, Yuying Chen, Zai Huang, Yang Liu, Zhou Zhao, Dan Zhang, and Shijin Wang. 2019. Hierarchical multi-label text classification: An attention-based recurrent network approach. In *Proceedings of the 28th ACM international conference on information and knowledge management*, pages 1051–1060.

Ke Ji, Yixin Lian, Jingsheng Gao, and Baoyuan Wang. 2023. Hierarchical verbalizer for few-shot hierarchical text classification. In *Proceedings of the 61st Annual Meeting of the Association for Computational Linguistics (Volume 1: Long Papers)*, pages 2918–2933, Toronto, Canada. Association for Computational Linguistics.

Ting Jiang, Deqing Wang, Leilei Sun, Zhongzhi Chen, Fuzhen Zhuang, and Qinghong Yang. 2022. Exploiting global and local hierarchies for hierarchical text classification. In *Proceedings of the 2022 Conference on Empirical Methods in Natural Language Processing*, pages 4030–4039, Abu Dhabi, United Arab Emirates. Association for Computational Linguistics.

Svetlana Kiritchenko, Stan Matwin, Richard Nock, and A. Fazel Famili. 2006. Learning and evaluation in the presence of class hierarchies: Application to text categorization. In *Advances in Artificial Intelligence*, pages 395–406, Berlin, Heidelberg. Springer Berlin Heidelberg.

Aris Kosmopoulos, Ioannis Partalas, Eric Gaussier, Georgios Paliouras, and Ion Androutsopoulos. 2014. Evaluation measures for hierarchical classification: a unified view and novel approaches. *Data Mining and Knowledge Discovery*, 29(3):820–865.

Kamran Kowsari, Donald Brown, Mojtaba Heidarysafa, Kiana Jafari Meimandi, Matthew Gerber, and Laura Barnes. 2018. Web of science dataset.

D. D. Lewis, Y. Yang, T. G. Rose, and F. Li. 2004. Rcv1: A new benchmark collection for text categorization research. *Journal of Machine Learning Research*, 5(Apr):361–397.

Volodymyr Lyubinets, Taras Boiko, and Deon Nicholas. 2018. Automated labeling of bugs and tickets using attention-based mechanisms in recurrent neural networks. In *2018 IEEE Second International Conference on Data Stream Mining and Processing (DSMP)*, pages 271–275.

Yuning Mao, Jingjing Tian, Jiawei Han, and Xiang Ren. 2019. Hierarchical text classification with reinforced label assignment. In *Proceedings of the 2019 Conference on Empirical Methods in Natural Language Processing and the 9th International Joint Conference on Natural Language Processing (EMNLP-IJCNLP)*, pages 445–455, Hong Kong, China. Association for Computational Linguistics.

Aditya Krishna Menon, Andreas Veit, Ankit Singh Rawat, Himanshu Jain, Sadeep Jayasumana, and Sanjiv Kumar. 2021. Long-tail learning via logit adjustment. In *International Conference on Learning Representations (ICLR) 2021*.

Roman Plaud, Matthieu Labeau, Antoine Saillenfest, and Thomas Bonald. 2024. Revisiting hierarchical text classification: Inference and metrics. ArXiv preprint.

Joseph Redmon and Ali Farhadi. 2017. Yolo9000: Better, faster, stronger. In *Proceedings of the IEEE Conference on Computer Vision and Pattern Recognition (CVPR)*.

Evan Sandhaus. 2008. The new york times annotated corpus. *Linguistic Data Consortium*, 6(12):e26752.

Kazuya Shimura, Jiyi Li, and Fumiyo Fukumoto. 2018. HFT-CNN: Learning hierarchical category structure for multi-label short text categorization. In *Proceedings of the 2018 Conference on Empirical Methods in Natural Language Processing*, pages 811–816, Brussels, Belgium. Association for Computational Linguistics.

Carlos Silla and Alex Freitas. 2011. A survey of hierarchical classification across different application domains. *Data Mining and Knowledge Discovery*, 22:31–72.

Hyun-Je Song, Jeong-Woo Son, Tae-Gil Noh, Seong-Bae Park, and Sang-Jo Lee. 2012. A cost sensitive part-of-speech tagging: Differentiating serious errors from minor errors. In *Proceedings of the 50th Annual Meeting of the Association for Computational Linguistics (Volume 1: Long Papers)*, pages 1025–1034, Jeju Island, Korea. Association for Computational Linguistics.

Junru Song, Feifei Wang, and Yang Yang. 2023. Peer-label assisted hierarchical text classification. In *Proceedings of the 61st Annual Meeting of the Association for Computational Linguistics (Volume 1: Long Papers)*, pages 3747–3758, Toronto, Canada. Association for Computational Linguistics.

Aixin Sun and Ee-Peng Lim. 2001. Hierarchial text classification and evaluation. pages 521–528.

Jack Valmadre. 2022. Hierarchical classification at multiple operating points. In *Advances in Neural Information Processing Systems*, volume 35, pages 18034–18045. Curran Associates, Inc.

Ashwin Vaswani, Gaurav Aggarwal, Praneeth Netrapalli, and Narayan G Hegde. 2022. All mistakes are not equal: Comprehensive hierarchy aware multi-label predictions (champ).

Boyan Wang, Xuegang Hu, Peipei Li, and Philip S. Yu. 2021. Cognitive structure learning model for hierarchical multi-label text classification. *Knowledge-Based Systems*, 218:106876.

Zihan Wang, Peiyi Wang, Lianzhe Huang, Xin Sun, and Houfeng Wang. 2022a. Incorporating hierarchy into text encoder: a contrastive learning approach for hierarchical text classification. In *Proceedings of the 60th Annual Meeting of the Association for Computational Linguistics (Volume 1: Long Papers)*, pages 7109–7119, Dublin, Ireland. Association for Computational Linguistics.

Zihan Wang, Peiyi Wang, Tianyu Liu, Binghuai Lin, Yunbo Cao, Zhifang Sui, and Houfeng Wang. 2022b. HPT: Hierarchy-aware prompt tuning for hierarchical text classification. In *Proceedings of the 2022 Conference on Empirical Methods in Natural Language Processing*, pages 3740–3751, Abu Dhabi, United Arab Emirates. Association for Computational Linguistics.

Zihan Wang, Peiyi Wang, and Houfeng Wang. 2024. Utilizing local hierarchy with adversarial training for hierarchical text classification. In *Proceedings of the 2024 Joint International Conference on Computational Linguistics, Language Resources and Evaluation (LREC-COLING 2024)*, pages 17326–17336, Torino, Italia. ELRA and ICCL.

Jonatas Wehrmann, Ricardo Cerri, and Rodrigo Barros. 2018. Hierarchical multi-label classification networks. In *Proceedings of the 35th International Conference on Machine Learning*, volume 80 of *Proceedings of Machine Learning Research*, pages 5075–5084. PMLR.

Thomas Wolf, Lysandre Debut, Victor Sanh, Julien Chaumond, Clement Delangue, Anthony Moi, Pierric Cistac, Tim Rault, Remi Louf, Morgan Funtowicz, Joe Davison, Sam Shleifer, Patrick von Platen, Clara Ma, Yacine Jernite, Julien Plu, Canwen Xu, Teven Le Scao, Sylvain Gugger, Mariama Drame, Quentin Lhoest, and Alexander Rush. 2020. Transformers: State-of-the-art natural language processing. In *Proceedings of the 2020 Conference on Empirical Methods in Natural Language Processing: System Demonstrations*, pages 38–45, Online. Association for Computational Linguistics.

Xi-Zhu Wu and Zhi-Hua Zhou. 2016. A unified view of multi-label performance measures. In *International Conference on Machine Learning*.

Bishan Yang and Claire Cardie. 2013. Joint inference for fine-grained opinion extraction. In *Proceedings of the 51st Annual Meeting of the Association for Computational Linguistics (Volume 1: Long Papers)*, pages 1640–1649, Sofia, Bulgaria. Association for Computational Linguistics.

Chao Yu, Yi Shen, and Yue Mao. 2022. Constrained sequence-to-tree generation for hierarchical text classification. In *Proceedings of the 45th International ACM SIGIR Conference on Research and Development in Information Retrieval*, SIGIR '22, page 1865–1869, New York, NY, USA. Association for Computing Machinery.

Simon Chi Lok Yu, Jie He, Victor Basulto, and Jeff Pan. 2023. Instances and labels: Hierarchy-aware joint supervised contrastive learning for hierarchical multi-label text classification. In *Findings of the Association for Computational Linguistics: EMNLP 2023*, pages 8858–8875, Singapore. Association for Computational Linguistics.

Alessandro Zangari, Matteo Marcuzzo, Matteo Rizzo, Lorenzo Giudice, Andrea Albarelli, and Andrea Gasparetto. 2024. Hierarchical text classification and its foundations: A review of current research. *Electronics*, 13(7).

Xinyi Zhang, Jiahao Xu, Charlie Soh, and Lihui Chen. 2022. La-hcn: Label-based attention for hierarchical multi-label text classification neural network. *Expert Systems with Applications*, 187:115922.

Yu Zhang, Zhihong Shen, Yuxiao Dong, Kuansan Wang, and Jiawei Han. 2021. Match: Metadata-aware text classification in a large hierarchy. In *Proceedings of the Web Conference 2021*, pages 3246–3257.

Jie Zhou, Chunping Ma, Dingkun Long, Guangwei Xu, Ning Ding, Haoyu Zhang, Pengjun Xie, and Gongshen Liu. 2020. Hierarchy-aware global model for hierarchical text classification. In *Proceedings of the 58th Annual Meeting of the Association for Computational Linguistics*, pages 1106–1117, Online. Association for Computational Linguistics.

He Zhu, Junran Wu, Ruomei Liu, Yue Hou, Ze Yuan, Shangzhe Li, Yicheng Pan, and Ke Xu. 2024. HILL:

Hierarchy-aware information lossless contrastive learning for hierarchical text classification. In *Proceedings of the 2024 Conference of the North American Chapter of the Association for Computational Linguistics: Human Language Technologies (Volume 1: Long Papers)*, pages 4731–4745, Mexico City, Mexico. Association for Computational Linguistics.

He Zhu, Chong Zhang, Junjie Huang, Junran Wu, and Ke Xu. 2023. HiTIN: Hierarchy-aware tree isomorphism network for hierarchical text classification. In *Proceedings of the 61st Annual Meeting of the Association for Computational Linguistics (Volume 1: Long Papers)*, pages 7809–7821, Toronto, Canada. Association for Computational Linguistics.

NeLLCom-X: A Comprehensive Neural-Agent Framework to Simulate Language Learning and Group Communication

Yuchen Lian[◇ †] **Tessa Verhoef**[†*] **Arianna Bisazza**[‡*]

[◇]Faculty of Electronic and Information Engineering, Xi'an Jiaotong University
[†]Leiden Institute of Advanced Computer Science, Leiden University
{y.lian, t.verhoef}@liacs.leidenuniv.nl
[‡]Center for Language and Cognition, University of Groningen
a.bisazza@rug.nl

Abstract

Recent advances in computational linguistics include simulating the emergence of human-like languages with interacting neural network agents, starting from sets of random symbols. The recently introduced NeLLCom framework (Lian et al., 2023) allows agents to first learn an artificial language and then use it to communicate, with the aim of studying the emergence of specific linguistics properties. We extend this framework (NeLLCom-X) by introducing more realistic role-alternating agents and group communication in order to investigate the interplay between language learnability, communication pressures, and group size effects. We validate NeLLCom-X by replicating key findings from prior research simulating the emergence of a word-order/case-marking trade-off. Next, we investigate how interaction affects linguistic convergence and emergence of the trade-off. The novel framework facilitates future simulations of diverse linguistic aspects, emphasizing the importance of interaction and group dynamics in language evolution.

1 Introduction

Human language can be viewed as a complex adaptive dynamical system (Fitch, 2007; Steels, 2000; Beckner et al., 2009), in which individual behaviours of language users drive linguistic emergence and change at the population level. Languages are shaped by the brains of individuals who are learning them (Christiansen and Chater, 2008; Kirby et al., 2014) and novel conventions and meanings are negotiated during interaction and language use (Fusaroli and Tylén, 2012; Namboodiripad et al., 2016; Garrod et al., 2007). The effect of these mechanisms on linguistic patterns has been studied extensively, and it is recognized that language systems do not spring from the mind of a single individual, but are the result of constant reinterpretation and filtering through populations of human minds. As such, language users are not mere passive learners, but unconsciously and gradually contribute to language change.

Recently, this interactive and dynamic property of human language was recognized as a key factor to improve AI (Mikolov et al., 2018), leading to a large interest in simulating the emergence of human-like languages with neural network agents (Havrylov and Titov, 2017; Kottur et al., 2017; Lazaridou et al., 2017; Lazaridou and Baroni, 2020). Typically, a pair of agents is simulated where a speaking agent tries to help a listener recover an intended meaning by generating a message the listener can interpret. Early frameworks have been progressively expanded to display important aspects of human language and communication, like generational transmission (Li and Bowling, 2019; Chaabouni et al., 2019; Lian et al., 2021; Chaabouni et al., 2022), group interaction (Tieleman et al., 2019; Chaabouni et al., 2022; Rita et al., 2022; Michel et al., 2023; Kim and Oh, 2021) and other aspects (Galke and Raviv, 2024). Within this body of work, most studies start from *sets of random symbols*, with a strong focus on tracking the emergence of human-like language properties such as compositionality (Chaabouni et al., 2020, 2022; Li and Bowling, 2019; Conklin and Smith, 2022) or principles of lexical organization like Zipf's law of abbreviation (Rita et al., 2020).

However, neural agent emergent communication frameworks could also be a valuable tool to simulate the evolution of more specific aspects of language. Studies with human participants have addressed many other aspects such as specific syntactic patterns like word order or morphology (Saldana et al., 2021b; Culbertson et al., 2012; Christensen et al., 2016; Motamedi et al., 2022), a tendency to reduce dependency lengths (Fedzechkina et al., 2018; Saldana et al., 2021a), colexification patterns and the role of iconicity or metaphor in the emer-

*Shared senior authorship.

Proceedings of the 28th Conference on Computational Natural Language Learning, pages 243–258
November 15-16, 2024 ©2024 Association for Computational Linguistics

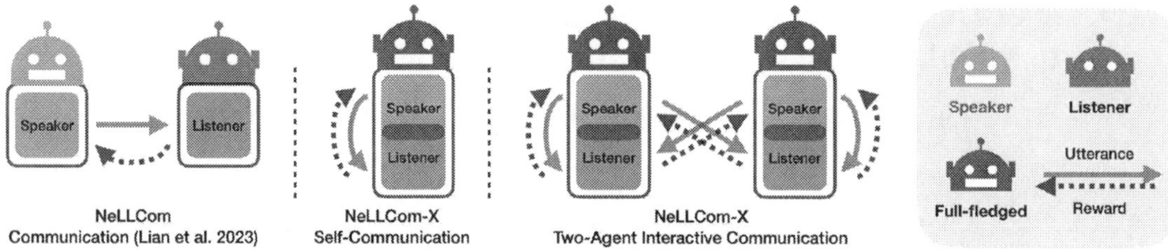

Figure 1: Overview of the NeLLCom-X framework.

gence of new meanings (Karjus et al., 2021; Verhoef et al., 2015, 2016, 2022; Tamariz et al., 2018), and combinatorial organisation of basic building blocks (Roberts and Galantucci, 2012; Verhoef, 2012; Verhoef et al., 2014). What most of these studies have in common is that participants are asked to learn and/or interact with *pre-defined artificial languages* specifically designed by the experimenters to study the linguistic property of interest. However, the existing neural-agent communication frameworks (often based on EGG (Kharitonov et al., 2019)), do not enable training agents on pre-defined languages. A different body of work has studied the *learnability* by neural networks of various types of artificial languages (Lupyan and Christiansen, 2002; Wang and Eisner, 2016; Bisazza et al., 2021; White and Cotterell, 2021; Hopkins, 2022; Kallini et al., 2024). This paradigm has led to important insights, revealing inductive biases of neural models, but is limited to studying learnability in a passive supervised learning setting, unlike the dynamic and interactive setting in which human language has evolved.

A framework combining agent communication with the ability to learn pre-defined artificial languages was recently introduced by Lian et al. (2023). In NeLLCom (Neural agent Language Learning and Communication), agents are first trained on an initial language through Supervised Learning, followed by a communication phase in which a speaking and listening agent continue learning together through Reinforcement Learning by optimizing a shared communicative reward.

In this paper, we extend NeLLCom with group interaction with the aim of studying the interplay between learnability of specific pre-defined languages, communication pressures, and group size effects under the same framework. To this end, we first extend the vanilla NeLLCom agent to act as both listener and speaker (i.e. role alteration, cf. Figure 1), which was identified as an important gap in the emergent communication literature by Galke et al. (2022). Then, we design a procedure to let such 'full-fledged' agents interact in pairs with either similar or different initial language exposure, or in groups of various sizes. With the extended framework, NeLLCom-X, we replicate the key findings of Lian et al. (2023) and additionally show that (i) pairs of agents trained on different initial languages quickly adapt their utterances towards a mutually understandable language, (ii) languages used by agents in larger groups become more optimized and less redundant, and (iii) a word-order/case-marking trade-off emerges not only in individual speakers, but also at the group level.

We release NeLLCom-X to promote simulations of other language aspects where interaction and group dynamics are expected to play a key role.[1]

2 Related Work

Role-alternating agents Initially, most work on emergent communication modeled agents to fulfill separate, complimentary roles (i.e. one agent always speaks, the other always listens). Human language users are, of course, able to take both roles. When listing a set of "design features" of human language, Hockett (1960) refered to *interchangeability* as the ability of language speakers to reproduce any linguistic message they can understand. In experiments with humans communicating via artificial languages, participants also usually take turns being the speaker and listener (Kirby et al., 2015; Namboodiripad et al., 2016; Roberts and Galantucci, 2012; Verhoef et al., 2015, 2022). Therefore, Galke et al. (2022) named role-alternation as a missing key ingredient to close the gap between outcomes of simulations and findings from human language evolution data.

Exceptions to this trend include the role-alternating architectures of Kottur et al. (2017), Harding Graesser et al. (2019), and Taillandier et al.

[1]https://github.com/Yuchen-Lian/NeLLCom-X

(2023). Recently, Michel et al. (2023) propose a method to couple a speaker and listener among a group of speaking and listening agents. By what they call "partitioning", the listener-part is only trained to adapt to its associated speaker, while the listener parameters are frozen during communication with other speakers. Hence, the speaking and listening parts of an agent are tied softly, i.e. no "physical" link via shared modules. While being workable, this partitioning seems less realistic in terms of cognitive plausibility and communication, as human listeners continually refine their understanding during all kinds of interactions (speaking as well as listening). What all these studies have in common is their focus on protocols emerging from scratch, i.e. starting from random symbols, which does not allow for simulations with pre-defined languages. Closer to our goal, Chaabouni et al. (2019) train agents on artificial languages and observe them drift in a simple iterated learning setup that does not model communication success. They use sequence-to-sequence networks that can function both as speaker and listener by representing both utterances and meanings as sequences and merging meaning and word embeddings into a single weight matrix, tied between input and output.

We combine elements of the above techniques to design agents that can learn artificial languages and use them to interact in a realistic manner.

Group communication Natural languages typically have more than two speakers, and language structure is shaped by properties of the population. According to the Linguistic Niche hypothesis, for example, languages used by larger communities tend to be simpler than those used in smaller, more isolated groups (Wray and Grace, 2007; Lupyan and Dale, 2010). Similarly, experiments with human participants have shown that interactions in larger groups can result in more systematic languages (Raviv et al., 2019). Various emergent communication simulations have been designed to investigate group effects, revealing the emergence of natural language phenomena. Tieleman et al. (2019), for example, found that representations emerging in groups are less idiosyncratic and more symbolic. They model a population of community-autoencoders and since the identities of the encoder and decoder are not revealed within a pair, the emerging representations develop in such way that all decoders can use them to successfully reconstruct the input, resulting in a more simple language as also found in humans. Michel et al. (2023) found that larger agent groups develop more compositional languages. Harding Graesser et al. (2019) investigated various language contact scenarios with populations of agents that have first developed distinct languages within their own groups, and could observe the emergence of simpler 'creole' languages, resembling findings from human language contact. Kim and Oh (2021) vary the connectivities between agents in groups, and find the spontaneous emergence of linguistic dialects in large groups with over a hundred agents having only local interactions. Again, none of these frameworks support training agents on pre-defined languages, limiting the extent to which they can be applied to specific human-like linguistic features.

In this work, we showcase how NeLLCom-X agents can interact in groups using artificial languages that were specifically designed to study the emergence of word-order/case-marking patterns.

3 NeLLCom-X

We summarize the original NeLLCom framework (Lian et al., 2023) and then explain how we extend it with role alternation and group communication.

3.1 Original Framework

NeLLCom agents exchange simple meanings using pre-defined artificial languages. To achieve this, the framework combines: (i) a supervised learning (SL) phase, during which agents are taught a language with specific properties, and (ii) a reinforcement learning (RL) phase, during which agent pairs interact via a meaning reconstruction game.

Meanings are triplets $m = \{A, a, p\}$ representing simple scenes with an action, agent, and patient, respectively (e.g. PRAISE, FOX, CROW). An artificial **language** defines a mapping between any given meaning m and utterance u which is a variable-length sequence of symbols from a fixed-size vocabulary (e.g. *'Fox praises crow'*). According to the language design, the same meaning may be expressed by different utterances, and vice versa, the same utterance may signal different meanings.

The **speaking** function $\mathcal{S} : m \mapsto u$ is implemented by a linear-to-RNN network, whereas the **listening** function $\mathcal{L} : u \mapsto m$ is implemented by a symmetric RNN-to-linear network.[2] The sequen-

[2]To make the two networks fully symmetric, we slightly modify the original listener architecture of Lian et al. (2023) by adding a meaning embedding layer before the final softmax. Preliminary experiments show no visible effect on the results.

tial components are implemented as a single-layer Gated Recurrent Unit (Chung et al., 2014). In both directions, meanings are represented by unordered tuples instead of sequences to avoid any ordering bias, differently from Chaabouni et al. (2019) who also represent meanings as sequences.

The **SL** phase minimizes the cross-entropy loss of the predicted words given meaning (speaker) or the predicted meaning tuple given utterance (listener) with respect to a gold-standard dataset $D = (m, u)$. The **RL** phase maximizes a shared reward $r(m, \hat{u})$ evaluated by the listener's prediction $\mathcal{L}(\hat{u})$ given the speaker-generated utterance $\hat{u} = \mathcal{S}(m)$. More details on the SL and RL procedures, the respective training objectives, and network architectures are given in Appendix A.

Crucially, each agent in the original NeLL-Com can either function as listener (utterance-to-meaning) or as speaker (meaning-to-utterance), but not as both, see Figure 1. While this minimal setup was sufficient to simulate the emergence of the word-order/case-marking trade-off (Lian et al., 2023), it does not allow for role alternation –a missing key ingredient for realistic simulations of emergent communication (Galke et al., 2022) and a necessary condition to simulate group communication.

3.2 Full-fledged Agent

To realize a full-fledged agent (α) that can speak *and* listen while interacting with other agents, we pair two networks $\alpha_i = (N_i^{\mathcal{S}}, N_i^{\mathcal{L}})$ using two strategies: parameter sharing and self-play (Fig. 1).

Parameter sharing A common practice in NLP is tying the weights of the embedding (input) and softmax (output) layers to maximize performance and reduce the number of parameters in large language models (Press and Wolf, 2017). Chaabouni et al. (2019) applied this technique to their sequence-to-sequence utterance↔meaning architecture. However in our setup, listening and speaking are implemented by two separate, symmetric networks. We then tie the input embedding of the speaking network to the output embedding of the listening network $\mathbf{X}(N_i^{\mathcal{S}}) = \mathbf{O}(N_i^{\mathcal{L}})$ (both representing meanings). Likewise, we tie the input embedding of the listener to the output embedding of the speaker $\mathbf{X}(N_i^{\mathcal{L}}) = \mathbf{O}(N_i^{\mathcal{S}})$ (both representing words). Because of these shared parameters, the speaker training process will also affect the listener, and vice versa. To balance listener and speaker optimization during supervised learning, we alternate between the two after each epoch.[3]

Self-play Even when word and meaning representations are shared, the rest of the speaking and listening networks remain disjoint, potentially causing the speaking and listening abilities to drift in different directions. As discussed in Section 2, a realistic full-fledged agent should be able to understand itself at any moment. To ensure this, we let the agent's speaking network send messages to its own listening network while optimizing the shared communicative reward r, a procedure known as self-play in emergent communication literature (Lowe et al., 2020; Lazaridou et al., 2020). In Section 6.1, we show empirically that self-play is indeed necessary to preserve the agents' self-understanding while their language evolves in interaction.

3.3 Interactive Communication

Given the new full-fledged agent definition, communication becomes possible between two or more role-alternating agents. We introduce the notion of *turn* to denote a minimal communication session where RL weight updates take place between an agent's speaker and either its own listener or another agent's listener:

$$\mathsf{self\_turn}(\alpha_i) = \mathsf{RL}(N_i^{\mathcal{S}}, N_i^{\mathcal{L}}) \quad (1)$$

$$\mathsf{inter\_turn}(\alpha_i, \alpha_j) = \mathsf{RL}(N_i^{\mathcal{S}}, N_j^{\mathcal{L}}) \quad (2)$$

For example, in our experiments, a turn corresponds to 10 batches of 32 meanings. Note that interaction can involve agents that were trained on the same language, or on different initial languages, as we will show in Section 6.

[3] As verified in preliminary experiments, results are similar whether the last epoch is a listening or speaking one.

Algorithm 1: Group Communication

Input: set of SL-trained agents: $Agents$,
edges in the connectivity graph: $\mathcal{G}$,
n_rounds, σ

for $r = 1 : n\_rounds$ **do**
  $comm\_turns$ = shuffle($\mathcal{G}$)
  for $turn_i \in comm\_turns$ **do**
    i_{spk}, i_{lst} = $turn_i$
    α_{spk} = $Agents[i_{spk}]$, α_{lst} = $Agents[i_{lst}]$
    inter_turn(α_{spk}, α_{lst})
    for $\alpha = \{\alpha_{spk}, \alpha_{lst}\}$ **do**
      α.activation += 1
      if α.*activation* >= σ **then**
        self_turn(α)
        α.activation = 0

Turn scheduling During group communication, a connectivity graph $\mathcal{G}$ is used to define which agents can communicate with another, and which cannot. Within $\mathcal{G}$, a node i represents an agent and a directed edge (i, j) represents a connection whereby α_i can speak to α_j, but not necessarily vice versa. Turn scheduling then proceeds as shown in Algorithm 1: Before each turn, an edge (i, j) is sampled without replacement from $\mathcal{G}$. Then α_i and α_j perform an inter_turn of meaning reconstruction game, with α_i acting as the speaker and α_j as the listener. Interactive turns are interleaved with self-play turns at fixed intervals, i.e. every time an agent has participated in $\sigma \times$ inter_turn, it performs one self_turn. Once all edges in $\mathcal{G}$ have been sampled, a communication *round* is complete. In this work, we only consider a setup where all agents can interact with all other agents ($\mathcal{G}$ is a complete directed graph). We leave an exploration of more complex configurations such as those studied by Harding Graesser et al. (2019); Kim and Oh (2021); Michel et al. (2023) to future work. We set $\sigma = 10$ in all interactive experiments, unless differently specified. Interaction between two agents follows the same procedure as group communication.

4 Experimental Setup

As our use case, we adopt the same artificial languages as Lian et al. (2023). These simple verb-final languages vary in their use of word order and/or case marking to denote subject and object, and were originally proposed by Fedzechkina et al. (2017) to study the existence of an effort-informativeness trade-off in human learners.

Artificial languages The meaning space includes 10 entities and 8 actions, resulting in a total of $10\times(10-1)\times8=720$ possible meanings. Utterances can be either SOV or OSV. The order profile of a language is defined by the proportion of SOV, e.g. 100% fixed, 80% dominant, 50% maximally flexible-order. Objects are optionally followed by a special token 'mk' while subjects are never marked. To simplify the vocabulary learning problem, each meaning item correspond to exactly one word, leading to a vocabulary size of $10+8+1=19$. Two example languages are shown in Table 1.

Evaluation Following Lian et al. (2023), agents are evaluated on a held-out set of meanings unseen during any training phase. The SL phase is evaluated by listening/speaking accuracy computed against gold dataset D, while the RL phase is evaluated by meaning reconstruction accuracy, or communication success. In NeLLCom-X, communication success denotes two different aspects: self-understanding when measured between the same agent's speaker and listener network, or interactive communication success when measured between a speaking agent and a different listener agent:

language	properties	possible utterances
100s+0m	100% SOV; 0% marker	*Tom Jerry chase*
80s+100m	80/20% SOV/OSV 100% marker	*Tom Jerry mk chase* *Jerry mk Tom chase*

Table 1: Two example languages with varying order and marking proportions, and corresponding utterances for the meaning m={A: CHASE, a: TOM, p: JERRY}.

$$acc_{self}(m, \alpha_i) = acc(m, \mathcal{L}_{\alpha_i}(\mathcal{S}_{\alpha_i}(m))) \quad (3)$$

$$acc_{inter}(m, \alpha_i, \alpha_j) = acc(m, \mathcal{L}_{\alpha_j}(\mathcal{S}_{\alpha_i}(m))) \quad (4)$$

where $acc(m, \hat{m})$ is 1 iff the entire meaning is matched. Interactive success is not symmetric.

Production preferences Besides accuracy, our main goal is to observe *how* the properties of a given language evolve throughout communication. This is done by recording the proportion of markers and different orders in a set of utterances generated by an agent for a held-out meaning set, after filtering out utterances that are not recognized by the initial grammar. When the focus is on the trade-off, rather than on a specific word order, we measure *order entropy*. Production preferences can be aggregated over an individual agent, a group, or the entire population.

5 Replicating the Trade-off with Full-fledged Agents

Before moving to interactive communication, we validate the new NeLLCom-X framework through a replication of Lian et al. (2023)'s main findings. The simple speaker-listener communication setup of NeLLCom could be seen as a speaker-internal monitoring mechanism predicting the utterance understandability (Ferreira, 2019). Here, we compare NeLLCom results to those of NeLLCom-X full-fledged agents only engaging in self-play. We use SL to train two sets of agents on the exact same languages as Lian et al. (2023), respectively: 100s+67m for fixed-order and 50s+67m for flexible-order. Then, every agent performs 60 self_turn iterations causing its production preferences to drift.

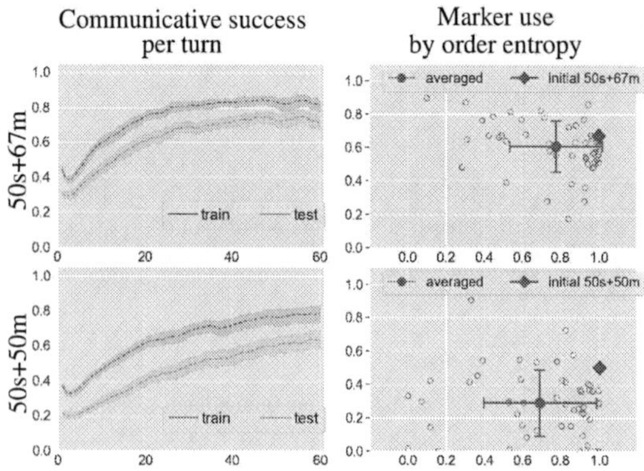

Figure 2: Two populations of 50 agents engaging in self-play (no interaction) after having learned two flexible-order, optional-marker languages: one with 67% the other with 50% marking. Left column: Average communication success across self-play turns. Right column: Production preferences: solid diamonds mark the initial language; each empty circle denotes a full-fledged agent at the end of self-play; solid circles are the average of all agents, with error bars showing standard deviation.

After SL, our agents have successfully learnt both languages but no regularization happens, as expected. By contrast, the results of self-play averaged over each 50-agent set indicate that both languages progressively lose markers. Crucially, the fixed-order language does so faster than the flexible one, where markers are often necessary for agent/patient disambiguation. In sum, self-play in NeLLCom-X results in very similar trends as the simple NeLLCom setup, confirming the emergence of a human-like order/marking trade-off (Fedzechkina et al., 2017). Detailed replication results are provided in Appendix B. Here, we report communication success during self-play and production preferences at the end of self-play for the flexible language (Figure 2, top row). Self-understanding increases through RL leading to a much more informative language, while production preferences reveal that this spans from an overall decrease in order entropy with marking proportion remaining almost the same on average (solid circle). While some agents approach the optimal points of fixed-order/no-marking (bottom-left corner) or flexible-order/full-marking (top-right), the large variability in production preferences suggests many agents settle on less optimized, redundant languages, as also found by Lian et al. (2023).

Initial marking proportion We reconsider here a language design choice of Lian et al. (2023) who, in turn, inherited it from the human study of Fedzechkina et al. (2017). It was recently found that human learners exposed to a fixed-order language with 75% marking tend to regularize by increasing marker use even though this would make the language less efficient (Tal et al., 2022). Similarly, the dominant proportion (67%) of marking utterances in our initial languages may push the agents to prefer marking even when it may be a redundant strategy. Hence, we propose that a more balanced distribution of 50% markers and 50/50% word order may be a better choice to reveal the intrinsic preferences of the learners, if there are any, without biasing them to regularize markers. Results in Figure 2 (bottom row) show that this language has overall lower communicative success, as expected given the higher amount of ambiguous sentences. However, success increases substantially during interaction while production preferences reveal a larger variability in solutions including those with more fixed order and less markers. We use this more neutral combination as the default language in all remaining experiments.

6 Interactive Communication Results

This section presents our main results: in Section 6.1 we focus on pairwise interaction and show how NeLLCom-X can be used to simulate communication between speakers of different languages, which was not possible in the original framework; in Section 6.2 we move to group communication and study the effect of group dynamics on communication success and production preferences. Training details for this section are given in Appendix C.

6.1 Speakers of Different Languages

We study a simple setup with two full-fledged agents interacting with each other in both ways $\alpha_{base} \leftrightarrow \alpha_{other}$. The first ($\alpha_b$ for *base*) is always trained on the neutral language 50s+50m, while the second (α_o for *other*) is trained on one of four languages with different properties. If interaction works, we expect (i) agent pairs to negotiate a mutually understandable language and (ii) α_b's language to drift in different directions according to its interlocutor. For production preferences, we are interested here in the specific word order of the evolving languages so we plot proportion of markers against *proportion of SOV* instead of order entropy.

The communication success plots in Figure 3 (left column) show a faster convergence and higher

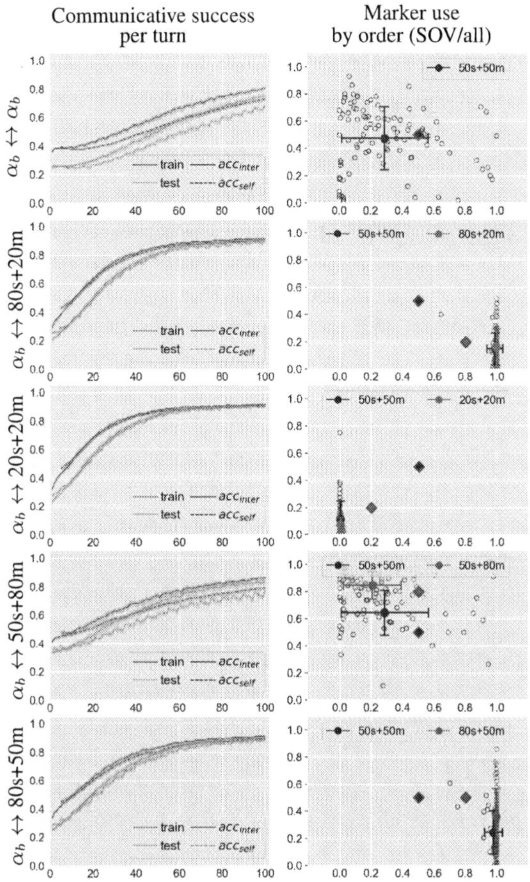

Figure 3: Interactive communication between different language speakers. The first agent is always trained on 50s+50m (α_b). Each experiment is repeated with 50 agent pairs.

final accuracy when α_o has a stronger order preference. As for production preferences (Figure 3, right column), in the control setting where two neutral agents interact with each other, most agents move towards either side of the plot, representing order regularization. A larger portion of agents regularize towards OSV rather than SOV, which was also observed by Lian et al. (2023) and might be due to OSV being the order where the disambiguating marker appears earlier. Marking decreases only slightly on average. The next two settings involve initial languages with few markers and different order preferences but equally low order entropy (20s+20m and 80s+20m). As shown by the highly symmetric trends, these pairs strongly converge by regularizing towards the dominant order of α_o and further reducing markers. The fourth setting involves a language where marking is widespread and informative due to high order entropy (50s+80m).

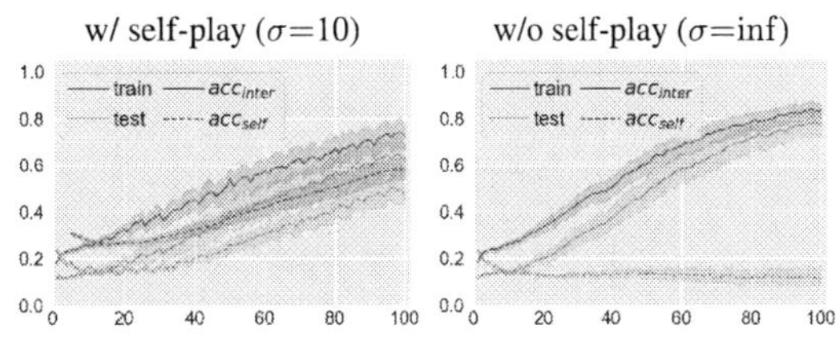

Figure 4: Impact of self-play during interaction in pairs of agents speaking 80s+20m and 20s+20m respectively. Each experiment is repeated with 20 agent pairs, and the average communication per turn is shown.

Here, α_b shows on average a similar order regularization as in the control setting $\alpha_b \leftrightarrow \alpha_b$, but with a marking increase instead of decrease. Finally, when involving a dominant-order language with no clear marking preference (80s+50m), agents strongly regularize the dominant order, with a majority of them reducing marker use.

Taken together, these results demonstrate that (i) pairs of different-language agents succeed in negotiating a mutually understandable language in most cases, and (ii) the evolution of an agent's language strongly depends on whom they interact with, thereby matching the expectations for a realistic simulation of interactive communication.

Impact of self-play during interactions As explained in Section 3.3, each agent performs a turn of self-play after completing $\sigma = 10$ turns of interactive communication, based on preliminary experiments. We compare this to a setup where no self-play is performed during interaction ($\sigma = \text{inf}$), in the case where two agents start from a state of poor mutual understanding due to limited marking and strongly diverging order preferences (80s+20m vs. 20s+20m). As shown in Figure 4, disabling self-play leads to extremely low self-understanding even though communication *between* the two agents is successful. To explain this result, we inspect the production preferences of individual agent pairs and find that many regularize their language in opposite directions (e.g. dominant SOV vs. dominant OSV, both with no markers), indicating a total decoupling of the speaking and listening ability. Thus, we confirm that embedding tying alone does not allow for a realistic interaction simulation, making self-play necessary in our framework.

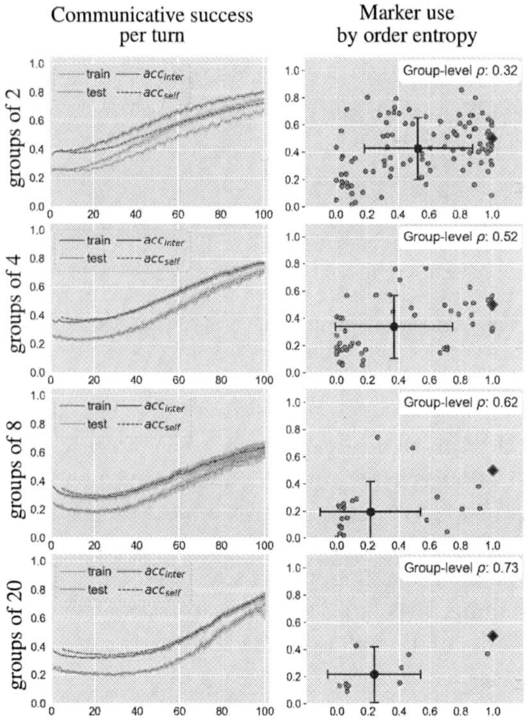

Figure 5: Interactive communication in groups of same-language speakers (50s+50m). Right column: Group-level production preferences (each point is a group) and Spearman's correlation ρ between marker use and order entropy.

6.2 Effect of Group Size

Here we move back to a setup where all agents are trained on the same neutral and unstable initial language (50s+50m), but this time they interact in groups of different sizes (2, 4, 8, 20) using the standard self-play frequency ($\sigma = 10$). To make results comparable, we ensure the *total* number of interactive turns per agent is the same ($\approx$200) in all setups, by setting *comm_round* to 100, 34, 15, and 6 respectively. A total of 200 agents are trained in each group size setting.[4]

Figure 5 (left column) shows similar learning curves for all group sizes, demonstrating that communication is successful even in larger groups. In all cases, interactive and self-communication test accuracy start low (25%), but agents collaborate and end up between 60% and 80% success at `inter_turn` = 100.

[4]100 runs of group of 2, 50 of 4, 25 of 8, and 10 of 20. See all group-specific training details in Appendix C. In this paper, we only consider fully connected communication graphs and fix the total amount of trained agents to enable comparison. We leave an exploration of other group communication factors, such as density and connectivity, to future work.

For production preferences, we plot proportion of marking by *order entropy* as we are again interested in order flexibility rather than the specific order chosen by the agents (Figure 5, right column). Here, each circle denotes the average production preferences of an entire group, as opposed to those of a single agent. When comparing results across different group sizes, we see that the variability observed in self-playing agents (Section 5) including less optimal and redundant strategies, gets smaller as group size increases. The average entropy in groups of 8 and 20 is also lower than in groups of 4 or 2. In the group setting, an agent's choice to use a marker does not only depend on its own order entropy but on that of the entire group. As a measure of the order/marking trade-off at group level, we therefore calculate Spearman's correlation (ρ) between order entropy and marker use, both computed over all (categorizable) utterances produced by all agents in a group. As shown in Figure 5, ρ steadily increases with group size from relatively weak (0.32) in pairs to strong (0.73) in groups of 20. This confirms that pairs, like self-playing agents, still often settle on redundant strategies, while larger groups develop more optimized languages in which stronger order consistency at the group level leads to a drop in marker use, confirming the emergence of the trade-off also at the group level.[5]

7 Discussion and conclusion

We introduced NeLLCom-X, a framework for simulating neural agent language learning and communication in groups, starting from pre-defined languages. Agents in this framework display the cognitively plausible property of interchangeability (Hockett, 1960), by which anything they can understand, they can say and vice versa, while also having the ability to align to other individuals. We replicated an earlier finding by Lian et al. (2023) and showed that a word-order/case-marking trade-off still appears with the adjusted full-fledged agent architecture. Subsequently, we simulated interactions between agents trained on different languages. We found that pairs quickly adapt their utterances towards a mutually understandable language and that the neutral language drifts in different directions depending on the preferences of the other

[5]Even when trained for much longer, the results of pairs remain similar, suggesting they indeed settle on less optimized solutions which is not overcome simply by more interactions (e.g. 200 rounds, $\rho = 0.33$). See Appendix D.

agent. Moreover, agents converge on a shared language faster, and reach higher accuracy in cases where one of the two agents has a stronger word order preference. We then assessed the effect of performing self-play during interactive communication and found it necessary to ensure our full-fledged agents continue to understand themselves, while also realistically adapting to other individuals. Lastly, we studied group dynamics and found that NeLLCom-X agents manage to establish a successful communication system even in larger groups (up to size 20). Moreover, we generally see a larger entropy reduction in the languages developed by larger groups as compared to the languages used by pairs of agents. This finding aligns with previous work on group-level emergent communication, where it was shown that groups developed less idiosyncratic languages than pairs (Tieleman et al., 2019) as well as with human experiments which demonstrated more systematic languages to emerge in larger groups (Raviv et al., 2019). In our simulations, pairs and smaller groups sometimes settle on less optimized and partly still redundant solutions, while large groups end up with more efficient communication systems.

In the future, NeLLCom-X can be used to study the influence of learning and group dynamics on many other language universals. We plan to keep refining the framework to allow studying different connectivities between the agents, multilingual populations and generational transmission of emerged languages to new agents.

Limitations

Although the use of miniature artificial languages in our work allows for easily interpretable results due to abstractions and simplifications that are hard to achieve with natural human languages, the languages used currently are very small. This may limit the possibility of drawing conclusions beyond proof-of-concept demonstrations. Future work should increase the size and complexity of the languages to see if results hold on a larger scale and compare to patterns found in real human languages, such as those reported by Levshina et al. (2023).

The meanings in our simulations are also strongly abstracted away from reality. While our design is well suited for an investigation of the word-order/case-marking trade-off, future simulations may need a less constrained meaning space, possibly using images to represent meanings.

All experiments conducted so far with NeLLCom-X use the same neural agent architecture (GRU), but we know that different architectures exhibit different inductive biases (Kuribayashi et al., 2024) or memory constraints and these factors may influence the findings. Different types of neural learners, however, can be easily plugged into NeLLCom-X.

Interaction between individuals in groups is not the only population factor that shapes language, but linguistic structure is shaped by both interaction and learning (Kirby et al., 2015). Especially when languages are learned and transmitted to subsequent generations repeatedly, even small inductive biases may have a large effect on emerging properties (Thompson et al., 2016). We therefore plan to augment NeLLCom-X with iterated learning so that new agents learn from the utterances of others and become teachers to agents in the next generation.

Finally, our agents are interacting in groups with multiple individuals, but they currently do not have any awareness of agent identities. A more realistic simulation should take into account that individuals know who they are interacting with, which becomes even more important when different network structures and connectivities will be explored.

Acknowledgements

Arianna Bisazza acknowledges the support of the Dutch Research Council (NWO) within the InDeep project (NWA.1292.19.399) and the Talent Programme (VI.Vidi.221C.009).

References

Clay Beckner, Nick C Ellis, Richard Blythe, John Holland, Joan Bybee, Jinyun Ke, Morten H Christiansen, Diane Larsen-Freeman, William Croft, and Tom Schoenemann. 2009. Language is a complex adaptive system: Position paper. *Language Learning*, 59:1–26.

Arianna Bisazza, Ahmet Üstün, and Stephan Sportel. 2021. On the difficulty of translating free-order case-marking languages. *Transactions of the Association for Computational Linguistics*, 9:1233–1248.

Rahma Chaabouni, Eugene Kharitonov, Diane Bouchacourt, Emmanuel Dupoux, and Marco Baroni. 2020. Compositionality and generalization in emergent languages. In *Proceedings of the 58th Annual Meeting of the Association for Computational Linguistics*, pages 4427–4442.

Rahma Chaabouni, Eugene Kharitonov, Alessandro Lazaric, Emmanuel Dupoux, and Marco Baroni. 2019. Word-order biases in deep-agent emergent communication. In *Proceedings of the 57th Annual Meeting of the Association for Computational Linguistics*, pages 5166–5175, Florence, Italy. Association for Computational Linguistics.

Rahma Chaabouni, Florian Strub, Florent Altché, Eugene Tarassov, Corentin Tallec, Elnaz Davoodi, Kory Wallace Mathewson, Olivier Tieleman, Angeliki Lazaridou, and Bilal Piot. 2022. Emergent communication at scale. In *International Conference on Learning Representations*.

Peer Christensen, Riccardo Fusaroli, and Kristian Tylén. 2016. Environmental constraints shaping constituent order in emerging communication systems: Structural iconicity, interactive alignment and conventionalization. *Cognition*, 146:67–80.

Morten H Christiansen and Nick Chater. 2008. Language as shaped by the brain. *Behavioral and brain sciences*, 31(5):489–509.

Junyoung Chung, Çaglar Gülçehre, KyungHyun Cho, and Yoshua Bengio. 2014. Empirical evaluation of gated recurrent neural networks on sequence modeling. *CoRR*, abs/1412.3555.

Henry Conklin and Kenny Smith. 2022. Compositionality with variation reliably emerges in neural networks. In *The Eleventh International Conference on Learning Representations*.

Jennifer Culbertson, Paul Smolensky, and Géraldine Legendre. 2012. Learning biases predict a word order universal. *Cognition*, 122(3):306–329.

Maryia Fedzechkina, Becky Chu, and T Florian Jaeger. 2018. Human information processing shapes language change. *Psychological science*, 29(1):72–82.

Maryia Fedzechkina, Elissa L. Newport, and T. Florian Jaeger. 2017. Balancing effort and information transmission during language acquisition: Evidence from word order and case marking. *Cognitive Science*, 41(2):416–446.

Victor S. Ferreira. 2019. A mechanistic framework for explaining audience design in language production. *Annual Review of Psychology*, 70(1):29–51. PMID: 30231000.

W Tecumseh Fitch. 2007. An invisible hand. *Nature*, 449(7163):665–667.

Riccardo Fusaroli and Kristian Tylén. 2012. Carving language for social coordination: A dynamical approach. *Interaction studies*, 13(1):103–124.

Lukas Galke, Yoav Ram, and Limor Raviv. 2022. Emergent communication for understanding human language evolution: What's missing? In *Emergent Communication Workshop at ICLR 2022*.

Lukas Galke and Limor Raviv. 2024. Emergent communication and learning pressures in language models: a language evolution perspective. *arXiv preprint arXiv:2403.14427*.

Simon Garrod, Nicolas Fay, John Lee, Jon Oberlander, and Tracy MacLeod. 2007. Foundations of representation: where might graphical symbol systems come from? *Cognitive science*, 31(6):961–987.

Laura Harding Graesser, Kyunghyun Cho, and Douwe Kiela. 2019. Emergent linguistic phenomena in multi-agent communication games. In *Proceedings of the 2019 Conference on Empirical Methods in Natural Language Processing and the 9th International Joint Conference on Natural Language Processing (EMNLP-IJCNLP)*, pages 3700–3710, Hong Kong, China. Association for Computational Linguistics.

Serhii Havrylov and Ivan Titov. 2017. Emergence of language with multi-agent games: Learning to communicate with sequences of symbols. In *Proceedings of the 31st International Conference on Neural Information Processing Systems*, NIPS'17, page 2146–2156. Curran Associates Inc.

Charles F Hockett. 1960. The origin of speech. *Scientific American*, 203(3):88–97.

Mark Hopkins. 2022. Towards more natural artificial languages. In *Proceedings of the 26th Conference on Computational Natural Language Learning (CoNLL)*, pages 85–94, Abu Dhabi, United Arab Emirates (Hybrid). Association for Computational Linguistics.

Julie Kallini, Isabel Papadimitriou, Richard Futrell, Kyle Mahowald, and Christopher Potts. 2024. Mission: Impossible language models. *arXiv preprint arXiv:2401.06416*.

Andres Karjus, Richard A Blythe, Simon Kirby, Tianyu Wang, and Kenny Smith. 2021. Conceptual similarity and communicative need shape colexification: An experimental study. *Cognitive Science*, 45(9):e13035.

Eugene Kharitonov, Rahma Chaabouni, Diane Bouchacourt, and Marco Baroni. 2019. EGG: a toolkit for research on emergence of lanGuage in games. In *Proceedings of the 2019 Conference on Empirical Methods in Natural Language Processing and the 9th International Joint Conference on Natural Language Processing (EMNLP-IJCNLP): System Demonstrations*, pages 55–60, Hong Kong, China. Association for Computational Linguistics.

Jooyeon Kim and Alice Oh. 2021. Emergent communication under varying sizes and connectivities. *Advances in Neural Information Processing Systems*, 34:17579–17591.

Simon Kirby, Tom Griffiths, and Kenny Smith. 2014. Iterated learning and the evolution of language. *Current opinion in neurobiology*, 28:108–114.

Simon Kirby, Monica Tamariz, Hannah Cornish, and Kenny Smith. 2015. Compression and communication in the cultural evolution of linguistic structure. *Cognition*, 141:87–102.

Satwik Kottur, José Moura, Stefan Lee, and Dhruv Batra. 2017. Natural language does not emerge 'naturally'in multi-agent dialog. In *Proceedings of the 2017 Conference on Empirical Methods in Natural Language Processing*, pages 2962–2967.

Tatsuki Kuribayashi, Ryo Ueda, Ryo Yoshida, Yohei Oseki, Ted Briscoe, and Timothy Baldwin. 2024. Emergent word order universals from cognitively-motivated language models. *arXiv preprint arXiv:2402.12363*.

Angeliki Lazaridou and Marco Baroni. 2020. Emergent multi-agent communication in the deep learning era. *arXiv preprint arXiv:2006.02419v2*.

Angeliki Lazaridou, Karl Moritz Hermann, Karl Tuyls, and Stephen Clark. 2018. Emergence of linguistic communication from referential games with symbolic and pixel input. In *International Conference on Learning Representations*.

Angeliki Lazaridou, Alexander Peysakhovich, and Marco Baroni. 2017. Multi-agent cooperation and the emergence of (natural) language. In *International Conference on Learning Representations*.

Angeliki Lazaridou, Anna Potapenko, and Olivier Tieleman. 2020. Multi-agent communication meets natural language: Synergies between functional and structural language learning. In *Proceedings of the 58th Annual Meeting of the Association for Computational Linguistics*, pages 7663–7674, Online. Association for Computational Linguistics.

Natalia Levshina, Savithry Namboodiripad, Marc Allassonnière-Tang, Mathew Kramer, Luigi Talamo, Annemarie Verkerk, Sasha Wilmoth, Gabriela Garrido Rodriguez, Timothy Michael Gupton, Evan Kidd, et al. 2023. Why we need a gradient approach to word order. *Linguistics*, 61(4):825–883.

Fushan Li and Michael Bowling. 2019. Ease-of-teaching and language structure from emergent communication. In *Advances in Neural Information Processing Systems*, volume 32. Curran Associates, Inc.

Yuchen Lian, Arianna Bisazza, and Tessa Verhoef. 2021. The effect of efficient messaging and input variability on neural-agent iterated language learning. In *Proceedings of the 2021 Conference on Empirical Methods in Natural Language Processing*, pages 10121–10129.

Yuchen Lian, Arianna Bisazza, and Tessa Verhoef. 2023. Communication drives the emergence of language universals in neural agents: Evidence from the word-order/case-marking trade-off. *Transactions of the Association for Computational Linguistics*, 11:1033–1047.

Ryan Lowe, Abhinav Gupta, Jakob Foerster, Douwe Kiela, and Joelle Pineau. 2020. On the interaction between supervision and self-play in emergent communication. In *International Conference on Learning Representations*.

Gary Lupyan and Morten H Christiansen. 2002. Case, word order, and language learnability: Insights from connectionist modeling. In *Proceedings of the Twenty-Fourth Annual Conference of the Cognitive Science Society*, pages 596–601. Routledge.

Gary Lupyan and Rick Dale. 2010. Language structure is partly determined by social structure. *PloS one*, 5(1):e8559.

Paul Michel, Mathieu Rita, Kory Wallace Mathewson, Olivier Tieleman, and Angeliki Lazaridou. 2023. Revisiting populations in multi-agent communication. In *The Eleventh International Conference on Learning Representations*.

Tomas Mikolov, Armand Joulin, and Marco Baroni. 2018. A roadmap towards machine intelligence. In *Computational Linguistics and Intelligent Text Processing: 17th International Conference*, pages 29–61. Springer.

Yasamin Motamedi, Lucie Wolters, Danielle Naegeli, Simon Kirby, and Marieke Schouwstra. 2022. From improvisation to learning: How naturalness and systematicity shape language evolution. *Cognition*, 228:105206.

Savithry Namboodiripad, Daniel Lenzen, Ryan Lepic, and Tessa Verhoef. 2016. Measuring conventionalization in the manual modality. *Journal of Language Evolution*, 1(2):109–118.

Ofir Press and Lior Wolf. 2017. Using the output embedding to improve language models. In *Proceedings of the 15th Conference of the European Chapter of the Association for Computational Linguistics: Volume 2, Short Papers*, pages 157–163, Valencia, Spain. Association for Computational Linguistics.

Limor Raviv, Antje Meyer, and Shiri Lev-Ari. 2019. Larger communities create more systematic languages. *Proceedings of the Royal Society B*, 286(1907):20191262.

Mathieu Rita, Rahma Chaabouni, and Emmanuel Dupoux. 2020. "lazimpa": Lazy and impatient neural agents learn to communicate efficiently. In *Proceedings of the 24th Conference on Computational Natural Language Learning*, pages 335–343.

Mathieu Rita, Corentin Tallec, Paul Michel, Jean-Bastien Grill, Olivier Pietquin, Emmanuel Dupoux, and Florian Strub. 2022. Emergent communication: Generalization and overfitting in lewis games. In *Advances in Neural Information Processing Systems*.

Gareth Roberts and Bruno Galantucci. 2012. The emergence of duality of patterning: Insights from the laboratory. *Language and cognition*, 4(4):297–318.

Carmen Saldana, Yohei Oseki, and Jennifer Culbertson. 2021a. Cross-linguistic patterns of morpheme order reflect cognitive biases: An experimental study of case and number morphology. *Journal of Memory and Language*, 118:104204.

Carmen Saldana, Kenny Smith, Simon Kirby, and Jennifer Culbertson. 2021b. Is regularization uniform across linguistic levels? comparing learning and production of unconditioned probabilistic variation in morphology and word order. *Language Learning and Development*, 17(2):158–188.

Luc Steels. 1997. The synthetic modeling of language origins. *Evolution of communication*, 1(1):1–34.

Luc Steels. 2000. Language as a complex adaptive system. In *International Conference on Parallel Problem Solving from Nature*, pages 17–26. Springer.

Valentin Taillandier, Dieuwke Hupkes, Benoît Sagot, Emmanuel Dupoux, and Paul Michel. 2023. Neural agents struggle to take turns in bidirectional emergent communication. In *The Eleventh International Conference on Learning Representations*.

Shira Tal, Kenny Smith, Jennifer Culbertson, Eitan Grossman, and Inbal Arnon. 2022. The impact of information structure on the emergence of differential object marking: an experimental study. *Cognitive Science*, 46(3):e13119.

Mónica Tamariz, Seán G Roberts, J Isidro Martínez, and Julio Santiago. 2018. The interactive origin of iconicity. *Cognitive Science*, 42(1):334–349.

Bill Thompson, Simon Kirby, and Kenny Smith. 2016. Culture shapes the evolution of cognition. *Proceedings of the National Academy of Sciences*, 113(16):4530–4535.

Olivier Tieleman, Angeliki Lazaridou, Shibl Mourad, Charles Blundell, and Doina Precup. 2019. Shaping representations through communication: community size effect in artificial learning systems. *arXiv preprint arXiv:1912.06208*.

Tessa Verhoef. 2012. The origins of duality of patterning in artificial whistled languages. *Language and cognition*, 4(4):357–380.

Tessa Verhoef, Simon Kirby, and Bart De Boer. 2014. Emergence of combinatorial structure and economy through iterated learning with continuous acoustic signals. *Journal of Phonetics*, 43:57–68.

Tessa Verhoef, Simon Kirby, and Bart De Boer. 2016. Iconicity and the emergence of combinatorial structure in language. *Cognitive science*, 40(8):1969–1994.

Tessa Verhoef, Seán G Roberts, and Mark Dingemanse. 2015. Emergence of systematic iconicity: Transmission, interaction and analogy. In *Proceedings of the 37th Annual Meeting of the Cognitive Science Society (CogSci 2015)*, pages 2481–2486. Cognitive Science Society.

Tessa Verhoef, Esther Walker, and Tyler Marghetis. 2022. Interaction dynamics affect the emergence of compositional structure in cultural transmission of space-time mappings. In *Proceedings of the 44th Annual Meeting of the Cognitive Science Society*, pages 2133–2139. Cognitive Science Society.

Dingquan Wang and Jason Eisner. 2016. The galactic dependencies treebanks: Getting more data by synthesizing new languages. *Transactions of the Association for Computational Linguistics*, 4:491–505.

Jennifer C. White and Ryan Cotterell. 2021. Examining the inductive bias of neural language models with artificial languages. In *Proceedings of the 59th Annual Meeting of the Association for Computational Linguistics and the 11th International Joint Conference on Natural Language Processing (Volume 1: Long Papers)*, pages 454–463, Online. Association for Computational Linguistics.

Ronald J Williams. 1992. Simple statistical gradient-following algorithms for connectionist reinforcement learning. *Machine learning*, 8(3):229–256.

Alison Wray and George W Grace. 2007. The consequences of talking to strangers: Evolutionary corollaries of socio-cultural influences on linguistic form. *Lingua*, 117(3):543–578.

A More Details about NeLLCom

We list here additional details on the original NeLL-Com framework (Lian et al., 2023) that also apply to our extended NeLLCom-X framework.

Speaker and Listener Architectures Both speaking and listening networks have a single 16-dim GRU layer. The shared meaning embeddings have 8-dim and the shared word embeddings have 16-dim. The maximum utterance length for the speaking decoder is set to 10 words.

Supervised Language Learning During supervised learning, the speaker learns the mapping from the meaning inputs to utterances and vice versa for the listener. Dataset D is composed of meaning-utterance pairs (m, u) where u is the gold-standard generated for m by a predefined grammar. Given training sample (m, u), speaker's parameters $\theta_{\mathcal{S}}$ and listener's parameters $\theta_{\mathcal{L}}$ are optimized by minimizing the cross-entropy loss of the predicted words and the predicted meaning tuples respectively:

$$Loss^{sup}_{(\mathcal{S})} = -\sum_{i=1}^{I} \log p_{\theta_{\mathcal{S}}}(w^i | w^{<i}, m) \quad (5)$$

$$Loss^{sup}_{(\mathcal{L})} = -(\log p_{\theta_{\mathcal{L}}}(A|u) + \log p_{\theta_{\mathcal{L}}}(a|u) + \log p_{\theta_{\mathcal{L}}}(p|u)) \quad (6)$$

where $w_i...w_I$ are the words composing utterance u, whereas A, a, p are respectively the action, agent and patient of meaning m.

Communicative Reward Optimization Communication is implemented by a meaning reconstruction game following common practice in the artificial agent communication literature (e.g. Steels, 1997; Lazaridou et al., 2018). The speaker generates an utterance $\hat{u}$ given a meaning m, and the listener needs to reconstruct meaning m given $\hat{u}$. The policy-based algorithm REINFORCE (Williams, 1992) is used to maximize a shared reward $r^{\mathcal{L}}(m, \hat{u})$, defined as the log likelihood of m given $\hat{u}$ according to the listener's model:

$$r^{\mathcal{L}}(m, \hat{u}) = \sum_{e \in m=\{A,a,p\}} \log p_{\theta_{\mathcal{L}}}(e|\hat{u}) \quad (7)$$

Thus, the communication loss becomes:

$$Loss^{comm}_{(\mathcal{S},\mathcal{L})} = -r^{\mathcal{L}}(m, \hat{u}) * \sum_{i=1}^{I} \log p_{\theta_{\mathcal{S}}}(w^i | w^{<i}, m) \quad (8)$$

B Replicating NeLLCom Results with NeLLCom-X Full-fledged Agents

B.1 Training details for the replication

For this replication (discussed in Section 5), we make the training configuration as consistent as possible with Lian et al. (2023). Specifically, we split the data into 66.7/20% training/testing. The testing proportion is different from the 33.3% used in NeLLCom as we would like to match the test set size we use for interactive communication in this work. All entities and actions are required to appear at least once in the training set. The default Adam optimizer is applied with a learning rate of 0.01. Both SL and self_turn iterate 60 times.[6] Each replication setup is repeated with 50 random seeds.

B.2 Results

Fixed-order self-communication Starting from the initial marker proportion (66.7%), fixed-order language learners start to drop the marker (50% at round 60) during self-communication while maintaining high understandability (95%) (Figure 6 (a1) and (a4)). This aligns with the results of Lian et al. (2023).

Flexible-order self-communication The self-communication accuracy in the flexible-order language (Figure 6 (c1)) starts from a relatively low success rate as expected, but increases with more communication rounds. In particular, agents exceed the communication success they had achieved at the end of SL on new meanings and finally reach a much higher accuracy on new meanings at the end of self-communication (around 75%) comparing to the communication success they had achieved at the end of SL.

The average ordering and marking proportions also show that flexible-order language self-communication results in a very similar pattern as was found by Lian et al. (2023): (i) The average word order production (Figure 6 (c2)) shows a strong preference for OSV, (ii) Although the overall marking system ends with a similar marker proportion as the initial condition (Figure 6 (c4)), i.e., the proportion of with-marker utterances is twice the proportion of no-marker utterances, we can see a clear shift to conditional marking (Figure 6 (c3)) with an asymmetric use of markers: at round 60,

[6] As the 66.7% trainset results in 480 samples, which equals 15 batches of 32 samples per turn. This is slightly different than 10 batches per turn during interactive communication.

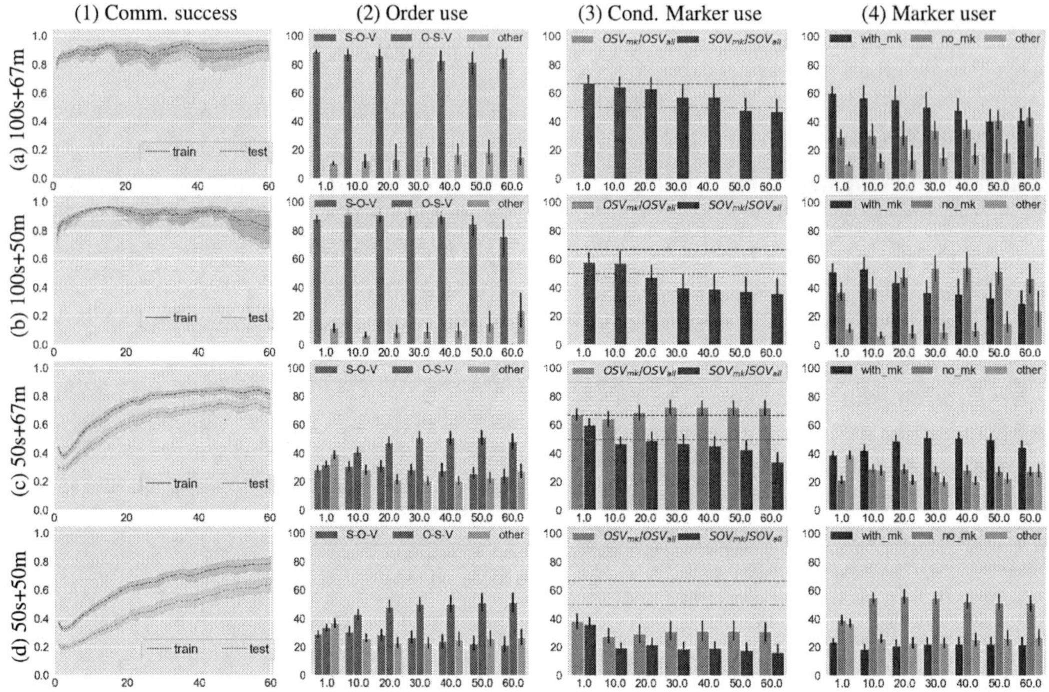

Figure 6: Replicating the results from Lian et al. (2023) with NeLLCom-X full-fledged self-communicating agents with fixed-order (a) and flexible order (c) languages. Comparing the original results with a new, more neutral, initial languages with 50% markers in (b) and (d).

the marker proportion on utterances with OSV order (70%) remains similar to the initial proportion (66.7%), while the proportion of markers use with SOV drops to 35%. This order preference and asymmetric marking system align with the flexible-order language results of Lian et al. (2023).

Figure 7d shows the production preferences of individual agents where the distributions of utterance type usage diverge over time, similar to the independent speaker and listener communication results in Lian et al. (2023).

Uncertainty vs. Effort Lian et al. (2023) found that agents balanced uncertainty and effort in a similar way to human participants in an artificial language learning task (Fedzechkina et al., 2017). To evaluate whether a similar uncertainty-effort trade-off is found with our full-fledged agents, we apply the same measurement on both fixed and flexible languages in Figure 7a. Besides the results from our new framework, we also reproduce the independent listener-speaker communication result from Lian et al. (2023) (Figure 7b) and human results from Fedzechkina et al. (2017) (Figure 7c) for comparison.

For the fixed-order language, the obvious drop of the averaged effort fits both Lian et al. (2023) and Fedzechkina et al. (2017). Among 50 agents, only one agent significantly increases the use of markers and ends at around 3.8 words per utterance. Others reduce the marker, and two agents even end with 3.0 and 3.05 words per utterance which means almost no markers are produced. For the flexible-order language, uncertainty is reduced slightly less strongly as in the human results, which was also the case in (Lian et al., 2023).

50% marking in initial language As described in Section 5, the initial proportion of marker use of 67%, which was used in Lian et al. (2023) and inherited from Fedzechkina et al. (2017), may create a bias for the agents to regularize towards more marker use, settling on more redundant languages. We therefore switched to the more neutral value of 50% markers in the initial language. In Figure 6, the self-communication results of this new setting can be directly compared to the original set-up. As expected, markers are dropped more rapidly in the fixed-order 50% marker language than in the 67% marker language (Figure 6 (a3) versus Figure 6 (b3)). In the flexible-order languages, agents trained on the 67% marker language mostly kept

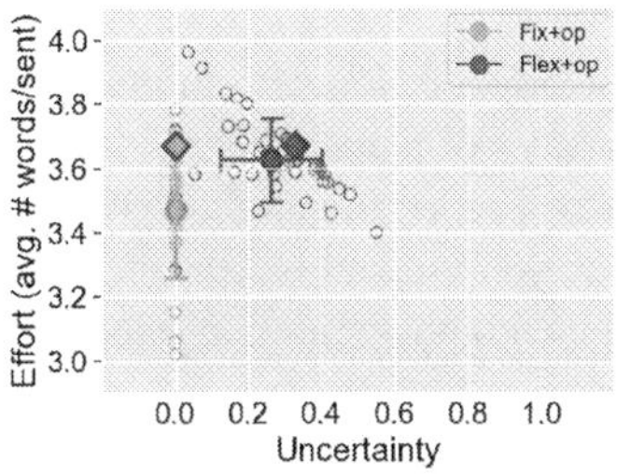

(a) NeLLCom-X self-communication

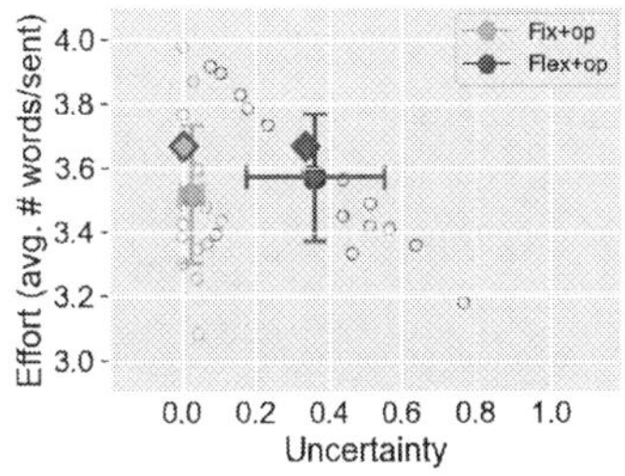

(b) Lian et al. (2023) communication

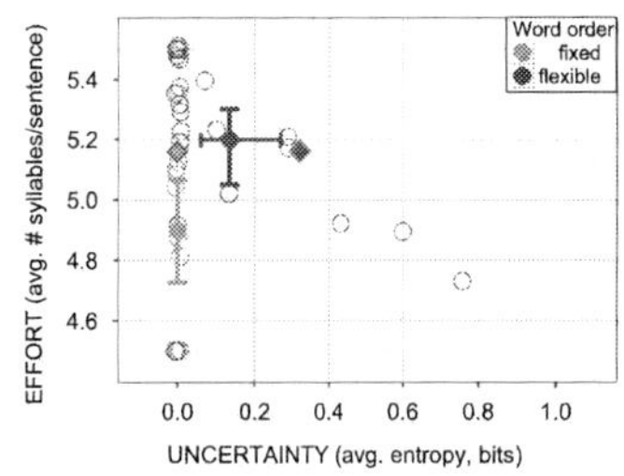

(c) Humans (Fedzechkina et al., 2017)

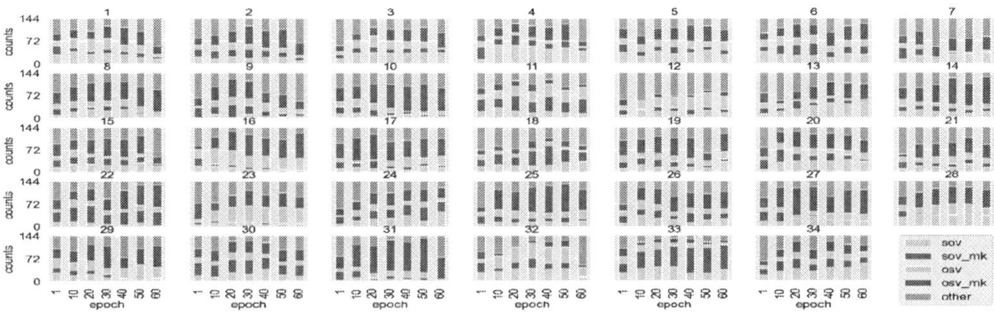

(d) flex-mk67: Individual production patterns during self-communication.

Figure 7: Replicating the results of Lian et al. (2023): Supervised learning followed by Self-communication with NeLLCom-X full-fledged agents. All results are averaged over 50 random seeds.

group size	# comm_edges	# comm_rounds	# repeated groups
2	$2 = 2 * (2 - 1)$	$100 = \lceil 100/(2 - 1) \rceil$	$100 = 200/2$
4	$12 = 4 * (4 - 1)$	$34 = \lceil 100/(4 - 1) \rceil$	$50 = 200/4$
8	$56 = 8 * (8 - 1)$	$15 = \lceil 100/(8 - 1) \rceil$	$25 = 200/8$
20	$380 = 20 * (20 - 1)$	$6 = \lceil 100/(20 - 1) \rceil$	$10 = 200/20$

Table 2: Number of communication edges, number of rounds, and number of repeated groups for each group-size setting. Theaw settings were selected to ensure a fair comparison (i.e. similar amount of computation) across different group sizes.

using the marker, even though they also developed a clear preference for one word order, resulting in redundant strategies. With 50% markers in the initial language, however, agents drop the marker when they develop a word order preference despite being trained on a flexible word order language (Figure 6 (c3) versus Figure 6 (d3)).

C Training Details for Interactive Communication Experiments

We explain here the detailed setup for the main experiments discussed in Section 6.1 and Section 6.2. This setup was determined based on preliminary experiments to yield optimal results in terms of learning accuracy (during SL) and communication success (during RL).

Data splits We first split the data into 80/20% training/test. The test split is used thoughout the whole training. We resample 66.7% meanings out of the first train set (resulting in 480 meaning-utterance pairs) for the SL training phase. All entities and actions are required to appear at least once in the training set.

Then, for each communication turn, 50% meanings are sampled from the first train set (resulting in 320 meanings) and used as the training samples for this RL turn. Because interactive communication is always preceded by SL, agents have already learnt the mapping between words and entities and actions in the meaning space. Thus we do not enforce the all-seen-entities/actions rule in RL sampling.

Communication turns and rounds During interactive communication, the RL learning rate is set to

0.005. For each communication turn, 1 epoch is applied corresponding to 10 batches of 32 meanings. We fix the total number of inter_turn per agent to (approximately) 200 (both speaking and listening are considered). The total round is then computed as:

$$comm\_rounds = \left\lceil \frac{200 * group\_size}{2 * |commu\_edges|} \right\rceil,$$

or to simplify the equation in fully connected communication graphs:

$$comm\_rounds = \left\lceil \frac{100}{group\_size - 1} \right\rceil.$$

For a group of 2, a communication round includes 2 communication edges to be sampled: $\mathcal{G}_{g2} = \{\alpha_0 \rightarrow \alpha_1, \alpha_1 \rightarrow \alpha_0\}$. For a group of 4, a communication round includes $12 = 4 \times (4-1)$ communication edges $\mathcal{G}_{g4} = \{A_0 \rightarrow A_1, A_0 \rightarrow A_2, A_0 \rightarrow A_3, A_1 \rightarrow A_0, A_1 \rightarrow A_2, A_1 \rightarrow A_3, A_2 \rightarrow A_0, A_2 \rightarrow A_1, A_2 \rightarrow A_3, A_3 \rightarrow A_0, A_3 \rightarrow A_1, A_3 \rightarrow A_2\}$. Similarly, $|\mathcal{G}_{g8}| = 8 \times (8-1) = 56$ and $|\mathcal{G}_{g20}| = 20 \times (20-1) = 380$. As for self-play, each agent performs 200/σ self-play turns in total during interaction, that is 200/10=20 in the standard case where $\sigma = 10$.

Number of random seeds In Section 6.1 we repeat each language combination experiment with 50 pairs of agents (i.e. 100 random seeds). In Section 6.2, we set the total number of trained agents to 200 in each setup, (i.e. number of groups = $200/group\_size$). The details of rounds and repeated groups are listed in Table 2.

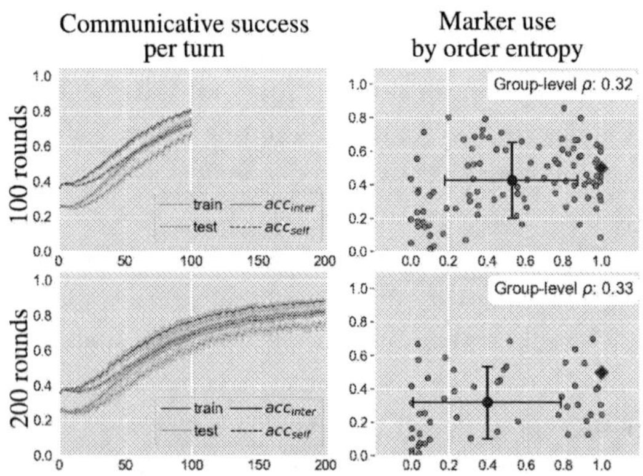

Figure 8: Interactive communication in pairs of same-language speakers (50s+50m): Production preferences (right column) do not change much when training for 200 rounds (bottom row) instead of 100 (top).

D Additional Group Experimennts

Figure 8 shows the effect of longer training on the production preferences of pairs of same-language speakers (50s+50m). Production preferences (right column) do not change much after 100 additional turns (bottom row), and the correlation ρ increases only marginally from 0.32 to 0.33.

A Novel Instruction Tuning Method for Vietnamese Mathematical Reasoning using Trainable Open-Source Large Language Models

Quang-Vinh Nguyen[1†], Thanh-Do Nguyen[1†], Van-Vinh Nguyen[2], Khac-Hoai Nam Bui[1*]
[1]Viettel AI, Viettel Group, Vietnam
[2]Vietnam National University of Hanoi, Hanoi, Vietnam
{vinhnq29, dont15}@viettel.com.vn , vinhvn@vnu.edu.vn, nambkh@viettel.com.vn

Abstract

This study introduces **Si**mple **R**easoning with **C**ode (**SiRC**), a novel instruction fine-tuning method for solving mathematical reasoning problems, particularly designed for Vietnamese, which is considered a low-resource language. Specifically, solving mathematical problems requires strategic and logical reasoning, which remains challenging in this research area. This paper presents a simple yet effective instruction fine-tuning method for mathematical reasoning. Unlike previous approaches, our proposed method effectively combines chain-of-thought reasoning with code generation without requiring a sophisticated inference procedure. Furthermore, we focus on exploiting small open-source large language models (LLMs) for the Vietnamese language. In this regard, we first introduce a trainable Vietnamese mathematical reasoning dataset, which is named `ViMath-InstructCode`. The proposed dataset is then used for fine-tuning open-source LLMs (e.g., less than 10 billion parameters). Experiments conducted on our custom `ViMath-Bench` dataset, the largest benchmarking dataset focusing on Vietnamese mathematical problems, indicate the promising results of our proposed method. Our source code and dataset are available for further exploitation[1].

1 Introduction

Large language models (LLMs), including closed sources (e.g., GPT series (OpenAI, 2023)) and open sources (e.g., Llama series (Touvron et al., 2023)) have become fundamental in advancing natural language processing (NLP). These models achieve remarkable language comprehension and generation abilities, which advances many applications in text generation, code assistance, and mathematical reasoning. Notably, leading proprietary LLMs like GPT-4 and Claude excel in mathematical tasks, as evidenced by their top rankings on benchmarks such as GSM8K and MATH. However, smaller open-source models (fewer than 10 billion parameters) significantly lag in performance. It is challenging for open source to achieve similar capabilities due to the nature of mathematical problem-solving, which requires precise multiple reasoning steps, symbolic manipulation, and complex computation (Ahn et al., 2024).

Technically, a potential solution is to special-

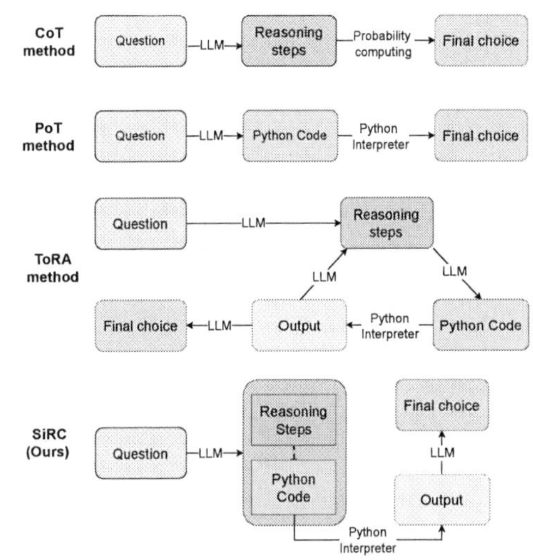

Figure 1: Comparative analysis of previous works with our approach for mathematical reasoning task using LLM with finetune instruction: Traditional method using reasoning step (CoT method); PoT uses Codex to generate text to programming language statements; ToRA employing multiple LLM calls within an LLM agent setting; Our proposed method uses LLM to generate both reasoning step and code generation within a single call LLM.

[1]https://github.com/quangvinh2110/vietnamese-math-reasoning
† Equal contribution
* Corresponding author

Proceedings of the 28th Conference on Computational Natural Language Learning, pages 259–268
November 15-16, 2024 ©2024 Association for Computational Linguistics

ize general-purpose LLMs in mathematics via supervised fine-tuning by distilling the knowledge from larger teacher models into smaller student models (Fu et al., 2023; Liang et al., 2023). An early approach uses chain-of-thought (CoT) explanations of existing data or extra CoT-style data generated by the larger models to train the smaller student model (Liu et al., 2023). Sequentially, (Chen et al., 2022a) proposes Program of Thoughts (PoT), which uses Codex (Chen et al., 2021) to generate text-to-programming language statements to find the answer. A recent approach uses the emerging LLM agent concept (Xi et al., 2023) to combine the two aforementioned approaches to improve the performance of mathematical reasoning (Gou et al., 2023a).

Despite various attempts to narrow the gap between closed-source and open-source models, the most cost-effective method for solving mathematical problems remains unresolved. Naively applying strategies like using chain-of-thought (CoT) or code generation to solve problems has not produced optimal results. Furthermore, employing multiple LLM calls within an agent setting (Gou et al., 2023a) incurs higher costs. Additionally, research on solving mathematical problems in Vietnamese, a low-resource language, is still nascent due to a lack of studies in this area.

In this regard, this study proposes **SiRC**, a simple effective instruction finetuning approach by combining chain-of-thought reasoning with code generation. Conceptual comparisons among **SiRC** and other previous approaches in this research field are illustrated in Figure 1. Generally, our main contributions in this study are threefold as follows:

- We propose **SiRC** framework, a simple and novel approach for solving elementary-level mathematical problems using a mixture of chain-of-thought reasoning and code generation (Figure 1). Empirical studies have demonstrated that this approach is effective for Vietnamese mathematical problems at this level and outperforms the naive implementation of CoT and code transferring.

- We present the first large-scale Vietnamese elementary mathematical dataset of 8k samples collected from various trusted sources, which we called **`ViMath-Bench`**. Furthermore, we augment this dataset using strong teacher models (`Llama3-70B-Instruct`[2] and `Qwen2-72B-Instruct`[3]), resulting in **`ViMath-InstructCode`** dataset consisting of 14k training samples. We also explored other synthetic data construction approaches. To the best of our knowledge, this is the first comprehensive study of Vietnamese mathematical reasoning.

- We release a series of models finetuned with **`ViMath-InstructCode`** dataset, which yield superior performance on **`ViMath-Bench`** test set. We hope that these models will establish a solid baseline for future research in mathematical reasoning in Vietnamese.

2 Literature Review

Human-annotated Math Datasets: Solving math word problems using Large Language Models (LLMs) has attracted extensive research efforts to create diverse datasets that enhance the model's mathematical reasoning capabilities, particularly in the English language. While early large-scale datasets like Dolphin18K (Huang et al., 2016) provided a foundation, they lacked detailed information on deriving the final answer, limiting their usefulness in teaching mathematical reasoning to models. Similarly, the AQuA-RAT dataset (Ling et al., 2017) has quality issues, including over-templatization and incorrect solutions. More recent math datasets have been designed with a focus on including detailed explanations and a diverse range of natural language expressions to provide more useful signals during model training. Notable examples are MathQA (Amini et al., 2019), GSM8K (Cobbe et al., 2021), and MATH (Hendrycks et al., 2021), which have improved the quality of the data by including questions requiring multiple solving steps as well as providing correct solutions. However, the language barrier presents a challenge, as these datasets are primarily in English, making them less directly beneficial for low-resource language research. Especially in Vietnamese, as far as we know, there has not been any large-scale dataset dedicated to math word problems.

Synthetic Data Construction: Some LLMs exhibit advanced mathematical reasoning and

[2]`https://huggingface.co/meta-llama/Meta-Llama-3-70B-Instruct`

[3]`https://huggingface.co/Qwen/Qwen2-72B-Instruct`

tool use abilities, making the idea of distilling knowledge from these models to student model highly attractive. `nvidia/OpenMathInstruct-1`[4] extracts problems from GSM8K and MATH training subsets and synthetically generate solutions by using `Mixtral 8x7b`[5] model to use a mix of text reasoning and code blocks executed by Python interpreter. `Tiger-Lab/MathInstruct`[6] compiles a list of high-quality and diverse math instruction-tuning datasets augmented by GPT-4. Several other approaches use capable LLMs to augment existing math datasets, such as evolving the difficulties of the questions (Luo et al., 2023) or deriving detailed solution trajectories interleaving rationales and code (Gou et al., 2023b).

Mathematical Reasoning and Tool Integration: The chain-of-thought (Wei et al., 2022) prompting technique, which instructs a model to divide a problem into smaller, manageable subproblems, enhances reasoning tasks significantly (referenced in CoT and least-to-most papers). This method has its merits in mathematical reasoning as well (as seen in wizard math studies), but its effectiveness diminishes when tasks require symbolic manipulation and computations. An alternative strategy involves training models to create code that solves problems, then utilizing computational tools like a Python interpreter to execute the code (Chen et al., 2022b). However, relying solely on code generation is not effective for theoretical questions or in scenarios with complex natural language, as it may lack sufficient rationale. (Gou et al., 2023b) combines chain-of-thought with code generation to improve performance, though it requires multiple interactions with large language models (LLM). All mentioned approaches are actively explored with English datasets in focus, however there has been no study on this subject in Vietnamese.

3 ViMath-Bench Dataset

In this section, we present the construction procedure of the Vietnamese mathematical reasoning dataset, **ViMath-Bench**. To the best of our knowledge, this is the first dataset created for Vietnamese mathematical reasoning. The pipeline of the data construction is illustrated in the Figure 2, which are sequentially described as follows:

3.1 Data Sources

Our dataset is derived from three prominent Vietnamese online educational platforms: Tailieumoi[7], Hamchoi[8], and Vietjack[9]. These websites serve as comprehensive resources for general education in Vietnam, catering to a diverse audience including students, teachers, and parents. They provide solutions to textbook and workbook problems, reference materials for grades 1 to 12 across various subjects, and lesson plans for teachers. Notably, all content on these websites is freely accessible. For our study, we specifically targeted multiple-choice questions (MCQs) from grades 3 to 5, collecting approximately 20,000 questions. The Vietjack website provided fields such as `question`, `choices`, `full answer`, and `right choice`. However, Tailieumoi and Hamchoi did not offer the `right choice` field, necessitating additional steps to complete the dataset.

3.2 Preprocessing

To ensure the quality of the data, we implemented a multi-step preprocessing pipeline. First, we normalize the data to follow a consistent and standardized representation:

- **Text Normalization**: All text data was normalized to the NFC standard to ensure consistent character encoding. Vietnamese tones were also standardized to maintain uniformity across the dataset.
- **Format Conversion**: We converted HTML formats to Markdown using the Pandoc[10] library. This conversion not only saved tokens during the model training and inference process but also facilitated easier processing and analysis.

Subsequently, we implemented a rigorous filtering process to ensure the data was of the highest quality:

- **Exclusion of Non-Relevant Samples:** We filtered out samples containing tables and images, as our current focus does not include multimodal data.

[4]https://huggingface.co/datasets/nvidia/OpenMathInstruct-1

[5]https://huggingface.co/mistralai/Mixtral-8x7B-v0.1

[6]https://huggingface.co/datasets/TIGER-Lab/MathInstruct

[7]https://tailieumoi.vn/

[8]https://hamchoi.vn/

[9]https://www.vietjack.com/

[10]https://pandoc.org/

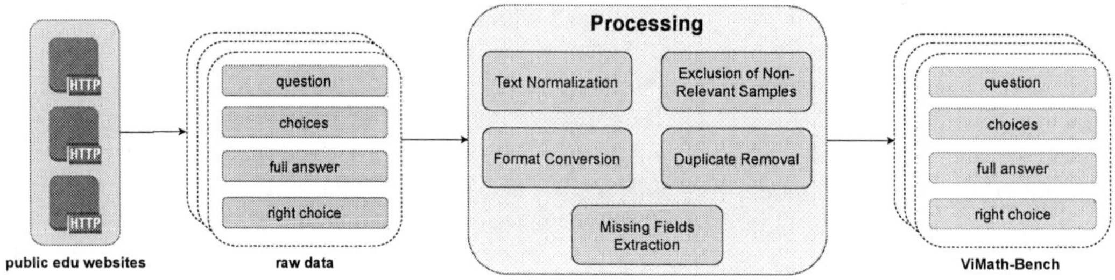

Figure 2: ViMath-Bench Dataset.

- **Duplicate Removal:** We employed an edit distance metric to identify and remove duplicate questions. Specifically, if two samples had an edit distance of greater than 90, one sample was discarded. Preference was given to retaining samples due to the completeness of its data fields.
- **Missing Fields Extraction:** For the remaining data from the available resources, we employed a set of rules to extract the `correct choice` field for `full answer`. This method allowed us to successfully retrieve the correct answers for approximately 70% of the samples. The remaining 30% of the data, which lacked this critical field, were subsequently removed.

After these preprocessing steps, the dataset contains 8.4K samples, which we name **ViMath-Bench**. Each sample of the dataset contains four fields: `question`, `choices`, `correct_choice`, and `full_answer`, which are beneficial for both training and evaluation. This dataset is then divided into 7.1K training samples and 1.3K test samples to facilitate the evaluation of our models.

4 Methodology

We introduce **Simple Reasoning with Code (SiRC)** framework, which is a simplified approach to solving elementary mathematical problems using both CoT reasoning and code generation. We leverage a teacher-student framework to distill knowledge from larger open-source LLMs to smaller, more resource-efficient models, tailored specifically for Vietnamese mathematical reasoning tasks.

4.1 SiRC Inference Procedure

We propose a novel, efficient approach to address the arithmetic and calculation challenges faced by large language models (LLMs), described in Algorithm 1. Our method integrates Python code generation into the problem-solving process in a unique way. Unlike previous studies that either generated only code all at once or used iterative reasoning and code generation (which can be cost-inefficient because of multiple LLM calls), our approach simplifies the process by combining reasoning and coding in a single, structured LLM response:

- **Step-by-Step Reasoning:** The LLM first outlines all necessary steps to solve the math problem without performing any calculations.
- **Python Code:** Immediately following the reasoning, the LLM generates Python code to execute the required calculations.

This seemingly two-step process is completed in a single LLM call, which not only simplifies the reasoning-code generation in a chained multi-agent setup but also enhances the effectiveness of the solution. By separating the logical problem-solving steps from the actual computation, our method provides a clear, executable pathway to solve complex mathematical problems. After finishing the reasoning-code generation and code execution, **SiRC** makes the last LLM call to generate the final answer to the question.

4.2 Teacher-Student Framework

To implement our **SiRC** approach effectively, we develop **`ViMath-InstructCode`**, a synthetic dataset designed to enable trainable open-source LLMs to adopt our proposed method. We employ a knowledge distillation approach (Semnani et al., 2023), utilizing larger models as teachers to transfer knowledge to smaller, more resource-efficient student models. In the most general case, this framework allows multiple strong larger models to act as teachers, enabling the available smaller models to learn from all of them and obtain combined capabilities. This process allows us to create

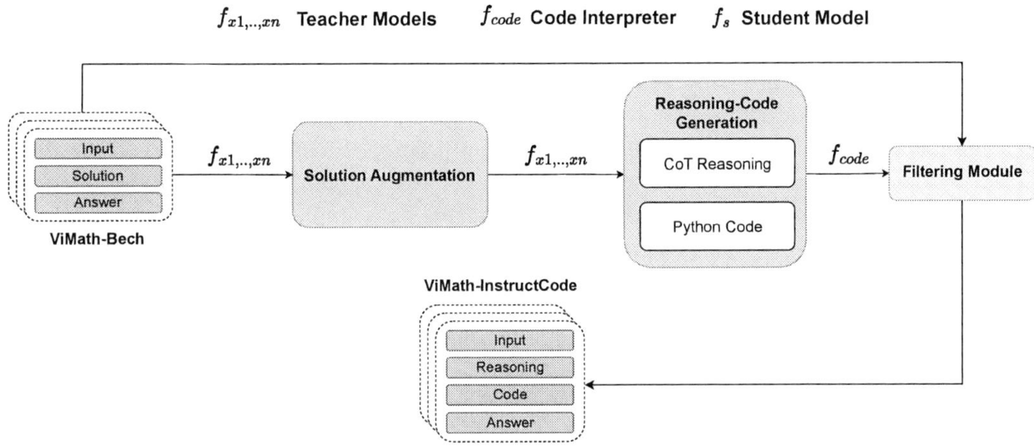

Figure 3: Overview of ViMath-Instruct-Code dataset construction

---

Algorithm 1 SiRC Inference Procedure

Require: Multiple-choice question of problem P
Ensure: Solution to P

1: **Reasoning-Code Generation (LLM call):** Generate all necessary steps to solve P as textual guidance only + Python code to execute the required calculations based on the outlined steps.
2: **Execution (Python interpreter):** Extract the generated Python code and execute to obtain the solution to P.
3: **Answer Generation (LLM call):** Generate final choice for P based on the output of previous steps.

---

more compact versions of the LLMs that are tailored for Vietnamese mathematical reasoning tasks while maintaining the ability to perform both step-by-step reasoning and code generation as outlined in our SiRC framework.

4.3 Construction of `ViMath-InstructCode` Dataset

Following the Teacher-Student framework, we specifically use `Llama-3-70B` and `Qwen-2-72B` as the teacher models, with publicly available small models serving as the distilled versions. We selected these two models because they usually demonstrate different reasoning responses to the same math problem, making it advantageous to learn from both. However, due to resource limitations, we could not extend our experiments to other large models or closed-source LLM APIs. Specifically, **`ViMath-InstructCode`** is constructed based on the **`ViMath-Bench`** training set, which is sequentially illustrated as follows (Figure 3)):

- **Input Data:** The input data consists of math problems collected and preprocessed as detailed in section 3. This dataset, referred to as **`ViMath-Bench`**, serves as the foundation for generating step-by-step solutions. Specifically, we extracted the training split and augmented it in subsequent steps to ensure it can be efficiently trained by language models.

- **Solution Augmentation**: Upon reviewing the full answer fields of the crawled data, we observed that the solutions often have an undesirable format where the conclusion precedes the explanation. This format may be unintuitive for the model to learn from, as learning from data of this format would teach the model to predict the answer before reasoning about the question. Additionally, the solutions lack depth, as they do not provide step-by-step explanations, thereby failing to offer a rich signal in reasoning for the model to learn. To address these issues, we decided to augment the crawled solutions using the teacher models. These models enhance the solutions in two ways: firstly, by adding a detailed explanation that outlines every step and computation involved in solving the problem; and secondly, by formatting the augmented solution so that the explanation precedes the final answer. At the end of this step, we obtain a dataset of pure Chain-of-Thought fashion.

- **Reasoning-Code Generation:** In this step,

we further augment the detailed step-by-step solutions from the previous step to obtain data with the desired structure. This structure contains reasoning followed by code, which are central to our **SiRC** framework. Specifically, we prompted the teacher models to first reformat the solutions from the previous step by eliminating all computations and preserving only the reasoning steps. After completing the reformatting, the models then continue to generate Python code to solve problems that require calculations. The input of this process is a *detailed solution* (with chain-of-thought fashion which details on both reasoning and computation), and the output is *textual guidance* (without computation) and *Python code* (that executes necessary computations).

- **Data Filtering:** The generated data from the previous step are passed through a filtering module. This module extracts and executes the Python code, then compares the extracted answer from the code's output with the provided correct answer to verify its correctness. Samples with incorrect output are discarded. Additionally, edit distance is used to deduplicate the generated solutions and code snippets.

5 Experimental Setup

5.1 Evaluation Metrics

The primary metric for evaluating the performance of the models was accuracy. This metric measures the percentage of questions q where the model gives the correct final answer. The accuracy is calculated as follows:

$$Accuracy(Q) = \frac{1}{|Q|} \sum_{i=1}^{|Q|} \{\texttt{SiRC}(q_i, C_i) == a_i\}$$

where q_i is the i-th question in a set of questions Q, C_i is the set of corresponding choices for question q_i. $\texttt{SiRC}(q_i, C_i)$ is the final answer concluded by running the **SiRC** inference procedure on q_i, which is compared with the correct choice a_i of q_i. Accuracy provides a straightforward and intuitive measure of the model's effectiveness in solving mathematical reasoning tasks.

5.2 Training datasets

We conducted extensive experiments using multiple training datasets, each representing a different approach to solving math problems with large language models (LLMs). These approaches include fine-tuning with an unprocessed crawled dataset as a baseline, Chain-of-Thought (CoT) reasoning, Programming-of-Thought (PoT), and our proposed **SiRC** framework. This diverse collection of training datasets allows for a comprehensive comparison, showcasing the effectiveness of our **SiRC** framework across various methodologies. Table 1 provides detailed information on the construction of each dataset, their characteristics, and the number of samples included. Notably, while the `ViMath-Bench` dataset contains only 7k training samples, its derivatives—`ViMath-Reasoning`, `ViMath-Code`, and most importantly, `ViMath-InstructCode`—each contains 14k training samples. This increase is due to the use of two teacher models, `Llama-3-70B` and `Qwen2-72B`, in generating these datasets.

Dataset	Description	#Num.
`ViMath-Bench`	Crawled dataset, described in section 3	7K
`ViMath-Reasoning`	Detailed Step-by-step reasoning with textual computation, generated by teacher models	14K
`ViMath-Code`	Only using code to solve the problem, generated by using teacher models	14K
`ViMath-InstructCode`	Structured reasoning followed by code, described in section 4.3	14K

Table 1: Details of Training Datasets for Different Approaches

5.3 Implementation

Hyperparameter	Values
batch size	128
epoch	3
learning rate	2e-4
learning rate scheduler	cosine
weight decay	0
cutoff-len	2048
lora-r	64
lora-alpha	128
lora-dropout	0.05
lora-target-modules	all linear

Table 2: Hyperparameters for the model fine-tuning

Model	No finetuning		Baseline Finetuning				Finetuning w/ SiRC (ours)	
	w/o CoT	w/ CoT	ViMath-Bench	ViMath-Reasoning	ViMath-Code	ViMath-Reasoning +Code	ViMath-InstructCode	ViMath-Reasoning +InstructCode
WizardMath-7B-V1.1	46.01	53.44	52.25	78.97	-	-	-	-
MetaMath-Mistral-7B	51.46	52.41	52.96	77.00	-	-	-	-
vinallama-7b-chat	40.79	38.97	38.26	57.87	-	-	-	-
Vistral-7B-Chat	44.98	63.56	51.30	74.31	-	-	-	-
Llama-3-8B-Instruct	75.97	67.98	73.60	83.32	85.22	86.01	**86.4**	**87.27**
Qwen2-7B-Instruct	83.4	84.82	79.68	88.38	87.98	88.14	**90.83**	**91.15**
deepseek-math-7b-rl	89.49	89.57	82.53	88.38	88.93	**89.64**	89.49	**90.59**
Llama-3-70B-Instruct	89.80	90.28	-	-	-	-	-	-
Qwen2-72B-Instruct	92.09	92.09	-	-	-	-	-	-

Table 3: Performance comparison of models under different finetuning conditions. The two best results in each row are in **bold**.

Backbone Model: In our experiments, we use a diverse selection of open-source language models as backbones. Firstly, we choose models specifically trained for mathematical problem-solving: `WizardMath-7B-V1.1` and `MetaMath-Mistral-7B`. However, these models lack native support for Vietnamese. To address this, we then select models trained with a sufficient amount of Vietnamese data: `vinallama-7b-chat` and `vistral-7b-chat`, though these are not specifically designed for solving math problems. Finally, we include some of the latest multilingual models which also show strong coding and mathematical capabilities: `Qwen2-7B-Instruct`, `Llama-3-8B-Instruct`, and `deepseek-math-7b-rl`. In total, we utilize seven models as our backbones.

Hyperparameters: For fine-tuning the backbones, we employed the Low-Rank Adaptation (LoRA) technique across all models. To ensure a fair comparison, we kept the hyperparameters consistent for every model. Detailed information regarding these hyperparameters is provided in Table 2.

6 Results

Table 3 presents a detailed performance comparison of various models under different conditions. The effectiveness of the proposed **SiRC** framework is highlighted, demonstrating its impact on enhancing model accuracy in mathematical reasoning tasks.

6.1 Baselines

No Fine-Tuning Among the models evaluated without any fine-tuning, `deepseek-math-7b-rl` and `Qwen2-7B-Instruct` exhibited the highest accuracies without CoT prompting, achieving 89.49% and 83.4%, respectively. This underscores these models' robust baseline capabilities in mathematical reasoning when used out of the box.

CoT prompting had varied effects on model performance. For some models, such as `vistral-7b-chat` and `WizardMath-7B-V1.1`, it significantly boosted accuracy by nearly 19% and 7%, respectively. However, for other models, CoT prompting had little to no effect or even decreased performance. This indicates that the benefits of CoT prompting are not consistent across all models and may depend on specific model architectures or underlying training data.

Baseline Fine-Tuning When models were fine-tuned with the baseline **`ViMath`** datasets (as detailed in Table 1), there were notable improvements in performance compared with no finetuning setting. Augmented datasets, namely **`ViMath-Reasoning`** and **`ViMath-Code`** consistently outperform raw dataset **`ViMath-Bench`**, showing the clear advantage of using teacher models to generate synthetic training data. Notably, for all models, we experimented with finetuning by combining these two augmented datasets yielded the highest accuracies across all baseline configurations. However, we did not conduct training experiments with code-related data on the first four models, because they were not sufficiently trained with code data.

6.2 Main results

Finetuning with SiRC framework To enable models to follow the SiRC inference framework, we trained them on datasets that include our proposed **`ViMath-InstructCode`** dataset. Finetuning with only **`ViMath-InstructCode`** dataset enabled models to consistently surpass performance when trained with only **`ViMath-Reasoning`** or

Model	Qwen2-7B-Instruct	Llama-3-8B-Instruct	deepseek-math-7b-rl
w/o Solution Augmentation	89.80	83.64	**89.72**
w/o Filtering Module	87.83	85.69	89.49
use only `Llama3-70B-Instruct`	88.46	84.19	87.98
use only `Llama3-70B-Instruct` (sampled twice)	87.91	84.11	87.91
use only `Qwen2-72B-Instruct`	89.25	83.79	88.14
use only `Qwen2-72B-Instruct` (sampled twice)	90.75	84.58	89.17
full pipeline (ours)	**90.83**	**86.40**	89.49

Table 4: Ablation study results

ViMath-Code. Additionally, finetuning using the combined **ViMath-{Reasoning+InstructCode}** dataset yielded the highest accuracies observed, with `Qwen2-7B-Instruct` achieving an impressive 91.15%, outperforming all other configurations. This highlights the synergistic effect of integrating reasoning data with our proposed **ViMath-InstructCode** data, which collectively enhances model performance more effectively than using either dataset in isolation.

Finally, we ran inference on the teacher models, `Llama3-70B-Instruct` and `Qwen2-72B-Instruct`, achieving the highest no-finetuning inference accuracy of 92.09% with `Qwen2-72B-Instruct` when using CoT prompting. Although `Qwen2-72B-Instruct` outperformed `Qwen2-7B-Instruct` (finetuned with our **ViMath-InstructCode** and follow **SiRC** inference procedure), our model closely followed by only less than 1% accuracy. This again demonstrates the robustness of the teacher-student methodology and the effectiveness of our **SiRC** framework.

6.3 Ablation Study

To further understand the contribution of each component in our proposed **SiRC** framework and the **ViMath-InstructCode** dataset, we conducted an ablation study. This study helps to isolate and evaluate the impact of different components and steps in our dataset construction pipeline. The configurations tested and their corresponding results are summarized in Table 4.

The full pipeline, including solution augmentation, filtering steps, and utilizing two teachers (`Llama3-70B-Instruct` and `Qwen2-72B-Instruct`, each sampled once), achieved the highest performance for both `Qwen2-7B-Instruct` (90.83%) and `Llama-3-8B-Instruct` (86.40%), demonstrating the effectiveness of the complete process. Excluding the solution augmentation step, which provides detailed explanations and formatting by the teacher models, resulting in a performance drop across almost all models. Using only `Llama3-70B-Instruct` or `Qwen2-72B-Instruct` for generating data also led to lower performance, underscoring the need for diversity provided by multiple teacher models. Sampling twice with either teacher model showed negligible improvement, indicating that the added diversity from another teacher model is crucial. Excluding the filtering step resulted in decreased accuracy for `Qwen2-7B-Instruct` (87.83%) and `Llama-3-8B-Instruct` (85.69%), emphasizing the role of data quality control in enhancing model reliability and accuracy. Interestingly, `deepseek-math-7b-rl` maintains stable performance even without the filtering step, suggesting that this model may be more resilient to noise in the training data compared to others. Overall, these results demonstrate that each component of our **ViMath-InstructCode** construction pipeline, including solution augmentation, the use of multiple teacher models, and filtering, significantly contributes to the overall performance of the models, with the full pipeline consistently yielding the best results, confirming the robustness and effectiveness of our approach.

7 Conclusion

This study proposes a novel fine-tuning instruction approach for mathematical reasoning, which is specified for the Vietnamese language. Specifically, we present SiRC, an effective framework, which significantly enhances the mathematical reasoning capabilities of language models with minimal cost. Furthermore, by leveraging the **ViMath-InstructCode** dataset and combining it with reasoning datasets, the proposed framework achieves superior performance, underscoring the effectiveness of our approach. Accordingly, the experimental results indicate that diverse and comprehensive training data is crucial for improving model accuracy in complex tasks such as mathematical reasoning.

Limitations

While our study successfully constructs the `ViMath-InstructCode` dataset using the **SiRC** framework, it is important to acknowledge some limitations in our approach: i) Firstly, the generalization to other languages of **SiRC**, though promising, is still unclear. The **SiRC** framework and `ViMath-InstructCode` dataset have been specifically designed for Vietnamese. Adapting this framework to other languages, particularly those with even fewer resources, necessitates additional efforts in constructing datasets as well as running experiments; ii) Secondly, the proposed `ViMath-InstructCode` is still prone to noises. The construction of this dataset, despite relying on trusted open sites and undergoing several preprocessing steps to ensure its quality, is completed without any human verification. This could result in a small proportion of faulty samples in our training dataset.

Ethical considerations

Regarding concerns related to the sources of the datasets in our research, they are built from publicly accessible sources, guaranteeing no privacy issues or violations. We do not gather any personally identifiable information, and all data is acquired in compliance with legal and ethical guidelines.

References

Janice Ahn, Rishu Verma, Renze Lou, Di Liu, Rui Zhang, and Wenpeng Yin. 2024. Large language models for mathematical reasoning: Progresses and challenges. In *Proceedings of the 18th Conference of the European Chapter of the Association for Computational Linguistics, EACL 2024: Student Research Workshop, St. Julian's, Malta, March 21-22, 2024*, pages 225–237. Association for Computational Linguistics.

Aida Amini, Saadia Gabriel, Shanchuan Lin, Rik Koncel-Kedziorski, Yejin Choi, and Hannaneh Hajishirzi. 2019. Mathqa: Towards interpretable math word problem solving with operation-based formalisms. In *Proceedings of the 2019 Conference of the North American Chapter of the Association for Computational Linguistics: Human Language Technologies, NAACL-HLT 2019, Minneapolis, MN, USA, June 2-7, 2019, Volume 1 (Long and Short Papers)*, pages 2357–2367. Association for Computational Linguistics.

Mark Chen, Jerry Tworek, Heewoo Jun, Qiming Yuan, Henrique Pondé de Oliveira Pinto, Jared Kaplan, Harrison Edwards, Yuri Burda, Nicholas Joseph, Greg Brockman, Alex Ray, Raul Puri, Gretchen Krueger, Michael Petrov, Heidy Khlaaf, Girish Sastry, Pamela Mishkin, Brooke Chan, Scott Gray, Nick Ryder, Mikhail Pavlov, Alethea Power, Lukasz Kaiser, Mohammad Bavarian, Clemens Winter, Philippe Tillet, Felipe Petroski Such, Dave Cummings, Matthias Plappert, Fotios Chantzis, Elizabeth Barnes, Ariel Herbert-Voss, William Hebgen Guss, Alex Nichol, Alex Paino, Nikolas Tezak, Jie Tang, Igor Babuschkin, Suchir Balaji, Shantanu Jain, William Saunders, Christopher Hesse, Andrew N. Carr, Jan Leike, Joshua Achiam, Vedant Misra, Evan Morikawa, Alec Radford, Matthew Knight, Miles Brundage, Mira Murati, Katie Mayer, Peter Welinder, Bob McGrew, Dario Amodei, Sam McCandlish, Ilya Sutskever, and Wojciech Zaremba. 2021. Evaluating large language models trained on code. *CoRR*, abs/2107.03374.

Wenhu Chen, Xueguang Ma, Xinyi Wang, and William W. Cohen. 2022a. Program of thoughts prompting: Disentangling computation from reasoning for numerical reasoning tasks. *CoRR*, abs/2211.12588.

Wenhu Chen, Xueguang Ma, Xinyi Wang, and William W. Cohen. 2022b. Program of thoughts prompting: Disentangling computation from reasoning for numerical reasoning tasks. *CoRR*, abs/2211.12588.

Karl Cobbe, Vineet Kosaraju, Mohammad Bavarian, Mark Chen, Heewoo Jun, Lukasz Kaiser, Matthias Plappert, Jerry Tworek, Jacob Hilton, Reiichiro Nakano, Christopher Hesse, and John Schulman. 2021. Training verifiers to solve math word problems. *CoRR*, abs/2110.14168.

Yao Fu, Hao Peng, Litu Ou, Ashish Sabharwal, and Tushar Khot. 2023. Specializing smaller language models towards multi-step reasoning. In *International Conference on Machine Learning, ICML 2023, 23-29 July 2023, Honolulu, Hawaii, USA*, volume 202 of *Proceedings of Machine Learning Research*, pages 10421–10430. PMLR.

Zhibin Gou, Zhihong Shao, Yeyun Gong, Yelong Shen, Yujiu Yang, Minlie Huang, Nan Duan, and Weizhu Chen. 2023a. Tora: A tool-integrated reasoning agent for mathematical problem solving. *CoRR*, abs/2309.17452.

Zhibin Gou, Zhihong Shao, Yeyun Gong, Yelong Shen, Yujiu Yang, Minlie Huang, Nan Duan, and Weizhu Chen. 2023b. Tora: A tool-integrated reasoning agent for mathematical problem solving. *CoRR*, abs/2309.17452.

Dan Hendrycks, Collin Burns, Saurav Kadavath, Akul Arora, Steven Basart, Eric Tang, Dawn Song, and Jacob Steinhardt. 2021. Measuring mathematical problem solving with the MATH dataset. In *Proceedings of the Neural Information Processing Systems Track on Datasets and Benchmarks 1, NeurIPS Datasets and Benchmarks 2021, December 2021, virtual.*

Danqing Huang, Shuming Shi, Chin-Yew Lin, Jian Yin, and Wei-Ying Ma. 2016. How well do computers solve math word problems? large-scale dataset construction and evaluation. In *Proceedings of the 54th Annual Meeting of the Association for Computational Linguistics, ACL 2016, August 7-12, 2016, Berlin, Germany, Volume 1: Long Papers*. The Association for Computer Linguistics.

Zhenwen Liang, Wenhao Yu, Tanmay Rajpurohit, Peter Clark, Xiangliang Zhang, and Ashwin Kalyan. 2023. Let GPT be a math tutor: Teaching math word problem solvers with customized exercise generation. In *Proceedings of the 2023 Conference on Empirical Methods in Natural Language Processing, EMNLP 2023, Singapore, December 6-10, 2023*, pages 14384–14396. Association for Computational Linguistics.

Wang Ling, Dani Yogatama, Chris Dyer, and Phil Blunsom. 2017. Program induction by rationale generation: Learning to solve and explain algebraic word problems. In *Proceedings of the 55th Annual Meeting of the Association for Computational Linguistics, ACL 2017, Vancouver, Canada, July 30 - August 4, Volume 1: Long Papers*, pages 158–167. Association for Computational Linguistics.

Hanmeng Liu, Zhiyang Teng, Leyang Cui, Chaoli Zhang, Qiji Zhou, and Yue Zhang. 2023. Logicot: Logical chain-of-thought instruction tuning. In *Findings of the Association for Computational Linguistics: EMNLP 2023, Singapore, December 6-10, 2023*, pages 2908–2921. Association for Computational Linguistics.

Haipeng Luo, Qingfeng Sun, Can Xu, Pu Zhao, Jianguang Lou, Chongyang Tao, Xiubo Geng, Qingwei Lin, Shifeng Chen, and Dongmei Zhang. 2023. Wizardmath: Empowering mathematical reasoning for large language models via reinforced evol-instruct. *CoRR*, abs/2308.09583.

OpenAI. 2023. GPT-4 technical report. *CoRR*, abs/2303.08774.

Sina J. Semnani, Violet Z. Yao, Heidi C. Zhang, and Monica S. Lam. 2023. Wikichat: Stopping the hallucination of large language model chatbots by few-shot grounding on wikipedia. In *Findings of the Association for Computational Linguistics: EMNLP 2023, Singapore, December 6-10, 2023*, pages 2387–2413. Association for Computational Linguistics.

Hugo Touvron, Thibaut Lavril, Gautier Izacard, Xavier Martinet, Marie-Anne Lachaux, Timothée Lacroix, Baptiste Rozière, Naman Goyal, Eric Hambro, Faisal Azhar, Aurélien Rodriguez, Armand Joulin, Edouard Grave, and Guillaume Lample. 2023. Llama: Open and efficient foundation language models. *CoRR*, abs/2302.13971.

Jason Wei, Xuezhi Wang, Dale Schuurmans, Maarten Bosma, Brian Ichter, Fei Xia, Ed H. Chi, Quoc V. Le, and Denny Zhou. 2022. Chain-of-thought prompting elicits reasoning in large language models. In *Advances in Neural Information Processing Systems 35: Annual Conference on Neural Information Processing Systems 2022, NeurIPS 2022, New Orleans, LA, USA, November 28 - December 9, 2022.*

Zhiheng Xi, Wenxiang Chen, Xin Guo, Wei He, Yiwen Ding, Boyang Hong, Ming Zhang, Junzhe Wang, Senjie Jin, Enyu Zhou, Rui Zheng, Xiaoran Fan, Xiao Wang, Limao Xiong, Yuhao Zhou, Weiran Wang, Changhao Jiang, Yicheng Zou, Xiangyang Liu, Zhangyue Yin, Shihan Dou, Rongxiang Weng, Wensen Cheng, Qi Zhang, Wenjuan Qin, Yongyan Zheng, Xipeng Qiu, Xuanjing Huang, and Tao Gui. 2023. The rise and potential of large language model based agents: A survey. *CoRR*, abs/2309.07864.

Generalizations across filler-gap dependencies in neural language models

Katherine Howitt[1] **Sathvik Nair**[1,3] **Allison Dods**[1] **Robert Melvin Hopkins**[1,2]
[1]Department of Linguistics, University of Maryland
[2]Department of Computer Science, University of Maryland
[3]University of Maryland Institute for Advanced Computer Studies
{kghowitt,sathvik}@umd.edu

Abstract

Humans develop their grammars by making structural generalizations from finite input. We ask how filler-gap dependencies, which share a structural generalization despite diverse surface forms, might arise from the input. We explicitly control the input to a neural language model (NLM) to uncover whether the model posits a shared representation for filler-gap dependencies. We show that while NLMs do have success differentiating grammatical from ungrammatical filler-gap dependencies, they rely on superficial properties of the input, rather than on a shared generalization. Our work highlights the need for specific linguistic inductive biases to model language acquisition.

1 Introduction

Human learners use their linguistic environment to acquire a grammar. At the same time, they come to generalizations that are not obviously signaled in the input. The central puzzle in language acquisition is to characterize the system that allows for human-like generalizations from finite input. Linguists posit that these generalizations are achieved through shared representations that allow learners to treat superficially distinct phenomena as a class (Chomsky, 1977; Kaplan and Bresnan, 1982; Gazdar, 1982; Gazdar et al., 1985; Pollard and Sag, 1987; Postal, 1999). The recent success of neural language models (NLMs) has caused many to question the necessity of linguistically-specific representational systems in language learning (Wilcox et al., 2018, 2023; Piantadosi, 2023).

We address this renewed controversy by conducting two experiments to uncover whether NLMs posit a shared representation for a particular syntactic dependency: filler-gap dependencies. We consider whether an NLM recognizes filler-gap dependencies in superficially distinct constructions, as humans do (Crain and Fodor, 1985; Stowe, 1986; Bever and McElree, 1988; Traxler and Pickering, 1996; Sprouse et al., 2016). We further ask whether the NLM posits a shared representation for filler-gap dependencies, and thus systematically applies constraints across them.

Recent research shows NLMs can differentiate between grammatical and ungrammatical instances of filler-gap dependencies in individual constructions, but our study asks whether filler-gap dependencies are treated as a *class* by the NLM. If a shared structural relation is learnable by an NLM, which lacks language-specific biases, then, in principle, a learner does not need to have such biases to learn that relation. Although one could learn the correct pattern through piecemeal learning of each construction individually (given enough input), a shared representation across filler-gap dependencies would allow a learner to generalize from only a subset of constructions containing filler-gap dependencies. Whether an NLM posits this shared representation is the question.

We provide an NLM with direct evidence for a filler-gap dependency in one construction and test whether it generalizes to other constructions. In our first experiment, we augment an NLM's training data with specific instances of clefting, and in our second, topicalization. We compare performance on four constructions containing filler-gap dependencies: Wh-movement, clefting, tough-movement, and topicalization. The NLM treating filler-gap dependencies systematically would be evidence that this shared representation is learnable without language-specific inductive biases.

2 Filler-gap dependencies

Filler-gap dependencies share a set of properties across superficially distinct constructions, including sensitivity to islands(Chomsky, 1977). These

Proceedings of the 28th Conference on Computational Natural Language Learning, pages 269–279
November 15-16, 2024 ©2024 Association for Computational Linguistics

properties persist across constructions, despite variation in semantic contribution and discourse function (Schütze et al., 2015). In psycholinguistic experiments, humans have been shown to be sensitive to gaps across filler-gap dependencies, including wh-movement (Crain and Fodor, 1985; Stowe, 1986), tough-movement (Bever and McElree, 1988), and clefting (Traxler and Pickering, 1996), though see Sprouse et al. (2016) for variation in English relative clauses. These effects are sensitive to locality constraints, and appear to be mediated by the presence of islands (Phillips, 2006; Traxler and Pickering, 1996; McElree and Griffith, 1998; Omaki et al., 2015). Generalizing from surface forms on the basis of a shared representation could be critical to learning, especially if some constructions containing filler-gap dependencies do not occur frequently in the input.

Clefting (1) is one construction that contains a filler-gap dependency. In (1a), the filler *these snacks* forms a dependency with the gap site, marked with __ for readability, but silent in natural language. The filler is interpreted as the object of *bought*, despite not appearing linearly beside *bought* in the string. Strings lacking a filler but containing a gap (1b) are ungrammatical, and when the gap is filled (i.e., an object, such as *cheese*, immediately follows the verb), the acceptability pattern reverses (1c-d). In other words, neither a filler nor a gap can occur without the other. Importantly, clefts are superficially similar to sentences like (1d) which lack a filler-gap dependency, and thus are structurally quite distinct. A learner must distinguish between instances of clefting (1a) and other superficially similar sentences (1d).

(1) a. It is *these snacks* that Mary bought __ today.
b. * It is *apparent* that Mary bought __ today.
c. * It is *these snacks* that Mary bought cheese today.
d. It is *apparent* that Mary bought cheese today.

Filler-gap dependencies occur in many constructions, including Wh-movement (2), topicalization (3), and tough-movement (4), which differ in surface form but share the filler-gap dependency and its properties.

(2) I know *what* Mary bought __ today.

(3) *These snacks*, Mary bought __ today.

(4) *These snacks* are tough to buy __ here.

While it might initially appear that learning could occur from simply expecting a gap when presented with a filler, properties of this dependency also include specific constraints on when they can be formed. Some structural configurations, called *islands*, block the formation of a filler-gap dependency. For example, a filler-gap dependency cannot be formed inside a relative clause (e.g., *that carried* __) despite the fact that *carried* lacks an object (i.e., is followed by a gap). The relative clause blocks the dependency, and so a gap is unacceptable regardless of the presence of a filler. Examples (5)-(8) show that all filler-gap dependencies are subject to this same restriction.

(5) * It is *these snacks* that Mary bought [the bag that carried __] today.

(6) * I know what Mary bought [the bag that carried __] today.

(7) * *These snacks,* Mary bought [the bag that carried __] today.

(8) * *These snacks* are tough to buy [the bag that carried __] here.

One task for a learner is to recognize, on the basis of grammatical examples only (e.g., (1a) and (1d), but not (1b), (1c), or (5)), when each filler-gap dependency can and cannot occur. A further task is to recognize that the same properties apply to each construction containing a filler-gap dependency (2-4), and thus posit a shared representation underlying all filler-gap dependencies.

An alternative method to generalizing would be a piecemeal learning process: learning each construction separately. For the piecemeal process to work, sufficient examples of each construction must occur in the input, and similar constraints across these constructions would arise from distinct observations. NLMs here provide an opportunity to test whether a shared representation can *in principle* be extracted from the input without linguistic biases.

2.1 NLMs and Filler-gap dependencies

NLMs can learn at least some syntactic representations involving locality (see Linzen and Baroni (2021) for a review). NLMs have been shown to represent shared syntactic structure across different constructions in simulated priming (Prasad et al., 2019) and simulated satiation (Lu et al., 2024) experiments, which compare measures from NLMs before and after exposing them to sentences with similar syntactic structures. Similarly, NLMs have been shown to generalize over syntactic structures that have been excluded from their training data (Jumelet et al., 2021; Warstadt, 2022; Misra and Mahowald, 2024; Patil et al., 2024). How human-like these generalizations are is still an open question.

With respect to filler-gap dependencies, NLMs capture language-specific island constraints in English (Wilcox et al., 2018; Ozaki et al., 2022; Wilcox et al., 2023) and Norwegian (Kobzeva et al., 2023) in sentences with embedded Wh-movement. Ozaki et al. (2022) analyze other constructions with filler-gap dependencies (clefting, topicalization, and tough-movement) and find that model performance varies by construction and is associated with the relative frequency of the constructions in texts resembling the training corpus. In other words, Ozaki et al. (2022) argue the model's ability to approximate human behavior is dependent on the availability of each construction type in the input. Whether this ability is modulated by a shared representation *across* different constructions is not known.

Finally, Lan et al. (2024) investigate the extent to which NLM performance with double gap phenomena (parasitic gaps and across the board movement) is in line with human judgments. In these constructions, a gap *can* occur inside an island, only if another gap is present. While they find that pretrained NLM performance is low for constructions with parasitic gaps or across the board movement, the authors show that adding examples of parasitic gaps and across the board movement to an NLM's training data adjusts its performance to be in line with human expectations, showing directly the relationship between NLM performance and surface forms in the training data. Thus, if the training data of an NLM does not contain sufficient instances of a particular construction, its ability to correctly capture the pattern of grammaticality suffers, strengthening Ozaki et al. (2022)'s claim that input frequency matters.

The methodology introduced by Lan et al. (2024) provides a path for exploring whether NLMs make generalizations that are not apparent from simply testing a pretrained model: if the model can improve on one construction from direct training on that construction, we can ask what other effects such training might have. Does training a model on one construction containing a filler-gap dependency affect its performance on *other* constructions containing filler-gap dependencies, the way one might expect given a shared representation?

3 Methods

3.1 Measuring Filler-gap dependencies and Island Effects

Psycholinguistic findings show structural constraints affect human expectations for gaps inside islands (Phillips, 2006; Traxler and Pickering, 1996; Stowe, 1986). One way to evaluate whether an NLM's predictions align with these effects is to measure its *surprisal*, the negative log probability of a word given context; less surprising words have higher probabilities. Surprisal quantifies the effect of processing difficulty (Levy, 2008). Investigating NLM surprisal at particular points in a sentence effectively treats the models like psycholinguistic subjects (Futrell et al., 2019).[1]

To determine whether the NLMs capture syntactically relevant knowledge, we evaluate surprisal at critical regions of grammatical and ungrammatical variants of superficially similar sentences, as in (1). We compute surprisal of the region following a verb, which can either consist of a direct object (a filled gap, **-gap**) or an adverb (a gap, i.e., no direct object, **+gap**). Each string also either contains a filler (**+filler**) or does not (**-filler**). This 2x2 design is illustrated in Table 1, with the critical region marked in bold. For example, the surprisal at *today* in (1a) should be lower than the surprisal at *cheese* in (1c) because in the latter case, given the filler *these snacks*, the reader expects a gap in the object position of *bought*. If the critical region consists of multiple words, we sum their surprisals.

If the NLM has learned the dependency, we expect to see high surprisal in the critical regions of ungrammatical sentences: both when it encounters a gap without having seen a prior filler (1b, +gap/-filler), as well as if it has seen a filler but then encounters a filled gap (1c, -gap/+filler). Likewise, we expect low surprisal in the critical regions of

[1] However, see Van Schijndel and Linzen (2021) and Huang et al. (2024) for arguments that surprisal is not always a good estimate of human behavior for some types of syntactically complex sentences.

	+filler	-filler	expected effect
+gap	It is these snacks that Mary bought _ **last week.**	*It is apparent that Mary bought _ **last week.**	negative
-gap	*It is these snacks that Mary bought **the cheese** last week.	It is apparent that Mary bought **the cheese** last week.	positive

Table 1: The expected effect is the difference in the LM's surprisal for versions of the same simple (non-island) construction with and without a filler.

	+filler	-filler	expected effect
+gap	*It is these snacks that Mary bought the bag that held _ **last week.**	*It is apparent that Mary bought the bag that held _ **last week.**	Closer to zero than simple effect
-gap	*It is these snacks that Mary bought the bag that held **the cheese** last week.	It is apparent that Mary bought the bag that held **the cheese** last week.	Closer to zero than simple effect

Table 2: For sentences containing islands, the expected effect is a reduction of the filler effect compared to the effect in simple sentences.

grammatical sentences: if it encounters a gap after having seen a filler (1a, +gap/+filler), as well as if it sees neither filler nor gap (1d, -gap/-filler).

To summarize these predictions, we calculate the **filler effect**: the *difference* in surprisal between two sentences that are identical except for the presence of a filler (Wilcox et al., 2018, 2023). We take the surprisal for a +filler sentence and subtract the surprisal of its -filler counterpart. Based on the predictions from the previous paragraph, our filler effect predictions for **simple** (non-island) sentences are as follows: a negative filler effect in the +gap condition and a positive filler effect in the -gap condition. These predictions are in Table 1.

The filler effect prediction for sentences with **islands** differs from the prediction for simple sentences. Filler-gap dependencies are not licensed into islands; sentences with islands are ungrammatical if they possess either a filler, a gap, or both. Only the sentences with no filler and no gap should be grammatical. Following Wilcox et al. (2023), we predict an NLM with human-like performance on island effects should show filler effects around zero in sentences with islands. If the NLM has learned that filler-gap dependencies are always unlicensed inside an island, the presence or absence of a filler should not affect the NLM's surprisal at a gap inside an island. Therefore, there should be no difference between the surprisal in the +filler and -filler conditions, i.e., a filler effect of zero. These predictions are summarized in Table 2. It is worth noting that Ozaki et al. (2022) have a different prediction for islands: they assume that grammaticality affects surprisal and that the NLM's surprisal will be different at the filled gap in the grammatical -gap, -filler condition. We discuss islandhood and surprisal further in Section 5.

3.2 Language Model

We estimate surprisal from a recurrent neural network (RNN) from Gulordava et al. (2018), which is a Long-Short-Term Memory (LSTM) RNN (Hochreiter and Schmidhuber, 1997) with two hidden layers with 650 units in each layer, trained on data from an English Wikipedia corpus (90 million tokens, or around 3 million sentences). We chose to use this model because prior research evaluating it on filler-gap dependencies has shown success in capturing human-like knowledge of filler-gap dependencies, even relative to larger models (Wilcox et al., 2018; Ozaki et al., 2022; Lan et al., 2024; Wilcox et al., 2023; Kobzeva et al., 2023). Because it has transparent training data, we could carefully compare the pretrained RNN with models augmented with instances of different constructions, which we call Cleft-RNN and Topic-RNN. Details of the augmented training data for these models are explained in Section 4. [2]

[2]Transformers and LSTMs perform similarly on syntactic generalization tasks when trained on the same amounts of data, despite the transformers' lower perplexity (Patil et al., 2024). We did, however, replicate the results of our baseline for each construction with a pretrained GPT-2 model. See Appendix C1 for these results and more discussion on modeling choices.

3.3 Statistical Analysis

We test for two effects: the first is whether the models recognize that a filler must be associated with a gap in simple sentences, and the second is whether this expectation is modulated by the presence of an island. To determine whether the RNN learned the filler-gap dependency in simple sentences, we fit a linear mixed-effects regression model following Wilcox et al. (2023) using surprisal as the dependent variable, sum-coded features for the presence or absence of fillers and gaps which were fixed effects. If the RNNs learn the filler-gap dependency for a particular construction, we expect to see a negative interaction term between the presence of fillers and gaps, in line with Wilcox et al. (2023).

Additionally, Wilcox et al. (2023) fit mixed-effects models including islandhood as a fixed effect, claiming that a positive three-way interaction between the presence of fillers, gaps, and islands reflects the successful learning of island constraints. We apply this analysis, but also consider both directions of the dependency separately: unlicensed gap effects (UGE) in sentences containing a gap, and filled gap effects (FGE) in sentences without a gap (Kobzeva et al., 2023). We fit separate linear mixed-effects models for the surprisals of sentences with and without gaps, with fixed effects for fillers and islands.[3] This analysis allows us to tease apart the two-way nature of the dependency and analyze whether the RNNs' failures or successes are driven by only one direction of the dependency. Success requires the regression models' coefficients to all be negative for UGEs and all be positive for FGEs for both main effects and interactions. These analyses were repeated separately for the pretrained and augmented RNNs. All regression models were sum-coded, included random effects for each item (Barr et al., 2013), and fit using the `Pymer` library in Python (Jolly, 2018). All formulas and results are reported in Appendix B.

4 Experiments

We evaluate an RNN's behavior on four filler-gap dependency constructions in both simple sentences and sentences with an island. We augment the NLM's training data with instances of a single construction and then observe the effects of that augmentation on its performance on tests of *other* constructions. In other words, we ask whether "teaching" an NLM filler-gap dependencies in one construction helps it "learn" the dependency in other constructions. If and only if the NLM acts consistently with linguists' conclusion that these constructions share an underlying representation, an improvement in performance on one construction should generalize to others. Our implementation [4] and models [5] are both publicly available.

4.1 Materials

For embedded Wh-movement, we use the materials from Wilcox et al. (2023)'s experiment on complex NP islands. For each of the other 4 constructions in (1)-(4), we test a "simple" version (no island) - where a dependency can be formed - and an island version - which does not allow for the formation of a filler-gap dependency. For topicalization, we test two versions: one ("topicalization without intro"), to closely match the materials used by Ozaki et al. (2022), in which the topicalized element has no analog in the no filler sentences, and one ("topicalization with intro") in which the filler is replaced with an introductory string to control for the length of the sentence and the presence of a comma. See Tables 1 and 2 for a schema of the design using one construction, clefting. For each construction, we generate a set of items with a fixed syntactic template and a vocabulary that varies across the set. We ensure that the lexical items are all in the RNN's vocabulary. For each item, we modulate the presence of a filler, a gap, and an island structure, generating 8 sentence types per item. Our final testing set contains 486 clefting items, 486 topicalization with intro, 161 topicalization without intro, and 243 tough-movement items.

4.2 Predictions

Each graph shows the average filler effect with 95% confidence intervals for simple and island sentences for each construction, before and after augmentation. For **simple** constructions, we expect to see a negative filler effect when the gap is present (blue bars) and a positive effect when

[3] Since Kobzeva et al. (2023) were only testing for island effects, their regression models were fit on filler effects rather than raw surprisals based on the presence of an island. We consider the joint presence of filler and island in our analysis.

[4] `https://github.com/umd-psycholing/lm-syntactic-generalization`

[5] `https://huggingface.co/sathvik-n/augmented-rnns`

the gap is absent (orange bars). This is because a human-like learner should find a gap less surprising when a filler is present than when there is no filler, and vice versa when there is no gap. (See Section 3.1 for more detail.) For **island** constructions, we expect that the confidence interval for the filler effect should overlap with zero because a human-like knowledge of islands suggests that a gap should be equally surprising regardless of the upstream presence of a filler; the same is true in the no-gap condition, using one of Wilcox et al. (2023)'s criteria. A less stringent relative metric for learning islands is a reduced effect relative to the filler effect in simple sentences (Wilcox et al., 2023); in other words, the difference in surprisal at the critical region decreases rather than disappears entirely.[6]

4.3 Experiment 1: Training on clefting

Our initial test of the pretrained RNN yielded variation across constructions consistent with Ozaki et al. (2022). Based on these results, we chose to augment the pretrained RNN's training data with instances of clefting because it fails to demonstrate knowledge of islands in clefting; also, clefting is reported as less frequent compared to Wh-movement in Ozaki et al. (2022). We hypothesize that Wilcox et al. (2023)'s robust effects with embedded Wh-movement may be due to the relative frequency of the construction in the training corpus.

We create a training set for clefting, using the same syntactic template for test sentences but with different lexical items. We then retrain the RNN following the same configurations in Gulordava et al. (2018), with training data that include all original training material and 864 additional examples of grammatical simple clefting. Half the examples contain a gap, as in (1a), half do not, as in (1d). We refer to this model as Cleft-RNN.

4.3.1 Results

Simple constructions. We first present the filler effects for the simple sentences of each construction of the pretrained RNN (before augmentation) and Cleft-RNN, plotted in Figure 1. Testing the pretrained RNN on simple constructions, we replicate Wilcox et al. (2023)'s findings for embedded Wh-movement. The pretrained RNN also shows the desired filler effect pattern in simple sentences for clefting and tough-movement, but not for either form of topicalization. For each construction type, we looked at the two-way interaction of filler and gap, confirming a positive result for Wh-movement, clefting, and tough-movement (negative interaction terms with $p < 0.001$). The interaction effects for topicalization were positive, indicating that the pretrained RNN did not learn the dependency in either type of topicalization constructions.

Training on clefting had no significant effect on knowledge of the dependency in simple sentences of any construction, confirmed both by the qualitative appearance of the graphs and by the mixed-effects models for each construction type (negative interaction terms with $p < 0.001$). [7] Since Cleft-RNN did not learn the dependency in either form of topicalization, we do not report island effects.

Island constructions. The results for constructions containing islands before and after augmentation, presented in Figure 2, are less straightforward. For no construction did the pretrained RNN meet the most stringent criteria for recognizing island constraints: that is, both filler effects in the island condition equaling zero. We do see varying degrees of *reduction* in the filler effects for each construction in the island vis-a-vis the simple condition. We consider each direction of the dependency separately: filled gap effects (FGE, orange) and unlicensed gap effects (UGE, blue).

The mixed-effects model using Wilcox et al. (2023)'s methods shows negative filler-gap interaction terms and positive three-way interaction terms for Wh-movement, clefting, and tough-movement, suggesting that the pretrained RNN correctly captures island constraints for all constructions where it knows the simple dependency. However, this result is at odds with our qualitative findings, which suggest the model did not learn the relevant generalization in clefting. We observe that in the -gap condition (orange bars), the filler effect is equal in magnitude in both the simple and island conditions. In fact, the filler effect is negative, suggesting high surprisal in the grammatical (-filler, -gap) sentence (see Table 2). This qualitative result is confirmed by our separate mixed-effects model for FGEs, which shows sta-

[6]For an alternative view on capturing island effects in NLMs, see Section 5 and Ozaki et al. (2022)

[7]We did observe changes in effect size, but because we consider knowledge of filler-gap dependencies to be binary (either learned or not learned), it is difficult to draw conclusions from minor changes in the effect size that do not change the status of the significant interaction.

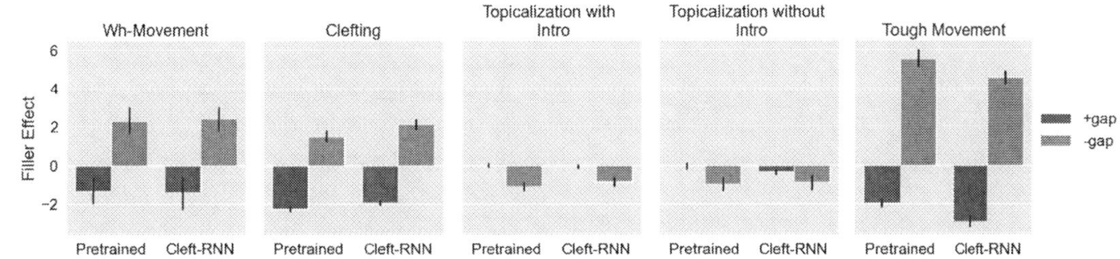

Figure 1: Filler effects for simple constructions for the pretrained model and Cleft-RNN.

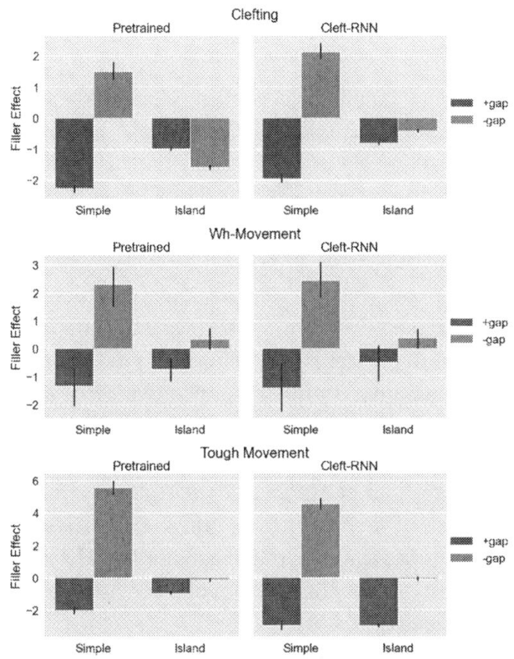

Figure 2: Filler effects for simple and island constructions for the pretrained model and Cleft-RNN. Since this dependency was not learned for topicalization, we do not display these results.

tistically significant positive coefficients for Wh-movement and tough-movement ($p < 0.001$), but not for clefting. In the regression models for UGE, we observe statistically significant negative coefficients for all three constructions ($p < 0.001$). In other words, the pretrained RNN is not sensitive to FGEs for clefting constructions, consistent with the qualitative pattern.

We now review Cleft-RNN's behavior with island constructions. The direction and magnitude of the effects in the three-way interaction model are consistent with the conclusion that Cleft-RNN captures island constraints in clefting and Wh-movement. For the clefting construction (in other words, when presented with examples structurally identical to those it was trained on), our regression models for FGEs and UGEs support this result. All coefficients for the UGEs are negative, and all coefficients for the FGEs are positive. Cleft-RNN is less sensitive to the presence of an upstream filler at a filled gap in an island construction than the pretrained RNN, though qualitatively the grammatical form is still more surprising than the ungrammatical form. For Wh-movement, Cleft-RNN's confidence interval of the filler effect for islands in the +gap condition overlaps with zero, achieving our most stringent criterion for displaying knowledge of island constraints. Results were statistically significant, both for clefting ($p < 0.001$) and for Wh-movement ($p < 0.01$), which was tested on a smaller stimulus set.

In tough-movement, however, augmentation has a detrimental effect. The magnitude of the filler effect in the +gap condition for islands is equivalent to that in the simple cases. The positive, non-significant interaction term for the regression model for UGEs in tough-movement supports this observation; Cleft-RNN lacks sensitivity to islands in tough-movement constructions.

For topicalization, our regression models do not have the correct signs for either construction type, confirming, as a qualitative inspection of Figure 1 suggests, that Cleft-RNN does not learn the dependency in these constructions.

4.4 Experiment 2: Training on topicalization

Since neither the pretrained RNN nor Cleft-RNN are able to arrive at the correct generalization for cases of topicalization, we now determine if providing the pretrained RNN with positive direct evidence of topicalization is sufficient for learning this dependency. We follow a similar procedure to the previous experiment, generating sentences from the same syntactic template for topicalization with intro and ensuring the lexical items do not appear in the testing sentences. We augment the RNN's Wikipedia corpus with 864 grammati-

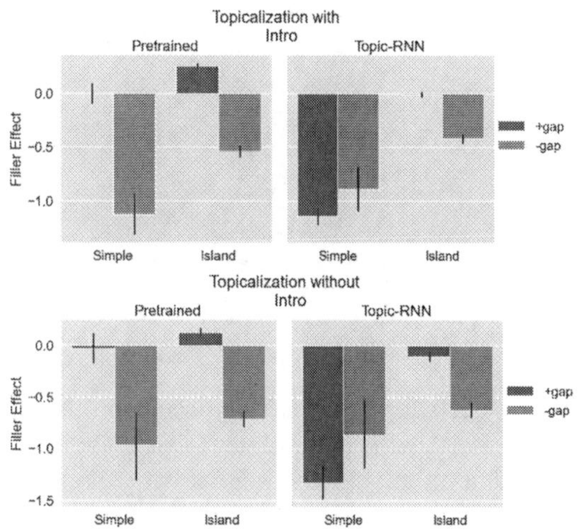

Figure 3: Filler effects for simple and island constructions for the pretrained model and Topic-RNN.

cal examples of topicalization, half with a gap and half without a gap, and train it using the hyperparameters in Gulordava et al. (2018). The augmented model is referred to here as Topic-RNN.

4.4.1 Results

Figure 3 shows filler effects in the pretrained RNN and Topic-RNN. Training explicitly on simple instances of topicalization does not lead the model to posit the dependency in both directions. Here, positive evidence is not enough to learn even the simple dependency. The regression model does not show significant effects for basic filler-gap licensing in Topic-RNN.

Topic-RNN *does* learn that the presence or absence of an upstream filler should modulate surprisal at a gap (UGEs, blue bars), but it fails to learn the correct relationship between a filled gap and the absence of an upstream filler (FGEs, orange bars). In fact, Topic-RNN's surprisal is consistent with the non-human-like hypothesis that *the cheese* in the sentence *The snacks, Mary bought the cheese last week* is less surprising than in the sentence *In fact, Mary bought the cheese last week.*

5 Discussion

In this paper, we test whether NLMs can generalize knowledge of filler-gap dependencies across different constructions when their input is augmented with only one construction containing a filler-gap dependency. The pattern of knowledge of the pretrained RNN potentially reflects piecemeal learning, where the frequency of particular constructions modulates the model's recognition of the filler-gap dependency for each construction type individually (Ozaki et al., 2022). However, based on the pretrained results alone we cannot determine whether the NLM's inferences for one construction are based on others, hence the need for an augmentation-based procedure. Experiment 1 found that while Cleft-RNN behaves differently than the pretrained RNN on clefting, Wh-movement, and tough-movement, it fails to generalize systematically across all the types of filler-gap dependencies we test. Cleft-RNN's failure to learn the relevant dependency for simple topicalization sentences further confirms that these models do not arrive at their knowledge of filler-gap dependencies through a shared representation.

Cleft-RNN does improve its representation of island constraints in clefting, the construction it was augmented with. However, this improvement still preserves the incorrect prediction for grammaticality. In this case, positive evidence of grammatical forms is still insufficient for human-like learning. This finding supports a conclusion drawn by Lan et al. (2024): that given sufficient evidence of a construction, NLMs can arrive at a correct representation of the constraints. However, the ability to generalize from one construction appears weak at best.

Cleft-RNN's filler effect for Wh-movement is the only instance among our findings where an NLM achieves the most stringent measure of islands: a confidence interval overlapping with zero. However, we are cautious to over-interpret this finding: our test set for Wh-movement was far smaller than that of the other construction types.

Further, the failure of Cleft-RNN to capture islands in tough-movement relative to the pretrained RNN highlights a more pressing issue with NLMs that rely only on surface distributions: exposure to one construction type can cause a degradation in an NLM's knowledge of a different type, when the two share superficially similar characteristics at odds with the dependency. The learner would then need even more positive direct evidence of the other type to offset such erroneous conclusions.

We found that the NLM we tested fares worse at recognizing island constraints than past studies would suggest: both the pretrained RNN and our augmented models failed to arrive at the most stringent measure of islandhood in all cases but

Wh-movement in Cleft-RNN. We suspect this is greatly influenced by the frequency of surface forms of particular constructions, as hypothesized by Ozaki et al. (2022).

Why, then, did Wilcox et al. (2023)'s method of using the presence of fillers, gaps, *and* islands as predictors of surprisal yield a significant interaction for islandhood in instances where the filler effect suggested otherwise? We believe that the interaction collapses effects across different combinations of features. Our NLMs succeed with UGEs, which likely obscures their corresponding failure to recognize FGEs. However, the failure in FGEs suggests that the NLM is recognizing neither grammaticality nor the presence of an island. For FGEs, the filler effect is in the wrong direction; grammatical continuations (i.e., those without a filler or a gap) are more surprising than ungrammatical ones (a filler and no gap). This contradicts both the measures for islands proposed by Wilcox et al. (2023) and Ozaki et al. (2022), who suggest that rather than no difference at the gap site, surprisal should align with grammaticality. Here we find that surprisal does not align with either measure and is in fact showing the reverse pattern for grammaticality.

The results of Experiment 1 strongly suggest that the NLM arrives at its knowledge of filler-gap dependencies through piecemeal learning and that positive direct evidence of a filler-gap dependency in each construction is required to learn the dependency for that construction. We conducted Experiment 2 to explore whether positive evidence of simple topicalization sentences is sufficient for Topic-RNN to make predictions consistent with a human-like understanding of both the simple dependency and islands. Topic-RNN learns to expect a gap given a filler, but fails to learn the other direction of the dependency: that in the absence of a filler, there should be no gap. The model's failure to learn the simple topicalization dependency even in the face of direct evidence is an additional challenge to claims that language-specific biases are not necessary to learn such dependencies.

Taken together, the results from Experiments 1 and 2 show that NLMs do not generalize from a shared representation to learn filler-gap dependencies. Instead, they rely heavily on input that closely aligns with individual constructions. Further, in cases such as topicalization, NLMs appear to struggle with learning the dependency. Our findings are particularly important as researchers consider in what ways NLMs might and might not serve as good proxies for language learners. Our work reiterates the importance of specific linguistic inductive biases to model language acquisition.

Acknowledgements

We appreciate feedback from Jeff Lidz, Colin Phillips, Philip Resnik, Naomi Feldman, Hal Daumé III, Bill Idsardi and other members of the UMD Psycholinguistics Workshop, Computational Cognitive Science group, and CLIP labs. Jiayi Lu, Nur Lan, and Suhas Arehalli provided insightful suggestions regarding our methodology. Sathvik Nair was supported by the ONR MURI Award N00014-18-1-2670 and NSF GRFP Grant No. DGE 2236417.

References

Dale J Barr, Roger Levy, Christoph Scheepers, and Harry J Tily. 2013. Random effects structure for confirmatory hypothesis testing: Keep it maximal. *Journal of memory and language*, 68(3):255–278.

Thomas G. Bever and Brian McElree. 1988. Empty categories access their antecedents during comprehension. *Linguistic Inquiry*, 19(1):35–43. Publisher: The MIT Press.

Noam Chomsky. 1977. On Wh-Movement. *Formal Syntax*, pages 71–132. Publisher: Academic Press.

Stephen Crain and Janet Dean Fodor. 1985. Rules and constraints in sentence processing. *North East Linguistics Society*, 15(1).

Richard Futrell, Ethan Wilcox, Takashi Morita, Peng Qian, Miguel Ballesteros, and Roger Levy. 2019. Neural language models as psycholinguistic subjects: Representations of syntactic state. In *Proceedings of the 2019 Conference of the North American Chapter of the Association for Computational Linguistics: Human Language Technologies, Volume 1 (Long and Short Papers)*, pages 32–42, Minneapolis, Minnesota. Association for Computational Linguistics.

Gerald Gazdar. 1982. Phrase Structure Grammar. In Pauline Jacobson and Geoffrey K. Pullum, editors, *The Nature of Syntactic Representation*, Synthese Language Library, pages 131–186. Springer Netherlands, Dordrecht.

Gerald Gazdar, Ewan Klein, Geoffrey Pullum, and Ivan Sag. 1985. *Generalized Phrase Structure Grammar*. Harvard Univ. Press, Cambridge, Mass.

Kristina Gulordava, Piotr Bojanowski, Edouard Grave, Tal Linzen, and Marco Baroni. 2018. Colorless Green Recurrent Networks Dream Hierarchically.

In *Proceedings of the 2018 Conference of the North American Chapter of the Association for Computational Linguistics: Human Language Technologies, Volume 1 (Long Papers)*, pages 1195–1205, New Orleans, Louisiana. Association for Computational Linguistics.

Sepp Hochreiter and Jürgen Schmidhuber. 1997. Long short-term memory. *Neural computation*, 9(8):1735–1780.

Kuan-Jung Huang, Suhas Arehalli, Mari Kugemoto, Christian Muxica, Grusha Prasad, Brian Dillon, and Tal Linzen. 2024. Large-scale benchmark yields no evidence that language model surprisal explains syntactic disambiguation difficulty. *Journal of Memory and Language*, 137:104510.

Eshin Jolly. 2018. Pymer4: Connecting r and python for linear mixed modeling. *Journal of Open Source Software*, 3(31):862.

Jaap Jumelet, Milica Denic, Jakub Szymanik, Dieuwke Hupkes, and Shane Steinert-Threlkeld. 2021. Language models use monotonicity to assess NPI licensing. In *Findings of the Association for Computational Linguistics: ACL-IJCNLP 2021*, pages 4958–4969. Association for Computational Linguistics.

Ronald Kaplan and Joan Bresnan. 1982. Lexical-Functional Grammar: A Formal System for Grammatical Representation. In Joan Bresnan, editor, *The Mental Representation of Grammatical Relations*, pages 173–281. MIT Press.

Anastasia Kobzeva, Suhas Arehalli, Tal Linzen, and Dave Kush. 2023. Neural Networks Can Learn Patterns of Island-insensitivity in Norwegian. In *Proceedings of the Society for Computation in Linguistics 2023*, pages 175–185, Amherst, MA. Association for Computational Linguistics.

Nur Lan, Emmanuel Chemla, and Roni Katzir. 2024. Large language models and the argument from the poverty of the stimulus. *Linguistic Inquiry*, pages 1–28.

Roger Levy. 2008. Expectation-based syntactic comprehension. *Cognition*, 106(3):1126–1177.

Tal Linzen and Marco Baroni. 2021. Syntactic structure from deep learning. *Annual Review of Linguistics*, 7:195–212.

Jiayi Lu, Jonathan Merchan, Lian Wang, and Judith Degen. 2024. Can syntactic log-odds ratio predict acceptability and satiation? In *Proceedings of the Society for Computation in Linguistics 2024*, pages 10–19, Irvine, CA. Association for Computational Linguistics.

Brian McElree and Teresa Griffith. 1998. Structural and lexical constraints on filling gaps during sentence comprehension: A time-course analysis. *Journal of Experimental Psychology: Learning, Memory, and Cognition*, 24(2):432–460.

Kanishka Misra and Kyle Mahowald. 2024. Language models learn rare phenomena from less rare phenomena: The case of the missing aanns. *arXiv preprint arXiv:2403.19827*.

Shikhar Murty, Pratyusha Sharma, Jacob Andreas, and Christopher Manning. 2023. Grokking of hierarchical structure in vanilla transformers. In *Proceedings of the 61st Annual Meeting of the Association for Computational Linguistics (Volume 2: Short Papers)*, pages 439–448, Toronto, Canada. Association for Computational Linguistics.

Akira Omaki, Ellen F. Lau, Imogen Davidson White, Myles L. Dakan, Aaron Apple, and Colin Phillips. 2015. Hyper-active gap filling. *Frontiers in Psychology*, 6.

Satoru Ozaki, Dan Yurovsky, and Lori Levin. 2022. How Well Do LSTM Language Models Learn Filler-gap Dependencies? *Proceedings of the Society for Computation in Linguistics*, 5(1):76–88.

Abhinav Patil, Jaap Jumelet, Yu Ying Chiu, Andy Lapastora, Peter Shen, Lexie Wang, Clevis Willrich, and Shane Steinert-Threlkeld. 2024. Filtered corpus training (fict) shows that language models can generalize from indirect evidence. *arXiv preprint arXiv:2405.15750*.

Colin Phillips. 2006. The Real-Time Status of Island Phenomena. *Language*, 82(4):795–823.

Steven Piantadosi. 2023. Modern language models refute Chomsky's approach to language. *LingBuzz Preprint*.

Carl Jesse Pollard and Ivan A. Sag. 1987. *Information-Based Syntax and Semantics: Volume 1, Fundamentals*. Number no. 13 in CSLI lecture notes. Cambridge University Press, Stanford, CA.

Paul M. Postal. 1999. *Three Investigations of Extraction*. The MIT Press.

Grusha Prasad, Marten van Schijndel, and Tal Linzen. 2019. Using priming to uncover the organization of syntactic representations in neural language models. In *Proceedings of the 23rd Conference on Computational Natural Language Learning (CoNLL)*, pages 66–76.

Alec Radford, Jeffrey Wu, Rewon Child, David Luan, Dario Amodei, Ilya Sutskever, et al. 2019. Language models are unsupervised multitask learners. *OpenAI blog*, 1(8):9.

Carson T. Schütze, Jon Sprouse, and Ivano Caponigro. 2015. Challenges for a theory of islands: A broader perspective on ambridge, pine, and lieven. *Language*, 91(2):31–39.

Jon Sprouse, Ivano Caponigro, Ciro Greco, and Carlo Cecchetto. 2016. Experimental syntax and the variation of island effects in english and italian. *Natural Language & Linguistic Theory*, 34(1):307–344.

Laurie A. Stowe. 1986. Parsing wh-constructions: Evidence for on-line gap location. *Language and Cognitive Processes*, 1:227–245.

Matthew J. Traxler and Martin J. Pickering. 1996. Plausibility and the processing of unbounded dependencies: An eye-tracking study. *Journal of Memory and Language*, 35:454–475.

Marten Van Schijndel and Tal Linzen. 2021. Single-stage prediction models do not explain the magnitude of syntactic disambiguation difficulty. *Cognitive science*, 45(6):e12988.

Marten van Schijndel, Aaron Mueller, and Tal Linzen. 2019. Quantity doesn't buy quality syntax with neural language models. In *Proceedings of the 2019 Conference on Empirical Methods in Natural Language Processing and the 9th International Joint Conference on Natural Language Processing*, pages 5831–5837.

Alex Warstadt. 2022. *Artificial Neural Networks as Models of Human Language Acquisition*. New York University.

Ethan Wilcox, Richard Futrell, and Roger Levy. 2023. Using Computational Models to Test Syntactic Learnability. *Linguistic Inquiry*, pages 1–44.

Ethan Wilcox, Roger Levy, Takashi Morita, and Richard Futrell. 2018. What do rnn language models learn about filler–gap dependencies? In *Proceedings of the 2018 EMNLP Workshop BlackboxNLP: Analyzing and Interpreting Neural Networks for NLP*, pages 211–221.

Of Models and Men: Probing Neural Networks for Agreement Attraction with Psycholinguistic Data

Maxim Bazhukov[🤖], **Ekaterina Voloshina, Sergey Pletenev**[✍️, 🧑‍🏫, 🤖]
Arseny Anisimov[🤖] **Oleg Serikov**[🖥️], **Svetlana Toldova**[🤖]
[🤖]HSE University, [🧑‍🏫]AIRI, [✍️]Skoltech, [🖥️]KAUST

Abstract

Interpretability studies have played an important role in the field of NLP. They focus on the problems of how models encode information or, for instance, whether linguistic capabilities allow them to prefer grammatical sentences to ungrammatical. Recently, several studies examined whether the models demonstrate patterns similar to humans and whether they are sensitive to the phenomena of interference like humans' grammaticality judgements, including the phenomenon of agreement attraction.

In this paper, we probe BERT and GPT models on the syntactic phenomenon of agreement attraction in Russian using the psycholinguistic data with syncretism. Working on the language with syncretism between some plural and singular forms allows us to differentiate between the effects of the surface form and of the underlying grammatical feature. Thus we can further investigate models' sensitivity to this phenomenon and examine if the patterns of their behaviour are similar to human patterns. Moreover, we suggest a new way of comparing models' and humans' responses via statistical testing. We show that there are some similarities between models' and humans' results, while GPT is somewhat more aligned with human responses than BERT. Finally, preliminary results suggest that surface form syncretism influences attraction, perhaps more so than grammatical form syncretism. [1]

1 Introduction[2]

With the fast development of large language models (LLMs), interpretability has become (Belinkov et al., 2023) an important issue in Natural Language Processing. Interpretability studies aim to explain what LLMs learn during pre-training, for instance, whether they pick up factual information or develop language skills. One of the promising directions of interpretability research is comparing model responses to human acceptability judgements (Lau et al., 2017; Warstadt et al., 2018). A case in point is the research on the phenomenon of agreement attraction.

In this paper, we investigate models' sensitivity to agreement attraction in light of morphological syncretism. We design a probing experiment based on the data from a previous psycholinguistic experiment on humans (Slioussar, 2018). The focus is on Russian, a language with rich morphology, which allows us to investigate agreement attraction interacting with different types of *syncretism*. *Syncretism* is a surface formal identity of grammatically distinct forms like genitive singular *polja* 'of field (GEN.SG)' and nominative plural *polja* 'fields (NOM.PL)' being formally identical. This kind of identity occurs in genitive case and it differs from accusative case syncretism of some other nouns, where it is simply the nominative and accusative case forms that coincide (separately in singular and in plural): *lug* 'meadow(NOM.SG=ACC.SG)' and *luga* 'meadows(NOM.PL=ACC.PL)'. Distinguishing accusative and genitive syncretisms is a unique setup that helps to disentangle the effects of structure (underlying features) from the effects of surface forms.

(1) a. *Trass-**a*** *čerez* *polje* *byl-**a*** *nov-**oj***
path-SG across field be.PST-SG new-SG
'The highway across the field was new'

b. *Trass-**y*** *čerez* *polje* *byl-**i*** *nov-**ymi***
path-PL across field be.PST-SG new-PL
'The highways across the field were new'

[1] The code for the experiments is available here: `https://github.com/bamaxi/agreement-probing`.

[2] For brevity we use the following abbreviations (glosses): SG – singular number; PL – plural number; NOM – nominative case; ACC – accusative case; GEN – genitive case; genders: M – masculine, F – feminine, N – neuter

Proceedings of the 28th Conference on Computational Natural Language Learning, pages 280–290
November 15-16, 2024 ©2024 Association for Computational Linguistics

Agreement is a grammar rule where grammatical features like number or gender of one linguistic element, the controller, license corresponding features on a syntactically related element, the target. In (1a) singular subject *trassa* is the controller and requires singular on the verb 'be' and adjective. Similarly, in (1b), plural *trassy* requires plural. This type of phenomena is well acquired by people (Guasti, 2017), who easily recognize errors in agreement (see e.g. (Slioussar, 2018)). However, the task becomes more complicated if the controller and the target of agreement are separated by some linguistic material. It is yet more complicated, if the surface form of the intervening material coincides with the form of a potential controller due to *syncretism*. The agreement errors are not recognised so easily in this case. The higher acceptability of incorrect sentences of this type is called *agreement attraction* and has been under research in psycholinguistics (Wagers et al., 2009) and in NLP. In NLP similar studies have already been widely conducted on the English language, revealing the inner workings of language models (Gulordava et al., 2018; Arehalli and Linzen, 2020), as well as the relationship between model errors and human errors (Linzen and Leonard, 2018).

We tackle a more complex question of whether and how the models parse two kinds of syncretism that could potentially cause agreement attraction for Russian. This allows us to finely distinguish the effect of the surface form from the effect of the underlying syntactical structure. We employ the data from a psycholinguistic study of (Slioussar, 2018), measuring Russian speakers reading times and cloze test completion. This further allows us to compare model's behaviour to that of humans.

Our contributions can be stated as following:

- We probe models on the task of agreement attraction with a new type of data. While recent studies were done for English, we work with a morphologically rich language with case-number syncretism, namely Russian;
- We compare the effect of syncretism to the effect of the underlying grammatical features
- We supply linguistic research with extra-human knowledge, showing to what extent neural networks' linguistic capabilities are similar to those of humans on the example of agreement attraction phenomenon;
- We propose a new way of comparing models' responses to the results of psycholinguistic experiments, as we perform more robust statistical analysis.

2 Related Work

2.1 Probing methodology

The interpretation of behaviour and learned representations of language models has been studied extensively. Belinkov et al. (2020) suggests classifying probing methods into *structural* and *behavioural*. *Structural* methods involve a diagnostic classifier, i.e. a simpler model, such as logistic regression, trained atop of embeddings from a bigger model. Such methods were criticised (Hewitt and Liang, 2019; Voita and Titov, 2020) for overrelying on an external classifier: it is not clear if the overall results of the studies depend on how well a model encoded linguistic information, and not on how well a classifier has been trained. *Behavioural* methods, on the other hand, involve no such external classifier and exploit models' inherit architecture. For example, Salazar et al. (2020) adapt masked language modelling task to probe internal linguistic knowledge of BERT.

2.2 Acceptability judgements

In linguistic theorizing, human acceptability judgements are an important tool. These are scores proxying grammaticality of the sentences (Chomsky, 1965; Schütze, 1996), binary (acceptable / unacceptable) or scalar. These were picked up in NLP (Lau et al., 2017) and, among other things, led to the creation of acceptability datasets like (Warstadt et al., 2018). Similarly, Warstadt et al. (2020) introduce a probing suite based on minimal pairs of grammatical and ungrammatical sentences. The suite covers several semantic, morphological and syntactic phenomena, such as negative polarity items, agreement and verb conjugation. It is shown that various behavioural model metrics can be chosen as analogues to human acceptability scores to establish preference of one sentence over another, and Warstadt et al. (2020) choose to compare full sentence likelihood. A similar work was recently done for Russian by Taktasheva et al. (2024). Indeed, this benchmark included sentences with attractor under subject-predicate agreement phenomenon, and models scored lower on such sentences than on similar sentences with no attractor. Our present work differs in that we compare human and models' performance on *psycholinguistic data*, designed for controlled experimental studies on human, with focus on syncretism-grammar comparison.

2.3 Psycholinguistics and neural networks

Since interpretation has become an important part of NLP research, several works have adapted psycholinguistic data to study how models acquire language. For example, Li et al. (2021) use psycholinguistic stimuli to study the effect of surprisal in RoBERTa layerwise showing that the best performing model shows surprisal already in the early layers. Other works adapt psycholinguistic concepts for better explanation of language model behaviour. Sinclair et al. (2022) use the effect of priming, studied earlier for humans, to see what can affect LLM's responses.

Other works directly or indirectly compare results of the models to human responses. Ettinger (2020) introduces a suite of several tasks taken from psycholinguistics to evaluate linguistic abilities of BERT. The author compares humans and the model on the basis of surface responses, such as sentence completion. Similarly, Li et al. (2022) adapt experiments based on the theory of Construction Grammar to study how different constructions are perceived by humans and models showing that transformers can detect constructions. They compare how the results of humans differ from the results of neural networks on such tasks as sorting preferable constructions. Wilcox et al. (2021) compare models' responses to human reaction time for a suite of syntactic tasks. They show that models resemble humans in their predictions although they do not achieve human-like level. Lampinen (2022) provides detailed discussion of how using proper psycholinguistic analysis of human evaluation allows drawing clearer insights from comparing LLMs to humans while bringing up the question of fair comparison of human and model responses.

2.4 Studies of attraction in agreement

Agreement is a phenomenon of licensing grammatical features like number or gender by one linguistic element, the controller, on another syntactically related element, the target. In general, while proper agreement requires understanding underlying hierarchic structure, subject-verb agreement is acquired early by human speakers (Guasti, 2017). Nonetheless, agreement is vulnerable to errors, particularly in the presence of "attractors" – subject noun dependents that are not subjects, but could be erroneously construed as subjects (see 2, 3 below).

(2) a. *The key to the cabinets were rusty
b. **The key to the cabinet were rusty

(3a) **Trass-a čerez polj-a byl-i nov-ymi*
path-SG across field-PL be.PST-PL new-PL
'The highway across the fields were new'

(3b)***Trassa čerez pol-e byli novymi*
path-SG across field-SG be.PST-PL new-PL
'The highway across the field were new'

Both sentences have longer reading times compared to fully grammatical sentences. However, sentences (2a) and (3a) show a reduced effect due to the presence of attractor nouns (*cabinets* and *polja* 'fields'). Here, these nouns could be construed as subjects and underlined parts could be proper sentences (see also Figure 1). This creates an illusion of grammaticality and mitigates the processing difficulty arising from the actual violation of grammar. Attraction of agreement is thus a grammatical notion, although similar interference effects are discussed for semantics, too (Timkey and Linzen, 2023). Hierarchy understanding by the models has been studied extensively for English (Gulordava et al., 2018; Arehalli and Linzen, 2020) and agreement attraction in particular has been compared in models and humans in a work similar to ours (Arehalli and Linzen, 2020).

One of the main sources of our data comes from Slioussar (2018). This study explores the role of *syncretism* (morphological ambiguity) in inducing attraction errors in number agreement, in Russian speakers. *Syncretism* is a phenomenon where two distinct moprhological categories are realized in the same way (Caha, 2019; Baerman et al., 2005). Unlike English, Russian nouns inflect for two categories: number and case, thus could potentially exhibit syncretism. Indeed, genitive singular *polja* 'of field (GEN.SG)' and accusative plural *polja* 'fields (ACC.PL)' are formally the same. Both are, in turn, identical to nominative plural *polja* 'fields (NOM.PL)' (all of these are, of course, distinguished in a context). Slioussar (2018) shows that surface syncretism in itself, independently of the underlying grammatical number feature, explains attraction effects. Thus ACC.PL and GEN.SG, surface forms both identical to what plural subject would be (=NOM.PL), show attraction effects, although GEN.SG is underlyingly singular (which is deducible from the syntactic structure of the full sentence). Crucially, Slioussar (2018) believes such data to be difficult for existing theories of attraction. We test whether the effect holds for models.

3 Experimental Setup

We study the attraction phenomenon in LLMs and compare it to human data available from (Slioussar, 2018). In these experiments, humans' reading time has been measured in relation to the grammatical pattern of the sentence. We follow this approach in our experimental setting, yet we also propose a model-specific interpretability analysis. We reproduce the reading time analysis performed on humans' data, by introducing the readability-like metrics for LLM. We offer deeper insights into how LLMs process sentences of every grammatical pattern, by analyzing their attention maps.

Our statistical analysis methodology mostly follows the one of Slioussar (2018), with a few changes made for the sake of results' interpretability. Since we test the models on the exact same data on which humans have been tested, we manage to avoid uneven comparisons, yet support the theoretical findings of the original work.

3.1 Models

We work with transformer-based models of different architectures: ruBERT[3], an encoder-only model, and ruGPT[4], a decoder-only architecture.

ruBERT (Kuratov and Arkhipov, 2019) was trained on the Russian part of Wikipedia and news data with pretraining objectives of Masked Language Modelling (MLM) and Next Sentence Prediction (NSP), following the original BERT architecture (Devlin et al., 2019).

ruGPT-3.5 (Zmitrovich et al., 2024) was trained on data from various domains (Wikipedia, books, and news) with a language modelling pretraining objective. The model is based on the original architecture of the GPT-3 model (Brown et al., 2020).

3.2 Data

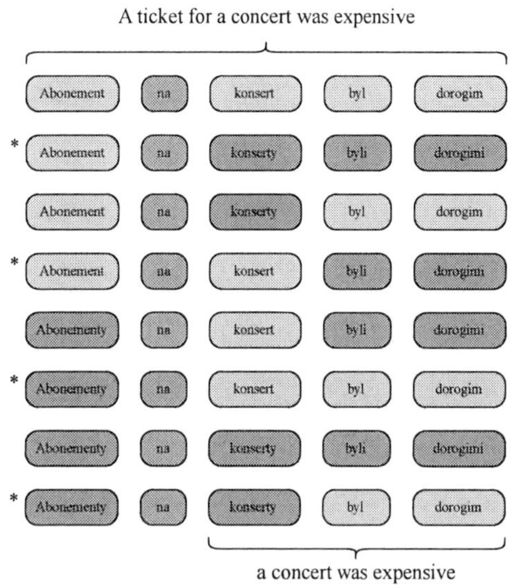

Figure 1: Example of one set of data: Each sentence exists in 8 variants, formed by different combinations of the number of the subject (the first word), the attractor (third word), and the predicate (fourth and fifth words). Words in the singular are highlighted in blue, and words in the plural are highlighted in purple. Sentences marked with an asterisk (∗) are ungrammatical.

To compare how perception of the attraction phenomenon differs in humans and models, we use the dataset prepared for a psycholinguistic study by Slioussar (2018), provided by the author upon our request.

The dataset includes in total 80 sentences with subject-verb agreement, full text is available for 64 of them. All our experiments with the models use this subset of 64 sentences, while fuller 80 sentence data is available for human response times (on these see the Section 4.3). All the sentences had the same syntactic structure: `subject + attractor + verb + other_verb_dependents`. The attractor is either in accusative case or in genitive case, splitting the data in halves. Also, in each of the 64 sentences, the subject, the attractor and the verb can have a singular or a plural marker amounting to 8 variants, as Figure 1 illustrates for a

[3]`https://huggingface.co/DeepPavlov/rubert-base-cased`

[4]`https://huggingface.co/ai-forever/ruGPT-3.5-13B`

condition with an attractor in accusative case. The total number of items is thus $64 * 8 = 512$. Notably, in all sentences the predicate is an adjective with *byt'* 'to be', the verb under examination, as an auxillary. We concur that using single lemma limits empirical coverage, but here it facilitates comparison.

As mentioned, sentences of Slioussar (2018) each belong to one of the two types. In half the sentences, the context demands that attractor be in the accusative case and in the other half that it be in the genitive case. Such setup allowed Slioussar to disentangle the effects of the underlying grammatical number from the effects of the surface form. This is because nominative plural is the form that could attract predicate agreement, and *accusative plural* is syncretic (has the same surface form) with nominative plural, while the reverse is true for genitive: it is *genitive singular*, that is syncretic with plural, while genitive plural is not (see Examples 4, 5). This is the unique property allowing to distinguish attraction by grammatical features and attraction by surface form. If attraction errors pattern the same way in accusative as in genitive, that would mean that only grammatical number is important. On the other hand, if these patterns were different depending on the case, surface form must matter too.

(4) ACCusative: ACC.**PL** = NOM.**PL**, ACC.SG ≠ NOM.PL

a. *tropinka cherez lug*[ACC.SG] *byla/*byli*
'a path trough the meadow was/*were'

b. *tropinka cherez **luga***[ACC.PL] *byla/*byli*
'a path trough the meadow was/*were'

c. ***luga***[NOM.PL] *byli*
'the meadows were'

(5) GENitive: GEN.PL ≠ NOM.PL, GEN.**SG** = NOM.**PL**

a. *korobka dlya **kraski***[GEN.SG] *byla/*byli*
'a box for the paints was/*were'

b. *korobka dlya krasok*[GEN.PL] *byla/*byli*
'a box for the paints was/*were'

c. ***kraski***[NOM.PL] *byli*
'paints were'

3.3 Methods

To evaluate models' behavior on the agreement attraction, we collect vectors representing model's activity when processing each of these 512 items. Then, inspired by (Slioussar, 2018), we employ statistical analysis to learn if observed features somehow reflect the sentence structure.

We hypothesize that eight groups of sentences can be meaningfully ranked by model's perplexity: sentences where attraction does happen as described above (e.g., 2a, 33a, 4b) should be more natural than the respective purely ungrammatical variants (2b, 33b, 4a), but less natural than correct sentences (6). Moreover, this effect should be reflected in human reading times.

(6) Predicted ranking of sentence types:
grammatical > attractor > ungrammatical

Most importantly, we expect to see one of three scenarios Slioussar (2018) outlined regarding the distinction between syncretism and underlying features. To test our hypotheses, we use two methods: perplexity-based and attention-based methods described below.

3.3.1 Estimation of models' certainty

Due to the differences in architectures and objectives of ruGPT and ruBERT, a direct comparison of the models' performance is not feasible. As the analysis of human behaviour in Slioussar (2018) was focused on word-level reading times, our analysis also focuses on word-level rather than sentence-level predictions.

In general, we want to estimate for each item how likely the verb is, given a prefix of subject and attractor (for grammatical items this is the correct verb form that agrees well with subject, and for ungrammatical ones — an incorrect form that does not). Such approach has already been shown to be effective for the study of attraction in GPT-like models (Arehalli and Linzen, 2020). Since this does not translate straightforwardly to BERT, to facilitate the comparison we establish the following methodological adjustments:

- **ruGPT**: we calculate the logarithmic probability of the first verb after the attractor word as an estimate of the model's generation.

$$Score_{GPT}(X) = logp_\theta(x_{i_{verb}}|x_{<i_{verb}})$$

where $x_{<i_{verb}}$ is tokens before verb.

- **ruBERT**: we use a masked language modeling approach. Specifically, we mask all tokens succeeding the attractor word. The generation estimate is then determined by subtracting the probability of the first masked token from the overall masked sequence probability.

$$Score_{BERT}(X) = logp_\theta(x_{verb}|context)$$

where $context$ is left part of the sentence $(x_0, x_1, ..., x_{verb-1})$.

This approach allows for a relative comparison of GPT and BERT's generation capabilities, focusing on the influence of the attractor word on subsequent word prediction, despite their distinct architectures and training objectives.

Both score estimates based on probability for BERT and GPT are naive implementations in this case. They may not work for other models or words (Kauf and Ivanova, 2023) (Pimentel and Meister, 2024). For some models word prediction estimation is made more difficult due to the tokenization step, where target word may be split into several tokens. In our case, however, we only predict one of four forms of 'to be' word: $byl(was)_{SG,masc}$ and all its variations $byla(was)_{SG,femn}$, $bylo(was)_{SG,neut}$, $byli(were)_{PL}$, which are tokenized as a single token for GPT and BERT.

3.3.2 Appoximating effect from a subject and an attractor

Apart from perplexity, we extract attention head projections and compare the attention distributions between different types of sentences. We take attention scores from each head and layer and then extract attention used to predict a predicate (an auxilary verb and an adjective) that comes from a subject and from an attractor. Therefore, we get two arrays representing attention from a predicate on a subject and an attractor respectively. These scores are averaged across attention heads for each layer. In other words, we calculate how much impact the subject had on prediction of a predicate and how much impact the attractor had on prediction of the same predicate. To compare the results on different sentence types, we use Student's T-test with Bonferroni correction.

4 Results and Discussion

4.1 How models perceive different types of ungrammatical sentences

To check whether models are sensitive to agreement errors in general, we evaluate their quality with adapted masked language model scoring (Salazar et al., 2020): we first calculate the scores (see Section 3.3.1) for each of our sentences and then we compare two sentences (grammatical and ungrammatical) that share the same subject and attractor and differ only in the number of the predicate. The sentence is grammatical if the number of the subject and the predicate match. We count the model as answering correctly, if the score for the grammatical sentence is higher than for the ungrammatical sentence. The results are summarised in Table 1, with the results for humans taken from the experiment 2 in (Slioussar, 2018) where participants were asked to complete a sentence. The tasks for models and humans are rather distinct and the data doesn't warrant a direct comparison. Rather, we are interested in comparing models' performance on different structures and their trend to the human trend.

As seen from the table, both ruGPT and ruBERT perform very well. Moreover, they show similar error patterns to humans. The sentences where it was easier to distinguish the correct sentence from an incorrect one were sentences where both the subject and the attractor were of the same number, especially in the singular. Humans show better results on completing such sentences as well. However, when the subject and the attractor differ in number, for humans it was easier when the subject was in plural, while for both ruBERT and ruGPT this was more difficult and they made less mistakes in singular subject + plural attractor structure.

4.2 Comparison of attention scores

We compare attention scores between sentences of different structures. We calculate paired Student's test; Figure 2 shows p-values of such tests after Bonferronni correction for ruBERT and ruGPT respectively. As seen from the figure, for ruBERT model, the main significant differences ($p < 0.05$) are mostly between correct sentences and similar sentences with attractors. For example, a correct sentence of type P_P-P (predicate, subject and attractor are in plural) is significantly different from structures P_S-P (predicate in plural, subject in singular and attractor in plural) and S_P-S (predicate in singular, subject in plural and attractor in singular). However, grammatical sentences do not differ in attention with ungrammatical sentences

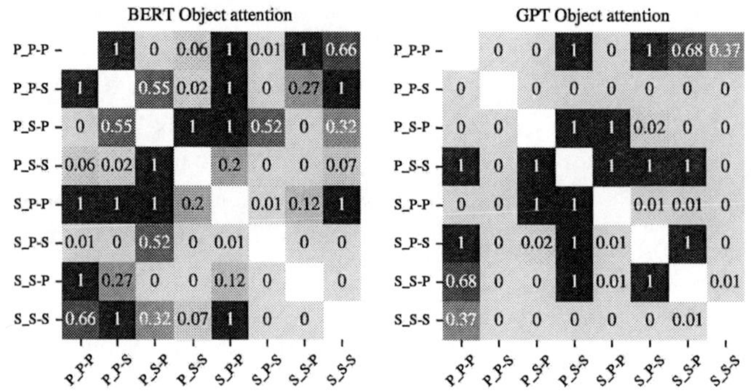

Figure 2: Results of Student's pairwise t-test (p-values) for ruBERT and ruGPT verb-to-attractor attention scores respectively between 8 variants of the sentence. The first letter encodes the number of a predicate (*S* for singular and *P* for plural), the second letter encodes the number of a subject and the third letter encodes the number of an attractor, for example, *P_S-P* stands for a sentence where a subject is in singular but an attractor and a predicate are in plural.

where attractors differ in number with predicates.

Attention scores in ruGPT do not follow a clear pattern and are most probably affected by other factors that we do not control as we focus on difference in number.

Structure	ruGPT	ruBERT	Humans
S-S	**1.0**	**1.0**	**0.83**
S-P	**1.0**	0.94	0.77
P-S	0.95	0.86	0.79
P-P	**1.0**	0.97	0.8

Table 1: Comparison of accuracy *scores* of ruGPT and ruBERT to the *percentage* of successfully completed tasks in the psycholinguistic experiment (figures for humans are taken from Slioussar (2018)

4.3 Comparison with human results

We employ statistical models similar to those of Slioussar (2018) and perform regression analysis in R (R Core Team, 2023) with mixed models from *lme4* package (Bates et al., 2015). We employed package *lmerTest* Kuznetsova et al. (2017), and also *pbkrtest* Halekoh and Højsgaard (2014), where applicable, to obtain the p-values of variables in these mixed models. Below we report p-value of *lmerTest* but Kenwald-Roger test of *pbkrtest* yields very similar p-values numerically. The R code for these calculations is also available in our project repository.

The following comparison is made to data on human reading times (RT) (Slioussar, 2018), on which we fit a new model. We evaluate the performance of both language models with the following mixed-effects statistical model (7). The dependent variable is the score (or RT in humans) of a singular and of a plural predicate given a certain subject-attractor prefix. Recall, that for every sentence, there are 4 possible prefixes and 2 possible numbers for the predicate, thus we have 8 sentence variants. This is a setup similar to Slioussar experiments with humans' RTs when reading such sentences word-by-word. We thus compare RT for humans with scores for our models. Although these are, of course, quite disparate values, we deem them to be the most optimal values for comparison in the available data. These are both numeric variables, which we take to be proxying 'surprisal' by a given sentence.

Slioussar shows that RTs are, in a sense, delayed and that predictor variables (described below) are not significant on the word 4, the verb, first word of the predicate, but significant on word 5, the participle, second word of the predicate. Our model fitted on word 4 is indeed not significant, thus for humans we analyze RTs on word 5. We reiterate that for models we test verb/word 4 scores. Models and humans are different in how they process sentences, and we consider such setup to be a fair comparison.

(7) $\text{lmer}(\text{Score} \sim N_1 + N_2 + \text{kind} + (1|\text{Sent}))$

As random effects we use sentence number (and participant number for humans, too). Our predictor variables are the number of the sub-

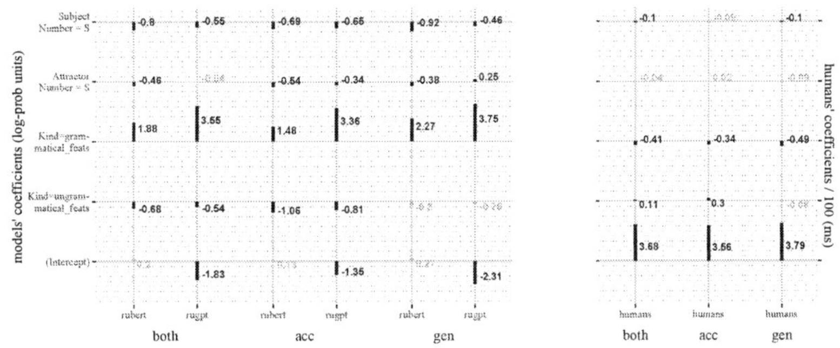

Figure 3: Estimates of variables predicting score for models (3.3.1), and reaction time (ms) for humans in data from (Slioussar, 2018). These proxy 'surprisal' but differently: *lower model score* $\rightarrow$ more surprisal, *higher human reaction time* $\rightarrow$ more surprisal. Coefficients are in **dark blue**, when p-values computed with *lmerTest* package (Kuznetsova et al., 2017) are significant with p-value $< \alpha = 0.05$.

ject and of the attractor, similarly to Slioussar (2018), but unlike Slioussar we do not include interaction terms into the model, opting instead for three-way encoding of sentence 'grammaticality' judged by *grammatical features*. We distinguish *gram*matical sentences, where verb number matches subject number, *attr*actor sentences, where verb number does not match subject number but matches attractor number and *ungram*matical sentences, where verb number matches neither. We encode contrasts, such that $kind = attractor$ falls into intercept, and $kind = grammatical$ and $kind = ungrammatical$ remain as (one-hot encoded) variables. Thus, while we also test attraction effects as does Slioussar, our approach allows us to test the ranking hypothesis. Recall, that we predict the ranking in (6) for 'surprisal'. For models this should be exactly the ranking of scores and for humans this should be the reverse ranking of RTs (least time spent on grammatical sentences and most on ungrammatical). We show below, that this is mostly borne out.

Finally, recall that sentences of Slioussar (2018) each belong to one of the two types: in half of the sentences the attractor is in accusative case and in the other half in the genitive case, and case determines surface syncretism (Section 3.2). Thus syncretism is captured differently: for accusative, where ACC.PL = NOM.PL – by 'kind' variable above, for genitive, where GEN.SG = NOM.PL – by 'attractor number' variable.

We thus perform regression analysis analysis for three sets of data: all sentences, accusative case only sentences, genitive case only sentences. The first model would inform us of grammatical tendencies, while the other two models isolating case would inform us of the effect of surface syncretism. These three regressions are fit on each of ruBERT, ruGPT and humans data, totalling in 9 experiments.

P-values and coefficients are shown in Figure 3. On full data, for ruBERT all variables achieve significance and for ruGPT all variables except attractor number achieve significance. This correlates with investigation into attention heads: there, similarly, ruBERT seems to attend to the attractor, while ruGPT does not. The ranking hypothesis in 6 holds, and grammatical sentences receive higher scores (W > 0) than baseline, attractor sentences, while absolutely bad sentences (non-grammatical and without attraction) receive scores lower (W < 0) than baseline attractor sentences. Importantly, for ruGPT the bigger coefficients indicate stronger distinction between sentence kinds. This is in line with its higher accuracy (Table 1). As for the human data, the result is similar to ruGPT, rather than ruBERT, with attractor number not achieving significance. However, the ranking holds for humans too: RTs to grammatical sentences are lower (W < 0) than for attractor sentences (interpreted as less surprisal) while they are higher (W > 0) for totally ungrammatical sentences.

We now consider two subsets by case independently. For accusative case sentences, where syncretism is exactly the (PL = NOM.PL) the results are very similar to full data results. The ranking hypothesis holds. This is because exactly this type of syncretism (deep, grammatical) is captured well by feature *kind* variable. As such, for ruBERT and ruGPT all variables achieve significance, even attractor number for ruGPT. Again, GPT coefficients are higher indicating stronger distinction between sentence kinds. As for human RTs, they are significantly different between sentence kinds and follow the hypothesis. However, the precise numbers of subject and attractor are insignificant, which would mean there is no assymetry in agreement with singular or plural nouns for humans.

Finally, we consider only the sentences with genitive, where syncretism is GEN.SG=NOM.PL, so if surface form matters in attraction, singular would be more "attractive" here than grammatical plural. This is not captured by *kind* variable, which is oriented on grammatical feature rather than surface form. Thus featurally ungrammatical sentences are not significantly different from feature attracting sentences. However, the attractor number being singular increases the score of ruGPT, while for full data and accusative data the reverse was true. Put more explicitly, it means that grammatical attraction in genitive plural (*P_S-P*: *Subject* =S, *kind=attractor*, *Attractor*=P $\implies$ *Attractor=Verb*=PL) is scored at $-2.31 + (-0.46) = -2.77$, *lower* than surface form attraction in genitive singular (*S_S-P*, techinically *kind=ungram*, *Subject* = *Attractor* =S $\implies$ *Verb*=PL) $-2.31 + (-0.46) + 0.25 = -2.52$ (not counting the insignificant *kind=ungram* = -0.26). Although ruBERT result is inconclusive (perhaps due to intercept not being significant) we take this to indicate that at least for GPT it is formal syncretism and not grammatical features, that predicts the attraction. This is a result similar to (Slioussar, 2018). Our model on her human data shows similar result: RT is not significantly different between featurally "attractive" and ungrammatical sentences, while singular attractor reduces RT.

Overall, models seem more sensitive to attractor number than humans, meaning singular and plural attractors are treated differently in a setup where attraction by grammatical number could happen.

5 Conclusion

We explored how models react to errors in subject-verb agreement, where humans are prone to mistakes of *attraction*. These are ungrammatical contexts that look as if agreement happens not with the subject as a whole, but with subject's dependent (2a, 33a).

We find that indeed, like humans, models see such sentences as more acceptable than ungrammatical sentences with no attraction, i.e. the ranking in (6) holds for humans and models alike. Most importantly, we find in genitive, a pattern similar to what Slioussar (2018) finds, where surface syncretism is more predictive of attraction than grammatical number. Recall that in our case attraction by surface syncretism obtains for genitive singular, where the attractor is neither nominative nor plural, while grammatical attraction is expected for genitive plural. This is a somewhat puzzling result for humans (Slioussar, 2018) and models alike, because other tasks show that both are sensitive to deeper structure.

As for overall accuracy, ruGPT, a decoder model, was more likely to choose correct sentence continuation, assigning higher probability to the verb form with the correct number. BERT, an encoder model, did worse here.

Attention scores investigation does not present a clear picture, but for ruBERT comparison between sentences that differ only in attractor are significant. This may be the reason for why its scores are significantly determined by attractor number.

We examined a single phenomenon of agreement attraction in subject-verb agreement on a constrained dataset from a psycholinguistic study of Slioussar (2018). We confirmed that ruBERT and ruGPT exhibit agreement attraction by grammatical number. An intriguing preliminary finding, resembling Slioussar (2018)'s results is that for ruGPT agreement attraction seems more sensitive to formal identity than to grammatical number, which could be distinguished in Russian genitive forms.

6 Limitations

This study presents several limitations that necessitate further investigation. The study's findings are based on a single experiment focusing on grammatical number agreement and only on one language. Moreover, a single and frequent verb lemma is tested. This narrow scope limits the generalizability of the results to other grammatical phenomena.

Future research should explore the observed effects across a wider range of grammatical structures.

The study compared human performance to that of language models based on the assumption that these models demonstrate sensitivity to probabilistic relationships at the word level. However, this comparison remains indirect. Although the selected models allowed direct comparisons under specific experimental conditions and successfully reproduced previously observed grammaticality effects, other models, even within the same architecture may show different results. Future research would benefit from exploring the nuances of different language model architectures in relation to human performance in grammaticality tasks.

Additionally, large language models are used for research, which implies that even inference on such models can be difficult with a limited computational budget.

7 Ethics Statement

In the implementation and evaluation of our proposed approach, we use only publicly available code to avoid any ethical concerns. We use data acquired upon request (to Slioussar). The data did not include any personal data, as each participant was encoded with a label. i.e. participant 1, 2 etc. To the best of our knowledge, all participants gave an informed consent to the author of original studies.

References

Suhas Arehalli and Tal Linzen. 2020. Neural language models capture some, but not all, agreement attraction effects.

M. Baerman, D. Brown, and G.G. Corbett. 2005. *The Syntax-Morphology Interface: A Study of Syncretism*. Cambridge Studies in Linguistics. Cambridge University Press.

Douglas Bates, Martin Mächler, Ben Bolker, and Steve Walker. 2015. Fitting linear mixed-effects models using lme4. *Journal of Statistical Software*, 67(1):1–48.

Yonatan Belinkov, Sebastian Gehrmann, and Ellie Pavlick. 2020. Interpretability and analysis in neural nlp. In *Proceedings of the 58th annual meeting of the association for computational linguistics: tutorial abstracts*, pages 1–5.

Yonatan Belinkov, Sophie Hao, Jaap Jumelet, Najoung Kim, Arya McCarthy, and Hosein Mohebbi, editors. 2023. *Proceedings of the 6th BlackboxNLP Workshop: Analyzing and Interpreting Neural Networks for NLP (Organizing committee message)*. Association for Computational Linguistics, Singapore.

Tom Brown, Benjamin Mann, Nick Ryder, Melanie Subbiah, Jared D Kaplan, Prafulla Dhariwal, Arvind Neelakantan, Pranav Shyam, Girish Sastry, Amanda Askell, et al. 2020. Language models are few-shot learners. *Advances in neural information processing systems*, 33:1877–1901.

Pavel Caha. 2019. Syncretism in morphology.

Noam Chomsky. 1965. Aspects of the theory of syntax cambridge. *Multilingual Matters: MIT Press*.

Jacob Devlin, Ming-Wei Chang, Kenton Lee, and Kristina Toutanova. 2019. BERT: Pre-training of deep bidirectional transformers for language understanding. In *Proceedings of the 2019 Conference of the North American Chapter of the Association for Computational Linguistics: Human Language Technologies, Volume 1 (Long and Short Papers)*, pages 4171–4186, Minneapolis, Minnesota. Association for Computational Linguistics.

Allyson Ettinger. 2020. What bert is not: Lessons from a new suite of psycholinguistic diagnostics for language models. *Transactions of the Association for Computational Linguistics*, 8:34–48.

Maria Teresa Guasti. 2017. *Language acquisition: The growth of grammar*. MIT press.

Kristina Gulordava, Piotr Bojanowski, Edouard Grave, Tal Linzen, and Marco Baroni. 2018. Colorless green recurrent networks dream hierarchically. In *Proceedings of the 2018 Conference of the North American Chapter of the Association for Computational Linguistics: Human Language Technologies, Volume 1 (Long Papers)*, pages 1195–1205, New Orleans, Louisiana. Association for Computational Linguistics.

Ulrich Halekoh and Søren Højsgaard. 2014. A kenward-roger approximation and parametric bootstrap methods for tests in linear mixed models – the R package pbkrtest. *Journal of Statistical Software*, 59(9):1–30.

John Hewitt and Percy Liang. 2019. Designing and interpreting probes with control tasks. In *Proceedings of the 2019 Conference on Empirical Methods in Natural Language Processing and the 9th International Joint Conference on Natural Language Processing (EMNLP-IJCNLP)*, pages 2733–2743, Hong Kong, China. Association for Computational Linguistics.

Carina Kauf and Anna Ivanova. 2023. A better way to do masked language model scoring. In *Proceedings of the 61st Annual Meeting of the Association for*

Computational Linguistics (Volume 2: Short Papers), pages 925–935, Toronto, Canada. Association for Computational Linguistics.

Yuri Kuratov and Mikhail Arkhipov. 2019. Adaptation of deep bidirectional multilingual transformers for russian language.

Alexandra Kuznetsova, Per B. Brockhoff, and Rune H. B. Christensen. 2017. lmerTest package: Tests in linear mixed effects models. *Journal of Statistical Software*, 82(13):1–26.

Andrew Kyle Lampinen. 2022. Can language models handle recursively nested grammatical structures? a case study on comparing models and humans. *arXiv preprint arXiv:2210.15303*.

Jey Han Lau, Alexander Clark, and Shalom Lappin. 2017. Grammaticality, acceptability, and probability: A probabilistic view of linguistic knowledge. *Cognitive science*, 41(5):1202–1241.

Bai Li, Zining Zhu, Guillaume Thomas, Frank Rudzicz, and Yang Xu. 2022. Neural reality of argument structure constructions. In *Proceedings of the 60th Annual Meeting of the Association for Computational Linguistics (Volume 1: Long Papers)*, pages 7410–7423, Dublin, Ireland. Association for Computational Linguistics.

Bai Li, Zining Zhu, Guillaume Thomas, Yang Xu, and Frank Rudzicz. 2021. How is BERT surprised? layerwise detection of linguistic anomalies. In *Proceedings of the 59th Annual Meeting of the Association for Computational Linguistics and the 11th International Joint Conference on Natural Language Processing (Volume 1: Long Papers)*, pages 4215–4228, Online. Association for Computational Linguistics.

Tal Linzen and Brian Leonard. 2018. Distinct patterns of syntactic agreement errors in recurrent networks and humans.

Tiago Pimentel and Clara Meister. 2024. How to compute the probability of a word.

R Core Team. 2023. *R: A Language and Environment for Statistical Computing*. R Foundation for Statistical Computing, Vienna, Austria.

Julian Salazar, Davis Liang, Toan Q. Nguyen, and Katrin Kirchhoff. 2020. Masked language model scoring. In *Proceedings of the 58th Annual Meeting of the Association for Computational Linguistics*, pages 2699–2712, Online. Association for Computational Linguistics.

Carson T. Schütze. 1996. *The Empirical Base of Linguistics: Grammaticality Judgments and Linguistic Methodology*. University of Chicago Press.

Arabella Sinclair, Jaap Jumelet, Willem Zuidema, and Raquel Fernández. 2022. Structural persistence in language models: Priming as a window into abstract language representations. *Transactions of the Association for Computational Linguistics*, 10:1031–1050.

Natalia Slioussar. 2018. Forms and features: The role of syncretism in number agreement attraction. *Journal of Memory and Language*, 101:51–63.

Ekaterina Taktasheva, Maxim Bazhukov, Kirill Koncha, Alena Fenogenova, Ekaterina Artemova, and Vladislav Mikhailov. 2024. Rublimp: Russian benchmark of linguistic minimal pairs.

William Timkey and Tal Linzen. 2023. A language model with limited memory capacity captures interference in human sentence processing. In *Findings of the Association for Computational Linguistics: EMNLP 2023*, pages 8705–8720, Singapore. Association for Computational Linguistics.

Elena Voita and Ivan Titov. 2020. Information-theoretic probing with minimum description length. In *Proceedings of the 2020 Conference on Empirical Methods in Natural Language Processing (EMNLP)*, pages 183–196, Online. Association for Computational Linguistics.

Matthew W. Wagers, Ellen F. Lau, and Colin Phillips. 2009. Agreement attraction in comprehension: Representations and processes. *Journal of Memory and Language*, 61(2):206–237.

Alex Warstadt, Alicia Parrish, Haokun Liu, Anhad Mohananey, Wei Peng, Sheng-Fu Wang, and Samuel R Bowman. 2020. Blimp: The benchmark of linguistic minimal pairs for english. *Transactions of the Association for Computational Linguistics*, 8:377–392.

Alex Warstadt, Amanpreet Singh, and Samuel R Bowman. 2018. Neural network acceptability judgments. *arXiv preprint arXiv:1805.12471*.

Ethan Wilcox, Pranali Vani, and Roger Levy. 2021. A targeted assessment of incremental processing in neural language models and humans. In *Proceedings of the 59th Annual Meeting of the Association for Computational Linguistics and the 11th International Joint Conference on Natural Language Processing (Volume 1: Long Papers)*, pages 939–952, Online. Association for Computational Linguistics.

Dmitry Zmitrovich, Aleksandr Abramov, Andrey Kalmykov, Vitaly Kadulin, Maria Tikhonova, Ekaterina Taktasheva, Danil Astafurov, Mark Baushenko, Artem Snegirev, Tatiana Shavrina, Sergei S. Markov, Vladislav Mikhailov, and Alena Fenogenova. 2024. A family of pretrained transformer language models for Russian. In *Proceedings of the 2024 Joint International Conference on Computational Linguistics, Language Resources and Evaluation (LREC-COLING 2024)*, pages 507–524, Torino, Italia. ELRA and ICCL.

Is Structure Dependence Shaped for Efficient Communication?: A Case Study on Coordination

Kohei Kajikawa[1,2], **Yusuke Kubota**[2], **Yohei Oseki**[1]
[1]The University of Tokyo, [2]NINJAL
{kohei-kajikawa, oseki}@g.ecc.u-tokyo.ac.jp
kubota@ninjal.ac.jp

Abstract

Natural language exhibits various universal properties. But why do these universals exist? One explanation is that they arise from functional pressures to achieve *efficient communication*, a view which attributes cross-linguistic properties to domain-general cognitive abilities. This hypothesis has successfully addressed some syntactic universal properties such as compositionality and Greenbergian word order universals. However, more abstract syntactic universals have not been explored from the perspective of efficient communication. Among such universals, the most notable one is *structure dependence*, that is, grammar-internal operations crucially depend on hierarchical representations. This property has traditionally been taken to be central to natural language and to involve domain-specific knowledge irreducible to communicative efficiency.

In this paper, we challenge the conventional view by investigating whether structure dependence realizes efficient communication, focusing on coordinate structures. We design three types of artificial languages: (i) one with a structure-dependent reduction operation, which is similar to natural language, (ii) one without any reduction operations, and (iii) one with a linear (rather than structure-dependent) reduction operation. We quantify the communicative efficiency of these languages. The results demonstrate that the language with the structure-dependent reduction operation is significantly more communicatively efficient than the counterfactual languages. This suggests that the existence of structure-dependent properties can be explained from the perspective of efficient communication.

1 Introduction

To understand the universals of natural language, it is crucial to address *why* such universals exist, as well as *how* such universals can be theoretically described. This raises the question: what kinds of pressures shape these universals?

One explanation is that the universals of natural language are shaped as a result of functional pressures to achieve *efficient communication* (Zipf, 1949; Jaeger and Tily, 2011; Christiansen and Chater, 2016; Kemp et al., 2018; Gibson et al., 2019; Futrell and Hahn, 2022; Fedorenko et al., 2024). Efficient communication refers to a situation where the amount of information conveyed is maximized while the effort required for production and comprehension is minimized under human cognitive constraints. If some structural property of languages is shaped to achieve efficient communication, it can be optimized under two competing functional pressures: the need to be as *simple* as possible and the need to be as *informative* as possible.

The hypothesis that two competing pressures for utilities shape the form of human language has long been assumed in linguistics (Hawkins, 1994, 2004; Haspelmath, 2008). In recent years, methodologies have been established to examine this hypothesis by quantifying the *simplicity* and *informativeness* of languages by using information-theoretic criteria (Kemp et al., 2018; Gibson et al., 2019; Futrell and Hahn, 2022). To date, this hypothesis has been successfully examined at the lexical level (Ferrer i Cancho and Solé, 2003; Kemp and Regier, 2012; Piantadosi et al., 2011, 2012; Regier et al., 2015; Zaslavsky et al., 2018; Mollica et al., 2021; Steinert-Threlkeld, 2021; Denić et al., 2022; Trott and Bergen, 2022; Uegaki, 2022; Chen et al., 2023; Pimentel et al., 2023; van de Pol et al., 2023; Denić and Szymanik, 2024, *inter alia*). At the syntactic level, there are pieces of empirical evidence that grammar itself is shaped to achieve efficient communication (Gildea and Jaeger, 2015; Futrell et al., 2020a,b; Hahn et al., 2020, 2021; Clark et al., 2023), and it has been shown that the existence of syntactic universals such as compositionality and

Proceedings of the 28th Conference on Computational Natural Language Learning, pages 291–302
November 15-16, 2024 ©2024 Association for Computational Linguistics

Greenbergian word order universals (Greenberg, 1963) can be explained by this hypothesis (Kirby et al., 2015; Hahn et al., 2020).

But we do not yet know whether this type of competition-based account can be extended to more abstract types of linguistic knowledge that go beyond mere sensitivity to structure such as compositionally and word order. A representative type of such abstract knowledge comes from cases of what one might call *structure dependence*, by which we broadly refer to operations that directly manipulate structural representations at some level of linguistic representation. Structure dependence has traditionally been taken to be a characteristic and central property of human language (Chomsky, 1957, 1965; Everaert et al., 2015); in fact, a key underlying theme throughout the whole history of mainstream generative grammar is extreme skepticism of the idea that such properties can be reduced to communicative principles. The dogma in this line of thought has it that abstract syntactic properties of language are thought to be governed by domain-specific efficient computation necessary for deriving the structure of language (Hauser et al., 2002; Chomsky, 2005; Berwick and Chomsky, 2016), while communication is viewed as *not* essential to the core linguistic competence (Chomsky, 2002; Hauser et al., 2002). It is thus crucial to investigate whether even such syntactic properties can be accounted for from the perspective of domain-general efficient communication.

In this paper, we directly address this issue by examining structure dependence. Specifically, we investigate whether structure dependence realizes efficient communication by focusing on coordinate structures. We design three types of languages: (i) one with a structure-dependent reduction operation, which has coordinate structures similar to those in natural language, (ii) one without any reduction operations, and (iii) one with a linear (rather than structure-dependent) reduction operation. The latter two are conceptually possible but counterfactual languages. We adopted White and Cotterell's (2021) artificial probabilistic context-free grammars (PCFGs) to create the three languages. Then we quantify the *simplicity* and *informativeness* of these languages and compare their communicative efficiency. The results demonstrate that the languages with a structure-dependent reduction operation are significantly more communicatively efficient than their counterfactual counterparts. This suggests that the structure-dependent properties in human language can be explained in terms of efficient communication.

2 Background

2.1 Efficient communication hypothesis

In recent years, many researchers in cognitive science and computational psycholinguistics have increasingly focused on attributing cross-linguistic properties to domain-general cognitive functions. The central thesis of this strand of research is that natural language is shaped to achieve efficient communication (Zipf, 1949; Jaeger and Tily, 2011; Christiansen and Chater, 2016; Kemp et al., 2018; Gibson et al., 2019; Futrell and Hahn, 2022; Fedorenko et al., 2024). Communicatively efficient structures are more likely to be learned because they may be used more frequently and are easier to process during learning. This can drive changes in the language that further enhance communicative efficiency (Jaeger and Tily, 2011; Fedzechkina et al., 2012). Alternatively, the intergenerational transmission bottleneck in cultural evolution might lead to the selection of communicatively efficient languages (Christiansen and Kirby, 2003; Kirby et al., 2015). In either case, if functional pressures for efficient communication are at work, languages are expected to be optimized for efficient communication.

To test this hypothesis, one approach is to quantify and compare the communicative efficiency of real languages with logically possible but unattested counterfactual languages. For example, Hahn et al. (2020) showed that real languages reach an optimal word order under the trade-off between simplicity and informativeness. Simplicity refers to how simple the sentences of a language are as strings, while informativeness indicates how accurately the meaning can be reconstructed from the sentences of that language. The communicative efficiency of a language is then defined as the weighted sum of simplicity and informativeness. They created counterfactual languages for each of the 51 natural languages by changing word order patterns while maintaining the projectivity of dependency structures and calculated the communicative efficiency of all the languages. They found that almost all of the real languages had significantly higher communicative efficiency than their counterparts. This indicates that natural language is shaped by the pressure to enhance communicative efficiency.

2.2 Structure dependence

It has long been argued that natural language syntax exhibits structure dependence, the sensitivity to a hierarchical syntactic structure rather than a linear sequence of words (Chomsky, 1957, 1965; Everaert et al., 2015). Grammatical operations are thus applied based on syntactic structures, not on linear strings. For instance, yes-no questions in English are a well-known syntactic phenomenon that requires a structure-dependent grammatical rule. In English yes-no questions, the auxiliary of the main clause moves to the front of the sentence. If we were to formulate the rule for forming yes-no questions as *move the leftmost auxiliary verb to the front*, which is not structure-dependent, we would incorrectly transform a sentence *The man who is running is happy* into *Is the man who running is happy?* The correct transformation should move the second *is* from the main clause, resulting in *Is the man who is running happy?*

In the same way, it has traditionally been assumed that coordination, which is the focus of this study, also requires a structure-dependent grammatical operation (Chomsky, 1957, 1975 (=1955); Ross, 1967). For example, the coordinated sentence *John ran and swam* is derived from *John ran and John swam*, and *Mary called and praised John* is derived from *Mary called John and Mary praised John*, through a structure-dependent grammatical operation known as *Conjunction Reduction* (Figure 1). Conjunction Reduction is formulated as follows:

$$(Y + X_1 + Z) + \text{CC} + (Y + X_2 + Z) \\ \rightarrow Y + (X_1 + \text{CC} + X_2) + Z,$$

(Chomsky, 1957, p.113, with slight modifications)

where X represents any syntactic category, Y and Z represent any syntactic category or string, CC represents any conjunction, and $+$ denotes concatenation. Conjunction Reduction captures the fact that coordination is possible between identical syntactic categories for any syntactic category.[1]

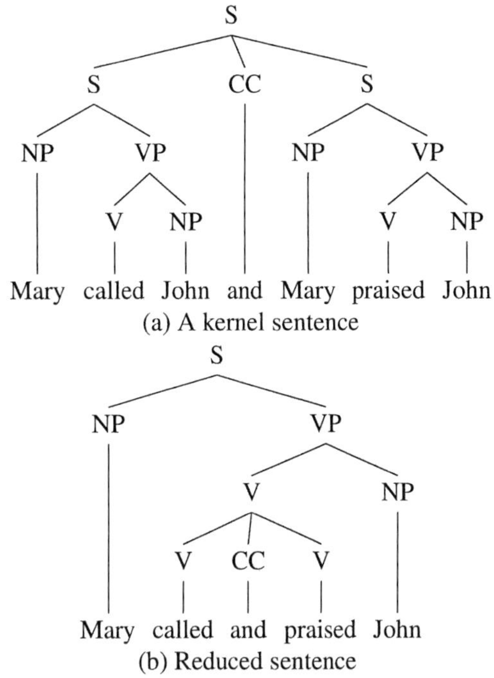

Figure 1: A coordinate structure (b) is derived by applying Conjunction Reduction, a structure-dependent reduction operation to a sentence-level coordinated kernel sentence (a).

We aim to investigate whether this structure-dependent reduction operation contributes to communicative efficiency in natural language.

3 Experiment

3.1 Data

Design of languages We designed the following three types of languages to investigate the impact on communicative efficiency when a language does not have a structure-dependent reduction operation at all:

1. `No-reduction` language: A language with no reduction. Only sentence-level coordination is possible.

2. `Structure-reduction` language: A language with structure-dependent reduction. Coordination is possible between identical syntactic categories.

[1] In the subsequent linguistic literature, Conjunction Reduction has been replaced by a more sophisticated approach known as *Generalized Conjunction* (Gazdar, 1980; Partee and Rooth, 1983), which overcomes some important limitations of Conjunction Reduction (e.g., Partee, 1970). However, the fundamental insight of structure dependence in the classical formulation of Conjunction Reduction is fully retained in Generalized Conjunction, since the latter can essentially be viewed as a reformulation of the former at the level of semantic representation using lambda calculus and higher-order functions. This study focuses on the operations applied to structures at any level. Therefore, the difference between Conjunction Reduction and Generalized Conjunction is orthogonal to the following discussion.

CFG rules		
S	$\rightarrow$	NP_{Subj} VP
VP	$\rightarrow$	IVerb | TVerb NP_{Obj} | $Verb_{Comp}$ S_{Comp}
S_{Comp}	$\rightarrow$	Comp S
NP	$\rightarrow$	Adj NP | NP PP | NP Rel VP
NP_{Subj}	$\rightarrow$	Noun $Case_{Subj}$ | $Pronoun_{Subj}$
NP_{Obj}	$\rightarrow$	Noun $Case_{Obj}$ | $Pronoun_{Obj}$
PP	$\rightarrow$	Prep NP
X	$\rightarrow$	X CC X, where X ={NP, Adj, IVerb, TVerb}

Table 1: Overview of the grammatical rules equipped in White and Cotterell's (2021) PCFG. For simplicity, features such as tense and number are omitted.

3. `Linear-reduction` language: A language with linear (rather than structure-dependent) reduction where repeated expressions in the same sentence are deleted in a coordinate structure.

Data generation For each language, the sentences to be evaluated were created using a set of PCFGs defined by White and Cotterell (2021). The PCFGs are equipped with six switches to reverse the linear order of specific heads and dependents, which results in a total of $2^6 = 64$ word order patterns in the artificial languages.

The PCFG includes the following basic syntactic categories: verb, noun, pronoun, adjective, conjunction, preposition, particle, sentential complementizer, and relativizer. Some features such as tense (present and past), number (singular and plural), and grammatical relation (subject and object) are assigned to categories. The grammatical rules are defined by the categories, as shown in Table 1. The combination of categories and features results in a total of 44 syntactic categories and a lexicon consists of 1,254 words. Although this grammar is much simpler than that of real natural languages, it is sufficiently sophisticated for our purpose of comparing structurally different languages. Moreover, it allows us to simultaneously take into consideration typologically diverse word order patterns.

We used this PCFG to create corpora of the artificial languages with 64 different word orders. We then constructed the `no-reduction`, `structure-reduction`, and `linear-reduction` languages defined above for each of these word orders. The `structure-reduction` language is the direct output of the PCFG. We then expanded all of the coordinate structures in the `structure-reduction` language to a sentence level to create the `no-reduction` language. Furthermore, we applied a linear reduction to the `no-reduction` language by deleting all repeated words in the same coordinate structure to create the `linear-reduction` language. The examples of the tree structures of the three types of artificial languages are shown in Figure 2.

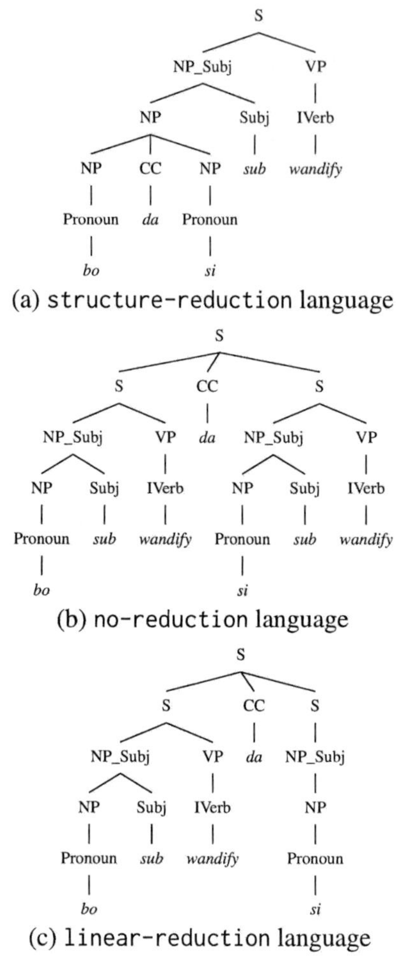

Figure 2: Examples of the three languages expressing the same meaning. The word order is set with all six switches being strictly head-final as in Japanese. For simplicity, information on number and tense has been omitted from the syntactic categories in these figures.

We measure the communicative efficiencies for these 64 word orders $\times$ 3 types $=$ 192 kinds of languages.

3.2 Estimating communicative efficiency

Definition of communicative efficiency For the simplicity/informativeness trade-off, following Hahn et al. (2020), we evaluate simplicity as a property of the linear sequence, in terms of how easily the next word in an utterance can be predicted, i.e., *predictability*, and informativeness in terms of how well the syntactic structure behind an utterance can be reconstructed, i.e., *parsability*.

Predictability is specifically defined as the negative entropy, $-H(\mathcal{U})$, of all utterances u in a language:

$$-H(\mathcal{U}) = \sum_{u \in \mathcal{U}} p(u) \log p(u). \tag{1}$$

Here, we define the probability of utterance u as the product of the probabilities of the words that constitute the utterance. When the sample size is sufficiently large, entropy can be estimated as the mean word-by-word surprisal. Surprisal is a metric that empirically predicts human behavioral (e.g., Demberg and Keller, 2008; Smith and Levy, 2013; Shain et al., 2024) and neural (e.g., Frank et al., 2015; Lopopolo et al., 2017; Brennan and Hale, 2019; Shain et al., 2020) data. The mean negative word-by-word surprisal represents the ease of incremental sentence processing on average under surprisal theory (Hale, 2001; Levy, 2008).

Parsability is defined as the negative conditinal entropy, $-H(\mathcal{T}|\mathcal{U})$, of the underlying syntactic structure t given an utterance u:[2]

$$-H(\mathcal{T}|\mathcal{U}) = \sum_{t \in \mathcal{T}, u \in \mathcal{U}} p(t, u) \log p(t|u). \tag{2}$$

Since semantic calculation in compositional semantics crucially depends on the building of syntactic structures (Montague, 1970; Heim and Kratzer, 1998), we employ a metric of informativeness that captures how unambiguously the underlying syntactic structure can be reconstructed—both temporally and globally—as an indicator of how accurately the intended meanings of utterances can be recovered.

Then, following Ferrer i Cancho and Solé (2003) and Hahn et al. (2020), we defined a communicative efficiency function as the weighted sum of predictability and parsability:

$$\Omega(\lambda) := \lambda \text{predictability} + (1 - \lambda) \text{parsability} \tag{3}$$

$$= -\lambda H(\mathcal{U}) - (1 - \lambda) H(\mathcal{T}|\mathcal{U}), \tag{4}$$

where λ is a trade-off parameter ranging from 0 to 1, which represents the contribution of each term. The objective function that captures the trade-off between the cost of linguistic expressions and the likelihood of meaning given the expression has been used in previous studies (e.g., Ferrer i Cancho and Solé, 2003; Frank and Goodman, 2012; Kemp and Regier, 2012; Regier et al., 2015; Hahn et al., 2020).

Recurrent Neural Network Grammars To obtain the values of predictability and parsability, we adopted Recurrent Neural Network Grammars (RNNGs; Dyer et al., 2016). RNNGs are a generative model of sentences that explicitly models hierarchical structures by processing the action sequence of shift-reduce parsing. RNNGs can be used for both language modeling and parsing with the same model parameters, which is suitable for our purpose here.

In this study, we used the left-corner stack-only RNNGs (Kuncoro et al., 2018) implemented with PyTorch[3] by Noji and Oseki (2021). We used a two-layer LSTM, where both the hidden layer and the input layer have 256 dimensions.[4]

Left-corner parsing is considered reasonable for human incremental sentence processing from the perspective of memory capacity (Abney and Johnson, 1991; Resnik, 1992) and is often assumed as a model of human sentence processing (e.g., Lewis and Vasishth, 2005; van Schijndel et al., 2013). Additionally, it has already been pointed out that a simple bottom-up strategy without a predictive process cannot explain the human incremental processing of coordinate structures in English at least when the parser conducts a serial parsing (Sturt and Lombardo, 2005; Stanojević et al., 2023). This motivates our choice of a left-corner as a parsing strategy.

We performed a beam search with a beam size of 100 for inference. We also used word-synchronous beam search (Stern et al., 2017) with a size of 10.

[2]Hahn et al. (2020) cenceptually defined parsability as mutual information $I(\mathcal{U}; \mathcal{T}) = H(\mathcal{T}) - H(\mathcal{T}|\mathcal{U})$ between an utterance and its syntactic structure. However, they actually estimated the value of parsability as $-H(\mathcal{T}|\mathcal{U})$ on the assumption that $H(\mathcal{T})$ is constant.

[3]`https://github.com/pytorch/pytorch/releases/tag/v1.12.1`

[4]Other hyperparameters are as follows: random seeds are $\{3435, 3436, 3437\}$, optimizer is Adam (Kingma and Ba, 2015), learning rate is 0.001, dropout is 0.3, and batch size is 128. The code of RNNGs we employed (Noji and Oseki, 2021) is available at `https://github.com/aistairc/rnng-pytorch`.

Estimation of communicative efficiency Predictability for the languages can be obtained by

$$-H(\mathcal{U}) = \sum_{u \in \mathcal{U}} p(u) \log p_\phi(u), \quad (5)$$

and following Hahn et al. (2020), we define the log-likelihood of each utterance u as

$$\log p_\phi(u) := \sum_{i=1}^{N} \log p_\phi(w_i | w_{<i}), \quad (6)$$

where w_i represents the i-th word composing the utterance and ϕ represents the parameters of the RNNGs. We can approximate the negative entropy of u with its Monte Carlo estimate on test data:

$$-H(\mathcal{U}) \approx \frac{1}{|\text{Test Data}|} \sum_{u \in \text{Test Data}} \log p_\phi(u). \quad (7)$$

We calculated the values of predictability according to the formula above.

Parsability can be calculated by

$$-H(\mathcal{T}|\mathcal{U}) = \sum_{t \in \mathcal{T}, u \in \mathcal{U}} p(t, u) \log p_\phi(t|u), \quad (8)$$

and in the same way, the conditional entropy can be approximated with its Monte Carlo estimate on test data:

$$-H(\mathcal{T}|\mathcal{U}) \approx \frac{1}{|\text{Test Data}|} \sum_{t, u \in \text{Test Data}} \log p_\phi(t|u). \quad (9)$$

Here, we define the log-likelihood of the conditional probability of the tree structure t given each utterance u as

$$\log p_\phi(t|u) := \sum_{i=1}^{N} \log p_\phi(t_{\text{best}} | w_{\leq i}). \quad (10)$$

Again, w_i and ϕ represent the i-th word of the utterance and the parameters of RNNGs, respectively. t_{best} refers to the most likely constituency parse in the word-synchronous beam at each word.

For 192 types of artificial languages, we generated 20,000 sentences for each and divided them into an 8-1-1 train-dev-test split for training and evaluation. For all languages, we trained RNNGs on word-by-word using Adam (Kingma and Ba, 2015) for 10 epochs each with multiple random seeds. Then, we calculated the values of predictability and parsability, normalized by the number of words, to ensure valid comparisons across languages with inherently different sentence lengths.

4 Results

A distribution of the values of communicative efficiency for the three types of languages, as calculated by RNNGs, is shown in Figure 3. For an interpretation of the trade-off parameter λ, the predictability and parsability values of all languages are z-transformed (i.e., centered and divided by the standard deviation) before being substituted into Eq 4. The lines in the figure show the transitions of the value of communicative efficiency for λ with a 95% confidence interval (CI). By finding the coordinates where the lines intersect, we can observe the behavior of communicative efficiency for each language depending on the value of λ. The lower bound of the 95% CI for `structure-reduction` intersects with the upper bound of the 95% CI for `linear-reduction` at $\lambda = 0.18$. In the same way, the upper bound of the 95% CI for `structure-reduction` intersects with the lower bound of the 95% CI for `linear-reduction` at $\lambda = 0.93$. This indicates that `structure-reduction` languages are the most communicatively efficient, at least within the range of λ values between 0.18 and 0.93.

Additionally, when we examine only predictability or parsability, their distributions are shown in Figure 4 and Figure 5, respectively. The mean values for predictability were ordered as `no-reduction` > `structure-reduction` > `linear-reduction`, while for parsability, the order was `linear-reduction` > `structure-reduction` > `no-reduction`, in which all of the pairs have a statistically significant difference ($p < 0.05/3$ by paired t-test with Bonferroni correction). This indicates that when only predictability or parsability is individually considered, the `structure-reduction` language may not always be the best option. However, to satisfy both criteria simultaneously, i.e., to consider the weighted sum of predictability and parsability under the parameter $\lambda \in [0.18, 0.93]$, the `structure-reduction` language achieves the highest score of communicative efficiency as shown in Figure 3.

To further interpret the results of predictability and parsability, we plotted least squares regression lines between word position in the sentence and each word-by-word value (Figure 6). For predictability, only the `linear-reduction` languages significantly decline towards the latter part of the sentence. As for parsability, although the

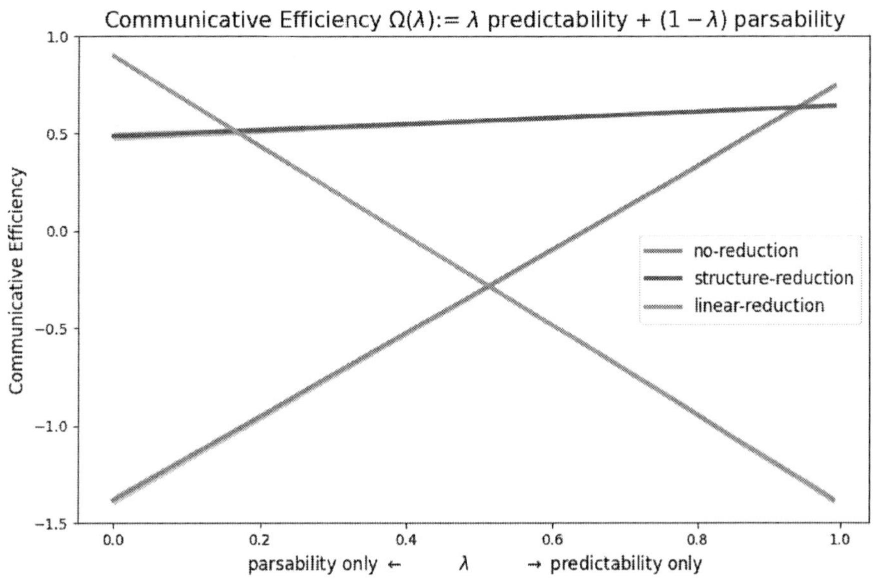

Figure 3: Distribution of **communicative efficiency** for the three types of languages with 95% CI. The x-axis and y-axis represent the trade-off parameter λ and communicative efficiency, respectively. Both predictability and parsability are z-transformed for an interpretation of λ. The `structure-reduction` languages are the most communicatively efficient under the parameter $\lambda \in [0.18, 0.93]$ for 95% CI.

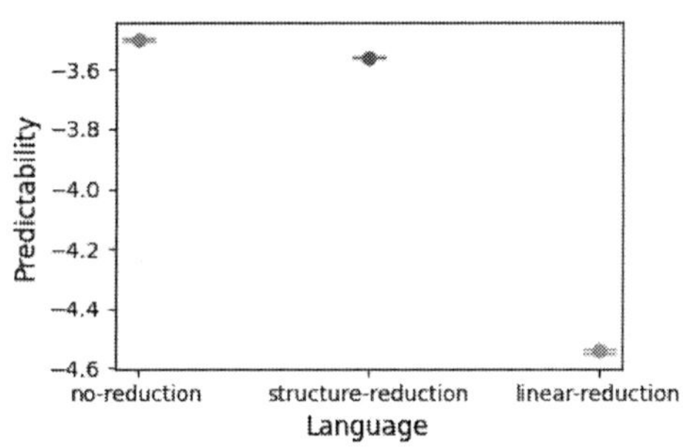

Figure 4: Distribution of **predictability** for the three types of languages. Error bars indicate 95% CI.

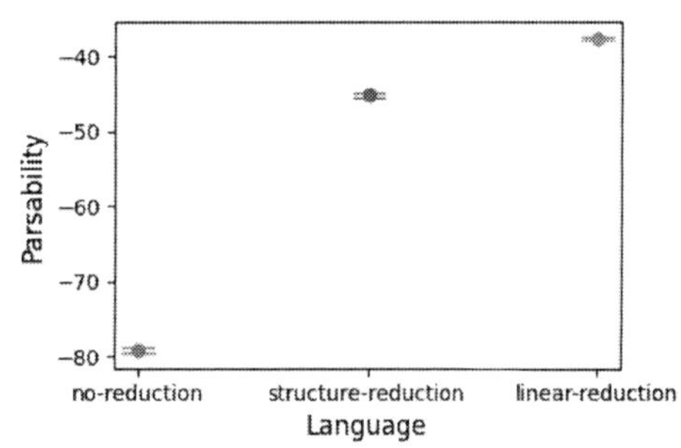

Figure 5: Distribution of **parsability** for the three types of languages. Error bars indicate 95% CI.

`linear-reduction` languages experience a faster decrease, the other two languages, which have longer expression lengths, achieve a lower overall score.

5 Discussion

We demonstrated that the `structure-reduction` languages, which have the same structure-dependent reduction operation as natural language, had significantly higher communicative efficiency compared to the conceptually possible but counterfactual `no-reduction` and `linear-reduction` languages when we calculated the scores by RNNGs with a trade-off parameter $\lambda \in [0.18, 0.93]$. This suggests that the structure-dependent reduction operation prevalent in the natural language syntax may exist due to functional pressures to support efficient communication along lines discussed in Section 2.1. It should be noted that, as Figure 3 shows, when λ is extremely small or large, the `no-reduction` or `linear-reduction` languages achieve the highest efficiency scores. However, λ represents the relative contribution of the two terms to the overall efficiency score. It is difficult to assume a reasonable scenario where only one term is emphasized. While we do not aim to estimate a spe-

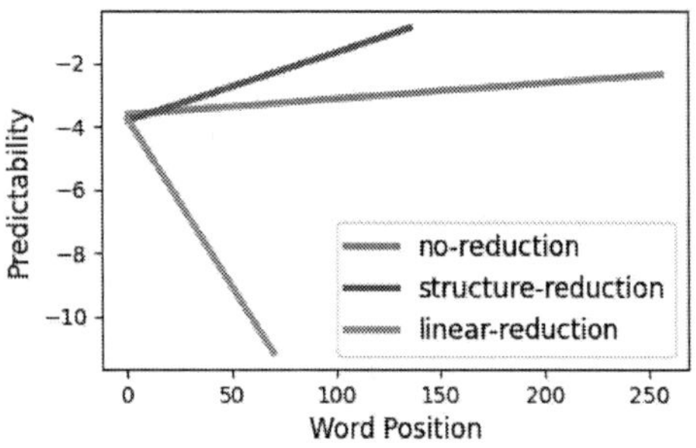

(a) Relationship between **predictability** and word position.

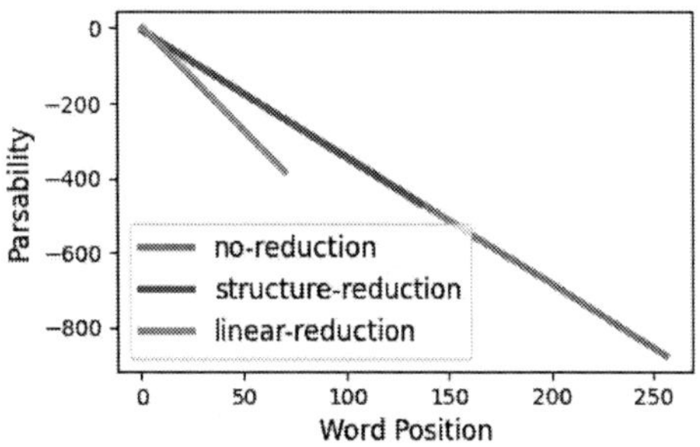

(b) Relationship between **parsability** and word position.

Figure 6: Relationship between predictability/parsability and word position for the three types of languages. Predictability and parsability here refer to the negative surprisal and the negative log-likelihood of the best parse for each word, respectively. The lines represent the fit of a least squares regression model for these data.

cific value of λ, empirically, Ferrer i Cancho and Solé (2003) found in their simulation experiment that Zipf's law emerged when $\lambda \approx 0.41$. In addition, Hahn et al. (2020) demonstrated that grammars optimized at $\lambda \approx 0.47$ captured all 8 of the Greenberg correlations they investigated, whereas optimizing solely for predictability or parsability did not account for all of them.[5]

When we consider only one of the terms constituting communicative efficiency, that is, predictability (simplicity) or parsability (informativeness), one of the two counterfactual languages achieves the highest score. The `no-reduction` language is the easiest in terms of prediction, i.e., the estimation of the next word, among the three types. This is because the language has no reduction, and all sentences are fully represented, so the number of local patterns for the next word is limited, which makes prediction easier. For example, in a `no-reduction` language where the part of speech at the beginning of a sentence is always X in its word order pattern, the part of speech following a conjunction must be X, while `structure-reduction` and `linear-reduction` languages have more variations, which lead to higher entropy of strings. However, the `no-reduction` language is not well-suited for parsing. As sentence length increases, the number of potential parses grows exponentially (Church and Patil, 1982). Since this language lacks reduction and results in longer overall expressions, the possible parses at each word position rapidly increase, as shown in Figure 6(b). Consequently, it is not an optimal design from the perspective of estimating the underlying structure of an utterance. In contrast, the `linear-reduction` language has shorter overall expressions, resulting in fewer possible parses at each word position.[6] As a result, it is superior in terms of estimating tree structures. However, the reduction is too radical, making it challenging to maintain predictability. As shown in Figure 6(a), this issue is evident in the latter parts of sentences in this language, where predictions become increasingly difficult due to the need to consider the possibility that previously mentioned words might have been reduced. In short, a reduction operation is necessary to enhance parsability, but it should be applied *restrictively* so as not to sacrifice next-word predictability. Balancing the trade-off between the two, a structure-dependent reduction is the most preferred design for maximizing communicative efficiency.

It should be noted that even in natural language, there are instances of linear reduction operations such as *stripping* (Hankamer and Sag, 1976), for instance shown below, or sentences that retain sentence-level coordination without reduction for pragmatic purposes such as emphasis.

(11) Mary took a walk in the park, and Bill too.

However, these phenomena occur as alternative choices in a language that has a structure-dependent

[5]Hahn et al. defined a communicative efficiency function as $\Omega(\lambda) := \lambda$predictability + parsability and set $\lambda = 0.9$. In other words, while we assigned weights of λ and $1 - \lambda$ to predictability and parsability, respectively, they assigned weights of 0.9 and 1. Solving the equation $\lambda/(1-\lambda) = 0.9/1$ gives $\lambda \approx 0.47$.

[6]The parsability metric used here may overestimate the informativeness of `linear-reduction` languages. This metric does not account for whether the estimated tree structure is correct, nor does it fully capture the inherent ambiguity in the language. A more accurate approach could involve quantifying informativeness using mutual information (e.g., Ferrer i Cancho, 2005; Futrell, 2017; Zaslavsky et al., 2018; Hahn et al., 2020), though this would not change our conclusion.

reduction operation. Our claim is that a language lacking a structure-dependent reduction operation entirely is not preferable from the perspective of efficient communication.

The results of this study have interesting implications for theoretical linguistics research. Structure dependence, a syntactic universal property we addressed here, has traditionally been argued to be one of the characteristic features of human language (Chomsky, 1957, 1965; Everaert et al., 2015). A prominent view in the mainstream generative grammar argues that natural language involves domain-specific predispositions and that syntactic properties of language—including structure dependence—are best explained from the perspective of 'efficient *computation*' reflecting such predispositions genetically hard-wired in the human brain (Hauser et al., 2002; Chomsky, 2005; Everaert et al., 2015; Berwick and Chomsky, 2016). Under this view, communication is taken to be a kind of epiphenomenon, not essential to the core linguistic competence (Chomsky, 2002; Hauser et al., 2002). However, our results suggest that at least some structure-dependent properties present in natural language (such as coordination) can be explained from the perspective of efficient *communication*. This does not immediately refute the dominant research program attempting to explain linguistic properties from a 'computational' perspective, but it does indicate that abstract properties in syntax may not necessarily need to be explained solely from that perspective. This aligns with the existing body of research that attempts to explain various aspects of natural language from the perspective of efficient communication (Gibson et al., 2019; Fedorenko et al., 2024).

6 Conclusion

In this paper, we investigated whether structure dependence, one of the syntactic universals, reflects the optimization for efficient communication. To address this issue, we focused on coordinate structures and designed three types of artificial languages: (i) one with a structure-dependent reduction operation, (ii) one without any reduction operations, and (iii) one with a linear (rather than structure-dependent) reduction operation. We quantified the communicative efficiency of these languages and compared them. The results demonstrated that the languages with a structure-dependent reduction operation were significantly more communicatively efficient than their counterfactual counterparts. This suggests that the structure-dependent properties of natural language can be explained from the functional perspective of efficient communication.[7]

Limitations

There is room for improvement in the objective function for communicative efficiency. Although we used the mean word-by-word surprisal, conditioned on all preceding words, as a measure of predictability, human language processing is subject to short-term memory constraints (Gibson, 1998; Lewis and Vasishth, 2005; Isono, 2024). Thus, it is preferable to model predictability in a way that incorporates *lossy memory representation* (Futrell et al., 2020a; Hahn et al., 2021, 2022). Moreover, the psychological plausibility of the parsability metric should be critically evaluated, both conceptually and empirically. Since parsability relies on an intermediate representation—syntactic structures—it does not fully capture the direct relationship between linguistic expressions and their meanings, suggesting that there is room for further conceptual refinement.

To the best of our knowledge, this study is the first to investigate communicative efficiency with respect to structure dependence. We focused on coordinate structures with the artificial language paradigm as a starting point. Of course, a deeper understanding of structure dependence in language will require using natural language data and extending the analysis to phenomena such as agreement and movement that are argued to be relevant to structure dependence. In future work, we plan to test the relationship between structure dependence and communicative efficiency by applying the methodology proposed here to a broader range of syntactic constructions, using treebanks like Universal Dependencies (Nivre et al., 2020).

Ethical considerations

We used all tools and datasets following their respective terms and licenses. We employed ChatGPT and Grammarly for writing assistance and utilized ChatGPT for writing experimental code. We used these tools in compliance with the ACL 2023 Policy on AI Writing Assistance.

[7]Code for reproducing our experiments is available at `https://github.com/kohei-kaji/coordination`.

Acknowledgments

We are grateful to the anonymous reviewers for their insightful comments and suggestions. We also thank Ryo Yoshida for providing the code to calculate the log-likelihood of each parse in RNNGs. We sincerely appreciate Shinnosuke Isono, Douglas Roland, Yushi Sugimoto, Asa Tomita, and members of the computational linguistics community at The University of Tokyo for their valuable feedback. This work was supported by JSPS KAKENHI Grant Numbers 21K00541 and 24H00087, JST PRESTO Grant Number JPMJPR21C2, and the NINJAL collaborative research project 'Toward a Computationally-Informed Theoretical Linguistics'.

References

Steven P. Abney and Mark Johnson. 1991. Memory requirements and local ambiguities of parsing strategies. *Journal of Psycholinguistic Research*, 20(3):233–250.

Robert C. Berwick and Noam Chomsky. 2016. *Why Only Us: Language and Evolution*. The MIT Press, Cambridge, MA.

Jonathan R. Brennan and John T. Hale. 2019. Hierarchical structure guides rapid linguistic predictions during naturalistic listening. *PLoS ONE*, 14(1):e0207741.

Sihan Chen, Richard Futrell, and Kyle Mahowald. 2023. An information-theoretic approach to the typology of spatial demonstratives. *Cognition*, 240:105505.

Noam Chomsky. 1957. *Syntactic Structures*. Mouton.

Noam Chomsky. 1965. *Aspects of the Theory of Syntax*. MIT Press.

Noam Chomsky. 1975 (=1955). *The Logical Structure of Linguistic Theory*. Springer New York, NY.

Noam Chomsky. 2002. An interview on minimalism. In Adriana Belletti and Luigi Rizzi, editors, *On Nature and Language*, pages 92–161. Cambridge University Press.

Noam Chomsky. 2005. Three Factors in Language Design. *Linguistic Inquiry*, 36(1):1–22.

Morten H. Christiansen and Nick Chater. 2016. The Now-or-Never bottleneck: A fundamental constraint on language. *Behavioral and Brain Sciences*, 39:e62.

Morten H. Christiansen and Simon Kirby. 2003. Language evolution: consensus and controversies. *Trends in Cognitive Sciences*, 7(7):300–307.

Kenneth Church and Ramesh Patil. 1982. Coping with syntactic ambiguity or how to put the block in the box on the table. *American Journal of Computational Linguistics*, 8(3-4):139–149.

Thomas Hikaru Clark, Clara Meister, Tiago Pimentel, Michael Hahn, Ryan Cotterell, Richard Futrell, and Roger Levy. 2023. A cross-linguistic pressure for Uniform Information Density in word order. *Transactions of the Association for Computational Linguistics*, 11:1048–1065.

Vera Demberg and Frank Keller. 2008. Data from eye-tracking corpora as evidence for theories of syntactic processing complexity. *Cognition*, 109(2):193–210.

Milica Denić, Shane Steinert-Threlkeld, and Jakub Szymanik. 2022. Indefinite pronouns optimize the simplicity/informativeness trade-off. *Cognitive Science*, 46(5):e13142.

Milica Denić and Jakub Szymanik. 2024. Recursive numeral systems optimize the trade-off between lexicon size and average morphosyntactic complexity. *Cognitive Science*, 48(3):e13424.

Chris Dyer, Adhiguna Kuncoro, Miguel Ballesteros, and Noah A. Smith. 2016. Recurrent neural network grammars. In *Proceedings of the 2016 Conference of the North American Chapter of the Association for Computational Linguistics: Human Language Technologies*, pages 199–209, San Diego, California. Association for Computational Linguistics.

Martin B.H. Everaert, Marinus A.C. Huybregts, Noam Chomsky, Robert C. Berwick, and Johan J. Bolhuis. 2015. Structures, not strings: Linguistics as part of the cognitive sciences. *Trends in Cognitive Sciences*, 19:729–743.

Evelina Fedorenko, Steven T. Piantadosi, and Edward A. F. Gibson. 2024. Language is primarily a tool for communication rather than thought. *Nature*, 630:575–586.

Maryia Fedzechkina, T. Florian Jaeger, and Elissa L. Newport. 2012. Language learners restructure their input to facilitate efficient communication. *Proceedings of the National Academy of Sciences*, 109(44):17897–17902.

Ramon Ferrer i Cancho. 2005. Zipf's law from a communicative phase transition. *The European Physical Journal B - Condensed Matter and Complex Systems*, 47:449–457.

Ramon Ferrer i Cancho and Ricard V. Solé. 2003. Least effort and the origins of scaling in human language. *Proceedings of the National Academy of Sciences*, 100(3):788–791.

Michael C. Frank and Noah D. Goodman. 2012. Predicting pragmatic reasoning in language games. *Science*, 336(6084):998–998.

Stefan L. Frank, Leun J. Otten, Giulia Galli, and Gabriella Vigliocco. 2015. The ERP response to the amount of information conveyed by words in sentences. *Brain and Language*, 140:1–11.

Richard Futrell. 2017. *Memory and Locality in Natural Language*. Ph.D. thesis, MIT.

Richard Futrell, Edward Gibson, and Roger P Levy. 2020a. Lossy-context surprisal: An information-theoretic model of memory effects in sentence processing. *Cognitive Science*, 44(3):e12814.

Richard Futrell and Michael Hahn. 2022. Information theory as a bridge between language function and language form. *Frontiers in Communication*, 7.

Richard Futrell, Roger P. Levy, and Edward Gibson. 2020b. Dependency locality as an explanatory principle for word order. *Language*, 96(2):371–412.

Gerald Gazdar. 1980. A cross-categorial semantics for coordination. *Linguistics and Philosophy*, 3(3):407–409.

Edward Gibson. 1998. Linguistic complexity: locality of syntactic dependencies. *Cognition*, 68(1):1–76.

Edward Gibson, Richard Futrell, Steven T. Piantadosi, Isabelle Dautriche, Kyle Mahowald, Leon Bergen, and Roger Levy. 2019. How efficiency shapes human language. *Trends in Cognitive Sciences*, 23(5):389–407.

Daniel Gildea and T. Florian Jaeger. 2015. Human languages order information efficiently. *Preprint*, arXiv:1510.02823.

Joseph H. Greenberg. 1963. *Universals of language*. MIT press.

Michael Hahn, Judith Degen, and Richard Futrell. 2021. Modeling word and morpheme order in natural language as an efficient tradeoff of memory and surprisal. *Psychological Review*, 128:726–756.

Michael Hahn, Richard Futrell, Roger Levy, and Edward Gibson. 2022. A resource-rational model of human processing of recursive linguistic structure. *Proceedings of the National Academy of Sciences*, 119(43):e2122602119.

Michael Hahn, Dan Jurafsky, and Richard Futrell. 2020. Universals of word order reflect optimization of grammars for efficient communication. *Proceedings of the National Academy of Sciences*, 117(5):2347–2353.

John Hale. 2001. A probabilistic Earley parser as a psycholinguistic model. In *Second Meeting of the North American Chapter of the Association for Computational Linguistics*.

Jorge Hankamer and Ivan A. Sag. 1976. Deep and surface anaphora. *Linguistic Inquiry*, 7:391–428.

Martin Haspelmath. 2008. Parametric versus functional explanations of syntactic universals. *The Limits of Syntactic Variation*, 132:75–107.

Marc D. Hauser, Noam Chomsky, and W. Tecumseh Fitch. 2002. The faculty of language: What is it, who has it, and how did it evolve? *Science*, 298(5598):1569–1579.

John A. Hawkins. 1994. *A Performance Theory of Order and Constituency*. Cambridge University Press.

John A. Hawkins. 2004. *Efficiency and Complexity in Grammars*. Oxford University Press.

Irene Heim and Angelika Kratzer. 1998. *Semantics in Generative Grammar*. Wiley-Blackwell.

Shinnosuke Isono. 2024. Category locality theory: A unified account of locality effects in sentence comprehension. *Cognition*, 247:105766.

T. Florian Jaeger and Harry Tily. 2011. On language 'utility': processing complexity and communicative efficiency. *WIREs Cognitive Science*, 2(3):323–335.

Charles Kemp and Terry Regier. 2012. Kinship categories across languages reflect general communicative principles. *Science*, 336(6084):1049–1054.

Charles Kemp, Yang Xu, and Terry Regier. 2018. Semantic typology and efficient communication. *Annual Review of Linguistics*, 4(1):109–128.

Diederik P. Kingma and Jimmy Ba. 2015. Adam: A method for stochastic optimization. In *Proceedings of the International Conference Learning Representations*, San Diego, CA, USA. Conference Track Proceedings.

Simon Kirby, Monica Tamariz, Hannah Cornish, and Kenny Smith. 2015. Compression and communication in the cultural evolution of linguistic structure. *Cognition*, 141:87–102.

Adhiguna Kuncoro, Chris Dyer, John Hale, Dani Yogatama, Stephen Clark, and Phil Blunsom. 2018. LSTMs can learn syntax-sensitive dependencies well, but modeling structure makes them better. In *Proceedings of the 56th Annual Meeting of the Association for Computational Linguistics (Volume 1: Long Papers)*, pages 1426–1436, Melbourne, Australia. Association for Computational Linguistics.

Roger Levy. 2008. Expectation-based syntactic comprehension. *Cognition*, 106(3):1126–1177.

Richard L. Lewis and Shravan Vasishth. 2005. An activation-based model of sentence processing as skilled memory retrieval. *Cognitive Science*, 29(3):375–419.

Alessandro Lopopolo, Stefan L. Frank, Antal van den Bosch, and Roel M. Willems. 2017. Using stochastic language models (SLM) to map lexical, syntactic, and phonological information processing in the brain. *PLoS ONE*, 12(5):e0177794.

Francis Mollica, Geoff Bacon, Noga Zaslavsky, Yang Xu, Terry Regier, and Charles Kemp. 2021. The forms and meanings of grammatical markers support efficient communication. *Proceedings of the National Academy of Sciences*, 118(49):e2025993118.

Richard Montague. 1970. Universal grammar. *Theoria*, 36(3):373–398.

Joakim Nivre, Marie-Catherine de Marneffe, Filip Ginter, Jan Hajič, Christopher D. Manning, Sampo Pyysalo, Sebastian Schuster, Francis Tyers, and Daniel Zeman. 2020. Universal Dependencies v2: An evergrowing multilingual treebank collection. In *Proceedings of the Twelfth Language Resources and Evaluation Conference*, pages 4034–4043, Marseille, France. European Language Resources Association.

Hiroshi Noji and Yohei Oseki. 2021. Effective batching for recurrent neural network grammars. In *Findings of the Association for Computational Linguistics: ACL-IJCNLP 2021*, pages 4340–4352, Online. Association for Computational Linguistics.

Barbara Partee and Mats Rooth. 1983. Generalized conjunction and type ambiguity. *Formal semantics: The essential readings*, pages 334–356.

Barbara Hall Partee. 1970. Negation, conjunction, and quantifiers: Syntax vs. semantics. *Foundations of Language*, 6:153–165.

Steven T. Piantadosi, Harry Tily, and Edward Gibson. 2011. Word lengths are optimized for efficient communication. *Proceedings of the National Academy of Sciences*, 108(9):3526–3529.

Steven T. Piantadosi, Harry Tily, and Edward Gibson. 2012. The communicative function of ambiguity in language. *Cognition*, 122(3):280–291.

Tiago Pimentel, Clara Meister, Ethan Wilcox, Kyle Mahowald, and Ryan Cotterell. 2023. Revisiting the optimality of word lengths. In *Proceedings of the 2023 Conference on Empirical Methods in Natural Language Processing*, pages 2240–2255, Singapore. Association for Computational Linguistics.

Terry Regier, Charles Kemp, and Paul Kay. 2015. Word meanings across languages support efficient communication. In *The Handbook of Language Emergence*, chapter 11, pages 237–263. John Wiley & Sons, Ltd.

Philip Resnik. 1992. Left-corner parsing and psychological plausibility. In *COLING 1992 Volume 1: The 14th International Conference on Computational Linguistics*.

John R. Ross. 1967. *Constraints on variables in syntax*. Ph.D. thesis, MIT.

Cory Shain, Idan Asher Blank, Marten van Schijndel, William Schuler, and Evelina Fedorenko. 2020. fMRI reveals language-specific predictive coding during naturalistic sentence comprehension. *Neuropsychologia*, 138:107307.

Cory Shain, Clara Meister, Tiago Pimentel, Ryan Cotterell, and Roger Levy. 2024. Large-scale evidence for logarithmic effects of word predictability on reading time. *Proceedings of the National Academy of Sciences*, 121(10):e2307876121.

Nathaniel J. Smith and Roger Levy. 2013. The effect of word predictability on reading time is logarithmic. *Cognition*, 128(3):302–319.

Miloš Stanojević, Jonathan R. Brennan, Donald Dunagan, Mark Steedman, and John T. Hale. 2023. Modeling structure-building in the brain with CCG parsing and Large Language Models. *Cognitive Science*, 47(7):e13312.

Shane Steinert-Threlkeld. 2021. Quantifiers in natural language: Efficient communication and degrees of semantic universals. *Entropy*, 23(10).

Mitchell Stern, Daniel Fried, and Dan Klein. 2017. Effective inference for generative neural parsing. In *Proceedings of the 2017 Conference on Empirical Methods in Natural Language Processing*, pages 1695–1700, Copenhagen, Denmark. Association for Computational Linguistics.

Patrick Sturt and Vincenzo Lombardo. 2005. Processing coordinated structures: Incrementality and connectedness. *Cognitive Science*, 29(2):291–305.

Sean Trott and Benjamin Bergen. 2022. Languages are efficient, but for whom? *Cognition*, 225:105094.

Wataru Uegaki. 2022. The Informativeness/Complexity Trade-Off in the Domain of Boolean Connectives. *Linguistic Inquiry*, pages 1–23.

Iris van de Pol, Paul Lodder, Leendert van Maanen, Shane Steinert-Threlkeld, and Jakub Szymanik. 2023. Quantifiers satisfying semantic universals have shorter minimal description length. *Cognition*, 232:105150.

Marten van Schijndel, Andy Exley, and William Schuler. 2013. A model of language processing as hierarchic sequential prediction. *Topics in Cognitive Science*, 5(3):522–540.

Jennifer C. White and Ryan Cotterell. 2021. Examining the Inductive Bias of Neural Language Models with Artificial Languages. In *Proceedings of the 59th Annual Meeting of the Association for Computational Linguistics and the 11th International Joint Conference on Natural Language Processing (Volume 1: Long Papers)*, pages 454–463, Online. Association for Computational Linguistics.

Noga Zaslavsky, Charles Kemp, Terry Regier, and Naftali Tishby. 2018. Efficient compression in color naming and its evolution. *Proceedings of the National Academy of Sciences*, 115(31):7937–7942.

George K. Zipf. 1949. *Human behavior and the principle of least effort*. Addison-Wesley.

Large Language Model Recall Uncertainty is Modulated by the Fan Effect

Jesse Roberts
Tennessee Tech University
jtroberts@tntech.edu

Kyle Moore
Vanderbilt University
kyle.a.moore@vanderbilt.edu

Thao Pham
Berea College

Oseremhen Ewaleifoh
Vanderbilt University

Doug Fisher
Vanderbilt University

Abstract

This paper evaluates whether large language models (LLMs) exhibit cognitive fan effects, similar to those discovered by Anderson in humans, after being pre-trained on human textual data. We conduct two sets of in-context recall experiments designed to elicit fan effects. Consistent with human results, we find that LLM recall uncertainty, measured via token probability, is influenced by the fan effect. Our results show that removing uncertainty disrupts the observed effect. The experiments suggest the fan effect is consistent whether the fan value is induced in-context or in the pre-training data. Finally, these findings provide *in-silico* evidence that fan effects and typicality are expressions of the same phenomena.

1 Introduction

Some subfields of AI are explicitly interested in understanding and mimicking the nature of human cognition (cognitive modeling, computational psychology, affective computing) but even more implicitly rely on models of human cognition (human-computer interaction, embodied robotics, collaborative robotics, AI assistive technology, computational game theory). A model that, through training, learned to implicitly exhibit human-like cognitive behaviors could be of tremendous value both to the explicit study of human cognition as an ethical test subject, and as a more faithful model of human behavior to those fields that seek to develop systems to work along side human counterparts. We believe that some large language models (LLM) may be excellent candidates for such a role.

LLMs process information in a manner that is fundamentally different from humans. The matrix multiplications, maximum inner product search, and perceptron networks may have, at some level, been inspired by the biological neuronal system. But beyond the superficial, the systems bear no similarities. In spite of algorithmic and mechanistic dissimilarity, a growing body of work suggests that by merely training on human-language data, large language models learn to exhibit human-like cognitive behaviors as shown in Table 1.

In this paper, we survey the work applying cognitive science inspired evaluations to LLMs to analyze, understand, and catalog their relation to human cognition. We extend the existing work by providing the first investigation of human-like fan effects à la Anderson and Reder (1999) in LLMs. This effect is specifically interesting because it has a relation to the previously studied typicality effect, and it is understood to be an expression of human categorization uncertainty that has been precisely measured through response time delay.

Our results show that (1) some LLMs exhibit human-like fan effects based on the typicality of categorical items learned in pre-training; (2) some LLMs exhibit human-like fan effects based on the relative frequency of items in the model context; and (3) with uncertainty mitigated, the observed fan effect is disrupted. Of the models tested, Mistral (Jiang et al., 2023) and SOLAR (Kim et al., 2023) exhibit noteworthy human-like fan effects, including nuanced differential fan effects previously observed in humans (Radvansky, 1999).

The results have two practical implications: LLMs learn to exhibit human-like uncertainty and that uncertainty may interfere with recall tasks. Our results additionally provide *in-silico* evidence that the fan effect is a special case of typicality as is true in COBWEB models (Silber and Fisher, 1989).

Understanding the cognitive behaviors acquired from language is essential to the successful application of LLMs in human-adjacent scenarios. Generally speaking, human-like cognitive effects may serve to smooth interactions between machine and human. Alternatively, a minority of discrepancies may serve to undermine the interactions.

https://github.com/JesseTNRoberts/Large-Language-Model-Recall-Uncertainty-is-Modulated-by-the-Fan-Effect

Proceedings of the 28th Conference on Computational Natural Language Learning, pages 303–313
November 15-16, 2024

Phenomena	Study by	Measure(s)	Statistic	Significance	Systematic Perturbation
Theory of Mind	Bubeck et al. (2023)	qualitative	—	—	—
	Kosinski (2023)	frequency	—	—	—
	Sap et al. (2022)	frequency	—	—	—
	Ullman (2023)	frequency	—	—	—
	Trott et al. (2023)	token probs	$\chi^2 + \beta$	reported	—
	Ma et al. (2023)	frequency	—	—	—
	Li et al. (2023)	frequqncy	—	—	—
Logical Reasoning	Binz and Schulz (2023)	token probs	$\chi^2 + t + \beta$	reported	—
	McCoy et al. (2019)	frequency	—	—	—
	Lamprinidis (2023)	frequency	—	—	—
	Yax et al. (2024)	token probs	χ^2	reported	—
	Lampinen et al. (2023)	frequency	$\chi^2 + t$	reported	—
Framing & Anchoring	Binz and Schulz (2023)	token probs	$\chi^2 + t + \beta$	reported	—
	Jones and Steinhardt (2022)	frequency	—	—	—
	Suri et al. (2023)	frequency	—	reported	—
Decision-Making	Binz and Schulz (2023)	token probs	$\chi^2 + t + \beta$	reported	—
	Jones and Steinhardt (2022)	frequency	—	—	—
	Coda-Forno et al. (2024)	frequency	β	reported	—
	Hagendorff et al. (2023)	frequency	χ^2	reported	—
Typicality	Misra et al. (2021)	token probs	$r + \rho$	reported	—
	Roberts et al. (2024b)	token probs	r	reported	model
Priming	Sinclair et al. (2022)	token probs	—	—	data
	Roberts et al. (2024b)	token probs	w	reported	data + model
	Michaelov et al. (2023)	token probs	—	—	data
Emotion Induction	Coda-Forno et al. (2023)	frequency	$r + t +$ probit β	reported	—

Table 1: Review summary of large language model behavioral studies. r = Pearson, ρ = Spearman, β = β-regression, t = t-test, w = Wilcoxon. Systematic perturbation refers to the presence of noise injected into the model or data to improve result robustness.

2 Background

The ***fan effect*** is a psychological effect in human categorization behavior, first identified in Anderson (1974), where subjects take longer to recognize and accept or reject concepts that have overlapping features with concepts previously presented in a learning set. This has most commonly been studied using concepts made up of person-place pairs. More formally, given some training concept set $S = \{< X_1, Y_1 >, ..., < X_n, Y_n >\}$, where X and Y are features of the concepts, response time when performing recognition tasks for an arbitrarily chosen query concept $< X_q, Y_q >$ is correlated with the number of times that X_q and Y_q occur in S. The effect is apparent regardless of whether or not $< X_q, Y_q > \in S$.

Fan effects have subsequently been found to present with varying strength across different contexts. This tendency is dubbed the ***differential fan effect***. Differential fan effects have been investigated across object type and concept presentation modality. It was first identified by Radvansky and Zacks (1991), in which the fan effect was found to occur in instances where presented concepts have the same object associated with multiple places (that is to say, the object feature had a high fan value) but not when multiple persons were associated with a single place (i.e. the place feature had a high fan value). Radvansky et al. (1993) later extended this to different object types, specifically small locations and inanimate objects. Stopher and Kirsner (1981) found that fan effects do not seem to present when concepts are presented via images rather than text, suggesting that differential fan effect context is affected by modality in addition to content.

There remains some debate on the mechanism of the fan effect in human subjects, particularly in regard to explaining differential fan effects. Radvansky et al. (1993) proposed a mechanism, based on the concept of mental models, by which subjects create and maintain models of the world based on learned facts and that some types of overlap in presented concepts necessitate the creation of more models than less overlapping concept sets of the same size. Anderson and Reder (1999) proposes a different mechanism, derived from a cognitive architecture in which fan effects are mediated by changing weights of edges in the concept network. This mechanism was further supported experimentally in Sohn et al. (2004) but challenged for larger datasets in Radvansky (1999).

Fan effects are found by Silber and Fisher (1989) in probabilistic categories created by COBWEB to be a special case of another phenomenon known as the ***typicality effect***. This would seem to suggest that fan effects may arise as a consequence of categorization, with a potential explanation being that items closer to the categorical center are more likely to collide with other items, leading to recall uncertainty, while items further from the center are less likely to experience aliasing.

Typicality, first formalized and identified in humans by Rosch (1975), refers to a tendency of humans to perform categorization tasks quicker when prompted with a more typical member of a category than with a less typical member of a category, with level of typicality determined by how common the features of an instance of a category are among all members of the same category and among contrasting categories. That is, both an item's intra-category similarity and its inter-category similarity affect typicality assessments. For example, given pictures of two birds, a robin and a penguin, human subject response time will be higher when answering whether the penguin is a bird than whether the robin is a bird.

2.1 Prior Work

In Table 1, the results of a comprehensive survey of current work in LLM cognitive behavior studies is provided. No works could be found that study language model fan effects. Though Tung (2024) studied memory interference behavior in LLMs and use fan values in their analysis, they do not explicitly consider the fan effect or its presence.

On the other hand, work has been done that establishes the presence of typicality effects in LLMs (Misra et al., 2021; Bhatia and Richie, 2022; Roberts et al., 2024b) as well as vision models (Upadhyay et al., 2022). Bhatia and Richie (2022) found that BERT shows evidence of typicality effects, including consistency with typicality violations common to humans. Misra et al. (2021) recreated a subset of the experiments conducted by Rosch (1975) which were used to identify typicality effects in humans, identifying typicality effects across numerous categories and models. Roberts et al. (2024b) replicated Misra et al. (2021) with PopulationLM, establishing that the effect was not eroded when studied in a population.

Roberts et al. (2024b) found that the population standard deviations tended to positively correlate with typicality in encoder-only models, though not in decoder-only models. This suggests that the uncertainty captured by LLM variance may not be analogous to human uncertainty since LLMs are overwhelmingly based on the decoder-only architecture (Roberts, 2024).

3 In-Pretraining (Typicality) Fan Effect

Anderson originally observed the fan effect in the response times of humans when **correctly responding** to questions. However, in Silber and Fisher (1989), the authors observed human-like fan effects in a COBWEB model and found they were consistent with a special case of typicality. Based on this observation and extant work regarding the presence of typicality effects in LLMs, we hypothesize that LLMs may exhibit a fan effect induced by the relative typicality of categorical items acquired from pretraining. Specifically we formulate RQ3.1.

Research Question 3.1. *Given a partial list of items drawn from a category and presented to an LLM, are absence/presence prediction probabilities modulated by item typicality such that probabilities conditioned on typical items tend to be lower than those conditioned on less typical items?*

Expanding on this, based on results from (Roberts et al., 2024b), more typical items tend to have increased predicted word probability even when counterfactual prompting is used, most likely due to base rate probability effects (Moore et al., 2024). However, if a fan effect is present, the probability should tend to decrease with increasing typicality.

It is important to note that LLM probabilities are not necessarily analogous to human response times. However, existing work (Misra et al., 2021; Roberts et al., 2024b) has shown that typicality judgments, which have been measured via response time in humans (Rosch, 1975), are correlated with LLM probabilities.

3.1 Methodology

Models: All experimental trials are conducted among a systematically perturbed population formed from each base model using PopulationLM (Roberts et al., 2024b) to decrease the likelihood that obtained results are anomalous. The median value is the preferred aggregation when random sampling for the purpose of estimating a true value (Doerr and Sutton, 2019). Therefore, the median

In-pretraining Fan Effect Prompt
Following is a list that contains a number of birds. After the list, a bird will be judged as either present or absent in the list. If the list contains the bird, answer with present. If the list does not contain the bird, answer with absent. The list of birds is: toucan, magpie, swan, flamingo, duck, goose, blackbird, pelican, woodpecker, condor, canary, ostrich, redbird, catbird, lark, parakeet, hummingbird, bluejay, bluebird, sparrow, crow, vulture, cardinal, turkey, chicken, goldfinch, wren. According to the list, magpie is present. According to the list, kingfisher is absent. According to the list, robin is____

LLM
$P(present)$ and $P(absent)$

Figure 1: Prompt to measure presence/absence belief.

across each base model population is taken as the group prediction.

We choose RoBERTa (Liu et al., 2019), GPT-2 (Radford et al., 2019), Llama-2 (Touvron et al., 2023), Llama-3 (Meta, 2024), Mistral (Jiang et al., 2023), and SOLAR (Kim et al., 2023) as the base models for the experiments. RoBERTa and GPT-2 are chosen as representatives of models previously studied and found to exhibit typicality effects (Roberts et al., 2024b). However, past work has found that higher order human-like behaviors may not be exhibited in smaller models (Roberts et al., 2024a). We therefore include large open source LLMs (Llama-2, Llama-3, Mistral, and SOLAR) that may be more likely to exhibit more nuanced recall effects.

Data Presentation: Based on work by Rosch (1975) regarding human typicality judgments across items in ten categories, we construct lists for each of the ten categories in Figure 3 by randomly selecting half of the items in a category. Selected items are included precisely once in a comma separated list with instructional content and two in-context examples. The in-context examples are not randomly sampled and are instead consistent across all experiments.

For each item (N≈60) in each category and every model population member (N=50) we obtain a probability of absence and a probability of presence via counterfactual prompting (Moore et al., 2024). The probability is measured by obtaining the probability assigned to the *canary* words "present" and "absent" given each constructed prompt. We repeat each experiment for each base model for each category 10 times without reuse of populations or item lists. An example interaction for the category *bird* and the item *robin* is shown in Figure 1.

Human Comparison: The values for human typicality ratings are taken from Rosch (1975) and compared to the generated model probabilities to understand how typicality, as understood from human studies, impacts model behavior when performing recall.

Other Hardware and Software: All experiments used an A100 GPU Google Colab environment. Token likelihoods were obtained using a fork of the minicons Python library (Misra, 2022).

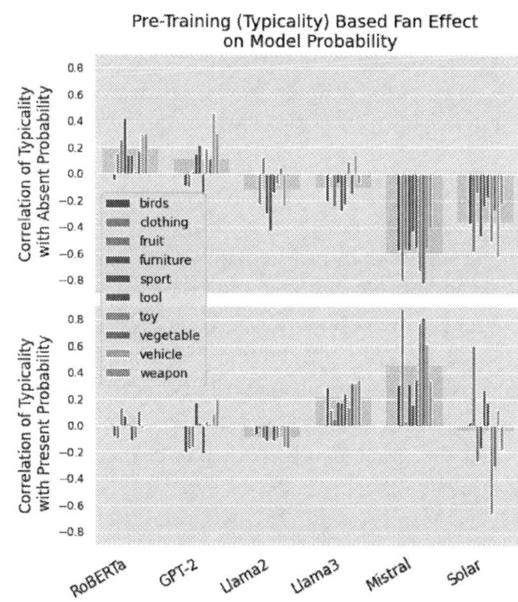

Figure 2: **Top row:** Mistral and SOLAR show significant negative Pearson correlations consistent with fan effects across a range of categories. **Bottom row:** Items present in the context do not elicit a human-like fan effect.

3.2 Results

As noted, the fan effect was only observed by Anderson in humans when responding correctly to questions. Thus, only the true absence group (TAG)

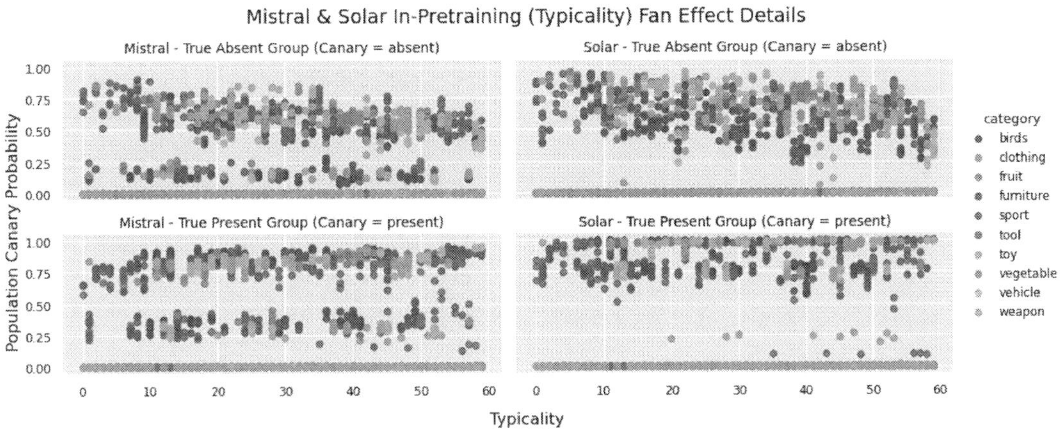

Figure 3: **Left col:** Predictions are made using Mistral. **Right col:** Predictions are made using SOLAR. **Bottom row:** queried item is present (w/o uncertainty). **Top row:** queried item is absent (with uncertainty). Fan effects are evident in the negative Pearson correlation (shown in Figure 2) in the natural group above the noise floor.

and true presence group (TPG) should be considered candidate scenarios that may exhibit a human-like fan effect.

In the upper left plot in Figure 3, there is an obviously distinct group which resides above the threshold (0.35), which we refer to as the probability noise floor. We interpret the group above the noise floor to be the TAG, that is the subset of absent items which the model regards as absent. The TPG, the subset of present items which the model regards as present, can be analogously seen in the bottom left with a noise floor at (0.5). Among predictions in the TAG, the probabilities have an obvious negative correlation with typicality, showing that more typical items tend to induce lower "absent" probabilities. We find that SOLAR (Kim et al., 2023) shows a similar fan effect, with TAG and TPG noise floor at (0.2).

The noise floor observed in both SOLAR and Mistral is an empirical observation which warrants additional consideration. From our investigation, the fan effect in LLMs is modulated by the probability magnitude. Therefore, low probability outputs induce noise in the observation of the fan effect in the model probabilities which are shown for completeness in Figure 3 but filtered in the correlation analysis shown in Figure 2.

Interestingly, in the lower left of Figure 3 the TPG for Mistral has positive correlations which are inconsistent with the fan effect. This is reflected in the bottom of Figure 2 as well. SOLAR, on the other hand, tends toward inter-category randomness in the bottom of Figure 2.

3.3 Discussion

In response to RQ3.1, we find in Figure 3 that items absent from the list elicit a human-consistent fan effect evident in the canary probabilities in Mistral (Jiang et al., 2023) and SOLAR (Kim et al., 2023). The probabilities show a significant (r>0.3) (Hinkle et al., 2003) correlation with intra-category typicality in Figure 2 consistent with the fan effects discovered in COBWEB and theorized in humans. This result shows that LLMs exhibit fan effects based on the effects of typicality present in the pretraining data.

RoBERTa (Liu et al., 2019), GPT-2 (Radford et al., 2019), Llama-2 (Touvron et al., 2023), and Llama-3 (Meta, 2024) were equivalently evaluated but showed no significant correlation, though Llama-3 does show a similar, slight effect. We additionally conducted the correlation investigation presented using the population variance in place of the token probabilities and found no significant correlations. This reinforces the possibility put forth in Roberts et al. (2024b) that decoder-only LLM variance may not capture human-like uncertainty given fan effects are understood as an expression of human uncertainty.

Interpretation: We were surprised to find the fan effect exhibited in the TAG but not the TPG. However, in retrospect this could have been anticipated based on nuanced consideration of the experiment.

The fan effect is canonically explained as a modulation of human uncertainty based on the categorical distance from an exemplar. When evaluating the TPG, the model is able to judge with near certainty by retrieving the queried item. On the other hand when judging the absence of a TAG item, the model can only know that the item has not been retrieved. The model assigns the probability of absence although it may actually be that the item is present but overlooked, inducing uncertainty. We hypothesize this uncertainty is precisely what the fan effect is modulating. So, when queried about an absent atypical item, the model responds confidently as if implying, "I definitely didn't see *that*".

The above scenario in which the fan effect is only observed in the absent case seems plausibly consistent with human cognitive behavior. Imagine a context in which a human has a deck of cards and is asked if a card is present. If the card is found, then the person will have no uncertainty about their response. On the other hand, if the card is not found, the certainty of the response would be expected to be modulated by the fan effect. That is, if an unusual or outlier card is being searched for then it is likely that the person would notice if it had been present. However, it is reasonable that a human could more easily overlook a common card.

We hypothesize that the uncertainty mitigation due to access to the queried items in the TPG leads to the disruption of the fan effect in Mistral and SOLAR. Our results leave unclear the nature of the fan effect under mitigated uncertainty in the TPG.

3.4 Next Steps

Future work should consider creating long context lists that prevent models from retrieving TPG items with high fidelity to attempt to induce uncertainty and fan effects in the TPG. This was not possible currently since no extant lists of intra-category typical items in humans are sufficiently long. However, it may be possible to use LLMs to augment the typicality datasets to create a sufficiently large list.

Results from Mistral suggest that fan effects without uncertainty tend toward a typicality effect response with increasing probability as typicality increases. However, results from SOLAR suggest that they tend toward noise. Future work should additionally attempt to disambiguate the nature of the fan effect when uncertainty is mitigated.

Future work should investigate human behavior in a scenario similar to the described card experiment to understand human fan effect behavior under mitigated uncertainty.

4 In-Context Fan Effect

We investigate the presence of fan effects as originally defined in Anderson (1974) in the context of concepts composed of categorical features. This addresses the question of whether fan effects show up in concepts defined and fan values induced exclusively in-context. We formulate this as RQ4.1. We augment our analysis to investigate the presence of differential fan effect as described in Radvansky and Zacks (1991), providing RQ4.2.

Research Question 4.1. *Given a list of simple concepts defined by their composite features that is presented to an LLM, are absence/presence prediction probabilities modulated by feature fan values such that probabilities conditioned on high fan features tend to be lower than probabilities conditioned on low fan features?*

Research Question 4.2. *Given a list of simple concepts defined by their composite features that is presented to an LLM, is correlation of absence/presence prediction probability with fan value modulated by the fan values of one feature more strongly than another feature?*

4.1 Methodology

We closely recreate the experimental methodology of Anderson (1974), with methods similar to those described in section 3.1 for in-pretraining fan effects.

Models: Based on the results regarding in-pretraining fan effects, we conduct in-context fan effect experiments with populations formed from Mistral and SOLAR using PopulationLM. The experiment uses a generated model population of size $N = 50$ with median aggregation across population to determine group prediction. As before, probabilities are obtained using the *canary* words "present" and "absent".

Data Presentation: Concepts are defined as natural language facts that pair persons, in the form of occupation labels, with places. Each fact is presented as a sentence of the form "The <occupation> is in the <place>". Features are sampled from predefined person and place lists, each of size 20. The fan value is defined as the number of concepts that contain a given feature value. For example, if three distinct concepts indicate a person is present in the place "School", the fan value of "School" is 3. Concept lists are randomly generated to control for ordering effects and feature combination base rates due to semantically connected features (e.g. <Priest, Church>).

No. of Concepts per Place		No. of Concepts per Person: 1	2	3
1		aA	dD	gG
		bB	eE	hH
		cC	fF	iI
2		jJ	eK	gJ
		kK	rR	hR
		lL		iL
3		mM	dM	gM
		nN	rN	hN
		oO	fO	iO

Table 2: Feature assignment pattern used in Anderson and Reder (1999) and replicated in the in-context fan effect experiment.

The concepts in the recreation of Anderson are generated exactly as in Anderson (1974). A predefined set of feature combinations are used, as summarized in Table 2, which are designated by lowercase letters for persons and uppercase letters for places. The person and place assigned to each letter is randomly selected without replacement at the beginning of each trial. The result is N=26 concepts presented to the model in each trial, with a total of 16 fan value combinations (including fan = 0 for features not present in the set).

Prompts presented to the model follow prompt design similar to that in section 3.1. The prompt is composed of four sections: An instructional preamble, the concept list, a two-shot ICL example, and the test query. The ICL examples include a concept that is appended to the end of the concept list that is guaranteed to not be generated. This guaranteed concept is followed by two example queries and simulated outputs, one where the concept is the guaranteed present concept and one with a guaranteed absent concept.

An example prompt in which the concept <Doctor, Park> is shown in Figure 4. Note that <Mechanic, Mall> is included in all trials and has a guaranteed fan value of 1 for both features, while <Airport, Pilot> is absent in all trials.

Human Comparison: The data pairings generated are based on the data presented to humans in Anderson and Reder (1999) which were shown to illicit the fan effect in human recall.

In-Context Fan Effect Prompt

Following is a list that contains a number of people and the places in which they are located. After the list, a person will be judged as either present or absent in a specified place. When asked about person A in place B, if the list says that person A is in place B, answer with present. If the list does not say that person A is in place B, answer with absent. The list of people and places is: The Nurse is in the Studio. The Police Officer is in the Bank. ... The Mechanic is in the Mall. According to the list, in the Mall, the Mechanic is present. According to the list, in the Airport, the Pilot is absent. According to the list, in the Park, the Doctor is____

LLM

$P(present)$ and $P(absent)$

Figure 4: Prompt to measure presence/absence belief.

Other Hardware and Software: All experiments are conducted on an A100 GPU Google Colab environment. Token likelihoods were again obtained with a modified version of the minicons library (Misra, 2022).

4.2 Results

The results for both models are shown in Figure 5. As was the case in the in-pretraining experiments, a probability noise floor was noted in the data for both canary completions (Mistral-absent: 0.3; Mistral-present: 0.4; SOLAR-absent: 0.45; SOLAR-present: 0.4), providing a TAG and TPG. The figures are truncated to show only the TPG and TAG datapoints. Correlation statistics of the results are shown in Figure 6, with solid columns indicating correlations with a $p \leq 0.01$.

In Mistral, we once again see an obvious negative correlation between canary probability and fan value in the TAG predictions. This is consistent with a fan effect when evaluating absence of a concept (RQ 4.1). In the TAG, we see a stronger correlation with the fan value of the person feature than with the fan value of the place feature,

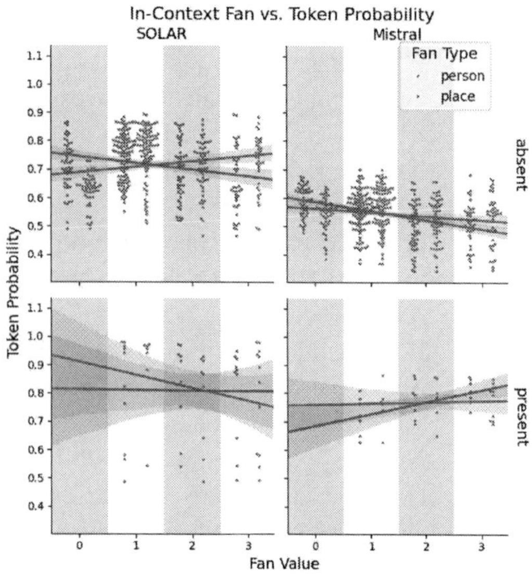

Figure 5: Results of the Anderson recreation experiments on SOLAR and Mistral **Top row:** queried item is absent with the model predicting true absence (with uncertainty). **Bottom row:** queried item is present with the model predicting true presence (w/o uncertainty). Lines of best fit are included. Pearson correlations shown in Figure 6.

supporting a positive result for RQ 4.2. This is consistent with results regarding differential fan effects in Radvansky and Zacks (1991), which found that the fan effect is mediated more by the fan of a particular object than the fan of a particular location.

SOLAR shows a slightly different story. For the TAG predictions, we still see a significant negative correlation when correlating with the fan of person, but a positive correlation with fan of place. TPG predictions instead show a negative correlation against fan of place and no correlation against fan of person. While this seems inconsistent with our Mistral results, it is consistent with our prior interpretations when properly analyzed. Based on these results, SOLAR and Mistral both show evidence of the fan effect in, at minimum, the same situations as in humans, which is to say uncertain contexts and based on the fan of person.

From the in-pretraining experiment, we expect that mitigated uncertainty in the TPG may lead to disruption of the fan effect. In confirmation, among TPG items all correlations fail to achieve a significant p value for fan value and canary probability Pearson correlation, again suggesting that mitigated uncertainty disrupts the fan effect.

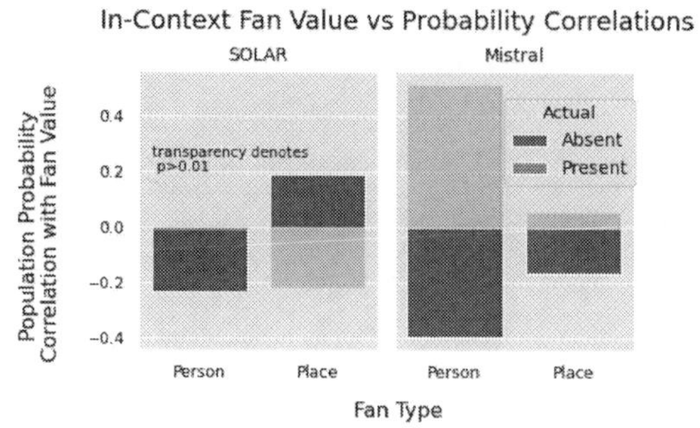

Figure 6: Negative correlations when the queried item is absent suggests items are recalled with higher certainty when the item has fewer in-context appearances (low fan value). Fan values derived from the queried person show fan effects while place fan values cause a distruption of the fan effect. No "present" item queries have significant p values though all "absent" item queries do.

4.3 Next Steps

There are numerous enhancements that could be applied to these experiments. While occupations were chosen as proxies for persons to be consistent with Anderson (1974), more unique identifiers like names may yield a stronger differential fan effect if the mental models mechanism proposed by (Radvansky and Zacks, 1991) is present in language models. This should be tested empirically in future work to investigate the nature of differential fan effects. Additionally, other feature types that are not related to persons and places should be investigated.

Human cognitive experiments often include a dimension of elapsed time between training and testing time when studying memory-sensitive behaviors. Future work should consider simulating this time separation in language models. Though language models do not possess a directly analogous temporal dimension, experiments could evaluate the injection of semantic noise of varying length as a potential proxy. In fact such an experiment may suggest that time, to humans, is itself a form of semantic noise.

5 Conclusions

Our experiments are the first to evaluate LLMs for the presence of human-like fan effects. We have shown that Mistral and SOLAR have learned to exhibit fan effects from training on human language data. This paper is not the first to identify SOLAR and Mistral as important human-like LLMs. Roberts et al. (2024a) found SOLAR and Mistral to be significantly more human-like than a large body of other open-source models when evaluated in a game theoretic context. Given Mistral was built from Llama-2 and SOLAR was built from Mistral, the authors propose the more human-like behavior may be the result of an improved representation acquired through additional training of Mistral with sliding window attention.

Our results show that fan effects are present both when the fan value is induced in-pretraining in the form of intra-category typicality and when the fan value is induced in-context in the form of repeated items within a list. The presence of typicality-based fan effects in language models lends further credence to the findings of Silber and Fisher (1989) suggesting that fan effects are a special case of typicality effects.

Additionally, we find that when uncertainty is mitigated, the fan effect is disrupted with divergent disruption patterns across LLMs. The divergent patterns across Mistral and SOLAR beg further investigation. However, we are unaware of any cognitive science literature that addresses fan effects in a disruptive scenario with mitigated uncertainty. Therefore, it is unclear how a human may behave in a similar context. We therefore call for human experiments.

Similarly, when the fan value is derived from place instead of person in the Anderson experiment, both Mistral and SOLAR exhibit a disruption of the fan effect in agreement with nuanced work regarding differential fan effects (Radvansky and Zacks, 1991). Again, each of these models diverges in the nature of the disruption but shows a consistent pattern of fan effects in the case of true absence when the fan value is calculated on the person feature.

Finally, we hope this paper will prove synergistic with the wider cognitive science and computational linguistic communities. By adapting experiments to evaluate the presence of known human cognitive effects in LLMs, we may gain new insight into cognitive effects. These insights not only help to explain the factors which influence the behavior of complex language models but also provide new potential hypotheses regarding the cognitive behavior of humans.

6 Practical Implications

Human-like uncertainty is shown to be present in Mistral and SOLAR in the form of a fan effect both when the fan value is induced in the pretraining of the model and in the context. However, just as found in Roberts et al. (2024b), the common measures of model uncertainty, variance and standard deviation, may not tend to correlate well with human uncertainty as quantified by the fan effect. This suggests that more work needs to be done to develop a human-consistent measure of LLM uncertainty.

Additionally, the fan effect should be considered when engaging LLMs in applications that require recall. The results here suggest that LLMs may have more trouble correctly evaluating the presence or absence of (1) items when the item is frequently present in the pretraining data and (2) coincident items when the base item is frequently present in the context of the model.

Acknowledgments

We appreciate the helpful recommendations of reviewers that led to improved presentation clarity and the insightful evaluation of the area chair.

Limitations

While this paper demonstrates that LLMs exhibit fan effects. It may be the case that the observed effects tend to be weak in comparison to the probability magnitude. So, it is unclear if LLMs fail in recall scenarios in manners consistent with fan effects.

References

John R Anderson and Lynne M Reder. 1999. The fan effect: New results and new theories. *Journal of Experimental Psychology: General*, 128(2):186.

John Robert Anderson. 1974. Retrieval of propositional information from long-term memory. *Cognitive psychology*, 6(4):451–474.

Sudeep Bhatia and Russell Richie. 2022. Transformer networks of human conceptual knowledge. *Psychological Review*.

Marcel Binz and Eric Schulz. 2023. Using cognitive psychology to understand gpt-3. *Proceedings of the National Academy of Sciences*, 120(6):e2218523120.

Sébastien Bubeck, Varun Chandrasekaran, Ronen Eldan, Johannes Gehrke, Eric Horvitz, Ece Kamar, Peter Lee, Yin Tat Lee, Yuanzhi Li, Scott Lundberg, et al. 2023. Sparks of artificial general intelligence: Early experiments with gpt-4. *arXiv preprint arXiv:2303.12712*.

Julian Coda-Forno, Marcel Binz, Jane X Wang, and Eric Schulz. 2024. Cogbench: a large language model walks into a psychology lab. In *Forty-first International Conference on Machine Learning*.

Julian Coda-Forno, Kristin Witte, Akshay K Jagadish, Marcel Binz, Zeynep Akata, and Eric Schulz. 2023. Inducing anxiety in large language models increases exploration and bias. *arXiv preprint arXiv:2304.11111*.

Benjamin Doerr and Andrew M Sutton. 2019. When resampling to cope with noise, use median, not mean. In *Proceedings of the Genetic and Evolutionary Computation Conference*, pages 242–248.

Thilo Hagendorff, Sarah Fabi, and Michal Kosinski. 2023. Human-like intuitive behavior and reasoning biases emerged in large language models but disappeared in chatgpt. *Nature Computational Science*, 3(10):833–838.

Dennis E Hinkle, William Wiersma, Stephen G Jurs, et al. 2003. *Applied statistics for the behavioral sciences*, volume 663. Houghton Mifflin Boston.

Albert Q Jiang, Alexandre Sablayrolles, Arthur Mensch, Chris Bamford, Devendra Singh Chaplot, Diego de las Casas, Florian Bressand, Gianna Lengyel, Guillaume Lample, Lucile Saulnier, et al. 2023. Mistral 7b. *arXiv preprint arXiv:2310.06825*.

Erik Jones and Jacob Steinhardt. 2022. Capturing failures of large language models via human cognitive biases. *Advances in Neural Information Processing Systems*, 35:11785–11799.

Dahyun Kim, Chanjun Park, Sanghoon Kim, Wonsung Lee, Wonho Song, Yunsu Kim, Hyeonwoo Kim, Yungi Kim, Hyeonju Lee, Jihoo Kim, et al. 2023. Solar 10.7 b: Scaling large language models with simple yet effective depth up-scaling. *arXiv preprint arXiv:2312.15166*.

Michal Kosinski. 2023. Theory of mind may have spontaneously emerged in large language models. *arXiv preprint arXiv:2302.02083*.

Andrew K Lampinen, Ishita Dasgupta, Stephanie CY Chan, Hannah R Sheahan, Antonia Creswell, Dharshan Kumaran, James L McClelland, and Felix Hill. 2023. Language models show human-like content effects on reasoning tasks. *arXiv preprint arXiv:2207.07051*.

Sotiris Lamprinidis. 2023. Llm cognitive judgements differ from human. *arXiv preprint arXiv:2307.11787*.

Huao Li, Yu Quan Chong, Simon Stepputtis, Joseph Campbell, Dana Hughes, Michael Lewis, and Katia Sycara. 2023. Theory of mind for multi-agent collaboration via large language models. *arXiv preprint arXiv:2310.10701*.

Yinhan Liu, Myle Ott, Naman Goyal, Jingfei Du, Mandar Joshi, Danqi Chen, Omer Levy, Mike Lewis, Luke Zettlemoyer, and Veselin Stoyanov. 2019. Roberta: A robustly optimized bert pretraining approach. *arXiv preprint arXiv:1907.11692*.

Ziqiao Ma, Jacob Sansom, Run Peng, and Joyce Chai. 2023. Towards a holistic landscape of situated theory of mind in large language models. *arXiv preprint arXiv:2310.19619*.

R Thomas McCoy, Ellie Pavlick, and Tal Linzen. 2019. Right for the wrong reasons: Diagnosing syntactic heuristics in natural language inference. *arXiv preprint arXiv:1902.01007*.

AI Meta. 2024. Introducing meta llama 3: The most capable openly available llm to date. *Meta AI*.

James Michaelov, Catherine Arnett, Tyler Chang, and Ben Bergen. 2023. Structural priming demonstrates abstract grammatical representations in multilingual language models. In *Proceedings of the 2023 Conference on Empirical Methods in Natural Language Processing*, pages 3703–3720, Singapore. Association for Computational Linguistics.

Kanishka Misra. 2022. minicons: Enabling flexible behavioral and representational analyses of transformer language models. *arXiv preprint arXiv:2203.13112*.

Kanishka Misra, Allyson Ettinger, and Julia Taylor Rayz. 2021. Do language models learn typicality judgments from text? *arXiv preprint arXiv:2105.02987*.

Kyle Moore, Jesse Roberts, Thao Pham, Oseremhen Ewaleifoh, and Doug Fisher. 2024. The base-rate effect on llm benchmark performance: Disambiguating test-taking strategies from benchmark performance. *arXiv preprint arXiv:2406.11634*.

Alec Radford, Jeffrey Wu, Rewon Child, David Luan, Dario Amodei, Ilya Sutskever, et al. 2019. Language models are unsupervised multitask learners. *OpenAI blog*, 1(8):9.

GA Radvansky and RT Zacks. 1991. Mental models and fact retrieval. *Journal of Experimental Psychology: Learning, Memory, and Cognition*, 17:940–953.

Gabriel A Radvansky. 1999. The fan effect: a tale of two theories.

Gabriel A Radvansky, Daniel H Spieler, and Rose T Zacks. 1993. Mental model organization. *Journal of Experimental Psychology: Learning, Memory, and Cognition*, 19(1):95.

Jesse Roberts. 2024. How powerful are decoder-only transformer neural models? In *2024 International Joint Conference on Neural Networks (IJCNN)*, pages 1–8. IEEE.

Jesse Roberts, Kyle Moore, and Doug Fisher. 2024a. Do large language models learn human-like strategic preferences? *arXiv preprint arXiv:2404.08710*.

Jesse Roberts, Kyle Moore, Drew Wilenzick, and Douglas Fisher. 2024b. Using artificial populations to study psychological phenomena in neural models. *Proceedings of the AAAI Conference on Artificial Intelligence*, 38(17):18906–18914.

Eleanor Rosch. 1975. Cognitive representations of semantic categories. *Journal of experimental psychology: General*, 104(3):192.

Maarten Sap, Ronan LeBras, Daniel Fried, and Yejin Choi. 2022. Neural theory-of-mind? on the limits of social intelligence in large lms. *arXiv preprint arXiv:2210.13312*.

J Silber and DH Fisher. 1989. A model of natural category structure and its behavioral implications. In *Proceedings of the eleventh annual conference of the Cognitive Science Society*, pages 884–891. Erlbaum Hillsdale, NJ.

Arabella Sinclair, Jaap Jumelet, Willem Zuidema, and Raquel Fernández. 2022. Structural persistence in language models: Priming as a window into abstract language representations. *Transactions of the Association for Computational Linguistics*, 10:1031–1050.

Myeong-Ho Sohn, John R Anderson, Lynne M Reder, and Adam Goode. 2004. Differential fan effect and attentional focus. *Psychonomic Bulletin & Review*, 11:729–734.

Kerry Stopher and Kim Kirsner. 1981. Long-term memory for pictures and sentences. *Memory & Cognition*, 9:34–40.

Gaurav Suri, Lily R Slater, Ali Ziaee, and Morgan Nguyen. 2023. Do large language models show decision heuristics similar to humans? a case study using gpt-3.5. *arXiv preprint arXiv:2305.04400*.

Hugo Touvron, Louis Martin, Kevin Stone, Peter Albert, Amjad Almahairi, Yasmine Babaei, Nikolay Bashlykov, Soumya Batra, Prajjwal Bhargava, Shruti Bhosale, et al. 2023. Llama 2: Open foundation and fine-tuned chat models. *arXiv preprint arXiv:2307.09288*.

Sean Trott, Cameron Jones, Tyler Chang, James Michaelov, and Benjamin Bergen. 2023. Do large language models know what humans know? *Cognitive Science*, 47(7):e13309.

Tzu-Yun Tung. 2024. *Prediction and Memory Retrieval in Dependency Resolution*. Ph.D. thesis.

Tomer Ullman. 2023. Large language models fail on trivial alterations to theory-of-mind tasks. *arXiv preprint arXiv:2302.08399*.

Neha Upadhyay, Kritika Mittal, and Sashank Varma. 2022. Typicality gradients in computer vision models. In *Proceedings of the Annual Meeting of the Cognitive Science Society*, volume 44.

Nicolas Yax, Hernan Anlló, and Stefano Palminteri. 2024. Studying and improving reasoning in humans and machines. *Communications Psychology*, 2(1):51.

Continuous Attentive Multimodal Prompt Tuning for Few-Shot Multimodal Sarcasm Detection

Soumyadeep Jana, **Animesh Dey**, and **Sanasam Ranbir Singh**
Department of Computer Science and Engineering
Indian Institute of Technology Guwahati
{sjana, d.animesh ,ranbir}@iitg.ac.in

Abstract

With the steep rise in multimodal content on social media, multimodal sarcasm detection has gained widespread attention from research communities. Existing studies depend on large-scale data, which is challenging to obtain and expensive to annotate. Thus, investigating this problem in a few-shot scenario is required. Overtly complex multimodal models are prone to overfitting on in-domain data, which hampers their performance on out-of-distribution (OOD) data. To address these issues, we propose **C**ontinuous **A**ttentive **M**ultimodal **P**rompt Tuning model (CAMP), that leverages the prompt tuning paradigm to handle few-shot multimodal sarcasm detection. To overcome the siloed learning process of continuous prompt tokens, we design a novel, continuous multimodal attentive prompt where the continuous tokens intricately engage with both image and text tokens, enabling the assimilation of knowledge from different input modalities. Experimental results indicate that our method outperforms other multimodal baseline methods in the few-shot setting and OOD scenarios. Our few-shot dataset and code is available at `https://github.com/mr-perplexed/camp`.

1 Introduction

Sarcasm is a figurative language where the utterance conveys a meaning opposite to the literal meaning of the words used. Detecting sarcasm is important for effectively understanding sentiment (Maynard and Greenwood, 2014; Badlani et al., 2019), hate speech (Frenda, 2018; Yang et al., 2022a), and users' opinions on social media (Tindale and Gough, 1987; van Eemeren and Grootendorst, 1992; Averbeck, 2013; Ghosh et al., 2021). With the rise in multimodal content on social media platforms, multimodal sarcasm detection has gained widespread attention from research communities. Multiple modalities provide a crucial clue to ascertain the sarcastic nature of a post since deciphering sarcasm from uni-modal (only text or image) content may be highly ambiguous or unspecified.

Current approaches for multimodal image-text sarcasm detection (Cai et al., 2019; Pan et al., 2020; Xu et al., 2020; Liang et al., 2021; Liu et al., 2022a; Liang et al., 2022; Tian et al., 2023; Wen et al., 2023) suffer from some major challenges. These models primarily rely on large annotated datasets to achieve good performance. However, these datasets are difficult to obtain, and annotation is expensive and highly challenging due to socio-cultural and contextual dependencies (Rockwell and Theriot, 2001; Ivanko and Pexman, 2003; Dress et al., 2008; Oprea and Magdy, 2019). Distant supervision techniques for labeling, like the use of special markers such as #sarcasm on Twitter, introduce additional noise in the form of wrong labels (Davidov et al., 2010; González-Ibáñez et al., 2011). Due to the complex structure of these multimodal models, they tend to overfit on in-domain data causing a reduction in performance for out-of-distribution (OOD) data.

Prompt-based methods have gained popularity in few-shot learning as they enable Pretrained Language Models (PLMs) to generalize to new tasks with minimal or no training data as PLMs can serve as knowledge bases (Petroni et al., 2019; Jiang et al., 2020) due to their large-scale training on huge corpora. Hence, it is imperative to use prompt-based method for our task.

Most of the existing prompt-based works on downstream tasks are based on prompt-based fine-tuning (Cao et al., 2022; Yang et al., 2022a,b; Yu and Zhang, 2022), where discrete prompts are given as inputs to PLMs, and the entire PLM is fine-tuned to fill up the mask token. This poses three main challenges. First, finding the right prompt in the discrete token space is difficult and often yields sub-optimal performance. Changes in token count drastically impact results (Liu et al., 2021).

Proceedings of the 28th Conference on Computational Natural Language Learning, pages 314–326
November 15-16, 2024 ©2024 Association for Computational Linguistics

Second, training all model weights increases parameters, memory use, and training time. Lastly, fine-tuning pre-trained language models often leads to catastrophic forgetting (Wang et al., 2022; Zhai et al., 2023), reducing generalizability and performance on out-of-distribution data due to changes in the pre-trained weights.

Motivated by the shortcomings of traditional multimodal approaches and discrete prompt-based techniques, we explore the idea of Prompt Tuning (Li and Liang, 2021; Lester et al., 2021), a new paradigm involving PLMs where task-specific continuous prompts are learned during training, keeping the parameters of the PLM frozen. Further, in the vanilla Prompt Tuning approach, a significant limitation arises from the frozen nature of the pre-trained language model (PLM). This constraint results in independent learning of continuous prompt tokens without integrating knowledge on how to attend to both image and text tokens effectively. To address this challenge, we propose a novel model: **CAMP** (**C**ontinuous **A**ttentive **M**ultimodal **P**rompt Tuning) model for few-shot multimodal sarcasm detection. To begin with, we design multimodal continuous prompts with text and image modalities. We also use captions of the images as the third modality to bridge the semantic gap between image and text. Our approach enhances the model's ability to better learn the continuous prompt tokens by incorporating multimodal information and introducing attentive mechanisms, thereby significantly improving its capacity to attend to both image and text tokens seamlessly.

Our results show that using only 0.3 fraction of the entire PLM parameters, CAMP can achieve state-of-the-art results in few-shot multimodal sarcasm detection. CAMP also shows strong performance on the OOD setting. In summary, the main contributions and findings of this paper are listed below:

1. To the best of our knowledge, this study is the first to investigate multimodal sarcasm detection in a few-shot setup using continuous prompt tuning paradigm.

2. We propose **CAMP**, a parameter efficient model leveraging novel continuous attentive multimodal prompt.

3. Our extensive experiments on two benchmark datasets showcase our model's superiority over strong multimodal baselines in a few-shot and OOD setting.

4. We present a comprehensive analysis of different prompt-based techniques including prompting, prompt-based finetuning, and prompt tuning on our task.

2 Related Work

2.1 Multimodal Image-Text Sarcasm Detection

The field of sarcasm detection started with text as the sole modality. Prior works (Joshi et al., 2015; Khattri et al., 2015; Joshi et al., 2016; Amir et al., 2016; Zhang et al., 2016; Poria et al., 2016; Ghosh et al., 2017; Agrawal and An, 2018; Agrawal et al., 2020; Babanejad et al., 2020; Lou et al., 2021; Liu et al., 2022b) use different sequence modeling techniques, along with external cues like author information, conversation context, etc, to detect the incongruity present in the text. With the rise in the usage of multimodal content on social media, researchers shifted their attention towards multimodal sarcasm detection. (Schifanella et al., 2016) was the first to perform the task of multimodal sarcasm detection with text and image modality. This work used manually designed features to detect incongruity between the two modalities. (Cai et al., 2019) released a new image-text dataset based on Twitter and proposed a hierarchical early and late fusion method to combine the two modalities. Work by (Xu et al., 2020) employed decomposition and relation network to identify cross-modality incongruity and semantic association. Study by (Pan et al., 2020) showed that sarcasm could arise from either intra-modal or inter-modal associations. So, they proposed a self-attention-based model to capture intra and inter-modal incongruity. (Liang et al., 2021, 2022) used graph neural networks over in-modal and cross-modal graphs to detect sarcasm. To model both granular-level and abstract-level incongruities, (Liu et al., 2022a) used hierarchical semantic interactions between image-text modalities. (Wen et al., 2023) proposed a Dual Incongruity Perceiving (DIP) network, which combines semantic intensified distribution modeling and siamese sentiment contrastive learning modules to distinguish between sarcastic and non-sarcastic samples. (Tian et al., 2023) proposed a Dynamic Routing Transformer model to adaptively capture the inter-modal contrast between image and text to identify sarcasm.

Unlike traditional methods relying on extensive annotated data and training of PLMs like BERT (Devlin et al., 2019) as foundational components, our approach operates in a few-shot learning scenario, utilizing a frozen PLM. This strategy proves effective in handling the scarcity of sarcasm annotations while achieving state-of-the-art performance with only a fraction of the PLM parameters.

2.2 Multimodal Prompt-Based Approaches

Recent studies have used prompt-based methods for various multimodal NLP downstream tasks like visual QA (Liu et al., 2022c; Chappuis et al., 2022; Guo et al., 2022; Ossowski and Hu, 2023), sentiment analysis (Gao et al., 2021; Yang et al., 2022b; Yu et al., 2022; Yu and Zhang, 2022; Hosseini-Asl et al., 2022), and hate speech detection (Cao et al., 2022; Ji et al., 2023; García-Díaz et al., 2023; Cao et al., 2023).

Most of these approaches have either focused on prompting or prompt-based finetuning paradigms. However, a detailed study on using continuous prompts for multimodal sarcasm detection is yet to be explored. To this end, we propose a continuous prompt tuning approach to tackle multimodal sarcasm detection with attentive prompts.

3 Proposed Approach

3.1 Problem Definition

Given a multimodal sample $x_j = (T_j, I_j)$, where $T_j = \{t_j^1, t_j^2, ..., t_j^n\}$ is the text and I is the associated image, the task is to assign x_j a label $y_j \in Y = \{sarcastic, nonsarcastic\}$. Traditionally, the task of multimodal sarcasm detection has been formulated as a binary classification task, wherein the model outputs two probabilities corresponding to the label space $Y = \{sarcastic, nonsarcastic\}$. The sample is classified based on the higher probability label. We reformulate the task as a Masked Language Modeling Problem. Given a PLM M, M is prompted with multimodal input to fill the $[MASK]$ token, which represents the labels Y.

3.2 Multimodal Prompt Tuning

We propose a novel model called **CAMP** (**C**ontinuous **A**ttentive **M**ultimodal **P**rompt Tuning) model for few-shot multimodal sarcasm detection. Figure 1 shows the overall architecture of our proposed model. In this sub-section, we elaborate on the design of continuous multimodal prompt, while in the next sub-section, we delve into incorporating attention mechanism into the continuous prompt tokens to generate continuous attentive multimodal prompt.

Given a multimodal sample consisting of text T_j and an associated image I_j, text modality T_j can be directly fed to the PLM. However, PLMs are not designed to accommodate image modality information. To curb this, following (Yang et al., 2022b), we generate pseudo-visual tokens. First, the original image I_j is passed through ResNet, and it is then projected into the text feature space using a weight matrix W^t and bias vector b^t, as depicted by the equation:

$$V_j = W^t * ResNet(I_j) + b^t \qquad (1)$$

The V_j is then reshaped, $V_j = reshape(V_j) = \{v_j^1, v_j^2, ..., v_j^p\}$, where $V_j \in \mathbb{R}^{p \times v_{dim}}$ to generate the final visual tokens where p is the number of image token slots and is kept as a hyperparameter. After introducing the visual tokens, to further reduce the gap between image and text modalities, we generate caption C_j using a vision-language model BLIP-2 (Li et al., 2023), where $C_j = BLIP2(I_j)$. BLIP-2 combines frozen pre-trained image models with language models for representation and generative learning. This helps BLIP to achieve state-of-the-art performance in image captioning task. With these at our disposal, we design our multimodal prompt template Z as follows which can be fed to the PLM for it to generate the $[MASK]$ token:

$Z(T_j, C_j, V_j) = [V_j]\ Tweet\ text : [T_j]$
$Caption : [C_j].\ [MASK]$

Subsequently, the PLM embeds Z as a series of m discrete tokens by passing through its encoder, creating an embedding matrix $F \in \mathbb{R}^{m \times h_{dim}}$.

Now, we design our continuous prompts. In the prompt tuning paradigm introduced in (Li and Liang, 2021), learnable vectors called continuous prompt tokens are added to the prompt being fed to PLM. These continuous tokens are generated from a prompt encoder, particularly multilayer perceptron or LSTM networks. During training, instead of fine-tuning the PLM, these continuous tokens are learned for the task at hand. This differs from the approach of prompting or prompt-based finetuning. In prompting, discrete prompt tokens are employed to query the PLM without modifying the PLM, while in prompt-based finetuning, all the PLM weights are updated. Figure 2 presents a schematic difference between the paradigms.

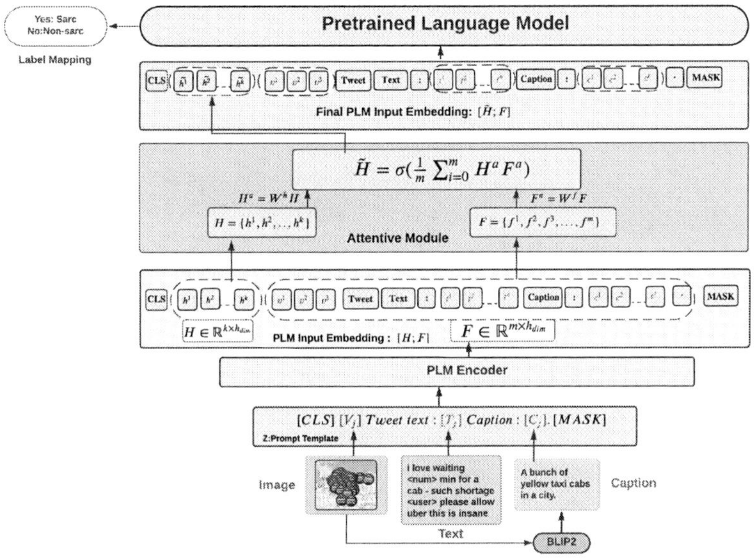

Figure 1: Architecture of our CAMP model.

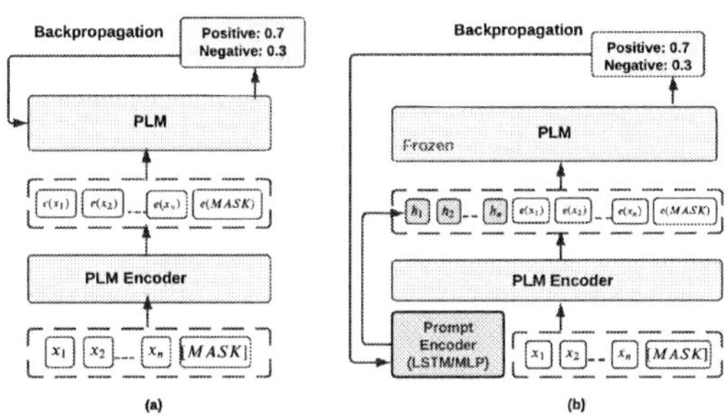

Figure 2: Schematic Representation of a) Prompt-Based Finetuning strategy and b) Prompt Tuning strategy.

We prepend the continuous learnable tokens to the prompt, which are represented by the matrix $H = \{h_1, h_2, ..., h_k\} \in \mathbb{R}^{k \times h_{dim}}$, where k is the number of continuous prompt tokens. The parameters of the underlying prompt encoder is represented by ϕ. H is then combined with the embedded input F, resulting in a unified matrix $[H; F]$ of dimensions $\mathbb{R}^{(k+m) \times h_{dim}}$. This combined matrix called the PLM input embedding matrix, forms the input for the PLM.

3.3 Attentive Multimodal Prompt Tuning

A significant drawback of the vanilla continuous prompt tuning approach is the siloed learning process for continuous prompt tokens, overlooking the essential integration of knowledge required for effectively attending to both image and text tokens. This happens because the weights of the PLM are frozen in prompt tuning, hindering the function of the attention mechanism. Thus the model cannot focus on specific parts of the input sequence when generating outputs, failing to capture dependencies and relationships between different tokens.

To address this issue, we design a continuous attentive multimodal prompt, where the learnable vectors can attend to the non-learnable or fixed tokens before passing through the PLM layers. We reason that this would capture the dependencies between the learnable and fixed tokens, and act as a substitute for the frozen attention layers of the PLM. We segregate the PLM input embedding matrix $[H; F]$ into two parts, learnable tokens H and non-learnable or fixed token embeddings F, where $H = \{h^1, h^2, .., h^k\}$ and $F = \{f^1, f^2, .., f^m\}$. $[CLS]$ and $[MASK]$ token embeddings are ignored. To find out which learnable tokens attend to which fixed tokens, we parameterize the token embeddings and find out their dot product using the following equations.

$$H^a = W^h H \tag{2}$$

$$F^a = W^f F \tag{3}$$

$$S = H^a F^a, \quad S \in \mathbb{R}^{k \times m} \tag{4}$$

S denotes the attention scores of the learnable tokens with each of the other fixed tokens.

For learnable token h^l, we calculate its relative attention score $attn^l$ from S.

$$attn^l = \sigma(\frac{1}{m}\sum_{i=0}^{m} S_{li}) \quad (5)$$

We define the new set of learnable tokens as $\tilde{H} = \{\tilde{h}^1, \tilde{h}^2, ..., \tilde{h}^k\}$, where,

$$\tilde{h}^l = attn^l h^l \quad (6)$$

The attentive learnable token matrix $\tilde{H}$ is then combined with the embedded input F, resulting in a unified matrix $[\tilde{H}; F]$ of dimensions $\mathbb{R}^{(k+m)\times h_{dim}}$. This combined matrix forms the final input and is passed through the PLM to generate the $[MASK]$ token.

3.4 Model Training and Prediction

We feed our final input embedding matrix $E = [\tilde{H}; F]$ to the PLM M. The $[MASK]$ token in E helps to recast the problem into a cloze-filling task. The objective of M is to model the probability of predicting class $y_j \in Y$ as:

$$P(([MASK] = y_j)|E) = \frac{e^{W_{y_j} O_{[MASK]}}}{\sum_{y_j \in Y} e^{W_{y_j} O_{[MASK]}}} \quad (7)$$

where $O_{[MASK]}$ is the hidden representation of $[MASK]$ token and W_{y_j} is the final layer weight of the PLM M. The parameters are optimized by using cross-entropy loss. We update the parameters of the continuous vector tokens ϕ, the projection weights, W^h, and W^f during the training process, while the entire set of weights for M is frozen.

4 Experiments

4.1 Datasets

We evaluate our model CAMP on two benchmark datasets MMSD (Cai et al., 2019) and MMSD2.0 (Qin et al., 2023). MMSD2.0 builds upon MMSD by removing spurious cues and re-annotating the unreasonable negative samples. Following (Yu and Zhang, 2022), we randomly sample 1% of the training data with two different seeds for our few-shot setting, keeping the number of samples equal for each category. We maintain $|valid| = |train|$, while the number of samples in the test set is kept the same. The statistics of the dataset are presented in Table 1.

4.2 Experimental Settings

We use BERT-base-uncased as our PLM and NF-ResNet-50 (Brock et al., 2021) as our visual encoder. Both these backbone networks are kept frozen while training. We map the label space of both MMSD and MMSD2.0 datasets from $\{0, 1\}$ to $\{No, Yes\}$, where the label Yes denotes a sarcastic sample. Following (Yu and Zhang, 2022), to account for variation in performance, we experiment three times for each split, totaling 6 (3×2) training runs for each dataset. We report the mean Accuracy (Acc), mean Macro-F1 (F1), and the standard deviation across the 6 runs. We set the batch size to 16 and the learning rate to 1e-4 for both datasets. The number of continuous prompt tokens is set to 50 for MMSD and 80 for MMSD2.0, while image token slots are fixed at 3 for both datasets. The maximum token length for the PLM is 128. We run our model for 20-100 epochs and pick the model that performs best for the validation set for testing. Additional hyperparameter details are in the Appendix section A.1

4.3 Baselines

We compare our proposed model CAMP with four groups of baselines in a few-shot setting.

1. **Text Modality**: We compare with **TextCNN** (Kim, 2014), a CNN based text classification model, and **BiLSTM** (Graves and Schmidhuber, 2005). We finetune standard **BERT** (Devlin et al., 2019) to compare with our model as it uses a BERT-based adaptation. **LM-BFF** (Gao et al., 2021) uses generated text prompts tailored to each dataset and text demonstrations to address few-shot text classification tasks. **LM-SC** (Jian et al., 2022) builds on LM-BFF by incorporating supervised contrastive learning for few-shot text tasks. We also compare a variant of our model **CAMP(w/o img)** without the image and caption tokens.

2. **Image Modality**: Similar to (Cai et al., 2019), we use the image embedding of the pooling layer of **ResNet** (He et al., 2015) for sarcasm classification. We also benchmark on **ViT** (Dosovitskiy et al., 2020), a transformer-based vision model. We also compare a variant of our model **CAMP(w/o txt)** without the text and caption tokens.

3. **Image + Text Modality (Full-Shot)**: We compare our model with state-of-the-art multimodal models for sarcasm detection designed for full dataset setting. **HFM** (Cai et al., 2019) used hierarchical early and late fusion to fuse

Dataset	Train			Valid			Test		
	Pos	Neg	Total	Pos	Neg	Total	Pos	Neg	Total
MMSD	**99** / 8642	**99** / 11174	**198** / 19816	**99** / 959	**99** / 1459	**198** / 2410	**959** / 959	**1450** / 1450	**2409** / 2409
MMSD2.0	**99** / 9572	**99** / 10240	**198** / 19816	**99**/1042	**99** / 1368	**198** / 2410	**1037** / 1037	**1072** / 1072	**2409** / 2409

Table 1: Statistics of MMSD and MMSD2.0 dataset in the few shot setting. For splits presented as **X/Y**, **X** represents the few-shot data sampled while Y represents the total data. The total train split represents approximately 1% of the total training data with $|valid| = |train|$, while the number of samples in the test set is kept the same.

Modality	Method	MMSD		MMSD2.0	
		Acc	F1	Acc	F1
Image	ResNet	0.664 (0.1)	0.602 (1.2)	0.638 (1.3)	0.625 (0.5)
	ViT	0.611 (1.6)	0.522 (1.7)	0.560 (2.8)	0.614 (0.5)
	CAMP(w/o txt)	0.664 (2.7)	0.635 (3.2)	0.659 (1.9)	0.645 (2.2)
Text	TextCNN	0.631 (2.8)	0.549 (2.5)	0.568 (0.7)	0.570 (1.6)
	BiLSTM	0.602 (1.7)	0.560 (2.3)	0.499 (2.1)	0.595 (2.1)
	BERT	0.667 (2.2)	0.665 (3.1)	0.590 (2.9)	0.623 (2.4)
	LM-BFF	0.695 (2.7)	0.688 (2.3)	0.637 (1.4)	0.626 (2.5)
	LM-SC	0.698 (1.4)	0.681 (0.8)	0.640 (0.7)	0.632 (1.5)
	CAMP(w/o img)	0.696 (1.7)	0.678 (1.5)	0.613 (0.3)	0.560 (2.0)
Image+Text (Full-Shot)	HFM	0.612 (1.3)	0.598 (1.1)	0.561 (0.2)	0.361 (0.3)
	Attn-BERT	0.707 (1.7)	0.696 (1.3)	0.659 (1.6)	0.683 (1.8)
	HKE	0.503 (2.3)	0.667 (2.8)	0.408 (1.5)	0.579 (1.3)
	DIP	0.704 (2.7)	0.698 (2.3)	0.685 (2.8)	0.658 (2.6)
	DynRT	0.583 (0.1)	0.487 (0.6)	0.518 (2.9)	0.513 (3.2)
Image+Text (Few-Shot)	PVLM	0.712 (0.6)	0.699 (0.2)	0.665 (2.2)	0.658 (2.1)
	UP-MPF	0.707 (2.4)	0.701 (2.6)	0.669 (0.4)	0.663 (0.1)
	CAMP(w/o attn)	0.716 (0.5)	0.697 (0.7)	0.662 (0.2)	0.652 (0.4)
	CAMP	**0.729** (0.9)	**0.717** (1.0)	**0.692** (2.8)	**0.681** (2.3)

Table 2: Performance comparison of existing methods with our proposed model CAMP. The best results across metrics are highlighted in bold. Numbers in bracket indicate standard deviation.

image, text, and image attributes. **D&R Net** (Xu et al., 2020) uses semantic association. **Attn-BERT** (Pan et al., 2020) used a self-attention mechanism to model intra and inter-modal incongruity. **InCrossMGs** (Liang et al., 2021) used GCN to model self and cross-modal interaction. A cross-modal image-text GCN is used by **CMGCN**. (Liang et al., 2022) **HKE** (Liu et al., 2022a) used a hierarchical interaction network to model both granular and abstract level incongruities. **DIP** (Wen et al., 2023) network integrates sentiment contrastive learning with semantic modeling. **DynRT** (Tian et al., 2023) used a Dynamic Routing Transformer model.

4. **Image + Text Modality (Few-Shot)**: Due to the lack of few-shot multimodal baselines for our task, we adopt two state-of-the-art baselines from the Multimodal Sentiment Analysis task. **PVLM** (Yu and Zhang, 2022) directly introduces the image features to pre-trained language. **UP-MPF** (Yu et al., 2022) uses pre-training data with tasks based on PVLM. We also compare a variant of our model named as **CAMP(w/o attn)** without the attention module.

We run all the baseline models in their original settings on our few-shot data splits and report the results. The original codes for some of the baselines are not available, and hence we don't include them in our comparisons.[1]

4.4 Main Results

Following (Yu and Zhang, 2022), we report the results on the randomly sampled 1% of the training data in Table 2. Our findings are as follows: (1) CAMP outperforms all other baseline methods for both datasets in unimodal as well as multimodal settings. This demonstrates the efficacy of continuous attentive prompts to leverage pretrained knowledge to classify instances accurately. It can be observed that the performance of CAMP, along with all other baselines, decreases for the MMSD2.0 dataset. This is because certain cues important for sarcasm, like hashtags and emojis, have been completely removed from the text in MMSD2.0. (2) For the unimodal methods, text modality methods perform better than image modality methods in MMSD. This shows that textual features provide more sarcastic cues. (3) For the image modality

[1]Original codes for D&R Net and InCrossMGs are not publicly available, while CMGCN uses extra attributes which is not available.

		MCMD	
Strategy	**Method**	**Acc**	**F1**
Multimodal Baselines	Attn-BERT	0.477 (0.3)	0.474 (0.1)
	DIP	0.545 (1.2)	0.545 (0.8)
	DynRT	0.519 (1.6)	0.518 (1.4)
	PVLM	0.564 (1.8)	0.541 (1.3)
	UP-MPF	0.582 (2.1)	0.577 (1.9)
Prompt-Based Finetuning	PT_1^d	0.578 (0.5)	0.509 (0.8)
	PT_2^d	0.584 (1.7)	0.374 (1.9)
Prompt-Tuning	CAMP(w/o attn)	0.588 (0.4)	0.516 (0.7)
	CAMP	**0.601** (1.3)	**0.591** (1.6)

Table 3: Performance comparison on OOD setting. Discrete Templates PT_i^d used in Prompt-Based Finetuning are listed in Table 6.

	MMSD		MMSD2.0	
Method	**Acc**	**F1**	**Acc**	**F1**
w/o cap	0.694 (1.3)	0.671 (0.2)	0.655 (1.2)	0.636 (1.7)
w cap	**0.729** (0.9)	**0.717** (1.0)	**0.692** (2.8)	**0.681** (2.3)

Table 4: Ablation on caption tokens for CAMP model

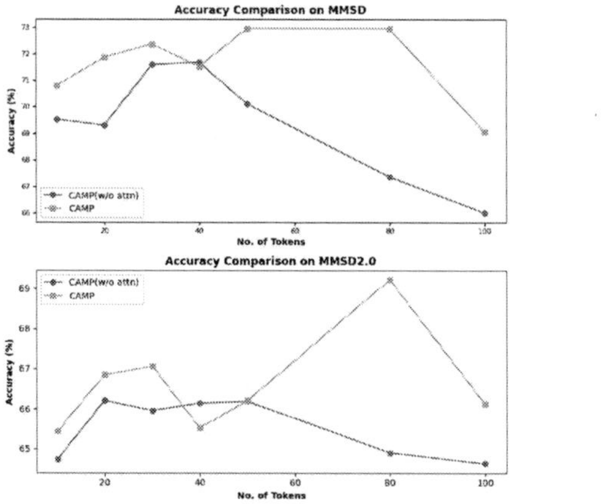

Figure 3: Performance comparison of CAMP and CAMP(w/o attn) over MMSD and MMSD2.0 datasets for various token lengths.

methods, CAMP(w/o text) outperforms other baselines across both the datasets. This observation is interesting because although PLMs are pretrained on text, our attentive, continuous prompt can still effectively attend to the visual tokens and guide the PLM to classify sarcastic samples correctly. (4) Contrary to the general perception that multimodal methods should outperform unimodal ones, we find that this does not always hold true for few-shot scenarios. We hypothesize that in a multimodal scenario, the baseline models necessitate a larger parameter count for training, with only a limited amount of supervised data, which directly results in subpar performance. Our model CAMP outperforms the best multimodal baseline by 1.7% in MMSD and 0.7% in MMSD2.0 dataset. This is because CAMP only learns instance-specific continuous prompts while keeping the PLM frozen. Thus, CAMP can effectively utilize the knowledge base of the PLM while generating dynamic prompts that guide the PLM for better classification.

4.5 Out-of-Domain Evaluation

To assess the generalization ability of CAMP, we evaluate it on a new dataset, which we call **MCMD** (Multi-modal Code-Mixed Memes Dataset), introduced by (Maity et al., 2022). As there are only two publicly available multimodal sarcasm datasets, we opt for this dataset due to its similarity in nature and the presence of labeled sarcasm. To construct MCMD, we filter out memes without sarcasm labels or those that are code-mixed, resulting in 306 samples (183 sarcastic and 123 non-sarcastic). Since MMSD2.0 is a more balanced dataset, we train all models with it and test on MCMD.

It can be observed from Table 3 that our model shows a stronger generalization ability than other multimodal baselines[2] and methods in prompt-based finetuning strategy. We reason that since we don't change the PLM weights for CAMP during training, the PLM can retain its inherent knowledge of language understanding, which results in better performance for cross-dataset setup. We also observe that within the prompt tuning strategy, CAMP outperforms CAMP(w/o attn) because the continuous prompt vectors in CAMP can attend to the input modality tokens and thus can adapt to generate different continuous prompts based on the input instance.

5 Ablation Experiments

With our ablation experiments, we try to answer the following research questions. (1) *Is continuous attentive multimodal prompt better than its non-attentive counterpart?* (2) *How effective are continuous prompt tokens over their discrete counterparts for multimodal sarcasm detection?* (3) *Do captions reduce the semantic gap between image and text modalities?*

5.1 Attentive vs Non-Attentive

We evaluate CAMP and CAMP(w/o attn) on various continuous token lengths namely {10, 20, 30, 40, 50, 80, 100}. Figure 3 shows that accuracy increases for both models across both datasets as the

[2]HFM and HKE cannot be compared as they required external attributes which is not present for MCMD dataset.

		MMSD		MMSD2.0	
Strategy	**Method**	**Acc**	**F1**	**Acc**	**F1**
Prompting	PT_1^d	0.601	0.375	0.569	0.362
	PT_2^d	0.574	0.504	0.551	0.474
Prompt-Based	PT_1^d	0.735 (0.4)	0.722 (0.3)	**0.692** (1.6)	0.680 (1.6)
Finetuning	PT_2^d	**0.746** (0.9)	**0.731** (0.8)	0.688 (1.9)	0.687 (1.9)
Prompt	CAMP(w/o attn)	0.716 (0.5)	0.697 (0.7)	0.662 (0.2)	0.652 (0.4)
Tuning	CAMP	0.729 (0.9)	0.717 (1.0)	**0.692** (2.8)	**0.681** (2.3)

Table 5: Performance comparison of discrete vs continuous prompt-based methods. For Prompting approach, we only prompt the model on test set using the templates in Table 6. Hence, we do not report any standard deviation.

Discrete Prompt Templates	Label Words
$PT_1^d = [V_j]$ Tweet Text: $[T_j]$ Caption: $[C_j]$ Is the sentence sarcastic? $[MASK]$	Yes/No
$PT_2^d = [V_j]$ Tweet Text: $[T_j]$ Caption: $[C_j]$ The sentence is $[MASK]$	Sarcastic/Neutral

Table 6: Description of various discrete prompt templates that we design for ablation experiments. Here PT_i^d is the discrete prompt template i. Here $[V_j]$ stands for visual token slots, $[T_j]$ stands for textual token slots while C_j represents caption token slots.

number of tokens increases up to a certain point, after which the performance degrades. We reason that as prompt length increases, the PLM's ability to effectively capture the contextual nuances of the task at hand increases. However, after a certain point, the information learned by these tokens becomes redundant, which leads to overfitting. We find that CAMP performs superiorly over almost all continuous prompt token lengths than CAMP(w/o attn), with an average accuracy gain of +2.2% for MMSD and +1.33% for MMSD2.0 datasets. This shows the effectiveness of our attention module, which potently captures the dependencies between continuous tokens and the input tokens of text and image modalities.

5.2 Discrete vs Continuous

To demonstrate the effectiveness of continuous attentive multimodal prompt over its discrete counterparts, we formulate two discrete prompt templates, one in the declarative form and the other as an interrogative sentence, presented in Table 6. We also perform experiments with other templates and label words which are presented in Appendix section A.3. It can be seen from Table 5 that our proposed model CAMP which is based on prompt tuning strategy, outperforms prompting-based approaches by a very significant margin. This is because sarcastic utterances are less common in the general corpora on which these PLMs have been trained. We can also observe that a slight change in discrete prompts induces a significant difference in accuracy ($\triangle$2.7% for MMSD and $\triangle$1.8% for MMSD2.0) for prompting strategy. While prompt-based finetuning methods demonstrate a moderate performance advantage (+1.7% Acc in MMSD while no improvement in MMSD2.0) over our model, this outcome aligns with expectations, given that we do not finetune the entire PLM. Our model's strength lies in its parameter efficiency and consequently reduced training time, as we update only 30% of the entire model weights, compared to fine-tuning the entire model weights of the PLM.

5.3 Importance of Caption Tokens

The importance of caption tokens to bridge the semantic gap between image and text modalities can be seen from the reduced performance of the CAMP(w/o cap) variant in Table 4. This suggests that captions provide additional semantic information that enriches the context of an image. This additional layer of information helps the model better understand and interpret the image, leading to improved performance.

6 Conclusion

In this paper, we tackled the problem of few-shot multimodal sarcasm detection. Unlike traditional approaches that rely on early or late image-text fusion to learn the subtle interaction between the image and text modalities, we reformulate the problem as a cloze-filling task. To this end, we propose a novel approach of using continuous attentive multimodal prompt for this task. These attentive, continuous prompt tokens can effectively attend to the image and text modalities tokens and can dynamically adapt according to the input instance. Our extensive experiments over two datasets demonstrate the effectiveness of our model, which outperforms strong baselines in few-shot and Out-of-Distribution (OOD) settings. We also demonstrate the efficacy of our model CAMP over other discrete token-based techniques, including prompting and prompt-based finetuning, through several ablation experiments.

Limitations

Firstly, for our few-shot setting, we randomly sample 1% of the entire training dataset, which is an experimental choice. To account for the variability in sample diversity, we randomly sample two 1% splits of the training data and report the average performance. However, we believe that an alternate sampling strategy, in which more diverse samples can be collected, needs exploration. Secondly, some of the images have embedded text which we did not consider. Incorporating the text information present in the images could provide additional contextual cues and improve the overall understanding and analysis of the image content. For this study, we experimented with a BERT-base model. It will be interesting to see how other encoder or encoder-decoder architectures perform for the multimodal sarcasm detection task in the prompt-tuning paradigm.

References

Ameeta Agrawal and Aijun An. 2018. Affective representations for sarcasm detection. *The 41st International ACM SIGIR Conference on Research & Development in Information Retrieval.*

Ameeta Agrawal, Aijun An, and Manos Papagelis. 2020. Leveraging transitions of emotions for sarcasm detection. *Proceedings of the 43rd International ACM SIGIR Conference on Research and Development in Information Retrieval.*

Silvio Amir, Byron C. Wallace, Hao Lyu, Paula Carvalho, and Mário J. Silva. 2016. Modelling context with user embeddings for sarcasm detection in social media. In *Proceedings of the 20th SIGNLL Conference on Computational Natural Language Learning*, Berlin, Germany.

Joshua M. Averbeck. 2013. Comparisons of ironic and sarcastic arguments in terms of appropriateness and effectiveness in personal relationships. *Argumentation and Advocacy*, 50:47 – 57.

Nastaran Babanejad, Heidar Davoudi, Aijun An, and Manos Papagelis. 2020. Affective and contextual embedding for sarcasm detection. In *Proceedings of the 28th International Conference on Computational Linguistics*, Barcelona, Spain (Online).

Rohan Badlani, Nishit Asnani, and Manan Rai. 2019. An ensemble of humour, sarcasm, and hate speech-for sentiment classification in online reviews. In *Proceedings of the 5th Workshop on Noisy User-generated Text (W-NUT 2019)*, Hong Kong, China. Association for Computational Linguistics.

Andrew Brock, Soham De, and Samuel L. Smith. 2021. Characterizing signal propagation to close the performance gap in unnormalized resnets. *ArXiv*, abs/2101.08692.

Yitao Cai, Huiyu Cai, and Xiaojun Wan. 2019. Multi-modal sarcasm detection in Twitter with hierarchical fusion model. In *Proceedings of the 57th Annual Meeting of the Association for Computational Linguistics*, Florence, Italy. Association for Computational Linguistics.

Rui Cao, Ming Shan Hee, Adriel Kuek, Wen-Haw Chong, Roy Ka-Wei Lee, and Jing Jiang. 2023. Pro-cap: Leveraging a frozen vision-language model for hateful meme detection. *Proceedings of the 31st ACM International Conference on Multimedia.*

Rui Cao, Roy Ka-Wei Lee, Wen-Haw Chong, and Jing Jiang. 2022. Prompting for multimodal hateful meme classification. In *Proceedings of the 2022 Conference on Empirical Methods in Natural Language Processing*, Abu Dhabi, United Arab Emirates. Association for Computational Linguistics.

Christine Chappuis, Valérie Zermatten, Sylvain Lobry, B. L. Saux, and Devis Tuia. 2022. Prompt–rsvqa: Prompting visual context to a language model for remote sensing visual question answering. *2022 IEEE/CVF Conference on Computer Vision and Pattern Recognition Workshops (CVPRW).*

Dmitry Davidov, Oren Tsur, and Ari Rappoport. 2010. Semi-supervised recognition of sarcasm in Twitter and Amazon. In *Proceedings of the Fourteenth Conference on Computational Natural Language Learning*, Uppsala, Sweden. Association for Computational Linguistics.

Jacob Devlin, Ming-Wei Chang, Kenton Lee, and Kristina Toutanova. 2019. Bert: Pre-training of deep bidirectional transformers for language understanding. In *North American Chapter of the Association for Computational Linguistics.*

Alexey Dosovitskiy, Lucas Beyer, Alexander Kolesnikov, Dirk Weissenborn, Xiaohua Zhai, Thomas Unterthiner, Mostafa Dehghani, Matthias Minderer, Georg Heigold, Sylvain Gelly, Jakob Uszkoreit, and Neil Houlsby. 2020. An image is worth 16x16 words: Transformers for image recognition at scale. *ArXiv*, abs/2010.11929.

Megan L. Dress, Roger J. Kreuz, Kristen E. Link, and Gina M. Caucci. 2008. Regional variation in the use of sarcasm. *Journal of Language and Social Psychology*, 27:71 – 85.

Simona Frenda. 2018. The role of sarcasm in hate speech.a multilingual perspective.

Tianyu Gao, Adam Fisch, and Danqi Chen. 2021. Making pre-trained language models better few-shot learners. In *Proceedings of the 59th Annual Meeting of the Association for Computational Linguistics and the 11th International Joint Conference on Natural Language Processing (Volume 1: Long Papers)*, Online. Association for Computational Linguistics.

José Antonio García-Díaz, Ronghao Pan, and Rafael Valencia-García. 2023. Leveraging zero and few-shot learning for enhanced model generality in hate speech detection in spanish and english. *Mathematics*.

Debanjan Ghosh, Alexander Richard Fabbri, and Smaranda Muresan. 2017. The role of conversation context for sarcasm detection in online interactions. In *Proceedings of the 18th Annual SIGdial Meeting on Discourse and Dialogue*, Saarbrücken, Germany.

Debanjan Ghosh, Ritvik Shrivastava, and Smaranda Muresan. 2021. "laughing at you or with you": The role of sarcasm in shaping the disagreement space. In *Proceedings of the 16th Conference of the European Chapter of the Association for Computational Linguistics: Main Volume*, Online. Association for Computational Linguistics.

Roberto I. González-Ibáñez, Smaranda Muresan, and Nina Wacholder. 2011. Identifying sarcasm in twitter: A closer look. In *Annual Meeting of the Association for Computational Linguistics*.

Alex Graves and Jürgen Schmidhuber. 2005. 2005 special issue: Framewise phoneme classification with bidirectional lstm and other neural network architectures. *Neural Networks*, 18.

Jiaxian Guo, Junnan Li, Dongxu Li, Anthony Meng Huat Tiong, Boyang Li, Dacheng Tao, and Steven C. H. Hoi. 2022. From images to textual prompts: Zero-shot visual question answering with frozen large language models. *2023 IEEE/CVF Conference on Computer Vision and Pattern Recognition (CVPR)*.

Kaiming He, X. Zhang, Shaoqing Ren, and Jian Sun. 2015. Deep residual learning for image recognition. *2016 IEEE Conference on Computer Vision and Pattern Recognition (CVPR)*.

Ehsan Hosseini-Asl, Wenhao Liu, and Caiming Xiong. 2022. A generative language model for few-shot aspect-based sentiment analysis. In *Findings of the Association for Computational Linguistics: NAACL 2022*, Seattle, United States. Association for Computational Linguistics.

Stacey L. Ivanko and Penny M. Pexman. 2003. Context incongruity and irony processing. *Discourse Processes*, 35:241 – 279.

Junhui Ji, Wei Ren, and Usman Naseem. 2023. Identifying creative harmful memes via prompt based approach. *Proceedings of the ACM Web Conference 2023*.

Yiren Jian, Chongyang Gao, and Soroush Vosoughi. 2022. Contrastive learning for prompt-based few-shot language learners. In *Proceedings of the 2022 Conference of the North American Chapter of the Association for Computational Linguistics: Human Language Technologies*, Seattle, United States. Association for Computational Linguistics.

Zhengbao Jiang, Frank F. Xu, Jun Araki, and Graham Neubig. 2020. How can we know what language models know? *Transactions of the Association for Computational Linguistics*, 8:423–438.

Aditya Joshi, Vinita Sharma, and Pushpak Bhattacharyya. 2015. Harnessing context incongruity for sarcasm detection. In *Proceedings of the 53rd Annual Meeting of the Association for Computational Linguistics and the 7th International Joint Conference on Natural Language Processing (Volume 2: Short Papers)*, Beijing, China. Association for Computational Linguistics.

Aditya Joshi, Vaibhav Tripathi, Kevin Patel, Pushpak Bhattacharyya, and Mark Carman. 2016. Are word embedding-based features useful for sarcasm detection? In *Proceedings of the 2016 Conference on Empirical Methods in Natural Language Processing*, Austin, Texas.

Anupam Khattri, Aditya Joshi, Pushpak Bhattacharyya, and Mark Carman. 2015. Your sentiment precedes you: Using an author's historical tweets to predict sarcasm. In *Proceedings of the 6th Workshop on Computational Approaches to Subjectivity, Sentiment and Social Media Analysis*, Lisboa, Portugal.

Yoon Kim. 2014. Convolutional neural networks for sentence classification. In *Conference on Empirical Methods in Natural Language Processing*.

Brian Lester, Rami Al-Rfou, and Noah Constant. 2021. The power of scale for parameter-efficient prompt tuning. In *Conference on Empirical Methods in Natural Language Processing*.

Junnan Li, Dongxu Li, Silvio Savarese, and Steven C. H. Hoi. 2023. Blip-2: Bootstrapping language-image pre-training with frozen image encoders and large language models. In *International Conference on Machine Learning*.

Xiang Lisa Li and Percy Liang. 2021. Prefix-tuning: Optimizing continuous prompts for generation. *Proceedings of the 59th Annual Meeting of the Association for Computational Linguistics and the 11th International Joint Conference on Natural Language Processing (Volume 1: Long Papers)*, abs/2101.00190.

Bin Liang, Chenwei Lou, Xiang Li, Lin Gui, Min Yang, and Ruifeng Xu. 2021. Multi-modal sarcasm detection with interactive in-modal and cross-modal graphs. *Proceedings of the 29th ACM International Conference on Multimedia*.

Bin Liang, Chenwei Lou, Xiang Li, Min Yang, Lin Gui, Yulan He, Wenjie Pei, and Ruifeng Xu. 2022. Multi-modal sarcasm detection via cross-modal graph convolutional network. In *Annual Meeting of the Association for Computational Linguistics*.

Hui Liu, Wenya Wang, and Haoliang Li. 2022a. Towards multi-modal sarcasm detection via hierarchical congruity modeling with knowledge enhancement. In *Proceedings of the 2022 Conference on Empirical Methods in Natural Language Processing*, Abu Dhabi, United Arab Emirates. Association for Computational Linguistics.

Xiao Liu, Yanan Zheng, Zhengxiao Du, Ming Ding, Yujie Qian, Zhilin Yang, and Jie Tang. 2021. Gpt understands, too. *ArXiv*, abs/2103.10385.

Yiyi Liu, Yequan Wang, Aixin Sun, Xuying Meng, Jing Li, and Jiafeng Guo. 2022b. A dual-channel framework for sarcasm recognition by detecting sentiment conflict. In *Findings of the Association for Computational Linguistics: NAACL 2022*, Seattle, United States.

Yuhang Liu, Wei Wei, Daowan Peng, and Feida Zhu. 2022c. Declaration-based prompt tuning for visual question answering. In *International Joint Conference on Artificial Intelligence*.

Chenwei Lou, Bin Liang, Lin Gui, Yulan He, Yixue Dang, and Ruifeng Xu. 2021. Affective dependency graph for sarcasm detection. *Proceedings of the 44th International ACM SIGIR Conference on Research and Development in Information Retrieval*.

Krishanu Maity, Prince Jha, Sriparna Saha, and Pushpak Bhattacharyya. 2022. A multitask framework for sentiment, emotion and sarcasm aware cyberbullying detection from multi-modal code-mixed memes. *Proceedings of the 45th International ACM SIGIR Conference on Research and Development in Information Retrieval*.

Diana Maynard and Mark Greenwood. 2014. Who cares about sarcastic tweets? investigating the impact of sarcasm on sentiment analysis. In *Proceedings of the Ninth International Conference on Language Resources and Evaluation (LREC'14)*, Reykjavik, Iceland.

Silviu Oprea and Walid Magdy. 2019. Exploring author context for detecting intended vs perceived sarcasm. In *Proceedings of the 57th Annual Meeting of the Association for Computational Linguistics*, Florence, Italy. Association for Computational Linguistics.

Timothy Ossowski and Junjie Hu. 2023. Multimodal prompt retrieval for generative visual question answering. *ArXiv*, abs/2306.17675.

Hongliang Pan, Zheng Lin, Peng Fu, Yatao Qi, and Weiping Wang. 2020. Modeling intra and inter-modality incongruity for multi-modal sarcasm detection. In *Findings of the Association for Computational Linguistics: EMNLP 2020*, Online. Association for Computational Linguistics.

Fabio Petroni, Tim Rocktäschel, Sebastian Riedel, Patrick Lewis, Anton Bakhtin, Yuxiang Wu, and Alexander Miller. 2019. Language models as knowledge bases? In *Proceedings of the 2019 Conference on Empirical Methods in Natural Language Processing and the 9th International Joint Conference on Natural Language Processing (EMNLP-IJCNLP)*, Hong Kong, China. Association for Computational Linguistics.

Soujanya Poria, Erik Cambria, Devamanyu Hazarika, and Prateek Vij. 2016. A deeper look into sarcastic tweets using deep convolutional neural networks. In *Proceedings of COLING 2016, the 26th International Conference on Computational Linguistics: Technical Papers*, Osaka, Japan.

Libo Qin, Shijue Huang, Qiguang Chen, Chenran Cai, Yudi Zhang, Bin Liang, Wanxiang Che, and Ruifeng Xu. 2023. MMSD2.0: Towards a reliable multi-modal sarcasm detection system. In *Findings of the Association for Computational Linguistics: ACL 2023*, Toronto, Canada. Association for Computational Linguistics.

Patricia Rockwell and Evelyn M. Theriot. 2001. Culture, gender, and gender mix in encoders of sarcasm: A self-assessment analysis. *Communication Research Reports*, 18:44 – 52.

Rossano Schifanella, Paloma de Juan, Joel R. Tetreault, and Liangliang Cao. 2016. Detecting sarcasm in multimodal social platforms. *Proceedings of the 24th ACM international conference on Multimedia*.

Yuan Tian, Nan Xu, Ruike Zhang, and Wenji Mao. 2023. Dynamic routing transformer network for multimodal sarcasm detection. In *Proceedings of the 61st Annual Meeting of the Association for Computational Linguistics (Volume 1: Long Papers)*, Toronto, Canada. Association for Computational Linguistics.

Christopher W. Tindale and James Gough. 1987. The use of irony in argumentation. *Philosophy and Rhetoric*, 20:1–17.

Frans H. van Eemeren and Rob Grootendorst. 1992. Argumentation, communication, and fallacies: A pragma-dialectical perspective.

Yihan Wang, Si Si, Daliang Li, Michal Lukasik, Felix X. Yu, Cho-Jui Hsieh, Inderjit S. Dhillon, and Sanjiv Kumar. 2022. Two-stage llm fine-tuning with less specialization and more generalization.

Chan Shao Wen, Guoli Jia, and Jufeng Yang. 2023. Dip: Dual incongruity perceiving network for sarcasm detection. *2023 IEEE/CVF Conference on Computer Vision and Pattern Recognition (CVPR)*.

Nan Xu, Zhixiong Zeng, and Wenji Mao. 2020. Reasoning with multimodal sarcastic tweets via modeling cross-modality contrast and semantic association. In *Proceedings of the 58th Annual Meeting of the Association for Computational Linguistics*, Online. Association for Computational Linguistics.

Chuanpeng Yang, Fuqing Zhu, Guihua Liu, Jizhong Han, and Songiln Hu. 2022a. Multimodal hate speech detection via cross-domain knowledge transfer. *Proceedings of the 30th ACM International Conference on Multimedia.*

Xiaocui Yang, Shi Feng, Daling Wang, Pengfei Hong, and Soujanya Poria. 2022b. Few-shot multimodal sentiment analysis based on multimodal probabilistic fusion prompts. *Proceedings of the 31st ACM International Conference on Multimedia.*

Yang Yu and Dong Zhang. 2022. Few-shot multi-modal sentiment analysis with prompt-based vision-aware language modeling. *2022 IEEE International Conference on Multimedia and Expo (ICME).*

Yang Yu, Dong Zhang, and Shoushan Li. 2022. Unified multi-modal pre-training for few-shot sentiment analysis with prompt-based learning. *Proceedings of the 30th ACM International Conference on Multimedia.*

Yuexiang Zhai, Shengbang Tong, Xiao Li, Mu Cai, Qing Qu, Yong Jae Lee, and Y. Ma. 2023. Investigating the catastrophic forgetting in multimodal large language models. *ArXiv*, abs/2309.10313.

Meishan Zhang, Yue Zhang, and Guohong Fu. 2016. Tweet sarcasm detection using deep neural network. In *Proceedings of COLING 2016, the 26th International Conference on Computational Linguistics: Technical Papers*, Osaka, Japan.

A Appendix

A.1 Hyperparameter Details

We run all our experiments on a Nvidia RTX A5000 GPU with 24GB of memory. We use the pre-trained blip-opt-2.7b [3] model for generating captions. We employ the OpenPrompt[4] library to build our prompt learning model. All our experiments use AdamW optimizer with a weight decay of 0.01. We run our model for 20-100 epochs and pick the model that performs best for the validation set for testing. In all experiments, we use a learning rate of 0.0001 and a batch size of 16. The value of h_{dim} is 768, which is the default embedding dimension for BERT. The number of continuous prompt tokens is set to 50 for MMSD and 80 for MMSD2.0, while image token slots are fixed at 3 for both datasets. The maximum token length for the PLM is 128.

A.2 Performance on Different Discrete Tokens

In this section, we experiment with different discrete tokens shown in Table 7 and present their comparative analysis in Table 10 in both prompting and prompt-based finetuning techniques. Sarcasm detection, being a difficult task, simple prompting with discrete tokens yields sub-optimal performance while showing a lot of variation in performance. However, finetuning the entire parameter set of BERT demonstrates a significant jump in performance, which is expected.

[3]https://huggingface.co/Salesforce/blip2-opt-2.7b

[4]https://github.com/thunlp/OpenPrompt

Discrete Prompt Templates	Label Words
$PT_1^d = [V_j]$ Tweet Text: $[T_j]$ Caption: $[C_j]$ Is the sentence positive? $[MASK]$	Yes/No
$PT_2^d = [V_j]$ Tweet Text: $[T_j]$ Caption: $[C_j]$ So the meme is: $[MASK]$	Sarcastic/Neutral
$PT_3^d = [V_j]$ Tweet Text: $[T_j]$ Caption: $[C_j]$ This post can be termed as: $[MASK]$	Funny/Serious

Table 7: Description of Various Discrete Prompt Templates. Here PT_i^d is the discrete prompt template i. Here $[V_j]$ stands for visual token slots, $[T_j]$ stands for textual token slots while C_j represents caption token slots.

	MMSD	
Method	Acc	F1
ResNet	0.715	0.696
ViT	0.663	0.659
NF-ResNet-50	**0.729**	**0.717**

Table 8: Performance comparison of different visual encoders for our CAMP model.

A.3 Effect of Different Visual Encoders

We experimented with different visual encoders, including ResNet and ViT, for our CAMP model. The experimental results on MMSD dataset are presented in Table 8. However, we found NF-ResNet-50 performs the best among them and hence we use this for all our experiments.

	MMSD	
Image Token Length	Acc	F1
1	0.710	0.671
3	**0.729**	**0.717**
5	0.724	0.702
7	0.716	0.699

Table 9: Ablation experiment on different image tokens for CAMP.

A.4 Impact of Different Image Token Lengths

To find out how much image information is required for CAMP to achieve best performance, we conduct experiments with varied image token lengths on MMSD dataset. The length of continuous prompt token is kept at 50 since we achieve best performance for MMSD dataset. It can be observed from Table 9 that the when image token

		MMSD		MMSD2.0	
Strategy	**Method**	**Acc**	**F1**	**Acc**	**F1**
Prompting	PT_1^d	0.601	0.377	0.567	0.364
	PT_2^d	0.603	0.501	0.554	0.497
	PT_3^d	0.436	0.435	0.491	0.491
Prompt-Based Finetuning	PT_1^d	0.732 (0.1)	0.727 (0.4)	0.686 (0.1)	0.664 (0.1)
	PT_2^d	0.721 (0.5)	0.718 (0.6)	0.702 (0.8)	0.691 (0.1)
	PT_3^d	0.738 (0.8)	0.718 (0.3)	0.694 (2.4)	0.691 (2.4)

Table 10: Performance comparison of discrete prompts under prompting and prompt-based finetuning strategy. Numbers in bracket indicate standard deviation. For Prompting approach, we only prompt the model on test set using the templates in Table 7. Hence, we do not report any standard deviation.

length is 1, the utilization of image information becomes incomplete, whereas increasing it beyond 3 introduces redundancy to the model.

Aligning Alignments: Do Colexification and Distributional Similarity Align as Measures of cross-lingual Lexical Alignment?

Taelin Karidi, Eitan Grossman, Omri Abend
Hebrew University of Jerusalem
{taelin.karidi,eitan.grossman,omri.abend}@mail.huji.ac.il

Abstract

The data-driven investigation of the extent to which lexicons of different languages align has mostly fallen into one of two categories: colexification-based and distributional. The two approaches are grounded in distinct methodologies, operate on different assumptions, and are used in diverse ways. This raises two important questions: (a) are there settings in which the predictions of the two approaches can be directly compared? and if so, (b) what is the extent of the similarity and what are its determinants? We offer novel operationalizations for the two approaches in a manner that allows for their direct comparison, and conduct a comprehensive analysis on a diverse set of 16 languages.

Our analysis is carried out at different levels of granularity. At the word-level, the two methods present different results across the board. However, intriguingly, at the level of semantic domains (e.g., kinship, quantity), the two methods show considerable convergence in their predictions. Our findings also indicate that the distributional methods likely capture a more fine-grained alignment than their counterpart colexification-based methods, and may thus be more suited for settings where fewer languages are evaluated.[1]

1 Introduction

To what degree do translation equivalents in different languages – for example, English *red* and French *rouge* – encode the same meaning? This question, in various forms, has long been a topic of interest in the cognitive sciences (Whorf, 1956; Fodor, 1975; Frawley, 1998; Burns, 1994; Snedeker and Gleitman, 2004; Majid et al., 2008; Croft, 2010). Indeed, lexicons are often viewed as reflecting the structure of human cognition; understanding how meaning is expressed across languages helps understand how humans categorize and represent the world.

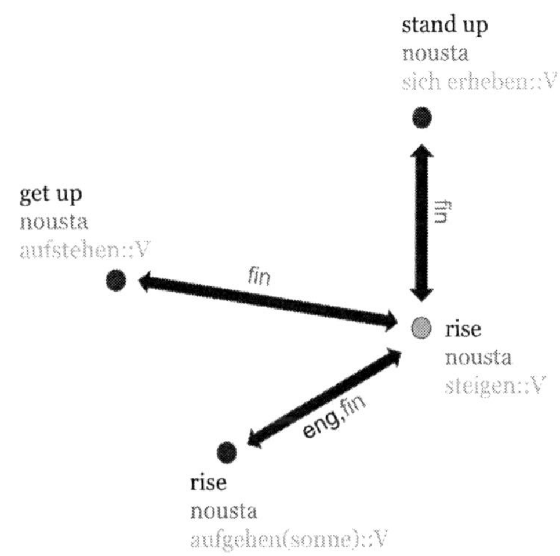

Figure 1: Colexification graph for the target concept "steigen::V" (which corresponds to the word *rise* in English, and *nousta* in Finnish. Each vertex corresponds to a concept that is colexified with the target concept either in English or Finnish. The English lexicalizations of the target concept are in black and the Finnish lexicalizations are in Blue. The concepts themeselves are in Green. Each edge (marked by an arrow) denotes that a colexification exists in English/Finnish (as labeled).

A building block in answering such a question is the ability to evaluate the similarity between words that seemingly express a similar meaning (henceforth, *translation pairs*) across different languages.

Traditionally, in linguistic and cognitive research, comparing the meaning of words across languages involves methodologies and approaches that are less data-driven in nature, prioritizing in-depth, relatively small-scale exploration of meaning, such as descriptive comparisons (Karidi et al., 2024; Wierzbicka, 1972), elicitation studies (Barnett, 1977; Tokowicz et al., 2002; Moldovan et al., 2012; Allen and Conklin, 2013; Purves et al., 2023) and semantic maps (Haspelmath, 2003; Croft, 2022).

[1] Our code and data is available at https://github.com/tai314159/Aligning_Alignments.

Proceedings of the 28th Conference on Computational Natural Language Learning, pages 327–341
November 15-16, 2024 ©2024 Association for Computational Linguistics

The difficulty in defining lexical similarity between concepts, let alone translation equivalents, has motivated a transition from theoretical frameworks to data-driven approaches. Indeed, a significant amount of recent works has focused on using data-driven methods to measure the equivalence of word pairs across different languages (Majid et al., 2014; Youn et al., 2016; Thompson et al., 2018; Jackson et al., 2019; Thompson et al., 2020; Rabinovich et al., 2020; Beinborn and Choenni, 2020; Georgakopoulos et al., 2022). All work on this question inherits an even more fundamental set of questions: how is meaning defined and how is the meaning of words captured? Within this rich body of work, we can identify two main methodological approaches.

The first approach is based on **colexification patterns**, which aims to compare the association between lexical form and senses across languages. Colexification is the case where two or more concepts are lexicalized with a single form in a given language (François, 2008; Rzymski et al., 2020) (see Table 2). For example, both English *right* and German *recht* colexify (i) a sense related to the correctness of a fact and (ii) a sense related to location or direction in space, while the Arabic *yamin* is associated with the spatial sense, but not the correctness sense. According to this approach, the degree to which words or sets of words in a certain domain in different languages align, can be defined as the degree to which the words colexify the same concepts. For example, the English *right* may be said to be more similar to the German *recht* than the Arabic *yamin* (cf. Haspelmath, 2003). Recently, a large-scale cross-lingual database of colexifications has been compiled (CLICS; Rzymski et al., 2020)[2]. This database provides a valuable resource for exploring the relationships between words and concepts across a wide range of languages, and enables the quantitative comparison of colexification patterns in different languages (Youn et al., 2016; Jackson et al., 2019; Xu et al., 2020; Georgakopoulos et al., 2022; Karjus et al., 2021a; Bao et al., 2021).

The second approach is based on **distributional word embeddings** (here, DISTA). This approach was recently proposed as a viable data-driven method for cross-lingual lexical semantic investigations (Thompson et al., 2018, 2020; Beinborn and Choenni, 2020; Rabinovich et al., 2020; Karidi et al., 2024), for improving cross-lingual transfer (Sun et al., 2021) and for investigating multicultural knowledge in LLMs (Havaldar et al., 2023). While all distributional methods use the word embeddings of translation pairs for computing similarity, many different operationalizations of this general approach are possible. See §2.1.

Both approaches have had a substantial impact on the computational cognitive science literature (Youn et al., 2016; Jackson et al., 2019; Thompson et al., 2020). These approaches seek to reveal an abstract structure that underlies the relation between words and their meanings (e.g, languages from different language families might have the same structure of kinship terms). However, while both are data-driven and aim to capture similar phenomena, they rely on different data and methodologies, and in fact likely capture different aspects of linguistic meaning. Colexification-based approaches set out to quantify similarity in lexicographical resources, while distributional embeddings use any signal that can be reliably extracted from the data. For example, DISTA may not represent rare senses, while colexification does not take frequency into account at all. They are also applied differently: colexification-based approaches often constructs intricate cross-lingual networks to explore meaning universality (Youn et al., 2016; Jackson et al., 2019), while distributional alignment methods operate at the word level and can then be extended to larger word sets (Thompson et al., 2020).

In this work we seek to empirically compare the predictions of these two approaches. However, given the divergence in methodologies and underlying assumptions adopted by these various approaches, it is not clear if it is sound, or even possible, to compare them. Moreover, obtaining a meaningful signal from colexification data typically requires aggregating information across thousands of languages (Youn et al., 2016; Jackson et al., 2019) and is rarely used for analysis at the word-pair level; instead, its strength lies in the analysis of intricate networks. Therefore, working with a substantially smaller set of languages or even comparing a single language pair at a time, as is often the case in multilingual NLP research, requires adapting the approaches so they will yield compa-

[2]Another valuable resource for lexical semantics is Babelnet (Navigli and Ponzetto, 2012). In this work we choose CLICS over BabelNet because BabelNet's fine-grained sense distinctions, such as separating "apple" as a fruit from "apple" as a tree, introduce excessive noise, whereas CLICS provides more manageable colexifications for our purposes.

rable predictions. We ask whether these distinct approaches converge at *interface settings* – settings in which the two approaches offer coherent similarity measures that can be compared. We show that such cases of convergence exist (§5) and, in these cases, ask whether – and when – the different approaches yield similar predictions. This is, to the best of our knowledge, the first time that these questions have been tackled within NLP.[3]

Analysis at various levels of granularity reveals that at the word-level, the two methodologies yield different results across the board. However, at the domain-level[4], the trends presented by the two methods show substantially higher correlation. In general, there is an overall greater similarity across different distributional methods than between the two families of approaches, in terms of their predictions and the factors that influence them (§5). Moreover, while distributional methods are correlated in their alignment predictions with external similarity measures (§5.4), the colexification approach is not. This suggests that the distributional approach captures more fine-grained aspects of meaning and is better suited for either delicate analysis of the results or when using a smaller set of languages. Also, the domain-level might be a more robust level to report alignment than the word-level. Additonally, we find that rate of lexical change is a significant predictor for cross-lingual alignment, across all methodologies. We discuss the implications of these results in §7.

To recap, we (i) operationalize distribution-based and colexification-based approaches so as to enable a direct empirical comparison between them, (ii) perform in-depth comparison of different operationalizations of the two approaches, (iii) study the ramifications of different design choices that they incorporate.

Concept	Languages
CLAW, FINGERNAIL	Japanese, Finnish, Estonian
SNOW, ICE	Hindi
DUST, ASH	German, French, Dutch Polish, Finnish
MONTH, MOON	Japanese, Korean Estonian, Turkish
DREAM, SLEEP (STATE)	Spanish, Polish, Finnish Italian
BABY, CHILD	French, Dutch, Hindi Polish
NEPHEW, NIECE	Italian

Figure 2: Colexifications. Examples of concepts from the CLICS dataset and their colexifications. Each colexification indicates the languages in which these concepts colexify, drawn from 16 languages used in this paper.

2 cross-lingual Lexicon Alignment

Much research on cross-lingual alignment between lexicons has sought to uncover whether certain concepts, notably in domains perceived as basic to the human experience, such as space, time, color, quantity, and family relations, are universal, on the one hand, or culturally- or historically-contingent, on the other hand (Fodor, 1975; Brown and Witkowski, 1983; Burns, 1994; Frawley, 1998; Evans and Levinson, 2009; Wierzbicka, 2010; Åke Viberg, 1983; Majid et al., 2014). Alignment can either be defined with respect to individual words (i.e, word-level alignment) or with respect to domains (i.e, domain-level alignment). For example, we might expect the word *Sunday* in English not to align well with the Hebrew multiword expression denoting the same day of the week *yom rishon*, as the latter does not bear any of the religious connotations of *Sunday* in English. The degree of their alignment is a **word-level alignment**. One can also compare the extent to which the concepts of time align more generally, in which case we might expect Hebrew and English to be relatively similar, given that Hebrew, spoken in Israel, *prima facie* has a Western conception of time, with, for example, a division of the year into twelve months, a division of the week into seven days, and so on. This is termed **domain-level alignment**.

2.1 Distribution-based Alignment

Distribution-based alignment measures leverage NLP tools to evaluate cross-lingual similarity (Artetxe et al., 2018; Conneau et al., 2017; Vulić et al., 2021; Rabinovich et al., 2020; Thompson et al., 2020; Karidi et al., 2024). Traditionally, these assessments have been performed using *global methods*, which align whole language spaces simultaneously and then assess their similarity using downstream tasks, such as Bilingual Lexicon Induction (Artetxe et al., 2018; Conneau et al., 2017).

[3]Recently, (Liu et al., 2023a) used co-occurrences to discover colexification patterns . However, their focus was primarily on reconstructing the colexifications from textual data, rather than analyzing colexification as a measure of cross-lingual semantic similarity and comparing it against methodologies that are based on word embeddings.

[4]A semantic domain is a way of grouping words together based on common aspects of meaning or function.

This approach typically includes techniques like linear transformations or joint model training across multiple languages (Pires et al., 2019; Gonen et al., 2020). [5] However, for identifying patterns of divergence and convergence in the usage of specific words and domains, this approach is suboptimal, as globally optimal alignment (one that minimizes the distance between the image of one language in the space of another language) may completely distort the alignment of specific words or subsets, in the interest of improving the alignment of other, larger word sets (Karidi et al., 2024).

On the other hand, *local methods* take a more granular approach, comparing the similarity of individual word meanings one at a time.

Intuitively, a naïve approach to comparing the meaning of a concept across languages is to compare the number of overlapping nearest neighbors of a word and its direct translation across languages (Thompson et al., 2018). This approach is intuitive and stems from the distributional definition of meaning as the semantic neighborhood of the concept. However, the current method falls short in considering the intricate semantic relations within the groups of neighbors. To address this drawback, metrics for historical semantic change (Hamilton et al., 2016) have been adopted (Thompson et al., 2020; Beinborn and Choenni, 2020; Karidi et al., 2024). This is done by comparing the vectors of distances between a word and its neighbors across languages. Our computational approach is fully adapted from (Karidi et al., 2024).

2.2 Colexification-based Methods

The most extensive resource on colexification is the CLICS database (Rzymski et al., 2020). It provides information on colexification patterns for a wide range of concepts (a notion of a word sense; see §4), such as individual terms in domains like basic colors, body parts, and kinship, as well as more complex conceptual domains like emotion, time, and space, across 3156 languages. Each concept is linked to a set of words in different languages that are used to express that concept.

Colexification patterns are frequently used by cognitive scientists to estimate word similarity, working under the assumption that colexification

[5]We are aware of one study of cross-lingual lexical comparison that used global alignment to project languages to a shared space, and defined the degree of alignment between a translation pair to be the distance of the image of one word to the embedding of the other (Rabinovich et al., 2020).

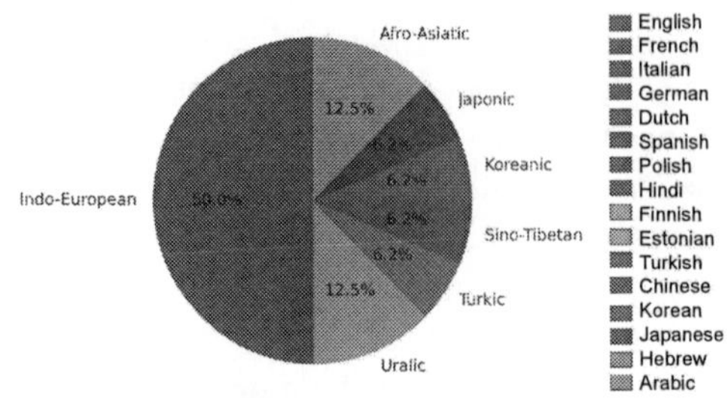

Figure 3: Distribution of languages by family. The 16 languages used in our analysis, color-coded by their language family. Each segment represents the proportion of languages within their respective families.

of two concepts reflects similarity between them (François, 2008; Xu et al., 2020; Harvill et al., 2022). For example, the word *ka-um* in Tagalog can be linked to the concepts FATHER and ELDER BROTHER. This colexification is taken to reflect the cultural concept of the importance and authority of older male relatives in Tagalog society. Youn et al. (2016) analyzed a subset of 22 basic concepts from the Swadesh list, and showed that they exhibit patterns of meaning universality across languages. Jackson et al. (2019) conducted the first large-scale analysis using colexification patterns to assess cultural variability in people's conceptualization of emotions. However, the hypothesis that colexification and semantic similarity are tightly related is still missing direct empirical validation at scale (Natale et al., 2021).

Recently, colexification has also been utilized in NLP to study cross-lingual transfer (Liu et al., 2023a,b; Chen et al., 2023).

3 Experimental Setup

We briefly describe our experimental setup, with full details in Appendix §A.

Data & Languages. We perform our analysis on a diverse set of 16 **languages**, spanning 7 different language families from many geographical areas across Eurasia (see Figure 3): English, French, Italian, German, Dutch, Spanish, Polish , Finnish, Estonian, Turkish, Chinese, Korean, Japanese , Hebrew, Hindi and Arabic.

The lexicon used in our analysis consists of 1,016 **concepts** sourced from NorthEuraLex (NEL) (Dellert et al., 2020), a comprehensive linguistic resource containing these concepts with their word forms in 107 different languages.

We map the concepts in NEL to **domains**, using Concepticon.[6] There are 20 domains (e.g, animals, kinship; full list is in Appendix §A), each containing $22-136$ concepts.

Models & Settings. For static word embeddings we use fastText[7] 300-dimension word embeddings, trained on Wikipedia using the skip-gram model (Bojanowski et al., 2017). For contextualised word embeddings (CWE) we use mBERT[8] (*bert-base-multilingual-uncased* model) 768-dimension vectors for the 16 languages. To extract sentences to use with contextualised models, we use the Leipzig corpus.[9] We replicate our experiments with other architectures and datasets (see Appendix D).

4 Alignment Metrics

We now turn to presenting the metrics we use in the paper. Each metric either follows the distribution-based Alignment (DISTA) or the Colexification-based Alignment (COLEXA) approach. For DISTA we follow the metrics and notations outlined in (Karidi et al., 2024).

Notation. Let $\mathcal{C}$ be the set of concepts in the NEL dataset (Dellert et al., 2019, see §3). We adopt the notion of a concept from the lexical typology literature (e.g., Dellert et al., 2019; Rzymski et al., 2020), and take it to mean a word sense defined independently of any specific language. Let Ω be a set of languages. A language $L \in \Omega$ may or may not lexicalize a concept $c \in \mathcal{C}$, and may lexicalize several concepts with one word (colexification). We denote the lexicon corresponding to $\mathcal{C}$ in a given language L with $\mathcal{L}$, and note that $|\mathcal{L}| \leq |\mathcal{C}|$ for every language. We assume that $\mathcal{C}$ is partitioned into domains, and denote the (non-overlapping) domains with $\mathcal{D}_1, \ldots, \mathcal{D}_m$.

Given a concept $c \in \mathcal{C}$, we denote its lexicalization (the word expressing that concept) in language L with $r_L(c) \in \mathcal{L}$. A translation pair between languages L_1 and L_2 is a pair of words $(w_1, w_2) \in \mathcal{L}_1 \times \mathcal{L}_2$, such that there exists $c \in \mathcal{C}$ such that $r_{L_1}(c) = w_1$ and $r_{L_2}(c) = w_2$. For example, the concept SONG gives rise to the English-French translation pair *(song,chanson)*. In principle, several translation pairs may correspond to a concept and language pair, but in the data we experiment with, this does not occur.

For a given word w in a given language L, we denote its embedding with $emb(w, L)$. We denote the embedding space corresponding to L with ℓ.

4.1 Colexification-based Alignment

We operationalize the notion of colexification-based alignment (COLEXA) to establish a common ground that facilitates a valid empirical comparison between DISTA and COLEXA. We experiment with a lexical alignment method that is based on colexification data (Rzymski et al., 2020). This method measures the alignment of a single concept across multiple languages. We furthermore extend it to measure the alignment of an entire domain across multiple languages. We note that different works that used COLEXA have used different methodologies, since there is no standard methodology for them. We therefore define measure that in our view captures the core statistics used by these papers.

Concept-Level Colexification-based Alignment. For every concept $c \in \mathcal{C}$ and language L_i $(i = 1, 2)$, let ${Z_c}^{(i)}$ the inverse image of $r_{L_i}(c)$:

$$Z_c^{(i)} = \{c' \in \mathcal{C} | r_{L_i}(c) = r_{L_i}(c')\}$$

We define:

$$\vartheta(c)_{L_1,L_2} = \frac{1}{2}\left(\frac{|{Z_c}^{(1)} \cap {Z_c}^{(2)}|}{|{Z_c}^{(1)}|} + \frac{|{Z_c}^{(2)} \cap {Z_c}^{(1)}|}{|{Z_c}^{(2)}|}\right)$$

Intuitively, this is a measure of the joint colexifications of the concept. For example, in Figure 1,the concept *steigen::V* is colexified with *aufgehen(sonne)::V* in English, and lexicalized as the word form *rise*, while in Finnish, an additional two concepts (*aufstehen::V* and *sich erheben::V*) are colexified (lexicalized as the word form *nousta*).

Domain-Level Colexification Based Alignment. Given the scarcity of colexifications that occur at the level of individual concepts (as many concepts are not colexified with any other concept), it is reasonable to extend the concept-level measure to quantify the alignment of a semantic domain across languages. For this we aggregate the concept-level alignment.This is done by aggregating ϑ over the concepts in $\mathcal{D}$.[10]

[6] https://concepticon.clld.org/

[7] https://fasttext.cc/docs/en/unsupervised-tutorial.html

[8] https://huggingface.co/bert-base-multilingual-uncased

[9] https://corpora.uni-leipzig.de/en?corpusId=deu_news_2021

[10] We note that both concept-level and domain-level measures obtain values in [0, 1], where a value of 1 is obtained in the case of identity in the colexifications in the domain and 0 is obtained where there are no joint colexifications.

4.2 Distribution-based Alignment

In this section, we first present the computational framework we adopt in this paper, namely Semantic Neighborhood Comparison; a standard approach for comparing embeddings in different spaces, used for both computational historical linguistics and lexical similarity tasks (Hamilton et al., 2016; Thompson et al., 2020; Beinborn and Choenni, 2020), that has recently been facilitated as an NLP task and extended to architectures beyond static representations (Karidi et al., 2024). We present several variants of this approach, including one based on contextualized word embeddings.[11]

Semantic Neighborhood Comparison (SNC). Let $c \in \mathcal{C}$ be a concept and $w_1 = r_{L_1}(c) \in \mathcal{L}_1$, $w_2 = r_{L_2}(c) \in \mathcal{L}_2$ its lexicalizations, and $v_1 = emb(w_1, L_1) \in \ell_1$, $v_2 = emb(w_2, L_2) \in \ell_2$ their respective embeddings. We compute its k nearest neighbors in ℓ_1 with $\{n_1^{(1)}, ..., n_k^{(1)}\}$ ($k = 100$ in our experiments[12]; see §3). We then translate the nearest neighbors to L_2 (§3 for translation retrieval method), by taking their translation pairs, and denote the resulting vectors with $\{n_1^{(2)}, ..., n_k^{(2)}\} \in \ell_2$. We define the unidirectional metric as

$$a_{L_1 \to L_2}(c) = \rho\left(\left(cos(v_1, n_i^{(1)})\right)_{i=1}^{k}, \left(cos(v_2, n_i^{(2)})\right)_{i=1}^{k}\right)$$

ρ is the Pearson correlation coefficient [13]. The bidirectional metric as the arithmetic mean over the two directions:

$$a_{L_1 \leftrightarrow L_2}(c) = \frac{a_{L_1 \to L_2}(c) + a_{L_2 \to L_1}(c)}{2}$$

We refer to this alignment strategy as DISTA-STATIC.

Contextualised Word Embeddings. We now turn to detailing metrics that are analogous to DISTA-STATIC, but instead use CEs [14].

[11]In a subsequent paper (Karidi et al., 2024), we present the variants of the standard approach, for contextualised word embeddings, and perform extensive evaluation on them. Here, we choose two variants (DISTA-AVE and DISTA-CLOUD) to use in our analysis.

[12]We experimented with other values of k and selected the one that overall correlated the most with human-judgment based evaluations (see §5.4).

[13]We conducted experiments with Spearman correlation, as well as Kendall τ. They present similar trends and are omitted due to space considerations.

[14]We denote contextualised word embeddings by CEs.

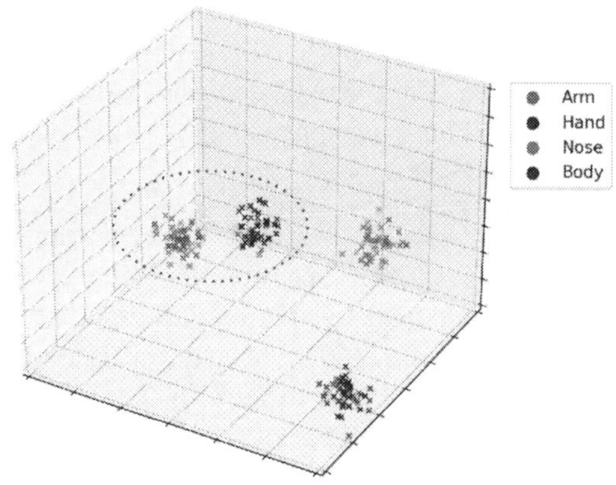

Figure 4: Illustration of nearest neighbors in the contextualized space. t-SNE plot in 2D of point clouds for the words: *arm*, *hand*, *nose*, and *body*. The nearest neighbor of *hand* is *arm*, as they have the minimal distance among all pairs of points from distinct clouds.

DISTA-AVE. For word $w \in \mathcal{L}$, we extract its representation from all layers (if w is tokenized to multiple subwords, we average over the subword representations). We average the outputs from layers 1-12 to define the final vector for w.[15] We then proceed with the SNC process, as described with DISTA-STATIC.

DISTA-CLOUD. For word $w \in \mathcal{L}$, we extract all sentences (with a threshold of 1000) that w appears in, from an auxiliary corpus (see §3). We extract the CEs (from layer 12, if it is tokenized to subwords, we average over them) for w from each of the sentences. Denote these vectors with $V_w = \{v_{1_w}, ..., v_{k_w}\} \subseteq \mathbb{R}^{768}$. In this setting, each word w is represented by a point cloud of vectors V_w. Hence, the distance between two words is the distance between their corresponding point clouds (see Figure 4). We define *point-cloud distance* as follows:

$$d(w, \tilde{w}) = min_{i,j}\ cos(v_{i_w}, v_{j_{\tilde{w}}})$$

We follow the SNC procedure (defined above) under this definition of distance [16].

[15]We follow the approach of averaging over layers as described in (Karidi et al., 2024), consistent with the method used in (Vulić et al., 2020).

[16]We experiment with various pooling strategies and computational methods for building the contextualised spaces. For example, we experiment with pooling from different layers or combination of layers, similarly to DISTA-AVE. We also experiment with several definitions for the point-cloud distance, and several processing steps for generating the point-cloud itself, such as averaging the vectors within the point-cloud or clustering the set into clusters using a Gaussian Mixture

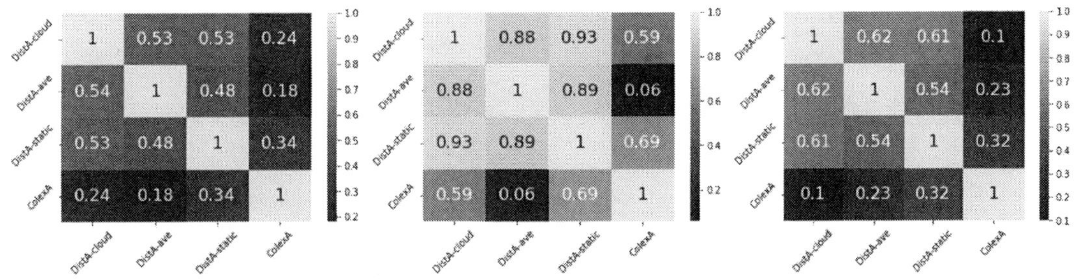

Figure 5: Correlation between DISTA and COLEXA. Correlation (Pearson) is computed for various aggregation methods: (a) concept-level, (b) domain-level and (c) language-level. All correlation values are significant with $p < 0.05$.

	COLEXA	DIST-STATIC	DIST-CLOUD
Top 3	fingernail	March	thirty
	sweep	August	fifty
	cover	January	twelve
Bottom 3	recognize	rise	corner
	endure	groan	soft
	wool	set	round

Table 1: Most and least aligned words. Word-level alignment, averaged across languages.

5 Comparing COLEXA and DISTA

The main goal of this paper is to asses the feasibility of applying two key types of alignment metrics, colexification-based (COLEXA §4.1) and distribution-based (DISTA §4.2) , within an interface setting, allowing for a direct empirical comparison of their outcomes. To this end, we initially establish the metrics in a manner that allows for a technically viable comparison (§2). We examine the convergence of their empirical findings as well as compare different metrics within the same category, that represent different operationalizations of a similar approach and data to account for.

5.1 Word-level Comparison

We start with the most straightforward level of comparison between metrics, which is their word-level correlation.[17]. Table 1 shows examples of the most and least aligned words.

Figure 5 shows that: (1) COLEXA is in low correlation with all of the DISTA methods (highest correlation is achieved between COLEXA and DISTA-STATIC, $r = 0.34$); and (2) DISTA methods are moderately correlated among themselves ($r \approx 0.5$).

Another natural question to ask is whether COLEXA and DISTA make similar predictions in terms of what concepts are more or less aligned across languages on average. That is, we investigate the correlation between COLEXA and DISTA over the set of concepts $\mathcal{C}$, where we average the score over all language pairs.

To conclude, by directly examining the statistical relation between the scores, we find that although there are similarities in the trends presented by the two methodologies, they yield different results across the board.

5.2 Domain-level Comparison

Alignment metrics between languages are often used to compare the degree of alignment across different domains. For example, Thompson et al. (2020) argue, based on findings with a DISTA-STATIC metric, that more structured domains tend to be better aligned across languages. To examine the alignment at the domain level, we aggregate the word-level alignment over each domain (without aggregating over languages; see Figure 5). Strikingly, as opposed to the concept-level comparison, here the similarity between the DISTA methods is very high, reaching $r = 0.93$ (between DISTA-CLOUD and DISTA-STATIC). In addition, the correlaton between COLEXA and DISTA highly increases (reaching $r = 0.65$ with DISTA-STATIC). The differentiation both amongst the DISTA methods themselves and between DISTA and COLEXA has become less distinct. This finding encourages the formulation of conclusions at the domain level, as it presents to be more stable.

Model. They all yield similar trends, and are not reported due to space limitations.

[17]A metric and a language pair give rise to a vector of alignment scores. Full details on how we compute the correlations at the word, domain, and language levels can be found in Appendix §B.

	COLEXA	DISTA-STATIC	DISTA-CLOUD
Top 3	Quantity The House Social Politics	Quantity Time Kinship	Quantity Kinship Time
Bottom 3	Basic actions Sense perception Motion	Basic actions Motion The house	Agriculture Spatial relations The house

Table 2: Most and least aligned domains for various metrics. Alignment computed by aggregating over languages and over domains. "Basic actions." refers to "Basic actions and technology" and "Agriculture" refers to "Agriculture and vegetation".

Most and Least Aligned Domains. For DISTA, the most aligned domains are Quantity, Time and Kinship (Figure 6, for DISTA-CLOUD)[18], whereas the least aligned domains are Motion, Basic Actions, and Technology and Possession. Similar trends are reported by Thompson et al. (2020), who argue that the high degree of alignment of these domains is related to their structure and organization along explicit dimensions (e.g., generation: grandmother/mother/daughter, in the Kinship domain). This robust effect exhibited in DISTA is partially preserved with COLEXA; Quantity the most aligned domain, whereas Time is the 4th aligned. However, Kinship is the 7th most aligned (out of the 20 domains). Table 2 presents a few examples of the differences.

5.3 Factors Influencing Alignment

We turn to analyse whether similar factors influence the alignment results for DISTA and COLEXA (full analysis is available in Appendix §C). Examining both lexical features, such as frequency, concreteness, and rate of change, alongside environmental features, such as cultural and geographical distance, we find that at the word level, the correlation between alignment measures and these features ranges from none to weak. However, at the domain level, an interesting finding emerges: the **rate of lexical change** is a strong predictor for both DISTA and COLEXA. Specifically, we observe a correlation of approximately $r \approx -0.6$ for DISTA and $r = -0.81$ for COLEXA. This interesting result means that words that undergo faster lexical change are less aligned across languages. This aligns with findings that polysemy plays a significant role in the rate of lexical change (Brown and Witkowski, 1983; Thompson et al., 2020), and corresponds with observations that the rate of change is negatively correlated with prototypicality (how representative a word is of its category) (Dubossarsky et al., 2017).

5.4 Comparing Against A Reference Point

Unlike many NLP tasks, when comparing the meanings of translation equivalents across languages, there is no ground truth to reference against. Instead, datasets and tasks from cognitive science literature, such as similarity in picture naming or translation norms, can serve as converging evidence for validating different measures.

This comparison has several caveats: first, it applies to a limited set of languages and stimuli; second, it is not clear that this measure captures the same notion of similarity we aim to quantify using metrics for cross-lingual lexical similarity. We hereby detail these measures and use them as a reference point for comparison.

Multipic. MultiPic is a standardized set of 750 drawings of concrete objects with name agreement norms for six European languages (English, Spanish, Netherlands Dutch, German, French and Italian). For each picture and language, the norm is an information statistic that reflects the level of agreement across participants.

We filter the pictures in the Multipic dataset to only include pictures with concepts from NEL, which results in a total of 194 pictures. We compute the correlation between the agreement scores (average agreement score over all languages) for these pictures and the different DISTA and COLEXA metrics for the corresponding concepts. Results show that while DISTA-AVE and DISTA-STATIC are moderately correlated with Multipic ($r \approx 0.3$, $p < 0.05$), the other methods are weakly to not correlated with the dataset.

TransSim. TransSim is a dataset of 562 Dutch-English translation pairs together with a human similarity rating between each pair. We again filter the dataset to include word pairs that are covered by NEL, resulting in 187 Dutch–English translation similarity judgment scores. We compute the correlation between English-Dutch translation similarity judgements and the alignment metrics for English-Dutch, aggregated by domain (domain-level). A relatively high correlation is presented, where DISTA-STATIC ($r = 0.59$, $p < 0.05$) and DISTA-AVE ($r = 0.51$, $p < 0.05$) rank highest.

[18]This trend persists for all DISTA methods and various k values.

However, COLEXA is only weakly correlated with TransSim ($r \approx 0.1, p < 0.05$).

To conclude, when comparing both DISTA and COLEXA to norm-based measures, we find that DISTA shows a moderate correlation with some measures, whereas COLEXA does not. This distinction suggests that DISTA may be more suitable for detailed analysis of cross-lingual similarity as it is better aligned with human judgements, while COLEXA might be better suited for coarse-grained analysis. However, since these external measures apply only to a subset of languages and concepts, this limitation should be considered. Therefore, we defer a more comprehensive multi-approach comparison to future work.

6 Qualitative Analysis

To further understand the nature of alignment and convergence of the various approaches, we manually examine data from four randomly-selected languages pairs (English-German, German-Arabic, Arabic-Hebrew and Spanish-Hindi); specifically, for each method and language pair we take the top/bottom aligned 100 words, together with their 10 nearest neighbors in each language (for COLEXA we consider colexifications instead of neighbors). Even within the most aligned domains, there is variability in the order of aligned words (e.g., in DISTA-CLOUD numbers such as *seven* and *fifty* are the most aligned, whereas in DISTA-STATIC it is months, such as *March*). However, words in highly aligned domains tend to greatly overlap in their neighbors, and somewhat preserve their order of distances.

It is difficult to draw conclusions at the word-level just by looking at the raw data (this is also reflected in our empirical analysis in disagreement between the methodologies, §5.1). This is especially true for COLEXA or for the least aligned words. We do find, however, that certain words exhibit highly consistent colexification patterns across languages. For instance, the word *fingernail* frequently colexifies with the word *nail*. Based on this analysis, we hypothesize that words that colexify conceptualy similar senses (e.g., *fingernail* and *nail/hand* and *claw*/etc.) tend to have more universal colexification patterns and in turn more aligned (this echoes the finding that conceptual similarity shape colexification (Karjus et al., 2021b)), and that this is also reflected by high alignment in DISTA as this type of polysemy is less prone to affect the dissimilarity of neighbors across languages. Conversely, when two distinct senses are colexified (e.g., *bank* in English colexifies a sense of *financial institution* and a sense of *terrain*), the neighbors are likely a mix of words relating to each sense, leading to lower distributional alignment.

7 Discussion

Distribution-based and colexification-based approaches both capture a data-driven notion of similarity between the lexicons of different languages. However, they rely on different methodologies and assumptions about the data that should be accounted for, and are commonly applied in distinct ways. This raises the question of whether they are comparable, and if so – whether their predictions converge.

We find that despite the inherent differences between the methods, when viewed at the level of domains, the two appraoches show similar trends. We also find that the rate of lexical change is a strong predictor for alignment, words that change less have more stable meaning across languages. In contrast to COLEXA, DISTA is significantly correlated with extrinsic measures for meaning alignment across languages. A possible explanation is that COLEXA captures coarser aspects of meaning or that it is more suitable for scenarios which require aggregation across a more extensive range of languages. We still find this resource highly valuable, especially for investigations of high-level patterns of lexical similarity (e.g., variation in emotion concepts over the worlds languages (Jackson et al., 2019)), since it is less prone to noise stemming from the training data than DISTA. However, for a more fine-grained analysis or when less languages are available, we encourage the use of DISTA.

In this paper we lay the ground for a direct comparison of DISTA and COLEXA. Our findings call for a more nuanced discussion of lexical alignment, and also underscore the importance of taking into account multiple approaches for similarity when drawing empirical conclusions about lexical similarity. Different approaches and settings may well lead to different conclusions, which highlights the importance of justifying the technical approach taken in each paper.

References

David Allen and Kathy Conklin. 2013. Cross-linguistic similarity norms for japanese-english translation equivalents. *Behavior research methods*, 46.

Mikel Artetxe, Gorka Labaka, and Eneko Agirre. 2018. A robust self-learning method for fully unsupervised cross-lingual mappings of word embeddings. In *Proceedings of the 56th Annual Meeting of the Association for Computational Linguistics (Volume 1: Long Papers)*, pages 789–798, Melbourne, Australia. Association for Computational Linguistics.

Hongchang Bao, Bradley Hauer, and Grzegorz Kondrak. 2021. On universal colexifications. In *Proceedings of the 11th Global Wordnet Conference*, pages 1–7, University of South Africa (UNISA). Global Wordnet Association.

George Barnett. 1977. Bilingual semantic organizationa multidimensional analysis. *Journal of Cross-cultural Psychology*, 8:315–330.

Lisa Beinborn and Rochelle Choenni. 2020. Semantic drift in multilingual representations. *Computational Linguistics*, 46:1–34.

Piotr Bojanowski, Edouard Grave, Armand Joulin, and Tomas Mikolov. 2017. Enriching word vectors with subword information. *Transactions of the Association for Computational Linguistics*, 5:135–146.

Cecil Brown and Stanley Witkowski. 1983. Polysemy, lexical change and cultural importance. *Man*, 18:72.

Allan Burns. 1994. Review of John A. Lucy, grammatical categories and cognition: A case study of the linguistic relativity hypothesis. *Language in Society - LANG SOC*, 23:445–448.

Yiyi Chen, Russa Biswas, and Johannes Bjerva. 2023. Colex2Lang: Language embeddings from semantic typology. In *Proceedings of the 24th Nordic Conference on Computational Linguistics (NoDaLiDa)*, pages 673–684, Tórshavn, Faroe Islands. University of Tartu Library.

Alexis Conneau, Guillaume Lample, Marc'Aurelio Ranzato, Ludovic Denoyer, and Hervé Jégou. 2017. Word translation without parallel data. *The International Conference on Learning Representations (ICLR)*.

William Croft. 2010. Relativity, linguistic variation and language universals. *CogniTextes*, 4.

William Croft. 2022. On two mathematical representations for "semantic maps". *Zeitschrift für Sprachwissenschaft*, 41.

Johannes Dellert, Thora Daneyko, Alla Münch, Alina Ladygina, Armin Buch, Natalie Clarius, Ilja Grigorjew, Mohamed Balabel, Hizniye Isabella Boga, Zalina Baysarova, et al. 2020. Northeuralex: A wide-coverage lexical database of northern eurasia. *Language resources and evaluation*, 54:273–301.

Johannes Dellert, Thora Daneyko, Alla Münch, Alina Ladygina, Armin Buch, Natalie Clarius, Ilja Grigorjew, Mohamed Balabel, Hizniye Boga, Zalina Baysarova, Roland Mühlenbernd, Johannes Wahle, and Gerhard Jäger. 2019. NorthEuraLex: a wide-coverage lexical database of Northern Eurasia. *Language Resources and Evaluation*, 54:1–29.

Haim Dubossarsky, Daphna Weinshall, and Eitan Grossman. 2017. Outta control: Laws of semantic change and inherent biases in word representation models. In *Proceedings of the 2017 Conference on Empirical Methods in Natural Language Processing*, pages 1136–1145, Copenhagen, Denmark. Association for Computational Linguistics.

Nicholas Evans and Stephen Levinson. 2009. The myth of language universals: Language diversity and its importance for cognitive science. *The Behavioral and Brain Sciences*, 32:429–48; discussion 448.

Jerry Fodor. 1975. *The Language of Thought*. Harvard University Press.

Alexandre François. 2008. Semantic maps and the typology of colexification. In Martine Vanhove, editor, *From Polysemy to Semantic change: Towards a Typology of Lexical Semantic Associations*, pages 163–215.

William Frawley. 1998. Review of Anna Wierzbicka, Semantics: primes and universals. *Journal of Linguistics*, 34:227–297.

Thanasis Georgakopoulos, Eitan Grossman, Dmitry Nikolaev, and Stéphane Polis. 2022. Universal and macro-areal patterns in the lexicon: A case-study in the perception-cognition domain. *Linguistic Typology*, 26:439–487.

Hila Gonen, Shauli Ravfogel, Yanai Elazar, and Yoav Goldberg. 2020. It's not greek to mbert: inducing word-level translations from multilingual bert. *arXiv preprint arXiv:2010.08275*.

William L. Hamilton, Jure Leskovec, and Dan Jurafsky. 2016. Diachronic word embeddings reveal statistical laws of semantic change. In *Proceedings of the 54th Annual Meeting of the Association for Computational Linguistics (Volume 1: Long Papers)*, pages 1489–1501, Berlin, Germany. Association for Computational Linguistics.

John Harvill, Roxana Girju, and Mark Hasegawa-Johnson. 2022. Syn2Vec: Synset colexification graphs for lexical semantic similarity. In *Proceedings of the 2022 Conference of the North American Chapter of the Association for Computational Linguistics: Human Language Technologies*, pages 5259–5270, Seattle, United States. Association for Computational Linguistics.

Martin Haspelmath. 2003. The geometry of grammatical meaning: Semantic maps and cross-linguistic comparison. In Michael Tomasello, editor, *The new psychology of language*, pages 217–248. Erlbaum.

Shreya Havaldar, Sunny Rai, Bhumika Singhal, Langchen Liu Sharath Chandra Guntuku, and Lyle Ungar. 2023. Multilingual language models are not multicultural: A case study in emotion. *arXiv preprint arXiv:2307.01370*.

Joshua Jackson, Joseph Watts, Teague Henry, Johann-Mattis List, Robert Forkel, Peter Mucha, Simon Greenhill, Russell Gray, and Kristen Lindquist. 2019. Emotion semantics show both cultural variation and universal structure. *Science*, 366.

Mathilde Josserand, Emma Meeussen, Asifa Majid, and Dan Dediu. 2021. Environment and culture shape both the colour lexicon and the genetics of colour perception. *Scientific Reports*, 11:19095.

Taelin Karidi, Eitan Grossman, and Omri Abend. 2024. Locally measuring cross-lingual lexical alignment: A domain and word level perspective. In *Empirical Methods in Natural Language Processing Findings (EMNLP 2024)*.

Andres Karjus, Richard Blythe, Simon Kirby, Tianyu Wang, and Kenny Smith. 2021a. Conceptual similarity and communicative need shape colexification: An experimental study. *Cognitive Science*, 45.

Andres Karjus, Richard A Blythe, Simon Kirby, Tianyu Wang, and Kenny Smith. 2021b. Conceptual similarity and communicative need shape colexification: An experimental study. *Cognitive Science*, 45(9):e13035.

Yihong Liu, Haotian Ye, Leonie Weissweiler, and Hinrich Schuetze. 2023a. Transfer learning for low-resource languages based on multilingual colexification graphs. *arxiv*.

Yihong Liu, Haotian Ye, Leonie Weissweiler, Philipp Wicke, Renhao Pei, Robert Zangenfeind, and Hinrich Schuetze. 2023b. A crosslingual investigation of conceptualization in 1335 languages. In *Proceedings of the 61th Annual Meeting of the Association for Computational Linguistics (Volume 1: Long Papers)*, Toronto, Canada. Association for Computational Linguistics.

Asifa Majid, James Boster, and Melissa Bowerman. 2008. The cross-linguistic categorization of everyday events: A study of cutting and breaking. *Cognition*, 109:235–250.

Asifa Majid, Fiona Jordan, and Michael Dunn. 2014. Semantic systems in closely related languages. *Language Sciences*, 49.

Cornelia Moldovan, Rosa Sanchez-Casas, Josep Demestre, and Pilar Ferré. 2012. Interference effects as a function of semantic similarity in the translation recognition task in bilinguals of catalan and spanish. *PSICOLOGICA*, 33:77–110.

Anna Natale, Max Pellert, and David Garcia. 2021. Colexification networks encode affective meaning. *Affective Science*, 2.

Roberto Navigli and Simone Paolo Ponzetto. 2012. Babelnet: The automatic construction, evaluation and application of a wide-coverage multilingual semantic network. *Artificial intelligence*, 193:217–250.

Mark Pagel, Quentin Atkinson, and Andrew Meade. 2007. Frequency of word-use predicts rates of lexical evolution throughout indo-european history. *Nature*, 449:717–20.

Telmo Pires, Eva Schlinger, and Dan Garrette. 2019. How multilingual is multilingual BERT? In *Proceedings of the 57th Annual Meeting of the Association for Computational Linguistics*, pages 4996–5001, Florence, Italy. Association for Computational Linguistics.

Ross Purves, Philipp Striedl, Inhye Kong, and Asifa Majid. 2023. Conceptualizing landscapes through language: The role of native language and expertise in the representation of waterbody related terms. *Topics in cognitive science*, 15.

Ella Rabinovich, Yang Xu, and Suzanne Stevenson. 2020. The typology of polysemy: A multilingual distributional framework. *(Annual Meeting of the Cognitive Science Society (CogSci)*.

Christoph Rzymski, Tiago Tresoldi, Simon Greenhill, Mei-Shin Wu, Nathanael Schweikhard, Maria Koptjevskaja-Tamm, Volker Gast, Timotheus Bodt, Abbie Hantgan, Gereon Kaiping, Sophie Chang, Yunfan Lai, Natalia Morozova, Heini Arjava, Nataliia Hübler, Ezequiel Koile, Steve Pepper, Mariann Proos, Briana Epps, and Johann-Mattis List. 2020. The database of cross-linguistic colexifications, reproducible analysis of cross-linguistic polysemies. *Scientific Data*, 7.

Jesse Snedeker and Lila Gleitman. 2004. *Weaving a Lexicon*. MIT Press.

Jimin Sun, Hwijeen Ahn, Chan Young Park, Yulia Tsvetkov, and David R. Mortensen. 2021. Cross-cultural similarity features for cross-lingual transfer learning of pragmatically motivated tasks. In *Proceedings of the 16th Conference of the European Chapter of the Association for Computational Linguistics: Main Volume*, pages 2403–2414, Online. Association for Computational Linguistics.

B. Thompson, S. G. Roberts, and G Lupyan. 2018. Quantifying semantic similarity across languages. *(Annual Meeting of the Cognitive Science Society (CogSci)*.

Bill Thompson, Seán Roberts, and Gary Lupyan. 2020. Cultural influences on word meanings revealed through large-scale semantic alignment. *Nature Human Behaviour*, 4:1–10.

Natasha Tokowicz, Judith Kroll, Annette Groot, and Janet van Hell. 2002. Number-of-translation norms for dutch–english translation pairs: A new tool for examining language production. *Behavior research methods, instruments, & computers : a journal of the Psychonomic Society, Inc*, 34:435–51.

Åke Viberg. 1983. The verbs of perception: a typological study. 21(1):123–162.

Ivan Vulić, Edoardo Maria Ponti, Anna Korhonen, and Goran Glavaš. 2021. LexFit: Lexical fine-tuning of pretrained language models. In *Proceedings of the 59th Annual Meeting of the Association for Computational Linguistics and the 11th International Joint Conference on Natural Language Processing (Volume 1: Long Papers)*, pages 5269–5283, Online. Association for Computational Linguistics.

Ivan Vulić, Edoardo Ponti, Robert Litschko, Goran Glavaš, and Anna Korhonen. 2020. Probing pretrained language models for lexical semantics.

Benjamin Lee Whorf. 1956. *Thought and Reality: Selected Writing*, first edition. MIT Press.

Anna Wierzbicka. 1972. Semantic primitives. *Frankfurter anthropologische Blätter*, 11:1–16.

Anna Wierzbicka. 2010. Lexical universals of kinship and social cognition. *Behavioral and Brain Sciences*, 33:403 – 404.

Yang Xu, Khang Duong, Barbara Malt, Serena Jiang, and Mahesh Srinivasan. 2020. Conceptual relations predict colexification across languages. *Cognition*, 201.

Hyejin Youn, Logan Sutton, Eric Smith, Cristopher Moore, Jon Wilkins, Ian Maddieson, William Croft, and Tanmoy Bhattacharya. 2016. On the universal structure of human lexical semantics. *Proceedings of the National Academy of Sciences*, 113.

A Experimental Setup

Languages. We perform our analysis on a diverse set of 16 languages, spanning 7 different top-level language families from many geographical areas across Eurasia: English (eng), French (fra), Italian (ita), German (deu), Dutch (nld), Spanish (spa), Polish (pol), Finnish (fin), Estonian (est), Turkish (tur), Chinese (chn), Korean (kor), Japanese (jap), Hebrew (heb), Hindi (hin) and Arabic (arb).

NorthEuraLex (**NEL**) is a lexical resource compiled from dictionaries and other linguistic resources available for individual languages in Northern Eurasia. NEL comprises a list of 1016 distinct *concepts* together with their word forms in 107 languages (Table 5). Rare cases where a concept does not have a realization in a given language are excluded for that language.

Semantic Domains. We map the concepts in NEL to domains, using Concepticon.[19] There are 20 domains, each containing 22 – 136 concepts: animals, Agriculture and vegetation, time, quantity, kinship, basic actions and technology, clothing and grooming, cognition, emotions and values, food and drink, modern world, motion, posession, sense perception, social and political relations, spatial relations, speech and language, the body, the house and the physical world.

Lexical and Language Features. We report results while controlling for a variety of lexical features and features of the languages compared. Geographic distance between languages is computed as the geodesic distance (distance in an ellipsoid) between their latitude and longitude coordinates (taken from Glottolog[20]). Cultural distance is computed as the proportion of common cultural traits from a set of 92 non-linguistic cultural traits for 16 societies representing the languages in our analysis, taken from D-PLACE[21] (Thompson et al., 2020). We use the *wordfreq* library[22] for word frequencies. We then compute the log-transformed frequency (to reduce the impact of outliers and extreme values). Realizations of some concepts, such as *tail*, evolve rapidly, while others, such as *two* evolve at a much slower rate. This phenomenon is referred to as the *rate of (lexical) change*. We use lexical change rates derived from (Pagel et al., 2007), available for Russian, Greek, English and Spanish.

Word Embeddings. For static word embeddings we use fastText[23] 300-dimension word embeddings, trained on Wikipedia using the skip-gram model (Bojanowski et al., 2017). For contextualised word embeddings (CWE) we use mBERT[24] (*bert-base-multilingual-uncased* model) 768-dimension vectors for the 16 languages. To extract sentences for DISTA-CLOUD, we use the Leipzig corpus.[25] We additionally conduct our experiments using XLM-RoBERTa-base [26] for DISTA-CLOUD and DISTA-AVE and on 300-dim word2vec multilingual embeddings [27] for DISTA-STATIC. Moreover, we run all of the computations for DISTA-CLOUD and DISTA-AVE with a differ-

[19] https://concepticon.clld.org/

[20] https://glottolog.org/

[21] https://d-place.org/

[22] https://pypi.org/project/wordfreq

[23] https://fasttext.cc/docs/en/unsupervised-tutorial.html

[24] https://huggingface.co/bert-base-multilingual-uncased

[25] https://corpora.uni-leipzig.de/en?corpusId=deu_news_2021

[26] https://huggingface.co/xlm-roberta-base

[27] https://github.com/Kyubyong/wordvectors

ent dataset; the Wikipedia section in the Leipzig Corpus, for the latest year available in each language [28]. The trends closely match those described in the paper.[29].

Hyperparameters. For our distributional based alignments (§4.2), we set $k = 100$. We experimented with other values of k and selected the one that overall correlated the most with human-judgment based evaluations (see §5.4).

B Word, Domain and Language Level Alignment

We describe here our method for computing correlations at three levels of granularity: word-level, domain-level, and language-level.

Let $\mathcal{M}$ be the set of alignment metrics. We denote the raw data as follows:

$$\mu(m, L_p, L_j) \quad \forall\, m \in \mathcal{M}, L_p \times L_j \in \Omega^2$$

For a pair of languages L_p, L_j and a metric m, $\mu(m, L_p, L_j) \in \mathbb{R}^{|\mathcal{C}|}$ is a vector whose i-th coordinate is the alignment value of concept c_i under metric m between L_p and L_j.

We use Pearson's r (with a two-tailed test for significance) for computing correlation, unless stated otherwise.

Word-level Correlation. The most direct level of comparison between metrics is their word-level correlation. Let $\binom{\Omega}{2}$ be the set of all language pairs (without repetitions), and denote its size with $l{=}\binom{|\Omega|}{2}$. For $m \in \mathcal{M}$, define $\hat{\mu}(m) \in \mathbb{R}^{l|\mathcal{C}|}$ the concatenation of $\mu(m, L_p, L_j)$ for all language pairs. Word-level correlation is the Pearson correlation between $\hat{\mu}(m)$, for $m \in \mathcal{M}$ (See Figure 5).

Domain-level Correlation. Alignment metrics between languages are often used to compare the degree of alignment across different domains. For example, Thompson et al. (2020) argue, based on findings with DISTA-STATIC , that more structured domains, such as Quantity and Time, tend to be better aligned across languages. To examine the alignment at the domain level, for every measure $m \in \mathcal{M}$, we aggregate the word-level alignment over each domain (without aggregating over languages). We get $\hat{\mu}(m) \in \mathbb{R}^{lm}$ (m is the number of semantic domains).

[28]https://wortschatz.uni-leipzig.de/en

[29]See Appendix §D for experiments on other architectures than the ones presented in the main paper.

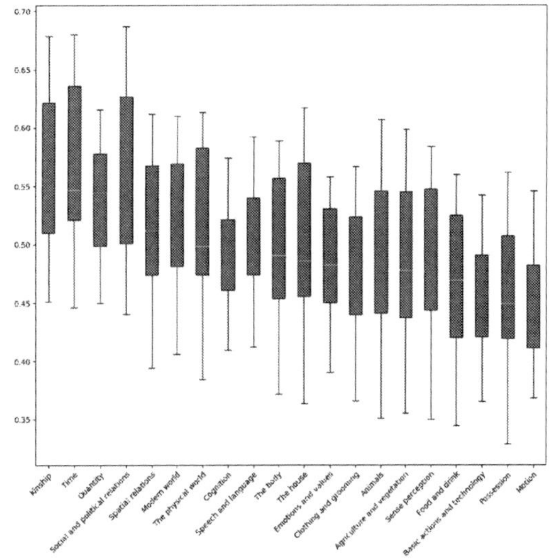

Figure 6: Alignment of domains under DISTA-AVE. The domains are ranked according to the mean value of the alignment. Each box represents the distribution of alignment values (per language pair), for a specific domain (concepts-level alignment is aggregated within each domain). The centre line is the median, the box limits are the upper and lower quartiles, and the whiskers represents the $1.5\times$ interquartile range.

Language-level Correlation. Another natural question to ask is whether COLEXA and DISTA make similar predictions in terms of what concepts are more or less aligned across languages on average. That is, we investigate the correlation between COLEXA and DISTA over the set of concepts $\mathcal{C}$, where we average the score over all language pairs. Formally, for each alignment measure $m_i \in \mathcal{M}$: $(\hat{\mu}(m_i))_j = \frac{1}{l} \sum_{(L_j, L_p) \in P} \mu(m_i, L_j, L_p)$ (we average over languages, not over concepts). Results are similar in this setting (Figure 5).

C Factors Influencing the Alignment

We examine factors influencing alignment and control for various features — lexical features like frequency, concreteness, and rate of lexical change, as well as environmental features such as geographical and cultural distance — and compare their effects on different alignment methodologies (see Section 5.3)[30]. Full results are presented in Table 3.

Correlation With Lexical Features. At the word-level ($\mu(m_i) \in \mathbb{R}^{|\mathcal{C}|l}$), there is no correlation

[30]We follow the analysis done in (Karidi et al., 2024) and extend it to other methodologies.

between both DISTA and COLEXA with respect to frequency and concreteness. There is a weak-moderate negative correlation with rate of lexical change (strongest for DISTA-STATIC, $r = -0.32$). When aggregating over domains ($\mu(m_i) \in \mathbb{R}^{lm}$) concreteness is still not correlated with any of the alignment methods; however, the correlation goes up for frequency (albeit still weakly) and jumps for rate of change ($r \approx -0.6$ for DISTA and $r = -0.81$ for COLEXA). This interesting result means that words that undergo faster lexical change are less aligned across languages.

Correlation With Environmental Features. The question of how **geographical** and **cultural** factors influence the alignment of words across languages is a matter of ongoing discussion among scholars (Youn et al., 2016; Josserand et al., 2021, e.g.,). Table 3 shows a significant correlation with geographic and cultural distance for DISTA, with cultural distance playing a more prominent role. However, COLEXA metrics only present a weak correlation with environmental methods. These results indicate yet another point of divergence between COLEXA and DISTA.

Controlling for Lexical and Enviromental Features. To further examine the influence of lexical and environmental features on the alignment methods, we perform partial correlation tests to control for the various features, and multiple regression analysis to account for the overall variance that is explained by them. We compute the partial correlation[31] between DISTA and COLEXA, while controlling for the lexical and environmental features.

We find that at the concept-level the two measures are still moderately correlated with $r \approx 0.4$. At the domain-level, DISTA methods are still highly correlated with one another ($r \approx 0.9$), with a moderate correlation between DISTA and COLEXA ($r \approx 0.5$). We use multiple linear regression to compute the adjusted R-squared value, with the environmental and lexical features as response variables. While the features explain $\approx 20\%$ of the variance for DISTA, they only explain a negligible amount of the variance for COLEXA. However, when aggregating over domains, the features explain up to 44% of the variance for DISTA, and 69% for ColexA. This suggests that the analysis is more suitable at the domain-level.

[31]For the partial correlation computations we use the *pingouin* package `https://pingouin-stats.org/build/html/generated/pingouin.partial_corr.html`

		DISTA CLOUD	DISTA AVE	DISTA STATIC	CA
CLT	C	0.14⋆	0.1⋆	0.25⋆	-0.04
	D	0.2⋆	0.49⋆	0.13⋆	0.13⋆
GEO	C	0.03⋆	0.09⋆	0.22⋆	-0.02
	D	0.16⋆	0.41⋆	0.05	0.05
frequency	C	0.04⋆	0.06	0.06	0.01
	D	0.33⋆	0.18⋆	0	0
concreteness	C	0.03	0	0	0.02
	D	0.18⋆	0.06	0.1⋆	0.15⋆
rate-change	C	-0.32⋆	-0.22⋆	-0.25⋆	-0.14⋆
	D	-0.57⋆	-0.62⋆	-0.62⋆	-0.81⋆

Table 3: Correlation with lexical and enviromental features. Columns represent the features (CA represents ColexA, CLT denotes cultural distance and GEO denotes geographical distance) and subcolumns represents concept-level aggregation (C) vs. domain-level aggregation (D). significant correlation with $p < 0.05$ are marked by $\star$.

		DISTA CLOUD	DISTA AVE	DISTA STATIC	CA
CLT	C	0.1⋆	0.08	0.27⋆	0
	D	0.23⋆	0.31⋆	0.11⋆	0.11⋆
GEO	C	0.1	0.08⋆	0.15⋆	0
	D	0.2⋆	0.39⋆	0.1⋆	−0.03
frequency	C	0	−0.04	0.01	0
	D	0.35⋆	0.15⋆	0	0.01
concreteness	C	0	0	0	0
	D	0.15⋆	0.1⋆	0.15⋆	0.1⋆
rate-change	C	-0.25⋆	-0.27⋆	-0.3⋆	-0.1⋆
	D	-0.55⋆	-0.48⋆	-0.65⋆	-0.73⋆

Table 4: Correlation with lexical and enviromental features (other architectures). Columns represent the features (CA represents ColexA, CLT denotes cultural distance and GEO denotes geographical distance) and subcolumns represents concept-level aggregation (C) vs. domain-level aggregation (D). NO represents Neighbors Overlap metric. significant correlation with $p < 0.05$ are marked by $\star$.

D Other Architectures

In the main paper, we conduct our analysis using the following models and data: for static word embeddings, we use fastText[32] 300-dimension word embeddings, trained on Wikipedia using the skip-gram model (Bojanowski et al., 2017). For

[32]`https://fasttext.cc/docs/en/unsupervised-tutorial.html`

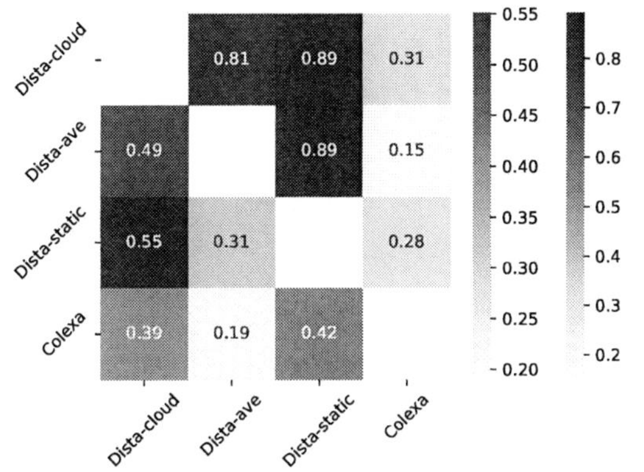

Figure 7: Correlation between DISTA and COLEXA (other architectures). Pearson correlation is computed for different aggregation methods. The **upper** matrix represents concept-level correlations, while the **bottom** matrix represents domain-level correlations. All correlation values are significant with $p < 0.05$.

contextualised word embeddings (CWE) we use mBERT[33] (*bert-base-multilingual-uncased* model) 768-dimension vectors for the 16 languages.To extract sentences for DISTA-CLOUD, we use the Leipzig corpus.[34]

We additionally conduct our experiments using XLM-RoBERTa-base [35] for DISTA-CLOUD and DISTA-AVE and on 300-dim word2vec multilingual embeddings [36] for DISTA-STATIC.

Moreover, we run all of the computations for DISTA-CLOUD and DISTA-AVE with a different dataset; the Wikipedia section in the Leipzig Corpus, for the latest year available in each language [37]. The trends closely match those described in the paper (see Figure 7 and Table 4).[38].

ENGLISH FORM	CONCEPT	DOMAIN
mother	mutter::N	Kinship
mind	verstand::N	Cognition
go	gehen::V	Motion

Table 5: Concepts and their domains. Examples of concepts, labled according to the NEL dataset (§3). Each concept belongs to a semantic domain ("Domain" column). The "English Form" column contains the lexicalization of each concept in English.

[33]https://huggingface.co/bert-base-multilingual-uncased

[34]https://corpora.uni-leipzig.de/en?corpusId=deu_news_2021

[35]https://huggingface.co/xlm-roberta-base

[36]https://github.com/Kyubyong/wordvectors

[37]https://wortschatz.uni-leipzig.de/en

[38]See Appendix §D for experiments on other architectures than the ones presented in the main paper.

TEXT2AFFORD: Probing Object Affordance Prediction abilities of Language Models solely from Text

Sayantan Adak, Daivik Agrawal, Animesh Mukherjee* and **Somak Aditya***
IIT, Kharagpur
West Bengal – 721302

Abstract

We investigate the knowledge of object affordances in pre-trained language models (LMs) and pre-trained Vision-Language models (VLMs). A growing body of literature shows that PTLMs fail inconsistently and non-intuitively, demonstrating a lack of reasoning and *grounding*. To take a first step toward quantifying the effect of grounding (or lack thereof), we curate a novel and comprehensive dataset of object affordances – TEXT2AFFORD, characterized by 15 affordance classes. Unlike affordance datasets collected in vision and language domains, we annotate *in-the-wild* sentences with objects and affordances. Experimental results reveal that PTLMs exhibit limited reasoning abilities when it comes to uncommon object affordances. We also observe that pre-trained VLMs do not necessarily capture object affordances effectively. Through few-shot fine-tuning, we demonstrate improvement in affordance knowledge in PTLMs and VLMs. Our research contributes a novel dataset for language grounding tasks, and presents insights into LM capabilities, advancing the understanding of object affordances. [1]

1 Introduction

Object affordance refers to the properties of an object that determine what actions a human can perform on them (Gibson, 1979). Gaining the knowledge of object affordances while learning textual representation from large corpora maybe hard; as in NLP, we lack corresponding images (or videos) which provides necessary visual cues such as shape, color, and texture to predict affordances. This lack of mapping or rather *grounding* ability has been noted by many researchers in the context of large pretrained language models (PTLMs). Authors in Bender and Koller (2020) have pointed the

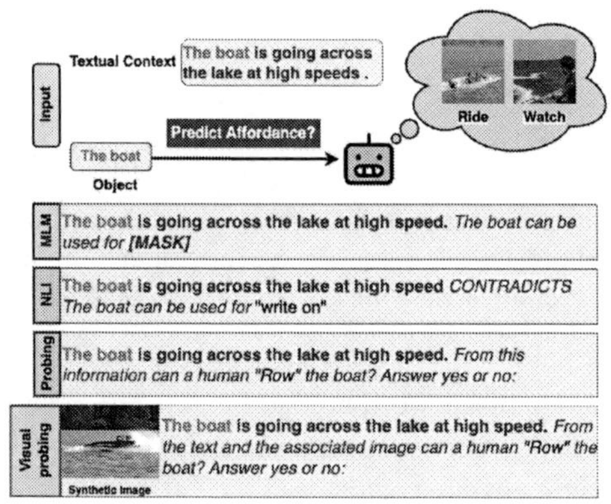

Figure 1: Overview of TEXT2AFFORD with its derived tasks.

lack of symbol grounding to be a fundamental factor behind PTLMs failing to grasp *meaning* from *form* (surface form text). The authors argue that language models which are exposed to only text (surface form) may never truly understand *meaning*, as PTLMs are unaware of possible *groundings* of the surface text. Most current NLP datasets and tasks are not designed to evaluate *grounding*, as it is hard to evaluate *grounding* without any visual context. Here, we aim to *quantify* the ability of pretrained models to learn *affordances* – which in turn requires the ability to *ground* symbols in text to real-world objects. In other words, *grounding* ability from text can enable understanding and reasoning about the physical properties of an object, which may help predict affordances.

As another example, for the sentence "an apple in the tree", we should infer that the "apple" can be eaten, and is rollable. However we cannot roll an "apple logo". In computer vision and robotics efforts, an accompanying image (or video) often provides necessary information about shape and physical properties of the entity, which can be used to predict affordances (Zhu et al., 2014). However such information is absent in NLP tasks. To capture this nuance, we annotate crowdsourced text intended for other tasks (such as NLI) with the

*Equal advising

[1]Code and Data are available at https://github.com/sayantan11995/Text2Afford

Proceedings of the 28th Conference on Computational Natural Language Learning, pages 342–364
November 15-16, 2024 ©2024 Association for Computational Linguistics

Dataset	Train size	Dev size	Test size	Reasoning type	Source	Image-dependent	Targeted affordance	Publicly available
PaCo (Qasemi et al., 2022a)	5,580	1,860	4,960	Preconditioned commonsense	Crowd-sourced	✗	✗	✓
WINOVENTI (Do and Pavlick, 2021)	-	-	4,352	Commonsense with exceptions	Crowd-sourced	✗	✗	✓
PVLIR (Qasemi et al., 2023)			34,000	Preconditioned visual commonsense	Other dataset	✓	✗	✗
Normlense (Han et al., 2023)	-	-	10,000	Defeasible visual commonsense	Crowd-sourced	✓	✗	✓
WinoViz (Jin et al., 2024)	-	-	1,380	Reasoning object's visual property	Crowd-sourced	✗	✗	✗
PROST (Aroca-Ouellette et al., 2021)	-	-	18,736	Reasoning object's physical property	Other dataset	✗	✗	✓
NEWTON (Wang et al., 2023)	-	-	2,800	Reasoning object's physical property	Crowd-sourced	✗	✗	✓
Persiani and Hellström (2019)	734,002	-	314,572	Object affordance without context	Synthetic	✗	✓	✗
TEXT2AFFORD (Ours)	-	-	35,520 (2368 * 15)	**Contextual object affordance**	Crowd-sourced	✗	✓	✓

Table 1: Comparison of TEXT2AFFORD with other reasoning datasets. A larger version is in Appendix A.3 Table 9.

objects and affordances. We use 15 affordance classes from Zhu et al. (2014). Through extensive pilot studies, we train a set of annotators using the `toloka.ai` platform. We choose 25 highly-skilled annotators who annotated a total of 2368 sentence-object pairs with 15 affordance classes, on a 0-3 Likert-like scale. For each sentence-object pair and each affordance class we ensure annotations from three annotators to enable majority votings. We name this novel dataset TEXT2AFFORD. We use the dataset for zero-shot evaluations of small LMs, open-source LLMs and also some VLMs by forming different task setups. Figure 1 presents an example from TEXT2AFFORD and the derived tasks (detailed in Section 4). We evaluate the effect of few-shot fine-tuning on few PTLMs and VLM. Our contributions can be summarized as follows.

• We curate a novel large scale crowdsourced text to affordance dataset – TEXT2AFFORD, consisting of 35,520 test data points (2368 sentence-object pairs with 15 unique affordance classes per pair). We ensure at least three annotations for each sentence-object pair for each class.

• Using TEXT2AFFORD, we perform zero-shot evaluation of several state-of-the-art PTLMs along with a few VLMs in different settings to identify the extent to which they gain the knowledge of affordance during pretraining. We further ensemble the VLM and the PTLM predictions to examine whether pre-training with images can enrich affordance prediction from text. Overall, we observe that the SOTA LLMs face difficulties predicting contextual object affordances solely from text (accuracy $< 55\%$) and the performance gets slightly enhanced when using powerful VLMs in presence of synthetic images.

• We also fine-tune few PTLMs on a small subset of our data as well as on some commonsense reasoning tasks to understand how quickly the affordance knowledge get scaled up and how far the affordances are related to commonsense knowledge. In addition, we examine the in-context learning (ICL) ability of few of the SOTA generative LLMs and VLMs in affordance prediction task. We find that the pre-trained encoder based models gain some knowledge about object affordance during fine-tuning using the commonsense reasoning dataset.

• Additionally through finetuning on our dataset, we show that knowledge of affordance can improve model's physical reasoning capability.

2 Related work

Reasoning about object affordances. Object affordances has been extensively studied in Computer Vision and Robotics (Sun et al. (2014); Zhu et al. (2014)). Recent methods employ deep learning approaches to detect object affordance. Nguyen et al. (2017) applies an object detector, CNN and dense conditional random fields to detect object affordance from RGB images. Persiani and Hellström (2019) extracts object-action pairs from web corpora using semantic role labelling. In contrast, we propose a crowd-sourced text only affordance dataset to audit the strength of SOTA LLMs and VLMs to reason about contextualized object affordance.

Probing methods. Talmor et al. (2020) utilizes probing and employs Multi-choice MLM (Masked Language Modelling) and Multi-choice QA (Question Answering) setup to capture reasoning capabilities of pre-trained Language Models. Yang et al. (2022) examines zero-shot prediction performances on different tasks by LLM through novel visual imagination. Aroca-Ouellette et al. (2021) highlights the shortcomings of state-of-the-art pre-trained models in physical reasoning, with a further performance decline observed when incorporating option shuffling and superlatives in reasoning questions. Liu et al. (2022) proposes a novel spatial commonsense probing framework to investigate object scales and positional relationship knowledge in text-based pre-trained models and models with visual signals. Joshi et al. (2020) uses probing methods to investigate a more fine-grained logical reasoning capabilities of pre-trained models.

Reasoning tasks and dataset. Reasoning about object affordance require a sort of commonsense reasoning. A series of works (Singh et al. (2021), et al. (2023), Bisk et al. (2019), Huang et al. (2019), Talmor et al. (2019), Talmor et al. (2021), Zellers et al. (2018)) study the text based commonsense knowledge of language models. Dataset such as δ-NLI (Rudinger et al., 2020) focuses on defeasible inference of commonsense knowledge; PaCo (Qasemi et al., 2022a) and PInKS (Qasemi et al., 2022b) deal with preconditioned commonsense inference of language models. PVLIR (Qasemi et al., 2023), Normlense (Han et al., 2023) use images as precoditions to reason about defeasible commonsense norms. However, none of these specifically focus on reasoning of object affordance. Wang et al. (2023) proposes a benchmark of object-attribute pairs plus a diverse set of questions to reason object's physical properties. Aroca-Ouellette et al. (2021) tackles physical and affordance reasoning from an object-centric approach. Persiani and Hellström (2019) attempts to extract common object-action pairs from web corpora. In Table 1, we demonstrate the comparison of TEXT2AFFORD with other datasets which perform different kind of reasoning tasks. We emphasize that, TEXT2AFFORD is the largest crowdsourced publicly available text based contextualized affordance dataset with a test size of 35,520 (2368 sentence-object pairs and 15 affordance classes).

Present work. Although a substantial number of work study the reasoning capabilities of language models and propose commonsense reasoning datasets, however, none of these work concentrate specifically on evaluating the knowledge of affordance and contextual affordance prediction *solely* from text. To bridge this gap, we present a reliable crowdsourced test dataset for identifying the contextualized affordance prediction capability of LLMs as well as VLMs. Our results show that the advanced large language models fail to understand an object's physical properties aka the affordances from texts, and there is significant room for improvement which may further motivate researchers to explore models that explicitly learns to *ground* objects in text to predict its physical properties and affordances.

3 TEXT2AFFORD dataset construction

We select $20,000$ sentences from a crowdsourced English dataset (XNLI English) (Conneau et al., 2018)[2] and extract the noun phrases using the Stanford CoreNLP tool. As we restrict to the affordances that humans can directly perform, we filter the phrases which do not represent a tangible object (using ConceptNet). We manually filter out objects that cannot be acted upon directly by humans (such as school, building). After this preprocessing, we obtain a set of sentence-object pairs $(\langle x_i, o_i \rangle)$, where the sentence acts as the context for the corresponding object. Each sentence on average has 2-3 such objects. We use the 15 predefined affordance classes from Zhu et al. (2014) to label each sentence-object pair for annotation.

We utilize the Toloka platform[3] for conducting the data annotation. We design an interface on this platform, containing clear instructions and examples for annotating the data. We conduct two rounds of pilot studies along with additional AMA (Ask Me Anything) sessions to analyze the subjective understanding of the annotators and, thereby, only select the high quality, serious annotators. A total of 114 annotators participated in the pilot study, and out of that we finally engage 25 skilled annotators to annotate a total of 2,368 sentence-object pairs each containing 15 affordance classes. Each datapoint (i.e., sentence-object pair along with an affordance class) has been annotated by *three* different annotators. We provide the details of the *pilot studies & annotator training* in Appendix A.1. By evaluating the complexity of the task for the annotators from the pilot studies, we intentionally consider a relatively small number of datapoints at a point for the annotation. This leads us to a total of 10 phases to complete the final annotation. We carefully reviewed each annotation and provided feedback with guidance in case of mistakes. For instance, annotators initially got confused with the affordance 'Watch' as human can *watch* any visual objects. In another instance, some annotators asked whether 'Throw' can be valid affordance for the object 'Kittens' as humans can perform 'Lift', 'Throw' to the object 'Kitten'. We discussed these types of ambiguities with the annotators after each phase. Throughout each of the data annotation phases, we put scrupulous attention to quality con-

[2]We choose XNLI as a source to facilitate multilingual extensions of our dataset.

[3]https://toloka.ai/

Agreement category	Affordance classes	Objects	Object-affordance pair
High agreement (>0.75)	Row, Feed, Ride, Fix	the horse, striped white shirts, a brown paper sack, Chinese lanterns, Adrin's sword, The movie	breakfast-Feed, a horse-Watch, crops-Fix, sports-Grasp, sports-Lift, sports-Push, the phone-Feed, football-Ride
Medium agreement (>0.4 & <0.75)	Throw, PourFrom, WriteWith, LookThrough, Lift, Grasp, Play, Push	A red flag, An arrow, Art, Automatic weapons, Babies, Black-and-white TV	computers-WriteWith, cats-Feed, football-Play, book-WriteWith, the door-Push
Low agreement (<0.4)	Watch, SitOn, TypeOn	Brandy from Spain, stone circles, iron, batteries, his fist, historical artifact, gift, olive oil, outdoor tables, bumper sticker on a car	weapon-Push, The table-Lift, boat-Fix, paintings-LookThrough, cats-Throw

Table 2: Agreement based on difficulty in disambiguating different affordance classes, objects and object-affordance pairs.

# of sentence-object pairs annotated	2368
# of affordance class	15
# of instances annotated	106560 (2368 $\times$ 15 $\times$ 3)
Avg # of objects / class	333
Most prominent class	Lift (851 objects)
Least prominent class	WriteWith (3 objects)
Total skilled annotators used	25
Avg agreement (Kripendorff's α)	0.68

Table 3: TEXT2AFFORD dataset statistics. # of instances annotated: (# of <s-o> pairs) * (# of classes) * (# of annotations per class).

trol, including iterative annotation refinement, and manual evaluation. The overall statistics for this *currently* constructed dataset – TEXT2AFFORD is in Table 3. The TEXT2AFFORD dataset consists of 2368 sentence-object pairs having $\sim 100k$ annotations (2368 $\times$ 15 $\times$ 3). For further details of the dataset construction, and our method of handling ambiguous scenarios, we refer the reader to Appendix A.1.

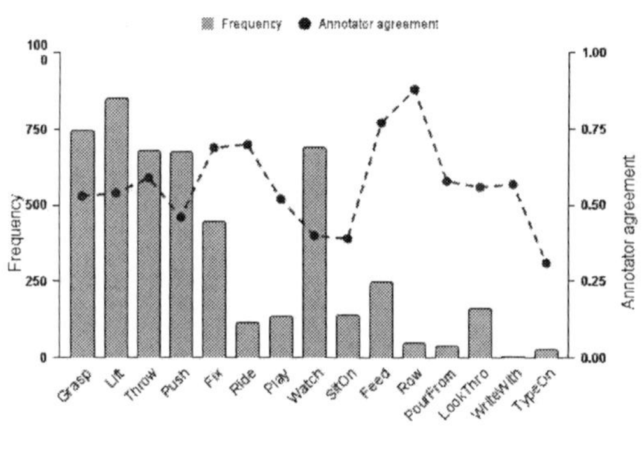

Figure 2: Classwise distribution of the number of objects and the annotator agreement.

TEXT2AFFORD data exploration. We observe that classes such as 'Grasp', 'Lift', 'Throw', 'Push', and 'Watch' are the most common affordances for the objects present in the dataset (see Figure 2). Most frequent objects and their corresponding agreement scores are shown in Appendix A.10 Fig. 8. We observe, agreement scores are fairly uniform (0.5-0.6) for frequent objects, with high agreement for some frequent objects (0.8 for "the movie"). In Figure 9 (see Appendix A.9), we also see that 'Grasp', 'Lift', and 'Throw' are highly correlated classes. There is similar positive correlation between the class 'SitOn' and 'Ride', and some correlation between 'Watch' and 'LookThrough'. In Table 2, we list down the affordance classes based on the annotator agreement score, and divide it into *three* categories to understand which of the affordance classes pose the most and least difficulties for the human annotators. We observe that the classes - 'Watch', 'SitOn', and 'TypeOn' are the most difficult to disambiguate. Further, to explore the difficulty of understanding contextual object affordance, we employ three *naïve annotators* to annotate some samples of the TEXT2AFFORD, and we observe that on an average in 88% cases the humans are able to predict affordance correctly, and in some cases the *context* introducing inherent difficulty for predicting affordance. Details of the study is provided in Appendix A.2.

4 Task description

Our first objective is to *audit* the strength of Large Language Models in identifying the pre-defined affordance classes of objects from text in zero-shot settings. Given a textual context, and the object, the task is to predict whether a particular affordance class is applicable to that object conditioned on the context. We majorly leverage 4 types of task setup for the experiments. For the encoder based models (e.g., RoBERTa, BERT) we choose Masked Language Modelling (MLM) and Natural Language Inference (NLI) based setup, and for the generative models we adopt 2 types of probing setup (text only, text+image) to formalize the task. Table 4 demonstrates different types of tasks that we engage for conducting the experiments from the TEXT2AFFORD dataset.

5 Experiments

We explore various state-of-the-art baselines using pre-trained language models (RoBERTa-large, BART-large), instruction-fine-tuned large language models (e.g., FLAN-T5, Falcon, ChatGPT, Llama-3), pre-trained multi-modal vision and language architectures (CLIP-ViT, ViLT, InstructBLIP,

Model architecture	Tasks	Input instance	Output
Encoder based	MLM	All the women in India wear bangles [SEP_TOKEN] bangles can be used for [MASK_TOKEN] by human	Probabilities of each affordance classes as the [MASK_TOKEN]
	NLI	premise: All the women in India wear bangles hypothesis: bangles can be used for <Affordance> by human	Entailment scores for each affordance classes
Generation based	Probing with text	Consider the sentence - 'All the women in India wear bangles'. Now, from this information can a human <Affordance> bangles? Answer YES or NO:	YES\NO
	Probing with text and image	 Consider the sentence - 'All the women in India wear bangles'. Now, from this information can a human <Affordance> bangles? Accompanying this query is an image of the bangles. Answer YES or NO:	YES\NO

Table 4: Overview of the tasks using TEXT2AFFORD. For detailed prompting see Appendix 10.

IDEFICS, LLaVA). We observe whether these models gain the knowledge of affordances through their pre-training, fine-tuning on commonsense tasks (NLI, PIQA), or few-shot fine-tuning scenarios.

5.1 Zero-shot affordance prediction

5.1.1 Pre-trained language models

We frame the zero-shot prediction task in different ways.

MLM based approach. Here, we pose the zero-shot task as masked word prediction problem. We choose BERT-large-uncased, RoBERTa-large (Zhuang et al., 2021), and BART-large (Lewis et al., 2020) models for the experiment. We pass the sentence and prompt separated by a `[SEP]` token as an input to the model. We use the prompt "`<Object> can be used for <MASK_TOKEN> by human`" and obtain the probability of each affordance label using the logit corresponding to the `<MASK_TOKEN>`.

Predictions from generative LLMs. We pose the task as 'YES\NO' questions-answering format and apply autoregressive language models such as FLAN-T5 (Chung et al., 2022) (large, xl, and xxl), Falcon (Almazrouei et al., 2023) (7b and 40b), Llama-3 [4], ChatGPT to get the predictions. We provide with a 'YES\NO' question-answer based prompt to the LLMs to predict whether a particular affordance can be performed on the given object. Based on rigorous prompt engineering we choose specific prompts for the different models as shown in the Appendix Table 10. We map 'YES\NO' predictions to 1\0 labels respectively.

5.1.2 Commonsense reasoning tasks

To understand whether the injection of the common sense knowledge in the pre-trained models can enhance the performance of the affordance prediction, we first fine-tune the pre-trained models on common sense reasoning dataset such as PIQA (Bisk et al., 2019). Then we run the fine-tuned models on our dataset using the MLM setup. We use BERT-base, BERT-large, RoBERTa-large, and BART-large models.

Apart from this, we leverage RoBERTa-large and BART-large fine-tuned on the Multi-genre NLI (MNLI) corpus (Williams et al., 2018) to evaluate on NLI setup. We utilize the sentence as premise and use the hypothesis as "*<object> can be used for <affordance> by human*" for each object-affordance pair, and use the entailment score to rank the affordance classes and report mAP and accuracy. Details of the experiment can be found in Appendix B.2.1.

5.1.3 Multimodal models

We explore both unimodal and multi-modal task setup for pre-trained vision and language models.

Text-only MLM setup

VLMs are pre-trained on large datasets having both image and text. The main goal of their pre-training is to capture some visual knowledge corresponding to the text while pre-training on multi-modal dataset such as image-caption pairs. To examine this, we first use the vision-language model CLIP, by providing only text prompt as the input and predict the affordance in an MLM setup.

Multimodal task setup

Images contain necessary information about shape, texture, and size of objects that can be utilized to effectively predict an object affordance (such as the handle of the bucket can be used to grasp and lift). Hence, we also convert the problem into a multi-modal task by synthesizing corresponding images from the context sentence, and predict the affordance of an object (mentioned in the sentence) based on the input.

Synthesizing images. In this setup, we use two different techniques to synthesize *semantically close* images to corresponding context sentences using 1) retrieval and 2) generation. We further use top five images for both, to get an accurate estimation.

Image retrieval: We use the CLIP (Radford et al.,

[4]`https://github.com/meta-llama/llama3`

2021) based sentence-transformers architecture to search for top five semantically similar images for each of the contexts from the Visualgenome (Krishna et al., 2017) dataset.

Image generation: We adopt the generative *StableDiffusion* (Rombach et al., 2022) model to generate top five images based on the sentence as a text prompt. Details can be found in the Appendix B.4.1.

We use the top five retrieved images by using retrieval and generation methods each. We use *CLIP* (Radford et al., 2021) and *ViLT* (Kim et al., 2021) as our vision-text models. CLIP has a text encoder f_T and a visual encoder f_V, which can project text and image into the shared latent space. We aggregate the k (=5) corresponding images and use CLIP to compute the relevance score of (x, y): $Score_{VI}(x, y) = \frac{1}{k}\sum_{i=1}^{K}\cos\left(f_T(x), f_v(I_y^k)\right)$, where I_y^k is the kth image for the input text y. In the ViLT model, we provide the text prompt along with the representative images as input to predict the masked token. We use the same prompt as the previous MLM task (i.e., "*<Object> can be used for <MASK_TOKEN> by human.*") and get the probability of each affordance class as the logit corresponding to the <MASK_TOKEN>.

Text generation based. Similar to section 5.1.1, we utilize state-of-the-art VLMs to make predictions regarding object affordances. We provide with a 'YES\NO' question answering based text prompt along with the aligned images as input to the VLMs, and the model should generate an answer whether a particular affordance can be performed on the given object. We use state-of-the-art VLMs such as IDEFICS (Laurençon et al., 2023), LLaVA (Liu et al., 2023b), InstructBLIP (Dai et al., 2023) for this task. The text prompt used for the models can be found in the Appendix D, Table 10.

Ensemble language and vision prediction. Following Yang et al. (2022), we use the weighted sum as the late fusion over the final output probabilities of each affordance class from the language and multi-modal models. Experimental details can be found in Appendix B.3.

5.2 Few-shot prediction

We conduct few-shot experiments by 1) fine-tuning the encoder based models, 2) randomly selecting 5 demonstration examples for the generative models to perform few-shot in-context learning (ICL). We consider the 62 annotated objects and corresponding 15 affordance classes by Zhu et al. (2014) for the few-shot based experiments.

Training data To create few-shot training examples for fine-tuning encoder based PTLMs, we take all the 62 objects, and for each object we randomly select exactly 1 positive affordance class (i.e., the class label annotated as 1) and 1 negative affordance class (i.e., the class label annotated as 0) for generating the training prompt. Overall they constitute 124 training examples (62 sentence-object pairs and 2 selected classes for each) for the few-shot experiment. For more details of the training data curation and the selection of examples for in-context learning, refer to Appendix B.4

Experimental setup. We fine-tune the encoder based language models using the training data, and for the generative LLMs and the VLMs, we utilize the training data to select in-context demonstration examples.

Fine-tuning PTLM: We fine-tune the encoder based PTLMs in NLI based setup having the context sentence as premise and use same hypothesis (i.e., "<object> can be used for <affordance> by human") which we use in the zero-shot settings. We use BERT-large-uncased, RoBERTa-large and BART-large for fine-tuning in this setup. For implementation details refer to Appendix B.4

In-context learning for generative models: We employ the same generative LLMs as well as VLMs to perform affordance prediction using *five* demonstration examples from the training data. We use the same text prompt as zero-shot setting and concatenate the five demonstration examples along with corresponding label (i.e., 'NO' for positive class, and 'NO' for the negative class) to the prompt and ask the LLMs and VLMs to predict the affordance. In case of the VLMs, we do not provide any additional image example here.

6 Benchmarking TEXT2AFFORD prediction

Evaluation metric. To assess the performance of the zero-shot affordance prediction, we calculate accuracy in the following way. Each affordance class is treated as a binary classification problem, where a value of 1 represents a positive class indicating that the affordance can be performed on the object, and a value of 0 represents a negative class indicating that the affordance cannot be performed. For each positive class $\in \{P_1, P_2, ..P_n\}$, we compare the predicted scores of that affordance class with the predicted scores of the negative classes $\in \{N_1, N_2, ..N_m\}$. If the predicted score of the positive class is higher than the predicted score of all the negative classes (i.e., $p(P_i) > p(N_j)_{\forall j}$), we increment the correct count by 1[5]. Conversely, if the predicted score of the negative class is higher, we increment the wrong count by 1. The final accuracy is calculated by dividing the total number of correct counts by the total number of the instances. To rank the affordance classes based on the predicted score, we also report the Mean Average Precision (mAP@K, where K is the number of affordance classes).

Model	Actual		Fine-tuned		LM + VI (CLIP)		LM + VI (ViLT)	
Encoder based								
NLI based								
	Acc	mAP	Acc	mAP	Acc	mAP	Acc	mAP
RoBERTa-large-mnli	0.64	0.43	0.72	0.49	**0.79**	0.52	**0.79**	**0.54**
BART-large-mnli	0.65	0.38	0.69	0.48	0.62	0.4	0.64	0.43
MLM based								
BERT-large-uncased	0.46	0.26	0.58	0.33	0.55	0.38	0.53	0.37
RoBERTa-large	0.55	0.36	**0.77**	**0.49**	0.61	0.41	0.62	0.43
BART-large	0.47	0.28	0.65	0.38	0.56	0.35	0.52	0.34
Multi-modal models (zero-shot)								
CLIP-VIT (text-only)	0.47	0.34	-	-	-	-	-	-
CLIP-VIT (retrieval)	0.56	0.35	-	-	-	-	-	-
CLIP-VIT (generation)	**0.61**	**0.4**	-	-	-	-	-	-
ViLT (retrieval)	0.41	0.31	-	-	-	-	-	-
ViLT (generation)	0.44	0.32	-	-	-	-	-	-

Table 5: Performance for affordance prediction using encoder based models. Acc: Accuracy, LM: Language model, VI: Vision. Only LMs are ensembled with VI. The best results are in bold.

Generation based		
Predictions from generative LLM		
Model	**Acc (zero-shot)**	**Acc (ICL)**
Random baseline	0.18	-
FLAN-T5-large	0.06	0.13±0.04
FLAN-T5-xl	0.07	0.21±0.03
FLAN-T5-xxl	0.33	0.39±0.04
Falcon-7b-instruct	0.19	0.24±0.03
Falcon-40b-instruct	**0.43**	**0.47**±0.06
Llama-3-8b-instruct	0.36	0.43±0.05
ChatGPT (GPT-3.5 turbo)	0.41	0.44±0.05

Multi-modal models				
Model	**Acc (zero-shot)**		**Acc (ICL)**	
	IR based	**IG based**	**IR based**	**IG based**
Idefics-9b-instruct	0.26	0.25	0.36±0.02	0.37±0.03
Llava-1.5-7b	0.32	0.34	0.36±0.03	0.40±0.04
InstructBlip-vicuna-13b	0.37	0.39	0.43±0.03	0.45±0.03
InstructBlip-flan-t5-xl	0.12	0.16	0.15±0.02	0.18±0.02
InstructBlip-flan-t5-xxl	0.39	**0.45**	0.48±0.04	**0.53**±0.05

Table 6: Zero-shot and in-context learning (ICL) performance for affordance prediction using generative models. IR: Image Retrieval; IG: Image Generation. Number of demonstration examples used for ICL = 5. We also mention the variance over different selections of examples. The best results are in bold.

Zero-shot performance. Table 5 shows the results of the zero-shot affordance predictions from the mentioned models. The second column (i.e., Actual) indicates the values from the original LM and multi-modal models. The third and fourth columns (i.e., LM + VI) indicate the performances of ensembling language models with two of the multi-modal models we used. We observe that, the PTLMs have some knowledge about object affordances, but they still lack the comprehensive reasoning ability about these affordances, which is reflected in the low mAP values. Further, the performances vary across different settings. In case of NLI based setup, the fine-tuned RoBERTa and BART models show improvement in the performance, which indicates that *during fine-tuning on MNLI dataset, those models gain some reasoning ability.* In Table 6 we show the generation based results in a zero-shot setting. In case of FLAN-T5-large model, where we use it to predict a binary label (YES\NO) for an affordance class, the performance drops significantly (the accuracy is less than 7%). This shows that there are still some challenges for the text-to-text models in general reasoning ability about the object affordances. In addition, we find that, the multi-modal models do not perform well in text-only settings, despite being pretrained on text and image data. The performances of the language models get boosted when ensembling with the multi-modal models, which indicates that the prediction of object affordance from sentence is a difficult task, and can be enhanced in presence of images. In addition to evaluating generative models, we establish a random baseline (Detailed in Appendix B.1). Interestingly, we find that models like Flan-T5-large and Flan-T5-XL underperform compared to this random baseline in zero-shot settings.

MLM based		
Model	**Accuracy**	**mAP**
BERT-base-uncased-finetuned-piqa	0.45	0.26
BERT-large-uncased-finetuned-piqa	0.56	0.29
RoBERTa-large-finetuned-piqa	**0.64**	**0.45**
BART-large-finetuned-piqa	0.59	0.35

Table 7: Affordance prediction using models trained on commonsense data. Best results are marked in bold.

Finetuning on commonsense datasets. We observe that the fine-tuned model on commonsense reasoning task (Table 7) show improved performance for the affordance prediction task. This indicates that the pre-trained models lack the reasoning of object affordance. Interestingly, we find that the smallest BERT-base model fine-tuned on PIQA, performs almost similar to that of the BERT-large or BART-large models (see Table 5).

Few-shot performance. We find that, in presence of few examples from our affordance dataset, the

[5]During calculation we discard the cases when there is no positive class for a sentence-object pair in the ground truth. We do not find any instance where no negative class is present.

reasoning capability about object affordances can be enhanced for the PTLMs. The results with 124 shots (62 pairs as discussed earlier) are noted in Table 5. In Table 6, we note the results for the in-context learning performance of the generative LLMs and VLMs. We observe a significant performance gain over zero-shot settings. Having said that, we also observe that, even with the in-context learning, the performance of the generative models (with more than 7b parameters) do not reach even close to the performance of the fine-tuned BERT-large model (340M parameters). This suggests that, for the specific affordance prediction tasks from text, finetuning is absolutely essential even for the state-of-the-art LLMs and VLMs.

Error analysis

Encoder based models. We conducted a qualitative analysis of the erroneous cases for the two models (BART-large and RoBerta-large) in MNLI settings to understand what are the typical causes of errors. We take examples where accuracy is below 0.3. Consider the representative example below.

> *Sentence: The salt from La Mata is often used as table salt. Object: table salt*
> Top 5 predicted affordances (according to the probability score) - ['sitOn', 'pourFrom', 'grasp', 'fix', 'lookThrough']

The model predicts 'SitOn' as the top affordance for table salt, implying that the model misinterprets "table salt" with "table". Similarly, for the object "the window sill", the model predicts 'lookThrough', 'watch' as top affordances, which again suggests that the model is confused between "the window sill" and a "window". In another case, the model predicts ['grasp', 'writing', 'typing', 'lookThrough', 'throw'] as the top affordance labels for the object "any rock concerts".

Analysis of generative models. In Appendix Figure 6a, we plot the correlation between error rate made by chatGPT for each affordance classes and the classwise annotator agreement. We observe a moderately negative correlation ($\rho = -0.29$) which suggests that there is a chance that the model is making higher mispredictions where the agreement is low. Similarly we observe that the mispredictions made by chatGPT for the most frequent objects has a moderately negative correlation ($\rho = -0.58$) with the annotator agreement. The correlation is shown in Figure 6b. The trends are similar for the other LLMs. These results together indicate that those objects and affordance classes which are hard to disambiguate by humans also pose a challenge to the most sophisticated GenAI models in predicting the correct answer.

7 TEXT2AFFORD for physical reasoning

Apart from benchmarking LLMs and VLMs, we observe whether Text2Afford can be used as a source of affordance knowledge. We choose the physical commonsense reasoning as a target as the 'Object affordance' represents an innate physical property of an object, and we believe that any language model having strong affordance reasoning capability can enhance the physical reasoning capability. To explore this, we perform an 'instruction fine-tuning' on the TEXT2AFFORD dataset (although it is not meant for training) using few open-source LLMs (`llama-3-8b-instruct`, `flan-t5`), and test on two physical reasoning dataset - (1) PROST (Aroca-Ouellette et al., 2021), which contains 10 types of different physical properties of an object (including 6 affordance properties - rolling, breaking, stacking, grasping, sliding, bouncing) along with complex reasoning questions, and (2) PIQA (Bisk et al., 2019) which, focuses on selecting appropriate option given a situation that requires physical commonsense.

For PROST, using `llama-3` the accuracy boosts from 0.36 to 0.42 after instruct fine-tuning with TEXT2AFFORD. Moreover, out of the 6 affordance properties from PROST, the accuracy got boosted for the reasoning of 5 affordance properties. For the PIQA, the same LLM gives a maximum of 4% accuracy boost. The full result is shown in Table 8. This suggest the generalizability of TEXT2AFFORD in physical reasoning tasks.

Model	Dataset			
	PROST		PIQA	
	Zero-shot	+TEXT2AFFORD	Zero-shot	+TEXT2AFFORD
`Llama-3-8b`	0.36	0.42(**+.06**)*	0.74	0.78(**+.04**)*
`FLAN-T5-xl`	0.13	0.16(**+.03**)	0.57	0.59(**+.02**)
`FLAN-T5-xxl`	0.34	0.38(**+.04**)*	0.72	0.75(**+.03**)

Table 8: Text-only physical reasoning dataset evaluation using different LLMs fine-tuned on TEXT2AFFORD. +TEXT2AFFORD: instruction fine-tuned on TEXT2AFFORD. * indicates p-value (< 0.05) using Mann-Whitney U-Test.

8 Additional details

Reason for choosing XNLI. We select XNLI to incorporate object references from less conventional and commonly explored scenarios. Unlike typical object identification datasets, XNLI offers sentences derived from novels, thus presenting a more in-the-wild textual context, which adds complexity and diversity to our dataset. Specifically, we choose the hypothesis portion of the XNLI sentences due to its shorter context length. This choice intentionally poses a challenge to LLMs, allowing us to better evaluate their reasoning capabilities, especially when dealing with minimal contextual information.

Non-explicit mention about contextual object affordance in the instruction. The instructions shown in Appendix Figure 3 represent the initial guidance provided to annotators as an introduction to the task. Since understanding contextual object affordance can be challenging for non-expert annotators, this initial step was designed to give a basic idea of the task. However, we follow this up with a comprehensive training process and conduct two AMA (Ask Me Anything) sessions to ensure that annotators fully understood the need to base their judgments on the provided context. These efforts are key in ensuring high-quality annotations throughout the dataset creation.

Reason for choosing 0-3 Likert scale in data annotation. We opt for a 0-3 Likert scale (4-point) to minimize the potential for neutral or noncommittal responses, which can often arise when a midpoint option is available. Our initial observations indicated that some annotators tended to select an "average" value without fully considering the contextual affordance of the objects, which diminished the depth of their evaluations and limited the discussion around ambiguities. By adopting a 4-point scale, we aim to encourage more decisive judgments. In addition, we provide a textbox (see Appendix Figure 3) for annotators to express any uncertainties or ambiguities they encountered, which has helped us in capturing more nuanced feedback.

Reason for choosing visual genome. We chose visual genome as a primary source for real images due to its rich, complex scenes, which are widely used in visual reasoning tasks. The complexity of the images in visual genome provides diverse contexts that align well with the goals of our study, which focuses on contextual object affordances. While other methods, such as using search engines like Bing, have been employed in prior work to retrieve images, we opt for visual genome to ensure that the images contain sufficient contextual and visual detail to support affordance prediction, even if there are minor limitations in reasoning.

Reason for choosing stable diffusion. Regarding the use of stable diffusion, we have been inspired by its demonstrated capability to generate high-quality, realistic images, particularly in prior studies where it was effective in reasoning tasks. While CLIP is primarily trained on real-world images, we hypothesize that stable diffusion could generate contextual images with sufficient accuracy to complement the real images. The generated images provide additional diversity, which helps us explore the affordance prediction task from a different angle. The benefit of using stable diffusion lies in its ability to create controlled, context-specific images that may not always be available in existing datasets, providing a broader range of testing scenarios for our models.

Reason for framing generative tasks as a binary decision problem. In the generative setting, we opt for a binary yes/no classification to evaluate the affordance of individual context-object-affordance triples. We decide this based on the observation of the tendency of smaller LLMs to hallucinate, which can make direct affordance prediction challenging, particularly in zero-shot scenarios. By framing it as a binary classification task, we aim to simplify the evaluation and obtain more reliable results. In addition, our approach allows for a comprehensive evaluation of both positive and negative affordances. This is critical for our dataset, as it is designed to assess affordances that are applicable, as well as those that are not, in a given context.

9 Conclusion

In this paper we introduced a novel text-based affordance dataset TEXT2AFFORD to investigate the affordance knowledge of PTLMs and pre-trained VLMs in different zero-shot settings. Our findings suggest that, the state-of-the-art language models, particularly text-to-text models, still exhibit limitations in their ability to reason about object affordances. In this seemingly easy task, we observe how context can introduce various levels of ambiguity and difficulty. We also observe, that even in the presence of such difficulty, human performance is superior and LLMs/VLMs still face difficulty in gaining such knowledge during their pretraining. Additionally, we observe how our dataset provides some additional knowledge that can be useful for physical commonsense reasoning – stressing its orthogonality more with respect to the pretraining knowledge LLMs and VLMs possess.

Acknowledgments

We would like to express our sincere gratitude to our co-authors for their invaluable contributions throughout this work. We also extend our thanks to the reviewers for their constructive feedback, which significantly helped improve the quality of the paper. Additionally, we gratefully acknowledge the support of the Toloka Research Grant program, which partially funded the data annotation process.

Limitations

All of our experiments were conducted for English language. The models may act differently in multilingual settings. Our dataset is curated based on a specific set of affordance classes, which may introduce bias in terms of affordance representation. This could limit the generalizability of our findings to other domains or contexts. Despite efforts to train annotators and ensure agreement, subjective interpretations of affordance classes, can introduce noise. Our study primarily relies on textual information for affordance prediction. The absence of grounded visual information may limit the model's ability to accurately predict affordances, as some affordances may be more visually dependent.

Ethics Statement

We used the publicly available XNLI corpus to curate our TEXT2AFFORD dataset. Our dataset does not contain any harmful or offensive contents. Any personal or sensitive information is anonymized and treated with utmost confidentiality. We ensure the protection of participants' privacy and obtain informed consent for data collection, annotation, and analysis. We incentivized all the annotators uniformly throughout the annotation process.

References

Ebtesam Almazrouei, Hamza Alobeidli, Abdulaziz Alshamsi, Alessandro Cappelli, Ruxandra Cojocaru, Mérouane Debbah, Étienne Goffinet, Daniel Hesslow, Julien Launay, Quentin Malartic, Daniele Mazzotta, Badreddine Noune, Baptiste Pannier, and Guilherme Penedo. 2023. The falcon series of open language models.

Stéphane Aroca-Ouellette, Cory Paik, Alessandro Roncone, and Katharina Kann. 2021. PROST: Physical reasoning about objects through space and time. In *Findings ACL-IJCNLP 2021*.

Emily M. Bender and Alexander Koller. 2020. Climbing towards NLU: On meaning, form, and understanding in the age of data. In *ACL*.

Chandra Bhagavatula, Ronan Le Bras, Chaitanya Malaviya, Keisuke Sakaguchi, Ari Holtzman, Hannah Rashkin, Doug Downey, Wen tau Yih, and Yejin Choi. 2020. Abductive commonsense reasoning. In *International Conference on Learning Representations*.

Yonatan Bisk, Rowan Zellers, Ronan Le Bras, Jianfeng Gao, and Yejin Choi. 2019. Piqa: Reasoning about physical commonsense in natural language. In *AAAI Conference on Artificial Intelligence*.

Hyung Won Chung, Le Hou, Shayne Longpre, Barret Zoph, Yi Tay, William Fedus, Yunxuan Li, Xuezhi Wang, Mostafa Dehghani, Siddhartha Brahma, Albert Webson, Shixiang Shane Gu, Zhuyun Dai, Mirac Suzgun, Xinyun Chen, Aakanksha Chowdhery, Alex Castro-Ros, Marie Pellat, Kevin Robinson, Dasha Valter, Sharan Narang, Gaurav Mishra, Adams Yu, Vincent Zhao, Yanping Huang, Andrew Dai, Hongkun Yu, Slav Petrov, Ed H. Chi, Jeff Dean, Jacob Devlin, Adam Roberts, Denny Zhou, Quoc V. Le, and Jason Wei. 2022. Scaling instruction-finetuned language models.

Alexis Conneau, Ruty Rinott, Guillaume Lample, Adina Williams, Samuel R. Bowman, Holger Schwenk, and Veselin Stoyanov. 2018. Xnli: Evaluating cross-lingual sentence representations. In *EMNLP*.

Wenliang Dai, Junnan Li, Dongxu Li, Anthony Meng Huat Tiong, Junqi Zhao, Weisheng Wang, Boyang Li, Pascale Fung, and Steven Hoi. 2023. Instructblip: Towards general-purpose vision-language models with instruction tuning.

Nam Do and Ellie Pavlick. 2021. Are rotten apples edible? challenging commonsense inference ability with exceptions. In *Findings of the Association for Computational Linguistics: ACL-IJCNLP 2021*.

Srivastava et al. 2023. Beyond the imitation game: Quantifying and extrapolating the capabilities of language models. *Transactions on Machine Learning Research*.

James J. Gibson. 1979. *The Ecological Approach to Visual Perception*. Houghton Mifflin, Boston.

Seungju Han, Junhyeok Kim, Jack Hessel, Liwei Jiang, Jiwan Chung, Yejin Son, Yejin Choi, and Youngjae Yu. 2023. Reading books is great, but not if you are driving! visually grounded reasoning about defeasible commonsense norms. In *EMNLP*.

Simeng Han, Hailey Schoelkopf, Yilun Zhao, Zhenting Qi, Martin Riddell, Luke Benson, Lucy Sun, Ekaterina Zubova, Yujie Qiao, Matthew Burtell, David Peng, Jonathan Fan, Yixin Liu, Brian Wong, Malcolm Sailor, Ansong Ni, Linyong Nan, Jungo Kasai, Tao Yu, Rui Zhang, Shafiq Joty, Alexander R. Fabbri, Wojciech Kryscinski, Xi Victoria Lin, Caiming

Xiong, and Dragomir Radev. 2022. Folio: Natural language reasoning with first-order logic.

Weinan He, Canming Huang, Yongmei Liu, and Xiaodan Zhu. 2021. WinoLogic: A zero-shot logic-based diagnostic dataset for Winograd Schema Challenge. In *Proceedings of the 2021 conference on empirical methods in natural language processing*.

Lifu Huang, Ronan Le Bras, Chandra Bhagavatula, and Yejin Choi. 2019. Cosmos QA: Machine reading comprehension with contextual commonsense reasoning. Hong Kong, China.

Woojeong Jin, Tejas Srinivasan, Jesse Thomason, and Xiang Ren. 2024. Winoviz: Probing visual properties of objects under different states.

Pratik Joshi, Somak Aditya, Aalok Sathe, and Monojit Choudhury. 2020. Taxinli: Taking a ride up the nlu hill. In *Proceedings of the 24th Conference on Computational Natural Language Learning*, pages 41–55.

Wonjae Kim, Bokyung Son, and Ildoo Kim. 2021. Vilt: Vision-and-language transformer without convolution or region supervision. In *International Conference on Machine Learning*, pages 5583–5594. PMLR.

Ranjay Krishna, Yuke Zhu, Oliver Groth, Justin Johnson, Kenji Hata, Joshua Kravitz, Stephanie Chen, Yannis Kalantidis, Li-Jia Li, David A Shamma, et al. 2017. Visual genome: Connecting language and vision using crowdsourced dense image annotations. *International journal of computer vision*, 123:32–73.

Hugo Laurençon, Lucile Saulnier, Léo Tronchon, Stas Bekman, Amanpreet Singh, Anton Lozhkov, Thomas Wang, Siddharth Karamcheti, Alexander M Rush, Douwe Kiela, et al. 2023. Obelisc: An open web-scale filtered dataset of interleaved image-text documents. *arXiv preprint arXiv:2306.16527*.

Mike Lewis, Yinhan Liu, Naman Goyal, Marjan Ghazvininejad, Abdelrahman Mohamed, Omer Levy, Veselin Stoyanov, and Luke Zettlemoyer. 2020. Bart: Denoising sequence-to-sequence pre-training for natural language generation, translation, and comprehension. In *ACL*, pages 7871–7880.

Hanmeng Liu, Jian Liu, Leyang Cui, Zhiyang Teng, Nan Duan, Ming Zhou, and Yue Zhang. 2023a. Logiqa 2.0—an improved dataset for logical reasoning in natural language understanding. *IEEE/ACM Transactions on Audio, Speech, and Language Processing*, 31:2947–2962.

Haotian Liu, Chunyuan Li, Qingyang Wu, and Yong Jae Lee. 2023b. Visual instruction tuning. In *NeurIPS*.

Jian Liu, Leyang Cui, Hanmeng Liu, Dandan Huang, Yile Wang, and Yue Zhang. 2021. Logiqa: a challenge dataset for machine reading comprehension with logical reasoning. In *Proceedings of the Twenty-Ninth International Conference on International Joint Conferences on Artificial Intelligence*, IJCAI'20.

Xiao Liu, Da Yin, Yansong Feng, and Dongyan Zhao. 2022. Things not written in text: Exploring spatial commonsense from visual signals. *arXiv preprint arXiv:2203.08075*.

Anh Nguyen, Dimitrios Kanoulas, Darwin G Caldwell, and Nikos G Tsagarakis. 2017. Object-based affordances detection with convolutional neural networks and dense conditional random fields. In *2017 IEEE/RSJ International Conference on Intelligent Robots and Systems (IROS)*, pages 5908–5915. IEEE.

Yixin Nie, Adina Williams, Emily Dinan, Mohit Bansal, Jason Weston, and Douwe Kiela. 2020. Adversarial NLI: A new benchmark for natural language understanding.

Timothy Niven and Hung-Yu Kao. 2019. Probing neural network comprehension of natural language arguments.

Michele Persiani and Thomas Hellström. 2019. Unsupervised inference of object affordance from text corpora.

Ehsan Qasemi, Filip Ilievski, Muhao Chen, and Pedro Szekely. 2022a. PaCo: Preconditions attributed to commonsense knowledge.

Ehsan Qasemi, Piyush Khanna, Qiang Ning, and Muhao Chen. 2022b. PInKS: Preconditioned commonsense inference with minimal supervision. Online only.

Ehsan Qasemi, Amani R. Maina-Kilaas, Devadutta Dash, Khalid Alsaggaf, and Muhao Chen. 2023. Preconditioned visual language inference with weak supervision.

Alec Radford, Jong Wook Kim, Chris Hallacy, Aditya Ramesh, Gabriel Goh, Sandhini Agarwal, Girish Sastry, Amanda Askell, Pamela Mishkin, Jack Clark, et al. 2021. Learning transferable visual models from natural language supervision. In *International conference on machine learning*, pages 8748–8763. PMLR.

Aditya Ramesh, Prafulla Dhariwal, Alex Nichol, Casey Chu, and Mark Chen. 2022. Hierarchical text-conditional image generation with clip latents.

Robin Rombach, Andreas Blattmann, Dominik Lorenz, Patrick Esser, and Björn Ommer. 2022. High-resolution image synthesis with latent diffusion models. In *Proceedings of the IEEE/CVF Conference on Computer Vision and Pattern Recognition*, pages 10684–10695.

Rachel Rudinger, Vered Shwartz, Jena D. Hwang, Chandra Bhagavatula, Maxwell Forbes, Ronan Le Bras, Noah A. Smith, and Yejin Choi. 2020. Thinking like a skeptic: Defeasible inference in natural language. In *Findings EMNLP 2020*.

Chitwan Saharia, William Chan, Saurabh Saxena, Lala Li, Jay Whang, Emily Denton, Seyed Kamyar Seyed Ghasemipour, Burcu Karagol Ayan, S. Sara Mahdavi, Rapha Gontijo Lopes, Tim Salimans, Jonathan Ho, David J Fleet, and Mohammad Norouzi. 2022. Photorealistic text-to-image diffusion models with deep language understanding.

Shikhar Singh, Nuan Wen, Yu Hou, Pegah Alipoormolabashi, Te-lin Wu, Xuezhe Ma, and Nanyun Peng. 2021. COM2SENSE: A commonsense reasoning benchmark with complementary sentences. Online.

Yu Sun, Shaogang Ren, and Yun Lin. 2014. Object–object interaction affordance learning. *Robotics and Autonomous Systems*, 62(4):487–496.

Alon Talmor, Yanai Elazar, Yoav Goldberg, and Jonathan Berant. 2020. olmpics-on what language model pre-training captures. *TACL*, 8:743–758.

Alon Talmor, Jonathan Herzig, Nicholas Lourie, and Jonathan Berant. 2019. CommonsenseQA: A question answering challenge targeting commonsense knowledge.

Alon Talmor, Ori Yoran, Ronan Le Bras, Chandra Bhagavatula, Yoav Goldberg, Yejin Choi, and Jonathan Berant. 2021. CommonsenseQA 2.0: Exposing the limits of AI through gamification.

Yi Wang, Jiafei Duan, Dieter Fox, and Siddhartha Srinivasa. 2023. NEWTON: Are large language models capable of physical reasoning? In *Findings EMNLP 2023*.

Adina Williams, Nikita Nangia, and Samuel Bowman. 2018. A broad-coverage challenge corpus for sentence understanding through inference. In *Proceedings of the 2018 Conference of the North American Chapter of the Association for Computational Linguistics: Human Language Technologies, Volume 1 (Long Papers)*, pages 1112–1122, New Orleans, Louisiana. Association for Computational Linguistics.

Yue Yang, Wenlin Yao, Hongming Zhang, Xiaoyang Wang, Dong Yu, and Jianshu Chen. 2022. Z-LaVI: Zero-shot language solver fueled by visual imagination. In *Proceedings of the 2022 Conference on EMNLP*.

Rowan Zellers, Yonatan Bisk, Roy Schwartz, and Yejin Choi. 2018. SWAG: A large-scale adversarial dataset for grounded commonsense inference. In *Proceedings of the 2018 Conference on EMNLP*.

Yuke Zhu, Alireza Fathi, and Li Fei-Fei. 2014. Reasoning about object affordances in a knowledge base representation. In *ECCV*, pages 408–424. Springer.

Liu Zhuang, Lin Wayne, Shi Ya, and Zhao Jun. 2021. A robustly optimized BERT pre-training approach with post-training. In *Proceedings of the 20th Chinese National Conference on Computational Linguistics*.

Appendices

A Data annotation

A.1 Details of the TEXT2AFFORD dataset construction

Preprocessing. We select $20,000$ sentences from a crowdsourced English dataset (XNLI English) (Conneau et al., 2018)[6] and extract the noun phrases using the Stanford CoreNLP tool. As we restrict to the affordances that humans can directly perform, we filter the phrases which do not represent a tangible object (using ConceptNet). We manually filter out objects that cannot be acted upon directly by humans (such as school, building). After this preprocessing, we obtain a set of sentence-object pairs ($\langle x_i, o_i \rangle$), where the sentence acts as the context for the corresponding object. Each sentence on average has 2-3 such objects. We use the 15 predefined affordance classes from Zhu et al. (2014) to label each sentence-object pair for annotation.

We further expand our dataset with the labeled dataset provided by Zhu et al. (2014). Authors present 62 common objects and their corresponding 15 affordance labels. Given that our task is *context-based affordance* prediction, we require to have sentence-object pairs for labelling. To generate diverse context for this dataset, we utilize the ChatGPT UI[7 8] model to generate synthetic sentences for each of the objects, followed by careful manual correction.

Pilot studies & annotator training. We annotate the dataset using the Toloka platform[9]. We design an interface on this platform, which contained clear instructions and examples for annotating the data. We conduct two rounds of pilot studies to analyze the subjective understanding of the annotators and, thereby, filter out the high quality, serious annotators. For the first pilot study, we present the annotators with the smaller 62 sentence-object pairs and ask them to label the instance with each affordance class on a scale of 0 to 3, indicating whether or not the affordance can be performed on the object. Here, 0-1 indicates that the affordance cannot be performed (high-low) and 2-3 indicates that the affordance can be performed low-high). We will further use these 62 synthetic sentence-object pairs for few-shot training. For quality control, we select the top 90% of the available annotators in the platform, who are proficient in English, and use computers to complete the tasks[10]. A total of 15 annotators labelled the data, and all of them were incentivized uniformly. After the first pilot, we find that there is an extremely poor agreement among the annotators, and the overall precision is around 28%. Therefore, we moved on to a second pilot study. Here, we use all the 62 sentence-object pairs from the previous study, along with 32 randomly selected sentence-object pairs from the XNLI data. We use the top 30% of the annotators (based on the quality determined by the platform) available on the platform, while other criteria remained the same. We annotate 32 sentence-object pairs ourselves, and use all the labelled examples as *control* data points to guide the annotators while labelling. A total of 114 annotators (including the 14 annotators from the first pilot study) participated in this version of the pilot study. We assign a specific skill to the annotators who attained more than 30% precision and 30% recall. In total, 48 annotators passed this criteria. Through initial pilot studies, we learnt that without grounded images, the task appears quite subjective to annotators. The main goal of the pilot studies have been to understand the annotators' quality, their comprehension of the task, and their preferences for incentives per task. We have also conducted two additional AMA (Ask Me Anything) sessions with interested annotators to further clarify the task.

Final annotation. In the final phase, we conduct the annotation on a larger set of sentence-object pairs, carefully selecting a total of 2,368 pairs. To ensure diverse perspectives and minimize bias, we engage 25 skilled annotators in this phase. Three annotators independently annotated each of the sentence-object pairs. Each annotator meticulously evaluated the affordance classes for every pair, contributing to a comprehensive annotation of the dataset. We perform the annotations in phases and complete the full task over 10 phases.

Reason for multiple annotation phases. We intentionally consider relatively small number of data points for annotation in a single phase to make the review process easier. We carefully reviewed each annotation and provided feedback with guidance

[6] We choose XNLI as a source to facilitate multilingual extensions of our dataset.

[7] https://chat.openai.com

[8] Prompt used: Can you make realistic sentences with the following objects? Followed by the list of object names.

[9] https://toloka.ai/

[10] We exclude mobile-users as we believe the instructions may not appear clearly on mobile devices.

in case of mistakes. For instance, annotators initially got confused with the affordance 'Watch' as human can *watch* any visual objects. In another instance, some annotators asked whether 'Throw' can be valid affordance for the object 'Kittens' as humans can perform 'Lift', 'Throw' to the object 'Kitten'. We discussed these types of ambiguities with the annotators after each phase. We measured class-wise agreement and average agreement across all classes after each annotation phase to ensure the quality of the annotations. The overall statistics for this *currently* constructed dataset – TEXT2AFFORD is in Table 3. Throughout the data processing pipeline, we put scrupulous attention to the quality control, including the use of pilot studies, iterative annotation refinement, and manual filtering. These measures ensure that the dataset is comprehensive, accurate, aligned with the objectives of the study and can be reliably reused in future. Overall, our TEXT2AFFORD dataset consists of 2368 sentence-object pairs having $\sim 100k$ annotations ($2368 \times 15 \times 3$).

A.2 Additional analysis on the datapoints by human

To further interpret the difficulty (or ambiguity) of the datapoints, we filter out the "sentence-object-affordance" triples based on the percentage annotator agreement. We categorize the triples into 3 sections:

Agreement $>$ 0.75: Total 26,411 triples
0.4<Agreement $<$ 0.75: Total 7,084 triples
Agreement $<$ 0.4: Total 2,025 triples

In general, the average agreement is higher for negative affordance classes than that of positive classes, which implies that it is easier for humans to tell which 'affordance' is not applicable to a particular object.

We employ three postgraduate students and provide them with the same set of instructions. We randomly sample 200 datapoints from the high agreement category (>0.75), and 200 samples from the low agreement category (<0.4) and ask to annotate independently. For the high agreement category scenario, we observe that in 86%, 87%, 91% of the cases their answers aligned with the majority voted answers. For the low agreement category, in most of the cases they feel there is not enough information in the context to answer about affordance. In some cases, it was easier to tell the affordance of the object alone, but the context made it difficult to answer. For example:
Context: "SCR systems are primarily made from tree branches , lime and sawdust ." Can a human "Sit On" tree branches?
Without the context, it is easier to say "Yes".

A.3 Comparison with other reasoning dataset

A.4 Instruction page on the Toloka platform

Figure 3 shows the guidelines/instructions, that the annotators had to follow for labelling.

A.5 Interface for labelling

A sample task interface is shown in Figure 4.

A.6 Annotators demographics

Figure 5 provides the demographic information about the annotators. We can observe that a large number of annotators (36%) are from Russia and most of the annotators having the age in between 20-35.

A.7 Phasewise annotator agreement

We plot the soft agreement[11], hard agreement[12] in Figure 7, which shows gradual increase in agreement scores.

A.8 Incentive details

During the pilot study, we provided USD 0.05 per task-suite where in each task-suite, there were 10 examples (15 affordance labels for each example) to be answered. We attempted to take feedback from the tolokers who had answered randomly (e.g., mark all the values as 0), to understand their requirements properly. Most of them suggested that a wage of $0.1 to $0.15 would be ideal for the survey.

During the main study we provided USD 0.25 per task-suite, where in each task-suite there were 5 examples to be answered. Some of them were consistently providing good answers and few of them also suggested improvement on the objects. We awarded them with an additional bonus of USD 0.5. Overall, we spent USD 777 for the annotation process.

[11]Soft agreement: Mapping Likert scale ratings to binary labels for measuring agreement by applying a threshold value.

[12]Hard agreement: Treating each Likert scale rating as a distinct label.

Dataset	Train size	Dev size	Test size	Reasoning type	Source	Image-dependent	Targeted affordance	Publicly available
αNLI (Bhagavatula et al., 2020)	169,654	-	1,532	Abductive logical reasoning	Crowd-sourced	✗	✗	✔
αARCT (Niven and Kao, 2019)	2420	632	888	Abductive logical reasoning	Crowd-sourced	✗	✗	✔
FOLIO (Han et al., 2022)	1004	204	227	Deductive logical reasoning	Expert written	✗	✗	✔
ANLI (Nie et al., 2020)	162,865	3,200	3,200	Deductive logical reasoning	Synthetic	✗	✗	✔
WinoLogic (He et al., 2021)	-	-	562	Deductive logical reasoning	Crowd-sourced	✗	✗	✔
LogiQA (Liu et al., 2021)	7,376	651	651	Mixed logical reasoning	Crowd-sourced	✗	✗	✔
LogiQA 2.0 (Liu et al., 2023a)	-	-	3,238	Mixed logical reasoning	Crowd-sourced	✗	✗	✔
PaCo (Qasemi et al., 2022a)	5,580	1,860	4,960	Preconditioned commonsense	Crowd-sourced	✗	✗	✔
δ-NLI(Rudinger et al., 2020)	36,999	3,329	3,512	Defeasible commonsense	Other dataset	✗	✗	✔
WINOVENTI (Do and Pavlick, 2021)	-	-	4,352	Commonsense with exceptions	Crowd-sourced	✗	✗	✔
PVLIR (Qasemi et al., 2023)			34,000	Preconditioned visual commonsense	Other dataset	✔	✗	✗
Normlense (Han et al., 2023)	-	-	10,000	Defeasible visual commonsense	Crowd-sourced	✔	✗	✔
WinoViz (Jin et al., 2024)	-	-	1,380	Reasoning object's visual property	Crowd-sourced	✗	✗	✗
PROST (Aroca-Ouellette et al., 2021)	-	-	18,736	Reasoning object's physical property	Other dataset	✗	✗	✔
NEWTON (Wang et al., 2023)	-	-	2,800	Reasoning object's physical property	Crowd-sourced	✗	✗	✔
Persiani and Hellström (2019)	734,002	-	314,572	Object affordance without context	Synthetic	✗	✔	✗
TEXT2AFFORD (Ours)	-	-	35,520 (2368 * 15)	**Contextual object affordance**	Crowd-sourced	✗	✔	✔

Table 9: Comparison of TEXT2AFFORD with other reasoning datasets.

A.9 Correlation of affordances

In Figure 9 we show the correlation between the different affordance classes.

A.10 Most frequent objects

Figure 8a shows the most frequent 15 objects in the TEXT2AFFORD dataset.

B Experimental setup

B.1 Random baseline

In addition to evaluating generative models, we establish a random baseline. For this baseline, we randomly assign "yes" to the 15 affordance classes for each sentence-object pair, with random selections made from 0 to 9 (based on the observation that the maximum number of positive affordances per pair is 9). Interestingly, we find that models like Flan-T5-large and Flan-T5-XL underperform compared to this random baseline in zero-shot settings, highlighting the inherent difficulty of the task in such scenarios.

B.2 Zero-shot experiments

B.2.1 Commonsense reasoning tasks

To understand whether the injection of the common sense knowledge in the pre-trained models can enhance the performance of the affordance prediction, we first fine-tune the pre-trained models on common sense reasoning dataset such as PIQA (Bisk et al., 2019). Then we run the fine-tuned models on our dataset using the MLM setup. We use BERT-base, BERT-large, RoBERTa-large, and BART-large finetuned on MNLI.

NLI based approach. The NLI task considers a premise and a hypothesis as input pair $\langle p, h \rangle$, and the models are trained to predict the probability whether the hypothesis is entailed by, contradicts or neutral with respect to the premise. Here we use the entailment probability from the models: $p_{La}(h|p) = p(l = \text{“}ENTAILMENT\text{”}|(p, h))$. This approach requires language models to be fine-tuned on premise-hypothesis pairs with the corresponding labels. Here we use RoBERTa-large and BART-large fine-tuned on the Multi-genre NLI (MNLI) corpus (Williams et al., 2018) consisting of 433k sentence pairs. For each sentence-object pair in our dataset as the premise, and use the hypothesis as “*<object> can be used for <affordance> by human*” for each object present in the sentence and 15 affordance classes. Using the NLI setting, we predict the entailment score for each affordance class for the given sentence-object pair. We use these scores for ranking the affordance classes and report mAP scores as well as accuracy.

B.3 Ensemble language and vision prediction

Following Yang et al. (2022), we use the weighted sum as the late fusion over the final output probabilities of each affordance class from the language and multi-modal models. Before late fusion, we normalize the output probability scores from different models. We calculate the score as: $P_{ens}(y|x) = (1 - w)p_{L_a}(y|x) + wp_{V_I}(y|x)$ where w is the relative size of the vision-text model and the language model (following Yang et al. (2022)): $w = Sigmoid\left(\frac{\rho_{V_I}}{\rho_{L_a}}\right)$. Here ρ_{V_I} and ρ_{L_a} denote the number of parameters of the multi-modal and language models respectively.

Introduction

Mike has bought a Robot to do simple household tasks such as writing on a paper, playing a guitar, throwing garbage outside based on what Mike says to the Robot. However, the Robot is not accustomed with the Mike's household objects, so it does not know which thing can be used for which of the tasks. For example, the Robot is not aware that a pen or a pencil can be used for writing on a paper, but can not be played. A guitar or a banjo can be played, but not used for writing. This is important for the Robot to know before acting on instructions such as "clean the dishes for me".
However, the good-news is that the Robot can be taught about any object and its corresponding action. You, as a trainer, have been asked to teach the Robot about the household objects. Your task is simple -- there are few common objects (or things) in the house and you need to tell the Robot what actions (i.e. tasks) can be performed with each of those from a set of selected actions (tasks). This will help the Robot learn about what action can be performed on what type of objects.

See the below figure to understand which kind of action can be performed on which objects.

Task Description

You are given a **sentence** and the **object name** present in the sentence. You are required to mark the actions that can be performed from a given list of 15 actions.

For example:

Sentence: The tennis shoes have a range of prices.
Object: The tennis shoes

Out of the 15 given actions: **Grasp, Lift, Throw, Push, Fix, Ride, Play, Watch, SitOn, Feed, Row, PourFrom, LookThrough, WriteWith, TypeOn**
Select: Grasp, Lift, Throw, Push, Fix as that is something we typically do/is done/can be done with "The tennis shoe".

For each of the given actions, you are given a scale ranging from **0 to 3**. **The selection of a score of "0" means you strongly believe the action cannot be done, while a score of "3" means you strongly believe the action can be done. Scores of "1" and "2" are for cases where you are less sure about whether or not the action can be done.** One example of selections is given below for the object "The tennis shoes"

Object:
The tennis shoes

Select the below actions:

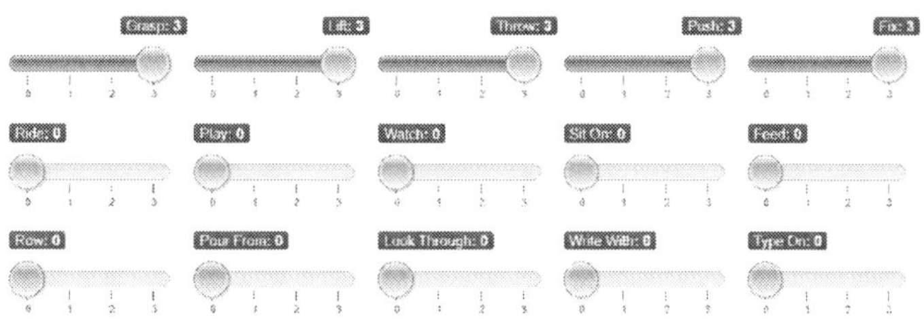

Additional Examples:

1. Objects that can be **grasped**: Pencil, tennis ball
2. Objects that can be **Lift**: a book, a box, a chair
3. Objects that can be **Thrown**: a baseball, a frisbee, a rock
4. Objects that can be **Pushed**: table, brakes of a car
5. Objects that can be **Fixed**: machines, vehicles, electronics
6. Objects that can be **Ride**: bicycles, motorcycles, horses, roller coasters
7. Objects that can be **Play**: musical instruments (guitar, piano, violin), sports equipment (tennis racket, soccer ball), electronic devices (video game console)
8. Objects that can be **Watch**: televisions, computer screens, movie screens
9. Objects that can be **SitOn**: chairs, benches, sofas
10. Objects that can be **Feed**: animals such as dogs and cats, as well as birds
11. Objects that can be **Row**: boats, canoes, kayaks, and rowboats
12. Objects that can be **PourFrom**: a pitcher, a bottle, a jug, a teapot
13. Objects that can be **looked through**: windows, telescopes, binoculars
14. Objects that can be **WriteWith**: pens, pencils, markers
15. Objects that can be **TypeOn**: computers, laptops, tablets, smartphones

Figure 3: The instruction used for annotators in the Toloka platform

B.4 Few-shot experiments

Training data To create few-shot training examples for fine-tuning encoder based PTLMs, we take all the 62 objects, and for each object we randomly select exactly 1 positive affordance class (i.e., the class label annotated as 1) and 1 negative affordance class (i.e., the class label annotated as 0) for generating the training prompt. As this dataset does not contain any context sentences for a corresponding object, we use ChatGPT UI

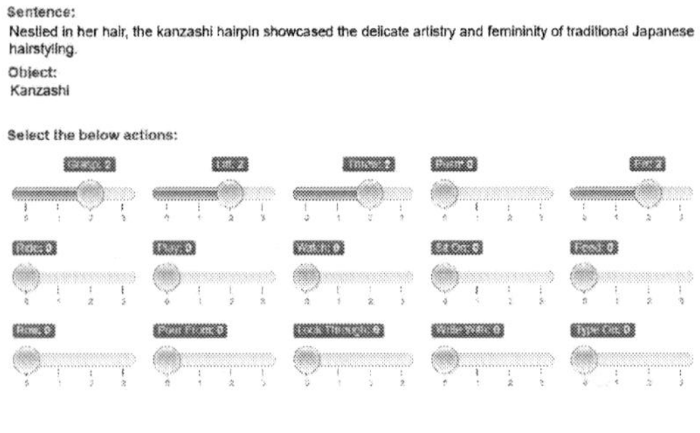

Figure 4: The sample task interface used for the annotators in the Toloka platform

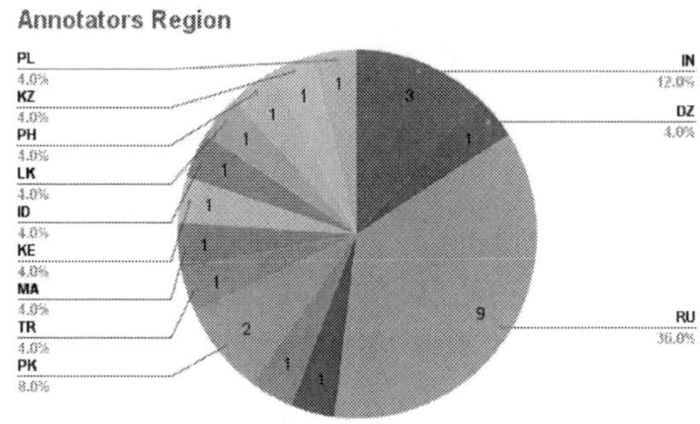

(a) Country distribution of the annotators

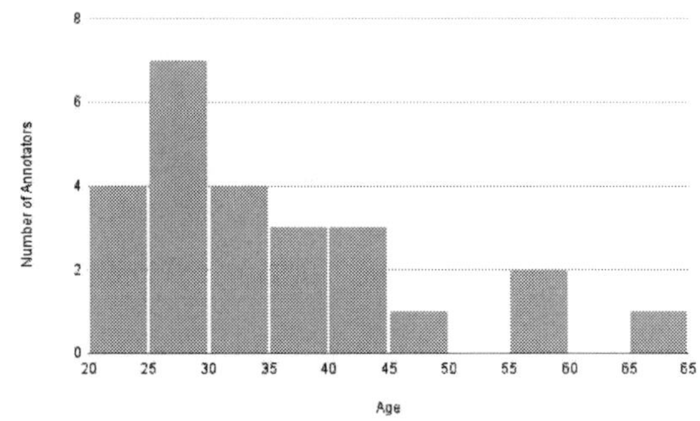

(b) Age distributions of the annotators

Figure 5: The Annotators Demographics

to generate the sentences for the corresponding objects and manually verify the sentences, so that it does not contain any invalid information. Finally, we have 62 sentence-object pairs and 2 classes (one positive and one negative) per pair, which we use to generate training examples. Each training example consists of a prompt and a label. They constitute 124 training examples (62 sentence-object pairs and 2 selected classes for each) for the few-shot experiment.

Selecting examples for in-context learning : We randomly sample five sentence-object-affordance triples from the above training data as the incontext demonstration examples in such a way that there should be k positive affordance classes. We vary the number of positive affordance classes $k \in \{1, 2, 3\}$ and report the average accuracy.

Experimental setup. We fine-tune the encoder based language models using the training data, and for the generative LLMs and the VLMs, we utilize the training data to select in-context demonstration examples.

Fine-tuning PTLM: We fine-tune the PTLMs in two different setups - NLI based and prompt based. For the NLI based setup we have the context sentence as premise and use same prompt (i.e., "<object> can be used for <affordance> by human") which we use in the zero-shot settings as hypothesis. We use label as 1 for the positive affordance and label as 0 for the negative affordance. We use BERT-large-uncased, RoBERTa-large and BART-large for fine-tuning in this setup. We reuse these fine-tuned models for few-shot predictions in MLM setup. We use Adam optimizer with a learning rate of 2×10^{-5}. We fine-tune the model for 5 epochs for each case.

In-context learning for generative models: We employ the same generative LLMs as well as VLMs to perform affordance prediction using *five* demonstration examples from the training data. We use the same text prompt as zero-shot setting and concatenate the five demonstration examples along with corresponding label (i.e., 'YES' for positive class, and 'NO' for the negative class) to the prompt and ask the LLMs and VLMs to predict the affordance. In case of the VLMs, we do not provide any additional image example here.

B.4.1 Multimodal task setup

Images contain necessary information about shape, texture, and size of objects that can be utilized to effectively predict an object affordance (such as the handle of the bucket can be used to grasp and lift). Hence, we also convert the problem into a multi-modal task by retrieving (or generating) a corresponding image from the context sentence, and predict the affordance of an object (mentioned in the sentence) based on the input.

Synthesizing images. In this setup, we use two different techniques to synthesize *semantically*

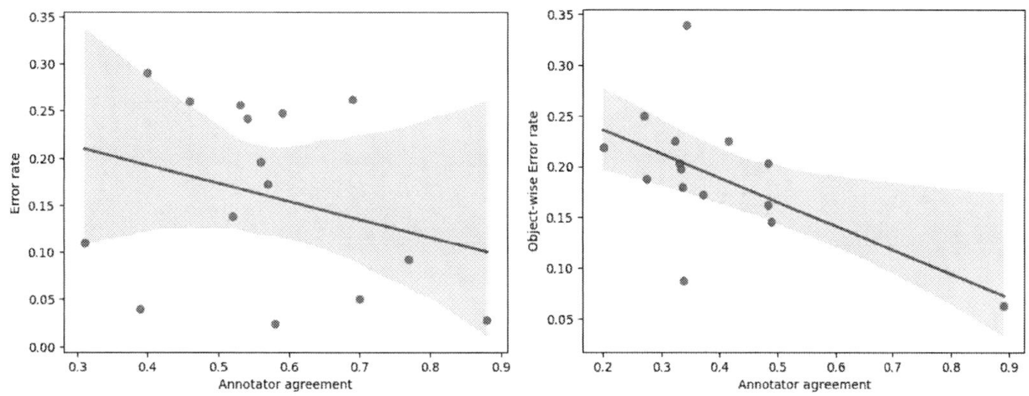

(a) (b)

Figure 6: (a) Correlation between average classwise error rate made by chatGPT and the annotator agreement. ($\rho = -0.29$) (b) Correlation between frequent object wise error rate made by chatGPT and the annotator agreement. ($\rho = -0.58*$). *indicates a p-value < 0.05.

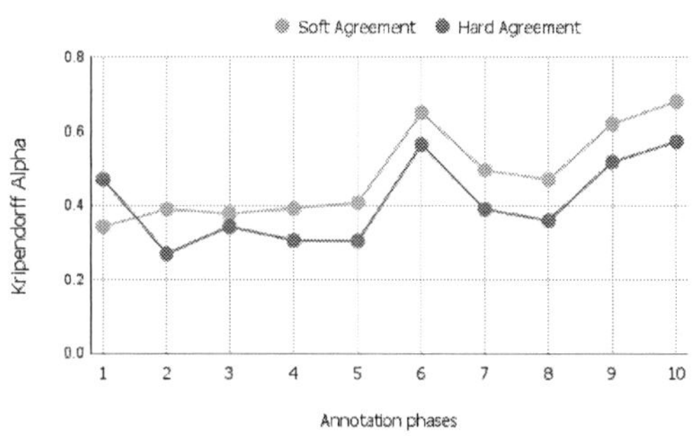

Figure 7: Phase-wise annotator agreement.

close images to corresponding context sentences using 1) retrieval and 2) generation. We further use top five images for both, to get an accurate estimation.

Retrieval based: We employ Visualgenome (Krishna et al., 2017) dataset, consisting of 108,077 images and 3.8 million object instances as the image database. We first encode the images using multi-modal CLIP (Radford et al., 2021) based sentence-transformers architecture, and index those image embeddings using Approximate Nearest Neighbour search (ANN)[13], for making the search efficient. Now, for each sentence, we search for top five images from the database to be used further.

Generation based: Recently, the multi-modal generative models (Ramesh et al., 2022; Saharia et al., 2022) have shown incredibly good performance for text based image generation tasks. We adopt the recent *StableDiffusion* (Rombach et al., 2022) model to generate top five images based on the sentence as a text prompt.

We use the top five retrieved images by using retrieval and generation methods each. We use *CLIP* (Radford et al., 2021) and *ViLT* (Kim et al., 2021) as our vision-text models. CLIP is pre-trained on 400M image-caption pairs with the contrastive learning strategy. CLIP has a text encoder f_T and a visual encoder f_V, which can project text and image into the shared latent space. We aggregate the k (=5) corresponding images and use CLIP to compute the relevance score of (x, y): $Score_{VI}(x, y) = \frac{1}{k}\sum_{i=1}^{K} \cos(f_T(x), f_v(I_y^k))$, where I_y^k is the kth image for the input text y. In the ViLT model we provide the text prompt along with the representative images as input to predict the masked token. We use the same prompt as the previous MLM task (i.e., "*<Object> can be used for <MASK_TOKEN> by human.*") and get the probability of each affordance class as the logit corresponding to the <MASK_TOKEN>.

Text generation based. Similar to section 5.1.1, we utilize state-of-the-art VLMs to make predictions regarding object affordances. We provide with a 'YES\NO' question answering based text prompt along with the aligned images as input to the VLMs, and the model should generate an answer whether a particular affordance can be performed on the given object. We use state-of-the-art VLMs such as IDEFICS (Laurençon et al., 2023), LLaVA (Liu et al., 2023b), InstructBLIP (Dai et al.,

[13]`https://pypi.org/project/annoy/`

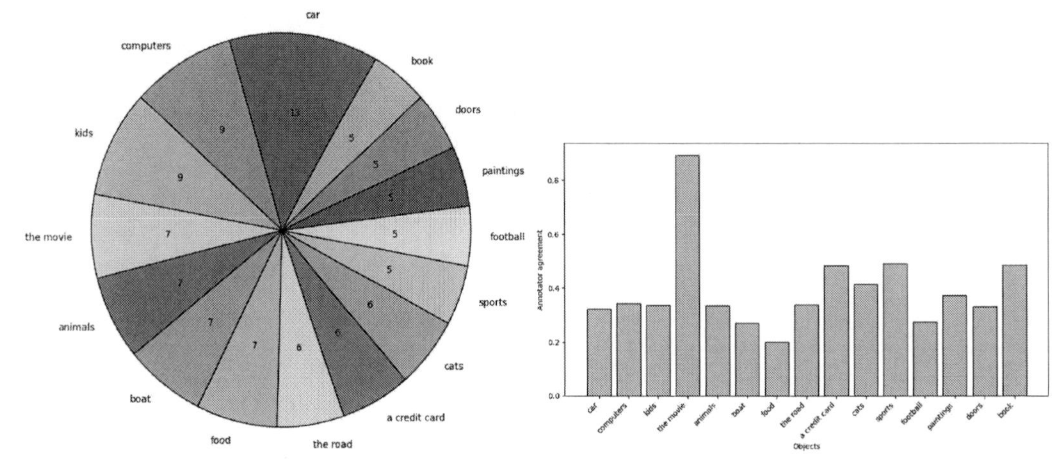

(a) (b)

Figure 8: (a) Most frequent 15 objects and their corresponding frequency in the TEXT2AFFORD dataset. (b) Annotator agreement for the most frequent 15 objects.

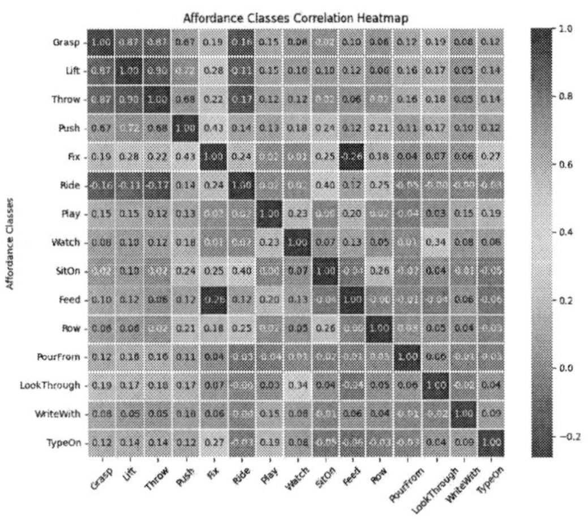

Figure 9: Correlation between each of the affordance classes.

2023) for this task. The text prompt used for the models can be found in the Appendix D, Table 10.

C Additional (mis)prediction analysis

C.1 Affordance classwise mis-prediction

We analyze the mis-prediction rates for each class using the best LLMs (chatGPT, llama-3-8b). We observe that, the classwise mis-prediction rate is similar to the distribution of each class in the original data, i.e., the classes such as 'grasp', 'lift' having higher mis-predictions compared to 'typeOn', 'row'.

C.2 Objects with multiple positive affordances

We conduct an analysis to determine whether the frequency of positive affordances for an object impacts model accuracy. Our findings indicate that the accuracy is highest when an object has a single positive affordance. Beyond this point, the number of positive affordances does not significantly influence the model's performance. Specifically, we observe that as the number of positive affordances increases, the accuracy fluctuates without a clear pattern, suggesting that additional positive affordances do not contribute to a consistent improvement or decline in model accuracy.

C.3 Correlation of ChatGPT accuracy and average human agreement

We provide the figures corresponding to the generative model analysis in Figure 6.

D Prompt selection

We use intuitive prompts for each of the setups, which are suitable for affordance related to object.

E Instruction fine-tuning setup

Data sample selection. We select sentence-object pairs from the TEXT2AFFORD dataset where at least one positive affordance is present. For each selected sentence-object pair, we randomly assign one positive affordance and one negative affordance, yielding a balanced dataset of 1819 training instances (positive and negative classes). To incorporate additional domain knowledge and

Model	Prompt used
FLAN-T5	consider {sentence}. Now, from this information can human {affordance} the {object_name}? Answer YES or NO:
Falcon	"""You are a helpful AI assistant. Answer only "YES" or "NO" for the question based on the given context. Context:sentence \n »QUESTION« Can human {affordance} the {object_name}? \n »ANSWER«""".strip()
I-BLIP, IDEFICS, LLaVA	consider the sentence {sentence}. Now from this information, can human {affordance} the {object_name}? Accompanying this query is an image of the object_name. Note that the image may contain noise or variations in appearance. Given the textual description and the image, answer YES or NO whether the human can {affordance} the {object_name}. Answer: "

Table 10: Prompt format used by different models for the prediction. I-BLIP: InstructBLIP.

reduce the likelihood of generating hallucinated answers, we include 500 randomly sampled instances from the training set of the target task (i.e., PIQA). For the PROST task, as the training set is not explicitly available, we sample from the test set and ensure these samples are removed from the evaluation set during testing. The training instances are framed in a multiple-choice question answering format.

Fine-tuning setup. We utilize Alpaca-formatted prompts (shown in Table 11, Table 12 and Table 13 for the TEXT2AFFORD, PIQA and PROST tasks, respectively). We fine-tune 4-bit quantized models with PEFT, focusing on the adapter layers. We perform the fine-tuning over 5 epochs with a batch size of 8, a learning rate of 2e-10, weight decay, and a maximum sequence length of 256.

F Model implementation details

The language models and the ViLT are built on top of the huggingface API[14]. For NLI based zero-shot prediction, we use the zero-shot classification pipeline [15]. We adapted the CLIP model from the OpenAI's public repo [16], and we select the ViT/B32 as the image encoder. For ViLT, we select the vilt-b32-mlm [17] model. For generative LLMs and VLMs we apply the models available on huggingface [18]. All the experiments were conducted on 2x NVIDIA RTX 4090 GPU server.

[14]https://huggingface.co/

[15]https://huggingface.co/docs/transformers/main_classes/pipelines

[16]https://github.com/openai/CLIP

[17]dandelin/vilt-b32-mlm

[18]https://huggingface.co/models

G Details of evaluation metric

For a 'Sentence-Object' pair we calculate accuracy in the following way. In the ground-truth, each affordance class is treated as a binary value, where a value of 1 represents a 'positive affordance' indicating that the affordance can be performed on the object, and a value of 0 represents a 'negative affordance' indicating that the affordance cannot be performed. Now, for a particular 'Sentence-Object' pair, let's assume there are two positive affordances (P1, P2) in the ground truth; then there will be 13 negative affordances (as we have a total 15 affordance classes). In case of encoder-based models, for each positive affordance, we compare its prediction score against each negative affordance's score. If a positive affordance's score is higher, we increase the Correct count; otherwise, the Wrong count. Accuracy is calculated as Correct / (Correct + Wrong).

In case of encoder-decoder or decoder-only models, Due to the inherent difficulty in automatic evaluation, we predict 'YES\NO' for each affordance class, mapping 'YES' to 1 and 'NO' to 0. Accuracy is then measured in the same way as for encoder-based models (assuming 1 or 0 as the score for each affordance class).

H Dataset creation time

Annotating affordances about the object from a text itself is a difficult and very subjective task. It took approximately 5 months for completing the extraction of noun-phrases from xnli data, filtering objects, selecting skillful tolokers and training, and then final phase-wise annotation after rigorous review process.

I Sample dataset

Figure 10 shows a sample of TEXT2AFFORD dataset

J Additional experiments

J.1 Qualitative analysis of generated images

We conducted a qualitative analysis on 50 randomly sampled objects and their corresponding generated images. Two annotators (one Phd student and one undergrad student) marked each of the 5 generated images as 1 or 0 according to their relevance and non-relevance to the object respectively. We considered the image as relevant if both of the annotators marked that image as 1. We achieved an

Instruction to fine-tune TEXT2AFFORD

Below is an instruction that describes a task. Write a response that appropriately completes the request.

Instruction:
You are an AI assistant that has strong reasoning capability. You are given a context containing an object, and you are asked to answer a question about the object based on the context. Just response 'Yes' or 'No'.

Context:
{context}

Object:
{object}

Question:
Can human {affordance} the {object}?

Answer:
{answer}

Table 11: Instruction to fine-tune TEXT2AFFORD.

Instruction to fine-tune PIQA

Below is an instruction that describes a task. Write a response that appropriately completes the request.

Instruction:
You are an AI assistant that has strong reasoning capability. You are given a situation and asked to choose the most appropriate option from given two options.

Situation:
{situation}

Options:
[0] {option0}
[1] {option1}

Only response the 'answer id'. For example if the answer is [0] then response 0. DO NOT respond anything other than <0, 1>.

Answer:
{answer}

Table 12: Instruction to fine-tune PIQA.

Instruction to fine-tune PROST

Below is an instruction that describes a task. Write a response that appropriately completes the request.

Instruction:
You are an AI assistant that has strong reasoning capability. You are given a question with 4 options and you have to choose the right option.

Question:
{question}

Options:
[0] {option_A}
[1] {option_B}
[2] {option_C}
[3] {option_D}

Only response the 'answer id'. For example if the answer is [0] then response 0. DO NOT respond anything other than <0, 1, 2, 3>.

Answer:
{answer}

Table 13: Instruction to fine-tune PROST.

Sentence	Object	Grasp	Lift	Throw	Push	Fix	Ride	Play	Watch	SitOn	Feed	Row	PourFrom	LookThrough	WriteWith	TypeOn
This diablo only comes out to slaughter the cattle .	cattle	0	0	0	1	0	0	0	1	0	1	0	0	0	0	0
Delivery points should include at least a bench and a locked storage compartment .	bench	1	1	0	0	0	0	0	1	1	0	0	0	0	0	0
There are four fences , and you can only go past the second one if you are a member of the imperial family , or a high-ranking priest .	fences	1	0	1	1	0	0	0	1	0	0	0	0	0	0	0
Users are excited about being able to share their own events on the calendar page .	calendar page	1	1	1	1	0	0	0	1	0	0	0	0	1	0	0
White ran towards where the people were hitting each other with swords .	swords	1	1	1	1	0	0	0	0	0	0	0	0	0	0	0
The cat ate every kind of fish except tuna .	fish	1	1	0	0	0	0	0	0	0	1	0	0	0	0	0
The snake was hissing underneath the deck .	deck	0	0	0	0	0	0	0	0	1	0	0	0	0	0	0
On the higher levels of the town hall , Umbrian and Tuscan paintings are on show .	the town hall	0	0	0	0	0	0	0	1	0	0	0	0	0	0	0
He couldn 't follow up because his mouth was gagged by a group of mercenaries .	mercenaries	1	0	0	0	0	0	0	1	0	1	0	0	0	0	0
A gristle gun is featured .	gristle gun	1	1	0	0	0	0	0	0	0	0	0	0	0	0	0

Figure 10: Example snapshot of TEXT2AFFORD dataset.

Acc@1 of 0.2, Acc@5 of 0.88 and an MAP@5 of 0.36. Which suggests that in most of the cases there are relevant images in the top-5 generated images. In our pursuit of assessing the statistical significance of our sampled data (i.e., the 50 examples), we embarked upon a rigorous hypothesis testing procedure utilizing the binomial distribution. Within our specific context, we accorded greater significance to the top-5 accuracy metric, which demonstrated an impressive achievement of 0.88. This signifies that among the 50 selected examples, in 44 instances, at least one of the five generated images displayed relevance to the object under consideration.

Guided by this success rate, we proceeded to conduct a meticulous hypothesis test employing the binomial distribution. We assumed an expectation of success at 0.75. The outcome of this statistical analysis revealed a p-value of less than 0.02, thereby underscoring the statistical significance of our success rate.

How Are Metaphors Processed by Language Models? The Case of Analogies

Joanne Boisson[1], **Asahi Ushio**[2], **Hsuvas Borkakoty**[1], **Kiamehr Rezaee**[1],
Dimosthenis Antypas[1], **Zara Siddique**[1], **Nina White**[1] and **Jose Camacho-Collados**[1]
[1]Cardiff NLP, School of Computer Science and Informatics
Cardiff University, United Kingdom
[2]Amazon, Japan
{boissonjc,borkakotyh,rezaeek,antypasd,siddiquezs2,camachocolladosj}
@cardiff.ac.uk

Abstract

The ability to compare by analogy, metaphorically or not, lies at the core of how humans understand the world and communicate. In this paper, we study the likelihood of metaphoric outputs, and the capability of a wide range of pretrained transformer-based language models to identify metaphors from other types of analogies, including anomalous ones. In particular, we are interested in discovering whether language models recognise metaphorical analogies equally well as other types of analogies, and whether the model size has an impact on this ability. The results show that there are relevant differences using perplexity as a proxy, with the larger models reducing the gap when it comes to analogical processing, and for distinguishing metaphors from incorrect analogies. This behaviour does not result in increased difficulties for larger generative models in identifying metaphors in comparison to other types of analogies from anomalous sentences in a zero-shot generation setting, when perplexity values of metaphoric and non-metaphoric analogies are similar.

1 Introduction

Analogical reasoning is critical to deep language understanding, as it is a core mechanism of human generalization and creativity (Holyoak and Thagard, 1996; Hofstadter, 2001). Analogical thinking includes figurativeness (e.g. The mind is a *sponge*.), in which humans naturally express relationships based on non-literal connections. Traditionally, metaphors have been challenging to model from a computational perspective (Veale et al., 2016) and in the context of NLP. This is due to their proteiform nature, conventional or creative, concise or structurally more complex.

Some limitations might have been lifted given the new wave of language models (LMs) that have revolutionalised the field of NLP and beyond (Chowdhery et al., 2022; Ouyang et al., 2022; Touvron et al., 2023). Indeed, recent studies on the last generation of large transformer-based LMs show enhanced abilities to perform analogical reasoning (Webb et al., 2023), suggesting that models of a larger size may gain the ability to process complex analogies.

As a conceptual innovation device, figurative analogies have also been studied in relation to the fluency, creativity and originality of students' writing (Kao, 2020). Creative writing support tools specialising in metaphor generation have been developed, such as Metaphoria (Gero and Chilton, 2019). The emergence of LLMs as writing assistants has further highlighted the importance of understanding how metaphors are processed by LMs, especially given some limitations pointed by their users related to the generation of poor metaphors and overly predictable endings, to name a few (Chakrabarty et al., 2024).

Motivated by the recent advances in language modeling and the need for understanding how LMs process metaphors, we establish the following two research questions:

Research Question 1 (RQ1). How do language models distinguish metaphors from literal and anomalous sentences? In particular, we are interested in determining if the likelihood of metaphors compared to both literal and anomalous sentences is consistent across models. For this, we are also interested in analysing the differences among model families and, particularly, sizes. This research question is addressed in Section 5.

Research Question 2 (RQ2). Assuming differences in the answer to RQ1, we aim to address the following complementary questions: how do metaphors impact the performance of language models in general analogy tests? Are language models capable of solving analogies when metaphors are involved? Our findings are presented

Proceedings of the 28th Conference on Computational Natural Language Learning, pages 365–387
November 15-16, 2024 ©2024 Association for Computational Linguistics

in Section 6.

In order to answer both research questions, we evaluate a broad range of language models on their ability to distinguish anomalous, metaphoric and non-metaphoric sentences on datasets from psycholinguistics, that were, to our knowledge, previously unused in NLP studies. The results clearly show the marked differences in terms of perplexity between attributive metaphors and other literal attributive structures, where, in some cases metaphors are processed more similarly to anomalies, whereas in other cases, they are processed more similarly to literal examples. A last experiment on the SAT analogy test dataset allows a comparison of the models in open-generation tasks for challenging metaphors and analogies. We observed differences between perplexity and generation-based approaches, with an enhanced ability of the models to deal with metaphors in the generation setting[1].

2 Background

In this section, we provide more details on the relation between analogies and metaphors, and discuss other terminology used across the paper.

Analogies. Analogy is a type of similarity in which the same system of relations holds across different sets of elements (Gentner and Smith, 2012). The analogies that we consider express parallels across pairs of concepts captured minimally through attributive structures *A is-a B* or more explicitly with comparisons of the form *A is to B what C is to D*. Mapping conceptual structures to understand or create analogies comes naturally to humans, but it is generally challenging for computational models because it conveys implicit semantic attributes and relations. For example, understanding the statement *ketchup is to tomato what guacamole is to avocado* involves an internal representation of the relation *x is made of mashed y*.

In two-word analogies, the relation of interest is implicit. For example, from the sentence *His editing style was a chainsaw*, one can reconstruct an implicit 4-term analogy: *His editing style was to the text what a chainsaw is to a forest.*[2]

[1]The code and datasets used in our experiments can be found at https://github.com/Mionies/Metaphors_and_Analogies.

[2]Such reconstructions may leave room for interpretation as they are generally underdefined. For instance, *forest* may not be the only choice in the example.

Metaphors. Within Conceptual Metaphor Theory (CMT), a metaphor is defined as a mapping process between broad conceptual domains (Lakoff and Johnson, 1980), which occur at the level of thought and manifests through language. In order to study the ability of models to identify metaphoric mappings, we experiment on linguistic expressions constrained in form. In this paper, a metaphor is defined as a word (or a set of related words), that can be understood through the prism of another distant word (or another paired set of related words), without relying on additional explicit context. We feed minimal metaphoric sentences that almost only contain the words forming mappings into the models, to gain a better understanding of how they are represented by the LMs.

According to Black (1977), all metaphors mediate an analogy , but not all analogies are metaphors. The relation between metaphors and analogies has been much debated. Researchers who refer to shared features and structural analogies as the basis of metaphors disagreed with some conceptual mapping theorists who have argued that similarity is not the basis for metaphors (Grady, 1999). Gentner et al. (2001) and Bowdle and Gentner (2005) introduce a framework that intends to unify both views. The present study adopts this theoretical framework. Metaphors are treated here as a species of analogies. More recently, Wijesiriwardene et al. (2023a) proposed a taxonomy of analogies where the metaphors included in our dataset would be classified as *semantic and pragmatic analogies*, i.e. the two most complex types of analogies, which require good semantic representations, and sometimes pragmatic knowledge, to be processed accurately.

Among all analogies, we hypothesise that metaphors might be even harder to process, because they are more structurally variable than other types of analogy. The attribute and relation conveyed are partial matches. They can even violate structural consistency (Gentner et al., 1988). According to Tourangeau and Sternberg (1982), a good metaphor is one that involves two very different domains. It is not an absolute criterion, but good metaphors are often cross-domain (far) analogies, which adds to the complexity. Another specificity of metaphors is that the mapping is not reversible (Ortony, 1993), i.e., metaphors have directionality. For example *The acrobat is a hippopotamus* suggests a clumsy acrobat and *The hippopotamus is an acrobat* suggests a graceful hippopotamus.

For these two reasons, LMs may struggle to catch capture the parallelism between the concepts involved in a metaphor in comparison to other types of analogies.

Anomalies. Semantic anomalies can resemble metaphors in the sense that they may eventually bring together concepts that are distant from each other. Unlike metaphors, the two concepts do not share any obvious properties. For example, *A chair is a syllogism* can be considered to be an anomaly (Black, 1977). Fallacious analogies made of two word pairs in the *A is to B what C is to D* structures are constructed by mapping words that are not connected by the same relation. For example, having the first pair linked by a *part of* relation and the second pair by a *made of* relation.[3]

3 Related Work

Automatic metaphor processing research has seen a garnered increased in recent years, partially due to the encouraging performance of language models on existing benchmarks (Leong et al., 2020). However, there have been almost no studies on metaphors in the context of analogies.

3.1 Analogies

Czinczoll et al. (2022) compared the performance of transformer-based language models on near analogies and more creative ones. They reported a large gap in the performance of the LMs between the two categories and released the SCAN dataset of creative analogies. In the context of the recent multiplication of larger language models, we can now say that their study is limited to relatively small models, BERT and GPT2, and in the framework of fine-tuning experiments. In contrast, we study the zero-shot abilities of the model, which allows us to conveniently scale up the experiments with limited computing power. The SCAN dataset does not contain anomalies or distinguish between metaphoric and non-metaphoric analogies. Therefore, integrating it into our our experimental setting would require additional annotations.

Webb et al. (2023) studied the performance of the GPT3-davinci models on a large range of different analogies, from geometric patterns to short pieces of text. All the experiments are compared with the performance of humans on the same task. The authors observed a sudden improvement with the davinci-003 model, which corresponds to the beginning of the release of instruction-tuned models by OpenAI (Ouyang et al., 2022). These results also suggest that abstract analogical reasoning may be an emergent ability of the larger models. This was also demonstrated by Wei et al. (2022), who observed a sudden improvement in the classification of fine-grained figurative language when the models are scaled up. These works were a motivation for the present study in the context of metaphorical analogies. We tested a large number of models of different sizes, including open-source ones, to better understand how the sizes and model types impact their ability to recognise complex analogies.

Wijesiriwardene et al. (2023b) and Sultan and Shahaf (2023) recently released resources for the identification of analogical pairs of short texts. While Sultan and Shahaf (2023) do not distinguish metaphors from other analogies, Wijesiriwardene et al. (2023b) proposed a scale of complexity for analogical relations, with metaphors occupying the highest level. The open research topic of analogical reasoning between documents explored in this previous study beyond the scope of our study. Instead, we frame our experiments to explore the behavior of the models when they are provided with the minimal linguistic information necessary to create an analogy and a metaphor, in zero-shot settings.

While good performance can be achieved when the models are fine-tuned on analogy datasets, (Griciūtė et al., 2022; Yuan et al., 2023), we are interested in understanding how LMs represent metaphors without explicit fine-tuning. In this respect, the present work is more in line of perplexity-based experiments of Ushio et al. (2021b). In contrast, we do not focus on improving the perplexity metrics but on the comparison between vanilla perplexity scores across models.

3.2 Metaphors

Metaphor processing in NLP comprises many methods developed for metaphor identification (Turney et al., 2011; Tsvetkov et al., 2014; Mao et al., 2019; Wachowiak and Gromann, 2023), but also generation (Veale, 2016; Stowe et al., 2021; Chakrabarty et al., 2021b), textual (Mao et al., 2018) and multimodal (Kulkarni et al., 2024) interpretation, metaphor understanding through entailment (Agerri et al., 2008; Chakrabarty et al., 2021a; Stowe et al., 2022), among other tasks. Ge et al.

[3]In the rest of this paper, we refer to the sentences that are not figurative, and not semantically anomalous as literal. Table 1 shows examples of 2-terms literal sentences, that are not analogies, and 4-terms sentences that are analogies.

Dataset	Format	n_sent	n_set	n_ins	Labels	Example
Cardillo	2-term	520	2	260	Literal	The murder weapon was a chainsaw.
					Metaphor	His editing style was a chainsaw.
Jankowiak	2-term	360	3	120	Literal	These marks are bruises.
					Metaphor	Failures are bruises.
					Anomaly	Bottles are bruises.
Green	4-term	120	3	40	Literal	Answer is to riddle what solution is to problem
					Metaphor	Answer is to riddle what key is to lock
					Anomaly	Answer is to riddle what jersey is to number

Table 1: Analogy datasets included in the experiments: n_sent indicate the number of sentences; n_set, the number of sentences per instance; and n_ins, and the number of instances. All datasets are balanced in terms of labels.

(2023) provide a comprehensive recent survey on the topic.

An early approach to metaphoric mapping detection that resonates with our perplexity-based study is the measurement of the preference of predicates for semantic classes of arguments (Fass and Wilks, 1983), formalized by Resnik (1997) as a WordNet based selectional preference (SP) and SP strength measure. Mason (2004); Shutova et al. (2010); Li et al. (2013) rely on the assumption that metaphoric verb-object pairs will tend to appear with lower association strength than literal compositions. More recently, Zhang and Liu (2022) models SP violations as incongruity between target words and their contexts.

In a similar work to ours, Pedinotti et al. (2021) investigated the plausibility of metaphoric associations for LMs. BERT's ability to identify the boundaries of metaphoric creativity is studied with literal sentences, conventional metaphors, creative metaphors and nonsensical sentences, and observed that the average pseudo-likelihood scores decreases in this order for the four considered categories, in accordance with human ratings of semantic plausibility. We expand the analysis to additional models and datasets, including 4-term analogies, and compare perplexity-based results to generation-based results for instructed models.

4 Experimental Details: Model Selection and Perplexity Computation

Our aim in this paper is to evaluate a wide range of diverse LMs in terms of architecture and size, which are presented below.

Models. In our experiments, we consider the masked language models BERT (Devlin et al., 2019) and RoBERTa (Liu et al., 2019), decoder-only LM GPT-2 (Radford et al., 2019), GPT-J (Wang and Komatsuzaki, 2021), OPT (Zhang et al., 2022), OPT-IML (Iyer et al., 2022), Galactica (Taylor et al., 2022), Bloom (Hasanain and Elsayed, 2022) and Bloomz (Muennighoff et al., 2023) , Llama-2 and Llama-3 (Touvron et al., 2023) , and the encoder-decoder LM T5 (Raffel et al., 2020), Flan-T5 (Chung et al., 2022), Flan-UL2 (Tay et al., 2023). Finally, we consider the recent Mistral (Jiang et al., 2023) and Sparse Mixture of Experts Mixtral models (Jiang et al., 2024). All the model weights are taken from HuggingFace, where the complete list of the models we used can be found in Appendix 6. In addition to those open-source LMs, we consider the OpenAI commercial API models. We use GPT-3 (Brown et al., 2020a), GPT-3.5 Instruct (Ouyang et al., 2022), GPT-3.5 and GPT-4 (Bubeck et al., 2023).[4]

Perplexity. Perplexity measures how well a LM predicts a given sentence. In that respect, this measure can provide a good proxy to compare how natural or likely different types of sentences are. Following previous work (Brown et al., 2020a; Ushio et al., 2021b), for comparing the sentence likelihood we compute perplexity on each candidate sentence and choose the one with the lowest perplexity[5]. For decoder-only LMs such as GPT (Radford et al.), we compute the perplexity of a tokenized sentence $\boldsymbol{x} = [x_1 ... x_m]$ as

$$f(\boldsymbol{x}) = \exp\left(-\frac{1}{m}\sum_{j=1}^{m}\log P_{\mathrm{lm}}(x_j|\boldsymbol{x}_{j-1})\right) \quad (1)$$

where $P_{\mathrm{lm}}(x|\boldsymbol{x})$ is the likelihood of the next token given the precedent tokens. For masked language models (MLM) such as BERT (Devlin et al., 2019),

[4]In the main body of the paper we provide results for the largest models, as well as representative models for all families in the size experiments, but in the appendix we include results for all models.

[5]We use `https://github.com/asahi417/lmppl` to compute perplexity.

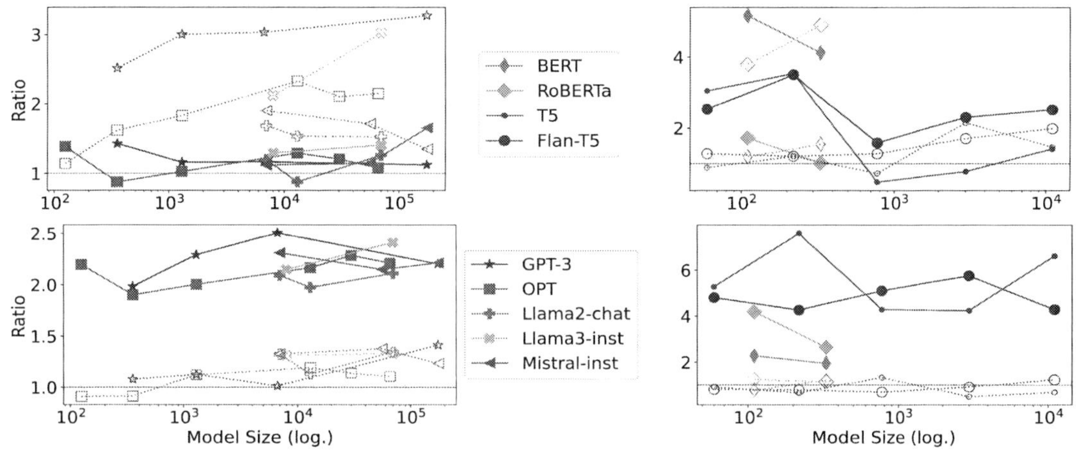

Figure 1: Medians of the ratios between the perplexities of the metaphoric and literal instances (solid lines) and between the anomalous and metaphoric instances (dashed lines) for decoder only models on the left, masked and encoder-decoder models on the right, for the Jankowiak dataset (upper plots) and Green dataset (lower plots).

pseudo-perplexity (Salazar et al., 2020) is used instead, which replaces the likelihood P in Equation 1 by $P_{\text{mask}}(x_j|\boldsymbol{x}_{\setminus j})$, the pseudo-likelihood (Wang and Cho, 2019) to predict the masked token x_j. For encoder-decoder LMs such as T5 (Raffel et al., 2020), we compute P_{lm} on the decoder, which is conditioned by the encoder. We should emphasize that perplexity values are model-dependent. Thus, in this work we have not attempted to measure perplexity values across LMs, but only for comparing sentences within the same LM. [6]

5 Language Model Representation of Metaphoric Analogies

In this section, we aim to understand how LMs identify metaphors in comparison to other types of analogies or literal statements, and how models can identify them from semantically anomalous sentences. To this end, we rely on three datasets containing sets of metaphoric and literal sentences, which are presented in Section 5.1. Following this, we rely exclusively on zero-shot experiments, first by computing perplexity scores (Section 5.2) and then by studying the abilities of the models to identify metaphors by following instructions (Section 5.3).

5.1 Metaphors and analogy datasets

In our evaluation, we focus on datasets that contain metaphors. Because of this, we exclude other well-known analogy datasets such as Google-analogies (Mikolov et al., 2013) or BATS (Gladkova et al., 2016), as they include analogies directly linked to well-defined lexical relations (e.g. capital-of). The three datasets considered in our experiments are summarized in Table 1. They are all composed of sets within which one element of the pairs remains identical and the second one varies.

Our data have two different formats. The Cardillo and Jankowiak datasets are sentences formed from two concepts based on the pattern x *is-a* y, where the problem to solve is the nature of the relation between x and y. The Green data are quadruples of the form $\{(x_i, x_j), (y_i, y_j)\}$ where the relation of interest stands between (x_i, x_j) and (y_i, y_j). Green and Jankowiak contain metaphoric, anomalous and literal sentences, while Cardillo only contains metaphoric and literal sentences.

Cardillo. This dataset (Cardillo et al., 2010, 2017) was initially created for studies within experimental psychology and contains 260 pairs of x is-a y instances. Each instance in the pair is composed of one literal and one metaphoric sentence.[7] We group the initial dataset from Cardillo et al. (2010) with the extension released in Cardillo et al. (2017). In addition to the set of instance pairs, each sentence has been annotated by a large number of participants on a scale of figurativeness that we also consider in our perplexity analysis.

[6] In the following experiments, due to computational resource limitation, we use the bitsandbytes python module to load the models larger than 13B parameters with quantization.

[7] Liu et al. (2022) created a large dataset of x is-a y metaphoric pairs but they do not contain negative examples.

Jankowiak. The Jankowiak dataset (Jankowiak, 2020) results from a similar study. In addition to literal and metaphorical sentences, it contains anomalous x is-a y sentences. It contains 120 sets of three sentences sharing the same concrete end word y, and the start words x are in the same range of frequencies.

Green. The Green dataset (Green et al., 2010) contains 120 quadruples organised in 40 sets. Each set contains one incorrect analogy (referred to as *anomaly*), one near analogy, and one far analogy (metaphor in our context). [8] For this dataset consisting of word pairs and not full sentences, we construct minimal sentences of the form A *is to* B *what* C *is to* D, where (A, B) is the first pair and (C, D) is the second pair.

5.2 Perplexity analysis

The metaphoric, anomalous and literal sentences from each dataset are fed into the model, and the perplexity is computed over each sentence, as explained in Section 4.

Results. For all datasets and for the vast majority of models, the median of the perplexities of metaphoric examples is higher than the median of literal ones, which is similar to the findings of Pedinotti et al. (2021) when analysing BERT-like models.[9] Full results and statistical significance of the difference in perplexity scores between the three classes are shown in Tables 7,8 and 9 in Appendix, Section B.2.

Figure 1 shows the variation of the perplexity ratios between metaphoric and literal examples and between anomalous and metaphoric examples, for the Jankowiak and the Green dataset. For the Green dataset, model perplexities are closer between metaphors and anomalies than between metaphors and literal instances. The ratios remain relatively stable when the size of the models increase, but we observe that the gap between metaphors and anomaly values increases for the largest decoder-only models. In contrast, in the Jankowiack dataset, metaphoric examples have closer perplexity scores to the literal ones than to the anomalous ones among most decoder-only models, and show unstable trends among the masked and encoder-decoder models.

Finally, as an example of the impact of instruction tuning on the representation of metaphors, we see that T5 and Flan-T5 models show different score distributions, particularly in the Jankowiak dataset. More comparison between instructed and non instructed version of the models can be found in Section B.2 of the Appendix. Across all the considered datasets, Flan-T5 models score the literal examples of each set lower than the other classes in a large majority of cases. This specificity on Flan-T5 models appears in the next experiment.

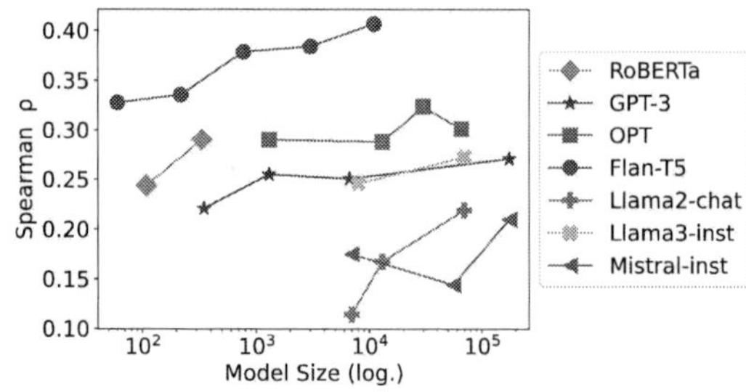

Figure 2: Correlation with human judgment for the perplexity setting on the Cardillo dataset.

Correlation between perplexity and figurativeness. Humans perceive sentences as more or less metaphoric, rather than merely as binary categories. As explained in Section 5.1, Cardillo et al. (2010, 2017) enriched their dataset with human ratings for each instance according to *figurativeness*. We study the correlation between all the previously obtained perplexities and the human judgments of figurativeness using Spearman correlation ρ. As shown in Figure 2, all models correlate positively with figurativeness. This means that sentences which are more figurative, tend to be have a lower pseudo log-likelihood according to the LMs.

FLAN-T5$_{XXL}$ obtains the highest Spearman correlation ρ of .41, and the Flan-T5 family correlation improves with the model size. BERT$_{BASE}$ and BERT$_{LARGE}$ also obtain competitive correlations, respectively .37 and .35. There is a weaker correlation for all other models including the largest ones (see the complete results in the Appendix, Table 11). The relatively low correlation between perplexity and figurativeness can be explained by the various levels of conventionality or creativity of the metaphors in the Cardillo dataset. Some frequently encountered metaphors are still perceived as very figurative. For example *The exhibition was a smash.* is both common and judged highly figurative.

[8] Kmiecik et al. (2019) released a similar corpus with 720 quadruples divided into near, far and incorrect analogies, but unlike Green, the far analogies were not all metaphors.

[9] Perplexity scores distributions for Llama3-Inst$_{70B}$ can be found in the Appendix Figure 5 as an example.

5.3 Can LMs identify metaphors from literal and anomalous sentences?

In this setting, we explicitly ask the models specialised in generation to produce a response to identify literal, metaphoric and anomalous sentences of each set at once with a prompt[10], in the form of multiple-choice question tasks. This allows us to integrate OpenAI models for which perplexity values are not accessible. We process the generated answers by each model[11] and provide the overall results based on accuracy. We run the experiments with all possible permutations of the sentences within each set (shuffling the order in which literal, metaphoric and anomalous sentences are presented in the prompt) because we identified a bias toward the generation of some sequences of labels in the models.[12]

Results. Accuracy scores for the models analysed in this setting are shown in Table 2. In this setting, Flan-T5$_{XXL}$ loses its advantage over the Llama2 and Mistral models. Unlike the other models, its generated answers do not always contain distinct labels for the elements of a set, especially for the Cardillo and Jankowiak datasets that contain three sentences per set. For those two datasets, the gap in accuracy with the other models is above 16 points. All the models have difficulties processing the Green dataset, made of 4-term instances, with the exception of GPT-4 that reaches an accuracy of 78.6%.

Error analysis. An error analysis of the results on the Green and Jankowiak datasets evaluated through the generation setting is shown in Table 3. For both datasets and all models, we observe that the confusion between literal and anomalous sentences is significantly less frequent than the confusion between metaphors and anomalies. With GPT-4, the confusion between metaphors and anomalies drops significantly for both datasets on all error types.

[10]An example prompt is available in Appendix C.1.

[11]The default hyper-parameters are used for all models. The minimum or maximum output length are adjusted to ensure a complete answer. Generation answers are processed semi-automatically, verifying manually those answers that do not conform exactly with the expected output.

[12]This bias is reported in the Appendix (Tables 12 and 13).

Model	Card.	Jank.	Green
FLAN-T5$_{XXL}$	78.9	57.4	37.6
Llama2-chat$_{70B}$	85.6	73.6	56.4
Llama3-Instr$_{70B}$	88.7	89	64.3
Mixtral-Instr$_{8x7B}$	76.5	84.1	55.3
Mixtral-Instr$_{8x22B}$	82	81.9	67.1
GPT-3.5$_{turbo\text{-}inst.}$	65.9	61.5	38.8
GPT-3.5$_{turbo}$	70.5	59.8	41.2
GPT-4	**91.8**	**91.4**	**78.6**
Random	50.0	33.3	33.3

Table 2: Accuracy of the generated answers for the three datasets Cardillo, Jankowiak and Green in the instruction generation setting (*gen*).

Model	Jank.			Green		
	LM	MA	LA	LM	MA	LA
FLAN-T5$_{XXL}$	282	**521**	116	214	**220**	15
Llama2-chat$_{70B}$	127	**345**	99	86	**111**	92
Llama3-Instr$_{70B}$	80	**117**	41	**111**	92	54
Mixtral-Instr$_{8x7B}$	127	**141**	75	**130**	123	60
Mixtral-Instr$_{8x22B}$	90	**253**	45	37	**153**	35
GPT-3.5$_{turbo\text{-}inst.}$	260	**433**	138	140	**165**	136
GPT-3.5$_{turbo}$	179	**450**	234	137	140	**143**
GPT-4	79	**89**	18	**92**	48	14

Table 3: Error analysis for the Jankowiak and Green datasets in the generation setting (*gen*). The non-directional confusion between *literal* and *metaphor* (LM), *metaphor* and *anomaly* (MA) and *literal* and *anomaly* (LA) labels are shown for all the models evaluation on generation.

6 Do Metaphors Have an Impact on How LMs Solve Analogies?

In the previous section, we tested the capabilities of language models in explicitly recognising metaphors. The results show how models find them less likely than literal sentences. A natural question that may arise is whether this behavior has an impact on how LMs solve analogies more generally. In particular, our aim is to understand whether LMs are capable of solving analogies irrespective of whether they are metaphorical or not.

6.1 Data

We rely on the SAT analogy dataset (Turney, 2006) for our experiments. SAT is composed of 374 multiple-choice word analogy questions from the SAT college entrance exam in the US. This dataset has been used in the context of NLP to evaluate how models recognise analogies (Brown et al., 2020b; Ushio et al., 2021b,a; Chen et al., 2022; Kumar and Schockaert, 2023). One advantage of this dataset

Input: *weave is to fabric what ...*	Label: Met.
1) illustrate is to manual	4) bake is to oven
2) hang is to picture	⇒ **5) write is to text**
3) sew is to thread	

Table 4: Example set of the SAT dataset where the correct analogy *5)* has been labeled as a metaphor.

over other benchmarks is that the dataset was not openly available on the internet, which mitigates possible concerns of data contamination in LMs. Each set in the SAT contains a stem word pair, and five other candidate pairs, forming a correct analogy and four anomalies with the stem pair. The task consists of selecting the correct analogy.

SAT annotation Each of the 374 questions of the SAT dataset contains a single correct analogy, and a subset of them are metaphoric analogies, as in the example presented Table 4. Our aim is to divide SAT correct analogies between metaphoric and non-metaphoric ones. This extended annotation enables a new experiment in which we assess the SAT performance of different types of analogies, metaphorical or not. Moreover, in the unlikely case that any of the closed language models that we analysed had been trained with the original SAT analogies, this information was not available to the model. Given the difficulty of the task, the annotation process required two rounds of annotation, detailed in the Appendix Section E.1.

A common reason for disagreement after the first round was that, sometimes, annotators could not think of a context in which two pairs of concepts could be used metaphorically. When one annotator had a clear example in mind, he or she was usually able to convince the others that an analogy was metaphoric during the discussions. For instance, the example *playwright is to actor what composer is to musician*, is easier to label after seeing the example *The playwright made him the gong in the symphony of his play*. Disagreement often occurred with the analogies when concrete domains were not very distant from each other[13]. We therefore asked all annotators to suggest and share examples prior to the second round of annotations. In total, 103 instances were labelled as metaphoric, and 239 as non-metaphoric.

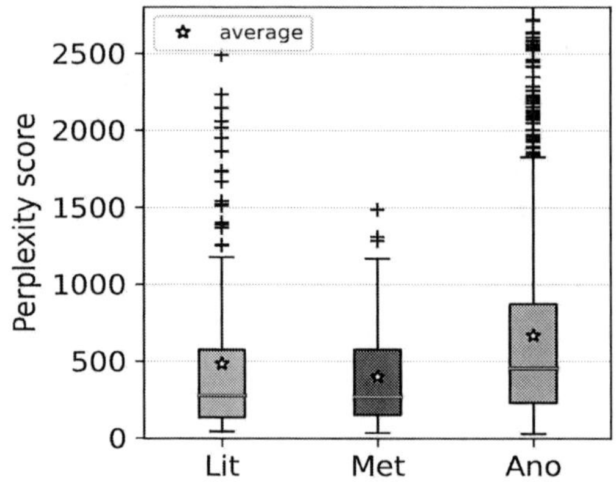

Figure 3: Boxplot showing the distribution of the perplexity scores for the three classes literal sentences (Lit), metaphor (Met) and anomalies (Ano) for the Llama3$_{70B\text{-}instr}$ model in SAT. Results for all models can be found in the Appendix, Table 10.

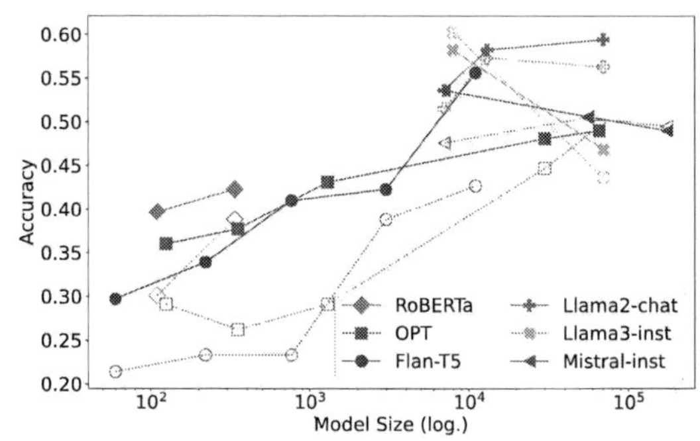

Figure 4: Accuracy results of the *perplexity* setting experiment on SAT. The results for the metaphoric class are displayed in the dashed lines, while the results for the non-metaphoric class are shown in the solid lines.

6.2 Experimental results

Experimental setting. The experimental setting is similar to the ones set out in the previous section. In particular, we test LMs using perplexity, following the same methodology outlined in Section 5.2. In this case, out of the five choices, the instance with the lowest perplexity is selected as the correct option. In addition, the large instructed LMs are tested through text generation, prompted to output the correct answer among the five choices[14]. Then, we simply report the accuracy on the metaphoric and non-metaphoric subsets of SAT.

[13]This difficulty is related to the practical delimitation and granularity of domains.

[14]As in Section 5, experiments are run on all possible permutations of the correct answer position to neutralise the effect of sentence position bias in the prompt. The prompt used for this experiment is available in Appendix E.3.

Perplexity analysis. The SAT* perplexity scores of the metaphoric and non-metaphoric analogies are in the same range of values for most models (Figure 3 shows the results for $\text{Llama3}_{\text{70B-instr}}$). A Mann-Whitney U rank test on two independent samples for the two classes (two-sided, $p<0.05$) shows significance in the difference between the two groups for only 6 of the 51 models tested (see Table 10 in the Appendix). In fact, a majority of models have slightly larger perplexity scores on average for the non-metaphoric analogies than for the metaphoric ones. The SAT dataset is designed to be a difficult test, containing infrequent words and non-obvious analogies. This allows us to study the behavior of the models and their ability to identify correct analogies when presented with metaphoric and non-metaphoric far analogies with a similar level of perplexity.

Results. Figure 4 shows the accuracy on the metaphorical and non-metaphorical subsets of SAT in the *perplexity* setting.[15] In general, model performance improves with size. Smaller models show a gap in accuracy between questions involving metaphors and other types. This gap diminishes when the model size increases until the accuracy for the metaphor class becomes similar to that of the simple analogy class in the larger models. We observe a decrease of the performance of the largest $\text{Llama3}_{\text{70B-inst}}$ and $\text{Mixtral}_{\text{8x22B}}$ models that might eventually be caused by more constrained expectations on the input format (e.g. special input tokens for Mixtral models and system prompt for Llama3).

Table 5 shows the results of the generation experiments for the large instructed models in comparison with the perplexity setting. While models tend to perform better for non-metaphoric analogies in the perplexity setting, they obtain better results on the metaphors in the generation setting. A possible explanation for this result is that the metaphors of SAT* have in fact more chances to appear in natural sentences than the artificially constructed non-metaphoric analogies. $\text{Llama3}_{\text{70B-inst}}$ and $\text{Mixtral}_{\text{8*22-inst}}$ perform better in the generation than in the perplexity setting, reinforcing the hypothesis that perplexity may not be the best metric when using these models in applications, even for the task of detecting plausible sentences or analogies. Moreover, we can observe again that GPT-4 performed better than the other models, although the conclusions that can be drawn from this model are limited due to its closed nature.

[15] See Table 10 in the Appendix for the full results.

Model	PPL		GEN	
	Lit	Met	Lit	Met
$\text{FLAN-T5}_{\text{XXL}}$	*55.6	42.7	41.6	44.5
$\text{Llama2-chat}_{\text{70B}}$	**59.4**	**56.3**	41.0	*49.5
$\text{Llama3-Instr}_{\text{70B}}$	46.9	43.7	55.8	*62.5
$\text{Mixtral-Instr}_{\text{8x7B}}$	50.6	50.5	45.4	47.6
$\text{Mixtral-Instr}_{\text{8x22B}}$	49.0	49.5	50.5	*55.7
$\text{GPT-3.5}_{\text{turbo}}$			28.5	32.6
GPT-4			**72.6**	**75.0**

Table 5: Accuracy results in the perplexity (PPL) and generation settings (GEN) for the literal and metaphor classes in SAT. Bold numbers show the highest accuracy scores overall. The statistical significance of the gap between literal and metaphoric accuracy scores is calculated with a two independent samples t-test ($p<0.05$), and indicated with * on the higher score in the table.

7 Conclusion

In this paper, we have analysed the capabilities of LMs to perceive and identify metaphors. Using perplexity as a proxy to measure plausibility in LMs, we observe that, in general, LMs perceive metaphors as less likely, and are often perceived closer to anomalous sentences than literal ones. In general, LMs struggle more often to distinguish metaphors from anomalous sentences even when instructed to do so, although this gap diminishes with newer and larger models.

As a result of this finding, we also investigated whether these results would be reflected in how models can distinguish metaphors from anomalies in a wider context. The results show that, at least for the new generation of LM-based conversational agents, this does not appear to be as problematic.

Several follow-up questions remain unaddressed in spite of these findings. What is the role of metaphors in generative models? Do LMs generate (new) metaphors in the context of a conversation, or do they resort to existing expressions and literal sentences? In the context of computational linguistics and semantics, it would be interesting to better understand how metaphors are internally represented or encoded in this new generation of LMs.

Limitations

There is a body of work in the literature that has questioned analogy evaluation as a reliable way to probe NLP models, and, in particular, word embeddings (Linzen, 2016; Schluter, 2018; Nissim et al., 2020). In our paper, we are not interested in analogy as an evaluation benchmark, and rather as input data to extract insights. Nonetheless, some of the criticism of the aforementioned papers with respect to word analogies can also be applied to language models. In relation to this, we have not attempted to perform extensive prompt engineering in this work, as we were interested in knowing the trends and raw behaviour of models rather than obtaining the best results. This was also prompted due to computational constraints (see Appendix F for details on the computational resources and time). It is likely, however, that some results may differ if other prompts or evaluation protocols were considered.

In this work, we did not study the model behavior in relation to the frequency of the semantic associations in corpora. Since some metaphors are more common than other literal associations, this extended control analysis may reveal other behavior patterns not captured in our experiments. Our experiments focus solely on English corpora, therefore findings may differ for other languages, especially less-resourced and languages from other families. Finally, data contamination may have an impact on the results, which we could not analyse extensively. To mitigate this, we considered datasets that are not openly available and enriched existing data, thereby ensuring that these new annotations had not been seen by any of the models.

Ethical considerations

We have not identified any potential misuse of this research. No personal data was required in the annotation of the SAT analogy dataset and all the annotators are co-authors of this paper.

Acknowledgments

We thank the anonymous reviewers for their invaluable feedback, Thomas Green at the Advanced Research Computing at Cardiff (ARCCA) for giving us access to the computational resources, Eileen Cardillo for authorizing us to re-share the datasets attached to Cardillo et al. (2010, 2017), Daniel Bouçanova Loureiro, Nico Potyca and Yi Zhou for the helpful discussions. Jose Camacho-Collados and Dimosthenis Antypas are supported by a UKRI Future Leaders Fellowship.

References

Rodrigo Agerri, John Barnden, Mark Lee, and Alan Wallington. 2008. Textual entailment as an evaluation framework for metaphor resolution: A proposal. In *Semantics in Text Processing. STEP 2008 Conference Proceedings*, pages 357–363. College Publications.

Max Black. 1977. More about metaphor. *Dialectica*, 31(3/4):431–457.

Brian Bowdle and Dedre Gentner. 2005. The career of metaphor. *Psychological review*, 112:193–216.

Tom B. Brown, Benjamin Mann, Nick Ryder, Melanie Subbiah, Jared Kaplan, Prafulla Dhariwal, Arvind Neelakantan, Pranav Shyam, Girish Sastry, Amanda Askell, Sandhini Agarwal, Ariel Herbert-Voss, Gretchen Krueger, Tom Henighan, Rewon Child, Aditya Ramesh, Daniel M. Ziegler, Jeffrey Wu, Clemens Winter, Christopher Hesse, Mark Chen, Eric Sigler, Mateusz Litwin, Scott Gray, Benjamin Chess, Jack Clark, Christopher Berner, Sam McCandlish, Alec Radford, Ilya Sutskever, and Dario Amodei. 2020a. Language models are few-shot learners. In *Proceedings of the Annual Conference on Neural Information Processing Systems*.

Tom B. Brown, Benjamin Mann, Nick Ryder, Melanie Subbiah, Jared Kaplan, Prafulla Dhariwal, Arvind Neelakantan, Pranav Shyam, Girish Sastry, Amanda Askell, Sandhini Agarwal, Ariel Herbert-Voss, Gretchen Krueger, Tom Henighan, Rewon Child, Aditya Ramesh, Daniel M. Ziegler, Jeffrey Wu, Clemens Winter, Christopher Hesse, Mark Chen, Eric Sigler, Mateusz Litwin, Scott Gray, Benjamin Chess, Jack Clark, Christopher Berner, Sam McCandlish, Alec Radford, Ilya Sutskever, and Dario Amodei. 2020b. Language models are few-shot learners.

Sébastien Bubeck, Varun Chandrasekaran, Ronen Eldan, Johannes Gehrke, Eric Horvitz, Ece Kamar, Peter Lee, Yin Tat Lee, Yuanzhi Li, Scott Lundberg, Harsha Nori, Hamid Palangi, Marco Tulio Ribeiro, and Yi Zhang. 2023. Sparks of artificial general intelligence: Early experiments with gpt-4.

Eileen R. Cardillo, Christine Watson, and Anjan Chatterjee. 2017. Stimulus needs are a moving target: 240 additional matched literal and metaphorical sentences for testing neural hypotheses about metaphor. *Behavior Research Methods*, 49(2):471–483.

E.R. Cardillo, G.L. Schmidt, A. Kranjec, and A. Chatterjee. 2010. Stimulus design is an obstacle course: 560 matched literal and metaphorical sentences for testing neural hypotheses about metaphor. *Behav. Res. Methods*, 42(3):651–664.

Tuhin Chakrabarty, Debanjan Ghosh, Adam Poliak, and Smaranda Muresan. 2021a. Figurative language in recognizing textual entailment. In *Findings of the Association for Computational Linguistics: ACL-IJCNLP 2021*, pages 3354–3361, Online. Association for Computational Linguistics.

Tuhin Chakrabarty, Vishakh Padmakumar, Faeze Brahman, and Smaranda Muresan. 2024. Creativity support in the age of large language models: An empirical study involving emerging writers.

Tuhin Chakrabarty, Xurui Zhang, Smaranda Muresan, and Nanyun Peng. 2021b. MERMAID: Metaphor generation with symbolism and discriminative decoding. In *Proceedings of the 2021 Conference of the North American Chapter of the Association for Computational Linguistics: Human Language Technologies*, pages 4250–4261, Online. Association for Computational Linguistics.

Jiangjie Chen, Rui Xu, Ziquan Fu, Wei Shi, Zhongqiao Li, Xinbo Zhang, Changzhi Sun, Lei Li, Yanghua Xiao, and Hao Zhou. 2022. E-KAR: A benchmark for rationalizing natural language analogical reasoning. In *Findings of the Association for Computational Linguistics: ACL 2022*, pages 3941–3955, Dublin, Ireland. Association for Computational Linguistics.

Aakanksha Chowdhery, Sharan Narang, Jacob Devlin, Maarten Bosma, Gaurav Mishra, Adam Roberts, Paul Barham, Hyung Won Chung, Charles Sutton, Sebastian Gehrmann, Parker Schuh, Kensen Shi, Sasha Tsvyashchenko, Joshua Maynez, Abhishek Rao, Parker Barnes, Yi Tay, Noam Shazeer, Vinodkumar Prabhakaran, Emily Reif, Nan Du, Ben Hutchinson, Reiner Pope, James Bradbury, Jacob Austin, Michael Isard, Guy Gur-Ari, Pengcheng Yin, Toju Duke, Anselm Levskaya, Sanjay Ghemawat, Sunipa Dev, Henryk Michalewski, Xavier Garcia, Vedant Misra, Kevin Robinson, Liam Fedus, Denny Zhou, Daphne Ippolito, David Luan, Hyeontaek Lim, Barret Zoph, Alexander Spiridonov, Ryan Sepassi, David Dohan, Shivani Agrawal, Mark Omernick, Andrew M. Dai, Thanumalayan Sankaranarayana Pillai, Marie Pellat, Aitor Lewkowycz, Erica Moreira, Rewon Child, Oleksandr Polozov, Katherine Lee, Zongwei Zhou, Xuezhi Wang, Brennan Saeta, Mark Diaz, Orhan Firat, Michele Catasta, Jason Wei, Kathy Meier-Hellstern, Douglas Eck, Jeff Dean, Slav Petrov, and Noah Fiedel. 2022. Palm: Scaling language modeling with pathways.

Hyung Won Chung, Le Hou, Shayne Longpre, Barret Zoph, Yi Tay, William Fedus, Eric Li, Xuezhi Wang, Mostafa Dehghani, Siddhartha Brahma, Albert Webson, Shixiang Shane Gu, Zhuyun Dai, Mirac Suzgun, Xinyun Chen, Aakanksha Chowdhery, Sharan Narang, Gaurav Mishra, Adams Yu, Vincent Zhao, Yanping Huang, Andrew Dai, Hongkun Yu, Slav Petrov, Ed H. Chi, Jeff Dean, Jacob Devlin, Adam Roberts, Denny Zhou, Quoc V. Le, and Jason Wei. 2022. Scaling instruction-finetuned language models.

Tamara Czinczoll, Helen Yannakoudakis, Pushkar Mishra, and Ekaterina Shutova. 2022. Scientific and creative analogies in pretrained language models. In *Findings of the Association for Computational Linguistics: EMNLP 2022*, pages 2094–2100, Abu Dhabi, United Arab Emirates. Association for Computational Linguistics.

Jacob Devlin, Ming-Wei Chang, Kenton Lee, and Kristina Toutanova. 2019. BERT: Pre-training of deep bidirectional transformers for language understanding. In *Proceedings of the 2019 Conference of the North American Chapter of the Association for Computational Linguistics: Human Language Technologies, Volume 1 (Long and Short Papers)*, pages 4171–4186, Minneapolis, Minnesota. Association for Computational Linguistics.

Dan Fass and Yorick Wilks. 1983. Preference semantics, ill-formedness, and metaphor. *American Journal of Computational Linguistics*, 9(3-4):178–187.

Mengshi Ge, Rui Mao, and Erik Cambria. 2023. A survey on computational metaphor processing techniques: From identification, interpretation, generation to application. *Artificial Intelligence Review*, 56(02):1829–1895.

D. Gentner, B. Falkenhainer, and J. Skorstad. 1988. Viewing metaphor as analogy.

Dedre Gentner, Brian Bowdle, Phillip Wolff, and Consuelo Boronat. 2001. Metaphor is like analogy. *Metaphor Is Like Analogy*.

Dedre Gentner and L. Smith. 2012. *Analogical Reasoning*, pages 130–136.

Katy Ilonka Gero and Lydia B. Chilton. 2019. Metaphoria: An algorithmic companion for metaphor creation. In *Proceedings of the 2019 CHI Conference on Human Factors in Computing Systems*, CHI '19, page 1–12, New York, NY, USA. Association for Computing Machinery.

Anna Gladkova, Aleksandr Drozd, and Satoshi Matsuoka. 2016. Analogy-based detection of morphological and semantic relations with word embeddings: what works and what doesn't. In *Proceedings of the NAACL Student Research Workshop*, pages 8–15, San Diego, California. Association for Computational Linguistics.

Joseph Grady. 1999. A typology of motivation for conceptual metaphor: correlation vs. resemblance. In *Metaphor in Cognitive Linguistics*. John Benjamins.

Adam E Green, David J M Kraemer, Jonathan A Fugelsang, Jeremy R Gray, and Kevin N Dunbar. 2010. Connecting long distance: semantic distance in analogical reasoning modulates frontopolar cortex activity. *Cereb Cortex*, 20(1):70–76.

Bernadeta Griciūtė, Marc Tanti, and Lucia Donatelli. 2022. On the cusp of comprehensibility: Can language models distinguish between metaphors and nonsense? In *Proceedings of the 3rd Workshop on Figurative Language Processing (FLP)*, pages 173–177, Abu Dhabi, United Arab Emirates (Hybrid). Association for Computational Linguistics.

Maram Hasanain and Tamer Elsayed. 2022. Cross-lingual transfer learning for check-worthy claim identification over twitter.

Douglas Hofstadter. 2001. Epilogue: Analogy as the core of cognition. In Dedre Gentner, Keith J. Holyoak, and Boicho N. Kokinov, editors, *The Analogical Mind: Perspectives from Cognitive Science*, pages 499–538. MIT Press.

Keith J Holyoak and Paul Thagard. 1996. *Mental leaps: Analogy in creative thought.* MIT press.

Srinivasan Iyer, Xi Victoria Lin, Ramakanth Pasunuru, Todor Mihaylov, Dániel Simig, Ping Yu, Kurt Shuster, Tianlu Wang, Qing Liu, Punit Singh Koura, et al. 2022. Opt-iml: Scaling language model instruction meta learning through the lens of generalization.

Katarzyna Jankowiak. 2020. Normative data for novel nominal metaphors, novel similes, literal, and anomalous utterances in polish and english. *Journal of Psycholinguistic Research*, 49(4):541–569.

Albert Q. Jiang, Alexandre Sablayrolles, Arthur Mensch, Chris Bamford, Devendra Singh Chaplot, Diego de las Casas, Florian Bressand, Gianna Lengyel, Guillaume Lample, Lucile Saulnier, Lélio Renard Lavaud, Marie-Anne Lachaux, Pierre Stock, Teven Le Scao, Thibaut Lavril, Thomas Wang, Timothée Lacroix, and William El Sayed. 2023. Mistral 7b.

Albert Q. Jiang, Alexandre Sablayrolles, Antoine Roux, Arthur Mensch, Blanche Savary, Chris Bamford, Devendra Singh Chaplot, Diego de las Casas, Emma Bou Hanna, Florian Bressand, Gianna Lengyel, Guillaume Bour, Guillaume Lample, Lélio Renard Lavaud, Lucile Saulnier, Marie-Anne Lachaux, Pierre Stock, Sandeep Subramanian, Sophia Yang, Szymon Antoniak, Teven Le Scao, Théophile Gervet, Thibaut Lavril, Thomas Wang, Timothée Lacroix, and William El Sayed. 2024. Mixtral of experts.

Chen-Yao Kao. 2020. How figurativity of analogy affects creativity: The application of four-term analogies to teaching for creativity. *Thinking Skills and Creativity*, 36:100653.

Matthew J. Kmiecik, Ryan J. Brisson, and Robert G. Morrison. 2019. The time course of semantic and relational processing during verbal analogical reasoning. *Brain and Cognition*, 129:25–34.

Shreyas Kulkarni, Arkadiy Saakyan, Tuhin Chakrabarty, and Smaranda Muresan. 2024. A report on the FigLang 2024 shared task on multimodal figurative language. In *Proceedings of the 4th Workshop on Figurative Language Processing (FigLang 2024)*, pages 115–119, Mexico City, Mexico (Hybrid). Association for Computational Linguistics.

Nitesh Kumar and Steven Schockaert. 2023. Solving hard analogy questions with relation embedding chains. In *Proceedings of the 2023 Conference on Empirical Methods in Natural Language Processing*, pages 6224–6236, Singapore. Association for Computational Linguistics.

George Lakoff and Mark Johnson. 1980. *Metaphors we Live by.* University of Chicago Press, Chicago.

Chee Wee (Ben) Leong, Beata Beigman Klebanov, Chris Hamill, Egon Stemle, Rutuja Ubale, and Xianyang Chen. 2020. A report on the 2020 VUA and TOEFL metaphor detection shared task. In *Proceedings of the Second Workshop on Figurative Language Processing*, pages 18–29, Online. Association for Computational Linguistics.

Hongsong Li, Kenny Q. Zhu, and Haixun Wang. 2013. Data-driven metaphor recognition and explanation. *Transactions of the Association for Computational Linguistics*, 1:379–390.

Tal Linzen. 2016. Issues in evaluating semantic spaces using word analogies. In *Proceedings of the 1st Workshop on Evaluating Vector-Space Representations for NLP*, pages 13–18, Berlin, Germany. Association for Computational Linguistics.

Emmy Liu, Chenxuan Cui, Kenneth Zheng, and Graham Neubig. 2022. Testing the ability of language models to interpret figurative language. In *Proceedings of the 2022 Conference of the North American Chapter of the Association for Computational Linguistics: Human Language Technologies*, pages 4437–4452, Seattle, United States. Association for Computational Linguistics.

Yinhan Liu, Myle Ott, Naman Goyal, Jingfei Du, Mandar Joshi, Danqi Chen, Omer Levy, Mike Lewis, Luke Zettlemoyer, and Veselin Stoyanov. 2019. Roberta: A robustly optimized bert pretraining approach. *arXiv preprint arXiv:1907.11692*.

Rui Mao, Chenghua Lin, and Frank Guerin. 2018. Word embedding and WordNet based metaphor identification and interpretation. In *Proceedings of the 56th Annual Meeting of the Association for Computational Linguistics (Volume 1: Long Papers)*, pages 1222–1231, Melbourne, Australia. Association for Computational Linguistics.

Rui Mao, Chenghua Lin, and Frank Guerin. 2019. End-to-end sequential metaphor identification inspired by linguistic theories. In *Proceedings of the 57th Annual Meeting of the Association for Computational Linguistics*, pages 3888–3898, Florence, Italy. Association for Computational Linguistics.

Zachary J. Mason. 2004. CorMet: A Computational, Corpus-Based Conventional Metaphor Extraction System. *Computational Linguistics*, 30(1):23–44.

Tomas Mikolov, Wen-tau Yih, and Geoffrey Zweig. 2013. Linguistic regularities in continuous space word representations. In *Proceedings of the 2013 Conference of the North American Chapter of the Association for Computational Linguistics: Human Language Technologies*, pages 746–751, Atlanta, Georgia. Association for Computational Linguistics.

Niklas Muennighoff, Thomas Wang, Lintang Sutawika, Adam Roberts, Stella Biderman, Teven Le Scao, M Saiful Bari, Sheng Shen, Zheng-Xin Yong, Hailey Schoelkopf, Xiangru Tang, Dragomir Radev, Alham Fikri Aji, Khalid Almubarak, Samuel Albanie, Zaid Alyafeai, Albert Webson, Edward Raff, and Colin Raffel. 2023. Crosslingual generalization through multitask finetuning.

Malvina Nissim, Rik van Noord, and Rob van der Goot. 2020. Fair is better than sensational: Man is to doctor as woman is to doctor. *Computational Linguistics*, 46(2):487–497.

Ortony. 1993. *Metaphor and Thought*, 2 edition. Cambridge University Press.

Long Ouyang, Jeff Wu, Xu Jiang, Diogo Almeida, Carroll L. Wainwright, Pamela Mishkin, Chong Zhang, Sandhini Agarwal, Katarina Slama, Alex Ray, John Schulman, Jacob Hilton, Fraser Kelton, Luke Miller, Maddie Simens, Amanda Askell, Peter Welinder, Paul Christiano, Jan Leike, and Ryan Lowe. 2022. Training language models to follow instructions with human feedback.

Paolo Pedinotti, Eliana Di Palma, Ludovica Cerini, and Alessandro Lenci. 2021. A howling success or a working sea? testing what BERT knows about metaphors. In *Proceedings of the Fourth BlackboxNLP Workshop on Analyzing and Interpreting Neural Networks for NLP*, pages 192–204, Punta Cana, Dominican Republic. Association for Computational Linguistics.

Alec Radford, Karthik Narasimhan, Tim Salimans, and Ilya Sutskever. Improving language understanding by generative pre-training.

Alec Radford, Jeffrey Wu, Rewon Child, David Luan, Dario Amodei, and Ilya Sutskever. 2019. Language models are unsupervised multitask learners. *OpenAI blog*, 1(8):9.

Colin Raffel, Noam Shazeer, Adam Roberts, Katherine Lee, Sharan Narang, Michael Matena, Yanqi Zhou, Wei Li, and Peter J Liu. 2020. Exploring the limits of transfer learning with a unified text-to-text transformer. *The Journal of Machine Learning Research*, 21(1):5485–5551.

Philip Resnik. 1997. Selectional preference and sense disambiguation. In *Tagging Text with Lexical Semantics: Why, What, and How?*

Julian Salazar, Davis Liang, Toan Q. Nguyen, and Katrin Kirchhoff. 2020. Masked language model scoring. In *Proceedings of the 58th Annual Meeting of the Association for Computational Linguistics*, pages 2699–2712, Online. Association for Computational Linguistics.

Natalie Schluter. 2018. The word analogy testing caveat. In *Proceedings of the 2018 Conference of the North American Chapter of the Association for Computational Linguistics: Human Language Technologies, Volume 2 (Short Papers)*, pages 242–246, New Orleans, Louisiana. Association for Computational Linguistics.

Ekaterina Shutova, Lin Sun, and Anna Korhonen. 2010. Metaphor identification using verb and noun clustering. In *Proceedings of the 23rd International Conference on Computational Linguistics (Coling 2010)*, pages 1002–1010, Beijing, China. Coling 2010 Organizing Committee.

Kevin Stowe, Tuhin Chakrabarty, Nanyun Peng, Smaranda Muresan, and Iryna Gurevych. 2021. Metaphor generation with conceptual mappings. In *Proceedings of the 59th Annual Meeting of the Association for Computational Linguistics and the 11th International Joint Conference on Natural Language Processing (Volume 1: Long Papers)*, pages 6724–6736, Online. Association for Computational Linguistics.

Kevin Stowe, Prasetya Utama, and Iryna Gurevych. 2022. IMPLI: Investigating NLI models' performance on figurative language. In *Proceedings of the 60th Annual Meeting of the Association for Computational Linguistics (Volume 1: Long Papers)*, pages 5375–5388, Dublin, Ireland. Association for Computational Linguistics.

Oren Sultan and Dafna Shahaf. 2023. Life is a circus and we are the clowns: Automatically finding analogies between situations and processes.

Yi Tay, Mostafa Dehghani, Vinh Q. Tran, Xavier Garcia, Jason Wei, Xuezhi Wang, Hyung Won Chung, Siamak Shakeri, Dara Bahri, Tal Schuster, Huaixiu Steven Zheng, Denny Zhou, Neil Houlsby, and Donald Metzler. 2023. Ul2: Unifying language learning paradigms.

Ross Taylor, Marcin Kardas, Guillem Cucurull, Thomas Scialom, Anthony Hartshorn, Elvis Saravia, Andrew Poulton, Viktor Kerkez, and Robert Stojnic. 2022. Galactica: A large language model for science.

Roger Tourangeau and Robert J. Sternberg. 1982. Understanding and appreciating metaphors. *Cognition*, 11(3):203–244.

Hugo Touvron, Louis Martin, Kevin Stone, Peter Albert, Amjad Almahairi, Yasmine Babaei, Nikolay Bashlykov, Soumya Batra, Prajjwal Bhargava, Shruti Bhosale, Dan Bikel, Lukas Blecher, Cristian Canton Ferrer, Moya Chen, Guillem Cucurull, David Esiobu, Jude Fernandes, Jeremy Fu, Wenyin Fu, Brian Fuller, Cynthia Gao, Vedanuj Goswami, Naman Goyal, Anthony Hartshorn, Saghar Hosseini, Rui Hou, Hakan Inan, Marcin Kardas, Viktor Kerkez, Madian Khabsa, Isabel Kloumann, Artem Korenev, Punit Singh Koura, Marie-Anne Lachaux, Thibaut Lavril, Jenya Lee, Diana Liskovich, Yinghai Lu, Yuning Mao, Xavier Martinet, Todor Mihaylov, Pushkar Mishra, Igor Molybog, Yixin Nie, Andrew Poulton, Jeremy Reizenstein, Rashi Rungta, Kalyan Saladi, Alan Schelten,

Ruan Silva, Eric Michael Smith, Ranjan Subramanian, Xiaoqing Ellen Tan, Binh Tang, Ross Taylor, Adina Williams, Jian Xiang Kuan, Puxin Xu, Zheng Yan, Iliyan Zarov, Yuchen Zhang, Angela Fan, Melanie Kambadur, Sharan Narang, Aurelien Rodriguez, Robert Stojnic, Sergey Edunov, and Thomas Scialom. 2023. Llama 2: Open foundation and fine-tuned chat models.

Yulia Tsvetkov, Leonid Boytsov, Anatole Gershman, Eric Nyberg, and Chris Dyer. 2014. Metaphor detection with cross-lingual model transfer. In *Proceedings of the 52nd Annual Meeting of the Association for Computational Linguistics (Volume 1: Long Papers)*, pages 248–258, Baltimore, Maryland. Association for Computational Linguistics.

Peter Turney, Yair Neuman, Dan Assaf, and Yohai Cohen. 2011. Literal and metaphorical sense identification through concrete and abstract context. In *Proceedings of the 2011 Conference on Empirical Methods in Natural Language Processing*, pages 680–690, Edinburgh, Scotland, UK. Association for Computational Linguistics.

Peter D. Turney. 2006. Similarity of semantic relations. *Computational Linguistics*, 32(3):379–416.

Asahi Ushio, Jose Camacho-Collados, and Steven Schockaert. 2021a. Distilling relation embeddings from pretrained language models. In *Proceedings of the 2021 Conference on Empirical Methods in Natural Language Processing*, pages 9044–9062, Online and Punta Cana, Dominican Republic. Association for Computational Linguistics.

Asahi Ushio, Luis Espinosa Anke, Steven Schockaert, and Jose Camacho-Collados. 2021b. BERT is to NLP what AlexNet is to CV: Can pre-trained language models identify analogies? In *Proceedings of the 59th Annual Meeting of the Association for Computational Linguistics and the 11th International Joint Conference on Natural Language Processing (Volume 1: Long Papers)*, pages 3609–3624, Online. Association for Computational Linguistics.

Tony Veale. 2016. Round up the usual suspects: Knowledge-based metaphor generation. In *Proceedings of the Fourth Workshop on Metaphor in NLP*, pages 34–41, San Diego, California. Association for Computational Linguistics.

Tony Veale, Ekaterina Shutova, and Beata Beigman Klebanov. 2016. *Metaphor: A computational perspective*. Morgan & Claypool Publishers.

Lennart Wachowiak and Dagmar Gromann. 2023. Does GPT-3 grasp metaphors? identifying metaphor mappings with generative language models. In *Proceedings of the 61st Annual Meeting of the Association for Computational Linguistics (Volume 1: Long Papers)*, pages 1018–1032, Toronto, Canada. Association for Computational Linguistics.

Alex Wang and Kyunghyun Cho. 2019. BERT has a mouth, and it must speak: BERT as a Markov random field language model. In *Proceedings of the Workshop on Methods for Optimizing and Evaluating Neural Language Generation*, pages 30–36, Minneapolis, Minnesota. Association for Computational Linguistics.

Ben Wang and Aran Komatsuzaki. 2021. GPT-J-6B: A 6 Billion Parameter Autoregressive Language Model. `https://github.com/kingoflolz/mesh-transformer-jax`.

Taylor Webb, Keith J. Holyoak, and Hongjing Lu. 2023. Emergent analogical reasoning in large language models.

Jason Wei, Yi Tay, Rishi Bommasani, Colin Raffel, Barret Zoph, Sebastian Borgeaud, Dani Yogatama, Maarten Bosma, Denny Zhou, Donald Metzler, Ed H. Chi, Tatsunori Hashimoto, Oriol Vinyals, Percy Liang, Jeff Dean, and William Fedus. 2022. Emergent abilities of large language models.

Thilini Wijesiriwardene, Amit Sheth, Valerie L. Shalin, Amitava Das, and Amit Sheth. 2023a. Why do we need neurosymbolic ai to model pragmatic analogies? *IEEE Intelligent Systems*, 38(5):12–16.

Thilini Wijesiriwardene, Ruwan Wickramarachchi, Bimal G. Gajera, Shreeyash Mukul Gowaikar, Chandan Gupta, Aman Chadha, Aishwarya Naresh Reganti, Amit Sheth, and Amitava Das. 2023b. Analogical – a novel benchmark for long text analogy evaluation in large language models.

Siyu Yuan, Jiangjie Chen, Changzhi Sun, Jiaqing Liang, Yanghua Xiao, and Deqing Yang. 2023. Analogykb: Unlocking analogical reasoning of language models with a million-scale knowledge base.

Shenglong Zhang and Ying Liu. 2022. Metaphor detection via linguistics enhanced Siamese network. In *Proceedings of the 29th International Conference on Computational Linguistics*, pages 4149–4159, Gyeongju, Republic of Korea. International Committee on Computational Linguistics.

Susan Zhang, Stephen Roller, Naman Goyal, Mikel Artetxe, Moya Chen, Shuohui Chen, Christopher Dewan, Mona Diab, Xian Li, Xi Victoria Lin, Todor Mihaylov, Myle Ott, Sam Shleifer, Kurt Shuster, Daniel Simig, Punit Singh Koura, Anjali Sridhar, Tianlu Wang, and Luke Zettlemoyer. 2022. Opt: Open pre-trained transformer language models.

A Language models used in our experiments

The models evaluated in the experiments, along with their sizes and corresponding HuggingFace links, are presented in Table 6.

	Model	Size	Name on HuggingFace
Masked LM	BERT$_{BASE}$	110M	bert-base-cased
	BERT$_{LARGE}$	355M	bert-large-cased
	RoBERTa$_{BASE}$	110M	roberta-base
	RoBERTa$_{LARGE}$	355M	roberta-large
Encoder-Decoder LM	T5$_{SMALL}$	60M	t5-small
	T5$_{BASE}$	220M	t5-base
	T5$_{LARGE}$	770M	t5-large
	T5$_{3B}$	3B	t5-3b
	T5$_{11B}$	11B	t5-11b
	Flan-T5$_{SMALL}$	60M	google/flan-t5-small
	Flan-T5$_{BASE}$	220M	google/flan-t5-base
	Flan-T5$_{LARGE}$	770M	google/flan-t5-large
	Flan-T5$_{XL}$	3B	google/flan-t5-xl
	Flan-T5$_{XXL}$	11B	google/flan-t5-xxl
	Flan-UL2	20B	google/flan-ul2
	UL2	20B	google/ul2
Decoder-only LM	GPT-2	124M	gpt2
	GPT-2$_{MEDIUM}$	355M	gpt2-medium
	GPT-2$_{LARGE}$	774M	gpt2-large
	GPT-2$_{XL}$	1.5B	gpt2-xl
	GPT-J$_{125M}$	125M	EleutherAI/gpt-neo-125M
	GPT-J$_{2.7B}$	2.7B	EleutherAI/gpt-neo-2.7B
	GPT-J$_{6B}$	6B	EleutherAI/gpt-j-6B
	GPT-J$_{20B}$	20B	EleutherAI/gpt-neox-20b
	OPT$_{125M}$	125M	facebook/opt-125m
	OPT$_{350M}$	350M	facebook/opt-350m
	OPT$_{1.3B}$	1.3B	facebook/opt-1.3b
	OPT$_{13B}$	13B	facebook/opt-13b
	OPT$_{30B}$	30B	facebook/opt-30b
	OPT$_{66B}$	66B	facebook/opt-66b
	OPT-IML$_{1.3B}$	1.3B	facebook/opt-iml-1.3b
	OPT-IML$_{30B}$	30B	facebook/opt-iml-30b
	OPT-IML$_{M\text{-}1.3B}$	1.3B	facebook/opt-iml-max-1.3b
	OPT-IML$_{M\text{-}30B}$	30B	facebook/opt-iml-max-30b
	Bloom$_{176B}$	176B	bigscience/bloom
	Bloomz$_{176B}$	176B	bigscience/bloomz
	Llama2$_{7B}$	7B	meta-llama/Llama-2-7b-hf
	Llama2$_{13B}$	13B	meta-llama/Llama-2-13b-hf
	Llama2$_{70B}$	70B	meta-llama/Llama-2-70b-hf
	Llama2-chat$_{7B}$	7B	meta-llama/ Llama-2-7b-chat-hf
	Llama2-chat$_{13B}$	13B	meta-llama/ Llama-2-13b-chat-hf
	Llama2-chat$_{70B}$	70B	meta-llama/ Llama-2-70b-chat-hf
	Llama3-Inst$_{8B}$	8B	meta-llama/ Meta-Llama-3-8b-Instruct
	Llama3-Inst$_{70B}$	70B	meta-llama/ Meta-Llama-3-70b-Instruct
	Mistral$_{7B}$	7B	mistralai/Mistral-7B-v0.1
	Mistral-Inst$_{7B}$	7B	mistralai/ Mistral-7B-Instr.-v0.2
sMoE	Mixtral$_{8x7B}$	56B	mistralai/Mixtral-8x7B-v0.1
	Mixtral-Inst$_{8x7B}$	56B	mistralai/ Mixtral-8x7B-Instr.-v0.1
	Mixtral-Inst$_{8x22B}$	176B	mistralai/ Mixtral-8x22B-Instr.-v0.1

Table 6: The model checkpoints used in the LM baselines on HuggingFace model hub. All the models can be obtained at `https://huggingface.co`.

B Perplexity setting experiments result

B.1 Graphics of the perplexity experiment results

The boxplots of the metaphoric, literal and anomalous instances for Llama3-Inst$_{70B}$ perplexity scores for the three datasets are shown Figure 5.

B.2 Result tables for all models

Tables 7, 8 and 9 include the full experimental results of Section 5.2. They show the proportions of sets where sentences with literal, metaphoric, and anomalous content exhibit the lowest perplexity for all the datasets, and the statistical significance test results for the differences in perplexity scores obtained by the metaphoric, literal and anomalous instances.

B.3 Correlation between perplexity scores and human ratings of figurativeness

Table 11 shows the correlation with human ratings of figurativeness for the Cardillo dataset with all studied models.

C Generation experiments

In this section we provide details for the generation experiments presented in Section 5.3.

C.1 Prompt used in the generation experiments

An example prompt used for text generation in order to label all the sentences of a set at once.

> **Example : Green**
>
> I will give you three sentences and I would like you to tell me which one is "anomalous", which one is "literal", and which one is a "metaphor". There is exactly one anomalous sentence, one metaphor, and one literal sentence among the three provided sentences. Here are the three sentences:
>
> 1. flock is to goose what wolfpack is to wolf
> 2. flock is to goose what constellation is to star
> 3. flock is to goose what pond is to turtle
>
> Please provide the answer in separate lines for each sentence.
> Answer:
> Sentence 1) is

C.1.1 Specificities of the Mixtral and Llama-3 models prompts.

Mixtral models. The use of special tokens is recommended in the Mixtral models prompts to obtain the best performances [16]. We modify the prompt according to the guideline.

> **<s> [INST]** I will give you three sentences and I would like you to tell me which one is "anomalous", which one is "literal", and which one is a "metaphor". There is exactly one anomalous sentence, one metaphor, and one "literal sentence among the three provided sentences. Here are the three sentences:
>
> **{SENTENCES LIST}**
>
> Please provide the answer in separate lines for each sentence. **[/INST]** Answer:
> Sentence 1) is

Llama3 models. The output of the Llama-3 models with the original prompt did not contain the expected answer to the task. We added the following system prompt to the original prompt. The results presented for Llama3 were all generated after the integration of this system prompt.

> You always answer in three lines, with one sentence index (for example "1)","2)" or "3)") followed by the words "is metaphoric", "is literal" or "is anomalous" on each line.

C.2 Bias of the models toward label sequences

We run a first batch of generation experiments using our generation prompt, and find that all the models are biased toward some sequences of sentence-label pairs. For example, in the case of the Cardillo dataset, all the models tend to answer that the first sentence of the set is *metaphoric* and the second is *literal* much more often than the opposite. This bias of the models is presented in Appendix Tables 12 and 13. As a consequence, we ran the experiments with all possible permutations of the sentences within each set, making distribution of label sequences uniform.

D Experiments on the SAT dataset

E Annotation Guidelines for Adding Metaphorical Labels in SAT

The proportional analogies to label are made of exactly four words x_i, x_j, y_i and y_j. The relation between the four words can be paraphrased by the sentence x_i *is to* x_j *what* y_i *is to* y_j. For example, *Dancing is to walking what singing is to talking.*

[16]see https://huggingface.co/mistralai/Mixtral-8x7B-Instruct-v0.1

Model Family	Model	% Lit. is lowest	p_{value}	p<0.05	Med. M/L
BERT	$BERT_{BASE}$	73.5	.0	T	2.14
	$BERT_{LARGE}$	72.3	.0	T	1.7
RoBERTa	$RoBERTa_{BASE}$	64.6	.0	T	2.22
	$RoBERTa_{LARGE}$	70.0	.0	T	2.31
T5	$T5_{SMALL}$	76.9	.0	T	2.62
	$T5_{BASE}$	66.5	.0	T	.36
	$T5_{LARGE}$	67.7	.0	T	.2
	$T5_{3B}$	42.3	.9992	F	0.0
	$T5_{11B}$	50.8	.2257	F	0.0
UL2	UL2	61.5	.0002	T	0.17
Flan-T5	Flan-$T5_{SMALL}$	78.8	.0	T	2.49
	Flan-$T5_{BASE}$	77.7	.0	T	2.35
	Flan-$T5_{LARGE}$	80.0	.0	T	2.44
	Flan-$T5_{XL}$	77.3	.0	T	2.14
	Flan-$T5_{XXL}$	82.3	.0	T	2.59
Flan-UL2	Flan-UL2	80.8	.0	T	2.37
GPT-2	GPT-2	60.8	.0	T	1.5
	GPT-2_{MEDIUM}	62.7	.0	T	1.45
	GPT-2_{LARGE}	61.9	.0	T	1.43
	GPT-2_{XL}	63.8	.0	T	1.49
GPT-J	GPT-J_{125M}	56.5	.0039	T	1.39
	GPT-$J_{2.7B}$	57.3	.019	T	1.3
	GPT-J_{6B}	62.7	.0	T	1.6
	GPT-J_{20b}	61.5	.0	T	1.45
GPT-3	GPT-3_{ada}	63.1	.0	T	1.54
	GPT-$3_{babbage}$	67.3	.0	T	1.63
	GPT-3_{curie}	67.7	.0	T	1.68
	GPT-$3_{davinci}$	67.7	.0	T	1.75
OPT	OPT_{125M}	64.2	.0	T	1.5
	OPT_{350M}	63.1	.0	T	1.4
	$OPT_{1.3B}$	68.5	.0	T	1.51
	OPT_{13B}	68.5	.0	T	1.53
	OPT_{30B}	68.5	.0	T	1.59
	OPT_{66B}	66.9	.0	T	1.54
OPT-IML	OPT-$IML_{1.3B}$	67.3	.0	T	1.54
	OPT-IML_{30B}	69.6	.0	T	1.54
OPT-IML (MAX)	OPT-$IML_{M-1.3B}$	65.8	.0	T	1.49
	OPT-IML_{M-30B}	70.4	.0	T	1.59
Bloom	$Bloom_{175B}$	61.9	.0	T	1.36
Bloomz	$Bloomz_{175B}$	66.5	.0	T	1.49
Llama2	$Llama2_{7B}$	63.1	.0	T	1.34
	$Llama2_{13B}$	63.5	.0	T	1.38
	$Llama2_{70B}$	60.8	.0	T	1.36
Llama2-Chat	Llama2-$Chat_{7B}$	57.3	.0007	T	1.26
	Llama2-$Chat_{13B}$	63.1	.0	T	1.32
	Llama2-$Chat_{70B}$	65.0	.0	T	1.45
Llama3-Inst	Llama3-$Inst_{8B}$	66.5	.0	T	1.51
	Llama3-$Inst_{70B}$	68.8	.0	T	1.88
Mistral	$Mistral_{7B}$	65.0	.0	T	1.4
	$Mixtral_{8x7B}$	62.7	.0	T	1.37
Mistral-Inst	Mistral-$Inst_{7B}$	64.6	.0	T	1.47
	Mixtral-$Inst_{8x7B}$	61.5	.0	T	1.28
	Mixtral-$Inst_{8x22B}$	66.9	.0	T	1.36

Table 7: Ratios of instances for which the literal sentences have a lower perplexity than the metaphoric sentences in the Cardillo dataset according to model family and size (*perplexity* setting). The following two columns show the significance in the difference of perplexity scores between the set of literal sentences and metaphoric sentences. A paired samples Wilcoxon test is used ($p<0.05$). The last column shows the median of the ratios between the score of the metaphoric and literal sentences in each set.

Model	%L is lowest	%M is lowest	%A is lowest	% L<M<A	p_{value} L-M	$p_{L\text{-}M}$ <0.05	p_{value} M-A	$p_{M\text{-}A}$ <0.05	Med. M/L	Med. A/M
BERT$_{BASE}$	85.8	9.2	5.0	47.5	.0	**T**	.102	F	5.156	1.192
BERT$_{LARGE}$	80.0	12.5	7.5	45.8	.0	**T**	.0362	**T**	4.118	1.543
RoBERTa$_{BASE}$	53.3	34.2	12.5	32.5	.0002	**T**	.0001	**T**	1.719	3.793
RoBERTa$_{LARGE}$	43.3	43.3	13.3	30.0	.2513	F	.0	**T**	1.012	4.894
T5$_{SMALL}$	70.8	11.7	17.5	35.0	.0	**T**	.6776	F	3.047	.887
T5$_{BASE}$	79.2	11.7	9.2	44.2	.0	**T**	.3309	F	3.541	1.209
T5$_{LARGE}$	29.2	34.2	36.7	7.5	.9918	F	.9646	F	.483	.728
T5$_{3B}$	33.3	40.8	25.8	19.2	.6729	F	.1363	F	.779	2.145
T5$_{11B}$	49.2	34.2	16.7	25.8	.0602	F	.0136	**T**	1.413	1.462
UL2	65.8	22.5	11.7	33.3	.0	**T**	.0667	F	2.58	1.322
Flan-T5$_{SMALL}$	85.8	9.2	5.0	56.7	.0	**T**	.0011	**T**	2.529	1.278
Flan-T5$_{BASE}$	84.2	9.2	6.7	47.5	.0	**T**	.0806	F	3.505	1.207
Flan-T5$_{LARGE}$	52.5	34.2	13.3	25.0	.002	**T**	.085	F	1.585	1.279
Flan-T5$_{XL}$	81.7	15.0	3.3	56.7	.0	**T**	.0	**T**	2.3	1.704
Flan-T5$_{XXL}$	77.5	19.2	3.3	55.0	.0	**T**	.0	**T**	2.518	1.986
Flan-UL2	73.3	21.7	5.0	45.0	.0	**T**	.0002	**T**	2.37	1.636
GPT-2	58.3	25.8	15.8	42.5	.0	**T**	.0	**T**	1.592	1.945
GPT-2$_{MEDIUM}$	36.7	50.8	12.5	26.7	.9724	F	.0	**T**	0.755	2.911
GPT-2$_{LARGE}$	41.7	44.2	14.2	30.0	.1797	F	.0	**T**	.979	2.698
GPT-2$_{XL}$	35.8	52.5	11.7	25.8	.6566	F	.0	**T**	.87	3.006
GPT-J$_{125M}$	21.7	62.5	15.8	15.8	.9999	F	.0	**T**	.662	3.269
GPT-J$_{2.7B}$	31.7	55.8	12.5	22.5	.9956	F	.0	**T**	.593	4.341
GPT-J$_{6B}$	38.3	52.5	9.2	28.3	.8928	F	.0	**T**	.763	3.795
GPT-J$_{20b}$	50.0	37.5	12.5	37.5	.2047	F	.0	**T**	1.047	2.885
GPT-3$_{ada}$	54.2	35.8	10.0	40.0	.0013	**T**	.0	**T**	1.427	2.517
GPT-3$_{babbage}$	50.0	40.0	10.0	40.0	.0474	**T**	.0	**T**	1.158	3.002
GPT-3$_{curie}$	51.7	41.7	6.7	35.8	.0399	**T**	.0	**T**	1.165	3.033
GPT-3$_{davinci}$	49.2	43.3	7.5	34.2	.0806	F	.0	**T**	1.122	3.273
OPT$_{125M}$	44.2	30.0	25.8	21.7	.0001	**T**	.3836	F	1.387	1.14
OPT$_{350M}$	36.7	45.8	17.5	19.2	.585	F	.0006	**T**	.876	1.62
OPT$_{1.3B}$	40.8	44.2	15.0	25.0	.3443	F	.0	**T**	1.025	1.83
OPT$_{13B}$	52.5	36.7	10.8	36.7	.0039	**T**	.0	**T**	1.291	2.332
OPT$_{30B}$	48.3	40.8	10.8	35.8	.0227	**T**	.0	**T**	1.205	2.107
OPT$_{66B}$	43.3	43.3	13.3	27.5	.2122	F	.0	**T**	1.077	2.151
OPT-IML$_{1.3B}$	40.0	42.5	17.5	26.7	.3224	F	.0	**T**	.99	1.684
OPT-IML$_{30B}$	44.2	42.5	13.3	27.5	.0519	F	.0	**T**	1.118	1.999
OPT-IML$_{M\text{-}1.3B}$	41.7	43.3	15.0	25.8	.3501	F	.0	**T**	1.016	1.794
OPT-IML$_{M\text{-}30B}$	46.7	42.5	10.8	30.8	.0476	**T**	.0	**T**	1.11	2.059
Bloom$_{175B}$	52.5	39.2	8.3	34.2	.0079	**T**	.0	**T**	1.225	2.524
Bloomz$_{175B}$	60.8	30.0	9.2	37.5	.0	**T**	.0041	**T**	1.928	1.558
Llama2$_{7b}$	52.5	33.3	14.2	29.2	.0022	**T**	.0021	**T**	1.334	1.229
Llama2$_{13B}$	47.5	35.8	16.7	25.8	.0926	F	.0012	**T**	1.192	1.398
Llama2$_{70B}$	50.0	35.0	15.0	27.5	.0283	**T**	.001	**T**	1.259	1.35
Llama2-Chat$_{7B}$	50.0	36.7	13.3	26.7	.0143	**T**	.0004	**T**	1.195	1.685
Llama2-Chat$_{13B}$	40.8	45.0	14.2	20.8	.8471	F	.0	**T**	.877	1.535
Llama2-Chat$_{70B}$	50.8	33.3	15.8	35.0	.0094	**T**	.0001	**T**	1.259	1.525
Llama3-Inst$_{8B}$	52.5	39.2	8.3	37.5	.0114	**T**	.0	**T**	1.293	2.119
Llama3-Inst$_{70B}$	51.7	38.3	10.0	37.5	.0012	**T**	.0	**T**	1.406	3.019
Mistral$_{7B}$	45.0	37.5	17.5	26.7	.1122	F	.006	**T**	1.133	1.413
Mixtral$_{8x7B}$	48.3	38.3	13.3	27.5	.079	F	.0065	**T**	1.171	1.473
Mistral-Inst$_{7B}$	45.0	36.7	18.3	30.0	.0727	F	.0006	**T**	1.118	1.901
Mixtral-Inst$_{8x7B}$	45.8	38.3	15.8	27.5	.2222	F	.0006	**T**	1.147	1.712
Mixtral-Inst$_{8x22B}$	54.2	27.5	18.3	33.3	.0	**T**	.0115	**T**	1.653	1.349

Table 8: The first three columns show the ratios of sets for which the literal (L), metaphoric (M) and anomalous (A) sentences have the lowest perplexity in the Jankowiak dataset according to model family and size (*perplexity* setting).%L<M<A shows the ratio of sets for which perplexity scores follow this order. The following four columns show the significance in the difference of perplexity scores between the set of literal and metaphoric sentences, and then between the set of metaphoric and anomalous sentences. A paired samples Wilcoxon test is used ($p<0.05$).

Model	%L is lowest	%M is lowest	%A is lowest	% L<M<A	p_{value} L-M	p_{L-M} <0.05	p_{value} M-A	p_{M-A} <0.05	Med. M/L	Med. A/M
BERT$_{BASE}$	65.0	15.0	20.0	30.0	.0	**T**	.592	F	2.277	0.765
BERT$_{LARGE}$	70.0	12.5	17.5	47.5	.0001	**T**	.0544	F	1.946	1.213
RoBERTa$_{BASE}$	80.0	2.5	17.5	52.5	.0	**T**	.4236	F	4.189	1.251
RoBERTa$_{LARGE}$	80.0	10.0	10.0	45.0	.0	**T**	.1702	F	2.654	1.139
T5$_{SMALL}$	95.0	0.0	5.0	45.0	.0	**T**	.6721	F	5.281	.907
T5$_{BASE}$	62.5	17.5	20.0	27.5	.0	**T**	.9016	F	7.618	.651
T5$_{LARGE}$	72.5	10.0	17.5	45.0	.0	**T**	.4709	F	4.287	1.335
T5$_{3B}$	70.0	7.5	22.5	25.0	.0	**T**	.8841	F	4.242	.487
T5$_{11B}$	80.0	5.0	15.0	32.5	.0	**T**	.9231	F	6.613	.677
UL2	57.5	12.5	30.0	32.5	.0	**T**	.8298	F	4.139	.907
Flan-T5$_{SMALL}$	87.5	0.0	12.5	40.0	.0	**T**	.8587	F	4.807	.805
Flan-T5$_{BASE}$	87.5	5.0	7.5	35.0	.0	**T**	.805	F	4.261	.78
Flan-T5$_{LARGE}$	85.0	5.0	10.0	30.0	.0	**T**	.9861	F	5.106	.684
Flan-T5$_{XL}$	92.5	2.5	5.0	40.0	.0	**T**	.823	F	5.756	.91
Flan-T5$_{XXL}$	80.0	7.5	12.5	45.0	.0	**T**	.255	F	4.288	1.24
Flan-UL2	85.0	7.5	7.5	55.0	.0	**T**	.0265	**T**	4.345	1.278
GPT-2	75.0	10.0	15.0	35.0	.0	**T**	.6624	F	1.937	.913
GPT-2$_{MEDIUM}$	70.0	15.0	15.0	42.5	.0	**T**	.2996	F	2.096	1.057
GPT-2$_{LARGE}$	72.5	12.5	15.0	45.0	.0	**T**	.075	F	2.299	1.202
GPT-2$_{XL}$	85.0	5.0	10.0	45.0	.0	**T**	.2101	F	2.211	.98
GPT-J$_{125M}$	60.0	12.5	27.5	27.5	.0	**T**	.8733	F	1.98	.864
GPT-J$_{2.7B}$	82.5	2.5	15.0	47.5	.0	**T**	.408	F	1.959	0.975
GPT-J$_{6B}$	87.5	5.0	7.5	55.0	.0	**T**	.1668	F	1.891	1.202
GPT-J$_{20b}$	85.0	7.5	7.5	47.5	.0	**T**	.0916	F	1.945	1.315
GPT-3$_{ada}$	77.5	12.5	10.0	45.0	.0	**T**	.3425	F	1.984	1.078
GPT-3$_{babbage}$	77.5	10.0	12.5	45.0	.0	**T**	.3573	F	2.292	1.125
GPT-3$_{curie}$	87.5	2.5	10.0	47.5	.0	**T**	.3184	F	2.506	1.014
GPT-3$_{davinci}$	92.5	2.5	5.0	62.5	.0	**T**	.0341	**T**	2.203	1.414
OPT$_{125M}$	77.5	7.5	15.0	37.5	.0	**T**	.7741	F	2.197	.911
OPT$_{350M}$	77.5	5.0	17.5	40.0	.0	**T**	.6957	F	1.901	.913
OPT$_{1.3B}$	92.5	2.5	5.0	52.5	.0	**T**	.195	F	2.004	1.123
OPT$_{13B}$	95.0	2.5	2.5	55.0	.0	**T**	.085	F	2.166	1.194
OPT$_{30B}$	97.5	.0	2.5	60.0	.0	**T**	.0385	**T**	2.286	1.141
OPT$_{66B}$	97.5	.0	2.5	57.5	.0	**T**	.0879	F	2.212	1.107
OPT-IML$_{1.3B}$	90.0	2.5	7.5	52.5	.0	**T**	.2423	F	1.964	1.032
OPT-IML$_{30B}$	90.0	2.5	7.5	52.5	.0	**T**	.1159	F	2.246	1.121
OPT-IML$_{M-1.3B}$	85.0	2.5	12.5	45.0	.0	**T**	.3279	F	1.951	.988
OPT-IML$_{M-30B}$	97.5	0.0	2.5	57.5	.0	**T**	.0624	F	2.166	1.136
Bloom$_{175B}$	80.0	5.0	15.0	52.5	.0	**T**	.1877	F	2.084	1.167
Bloomz$_{175B}$	87.5	2.5	10.0	55.0	.0	**T**	.0446	**T**	2.161	1.185
Llama-2$_{7b}$	80.0	15.0	5.0	50.0	.0	**T**	.0341	**T**	1.747	1.245
Llama-2$_{13B}$	82.5	10.0	7.5	60.0	.0	**T**	.0184	**T**	1.713	1.202
Llama-2$_{70B}$	77.5	17.5	5.0	55.0	.0001	**T**	.0011	**T**	1.785	1.322
Llama2-Chat$_{7B}$	82.5	10.0	7.5	60.0	.0	**T**	.0018	**T**	2.091	1.325
Llama2-Chat$_{13B}$	90.0	5.0	5.0	62.5	.0	**T**	.0204	**T**	1.975	1.132
Llama2-Chat$_{70B}$	80.0	15.0	5.0	62.5	.0	**T**	.0001	**T**	2.11	1.344
Llama3-Inst$_{8B}$	95.0	2.5	2.5	65.0	.0	**T**	.0043	**T**	2.147	1.314
Llama3-Inst$_{70B}$	82.5	10.0	7.5	60.0	.0	**T**	.0139	**T**	2.412	1.332
Mistral$_{7B}$	82.5	7.5	10.0	52.5	.0	**T**	.0191	**T**	2.153	1.136
Mixtral$_{8x7B}$	82.5	10.0	7.5	60.0	.0	**T**	.0041	**T**	1.976	1.313
Mistral-Inst$_{7B}$	82.5	10.0	7.5	62.5	.0	**T**	.0003	**T**	2.311	1.329
Mixtral-Inst$_{8x7B}$	80.0	12.5	7.5	52.5	.0	**T**	.0019	**T**	2.149	1.378
Mixtral-Inst$_{8x22B}$	77.5	7.5	15.0	60.0	.0	**T**	.0024	**T**	2.214	1.236

Table 9: The first three columns show the ratios of sets for which the literal (L), metaphoric (M) and anomalous (A) sentences have the lowest perplexity in the Green dataset according to model family and size (*perplexity* setting).%L<M<A shows the ratios of sets for which perplexity scores follow this order. The following four columns show the significance in the difference of perplexity scores between the set of literal and metaphoric sentences, and then between the set of metaphoric and anomalous sentences. A paired samples Wilcoxon test is used (p<0.05).

Model	p_{value} L<A	$p_{L<A}$ <0.05	p_{value} M<A	$p_{M<A}$ <0.05	p_{value} L<M	$p_{L<M}$ <0.05	p_{value} Acc. L-M	$p_{Acc. L-M}$ <0.05	%Lit. is lowest	%Met. is lowest
BERT$_{BASE}$	.0	**T**	.0	**T**	.6787	F	.3057	F	34.7	29.1
BERT$_{LARGE}$	.0	**T**	.0	**T**	.1583	F	.0879	F	34.3	25.2
RoBERTa$_{BASE}$	.0	**T**	.0001	**T**	.7688	F	.083	F	39.7	30.1
RoBERTa$_{LARGE}$	.0	**T**	.025	**T**	.1813	F	.555	F	42.3	38.8
T5$_{SMALL}$	.0	**T**	.0	**T**	.4271	F	.6919	F	29.3	27.2
T5$_{BASE}$	.0	**T**	.0	**T**	.0973	F	.0742	F	29.3	20.4
T5$_{LARGE}$	.0	**T**	.0	**T**	.6088	F	.4069	F	32.6	28.2
T5$_{3B}$	.0	**T**	.0	**T**	.862	F	.2241	F	36.8	30.1
T5$_{11B}$	.0	**T**	.0	**T**	.1066	F	.0216	**T**	39.7	27.2
Flan-T5$_{SMALL}$	.0	**T**	.0	**T**	.2046	F	.0981	F	29.7	21.4
Flan-T5$_{BASE}$	.0	**T**	.0	**T**	.0135	**T**	.0425	**T**	33.9	23.3
Flan-T5$_{LARGE}$	.0	**T**	.0	**T**	.0024	**T**	.0009	**T**	41.0	23.3
Flan-T5$_{XL}$	.0001	**T**	.0016	**T**	.8248	F	.555	F	42.3	38.8
Flan-T5$_{XXL}$	.169	F	.0473	**T**	.9573	F	.0286	**T**	55.6	42.7
Flan-UL2	.1298	F	.2246	F	.0963	F	.606	F	50.6	47.6
GPT-2	.0	F	.0	**T**	.0398	**T**	.1305	F	34.3	26.2
GPT-2$_{MEDIUM}$	.0	**T**	.0	**T**	.235	F	.3371	F	36.4	31.1
GPT-2$_{LARGE}$	.0	**T**	.0	**T**	.2262	F	.1503	F	38.1	30.1
GPT-2$_{XL}$	.0	**T**	.0001	**T**	.3808	F	.6338	F	37.7	35.0
GPT-J$_{125M}$	.0	**T**	.0	**T**	.085	F	.0342	**T**	37.7	26.2
GPT-J$_{1.3B}$	.0	**T**	.0	**T**	.236	F	.3456	F	39.3	34.0
GPT-J$_{6B}$	.0127	**T**	.0168	**T**	.132	F	.0609	F	49.8	38.8
GPT-J$_{20b}$	.0077	**T**	.0153	**T**	.4348	F	.207	F	45.2	37.9
GPT-3$_{davinci}$	.0604	F	.5223	F	.7779	F	.4249	F	50.6	55.3
OPT$_{125M}$	.0	**T**	.0	**T**	.9119	F	.2114	F	36.0	29.1
OPT$_{350M}$	.0	**T**	.0	**T**	.293	F	.0342	**T**	37.7	26.2
OPT$_{1.3B}$	.0024	F	.0002	**T**	.5922	F	.0122	**T**	43.1	29.1
OPT$_{30B}$	.096	F	.147	F	.7362	F	.5581	F	48.1	44.7
OPT$_{66B}$	.1401	F	.3924	F	.9563	F	.9246	F	49.0	49.5
OPT-IML$_{1.3B}$	.0006	**T**	.0003	**T**	.7934	F	.2951	F	43.9	37.9
OPT-IML$_{30B}$	.0666	F	.0781	F	.5541	F	.3125	F	50.6	44.7
OPT-IML$_{M-1.3B}$	.0003	**T**	.0004	**T**	.7761	F	.1552	F	43.1	35.0
OPT-IML$_{M-30B}$	.1221	F	.0676	F	.4202	F	.2218	F	51.9	44.7
Llama-2$_{7b}$	.5361	F	.0685	F	.0053	**T**	.3357	F	52.3	46.6
Llama-2$_{13B}$	.8903	F	.3698	F	.0985	F	.3682	F	57.7	52.4
Llama-2$_{70B}$	.7528	F	.4882	F	.0565	F	.8109	F	54.8	53.4
Llama2-Chat$_{7B}$	.5661	F	.4373	F	.1395	F	.7228	F	53.6	51.5
Llama2-Chat$_{13B}$	.9327	F	.9185	F	.298	F	.8809	F	58.2	57.3
Llama2-Chat$_{70B}$	.946	F	.6535	F	.1786	F	.5965	F	59.4	56.3
Llama3-Inst$_{8B}$	.8849	F	.9923	F	.7068	F	.7263	F	58.2	60.2
Llama3-Inst$_{70B}$	.0089	**T**	.0454	**T**	.9355	F	.5902	F	46.9	43.7
Mistral$_{7B}$	.2952	F	.2511	F	.0561	F	.9628	F	49.8	49.5
Mixtral$_{8x7B}$	.1081	F	.1586	F	.0164	**T**	.8135	F	48.1	49.5
Mistral-Inst$_{7B}$	.3453	F	.4334	F	.0385	**T**	.3124	F	53.6	47.6
Mixtral-Inst$_{8x7B}$	.2714	F	.3441	F	.1188	F	.9809	F	50.6	50.5
Mixtral-Inst$_{8x22B}$	.2538	F	.2993	F	.7561	F	.9246	F	49.0	49.5

Table 10: The first four columns shows significance in the gap of perplexity scores between the anomalies that has the lowest perplexity of the four incorrect options in each set (A) and the literal instances (L) or the metaphoric instances (M). A paired samples Wilcoxon test is used ($p<0.05$). The next two columns show the the statistical significance between the set of perplexity values of the literal and the metaphoric instances using a Mann-Whitney U test. This test is used because metaphoric and non-metaphoric analogies are not paired in the SAT. The following two columns , p_{value} Acc. L-M show the result of two independent samples t-tests to show if the accuracy of the models for non-metaphoric examples is significantly better than its accuracy on metaphoric examples. The last two columns show the ratios of instances for which the non-metaphoric analogy on the left, and the metaphoric analogy on the right, have the lowest perplexity of their set in the SAT dataset, according to model family and size (perplexity setting).

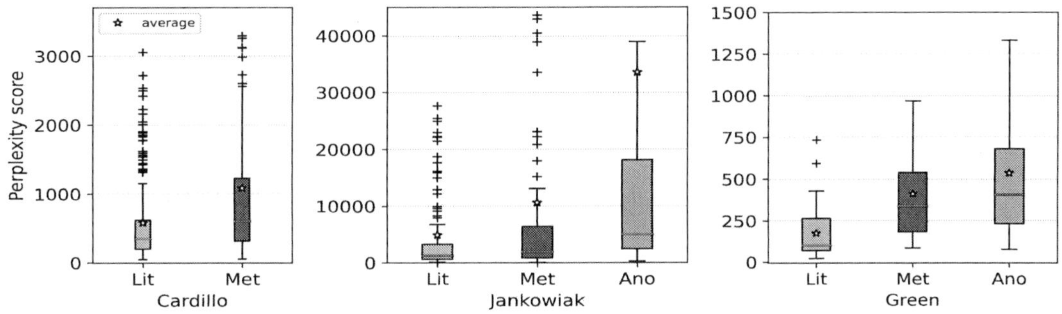

Figure 5: Boxplots of the Llama3-Inst$_{70B}$ perplexity scores for the three datasets and three classes: literal (Lit), metaphoric (Met) and anomalous (Ano). Outliers with the highest scores do not appear in the plots.

We want to decide if x_i and x_j can form a metaphoric mapping with $y_i$and y_j.

Given four words x_i, x_j, y_i and y_j :

1. Find the relation between the two elements of each pair. You can imagine relevant contexts in which they can be used. For example, *dancing* implies steps that follow a music, and *singing* often implies saying words following a music.

   If a word has multiple senses, consider its meaning in the context of the pair. For example, in the following analogy, *Abash is to embarrassment what annoy is to irritation*, the word *irritation* is polysemic. It it may take the meaning of an inflammation of the skin or be a near synonym of annoyance. Here, in the context of the word *annoy*, its emotional meaning is the only one to consider. This usage of the word may be a metaphoric sense, but it should not influence the label. We are only interested in the relation between the provided words.

   (a) Try to infer the relation between x_i and x_j

   (b) Try to infer the relation between y_i and y_j

   The relations should be similar.

2. Consider the relation between the two pairs (x_i, x_j) and (y_i, y_j).

   - Do they belong to the same domain? If x_i and y_i or x_j and y_j are either near synonyms or antonyms, then it is not a metaphor. For example, *worry is to panic what happiness is to bliss* is not a metaphor.
   - Try to recombine the pairs and form sentences using x_i and y_j or y_i and x_j. If one of the two combinations work, it may be a metaphor. For example, given *invest money* and *pour liquid*, you can construct the metaphor *pour money*.
   - Try to talk about x_i and x_j using y_i and y_j and then to talk about y_i and y_j using x_i and x_j. If you cannot think of a natural sentence, then do not label it as a metaphor.

3. Label the quadruple :

   - 0 : analogy that is not a metaphor
   - 2 : analogy that is also a metaphor
   - 1 : unsure

E.1 SAT annotations

First annotation round. Three annotators including two native speakers and two with a background in metaphor studies and linguistics labeled the 374 analogies of SAT after an initial training session and presentation of the guidelines (Appendix E). The labels were 0 for *non-metaphoric*, 1 for *unsure* and 2 for *metaphoric*. At the end of this process, in spite of the training sessions and provided guidelines, the pairwise agreement between annotators was low (Spearman $\rho = 0.17$; std$= 0.16$).

Second annotation round. In the second annotation round, we included an additional qualified native speaker and first asked all participants to place analogies in context. The source of disagreement was mainly due to the difficulty of imagining a relevant context where the 4-term analogy could be used to make a meaningful metaphor. The four participants were asked to create sentences whenever they thought that a metaphoric sentence

Model Familly	Model	Spearman ρ
BERT	$\text{BERT}_{\text{BASE}}$	.37
	$\text{BERT}_{\text{LARGE}}$	.35
RoBERTa	$\text{RoBERTa}_{\text{BASE}}$	.24
	$\text{RoBERTa}_{\text{LARGE}}$	.29
T5	T5_{SMALL}	.32
	T5_{BASE}	.11
	T5_{LARGE}	.23
	T5_{3B}	-.14
	T5_{11B}	-.05
UL2	UL2	.09
Flan-T5	$\text{Flan-T5}_{\text{SMALL}}$	.33
	$\text{Flan-T5}_{\text{BASE}}$	.34
	$\text{Flan-T5}_{\text{LARGE}}$	.38
	$\text{Flan-T5}_{\text{XL}}$	.38
	$\text{Flan-T5}_{\text{XXL}}$	**.41**
Flan-UL2	Flan-UL2	.39
GPT-2	GPT-2	.2
	$\text{GPT-2}_{\text{MEDIUM}}$	.19
	$\text{GPT-2}_{\text{LARGE}}$	.22
	GPT-2_{XL}	.21
GPT-J	$\text{GPT-J}_{\text{125M}}$	.1
	$\text{GPT-J}_{\text{2.7B}}$	.12
	GPT-J_{6B}	.21
	$\text{GPT-J}_{\text{20b}}$	.21
GPT-3	$\text{GPT-3}_{\text{ada}}$	.22
	$\text{GPT-3}_{\text{babbage}}$	.25
	$\text{GPT-3}_{\text{curie}}$	.25
	$\text{GPT-3}_{\text{davinci}}$	.27
OPT	OPT_{125M}	.29
	OPT_{13B}	.29
	OPT_{30B}	.32
	OPT_{66B}	.3
OPT-IML	$\text{OPT-IML}_{\text{1.3B}}$	.29
	$\text{OPT-IML}_{\text{30B}}$	.3
OPT-IML (MAX)	$\text{OPT-IML}_{\text{M-1.3B}}$	.28
	$\text{OPT-IML}_{\text{M-30B}}$	.31
Bloom	$\text{Bloom}_{\text{175B}}$	.19
Bloomz	$\text{Bloomz}_{\text{175B}}$	.27
Llama2	$\text{Llama-2}_{\text{7b}}$	.19
	$\text{Llama-2}_{\text{13B}}$	.19
	$\text{Llama-2}_{\text{70B}}$	.18
Llama2-Chat	$\text{Llama2-Chat}_{\text{7B}}$	.11
	$\text{Llama2-Chat}_{\text{13B}}$	.17
	$\text{Llama2-Chat}_{\text{70B}}$	.22
Llama3-Inst	$\text{Llama3-Inst}_{\text{8B}}$	.25
	$\text{Llama3-Inst}_{\text{70B}}$	.27
Mistral	$\text{Mistral}_{\text{7B}}$	.17
	$\text{Mixtral}_{\text{8x7B}}$	.18
Mistral-Inst	$\text{Mistral-Inst}_{\text{7B}}$	.17
	$\text{Mixtral-Inst}_{\text{8x7B}}$	.14
	$\text{Mixtral-Inst}_{\text{8x22B}}$	.21

Table 11: Spearman ρ correlation between human ratings of figurativeness and peplexity scores for the instances of the Cardillo dataset, according to model family and size (*perplexity* setting).

Answer	[M, L]	[L, M]	[M, M]	[L, L]
$\text{Flan-T5}_{\text{XXL}}$	**61.2**	29.4	9.4	0
$\text{Llama2-chat}_{\text{70B}}$	**57.1**	42.9	0	0
$\text{Llama3-Instr.}_{\text{70B}}$	**58.7**	38.3	3.1	0
$\text{Mixtral-Instr.}_{\text{8x7B}}$	**71.0**	24.6	3.5	0.6
$\text{Mixtral-Instr.}_{\text{8x22B}}$	**67.3**	31.3	1.3	0
$\text{GPT-3.5}_{\text{turbo-instr.}}$	**78.7**	15.8	0.2	0
$\text{GPT-3.5}_{\text{turbo}}$	**78.1**	21.7	0	0
GPT-4	**57.9**	41.5	0.6	0

Table 12: Imbalance of the models' answers on the Cardillo dataset. Experiments are run with all possible permutations of sentence within each set, with each correct sequence appearing an equal number of times in each position.

could be created. For example, given the two pairs $(sap, tree)$ and $(blood, mammal)$, one can imagine telling a kid who is damaging a tree *"Be careful, you are hurting it. Look, it is bleeding"*. The sentences were shared among all the participants and a new labelling task was completed, leading to a significant pairwise inter-annotator agreement (Spearman $\rho = 0.48$; std$= 0.17$).

The final SAT labels were obtained by averaging the scores of the four participants. We labeled as non-metaphoric all the quadruples scoring lower to 1 on average and metaphoric all those scoring above 1. 32 instances with an average score of 1 were filtered out. Table 4 contains an example of a metaphoric instance of the SAT dataset after annotation. In total, 103 instances were labelled as metaphoric, and 239 as non-metaphoric.

E.2 SAT* perplexity experiments

Table 10 shows a comparison of the models on the task of solving the analogy questions of SAT in the *perplexity* setting. The sentence in each set with the lowest perplexity is selected as the correct analogy. Accuracy is shown in two distinct columns for metaphoric and non-metaphoric analogies.

E.3 Generation experiment prompts

Prompt G2 . The correct answer of the example below is 1., it is classified as non-metaphoric in SAT. Identical modification to the prompt as the ones described in Appendix section C.1.1 are applied to Mixtral and Llama3 models.

Answer		[M, L, A]	[M, A, L]	[A, L, M]	[A, M, L]	[L, A, M]	[L, M, A]
Green	Flan-T5$_{XXL}$	0	0	0.4	7.5	0	0.4
	Llama2-chat$_{70B}$	16.2	6.2	14.6	4.2	**24.2**	17.9
	Llama3-Instr.$_{70B}$	23.8	**39.6**	14.6	18.3	0.8	0.8
	Mixtral-Instr.$_{8x7B}$	**42.5**	35.0	4.6	6.2	0.8	2.1
	Mixtral-Instr.$_{8x22B}$	**33.3**	19.6	1.7	0.4	12.9	16.2
	GPT-3.5$_{turbo\text{-}instr.}$	**75.8**	17.1	0.4	0.4	1.2	4.6
	GPT-3.5$_{turbo}$	**73.3**	3.3	7.9	5.0	0.4	8.8
	GPT-4	19.6	**28.8**	21.2	13.8	9.2	7.5
Jankowiak	Flan-T5$_{XXL}$	0.8	0.7	9.7	**34.2**	1.5	7.4
	Llama2-chat$_{70B}$	8.5	6.4	**34.0**	22.8	15.3	12.9
	Llama3-Instr.$_{70B}$	**19.2**	18.6	14.6	16.7	12.1	13.6
	Mixtral-Instr.$_{8x7B}$	20.1	18.5	18.9	16.9	8.1	13.9
	Mixtral-Instr.$_{8x22B}$	**27.9**	18.5	9.3	8.8	10.4	18.8
	GPT-3.5$_{turbo\text{-}instr.}$	**46.5**	25.6	1.7	3.1	6.7	11.5
	GPT-3.5$_{turbo}$	**53.5**	9.9	4.7	6.0	4.9	20.3
	GPT-4	22.4	21.5	13.5	13.5	13.8	14.0

Table 13: Imbalanced distribution of the sequence of labels in the models' answers on the Green and Jankowiak datasets. Experiments are run with all possible permutations of the sentences within each set, with each possible sequence of labels being the correct answer an equal number of times. Flan-T5$_{XXL}$ label distribution does not sum to 100 in the table because the model outputs a large proportion of incorrect sequences such as [M,M,M], not shown here.

Prompt 3: Find the correct analogy
Example: SAT

Answer the question by choosing the correct option. Which of the following is an analogy?

1. beauty is to aesthete what pleasure is to hedonist
2. beauty is to aesthete what emotion is to demagogue
3. beauty is to aesthete what opinion is to sympathizer
4. beauty is to aesthete what seance is to medium
5. beauty is to aesthete what luxury is to ascetic

The answer is

F Computational and Annotation Time

Computation time. In terms of experiments, we have run a wide range of models of different sizes and settings, leading to a high computational cost. Most of the experiments have been run on a 4 40GB A100 GPUs.

We estimate the total execution time to be 100 hours overall in this infrastructure, with some experiments for small models having been run on local GPUs as well.

Annotation time. In order to annotate the SAT dataset, four annotators that have contributed as authors of the paper have dedicated an overall 80 hours, which includes the annotation and discussion processes.

Further Compressing Distilled Language Models via Frequency-aware Partial Sparse Coding of Embeddings

Kohki Tamura[†] **Naoki Yoshianga**[‡] **Masato Neishi**[†*]

[†]The University of Tokyo [‡]Institute of Industrial Science, The University of Tokyo

[†]{tamura-k,neishi}@tkl.iis.u-tokyo.ac.jp [‡]ynaga@iis.u-tokyo.ac.jp

Abstract

Although pre-trained language models (PLMs) are effective for natural language understanding (NLU) tasks, they demand a huge computational resource, thus preventing us from deploying them on edge devices. Researchers have therefore applied compression techniques for neural networks, such as pruning, quantization, and knowledge distillation, to the PLMs. Although these generic techniques can reduce the number of internal parameters of hidden layers in the PLMs, the embedding layers tied to the tokenizer are hard to be compressed, occupying a non-negligible portion of the compressed model. In this study, aiming to further compress PLMs reduced by the generic techniques, we exploit frequency-aware sparse coding to compress the embedding layers of the PLMs fine-tuned to downstream tasks. To minimize the impact of the compression on the accuracy, we retain the embeddings of common tokens as they are and use them to reconstruct embeddings of rare tokens by locally linear mapping. Experimental results on the GLUE and JGLUE benchmarks for language understanding in English and Japanese confirmed that our method can further compress the fine-tuned DistilBERT models while maintaining accuracy.

1 Introduction

Transformer (Vaswani et al., 2017)-based language models (LMs) have been extensively used to solve natural language processing (NLP) tasks via pre-train and fine-tuning (Devlin et al., 2019); the accuracy of the fine-tuned LMs can be improved by scaling up the model and pre-training data sizes (Kaplan et al., 2020). Pre-trained LMs (PLMs) thereby became larger and larger, which prevents us from deploying them on resource-constrained environments. Thus, we cannot leverage powerful PLMs to text with privacy concerns in end-user devices or confidential documents in small businesses.

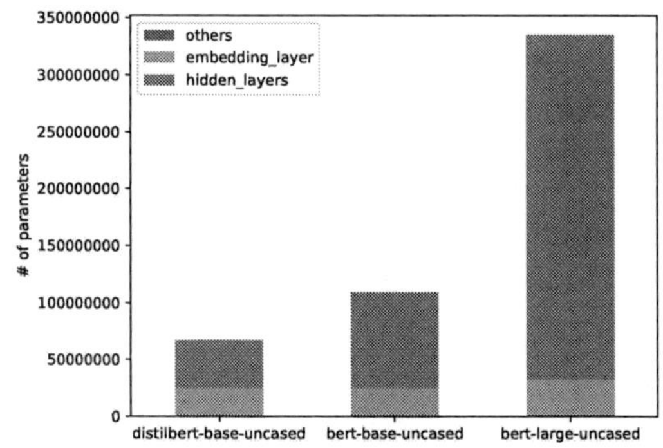

Figure 1: The number of parameters in BERT variants; these PLMs have similar numbers of parameters in the embedding layers, which become more dominant (34.9%) in `distilbert-base-uncased`.

To make PLMs faster and smaller while maintaining the accuracy, researchers have utilized common compression techniques for neural networks (surveyed in Zhu et al. (2023)); the techniques include pruning, quantization, and knowledge distillation, mainly focusing on compressing hidden layers which occupy the largest part in the PLMs with deep Transformer layers (Wan et al., 2024; Zhou et al., 2024). In the distilled PLMs, however, parameters in those other than hidden layers account for a large proportion of the entire parameters (Figure 1), and most of them are accounted for by the embedding layers. For instance, the parameters of the embedding layer account for about 34.9% of `distilbert-base-uncased`[1] (Sanh et al., 2019), whereas they occupy about 21.4% of the original 12-layer `bert-base-uncased`[2] (Devlin et al., 2019). Therefore, we subject the embedding layers to further compression.

In this study, given a PLM fine-tuned to the target downstream task, we propose to compress the

*Currently, he works for Mirai Translate, Inc.

[1]https://huggingface.co/distilbert/distilbert-base-uncased

[2]https://huggingface.co/google-bert/bert-base-uncased

Proceedings of the 28th Conference on Computational Natural Language Learning, pages 388–399
November 15-16, 2024 ©2024 Association for Computational Linguistics

embedding layer of the PLM by using sparse coding of embeddings, which represents embeddings with a sparse linear combination of basis embeddings (Faruqui et al., 2015). The issue here is that the sparse coding introduces approximation errors, or noises, into the fine-tuned embeddings. To reduce the impact of these noises on the PLM's outputs, we perform a frequency-aware partial sparse coding of embeddings; namely, we regard a small number of common token embeddings as basis embeddings to reconstruct the remaining rare token embeddings, as employed in Chen et al. (2016) for recurrent neural network LMs.

Since the embeddings of the recent PLMs will be contextualized through deep Transformer layers and noisy rare token embeddings will be supplemented by intact embeddings of surrounding common tokens, we adopt simple locally-linear embeddings (Roweis and Saul, 2000; Sakuma and Yoshinaga, 2019) to choose a few basis (common token) embeddings for each rare token embedding, thereby enabling sparser coding of embeddings. Each rare token embedding is thereby represented as a weighted linear sum of the nearest neighbor common token embeddings. Finally, we save the weight and the IDs of the common tokens to dynamically reconstruct embeddings during inference.

We applied our method to English and Japanese DistilBERT models fine-tuned to GLUE (Wang et al., 2018) and JGLUE datasets (Kurihara et al., 2022), respectively. We then compared our methods with three baselines; the two of them approximate the same rare token embeddings as our method, by <unk> token embedding in the target PLM and by common basis embeddings induced by principal component analysis, respectively. The other approximates the entire embedding layers using sparse vectors to select vectors to sum up from shared chunks of vectors (additive quantization).

The contributions of this paper are as follows:

- We present a simple, frequency-aware partial sparse coding to compress embedding layers in the PLMs fine-tuned to downstream tasks.
- We confirmed an advantage of our method on distilled LMs in two languages, fine-tuned to various natural language understanding tasks.
- We confirmed the robustness of our frequency-aware sparse coding of embeddings in that the PLM retains the original accuracy even when the reconstruction introduces noises.

2 Proposed Method

The major difficulty in compressing the embeddings of a fine-tuned Transformer-based PLM is that if the compression introduces some approximation (noises) in the embeddings, they will severely affect the latter processing in the deep Transformer layers. Fukuda et al. (2020) confirmed on sentiment classification that the accuracy of BERT decreased greatly (>10%) when one or more words take perturbations mimicking typos.

Motivated by this observation, we adopt partial sparse coding, which reconstructs only a subset of PLM's embeddings whose approximation errors (noises) will not severely affect the PLM's behavior. To reduce the memory footprint, we divert common token embeddings to the candidate of basis embeddings that represent the rare token embeddings.

Our partial sparse coding consists of the following two steps:

Step 1: Splitting vocabularies. We first split the vocabulary of the PLM, $\mathcal{V}$, into two portions, $\mathcal{V}_C$ (**source vocabularies**) and $\mathcal{V}_R = \mathcal{V} - \mathcal{V}_C$ (**target vocabularies**), in which the embeddings of the source vocabularies (**source embeddings** are used as basis embeddings in sparse coding to approximate the embeddings of the target vocabularies (**target embeddings**).

Step 2: Reconstructing target embeddings. We then compute compact representations for the target embeddings, $\mathcal{Y} = \{\boldsymbol{y}_i \in \mathbb{R}^d\}_{i=1}^{|\mathcal{V}_R|}$ (d is the number of embedding dimensions), by approximating them as a weighted linear sum of the source embeddings, $\mathcal{X} = \{\boldsymbol{x}_i \in \mathbb{R}^d\}_{i=1}^{|\mathcal{V}_C|}$. To facilitate the compression, we choose a small subset of size k, $\mathcal{N}_i$, among the source embeddings $\mathcal{X}$ to approximate each target embedding $\boldsymbol{y}_i \in \mathcal{Y}$. We then represent target embedding $\boldsymbol{y}_i$ by compact (sparse vector) representations, $\hat{\boldsymbol{y}}_i = \{(j, \alpha_{ij}) \mid \boldsymbol{x}_j \in \mathcal{N}_i\}$, namely, k pairs of embedding ID $j \in \mathcal{N}_i$ and the weight $\alpha_{ij} \in \mathbb{R}$ for the linear summation.

We then reduce the target embeddings $\mathcal{Y}$ by replacing them with their sparse vector representations and dynamically reconstruct the target embedding $\boldsymbol{y}_i$ during the inference by referring to $\hat{\boldsymbol{y}}_i$, thus obtaining a model with a smaller embedding layer. The resulting embedding layer is composed of the original parameters (embeddings) $\mathcal{X}$ for the source

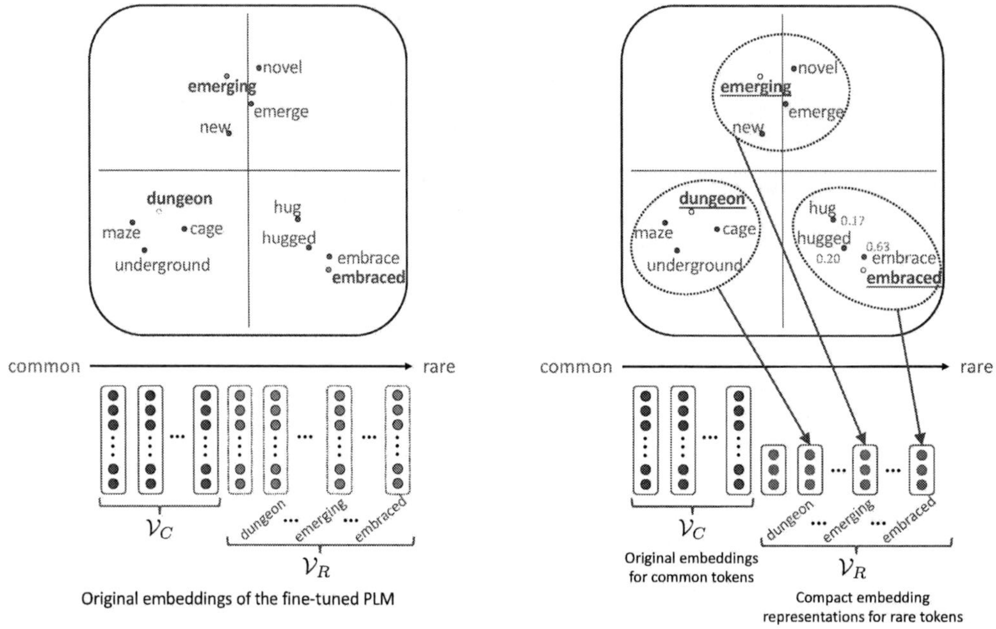

Figure 2: An overview of our frequency-aware partial sparse coding of embeddings. We represent embeddings of rare tokens (*e.g.*, "hugged") with their nearest neighbor embeddings of common tokens.

embeddings and the compact representations for the target embeddings $\mathcal{Y}$. The modified model has $(d-2k)|\mathcal{V}_R|$ fewer parameters,[3] which greatly reduces the number of parameters in the embedding layer when $k \ll d$ and $|\mathcal{V}_C| \ll |\mathcal{V}_R|$.

2.1 Step 1: Splitting vocabularies

To retain the inference accuracy of the fine-tuned PLMs, we need an effective criterion to split the LM's vocabulary into the source, basis embeddings, and the target embeddings for reconstruction. We thus leverage the frequency of tokens in the training data of the downstream task which are used to fine-tune the target PLM. Specifically, we count the frequency, f_i, for each token, $t_i \in \mathcal{V}$ in the training data which is tokenized with the target PLM's tokenizer. We set the top-n common tokens in $\mathcal{V}$ as $\mathcal{V}_C$ and the others as $\mathcal{V}_R$.

We should mention that a similar approach has been explored by Chen et al. (2016) to compress word embedding layers of recurrent neural network (RNN) LMs. The essential difference is that our method *explicitly* narrows down the candidate basis (common token) embeddings to reconstruct each rare token embedding, whereas Chen et al. (2016) used ℓ_1-regularization in learning a weight matrix for linear combinations to promote the sparseness of the weights implicitly, as described in § 2.2.

[3]Our method requires slightly more parameters (§ 2.2).

2.2 Step 2: Reconstructing target embeddings

To obtain the compact representations of the target embeddings, we want to use only a small subset of size k of the source embeddings to approximate the target embeddings. Because we want to explicitly control the required memory footprint and the PLM has a strong contextualization ability based on the surrounding intact embeddings for common tokens, we adopt a simple method of locally linear mapping (Roweis and Saul, 2000; Sakuma and Yoshinaga, 2019), which selects for each target embedding k nearest neighbor source embeddings for approximation.

In the original locally linear mapping for task-specific multilingual models (Sakuma and Yoshinaga, 2019), the authors first represent target embeddings (*e.g.*, Japanese word embeddings) with a weighted linear sum of top-k nearest neighbor source embeddings (*e.g.*, English word embeddings) in one semantic space (*e.g.*, the semantic space of the PLM), and use these weights to reconstruct target embeddings in another semantic space (*e.g.*, the semantic space of the fine-tuned PLM) to realize a task-specific multilingual model. In our setting, however, since the target semantic space (here, the semantic space of the fine-tuned PLM) also has the target embeddings for the target tokens, in contrast to Sakuma and Yoshinaga (2019), we do not need to consider two semantic spaces and can compute a linear weighted sum in the semantic space of the fine-tuned PLMs.[4]

In this study, we add a small fix to locally linear mapping to use normalized embeddings instead of raw embeddings, and force estimated embeddings to have the same length as the original just fine-tuned one. First, we normalize $\mathcal{Y}$ and $\mathcal{X}$ to make all embeddings e to be $\|e\| = 1$, and obtain the normalized embeddings as $\mathcal{X}^{\mathrm{n}}$ and $\mathcal{Y}^{\mathrm{n}}$. We set $\mathcal{N}_i$ as tokens with the top k nearest neighbor embeddings in $\mathcal{X}^{\mathrm{n}}$ from each embedding $\boldsymbol{y}_i^{\mathrm{n}}$ in $\mathcal{V}_R$ with cosine similarity, and compute the weights $\boldsymbol{\alpha}_i$ to estimate each $\hat{\boldsymbol{y}}_i^{\mathrm{n}}$ by $\sum_{j \in \mathcal{N}_i} \hat{\alpha}_{ij} \boldsymbol{x}_j^{\mathrm{n}}$. With locally linear mapping, we compute $\hat{\boldsymbol{\alpha}}_i$ which approximate $\boldsymbol{y}_i^{\mathrm{n}}$ the most by weighted linear sum of $\boldsymbol{x}_j^{\mathrm{n}}$ represented as

$$\hat{\boldsymbol{\alpha}}_i = \underset{\boldsymbol{\alpha}_i}{\arg\min} \left\| \boldsymbol{y}_i^{\mathrm{n}} - \sum_{j \in \mathcal{N}_i} \alpha_{ij} \boldsymbol{x}_j^{\mathrm{n}} \right\|^2 \quad (1)$$

using Lagrange multiplier from $\boldsymbol{x}_i^{\mathrm{n}}$, $\boldsymbol{y}_i^{\mathrm{n}}$ and a constraint of $\sum_j \alpha_{ij} = 1$ by compute

$$\hat{\alpha}_{ij} = \frac{\sum_l (C_i^{-1})_{jl}}{\sum_j \sum_l (C_i^{-1})_{jl}} \quad (2)$$

under $C_{ijl} = (\boldsymbol{y}_i^{\mathrm{n}} - \boldsymbol{x}_j^{\mathrm{n}}) \cdot (\boldsymbol{y}_i^{\mathrm{n}} - \boldsymbol{x}_l^{\mathrm{n}})$ to estimate whole $\hat{\mathcal{Y}}^{\mathrm{n}}$ $(l \in \mathcal{N}_i)$. We finally estimate each $\hat{\boldsymbol{y}}_i$ by adjusting the length of $\hat{\boldsymbol{y}}_i^{\mathrm{n}}$ same as $\boldsymbol{y}_i$ with

$$\hat{\boldsymbol{y}}_i = \|\boldsymbol{y}_i\| \frac{\hat{\boldsymbol{y}}_i^{\mathrm{n}}}{\|\hat{\boldsymbol{y}}_i^{\mathrm{n}}\|} \quad (3)$$

We save necessary parameters to reconstruct $\hat{\boldsymbol{y}}_i$ instead of the original embedding $\boldsymbol{y}_i$. To reconstruct $\hat{\boldsymbol{y}}_i$, we need ID of embeddings in $\mathcal{N}_i$, weights $\boldsymbol{\alpha}_i$ and the length of embedding $\|\boldsymbol{y}_i\|$. We save these $2k + 1$ parameters for every token in $\mathcal{V}_R$ as our compact representation, thus we reduce $(d - (2k + 1))|\mathcal{V}_R|$ parameters. In the inference, we dynamically reconstruct $\hat{\boldsymbol{y}}_i$ upon request when the tokenizer outputs those tokens.

3 Experimental Setup

We evaluate our frequency-aware sparse coding of embeddings on distilled PLMs fine-tuned to NLU tasks in terms of the model size and performance.

3.1 Datasets

For evaluation, we adopt GLUE (Wang et al., 2018) and JGLUE benchmark (Kurihara et al., 2022) for language understanding tasks in English and Japanese, respectively.

GLUE is a benchmark consisting of nine natural language understanding (NLU) tasks. It contains datasets of acceptability (CoLA), sentiment analysis (SST-2), paraphrase (MRPC, QQP), textual similarity (STS-B), and natural language inference (NLI; MNLI, QNLI, RTE, and WNLI). The sizes of the datasets range from $<$1k to over 500k. In the experiments, we adopted the common metrics used in the evaluation of BERT (Devlin et al., 2019) and DistilBERT (Sanh et al., 2019); F_1 for MRPC and QQP, Spearman Correlation for STS-B, and accuracy for the others.

Since we experimented on the diverse settings of k and $\mathcal{V}_R$ resulting in plenty of results, it was not possible to upload all of our results to test on the website[5] because of its limitation of submission. Hence, for every task, we used the original validation set as the test set. Instead of the original validation set, we split the train set into 90% and 10% shuffling randomly using a fixed random seed 42 and treated the latter as a validation set. We did not evaluate our method on QQP and WNLI since these tasks have different label distributions between the validation set and the test set, which means that the results of experiments on these datasets may be misleading.[6] In addition, we did not conduct experiments on MNLI due to the computational cost of running experiments on this large dataset.

JGLUE is a benchmark consisting of seven NLU tasks in Japanese. It contains datasets of text classification (MARC-ja and JCoLA), sentence pair classification (JSTS and JNLI), and QA (JSQuAD and JCommonsenseQA). Because the MARC-ja dataset is no longer available at this time, we evaluated our method on the other tasks. We used only Spearman's Correlation for the evaluation of JSTS following STS-B, and accuracy on the other tasks, following Kurihara et al. (2022).

Since the test sets of JGLUE have not been released yet, we employed the same process as we did for GLUE, except for JCoLA (we used the "`validation_out_of_domain`" subset as the test data). We experimented on JCoLA, JSTS, and JNLI datasets of the benchmark.

[4]Because the target rare token embeddings may not be updated for the target task and are in the semantic space of PLM instead of the fine-tuned PLM), we may be able to obtain better embeddings by computing weights for the summation in the semantic space of the PLM and by using the weights to reconstruct the target embeddings in the semantic space of the fine-tuned PLM. However, our preliminary experiments revealed that the fine-tuning did not change the embeddings much, this did not contribute to the accuracy improvements.

[5]`https://gluebenchmark.com`

[6]`https://gluebenchmark.com/faq`

3.2 PLMs for embedding compression

We applied our method to fine-tuned DistilBERT models whose hidden layer of BERT is compressed by knowledge distillation. Specifically, we experimented on `distilbert-base-uncased`[7] for English and `line-distilbert-base-japanese`[8] for Japanese. In what follows, we report the averages and standard deviations of three fine-tuning trials.

The English PLM has 23M parameters in the embedding layer, which consist of 30,522 token embeddings of 768 dimensions and account for 34.9% of the parameters (67M in total). This PLM employs WordPiece as the tokenizer. In fine-tuning, we trained for three epochs with a learning rate of 2e-5, except for five epochs on MRPC.

The Japanese PLM has 25M parameters of the embedding layer, which consist of 32,768 token embeddings of 768 dimensions and account for 36.6% of the parameters (68M in total). The tokenization of this model is done in two stages; pre-tokenization by MeCab[9] (unidic-lite) and tokenization by unigram LM of SentencePiece (Kudo and Richardson, 2018). In fine-tuning, we trained for four epochs with a learning rate of 5e-5.

3.3 Embedding compression

Threshold for common tokens We initially treat all PLM vocabularies that appear during the fine-tuning as $\mathcal{V}_C$ and the others as $\mathcal{V}_R$. Then, we transfer common tokens in $\mathcal{V}_C$ to $\mathcal{V}_R$ to see the trade-off between the compression rate and the performance. In these settings, the top 50% to 90% of the tokens with the higher frequency remain as $\mathcal{V}_C$, and the others are transferred to the $\mathcal{V}_R$. In the experiments, we compare our method while varying the retention rate of $\mathcal{V}_C$, $\mathrm{r}(\mathcal{V}_C)$, for each task; for example, $\mathrm{r}(\mathcal{V}_C) = 1.0$ means all the tokens that appeared during the fine-tuning are kept in $\mathcal{V}_C$ and $\mathrm{r}(\mathcal{V}_C) = 0.5$ means the half of the tokens that appeared during the fine-tuning are transferred to $\mathcal{V}_R$.

The number of the source embeddings We also compare our method while varying k, the number of the source embeddings used to represent each target embedding, ranging from one to five for each task. We tune k to minimize the inference error on the validation set and report the results of the best-performing k. We will later confirm that the choice of k does not affect the PLM performance, thanks to its strong contextualization capabilities.

3.4 Baselines

We compare our model with three baselines: i) replacing $\mathcal{V}_R$ with **<unk>** token learned by the PLM, ii) Principal Component Analysis (PCA)-based approximation and iii) Additive Quantization.

"unknown" token (<unk>) replaces all of the target tokens in $\mathcal{V}_R$ with a special token <unk> to leverage the unknown token embedding learned by the PLM.

Principal Component Analysis (PCA) uses the bases of the embedding space obtained by PCA as the source embeddings, instead of $\mathcal{V}_C$, to reconstruct $\mathcal{V}_R$. We compute the coordinate in k-dimensional space with this basis for each target token, and we treat the coordinate as the weight like our method. We save the same number of the source embedding, k, to reconstruct $\mathcal{V}_R$, and the coordinate of k dimension for each token in $\mathcal{V}_R$ instead of the original embeddings. We show the results from a single k selected with the same criteria as the proposed method, while ranging k from one to ten.

Additive Quantization (AQ) represents the original embeddings with the sum of basis embeddings which are shared across the target tokens with similar meanings (Babenko and Lempitsky, 2014; Shu and Nakayama, 2017). Although AQ reconstructs the original embeddings by a sum of a small subset of the basis embeddings as in our method, it is designed to reconstruct all embeddings using the independently-learned basis embeddings. We have used the official implementation of Shu's method (Shu and Nakayama, 2017)[10] with hyperparameters of $K = 16$ and $M = 32$.

The former two baselines approximate the same $\mathcal{V}_C$ as ours to see the effectiveness of choosing the source embeddings from the nearest neighbors, while the last baseline compresses the entire set of embeddings to see the impact of frequency-aware partial sparse coding.

[7]https://huggingface.co/distilbert/distilbert-base-uncased

[8]https://huggingface.co/line-corporation/line-distilbert-base-japanese

[9]https://taku910.github.io/mecab/

[10]https://github.com/zomux/neuralcompressor

$\|\mathcal{V}_C\|$	CoLA 5585	SST-2 11570	MRPC 11561	STS-B 10794	QNLI 26180	RTE 13863	Average
$r(\mathcal{V}_C) = 1.0$							
<unk>	37.16±1.12	**90.18**±0.23	**87.95**±0.39	83.67±0.15	86.96±0.10	57.76±1.42	73.95
PCA	41.79±0.48$^{k=2}$	89.72±0.05$^{k=7}$	87.72±0.54$^{k=1}$	81.08±0.41$^{k=1}$	86.97±0.09$^{k=1}$	53.19±2.20$^{k=2}$	73.41
proposed	**41.91**±0.20$^{k=5}$	89.87±0.40$^{k=4}$	87.75±0.47$^{k=3}$	**85.45**±0.14$^{k=1}$	**86.99**±0.09$^{k=2}$	**57.88**±0.53$^{k=1}$	**74.98**
$r(\mathcal{V}_C) = 0.5$							
<unk>	29.12±1.05	89.56±0.14	**88.18**±0.40	81.54±0.21	86.16±0.20	54.99±1.88	71.59
PCA	**33.29**±0.27$^{k=2}$	89.30±0.20$^{k=10}$	86.29±0.44$^{k=1}$	75.23±0.91$^{k=10}$	83.85±0.32$^{k=1}$	53.79±1.55$^{k=10}$	70.29
proposed	32.33±0.62$^{k=5}$	**90.18**±0.38$^{k=5}$	87.25±0.43$^{k=4}$	**82.67**±0.23$^{k=3}$	**86.19**±0.05$^{k=1}$	**56.92**±0.15$^{k=1}$	**72.59**
original	48.74±0.38	90.02±0.35	88.75±0.12	85.77±0.12	87.06±0.12	57.40±1.84	76.29

Table 1: The results of **GLUE** benchmark. The numbers in brackets show the number of the source embeddings, k, chosen by using the validation set.

$\|\mathcal{V}_C\|$	JCoLA 3558	JSTS 4576	JNLI 4403	Average
$r(\mathcal{V}_C) = 1.0$				
<unk>	74.60±0.58	84.70±0.09	87.69±0.36	82.33
PCA	75.33±0.00$^{k=1}$	**84.73**±0.12$^{k=8}$	87.83±0.28$^{k=2}$	82.63
proposed	**76.50**±0.10$^{k=2}$	84.65±0.11$^{k=1}$	**87.85**±0.24$^{k=2}$	**83.00**
$r(\mathcal{V}_C) = 0.5$				
<unk>	70.61±1.55	83.55±0.03	86.72±0.19	80.29
PCA	**75.67**±0.49$^{k=1}$	83.46±0.13$^{k=10}$	86.52±0.25$^{k=1}$	81.88
proposed	**75.67**±0.47$^{k=5}$	**84.30**±0.12$^{k=3}$	**87.47**±0.08$^{k=1}$	**82.48**
AQ	28.81±1.48	46.95±11.21	−2.34±1.14	24.47
original	77.08±0.31	84.67±0.10	87.96±0.29	83.24

Table 2: The results of **JGLUE** benchmark. The numbers in brackets show the number of the source embeddings, k, chosen by using the validation set.

4 Results

4.1 Main results

We first compared the results of the proposed method and the three baselines. <unk> and PCA baselines approximate the same target embeddings as ours, under the settings of $r(\mathcal{V}_C) = 1.0$ and $r(\mathcal{V}_C) = 0.5$. We also compared to AQ in JGLUE, it approximates the entire embeddings regardless of $r(\mathcal{V}_C)$.

Tables 1 and 2 show the results on the GLUE and JGLUE benchmark datasets, respectively. From the results, we can observe that our method outperforms the baselines on average and exhibits stable performance across tasks. Our method outperforms the PCA baseline in all tasks except for CoLA of $r(\mathcal{V}_C) = 0.5$ and JSTS of $r(\mathcal{V}_C) = 1.0$, thus confirming the importance of target-dependent source (basis) embeddings. Meanwhile, our method slightly underperforms the <unk> baseline in SST-2, MRPC, and JSTS of $r(\mathcal{V}_C) = 1.0$, and MRPC of $r(\mathcal{V}_C) = 0.5$. However, the token and sentence coverage by only common tokens are higher in those datasets as we will later confirm in Tables 5 and 6; all the three frequency-aware methods exhibit similar performance to the original model even under $r(\mathcal{V}_C) = 0.5$. Overall, our method mitigates performance degradation compared to only replacing such tokens with <unk> tokens, especially for $r(\mathcal{V}_C) = 0.5$ in both languages.

The relationship between performance and $|\mathcal{V}_C|$ Tables 3 and 4 show the results of our method while varying $r(\mathcal{V}_C)$. From the tables, there is a weak tendency that setting a lower value to $r(\mathcal{V}_C)$ results in lower performance. Thus, rare tokens weakly affect the PLM's performance, and it is reasonable to compress only rare token embeddings while keeping the original common token embeddings.

We compare the token and sentence coverage by $\mathcal{V}_C$ in the following three GLUE datasets: CoLA, which has the largest performance drop at small $r(\mathcal{V}_C)$, MRPC, which has a small performance drop despite being the similar training data size to CoLA, and QNLI, which has a small performance drop because more tokens are preserved (§ 4.2) at

$\mathrm{r}(\mathcal{V}_C)$	CoLA	SST-2	MRPC	STS-B	QNLI	RTE
0.5	$32.33{\pm}0.62^{k=5}$	$\mathbf{90.18}{\pm}0.38^{k=5}$	$87.25{\pm}0.43^{k=4}$	$82.67{\pm}0.23^{k=3}$	$86.19{\pm}0.05^{k=1}$	$56.92{\pm}0.15^{k=1}$
0.6	$35.27{\pm}0.32^{k=5}$	$89.68{\pm}0.29^{k=5}$	$87.80{\pm}0.42^{k=3}$	$83.80{\pm}0.17^{k=2}$	$86.27{\pm}0.12^{k=1}$	$56.80{\pm}0.30^{k=1}$
0.7	$37.50{\pm}0.12^{k=4}$	$89.60{\pm}0.25^{k=5}$	$88.09{\pm}0.45^{k=5}$	$84.03{\pm}0.16^{k=2}$	$86.63{\pm}0.10^{k=1}$	$57.04{\pm}0.26^{k=1}$
0.8	$39.56{\pm}0.15^{k=5}$	$89.99{\pm}0.26^{k=5}$	$\mathbf{88.55}{\pm}0.91^{k=4}$	$84.29{\pm}0.15^{k=3}$	$86.86{\pm}0.21^{k=1}$	$57.76{\pm}0.26^{k=1}$
0.9	$39.72{\pm}0.44^{k=5}$	$90.02{\pm}0.37^{k=3}$	$88.10{\pm}0.84^{k=5}$	$85.01{\pm}0.11^{k=1}$	$\mathbf{87.02}{\pm}0.09^{k=1}$	$\mathbf{58.24}{\pm}0.39^{k=1}$
1.0	$\mathbf{41.91}{\pm}0.20^{k=5}$	$89.87{\pm}0.40^{k=4}$	$87.75{\pm}0.47^{k=3}$	$\mathbf{85.45}{\pm}0.14^{k=1}$	$86.99{\pm}0.09^{k=2}$	$57.88{\pm}0.53^{k=1}$
original	$48.74{\pm}0.38$	$90.02{\pm}0.35$	$88.75{\pm}0.12$	$85.77{\pm}0.12$	$87.06{\pm}0.12$	$57.40{\pm}1.84$

Table 3: The results of modified models with our method under different $\mathrm{r}(\mathcal{V}_C)$ in the **GLUE** benchmark. The numbers in brackets show the number of the source embeddings, k, chosen by using the validation set.

$\mathrm{r}(\mathcal{V}_C)$	JCoLA	JSTS	JNLI
0.5	$75.67{\pm}0.47$	$84.30{\pm}0.12$	$87.47{\pm}0.08$
0.6	$76.79{\pm}0.36$	$84.50{\pm}0.14$	$87.55{\pm}0.23$
0.7	$76.93{\pm}0.10$	$84.53{\pm}0.14$	$87.57{\pm}0.31$
0.8	$76.45{\pm}0.47$	$\mathbf{84.66}{\pm}0.14$	$87.80{\pm}0.18$
0.9	$\mathbf{77.13}{\pm}0.33$	$\mathbf{84.65}{\pm}0.13$	$87.76{\pm}0.21$
1.0	$76.50{\pm}0.10$	$\mathbf{84.65}{\pm}0.11$	$\mathbf{87.85}{\pm}0.24$
original	$77.08{\pm}0.31$	$84.67{\pm}0.10$	$87.96{\pm}0.29$

Table 4: The results of modified models with our method under different $\mathrm{r}(\mathcal{V}_C)$ in the **JGLUE** benchmark.

$\mathrm{r}(\mathcal{V}_C)$	CoLA	MRPC	QNLI
0.5	99.37	96.00	98.27
0.6	99.47	96.66	98.72
0.7	99.55	97.06	99.14
0.8	99.60	97.52	99.52
0.9	99.64	97.92	99.74
1.0	99.69	98.30	99.90

Table 5: Token coverage in the **GLUE** test data by tokens in $\mathcal{V}_C$.

$\mathrm{r}(\mathcal{V}_C)$	CoLA	MRPC	QNLI
0.5	56.66	9.31	22.84
0.6	61.38	15.44	33.15
0.7	66.35	18.63	47.34
0.8	68.65	23.53	64.67
0.9	72.00	28.43	79.15
1.0	75.17	34.07	91.10

Table 6: Sentence coverage in the **GLUE** test data only by tokens in $\mathcal{V}_C$. In covered sentences, the model performs exactly the same as the original model.

$\mathrm{r}(\mathcal{V}_C)$	GLUE				JGLUE
	CoLA	MRPC	STS-B	QNLI	JSTS
0.5	10.15	19.05	17.71	43.13	10.17
1.0	18.85	36.76	34.16	85.88	16.65

Table 7: The rate of parameters (%) that our method requires compared to the original embedding layer. We also list the result of CoLA and MRPC, for the analysis related to Tables 5 and 6.

$\mathrm{r}(\mathcal{V}_C) = 0.5$.

Tables 5 and 6 show the token and sentence coverage by $\mathcal{V}_C$ for these three characteristic datasets, respectively. From the results, $\mathcal{V}_C$ of CoLA has high token and sentence coverage even though $\mathcal{V}_C$ of CoLA is much smaller than QNLI and MRPC (Table 7). CoLA, however, has a large performance drop despite high coverage. We guess that the differences in performance degradation are explained by differences in the information required by the tasks, rather than by the rate of affected sentences.

The overhead to recover rare token embeddings It requires 142 ms to recover rare token embedding ($r(V_C) = 1.0$, $k = 5$) for JCoLA "`validation`" datasets using a server with Intel Xeon 2.40-GHz CPU. This is negligible ($< 5\%$) against the inference time (3010 ms) of the same datasets with the original PLM, which uses an additional NVIDIA P6000 GPU for matrix multiplication.

4.2 Sensitivity to compression rate

Using our method, we can explicitly control the compression rate of embedding by varying $\mathrm{r}(\mathcal{V}_C)$. We thus investigate the relation between the compression rate of the fine-tuned PLMs by our method and the PLM's performance (Tables 1 and 2), among three datasets: STS-B and QNLI in GLUE, and JSTS in JGLUE. These datasets have different training data sizes (5.2k examples for STS-B, 94.3k for QNLI, and 11.2k for JSTS in our settings), as shown in Table 7.

We can see that the compression rates of CoLA and JSTS of $\mathrm{r}(\mathcal{V}_C) = 1.0$ and MRPC and STS-B of $\mathrm{r}(\mathcal{V}_C) = 0.5$ are similar but their performance drops differ greatly, as shown in Tables 1 and 2. This will be because individual tasks require different degrees of information, and we thus need to tune the compression rate depending on the target downstream tasks.

$r(\mathcal{V}_C)$	GLUE				JGLUE	
	STS-B		QNLI		JSTS	
	all	(emb.)	all	(emb.)	all	(emb.)
0.5	47.7M	(4.15M)	53.7M	(10.11M)	46.1M	(2.56M)
1.0	51.6M	(8.01M)	63.7M	(20.13M)	47.7M	(4.19M)
orig.	67.0M	(23.44M)	67.0M	(23.44M)	68.7M	(25.17M)

Table 8: The number of parameters in the DistilBERT models with vocabulary compressed by our method.

	CoLA	JCoLA
$r(\|\mathcal{V}_C\|) = 1.0$		
<unk>	35.55	5.63
$k = 1$	70.56	29.14
$k = 2$	75.60	34.59
$k = 3$	77.51	37.41
$k = 4$	78.53	39.21
$k = 5$	79.16	40.48
AQ ($\mathcal{V}_C \cup \mathcal{V}_R$)	77.89	65.27
AQ ($\mathcal{V}_C$)	70.16	54.73
AQ ($\mathcal{V}_R$)	79.55	66.55

Table 9: Cosine similarity of the approximated embeddings to the original embedding.

4.3 Sensitivity to k

In our method and the PCA baseline, we can obtain a better approximation by increasing the number of the source embeddings, k. In this section, we investigate the relation between the quality of approximation and the PLM's performance.

Table 9 shows the cosine similarity between the original and the reconstructed embeddings in the PLMs fine-tuned to the CoLA and JCoLA datasets. From the table, we can confirm that more similar embeddings to the original can be reconstructed when we increase the number of the source embedding, k, in both CoLA and JCoLA. However, the higher similarity does not always lead to higher performance as lower k are chosen in most datasets in Table 1 and 2. Meanwhile, AQ achieves comparable (CoLA) or much better (JCoLA) similarity for rare tokens but performs poorly (Table 2). These results confirm that the noises in common token embeddings are vital and the PLMs have a strong contextualized ability to guess the meanings of rare tokens from their surrounding contexts, we do not need to care much about tuning k to obtain a better approximation of embeddings.

5 Related Work

In the development of neural network-based NLP, how to embed a sequence of discrete symbols in languages into the continuous space has been an important issue, and various compact representations of embeddings have been explored. In what follows, we first review approaches to compressing word embeddings (§ 5.1). We next introduce finer-grained tokenization than words, which results in compact embedding layers (§ 5.2). We then discuss a method of predicting embeddings of out-of-vocabulary words (§ 5.3).

5.1 Compressing Word Embeddings

Classical approaches to neural language modeling leverage word-level embeddings such as CBoW (Mikolov et al., 2013) and GloVe (Pennington et al., 2014), which are learned via shallow neural networks. Since out-of-vocabulary (OOV) words cause serious issues in word-based embeddings, the embeddings are often trained to cover as many words as possible, which makes embedding layers larger. Hence, researchers have worked to compress word embeddings during or after training neural models.

Matrix (Tensor) factorization decomposes a large matrix (tensor) by a product of low-rank matrices (tensors) and has been used to compress word embeddings (Chen et al., 2018a; Acharya et al., 2019; Winata et al., 2019; Lan et al., 2020; Hrinchuk et al., 2020; Lioutas et al., 2020; Lee et al., 2021; Wang et al., 2023). In particular, ALBERT (Lan et al., 2020) learns to represent the embedding layer of a PLM with a product of two small matrices during pre-training; although the factorized vocabulary reduces the memory footprint, it involves matrix multiplications that slow the inference and is not adopted in other PLMs.

Sparse coding has been thereby explored to address the aforementioned issue in matrix factorization (Faruqui et al., 2015; Chen et al., 2016; Shu and Nakayama, 2017; Chen et al., 2018b; Tissier et al., 2019; Ma et al., 2019; Kim et al., 2020). The sparse coding represents embeddings using a sparse linear combination of basis embeddings; each embedding is represented by a short sparse vector, which has pairs of IDs for basis embeddings and weight (optional). In particular, Chen et al. (2016) adopted frequency-aware partial sparse coding as ours and applied it to embedding layers of RNN-LMs with word tokenization. To choose a small subset of basis (common token) embeddings for each rare token embedding, they used ℓ_1-regularization. However, the sparsity is limited since ℓ_1 regularization does not directly minimize the number of basis embeddings for reconstruction.

In this study, focusing on the recent subword-based Transformer-based PLMs that have strong contextualization abilities of embeddings, we develop a lightweight method that chooses a fixed number of basis embeddings to represent each rare embedding from its nearest-neighbor common token embeddings and confirms that it attains high sparsity while retaining the original accuracy.

5.2 Finer-grained Tokenization

To address the issue of OOV words, researchers leveraged finer-grained tokenization based on subwords (Sennrich et al., 2016; Kudo, 2018) to back-off embeddings of OOV words to those of subwords (ultimately, characters or bytes). The finer-grained tokenization allows us to reduce the vocabulary size dramatically. Furthermore, to handle massive vocabularies in multilingual models, character- (Clark et al., 2022) and byte-level tokenization (Xue et al., 2022) have been used. These finer-grained tokenizations, however, incur high computational costs, because they heavily rely on the hidden layers of PLMs to recover (sub)word-level representations. Meanwhile, recent large language models (LLMs) are trained with a larger set of subwords; Takase et al. (2024) reported that larger vocabulary contributes to the performance of LLMs. Meanwhile, when we adopt pretrain-and-fine-tune paradigm, we need to stick to the original tokenizer of the PLMs, since it is difficult to obtain a different set of fine-grained vocabularies that replace the existing subword-level vocabularies in the PLMs. We thus need to address large subword vocabularies of PLMs to compress PLMs.

5.3 Predicting OOV Embeddings

As stated in § 5.1, out-of-vocabulary (OOV) words had been a problem in the word-level embeddings, before the subword-based tokenization becomes a de-facto standard in neural text processing via Transformer-based PLMs. Several researchers thus attempted to reconstruct OOV embeddings from subword embeddings (Pinter et al., 2017; Zhao et al., 2018; Sasaki et al., 2019; Fukuda et al., 2020; Chen et al., 2022). Although these methods can compute OOV embeddings from subword embeddings, they usually leverage a neural network to accurately predict OOV embeddings, which not only requires an additional memory footprint but also slows down the inference. In this study, we resort to the strong contextualization abilities of PLMs to handle OOV words, and focus on reconstructing rare token embeddings by abusing common token embeddings, to minimize the space and time cost to compute the embeddings in the inference.

6 Conclusions

We proposed a simple yet effective sparse coding method to compress the embedding layer of a given fine-tuned PLM. We keep common tokens that appear frequently in the fine-tuning data and only compress the embeddings of rare tokens that do not appear in the fine-tuning data. We select only a small subset of the nearest neighbor source (common token) embeddings to approximate the target (rare token) embeddings so that we represent the target embeddings with only a small number of parameters. Our experimental results confirmed that our frequency-aware partial sparse coding can greatly compress the embedding layer while preventing performance degradation. Our method works effectively without carefully choosing the number of the source embedding for compression.

In future work, we will apply a method to select the target tokens for compression from the vocabulary while considering the easiness of reconstruction as well as the frequency. We also plan to apply our method to decoder-only and encoder-decoder LMs, although there are issues as stated in the Limitations section.

Limitations

Since our method discards the original embeddings for rare tokens and dynamically reconstructs those embeddings upon request, the application to decoder-only and encoder-decoder PLMs has some challenges. First, If the PLMs do not adopt the weight tying, which shares the weights of the embedding and softmax layers, then our method is applicable to the embedding layers. If the PLMs adopt the weight tying, a naive application of our method to those PLMs will result in outputs without rare tokens. However, we will be able to generate rare tokens, by remembering neighboring rare tokens for each common token with embeddings; we first choose a common token as the next token, by greedy decoding or some decoding strategy, and then reconstruct the neighboring rare token embeddings to include those rare tokens as the candidates of the next token. We will plan to evaluate this method on recent decoder-only large LMs.

Acknowledgements

This work was partially supported by the special fund of Institute of Industrial Science, The University of Tokyo and by JSPS KAKENHI Grant Number JP21H03494.

References

Anish Acharya, Rahul Goel, Angeliki Metallinou, and Inderjit Dhillon. 2019. Online embedding compression for text classification using low rank matrix factorization. In *Proceedings of the Thirty-Third AAAI Conference on Artificial Intelligence and Thirty-First Innovative Applications of Artificial Intelligence Conference and Ninth AAAI Symposium on Educational Advances in Artificial Intelligence*, AAAI'19/IAAI'19/EAAI'19. AAAI Press.

Artem Babenko and Victor Lempitsky. 2014. Additive quantization for extreme vector compression. In *2014 IEEE Conference on Computer Vision and Pattern Recognition*, pages 931–938. IEEE.

Lihu Chen, Gael Varoquaux, and Fabian Suchanek. 2022. Imputing out-of-vocabulary embeddings with LOVE makes LanguageModels robust with little cost. In *Proceedings of the 60th Annual Meeting of the Association for Computational Linguistics (Volume 1: Long Papers)*, pages 3488–3504, Dublin, Ireland. Association for Computational Linguistics.

Patrick Chen, Si Si, Yang Li, Ciprian Chelba, and Cho-Jui Hsieh. 2018a. Groupreduce: Block-wise low-rank approximation for neural language model shrinking. In *Advances in Neural Information Processing Systems*, volume 31. Curran Associates, Inc.

Ting Chen, Martin Renqiang Min, and Yizhou Sun. 2018b. Learning k-way d-dimensional discrete codes for compact embedding representations. In *Proceedings of the 35th International Conference on Machine Learning*, volume 80 of *Proceedings of Machine Learning Research*, pages 854–863. PMLR.

Yunchuan Chen, Lili Mou, Yan Xu, Ge Li, and Zhi Jin. 2016. Compressing neural language models by sparse word representations. In *Proceedings of the 54th Annual Meeting of the Association for Computational Linguistics (Volume 1: Long Papers)*, pages 226–235, Berlin, Germany. Association for Computational Linguistics.

Jonathan H. Clark, Dan Garrette, Iulia Turc, and John Wieting. 2022. Canine: Pre-training an efficient tokenization-free encoder for language representation. *Transactions of the Association for Computational Linguistics*, 10:73–91.

Jacob Devlin, Ming-Wei Chang, Kenton Lee, and Kristina Toutanova. 2019. BERT: Pre-training of Deep Bidirectional Transformers for Language Understanding. In *Proceedings of the 2019 Conference of the North American Chapter of the Association for Computational Linguistics: Human Language Technologies, Volume 1 (Long and Short Papers)*, pages 4171–4186, Minneapolis, Minnesota. Association for Computational Linguistics.

Manaal Faruqui, Yulia Tsvetkov, Dani Yogatama, Chris Dyer, and Noah A. Smith. 2015. Sparse overcomplete word vector representations. In *Proceedings of the 53rd Annual Meeting of the Association for Computational Linguistics and the 7th International Joint Conference on Natural Language Processing (Volume 1: Long Papers)*, pages 1491–1500, Beijing, China. Association for Computational Linguistics.

Nobukazu Fukuda, Naoki Yoshinaga, and Masaru Kitsuregawa. 2020. Robust Backed-off Estimation of Out-of-Vocabulary Embeddings. In *Findings of the Association for Computational Linguistics: EMNLP 2020*, pages 4827–4838, Online. Association for Computational Linguistics.

Oleksii Hrinchuk, Valentin Khrulkov, Leyla Mirvakhabova, Elena Orlova, and Ivan Oseledets. 2020. Tensorized embedding layers. In *Findings of the Association for Computational Linguistics: EMNLP 2020*, pages 4847–4860, Online. Association for Computational Linguistics.

Jared Kaplan, Sam McCandlish, Tom Henighan, Tom B. Brown, Benjamin Chess, Rewon Child, Scott Gray, Alec Radford, Jeffrey Wu, and Dario Amodei. 2020. Scaling laws for neural language models.

Yeachan Kim, Kang-Min Kim, and SangKeun Lee. 2020. Adaptive compression of word embeddings. In *Proceedings of the 58th Annual Meeting of the Association for Computational Linguistics*, pages 3950–3959, Online. Association for Computational Linguistics.

Taku Kudo. 2018. Subword Regularization: Improving Neural Network Translation Models with Multiple Subword Candidates. In *Proceedings of the 56th Annual Meeting of the Association for Computational Linguistics (Volume 1: Long Papers)*, pages 66–75, Melbourne, Australia. Association for Computational Linguistics.

Taku Kudo and John Richardson. 2018. SentencePiece: A simple and language independent subword tokenizer and detokenizer for neural text processing. In *Proceedings of the 2018 Conference on Empirical Methods in Natural Language Processing: System Demonstrations*, pages 66–71, Brussels, Belgium. Association for Computational Linguistics.

Kentaro Kurihara, Daisuke Kawahara, and Tomohide Shibata. 2022. JGLUE: Japanese general language understanding evaluation. In *Proceedings of the Thirteenth Language Resources and Evaluation Conference*, pages 2957–2966, Marseille, France. European Language Resources Association.

Zhenzhong Lan, Mingda Chen, Sebastian Goodman, Kevin Gimpel, Piyush Sharma, and Radu Soricut. 2020. Albert: A lite bert for self-supervised learning of language representations. In *International Conference on Learning Representations*.

Jong-Ryul Lee, Yong-Ju Lee, and Yong-Hyuk Moon. 2021. Block-wise word embedding compression revisited: Better weighting and structuring. In *Findings of the Association for Computational Linguistics: EMNLP 2021*, pages 4379–4388, Punta Cana, Dominican Republic. Association for Computational Linguistics.

Vasileios Lioutas, Ahmad Rashid, Krtin Kumar, Md. Akmal Haidar, and Mehdi Rezagholizadeh. 2020. Improving Word Embedding Factorization for Compression Using Distilled Nonlinear Neural Decomposition. In *Findings of the Association for Computational Linguistics: EMNLP 2020*, pages 2774–2784, Online. Association for Computational Linguistics.

Yukun Ma, Patrick H. Chen, and Cho-Jui Hsieh. 2019. MulCode: A multiplicative multi-way model for compressing neural language model. In *Proceedings of the 2019 Conference on Empirical Methods in Natural Language Processing and the 9th International Joint Conference on Natural Language Processing (EMNLP-IJCNLP)*, pages 5257–5266, Hong Kong, China. Association for Computational Linguistics.

Tomas Mikolov, Kai Chen, Gregory S. Corrado, and Jeffrey Dean. 2013. Efficient estimation of word representations in vector space. In *International Conference on Learning Representations*.

Jeffrey Pennington, Richard Socher, and Christopher Manning. 2014. GloVe: Global vectors for word representation. In *Proceedings of the 2014 Conference on Empirical Methods in Natural Language Processing (EMNLP)*, pages 1532–1543, Doha, Qatar. Association for Computational Linguistics.

Yuval Pinter, Robert Guthrie, and Jacob Eisenstein. 2017. Mimicking word embeddings using subword RNNs. In *Proceedings of the 2017 Conference on Empirical Methods in Natural Language Processing*, pages 102–112, Copenhagen, Denmark. Association for Computational Linguistics.

Sam T. Roweis and Lawrence K. Saul. 2000. Nonlinear dimensionality reduction by locally linear embedding. *Science*, 290(5500):2323–2326.

Jin Sakuma and Naoki Yoshinaga. 2019. Multilingual Model Using Cross-Task Embedding Projection. In *Proceedings of the 23rd Conference on Computational Natural Language Learning (CoNLL)*, pages 22–32, Hong Kong, China. Association for Computational Linguistics.

Victor Sanh, Lysandre Debut, Julien Chaumond, and Thomas Wolf. 2019. DistilBERT, a distilled version of BERT: smaller, faster, cheaper and lighter. In *Proceedings Fifth Workshop on Energy Efficient Machine Learning and Cognitive Computing*.

Shota Sasaki, Jun Suzuki, and Kentaro Inui. 2019. Subword-based Compact Reconstruction of Word Embeddings. In *Proceedings of the 2019 Conference of the North American Chapter of the Association for Computational Linguistics: Human Language Technologies, Volume 1 (Long and Short Papers)*, pages 3498–3508, Minneapolis, Minnesota. Association for Computational Linguistics.

Rico Sennrich, Barry Haddow, and Alexandra Birch. 2016. Neural machine translation of rare words with subword units. In *Proceedings of the 54th Annual Meeting of the Association for Computational Linguistics (Volume 1: Long Papers)*, pages 1715–1725, Berlin, Germany. Association for Computational Linguistics.

Raphael Shu and Hideki Nakayama. 2017. Compressing word embeddings via deep compositional code learning. In *Proceedings of the sixth International Conference on Learning Representations*.

Sho Takase, Ryokan Ri, Shun Kiyono, and Takuya Kato. 2024. Large vocabulary size improves large language models. *arXiv*, abs/2406.16508.

Julien Tissier, Christophe Gravier, and Amaury Habrard. 2019. Near-lossless binarization of word embeddings. In *Proceedings of the Thirty-Third AAAI Conference on Artificial Intelligence and Thirty-First Innovative Applications of Artificial Intelligence Conference and Ninth AAAI Symposium on Educational Advances in Artificial Intelligence*, AAAI'19/IAAI'19/EAAI'19. AAAI Press.

Ashish Vaswani, Noam Shazeer, Niki Parmar, Jakob Uszkoreit, Llion Jones, Aidan N Gomez, Ł ukasz Kaiser, and Illia Polosukhin. 2017. Attention is all you need. In *Advances in Neural Information Processing Systems*, volume 30. Curran Associates, Inc.

Zhongwei Wan, Xin Wang, Che Liu, Samiul Alam, Yu Zheng, Jiachen Liu, Zhongnan Qu, Shen Yan, Yi Zhu, Quanlu Zhang, Mosharaf Chowdhury, and Mi Zhang. 2024. Efficient large language models: A survey. *Transactions on Machine Learning Research*. Survey Certification.

Alex Wang, Amanpreet Singh, Julian Michael, Felix Hill, Omer Levy, and Samuel Bowman. 2018. GLUE: A multi-task benchmark and analysis platform for natural language understanding. In *Proceedings of the 2018 EMNLP Workshop BlackboxNLP: Analyzing and Interpreting Neural Networks for NLP*, pages 353–355, Brussels, Belgium. Association for Computational Linguistics.

Haoyu Wang, Ruirui Li, Haoming Jiang, Zhengyang Wang, Xianfeng Tang, Bin Bi, Monica Cheng, Bing Yin, Yaqing Wang, Tuo Zhao, and Jing Gao. 2023. Lighttoken: A task and model-agnostic lightweight token embedding framework for pre-trained language models. In *Proceedings of the 29th ACM SIGKDD Conference on Knowledge Discovery and Data Mining*, KDD '23, page 2302–2313, New York, NY, USA. Association for Computing Machinery.

Genta Indra Winata, Andrea Madotto, Jamin Shin, Elham J Barezi, and Pascale Fung. 2019. On the effectiveness of low-rank matrix factorization for LSTM model compression. In *Proceedings of the 33rd Pacific Asia Conference on Language, Information and Computation*, Hakodate, Japan.

Linting Xue, Aditya Barua, Noah Constant, Rami Al-Rfou, Sharan Narang, Mihir Kale, Adam Roberts, and Colin Raffel. 2022. ByT5: Towards a Token-Free Future with Pre-trained Byte-to-Byte Models. *Transactions of the Association for Computational Linguistics*, 10:291–306.

Jinman Zhao, Sidharth Mudgal, and Yingyu Liang. 2018. Generalizing word embeddings using bag of subwords. In *Proceedings of the 2018 Conference on Empirical Methods in Natural Language Processing*, pages 601–606, Brussels, Belgium. Association for Computational Linguistics.

Zixuan Zhou, Xuefei Ning, Ke Hong, Tianyu Fu, Jiaming Xu, Shiyao Li, Yuming Lou, Luning Wang, Zhihang Yuan, Xiuhong Li, Shengen Yan, Guohao Dai, Xiao-Ping Zhang, Yuhan Dong, and Yu Wang. 2024. A survey on efficient inference for large language models. *arXiv*, abs/2404.14294.

Xunyu Zhu, Jian Li, Yong Liu, Can Ma, and Weiping Wang. 2023. A survey on model compression for large language models. *arXiv*, abs/2308.07633.

Translating Across Cultures: LLMs for Intralingual Cultural Adaptation

Pushpdeep Singh, Mayur Patidar, Lovekesh Vig
TCS Research
{pushpdeep.singh, patidar.mayur, lovekesh.vig}@tcs.com

Abstract

LLMs are increasingly being deployed for multilingual applications and have demonstrated impressive translation capabilities between several low and high-resource languages. An aspect of translation that often gets overlooked is that of cultural adaptation, or modifying source culture references to suit the target culture. While specialized translation models still outperform LLMs on the machine translation task when viewed from the lens of correctness, they are not sensitive to cultural differences often requiring manual correction. LLMs on the other hand have a rich reservoir of cultural knowledge embedded within its parameters that can be potentially exploited for such applications. In this paper, we define the task of cultural adaptation and create an evaluation framework to evaluate the performance of modern LLMs for cultural adaptation and analyze their cross-cultural knowledge while connecting related concepts across different cultures. We also analyze possible issues with automatic adaptation. We hope that this task will offer more insight into the cultural understanding of LLMs and their creativity in cross-cultural scenarios.

NOTE: This paper contains examples that may be offensive.

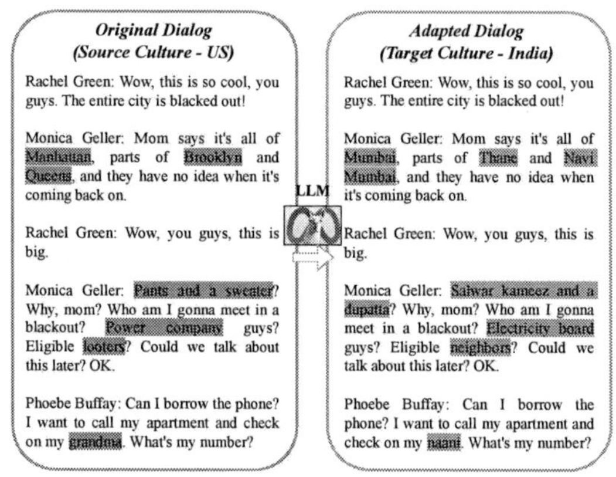

Figure 1: Cultural Adaptation using LLM

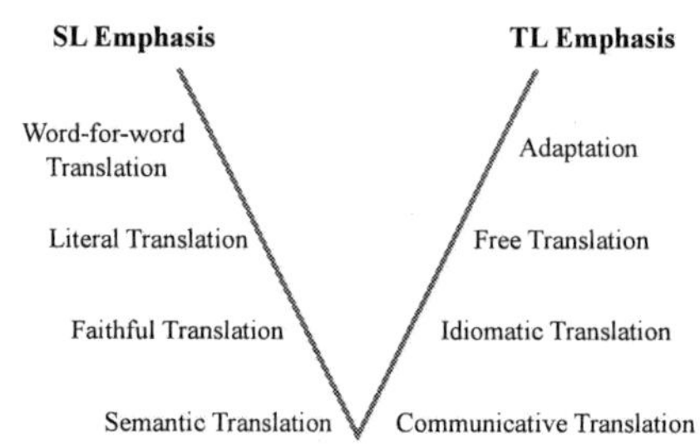

Figure 2: Newmark (1988)'s V diagram of translation methods. SL: Source Language, TL: Target Language

1 Introduction

Recent progress in NLP is largely driven via LLMs, which have shown great promise in a variety of tasks including text generation, language understanding, question answering, code generation, and even machine translation. Though LLMs have not achieved state-of-the-art performance for machine translation (Zhu et al., 2023), their instruction-following ability makes them suitable for tasks involving more creativity and customization during generation. Many translation applications require literal translations for which specialized transformer-based models trained on parallel data are ideal. However, there are other facets of translation (see Figure 2), such as adaptation, also called the 'freest' form of translation (Newmark, 1988) wherein the original text is rewritten to make it more appropriate for the target audience belonging to a specific age group or culture (See Figure 1). Applications of adaptation (Appendix E) include adapted transcriptions for plays, poetry, and movie subtitles where the plot, characters and central theme are usually kept intact but the text is rewritten to ensure the output is sensitive to the target culture. Adaptation can either be done within the same (intralingual adaptation) or in different languages (interlingual adaptation).

Proceedings of the 28th Conference on Computational Natural Language Learning, pages 400–418
November 15-16, 2024

Polizzotti (2018) in his book *"Sympathy for the Traitor: The Translation Manifesto"* describes how in 17th century France, a sexist term *belles infidèles* (the beautiful, unfaithful ones) was used to describe the prevalent approach to French translations at the time, which involved "updating" ancient Greek and Latin texts by removing vulgar language or sexual content and replacing outdated references with modern equivalents to make the texts more easily understandable and socially acceptable. These translations were considered "beautiful" because they were smooth to read and met contemporary expectations, but they were not faithful to the original texts in a strict sense. The debate between "literalism" and "adaptation" persists, with proponents of each arguing their merits. Yet, adaptations of existing texts continue to serve diverse purposes including cross-cultural communication.

In this study, we steer clear of this debate and explore this task purely from an NLP perspective particularly investigating the power of large language models. We define a specific version of the task along with clear goals and an evaluation framework for assessing the effectiveness of these adaptations considering factors such as localisation, preservation, naturalness, and appropriateness. The motivation behind this work stems from the need to transcend the constraints of literal translation and explore freer forms of translation such as adaptation. Due to the rising creativity, multilinguality, cross-cultural knowledge and instruction-following ability of modern language models, they have the potential to generate culturally resonant adaptations of the source text.

We limit our study to cultural adaptation with English as the source and target language i.e. Intralingual adaptation. As Hershcovich et al. (2022) argues, although language and culture are interconnected, they are not synonymous. For example, English, being the *lingua franca* for many parts of the world, can carry views and concepts from different parts of the world. By sticking to English, we can specifically evaluate how well cultural aspects are adjusted in adaptation without the added complexity of translating between languages. As LLMs become more multilingual (in generation and understanding), their ability can better be evaluated for interlingual adaptation and related aspects of this study can be applied there. We can also view Interlingual Cultural Adaptation as a combination of Intralingual Cultural Adaptation and Machine Translation.

We explore the following research questions and contribute along these: RQ 1) How do we define what constitutes adaptation in terms of modifications to the source text i.e. what is changed during adaptation and for what purpose? RQ 2) Based on the goals of adaptation, what are the optimal criteria/aspects for evaluation? RQ 3) Given the evaluation, how proficient are modern language models at adaptation? What strategies do they employ, and to what extent do they adapt based on provided instructions? RQ 4) What insights does this offer into their parametric cross-cultural knowledge?

2 Related Work

Yao et al. (2023) discusses the aspect of using cultural knowledge to support LLM-based translation. They focus on literal translation and create a culture-specific parallel corpus, to evaluate the cultural awareness of MT systems. They explored different prompting strategies using external and internal knowledge for LLM-based machine translation and created an automatic evaluation metric, to measure the translation quality of cultural concepts.

Recent works on evaluating cultural awareness in LLMs have centred primarily around measuring cultural value alignment (Durmus et al., 2023; Cao et al., 2023; Masoud et al., 2023; Ramezani and Xu, 2023). While this is important, it does not necessarily indicate that LLMs are aware of culture-specific items or concepts from different cultures. More research is needed to assess whether LLMs truly understand these culture-specific items and concepts and can use them coherently in text. Our research aims to address this question.

Jiang and Joshi (2023) created a ranking-based statistical QA task that compared cultural concept popularity across countries. Wang et al. (2024) examined the cultural dominance of concrete (e.g., holidays and songs) and abstract (e.g., values and opinions) cultural objects in LLM responses.

Peskov et al. (2021) introduced the idea of automatic cultural adaptation by adapting named entities across cultures and languages, however, it focused on simpler entities in standalone sentences. Cao et al. (2024) constructed resources for cultural adaptation of recipes and also evaluated their method against LLM-based adaptation. More recently, Zhang et al. (2024) created Chinese-English menu corpora and defined an evaluation for the task of adapting restaurant menus.

3 Task Definition

For the task of adaptation, we use a corpus of dialogs from a TV show and adapt it to the target culture. We choose adaptation of dialogs instead of standalone sentences as done by Peskov et al. (2021) since they provide richer context and are more representative of a true use case of adaptation. The original corpus of dialogues is denoted as $D_o = \{d_1^o, d_2^o, \ldots, d_n^o\}$. We obtain an adapted version of these dialogues denoted as $D_a = \{f(d_1^o, c), f(d_2^o, c), \ldots, f(d_n^o, c)\}$, where f represents the language model that adapts the original dialogues to the target culture and c is the specific cultural context or prompt representing the cultural context for adaptation. Each dialogue d consists of a number of utterances i.e. $d = \{u_1, u_2, \ldots, u_m\}$. Each utterance u_i = speaker(u_i) : text(u_i), where $speaker(u_i)$ is the speaker or participant name and (u_i) is the textual content for utterance u_i. Our task is to evaluate how well dialogues in the adapted set D_a are culturally aligned to the target culture while maintaining the intent and essence of the original dialogue. Section 4 provides details on the exact aspects along which we assess these adaptations.

4 Annotating Cultural References

Corpus Description: We choose the 'Friends Dialogs' corpus for this study. We filter the data to choose dialogues with utterances between 1 and 15. The corpus includes 1110 conversations (or dialogs) containing 11812 utterances by 363 speakers. The reason for choosing such a corpus is that 'Friends TV Show' is deeply rooted in American culture offering a distinct contrast that highlights the need for adaptation when targeting a new cultural context, specifically *India*[1] in our study. Here, adaptation ensures that the message is not only understood but also embraced and valued in a different cultural environment.

Culture is a multi-faceted concept. Many scholars have tried to define culture. One such theory which is very relevant here and is also mentioned in cultural translation studies is Hall's

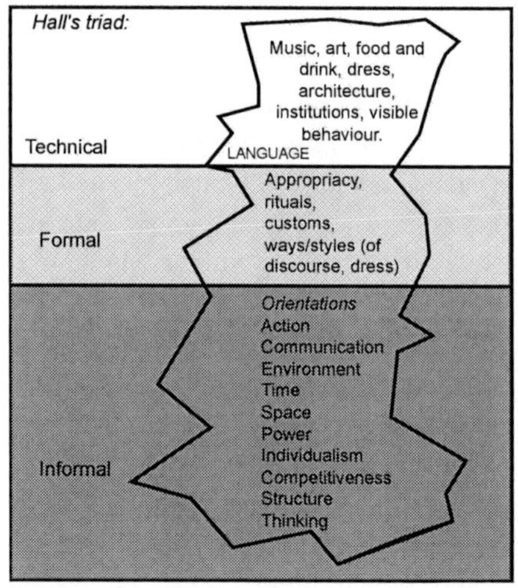

Figure 3: Hall's Iceberg Theory and Triads

Iceberg Model of Culture (or the Triad of Culture) which divides aspects of culture into three levels: visible (above the waterline), semi-visible and invisible (see Figure 3) which are referred as the technical, formal and informal level of culture, respectively. As Katan (2014) describes, these levels also relate to how we grasp culture: technical culture can be taught by an expert, formal culture through trial-and-error while informal culture is learned unconsciously.

At the tip of the iceberg i.e. the technical level, the goal of translation is to transfer the terms and concepts of the source text to the target text with minimal loss. The terms and concepts are usually referred to as "culture-bound" terms, or "culturemes". Hall's second level, i.e., the Formal level of culture focuses on rituals, customs, and accepted or appropriate ways of doing things. This level follows the 'Skopos Theory' (Vermeer, 1989) i.e translation should be oriented towards achieving the desired function in the target culture, rather than being faithful to the source text. Hall's third level, i.e., the Informal level cannot be taught or learned but is acquired 'out-of-awareness' or unconsciously. This is what makes a translation more artistic rather than mechanistic.

RQ 1: How do we define what constitutes adaptation in terms of modifications to the source text i.e. what is changed during adaptation and for what purpose? In this study, we mainly focus on the first two levels of culture. In order to evaluate whether an adaptation navigates different levels of culture, we need to annotate culture-related references in the source text and look at

[1]We choose country as a proxy for culture (Adilazuarda et al., 2024). While a country such as India has many subcultures, still, many aspects and items are still universal and are relatable to a national audience. Those remain the key focus of our study and our annotation task.

how they are being adapted in the corresponding adaptation. We call these items adaptable items or **Culture-Specific Items(CSI)** used by Newmark (1988).

Items which can undergo adaptation include references to concepts and realities which are foreign to the target culture, socially sensitive and taboo topics, colloquialisms, slang, idioms, figures of speech, humour, or content which can be considered offensive in the target culture. We manually annotate these items in our corpus of dialogues. We also categorise these items into the following categories : 1) Ecology ((flora, fauna, winds etc.) 2) Material Culture (artefacts, food, clothes, houses, towns, transport etc.) 3) Social Culture (work and leisure) 4) Institutions, Organizations and ideas (political, social, religious, social, artistic, administrative, ideas etc.) 5) Gestures and Habits (name of regular behaviour and movements), as proposed by Newmark (1988). Additionally, we introduce four more categories which reflect the need for adaptation: 6) Slang or Figure of Speech, 7) Offensive Content, 8) Socially Sensitive or Taboo Topics and 9) Humour (Since 'Friends' is a sitcom). We use the descriptions from Newmark (1988) plus descriptions of the other four categories as our annotation guidelines.

While Yao et al. (2023) demonstrates an automated approach to annotating culture-bound items, however, for our use case, we observed that it only identifies a fraction of items which can undergo adaptation. Also, CSI are culture-specific not due to their origin but also due to their foreignness to the target culture. For example, sausage is common in both the USA and the UK but still foreign in Indian culture, so manually annotating these items based on the foreignness to the target culture is desired. This is especially important due to the "McDonaldization of Society" (Ritzer, 1996) where cultural boundaries are becoming blurred and the notion of foreignness is constantly evolving due to migration and cultural exchange. Therefore, we also annotate the degree of foreignness to the target audience to provide a more accurate depiction and expectation since items that are more foreign to the target culture should be more likely to undergo adaptation. We define 3 foreignness levels: 1,2 and 3 for our annotation. Foreignness level 1 consists of items/behaviours which have traceable foreign origin/usage however they are common (in terms of familiarity, integration and perception) in the target culture. For example, pizza, chocolate, cricket and coffee are fairly common in India. We omit items in foreignness level 1 from our analysis. For items with foreignness level 2, they may be recognized in the target culture, but their usage or significance is somewhat foreign or less familiar. For example, sushi, tacos, k-pop and beer are not very common and not fully assimilated or mainstream in India. Items in foreignness level 3 are largely unfamiliar or perceived as distinctly foreign within the target culture. Some examples include *kimono*, rodeo, thanksgiving etc. which are largely unknown to the Indian audience.

Human annotation: We hired three human annotators from India for our study (both annotation and human evaluation (Section 7.2)), who were able to understand different aspects and sensitivities of Indian culture expressed through English. The annotators were aware of the source ("USA" as a proxy) culture and good at identifying what aspects of it are foreign to India and to what extent. They were instructed to annotate[2] for these cultural items in the corpus, their categories and foreignness level.
Recent studies (Schaekermann et al., 2018; Drapeau et al., 2016) have indicated that deliberation can enhance the quality of answers and even a small number of debates can outperform the wisdom of large crowds (Navajas et al., 2017). Therefore, in this study, annotations were carried out using deliberation through verbal discussion until a consensus was reached.

Some examples of CSI for different categories or foreignness levels are given in Table 1. The number of occurrences of these CSI for each category/foreignness is shown in Figure 4. The corpus is publicly accessible[3].

5 Evaluation of Cultural Adaptation

In order to design an evaluation framework for adaptation, we need to understand the motivation and goals behind it. In the following section, we mention some goals of adaptation which are aspects along which we assess the quality of cultural

[2]Although we acknowledge subjectivity in terms of annotation on aspects like foreignness, offensive content, taboo topics, etc., the instructions for annotations were made as specific and unambiguous as possible. Annotators were asked to consider a wider target audience to avoid any personal bias when annotating these cultural items in the corpus, their categories, and their level of foreignness.

[3]https://github.com/iampushpdeep/CulturalAdaptEval

CSI Category	CSI Examples
Ecology	sage branches, Vail, Alps, Grand Canyon, San Diego Zoo, Capuchin etc.
Material Culture	meatball sub, MonkeyShine Beer poster, hamburger, Soap Opera Digest etc.
Social Culture	Another World, Thanksgiving, Days of Our Lives, bridesmaids, Halloween etc.
Institutions, Organisations and Ideas	Alan Alda, Mattress King, Wendy's, FICA, Fortunata Fashions etc.
Gestures and Habits	"You licked and you put", "honk honk", "Cha-ching", "step-ity step and jazz hands" etc.
Offensive Content	"go to hell", dumb ass, bitch, "climb out of my butt", "third nipple" etc.
Socially Sensitive and Taboo topics	porn, naked, lust, have sex, undressing etc.
Humour	knock-knock jokes, "get him something like a wrecking ball, or a vile of smallpox" etc.
Foreignness Level	**CSI Examples**
2	Christmas, Superman, cheesecake, wok, "spill coffee grounds", Porsche etc.
3	graham cracker, Archie and Jughead Double Digest, barca lounger, Swing Kings etc.

Table 1: Examples of CSI along different categories/foreignness levels found in 'Friends' Corpus.

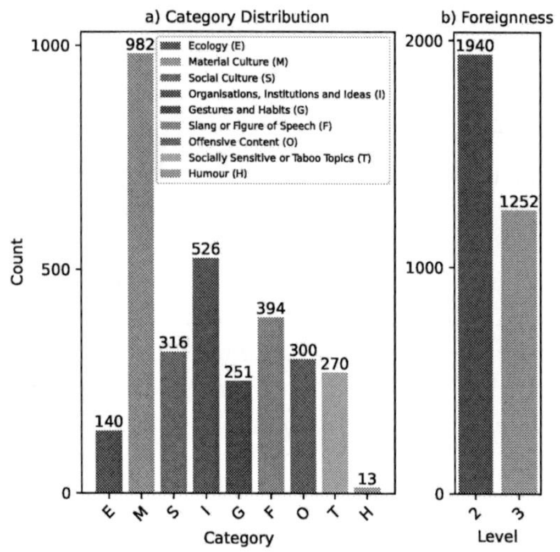

Figure 4: Number of Occurrences of CSI by a) Category, b) Foreignness level. A total of 3192 occurrences were found.

adaptation.

5.1 Aspects of Evaluation

RQ 2: Based on the goals of adaptation, what are the optimal criteria/aspects for evaluation? Adaptation can be used for a variety of applications[4] and the goals will vary for each application be it marketing, children's literature, or creative content translation. However, the main goal of adaptation is to serve the target audience, even if it means being unfaithful to the original text. This means that one of the goals is to achieve a shift in cultural levels to make the text more familiar and appropriate to the target culture by adapting more items in the source text. The greater the **Extent of Cultural Adaptation or Localisation**, the higher the chances it will be accepted by the target audience. Another obvious goal of adaptation is **Cultural Appropriateness and Sensitivity** i.e. respecting the sensitivities of the target culture without being *offensive* and avoiding propagation of harmful *stereotypes*. Sometimes, items adapted to the target culture may not fit well or might appear forced or unnatural. Thus, another goal is **Naturalness** i.e. that adaptation must appear natural and coherent. Changes done to the source text should not disrupt the flow of the text. As mentioned earlier, adaptation used for plays, poetry, drama etc keeps the characters and the central theme intact and only modifies cultural elements. This means that another goal of adaptation is **Content Preservation**. We want adaptation to preserve the original meaning and intent of the dialogue and it should not distort the main message. Since we are dealing with intralingual cultural adaptation, it is very similar to text style transfer (Mir et al., 2019) which also uses metrics like style transfer intensity (in our case, extent of cultural adaptation), content preservation and naturalness. In order to evaluate cultural adaptations along these aspects, we perform two types of analysis: *1) edit level analysis*, *2) dialogue level analysis*.

5.2 Edit Level Analysis

% CSI edited: We define a proxy metric to measure the extent of cultural adaptation i.e. % Of CSI edited. We use the annotations in our source corpus and using fuzzy string matching[5], we calculate what percentage of cultural elements that we have annotated in source text also appear in translation. If they do that means they aren't adapted/edited. Using this we can calculate % CSI edited as :

$$\% \text{ CSI edited} = 100 - \% \text{ of CSI found in adaptations}$$

This metric is not very informative of the

[4]In this study, we are exploring the creative side of adaptation however for more serious applications like adapting legal or medical content, factuality is the most important aspect of evaluation which these language models may not guarantee.

[5]https://github.com/seatgeek/thefuzz

quality of edits performed on items or whether that edit was correct or appropriate, however, it does quantify the extent of change or adaptation. We also report %CSI edited for each category and foreignness level.

Aspect Evaluation: For aspect-based evaluation at the edit level, we rate each individual edit on 3 aspects: localization, correctness in context and offensiveness. During adaptation, many edits are also performed on items which are culturally neutral. This is usually done to make the text more localized by creating new cultural items. Therefore we need to identify all edits whether they are on CSI or non-CSI. While there are libraries which can help to identify edits, we observed that LLMs are more suitable for such a task given their language understanding ability. We use **Mixtral**[6](Jiang et al., 2024) for automatic evaluation in our experiments including identifying edits in each utterance for all the dialogues. Then we ask the LLM to rate each edit on 3 aspects : 1) *Correctness* (0 or 1), 2) *Localization* (0 or 1 or 2), 3) *Offensiveness*(0 or 1) The prompts used for obtaining edits and rating them on these aspects are given in Appendix B. These aspects somewhat relate to the aspects described in Section 5.1. Correctness relates to Naturalness, Localization to Extent of Cultural Adaptation and Offensiveness to Cultural Appropriateness. However, it's important to note that aspect evaluation at the edit level may not account for the entire context of the dialog but for the edit and the context in which it is used. Once we obtain these ratings, we can analyze and compare adaptations from different LLMs in terms of 1) percentage of correct edits, 2) Average edit localization score and 3) percentage of offensive edits.

Translation Strategies: For each edit corresponding to source culture CSI, we determine the strategy used for adaptation. According to Davies (2003), the following strategies can be used while translating CSI: 1) Preservation, 2) Addition, 3) Omission, 4) Localisation, 5) Globalisation, 6) Transformation and 7) Creation. The prompt for determining the translation strategy for a given CSI edit is given in Appendix B, which also contains a description of these strategies. In the context of intralingual adaptation, 'preservation' corresponds to no edit. 'Creation' corresponds to edits where non-CSI are edited to CSI. We perform the analysis for CSI edits and classify them based on the strategy used.

5.3 Dialog Level Analysis

For dialog level analysis, we directly ask the LLM to rate the adapted dialog given the original dialog on a scale of 1 to 5, along five aspects : 1) Localization, 2) Naturalness, 3) Offensiveness, 4) Content Preservation and 5) Stereotypical behavior all of which fall under the aspects/goals of adaptation described in Section 5.1. The prompt used to score the adapted dialogs is given in Appendix B. We report average aspect scores over all dialogues.

6 Prompting for Cultural Adaptation

In this study, based on our goals, we use a simple prompt which includes our goals and exemplars to guide the LLM for expected adaptations of the dialogs. The adaptation prompt is given in Table 2.

You have to adapt the given dialogue to align with Indian culture and audience while keeping the response in English. Adapt culture-specific references/items (do not change character names) which are foreign to ***Indian culture*** to align with Indian cultural context, norms, and sensitivities, while maintaining the correctness, coherence and keeping original intent intact. Also adapt very foreign humour, slang or figure of speech unfamiliar to Indian English audiences, offensive and socially sensitive or taboo content while making sure that the intensity of emotions like humour don't get affected. Ensure that code-mixing is avoided, and output remains in English. Every utterance in the original dialogue should have a corresponding utterance in the adapted version, don't add or delete utterances or don't change speakers. {2 shot example (In Appendix C)} What is the adapted version for the following dialogue : {Dialog}

Table 2: Prompt for getting cultural adaptation

We experimented with a few prompts on a small scale to finally select the prompt for this study. We opine that the correct prompt can unlock certain dimensions and improve creativity, however, a detailed study involving large-scale experiments with different prompts would involve working at a deeper level of culture (especially the informal level) and evaluating related aspects as described in Section 4, which is beyond the scope of the present study.

Models: We explore adaptations obtained from

[6]https://huggingface.co/mistralai/Mixtral-8x7B-Instruct-v0.1

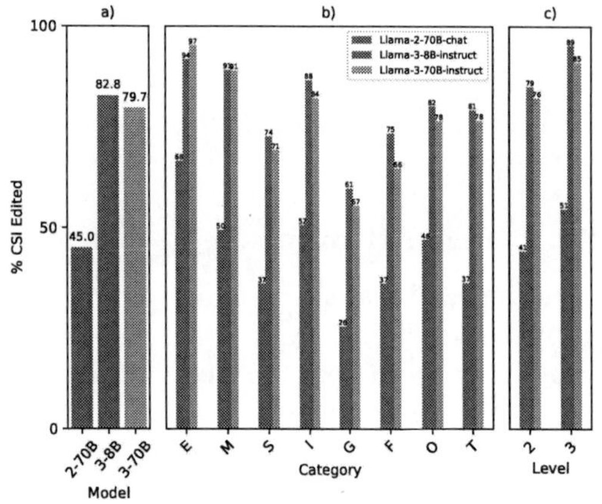

Figure 5: Percentage of CSI edited in a) total, b) along different categories and c) foreignness level.

Aspect	Llama-2 70B	Llama-3 8B	Llama-3 70B
# Edits	3256	12177	5747
Correctness(%)	99.05	99.79	**99.87**
Localisation(Average)	1.52	1.55	**1.74**
Localisation(%(0,1,2))	0.5, 46.7, 52.8	0.1, 54.5, 45.4	**0, 27.6, 72.4**
Offensiveness(%)	0.43	0.30	**0.00**

Table 3: Edit level scores

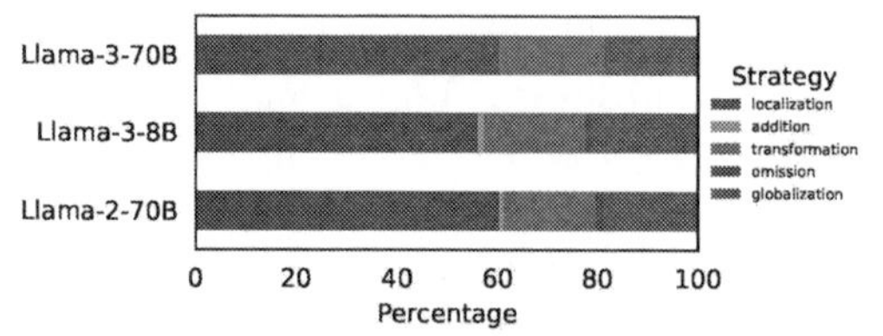

Figure 6: Translation strategies used for adapting CSI by percentage for different models

3 LLMs : Llama-2 70B[7](Touvron et al., 2023), Llama-3 8B[8] and Llama-3 70B[9]. These models are state-of-the-art open source LLMs and are cheaply available for inference.

Examples of adaptation from these models for a given dialog and several utterances are given in Appendix D (Table 12 and Table 14).

7 Results and Analysis

RQ 3: Given the evaluation, how proficient are modern language models at adaptation? What strategies do they employ, and to what extent do they adapt based on provided instructions?

7.1 Edit level Analysis

% CSI Edited As shown in Figure 5, %CSI Edited is lowest for Llama-2 70B (45%). This suggests a lower extent of adaptation. Llama-3 8B (82.8%) and Llama-3 70B (79.7%) seem to perform equally well in editing CSI. Items from the 'Ecology' category have the highest percentage of items edited due to items that are easier to edit. A higher fraction of items with foreignness level 3(very foreign) were edited compared to items with foreignness level 2 indicating that adaptation is prioritizing changing of more foreign items preferably into localized, more relatable items/expressions.

Aspect level evaluation : The results for aspect level evaluation are given in Table 3. Using Mixtral, we extracted significant edits (edits causing significant token change) from each adapted dialogue at an utterance level. Llama-3 8B, surprisingly, uses a large number of edits to get the adaptation, compared to other models. All models used in our evaluation have a high percentage of correct edits, the highest for Llama-3 70B, followed by Llama-3 8B and Llama-2 70B. Also, Llama-3 70B exhibits the highest average localization score per edit, primarily due to a larger proportion of edits being highly localized (score 2). Furthermore, Llama-3 70B displays no instances of offensive behaviour in our evaluation. Based on the edit-level analysis, Llama-2 70B performs slightly worse than other models. Nevertheless, LLMs are prone to perform incorrect edits, examples of which are given in Appendix D (Table 13). As shown, LLMs often struggle with instances that involve understanding and reasoning about cultural objects.

Translation Strategies used : We also obtain the type of strategy used for adapting CSI. Since the adaptation is intralingual, 'preservation' is already in use whenever CSI is not adapted, as captured by %CSI Edited. Figure 6 shows strategies used by percentage. We observe similar behaviour across all models: most percentage of CSI edits using localization, followed by transformation and then very closely, globalization. Addition and omission-related edits are very rare during adaptation. Some examples of CSI edits and the corresponding translation strategy used are given in Table 4.

[7]https://huggingface.co/meta-llama/Llama-2-70b-chat-hf

[8]https://huggingface.co/meta-llama/Meta-Llama-3-8B-Instruct

[9]https://huggingface.co/meta-llama/Meta-Llama-3-70B-Instruct

Edit	Strategy Used
sexually → romantically	globalisation
Jimmies → tamarind chutney	transformation
Poulet → Dhoni	transformation
FICA → Income Tax	localisation
predicament room → waiting lounge	globalisation
"Son of a bitch" is back → he is back	omission
Wendy's → Haldiram's	localisation
gumball ring → gumball ring. It's not even a real diamond!	addition

Table 4: Examples of extracted CSI edits and the translation strategy used

Aspect	Llama-2 70B	Llama-3 8B	Llama-3 70B
Localisation	3.53	4.36	**4.44**
Naturalness	**4.32**	3.97	4.05
Content Preservation	**4.56**	4.03	4.27
Offensiveness	1.01	1.01	**1.00**
Stereotypical	**1.18**	1.62	1.37

Table 5: Dialog level scores

7.2 Dialog level Analysis

Aspect level evaluation : Aspect level scores are shown in Table 5. We report average aspect scores over all the dialogs. In terms of localization, Llama-3 70B clearly outperforms other models. Llama-2 70B performs the worst in terms of localization, which was also indicated by a lower %CSI edited number as observed in Section 7.1. However, for other aspects like naturalness, content preservation and stereotypical behaviour, Llama-2 70B outperforms other models by a significant gap. One contributing factor to this gap is the comparatively lower score for localization and lower no of edits (also CSI edits) for Llama-2 70B. Since fewer items are localized, more content is likely to get preserved, fewer edits are less likely to disrupt the naturalness of the dialogue and cause stereotypical behaviour in outputs.

We verify this hypothesis based on the correlation score (using Kendall's τ[10]) between different aspects. Figure 7 shows that for Llama-2 70B, localization is significantly correlated to naturalness(negative) and stereotypical behaviour(positive). A strong correlation between content preservation and naturalness suggests that with content preserved, it is unlikely that the natural flow of the dialogue is compromised. However, Llama-3 70B shows no correlation between localization and naturalness indicating that more localized edits don't necessarily impact naturalness, which is desirable.

Human Evaluation: LLM-based evaluation correlates well with human evaluation in all aspects. Since we are using Mixtral (Jiang et al., 2024) to automatically evaluate edits and score adapted versions of dialogs on various aspects, to justify whether an automatic evaluation is plausible, we perform human evaluation on 100 dialogs ($\approx 9\%$ of total number of dialogs to ensure statistical significance of the test) from our corpus. Mixtral[11] has shown remarkable performance on a number of benchmarks often outperforming closed-source LLMs like GPT-3.5[12](Jiang et al., 2024). We take 100 dialog pairs (original and an adapted version from Llama 2 70B model) at random and ask human raters to score the adapted version given the original version on a scale of 1-5 on each aspect using the same criteria as given in the LLM prompt for dialog level aspect evaluation (Appendix B). Taking an average of scores from human annotators, we measure the correlation (Kendall's τ) between average human rating and LLM rating. Taking inspiration from Amidei et al. (2019), we opted to use correlation rather than agreement. The agreement primarily focuses on whether two annotators exactly agree on their ratings, whereas the correlation coefficient addresses whether, "when annotator A rates an adaptation higher on an aspect, annotator B also rates that adaptation higher." The results are shown in Table 6. For all aspects, human ratings significantly correlate with LLM ratings (all with *p-value* < 0.05), which validates the reliability of using LLM-based scoring in assessing dialog quality along these aspects for 'India' as the target culture.

For aspects like Naturalness and Content Preservation, this is not surprising due to the superior language understanding ability of these models, however for aspects like localisation, identifying stereotypes and offensiveness, a strong correlation can be attributed to the model's knowledge of *Indian culture* along with the specific instructions in the prompt. However, for target cultures with lower representation in NLP, better (culturally well-informed) models need to be used

[10]According to Botsch (2011), $|\tau| \in [0, 0.1)$ - very weak correlation, $|\tau| \in [0.1, 0.2)$ - weak correlation, $|\tau| \in [0.2, 0.3)$ - moderate correlation, and $|\tau| \in [0.3, 1.0]$ - strong correlation.

[11]https://huggingface.co/mistralai/Mixtral-8x7B-Instruct-v0.1

[12]GPT-3.5-Turbo-0125

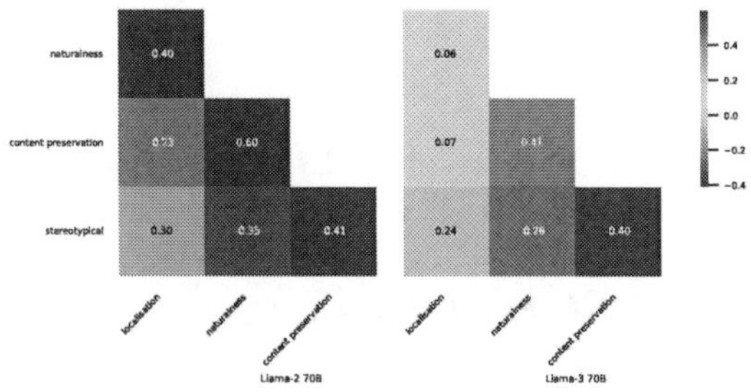

Figure 7: Correlation between aspects

in order to scale this evaluation and achieve better performance at this task.

Aspect	kendall's τ
Naturalness	0.63
Localisation	0.60
Content Preservation	0.39
Stereotypical	0.47
Offensiveness	1.00

Table 6: Correlation between Human and LLM dialog level scores

RQ 4: What insights does this offer into their parametric cross-cultural knowledge?
Through these results, it can be observed that LLMs can localize different CSI in a cross-cultural setting for the case of "USA to India" adaptation, although, the quality of content may be compromised. In many cases, efforts of localization compromise naturalness and content preservation which is not desired, and can introduce generalizations or stereotypes about the target culture. Models getting high localisation scores without much impact on other aspects like naturalness, stereotypical behaviour and content preservation indicate that the quality of localised edits is better i.e the edits are less stereotypical/offensive and they fit well in the context of the dialog, without changing the original intent or disrupting the flow of the dialog. The quality of localised edits is indicative of whether the model truly understands the technical aspects of a culture or just has a superficial knowledge of terms and concepts without much idea of how they can be used in cross-cultural scenarios such as this task of cultural adaptation.

8 Conclusion

In this paper, we explored the task of cultural adaptation within the realm of NLP. We defined the cultural elements likely to undergo transformation during adaptation. We curated a corpus of dialogues, annotating culture-specific elements across various categories and levels of foreignness, and defined the goals and aspects of cultural adaptation employing both edit-level analysis and broader, more contextual dialogue-level analysis for evaluation. We assess the performance of several open-source LLMs for cultural adaptation and analyse how these aspects tie together. We found that while modern language models are able to localise context to a target culture to a significant extent, they often struggle with reasoning over these cultural artefacts resulting in a lack of coherence within the context of dialogue which often leads to loss of original message. The ability of LLMs to localize text for a specific target culture provides a good starting point for adaptation experts to take ideas from and further refine and enhance.

References

Muhammad Farid Adilazuarda, Sagnik Mukherjee, Pradhyumna Lavania, Siddhant Singh, Ashutosh Dwivedi, Alham Fikri Aji, Jacki O'Neill, Ashutosh Modi, and Monojit Choudhury. 2024. Towards measuring and modeling "culture" in llms: A survey.

Jacopo Amidei, Paul Piwek, and Alistair Willis. 2019. Agreement is overrated: A plea for correlation to assess human evaluation reliability. In *Proceedings of the 12th International Conference on Natural Language Generation*, pages 344–354, Tokyo, Japan. Association for Computational Linguistics.

R Botsch. 2011. Chapter 12: Significance and measures of association. *Scopes and Methods of Political Science*.

Yong Cao, Yova Kementchedjhieva, Ruixiang Cui, Antonia Karamolegkou, Li Zhou, Megan Dare, Lucia Donatelli, and Daniel Hershcovich. 2024. Cultural adaptation of recipes. *Transactions of the Association for Computational Linguistics*, 12.

Yong Cao, Li Zhou, Seolhwa Lee, Laura Cabello, Min Chen, and Daniel Hershcovich. 2023. Assessing cross-cultural alignment between ChatGPT and human societies: An empirical study. In *Proceedings of the First Workshop on Cross-Cultural Considerations in NLP (C3NLP)*, pages 53–67, Dubrovnik, Croatia. Association for Computational Linguistics.

Eirlys E. Davies. 2003. A goblin or a dirty nose? *The Translator*, 9(1):65–100.

Ryan Drapeau, Lydia B. Chilton, Jonathan Bragg, and Daniel S. Weld. 2016. Microtalk: Using argumentation to improve crowdsourcing accuracy. In *AAAI Conference on Human Computation & Crowdsourcing*.

Esin Durmus, Karina Nyugen, Thomas I. Liao, Nicholas Schiefer, Amanda Askell, Anton Bakhtin, Carol Chen, Zac Hatfield-Dodds, Danny Hernandez, Nicholas Joseph, Liane Lovitt, Sam McCandlish, Orowa Sikder, Alex Tamkin, Janel Thamkul, Jared Kaplan, Jack Clark, and Deep Ganguli. 2023. Towards measuring the representation of subjective global opinions in language models.

Daniel Hershcovich, Stella Frank, Heather Lent, Miryam de Lhoneux, Mostafa Abdou, Stephanie Brandl, Emanuele Bugliarello, Laura Cabello Piqueras, Ilias Chalkidis, Ruixiang Cui, Constanza Fierro, Katerina Margatina, Phillip Rust, and Anders Søgaard. 2022. Challenges and strategies in cross-cultural NLP. In *Proceedings of the 60th Annual Meeting of the Association for Computational Linguistics (Volume 1: Long Papers)*, pages 6997–7013, Dublin, Ireland. Association for Computational Linguistics.

Albert Q. Jiang, Alexandre Sablayrolles, Antoine Roux, Arthur Mensch, Blanche Savary, Chris Bamford, Devendra Singh Chaplot, Diego de las Casas, Emma Bou Hanna, Florian Bressand, Gianna Lengyel, Guillaume Bour, Guillaume Lample, Lélio Renard Lavaud, Lucile Saulnier, Marie-Anne Lachaux, Pierre Stock, Sandeep Subramanian, Sophia Yang, Szymon Antoniak, Teven Le Scao, Théophile Gervet, Thibaut Lavril, Thomas Wang, Timothée Lacroix, and William El Sayed. 2024. Mixtral of experts.

Ming Jiang and Mansi Joshi. 2023. Cpopqa: Ranking cultural concept popularity by llms.

David Katan. 2014. *Translating Cultures: An Introduction for Translators, Interpreters and Mediators*. Routledge.

Reem I. Masoud, Ziquan Liu, Martin Ferianc, Philip Treleaven, and Miguel Rodrigues. 2023. Cultural alignment in large language models: An explanatory analysis based on hofstede's cultural dimensions.

Remi Mir, Bjarke Felbo, Nick Obradovich, and Iyad Rahwan. 2019. Evaluating style transfer for text. In *Proceedings of the 2019 Conference of the North American Chapter of the Association for Computational Linguistics: Human Language Technologies, Volume 1 (Long and Short Papers)*, pages 495–504, Minneapolis, Minnesota. Association for Computational Linguistics.

Joaquin Navajas, Tamara Niella, Gerry Garbulsky, Bahador Bahrami, and Mariano Sigman. 2017. Aggregated knowledge from a small number of debates outperforms the wisdom of large crowds.

Peter Newmark. 1988. *A textbook of translation*, volume 66. Prentice hall New York.

Denis Peskov, Viktor Hangya, Jordan Boyd-Graber, and Alexander Fraser. 2021. Adapting entities across languages and cultures. In *Findings of the Association for Computational Linguistics: EMNLP 2021*, pages 3725–3750, Punta Cana, Dominican Republic. Association for Computational Linguistics.

Mark Polizzotti. 2018. *Sympathy for the Traitor: A Translation Manifesto*. The MIT Press.

Aida Ramezani and Yang Xu. 2023. Knowledge of cultural moral norms in large language models.

G. Ritzer. 1996. *The McDonaldization of Society: An Investigation Into the Changing Character of Contemporary Social Life*. Pine Forge press titles of related interest. Pine Forge Press.

Mike Schaekermann, Joslin Goh, Kate Larson, and Edith Law. 2018. Resolvable vs. irresolvable disagreement: A study on worker deliberation in crowd work. *Proc. ACM Hum.-Comput. Interact.*, 2(CSCW).

Hugo Touvron, Louis Martin, Kevin Stone, Peter Albert, Amjad Almahairi, Yasmine Babaei, Nikolay Bashlykov, Soumya Batra, Prajjwal Bhargava, Shruti Bhosale, Dan Bikel, Lukas Blecher, Cristian Canton Ferrer, Moya Chen, Guillem Cucurull, David Esiobu, Jude Fernandes, Jeremy Fu, Wenyin Fu, Brian Fuller, Cynthia Gao, Vedanuj Goswami, Naman Goyal, Anthony Hartshorn, Saghar Hosseini, Rui Hou, Hakan Inan, Marcin Kardas, Viktor Kerkez, Madian Khabsa, Isabel Kloumann, Artem Korenev, Punit Singh Koura, Marie-Anne Lachaux, Thibaut Lavril, Jenya Lee, Diana Liskovich, Yinghai Lu, Yuning Mao, Xavier Martinet, Todor Mihaylov, Pushkar Mishra, Igor Molybog, Yixin Nie, Andrew Poulton, Jeremy Reizenstein, Rashi Rungta, Kalyan Saladi, Alan Schelten, Ruan Silva, Eric Michael Smith, Ranjan Subramanian, Xiaoqing Ellen Tan, Binh Tang, Ross Taylor, Adina Williams, Jian Xiang Kuan, Puxin Xu, Zheng Yan, Iliyan Zarov, Yuchen Zhang, Angela Fan, Melanie Kambadur, Sharan Narang, Aurelien Rodriguez, Robert Stojnic, Sergey Edunov, and Thomas Scialom. 2023. Llama 2: Open foundation and fine-tuned chat models.

H. Vermeer. 1989. Skopos and commission in translational action.

Wenxuan Wang, Wenxiang Jiao, Jingyuan Huang, Ruyi Dai, Jen tse Huang, Zhaopeng Tu, and Michael R. Lyu. 2024. Not all countries celebrate thanksgiving: On the cultural dominance in large language models.

Binwei Yao, Ming Jiang, Diyi Yang, and Junjie Hu. 2023. Empowering llm-based machine translation with cultural awareness.

Zhonghe Zhang, Xiaoyu He, Vivek Iyer, and Alexandra Birch. 2024. Cultural adaptation of menus: A fine-grained approach.

Wenhao Zhu, Hongyi Liu, Qingxiu Dong, Jingjing Xu, Shujian Huang, Lingpeng Kong, Jiajun Chen, and Lei Li. 2023. Multilingual machine translation with large language models: Empirical results and analysis.

A Limitations

English as a medium We acknowledge the fact that language strongly reflects culture. Our selection of English (for Intralingual adaptation) enabled us to focus on identifying culture-related modifications in adaptation without the complexities of translation.
Country as a proxy for culture In this study, we have selected "nation" as a proxy for culture as a proof of concept. While this choice is often made for addressing a broader national audience in such applications, it inevitably emphasizes popular aspects of culture while potentially neglecting local subcultures.
Prompt Analysis Our analysis of prompts is not exhaustive. This is due to evaluation limits as we go deeper down the levels of culture, where culture becomes less technical and more abstract as discussed in Section 4.
Single Source-Target Culture pair Our study is confined to a single source-target culture pair. While we hope to extend our study, it requires CSI annotations from people belonging to the target culture.
Evaluation on State-of-the-art LLMs We did not evaluate on state-of-the-art closed source models like GPT-3.5 and GPT-4. While comparing models is not the main goal of this study, due to our budgetary limitations as well as our commitment to open science, we decided not to evaluate on these models.
Human Evaluation Another limitation is limited human evaluation. While we have shown a correlation between human and LLM judgements on various aspects of evaluation, we still believe there is no substitute for human evaluation. However, the associated costs make large-scale studies across different cultures prohibitively expensive and unscalable.
Extent of Localisation For this study, we measured the extent to which LLMs can adapt cultural items, however, in many applications, not all CSI need to be adapted. The selective adaptation approach allows for a balance between preserving cultural authenticity and ensuring relevance and comprehension within new or diverse cultural settings.

B Prompts for LLM Evaluation

The prompt used to extract edits(at an utterance level) is given in Table 7. Using this prompt, we can find edits corresponding to all edited CSI along with the rest of the significant edits.

The prompt used for finding translation strategy for a given CSI edit is given in Table 8.

The prompt used for scoring edits is given in Table 9.

The prompt used for scoring adapted dialog given the original dialog is given in Table 10.

C Examples used in the prompt for obtaining adaptation

The examples used in the adaptation prompt as described in Table 2 are given in Table 11.

D Example adaptations and Edits

Examples of adaptations from different models for a single dialog are given in Table 12. Table 14 shows examples of original and adapted versions of several utterances. Table 13 shows examples of Incorrect Edits found in cultural adaptations using LLM evaluation.

E Applications of Adaptation

Following are some (non-exhaustive) applications of adaptation:

Literary Translation and Entertainment Media : Literary works and Entertainment Media (Subtitles and dubbing) are adapted to maintain the original's emotional impact, and humor while replacing cultural references with equivalents that make sense to the target audience.

Advertising or Marketing : Multinational companies adapt their marketing materials to align with local values and consumer behaviour.

Training and Education Materials : Corporate training materials are often adapted to suit the cultural context of international employees. Even educational materials like storybooks are adapted to cater to different age groups.

Legal and Healthcare Documents : Medical documents are adapted to ensure patients understand their rights and the procedures. Legal Contracts are often tailored to comply with local laws.

Identify all occurrences of the lexically edited words or phrases in original vs modified form :

Examples:

Original text : "Joey Tribbiani: What are you talking about? 'One woman'? That's like saying there's only one flavor of ice cream for you. Lemme tell you something, Ross. There's lots of flavors out there. There's Rocky Road, and Cookie Dough, and Bing! Cherry Vanilla. You could get 'em with Jimmies, or nuts, or whipped cream! This is the best thing that ever happened to you! You got married, you were, like, what, eight? Welcome back to the world! Grab a spoon!"

Modified text : "Joey Tribbiani: What are you talking about? 'One woman'? That's like saying there's only one flavor of biryani for you. Lemme tell you something, Ross. There's lots of flavors out there. There's Butter Chicken, and Paneer Tikka, and Paan! You could get 'em with Naan, or rice, or raita! This is the best thing that ever happened to you! You got married, you were, like, what, eight? Welcome back to the world! Grab a spoon!"
Edits:
ice cream → biryani
Rocky Road → Butter Chicken
Cookie Dough → Paneer Tikka
Bing! Cherry Vanilla → Paan
Jimmies → Naan
nuts → rice
whipped cream → raita

Original text : "Emily: Yes, I went there due to the crowd at the vegan cafe in the arts district."
Modified text : "Emily: Yes, I went there due to the crowd at the chai stall near the temple."
Edits:
vegan cafe → chai stall
in the arts district → near the temple

Original text : "Rason: Want to relax by the nude beach?"
Modified text : "Rason: Want to relax by the beach and do yoga?"
Edits:
nude → # deletion
→ and do yoga # addition

Original text : "Joey: What's the matter with you?"
Modified text : "Joey: What's the matter with you?
Edits:
No edit found.

Extract edits for following :
{Original utterance}
{Adapted utterance}

Table 7: Prompt for extracting relevant edits

You are a translator performing an adaptation from a foreign culture to Indian culture. Given an original dialog from a show called 'Friends' and an intralingual adapted version for the Indian audience, your task is to determine which translation strategy is used in the given edit in the context of adapted version.

In the translation of Culture-specific items, Davies defines the following translation strategies:

1. Addition is when more information is added simultaneously with the transfer from source culture to target culture, for example: eating at *Wendy's* $\rightarrow$ *eating at Wendy's, an American international fast food restaurant chain*

2. Omission is a strategy when a word or a phrase is omitted from the target culture when no equivalents can be found, for example: *getting a taco from taco bell* $\rightarrow$ *getting a taco*

3. Globalization is a strategy of exchanging cultural elements of the text with more general and neutral words, to match it with the target language culture, for example: *Kimono* $\rightarrow$ *Traditional garment*; *Hamburger* $\rightarrow$ *Burger*; *Greek yoghurt* $\rightarrow$ *Curd* etc.

4. Localization is trying to find an appropriate equivalent of the CSI in the target language, for example, *sausage* $\rightarrow$ *kebab*; *mentos* $\rightarrow$ *paan*; etc.

5. Transformation is an alteration of a CSI to another CSI which is not a local equivalent but an altered/distorted version, familiar to the target language audience, for example: *football game* $\rightarrow$ *Local cricket match*; *mentos* $\rightarrow$ *namkeen* (alteration of CSI); *pastry* $\rightarrow$ *halwa* (no close equivalent so altered the CSI); etc.

Original Dialog:
{o}

Adapted Dialog:
{a}

Based on the original dialog, adapted dialog and the given translation strategies, the strategy used in the following edit based on its context in the adapted dialog is:
{edit}

Table 8: Prompt for finding translation strategy used for a given edit

You are from India. Given an original dialog from a show called 'Friends' and an adapted version for Indian audience, your task is to **rate the given edit in the context of adapted version based on the given aspects** :

Scores for each aspect is either 0 or 1 except localisation (score can be 0,1 or 2), representing either that aspect is absent(0) or present(1) in the adapted version.

Aspects:

1. correctness (0 or 1): This aspect evaluates whether the edits made in the adapted version make sense in the context of the conversation. A score of 1 indicates that the edit seamlessly integrates into the dialogue, maintaining its natural flow, practicality and coherence. A score of 0 suggests that the edit feels out of place, forced, or does not fit well in the context.
2. localisation (0, 1, 2): This aspect assesses the degree to which the adapted version is tailored for the Indian audience. A score of 0 implies that the edit lacks any localization efforts and feels completely foreign or unrelated to the Indian context. A score of 1 signifies that the changes reflect some level of localization but are more of a globalized edit that resonates with the global audience beyond just the Indian context. A score of 2 indicates that the edit is highly localized, seamlessly integrating elements specific to the Indian culture.
3. offensiveness (0 or 1): This aspect determines whether the adapted version contains any offensive content(i.e score: 1) that is clearly inappropriate or disrespectful within the Indian cultural framework, such as mockery of Indian traditions or values, propagation of harmful stereotypes or depiction of sensitive topics without appropriate cultural sensitivity. A score of 0 indicates that no offensive content is present, while, an offensiveness score of 1 indicates the presence of offensive content that should be addressed or revised.

Original Dialog:
{}

Adapted Dialog:
{}

Based on the original dialog, adapted dialog and the aspects, please give the rating for the following edit based on its context in the adapted dialog along each aspect in Python dictionary format (no explanation) 'aspect1': scorevalue1,...,:
{Edit}

Table 9: Prompt for scoring edits on different aspects.

You are from India. Given an original dialog from a show called 'Friends' and an adapted version for the Indian audience, **your task is to rate the adapted version along the following aspects**, scores for each aspect ranges from 1 to 5.

Aspects:

1. naturalness(1-5): This aspect assesses the fluidity and coherence of the adapted dialogue within the context of the conversation. It evaluates whether the adapted version feels natural and seamlessly integrates cultural modifications without appearing forced or disrupting the flow of the conversation.
2. localisation(1-5): This aspect assesses the degree to which the adapted version is localized/adapted for the Indian audience. A high score signifies that the changes reflect cultural nuances, language preferences, and social norms relevant to the Indian setting. A lower score means more presence of foreign items or the edits are done in a globalised/generalised way.
3. offensiveness(1-5): This aspect determines whether the adapted version contains offensive content that is clearly inappropriate or disrespectful within the Indian cultural framework, such as mockery of Indian traditions or values, propagation of harmful stereotypes or depiction of sensitive topics without appropriate cultural sensitivity. The offensiveness score ranges from 1 (least offensive) to 5 (most offensive).
4. stereotypical(1-5): This aspect evaluates the presence of stereotypical representations of Indian culture or its people. A high score indicates a high degree of stereotypical content, while a low score suggests a more accurate and nuanced portrayal. Some common stereotypes about India and its people include - "All Indians are vegetarians.", "All Indian women wear sarees, and all Indian men wear turbans.", "All Indian cuisine is extremely spicy and hot.", "All Indians live in extreme poverty and deprivation.", "All Indians are obsessed with Bollywood movies and stars.", "All Indians work in call centres or IT support.", etc.
5. content preservation (1-5): This aspect gauges how effectively the essence, message, and emotional undertones of the original dialogue are maintained in the adapted version, irrespective of cultural style. A higher score reflects a faithful preservation of the original dialogue's message, humour, and emotional impact, while a lower score suggests significant alterations that may compromise the original intent or emotional resonance.

Scoring Criteria:

naturalness (1-5):
5: The adapted dialog flows seamlessly, maintaining a natural and coherent conversation.
4: The adapted dialog feels mostly natural and contextually fitting, with minor deviations.
3: Some parts of the adapted dialog may feel slightly forced or unnatural, affecting its coherence.
2: The coherence of the adapted dialog is disrupted by noticeable inconsistencies or unnatural phrasing.
1: The adapted dialog appears completely out of place or nonsensical, lacking coherence and natural flow.

localisation (1-5):
5: The adaptation demonstrates a deep understanding of Indian cultural nuances, language, and social norms, resulting in a highly localized portrayal.
4: Cultural elements are effectively integrated, enriching the adaptation with a blend of local flavour.
3: Localization attempts are noticeable, albeit with some inconsistencies in maintaining cultural authenticity.
2: Minimal localization efforts are evident, appearing globally adapted rather than localized.
1: The adaptation lacks any reflection of Indian culture, appearing very foreign rather than localized.

offensiveness (1-5):
5: Contains highly offensive material that is disrespectful and inappropriate within the Indian cultural framework.
4: Includes offensive content that is likely to offend or cause discomfort.
3: Some potentially offensive elements are present, requiring careful revision.
2: Minor offensive aspects that may need adjustment.
1: No offensiveness

stereotypical (1-5):
5: Contains highly stereotypical representations of Indian culture or its people.
4: Includes noticeable stereotypes that may perpetuate cultural biases.
3: Some stereotypical content is present, but not overly pervasive.
2: Minimal stereotypical content, with occasional instances.
1: No stereotypes present.

content preservation (1-5):
5: The adapted version faithfully retains the essence and significance of the original content.
4: The majority of the original content is preserved, albeit with minor adjustments.
3: While some changes are evident, the overall meaning remains largely intact.
2: Significantly altered content leads to a noticeable shift in meaning.
1: The original content is either lost entirely or severely distorted in the adaptation.

Original Dialog:
{}

Adapted Dialog:
{}

Based on the original dialog and the adapted dialog, please rate the adapted dialog, and give a score along each aspect with an explanation only in a JSON format {aspect: {score:, explanation:},...,}:

Table 10: Prompt for scoring adapted dialogs on different aspects.

Original Dialog 1:
Angela: Did you see the Beatles concert last night?
Mary: No, I was catching up baseball game last night on TV.
Angela: Oh! Did you eat the meatball spaghetti I made ?
Rosy: Totally! I also added some oregano and rosemary to it.
Mary: Ohkay Angela tell me, what should I wear for the date, is this skirt good?
Angela: Nope, wear the gown I gave you on last Thanksgiving.
Rosy: Yeah totally wear that. That was beautiful.
Angela: And where are you going for the date?
Mary: A nice restaurant near the White House.
Angela: Bring me gelato.
Rosy: Bye Mary!
Mary: Bye! Wish me luck, Hope I score tonight!
TRANSCRIPT NOTE: (Mary and her date meet and greet each other with a kiss)

Adapted Version 1:
Angela: Did you see Shreya Ghoshal's concert last night?
Mary: No, I was catching up cricket game last night on TV.
Angela: Oh! Did you eat the sevai I made? Rosy: Totally! I also added some gunpowder and coriander to it.
Mary: Ohkay Angela tell me, what should I wear for the date, is this kurta good?
Angela: Nope, wear the kurta I gave you on Diwali last time.
Rosy: Yeah totally wear that. That was beautiful.
Angela: And where are you going for the date?
Mary: A nice restaurant near the Red Fort.
Angela: Bring me kulfi.
Rosy: Bye Mary!
Mary: Bye! Wish me luck, Hope it goes well!
TRANSCRIPT NOTE: (Mary and her date meet and greet each other with a handshake)

Original Dialog 2:
Mark: Have you been to the new Italian restaurant downtown?
Emily: Yes, I went there due to the crowd at the vegan cafe in the arts district.
Mark: Oh! Did you try their tiramisu?
Emily: Yes, it was delicious! Nice touch of coco powder to it.
Mark: Good! Emily, I have been thinking about applying for the post of editor for Harvard Business Review.
Emily: Great Mark! Good luck, you totally deserve it.

Adapted Version 2:
Mark: Have you been to the new Kerala restaurant in the market?
Emily: Yes, I went there due to the crowd at the chai stall near the temple.
Mark: Oh! Did you try their Rava Kesari? Emily: Yes, it was delicious! Nice touch of cardamom to it.
Mark: Good! Emily, I have been thinking about applying for the post of editor for The Times of India.
Emily: Great Mark! Good luck, you totally deserve it.

Table 11: 2-shot example used in adaptation prompt

Original Dialog	Llama-2 70B	Llama-3 8B	Llama-3 70B
Franny: Hey, Monica! Monica Geller: Hey Frannie, welcome back! How was Florida? Franny: You had sex, didn't you? Monica Geller: How do you do that? Franny: Oh, I hate you, I'm pushing my Aunt Roz through Parrot Jungle and you're having sex! So? Who? Monica Geller: You know Paul? Franny: Paul the Wine Guy? Oh yeah, I know Paul. Monica Geller: You mean you know Paul like I know Paul? Franny: Are you kidding? I take credit for Paul. Y'know before me, there was no snap in his turtle for two years.	Franny: Hey, Monica! Monica Geller: Hey Frannie, welcome back! How was Goa? Franny: You had sex, didn't you? Monica Geller: How do you do that? Franny: Oh, I hate you, I'm pushing my Aunt Roz through Anjuna Flea Market and you're having sex! So? Who? Monica Geller: You know Rohan? Franny: Rohan the Yoga Guy? Oh yeah, I know Rohan. Monica Geller: You mean you know Rohan like I know Rohan? Franny: Are you kidding? I take credit for Rohan. Y'know before me, there was no spark in his chakra for two years.	Riya: Hey, Nalini! Nalini Goyal: Hey Riya, welcome back! How was Goa? Riya: You got married, didn't you? Nalini Goyal: How do you do that? Riya: Oh, I hate you, I'm pushing my Chachi through the beach and you're getting married! So? Who's the lucky guy? Nalini Goyal: You know Rohan? Riya: Rohan the IT guy? Oh yeah, I know Rohan. Nalini Goyal: You mean you know Rohan like I know Rohan? Riya: Are you kidding? I take credit for Rohan. Y'know before me, there was no spark in his eyes for two years.	Franny: Hey, Monica! Monica Geller: Hey Frannie, welcome back! How was Goa? Franny: You had a romantic getaway, didn't you? Monica Geller: How do you do that? Franny: Oh, I hate you, I'm pushing my Aunt Roz through the spice plantation and you're having a romantic time! So? Who? Monica Geller: You know Rohan? Franny: Rohan the Cafe Owner? Oh yeah, I know Rohan. Monica Geller: You mean you know Rohan like I know Rohan? Franny: Are you kidding? I take credit for Rohan. Y'know before me, there was no spark in his life for two years.

Table 12: Example of adaptations from different models for a single dialog

Original	Adaptation	Reason (LLM Verbal Rationale)
... Paul the Wine Guy: Well, you might try accidentally breaking something valuable of hers, say her- Monica Geller: -**leg**? Paul the Wine Guy: That's one way! Me, I- I went for the watch. ...	... Paul the Wine Guy: Well, you might try accidentally breaking something valuable of hers, say her- Monica Geller: -Bindi? Paul the Wine Guy: That's one way! Me, I- I went for the watch. ... # (Llama 2 70B)	A bindi is typically a decorative mark or dot applied to the forehead, commonly used in South Asian cultures. It is usually made from a small adhesive sticker, kumkum (vermilion), or other cosmetic materials. Technically, a bindi itself cannot be "broken". It might be peeled off or damaged, but not broken.
... Paul the Wine Guy: Ever since she walked out on me, I, uh... Monica Geller: What?..... What, you wanna spell it out with **noodles**? ...	... Raj: Ever since she walked out on me, I, uh... Monica: What?.. What, you want to spell it out with naan? ... # (Llama 2 70B, Llama 3 8B)	The original phrase "spell it out with noodles" is a humorous expression that makes sense as noodles might be used to spell out words as a playful or whimsical act. "Naan" is a type of bread commonly eaten in South Asian cuisine. Spelling out something with naan is not common or intuitive, making the adaptation feel forced.
	... Raj: Ever since she walked out on me, I, uh... Monica: What?.. What, you want to spell it out with gulab jaamun? ... # (Llama 3 70B)	Gulab jamun is a popular Indian dessert, but it is a round, syrup-soaked sweet that doesn't lend itself to being used to spell out words. This makes the phrase less intuitive and relatable.

Table 13: Few examples of Incorrect Edits (in red) found in cultural adaptations by LLM evaluator. These mistakes often arise due to a lack of understanding and reasoning about cultural objects.

Original Lines	Adapted Lines
... Chandler Bing: I can't believe you would actually say that. I would much rather be **Mr. Peanut** than **Mr. Salty**. Joey Tribbiani: No way! **Mr.Salty** is a sailor, all right, he's got to be, like, the toughest snack there is. Ross Geller: I don't know, you don't wanna mess with **corn nuts**. They're craaazy. ...	... Chandler Bing: I can't believe you would actually say that. I would much rather be Haldiram's than Bikano. Joey Tribbiani: No way! Bikano is a strong brand, all right, they've got to be, like, the toughest snack there is. Ross Geller: I don't know, you don't wanna mess with murmure. They're craaazy. ··· # (Llama 3 70B)
... Chandler Bing: **Dehydrated Japanese noodles** under fluorescent lights... does it get better than this? ...	... Chandler Bing: Maggi under the streetlights... does it get better than this? ··· # (Llama 3 8B)
... Monica Geller: Are these the **shoes**? Rachel Green: Yes. **Paolo** sent them from **Italy**. ...	... Monica Geller: Are these the sandals? Rachel Green: Yes. Rohan sent them from Jaipur. ··· # (Llama 3 8B)
... Joanna: Oh. And Rachel has been really incredible in getting my morning **bagel** for me. It's amazing how she gets it right almost every time! ···	... Joanna: Oh. And Rachel has been really incredible in getting my morning chai for me. It's amazing how she gets it right almost every time! ··· # (Llama 2 70B)
... Rachel Green: Alright, c'mon! Let's play **Twister**! ...	... Rachel Green: Alright, c'mon! Let's play Antakshari! ··· # (Llama 2 70B)
... Joey Tribbiani: Well, Chandler's old roommate was **Jewish**, and these are the only **candles** we have, so... Happy **Chanukah**, everyone. ···	... Joey Tribbiani: Well, Chandler's old roommate was Hindu, and these are the only diyas we have, so... Happy Diwali, everyone. ··· # (Llama 3 70B)
... Monica Geller: He is so cute. So, where did you guys grow up? Angela Delveccio: **Brooklyn Heights**. Bob: **Cleveland**. ...	... Monica Geller: He is so cute. So, where did you guys grow up? Angela Delveccio: Bandra. Bob: Ahmedabad. ··· # (Llama 3 70B)

Table 14: Few examples of original and adapted versions of several utterances in the corpus of dialogs. Major edits are highlighted.

Explaining the Hardest Errors of Contextual Embedding Based Classifiers

Claudio M. V. de Andrade[1], **Washington Cunha**[1], **Guilherme Fonseca**[2]
Ana Clara S. Pagano[1], **Luana de C. Santos**[1], **Adriana S. Pagano**[1]
Leonardo Rocha[2], **Marcos André Gonçalves**[1]
claudio.valiense@dcc.ufmg.br, washingtoncunha@dcc.ufmg.br,
guilhermefonseca8426@aluno.ufsj.edu.br, anapagano@ufmg.br, lcs2017@ufmg.br
apagano@ufmg.br, lcrocha@ufsj.edu.br, mgoncalv@dcc.ufmg.br
[1] Federal University of Minas Gerais, Brazil
[2] Federal University of São João Del-Rei, Brazil

Abstract

We seek to explain the causes for the misclassification of the most challenging documents, namely those that no classifier using state-of-the-art, very semantically-separable contextual embedding representations managed to predict accurately. To do so, we propose a taxonomy of incorrect predictions, which we used to perform qualitative human evaluation. We posed two research questions, considering three sentiment datasets in two different domains – movie and product reviews. Evaluators with two different backgrounds evaluated documents by comparing the predominant sentiment assigned by the model and the label in the gold dataset in order to decide on a likely misclassification reason. Based on a high inter-evaluator agreement (81.7%.), we observed significant differences between domains, such as the prevalence of ambivalence in product reviews and sarcasm in movie reviews. Our analysis also revealed an unexpectedly high rate of incorrect labeling in the gold dataset (up to 33%) and a significant amount of incorrect prediction by the model due to a series of linguistic phenomena (including amplified words, contrastive markers, comparative sentences, and references to world knowledge). Overall, our taxonomy and methodology allow us to explain between 80%-85% of the errors with high confidence (agreement) – enabling us to point out where future efforts to improve models should be concentrated.

1 Introduction

In a scenario where the amount of user-generated content is growing exponentially, automatic text classification (ATC) plays a vital role in enabling automatic categorization of texts into different semantic groups based on their distinctive characteristics (Li et al., 2022; Galke and Scherp, 2022). The state-of-the-art in ATC is currently provided by Attention-Based Transformer methods (e.g., BERT (Devlin et al., 2019), RoBERTa (Liu et al., 2019), BART (Lewis et al., 2020)), which produce contextual representations of words and documents. Indeed, in de Andrade et al. (2023), the authors show that these contextual representations are so (semantically) separable in the embeddings space that any classifier using them achieves similar effectiveness, no matter how simple (e.g., a Nearest-Centroid classifier) or complex it may be (e.g., a Gradient Boosted Decisions Tree or a Support Vector Machines). Some of the results obtained in that study are the highest (state-of-the-art) ever reported in the literature for effectiveness (e.g., Macro-F1) in several experimented datasets.

With such powerful text representations and results, sometimes achieving or even exceeding human parity (Hassan et al., 2018; Yan et al., 2023), a main question that arises is: *Are we approaching the limits of what can be automatically classified by a machine learning model?* This article delves deep into this question by analyzing the reasons for misclassification by classifiers using these powerful contextual representations. We go one step further to advance the literature and look into the **hardest cases**, i.e., documents that none of the strongest classifiers explored in the aforementioned study, using contextual embedding-based representations, was able to classify correctly.

A thorough review evidenced that this type of error or misclassification analysis is rarely performed in the literature, with a few exceptions (Martins et al., 2021). Misclassification analysis serves the purpose of revealing the how's and why's behind model (or human) failure. One of the main difficulties in performing such an analysis is the lack of standardized methodologies and methods for doing so. Accordingly, one of our contributions is the proposal of a **misclassification taxonomy** capable of categorizing incorrect predictions *upon classifiers application.*

We propose and evaluate an *error taxonomy* using a document sample for which no classifier

Proceedings of the 28th Conference on Computational Natural Language Learning, pages 419–434
November 15-16, 2024 ©2024 Association for Computational Linguistics

was able to produce correct predictions. Due to the very complex nature of the error analysis task, we adopt BERT to generate **contextual document representations**[1]. We evaluated the proposed taxonomy with a different sample of erroneous documents, using human evaluators with different backgrounds to assess how effective and useful the taxonomy is in explaining the errors.

Unlike previous work (Martins et al., 2021) – which focuses on assessing the impact of "hard" instances on the effectiveness of polarity detection using a single dataset (movie reviews) and not concerned with textual representation – here we focus on analyzing and quantifying the reasons for the misclassification of the **hardest** documents by all machine learning methods using some of the most separable representations in the literature. For this, we used datasets from two domains: movie and product reviews. We also compare and contrast the results in these two domains, gathering insights into the differences in the type of errors found in each of them.

The main questions we seek to answer are: [RQ1] *Is the proposed taxonomy effective for misclassification analysis?* To answer RQ1, we analyze evaluators' responses regarding their level of agreement – the higher the agreement, the more effective the taxonomy. We analyze inter-evaluator agreement and correlate that with hardness in classifying; and [RQ2] *Can the proposed taxonomy be used to reveal the main reasons for misclassification? Are there significant differences in the results between different domains?* In RQ2, drawing on the consensus achieved, we quantify and analyze the main reasons for the misclassification, highlighting the differences between domains.

Our experiments engaging eight human evaluators with two different backgrounds (Computer Science and Linguistics) and three datasets, two in the movie reviews domain and one in the product reviews domain, revealed that (i) the developed taxonomy proved effective, with an inter-evaluator agreement of over 81% for error category – this suggests that evaluators find it relatively easy to identify classification errors using the proposed taxonomy; (ii) between 50%-80% of the errors can be ascribed to the model for reasons further explained below; (iii) the evaluators found a significant amount of *incorrect labels in the dataset* –, i.e., there were incorrect labels in the gold datasets – around 33% of the documents in the product dataset and 16% in one of the movie datasets; (iv) in movie reviews, sarcasm[2] (> 23% of the cases) is considered a major reason for incorrect prediction by the model, while (v) in product reviews, the main reason is ambivalence (40% of the cases) – we believe this is a particular characteristic of this domain.

The remaining *model* errors were considered instances of *"incorrect prediction despite available textual cues"* ascribable to a series of language phenomena, including amplified words, contrastive markers, comparative sentences, and world-knowledge regarding named entities. While for product review, the model errors are mostly associated with comparisons and contrastive cases, for movie scenarios, world knowledge, use of amplifiers and idiomatic/new expressions are issues in the model's incorrect predictions. Our results can be potentially leveraged for model enhancement focused on the application domain.

In sum, our main contributions include: (i) the development and evaluation of a *taxonomy* for categorizing the main causes for misclassification of the *hardest* documents; ii) a *fine-grained analysis* of the results of a comprehensive qualitative experiment applying the taxonomy to 3 different datasets in 2 different domains, with relevant implications for the improvement of the next generation of textual classifiers and representations; and (iii) a release of a *new dataset* of challenging documents manually annotated by humans.

2 Related Work

In Lee et al. (2017), five categories for misclassification of objects in images are explored (See Appendix A.3 for Evaluation Schema). Meek (2016) categorized prediction failures in textual documents by defining four error categories (see Appendix A.3 for schema), focusing on the lack of training information. Pandey et al. (2022) assesses the impact on labeling of (i) time allocated to evaluators; and (ii) the order of annotations in the labeling task. Unlike these works, we propose a taxonomy for ATC test errors and investigate a more comprehensive set of reasons, focusing on the hardest cases for classifiers using state-of-the-art,

[1]We ran experiments in our datasets comparing BERT with other transformers such as RoBERTa (Liu et al., 2019) and BART (Lewis et al., 2020). The differences are minimal (if any) and potentially not influential in our work.

[2]Unlike (Frenda et al., 2023), we group irony and sarcasm under a single category as instances of figurative use of language intended to produce an effect on the reader.

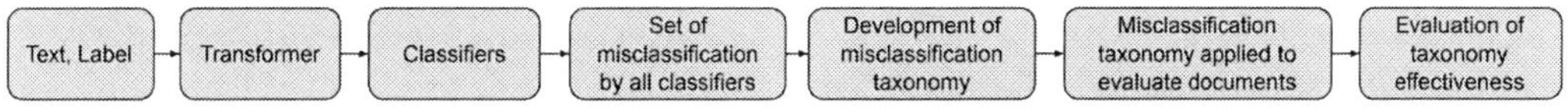

Figure 1: Methodological steps flowchart.

very separable (contextual) representations by means of qualitative human assessment.

Bras et al. (2020) remove bias in training to reduce misclassification. Pleiss et al. (2020) propose adapting the Area Under the Margin to identify training data that preclude generalization. Both focus on the training set to identify (challenging) documents that do not contribute to the learning process. Instead, we focus on misclassification at inference time (test set), aiming to identify common characteristics of misclassified documents.

Swayamdipta et al. (2020) present a tool to characterize and diagnose datasets regarding the behavior of the model on individual instances during training. Ethayarajh et al. (2022) seek to find challenging documents using V-usable information. Differently, we find challenging documents based on their incorrect classification by four classifiers using a very separable contextualized representation as input. Moreover, unlike Ethayarajh et al. (2022), who do not provide qualitative experiments involving human evaluation and Swayamdipta et al. (2020), who evaluate human mislabeling only, we evaluate both automatic and human mislabeling.

Martins et al. (2021) analyze a set of hard instances (evaluation schema in Appendix A.3) but, unlike ours, their study centers on evaluating the influence of challenging cases on the classifier's effectiveness when performing polarity detection using **one single movie review dataset**. Our study focuses on analyzing and quantifying the factors contributing to the misclassification of the hardest documents *using multiple datasets in two domains* with a more detailed taxonomy. We also have additional goals such as validating our taxonomy and contrasting the results in multiple different datasets and domains, running qualitative experiments engaging evaluators with different backgrounds.

Barnes et al. (2019) propose categories to understand model misclassifications. Unlike ours, their study: (i) did not focus on the hardest cases; (ii) did not detail how the data was evaluated; (iii) did not provide information on inter-rater agreement; and (iv) did not examine domain impact on results – all results for all datasets are analyzed in conjunction. We drew on their taxonomy, though, to develop the categories we used for focused (hierarchical) evaluation, as described in section 3.8.

3 Experimental Methodology

Our methodology, which comprises seven steps, is summarized in Figure 1. The text and label for each document are used as input for fine-tuning a Transformer model, resulting in an encoder that produces contextual embedding vectors representing the documents using the CLS approach. We employ various classifiers with these embeddings as input, exploring different underlying techniques. From this set of classifiers, we select the set of documents for which none of the classifiers was able to produce correct predictions (according to the labels assigned in the datasets). Within this set, we sample documents for analysis to outline misclassification categories ("Development of the misclassification taxonomy" in Figure 1), which human evaluators will apply to evaluate documents in a second sample different from the first one ("Application of the misclassification taxonomy to evaluate documents" in Figure 1). Upon applying the taxonomy, we quantify the results and evaluate its efficiency. A detailed account of the steps follows.

3.1 Datasets

Our study draws on 3 datasets developed for binary sentiment classification. Although this task is considered less complex than, for instance, multi-label topic classification, our choice was strategically purposeful due to the very complex endeavor we made in our work to identify the potential reasons for misclassifications of the hardest cases - those that no classifier is able to predict correctly using state-of-the-art representations. Thus, even though current solutions for sentiment analysis are highly effective, with some solutions achieving F1≐90, one of our main goals is precisely to evaluate the current technologies' limits. With such high effectiveness, what are the reasons for the few errors still made by the very effective sentiment classifiers? Answers to this question, which our methodology helps clarify by pointing out and quantifying the main sources of misclassifications, are what we believe will provide necessary grounds for the improvements of the next generation of methods.

Each dataset was constructed with text and an associated sentiment label. The first dataset comprises customers' reviews of purchased products on Amazon's website (Keung et al., 2020), which are assigned a rating from 1 to 5 stars by customers. We collected reviews containing ratings of 1 and 2 stars and labeled them as negative, while reviews containing ratings of 4 and 5 stars were labeled as positive. We discarded reviews with 3 stars (deemed neutral). The second (PangMovie (Pang and Lee, 2004)) and the third (VaderMovie (Ribeiro et al., 2016)) datasets were used in (de Andrade et al., 2023) and we obtained the representations directly from the authors. These datasets compile movie reviews comprising a text and a sentiment label (positive or negative). Table 3 in the Appendix presents some statistics of the datasets. As it can seen, class distribution into positive and negative instances is balanced in the three datasets.

3.2 Data Representation

We fine-tuned BERT, adapting this Transformer to the specific domain of sentiment classification using the texts and labels in our datasets. The aim is to improve the representation and enhance the model's effectiveness for sentiment classification. The model's fine-tuning produces an encoder, which generates CLS-based 768-dimensional embedding vectors to represent the documents. As discussed in (de Andrade et al., 2023), this fine-tuning process is fundamental to ensure the quality of the representation and the separability (into semantic classes) of the generated embedding space.

To perform fine-tuning, we used the literature´s suggested hyper-parameterization (Cunha et al., 2021), fixing the learning rate with the value $2x10^{-5}$, the batch size with 64 documents, adjusting the model to five epochs, and setting the maximum size of each document to 256 tokens. We used differentiable heads by fine-tuning with *AutoModelForSequenceClassification*. In our experiments, we employ a five-fold stratified cross-validation procedure – fine-tuning, training, and optimizing the classifiers' parameters with the validation sets that are repeated five times. The reported results correspond to the average of the five test folds.

Although we used BERT in our study, other Transformers can be easily applied within our methodology. Indeed, experiments in (de Andrade et al., 2023) showed that the contextual representations produced by different transformers (e.g., RoBERTa, BART) are quite similar in terms of class separability, the main aspect driving our evaluations. To confirm that, we run experiments of our own in the tested datasets comparing BERT with RoBERTa (Liu et al., 2019) and BART (Lewis et al., 2020). The results are shown in Appendix A.8. As we can see, the effectiveness of these transformers is very similar – BERT is statistically tied as the best method with Roberta in Amazon and marginally loses (by at most 1-2 pp) in the other two datasets[3]. These differences, which mean just a few documents in practice, are potentially not relevant in a qualitative study as ours, which uses a sample of the documents that all classifiers predicted incorrectly. We believe the intuitions and insights gathered with the current methodology, representations, and models would not be substantially different if we used other Transformers[4].

3.3 Text Classifiers Used along with Contextual Embeddings

For document classification, we used the textual representations generated by the Transformer as input to four of the strongest classifiers used in (de Andrade et al., 2023), namely KNN, Random Forests (RFs), Support Vector Machines (SVMs) and Logistic regression (LR), as well as BERT model with the classification head as one of the classifiers. Indeed, despite using different rules and heuristics, the effectiveness of these classifiers (and of all other classifiers tested in (de Andrade et al., 2023)) is basically the same in all tested datasets when using the contextual embedding representations. This is due to the fact that these representations are already so semantically separated (by class) in the embeddings space that the employed classifier has no little effect in the classification process. For a detailed comparison among these classifiers (taken from (de Andrade et al., 2023)) in two of the tested datasets check Appendix A.8.

We decided to explore classifiers based on different approaches – decision rules (RFs), local neighborhoods (kNN), global maximum margins (SVMs and LR) – so that if all of them misclassify the same document, this can be ascribed to the misclassified document being hard to classify. *And we do want to understand the reasons why!*.

Hence, we selected the set of documents that all classifiers misclassified in the three datasets, as presented in Table 6. A sub-sample from this set was used as a basis for devising our taxonomy, and a different (disjoint) sub-sample was used for actual

[3]Indeed, some benchmarks such as GLUE do not make clear even if recent LLMs are better than RoBERTa, a remarkable sentiment classifier, see a discussion in the Appendix.

[4]We will evaluate different pre-trained representations in future studies to find out if the same error type, in similar proportions, occurs across different representations.

evaluation, as described next. Table 6 in the Appendix shows the number of misclassified instances by all classifiers – there is no significant skewness in the distribution of positive and negative misclassified documents. We took a random sample of 60 misclassified documents from each dataset for evaluation, and the results are presented in Section 4.

3.4 Taxonomy Development

We conducted a preliminary round of assessment using a set of 15 randomly selected documents from PangMovie and Amazon. During this round, we convened to discuss potential sources of misclassification, aiming to better comprehend the reasons behind incorrect predictions. Drawing on the literature, we assumed that there could be incorrect labels in the gold datasets and hence decided to include human mislabelling as a potential reason for the mismatch between the model's prediction and our ground truth. Through this process, we agreed upon a set of potential reasons representing the bulk of the categories in our taxonomy of errors. We conducted a subsequent evaluation with another set of 15 documents from each dataset, refining definitions, instructions, and the evaluation process. Upon concluding this iteration, we excluded all documents used in the preliminary stage and proceeded with a new evaluation. We randomly selected 60 samples from each dataset for manual human evaluation.

3.5 Distribution of documents

To evaluate the selected texts, we recruited 8 participants, 4 with expertise in Computer Science and 4 in Linguistics, all with prior experience in NLP annotation tasks. The participants comprised two professors holding a PhD in CS, one with a PhD in Linguistics, and five students pursuing their bachelor's or master's degrees, who performed the work voluntarily out of curiosity and with learning goals.

Each participant was assigned 30 out of the 60 documents in each of the three datasets, totaling 90 documents per evaluator. Each document was assigned to be evaluated by four participants, two having a computer science background and the other two having a linguistics background. The decision to assess each document by two evaluators from each field was meant to enable quantification of agreement within the same background groups and between the two groups with different backgrounds. Section 4 presents results considering all four evaluators – the impact of evaluators' background is analyzed in Appendix A.6.

3.6 Evaluation Form

Individual forms were created for each evaluator and shared on a web cloud provider, ensuring evaluators could not access each other's forms. Our evaluation form comprised four tabs, the first containing instructions on how to evaluate the documents and the remaining ones having one sample of documents per tab, each line containing a document and the categories to be assigned to it.

The form provided to evaluators presents columns for text ID, text to be evaluated, label assigned by a human, and label assigned by the machine model. Two additional columns were assigned to be filled in by evaluators with their answer to two questions: (i) "Who misclassified the text? ", for which one out of three options could be chosen: "Model", "Human", and "I don't know"; and (ii) "Based on your answer to question 1, "why do you think the text was misclassified?", for which 1 out of 6 options could be chosen. Table 1 provides a description of the available options.

3.7 Categories To Evaluate Misclassification

The second question in our evaluation form required the evaluator to choose a category that could account for the misclassification. The instructions tab provided evaluators with examples of each category, some of which are presented in Table 1. The first row shows an example of a text misclassified due to the model's incorrect prediction despite available textual cues. In this case, the model assigned a negative sentiment, though the text contains positive cues: "precious increments artfully.....". The second row shows an example of misclassification due to an incorrect label in the dataset. The wording "completely broke off" indicates a negative opinion, but it is labeled as positive. The third row is a misclassification ascribed to sarcasm, where "seen it before" is a negative opinion ironically expressed. The fourth row exemplifies a misclassification due to *ambivalence*, having both negative ("expensive") and positive cues ("won't oxidize" and "better than soap").

It should be noted that the categories "Sarcasm" and "ambivalence" are designed to capture very different instances of language use. "Sarcasm" refers to instances of language use when a user makes a statement that is meant to be understood figuratively. For instance, if a movie is assessed as being "a sleeping pill that works wonders", the statement is meant to be understood as "a very boring film to the point it makes you fall

Category	Description and Example
Sarcasm	**Description**: Text contains irony (words that express the opposite of what one means), humorous expressions, and figurative language (metaphors) **Example**: Final verdict: you've seen it all before.
Ambivalence	**Description**: Text contains both positive and negative opinions, neither being predominant over the other **Example**: Expensive but won't oxidize metal. Maybe better than soap
Lack of textual cues for label prediction	**Description**: Text is very brief or provides no cues for a human and a model to assign a predominant sentiment **Example**: Big biggg large shoes as expected and loose fitting
Incorrect prediction despite available textual cues	**Description**: Text provides textual cues but model fails to correctly assign the predominant sentiment **Example**: A film of precious increments artfully camouflaged as everyday activities
Incorrect label in the dataset	**Description**: Text has an incorrect gold label in original dataset **Example**: Rope completely broke off after a couple of months (positive in the gold standard)
None of the above	**Description**: None of the above categories can account for the misclassification

Table 1: First-level categories and their description with examples

Category	Description and Example
Amplifier	**Description**: Words such "really", "very", "super", "incredibly", "so", "pretty", "definitely", "too" tend to co-occur with instances of very negative or very positive sentiment and can be interpreted by the model as conveying a sentiment contrary to what they actually amplify. **Example**: Secretary is just too original to be ignored.
Comparative	**Description**: Comparisons ("more", "less", "higher", "lower", etc.) establish a relationship of inequality between two elements, requiring the model to interpret which of the two is being evaluated as positive or negative. **Example**: LaBute was more fun when his characters were torturing each other psychologically and talking about their genitals in public.
Contrastive	**Description**: Two distinct sentiments are expressed and explicitly signaled by conjunctions ("but", "yet", "on the other hand", "however", "yet", "still", "though", "despite this", "all the same"), one sentiment being dominant over the other. **Example**: Uneven, self-conscious but often hilarious spoof.
Idiom	**Description**: Meaning cannot be inferred from the meaning of each individual word in an expression. **Example**: A pleasurably jacked-up piece of action moviemaking.
Modality	**Description**: Modal expressions such as may, could, should, must, can, might, etc. imply that something is other than expected or desired. **Example**: Cattaneo should have followed the runaway success of his first film, the full monty, with something different.
Negation	**Description**: Polarity and negative markers (no, not, never, neither, etc) as well as negative words may be used in texts with positive sentiment. **Example**: Can't turn off the unit the fast charger work perfect.
Non-standard spelling	**Description**: Symbols such as #, words written together instead of apart, use of all caps, etc., may not be recognized as words by the model. **Example**: Much monkeyfun for all.
Reducer	**Description**: Reducers such as "kind of", "less", "lot less", "sort of", "so so", "about", "more or less", may shift classification towards a particular sentiment. **Example**: A subtle variation on i spit on your grave in which our purported heroine pathologically avenges a hatred for men.
World knowledge	**Description**: Facts, events, people, characters, etc., associated to positive and negative sentiment. **Example**: Granddad of Le Nouvelle Vague, Jean Luc Godard continues to baffle the faithful with his games of hide and seek.
New word / expression	**Description**: Newly-coined, mostly hyphenated words and expressions that may not be recognized by the model. **Example**: Even in this less-than-magic kingdom, reese rules.
None of the above	**Description**: None of the above categories can account for the misclassification

Table 2: Categories for fine-grained analysis of "Incorrect prediction despite available textual cues"

asleep". "Ambivalence", on the other hand, refers to instances of language use where two contrasting sentiments are worded. Hence, if a movie is assessed as "having an excellent cast despite being very slow-paced," both a positive and negative sentiment are expressed. "Ambivalence" does not inherently implicate figurative language.

We created the taxonomy based on an extensive survey of works seeking to categorize misclassification and held discussions until we reached a consensus on the taxonomy´s categories. These categories may apply to several ATC tasks besides sentiment analysis when there is some type of opinionated comment. We believe that our methodology is robust enough to be applied to other tasks beyond sentiments, as several categories pertain to general ATC problems, regardless of the domain.

3.8 Focused (Hierarchical) Categorization

The final step in our methodology comprises further evaluation of some of the "most complex errors", namely, those identified in the previous step as being *incorrect prediction despite available textual cues* could have led to assigning the correct sentiment. In this final analysis, we aim to identify reasons for those incorrect predictions. We opted for an increasingly focused evaluation process in order to manage the complexity of the annotation task, cognizant of the effort required by assessing documents with increasingly fine-grained categories. Hence, our methodology moved from a general, binary query (Question 1) to a more distilled, six-category query (Question 2), concluding with a ten-category query (Focused categorization).

In this last assessment round, all instances of *incorrect prediction despite available textual cues* were evaluated using a fine-grained category set pertaining to linguistic phenomena reportedly not adequately captured by models. We designed a taxonomy based on ten particular linguistic phenomena potentially impacting a model's predictions. They cover words modifying the sentiment intensity (Amplifiers and Reducers); explicitly signaled comparisons which require identifying which of the two elements is decisive for a sentiment (Comparatives); explicitly contrasted arguments or aspects (Contrastive), with one of them being dominant; idiomatic expressions (Idiom); expressions of probability and obligation (Modality); negative polarity scope and negative words (Negation); symbols and characters rendering unrecognizable words (Non-standard spelling); newly-coined and idiosyncratic words unknown to the model (New word / Expression); and mentions to entities requiring world-knowledge to assign a correct sentiment (World-Knowledge). These categories are detailed described in Table 2 , along with the instructions provided to the evaluators, with a definition of each category and examples.

4 Results

Documents were assessed by 4 evaluators. Question 1 required selecting 1 out of 3 alternatives, whereas Question 2 had 6 alternatives. Focused categorization comprised 10 categories. Consensus was defined as one of the alternatives having the *majority* of votes – 4, 3, or 2 [5]. If there was no majority, a document was classified as "No consensus".

4.1 Taxonomy effectiveness

High consensus was achieved for the three levels of assessment: 86.7% for Question 1; 81.2% for Question 2 and 86.5% for focused assessment, allowing us to state that the taxonomy was effective for evaluation purposes[6]. We present a detailed effectiveness (consensus) analysis in the Appendix A.4.

4.2 Response Analysis

Given that a high consensus had been achieved, we proceeded to analyze the responses of the evaluators. Half of the misclassifications in the Amazon dataset were ascribed to the model (see Figure 5 in Appendix). This is even higher in the movie datasets, emerging as the main misclassification reason in 65% of the cases in PangMovie and almost 80% in VaderMovie. Percentages for the option "Don't know" were very low in all datasets. Together with the option "No consensus", they achieved at most 18.3% in PangMovie (and 16.3% and 15% in Amazon and VaderMovie, respectively) of all analyzed documents in all datasets.

Though lower than errors ascribed to the model, the percentage of errors ascribed to the "Human" category is significant, mainly in the Amazon dataset (33%) (See Appendix A.5). This means that in 33% of the misclassifications, 3 or 4 evaluators (majority of the cases) considered that the model classified the document correctly and there was an error in the gold dataset. Though lower in the movie domain, human mislabeling is not negligible – 16.7% in PangMovie and 6.7% in VaderMovie. This relatively high percentage of human mislabeling merits further investigation in future studies, though manual labeling has been acknowledged as a complex and prone to errors (Zhu et al., 2023).

Figure 2 presents the results for Question 2. Consensus cases show clear differences between the two domains. The main reason for misclassification in Amazon was "Ambivalence", with 30% of the cases, whereas "Sarcasm" is almost non-existent. This can be accounted for by the fact that in product reviews, texts tend to be more focused on features of a product, so-called *aspects*, there being less irony or sarcasm in the reviews. Most misclassifications occurred when the text concomitantly expressed both positive and negative opinions about product aspects ("Ambivalence"). This is a challenge both for the model and the human to predict the "correct polarity" for the document. This raises the question as to whether there is a single correct polarity label for these documents or whether different product aspects should be given different polarities (Brauwers and Frasincar, 2022).

We see a different result in the movie domain, with "Sarcasm" as the main reason for misclassification in VaderMovie and the second main one in PangMovie, almost tied with "Ambivalence". We believe sarcasm is a particular characteristic of the movie review domain, possibly due to the fact that reviewers assess artistic productions and feel the need to use figurative language to express their opinions about them. As in the Amazon dataset, "Ambivalence" is a major reason for misclassifications, especially in PangMovie. This

[5]In case of two votes, provided that the remaining two alternatives have one vote each.

[6]An effective taxonomy has high consensus among evaluators upon the defined categories and low consensus in a category that has no definition, in our case, "Don't know" for Question 1 and "None of the above" for Question 2

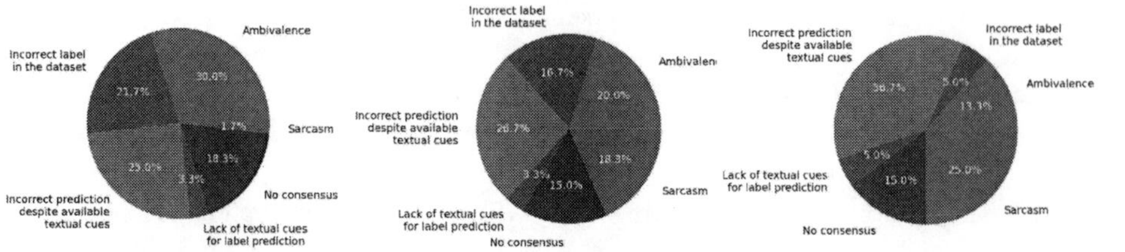

(a) Amazon (b) Pang Movie (c) Vader Movie

Figure 2: Percentages for answers to Question 2 in the three datasets.

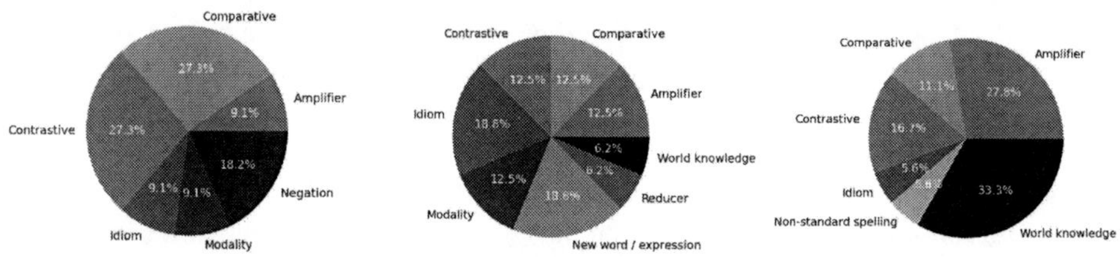

(a) Amazon (b) Pang Movie (c) Vader Movie

Figure 3: Percentages for answers when breaking down the category "Incorrect prediction despite available textual cues".

suggests that in the movie domain, reviewers also tend to point out both positive and negative aspects, bringing a challenge both for models and humans to ascribe polarity to the texts. In this sense, *sarcasm detection* (Verma et al., 2021) and *aspect analysis* (Brauwers and Frasincar, 2022) are both interesting lines of investigation worth pursuing.

4.2.1 Focused (Hierarchical) Analysis

A major reason for errors in both movie datasets (36.7% in Vader and 26.7% in PangMovie) and the second most frequent for products (25% of the cases) for Question 2 was "Incorrect Prediction Despite Available Textual Cues" (Figure 2). Indeed, if we look at the reasons why evaluators selected Model failure in Question 1 (Figure 10 in the Appendix), almost half of the errors are ascribed to this category for the three datasets. Evaluators considered textual cues were available to predict the correct sentiment, but for reasons other than "Ambivalence" or "Sarcasm", the model failed to do it.

The final step in our methodology was devoted precisely to understanding the reasons for those errors. In a new round of assessment, we evaluated 52 documents that had been assigned this category in the first round: 14 in Amazon, 16 in Pang Movie and 22 in VaderMovie. Like the first round, we also obtained a high overall percentage of agreement– 86.5% – which can be considered quite high considering that (i) there are more categories to assign (10 in total) and (ii) these are some of the hardest cases to evaluate.

Figure 3 shows the results of this final focused (hierarchical) analysis. As we can see, in Amazon, 54.6% of the model errors are due to explicit comparisons and contrastive cases where one aspect is dominant over the other. This is expected as these are product reviews. Negation (e.g., "Can't turn off the unit the fast charger work perfect." in Table 2) is also a major reason for errors. The remainder of the errors are roughly evenly spread over the categories related to idiomatic expressions, modality (e.g., "Cattaneo should have followed the runaway success of his first film with something different." in Table 2) and errors due to amplifiers.

The case is more complex in the Movie domain, where the errors evidence a different pattern. In the Vader dataset, lack of world knowledge (e.g. a movie name, a director/actor, a real-world event (e.g., "Granddad of Le Nouvelle Vague, Jean Luc Godard continues to baffle the faithful with his games of hide and seek." in Table 2) accounts for $\frac{1}{3}$ of the errors, followed by amplifiers, which are popular among movie reviewers. In the PangMovie dataset, we see a more complex, almost even distribution of errors among all categories with a high impact (37.6% of the cases) of idiomatic expressions (e.g. "A pleasurably jacked-up piece of action moviemaking." in Table 2) and newly coined words/expressions, also popular among movie reviewers, which may occur in a single or just a few documents and do not have enough support in the training data for the model to learn properly.

The few errors that remain unexplained may be due to distinct reasons, such as lack of training data and borderline cases. Although it is possible to perform this analysis in open models such as BERT, which is not the case for closed-source solutions such as GPT, it is hard due to Transformer complexity. We will devote our attention to this challenging issue in future work. Nevertheless, to give initial insights for analyses, Figure 12 (Appendix A.11) presents the TSNE visualization of the misclassified BERT-based document vectors – many of them lie on class borders.

In this work, we investigated the reasons for misclassification, highlighting the issues found and enabling the implementation of strategies to address these problems. For example, if an instance is found to be wrongly classified due to sarcasm, this implies that before the actual classification, the sentiment classifier should be given information that this message is possibly sarcastic (using, for instance, a sarcasm/irony classifier) so that the sentiment classifier can use this information in the decision process. If a document is found to be ambivalent, segments with polarity clash should be located and assigned a separate label for each polarity, or the full sentence be assigned the polarity of the stronger sentiment. If a sentence has two polarities and there is an overt contrasting connector, polarity inversion may be performed, as it is done in Vader's shell. If an instance is incorrectly classified due to idiomatic expressions, lack of world knowledge, or the occurrence of newly coined words, the solution involves enhancing the model with further training instances that provide the missing knowledge, including idioms and new expressions. Similar strategies can be developed regarding the other categories.

As a **final remark**, we would like to emphasize the *complexity* of the performed analysis. Our misclassification assessment prioritizes fine-grained analysis of a representative sample of documents. Several rounds of discussions were held till a taxonomy was reached. Our study is exploratory and involves human evaluation, demanding careful manual data analysis. Evaluators had to answer 2 questions for each document in 3 datasets in 2 domains and were requested to comment on dubious cases. The focused (hierarchical) categorization required yet, a new round of evaluation considering 10 linguistic categories. Each of the 8 evaluators was requested to evaluate 90 documents and compare the predominant (sentiment) model assignment to that in the gold human standard in order to decide whether misclassification was due to the model or the human and the likely reason for such misclassification. This very complex task constrains sample size and number of participants, a not uncommon issue in qualitative experiments (Sharp et al., 2019) and justifies our current choice of a single task - - sentiment analysis.

5 Conclusion

We addressed the hard task of unveiling the reasons why models misclassified the hardest documents, those which no classifier using very separable contextual representations could correctly classify. For this, we devised an error taxonomy and ran qualitative experiments requesting 8 evaluators with distinct backgrounds to use the taxonomy to qualify the errors using 3 datasets in 2 domains – prior work has been limited to a *single domain or dataset*. The high consensus among the evaluators emerged as an interesting finding. We have found significant differences regarding reasons for misclassification in the product and movie review domains. Sarcasm is very pronounced in movie reviews, while Ambivalence is more prevalent in product reviews. There is a high proportion of wrong labels in the gold dataset and a noteworthy number of incorrect model predictions due to various linguistic phenomena, including comparisons, contrastive constructions, negation and instances requiring world knowledge. No single category emerged as dominant.

Future work includes explaining the few remaining unexplained cases; applying our methodology/taxonomy to other domains (e.g., topic classification); and using acquired knowledge to improve models. Additionally, we intend to investigate current models, such as Large Language Models (LLMs), in classification tasks, assessing the potential of these models to address the issue of misclassification presented in this paper.

Acknowledgements

This work was partially supported by CNPq, CAPES, FAPEMIG, AWS, UNIMED, NVIDIA, CIIA-Saúde, and FAPESP.

References

Jun Bai, Xiaofeng Zhang, Chen Li, Hanhua Hong, Xi Xu, Chenghua Lin, and Wenge Rong. 2023. How to determine the most powerful pre-trained language model without brute force fine-tuning? an empirical survey. In *Findings of the EMNLP 2023*.

Jeremy Barnes, Lilja Øvrelid, and Erik Velldal. 2019. Sentiment analysis is not solved! assessing and probing sentiment classification. In *Proceedings of the 2019 ACL Workshop BlackboxNLP: Analyzing and Interpreting Neural Networks for NLP*. ACL.

Ronan Le Bras, Swabha Swayamdipta, Chandra Bhagavatula, Rowan Zellers, Matthew Peters, Ashish Sabharwal, and Yejin Choi. 2020. Adversarial filters of dataset biases. In *Proceedings of the 37th International Conference on Machine Learning*. PMLR.

Gianni Brauwers and Flavius Frasincar. 2022. A survey on aspect-based sentiment classification. 55(4).

Washington Cunha, Celso França, Guilherme Fonseca, Leonardo Rocha, and Marcos André Gonçalves. 2023a. An effective, efficient, and scalable confidence-based instance selection framework for transformer-based text classification. In *Proceedings of the 46th International ACM SIGIR'23*.

Washington Cunha, Vítor Mangaravite, Christian Gomes, Sérgio Canuto, Elaine Resende, Cecilia Nascimento, Felipe Viegas, Celso França, et al. 2021. On the cost-effectiveness of neural and non-neural approaches and representations for text classification: A comprehensive comparative study. *Information Processing & Management*, 58(3):102481.

Washington Cunha, Felipe Viegas, Celso França, Thierson Rosa, Leonardo Rocha, and Marcos André Gonçalves. 2023b. A comparative survey of instance selection methods applied to non-neural and transformer-based text classification. *ACM CSUR*.

Claudio M.V. de Andrade, Fabiano M. Belém, Washington Cunha, Celso França, Felipe Viegas, Leonardo Rocha, and Marcos André Gonçalves. 2023. On the class separability of contextual embeddings representations – or "the classifier does not matter when the (text) representation is so good!". *Information Processing & Management*, 60(4):103336.

Jacob Devlin, Ming-Wei Chang, Kenton Lee, and Kristina Toutanova. 2019. BERT: Pre-training of deep bidirectional transformers for language understanding. pages 4171–4186.

Kawin Ethayarajh, Yejin Choi, and Swabha Swayamdipta. 2022. Understanding dataset difficulty with $\mathcal{V}$-usable information. In *Proceedings of the 39th International Conference on Machine Learning*, pages 5988–6008. PMLR.

Simona Frenda, Alessandro Pedrani, Valerio Basile, Soda Marem Lo, Alessandra Teresa Cignarella, Raffaella Panizzon, Cristina Marco, Bianca Scarlini, Viviana Patti, Cristina Bosco, and Davide Bernardi. 2023. EPIC: multi-perspective annotation of a corpus of irony. In *Proceedings of the 61st Annual Meeting of the Association for Computational Linguistics*.

Lukas Galke and Ansgar Scherp. 2022. Bag-of-words vs. graph vs. sequence in text classification: Questioning the necessity of text-graphs and the surprising strength of a wide MLP. In *Proceedings of the 60th Annual Meeting of the Association for Computational Linguistics*, pages 4038–4051.

Hany Hassan, Anthony Aue, Chang Chen, Vishal Chowdhary, Jonathan Clark, Christian Federmann, Xuedong Huang, Marcin Junczys-Dowmunt, William D. Lewis, Mu Li, Shujie Liu, Tie-Yan Liu, Renqian Luo, Arul Menezes, Tao Qin, Frank Seide, Xu Tan, Fei Tian, Lijun Wu, Shuangzhi Wu, Yingce Xia, Dongdong Zhang, Zhirui Zhang, and Ming Zhou. 2018. Achieving human parity on automatic chinese to english news translation. *ArXiv*, abs/1803.05567.

Phillip Keung, Yichao Lu, György Szarvas, and Noah A. Smith. 2020. The multilingual amazon reviews corpus. In *Proceedings of the 2020 Conference on Empirical Methods in Natural Language Processing*.

Han S. Lee, Alex A. Agarwal, and Junmo Kim. 2017. Why do deep neural networks still not recognize these images?: A qualitative analysis on failure cases of imagenet classification. *CoRR*, abs/1709.03439.

Mike Lewis, Yinhan Liu, Naman Goyal, Marjan Ghazvininejad, Abdelrahman Mohamed, Omer Levy, Veselin Stoyanov, and Luke Zettlemoyer. 2020. BART: Denoising sequence-to-sequence pre-training for natural language generation, translation, and comprehension. In *Proceedings of the 58th Annual Meeting of the Association for Computational Linguistics*.

Qian Li, Hao Peng, Jianxin Li, Congying Xia, Renyu Yang, Lichao Sun, Philip S. Yu, and Lifang He. 2022. A survey on text classification: From traditional to deep learning. 13(2).

Yinhan Liu, Myle Ott, Naman Goyal, Jingfei Du, Mandar Joshi, Danqi Chen, Omer Levy, Mike Lewis, Luke Zettlemoyer, and Veselin Stoyanov. 2019. Roberta: A robustly optimized BERT pretraining approach. *CoRR*, abs/1907.11692.

Karen Martins, Pedro O.S Vaz-de Melo, and Rodrygo Santos. 2021. Why do document-level polarity classifiers fail? In *Proceedings of the 2021 Conference of the North American Chapter of the Association for Computational Linguistics*.

Christopher Meek. 2016. A characterization of prediction errors. *CoRR*, abs/1611.05955.

Rahul Pandey, Hemant Purohit, Carlos Castillo, and Valerie L. Shalin. 2022. Modeling and mitigating human annotation errors to design efficient stream processing systems with human-in-the-loop machine learning. *International Journal of Human-Computer Studies*, 160:102772.

Bo Pang and Lillian Lee. 2004. A sentimental education: Sentiment analysis using subjectivity summarization based on minimum cuts. page 271–es.

Geoff Pleiss, Tianyi Zhang, Ethan Elenberg, and Kilian Q Weinberger. 2020. Identifying mislabeled data using the area under the margin ranking. In *Advances in Neural Information Processing Systems*, volume 33, pages 17044–17056. Curran Associates, Inc.

Filipe N Ribeiro, Matheus Araújo, Pollyanna Gonçalves, Marcos André Gonçalves, and Fabrício Benevenuto. 2016. Sentibench-a benchmark comparison of state-of-the-practice sentiment analysis methods. *EPJ Data Science*, 5:1–29.

H. Sharp, J. Preece, and Y. Rogers. 2019. *Interaction Design: Beyond Human-Computer Interaction*. Wiley.

D. Silverman. 2004. *Qualitative Research: Theory, Method and Practice*. SAGE Publications.

Swabha Swayamdipta, Roy Schwartz, Nicholas Lourie, Yizhong Wang, Hannaneh Hajishirzi, Noah A. Smith, and Yejin Choi. 2020. Dataset cartography: Mapping and diagnosing datasets with training dynamics. In *Proceedings of the 2020 Conference on Empirical Methods in Natural Language Processing (EMNLP)*.

Palak Verma, Neha Shukla, and A.P. Shukla. 2021. Techniques of sarcasm detection: A review. In *2021 International Conference on Advance Computing and Innovative Technologies in Engineering (ICACITE)*, pages 968–972.

Ming Yan, Haiyang Xu, Chenliang Li, Junfeng Tian, Bin Bi, Wei Wang, Xianzhe Xu, Ji Zhang, Songfang Huang, Fei Huang, et al. 2023. Achieving human parity on visual question answering. *ACM Transactions on Information Systems*, 41(3):1–40.

Yu Zhu, Yingchun Ye, Mengyang Li, Ji Zhang, and Ou Wu. 2023. Investigating annotation noise for named entity recognition. *Neural Comput. Appl.*, 35(1):993–1007.

A Appendix

A.1 Limitations

Despite relevant contributions, our study has some limitations. Our evaluation targeted two domains, three datasets, and the task of sentiment analysis. Increasing the number of dataset domains and expanding our analysis to the task of Topic Classification will provide new valuable insights. The size of our evaluation group is relatively small, although this is common in qualitative studies (Silverman, 2004). We will increase the number of evaluators in future studies. Our work uses BERT's contextual representations. Although (de Andrade et al., 2023) shows BERT produces representations that are as (semantically) separable in the embedding space as representations produced by other Transformers (e.g., RoBERTa, BART), we intend to test our methodology with different Transformers in the future.

While our current work covers only one classification task, in our study, we devise a general-purpose taxonomy for text classification designed to be useful in more than one scenario. Our first question aims to answer whether the source of the misclassification is human or the model—a question that applies to any ATC task where we have a label and a model's prediction. Our second question inquires about the reason for the misclassification - Incorrect Prediction Despite Available Textual Cues; or incorrect label in the dataset - lack of textual cues for label prediction, ambivalence, and sarcasm. Likewise, the first two categories are not restricted to the sentiment analysis task but apply to other ATC tasks. At the first level of the proposed taxonomy, two categories (ambivalence and sarcasm) can be said to be task-related, but the taxonomy needs them for analytical purposes; otherwise, it would be too general. Nonetheless, if used for evaluation in other tasks, these two more task-oriented categories may be adapted, the core of the taxonomy remaining as it is.

Our spreadsheet validation only allowed annotators to choose a single category to answer each question. A column for annotators to freely state their Remarks was available in case the categories should present any annotation problem. No remarks were placed by annotators, which suggests no overlapping was felt by them. While theoretically some of the categories could be felt to overlap, our results did not support this.

A.2 Datasets Statistics

Table 3 presents statistics of the datasets in terms of the number of documents and average document length, and the class distribution into positive and negative instances is balanced in the three datasets.

Dataset	Documents	Avg words	Positive	Negative
Amazon	168000	33	84000	84000
PangMovie	10662	19	5331	5331
VaderMovie	10568	19	5242	5326

Table 3: Datasets Statistics

A.3 Summary of Evaluation Schemas Reported in Related Work

Table 4 shows a summary of the evaluation schemas reported in related work. Compared to them, our schema is much more robust and comprehensive.

Related Work	Taxonomy categories
(Meek, 2016)	**"Mislabeling errors"**: human labeling errors; **"Representation errors"**: limitations in the feature set used for evaluation; **"Learner errors"**: prediction errors when there is sufficient information for accurate classification; **"Boundary errors"**: correct predictions could be achieved by adding more examples, indicating an absence of labeled examples for a specific class in the training set.
(Lee et al., 2017)	**"Similar Labels"**: the term representing the predicted object in the image is not in the ground truth (GT) but is semantically similar to the GT. The set of true labels is the set of terms that textually describe the objects in the image. **"Not Salient"**: the predicted object exists in the image but is not present in the GT; **"Challenging Images"**: the GT is challenging even for a human being; **"Incorrect GT"**: incorrect annotation by humans; and 5) "incorrect prediction class": machine prediction is incorrect but with sufficient information in the image for humans to detect.
(Martins et al., 2021)	**"Neutral"**: when polarity is not clearly defined **"Discrepant"**: when polarity differs from its associated labeling

Table 4: Summary of Evaluation Schemas Reported in Related Work.

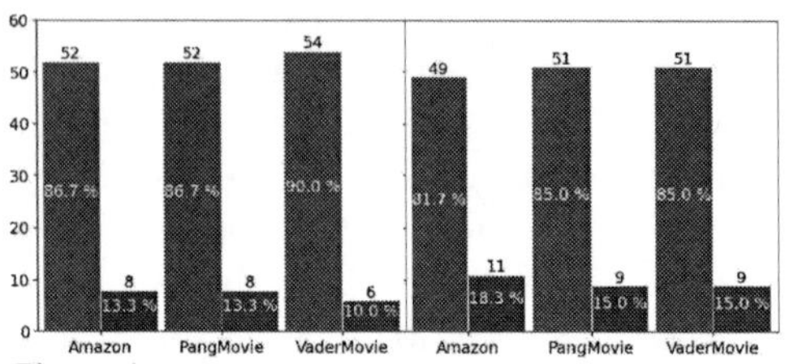

Figure 4: Consensus and No Consensus on Q1 (left) and Q2 (right).

A.4 Taxonomy Effectiveness (Consensus) Analysis

To answer our first research question: "Is the proposed taxonomy for misclassification effective to be used for misclassification analysis?", we analyzed the responses from questions 1 and 2 provided by the evaluators.

Figure 4 shows the consensus percentages obtained for Questions 1 and 2 in the three evaluated datasets. For Question 1, out of 60 documents, 54 attained high inter-evaluator agreement in VaderMovie, and 52 in Amazon and PangMovie. In other words, in at least 86.7% of the cases (52/60), consensus was achieved in some category defined for Question 1 in the three evaluated datasets, implying low difficulty for evaluators to define a type of misclassification. We break down those numbers in Section A.4.1 to show the consensus distribution per document and A.6 per evaluator background. As shown there, the vast majority of the documents had the same categorization assigned by 4 or 3 evaluators, emphasizing high agreement and taxonomy effectiveness.

Figure 4 (b) shows the consensus percentages for Question 2. It is important to bear in mind that in Question 2, six options were available, likely leading to a higher difficulty in achieving agreement. Nonetheless, we can observe a high consensus in all datasets for this question, with the lowest value being obtained in the Amazon dataset, 49 out of 60 documents reaching at least 81.7% consensus. As also shown in Figure 5, "No Consensus" was below 14% for Question 1 and below 19% for Question 2. In Section A.4.1, we show examples (in Table 5) of documents that posed difficulties for evaluators.

A.4.1 Consensus Distribution

This subsection presents the evaluator consensus distribution for Questions 1 and 2, which is analyzed in Section 4.1. Regarding Question 1, as can be seen in Figure 6a, out of the 52 documents that achieved evaluator consensus in the Amazon dataset, 33 reached full agreement among all four evaluators, 16 documents reached full agreement among three, and 3 documents reached full agreement between two evaluators. This points to documents with full agreement among three or four evaluators representing a significant portion of the total number of documents with consensus, demonstrating the robustness of our final results. Similar results were obtained for VaderMovie and PangMovie regarding the joint proportion (i.e., the sum of the proportions) of evaluations with 4 and 3 agreements.

Regarding Question 2, results show less consensus among the evaluators, which may be due to the number of categories they had to choose from. This is reflected in the graphs in Figure 7. The Amazon dataset showed higher consensus among a higher number of evaluators, possibly accounted for by the type of review - product review. As movie reviews assess artistic productions and implicate more sarcasm and figurative language, the full consensus is harder to achieve, though still attainable. Similarly to Figures 6 and 7, Figure 8 shows the distribution of consensus among evaluators for hierarchical categorization.

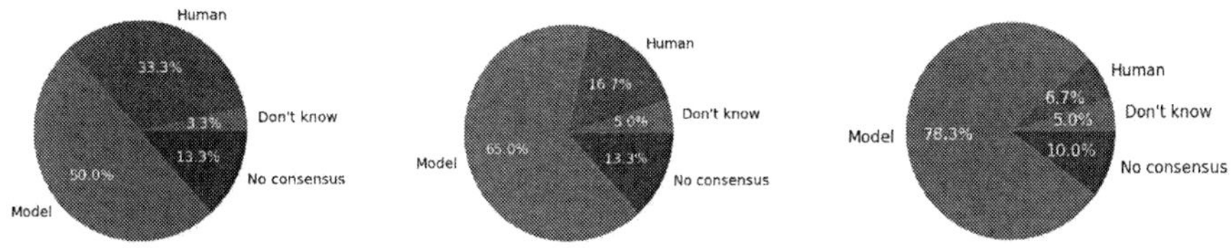

(a) Amazon (b) Pang Movie (c) Vader Movie

Figure 5: Percentages for answers to Question 1 in the three datasets.

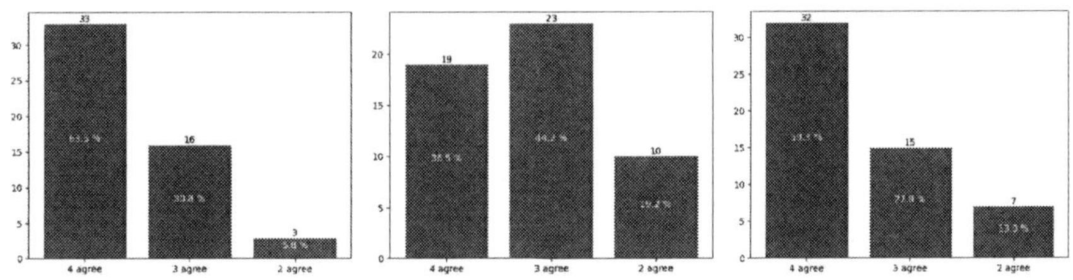

(a) Amazon (b) Pang Movie (c) Vader Movie

Figure 6: Consensus for Question 1.

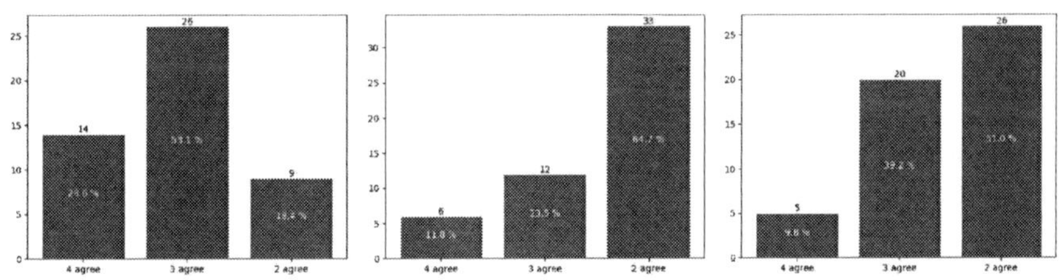

(a) Amazon (b) Pang Movie (c) Vader Movie

Figure 7: Consensus for Question 2.

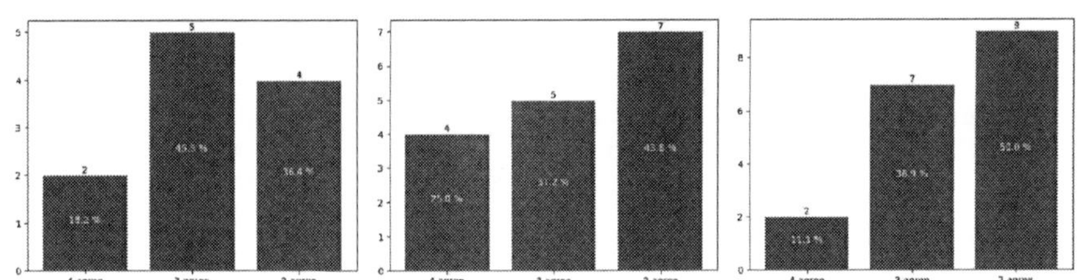

(a) Amazon (b) Pang Movie (c) Vader Movie

Figure 8: Consensus for hierarchical categories.

Text	**Dataset**
They are ok except. The fitted pops off.	Amazon
I tried a few LED harnesses and none were bright enough to see my black dog at night running through the woods. This vest, as long as not directly in front of head/tail, is super visable.	Amazon
Very short on the sides. Overall, good fit but I do not like to show my belly. Too bad lad got that. Fabric very soft.	Amazon
The script kicks in, and mr. hartley's distended pace and foot-dragging rhythms follow.	Pang Movie
Eastwood winces, clutches his chest and gasps for breath. it's a spectacular performance - ahem, we hope it's only acting.	Pang Movie
Parts seem like they were lifted from terry gilliam's subconscious , pressed through kafka's meat grinder and into buñuel's casings	Pang Movie
The recording session is the only part of the film that is enlightening and how appreciative you are of this depends on your level of fandom.	Vader Movie
It shows that some studios firmly believe that people have lost the ability to think and will forgive any shoddy product as long as there's a little girl on girl action.	Vader Movie
A light, engaging comedy that fumbles away almost all of its accumulated enjoyment with a crucial third act miscalculation.	Vader Movie

Table 5: Texts illustrating the "No consensus" category

Regarding documents for which there was no consensus among the evaluators (Figure 4 - Left), there are 8 for the Amazon dataset, 8 for the PangMovie dataset and 6 for the VaderMovie dataset. As for question 2 (Figure 4 - Right), there are 11, 9, and 9 documents without consensus for Amazon, Pang Movie, and Vader Movie datasets, respectively. To exemplify challenging documents, we provide three examples from each dataset in the "No consensus" category for Question 2, as shown in Table 5.

The first row in Table 5 shows an Amazon product review where the text begins positively but then brings in an issue with the product. Row 4 shows a movie review from the Pang Movie dataset, where the reviewer uses the words "distended" and "dragging", creating uncertainty for categorization. Row 6 shows a series of references to other movies and directors, which requires previous knowledge of those movies and their evaluations. Therefore, we believe that the methodology of this study serves to identify challenging documents based on evaluator agreement.

A.5 Inter-evaluator agreement for Question 2 in cases of "Human Mislabeling"

In Figure 9, similar to Figure 10, we have the quantification of Question 2, but now restricted to the documents that were evaluated as human mislabeling in Question 1. In other words, documents the evaluator considered to have been correctly classified by the Model but which had been incorrectly labeled by the human (positive or negative). We can observe that, in general, the number is lower; for instance, in the Amazon dataset, we have 20 documents evaluated as errors in the gold standard.

Additionally, we can observe a high prevalence of the category Incorrect label in the dataset, which corresponds to 65% in the Amazon and 70% in the Pang Movie datasets. This means that the evaluator considered the document to have been mislabeled by the human, despite there being sufficient information in the text for the human to choose the "right" label according to the evaluator's assessment.

Regarding the VaderMovie dataset, numbers are low, which may bias some proportions – there are only four mislabeled documents evaluated as human mislabeling, and only 1 sample was considered Incorrect label in the dataset.

A.6 Differences in Evaluation carried out by Computer Scientists and Linguists

We carried out an additional analysis focusing on the evaluators' backgrounds. Since two evaluators rated each document with a Linguistics background and two with a Computer Science one, we examined our data to investigate differences ascribable to evaluators' backgrounds. Figure 11 represents the quantification of the responses to question 1 by evaluators having a Computer Science background (11a, 11b, 11c) and a Linguistics one (11d, 11e, 11f), in which there was inter-evaluator agreement of the two evaluators. We can notice that evaluators' backgrounds had little impact on the results for all datasets.

A.7 Set of misclassifications by all classifiers

Dataset	Misclassification	Positive	Negative
Amazon	216	115	101
PangMovie	120	54	66
VaderMovie	85	37	48

Table 6: Set of misclassifications by all classifiers.

A.8 Comparison between BERT and the Classifiers using the Contextual Representations (from de Andrade et al. (2023))

For the sake of self-containedness, in Table 7, we show the results reported by (de Andrade et al., 2023) for the comparison between BERT and classifiers that used the textual representations generated by the Transformer as input. Here, we consider the results of four of the strongest classifiers used in (de Andrade et al., 2023), namely: KNN, Random Forests (RFs), Support Vector Machines (SVMs), and Logistic regression (LR) applied to two of the datasets we exploit – PangMovie and VaderMovie. Indeed, despite using different rules and heuristics, the effectiveness of these classifiers (and of all other classifiers tested in (de Andrade et al., 2023)) is basically the same in all tested datasets when using the contextual embedding representations. This is due to the fact that these representations are already so semantically separated (by class) in the embedding space that the employed classifier has little effect on the classification process.

A.9 Comparison Among Transformers

We run experiments in the tested datasets comparing BERT with RoBERTa (Liu et al., 2019) and BART (Lewis et al., 2020). Results are shown in

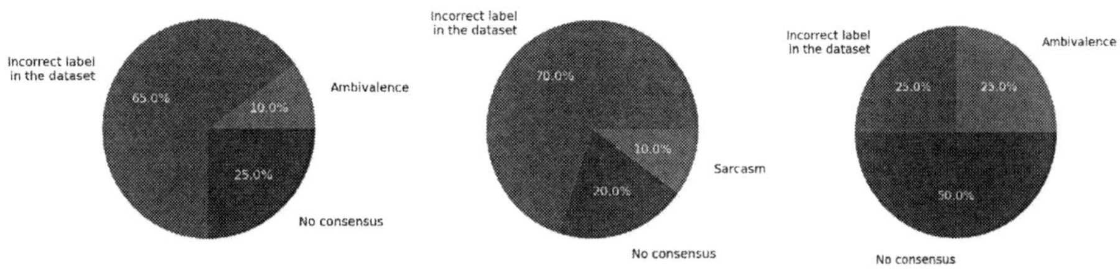

(a) Amazon (b) Pang Movie (c) Vader Movie

Figure 9: Results for Question 2 in cases where Response to Question 1 was "Human Failure".

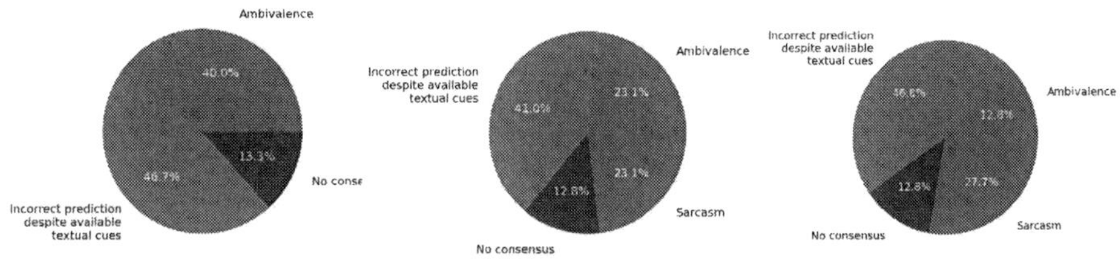

(a) Amazon (b) Pang Movie (c) Vader Movie

Figure 10: Response analysis for Question 2 in cases where "Model Failure" was selected for Question 1.

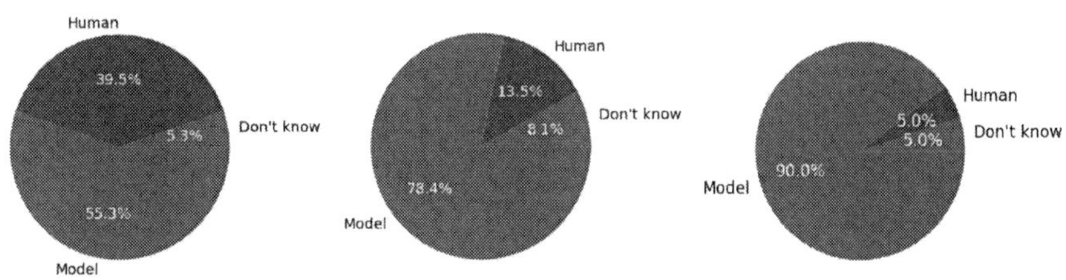

(a) Amazon (b) Pang Movie (c) Vader Movie

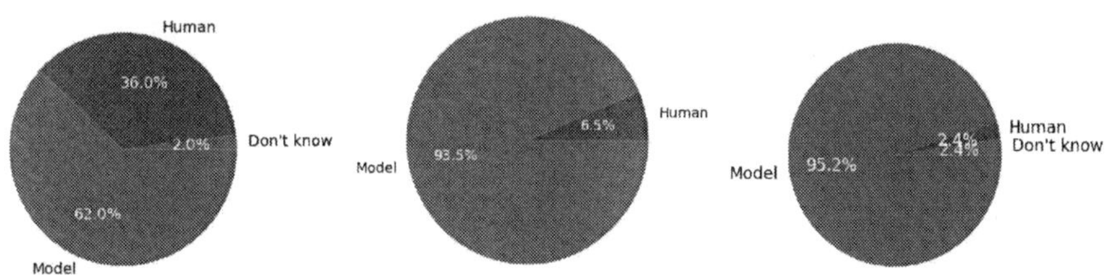

(d) Amazon (e) Pang Movie (f) Vader Movie

Figure 11: Percentages for answers to Question 1 by evaluators with a Computer Science background (a, b and c) and a Linguistics background (d, e and f).

Dataset	BERT	RF	SVM	KNN	LR
Amazon	**94.2(0.7)**	**94.2(0.1)**	**94.1(0.1)**	**94.3(0.1)**	**94.2(0.1)**
PangMovie	**87.0(0.6)**	**86.8(0.8)**	**87.2(1.0)**	**87.1(0.6)**	**87.1(0.8)**
VaderMovie	**89.1(0.7)**	**89.4(0.6)**	**89.4(0.5)**	**89.3(0.7)**	**89.5(0.6)**

Table 7: Macro-F1 (%) and confidence interval of 95%. Best results (including statistical ties) are marked in **bold**. BERT is the original method while the other columns correspond to the respective classifiers run using the contextual embeddings produced by BERT.

Table 8. As we can see, these transformers' effectiveness are very similar – BERT is statistically tied as the best method with Roberta in Amazon and marginally loses (by at most 1-2 pp) in the other two datasets. These differences, which means just a few documents in practice, are potentially irrelevant in a qualitative study as ours, which uses a sample of the documents that all classifiers predicted incorrectly. We believe that the intuitions and insights we got with the current methodology, representations, and models would not be substantially different if we used other Transformers.

Dataset	BART	BERT	RoBERTa
Amazon	93.0 (0.2)	94.2 (0.7)	94.5 (0.3)
PangMovie	88.1(0.5)	87.0(0.6)	89.0(0.4)
VaderMovie	90.4(0.6)	89.1(0.7)	91.3(0.5)

Table 8: Results regarding the evaluation metric Macro-F1.

A.10 Comparison between Transformers and LLM's

Applying our methodology to other stronger LLMs would be interesting and we will do it in the near future. However, we would like to call the reader's attention to the fact in GLUE's benchmark, for the sentiment analysis task, SST-2, a dataset similar to the ones used in our work, has an accuracy of 97.9 (Vega v1), whereas RoBERTa obtains 96.7 (Facebook AI). Without a statistical method for comparison, these results are not enough to claim that Vega V1 is clearly superior to RoBERTa. In other words, it is not always true that LLMs are better than 1st or 2nd generation Transformers for all tasks.

Several studies show that RoBERTa is a very strong model for sentiment analysis (Cunha et al., 2023b; Bai et al., 2023). Indeed, recent benchmarks (Cunha et al., 2023a) have shown that the differences among the latest versions of these Transformers (including RoBERTa, BERT, DistilBERT, BART, AlBERT, and XLNet) in some of the datasets we use in our experiments are very small. More specifically, in (Cunha et al., 2023b), RoBERTa achieved the highest effectiveness on 12 out of 22 datasets compared to other Transformer-based alternatives. On the remaining datasets, RoBERTa's performance was statistically equivalent to the best method, with marginal differences ranging from 0.10% to 1.09% (on average, 0.82%).

Furthermore, our proposed endeavor of analyzing the hardest misclassification cases (those that no classifier can correctly assign using very separable contextual embeddings (de Andrade et al., 2023)) is a challenging one. So we decided to start with strong methods for the (sentiment analysis) task, which is better documented, allowing us to understand certain premises, over which we also have better control regarding training and fine-tuning. Moreover, these analyses can be done at a much reduced cost than used Large Language Models.

A.11 TSNE Visualization of the Errors in the Dataset

Figure 12 presents the TSNE visualization of the documents in the analyzed datasets using the BERT-based vectors. We marked in red the misclassified documents. We can see that many misclassified documents lie on the class borders, but there are other cases demanding further investigation.

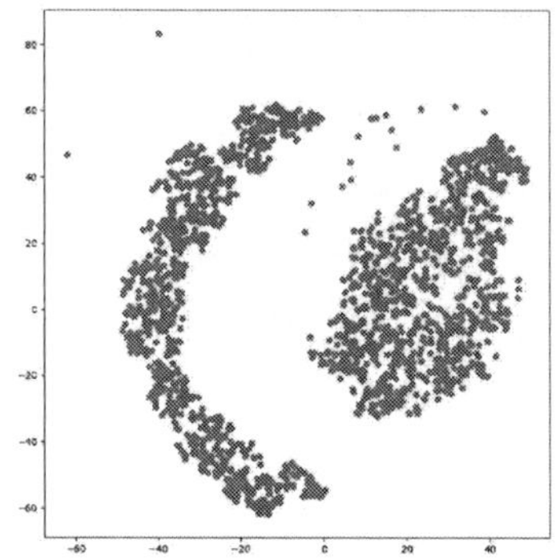

(a) Amazon

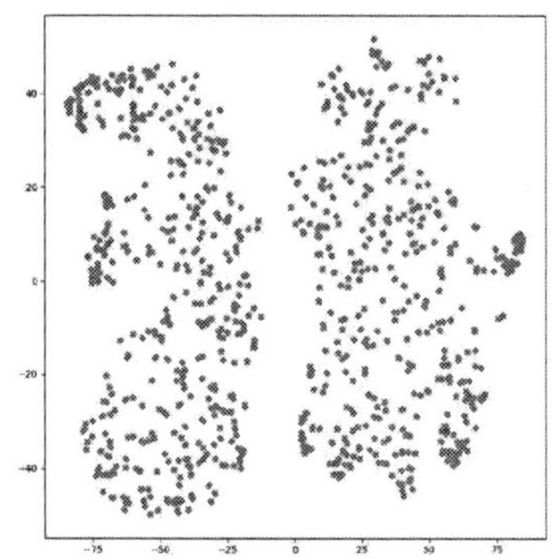

(b) Pang Movie

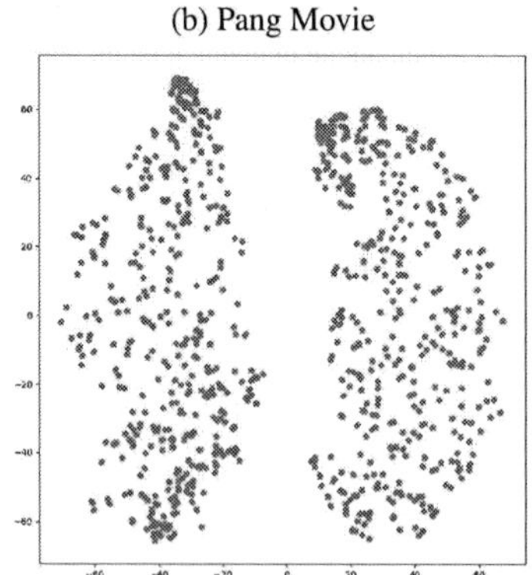

(c) Vader Movie

Figure 12: TSNE three datasets. In red, it is the set of documents misclassification by all classifiers used in this study.

A Multimodal Large Language Model "Foresees" Objects Based on Verb Information but Not Gender

Shuqi Wang* **Xufeng Duan*** **Zhenguang Cai**
Department of Linguistics and Modern Languages, CUHK
{shuqiwang, xufeng.duan}@link.cuhk.edu.hk, zhenguangcai@cuhk.edu.hk

Abstract

This study employs the classical psycholinguistics paradigm, the visual world eye-tracking paradigm (VWP), to explore the predictive capabilities of LLAVA, a multimodal large language model (MLLM), and compare them with human anticipatory gaze behaviors. Specifically, we examine the attention weight distributions of LLAVA when presented with visual displays and English sentences containing verb and gender cues. Our findings reveal that LLAVA, like humans, can predictively attend to objects relevant to verbs, but fails to demonstrate gender-based anticipatory attention. Layer-wise analysis indicates that the middle layers of the model are more related to predictive attention than the early or late layers. This study is pioneering in applying psycholinguistic paradigms to compare the multimodal predictive attention of humans and MLLMs, revealing both similarities and differences between them.

1 Introduction

Recent psycholinguistic research has shown that human language processing involves multimodal predictions, especially between language and vision (e.g., Altmann & Kamide, 1999; see Huettig et al., 2011, for a review). For instance, numerous visual world paradigm (VWP) studies have demonstrated that when people hear an utterance, they predict upcoming mentions, which direct their looks to the visual objects. For example, in Corps et al. (2022), participants heard a sentence featuring either male or female characters and looked at the visual display of four objects at the same time (Figure 1). They found that: (1) participants used

Figure 1: Sample visual display adapted from Corps et al. (2022)

verb semantics to predict upcoming mentions (e. g., looking at wearable objects such as a tie or dress at hearing *Tonight, James/Kate will wear ...*); (2) they further used the gender of the subject to refine their prediction (e.g., more looks to a tie than a dress following *James*, and more looks to a dress than a tie following *Kate*).

The finding that humans use linguistic (verb and gender) information to make predictive fixations of a visual scene led us to ask whether LLAVA (Liu et al., 2023), a multimodal large language model (MLLM), exhibits similar cross-modal predictive behaviors. Previous studies have found parallels between model attention weights and human attention (measured by eye-tracking movements) in text reading (Gao et al., 2023; Kewenig et al., 2024; Sood et al., 2020). Kewenig et al. (2024) recently provided tentative evidence that multimodal models like CLIP (Radford et al., 2021) may also resemble human predictive visual attention in video viewing. However, there is a gap in our understanding of whether MLLMs like LLAVA can predictively "look at" a target object

* Joint first authors.

Proceedings of the 28th Conference on Computational Natural Language Learning, pages 435–441
November 15-16, 2024 ©2024 Association for Computational Linguistics

(e.g., a wearable object like "dress") upon encountering relevant linguistic cues (e.g., the verb "wear") before the object is explicitly mentioned.

The current study employs the widely adopted VWP in psycholinguistics to investigate whether LLAVA, an open-source MLLM, shows similar linguistically-guided predictive visual attention as humans. By analyzing the model's attention weight distribution on the task used by Corps et al. (2022), we found that LLAVA can predictively attend to relevant objects based on verb information, similar to humans, but not gender information. In addition, layer-wise analysis shows that the middle layers of LLAVA are primarily responsible for the predictions. These findings indicate both similarities and differences between the model and humans in multimodal predictions.

2 Methods

2.1 Design and materials

Our study adapted the materials and experimental design of Corps et al. (2022). We used 28 pairs of sentences featuring either male or female characters (e.g., *Tonight, James/Kate will wear the nice tie/dress*), each with a visual display of four objects (Figure 1). We tested whether LLAVA can predictively attend to a visual object according to whether the object is verb-congruent (e.g., dress and tie for the verb *wear*) or verb-incongruent (e.g., drill and hairdryer), and whether this prediction (if any) is further modulated by the object's congruency with the gender of the sentential subject (e.g., for *James*, tie and drill are gender-congruent and dress and hairdryer are gender-incongruent; for *Kate*, the conditions are reversed). The object images are 200×200 pixels, with their locations counterbalanced across items.

2.2 Model

We utilized LLAVA 1.5 (7B parameters, Liu et al., 2023), a transformer-based MLLM that encodes images using CLIP's vision encoder and maps them into the linguistic embedding space of Vicuna (Chiang et al., 2023), allowing cross-modal attention to be computed. This model was chosen for its open-source availability and its state-of-the-art performance on 11 benchmarks (Liu et al., 2023).

2.3 Pre-tests

We first conducted three pre-tests to explore if LLAVA can recognize the basic information in sentences and pictures as humans do.

(1) Name gender detection. To investigate if the model can distinguish gender based on names (*James* vs. *Kate*), we asked the model to continue a sentence preamble (e.g., *Although James/Kate was sick...)* and calculated the proportions of female (*she/her/hers*) or male pronouns (*he/his*) used in the continuations following Cai et al. (2023, experiment 2). We found that all sentences with *James* were continued with male pronouns and all sentences with *Kate* were continued with female pronouns. This indicates that the model can perfectly distinguish between typical male and female names in sentences.

(2) Object gender evaluation. To assess whether the model can identify pictured objects as stereotypically male (e.g., tie, drill) or female (e.g., dress, hairdryer), we asked the model to evaluate the masculinity or femininity of each object on a 5-point Likert scale and calculated the "femininity score" of each object where 1 represents strongly masculine and 5 represents strongly feminine. The results show that the femininity score of stereotypically female objects is significantly higher than that of stereotypically male objects (3.13 vs. 2.67; $t(5641.6) = 11.20$, $p < .001$), indicating that the model can identify the stereotypical gender associations of the objects.

(3) Multimodal sentence completion. To examine whether the model can complete the sentence with verb-and-gender-congruent nouns in a multimodal setting, we removed the final noun from the sentence and asked the model to complete the fragments according to the sentence's corresponding visual display. As shown in Figure 4 in Appendix A, the model produced more verb-congruent completions than incongruent ones (83.77 vs. 12.52; $t(109.29) = -11.84$, $p < .001$), and also more gender-congruent completions than incongruent ones (64.61 vs. 29.52; $t(109.83) = -4.28$, $p < .001$). This indicates that the model can predict verb-and-gender-congruent nouns in a multimodal sentence completion task.

2.4 Procedure

To simulate human incremental sentence comprehension, we presented the sentence in an unfolding fashion, ending first with the name (e.g., *Tonight, James/Kate*), then with the verb (e.g., *Tonight, James/Kate will wear*), then with the pre-noun adjective (e.g., *Tonight, James/Kate will wear the nice*), and finally the whole sentence ending with the target noun (e.g., *Tonight, James/Kate will wear the nice tie/dress*). Each text presentation was accompanied by the same visual display of four objects. We used the prompt: "Please read carefully and look at the objects in the picture," which mirrors the instructions given to human participants, ensuring that the model's task closely parallels the one performed by human subjects.

3 Analyses and results

3.1 Analysis

We extracted the max-pooled attention weights of each layer mapping from the last word (name, verb, pre-noun adjective, or target noun) of each sentence segment to the four images in the visual display. Following Manning et al. (2020), if the last word had multiple tokens, we combined the weights across the tokens. We then calculated the proportion of attention allocated to each object relative to the total attention across all four objects, similar to fixation proportions in VWP studies (e.g., Corps et al., 2022).

For statistical analysis, we used linear mixed-effect models, with attention proportion as dependent variable, verb congruency and gender congruency as independent variables. For the whole-model analysis, we included both layer and item as random effects. In the layer-wise analysis, only item was treated as a random effect. Following Matuschek et al. (2017), we used forward model comparison with an alpha level of 0.2 to determine whether a random slope should be included in the final model.

3.2 Results

3.2.1 Main results of the whole model

Figure 2 (top panel) shows the attention proportions to four objects across sentence segments. Initially, when the name was read, LLAVA showed no preference for gender-congruent objects (β = 0.00, *SE* = 0.00, t = 0.33, p = 0.744), suggesting that the model did not associate specific objects with the gendered name in the absence of further contextual information.

As the sentence unfolded to the verb (e.g., *wear*), there is a significant preference for verb-congruent objects (e.g., tie and dress) over incongruent ones (e.g., drill and hairdryer; β = 0.01, *SE* = 0.00, t = 4.17, p < .001), indicating that LLAVA can use verb

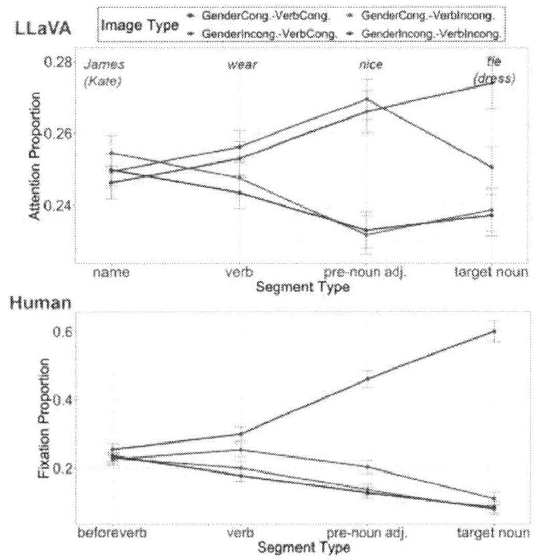

Figure 2: Compare attention proportion of LLAVA (top panel) and fixation proportion of humans (bottom panel; data from Corps et al., 2022)

semantics to direct attention similar to humans. Nevertheless, there was still no effect of gender congruency (β = 0.00, *SE* = 0.00, t = 0.19, p = .852), suggesting that the model still does not preferentially attend to gender-congruent objects at this stage.

As the model received more input (e.g., *Tonight, James/Kate will wear the nice* ...), the difference between verb-congruent and verb-incongruent objects remained (β = 0.04, *SE* = 0.00, t = 8.60, p < .001) and the absence of a gender congruency effect persisted (β = -0.00, *SE* = 0.00, t =- 0.86, p = .389).

Finally, when the sentence was fully presented , the pattern remained unchanged, with a significant effect of verb congruency (β = 0.02, *SE* = 0.00, t = 9.49, p < .001), but no evidence of a gender congruency effect (β = 0.01, *SE* = 0.02, t = 0.64, p = .527).

We compared LLAVA's attention with human eye fixation data in Corps et al. (2022) (see Appendix B for detailed methods). During the prediction window (verb and adjective before noun), we found a significant difference between humans and LLAVA in gender-specific attention (β = -0.59, *SE* = 0.18, t = -3.20, p < .001), but not in verb-related attention (β = 0.30, *SE* = 0.18, t = -1.66, p = .098). This is because humans predictively attended to both verb-relevant (β = 0.09, *SE* = 0.01, t = 9.11, p < .001) and gender-relevant objects (β = 0.03, *SE* = 0.02, t = 2.15, p = 0.040), while LLAVA only predictively attended to verb-relevant objects.

3.2.2 Results of layer-wise analysis

In addition to analyzing the overall behavior of the model across all layers, we conducted a more fine-grained, layer-wise analysis to identify the layers that were primarily responsible for the verb-based predictive visual attention in LLAVA. As shown in Figure 3, our results indicate that the middle layers of the model play a crucial role in generating visual predictions based on verb information.

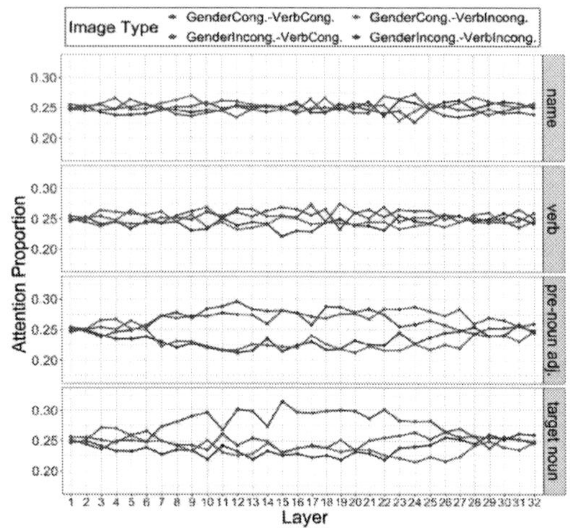

Figure 3: Attention results by layers

During the verb segment of the sentence (e.g., *James/Kate will wear*), we found a significant main effect of verb ($ps < .05$) in layers 10, 12, and 17 (see the second panel in Figure 3). As the sentence unfolds (e.g., *James/Kate will wear the nice*), the main effect of verb becomes more widespread, occurring in layers 7 through 26 ($ps < .05$, see the third panel in Figure 3). This indicates that a larger portion of the model's architecture is engaged in verb-based predictions as more linguistic context becomes available.

4 Discussion

This study uses the VWP to investigate the predictive capabilities of LLAVA, a specific MLLM. The findings reveal that the model exhibits human-like behavior in using verb information to predict the upcoming object in a visual display. This aligns with previous research demonstrating that both humans and models can utilize multimodal information to predictively attend to relevant features (Kewenig et al., 2024).

However, unlike humans, the model does not predictively attend to relevant objects based on gender information, consistent with the lack of gender bias in CLIP, which is the basis for LLAVA's vision encoder (Hall et al., 2024; Radford et al., 2021). However, attributing this lack of gender prediction solely to CLIP's characteristics requires further investigation. Future studies should conduct more fine-grained comparisons between unimodal (text-only) and multimodal models to isolate the source of this behavior and better understand the interplay between linguistic and visual information in gender-based predictions.

The difference between the model and humans may be explained by the nature of the stimuli, as our study used cartoon-like images while LLAVA is mainly trained and evaluated on real-world objects (Liu et al., 2023; Thrush et al., 2022). To investigate this hypothesis, we replaced the cartoon-like objects with real-world ones. As shown in Figure 7 in Appendix C, we observed a main effect of gender in the verb segment ($\beta = 0.01$, $SE = 0.00$, $t = 4.12$, $p < .001$), suggesting that the model processes real-world objects in a more human-like way than cartoon objects. This is consistent with the idea that models lack the perceptual flexibility of humans, leading to lower performance in recognizing atypical objects (Zang et al., 2023).

The study also found that the middle layers play a significant role in multimodal predictions, aligning with previous studies showing that attention weights in middle layers better fit neural signals (Lamarre et al., 2022). However, the discrepancy with some studies showing that late layers correlate most significantly with human eye-tracking data (Kewenig et al., 2024) may be attributed to task differences: comprehension tasks (as in our and Lamarre et al.'s studies) require more high-level semantic processing in middle layers, while production tasks (as in Kewenig et al., 2024) focus more on low-level features of individual words in later layers. Further detailed experiments are needed to explore this hypothesis.

5 Conclusion

In conclusion, our study utilizes the VWP from psycholinguistics to probe whether LLAVA shows similar multimodal predictive patterns to humans. We found that LLAVA can predictively attend to verb-relevant objects in visual displays similar to humans, but they do not show the same predictive attention for gender-relevant objects. These verb-related predictive behaviors are predominantly driven by the middle layers of the model.

Limitations

This study has several limitations that should be addressed in future research. Firstly, we investigated only one model — LLAVA-1.5 7B — and conducted a thorough comparison between its attention weights and human eye movements. With more MLLMs being released (see Yin et al., 2024 for a comprehensive review), it is crucial to compare different models horizontally to understand the key factors contributing to their differences and similarities with human cognition.

Secondly, our study lacks image variation due to our adherence to Corps et al. (2022)'s experimental design, as noted by an anonymous reviewer. Although we conducted complementary tests with real-world objects, future research should incorporate systematic image variations to thoroughly explore how image type influences LLAVA's predictions.

Lastly, caution is needed when comparing human and model attention. Although both use the term "attention," they may refer to different underlying mechanisms. For instance, model attention is more evenly dispersed, while human attention tends to be focused (Kewenig et al., 2024; also see Figure 2). More detailed studies are needed to explore the similarities and differences between model attention mechanism and human attention.

Ethical considerations

The authors declare no competing interests. The stimuli used are provided by the first author of Corps et al. (2022) via email. The human eye-tracking data used is publicly available (https://osf.io/nkud5/) and does not contain personal information about the subjects. The usage scenario of the model LLAVA conforms to its licensing terms. As this work focuses on comparing the multimodal predictions of models and humans, its potential negative impacts on society seem to be minimal.

Acknowledgments

We acknowledge Corps for generously sharing the stimuli of their study; We acknowledge Chi Fong Wong and Shixuan Li for helping with coding.

References

Gerry TM Altmann and Yuki Kamide. 1999. Incremental interpretation at verbs: Restricting the domain of subsequent reference. *Cognition*, 73(3):247–264.

Zhenguang G. Cai, David A. Haslett, Xufeng Duan, Shuqi Wang, and Martin J. Pickering. 2023. Does ChatGPT resemble humans in language use? *arXiv preprint* arXiv:2303.08014 [cs]. Version 2.

Wei-Lin Chiang, Zhuohan Li, Zi Lin, Ying Sheng, Zhanghao Wu, Hao Zhang, Lianmin Zheng, Siyuan Zhuang, Yonghao Zhuang, and Joseph E. Gonzalez. 2023. Vicuna: An open-source chatbot impressing gpt-4 with 90%* chatgpt quality. (accessed 14 April 2023), 2(3):6.

Ruth E. Corps, Charlotte Brooke, and Martin J. Pickering. 2022. Prediction involves two stages: Evidence from visual-world eye-tracking. *Journal of Memory and Language*, 122:104298.

Changjiang Gao, Shujian Huang, Jixing Li, and Jiajun Chen. 2023. Roles of Scaling and Instruction Tuning in Language Perception: Model vs. Human Attention. In *Findings of the Association for Computational Linguistics: EMNLP 2023*, pages 13042–13055, Singapore. Association for Computational Linguistics.

Siobhan Mackenzie Hall, Fernanda Gonçalves Abrantes, Hanwen Zhu, Grace Sodunke, Aleksandar Shtedritski, and Hannah Rose Kirk. 2023. Visogender: A dataset for benchmarking gender bias in image-text pronoun resolution. Advances in Neural Information Processing Systems 36 (NeurIPS 2023).

Falk Huettig, Joost Rommers, and Antje S. Meyer. 2011. Using the visual world paradigm to study language processing: A review and critical evaluation. *Acta psychologica*, 137(2):151–171.

Yuki Kamide, Gerry TM Altmann, and Sarah L. Haywood. 2003. The time-course of prediction in incremental sentence processing: Evidence from anticipatory eye movements. *Journal of Memory and language*, 49(1):133–156.

Viktor Kewenig, Andrew Lampinen, Samuel A. Nastase, Christopher Edwards, Quitterie Lacome DEstalenx, Akilles Rechardt, Jeremy I. Skipper, and Gabriella Vigliocco. 2024. Multimodality and Attention Increase Alignment in Natural Language Prediction Between Humans and Computational Models. *arXiv preprint* arXiv:2308.06035 [cs]. Version 3.

Mathis Lamarre, Catherine Chen, and Fatma Deniz. 2022. Attention weights accurately predict language representations in the brain. In *Findings of the Association for Computational Linguistics:*

EMNLP 2022, pages 4513–4529. Abu Dhabi, United Arab Emirates. Association for Computational Linguistics.

Haotian Liu, Chunyuan Li, Yuheng Li, and Yong Jae Lee. 2023a. Improved Baselines with Visual Instruction Tuning. *arXiv preprint* arXiv: 2310.03744 [cs].

Christopher D. Manning, Kevin Clark, John Hewitt, Urvashi Khandelwal, and Omer Levy. 2020. Emergent linguistic structure in artificial neural networks trained by self-supervision. *Proceedings of the National Academy of Sciences*, 117(48):30046–30054.

Hannes Matuschek, Reinhold Kliegl, Shravan Vasishth, Harald Baayen, and Douglas Bates. 2017. Balancing Type I error and power in linear mixed models. *Journal of memory and language*, 94:305–315.

Martin J. Pickering and Chiara Gambi. 2018. Predicting while comprehending language: A theory and review. *Psychological Bulletin*, 144(10):1002–1044. 113.

Alec Radford, Jong Wook Kim, Chris Hallacy, Aditya Ramesh, Gabriel Goh, Sandhini Agarwal, Girish Sastry, Amanda Askell, Pamela Mishkin, Jack Clark, Gretchen Krueger, and Ilya Sutskever. 2021.Learning Transferable Visual Models From Natural Language Supervision. In *Proceedings of the 38th International Conference on Machine Learning, PMLR 139.*

Ekta Sood, Simon Tannert, Diego Frassinelli, Andreas Bulling, and Ngoc Thang Vu. 2020. Interpreting Attention Models with Human Visual Attention in Machine Reading Comprehension. In Raquel Fernández and Tal Linzen, editors, *Proceedings of the 24th Conference on Computational Natural Language Learning*, pages 12–25, Online. Association for Computational Linguistics.

Tristan Thrush, Ryan Jiang, Max Bartolo, Amanpreet Singh, Adina Williams, Douwe Kiela, and Candace Ross. 2022. Winoground: Probing vision and language models for visio-linguistic compositionality. In *Proceedings of the IEEE/CVF Conference on Computer Vision and Pattern Recognition*, pages 5238–5248.

Shukang Yin, Chaoyou Fu, Sirui Zhao, Ke Li, Xing Sun, Tong Xu, and Enhong Chen. 2024. A Survey on Multimodal Large Language Models. *arXiv preprint* arXiv:2306.13549 [cs].

Yuhang Zang, Wei Li, Jun Han, Kaiyang Zhou, and Chen Change Loy. 2023. Contextual Object Detection with Multimodal Large Language Models. *arXiv preprint* arXiv:2305.18279 [cs].

A Prompts and results of pre-tests

(1) Name gender detection. The prompt is: "Repeat the sentence preamble and continue it into a full sentence. Use just one sentence. Here is the sentence:"

(2) Object gender evaluation. For half of the runs, the prompt is: "Evaluate the masculinity or femininity of the object, activity, or job depicted in the picture. Use the following scale: 1 = strongly masculine, 2 = moderately masculine, 3 = neutral, 4 = moderately feminine, 5 = strongly feminine. Only respond with a number." For the other half, the location of "feminine" and "masculine" is exchanged.

(3) Multimodal sentence completion. The prompt is: "Please carefully read the beginning of the sentence and examine the objects in the picture. The sentence will mention one of the four objects. Complete the sentence with one or two words based on the objects you see. Don't repeat the sentence. Only provide your answer."

The results of this test are shown in Figure 4.

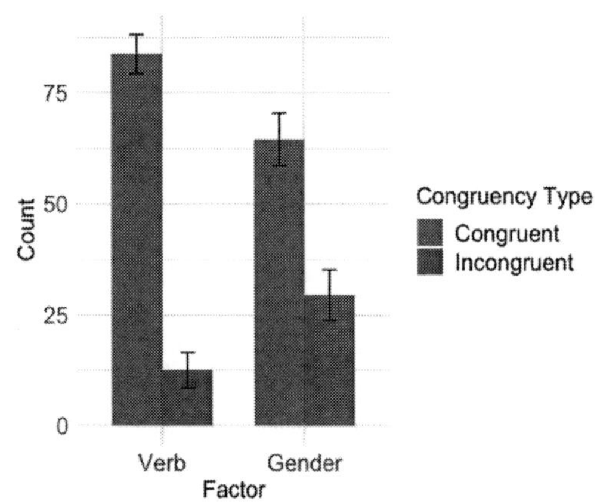

Figure 4: Results of sentence completion task

B Compare with human data

Since eye movement data in Corps et al. (2022, accessible at https://osf.io/nkud5) were analyzed at 50ms intervals, we need to transform the data into four segments to align with the model data. According to the R scripts available at https://osf.io/nkud5/, the four segments are defined as follows:

- Before verb: < 0ms (before verb onset)
- Verb: 0-350ms (from verb onset to verb offset)

- Pre-noun adjective: 350-850ms (from verb offset to target onset)
- Target: >850ms (after target onset)

Within each segment, we aggregated fixation points and calculated the fixation proportion of each object. These aggregated data were then used for further analysis and plotting. This transformation ensures the human data is comparable with the model data. From Figure 5, we can observe that the reshaped data exhibit a similar pattern to the original data.

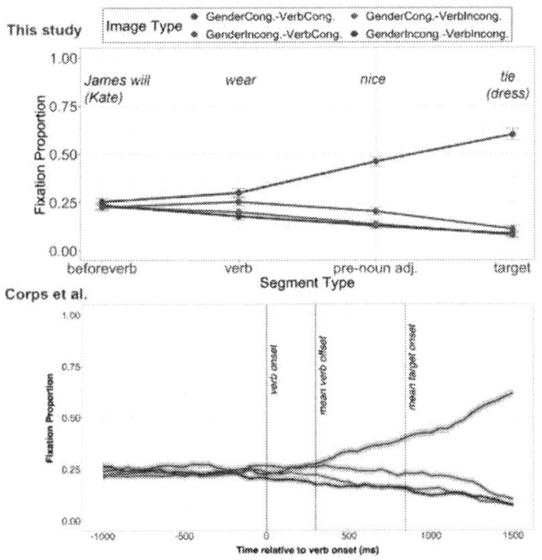

Figure 5: Compare plots of humans in our study (top panel) and Corps et al. (2022, bottom panel)

C Attention to real-world objects

For each object picture in the stimuli, we search for a similar picture in Google Images (the same source as Corps et al., 2022) but with a real-world object. We replaced each object picture with the new real-world one and conducted the experiment again. The results are shown as in. Figure 6 provides an example of the real-world images used in this follow-up study. The outcomes of this complementary experiment are presented in Figure 7.

Figure 6: Sample of visual display with real-world objects

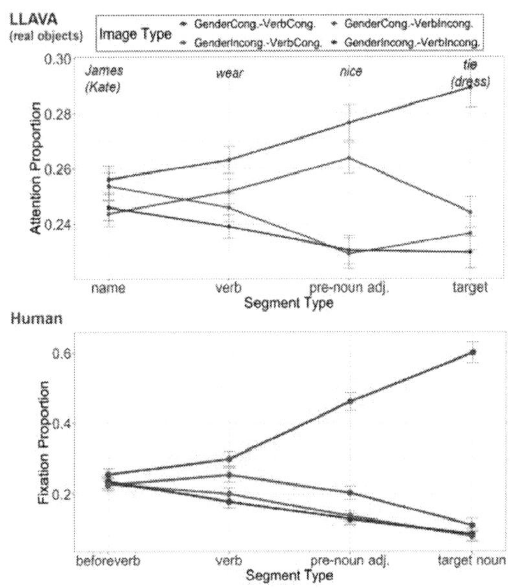

Figure 7: Compare model attention proportions using real-world stimuli in LLAVA (top) and fixation proportions of humans (bottom)

PRAct: Optimizing Principled Reasoning and Acting of LLM Agent

Zhiwei Liu[*], Weiran Yao[†], Jianguo Zhang, Rithesh Murthy, Liangwei Yang, Zuxin Liu, Tian Lan, Ming Zhu, Juntao Tan, Shirley Kokane, Thai Hoang, Juan Carlos Niebles, Shelby Heinecke, Huan Wang, Silvio Savarese and **Caiming Xiong**
Salesforce AI Research, USA

Abstract

We introduce the Principled Reasoning and Acting (PRAct) framework, a novel method for learning and enforcing action principles from trajectory data. Central to our approach is the use of text gradients from a reflection and optimization engine to derive these action principles. To adapt action principles to specific task requirements, we propose a new optimization framework, Reflective Principle Optimization (RPO). After execution, RPO employs a reflector to critique current action principles and an optimizer to update them accordingly. We develop the RPO framework under two scenarios: Reward-RPO, which uses environmental rewards for reflection, and Self-RPO, which conducts self-reflection without external rewards. Additionally, two RPO methods, RPO-Traj and RPO-Batch, is introduced to adapt to different settings. Experimental results across four environments demonstrate that the PRAct agent, leveraging the RPO framework, effectively learns and applies action principles to enhance performance.

1 Introduction

Large language model (LLM) agents enable the action execution (Gravitas, 2023; Goodman, 2023; Yao et al., 2023a; Wang et al., 2023a) and consecutive reasoning ability (Nakajima, 2023; Shinn et al., 2023; Yao et al., 2023b) of LLM. Specifically, an LLM agent has both memory (Shinn et al., 2023; Li et al., 2023; Liu et al., 2024) and action space (Chase, 2023; Wu et al., 2023; Liu et al., 2023). Adding those information into prompt extends the inference of LLM to be multi-turn action execution. Therefore, an LLM agent is able to decide next actions based on its previous execution observations (Wang et al., 2023b; Xu et al., 2023; Goodman, 2023; Song et al., 2023).

[*]zhiweiliu@salesforce.com
[†]Equal contribution.

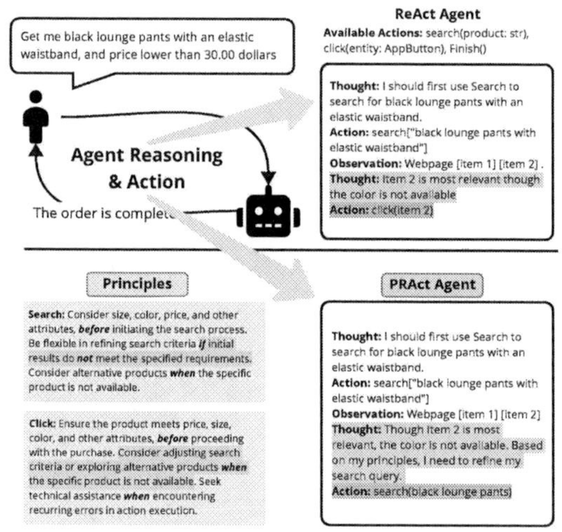

Figure 1: Comparison of ReAct and PRAct agents.

Optimizing the reasoning framework (Yao et al., 2023a; Liu et al., 2023; Wang et al., 2023b) of agent is crucial in generating correct action execution. As of now, customizing an LLM agent with existing open-source packages (Liu et al., 2024; Wu et al., 2023; Chase, 2023; Liu, 2022) requires the designing of action spaces, such as function calls (Patil et al., 2023) and code execution (Wu et al., 2023, 2024). Along with a well-designed agent reasoning framework, i.e. the prompts of agent, an LLM is able to consecutively generate correct actions. ReAct (Yao et al., 2023a) framework achieves wide successes via adding one-step *think* actions to enhance the reasoning ability of an agent. Additionally, Reflection (Shinn et al., 2023; Yao et al., 2023b; Paul et al., 2023) mechanism is proposed to improve the agent self-correction capability. *Plan* (Xu et al., 2023; Liu et al., 2023) before execution is also verified to be beneficial.

Despite many successes, agent execution can fail to make decisions when faced with contradictory observations, particularly during the execution of long-step tasks. To address it, we propose a new

Proceedings of the 28th Conference on Computational Natural Language Learning, pages 442–446
November 15-16, 2024 ©2024 Association for Computational Linguistics

type of reasoning strategy, *PRAct*, for the LLM agent. Intuitively, we associate each action with principles that describe the conditions for using that action. During execution, an agent can check these principles before generating the next action. Compared to simple action descriptions, principles provide more detailed conditions on when to use the action and offer specific instructions on how to generate the parameters for an action. We demonstrate the benefits of PRAct in Figure 1 via comparing with ReAct agent in WebShop (Yao et al., 2022) where an agent uses search and click actions to interact with a shopping website. The ReAct agent searches a query and, despite item 2 not having the available color, still clicks it as it appears most relevant. In contrast, the PRAct agent refines the search based on both search and click principles. Consequently, the PRAct agent decides to search with an improved query, enhancing its decision-making process.

To reduce the labor involved in prompt design and to cover more complex scenarios, we propose a new principle optimization framework, Reflective Principle Optimization (RPO). RPO operates in three stages: execution, reflection, and optimization. During the execution stage, an agent performs tasks using predefined or null principles and memorizes the task trajectories. In the reflection stage, the agent reviews its task executions, evaluating how actions were selected and whether they met the task requirements. Finally, in the optimization stage, an optimizer refines principles to enhance agent performance. We investigate two optimization methods: RPO-Traj, which individually optimizes principles for each trajectory, and RPO-Batch, which concatenates all reflections in a batch for optimization.

We summarize our contributions as follows: 1) PRAct is the first work that considers the action principles for LLM agent; 2) we propose two optimization methods to adapt the principles to tasks.

2 PRAct: Optimizing Principled Reasoning and Acting

2.1 Formulation

Given a task query, an agent is able to consecutively execute actions $[a_1, a_2, \ldots, a_n]$ and collects observations $[o_1, o_2, \ldots, o_n]$ from environments, where o_i is the execution results of a_i. A policy function $\pi(a_t|c_t)$ predicts the next action a_t given the execution trajectory context $c_t = [(a_1, o_1), (a_2, o_2), \ldots, (a_{t-1}, o_{t-1})]$. An Executor agent utilizes a language model to determine the policy function. It requires textual trajectory information for the prompt Intrinsically, those context information are text-based, including action names, action parameters and observations.

PRAct constraints the reasoning of LLM to follow a set of principles $\mathcal{P}$ as follows:

$$\pi(a_t|c_t) = \text{Executor}(a_t|\mathcal{T}(c_t); \mathcal{P}), \quad (1)$$

where $\mathcal{T}$ is the prompt template to organize context information and the principles $\mathcal{P}$ are guidelines that help shape the decision-making process of an LLM agent. Principles provide instructions on the usage of the action such as how to generate parameters for the action. Additionally, principles reduce the set of potential actions by eliminating those that do not conform to the defined guidelines, thereby narrowing the search within the action space. In this paper, we simplify the principles space to be the same as actions space, *i.e.* each $a_i \in \mathcal{A}$ associated with a $p_i \in \mathcal{P}$.

2.2 Reflective Principle Optimization (RPO)

Although the principles could be predetermined, as in the action descriptions, it is challenging to comprehensively cover all possible conditions without an automatic optimization paradigm. Therefore, we propose a new algorithm, Reflective Principle Optimization (RPO), to adapt principles for complex scenarios. RPO operates in three stages: 1) Execution, 2) Reflection, and 3) Optimization.

2.2.1 Execution

Given a set of tasks, the executor agent performs actions based on the current set of principles, collecting observations from the environment. This stage involves prompting the LLM agent to generate actions, which regressively calls Eq. (2) until reaching the final actions or maximum steps. Given a task query q, we denote the trajectory as $c_q = [(a_q^{(1)}, o_q^{(1)}), (a_q^{(2)}, o_q^{(2)}), \cdot, (a_q^{(n)}, o_q^{(n)})]$. Note that those actions may be some inner actions, such as *think* or *plan* (Yao et al., 2023a; Liu et al., 2024) , which do not forward to the environment and are associated with a default or null observation. Executor collects a set of trajectory context sequences $\mathcal{C}$ for those queries $\mathcal{Q}$ during execution stage.

2.2.2 Self-Reflection

After executing the actions, a reflector agent reflects on trajectories $\mathcal{C}$ by analyzing the collected

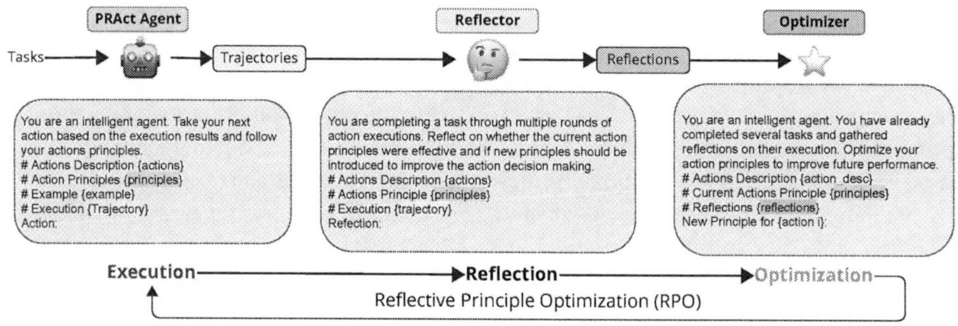

Figure 2: **PRAct and RPO overview.** Each iteration three stages: execution, reflection and optimization. During execution, an agent executes tasks with previous principles. The trajectories are saved. Then, the agent reflects on those tasks executions. Finally, the agent leverages those self-reflection results to optimize the principle.

Table 1: Overall comparison results. **Bold** denotes the best performance.

	GPT-3.5-turbo				GPT-4-turbo			
	WebShop	Academia	Movie	Weather	WebShop	Academia	Movie	Weather
Act	0.4542	0.5304	0.5483	0.5869	0.5257	0.6704	0.5875	0.6882
ReAct	0.4742	0.5504	0.5416	0.5973	0.5667	0.7428	0.5583	0.6990
Reflexion	0.5539	0.6024	0.5728	0.5876	0.5723	0.7796	0.6072	0.7197
ExpeL	0.5823	0.6318	0.6215	0.6475	0.6329	0.8084	0.6847	0.7583
PRAct-T	**0.6012**	0.6798	0.6595	0.6953	0.6323	**0.9207**	0.7132	0.7796
PRAct-B	0.5904	**0.7396**	**0.6625**	**0.7042**	**0.6413**	0.8254	**0.7250**	**0.8331**

observations. This stage involves evaluating the effectiveness of the actions in each trajectory and the adherence to the principles as follows:

$$r_q = \text{REFLECTOR}(c_q, \mathcal{P}), \tag{2}$$

for all $c_q \in \mathcal{C}$. The reflection process identifies conditions or guidelines where the principles need adjustment to better handle the observed tasks. If an environment provides rewards toward the execution, it is a reward-based reflector aligning the executions with reward feedback. Instead, if no rewards present for execution, it is a self-reflector.

2.2.3 Optimization

Based on the reflection results, we leverage the generation ability of LLM to refine the principles for improving the performance of agent in similar future scenarios. This stage involves refining the principles to better align with the observed conditions and enhance decision-making. We investigate two types of optimization methods.

RPO-Traj. This approach individually considers each trajectory and its reflection to optimize principles. Then a batch of principles are summarized as a new set of tailored principles $\mathcal{P}^*$. We formulate RPO-Traj as follows:

$$\mathcal{P}^* = \sum_{\mathcal{Q}} \text{OPT}(r_q, \mathcal{P}), \tag{3}$$

where $\sum_{\mathcal{Q}}$ denotes a summarizor of all principles generated from optimizer OPT for all queries $\mathcal{Q}$.

RPO-Batch. We use a prompt template to concatenate all the reflections in a batch. Then the optimizer directly generates new principles via considering all those reflections, which is formulated as follows:

$$\mathcal{P}^* = \text{OPT}(\text{CONCAT}\{r_q | q \in \mathcal{Q}\}, \mathcal{P}), \tag{4}$$

where CONCAT denotes using a prompt template to concat those reflections. In comparison, RPO-Traj requires generating principles for $|Q|+1$ times, while RPO-Batch only needs one time principles generation but with $|Q|$ times longer context length. Hence, long context reasoning ability is necessary for an optimizer in RPO-Batch method.

3 Experiment

3.1 Experiment Setup

Baselines. We compare our PRAct agent with existing Act, ReAct (Yao et al., 2023a), Reflexion (Shinn et al., 2023) agent reasoning methods and Expel (Zhao et al., 2024) prompt optimization framework. In this paper, we employ GPT-3.5-Turbo-0125 and GPT-4-Turbo-2024-04-09 (OpenAI, 2023) as two foundation LLMs. And for simplicity, the executor, reflector and optimizer in PRAct are of the same language model.

Benchmarks and Evaluation. Following AgentBoard (Ma et al., 2024), we evaluate PRAct agent on three tool environments and one WebShop environment. Tool environments support the designing of WEATHER, MOVIE, and ACADEMIA agents. Tasks are 60 queries and actions are a set of function calls. The reward score is the recall of ground truth actions. Webshop environment is a web browser simulation. Agent performs either *search* and *click* actions to complete 251 online shopping tasks. Reward is attributes coverage ratio between final shopped items and ground truth item.

3.2 Optimization setup

For optimizing the WebShop agent with a Reward-based reflector, we randomly split the query tasks into training, validation, and test tasks with a ratio of 3:1:1. During each training step, we sample a batch of training tasks to execute and use RPO to optimize the principles. Performance on validation tasks is used for early stopping, and results are reported on test tasks. For tool agents, we use a self-reflector without rewards, making reflection tasks the same as test tasks. Since there is no ground truth, no data leakage problem exists. We tune the training batch size in [10,20,40] for WebShop and [2,4,6] for tool environments.

3.3 Experiment Results

Overall Performance. We present comprehensive comparisons of our methods against the agent baselines in Table 1. PRAct-T and PRAct-B are our methods with RPO-Traj and RPO-Batch optimization methods, respectively. We observe consistently better performance of PRAct agent, which demonstrates the effectiveness of principles in improving agent performance. Between the two optimization methods, *i.e.* PRAct-T and PRAct-B, PRAct-B generally performs better than PRAct-T. The reason is that summarizing principles from a batch of reflections enables potential reasoning across trajectories. However, PRAct-T outperforms PRAct-B due to the potential weaker long context understanding ability of GPT-3.5-Turbo, which indicates batch-wise optimization is more suitable for larger models.

Reflector	GPT-3.5	GPT-4
Self-T	0.5871	0.6172
Self-B	0.5763	0.6238
Reward-T	**0.6012**	0.6323
Reward-B	0.5904	**0.6413**

Table 2: Different reflectors of PRAct. *Self* and *Reward* stand for self and reward-based reflectors, respectively. T and B denote RPO-Traj and RPO-Batch, respectively.

An additional variant is *PRAct with self-reflector* on Webshop. We compare it on both RPO-T and RPO-B optimization methods, and report the results in Table 2. Compared with both results, reward-based reflector, demonstrates its superiority in optimizing principles with rewards.

Optimization Curve. We present the training curves in Fig. 3. Although at each step, we did not pick the best principle out of the sampled action principles on the validation set, we still observe consistent improvement over time. Notably, with action principles optimized by PRAct, LLM agents under GPT-3.5-Turbo can match the performance of GPT-4-turbo in Webshop environment.

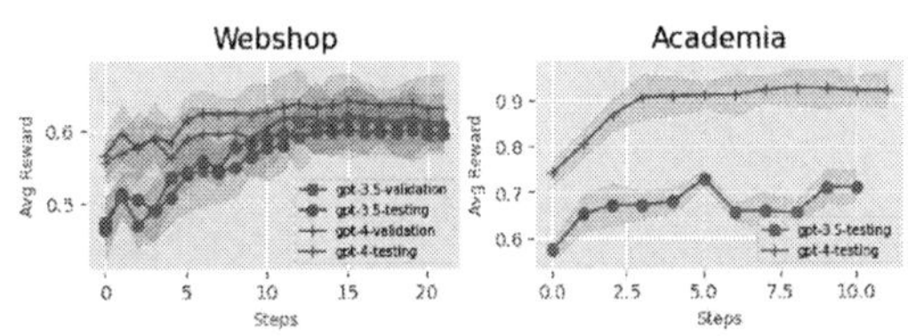

Figure 3: Training curves in Webshop and Academia with different LLMs and data splits. The reported scores are the average across 5 random seeds.

4 Conclusion

We propose a novel agent reasoning framework, PRAct, which provides principles of actions and thus benefits the action understanding of agent. Besides, we introduce two optimization algorithm, RPO-Traj and RPO-Batch for adapting the action principles with task executions. Experimental results on four environments demonstrates the effectiveness of PRAct framework. And the training curve illustrates the learning efficacy of RPO. In conclusion, PRAct opens a new discussion on how to regularize the agent actions while RPO shades the light on how to optimize the agent prompts.

References

Harrison Chase. 2023. Langchain. https://github.com/hwchase17/langchain.

Noah Goodman. 2023. Meta-prompt: A simple self-improving language agent. *noahgoodman.substack.com.*

Significant Gravitas. 2023. Autogpt. https://github.com/Significant-Gravitas/Auto-GPT.

Guohao Li, Hasan Abed Al Kader Hammoud, Hani Itani, Dmitrii Khizbullin, and Bernard Ghanem. 2023. Camel: Communicative agents for "mind" exploration of large language model society. In *Thirty-seventh Conference on Neural Information Processing Systems.*

Jerry Liu. 2022. LlamaIndex.

Zhiwei Liu, Weiran Yao, Jianguo Zhang, Le Xue, Shelby Heinecke, Rithesh Murthy, Yihao Feng, Zeyuan Chen, Juan Carlos Niebles, Devansh Arpit, et al. 2023. Bolaa: Benchmarking and orchestrating llm-augmented autonomous agents. *arXiv preprint arXiv:2308.05960.*

Zhiwei Liu, Weiran Yao, Jianguo Zhang, Liangwei Yang, Zuxin Liu, Juntao Tan, Prafulla K. Choubey, Tian Lan, Jason Wu, Huan Wang, Shelby Heinecke, Caiming Xiong, and Silvio Savarese. 2024. Agentlite: A lightweight library for building and advancing task-oriented llm agent system. *Preprint*, arXiv:2402.15538.

Chang Ma, Junlei Zhang, Zhihao Zhu, Cheng Yang, Yujiu Yang, Yaohui Jin, Zhenzhong Lan, Lingpeng Kong, and Junxian He. 2024. Agentboard: An analytical evaluation board of multi-turn llm agents. *Preprint*, arXiv:2401.13178.

Yohei Nakajima. 2023. Babyagi. https://github.com/yoheinakajima/babyagi.

OpenAI. 2023. Gpt-4 technical report. *ArXiv.*

Shishir G Patil, Tianjun Zhang, Xin Wang, and Joseph E Gonzalez. 2023. Gorilla: Large language model connected with massive apis. *arXiv preprint arXiv:2305.15334.*

Debjit Paul, Mete Ismayilzada, Maxime Peyrard, Beatriz Borges, Antoine Bosselut, Robert West, and Boi Faltings. 2023. Refiner: Reasoning feedback on intermediate representations. *arXiv preprint arXiv:2304.01904.*

Noah Shinn, Federico Cassano, Beck Labash, Ashwin Gopinath, Karthik Narasimhan, and Shunyu Yao. 2023. Reflexion: Language agents with verbal reinforcement learning. *arXiv preprint arXiv:2303.11366.*

Chan Hee Song, Jiaman Wu, Clayton Washington, Brian M Sadler, Wei-Lun Chao, and Yu Su. 2023. Llm-planner: Few-shot grounded planning for embodied agents with large language models. In *Proceedings of the IEEE/CVF International Conference on Computer Vision*, pages 2998–3009.

Lei Wang, Chen Ma, Xueyang Feng, Zeyu Zhang, Hao Yang, Jingsen Zhang, Zhiyuan Chen, Jiakai Tang, Xu Chen, Yankai Lin, et al. 2023a. A survey on large language model based autonomous agents. *arXiv preprint arXiv:2308.11432.*

Yu Wang, Zhiwei Liu, Jianguo Zhang, Weiran Yao, Shelby Heinecke, and Philip S Yu. 2023b. Drdt: Dynamic reflection with divergent thinking for llm-based sequential recommendation. *arXiv preprint arXiv:2312.11336.*

Qingyun Wu, Gagan Bansal, Jieyu Zhang, Yiran Wu, Beibin Li, Erkang Zhu, Li Jiang, Xiaoyun Zhang, Shaokun Zhang, Jiale Liu, Ahmed Hassan Awadallah, Ryen W White, Doug Burger, and Chi Wang. 2023. Autogen: Enabling next-gen llm applications via multi-agent conversation framework.

Yiran Wu, Tianwei Yue, Shaokun Zhang, Chi Wang, and Qingyun Wu. 2024. Stateflow: Enhancing llm task-solving through state-driven workflows. *arXiv preprint arXiv:2403.11322.*

Binfeng Xu, Zhiyuan Peng, Bowen Lei, Subhabrata Mukherjee, Yuchen Liu, and Dongkuan Xu. 2023. Rewoo: Decoupling reasoning from observations for efficient augmented language models. *arXiv preprint arXiv:2305.18323.*

Shunyu Yao, Howard Chen, John Yang, and Karthik Narasimhan. 2022. Webshop: Towards scalable real-world web interaction with grounded language agents. *Advances in Neural Information Processing Systems*, 35:20744–20757.

Shunyu Yao, Jeffrey Zhao, Dian Yu, Nan Du, Izhak Shafran, Karthik Narasimhan, and Yuan Cao. 2023a. ReAct: Synergizing reasoning and acting in language models. In *International Conference on Learning Representations (ICLR).*

Weiran Yao, Shelby Heinecke, Juan Carlos Niebles, Zhiwei Liu, Yihao Feng, Le Xue, Rithesh Murthy, Zeyuan Chen, Jianguo Zhang, Devansh Arpit, Ran Xu, Phil Mui, Huan Wang, Caiming Xiong, and Silvio Savarese. 2023b. Retroformer: Retrospective large language agents with policy gradient optimization. *Preprint*, arXiv:2308.02151.

Andrew Zhao, Daniel Huang, Quentin Xu, Matthieu Lin, Yong-Jin Liu, and Gao Huang. 2024. Expel: Llm agents are experiential learners. In *Thirty-Eighth AAAI Conference on Artificial Intelligence, AAAI 2024, Thirty-Sixth Conference on Innovative Applications of Artificial Intelligence, IAAI 2024, Fourteenth Symposium on Educational Advances in Artificial Intelligence, EAAI 2024, February 20-27, 2024, Vancouver, Canada*, pages 19632–19642. AAAI Press.

Image-conditioned human language comprehension and psychometric benchmarking of visual language models

Subha Nawer Pushpita
Masachusetts Institute of Technology
snpushpi@mit.edu

Roger Levy
Massachusetts Institute of Technology
rplevy@mit.edu

Abstract

Large language model (LLM)s' next-word predictions have shown impressive performance in capturing human expectations during real-time language comprehension. This finding has enabled a line of research on psychometric benchmarking of LLMs against human language-comprehension data in order to reverse-engineer humans' linguistic subjective probability distributions and representations. However, to date this work has exclusively involved unimodal (language-only) comprehension data, whereas much human language use takes place in rich multimodal contexts. Here we extend psychometric benchmarking to visual language models (VLMs). We develop a novel experimental paradigm, *Image-Conditioned Maze Reading*, in which participants first view an image and then read a text describing an image within the Maze paradigm, yielding word-by-word reaction-time measures with high signal-to-noise ratio and good localization of expectation-driven language processing effects. We find a large facilitatory effect of correct image context on language comprehension, not only for words such as concrete nouns that are directly grounded in the image but even for ungrounded words in the image descriptions. Furthermore, we find that VLM surprisal captures most to all of this effect. We used these findings to benchmark a range of VLMs, showing that models with lower perplexity generally have better psychometric performance, but that among the best VLMs tested perplexity and psychometric performance dissociate. Overall, our work offers new possibilities for connecting psycholinguistics with multimodal LLMs for both scientific and engineering goals.

1 Introduction

Human language comprehension is highly incremental. Our minds integrate linguistic input with context very rapidly: words within sentences, and even phonemes or letters within spoken or written words, to update our understanding of linguistic input (Tanenhaus et al., 1995; Rayner, 1998). This process involves the rapid update of expectations about the interpretation of what has already been said and predictions about what might be said next. These predictions affect how we process the language we encounter, helping us to recognize and correct errors (Marslen-Wilson, 1975; Levy, 2008b) and to analyze input more rapidly.

The fundamental operation of large language models (LLMs) is similar: LLMs put probability distributions over the next tokens given the preceding context. This convergence has made it natural to compare LLM distributions with human linguistic behavior. In unimodal language processing, LLM predictions have been shown to align fairly well with those generated by humans in the Cloze task (Goldstein et al., 2022). Furthermore, there is a linear relationship between the surprisal of a word in linguistic context (negative log-probability; (Hale, 2001; Levy, 2008a)) and how long comprehenders take to read it (Smith and Levy., 2013; Wilcox et al., 2023). These findings have generated interest in psychometric benchmarking of language models (LMs): comparing LMs in terms of how well their autoregressive probabilities predict human reading times or other types of linguistic behavior (Frank and Bod, 2011; Fossum and Levy, 2012; Goodkind and Bicknell, 2018; Oh and Schuler, 2023; Shain et al., 2024).

Psychometric benchmarking of LLMs has exclusively involved unimodal, language-only data and models. However, human language use generally involves a rich multimodal context. For this reason, there is growing interest in multimodal language models. The most advanced such type of model is vision-language models (VLMs), which relate visual content (most commonly static images) to linguistic content. For example, models like BLIP-2 (Li et al., 2023) can generate text associated with an image; to do this, it autoregressively places con-

Proceedings of the 28th Conference on Computational Natural Language Learning, pages 447–457
November 15-16, 2024 ©2024 Association for Computational Linguistics

ditional probability distributions over next linguistic tokens given an image in context plus preceding linguistic context. However, evaluation techniques for VLMs are less developed than for unimodal LLMs, and we are aware of no work to date on psychometric benchmarking for VLMs.

Here we present a framework and experimental results on psychometric evaluation of visual language models using a novel yet simple psycholinguistic experimental paradigm. In an experimental trial, a participant first previews an image, then reads a sentence describing an image, with word-by-word reading times measured (Figure 1). The image may be the one that the sentence describes (the **Correct Image** condition), a different image that the sentence does not describe (the **Wrong Image** condition), or simply a black screen (the **No Image** condition). Intuitively, previewing the correct image should prepare the participant for the sentence description and facilitate them reading it more quickly and accurately. However, there are different forms that this facilitation could take, corresponding to different theoretical accounts of how visual context shapes language processing. Additionally, we can compare VLMs in terms of how well they capture how different image contexts influence the participant's reading behavior. We can thus use this experimental paradigm both to gain insight into the role of visual context in language processing in the human mind and to psychometrically benchmark visual language models. All the experiment codes, analysis, and datasets used in the project are made available at the linked repository. [1].

2 Related Work

2.1 Human vision and language processing

There is considerable psycholinguistic literature on the vision-language interface, with emphasis on visual context effects on spoken word recognition, syntactic disambiguation, and predictive processing.Much of this work uses the Visual World Paradigm (VWP), which investigates eye movements in visual scenes during spoken language understanding. Allopenna et al. (1998) and Dahan et al. (2001) used the VWP to demonstrate rapid, fine-grained effects of sub-word phonetic information on word-level interpretations, demonstrating incrementality of spoken language processing at the sub-word level. (Tanenhaus et al., 1995) used the VWP to demonstrate that the language processing system utilizes visual context to quickly interpret an ambiguous prepositional phrase, integrating lexical, syntactic, visual, and pragmatic reasoning. (Altmann and Kamide, 1999) showed how visual context aids predictive processing, supporting the idea that sentence comprehension involves anticipating the relationships between verbs, their syntactic components, and the real-world context they describe. For a broader review see Huettig et al. (2011).

2.2 Psychometric benchmarking of LLMs

It has long been known that words predictable in context are read faster (Ehrlich and Rayner, 1981) and elicit distinctive brain responses (Kutas and Hillyard, 1980; Kutas and Federmeier, 2011). Smith and Levy. (2013) found a linear relationship between n-gram word surprisal (negative log-probability) and reading time, a relationship that has held up with neural language models (Goodkind and Bicknell, 2018; Wilcox et al., 2023) and has been widely used to psychometrically benchmark LLMs (Oh and Schuler, 2023; Shain et al., 2024). There is also some evidence for a linear relationship between surprisal and the N400 ERP response (Heilbron et al., 2022, though see Szewczyk and Federmeier, 2022), and the best alignment of LM internal representations with brain activation patterns during language comprehension seems to be achieved by autoregressive LM architectures (Schrimpf et al., 2021; Caucheteux and King, 2022; Antonello et al., 2023). These results raise the prospect of reverse-engineering human subjective probabilities active during language processing through psychometric LLM benchmarking.

2.3 The Maze paradigm

Our experiment involves a simple adaptation of the Maze paradigm for studying word-by-word reading (Forster et al., 2009; Witzel et al., 2012; Boyce et al., 2020). In the Maze paradigm, experimental participants read a text passage through a sequence of two-alternative forced-choice tasks, one per word in the passage. Each word is coupled with an alternative distractor, one randomly assigned on the left and the other on the right, and the participant has to choose which word is correct (i.e., fits with the preceding linguistic context). The participant's reaction time (RT) and whether they chose the correct word are recorded. These reaction times

[1]https://github.com/snpushpi/Image-creates-linguistic-expectation

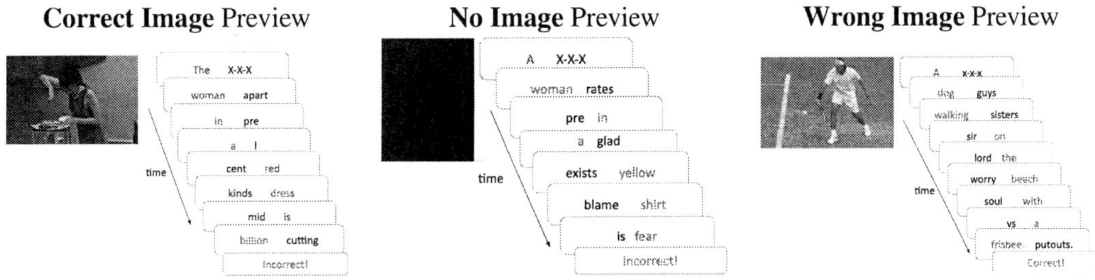

Figure 1: Schematic of image-description A-maze reading in each of the three experimental conditions. Participants first briefly view an image and then read a description by successively choosing the word fitting the preceding linguistic context and rejecting a foil word (example selections marked in blue). A mistake triggers an error message, and the participant moves on to the next trial sentence.

and accuracies carry information about the word's difficulty in a context that can be revealed through statistical analysis. The Maze paradigm has a number of methodological advantages: it is easily deployable over the web, it has a good signal-to-noise ratio, and processing difficulty is highly *localized*: that is, if a word is difficult for the comprehender, that difficulty shows up predominantly in RT and accuracy on that word, rather than "spilling over" to subsequent words as is often seen with other reading-time measurement techniques such as eye tracking or self-paced reading. Boyce and Levy (2023) showed that a linear relationship between surprisal and RT holds in the Maze paradigm as it does for other reading time-measuring paradigms.

3 Experimental Methodology

We developed an *Image-Conditioned Maze* experimental paradigm which is like the original Maze, but participants preview an image before reading each text passage. We chose 108 images and their corresponding descriptions from the validation split of Microsoft COCO (Lin et al., 2014). In each experimental trial, participants were first shown an image for 5 seconds, and then the image disappeared from the screen and they read an image description word by word in the Maze task. We generated distractor words using the A(uto)-Maze software of Boyce et al. (2020), which uses an LSTM RNN based model (Gulordava et al., 2018) to generate contextually unlikely words. Reaction time and response for each word choice (correct vs. distractor) were recorded. We recruited 69 US native English speaker participants (a quantity determined using power analysis based on a pilot study with a different set of images and descriptions) on Prolific, showed them some examples, and paid them 12$/hour for their participation. Each of them participated in 36 trials, 12 in each of the three conditions described before in figure (1), with trial order randomized for each participant. No participant saw the same image description twice.

In a separate study with different participants, we collected groundedness ratings for each word in each description in the context of the correct image associated with the description (Figure 2). We recruited 42 US native English speaker participants on Prolific for this study. Each sentence was rated by 7 participants on average. Participants used a slider to indicate how "present" each word was in the image, ranging from -10 (Not Present) to $+10$ (Surely Present).

4 Psycholinguistic hypotheses

Under wide circumstances, visual input automatically activates corresponding linguistic representations; a famous example is the Stroop effect, where a word naming one color but presented in another, such as blue, is difficult to say due to the interference between the words activated by the color versus orthographic information. We thus hypothesize that previewing the image will tend to activate at least some of the linguistic content in the image's description, so that reaction times will be faster and accuracy higher more quickly and accurately in the Correct Image condition than in the Wrong Image and No Image conditions. We also hypothesize that the Wrong Image condition may slow reaction times and reduce accuracy relative to the No Image condition, since the linguistic content that the image activates may conflict with the content in the subsequent text.

We distinguish between two versions of these hypotheses. One possibility is that activation of linguistic content may be restricted to content that is straightforwardly grounded in the image. For

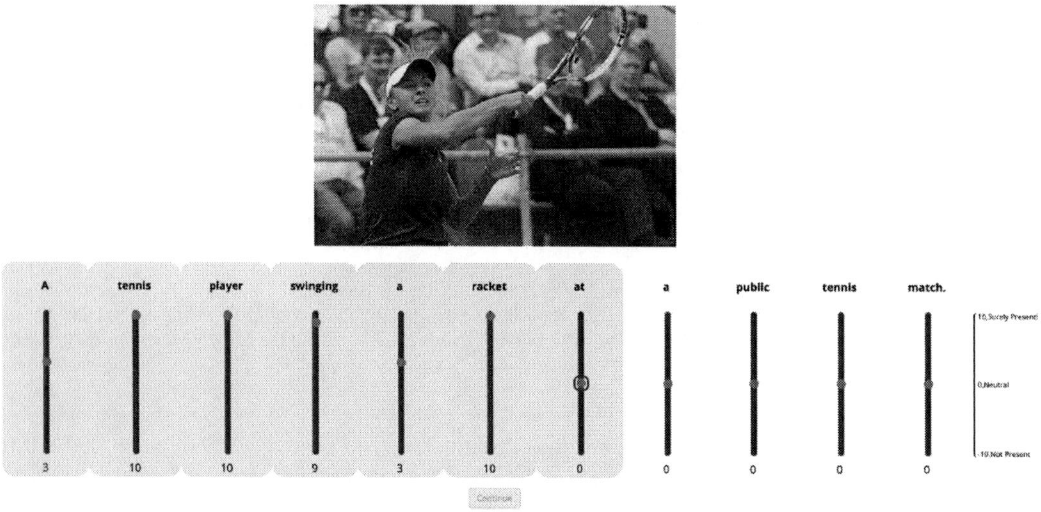

Figure 2: Example experiment page for a trial in the groundedness rating study. The circle indicates the slider the participant is currently manipulating. Once a participant chooses the vertical slider, the slider turns green. A participant must rate each word in the description to continue to the next trial. The scale on the right is a reminder of how the rating works.

example, in the Correct Image example of Figure 1, the words *woman*, *red*, and *dress* are straightforwardly grounded: the meaning of each word is prominent in the image without extensive reasoning or search for complex linguistic descriptions. In contrast, the rest of the words in that description are less straightforwardly grounded. Our **lexical-grounding hypothesis** is that linguistic facilitation or interference effects from the image will be limited to relatively straightforwardly grounded words. In cognitive terms, objects, properties, events, and states in the scene are visually identified, and the corresponding lemmas are activated so that when those lemmas are encountered in the image description, they are processed more effectively. We operationalize groundedness in two different ways: first as open-class (generally more grounded) versus closed-class (generally less grounded) parts of speech; second, through our grounding study as described in Section 3.

The second possibility, the **comprehensive-grounding hypothesis**, is that images evoke expectations over complete possible descriptions. This hypothesis predicts that facilitation or interference will affect all types of words in the sentence, regardless of part of speech or groundedness. A particularly strong version of the comprehensive-grounding hypothesis is that *all* facilitation and interference effects from the image will be mediated by this change in linguistic expectations. If this strong version of the hypothesis is correct, and if visual language models do a good job of capturing this shift in expectations, then visual language model surprisal should fully account for the effect of experimental conditions in the human behavioral data in our experiment.

5 Modelling Approach

We created a set of predictor variables including Condition_ID, frequency, word length, groundedness, open vs. closed part of speech, and surprisals from six Transformer-based LLMs: four visual language models with a variety of objectives regarding language-vision alignment (BLIP2, Li et al., 2023; KOSMOS2, Peng et al., 2023; LLAVA-7b, Liu et al., 2023; and IDEFICS-9b, Laurençon et al., 2024) and two language only models (GPT2, Radford et al., 2019; and LLAMA2 Touvron et al., 2023). Condition_ID indicates whether a certain image description was seen in Correct, Wrong, or No Image condition, which could be extracted from the experiment setup on IBEXZehr and Schwarz, 2018. For length, we used the length in characters excluding end punctuation. We obtain word frequencies from SUBTLEX_US (Brysbaert and New, 2009); for the words not in the database, we use the minimum frequency of any word in that database. Groundedness comes from our norming study. For open versus closed class part of speech, we ran the Stanford POS tagger on our image descriptions and considered all nouns, adjectives, adverbs, and non-auxiliary verbs, as open-class, and the rest as

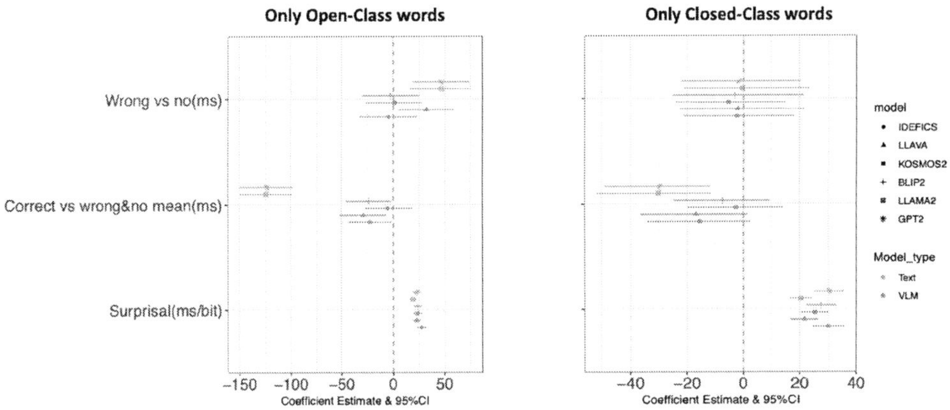

Figure 3: Coefficent Estimates and 95% CI of the fixed effects with theoretical interests for models fitted with open and closed class respectively. Condition_ID was Helmert encoded making comparisons between wrong vs no and correct vs wrong and no mean

closed-class. Surprisal does not vary across conditions for LLMs, but does so for VLMs for image conditioning. (Note that for the No Image condition, we used a black screen as the image, and additionally added "Ignore the image context" as a prompt preceding the description.) Using these predictors, for both testing our psycholinguistic hypotheses and psychometric benchmarking, we fitted mixed effects regression models to predict the reading time data that we collected, using the `brms` and `lmer` package in `R`. These models give us estimates and statistical significance of coefficients for all the predictor variables, which we can later analyze to distinguish between psycholinguistic hypotheses. For psychometric benchmarking, we fitted many models, each only varying at the kind of surprisal estimate it's using. For each fitted model, we then analyze the likelihood of the ground truth reading time data.

5.1 Regression predictor encoding

Unless otherwise specified, we used Helmert coding for Condition_ID, set up so that one coefficient encodes the **wrong** and **no** difference and another coefficient encodes the difference between **correct** and (**wrong** and **no**) mean. We used sum-encoding for open vs. closed part of speech (POS). Unless the model is condition specific, in which case Condition_ID can't be used as a predictor, we also assumed an interaction between Condition_ID and groundedness and Condition_ID and POS. Assuming this interaction makes sense since one would intuitively expect that one reads words in the correct condition even faster especially when the words are more highly grounded. For all the models, we use the maximal random effects structure justified by the design, so we have included correlated by-subject, by-sentence, by-word, and by-wordtoken random slopes for Condition_ID, the fixed effect of our primary theoretical interest. An example of a mixed effect model fitted for reading time prediction using data from all conditions and parts of speech(open vs. closed) is the following - `RT ~ Condition_ID.helm*POS + surprisal + Frequency + Length + (Condition_ID.helm*POS + surprisal | Subject_ID)+ (Condition_ID.helm | Group) + (Condition_ID.helm | WordToken) + (Condition_ID.helm | Word)`.

6 Results

6.1 Reading Time Prediction

Consider figure (3), which plots the coefficient estimates and 95% confidence interval of the effects of theoretical interests from the model fitted with equation `RT ~ Condition_ID.helm + surprisal + Frequency + Length + (Condition_ID.helm + surprisal | Subject_ID)+ (Condition_ID.helm | Group) + (Condition_ID.helm | WordToken) + (Condition_ID.helm | Word)`, individually for open and closed class words. Now note the second rows in both panels for models fitted with text-based surprisals(indicated in light blue in the figure). For the left panel, the second row is saying that on average people need 125 ms less to read an open class word in the correct condition compared to other conditions. Similarly, for the right panel, the second row indicates that on average people need 30ms less to read a closed class word in the correct condition compared to other conditions. So there is a very significant facilitation for both open and closed-class words when people get a preview of the relevant image compared to when they don't. This evidence strongly suggests that people's facilitation of reading image descriptions after having a relevant visual preview can be explained by **Comprehensive Grounding Hypothesis** and not by **Lexical Grounding Hypothesis**. Note that

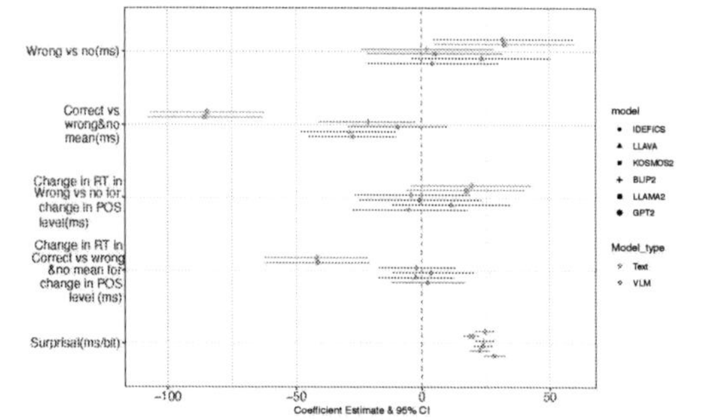

Figure 4: Coefficent Estimates and 95% CI of the fixed effects with theoretical interests. Note that the model had a Condition_ID*POS term, where Condition_ID was Helmert encoded making comparisons between wrong vs no and correct vs mean of wrong and no and POS was sum encoded with two levels, resulting in 2 interaction terms and 2 main effect terms for Condition_ID

we want to consider only the text surprisal fitted models' condition-related effects to distinguish between lexical and comprehensive grounding hypotheses. It is because in this scenario the only image-related information we want to use for RT prediction should be through Condition_ID/POS levels. In both panels of Figure (3), we can see that the impact of condition ID-related effects is noticeably smaller—or even non-existent—in VLM surprisal-fitted models compared to text surprisal-fitted models. However, the overall effect of surprisal itself is quite similar across both types of models. To gain a complete understanding of the differences between these models, we fit reading time data from all three conditions and parts of speech in Figure (4). From the coefficient estimates and their significance in the first and second rows, we observe significant facilitation—around 30 ms and 90 ms on average respectively in the "no" condition compared to the "wrong" condition, and in the "correct" condition compared to the others, in models fitted with text-based surprisals. This indicates that people are significantly faster in correct condition compared to other conditions and wrong condition significantly slows people down compared to not seeing any image at all. As before, we see that these effects, however, tend to shrink or disappear in models fitted with VLM surprisals(indicated with orange-pink on the diagram), while the impact of surprisal itself (along with other fixed predictors not shown in the figure) remains consistent across all models. **This strongly suggests that the notable difference in condition ID-related effects can only be explained by how the nature of surprisal changes when transitioning from text-based to multimodal models.** All this evidence also strongly indicates that Correct Image preview substantially affects comprehenders' expectations and that visual-language model surprisal captures a substantial part (though not all) of this effect.

6.2 Error Prediction

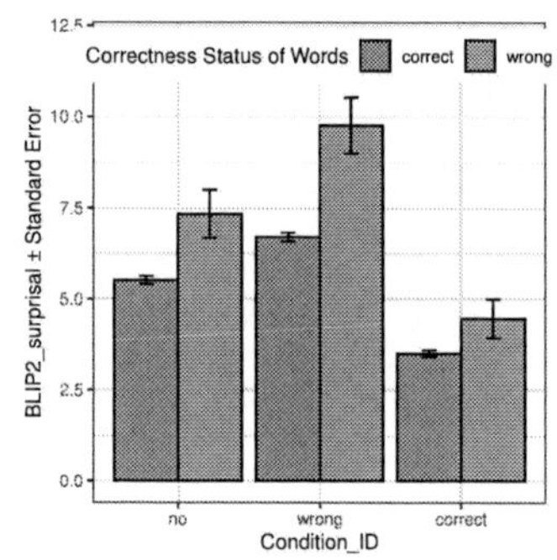

Figure 5: X axis indicates the conditions and correctness status of words(whether or not someone made a mistake in that word) and Y axis indicates mean and standard error of BLIP2 surprisal for words in a certain condition and correctness status

To investigate if the errors that people make have anything theoretically interesting to tell us, we first look into a univariate analysis showing the surprisal distribution across words in different conditions and correctness status. Consider the distribution of BLIP2 surprisal, which is a VLM, in figure (5). There is a very clear trend of high average contextual surprisal values for words that people got wrong. To prove this claim rigorously with a multivariate analysis, we fit a logistic regression model, so the goal is to predict the log-likelihood of making an error. Figure(6) shows the coefficient estimates and 95% confidence intervals of theoretically interesting predictors of this logistic regression model. From this figure, three things become evident - 1. From the first two rows, we see that the error occurrence likelihood does not vary much across different conditions, 2. From row

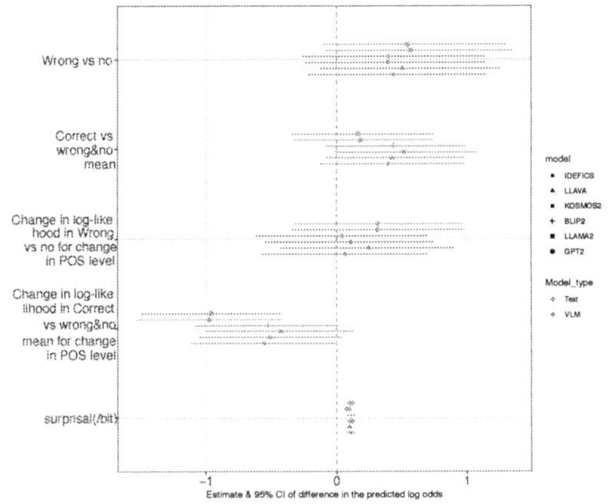

Figure 6: Estimate & 95% CI of difference in the predicted log odds of the fixed effects with theoretical interests. Note that the model had a Condition_ID*POS term, where the encoding of these terms is similar to before, resulting in 2 main effects of Condition_ID and 2 interaction terms, which is what we showed in the figure, along with surprisal.

4, we see that people are less likely to make errors for open parts of speech in the correct condition compared to other conditions (since the blue bars are on the negative side of the plot) and 3. From row 5, we see that the effect of surprisals is consistent across all models and increasing surprisal leads to more likelihood of error occurrence.

6.3 Can surprisal difference be explained as a function of groundedness?

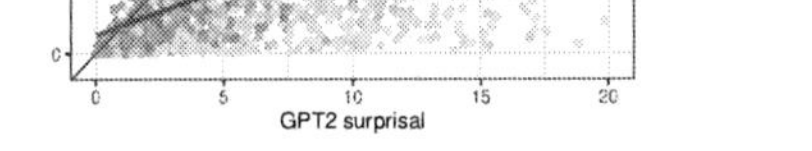

Figure 7: Every word token in every sentence in the dataset is indicated with a dot here. X coordinate of that dot indicates the GPT2 surprisal of that word given the previous words in that sentence and the Y coordinate of that dot indicates the KOSMOS2 surprisal of that word given the previous words and the image that sentence is describing, i.e, the KOSMOS2 surprisal in the correct condition. The color of the dot is determined by the groundedness rating of the word, noted as a scale to the right.

Consider the figure (7). We can notice that most dots below the dark blue line, the best-fitted linear relationship between GPT2 and KOSMOS2 surprisals, are light blue dots indicating highly grounded words. This motivation suggests that a lot of highly grounded words exhibit notably lower surprisal values in VLMs when contrasted with those derived solely from textual models. Intuitively speaking, ImageConditionedTextSurprisal minus TextSurprisal for a word roughly indicates the reduction of surprisal for the presence of the image. Hence, we expect that the more negative ImageConditionedTextSurprisal minus TextSurprisal is for a word, the more the effect of the image is on that word, hence the more grounded that word should be in the image. To formally analyze this nuance, in figure (8) we predicted the surprisal difference between two conditions from the same model using POS type, POS type and groundedness interaction, frequency and length as fixed effect predictors. In addition, we incorporated a random effect predictor that encompasses all fixed predictors, with the sentence type serving as the grouping variable. The significance of the groundedness effect on the surprisal difference for each type of POS is indicated such that "ns" means "not significant"; * means $p < 0.01$ and ** means $p < 0.001$.

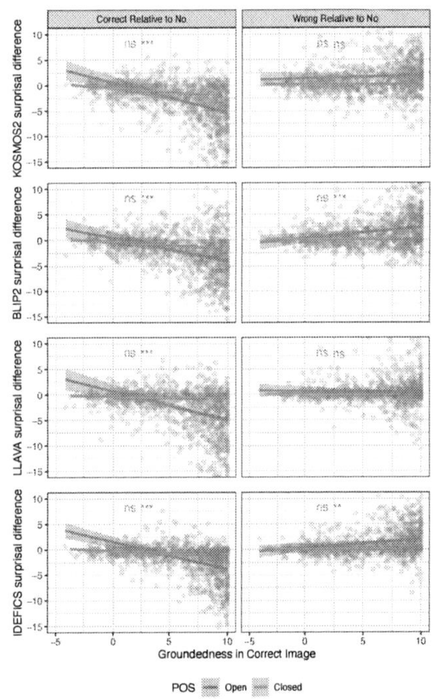

Figure 8: For each of the 4 VLMs we considered for this paper, the X axis indicates the groundedness value of a word and the Y axis indicates the difference between the surprisals of that word in correct condition and no condition (left panel) and wrong condition and no condition(right panel). The best linear fits for each type of POS(open/closed) are shown in the plots. The significance of groundedness contribution for each type of POS is also indicated in each plot.

Note that when comparing correct condition to no condition, we notice a consistent pattern of open class words' groundedness significantly contributing to the surprisal difference for all models. But we don't notice the same for closed class words, which makes sense given that they are mostly not strongly grounded in the image and hence the presence of an image doesn't give much extra information about them. **These findings highlight a strong correlation between human judgment of a word's degree of grounding in an image and the reduction in that word's surprisal for the presence of that image, as measured by recent VLMs.**

However, we notice a significant contribution of open class words' groundedness on surprisal difference between wrong and no conditions for BLIP2 and IDEFICS(but in the opposite direction of what we saw in the other comparison). At first, it might seem counter-intuitive but it just tells us that models like BLIP2 and IDEFICS struggle to ignore the image context in the wrong image condition, hence for the open class words in a sentence that would otherwise be grounded in the image in the 'Correct Image' context, they have significantly high surprisal due to those words' visual absence in the 'Wrong Image' context, resulting in the significance we observe in figure (8).

7 Perplexity and psychometric accuracy

In recent years, there has been an effort to study the increase of log-likelihood for including LLM surprisal estimate from models as a function of perplexity(Oh and Schuler, 2023). To investigate what traits in a VLM give them better predictive power for human RT, we ran a similar analysis with different-sized open-sourced versions of all the models we used in the work - two versions of all the VLMs except for KOSMOS-2 and a new VLM that improved upon Llava, Llava-Next. The baseline regression model was considered with all baseline predictors such as main effects of helmert encoded Condition_ID and sum encoded POS and interaction between them, frequency, length and full regression models additionally contained each LM surprisal predictor. Both the baseline and full regression models had the same random effects structure; a random intercept and slope for Condition_ID within each subject, sentence, word, and word token type was included. After fitting the regression models, we determined the increase in log-likelihood (ΔLL) for each model by subtracting the log-likelihood of the baseline model from that of the full model. Finally, the perplexity of each model type was calculated in our dataset of all items. Figure (9) shows the resultant plots.

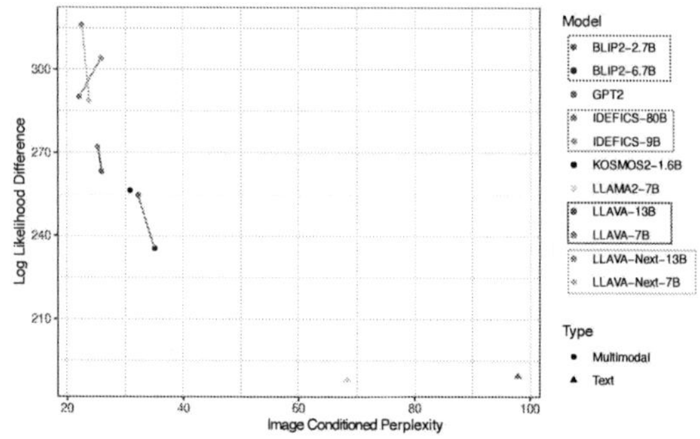

Figure 9: Increase in regression model log-likelihood fitted with data from all conditions for including each surprisal estimate as a function of **image-conditioned perplexity**, the different-sized versions of the same model are indicated with different shades of the same color and connected with a line for ease of interpretation.

Note that the increase of log-likelihood for adding surprisals from different-sized versions of the same model isn't very different, however different models can have very different predictive power regardless of the size, consider Llava and Llava-Next for example, both versions considered for these models have the same sizes(7B and 13B parameter) but Llava-Next has a lot more predictive power compared to Llava. This strongly indicates that training diet and objective are more important than the model size when it comes to psychometric predictive power. However, all the smaller-size versions except for Llava-Next are better than the bigger-size versions. Although this needs further exploration, the observations indicate that for each type of training objective and diet, there is possibly an optimal number of parameters that make the model most aligned with human expectations, and beyond that alignment decreases.

8 Conclusion

In this work, we have developed a novel experimental paradigm, Image-Conditioned Maze Reading, to study human linguistic expectations during real-time language comprehension when a visual context is involved. Our results demonstrate a substantial facilitatory effect of correct image context on language comprehension. This effect is evident not only for concrete nouns, adjectives, or verbs directly present in the image but also extends to words not explicitly grounded in the visual context. We extended psychometric benchmarking to visual language models and found that VLM surprisals capture most to all of the facilitator effect that occurs due to the presence of a relevant visual context. We discovered that as one goes from text based model surprisal to VLM surprisal, the effect of surprisal on reading time doesn't change much, but the huge Condition_ID related effects mostly disappear for VLM surprisal based models. So, the explanation is in how the nature of the surprisal changes. We also found a strong correlation between the human judgment of a word's degree of grounding in the image and the reduction of that word's surprisal for the presence of that image. We showed empirical support indicating that heightened contextual surprisal significantly contributes to errors in maze tasks. Finally, our findings reveal compelling evidence that the training objectives and diet of Vision-Language Models (VLMs) significantly impact their psychometric predictive power, more so than their size. However, this observation warrants further investigation.

9 Limitations

In this study, we used images and descriptions from the validation split of the COCO dataset. At that time, we were uncertain about the specifics of investigating Vision-Language Models (VLMs). Upon further examination down the line, we discovered that Llava and BLIP-2 had COCO in their pretraining data, indicating that these models may have encountered some of our items before. In future work, we plan to use images and descriptions from a dataset that has not been used for pre-training any of the models.

Another challenge we faced was the limited availability of different-sized versions of open-sourced VLMs for comprehensive analysis. There are typically only 2-3 versions available for each model. This limited our analysis compared to studies like (Oh and Schuler, 2023), which utilized many versions of Pythia models (Biderman et al., 2023) for interpretability analysis and understanding the development of knowledge in autoregressive transformers. The scarcity of multiple versions of open-sourced VLMs hindered our ability to perform a similarly comprehensive analysis.

References

Paul D. Allopenna, James S. Magnuson, and Michael K. Tanenhaus. 1998. Tracking the time course of spoken word recognition using eye movements: Evidence for continuous mapping models. *Journal of Memory and Language*, 38:419–439.

Gerry T.M. Altmann and Yuki Kamide. 1999. Incremental interpretation at verbs: restricting the domain of subsequent reference. *Cognition*, 73(3):247–264.

Richard Antonello, Aditya Vaidya, and Alexander Huth. 2023. Scaling laws for language encoding models in fmri. In *Advances in Neural Information Processing Systems*, volume 36, pages 21895–21907. Curran Associates, Inc.

S. Biderman, H. Schoelkopf, Q. G. Anthony, H. Bradley, K. O'Brien, E. ... Hallahan, and O. Van Der Wal. 2023. A suite for analyzing large language models across training and scaling. *In International Conference on Machine Learning (pp. 2397-2430). PMLR.*

V. Boyce and R. Levy. 2023. A-maze of natural stories: Comprehension and surprisal in the maze task. *Glossa Psycholinguistics, 2(1).*

Veronica Boyce, Richard Futrell, and Roger Levy. 2020. Maze made easy: Better and easier measurement of incremental processing difficulty. *Journal of Memory and Language*, 111:1–13.

M. Brysbaert and B. New. 2009. Moving beyond kucera and francis: A critical evaluation of current word frequency norms and the introduction of a new and improved word frequency measure for american english. *Behavior Research Methods, 41, 977-990.*

Charlotte Caucheteux and Jean-Rémi King. 2022. Brains and algorithms partially converge in natural language processing. *Communications Biology*, 5(1):134.

Delphine Dahan, James S Magnuson, and Michael K Tanenhaus. 2001. Time course of frequency effects in spoken-word recognition: Evidence from eye movements. *Cognitive Psychology*, 42(4):317–367.

Susan F. Ehrlich and Keith Rayner. 1981. Contextual effects on word perception and eye movements during reading. 20:641–655.

Kenneth I Forster, Christine Guerrera, and Lisa Elliot. 2009. The maze task: Measuring forced incremental sentence processing time. *Behavior Research Methods*, 41(1):163–171.

Victoria Fossum and Roger Levy. 2012. Sequential vs. hierarchical syntactic models of human incremental sentence processing. pages 61–69, Montreal, Quebec.

Stefan L. Frank and Rens Bod. 2011. Insensitivity of the human sentence-processing system to hierarchical structure. *Psychological Science*, 22(6):829–834.

Ariel Goldstein, Zaid Zada, Eliav Buchnik, Mariano Schain, Amy Price, Bobbi Aubrey, Samuel A Nastase, Amir Feder, Dotan Emanuel, Alon Cohen, Aren Jansen, Harshvardhan Gazula, Gina Choe, Aditi Rao, Catherine Kim, Colton Casto, Lora Fanda, Werner Doyle, Daniel Friedman, Patricia Dugan, Lucia Melloni, Roi Reichart, Sasha Devore, Adeen Flinker, Liat Hasenfratz, Omer Levy, Avinatan Hassidim, Michael Brenner, Yossi Matias, Kenneth Norman, Orrin Devinsky, and Uri Hasson. 2022. Shared computational principles for language processing in humans and deep language models. *Nature Neuroscience*, 25(3):369–380.

Adam Goodkind and Klinton Bicknell. 2018. Predictive power of word surprisal for reading times is a linear function of language model quality. In *Proceedings of the 8th Workshop on Cognitive Modeling and Computational Linguistics (CMCL 2018)*, pages 10–18.

Kristina Gulordava, Piotr Bojanowski, Edouard Grave, Tal Linzen, and Marco Baroni. 2018. Colorless green recurrent networks dream hierarchically. In *Proceedings of the 2018 Conference of the North American Chapter of the Association for Computational Linguistics: Human Language Technologies, Volume 1 (Long Papers)*, pages 1195–1205, New Orleans, Louisiana. Association for Computational Linguistics.

John Hale. 2001. A probabilistic Earley parser as a psycholinguistic model. pages 159–166, Pittsburgh, Pennsylvania.

Micha Heilbron, Kristijan Armeni, Jan-Mathijs Schoffelen, Peter Hagoort, and Floris P. de Lange. 2022. A hierarchy of linguistic predictions during natural language comprehension. 119(32):e2201968119.

Falk Huettig, Joost Rommers, and Antje S Meyer. 2011. Using the visual world paradigm to study language processing: A review and critical evaluation. *Acta Psychologica*, 137(2):151–171.

Marta Kutas and Kara D Federmeier. 2011. Thirty years and counting: finding meaning in the n400 component of the event-related brain potential (erp). *Annual review of psychology*, 62:621–647.

Marta Kutas and Steven A. Hillyard. 1980. Reading senseless sentences: Brain potentials reflect semantic incongruity. *Science*, 207(4427):203–205.

H. Laurençon, L. Saulnier, L. Tronchon, S. Bekman, A. Singh, ... Lozhkov, A., and V. Sanh. 2024. Obelics: An open web-scale filtered dataset of interleaved image-text documents. *Advances in Neural Information Processing Systems, 36.*

Roger Levy. 2008a. Expectation-based syntactic comprehension. *Cognition*, 106(3):1126–1177.

Roger Levy. 2008b. A noisy-channel model of rational human sentence comprehension under uncertain input. pages 234–243, Waikiki, Honolulu.

Junnan Li, Dongxu Li, Silvio Savarese, and Steven Hoi. 2023. BLIP-2: Bootstrapping language-image pre-training with frozen image encoders and large language models. *arXiv preprint arXiv:2301.12597.*

Tsung-Yi Lin, Michael Maire, Serge Belongie, James Hays, Pietro Perona, Deva Ramanan, Piotr Dollár, and C Lawrence Zitnick. 2014. Microsoft COCO: Common objects in context. In *Computer Vision–ECCV 2014: 13th European Conference, Zurich, Switzerland, September 6-12, 2014, Proceedings, Part V 13*, pages 740–755. Springer.

H. Liu, C. Li, Y. Li, and Y. J. Lee. 2023. Improved baselines with visual instruction tuning. *arXiv preprint arXiv:2310.03744.*

William Marslen-Wilson. 1975. Sentence perception as an interactive parallel process. *Science*, 189(4198):226–228.

B. D. Oh and W. Schuler. 2023. Transformer-based language model surprisal predicts human reading times best with about two billion training tokens. *Conference on Empirical Methods in Natural Language Processing.*

Z. Peng, W. Wang, L. Dong, Y. Hao, S. Huang, S. Ma, and F. Wei. 2023. Kosmos-2: Grounding multimodal large language models to the world. *arXiv preprint arXiv:2306.14824.*

Alec Radford, Jeffrey Wu, Rewon Child, David Luan, Dario Amodei, and Ilya Sutskever. 2019. Language models are unsupervised multitask learners.

Keith Rayner. 1998. Eye movements in reading and information processing: 20 years of research. 124(3):372–422.

Martin Schrimpf, Idan Asher Blank, Greta Tuckute, Carina Kauf, Eghbal A Hosseini, Nancy Kanwisher, Joshua B Tenenbaum, and Evelina Fedorenko. 2021. The neural architecture of language: Integrative modeling converges on predictive processing. *Proceedings of the National Academy of Sciences*, 118(45).

Cory Shain, Clara Meister, Tiago Pimentel, Ryan Cotterell, and Roger P. Levy. 2024. Large-scale evidence for logarithmic effects of word predictability on reading time. 121(10):e2307876121.

Nathaniel J. Smith and Roger Levy. 2013. The effect of word predictability on reading time is logarithmic. *Cognition, 128:302–319.*

Jakub M Szewczyk and Kara D Federmeier. 2022. Context-based facilitation of semantic access follows both logarithmic and linear functions of stimulus probability. *Journal of Memory and Language*, 123:104311.

Michael K. Tanenhaus, Michael J. Spivey-Knowlton, Kathleen Eberhard, and Julie C. Sedivy. 1995. Integration of visual and linguistic information in spoken language comprehension. *Science*, 268:1632–1634.

H. Touvron, L. Martin, K. Stone, P. Albert, A. Almahairi, Y. ... Babaei, and T. Scialom. 2023. Llama 2: Open foundation and fine-tuned chat models. *arXiv preprint arXiv:2307.09288*.

Ethan G. Wilcox, Tiago Pimentel, Clara Meister, Ryan Cotterell, and Roger P. Levy. 2023. Testing the Predictions of Surprisal Theory in 11 Languages. *Transactions of the Association for Computational Linguistics*, 11:1451–1470.

Naoko Witzel, Jeffrey Witzel, and Kenneth Forster. 2012. Comparisons of online reading paradigms: Eye tracking, moving-window, and maze. *Journal of Psycholinguistic Research*, 41:105–128.

J. Zehr and F. Schwarz. 2018. Penncontroller for internet based experiments (ibex). *https://doi.org/10.17605/OSF.IO/MD832*.

Self-supervised speech representations display *some* human-like cross-linguistic perceptual abilities

Joselyn Rodriguez[1], Kamala Sreepada[1],
Ruolan Leslie Famularo[1], Sharon Goldwater [2], Naomi H. Feldman[1]
[1] University of Maryland
[2] University of Edinburgh
Correspondence: jrodri20@umd.edu

Abstract

State of the art models in automatic speech recognition have shown remarkable improvements due to modern self-supervised (SSL) transformer-based architectures such as wav2vec 2.0 (Baevski et al., 2020). However, how these models encode phonetic information is still not well understood. We explore whether SSL speech models display a linguistic property that characterizes human speech perception: language specificity. We show that while wav2vec 2.0 displays an overall language specificity effect when tested on Hindi vs. English, it does not resemble human speech perception when tested on finer-grained differences in Hindi speech contrasts.

1 Introduction

Human listeners become attuned to the speech sounds of their native language already in their first year of life (Werker, 1995; Jusczyk, 2000; Kuhl et al., 2006). By adulthood, nonnative contrasts which they were once able to discriminate are no longer discriminable (Miyawaki et al., 1975; Cutler, 2000; Best and Tyler, 2007). Acquiring a second language as an adult can thus be marred by difficulty acquiring certain phonetic contrasts. This *language specificity* effect is a core property of human speech perception.

For human listeners, the difficulty of acquiring a particular non-native contrast depends both on whether the acoustic-phonetic dimension used to distinguish the contrasts is used in the native language and on the perceptual similarity of the nonnative categories to native categories (see Best and Tyler, 2007). For example, while English only has two categories for the coronal stop series (/t/ and /d/), Hindi has eight (/ɖ/,/ɖ^h/,/ʈ/,/ʈ^h/,/t̪/,/t̪^{h}/,/d̪/,/d̪^{h}/). Because of the relationship between the acoustic dimensions used and the perceptual similarity to existing English categories, Hindi contrasts that differ along aspiration (/t/ vs. /t^h/) are easier for English listeners to acquire than along place of articulation (dental vs. retroflex; /t/ vs. /ʈ/) or voicing (/t/ vs. /d/) (Werker et al., 1981; Tees and Werker, 1984; Pederson and Guion-Anderson, 2010; Hayes-Harb and Barrios, 2022).

Whether computational models of speech perception share certain properties with humans has been a subject of recent interest. Previous work has suggested that like humans, some speech models with non-transformer architectures display language specificity effects (Millet et al., 2019; Matusevych et al., 2020; Schatz et al., 2021).

However, less work has examined this effect in transformer architectures. Millet and Dunbar (2022) suggest that self-supervised speech transformers do not display a cross-linguistic difference in predicting human performance, but their measures aggregate across all contrasts, and given the complex relationship between native and non-native contrasts, this makes interpretation of the results difficult. In fact, previous work with non-transformer speech models found that for vowels, while the model displayed an overall language specificity effect, the direction of the effect was in the opposite direction than expected (Millet et al., 2019): a non-native model better predicted native speakers' discrimination. It is not known to what extent the specific perceptual similarity space in transformers is similar to humans.

In this paper, we test whether self-supervised transformer speech models (wav2vec 2.0) display an effect of language specificity. We do so by examining specific patterns of cross-linguistic differences, using Hindi contrasts as a case study. We explore a series of contrast that are known be be difficult for native English listeners. For these listeners, as noted above, place (/t/ vs. /ʈ/) and voicing (/t/ vs. /d/) are more difficult dimensions to discriminate along than aspiration (/t/ vs. /t^h/) (Werker et al., 1981; Tees and Werker, 1984; Pederson and Guion-Anderson, 2010; Hayes-Harb and Barrios,

Proceedings of the 28th Conference on Computational Natural Language Learning, pages 458–463
November 15-16, 2024

2022). These behavioral results provide a test case to explore targeted fine-grained categorization patterns of speech models to determine whether the models' representations are structured similarly to human listeners.

In Experiment 1, we find that wav2vec 2.0 displays an overall language specificity effect: a native-trained model performs better on native categorization task than a non-native model. In Experiment 2, we examine specific contrasts where second language learners are attested to struggle, and find that both the native and non-native model show high accuracy in categorization across the most difficult dimensions for humans – place and voicing. We additionally find that where human listeners have been shown to have the least difficulty overall, the models show the largest cross-linguistic difference in accuracy. This suggests that wav2vec 2.0 is encoding language specific information, but structured in ways that differ from human listeners.

2 Experiments

2.1 Models

The following experiments were performed on two models based on the wav2vec 2.0 architecture with 7 CNN encoder layers and 12 transformer layers (Baevski et al., 2020). Throughout this paper we display results from all 12 transformer layers, as previous work has shown that different layers may produce different results depending on the task (Pasad et al., 2021).

The first model we use is the English pre-trained wav2vec 2.0 base model available through the `fairseq` repository.[1] This model is pre-trained on approximately 1000 hours of English from the Librispeech Corpus of read English (this model is referred to as `wav2vec-english`).

The second is a Hindi pre-trained model available through the `Vakyansh` toolkit (Chadha et al., 2022).[2] The Hindi model is trained on 4200 hours of Hindi starting from the base fairseq wav2vec 2.0 model with continued pre-training (this model is referred to as `wav2vec-hindi`).

2.2 Data Preparation and Classifier Setup

For Hindi evaluation, we used the Hindi Common Voice corpus,[3] a crowd-sourced corpus of read speech. To acquire time-aligned phoneme transcriptions, we force-aligned the speech with the Montreal Forced Aligner (McAuliffe et al., 2017). We used the validated subset of the corpus which totaled 13 hours. For English evaluation, we used the Wall Street Journal corpus (Paul and Baker, 1992), a read corpus of English. To match the sizes of the corpora, we randomly sampled utterances until we reached 13 hours.

For each utterance in both Hindi and English, we extracted embeddings from each of the 12 transformer layers from both the Hindi-trained and English-trained models. For each embedding, we average over the frames composing a single phoneme according to the forced alignments. Thus, each phoneme is represented by a single embedding vector of size 768.

Given all the Hindi and English embedded phonemes, we additionally sub-sampled both datasets to get roughly an equal number of instances in each target category. We performed this step because the distribution of phonemes differs between English and Hindi, especially for the phonemes of interest. The number of individual tokens was determined by the smallest class of interest (N=67 for Hindi /$ɖ^h$/). Taking the entire set of embeddings and phoneme labels, we randomly sampled from the set of phoneme embeddings until the desired number of tokens was reached. In all experiments, each phone category contains at most 67 tokens.[4] This step was performed to ensure that any difference in classification accuracy was due to the learned representations, and not to a frequency effect in the classifier.

Classification was performed using `sklearns`'s Logistic Regression function with a multinomial loss to get a measure of overall phone multi-way classification accuracy across layers. The classifier is trained to predict the correct phone label from all possible labels (English=42 labels, Hindi=72 labels). In order to get a measure of standard error, we utilized 5-fold cross validation.

2.3 Experiment 1: Global Language Specificity

In the first experiment, we explored whether the models display an overall global language specificity effect by examining the cross-linguistic classification accuracy aggregated over all phonemes

[1] https://github.com/facebookresearch/fairseq/tree/main/examples/wav2vec

[2] https://github.com/Open-Speech-EkStep/vakyansh-models

[3] https://commonvoice.mozilla.org/en/datasets

[4] Some rare phonemes (e.g., /ʒ/) occurred fewer than 67 times but were not the focus of the current work

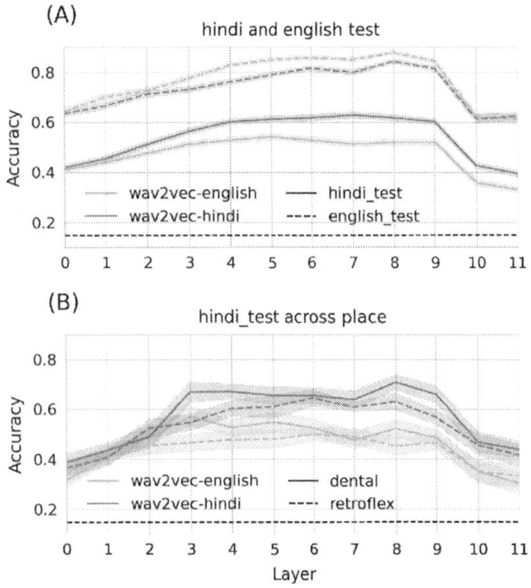

Figure 1: Wav2vec-hindi performs better than wav2vec-english on global multi-way classification for Hindi test (A) as well as for Hindi dental and retroflex sounds (B)

for the Hindi- and English-trained models' performance on both Hindi and English test data.

If the models display a native language specificity effect, we would expect that the aggregated classification accuracy across phonemes for the Hindi-trained model should be higher on Hindi test data than the English-trained model on Hindi test data and vice versa for English test data.

2.3.1 Results

Examining the overall classification accuracy in the best performing layer (layer=8), we find that the wav2vec-hindi has 10% higher categorization accuracy than wav2vec-english on Hindi test data. When tested on English, wav2vec-english outperforms wav2vec-hindi by 3% (Figure 1a). This suggests that the models do display a language specificity effect at a global level.

To determine whether the cross-linguistic differences are due to predicted difficulty in place of articulation for Hindi test data, we further examined the multi-way classification results averaged across only the set of Hindi dental and retroflex test phonemes (Figure 1b). As expected, the effect remains. The non-native wav2vec-english displays more difficulty with the dental and retroflex sounds in Hindi than the native model (wav2vec-hindi).

2.3.2 Discussion

In the global classification, we found an overall difference in wav2vec-english and wav2vec-hindi cross-linguistic classification accuracy collapsed across phonemes for Hindi and English test data. When we examined the aggregated classification accuracy of dental and retroflex sounds in the Hindi test data only, the effect remains – the Hindi model performs better on both dental and retroflex classification than the English model.

This suggests that through self-supervised training, wav2vec 2.0 is encoding language specific information. This has downstream consequences on phoneme encoding causing language-dependent patterns of categorization. However, the current experiment is limited to multi-way classification in which the model identifies the correct phoneme out of all possible labels (e.g., /d/ vs all other labels {/d^{h}/, /t^{h}/, /ɖ/, /b/, /p/,...}).

To determine whether the model is encoding information in a similar way to human listeners, it is of interest what the possible errors in this categorization are. For example, while the model makes errors in classification of dental or retroflex sounds, it is unknown whether the error is due to mistaking a dental sound as a retroflex sound or for some unrelated sound such as a vowel or fricative.

Therefore, in the following experiment, we examine finer-grained categorization performance limited to just the distinctions across dimensions of interest in the Hindi test data: place (dental or retroflex), voicing (voiced or unvoiced), and aspiration (aspirated or unaspirated). This task is also more directly comparable to the kind of perceptual tasks used with human listeners.

2.4 Experiment 2: Local Language Specificity

We simulate a two-alternative forced choice task where the model must categorize a sound into one of two categories while other features are kept constant. In a behavioral two-alternative forced choice task, listeners are given a sound, and asked to determine whether the sound belongs to category A or B. We simulate this by reducing the multi-way classification of Experiment 1 to a two-way classification task where the probability of a class y for a feature vector x_l from layer l is equal to

$$p(y = A) = \frac{exp(W_A^T x_l)}{exp(W_A^T x_l) + exp(W_B^T x_l)} \quad (1)$$

W_A refers to the classifier weights for class A and W_B refers to the weights for class B in the classifier trained on representations from a given layer l.

2.4.1 Results

If the models are encoding language specific information during training, we would expect the English model to struggle in classification of the Hindi sounds relative to the Hindi model primarily along the dimensions of place (dental vs. retroflex), secondarily along voicing, and rarely along aspiration, as these are the relative difficulties experienced by human second language learners of Hindi whose native language is English (Werker et al., 1981; Tees and Werker, 1984; Pruitt et al., 2006; Hayes-Harb and Barrios, 2022). What we found instead is that **both** the English and the Hindi trained models perform well in correctly categorizing sounds as either dental or retroflex (Figure 2, top plot). Thus, despite the cross-linguistic difference for the global multi-way classification task from Experiment 1, this effect is no longer present when we compare between only dental and retroflex sounds, where human data would most predict it. Similarly, both the Hindi and English models perform well when tested on categorization along voicing (Figure 2, middle plot). While voicing seems to be marginally easier to categorize along, this holds for both the English and the Hindi-trained models. Therefore, unlike human English listeners who perform worse than native Hindi listeners when categorizing these sounds, the monolingual native English model and the Hindi-trained model perform well overall on the Hindi contrasts *regardless* of training language.

Further, when testing categorization accuracy along aspiration, where we expect the least amount of language specificity (i.e., best performance for the wav2vec-english), we find the opposite effect. In the best performing layer (layer=7), we find the largest cross-linguistic difference in which the the categorization accuracy for wav2vec-hindi is 25% higher than the wav2vec-english. Further examination of the pattern of classification errors in the multi-way classification from Experiment 1 shows that the confusions for both wav2vec-hindi and wav2vec-english were indeed primarily across aspiration and only secondarily across place Figure 3.

2.4.2 Discussion

In this experiment, we limited the task to a two-alternative forced choice in order to explore classification accuracy across specific phonetic dimensions. We found that neither the monolingual wav2vec-english nor wav2vec-hindi displayed any

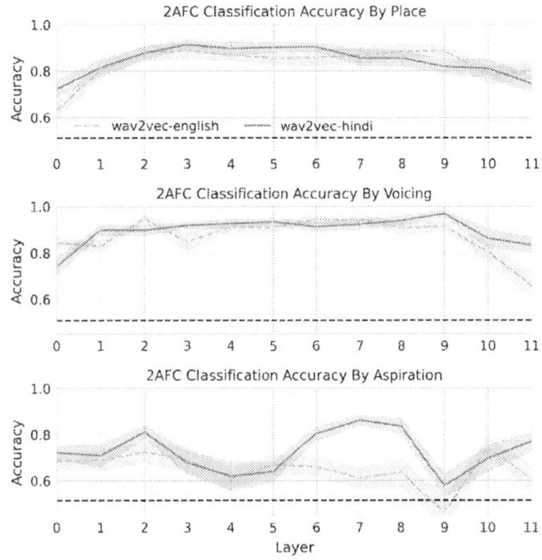

Figure 2: There is no difference in performance for the models on contrasts differing along place or voicing. Wav2vec-hindi outperforms wav2vec-english only on contrasts differing along aspiration.

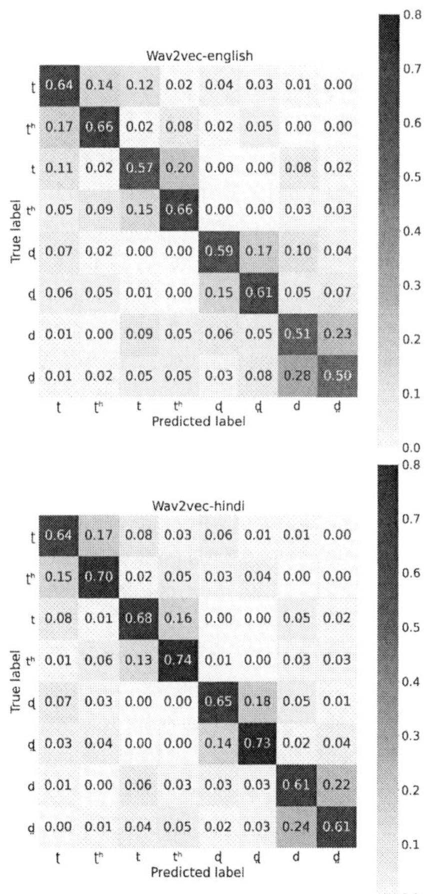

Figure 3: Confusion matrix of Hindi phoneme classification for English and Hindi trained models

difficulty in distinguishing between the Hindi contrasts of place (dental vs. retroflex) or voicing (voiced vs. unvoiced) in phoneme classification. We also found that for distinctions along aspiration (aspirated vs. unaspirasted), wav2vec-hindi outperforms wav2vec-english, displaying a fine-grained effect of language specificity. These results show that the effect of overall language specificity that was found in Experiment 1 was driven primarily by the wav2vec-english model's errors along aspiration when categorization the Hindi phonemes.

Native English listeners who are learning Hindi as a second language primarily struggle with place and voicing distinctions rather than aspiration (Werker et al., 1981; Tees and Werker, 1984; Pruitt et al., 2006; Pederson and Guion-Anderson, 2010; Hayes-Harb and Barrios, 2022). The difficulty in discrimination along place for native English listeners is thought to be due to issues in attending to the relevant acoustic cues differentiating the contrast (Flege and Bohn, 2021; Strange, 2011). The models' performance suggests they are not weighting the relevant cues to category identification in a way similar to humans. This is in line with recent work that has found that wav2vec 2.0 displays different weighting of dimensions than humans in noisy listening environments (Jurov, 2024).

While large speech models may have high performance on downstream speech recognition tasks, they are not learning speech representations in a way comparable to humans. The difference in the learned representations could be because the current pre-trained models are trained in a self-supervised manner without any information regarding category identity, unlike human learners who have knowledge the phonological structure of their native language. This could indicate that the necessary information for creating native-like cue-weighting patterns is guided by higher-level category knowledge that is not present in the current models. Of interest in future work is investigating this differential weighting of acoustic cues to better understand how the learned perceptual spaces differ between humans and speech models and how this may impact global and fine-grained cross-linguistic in categorization and discrimination performance.

3 Conclusion

In this work we explored both global and fine-grained cross-linguistic patterns of categorization in wav2vec 2.0. We found that models perform better overall at test on a language they have been trained on, displaying a global language specificity effect similar to humans. However, when we examined specific contrasts differing along certain phonetic features, the models pattern differently than humans. This result provides evidence of fundamental differences in the structure of representations learned by wav2vec 2.0 and human listeners.

4 Limitations

One limitation of the current work is the reliance on pre-trained models which limited the balance between amount and kind of training data for the wav2vec-hindi and wav2vec-english. Wav2vec-hindi was trained on a greater amount of data than wav2vec-english, but had been trained using the weights from the wav2vec BASE as the starting point for continued pre-training. Thus, the model may be better described as a bilingual Hindi-English model. The current work also displayed results from only wav2vec 2.0, leaving open the question of whether transformer models trained with a different objective would display the same patterns of language specificity.

5 Acknowledgements

We thank Bill Idsardi and the computational cognitive science group for helpful comments and discussion. This work was supported by NSF grant BCS-2120834.

References

Alexei Baevski, Henry Zhou, Abdelrahman Mohamed, and Michael Auli. 2020. wav2vec 2.0: A Framework for Self-Supervised Learning of Speech Representations.

Catherine T. Best and Michael D. Tyler. 2007. Nonnative and second-language speech perception: Commonalities and complementarities. In Ocke-Schwen Bohn and Murray J. Munro, editors, *Language Learning & Language Teaching*, volume 17, pages 13–34. John Benjamins Publishing Company, Amsterdam.

Harveen Singh Chadha, Anirudh Gupta, Priyanshi Shah, Neeraj Chhimwal, Ankur Dhuriya, Rishabh Gaur, and Vivek Raghavan. 2022. Vakyansh: Asr toolkit for low resource indic languages. *Preprint*, arXiv:2203.16512.

Anne Cutler. 2000. Listening to a second language through the ears of a first. *Interpreting. International Journal of Research and Practice in Interpreting*, 5(1):1–23.

James Emil Flege and Ocke-Schwen Bohn. 2021. The Revised Speech Learning Model (SLM-r). In Ratree Wayland, editor, *Second Language Speech Learning*, 1 edition, pages 3–83. Cambridge University Press.

Rachel Hayes-Harb and Shannon Barrios. 2022. Native English speakers and Hindi consonants: From cross-language perception patterns to pronunciation teaching. *Foreign Language Annals*, 55(1):175–197.

Nika Jurov. 2024. *Modeling Adaptability Mechanisms of Speech Perception*. Ph.D. thesis, University of Maryland.

Peter W. Jusczyk. 2000. *The Discovery of Spoken Language*. The MIT Press.

Patricia K. Kuhl, Erica Stevens, Akiko Hayashi, Toshisada Deguchi, Shigeru Kiritani, and Paul Iverson. 2006. Infants show a facilitation effect for native language phonetic perception between 6 and 12 months. *Developmental Science*, 9(2):F13–F21. Https://onlinelibrary.wiley.com/doi/pdf/10.1111/j.1467-7687.2006.00468.x.

Yevgen Matusevych, Thomas Schatz, Herman Kamper, Naomi H. Feldman, and Sharon Goldwater. 2020. Evaluating computational models of infant phonetic learning across languages. *arXiv:2008.02888 [cs, eess]*. ArXiv: 2008.02888.

Michael McAuliffe, Michaela Socolof, Sarah Mihuc, Michael Wagner, and Morgan Sonderegger. 2017. Montreal Forced Aligner: Trainable Text-Speech Alignment Using Kaldi. In *Proc. Interspeech 2017*, pages 498–502.

Juliette Millet and Ewan Dunbar. 2022. Do self-supervised speech models develop human-like perception biases? *arXiv preprint*. ArXiv:2205.15819 [cs, eess].

Juliette Millet, Nika Jurov, and Ewan Dunbar. 2019. Comparing unsupervised speech learning directly to human performance in speech perception. In *CogSci 2019 - 41st Annual Meeting of Cognitive Science Society*, Montréal, Canada.

Kuniko Miyawaki, James J. Jenkins, Winifred Strange, Alvin M. Liberman, Robert Verbrugge, and Osamu Fujimura. 1975. An effect of linguistic experience: The discrimination of [r] and [l] by native speakers of Japanese and English. *Perception & Psychophysics*, 18(5):331–340.

Ankita Pasad, Ju-Chieh Chou, and Karen Livescu. 2021. Layer-Wise Analysis of a Self-Supervised Speech Representation Model. In *2021 IEEE Automatic Speech Recognition and Understanding Workshop (ASRU)*, pages 914–921.

Douglas B. Paul and Janet M. Baker. 1992. The design for the Wall Street Journal-based CSR corpus. In *Speech and Natural Language: Proceedings of a Workshop Held at Harriman, New York, February 23-26, 1992*.

Eric Pederson and Susan Guion-Anderson. 2010. Orienting attention during phonetic training facilitates learning. *The Journal of the Acoustical Society of America*, 127(2):EL54–EL59.

John S. Pruitt, James J. Jenkins, and Winifred Strange. 2006. Training the perception of Hindi dental and retroflex stops by native speakers of American English and Japanese. *The Journal of the Acoustical Society of America*, 119(3):1684–1696. Publisher: Acoustical Society of America.

Thomas Schatz, Naomi H. Feldman, Sharon Goldwater, Xuan-Nga Cao, and Emmanuel Dupoux. 2021. Early phonetic learning without phonetic categories: Insights from large-scale simulations on realistic input. *Proceedings of the National Academy of Sciences*, 118(7):e2001844118.

Winifred Strange. 2011. Automatic selective perception (ASP) of first and second language speech: A working model. *Journal of Phonetics*, 39(4):456–466.

Richard C. Tees and Janet F. Werker. 1984. Perceptual flexibility: Maintenance or recovery of the ability to discriminate non-native speech sounds. *Canadian Journal of Psychology / Revue canadienne de psychologie*, 38(4):579–590.

Janet F. Werker. 1995. Exploring developmental changes in cross-language speech perception. In *An Invitation to Cognitive Science, Volume 1: Language*. The MIT Press. Https://direct.mit.edu/book/chapter-pdf/2306128/9780262273916_cad.pdf.

Janet F. Werker, John H. V. Gilbert, Keith Humphrey, and Richard C. Tees. 1981. Developmental Aspects of Cross-Language Speech Perception. *Child Development*, 52(1):349–355. Publisher: [Wiley, Society for Research in Child Development].

One-Vs-Rest Neural Network English Grapheme Segmentation: A Linguistic Perspective

Samuel Rose*, **Chandrasekhar Kambhampati** and **Nina Dethlefs**
School of Computer Science, University of Hull
Cottingham Road, Hull, HU6 7RX
*s.p.rose-2017@hull.ac.uk

Abstract

Grapheme-to-Phoneme (G2P) correspondences form foundational frameworks of tasks such as text-to-speech (TTS) synthesis or automatic speech recognition. The G2P process involves taking words in their written form and generating their pronunciation. In this paper, we critique the status quo definition of a *grapheme*, currently a forced alignment process relating a single character to either a phoneme or a blank unit, that underlies the majority of modern approaches. We develop a linguistically-motivated redefinition from simple concepts such as vowel and consonant count and word length and offer a proof-of-concept implementation based on a multi-binary neural classification task. Our model achieves competitive results with a 31.86% Word Error Rate on a standard benchmark, while generating linguistically meaningful grapheme segmentations.

1 Introduction

Segmenting words into graphemes is crucial for accurate and reliable text-to-speech systems (Le et al., 2020; Taylor, 2022; Ying et al., 2024), as well as providing a tokenisation framework for training language models for use by varied segments of society (Raškinis et al., 2019; Basher et al., 2023). The currently predominant approach to G2P, which extracts phonemes from a list of graphemes, is one of forced alignment (Williams et al., 2024; Gao et al., 2024; Cheng et al., 2016; Rao et al., 2015). In this approach, a grapheme is defined as a single character that either does or does not have a respective phoneme when using G2P correspondences. This process is illustrated in Table 1 (a) with blank units denoted as φ. However, from a linguistic perspective, a grapheme is not just a single character, but a representation of a phoneme, consisting of up to four characters (Brooks, 2019). Redefining the notion of grapheme could therefore change sub-word tokenisation, allowing for models to be trained on a set of compound graphemes in addition to providing a more linguistically correct method to split words into phonemes. This is shown in Table 1 (b).

The contributions of this paper are as follows:

- We redefine the concept of graphemes in G2P segmentation, aligning it with *Referential Conception* theory (Kohrt, 1986).
- We present a novel twin-staged method for (a) G2P segmentation and (b) phoneme correspondences that approaches the results of leading techniques on a standard CMUDict benchmark.
- We release a new dataset to the community, *EngGraph*, a subset of CMUDict, with 9,641 pre-transcribed British English graphemes to enable future grapheme segmentation research.

2 Related Work

LSTM-based G2P Significant advances in LSTM models for G2P have commonly relied on a one-to-one mapping between graphemes and phonemes. Rao et al. (2015) introduced a unidirectional LSTM with output delays, achieving a word error rate (WER) of 25.8% on the CMUDict benchmark by ensuring 1:1 phoneme-grapheme alignment (e.g., "google" transcribed to g, u, g, @, l, ϕ, where ϕ is a placeholder). Mousa and Schuller (2016) addressed the many-to-many alignment issue with a bidirectional LSTM (BLSTM), achieving a 23.23% WER on the same task by adding a linear projection layer, splicing window, and decoding beam to a 4-layer BLSTM network to improve alignment. Yao and Zweig (2015) achieved a 23.55% WER with a BLSTM and character-to-phoneme alignment that allowed for single, multiple, or no corresponding phonemes (e.g., "tangle" transcribed to T, AE, NG, G, AH: L, NULL).

Attention-based G2P Recent advances in attention mechanisms and transformers have largely

Proceedings of the 28th Conference on Computational Natural Language Learning, pages 464–469
November 15-16, 2024 ©2024 Association for Computational Linguistics

Word	Grapheme Transcription (a)	Phoneme Transcription (a)	Grapheme Transcription (b)	Phoneme Transcription (b)
accuse	a-c-c-u-s-e	@-k-φ-U-z-φ	a-cc-u-se	@-k-U-z
commercial	c-o-m-m-e-r-c-i-a-l	k-ah-m-φ-e-r-s-h-ah-l	c-o-mm-er-ci-a-l	k-ah-m-er-sh-ah-l
boulevard	b-o-u-l-e-v-a-r-d	b-φ-uh-lə-φ-v-φ-ar-d	b-ou-le-v-ar-d	b-ou-lə-v-ar-d

Table 1: Current (a) and proposed (b) linguistic Grapheme transcription examples

kept to the same definition of a grapheme. Toshniwal and Livescu (2016)'s early ensemble model with global attention achieved a 20.24% WER on the CMUDict task, struggling with foreign names, a common issue in G2P models (Waxmonsky and Reddy, 2012). Řezáčková et al. (2021)'s Text-to-Text Transfer Transformer showed a 0.96% WER, but similarly struggled with unseen words, increasing errors to 33.8%. Dong et al. (2022)'s BERT model had a 23.36% WER on Dutch due to English complexities, making it a less comparable baseline.

We advocate for a precise linguistic definition of graphemes, as accurate G2P conversion is vital for natural and clear speech synthesis. Mousa and Schuller (2016)'s models adopt a many-to-many alignment, but still miss the essential graphemic units of trigraphs (e.g., "ear" in "research" for the /ɛ:/ phoneme), quadgraphs (e.g., "ough" in "thought" for the /c:/ phoneme), and split digraphs, a non contigous two character grapheme, (e.g., "a.e" in "rationale" for the /eɪ/ phoneme).

3 Linguistic Definitions of Graphemes

In NLP areas, a grapheme is currently defined as a single character, with G2P models aligning each character with a phoneme or a blank unit. Outside of NLP research, there are two linguistic theories on graphemes. Referential conception (Kohrt, 1986) defines a grapheme as the smallest written unit corresponding with phonemes, like "ph" in "phonetics" for the /f/ phoneme. This theory suggests writing depicts speech. The analogical concept (Lockwood, 2000) uses minimal pairs to show phoneme differences based on spelling, such as "t" and "k" in "parts" and "parks," arguing that writing and speech should be studied separately.

G2P correspondences balance these theories by viewing graphemes as influencing pronunciation but also as distinct from phonemes in TTS research. This hybrid approach presents challenges. Given the focus on TTS in G2P models, we propose adopting the referential conception for computational linguistic applications as in these applications, writing is being used to mimic and create spoken language. We rely on Brooks (2019), who conducted a detailed analysis of British English spelling, identifying 284 graphemes: 89 in the 'main system' and 195 in the 'extended system,' corresponding to 43 phonemes. Brooks notes that while the number of graphemes remains the same in American English, correspondences differ to reflect pronunciation differences.

Grapheme Length	Main System	Extended System
Single Character	26	0
2 Characters	53	118
3 Characters	10	57
4 Characters	0	20

Table 2: Grapheme lengths for the main and extended system (Brooks, 2019)

Analysing grapheme lengths highlights flaws in current G2P models, see Table 2. Current models, which use only single or digraph graphemes, fail to handle the complexities of English, leading to mispronunciations. For instance, without recognising trigraphs, TTS systems can add an extra phoneme in the G2P stage, such as an additional /d/ in "acknowledge." Proper grapheme segmentation transcribes the word as "a-ck-n-o-w-le-dge" with the "dge" grapheme represented with a single /g/ sound with the d being silent, enhancing pronunciation accuracy for simple and complex words.

4 Case Study

4.1 Data Analysis

The initial task of this project was to compile a comprehensive corpus of English words along with their grapheme transcriptions. The Oxford English Dictionary states that the 7,000 most common English words account for 90% of word use (Oxford Dictionaries, 2023), which we used as lower bound of coverage for our resource. Given that there are no existing linguistically transcribed British English grapheme resources, we selected a large set of common English words, specifically, the 10,000 most indexed British English words on web-pages indexed by Google (WorldlyWisdom, 2021) as a basis for a new resource. All words were transcribed into grapheme form based on the guidelines in Brooks (2019). All words in this new British English dataset are also found in the American English CMUDict benchmark, although transcribed to British English pronunciation correspondences instead of American English correspondences.

Our new corpus *EngGraph* includes 9,641 words annotated with grapheme transcriptions, grapheme counts, and basic linguistic features such as word length, vowel and consonant count. In this dataset, all characters are consonants except for the vowels [a,e,i,o,u].[1] Figure 1 illustrates the number of graphemes against characters, consonants and vowels. While the feature counts plotted approximate Gaussian distributions, some grapheme distributions exhibit significant skew and overlap. These deviations pose challenges for mathematical models by distorting data representation and complicating decision boundaries. Specifically, skewness results in asymmetric distributions, affecting membership function evaluations, while overlap makes class distinction difficult, leading to less precise classification and increased ambiguity. This skew proved a challenge for classical mathematical modelling approaches such as Fuzzy Inference Systems (Rose and Kambhampati, 2024), having a grapheme count classification accuracy of 50.18%, with an accuracy of 95.51% if a margin of $\pm$ 1 is given, highlighting the issue of class overlapping.

4.2 One-vs-Rest (OvR) Model

As our key aim is to evaluate the effectiveness of our new linguistically-motivated definition of grapheme, we opt for a simple, easy-to-replicate One-vs-Rest (OvR) architecture: a set of ten identical binary feedforward neural networks. Each network has three inputs (word length, vowel count, consonant count), two dense layers with 128 units, and 30% dropout, with a binary output. The models were trained for 150 epochs with ADAM optimisation, a learning rate of 0.001, a batch size of 8, and early stopping with a patience of 20 epochs.

The architecture was trained on curated subsets of our EngGraph corpus, ensuring all elements are also present in the CMUDict benchmark dataset for comparability. We generated 10 balanced data subsets by selecting all examples with a specified number of graphemes (from 1 to 10) and augmenting each subset with an equal number of examples featuring a different number of graphemes. For instance, the subset for one grapheme includes all records with one grapheme, alongside an equal number of randomly selected records with 2-10 graphemes. This approach ensures an equal distribution of true and false records for each OvR model, with a random 30% of the data reserved as a testing set. Earlier experiments with a single multi-class architecture failed with low accuracy, arguably due to complexities shown in Figure 1.

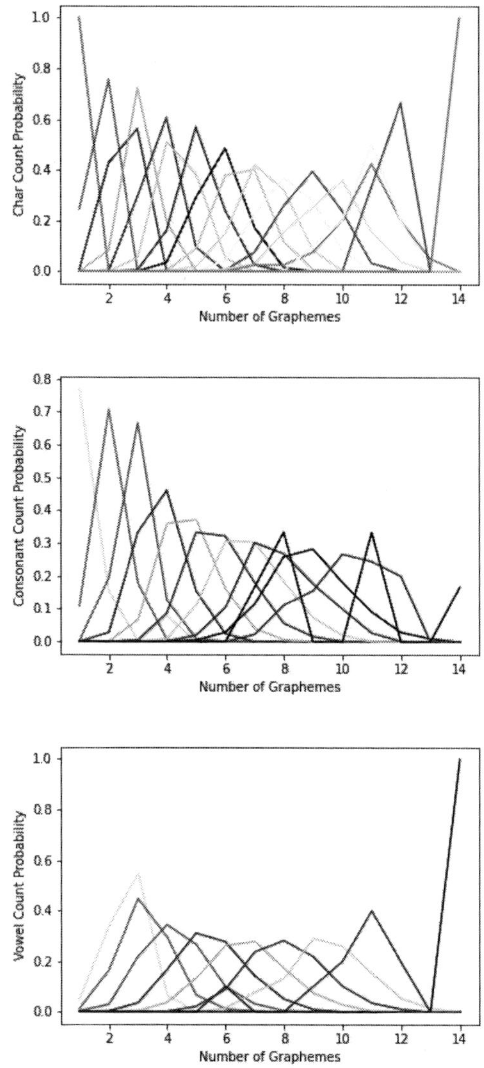

Figure 1: Character, consonant, and vowel count distributions for different numbers of graphemes.

Following the classification of grapheme counts, we developed a word-to-grapheme mapping method to established word error rates. This

[1]This dataset can be found at: `https://github.com/SamuelRoseAI/EngGraph-Dataset/tree/main`

Word	Input	One-vs-Rest Neural Network Outputs										Grapheme Count
		One	Two	Three	Four	Five	Six	Seven	Eight	Nine	Ten	
labelled	[8,3,5]	0.0002	0.0001	0.0217	0.3746	0.6110	0.8101	0.1190	0.0237	0.0097	0.0057	6
ribbon	[6,2,4]	0.0009	0.0028	0.1512	0.7157	0.7987	0.2549	0.0023	0.0021	0.0016	0.0018	5
study	[5,1,4]	0.0054	0.0129	0.5885	0.8390	0.3667	0.0003	0.0001	0.0002	0.0006	0.0006	4
strengthen	[10,2,8]	0.0001	0.0000	0.0001	0.0085	0.0611	0.4718	0.8796	0.8622	0.4068	0.6171	6

Table 3: One-vs-Rest Networks Input and Output Examples

OvR Model	$n = 1$	$n = 2$	$n = 3$	$n = 4$	$n = 5$	$n = 6$	$n = 7$	$n = 8$	$n = 9$	$n = 10$
Accuracy	0.9531	0.9238	0.8744	0.7976	0.7844	0.7855	0.8402	0.8878	0.9255	0.9466
F1-Score	0.95	0.93	0.86	0.82	0.81	0.80	0.85	0.89	0.93	0.95
Recall	0.94	0.99	0.88	0.91	0.89	0.89	0.96	0.97	0.94	0.98
Precision	0.97	0.88	0.85	0.74	0.74	0.73	0.77	0.83	0.92	0.93

Table 4: One-vs-Rest Neural Network classification results, where n equals the number of graphemes.

method uses the OvR classifier with the highest confidence to identify grapheme mappings. If no valid mapping of graphemes is possible using the classified number of graphemes, the class with the next highest confidence is selected. This process is repeated until a valid grapheme mapping and phonetic transcription are obtained. To achieve this, an iterative approach was employed. The list of graphemes was ordered from largest to smallest, and the largest grapheme matching the first n characters of the word was selected. This process continued with the remaining characters until all characters in the word were mapped to a valid grapheme representation. The procedure iterates recursively, ruling out certain grapheme combinations when a valid mapping is not found for the current branch. This approach was validated against the ground truth phonetic transcriptions, yielding a Word Error Rate (WER) of 31.86%, comparable to the models discussed in Sec. 2. This indicates a significant opportunity for future refinements to enhance the accuracy of G2P transcriptions using our proposed new redefinition of graphemes in NLP.

4.3 Results and Discussion

The performance of these ten networks is notably high, see Table 4, and approaching the WERs presented in Sec. 2, despite our simple architecture. The system is computationally efficient despite maintaining ten neural networks. Our OvR format ensures each model is trained on a balanced dataset, distinguishing the characteristics of words with a specified number of graphemes, which adds transparency to grapheme analyses. Our multi-network system is easily extendable, e.g. new datasets can accommodate longer, more linguistically complex words, and more complex neural architectures may further enhance classification performance. Table 3 shows examples of network inputs and outputs, where 3/4 predictions matched the correct grapheme count, while the fourth was off by one.

5 Conclusion

Our redefinition of *graphemes*, inspired by the referential conception theory, has profound implications for the task of G2P. Already approaching results given in state-of-the-art methods using a simple architecture, our research challenges current methodologies, highlighting the limitations of single-character graphemes, and offering a more inclusive framework for text representation and semantic research. This shift paves the way for more accurate, culturally-sensitive language processing systems. This paper advances NLP research by advocating for hybrid graphemes, addressing critical gaps in existing methods. It provides practitioners with tools to improve the performance and adaptability of their applications, and encourages exploration of the phonetics-semantics connection, influencing text tokenisation, segmentation, and feature extraction in NLG applications. Additionally, the application of hybrid graphemes will aid in speech recognition tasks, such as differentiating homophones, and modelling dialect differences in English, reflecting true linguistic diversity and additionally allowing for more culturally sensitive models.

Limitations

Our study has several limitations that should be noted. The dataset, while comprehensive, includes only 9,641 words and focuses on British English pronunciation, potentially limiting its applicability to other English dialects and languages. In addition, while all elements of EngGraph are present in the standard CMUDict Dataset, our study is looking at British English compared to American English and additionally our dataset is not as expansive as the CMUDict dataset which has over 134,000 words with their phonetic transcription. The preprocessing steps and basic feature set, including word length, vowel count, and consonant count, may not fully capture the nuances required for accurate grapheme segmentation, particularly for irregular, slang, borrowed, or complex words. Additionally, the model's simple architecture, though computationally efficient, may not perform as well as more advanced architectures like transformers.

The use of Word Error Rate (WER) as the primary evaluation metric, while standard, does not fully reflect linguistic accuracy, particularly for partial matches. Ethical considerations include potential biases in the dataset, which overlooks regional dialects and minority languages, impacting accessibility and fairness in applications. Furthermore, our study has not been extensively tested in real-world scenarios, which may present challenges not accounted for in controlled experiments. Future work should explore more advanced architectures, a wider range of linguistic features, and larger, more diverse datasets, as well as extend the approach to other languages, English dialects, and real-world applications.

References

Mohammad Jahid Ibna Basher, Mohammad Raghib Noor, Sadia Afroze, Ikbal Ahmed, and Mohammed Moshiul Hoque. 2023. BnGraphemizer: A Grapheme-based Tokenizer for Bengali Handwritten Text Recognition. In *2023 IEEE 9th International Women in Engineering (WIE) Conference on Electrical and Computer Engineering (WIECON-ECE)*, pages 183–188. ISSN: 2837-8245.

Greg Brooks. 2019. *Dictionary of the British English Spelling System*. Open Book Publishers. Accepted: 2021-02-11T11:23:40Z.

Jianpeng Cheng, Li Dong, and Mirella Lapata. 2016. Long Short-Term Memory-Networks for Machine Reading. In *Proceedings of the 2016 Conference on Empirical Methods in Natural Language Processing*, pages 551–561. Association for Computational Linguistics.

Lu Dong, Zhi-Qiang Guo, Chao-Hong Tan, Ya-Jun Hu, Yuan Jiang, and Zhen-Hua Ling. 2022. Neural Grapheme-To-Phoneme Conversion with Pre-Trained Grapheme Models. In *ICASSP 2022 - 2022 IEEE International Conference on Acoustics, Speech and Signal Processing (ICASSP)*, pages 6202–6206. ISSN: 2379-190X.

Heting Gao, Mark Hasegawa-Johnson, and Chang D. Yoo. 2024. G2PU: Grapheme-To-Phoneme Transducer with Speech Units. In *ICASSP 2024 - 2024 IEEE International Conference on Acoustics, Speech and Signal Processing (ICASSP)*, pages 10061–10065. ISSN: 2379-190X.

Manfred Kohrt. 1986. THE TERM 'GRAPHEME' IN THE HISTORY AND THEORY OF LINGUISTICS. In *THE TERM 'GRAPHEME' IN THE HISTORY AND THEORY OF LINGUISTICS*, pages 80–96. De Gruyter.

Duc Le, Thilo Koehler, Christian Fuegen, and Michael L. Seltzer. 2020. G2G: TTS-Driven Pronunciation Learning for Graphemic Hybrid ASR. In *ICASSP 2020 - 2020 IEEE International Conference on Acoustics, Speech and Signal Processing (ICASSP)*, pages 6869–6873. ISSN: 2379-190X.

David G. Lockwood. 2000. Phoneme and grapheme: how parallel can they be? *LACUS Forum*, 27:307–317. Publisher: Linguistic Association of Canada and the United States.

Amr El-Desoky Mousa and Björn Schuller. 2016. Deep Bidirectional Long Short-Term Memory Recurrent Neural Networks for Grapheme-to-Phoneme Conversion Utilizing Complex Many-to-Many Alignments. In *Interspeech 2016*, pages 2836–2840. ISCA.

Oxford Dictionaries. 2023. Oxford English Corpus - Facts About the Language.

Kanishka Rao, Fuchun Peng, Haşim Sak, and Françoise Beaufays. 2015. Grapheme-to-phoneme conversion using Long Short-Term Memory recurrent neural networks. In *2015 IEEE International Conference on Acoustics, Speech and Signal Processing (ICASSP)*, pages 4225–4229. ISSN: 2379-190X.

Gailius Raškinis, Gintarė Paškauskaitė, Aušra Saudargienė, Asta Kazlauskienė, and Airenas Vaičiūnas. 2019. Comparison of Phonemic and Graphemic Word to Sub-Word Unit Mappings for Lithuanian Phone-Level Speech Transcription. *Informatica*, 30(3):573–593. Publisher: Vilnius University Institute of Mathematics and Informatics.

Samuel Rose and Chandrasekhar Kambhampati. 2024. Classifying Graphemes in English Words Through the Application of a Fuzzy Inference System. ArXiv:2404.01953 [cs].

Jason Taylor. 2022. *Pronunciation modelling in end-to-end text-to-speech synthesis*. Ph.D. thesis, University of Edinburgh. Accepted: 2022-06-13T13:54:29Z Publisher: The University of Edinburgh.

Shubham Toshniwal and Karen Livescu. 2016. Jointly learning to align and convert graphemes to phonemes with neural attention models. In *2016 IEEE Spoken Language Technology Workshop (SLT)*, pages 76–82.

Sonjia Waxmonsky and Sravana Reddy. 2012. G2P Conversion of Proper Names Using Word Origin Information. In *Proceedings of the 2012 Conference of the North American Chapter of the Association for Computational Linguistics: Human Language Technologies*, pages 367–371, Montréal, Canada. Association for Computational Linguistics.

Samantha Williams, Paul Foulkes, and Vincent Hughes. 2024. Analysis of forced aligner performance on L2 English speech. *Speech Communication*, 158:103042.

WorldlyWisdom. 2021. Google 10000 English.

Kaisheng Yao and Geoffrey Zweig. 2015. Sequence-to-Sequence Neural Net Models for Grapheme-to-Phoneme Conversion. ArXiv:1506.00196 [cs].

Zelin Ying, Chen Li, Yu Dong, Qiuqiang Kong, Qiao Tian, Yuanyuan Huo, and Yuxuan Wang. 2024. A Unified Front-End Framework for English Text-to-Speech Synthesis. In *ICASSP 2024 - 2024 IEEE International Conference on Acoustics, Speech and Signal Processing (ICASSP)*, pages 10181–10185. ISSN: 2379-190X.

Markéta Řezáčková, Jan Švec, and Daniel Tihelka. 2021. *T5G2P: Using Text-to-Text Transfer Transformer for Grapheme-to-Phoneme Conversion*. International Speech Communication Association. Accepted: 2022-03-28T10:00:27Z ISSN: 2308-457X.

CrowdCounter: A benchmark type-specific multi-target counterspeech dataset

Punyajoy Saha[1], **Abhilash Datta**[1], **Abhik Jana**[2] and **Animesh Mukherjee**[1]
[1]Indian Institute of Technology, Kharagpur, [2]Indian Institute of Technology, Bhubaneswar
punyajoys@iitkgp.ac.in, abhilashdatta8224@gmail.com
abhikjana@iitbbs.ac.in, animeshm@cse.iitkgp.ac.in

Abstract

Counterspeech presents a viable alternative to banning or suspending users for hate speech while upholding freedom of expression. However, writing effective counterspeech is challenging for moderators/users. Hence, developing suggestion tools for writing counterspeech is the need of the hour. One critical challenge in developing such a tool is the lack of quality and diversity of the responses in the existing datasets. Hence, we introduce a new dataset - CrowdCounter containing 3,425 hate speech-counterspeech pairs spanning six different counterspeech types (empathy, humor, questioning, warning, shaming, contradiction), which is the first of its kind. The design of our annotation platform itself encourages annotators to write type-specific, non-redundant and high-quality counterspeech. We evaluate two frameworks for generating counterspeech responses - vanilla and type-controlled prompts - across four large language models. In terms of metrics, we evaluate the responses using relevance, diversity and quality. We observe that Flan-T5 is the best model in the vanilla framework across different models. Type-specific prompts enhance the relevance of the responses, although they might reduce the language quality. DialoGPT proves to be the best at following the instructions and generating the type-specific counterspeech accurately.

1 Introduction

The proliferation of hate speech and offensive language has become a significant problem in the current society (Israeli and Tsur, 2022). Efforts to moderate such content using banning and suspension are ineffective as users might shift to other platforms (Russo et al., 2023). Further, banning/suspension hampers the principles of freedom of speech (Ullmann and Tomalin, 2020). Hence, social scientists are focusing on alternative forms of mitigation strategies, one of which is *counterspeech*. It is a response to abusive or hateful language in the form of constructive and persuasive responses. While counterspeech presents itself as a viable alternative following the principles of freedom of expression, it comes with challenges. A major challenge is the onus on the moderators or the users to write a good counterspeech (Chung et al., 2021b).

Hence, researchers across the globe are attempting to develop NLG-based suggestion tools to help moderators craft counterspeech. One major challenge of building such tools is a good quality and diverse abusive speech-counterspeech pair dataset. Few of the past datasets use synthetically generated hate speech(Chung et al., 2019; Fanton et al., 2021), while others are not very diverse in terms of abusive speech targets (Chung et al., 2019) or types of counterspeech (Qian et al., 2019). Few of the approaches require experts (Chung et al., 2019; Fanton et al., 2021), which makes them less scalable. Hence, we prepare a dataset - CrowdCounter following the steps listed below.

- We use HateXplain (Mathew et al., 2021) to collect the abusive samples which has **diverse targets** and **social media dialect**.
- Our crowd-based annotation platform is designed to avoid common pitfalls, which reduces the dependence on **experts**.
- We encourage the annotators to write a particular type of counterspeech for each hate speech. This ensures **diversity** of responses.

Based on this, we curate a dataset having **3425** hate speech-counterspeech pairs from **1325** unique hate speech which amounts to **2.58** counterspeech per hate speech. The dataset contains six different types of counterspeech as suggested by Benesch (2014). To the best of our knowledge, this is the first benchmark for evaluating type-specific counterspeech generation across various types and targets.

Using this dataset, we built two prompting frame-

Proceedings of the 28th Conference on Computational Natural Language Learning, pages 470–488
November 15-16, 2024

works – vanilla and type-specific prompts, for generating counterspeech using four models. In the vanilla prompt approach, we also compare two parallel hatespeech-counterspeech datasets - Gab and Reddit (Qian et al., 2019). We evaluate the generated responses using three different categories of metrics - referential, diversity and quality. We make the following observations.

- Our dataset has a higher quality in terms of **diversity**, **readability** and **quality** metrics compared to other crowd-sourced datasets - Gab and Reddit.
- **Flan-T5-base** emerges as the top model in the vanilla generation - generating more relevant (meteor and gleu), better quality (gruen) and diverse responses (div, dist-2). The **Llama** models are better in terms of bleurt, while the **DialoGPT** generates counterspeech with high counter-argument quality.
- Type-specific generation enhances the counterspeech quality and relevance (bleurt), deteriorates the language quality, and increases toxicity. **Flan-T5-base** generates the most diverse counterspeech and has better language quality. **DialoGPT** responses follow the type to be generated more accurately in terms of precision and recall. (Examples in Appendix)

We make our annotation framework, code and dataset public at this link[1] for reproducibility and future research.

2 Related works

Counterspeech (Benesch, 2014) has been proposed as an effective mitigation strategy for hate speech (Cypris et al., 2022; Saha et al., 2022; Li et al., 2022; Zhu and Bhat, 2021). One of the earliest works (Qian et al., 2019) collected abusive language from Gab and Reddit and asked the crowd annotators to provide the counterspeech. Few other datasets (Chung et al., 2019; Fanton et al., 2021) rely on expert annotations. One of the key problems of both these datasets is that the hate speech instances are generated synthetically; hence, a counterspeech generation system built on this cannot be deployed on actual social media platforms.

As highlighted by Benesch et al. (2016), different strategies/types are helpful while writing an effective counterspeech. Mathew et al. (2019) curated a dataset of counterspeech, where each instance was annotated by the type(s) they corresponded to. Another dataset (Chung et al., 2019) also contains types annotated along with the counterspeech provided; however, it is only limited to Islamophobic content. Recently, Gupta et al. (2023) re-annotated the counterspeech instances from a past work (Fanton et al., 2021) with type-specific annotation. We had difficulty accessing the dataset for our benchmarking. The data was not available in the mentioned repository- `https://github.com/LCS2-IIITD/quarc-counterspeech`, and we did not receive responses to our emails requesting it. Another paper (Saha et al., 2024a) focused on creating counterspeech in zero-shot setting and tries to create type-specific counterspeech using type-specific prompts. Although this is a step in the right direction, prompt based control provides limited flexiibility. Finally, we were dismayed by not being able to retrieve the dataset and use it for our benchmarking experiments. We did not find the dataset (as claimed by the authors) in the repository associated with the paper - `https://github.com/LCS2-IIITD/quarc-counterspeech`; moreover, the authors did not respond to our e-mails requesting the data.

In our paper, we attempt to address the limitations of the past research and present a dataset of abusive speech-counterspeech pairs CROWDCOUNTER. The abusive speech in this dataset is naturally occurring (from either X or Gab) and is diverse in terms of the number of targets. While the counterspeech is crafted by crowd annotators, we introduced a series of techniques to avoid the pitfalls of crowd-based annotations. The annotators were tasked to craft the counterspeech instances of different types (*warning of consequences*, *shaming/labeling*, *empathy/affiliation*, *humor*, *contradiction* and *questions*) unlike in (Gupta et al., 2023) where the annotators had to label an existing counterspeech with a type thus severely limiting the expression of their own opinion.

3 Dataset curation

In this section, we discuss the details of how CROWDCOUNTER was curated. Specifically, we discuss how we sampled the abusive language dataset, the design of the annotation platform, the selection of annotators and the final dataset curation. We employ annotators from Amazon Mechanical Turk (https://www.mturk.com/), one of the popular annotation platforms. The following subsections provide an in-depth overview of the

[1] `https://github.com/hate-alert/CrowdCounter`

key steps and considerations in our dataset curation process.

3.1 Hate speech sampling

In order to create an abusive speech-counterspeech pairs dataset, we first need to sample the hate speech. Since we wanted the abusive speech to represent speech from the online world, we chose one of the past datasets – HateXplain (Mathew et al., 2021). This dataset has abusive speech from two different platforms and targets 10 different communities like African, Islamic, etc. To collect authentic abusive speech samples, we remove all the samples considered normal by two or more annotators. This amounts to around 12k data points already labeled as abusive, i.e., hate speech or offensive. We consider only the samples from Gab, around 9k data points, since Twitter recently put strict guidelines against making their data public[2]. Finally, we removed all the slur heavy posts (*"Nogs, jews and dykes >>> how enriching "*) having less than ten non-slur words. Slur-heavy posts have less context, discourage diversity and can be easily countered using template-based denouncing strategies. After applying these filtering conditions, we are left with 7474 samples, out of which we select around 1325 random samples for our annotation.

3.2 Definitions

Here, we note the definitions used in the annotation framework which includes the definitions used for identifying something as abusive, i.e., hate speech/offensive and writing counterspeech of different types.

3.2.1 Abusive language

This section outlines the definitions used in the annotation framework for identifying abusive content and writing counterspeech. The authors emphasize the importance of annotators personally identifying content as abusive before writing counterspeech, as this is crucial for effective moderation. We adopt definitions from a previous study (Mathew et al., 2021) who categorize abusive content into two types:

Hate speech: Hate speech is a language used to express hatred toward a targeted individual or group or is intended to be derogatory, to humiliate, or to insult the members of the group, based on sensitive attributes such as race, religion, ethnic origin, sexual orientation, disability, or gender.

Offensive speech: Offensive speech uses profanity, strongly impolite, rude or vulgar language expressed with fighting or hurtful words to insult a targeted individual or group.

3.2.2 Counterspeech

Counterspeech is an expression which aims to provide a positive response to hate speech with the aim to diffuse/dilute the conversation. In addition, counterspeech should further aim to influence the bystanders to act and the perpetrators to change their views using a counterspeech post (Benesch, 2014). Moreover, there are different recommended strategies to write a counterspeech as mentioned in the literature (Mathew et al., 2019; Benesch et al., 2016; Chung et al., 2021a). We summarise the strategies used in this work here (see Appendix section B for more details)

- *Warning of consequences* - Cautioning hate speakers about potential repercussions like harm caused, online consequences, etc.
- *Shaming* - Explicitly calling out hate speech as racist, bigoted, etc. and denouncing it.
- *Empathy/affiliation* - Responding with a friendly, empathetic tone to de-escalate hostility.
- *Humor* - Using humor to defuse tensions and shift the conversation dynamics.
- *Contradiction* - Highlighting contradictions in the hate speaker's stance to discredit them.
- *Questions* - Probing the hate speaker's sources and rationale to encourage self-reflection.

We add the examples of each of these types in the Appendix Table 9. We further ask the annotators not to write hostile counterspeech and not to include factual counterspeech as a type since it is not a recommended strategy (Benesch et al., 2016).

3.3 Design of the annotation platform

We developed an annotation platform which was a web page providing task descriptions, instructions, and examples. Annotators were shown ten examples of abusive speech samples. For each sample, they had to write a counterspeech of a specified required type (Benesch et al., 2016) if they found the sample abusive. They could additionally mark any other counterspeech types employed in their response, as one hate speech sample may warrant multiple counterspeech strategies. Several checks were implemented to ensure quality and

[2]https://developer.twitter.com/en/developer-terms/more-on-restricted-use-cases

diversity in the collected counterspeech. A word counter check requires the response to have more than five words to avoid single-word or very short responses. An open-source grammar checker [3] was used to verify the grammatical correctness of the counterspeech. Additionally, a similarity check was performed to prevent excessive repetition. Frequently occurring counterspeech (over ten times) were identified, and their embeddings were created using `bert-base-uncased` and indexed efficiently using FAISS (Douze et al., 2024). For each new counterspeech, if its cosine similarity to a frequent response exceeded 0.95, it was flagged as a repeated instance. If any of these three checks failed, the annotator had to re-write their counterspeech response. This rigorous annotation process and criteria aimed to collect diverse, grammatically sound, and substantive counterspeech responses, ensuring a high-quality dataset.

3.4 Selection of annotators

We employ annotators from Amazon Mechanical Turk (AMT)[4] using a pilot study. We design the pilot study by collecting the hate speech-counterspeech pairs from three of the past datasets (Qian et al., 2019; Chung et al., 2019). An expert selected these based on the complexity of the hate speech. We selected 10 for such pairs for the pilot study. Each annotator had to respond with a counterspeech if (s)he thinks the post is abusive. One expert manually checks the counterspeech in terms of relevance and the presence of the type mentioned. The expert is an experienced researcher in content moderation research, particularly experienced in counterspeech writing for a period of 5+ years. (S)he is selected if (s)he writes good counterspeech in at least $8 - 10$ posts. We only allow the annotators having a high approval rate (93%) and approved HITS (> 1000) to participate in this task. In this task, the annotators are paid 20 cents if they complete the pilot task. For the main task, we selected 91 annotators out of the 194 who participated in the pilot study.

3.5 Main annotation task

From the set of 1325 abusive samples, we select 50 samples in each batch for the main annotation task. For each sample, we choose three types of counterspeech. Each hate speech and type is shown to a different annotator, and the annotators are expected to write a counterspeech of the designated type. So, we should have three different counterspeech of three different types from three different annotators. For some of the cases, however, we did not get the annotators' responses; therefore, some of the hate speech instances have less than three responses. After completing each batch of such data, an expert checks three samples for quality control and adds the batch to the main dataset. The quality check further removes some of the annotators who still give wrong responses in the main task. The annotator has been paid \$ 1 if they completed one HIT.

3.6 Final dataset

Our final dataset contains 3435 abusive speech-counterspeech pairs obtained from 1325 abusive speech. Out of the 91 users selected, 44 annotators took part in the annotations. The annotators further added additional types to 1115 of their written counterspeech. Overall, the average length of the counterspeech is 20.64 words (with standard deviation $\sigma = 10.88$). Among the types, 980 are of type warning of consequences, 853 are of type questions, 803 are of type shaming, 699 are of type contradiction, 687 are of type empathy/affiliation, and 664 are of type humor. Based on the types, we perform multi-label stratification (Sechidis et al., 2011) to divide this dataset into train and test sets of sizes 2147 and 1288 data points. We make sure the hate speech in the test and train sets are mutually exclusive. We note the keyword distribution and targets of the abusive speech associated with different types of counterspeech in the Appendix (Tables 10 and 11 respectively).

4 Other datasets

Here, we note the other crowd-sourced hate speech-counterspeech pairs (HS-CS) datasets that were used to compare with our dataset. We also note the curation of an additional dataset, which was used to build the multilabel type classifier (section 7).

4.1 HS-CS datasets

In order to evaluate the effectiveness of CROWD-COUNTER as a benchmark dataset, we compare it with two crowd-sourced public datasets (Qian et al., 2019) - Reddit and Gab that contain hate speech and its corresponding counterspeech. Reddit and Gab datasets contain $5,257$ and $14,614$ hate speech instances, respectively. We randomly

[3] https://languagetool.org/

[4] https://www.mturk.com/

take 500 hate speech samples from both these datasets and collect the corresponding counter-speeches to make the test dataset. In order to maintain size parity across all the datasets, we sampled 2000 data points and used them for training for each of these datasets. The test sizes are left intact. The details of these datasets (in terms of HS-CS pairs) are noted in Table 1.

Dataset	#train	#test
Gab	40106	1474
Reddit	12839	1384
CROWDCOUNTER	2147	1288
Type data	4136	1018

Table 1: Training and testing splits for each dataset.

4.2 Type classification dataset

We use two datasets from Mathew et al. (2020) and Chung et al. (2021a) where each counterspeech is associated with one or more types. We merge these two datasets to create a pool of 9963 samples. We remove all the samples with one label as "*hostile*", primarily present in the dataset (Mathew et al., 2020). Finally, for each datapoint, we remove the labels which are not one of the six types that we have considered. Finally, we are left with 5154 samples. Based on the types, we perform a multi-label stratification (Sechidis et al., 2011) to divide the dataset into train, validation and test in the ratio of 60:20:20, respectively. We use this dataset to train a model that can classify the counterspeech type(s) given a (generated) counterspeech. We note the statistics in table 2.

5 Models

Here, we briefly mention the models utilized in this work for counterspeech generation or counterspeech-type classification.

BERT (Devlin et al., 2019):BERT is a pre-trained language model that has revolutionized natural language processing tasks. Developed by Google AI researchers, BERT's bidirectional training approach allows it to understand the context better, leading to improved performance (Devlin et al., 2019). We use the `bert-base-uncased`[5] model having 110M parameters. This model is used for counterspeech-type classification.

DialoGPT (Zhang et al., 2020): DialoGPT (Zhang et al., 2020) is a dialogue-centric language model developed by Microsoft, derived from the GPT-2 architecture and fine-tuned on a large dataset of Reddit conversations. It generates human-like, contextually relevant responses in multi-turn dialogues, making it well-suited for conversational AI applications like chatbots and dialogue systems. We use the `DialoGPT-medium`[6], which has 250M parameters. This model is used for counterspeech generation.

Flan-T5 (Chung et al., 2022): FlanT5 is a large language model developed by Google that builds upon the T5 encoder-decoder architecture. It was trained on a vast and diverse corpus using a unified text-to-text framework, enabling strong performance across a wide range of natural language processing tasks. FLAN-T5's massive scale and innovative training approach have pushed the boundaries of few-shot learning, allowing it to adapt quickly to new tasks with just a few examples. We use the `flan-t5-base`[7] having 250M parameters. This model was used for both counterspeech generation and counterspeech type classification.

Llama (Touvron et al., 2023): Llama is a finely-tuned generative text model designed by Meta. These are trained on a diverse mix of publicly available online data between January 2023 and July 2023, and this model utilizes supervised fine-tuning (SFT) and reinforcement learning with human feedback (RLHF) to align with human preferences for helpfulness and safety. We used the `Llama-2-7b-chat-hf`[8] and the recent `Meta-Llama-3-8B-Instruct`[9] for counterspeech generation. While the former is tuned for chat-specific scenarios, the latter is better in following instructions. We use the 4-bit quantized version of these models along with LoRA (Hu et al., 2021) to train these models.

6 Metrics

Broadly, the metrics in this paper can be divided into three parts - referential, diversity and quality metrics. Diversity and quality metrics do not require the ground truth.

[5] https://huggingface.co/google-bert/bert-base-uncased

[6] https://huggingface.co/microsoft/DialoGPT-medium

[7] https://huggingface.co/google/flan-t5-base

[8] https://huggingface.co/meta-llama/Llama-2-7b-chat-hf

[9] https://huggingface.co/meta-llama/Meta-Llama-3-8B-Instruct

Dataset	#hs	#hs-cn	len	fk (↓)	dc (↓)	div	arg	c-arg	cs	tox (↓)
Gab	13678	41580	15.54	8.67 (-13%)	8.55 (-2%)	0.73 (-14%)	0.17 (-19%)	0.47 (-17%)	0.48 (-6%)	0.15
Reddit	5203	14223	16.03	8.80 (-15%)	8.70 (-4%)	0.72 (-15%)	0.17 (-19%)	0.44 (-20%)	0.49 (-4%)	**0.14**
CROWDCOUNTER	1325	3435	20.65	**7.64**	**8.35**	**0.85**	**0.21**	**0.55**	**0.51**	0.16

Table 2: Comparison of dataset statistics using quality metrics like counterspeech (cs), argument (arg), counter-argument (c_arg), toxicity (tox) scores, readability metrics - Fleisch Kincaid (fk) and Dale Chall (dc) and semantic diversity (div).

6.1 Referential metrics

In terms of traditional referential metrics, we use `gleu` (Wu et al., 2016) and `meteor` (Banerjee and Lavie, 2005) to measure how similar the generated counterspeech are to the ground truth references. In addition, we also report two of the recent generation metrics, `bleurt` (Sellam et al., 2020) and `mover-score` (Zhao et al., 2019). These metrics correlate better with human ratings than traditional metrics like `gleu` or `meteor`.

6.2 Quality metrics

Argument quality: One basic characteristic of the counterspeech is that it should be argumentative. To measure this, we use the confidence score of a `roberta-base-uncased` model[10] fine-tuned on the argument dataset (Stab et al., 2018) on the generated counterspeech.
Counter-argument quality: One can say that a counterspeech should not only be an argument but, more appropriately, a counter-argument to the abusive speech. To measure this, we use the confidence score of a `bert-base-uncased`[11] model (Saha et al., 2024b) trained to identify if the reply to an argument is counter-argument or not.
Counterspeech quality: This metric is beneficial when either ground truth is absent or only a single ground truth is present, which might not be the only way to counter. We use the confidence score from a `bert-base-uncased` (Saha et al., 2024b)[12] model trained to identify something as counterspeech or not.
Toxicity: As highlighted by Howard (2021), counterspeech should aim to diffuse the toxic language. Hence, inherently, the language of the generated response should be non-toxic. We use the HateXplain model (Mathew et al., 2021) trained on two classes – toxic and non-toxic[13] to estimate toxicity of the generated response. We report the confidence in the toxic class. Higher scores in this metric correspond to a higher level of perceived toxicity.
Readability: Readability measures how easily and effectively a written text can be understood by its intended audience, which might determine its engagement (Pancer et al., 2019). We use two of the common metrics – Fleisch Kincaid (Flesch, 2007) and Dale Chall (Dale and Chall, 1948) that have been used in the previous literature and are shown to be correlated with social media engagement.
GRUEN: The GRUEN (GRammaticality, Uncertainty, and ENtailment) metric[14] (Zhu and Bhat, 2020) is designed to evaluate text quality by assessing four dimensions of language generation – grammaticalilty, focus, non-redundancy and coherence.

6.3 Diversity metrics

Diverse responses show their linguistic expanse. It is important as the abusive language has different targets, and various counterspeech types are possible. We employ two traditional diversity metrics: `dist-2` (Li et al., 2016) and `ent-2` (Baheti et al., 2018). While `dist-2` measures the proportion of distinct bigrams within the generated text, `ent-2`, or bigram entropy, calculates the text's unpredictability and richness of word pairings. Finally, we also employ a semantic diversity (`div`) metric. In this metric, we first calculate the average pairwise cosine-similarity across all the generated responses and subtract this value from 1.

6.4 Type-classification metrics

We utilized five metrics used in the previous work (Mathew et al., 2019) – accuracy, precision, recall, f1-score and hamming score for evaluating the type classification. We note the description of these metrics in the Appendix. The metrics are used in two different settings. In Table 3, we compare the predicted output with the ground truth of the test dataset of the counterspeech type data. In Table 6, we try to classify the responses generated by the models. Intuitively, if the type asked to be

[10]`https://huggingface.co/chkla/roberta-argument`
[11]`https://huggingface.co/Hate-speech-CNERG/argument-quality-bert`
[12]`https://huggingface.co/Hate-speech-CNERG/counterspeech-quality-bert`
[13]`https://huggingface.co/Hate-speech-CNERG/bert-base-uncased-hatexplain-rationale-two`
[14]`https://github.com/WanzhengZhu/GRUEN`

generated is the same as the type classified, then the model can generate that type accurately. We use the Flan-T5 (base) for calculating precision and GPT-4 for calculating recall based on the results of Table 3. While precision measures how accurately the model can generate the given type of counterspeech, the recall measures if the given type is one of the predicted types.

7 Experiments

Model	Ham. Loss (↓)	Accuracy	Precision	Recall	F1 Score
BERT	0.25	0.27	0.31	0.27	0.29
Flan-T5 (b)	**0.18**	**0.47**	**0.50**	0.47	**0.49**
GPT-4	0.27	0.37	0.38	**0.66**	**0.49**

Table 3: This table shows the comparison of different models trained and tested on the counterspeech type dataset for the task of type classification. GPT-4 is used in zero-shot setting. We use the accuracy, precision, hamming loss, recall, and F1-score.

Here, we discuss our experimental setup.
Data statistics: We compute different metrics to understand the quality and diversity of responses in our dataset. We compare our dataset's argument quality, counterspeech quality, toxicity, readability, and semantic diversity (div) with the Reddit and Gab datasets. For uniform comparison, we sample 3435 points from all datasets.
Type classification: To perform type classification, we use `bert-base-uncased`, `flan-t5-base` models trained on the training part of the type dataset. We use validation loss to select the best model. Hyperparameters and the instruction prompt for `flan-t5-base` are in Appendix. We also use GPT-4 [15] in a zero-shot setting on the test set. We report accuracy, precision, recall, f1-score, and hamming score.
Counterspeech generation: There are two frameworks for counterspeech generation. The **first** uses a vanilla prompt, training the model on the hate speech-counterspeech dataset from a particular dataset and testing on the same. We use 100 data points for validation and evaluate generated responses using *referential*, *diversity*, and *quality* metrics (Table 4). The **second** framework deals with type-specific counterspeech generation. We use type-specific prompts with both hate speech and counterspeech types. We train on the CROWDCOUNTER dataset, using 100 data points for validation. After training, we generate type-specific counterspeech for each hate speech and type. Hyperparameters and prompts are in Appendix. We evaluate using *reference-based* and *reference-free* settings. In the *reference-based* setting, we select responses matching ground truth counterspeech types for each hate speech. We report type-specific response scores and changes from vanilla responses for bleurt, gruen, argument/counter-argument quality, counterspeech score, and toxicity (Table 5). In the *reference-free* setting, we use semantic diversity (div), dist-2, ent-2, gruen, argument/counter-argument quality, counterspeech score, toxicity, and precision from Flan-T5 and recall from GPT-4 considering the generated type as ground truth.

[15] `https://openai.com/index/gpt-4-research/`

8 Results

Comparison among datasets: We find that CROWDCOUNTER has a higher average length of counterspeech and readability than Reddit and Gab datasets. Due to the mandatory type requirement, CROWDCOUNTER also has a higher diversity of counterspeech. CROWDCOUNTER scores higher on argument, counter-argument quality, and counterspeech quality. While toxicity is slightly higher, it is overall comparable. Table 2 demonstrates CROWDCOUNTER's superiority as a counterspeech benchmark.
Type classification: For type classification, Flan-T5 has the highest performance for hamming loss, accuracy, and precision, while GPT-4 has the highest recall (Table 3). BERT is the worst performer. We use Flan-T5 predictions for precision and GPT-4 for recall when evaluating generated responses (Table 6).
Vanilla generation: Across datasets and metrics (referential, diversity, quality in Table 4), Flan-T5 performs best for meteor, mover's score, div, `dist-2`, and gruen. Llama models are better for bleurt and generating novel counterspeech. DialoGPT excels in counter-argument quality and `ent-2` while having low counterspeech scores for Reddit and Gab.
Type-specific generation: For **reference-based** metrics (Table 5), bleurt improves for most types except humor for Llama models. Language quality decreases except for DialoGPT's contradiction. Counterspeech quality improves for contradiction, empathy, and shaming. Toxicity increases for contradiction, humor, and questions but decreases for empathy and shaming. If we further compare the performances of different models across types, we find that the Llama models produce better bleurt scores, hence generating more relevant counter-

Model	gleu	meteor	bleurt	mover	nov	div	dist-2	ent-2	gruen	arg	c-arg	cs	tox (↓)
						Gab							
DialoGPT	0.01	0.11	-0.62	0.01	0.68	0.65	0.60	**11.07**	0.61	0.15	**0.46**	0.42	0.17
Flan-T5 (b)	**0.03**	**0.18**	-0.59	**0.08**	0.51	**0.69**	**0.77**	10.84	**0.80**	**0.17**	0.42	**0.50**	**0.14**
Llama-2	0.02	0.13	**-0.59**	0.04	0.67	0.62	0.68	9.87	0.68	0.08	0.42	0.22	0.18
Llama-3	0.01	0.10	-0.63	0.00	**0.71**	0.66	0.57	10.42	0.54	0.09	0.42	0.23	0.19
						Reddit							
DialoGPT	0.01	0.10	-0.64	0.01	0.65	0.68	0.59	**11.32**	0.61	0.14	**0.47**	0.32	0.26
Flan-T5 (b)	**0.03**	**0.19**	-0.62	**0.08**	0.50	**0.68**	**0.78**	10.76	**0.80**	**0.17**	0.43	**0.44**	0.16
Llama-2	0.02	0.11	**-0.51**	0.04	**0.69**	0.60	0.62	9.72	0.70	0.11	0.41	0.24	0.20
Llama-3	0.01	0.10	-0.54	0.04	0.65	0.59	0.57	9.91	0.63	0.09	0.41	0.28	**0.16**
						CrowdCounter							
DialogGPT	0.01	0.10	-0.75	-0.03	0.70	0.81	0.59	**11.94**	0.67	0.20	**0.53**	**0.59**	0.15
Flan-T5 (b)	**0.02**	**0.14**	-0.94	-0.02	0.62	**0.85**	**0.75**	11.73	**0.79**	0.17	0.50	0.45	**0.15**
Llama-2	0.02	0.11	-0.75	**-0.02**	0.78	0.80	0.61	11.51	0.67	0.19	0.51	0.42	0.21
Llama-3	0.02	0.10	**-0.67**	-0.03	**0.80**	0.78	0.55	11.61	0.64	**0.20**	0.49	0.57	0.18

Table 4: Evaluation of vanilla responses in terms of referential, diversity and quality metrics. For evaluating referential metrics, we measure the average gleu, meteor (met), bleurt novelty (nov). For diversity, we measure average diversity (div), dist-2, ent-2. For quality, we utilize the counterspeech (cs), argument (arg), counter-argument (c_arg), and toxicity (tox) scores, and gruen. **Bold** denotes the best scores, and higher scores denote better performance except for toxicity.

Type	Model	bleurt	gruen	arg	c-arg	cs	tox(↓)
con	DialoGPT	-0.75 (2.6%)	0.65 (6.56%)	0.21 (-8.7%)	**0.55** (10.0%)	0.68 (9.68%)	**0.15** (7.14%)
	Flan-T5 (b)	-0.89 (7.29%)	**0.74** (-5.13%)	0.21 (31.25%)	0.55 (5.77%)	0.55 (19.57%)	0.17 (30.77%)
	Llama-2	**-0.65** (14.47%)	0.62 (-1.59%)	0.26 (36.84%)	0.54 (5.88%)	0.62 (31.91%)	0.21 (0.0%)
	Llama-3	-0.66 (5.71%)	0.54 (-6.9%)	**0.29** (31.82%)	0.5 (2.04%)	**0.72** (16.13%)	0.19 (26.67%)
emp	DialoGPT	-0.69 (8.0%)	0.65 (6.56%)	**0.22** (4.76%)	**0.57** (9.62%)	0.7 (20.69%)	0.17 (13.33%)
	Flan-T5 (b)	-0.77 (18.09%)	**0.75** (-3.85%)	0.18 (-5.26%)	0.55 (7.84%)	0.69 (76.92%)	0.16 (14.29%)
	Llama-2	**-0.54** (26.03%)	0.67 (6.35%)	0.21 (10.53%)	0.57 (11.76%)	0.67 (52.27%)	**0.1** (-54.55%)
	Llama-3	-0.59 (9.23%)	0.65 (10.17%)	0.2 (-4.76%)	0.52 (10.64%)	**0.73** (7.35%)	0.1 (-37.5%)
hum	DialoGPT	-0.8 (3.61%)	0.65 (4.84%)	**0.23** (15.0%)	0.57 (5.56%)	**0.67** (11.67%)	**0.17** (0.0%)
	Flan-T5 (b)	-0.94 (4.08%)	**0.73** (-7.59%)	0.18 (5.88%)	0.5 (-1.96%)	0.61 (38.64%)	0.18 (12.5%)
	Llama-2	-0.82 (-3.8%)	0.63 (5.0%)	0.21 (16.67%)	0.54 (3.85%)	0.42 (-16.0%)	0.25 (47.06%)
	Llama-3	**-0.79** (-9.72%)	0.59 (1.72%)	0.21 (-8.7%)	**0.59** (15.69%)	0.58 (-6.45%)	0.23 (35.29%)
que	DialoGPT	-0.76 (2.56%)	0.61 (0.0%)	**0.17** (-22.73%)	0.49 (-10.91%)	**0.58** (0.0%)	0.23 (76.92%)
	Flan-T5 (b)	-0.99 (-4.21%)	**0.77** (-1.28%)	0.09 (-52.63%)	0.48 (-11.11%)	0.53 (23.26%)	**0.19** (18.75%)
	Llama-2	-0.69 (8.0%)	0.6 (-1.64%)	0.14 (-22.22%)	0.52 (0.0%)	0.43 (-15.69%)	0.25 (25.0%)
	Llama-3	**-0.67** (4.29%)	0.52 (-11.86%)	0.17 (-22.73%)	**0.53** (6.0%)	0.46 (-25.81%)	0.3 (87.5%)
sha	DialoGPT	-0.72 (2.7%)	0.63 (1.61%)	0.21 (10.53%)	0.52 (0.0%)	**0.67** (11.67%)	**0.15** (7.14%)
	Flan-T5 (b)	-0.72 (21.74%)	**0.76** (-3.8%)	0.2 (11.11%)	0.51 (-1.92%)	0.63 (34.04%)	0.16 (14.29%)
	Llama-2	**-0.56** (22.22%)	0.6 (-3.23%)	0.22 (15.79%)	**0.53** (6.0%)	0.63 (53.66%)	0.15 (-28.57%)
	Llama-3	-0.59 (6.35%)	0.49 (-18.33%)	**0.23** (9.52%)	0.44 (-2.22%)	0.61 (5.17%)	0.15 (-16.67%)
war	DialoGPT	-0.64 (13.51%)	0.61 (0.0%)	0.19 (-9.52%)	**0.53** (-3.64%)	**0.63** (8.62%)	0.1 (-28.57%)
	Flan-T5 (b)	-0.81 (11.96%)	**0.77** (-1.28%)	0.16 (0.0%)	0.49 (-7.55%)	0.37 (-21.28%)	**0.06** (-60.0%)
	Llama-2	**-0.55** (25.68%)	0.62 (-1.59%)	0.17 (-5.56%)	0.47 (-9.62%)	0.52 (10.64%)	0.11 (-45.0%)
	Llama-3	-0.56 (16.42%)	0.51 (-15.0%)	**0.21** (0.0%)	0.46 (-11.54%)	0.59 (-6.35%)	0.06 (-64.71%)

Table 5: This table shows the evaluation of type specific responses with respect to vanilla responses for all the six categories of counterspeech. We report the type-specific scores and changes compared to vanilla generation. We measure bleurt, counterspeech (cs), argument (arg), counter-argument (c_arg), toxicity (tox) scores and gruen. **Bold** denotes the best scores, and higher scores denote better performance except for toxicity.

speech.

For **reference-free** metrics (Table 6), Flan-T5 has the best semantic diversity (div), dist-2, gruen, and precision. DialoGPT excels in ent-2. Llama-3 is best for argument quality except for empathy-affiliation. DialoGPT has the highest precision for questions and warning-of-consequences types. In terms of recall, DialoGPT has again the highest scores for empathy-affiliation, questions, shaming and warning-of-consequences. The Llama family models are less diverse which might highlight the issue of size vs steerability for such subjective tasks. Overall, we find that no model outperforms in all counterspeech metrics. One can choose Llama for relevancy, Llama/DialoGPT for high counterspeech scores, or Flan-T5 for language quality. Further research is needed to develop a more comprehensive solution.

Human judgement: We took 10 generated counterspeeches each with best and worst bleurt scores for each type thus making a set of 120 samples and got them annotated by 4 experts who have long experience of research and publications on this topic. Each annotator rated each generated counterspeech on a scale of 1-5 with 1 being the worst and 5 being the best. We did the exact same exercise for 10 generated counterspeeches, but now, each with best and worst cs-scores. We measure the Pearson's correlation between the bleurt/cs-scores and the human judgement ratings. The results from these evaluations are presented in Table 7. Not surprisingly we observe (as was also observed in (Saha

Type	Model	div	dist-2	ent-2	gruen	arg	c-arg	cs	tox(↓)	prec	rec
con	DialoGPT	0.79	0.54	**12.04**	0.64	0.22	0.55	0.67	**0.16**	0.04	0.82
	Flan-T5	**0.83**	**0.70**	12.00	**0.74**	0.21	0.54	0.57	0.19	0.05	**0.87**
	Llama-2	0.79	0.55	11.63	0.62	0.25	**0.57**	0.60	0.22	**0.05**	0.70
	Llama-3	0.78	0.50	11.53	0.54	**0.27**	0.52	**0.67**	0.18	0.02	0.79
aff	DialoGPT	0.78	0.54	**12.09**	0.64	**0.22**	0.56	**0.69**	0.16	**0.32**	**0.84**
	Flan-T5	**0.80**	**0.66**	11.62	**0.74**	0.16	**0.56**	0.65	0.16	0.20	0.66
	Llama-2	0.71	0.56	10.99	0.67	0.21	0.53	0.67	**0.13**	0.26	0.50
	Llama-3	0.71	0.54	11.23	0.64	0.19	0.52	0.68	0.11	0.11	0.37
hum	DialoGPT	0.79	0.54	**12.14**	0.64	0.21	0.55	**0.67**	**0.16**	0.28	0.13
	Flan-T5	**0.85**	**0.70**	12.10	**0.74**	0.18	0.53	0.60	0.17	**0.31**	**0.17**
	Llama-2	0.83	0.58	11.85	0.62	0.21	0.53	0.47	0.26	0.28	0.13
	Llama-3	0.82	0.53	11.96	0.57	**0.22**	**0.56**	0.58	0.21	0.25	0.06
que	DialoGPT	0.83	0.53	**11.84**	0.59	0.16	0.51	**0.56**	0.22	**0.92**	**0.96**
	Flan-T5	0.83	**0.76**	11.37	**0.77**	0.08	0.48	0.51	**0.19**	0.81	0.91
	Llama-2	**0.85**	0.54	11.56	0.60	0.15	**0.52**	0.42	0.27	0.84	0.95
	Llama-3	0.83	0.50	11.48	0.52	**0.16**	0.49	0.46	0.29	0.68	0.89
sha	DialoGPT	**0.78**	0.55	**12.02**	0.64	0.22	**0.57**	**0.68**	0.15	0.00	**0.43**
	Flan-T5	0.75	**0.70**	11.39	**0.76**	0.21	0.53	0.68	**0.13**	0.00	0.38
	Llama-2	0.72	0.54	11.17	0.60	0.23	0.53	0.64	0.17	0.00	0.27
	Llama-3	0.71	0.50	11.04	0.51	**0.25**	0.47	0.66	0.16	0.00	0.30
war	DialoGPT	0.71	0.53	**10.83**	0.61	0.19	**0.54**	**0.62**	0.10	**0.94**	**0.99**
	Flan-T5	**0.70**	**0.78**	9.26	**0.78**	0.17	0.49	0.38	**0.06**	0.85	0.98
	Llama-2	0.63	0.56	10.62	0.62	0.15	0.48	0.52	0.11	0.89	0.97
	Llama-3	0.59	0.49	9.91	0.49	**0.20**	0.46	0.61	0.06	0.76	0.92

Table 6: This table shows the evaluation of type specific responses. We measure semantic diversity (div), dist-2, ent-2, counterspeech (cs), argument (arg), counter argument (c_arg), toxicity (tox) scores, gruen, precision (prec) using Flan-T5 and recall (rec) using GPT-4. **Bold** denotes the best scores, and higher scores denote better performance except for toxicity.

Type	Bleurt	CS-score
con	0.66	0.66
aff	0.31	0.52
hum	0.18	0.77
que	0.17	0.77
sha	0.71	0.58
war	0.37	0.52

Table 7: This table shows the Pearson's correlation between the bleurt/cs-scores and the human judgement ratings.

et al., 2024a)) that across all the types the correlations are positive (always > 0.5 for at least one of the two metrics) thus reinforcing the utility of the automatic metrics we chose.

9 Conclusion

In conclusion, we create the first ever type-specific, diverse and crowd-sourced abusive-counterspeech pairs - CROWDCOUNTER. We trained four language models in two different frameworks i.e., vanilla and type-specific prompting. We evaluated the responses generated by these models along the dimensions of relevance, diversity and quality. We notice that compared to other crowd-sourced datasets, i.e., Gab and Reddit, CROWDCOUNTER has higher diversity and quality. In terms of vanilla generation, finetuned Flan-T5 is quite superior to even larger models from the Llama family while being 32x smaller than them. Constraining the models to generate a particular type of counterspeech does improve the relevance of their outputs but also reduces the language quality to some extent. Finally, DialoGPT is quite proficient at following the type-specific instructions better than all the other models. Examples of generations are added in Appendix table 12 and 13. Overall, this work opens up new avenues towards generating and evaluating type-specific counterspeech.

10 Limitations

Our work has a few limitations. Our dataset is only based on the English language, but our framework is general enough to extend to other languages as per requirement. We select the abusive content from only one specific platform - Gab, owing to various stringent policies regarding data-sharing in other platforms. Due to resource constraints, we had to run the Llama family models in quantized settings, which might have led to inferior performance compared to other models. Many of our automatic metrics are based on particular datasets, which might carry the bias of those datasets. However, we have to rely on these models to do a large-scale evaluation.

11 Ethics statement

As part of data ethics, we anonymize the worker IDs before sharing the data with the public. Although our paper proposes fine-tuned large language models as counterspeech generators, we advocate against the fully automated usage of such models. We built these models as an active aid for moderators or users who wish to write counterspeech. Even then, appropriate guardrails should be applied to these models before making them public for such a sensitive task. Further, we encourage active monitoring of such counterspeech suggestion tools if deployed.

References

Ashutosh Baheti, Alan Ritter, Jiwei Li, and Bill Dolan. 2018. Generating more interesting responses in neural conversation models with distributional constraints. In *Proceedings of the 2018 Conference on Empirical Methods in Natural Language Processing*, pages 3970–3980, Brussels, Belgium. Association for Computational Linguistics.

Satanjeev Banerjee and Alon Lavie. 2005. Meteor: An automatic metric for mt evaluation with improved correlation with human judgments. In *Proceedings of the acl workshop on intrinsic and extrinsic evaluation measures for machine translation and/or summarization*, pages 65–72.

Susan Benesch. 2014. Countering dangerous speech: New ideas for genocide prevention. *Washington, DC: United States Holocaust Memorial Museum*.

Susan Benesch, Derek Ruths, Kelly P Dillon, Haji Mohammad Saleem, and Lucas Wright. 2016. Considerations for successful counterspeech. *A report for Public Safety Canada under the Kanishka Project. Accessed November*, 25:2020.

Hyung Won Chung, Le Hou, Shayne Longpre, Barret Zoph, Yi Tay, William Fedus, Yunxuan Li, Xuezhi Wang, Mostafa Dehghani, Siddhartha Brahma, Albert Webson, Shixiang Shane Gu, Zhuyun Dai, Mirac Suzgun, Xinyun Chen, Aakanksha Chowdhery, Alex Castro-Ros, Marie Pellat, Kevin Robinson, Dasha Valter, Sharan Narang, Gaurav Mishra, Adams Yu, Vincent Zhao, Yanping Huang, Andrew Dai, Hongkun Yu, Slav Petrov, Ed H. Chi, Jeff Dean, Jacob Devlin, Adam Roberts, Denny Zhou, Quoc V. Le, and Jason Wei. 2022. Scaling instruction-finetuned language models.

Yi-Ling Chung, Marco Guerini, and Rodrigo Agerri. 2021a. Multilingual counter narrative type classification. *arXiv preprint arXiv:2109.13664*.

Yi-Ling Chung, Elizaveta Kuzmenko, Serra Sinem Tekiroglu, and Marco Guerini. 2019. CONAN - COunter NArratives through nichesourcing: a multilingual dataset of responses to fight online hate speech. In *Proceedings of the 57th Annual Meeting of the Association for Computational Linguistics*, pages 2819–2829, Florence, Italy. Association for Computational Linguistics.

Yi-Ling Chung, Serra Sinem Tekiroğlu, Sara Tonelli, and Marco Guerini. 2021b. Empowering ngos in countering online hate messages. *Online Social Networks and Media*, 24:100150.

Niklas Felix Cypris, Severin Engelmann, Julia Sasse, Jens Grossklags, and Anna Baumert. 2022. Intervening against online hate speech: A case for automated counterspeech. *IEAI Research Brief*, pages 1–8.

Edgar Dale and Jeanne S Chall. 1948. A formula for predicting readability: Instructions. *Educational research bulletin*, pages 37–54.

Tim Dettmers, Artidoro Pagnoni, Ari Holtzman, and Luke Zettlemoyer. 2023. Qlora: Efficient finetuning of quantized llms.

Jacob Devlin, Ming-Wei Chang, Kenton Lee, and Kristina Toutanova. 2019. BERT: Pre-training of deep bidirectional transformers for language understanding. In *Proceedings of the 2019 Conference of the North American Chapter of the Association for Computational Linguistics: Human Language Technologies, Volume 1 (Long and Short Papers)*, pages 4171–4186, Minneapolis, Minnesota. Association for Computational Linguistics.

Matthijs Douze, Alexandr Guzhva, Chengqi Deng, Jeff Johnson, Gergely Szilvasy, Pierre-Emmanuel Mazaré, Maria Lomeli, Lucas Hosseini, and Hervé Jégou. 2024. The faiss library. *arXiv preprint arXiv:2401.08281*.

Margherita Fanton, Helena Bonaldi, Serra Sinem Tekiroğlu, and Marco Guerini. 2021. Human-in-the-loop for data collection: a multi-target counter narrative dataset to fight online hate speech. In *Proceedings of the 59th Annual Meeting of the Association for Computational Linguistics and the 11th International Joint Conference on Natural Language Processing (Volume 1: Long Papers)*, pages 3226–3240, Online. Association for Computational Linguistics.

Rudolf Flesch. 2007. Flesch-kincaid readability test. *Retrieved October*, 26(3):2007.

Rishabh Gupta, Shaily Desai, Manvi Goel, Anil Bandhakavi, Tanmoy Chakraborty, and Md. Shad Akhtar. 2023. Counterspeeches up my sleeve! intent distribution learning and persistent fusion for intent-conditioned counterspeech generation. In *Proceedings of the 61st Annual Meeting of the Association for Computational Linguistics (Volume 1: Long Papers)*, pages 5792–5809, Toronto, Canada. Association for Computational Linguistics.

Jeffrey W Howard. 2021. Terror, hate and the demands of counter-speech. *British Journal of Political Science*, 51(3):924–939.

Edward J Hu, Yelong Shen, Phillip Wallis, Zeyuan Allen-Zhu, Yuanzhi Li, Shean Wang, Lu Wang, and Weizhu Chen. 2021. Lora: Low-rank adaptation of large language models. *arXiv preprint arXiv:2106.09685*.

Abraham Israeli and Oren Tsur. 2022. Free speech or free hate speech? analyzing the proliferation of hate speech in parler. In *Proceedings of the Sixth Workshop on Online Abuse and Harms (WOAH)*, pages 109–121, Seattle, Washington (Hybrid). Association for Computational Linguistics.

Jiwei Li, Michel Galley, Chris Brockett, Jianfeng Gao, and Bill Dolan. 2016. A diversity-promoting objective function for neural conversation models. In *Proceedings of the 2016 Conference of the North American Chapter of the Association for Computational Linguistics: Human Language Technologies*, pages 110–119, San Diego, California. Association for Computational Linguistics.

Yu Li, Baolin Peng, Yelong Shen, Yi Mao, Lars Liden, Zhou Yu, and Jianfeng Gao. 2022. Knowledge-grounded dialogue generation with a unified knowledge representation. In *Proceedings of the 2022 Conference of the North American Chapter of the Association for Computational Linguistics: Human Language Technologies*, pages 206–218, Seattle, United States. Association for Computational Linguistics.

Binny Mathew, Navish Kumar, Pawan Goyal, and Animesh Mukherjee. 2020. Interaction dynamics between hate and counter users on twitter. In *Proceedings of the 7th ACM IKDD CoDS and 25th COMAD*, CoDS COMAD 2020, page 116–124, New York, NY, USA. Association for Computing Machinery.

Binny Mathew, Punyajoy Saha, Hardik Tharad, Subham Rajgaria, Prajwal Singhania, Suman Kalyan Maity, Pawan Goyal, and Animesh Mukherjee. 2019. Thou shalt not hate: Countering online hate speech. In *Proceedings of the international AAAI conference on web and social media*, volume 13, pages 369–380.

Binny Mathew, Punyajoy Saha, Seid Muhie Yimam, Chris Biemann, Pawan Goyal, and Animesh Mukherjee. 2021. Hatexplain: A benchmark dataset for explainable hate speech detection. In *Proceedings of the AAAI conference on artificial intelligence*, volume 35, pages 14867–14875.

Ethan Pancer, Vincent Chandler, Maxwell Poole, and Theodore J Noseworthy. 2019. How readability shapes social media engagement. *Journal of Consumer Psychology*, 29(2):262–270.

Kishore Papineni, Salim Roukos, Todd Ward, and Wei-Jing Zhu. 2002. Bleu: a method for automatic evaluation of machine translation. In *Proceedings of the 40th annual meeting of the Association for Computational Linguistics*, pages 311–318.

Jing Qian, Anna Bethke, Yinyin Liu, Elizabeth Belding, and William Yang Wang. 2019. A benchmark dataset for learning to intervene in online hate speech. In *Proceedings of the 2019 Conference on Empirical Methods in Natural Language Processing and the 9th International Joint Conference on Natural Language Processing (EMNLP-IJCNLP)*, pages 4755–4764.

Giuseppe Russo, Luca Verginer, Manoel Horta Ribeiro, and Giona Casiraghi. 2023. Spillover of antisocial behavior from fringe platforms: The unintended consequences of community banning. In *Proceedings of the International AAAI Conference on Web and Social Media*, volume 17, pages 742–753.

Punyajoy Saha, Aalok Agrawal, Abhik Jana, Chris Biemann, and Animesh Mukherjee. 2024a. On zero-shot counterspeech generation by LLMs. In *Proceedings of the 2024 Joint International Conference on Computational Linguistics, Language Resources and Evaluation (LREC-COLING 2024)*, pages 12443–12454, Torino, Italia. ELRA and ICCL.

Punyajoy Saha, Aalok Agrawal, Abhik Jana, Chris Biemann, and Animesh Mukherjee. 2024b. On zero-shot counterspeech generation by llms. In *Proceedings of the 2024 Joint International Conference on Computational Linguistics, Language Resources and Evaluation (LREC-COLING 2024)*, pages 12443–12454.

Punyajoy Saha, Kanishk Singh, Adarsh Kumar, Binny Mathew, and Animesh Mukherjee. 2022. Countergedi: A controllable approach to generate polite, detoxified and emotional counterspeech. *arXiv preprint arXiv:2205.04304*.

Gerard Salton and Chris Buckley. 1988. Term-weighting approaches in automatic text retrieval. *Inf. Process. Manag.*, 24:513–523.

Konstantinos Sechidis, Grigorios Tsoumakas, and Ioannis Vlahavas. 2011. On the stratification of multi-label data. In *Machine Learning and Knowledge Discovery in Databases: European Conference, ECML PKDD 2011, Athens, Greece, September 5-9, 2011, Proceedings, Part III 22*, pages 145–158. Springer.

Thibault Sellam, Dipanjan Das, and Ankur Parikh. 2020. Bleurt: Learning robust metrics for text generation. In *Proceedings of the 58th Annual Meeting of the Association for Computational Linguistics*, pages 7881–7892.

Christian Stab, Tristan Miller, Benjamin Schiller, Pranav Rai, and Iryna Gurevych. 2018. Cross-topic argument mining from heterogeneous sources. In *Proceedings of the 2018 Conference on Empirical Methods in Natural Language Processing*, pages 3664–3674, Brussels, Belgium. Association for Computational Linguistics.

Hugo Touvron, Louis Martin, Kevin Stone, Peter Albert, Amjad Almahairi, Yasmine Babaei, Nikolay Bashlykov, Soumya Batra, Prajjwal Bhargava, Shruti Bhosale, Dan Bikel, Lukas Blecher, Cristian Canton Ferrer, Moya Chen, Guillem Cucurull, David Esiobu, Jude Fernandes, Jeremy Fu, Wenyin Fu, Brian Fuller, Cynthia Gao, Vedanuj Goswami, Naman Goyal, Anthony Hartshorn, Saghar Hosseini, Rui Hou, Hakan Inan, Marcin Kardas, Viktor Kerkez, Madian Khabsa, Isabel Kloumann, Artem Korenev, Punit Singh Koura,

Marie-Anne Lachaux, Thibaut Lavril, Jenya Lee, Diana Liskovich, Yinghai Lu, Yuning Mao, Xavier Martinet, Todor Mihaylov, Pushkar Mishra, Igor Molybog, Yixin Nie, Andrew Poulton, Jeremy Reizenstein, Rashi Rungta, Kalyan Saladi, Alan Schelten, Ruan Silva, Eric Michael Smith, Ranjan Subramanian, Xiaoqing Ellen Tan, Binh Tang, Ross Taylor, Adina Williams, Jian Xiang Kuan, Puxin Xu, Zheng Yan, Iliyan Zarov, Yuchen Zhang, Angela Fan, Melanie Kambadur, Sharan Narang, Aurelien Rodriguez, Robert Stojnic, Sergey Edunov, and Thomas Scialom. 2023. Llama 2: Open foundation and fine-tuned chat models.

Stefanie Ullmann and Marcus Tomalin. 2020. Quarantining online hate speech: technical and ethical perspectives. *Ethics and Information Technology*, 22:69–80.

Yonghui Wu, Mike Schuster, Zhifeng Chen, Quoc V Le, Mohammad Norouzi, Wolfgang Macherey, Maxim Krikun, Yuan Cao, Qin Gao, Klaus Macherey, et al. 2016. Google's neural machine translation system: Bridging the gap between human and machine translation. *arXiv preprint arXiv:1609.08144*.

Yizhe Zhang, Siqi Sun, Michel Galley, Yen-Chun Chen, Chris Brockett, Xiang Gao, Jianfeng Gao, Jingjing Liu, and William B Dolan. 2020. Dialogpt: Large-scale generative pre-training for conversational response generation. In *Proceedings of the 58th Annual Meeting of the Association for Computational Linguistics: System Demonstrations*, pages 270–278.

Wei Zhao, Maxime Peyrard, Yang Gao Fei Liu, Christian M. Meyer, and Steffen Eger. 2019. Moverscore: Text generation evaluating with contextualized embeddings and earth mover distance. In *Proceedings of the 2019 Conference on Empirical Methods in Natural Language Processing*, Hong Kong, China. Association for Computational Linguistics.

Wanzheng Zhu and Suma Bhat. 2020. Gruen for evaluating linguistic quality of generated text. In *Proceedings of the 2020 Conference on Empirical Methods in Natural Language Processing: Findings*, pages 94–108.

Wanzheng Zhu and Suma Bhat. 2021. Generate, prune, select: A pipeline for counterspeech generation against online hate speech. In *Findings of the Association for Computational Linguistics: ACL-IJCNLP 2021*, pages 134–149, Online. Association for Computational Linguistics.

A Annotation details

We note the pilot questions from the annotations tasks in the Table 8 and the examples of the particular counterspeech in the Table 9.

Hate speech	Counterspeech	Type
Minorities vote to strip wealth and power from White people and they are organised to do this by the J*ws	Where is the evidence for this claim ?	que
It is enough to burn down mosques and the Koran to solve all our problems.	That sounds a lot like terrorism to me.	sha
All Muslims are incompatible with any Western society.	Millions of Muslims live in western nations.	con
Our national flag cannot be shown as it could annoy a Muslim.#fitinorfuckoff.,	I am really good at making up stories, believing only the things I want to and then ranting about it too.	hum
We must send Islamics back to their native countries. They are too different from us.	I have met so many Muslim people adhering to British values. What do you base your view on?	emp
The Jews did: USS Liberty Attack, the King David hotel attack, New York 9/11, London 7/7	Where is the proof of this? Looks like assumptions as opposed to facts...	que
The world would be a better place without Muslims. They are only killing and raping our children.	There is a problem in every community, what are you doing to stop it in yours?	con
The vast majority of Muslims are unemployed and refuse to work.	All Muslim people I know are employed and hardworking individuals. Stereotyping much?	emp
Muslim invasion is the new plague of London. They must be repatriated to their home countries!	Invasion? Don't you think this expression is slightly over dramatic? People simply want to live in one of the best cities in the world!	sha
Never break bread with a Quranimal. You risk catching HIV and/or Ebola.	If you do not think Muslims have ever done anything for 'us' I think you need to do a quick google search. The evidence of Muslims contributions to society is everywhere!	con

Table 8: This table shows the expert-written hate speech and counterspeech pairs along with their types.

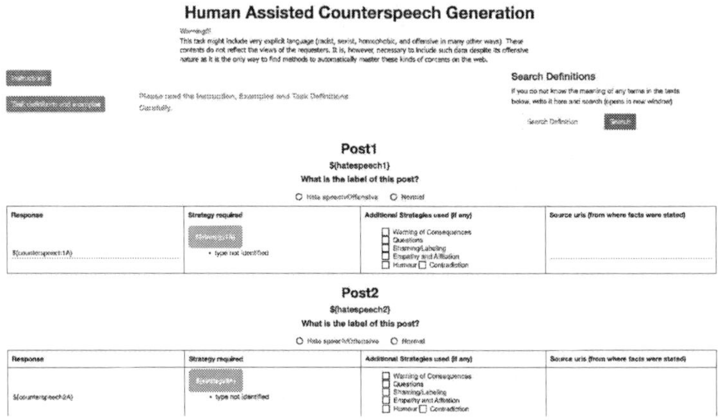

Figure 1: The annotation platform which was used in MTurk.

Type	Hate speech	Counterspeech
Warning of consequences	The world would be a better place without Muslims. They are only killing and raping our children.	Online communication is permanent, so please choose your words carefully.
	What if our entire ruling class consisted of J-controlled paedophiles? That would explain a lot.	You might be banned for making such harmful and questionable claims, so please be aware.
Shaming	Islam is characterized by hate! When the first Muslim set foot in Britain, racism started in England!	Perhaps you should monitor your own hate speech before pointing the finger at others?
	Islam is all about hate! When Muslims first set foot in Britain was when race hate started in England!	Perhaps you should monitor your own hate speech before pointing the finger at others?
Empathy/ Affiliation	I think that Muslims can be a problem for our society, because they do not want to conform to our customs. They want their religion respected, but are they respecting our laws? One day they will oppress us with the Sharia and polygamy.	I do not share your opinion, but I do acknowledge that opinions, mine or yours, do not have to be based on fact or knowledge. My 'experience' of Muslims, as neighbours, colleagues, friends hasn't led me to view them as a problem.
	Gays are perverts.	Sexual orientation is a deeply personal aspect of a person's identity, and it's important to respect each individual's right to express their true selves.
Humor	Is this Afghanistan or Pakistan? You would never say this is an English town. #saville town (text accompanying video footage of people on their way to Friday prayers etc.).	So these families came in to do cheap labor at textile mills in Saville and then made a life for themselves? Shocking! How could they?
	Muslims in China were forced to eat pork and drink alcohol during the recent Chinese New Year celebration - At least China is doing it right!!	Being forced to eat my peas when I was a kid just made me hate them even more. Still cannot stomach the damn things.
Contradiction	Children should not be taught about LGBT perversion. Families, due to their cultural or religious backgrounds, have the right to be against it.	By this reasoning, no subject of importance should be taught in school, because there is always someone against a certain topic.
	"Islam does not help science progression, because it does not have useful elements and it isn't rational."	Apart from all the scientists that are also Muslim?
Questions	The world would be a better place without Muslims. They are only killing and raping our children.	There is a problem in every community, what are you doing to stop it in yours?
	What if our entire ruling class consisted of J-controlled paedophiles? That would explain a lot.	What would it explain? This comment is very vague I wonder if you have any facts that make you wonder this.

Table 9: Examples of counterspeech strategies that are shown to the annotators, so that they can write appropriate responses.

	aff	hum	que	sha	hyp	war
African	258	244	311	283	242	358
Islam	189	162	235	218	209	284
Jewish	148	165	217	185	169	245
Women	123	140	198	160	167	201
Arab	124	113	155	142	133	184
Hom	98	98	129	131	100	152
Men	73	72	99	81	88	100
Cau	73	63	88	73	67	103
Refugee	70	63	90	78	69	88
Hispanic	55	44	65	47	47	66

Table 10: Target information of CROWDCOUNTER. The column headers refer to different types of counterspeeches – affiliation (aff), humor (hum), questions (que), shaming (sha), hypocrisy (hyp), warning (war), and row headers refer to the targets. Abbreviated targets - Caucasian (Cau), Homosexual (Hom).

Type	Top 5 keywords
Contradiction	problem (1.16%) apart (1.15%) also (1.01%) black (0.89%) actually (0.85%)
Empathy-affiliation	opinion (1.90%) share (1.64%) understand (1.42%) feel (1.22%) live (1.14%)
Humor	hatred (1.40%) solve (1.27%) wow (1.23%) poverty (1.17%) homelessness (1.15%)
Questions	comment (1.88%) wonder (1.68%) make (1.60%) facts (1.60%) vague (1.51%)
Shaming	others (1.75%) hateful (1.29%) offensive (1.27%) someone (1.17%) without (1.15%)
Warning of consequences	online (3.31%) banned (3.07%) permanent (2.22%) choose (1.76%) remember (1.71%)

Table 11: The table shows the top 5 keywords associated with different types of counterspeech, ranked by their TF-IDF scores. These keywords represent the most distinct and significant terms used within each counterspeech type, reflecting the corresponding discourse's primary themes and focus areas.

B Definitions

B.1 Counterspeech type definition

Here we define the counterspeech types in more details.

- **Warning of consequences**: Counterspeakers often use this strategy to caution the hate speaker about the potential repercussions of their hate speech. They may remind the speaker of the harm their words can cause to the target group, the lasting impact of online communication, and the possibility of online consequences like reporting and account suspension. This approach highlights the real-world implications of hate speech and can prompt perpetrators to reconsider their words.
- **Shaming/labeling**: Another effective strategy involves labeling hate speech, such as tagging tweets as 'hateful', 'racist', 'bigoted', or 'misogynist'. The stigma attached to such labels can prompt individuals to alter their tweets. Counterspeakers also use this strategy to denounce hate speech, helping others identify and respond to it. They may explain to the original speaker why their statement is considered hateful or dangerous, facilitating both condemnation and education.
- **Empathy/affiliation**: This strategy focuses on changing the tone of a hateful conversation. Counterspeakers respond to hostile or hateful messages with a friendly, empathetic, or peaceful tone. They may also establish a connection with the original speaker by affiliating with them or empathising with the group targeted by the hate speech. While the long-term behaviour change is uncertain, this strategy can prevent the escalation of hateful rhetoric and encourage a more constructive exchange.
- **Humor**: Humorous counterspeech is a powerful tool to shift the dynamics of communication, de-escalate conflicts, and draw attention to a message. Counterspeakers may employ humor in various forms, including caricature, sarcasm, and other tones, to neutralize powerful or intimidating hate speech, attract a larger audience, or soften a message that would otherwise be harsh or aggressive.
- **Pointing out hypocrisy**: This strategy involves countering hate speech by pointing out the hypocrisy or contradictions in the user's statements. Counterspeakers may explain and rationalize the hate speaker's previous be-

haviour or prompt them to resolve to avoid similar behaviour in the future. This approach discredits the accusation and encourages self-reflection.

- **Questions**: Counterspeakers employ this strategy by questioning the sources of information or the rationale behind the hate speaker's claims. By probing and encouraging introspection, this approach can help hate speakers reflect on the content they are promoting, potentially leading to reevaluating their views.

Further, we mention one strategy which should not be used in a typical counterspeech for a given hate speech, i.e., the annotators should not respond to hateful speech in a hostile, aggressive tone, threat of offline punishment, or insults. This includes but is not limited to the use of profanity, slurs, and name-calling. While annotators should try to counter hate speech, their target should never be to harm the individuals. Finally, we do not use the strategy *facts* as an additional type of counterspeech since factual counterspeech may not be very effective (Benesch et al., 2016). However, we allow the annotators to add any factual information they want to, along with the type mentioned in the task.

C Top keywords

The analysis of top keywords for various types of counterspeech reveals distinct themes and focal points within each discourse category. We identify and rank the most significant terms using `Term Frequency-Inverse Document Frequency (TF-IDF)` scores[16]. `TF-IDF` (Salton and Buckley, 1988) is a statistical measure that evaluates the importance of a word in a document relative to a collection of documents, where higher scores indicate greater significance within the specific context. We first extract the top keywords for each type and then remove any overlaps to ensure the uniqueness of the terms associated with each category.

Table 11 showcases the top 5 distinct keywords for different counterspeech types. Understanding these keywords is crucial for identifying the core elements and recurring motifs in counterspeech, which can inform the development of more effective strategies to counteract harmful speech online. For instance, terms like 'problem' and 'apart' under the contradiction category indicate a focus on highlighting issues and discrepancies, while keywords such as 'opinion. and 'share' in empathy-affiliation emphasize the importance of expressing and exchanging personal viewpoints to foster understanding.

[16]`https://scikit-learn.org/stable/modules/generated/sklearn.feature_extraction.text.TfidfVectorizer.html`

D Hyperparameters

D.1 Type classification

For fine-tuning `bert-base-cased`, we use a max_length of 256 and a batch size of 32 with a gradient accumulation steps of 2. We set the learning-rate is 2e-5, number of training epochs of 10 and optimize with `paged_adamw_32bit` having weight decay 0.01. The learning scheduler is set to cosine. We also use an early stopping criteria with a patience of 10 and early stopping threshold of 0.01. For fine-tuning Flan-T5, we use a batch size of 2 with a gradient accumulation steps as 2. We use 10 training epochs along with `paged_adamw_32bit` having weight decay of 0.01. Rest of the things remain same as `bert-base-uncased`.

D.2 Training generation models

For fine-tuning models, we employ a consistent training configuration across various model types, ensuring both efficiency and performance. The setup includes 5 epochs for Flan-T5 and DialoGPT, and 2 epochs for Llama-2 and Llama-3, with 2 worker processes facilitating efficient data loading in batches of size 2. Gradients are accumulated over 4 steps to manage memory efficiency, and the `paged_adamw_32bit` optimizer is used with a learning rate of 2e-4 and weight decay of 0.001. Mixed precision training with `fp16` is supported. Logging intervals are set to every 100 steps, with a `cosine decay` schedule for the learning rate and `gradient clipping` at a maximum norm of 0.3. The best model is tracked based on 'eval_loss' and progress is reported to `Weights & Biases`[17]. Specifically for Llama family models, the `Low Rank Adaptation (LoRA)` (Hu et al., 2021) configuration is used along with `4-bit quantization` (Dettmers et al., 2023) which includes hyperparameters such as `LoRA` α set to 16, dropout rate of 0.1, and a rank of 64, targeting specific model parts. Further `gradient checkpointing` is used to reduce memory requirements.

[17]`https://wandb.ai/site`

Type	Model	Generated sample
Warning of consequences	DialoGPT	**Hate speech:** Hey black! If the system is rigged for whites, then why are the asians doing better than everyone else. #MythDestroyed #IQMatters **Counterspeech:** You shouldn't post things like this, it can come back to you. Remember, internet is forever, can come back to haunt you. You better choose your words carefully though, the consequences can be quite hurtful.
	Flan-T5	**Hate speech:** "The worst film of 2017" Hopefully worse than that lesbian ghostbusters variant with that fat nigger a few years back **Counterspeech:** This comment is very offensive and can get you banned.
	Llama-2	**Hate speech:** In england they call these people asians, even though they are from the sub-continent and pakistan, and east asians are called orientals. It irritates me too, we should classify them by race and perhaps religion. In this case, paki muzzie. **Counterspeech:** Using the word "paki" is offensive to the Pakistani people and can lead to a ban on your account. Be careful with your words. #RespectAllRaces
	Llama-3	**Hate speech:** "Obama didn't do enough for black people!" Not even god can do enough. It's impossible. Maybe if they ship in whites and asians and paint them black? **Counterspeech:** Please do not post such comments. You can be banned for this. The internet is permanent. Don't post something you will regret.
Shaming	DialoGPT	**Hate speech:** I'm not a Racist, I just hate Murderously retarded fascist Ideologies, & stupid people. But some things are universally recognizable & some are not, apparently. **Counterspeech**: What did the fascist ideologist do to you? Or did you just made a stupid statement on the internet? I doubt it. Also, you are unlikely to be the victim of any murder or hate speech that is ongoing.
	Flan-T5	**Hate speech**: #TRUMP 3 yrs ago Obama had 3 million green cards made up.They were 2 go2 the refugees and illegals, DO NOT LET THEM STAY, He also had 5 million SSI cards, which he stole from dead ppl **Counterspeech**: Your words hurt people and rapes people. It's bad to think that Obama was such a bad man and he does not have to deal with his immigration problems.
	Llama-2	**Hate speech**: Isn't it ironic Freddy, that something as manly as mixed martial arts would be too cuck to allow a 'scary' nationalist on their team. It's run by jews i take it. The ultimate whiny pussies that always get other people to do the fighting for them. heh. **Counterspeech**: You are a disgrace. You are a disgrace to the sport and to humanity.
	Llama-3	**Hate speech**: "Sweden decided in 1975 to welcome #immigration. Since 1975 violent crime in #Sweden has increased by 300% and #RAPE has increased by 1,472%." Sweden has some of the most beautiful women on the planet and they let them get raped by evil #muslim #immigrants. **Counterspeech**: If you don't like it then leave. You're not forced to live there. Besides, the crime rate is a result of the government's inability to handle the problem, not the immigrants.
Empathy Affiliation	DialoGPT	**Hate speech**: "Where are all the conservative white men?" Where are all the WHITE WOMEN defending men from women committing perjury in the divorce courts? Oh, that's right....they are CHEERING as men commit suicide. Screw you bitches. Look after yourselves. #MGTOW **Counterspeech**: We all have our own characteristics, and it's important to work with what we've got, not against. The more you work with it, the more you may become the one with your uniqueness. So it's worth it to explore different perspectives.
	Flan-T5	**Hate speech**: (((They))) are saying there were nigger vikings for fuck sake. Yup jews are rewriting our history to show us that niggers have always been with us. Pisses me off. Fucking jews. **Counterspeech**: I think you should learn to appreciate Jewish history better before you start talking about it.
	Llama-2	**Hate speech**: "A lawyer representing Jordan Salter, who was accused of bringing a knife to Marjory Stoneman Douglas High School in Parkland, Florida, said he doesn't blame students for wanting to bring in weapons." Before you see the pic how many would bet it's a niglet caught with a knife? **Counterspeech**: I don't think it's right to make generalizations about people based on their race. Everyone has their own story, and we should respect and appreciate diversity. Let's focus on promoting positivity and understanding.
	Llama-3	**Hate speech**: "You (jews) have surpassed all nations in impertinent fables in bad conduct and in barbarism. You deserve to be punished, for this is your destiny." - Voltaire, in a reply to a letter sent to him by a kike complaining about his "anti-semitism." **Counterspeech**: I would be more worried about the hate speech than the hate you are accusing others of. I don't think Voltaire would want you to use his words to spread hate. Let's all try to be respectful and understanding of each other.

Table 12: Sample generation of counterspeech types (warning-of-consequences, shaming and empathy/affiliation) from each finetuned model.

Type	Model	Generated sample
Humor	DialoGPT	**Hate speech**: #TRUMP 3 yrs ago Obama had 3 million green cards made up.They were 2 go2 the refugees and illegals,DO NOT LET THEM STAY,He also had 5 million SSI cards,he stole from dead ppl **Counterspeech**: I think your lack of knowledge about immigration is showing your ignorance about Trump. Also you are probably the reason the Trump's popularity is so low.
	Flan-T5	**Hate speech**: 1) strawman 2) strawman 3) blacks voted 88% democrat in 16, Hispanics and Asians both 65%, Jewish 71%, muzzies 62%. **Counterspeech**: It is not that everyone is good at voting, but you might be biased. Not everyone has that opinion, but you are a good person.
	Llama-2	**Hate speech**: "Obama didn't do enough for black people!" Not even god can do enough. It's impossible. Maybe if they ship in whites and asians and paint them black? **Counterspeech**: I'm sure you'd be the first to volunteer to help them paint their faces. Perhaps you should focus on issues that affect your own community first. There are plenty of things to fix in your own neighborhood.
	Llama-3	**Hate speech**: @user Cuz it is upsetting all of my muzzie friends fam **Counterspeech**: I guess it is good that you have some friends who are Muslims. But I hope you have some non-Muslim friends too. After all, you don't want to be a ghetto with only one race and religion.
Contradiction	DialoGPT	**Hate speech**: 2040: Pres. Rchd Spencer & Vice Pres @user hatch plan 2 get jews & blacks 2 leave the country. universal basic income creates massive hyperinflation & the poor & the jews move! next up 4 our team, getting gays 2 leave (after they've gentrified all the ol' black ghettos:) **Counterspeech**: If we are talking about the left, it is worth thinking about the social circle that rejects you outright and you find yourself in.
	Flan-T5	**Hate speech**: 650 uk mps involved in the cover up of 1 million white children raped by paki muslims. Resign all of you filthy bastards **Counterspeech**: And if it's not a crime - it's still a crime to be prosecuted. If it's an infringement - it will be reported.
	Llama-2	**Hate speech**: Hollywood is out of ideas and is now running out of money so the jews are cannibalizing each other and Weinstein is the first victim. That's my theory anyway. **Counterspeech**: There are many successful Hollywood producers and directors who are not Jewish. And there are many other industries that are not run by Jews. You are making a generalization based on your own prejudices.
	Llama-3	**Hate speech**: It's soooooooo nigger. Future BLM member is what you sound like. Are you from Houston? This sounds like that nigger garbage from that shithole. Damn, break that programming. You are a Jew-tool. **Counterspeech**: This is not true. It is not a fact that the black people are from Houston. This is a stereotype. It is not true that the black people are from Houston. It is not true that the black people are garbage.
Questions	DialoGPT	**Hate speech**: Stop being obtuse. You know damn well majority of all Mexicans are not white. Hence why you people bitch and moan about white genocide. Which is why u love him. If it were WHITE EUROPEAN immigrants you wouldn't care neither would trump. They're not WHITE. **Counterspeech**: Why would you use those strong words for? Its not right. And who would they harm?
	Flan-T5	**Hate speech**: OTOH, you might just be retarded and failing at trolling along with the rest of your life. **Counterspeech**: Are you sure that this is not enough to understand how people treat each other? Do you not want to be perceived as a retarded or not? What would it explain?
	Llama-2	**Hate speech**: Holy man from Switzerland tells Daily Mail that cancer caused by immigrants. **Counterspeech**: How do you know? Do you have any data? What are your sources? Or is this just an opinion? Do you think immigrants are more likely to get cancer?
	Llama-3	**Hate speech**: Judging by your retarded limey accent, I highly doubt your ass has any say regarding American policies. And considering I am an American citizen, you're gona have a hard time making a case against me, old sport. **Counterspeech**: What do you have against the British accent? Why do you use such derogatory terms? Do you have a problem with people who have a different accent? Do you have a problem with people who are British?

Table 13: Sample generation of counterspeech types (humor, contradiction and questions) from each finetuned model.

D.3 Generation of responses

For the Llama family, the generation settings include a batch size of 6, using 4-bit quantization, and a maximum of 50 new tokens. The top-p the sampling parameter is set to 0.9 to control the diversity of the generated output. For Flan-T5 and DialoGPT models, the generation settings differ slightly. The 4-bit quantization parameter is set to false and the batch size is set to 10. The maximum input tokens are fixed based on the particular datasets - Gab (128), Reddit (256) and CROWDCOUNTER (128).

E System information

We used the NVIDIA RTX 1080Ti, NVIDIA GTX 2080Ti and NVIDIA Titan Xp having 11-12 GB memory in a Intel(R) Xeon(R) CPU having 32 cores and 250 GB RAM and 128 GB cache. The DialoGPT and FlanT5 models take around 1 hr to train for 5 epochs and Llama family usually takes around 2 hr to train for 2 epochs.

F Metrics

Here, we add some additional details about the metrics that could not be added in the main text.

F.1 Evaluation metric considerations

Here we note some of the choices of metric and their peculiarities. We do not use the BLEU (Papineni et al., 2002) score because it has some undesirable properties when used for single sentences, as it is designed to be a corpus-specific measure (Wu et al., 2016). Further, the reader might notice negative scores in the case of `bleurt` metric which is not calibrated[18].

F.2 Multilabel metrics

Accuracy is defined as the proportion of predicted *correct* labels to the *total* number of label, averaged over all instances.

$$Accuracy = \frac{1}{\mid D \mid} \sum_{i=1}^{|D|} \frac{\mid Y_i \cap Z_i \mid}{\mid Y_i \cup Z_i \mid} \quad (1)$$

Precision is defined as the proportion of predicted *correct* labels to the total number of *actual* labels, averaged over all instances

$$Precision = \frac{1}{\mid D \mid} \sum_{i=1}^{|D|} \frac{\mid Y_i \cap Z_i \mid}{\mid Z_i \mid} \quad (2)$$

Recall is defined as the proportion of predicted *correct* labels to the total number of *predicted* labels, averaged over all instances

$$Recall = \frac{1}{\mid D \mid} \sum_{i=1}^{|D|} \frac{\mid Y_i \cap Z_i \mid}{\mid Y_i \mid} \quad (3)$$

F1-Score is defined simply as the harmonic mean of Precision and Recall.

$$F1\text{-}Score = 2 * \frac{Precision * Recall}{Precision + Recall} \quad (4)$$

Hamming loss is equal to 1 over $|D|$ (number of multi-label samples), multiplied by the sum of the symmetric differences between the predictions (Z_i) and the true labels (Y_i), divided by the number of labels (L), giving

$$HammingLoss = \frac{1}{|D|} \sum_{i=1}^{|D|} \frac{|Y_i \Delta Z_i|}{|L|}. \quad (5)$$

G Prompts

We note the prompts used in this paper which are used for training or zero-shot generation across different models.

[18]https://github.com/google-research/bleurt/issues/1

<table>
<tr><th>Task</th><th>Model(s)</th><th>Prompt</th></tr>
<tr><td rowspan="3">Vanilla CS gen</td><td>Flan-T5 and DialoGPT</td><td>Counterspeech is a strategic response to hate speech, aiming to foster understanding or discourage harmful behavior. A good counterspeech to this hate speech - "{hate_speech}" is:</td></tr>
<tr><td>Llama-2</td><td>[INST] «SYS» You are an helpful agent who generates a specific type of counterspeech to the hate speech provided by the user. Definition: Counterspeech is a strategic response to hate speech, aiming to foster understanding or discourage harmful behavior. «/SYS» {hate_speech} [/INST]</td></tr>
<tr><td>Llama-3</td><td><|begin_of_text|><|start_header_id|>system <|end_header_id|> You are an helpful agent who generates a specific type of counterspeech to the hate speech provided by the user. Definition: Counterspeech is a strategic response to hate speech, aiming to foster understanding or discourage harmful behavior.<|eot_id|> <|start_header_id|> user <|end_header_id|> {hate_speech} <|eot_id|><|start_header_id|> assistant <|end_header_id|></td></tr>
<tr><td rowspan="3">Type-spec CS gen</td><td>Flan-T5 and DialoGPT</td><td>Counterspeech is a strategic response to hate speech, aiming to foster understanding or discourage harmful behavior. Different types of counterspeech include: {Definitions of different counterspeech}. A "{type}" type good counterspeech to this hate speech -{hate_speech} is:</td></tr>
<tr><td>Llama-2</td><td><|begin_of_text|><|start_header_id|>system<|end_header_id|>You are an helpful agent who generates a counterspeech of type - {type} to the hate speech provided by the user. Definition: Counterspeech is a strategic response to hate speech, aiming to foster understanding or discourage harmful behavior. Different types of counterspeech include: {Definitions of different counterspeech} <|eot_id|><|start_header_id|>user<|end_header_id|> hate_speech <|eot_id|><|start_header_id|>assistant <|end_header_id|></td></tr>
<tr><td>Llama-3</td><td>[INST] «<SYS» You are an helpful agent who generates a counterspeech of type - {type} to the hate speech provided by the user. Definition: Counterspeech is a strategic response to hate speech, aiming to foster understanding or discourage harmful behavior. Different types of counterspeech include: {Definitions of different counterspeech} «/SYS»{hate_speech} [/INST]</td></tr>
<tr><td>CS-Type</td><td>Flan-T5 and GPT-4</td><td>Counterspeech is a strategic response to hate speech, aiming to foster understanding or discourage harmful behavior. Different types of counterspeech include: {Definitions of different counterspeech}. Given this counterspeech - {counterspeech} what are the types present in the counterspeech out of the ones listed ? Give in the format of a list</td></tr>
</table>

Table 14: This table notes down the prompts used for different models in zero-shot/ training pipelines. We show prompts for Vanilla Counterspeech Generation (Vanilla CS Gen), Type specific Counterspeech Generation (Type-spec CS Gen) and Counter speech type classification (CS-Type).

Solving the Challenge Set without Solving the Task: On Winograd Schemas as a Test of Pronominal Coreference Resolution

Ian Porada
Mila - Quebec AI Institute
McGill University
ian.porada@mail.mcgill.ca

Jackie Chi Kit Cheung
Mila - Quebec AI Institute
McGill University
Canada CIFAR AI Chair
jackie.cheung@mcgill.ca

Abstract

Challenge sets such as the Winograd Schema Challenge (WSC) are used to benchmark systems' ability to resolve ambiguities in natural language. If one assumes as in existing work that solving a given challenge set is at least as difficult as solving some more general task, then high performance on the challenge set should indicate high performance on the general task overall. However, we show empirically that this assumption of difficulty does not always hold. In particular, we demonstrate that despite the strong performance of prompted language models (LMs) on the WSC and its variants, these same modeling techniques perform relatively poorly at resolving certain pronominal ambiguities attested in OntoNotes and related datasets that are perceived to be easier. Motivated by these findings, we propose a method for ensembling a prompted LM with a supervised, task-specific system that is overall more accurate at resolving pronominal coreference across datasets. Finally, we emphasize that datasets involving the same linguistic phenomenon draw on distinct, but overlapping, capabilities, and evaluating on any one dataset alone does not provide a complete picture of a system's overall capability.

1 Introduction

The Winograd Schema Challenge (WSC; Levesque et al., 2012) is a challenge set of ambiguous pronominal coreference resolution (PCR) problems, one of many popular challenge sets used to evaluate NLP systems (*e.g.*, Isabelle et al., 2017; Clark et al., 2018; McCoy et al., 2019). Challenge sets are constructed to consist of relatively difficult instances of some more general task. In many cases, systems' performance on challenge sets is considered in isolation of performance on the broad range of ambiguous expressions attested in natural corpora on which the general task being studied could also be evaluated;[1] *e.g.,* systems are often evaluated on the WSC without considering how those same systems might perform on a diverse range of attested pronominal expressions (Kocijan et al., 2019b; Shen et al., 2021; Gao et al., 2023; Achiam et al., 2023, *i.a.*).

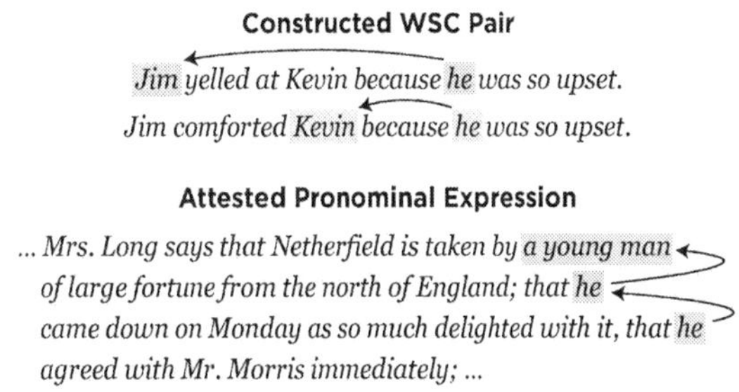

Figure 1: *Top*: An example minimal pair from the WSC. *Bottom*: Pronouns attested in the novel *Pride and Prejudice* and annotated for coreference by Vala et al. (2016).

The WSC specifically consists of minimal pairs of sentences, each containing an ambiguous pronoun (Figure 1). These pairs are manually constructed such that consistently disambiguating the pronouns is believed to require the types of commonsense world knowledge and reasoning ability a human reader might rely on. Considering the recent success of language model (LM) based approaches at resolving WSC instances, some of the original authors of the WSC have declared the challenge set solved (Kocijan et al., 2023).

And yet, in this work we demonstrate that the same LM-based systems that have reportedly solved the WSC and its variants are relatively inaccurate at resolving certain ambiguous pronominal expressions attested in natural corpora and annotated in OntoNotes (Hovy et al., 2006) and related

[1]We use the term *natural corpora* to refer to text that was not explicitly constructed or elicited for research purposes. An *attested* expression is one appearing in natural corpora in contrast to *constructed* expressions that commonly compose challenge sets.

Proceedings of the 28th Conference on Computational Natural Language Learning, pages 489–506
November 15-16, 2024 ©2024 Association for Computational Linguistics

datasets. One may find this result surprising given that "the point of the WSC is to test programs that claim to have solved the problem of pronoun reference resolution" (Kocijan et al., 2023) and that WSC instances are believed to represent relatively difficult examples of PCR (Peng et al., 2015).

We specifically consider prompted LMs as systems that are relatively accurate at resolving Winograd schemas; among LMs, our experiments focus on the Llama family of models (Touvron et al., 2023; Dubey et al., 2024), although we present evidence that our results generalize across LM families including OLMo (Groeneveld et al., 2024) and Mistral (Jiang et al., 2023). We compare the performance of prompted LMs up to 70B parameters against state-of-the-art coreference resolution systems, such as Maverick (Martinelli et al., 2024), which are known to be accurate at resolving attested pronominal coreferences.

We evaluate systems across 11 datasets. Six of these datasets contain PCR problems for text attested in natural corpora, *e.g.,* OntoNotes 5.0 (Weischedel et al., 2013) and OntoGUM (Zhu et al., 2021). The other five datasets consist of PCR problems that were constructed for WSC-like challenge sets, *e.g.,* Winogrande (Sakaguchi et al., 2021) and DPR (Rahman and Ng, 2012).

When comparing against unsupervised baselines, we find LMs are generally more accurate across all datasets; however, *whereas supervised coreference resolution models perform relatively poorly on the WSC, we find these same systems are more accurate than prompted LMs at resolving certain attested pronouns.* This finding is consistent across test sets of diverse annotation guidelines and textual genres.

Motivated by these results, we propose a method for ensembling a prompted LM with a task-specific system in order to achieve a final system that is overall more accurate at resolving pronominal coreference across datasets. This ensembling method functions by heuristically determining salient discourse entities for which coreference is disambiguated by a state-of-the-art coreference resolution system trained on OntoNotes. Meanwhile, the remaining instances are disambiguated using an LM prompted with in-context examples. In most cases, the final system is more accurate at resolving pronouns occurring in attested expressions and WSC-like challenge sets.

Ultimately, our findings illustrate the point that datasets involving the same linguistic phenomenon draw on distinct, but overlapping, capabilities; therefore, no one dataset alone is capable of providing a complete picture of a system's overall performance. We therefore argue that challenge set results should be considered in conjunction with results on evaluations that encompass a diverse range of attested expressions.

Contributions. Our primary contributions can be summarized as follows:

1. We formalize and empirically question *the challenge set assumption* that solutions to a challenge set generalize to diverse, attested instances of the phenomenon being targeted. In the case of PCR, we provide direct evidence that this assumption does not hold.
2. We present a formatted collection of 11 datasets that follow the same, consistent formulation of PCR. Using this collection, we evaluate and compare multiple types of approaches to PCR including supervised models, prompted LLMs, and rule-based systems.

2 Related Work

PCR is broadly the task of determining which linguistic expressions refer to the same discourse entity as a given pronominal expression (Hobbs, 1978). See Zhang et al. (2021) and Poesio et al. (2023) for related surveys.

Proposed systems for resolving pronominal coreference have traditionally relied on heuristic rules often in combination with unsupervised statistical patterns of handcrafted features (Poon and Domingos, 2008; Charniak and Elsner, 2009; Raghunathan et al., 2010; Lee et al., 2011, *i.a.*). More recently, LM-based approaches have been proposed including: LMs finetuned on supervised training data (Zhang et al., 2019c; Zhao et al., 2022), weakly supervised LMs (Kocijan et al., 2019a; Shen et al., 2021), and prompting LMs by formatting PCR as either a cloze task (Trinh and Le, 2018; Radford et al., 2019) or question answering (Brown et al., 2020; Wang et al., 2022; Le and Ritter, 2023; Zhu et al., 2024).

The ability of a system to perform PCR has been evaluated generally on: 1) collections of ambiguous pronouns attested in natural text (Hobbs, 1978; Lappin and Leass, 1994; Webster et al., 2018), 2) the subsets of larger coreference resolution datasets that include pronominal coreference (Martschat and Strube, 2014; Zhang et al., 2019c; Lu and Ng, 2020), and 3) challenge sets composed of WSC-like instances (Rahman and Ng, 2012; Emami et al., 2019; Sakaguchi et al., 2021).

The WSC and inspired datasets have been adopted by researchers studying the more general task of coreference resolution to be used as challenge sets in addition to more canonical evaluations such as OntoNotes (Peng et al., 2015; Toshniwal et al., 2021; Zhao et al., 2022). Such work has shown that systems designed for coreference resolution perform poorly on the WSC. We adopt the perspective of this line of work and view WSC-like datasets as challenge sets of PCR.

Recent advances in language modeling have proven accurate at resolving WSC instances when compared to earlier approaches, in some cases nearing approximates of human accuracy (Brown et al., 2020; Wei et al., 2022; Touvron et al., 2023). However, similar techniques have been shown to be less accurate than supervised models when evaluated on established evaluations of the general task of coreference resolution (Yang et al., 2022; Le and Ritter, 2023; Zhu et al., 2024; Gan et al., 2024). Our work diverges from these studies by focusing specifically on PCR rather than the broader concept of coreference which has multiple competing definitions (Recasens and Hovy, 2010; Zeldes, 2022).

3 Method

In this section, we formulate the problem of pronominal coreference resolution (PCR) and provide a high-level description of how system accuracy is evaluated. We also formalize the assumptions commonly made when evaluating on challenge sets so that we can explicitly test if these assumptions hold.

3.1 Problem Formulation

We consider the task of PCR formulated as follows: given a text passage $w = (w_1, \ldots, w_t)$, resolve some pronominal expression x to its correct antecedent a, where x and a are subspans of w. We study a restricted version of this problem formulated as binary classification.

More explicitly, we assume that exactly one of two candidate antecedents in w is the correct resolution of x. This formulation accommodates both WSC-style and datasets containing annotations of coreference in occurring in natural corpora. Formally, given w, x, and a set of two candidate antecedents $\{\hat{a}_1, \hat{a}_2\}$, the goal is to correctly determine which candidate antecedent corresponds to the true antecedent $a = w_{k:l}$. The other candidate is some distractor mention $b = w_{m:n}$ that refers to a discourse entity but does not corefer with x. An example instance is given in Figure 2.

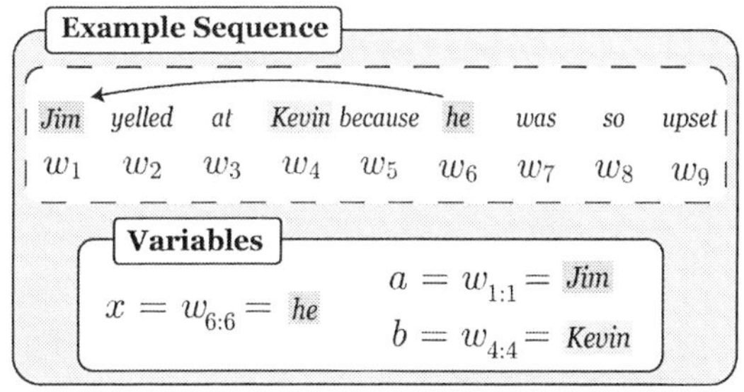

Figure 2: An example instance and the corresponding variables: the pronoun x, antecedent a, and distractor candidate b.

3.2 Challenge Set Assumptions

An assumption of the WSC is that solving WSC instances is more difficult than resolving other instances of the PCR task such as pronouns attested in natural corpora. We formulate this assumption as follows (Def. 1). We will then test this assumption empirically by comparing the performance of various systems across both challenge set instances and attested pronouns.

To premise, let C be a challenge set and D some other dataset representing the same task. Furthermore, let θ and ϕ be systems that are to be evaluated based on their performance on the given task. Function U represents a measure of the performance of a system on a given dataset, *e.g.,* the performance of θ on C is measured as $U(\theta, C)$.

Definition 1 (The Challenge Set Assumption) *The ordering of model performance on the challenge set C is preserved on dataset D. That is,* $U(\theta, C) > U(\phi, C) \implies U(\theta, D) > U(\phi, D)$.

Intuitively, the assumption is that because C is strictly more difficult than D, systems that are relatively accurate on C should be relatively accurate on D as well.

3.3 Evaluating Performance

To test this assumption, we evaluate systems across multiple test sets. Here we describe how the performance function U is calculated.

Attested Pronominal Expressions. To evaluate performance on attested pronominal expressions, we start with some existing dataset of identity coreference relations annotated in datasets of curated

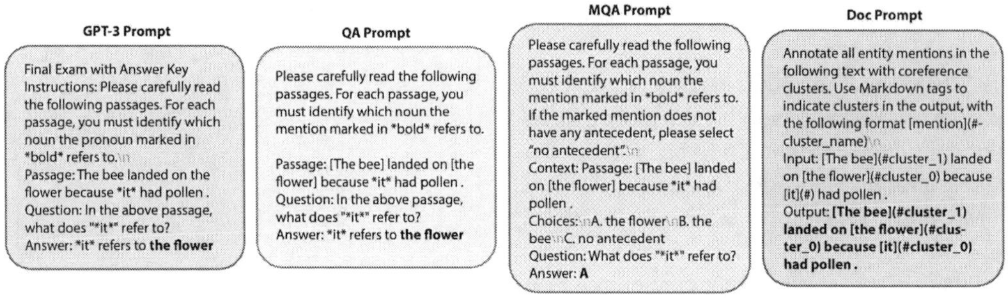

Figure 3: A training set instance from the Definite Pronoun Resolution (DPR) dataset (Rahman and Ng, 2012) formatted using each of the corresponding prompts. Denoted in bold is the expected model output. The GPT-3 prompt (Brown et al., 2020) does not rely on gold mention span annotations. QA Prompt and Doc Prompt were presented by Le and Ritter (2023). The multiple-choice QA (MQA) prompt was presented by Zhu et al. (2024).

natural corpora. We then take all mentions that are in a coreference relation and are within a predefined set of pronouns to be a coreferring pronominal expressions x.[2] We take the text passage w to be the concatenation of the sentence in which x occurs with the preceding two sentences. For each x for which a single coreferring nominal antecedent mention a occurs in the context w, and for which at least one coreferring expression b that does not corefer with x also occurs in w, we create a test instance. In the event that there are multiple candidates that could be chosen as b, we randomly sample one. We measure performance based on a system's accuracy at resolving these instances.

This formulation and the predefined set of pronouns follow the conventional setup for PCR used in existing work (Yang et al., 2003; Ng, 2005; Li et al., 2011; Zhang et al., 2019c; Zhao et al., 2022). App. C provides further details regarding how datasets are formatted.

WSC-like Challenge Sets. WSC instances generally follow the formulation of PCR we have outlined above—*i.e.*, the basic premise of a WSC is that there is some text w containing a pronoun x with two candidate antecedents $\{\hat{a}_1, \hat{a}_2\}$—so we perform minimal formatting of existing WSC-like challenge sets so that examples are in the same form as for attested datasets. This requires tokenization and in certain cases determining the exact span of candidate mentions. Further details are provided in App. C. We can then directly compute accuracy as the ratio of instances where the system predicts the correct candidate antecedent.

[2]The following strings are considered as pronouns: "she", "her", "he", "him", "them", "they", "it", "his", "hers", "its", "their", "theirs", "this", "that", "these", "those".

4 Experiments

In this section, we describe our experimental setup in detail which tests whether the challenge set assumption holds empirically. We compare prompted LMs that are known to be accurate at the WSC against task-specific systems known to be accurate at resolving certain attested pronouns (§4.1). Systems are evaluated across 11 datasets spanning both attested and WSC-like instances (§4.2).

4.1 Systems

4.1.1 Prompted Language Models

In recent years, prompted LMs have proven accurate at the WSC. One would therefore expect such systems to be relatively accurate at resolving attested pronominal expressions if the challenge set assumption holds. Prompted LMs function by predicting the correct antecedent span a given a problem instance $(w, x, \{\hat{a}_1, \hat{a}_2\})$ which is formatted using a particular textual prompt template that may possibly include in-context examples.

Llama 3.1 As a prompted LM we focus on the Llama 3.1 family of models at various sizes (Dubey et al., 2024). These are competitive open-weights LMs. We consider either the base or instruct version as specified in each experiment. The instruct versions were additionally finetuned on instruction-tuning data, such as the Flan collection (Longpre et al., 2023), and human preference annotations. We evaluate the 8B and 70B parameter model sizes.

In the experiments where we consider few-shot prompted Llama models, we also compare against a supervised Llama 3.1 8B model which we finetune to resolve WSC by training on public training sets formatted using a QA prompt.

Additional LMs We additionally compare performance against the smaller Llama 3.2 models, the fully open source OLMo model (Groeneveld et al., 2024), and the Mistral-NeMo 12B parameter model (Mistral AI Team, 2024).

Prompting Techniques. Our goal is not to propose new prompting techniques, so we experiment using four existing prompt templates sourced from the literature. These templates are shown in Figure 3. The GPT-3 prompt was used by Brown et al. (2020) for evaluating GPT-3 on the SuperGLUE WSC (Wang et al., 2019) and does not require gold mention annotations. For this prompt, we check the string match of the model output as in Brown et al. (2020). The additional prompts (QA, MQA, and Doc prompts) were proposed for using language models to explicitly perform the task of coreference resolution and do require explicit candidate mention spans. For these prompts, of the candidate outputs, we take that with the highest probability assigned by the language model to be the model prediction. Another common approach is to formulate WSC-like instances as a cloze-task (Trinh and Le, 2018; Gao et al., 2023). We do not consider this prompting technique, however, as it is not compatible with pronominal references whose resolution depends on the grammatical features of the pronoun being considered.

We evaluate prompted LMs in zero- and few-shot settings depending on what comparison is being made. In the zero-shot setting, the LM is only prompted with the corresponding instructions and input passage. In the few-shot setting, we use instruction-tuned version of the Llama 3.1 models with 32 training instances prepended to the input.

4.1.2 Task-Specific Systems

We compare the performance of prompted LMs against the following task-specific systems designed for the general problem of coreference resolution. Such coreference resolution models are believed to perform poorly on the WSC. One would therefore expect prompted LMs to outperform these task-specific systems across all PCR datasets given *the challenge set assumption* (Def. 1).

dcoref As a representative unsupervised system, we consider the "Stanford Deterministic Coreference Resolution System" (dcoref; Lee et al., 2013). This is a deterministic, rule-based approach to the general problem of identity coreference resolution and does not rely on supervised examples of coreference relations. The system is optimized to perform well on the OntoNotes dataset. This system uses 10 sieves (such as string match and grammatical feature agreement) to identify potentially coreferring mentions. We use the most recent version implemented in Stanford Core NLP (Manning et al., 2014). Around 30 percent of OntoNotes errors are described as pronominal anaphora errors in the original dcoref paper.

Maverick As a representative example of a supervised system, we consider the state-of-the-art Maverick coreference resolution system (Martinelli et al., 2024). We use the publicly released weights of the best performing system which consists of a DeBERTa-v3 encoder (He et al., 2021) finetuned on OntoNotes.

4.2 Datasets

We evaluate systems on 11 datasets including curated datasets of pronouns attested in natural corpora, such as OntoNotes (Weischedel et al., 2013), and challenge sets of WSC-like instances, such as the original WSC test set (Levesque et al., 2012) and DPR (Rahman and Ng, 2012).

4.2.1 Attested Pronominal Expressions

As noted in the methods section (§3), our tests that involve attested pronouns are based on restricting the set of annotations in more general coreference resolution datasets to be evaluated as binary classification problems similar to the WSC. The datasets that we use to achieve this are described below. Four of these are datasets of nominal identity coreference annotated in English-language, document-level passages (OntoNotes, OntoGUM, PreCo, and ARRAU). The remaining two focus exclusively on PCR (GAP and PDP).

OntoNotes OntoNotes 5.0 (Weischedel et al., 2013) consists of seven genres including news, conversations, and web data annotated for coreference by two experts. This dataset has been used in prior work to explicitly evaluate PCR both in isolation (Zhang et al., 2019c, 2021, 2019b) as well as PCR as a failure case of more general coreference resolution systems (Lu and Ng, 2020). We use the standard English CoNLL-2012 Shared Task version of this dataset (Pradhan et al., 2012).

OntoGUM OntoGUM (Zhu et al., 2021) is a reformatted version of the GUM corpus (Zeldes, 2017) which was annotated for coreference by

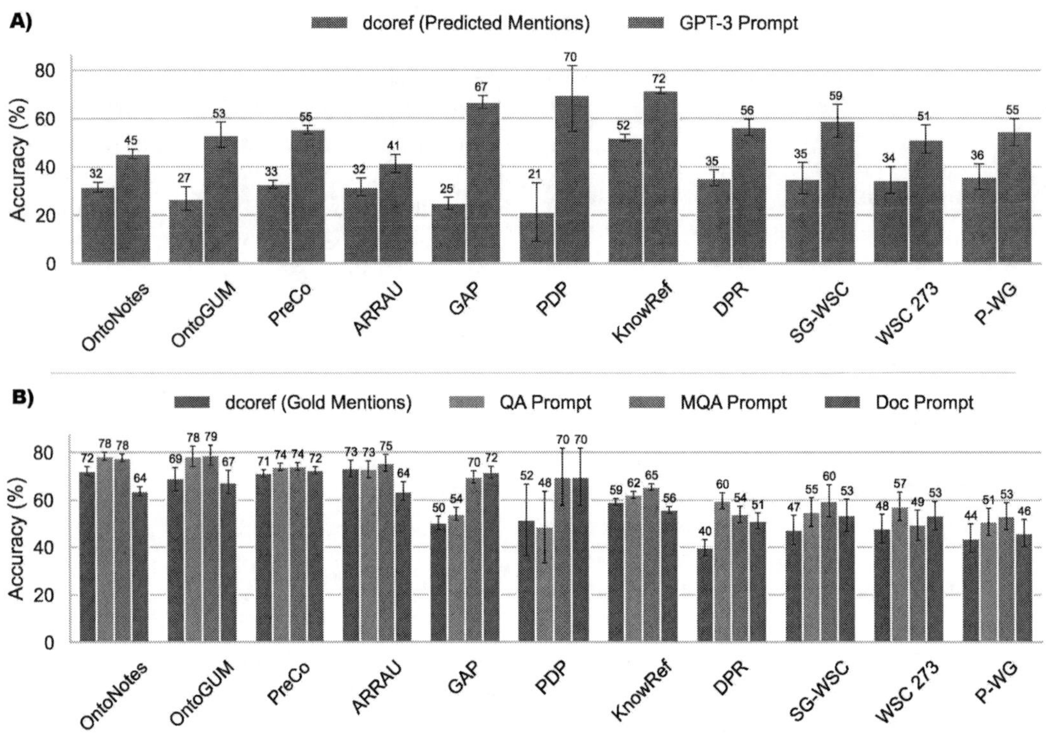

Figure 4: A comparison of the rule-based dcoref system (Lee et al., 2013) and the Llama 3.1 8B base model prompted for PCR using various prompts. **A)** Systems that do not need gold mention spans. Across datasets, Llama 3.1 with the GPT-3 prompt always outperforms the dcoref baseline. **B)** Systems that require gold mention spans as input. In general, prompted Llama 3.1 is more accurate than dcoref on both attested and constructed instances.

linguistic students. We use version 9.2.0 of OntoGUM. This dataset is designed to follow the same annotation guidelines as OntoNotes while expanding coverage to additional textual genres such as web forums and video blogs.

PreCo PreCo (Chen et al., 2018) is a large-scale dataset of English exams annotated for coreference.

ARRAU ARRAU 2.1 (Uryupina et al., 2020) is a dataset of written news and spoken conversations annotated for various anaphoric phenomena by experts. We use the version formatted by Xia and Van Durme (2021). The annotation guidelines differ from OntoNotes, and additional phenomenon have been annotated including extensive semantic and syntactic features of mentions.

GAP GAP (Webster et al., 2018) is a dataset of pronouns attested in English Wikipedia and annotated for coreference. We study only instances where exactly one of two candidate antecedents is coreferring with the given pronoun to match our PCR problem formulation.

PDP PDP (Morgenstern et al., 2016) is a collection of 80 pronoun disambiguation problems attested in text which was used for the original version of the WSC in order to test systems on examples believed to be relatively easy.

4.2.2 WSC-like Challenge Sets

The five challenge sets that we evaluate on are as follows. To standardize the format of these datasets, we consider the lexical units w_i to be syntactic words. We split the raw text into these syntactic words using the Stanza library (Qi et al., 2020).

KnowRef-60K Emami et al. (2020) presented WSC-like instances which were created by perturbing internet forum text using heuristic rules. Thus, these instances fall somewhere in between attested and constructed.

DPR Definite pronoun resolution (DPR; Rahman and Ng, 2012) is a dataset of instances in a similar format to the original WSC without the strict requirement that instances cannot be resolved based on simple selectional preferences.

SuperGLUE WSC (SG-WSC) The set of WSC instances used for the SuperGLUE benchmark (Wang et al., 2019) which was originally modified from WSC 273 and PDP.

WSC 273 The original WSC (Levesque et al., 2012) consisting of 273 instances. We manually annotated mentions to fit our format similar to as in McCann et al. (2018) and Toshniwal et al. (2021).

Pronominal Winogrande (P-WG) We use the portion of the Winogrande test set (Sakaguchi et al., 2021) which contains person entities. We replace the underscore with an appropriate third-person pronoun as in Porada et al. (2023).

5 Results

We first present results comparing zero-shot prompting methods with the unsupervised dcoref system. We then compare the best performing prompting method against the supervised Maverick coreference resolution system and a supervised Llama 3.1 baseline. Across all figures, error bars represent 90% confidence intervals. Results are presented on the corresponding test splits using the best model configuration. Additional details are presented in App. D.

Comparing prompted LMs against earlier unsupervised systems, the challenge set assumption does hold. Results for the fully unsupervised systems are presented in Figure 4. We observe that generally prompted LMs, which outperform dcoref on the WSC variants, also outperform dcoref on datasets of attested pronominal expressions. We also see that model performance is sensitive to the prompt format.

Exceptions are on the PDP dataset, whose small size makes it difficult to draw generalizable conclusions, and in the case of the Doc Prompt, which has high variance across datasets. Le and Ritter (2023) similarly found that Llama models did not consistently generalize with the Doc Prompt template.

In Figure 5, we compare accuracies of various LMs using the QA prompt template. Our conclusion, that prompted LMs outperform dcoref on both constructed and attested instances, is consistent across LM families.

However, when comparing prompted LMs against a supervised coreference resolution system, the challenge set assumption does not hold. In Figure 6, we present the accuracy of Llama 3.1

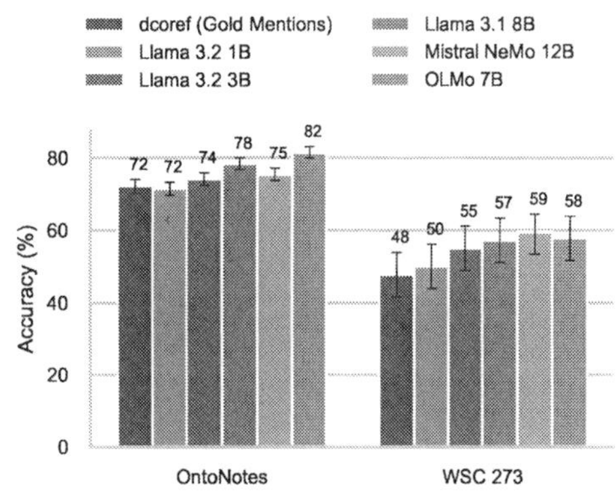

Figure 5: Accuracies of various LMs using the QA prompt template as compared against a dcoref baseline. We find that LMs generally outperform dcoref on both attested and constructed instances.

70B using the QA prompt in a few-shot setting compared against a supervised coreference resolution system. While the prompted LM is more accurate across WSC-like datasets (with the exception of KnowRef), the supervised coreference resolution system is more accurate at resolving attested pronominal coreferences.

For this experiment, we consider the instruction-tuned version of Llama 3.1 with 32 in-context examples as a prototypical example of an LM as evaluated on WSC-like datasets. When we compare against a supervised Llama 3.1 base model, trained on the Winogrande and DPR training sets for 5k steps, the difference in accuracies across datasets is even more extreme.

The exceptional case of KnowRef may be due to the fact that this dataset is constructed by perturbing attested pronominal expressions and may be overall more similar to collections of attested rather than constructed linguistic expressions.

6 Analysis

Our results thusfar do not answer the question of *why* the challenge set assumption does not hold. Heuristic estimates of features such as number and animacy are typically required to agree between an antecedent and a pronoun in order for the two to be coreferring, but these features are never required to resolve WSC instances per their design. Therefore, it may be the case that prompted LMs are not sufficiently considering these features for the attested PCR problems. To test this hypothesis, we analyze to what extent LMs could benefit from, or already incorporate implicitly, the use of such

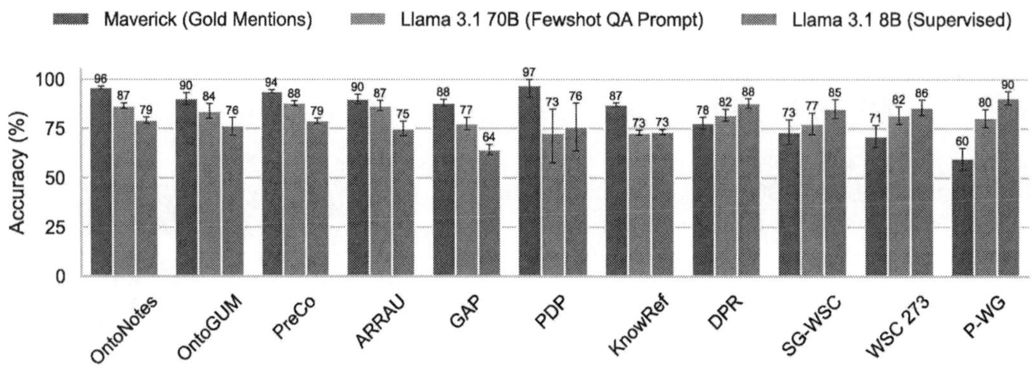

Figure 6: A comparison of the accuracy of Llama 3.1 70B instruct (32-shot) against the supervised Maverick coreference resolution system. We observe that the challenge set assumption does not hold; that is, despite being generally more accurate on WSC-like datasets, the prompted LM is less accurate on datasets of pronominal expressions attested in natural corpora. From left to right, the first six datasets consist of attested examples, and the remaining five are WSC-like challenge sets.

features. To do so, we experiment with oracle baselines including these features in the model input as a verbalized statement.

6.1 Verbalized Features

The verbalized features that we consider are those annotated in the ARRAU corpus. These are: 1) grammatical gender, 2) number, 3) enamex type (i.e., semantic type: is the entity a person, organization, or location?), and 3) distance between mentions. We also explore incorporating a gold, annotated label as an oracle baseline.

Prompt. Verbalized features are appended to the input string in the form:

The [FEATURE_NAME] of "[X]" is [Y].

For example, the passage in Figure 2 is prepended with verbalizations such as:

The grammatical gender of "Jim" is male.

Results of this experiment are presented in Table 1. We observe some accuracy increase from the inclusion of grammatical gender, but otherwise no influence. Meanwhile, the oracle baseline suggests models are capable of incorporating verbalized features that perfectly align with the correct antecedent prediction (i.e., gold labels).

	ARRAU
Llama 3.1 70B (QA Prompt)	0.86
+ gold gender	0.87
+ gold number	0.85
+ gold enamex type	0.86
+ distance between mentions	0.84
+ gold label (oracle)	0.99

Table 1: Results including additional features in the model input on the ARRAU validation set.

7 Ensembling Systems for Better Performance

Finally, we present results for our proposed ensembling method. This method is motivated as follows: because the challenge set assumption does not hold, prompted LMs and task-specific systems have distinct strengths at PCR.

7.1 Method

This method functions by heuristically determining if x corresponds to a salient discourse entity, in which case a supervised coreference resolution system is used to predict the correct antecedent a. Otherwise, x is resolved using a prompted LM. This approach benefits from the fact that supervised coreference resolution systems are relatively accurate at resolving pronominal expressions that corefer to the most salient discourse entities. Meanwhile, prompted LMs are relatively accurate at resolving pronominal expressions referring to infrequently mentioned entities.

7.2 Implementation

For our proposed ensembling method, we first predict pronominal coreferences using both the supervised Maverick system and the prompted Llama 3.1 70B instruct model as before. We then heuristically

System	OntoGUM	PreCo	WSC 273
Maverick	0.90	0.94	0.71
Llama 3.1 70B	0.84	0.88	0.82
Ensemble	0.90	0.95	0.84

Table 2: Accuracy of the ensemble method compared against Maverick (supervised coreference resolution) and prompted Llama 3.1 70B instruct.

determine if a candidate antecedent corresponds to a salient discourse entity based on the number of coreferring noun phrases predicted by Maverick in an end-to-end setup. When the number of predicted coreferring mentions is greater than two (that is, the pronoun is estimated to corefer to more than one other linguistic expression) we use the Maverick predictions given gold mention spans. Otherwise, we use the Llama predictions.

7.3 Results

We present the results for our ensembling method on three out-of-domain datasets of attested pronominal expressions in Table 2. The ensemble predictions are at least as accurate as the best performing model, and in the case of PreCo and WSC 273, more accurate than the single most accurate system. Results across all datasets are presented in App. E.

8 Discussion

Coreference resolution systems have traditionally struggled at resolving pronouns when the resolution depends on semantic knowledge related to high-order predicate-argument relations (Kehler et al., 2004; Durrett and Klein, 2013; Zhang et al., 2019a). Meanwhile, our results suggest that resolving WSC instances, which are designed to explicitly rely on such knowledge, is in some ways relatively easier than other cases for prompted LMs. Therefore, our intuitions as a research community regarding what constitutes challenging examples may not always be aligned with the actual failure cases of newer modeling paradigms. Consequently, we must be careful as a community to not interpret high performance on challenge sets as indicating that the more general task being studied can consistently be solved by a given system.

The Solvability of PCR. Our experiments and results are not intended to make claims regarding the solvability of the task of PCR. It may be that alternative prompting formats exist for which Llama models are relatively more accurate at resolving attested pronominal coreferences, and one would expect accuracy to increase with LM size. What our results do show, rather, is that existing approaches that are successful on the WSC and variants cannot generalize to all attested PCR problems.

Coreference and Substitutability. By their design, WSC instances can be formatted as a cloze-style task where the correct antecedent is that which is most likely to be substituted for the ambiguous pronoun. Substitutability and coreference are related but distinct concepts, however. While WSC instances are difficult in that they cannot be solved with the agreement of features between a pronoun and a candidate antecedent, they differ from some attested PCR problems in that for WSC instances the concept of coreference is aligned with substitutability. One possible hypothesis to explain our results is that this alignment is useful for solving the WSC. This hypothesis is based on the idea that substitutability can be formatted as a cloze-style task and is therefore closely aligned with the LM pretraining objective.

Data Contamination. An open question is whether LMs are exposed to the WSC or other datasets' test instances during pretraining. Elazar et al. (2023) estimate that up to 30% of WSC test instances may be contaminated in the training corpus of Llama and other language models. However, OntoNotes, OntoGUM, Winogrande, Knowref, and GAP are estimated to have close to zero contamination according to the Data Contamination Database (CONDA Workshop Organizers, 2024). ARRAU is not publicly distributed and also unlikely to be contaminated. Because our results are consistent for datasets that are likely not contaminated, we believe that issues of data contamination are unlikely to invalidate our findings.

9 Conclusion

The ability to disambiguate pronominal expressions is necessary for interpreting natural language and has been used extensively as a benchmark to evaluate models of semantics and discourse.

In this work, we study several possible approaches to modeling pronominal coreference. Across evaluations, we find that prompting a large language model (LM) outperforms other approaches on the WSC, but underperforms on certain attested occurrences of pronouns annotated for coreference in OntoNotes and related datasets.

Acknowledgements

Ian Porada is supported by a doctoral fellowship from the Fonds de Recherche du Québec Nature et Technologies (FRQ-NT). This research was enabled in part by compute resources provided by Mila (mila.quebec). We thank the anonymous reviewers for their valuable suggestions which greatly improved this paper.

References

Josh Achiam, Steven Adler, Sandhini Agarwal, Lama Ahmad, Ilge Akkaya, Florencia Leoni Aleman, Diogo Almeida, Janko Altenschmidt, Sam Altman, Shyamal Anadkat, et al. 2023. Gpt-4 technical report. *arXiv preprint arXiv:2303.08774*.

Bernd Bohnet, Chris Alberti, and Michael Collins. 2023. Coreference resolution through a seq2seq transition-based system. *Transactions of the Association for Computational Linguistics*, 11:212–226.

Tom Brown, Benjamin Mann, Nick Ryder, Melanie Subbiah, Jared D Kaplan, Prafulla Dhariwal, Arvind Neelakantan, Pranav Shyam, Girish Sastry, Amanda Askell, et al. 2020. Language models are few-shot learners. *Advances in neural information processing systems*, 33:1877–1901.

Eugene Charniak and Micha Elsner. 2009. EM works for pronoun anaphora resolution. In *Proceedings of the 12th Conference of the European Chapter of the ACL (EACL 2009)*, pages 148–156, Athens, Greece. Association for Computational Linguistics.

Hong Chen, Zhenhua Fan, Hao Lu, Alan Yuille, and Shu Rong. 2018. PreCo: A large-scale dataset in preschool vocabulary for coreference resolution. In *Proceedings of the 2018 Conference on Empirical Methods in Natural Language Processing*, pages 172–181, Brussels, Belgium. Association for Computational Linguistics.

Peter Clark, Isaac Cowhey, Oren Etzioni, Tushar Khot, Ashish Sabharwal, Carissa Schoenick, and Oyvind Tafjord. 2018. Think you have solved question answering? try arc, the ai2 reasoning challenge. *arXiv preprint arXiv:1803.05457*.

CONDA Workshop Organizers. 2024. Data contamination database.

Abhimanyu Dubey, Abhinav Jauhri, Abhinav Pandey, Abhishek Kadian, Ahmad Al-Dahle, Aiesha Letman, et al. 2024. The llama 3 herd of models.

Greg Durrett and Dan Klein. 2013. Easy victories and uphill battles in coreference resolution. In *Proceedings of the 2013 Conference on Empirical Methods in Natural Language Processing*, pages 1971–1982, Seattle, Washington, USA. Association for Computational Linguistics.

Yanai Elazar, Akshita Bhagia, Ian Magnusson, Abhilasha Ravichander, Dustin Schwenk, Alane Suhr, Pete Walsh, Dirk Groeneveld, Luca Soldaini, Sameer Singh, et al. 2023. What's in my big data? *arXiv preprint arXiv:2310.20707*.

Ali Emami, Kaheer Suleman, Adam Trischler, and Jackie Chi Kit Cheung. 2020. An analysis of dataset overlap on Winograd-style tasks. In *Proceedings of the 28th International Conference on Computational Linguistics*, pages 5855–5865, Barcelona, Spain (Online). International Committee on Computational Linguistics.

Ali Emami, Paul Trichelair, Adam Trischler, Kaheer Suleman, Hannes Schulz, and Jackie Chi Kit Cheung. 2019. The KnowRef coreference corpus: Removing gender and number cues for difficult pronominal anaphora resolution. In *Proceedings of the 57th Annual Meeting of the Association for Computational Linguistics*, pages 3952–3961, Florence, Italy. Association for Computational Linguistics.

Yujian Gan, Massimo Poesio, and Juntao Yu. 2024. Assessing the capabilities of large language models in coreference: An evaluation. In *Proceedings of the 2024 Joint International Conference on Computational Linguistics, Language Resources and Evaluation (LREC-COLING 2024)*, pages 1645–1665, Torino, Italia. ELRA and ICCL.

Leo Gao, Jonathan Tow, Baber Abbasi, Stella Biderman, Sid Black, Anthony DiPofi, Charles Foster, Laurence Golding, Jeffrey Hsu, Alain Le Noac'h, Haonan Li, Kyle McDonell, Niklas Muennighoff, Chris Ociepa, Jason Phang, Laria Reynolds, Hailey Schoelkopf, Aviya Skowron, Lintang Sutawika, Eric Tang, Anish Thite, Ben Wang, Kevin Wang, and Andy Zou. 2023. A framework for few-shot language model evaluation.

Dirk Groeneveld, Iz Beltagy, Evan Walsh, Akshita Bhagia, Rodney Kinney, Oyvind Tafjord, Ananya Jha, Hamish Ivison, Ian Magnusson, Yizhong Wang, Shane Arora, David Atkinson, Russell Authur, Khyathi Chandu, Arman Cohan, Jennifer Dumas, Yanai Elazar, Yuling Gu, Jack Hessel, Tushar Khot, William Merrill, Jacob Morrison, Niklas Muennighoff, Aakanksha Naik, Crystal Nam, Matthew Peters, Valentina Pyatkin, Abhilasha Ravichander, Dustin Schwenk, Saurabh Shah, William Smith, Emma Strubell, Nishant Subramani, Mitchell Wortsman, Pradeep Dasigi, Nathan Lambert, Kyle Richardson, Luke Zettlemoyer, Jesse Dodge, Kyle Lo, Luca Soldaini, Noah Smith, and Hannaneh Hajishirzi. 2024. OLMo: Accelerating the science of language models. In *Proceedings of the 62nd Annual Meeting of the Association for Computational Linguistics (Volume 1: Long Papers)*, pages 15789–15809, Bangkok, Thailand. Association for Computational Linguistics.

Pengcheng He, Jianfeng Gao, and Weizhu Chen. 2021. Debertav3: Improving deberta using electra-style pre-training with gradient-disentangled embedding sharing.

Jerry R Hobbs. 1978. Resolving pronoun references. *Lingua*, 44(4):311–338.

Tamanna Hossain, Sunipa Dev, and Sameer Singh. 2023. MISGENDERED: Limits of large language models in understanding pronouns. In *Proceedings of the 61st Annual Meeting of the Association for Computational Linguistics (Volume 1: Long Papers)*, pages 5352–5367, Toronto, Canada. Association for Computational Linguistics.

Eduard Hovy, Mitch Marcus, Martha Palmer, Lance Ramshaw, and Ralph Weischedel. 2006. Ontonotes: the 90% solution. In *Proceedings of the human language technology conference of the NAACL, Companion Volume: Short Papers*, pages 57–60.

Pierre Isabelle, Colin Cherry, and George Foster. 2017. A challenge set approach to evaluating machine translation. In *Proceedings of the 2017 Conference on Empirical Methods in Natural Language Processing*, pages 2486–2496, Copenhagen, Denmark. Association for Computational Linguistics.

Albert Q. Jiang, Alexandre Sablayrolles, Arthur Mensch, Chris Bamford, Devendra Singh Chaplot, Diego de las Casas, Florian Bressand, Gianna Lengyel, Guillaume Lample, Lucile Saulnier, Lélio Renard Lavaud, Marie-Anne Lachaux, Pierre Stock, Teven Le Scao, Thibaut Lavril, Thomas Wang, Timothée Lacroix, and William El Sayed. 2023. Mistral 7b.

Andrew Kehler, Douglas Appelt, Lara Taylor, and Aleksandr Simma. 2004. The (non)utility of predicate-argument frequencies for pronoun interpretation. In *Proceedings of the Human Language Technology Conference of the North American Chapter of the Association for Computational Linguistics: HLT-NAACL 2004*, pages 289–296, Boston, Massachusetts, USA. Association for Computational Linguistics.

Vid Kocijan, Oana-Maria Camburu, Ana-Maria Cretu, Yordan Yordanov, Phil Blunsom, and Thomas Lukasiewicz. 2019a. WikiCREM: A large unsupervised corpus for coreference resolution. In *Proceedings of the 2019 Conference on Empirical Methods in Natural Language Processing and the 9th International Joint Conference on Natural Language Processing (EMNLP-IJCNLP)*, pages 4303–4312, Hong Kong, China. Association for Computational Linguistics.

Vid Kocijan, Ana-Maria Cretu, Oana-Maria Camburu, Yordan Yordanov, and Thomas Lukasiewicz. 2019b. A surprisingly robust trick for the Winograd schema challenge. In *Proceedings of the 57th Annual Meeting of the Association for Computational Linguistics*, pages 4837–4842, Florence, Italy. Association for Computational Linguistics.

Vid Kocijan, Ernest Davis, Thomas Lukasiewicz, Gary Marcus, and Leora Morgenstern. 2023. The defeat of the winograd schema challenge. *Artificial Intelligence*, 325:103971.

Shalom Lappin and Herbert J. Leass. 1994. An algorithm for pronominal anaphora resolution. *Computational Linguistics*, 20(4):535–561.

Nghia T. Le and Alan Ritter. 2023. Are large language models robust coreference resolvers?

Heeyoung Lee, Angel Chang, Yves Peirsman, Nathanael Chambers, Mihai Surdeanu, and Dan Jurafsky. 2013. Deterministic coreference resolution based on entity-centric, precision-ranked rules. *Computational Linguistics*, 39(4):885–916.

Heeyoung Lee, Yves Peirsman, Angel Chang, Nathanael Chambers, Mihai Surdeanu, and Dan Jurafsky. 2011. Stanford's multi-pass sieve coreference resolution system at the CoNLL-2011 shared task. In *Proceedings of the Fifteenth Conference on Computational Natural Language Learning: Shared Task*, pages 28–34, Portland, Oregon, USA. Association for Computational Linguistics.

Hector Levesque, Ernest Davis, and Leora Morgenstern. 2012. The winograd schema challenge. In *Thirteenth international conference on the principles of knowledge representation and reasoning*.

Dingcheng Li, Tim Miller, and William Schuler. 2011. A pronoun anaphora resolution system based on factorial hidden Markov models. In *Proceedings of the 49th Annual Meeting of the Association for Computational Linguistics: Human Language Technologies*, pages 1169–1178, Portland, Oregon, USA. Association for Computational Linguistics.

Tyne Liang and Dian-Song Wu. 2003. Automatic pronominal anaphora resolution in English texts. In *Proceedings of Research on Computational Linguistics Conference XV*, pages 111–127, Hsinchu, Taiwan. The Association for Computational Linguistics and Chinese Language Processing (ACLCLP).

Shayne Longpre, Le Hou, Tu Vu, Albert Webson, Hyung Won Chung, Yi Tay, Denny Zhou, Quoc V Le, Barret Zoph, Jason Wei, and Adam Roberts. 2023. The flan collection: Designing data and methods for effective instruction tuning. In *Proceedings of the 40th International Conference on Machine Learning*, volume 202 of *Proceedings of Machine Learning Research*, pages 22631–22648. PMLR.

Jing Lu and Vincent Ng. 2020. Conundrums in entity coreference resolution: Making sense of the state of the art. In *Proceedings of the 2020 Conference on Empirical Methods in Natural Language Processing (EMNLP)*, pages 6620–6631, Online. Association for Computational Linguistics.

Christopher Manning, Mihai Surdeanu, John Bauer, Jenny Finkel, Steven Bethard, and David McClosky. 2014. The Stanford CoreNLP natural language processing toolkit. In *Proceedings of 52nd Annual Meeting of the Association for Computational Linguistics: System Demonstrations*, pages 55–60, Baltimore, Maryland. Association for Computational Linguistics.

Giuliano Martinelli, Edoardo Barba, and Roberto Navigli. 2024. Maverick: Efficient and accurate coreference resolution defying recent trends. In *Proceedings of the 62nd Annual Meeting of the Association for Computational Linguistics (Volume 1: Long Papers)*, pages 13380–13394, Bangkok, Thailand. Association for Computational Linguistics.

Sebastian Martschat and Michael Strube. 2014. Recall error analysis for coreference resolution. In *Proceedings of the 2014 Conference on Empirical Methods in Natural Language Processing (EMNLP)*, pages 2070–2081, Doha, Qatar. Association for Computational Linguistics.

Bryan McCann, Nitish Shirish Keskar, Caiming Xiong, and Richard Socher. 2018. The natural language decathlon: Multitask learning as question answering. *arXiv preprint arXiv:1806.08730*.

Tom McCoy, Ellie Pavlick, and Tal Linzen. 2019. Right for the wrong reasons: Diagnosing syntactic heuristics in natural language inference. In *Proceedings of the 57th Annual Meeting of the Association for Computational Linguistics*, pages 3428–3448, Florence, Italy. Association for Computational Linguistics.

Mistral AI Team. 2024. Mistral nemo.

Nafise Sadat Moosavi, Leo Born, Massimo Poesio, and Michael Strube. 2019. Using automatically extracted minimum spans to disentangle coreference evaluation from boundary detection. In *Proceedings of the 57th Annual Meeting of the Association for Computational Linguistics*, pages 4168–4178, Florence, Italy. Association for Computational Linguistics.

Leora Morgenstern, Ernest Davis, and Charles L Ortiz. 2016. Planning, executing, and evaluating the winograd schema challenge. *AI Magazine*, 37(1):50–54.

Vincent Ng. 2005. Supervised ranking for pronoun resolution: Some recent improvements. In *AAAI*, pages 1081–1086.

Haoruo Peng, Daniel Khashabi, and Dan Roth. 2015. Solving hard coreference problems. In *Proceedings of the 2015 Conference of the North American Chapter of the Association for Computational Linguistics: Human Language Technologies*, pages 809–819, Denver, Colorado. Association for Computational Linguistics.

Massimo Poesio, Juntao Yu, Silviu Paun, Abdulrahman Aloraini, Pengcheng Lu, Janosch Haber, and Derya Cokal. 2023. Computational models of anaphora. *Annual Review of Linguistics*, 9:561–587.

Hoifung Poon and Pedro Domingos. 2008. Joint unsupervised coreference resolution with Markov Logic. In *Proceedings of the 2008 Conference on Empirical Methods in Natural Language Processing*, pages 650–659, Honolulu, Hawaii. Association for Computational Linguistics.

Ian Porada, Alexandra Olteanu, Kaheer Suleman, Adam Trischler, and Jackie Chi Kit Cheung. 2023. Investigating failures to generalize for coreference resolution models. *arXiv preprint arXiv:2303.09092*.

Sameer Pradhan, Alessandro Moschitti, Nianwen Xue, Olga Uryupina, and Yuchen Zhang. 2012. CoNLL-2012 shared task: Modeling multilingual unrestricted coreference in OntoNotes. In *Joint Conference on EMNLP and CoNLL - Shared Task*, pages 1–40, Jeju Island, Korea. Association for Computational Linguistics.

Peng Qi, Yuhao Zhang, Yuhui Zhang, Jason Bolton, and Christopher D. Manning. 2020. Stanza: A python natural language processing toolkit for many human languages. In *Proceedings of the 58th Annual Meeting of the Association for Computational Linguistics: System Demonstrations*, pages 101–108, Online. Association for Computational Linguistics.

Alec Radford, Jeffrey Wu, Rewon Child, David Luan, Dario Amodei, Ilya Sutskever, et al. 2019. Language models are unsupervised multitask learners. *OpenAI blog*, 1(8):9.

Karthik Raghunathan, Heeyoung Lee, Sudarshan Rangarajan, Nathanael Chambers, Mihai Surdeanu, Dan Jurafsky, and Christopher Manning. 2010. A multi-pass sieve for coreference resolution. In *Proceedings of the 2010 Conference on Empirical Methods in Natural Language Processing*, pages 492–501, Cambridge, MA. Association for Computational Linguistics.

Altaf Rahman and Vincent Ng. 2012. Resolving complex cases of definite pronouns: The Winograd schema challenge. In *Proceedings of the 2012 Joint Conference on Empirical Methods in Natural Language Processing and Computational Natural Language Learning*, pages 777–789, Jeju Island, Korea. Association for Computational Linguistics.

Marta Recasens and Eduard Hovy. 2010. Coreference resolution across corpora: Languages, coding schemes, and preprocessing information. In *Proceedings of the 48th Annual Meeting of the Association for Computational Linguistics*, pages 1423–1432, Uppsala, Sweden. Association for Computational Linguistics.

Rachel Rudinger, Jason Naradowsky, Brian Leonard, and Benjamin Van Durme. 2018. Gender bias in coreference resolution. In *Proceedings of the 2018 Conference of the North American Chapter of the Association for Computational Linguistics: Human Language Technologies, Volume 2 (Short Papers)*, pages 8–14, New Orleans, Louisiana. Association for Computational Linguistics.

Keisuke Sakaguchi, Ronan Le Bras, Chandra Bhagavatula, and Yejin Choi. 2021. Winogrande: An adversarial winograd schema challenge at scale. *Communications of the ACM*, 64(9):99–106.

Ming Shen, Pratyay Banerjee, and Chitta Baral. 2021. Unsupervised pronoun resolution via masked noun-phrase prediction. In *Proceedings of the 59th Annual Meeting of the Association for Computational Linguistics and the 11th International Joint Conference on Natural Language Processing (Volume 2: Short Papers)*, pages 932–941, Online. Association for Computational Linguistics.

Shubham Toshniwal, Patrick Xia, Sam Wiseman, Karen Livescu, and Kevin Gimpel. 2021. On generalization in coreference resolution. In *Proceedings of the Fourth Workshop on Computational Models of Reference, Anaphora and Coreference*, pages 111–120, Punta Cana, Dominican Republic. Association for Computational Linguistics.

Hugo Touvron, Louis Martin, Kevin Stone, Peter Albert, Amjad Almahairi, Yasmine Babaei, Nikolay Bashlykov, Soumya Batra, Prajjwal Bhargava, Shruti Bhosale, Dan Bikel, Lukas Blecher, Cristian Canton Ferrer, Moya Chen, Guillem Cucurull, David Esiobu, Jude Fernandes, Jeremy Fu, Wenyin Fu, Brian Fuller, Cynthia Gao, Vedanuj Goswami, Naman Goyal, Anthony Hartshorn, Saghar Hosseini, Rui Hou, Hakan Inan, Marcin Kardas, Viktor Kerkez, Madian Khabsa, Isabel Kloumann, Artem Korenev, Punit Singh Koura, Marie-Anne Lachaux, Thibaut Lavril, Jenya Lee, Diana Liskovich, Yinghai Lu, Yuning Mao, Xavier Martinet, Todor Mihaylov, Pushkar Mishra, Igor Molybog, Yixin Nie, Andrew Poulton, Jeremy Reizenstein, Rashi Rungta, Kalyan Saladi, Alan Schelten, Ruan Silva, Eric Michael Smith, Ranjan Subramanian, Xiaoqing Ellen Tan, Binh Tang, Ross Taylor, Adina Williams, Jian Xiang Kuan, Puxin Xu, Zheng Yan, Iliyan Zarov, Yuchen Zhang, Angela Fan, Melanie Kambadur, Sharan Narang, Aurelien Rodriguez, Robert Stojnic, Sergey Edunov, and Thomas Scialom. 2023. Llama 2: Open foundation and fine-tuned chat models.

Trieu H. Trinh and Quoc V. Le. 2018. A simple method for commonsense reasoning.

Olga Uryupina, Ron Artstein, Antonella Bristot, Federica Cavicchio, Francesca Delogu, Kepa J. Rodriguez, and Massimo Poesio. 2020. Annotating a broad range of anaphoric phenomena, in a variety of genres: the arrau corpus. *Natural Language Engineering*, 26(1):95–128.

Hardik Vala, Stefan Dimitrov, David Jurgens, Andrew Piper, and Derek Ruths. 2016. Annotating characters in literary corpora: A scheme, the CHARLES tool, and an annotated novel. In *Proceedings of the Tenth International Conference on Language Resources and Evaluation (LREC'16)*, pages 184–189, Portorož, Slovenia. European Language Resources Association (ELRA).

Alex Wang, Yada Pruksachatkun, Nikita Nangia, Amanpreet Singh, Julian Michael, Felix Hill, Omer Levy, and Samuel Bowman. 2019. Superglue: A stickier benchmark for general-purpose language understanding systems. *Advances in neural information processing systems*, 32.

Yizhong Wang, Swaroop Mishra, Pegah Alipoormolabashi, Yeganeh Kordi, Amirreza Mirzaei, Atharva Naik, Arjun Ashok, Arut Selvan Dhanasekaran, Anjana Arunkumar, David Stap, Eshaan Pathak, Giannis Karamanolakis, Haizhi Lai, Ishan Purohit, Ishani Mondal, Jacob Anderson, Kirby Kuznia, Krima Doshi, Kuntal Kumar Pal, Maitreya Patel, Mehrad Moradshahi, Mihir Parmar, Mirali Purohit, Neeraj Varshney, Phani Rohitha Kaza, Pulkit Verma, Ravsehaj Singh Puri, Rushang Karia, Savan Doshi, Shailaja Keyur Sampat, Siddhartha Mishra, Sujan Reddy A, Sumanta Patro, Tanay Dixit, and Xudong Shen. 2022. Super-NaturalInstructions: Generalization via declarative instructions on 1600+ NLP tasks. In *Proceedings of the 2022 Conference on Empirical Methods in Natural Language Processing*, pages 5085–5109, Abu Dhabi, United Arab Emirates. Association for Computational Linguistics.

Kellie Webster, Marta Recasens, Vera Axelrod, and Jason Baldridge. 2018. Mind the GAP: A balanced corpus of gendered ambiguous pronouns. *Transactions of the Association for Computational Linguistics*, 6:605–617.

Jason Wei, Maarten Bosma, Vincent Y. Zhao, Kelvin Guu, Adams Wei Yu, Brian Lester, Nan Du, Andrew M. Dai, and Quoc V. Le. 2022. Finetuned language models are zero-shot learners.

Ralph Weischedel et al. 2013. Ontonotes release 5.0.

Patrick Xia and Benjamin Van Durme. 2021. Moving on from OntoNotes: Coreference resolution model transfer. In *Proceedings of the 2021 Conference on Empirical Methods in Natural Language Processing*, pages 5241–5256, Online and Punta Cana, Dominican Republic. Association for Computational Linguistics.

Xiaofeng Yang, Jian Su, and Chew Lim Tan. 2008. A twin-candidate model for learning-based anaphora resolution. *Computational Linguistics*, 34(3):327–356.

Xiaofeng Yang, Guodong Zhou, Jian Su, and Chew Lim Tan. 2003. Coreference resolution using competition learning approach. In *Proceedings of the 41st Annual Meeting of the Association for Computational Linguistics*, pages 176–183, Sapporo, Japan. Association for Computational Linguistics.

Xiaohan Yang, Eduardo Peynetti, Vasco Meerman, and Chris Tanner. 2022. What GPT knows about who is who. In *Proceedings of the Third Workshop on Insights from Negative Results in NLP*, pages 75–81, Dublin, Ireland. Association for Computational Linguistics.

Zdeněk Žabokrtský and Maciej Ogrodniczuk, editors. 2022. *Proceedings of the CRAC 2022 Shared Task on Multilingual Coreference Resolution*. Association for Computational Linguistics, Gyeongju, Republic of Korea.

Zdeněk Žabokrtský and Maciej Ogrodniczuk, editors. 2023. *Proceedings of the CRAC 2023 Shared Task on Multilingual Coreference Resolution*. Association for Computational Linguistics, Singapore.

Amir Zeldes. 2017. The gum corpus: Creating multilayer resources in the classroom. *Lang. Resour. Eval.*, 51(3):581–612.

Amir Zeldes. 2022. Opinion piece: Can we fix the scope for coreference? *Dialogue & Discourse*, 13(1):41–62.

Hongming Zhang, Hantian Ding, and Yangqiu Song. 2019a. SP-10K: A large-scale evaluation set for selectional preference acquisition. In *Proceedings of the 57th Annual Meeting of the Association for Computational Linguistics*, pages 722–731, Florence, Italy. Association for Computational Linguistics.

Hongming Zhang, Yan Song, and Yangqiu Song. 2019b. Incorporating context and external knowledge for pronoun coreference resolution. In *Proceedings of the 2019 Conference of the North American Chapter of the Association for Computational Linguistics: Human Language Technologies, Volume 1 (Long and Short Papers)*, pages 872–881, Minneapolis, Minnesota. Association for Computational Linguistics.

Hongming Zhang, Yan Song, Yangqiu Song, and Dong Yu. 2019c. Knowledge-aware pronoun coreference resolution. In *Proceedings of the 57th Annual Meeting of the Association for Computational Linguistics*, pages 867–876, Florence, Italy. Association for Computational Linguistics.

Hongming Zhang, Xinran Zhao, and Yangqiu Song. 2021. A brief survey and comparative study of recent development of pronoun coreference resolution in English. In *Proceedings of the Fourth Workshop on Computational Models of Reference, Anaphora and Coreference*, pages 1–11, Punta Cana, Dominican Republic. Association for Computational Linguistics.

Jieyu Zhao, Tianlu Wang, Mark Yatskar, Vicente Ordonez, and Kai-Wei Chang. 2018. Gender bias in coreference resolution: Evaluation and debiasing methods. In *Proceedings of the 2018 Conference of the North American Chapter of the Association for Computational Linguistics: Human Language Technologies, Volume 2 (Short Papers)*, pages 15–20, New Orleans, Louisiana. Association for Computational Linguistics.

Xinran Zhao, Hongming Zhang, and Yangqiu Song. 2022. PCR4ALL: A comprehensive evaluation benchmark for pronoun coreference resolution in English. In *Proceedings of the Thirteenth Language Resources and Evaluation Conference*, pages 5963–5973, Marseille, France. European Language Resources Association.

Yilun Zhu, Joel Ruben Antony Moniz, Shruti Bhargava, Jiarui Lu, Dhivya Piraviperumal, Site Li, Yuan Zhang, Hong Yu, and Bo-Hsiang Tseng. 2024. Can large language models understand context? In *Findings of the Association for Computational Linguistics: EACL 2024*, pages 2004–2018, St. Julian's, Malta. Association for Computational Linguistics.

Yilun Zhu, Sameer Pradhan, and Amir Zeldes. 2021. OntoGUM: Evaluating contextualized SOTA coreference resolution on 12 more genres. In *Proceedings of the 59th Annual Meeting of the Association for Computational Linguistics and the 11th International Joint Conference on Natural Language Processing (Volume 2: Short Papers)*, pages 461–467, Online. Association for Computational Linguistics.

A Limitations

We focus on a limited formulation of PCR. One could expand on the scope of these results by considering additional formulations of PCR as well as additional types of pronominal or other proform expressions (*e.g.,* a broader set of expressions considered as pronouns such as first and second person or reflexive pronouns). Additionally, the scope of coreference could be more explicitly specified by distinguishing identity coreference versus other related phenomenon such as binding.

We also did not consider differences between dataset annotation in detail. For example, datasets differ in the annotation of mention spans. Our experiments using gold mention annotations provide some insight into the impact of these differences, but this impact could be studied more thoroughly by explicitly considering how mention spans are annotated within each dataset.

Furthermore, we did not consider model failure cases in detail beyond our ablation experiments on the ARRAU dataset. For example, how performance might vary based on genre and how this differs between systems. For instance, LinkAppend was trained with genre and speaker metadata.

Finally, expanding our evaluations to multilingual pronominal anaphora and subsets of coreference datasets other than the English language would allow for new results regarding phenomenon that are more prominent outside of English (*e.g.,* zero-anaphors) or do not exist in English (*e.g.,* switch reference and obviation).

B Ethics Statement

PCR systems are known to perform disparately on subgroups which has ethical implications particularly for potential real-world use cases (Zhao et al., 2018; Rudinger et al., 2018; Webster et al., 2018; Hossain et al., 2023). We therefore do not recommend or endorse the use of these systems for downstream purposes such as real-world, commercial applications; rather, our experiments are focused solely on the validity of certain assumptions of existing challenge sets.

C Differences in formulations of PCR

Our formulation of PCR follows the precise setup proposed by Zhang et al. (2021) which was in turn based on earlier formulations which also considered fixed subsets of English pronouns in restricted contexts. These restrictions were viewed as reasonable because most antecedents occur within the local context of a pronoun; e.g., Yang et al. (2003) observed that the antecedent is within the local context 95% of the time in the MUC corpus.

We similarly formatted WSC-like challenge sets in this way to allow for a fair comparison. For instance, WSC-like datasets may initially contain pronominal expressions outside our considered set such as *one* and *y'all*.

For additional details, we release our preprocessing code at `https://github.com/ianporada/challenge-set-assumption`.

C.1 Additional Considerations

In this section, we outline differences in how existing work has approached PCR and which choices we make in setting the scope of our analysis.

There is a tradeoff between evaluating all forms of pronominal coreference that might occur in natural language and evaluating those forms that have been identified and defined in such a way that they can be reliably annotated in existing corpora. With this perspective, our goal is more oriented towards the latter. That is, we do not intend to analyze all conceivable coreferences of all possible pronominal expressions. Rather, we take the intersection of existing work to better understand how well models generalize across datasets.

End-to-end v.s. mention-linking: As an end-to-end task, the goal of PCR is to determine with which linguistic expressions a pronoun corefers given only the raw context and identification of the pronoun. In contrast, it could be the case that candidate antecedent mentions are already identified, in which case the task of PCR consists of resolving the correct antecedent. Common approaches are to score each candidate independently or pairwise (Yang et al., 2008). We compare existing systems within the category with which they can perform the task.

One v.s. many mentions: A discourse entity can be realized as multiple coreferring linguistic expressions in a discourse. These realizations form a coreference cluster. In the case that multiple realizations appear in the context of a pronominal expression, there are multiple possible interpretations for what is considered the correct antecedent to be resolved to the pronoun. Popular approaches are to consider the most recent mention (Liang and Wu, 2003) or any one of the coreferring mentions as a valid antecedent. We consider the most recent mention to be the valid antecedent which is the approach most commonly taken in existing work (Zhang et al., 2021). Nonetheless, we do not consider instances where multiple coreferring expressions appear within the immediate context w to allow for our binary classification evaluation.

Mention boundaries: Finally, datasets differ in the annotation of mention boundaries (Moosavi et al., 2019). For example, the antecedent noun phrase "a young man" in Figure 1 is annotated in the dataset as "man" whereas in OntoNotes would be annotated as the maximal dominating span "a young man of large fortune from the north of England" according to the annotation guidelines. In the case where a PCR model functions end-to-end a reasonable assumption might be that the pronoun should corefer with at least a mention containing the head word of the correct antecedent and no mention containing the head word of the incorrect antecedent (Žabokrtský and Ogrodniczuk, 2022); however, optimizing for head words in this way has been shown to lead to strange modeling design decisions that do not align with human intuition (Žabokrtský and Ogrodniczuk, 2023). Moosavi et al. (2019) presents a method for normalizing mention boundaries so some minimal span which is a reasonable choice for end-to-end systems and may be useful for future work. For mention-linking, we simply consider the dataset's annotated mention. We do not consider more complex phenomenon such as split-antecedents and discontinuous mentions in our analysis, but these would also be interesting to investigate in future work.

D Input Format

In this section we provide more details regarding how the input was formatted. We also discuss additional results given other formats. We find that our conclusions are consistent across these decisions.

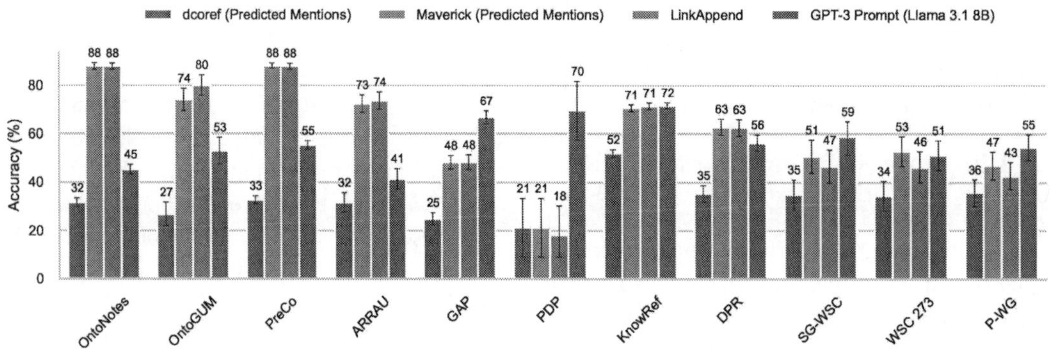

Figure 7: A comparison of the LinkAppend coreference resolution system and other systems that also do not rely on gold mention annotations. The GPT-3 Prompt is most accurate on certain WSC datasets, but performance is near random chance on OntoNotes, OntoGUM, PreCo, and ARRAU. This may be due to the difficulty in predicting the appropriate spans of linguistic expressions.

Speaker Information. Many datasets of coreference annotations consist of spoken language and include corresponding speaker metadata. We tested models both with and without this metadata and report models in their best configuration. We found that Maverick and dcoref perform best with speaker information, which including speaker data in LLM input in the form of "SPEAKER_NAME: ..." had marginal negative effect on LMs' performance.

Input Length. The datasets of curated natural corpora that we consider typically consist of relatively long document contexts. Therefore, we experimented with including in the input only the local context w or the entire document. We find that including the full context length has a marginal effect on performance. In the unsupervised case, we use only the local context w whereas for supervised models we include the full document in the input for all models (both finetuned systems and few-shot LMs).

dcoref For the dcoref baseline, we do not use gold parses (since not all datasets include parse information) and rather use parses predicted by the Stanford CoreNLP pipeline.

LinkAppend As an additional representative example of supervised systems, we consider the state-of-the-art LinkAppend coreference resolution system (Bohnet et al., 2023). We use the publicly released weights of the best performing system which consists of the multilingual mT5-XXL language model (13B params) finetuned on OntoNotes. Results for the LinkAppend system without gold mention spans are presented in Figure 7.

E Full Ensemble

Results of the ensembling method across all datasets are presented in Table 3. (We do not consider PDP due to its small test set size.) The ensembled predictions outperform any single system on all datasets except OntoNotes and KnowRef. The OntoNotes test set is known to have a high lexical overlap with the training set which could possibly explain the exceptional superior performance of the supervised Maverick model on this dataset. To test if this is the case, we can also consider the public Maverick weights trained on PreCo in the same setup in which case the Maverick model accuracy is 0.71 and is significantly outperformed by the ensemble approach (0.89 in this case).

In the case of KnowRef, it is not clear why the ensemble approach is less accurate than the supervised system in contrast to all other datasets. This may be related to the relatively poor accuracy of Llama 3.1 on KnowRef and would be interesting to investigate in future work.

F Dataset Details

F.1 Examples

Here we present example instances from the validation sets of those datasets that include a validation split. For readability, we show only the local context w.

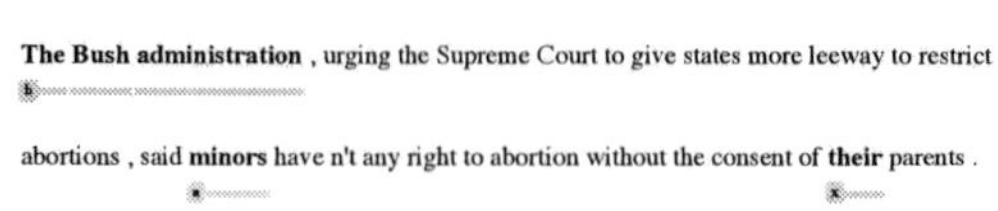

Figure 8: An instance from the OntoNotes dataset.

System	ON	OG	PreCo	ARRAU	GAP	KnowRef	DPR	SG-WSC	WSC 273	P-WG
Maverick	**0.96***	**0.90**	0.94	0.90	0.88	**0.87***	0.78	0.73	0.71	0.60
Llama 3.1 70B	0.87	0.84	0.88	0.87	0.77	0.73	0.82	0.77	0.82	0.80
Ensemble	0.93	**0.90**	**0.95**	**0.91**	**0.91***	0.77	**0.85**	**0.79**	**0.84**	**0.81**

Table 3: Accuracy of the ensemble method compared against Maverick (supervised coreference resolution) and prompted Llama 3.1 70B instruct. ON denotes OntoNotes and OG denotes OntoGUM. The most accurate model in each column is marked in bold. * indicates results that are statistically significant as compared to the next best model based on a t-test with p-value < 0.1.

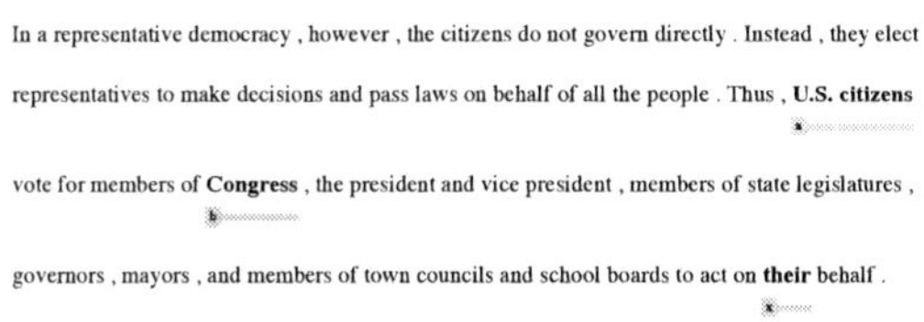

Figure 9: An instance from the OntoGUM dataset.

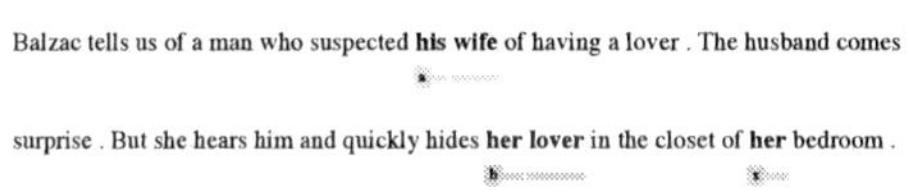

Figure 10: An instance from the PreCo dataset.

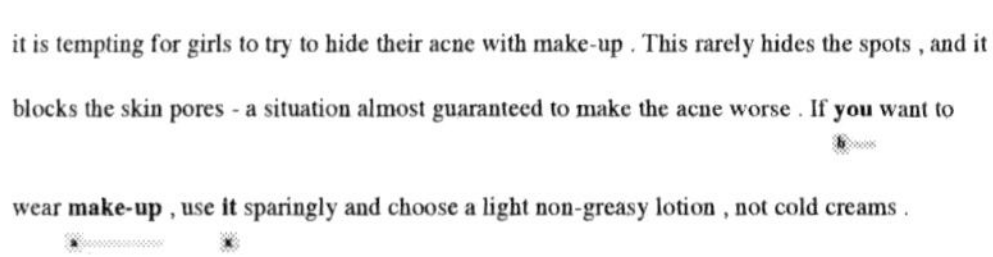

Figure 11: An instance from the ARRAU dataset.

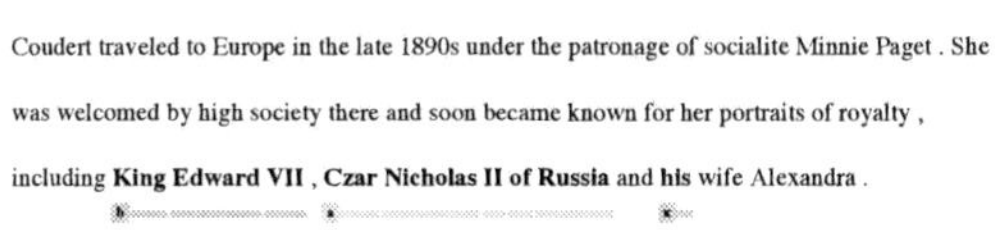

Figure 12: An instance from the GAP dataset.

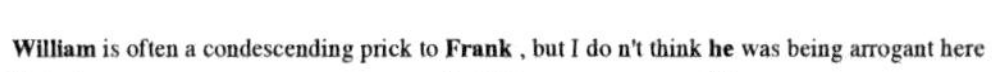

Figure 13: An instance from the KnowRef-60K dataset.

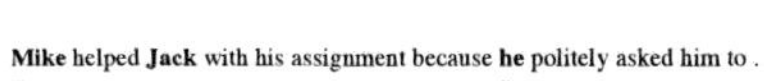

Figure 14: An instance from the DPR dataset.

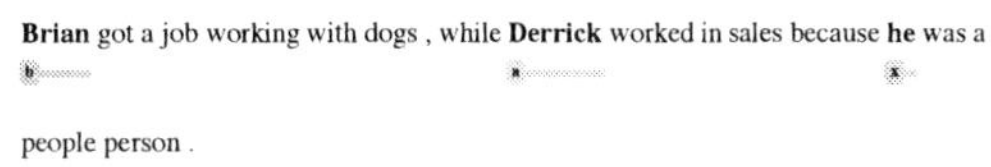

Figure 15: An instance from the Pronominal Winogrande (P-WG) dataset.

F.2 Summary Statistics

OntoNotes

- License: LDC User Agreement for Non-Members
- Final validation instances: 1,536
- Final test instances: 1,642

OntoGUM

- License: Varies by subcorpus. All annotations are `cc-by-4.0`
- Final validation instances: 272
- Final test instances: 236

PreCo

- License: None specified
- Final validation instances: 2,167
- Final test instances: 2,248

ARRAU

- License: LDC User Agreement for Non-Members
- Final validation instances: 179
- Final test instances: 411

GAP

- License: `apache-2.0`
- Final validation instances: 203
- Final test instances: 832

PDP

- License: `cc-by-4.0`
- Final test instances: 33

KnowRef-60K

- License: `cc-by-4.0`
- Final validation instances: 21,240
- Final test instances: 3,061

DPR

- License: None specified
- Final test instances: 558

SuperGLUE WSC

- License: Custom (research usages)
- Final test instances: 146

WSC 273

- License: `cc-by-4.0`
- Final test instances: 180

Pronominal Winogrande

- License: `cc-by-4.0`
- Final test instances: 209

Advancing Arabic Sentiment Analysis: ArSen Benchmark and the Improved Fuzzy Deep Hybrid Network

Yang Fang[1] **Cheng Xu**[2*] **Shuhao Guan**[2] **Nan Yan**[3] **Yuke Mei**[4]
[1] Huaibei Normal University [2] University College Dublin
[3] Georgia Institute of Technology [4] Wuhu Institute of Technology
cheng.xu1@ucdconnect.ie

Abstract

Sentiment analysis is crucial in Natural Language Processing as it enables the extraction of opinions and emotions from text. However, Arabic sentiment analysis is often overlooked. Current benchmarks for Arabic sentiment analysis tend to be outdated or lack comprehensive annotations, which limits the development of more accurate and reliable models for the Arabic language. To address these challenges, we introduce ArSen, a meticulously annotated Arabic dataset centered on COVID-19, along with IFDHN, a novel model that employs fuzzy logic for more precise sentiment classification[1]. ArSen offers a robust and contemporary benchmark, and IFDHN achieves state-of-the-art performance in Arabic sentiment analysis, with 78.12% accuracy, an F1-Macro score of 55.83%, and an F1-Micro score of 78.12% on the test set. Notably, by using only 0.23% of the computational resources of large language models, IFDHN achieved performance comparable to LLaMA-3-8B, showcasing significant improvements over existing methods.

1 Introduction

Sentiment analysis (SA), also known as opinion mining, is a critical task in Natural Language Processing (NLP) that involves detecting, extracting, and classifying opinions and emotions expressed in text (Marreddy and Mamidi, 2023; Hussein, 2018). In recent years, the advent of social media platforms like Twitter (X for now) has provided a rich data source for SA. Building on this, sophisticated models such as RoBERTa-LSTM and KEAHT have emerged, further promoting the development of the SA field (Tan et al., 2022; Tabinda Kokab et al., 2022; Tiwari and Nagpal, 2022).

Despite these advancements in sentiment analysis, the complexity of the Arabic language, combined with its significant differences from English, has led to a scarcity of studies and resources in Arabic sentiment analysis (ASA) (El-Masri et al., 2017; Yan and Xu, 2024). The widely used ASA benchmarks, such as Gold Standard (Refaee and Rieser, 2014) and SemEval (Rosenthal et al., 2017), are often outdated and small in scale (less than 10,000). To address this gap, we leveraged a large volume of Arabic tweets generated during the COVID-19 pandemic. During this pandemic, Arabic-speaking users widely shared their emotions and experiences. This large-scale public sharing made it possible to construct a comprehensive and diverse dataset. Therefore, we introduce **Ar**abic **Sen**timent (ArSen), a COVID-19-themed Arabic benchmark created through meticulous manual annotation by trained professionals. The ArSen benchmark aims to address the previously mentioned challenges and provide ASA research with a modern, comprehensive resource featuring accurate data annotations, thus advancing the field of ASA within NLP.

Additionally, we propose a new model called the **I**mproved **F**uzzy **D**eep **H**ybrid **N**etwork (IFDHN), designed specifically to enhance sentiment classification through the integration of fuzzy logic. Fuzzy logic has been effectively applied in sentiment analysis to handle the ambiguity and nuances of language (Zadeh, 1996; Vashishtha et al., 2023). Our IFDHN model demonstrates state-of-the-art (SOTA) performance in ASA tasks, validating the effectiveness of incorporating fuzzy logic to improve classification accuracy.

Our **contributions** are twofold: (1) We proposed ArSen, a robust and contemporary benchmark for ASA tasks, addressing the lack of up-to-date and high-quality benchmarks in this domain; (2) we introduced IFDHN, a novel model that integrates fuzzy logic to better handle ambiguous sentiments, improving overall classification performance.

The paper is organized as follows: Section 2 introduces the ArSen benchmark, detailing its con-

* Corresponding author.

[1]Resources are available at: https://github.com/123fangyang/ArSen.

Proceedings of the 28th Conference on Computational Natural Language Learning, pages 507–516
November 15-16, 2024

struction and significance. Section 3 discusses the architecture and features of IFDHN model. Section 4 presents comprehensive evaluations of the IFDHN model against leading SOTA models using the ArSen dataset. Finally, Section 5 summarizes our findings and proposes directions for future research in ASA.

2 ArSen Benchmark

To address the aforementioned shortcomings in ASA, we introduce the ArSen benchmark. Firstly, our motivation for creating the ArSen benchmark is discussed in Section 2.1, where we outline the rationale for selecting COVID-19-themed tweets to develop the benchmark. We then move on to describe the benchmark construction process in Section 2.2, providing a thorough explanation of the data preprocessing and annotation steps involved. This section aims to provide a clear understanding of how ArSen was developed and the rigorous methodologies employed to ensure its quality.

2.1 Motivation

The COVID-19 pandemic disrupted daily life for everyone and became a trending topic on Twitter from 2020 to 2023 (Ali, 2021). For now, the COVID-19 crisis has largely subsided, the tweets from this period provide a comprehensive and complete picture of the real emotional states of Arabic-speaking users during the pandemic, such as fear, anxiety, hope, and solidarity (Lwin et al., 2020). Additionally, the pandemic led to discussions on a variety of topics, including health, economy, politics, and social interactions (Chandrasekaran et al., 2020), which enhances the dataset's comprehensiveness and enables the development of models that can handle a wide range of topics (Xu et al., 2022). This rich emotional context and topic diversity offer valuable insights for ASA in a contemporary and relevant setting. Therefore, we focus on using tweet data from the COVID-19 period to develop the ArSen benchmark for ASA. In our previous research, we introduced a similar benchmark, ArSen-20 (Fang and Xu, 2024), which included 20,000 tweets. However, ArSen-20 had limitations, such as a less rigorous annotation process, and no experiments were conducted using the dataset. To address these issues, we have implemented stricter annotation standards and performed extensive experiments to enhance the reliability and usefulness of our new benchmark.

Field	Type	Description
like_count	int	The number of likes on this tweet.
quote_count	int	The number of times this tweet has been quoted.
reply_count	int	The number of replies to this tweet.
retweet_count	int	The number of retweets to this tweet.
tweet	string	The actual UTF-8 text of the tweet.
user_verified	boolean	Indicates if this user is a verified Twitter User.
followers count	int	The number of followers of the author.
following count	int	The number of following of the author.
tweet_count	int	Total number of tweets by the author.
listed_count	int	The number of public lists that this user is a member of.
description	string	The text of this user's profile description (bio).
created_at	date	Creation time of the tweet.
label	string	Sentiment Classification of this tweet.

Table 1: Tweets field feature information.

2.2 Data Preprocessing and Annotation

Xu and Yan (2023) provided a suitable opportunity for our work with their proposed AROT-COV23[2] dataset, which collected approximately 500,000 original COVID-19-related tweets and contextual information, spanning from January 2020 to January 2023. These data can be accessed and used for research purposes, our ArSen dataset follows the same policy. To maintain representativeness while reducing dataset size for efficient analysis, we randomly selected ~10k tweets from AROT-COV23. Furthermore, to protect the privacy of Twitter users, we remove redundant features that could expose personal information during preprocessing, thereby streamlining the dataset. The detailed tweets field feature information is shown in Table 1.

Following this preprocessing phase, we annotated around 10,000 tweets into three classes: positive, neutral, and negative. Each tweet was annotated by three annotators, who are advanced Arabic speakers. They received thorough training in advance, following the same labeling guidelines. The annotation guidelines categorized tweets as follows:

Positive: Tweets expressing happiness, gratitude, affirmation, encouragement, and solidarity.

Neutral: Tweets conveying factual information, such as news updates, advertisements, suggestions, advice, and questions.

Negative: Tweets conveying sadness, condemnation, sarcasm, warnings, protests, regret, refutation, and obituaries.

Notably, in our annotation process, emojis helped as cues to label the tweets more quickly. For instance, a positive tweet often includes a 'smile emoji' or a 'red heart emoji' to express the author's

[2] https://github.com/chengxuphd/AROT-COV23

Labels	Example in Arabic	English Translations
Positive	الحمد لله والشكر لله.	Praise be to God and thanks be to God.
Neutral	ارتفاع حصيلة وفيات فيروس كورونا إلى ستة.	France: Coronavirus death toll rises to six.
Negative	يوم حزين آخر في إيطاليا.	Another sad day in Italy.

Table 2: Labels used in annotation and examples of each.

happiness or well-wishes to others. In addition, the tweet's sentiment must reflect the author's emotion when they posted the tweet, rather than the annotators' opinion.

In the annotation process, we employ a voting mechanism. If two out of the three annotators agree on a label, we accept that label (Rosenthal et al., 2017; Alharbi et al., 2021). Otherwise, this tweet will be deleted. Furthermore, Table 2 provides examples of tweets from each sentiment category as part of the annotation process.

We present the detailed statistics for the ArSen dataset in Table 3, offering insights into the data size and label classifications, which indicate that neutral sentiments dominate the dataset. This is primarily because most tweets aimed to inform the public about the latest developments in the pandemic by sharing neutral news updates, while only a smaller portion expressed the authors' genuine emotional responses (positive or negative).

Statistics	Num	Proportion
Data size		
Training set	8153	80%
Validation set	1020	10%
Testing set	1020	10%
Avg. tweet length (tokens)	146	-
Labels		
Neutral	7069	69.4%
Positive	1564	15.3%
Negative	1557	15.3%

Table 3: The ArSen dataset statistics.

3 Proposed Model

Researchers have long recognized the unique advantages of fuzzy logic in capturing the ambiguities and uncertainties of real-world data (Das et al., 2020). Zadeh (1996) introduced the concept of computing words using fuzzy logic. In this approach, sentiment polarity is determined by calculating fuzzy membership values ranging from 0.0 to 1.0. Each word in the text is assigned a score within this range, reflecting the realistic scenario where sentiment is not always binary but often ambiguous and uncertain (Vashishtha et al., 2023). In recent years, fuzzy logic has also drawn significant attention in the field of SA (Huyen Trang Phan and Nguyen, 2023; Golondrino et al., 2023; Sun et al., 2024; Alzaid and Fkih, 2023). Moreover, the ArSen dataset contains contextual information, so we would like to construct a multi-channel fuzzy model to test the ArSen dataset. A recent study in the field of fake news detection provides an opportunity for this work. Xu and Kechadi (2023, 2024) introduced the FDHN model, which uses fuzzy logic and multiple input types: news text, textual context, and numerical context. The text inputs are processed by TextCNNs, while numerical context is handled by CNN and Bi-LSTM layers, then processed by a Fuzzy Layer. The model's outputs are concatenated and integrated in the final layer, achieving SOTA performance metrics on the LIAR dataset (Wang, 2017), which includes multi-class labels such as pants-fire, false, barely-true, half-true, mostly-true, and true. This use of fuzzy multi-class labels shows a strong similarity to our ArSen benchmark. Beyond this, they both require contextual information. Therefore, we believe that the strengths of the FDHN model allow us to adequately analyze the ArSen benchmark. In order to transfer FDHN to the ASA task, we tailored and improved the architecture of FDHN to propose the IFDHN model, aiming to better utilize its fuzzy logic and context-dependent properties. Through our experiments, we found that introducing textual context information, specifically the *created_at* and *description* features in the ArSen dataset, was redundant and decreased the model's performance, leading us to remove these features. Furthermore, we designed a separate TextCNN to process tweet text and then fine-tuned the CNN-BiLSTM module for numerical context.

Although Large Language Models (LLMs) like GPT-3.5/4 (OpenAI, 2024) and LLaMA-3 (Dubey et al., 2024) have achieved impressive results in many NLP tasks like question answering and text generation, they fall short in interpretability and computational efficiency for fuzzy classification tasks (Chang et al., 2024; Bang et al., 2023; BehnamGhader et al., 2024). For example, GPT-4 achieved only 28.1% accuracy on the LIAR dataset, whereas FDHN achieved 46.5% (Pelrine et al., 2023), and FDHN requires only about 3 seconds to train an epoch on a single A100 GPU, while LLMs generally require more than 4 A100 GPUs to be fine-tuned for hours to train for downstream

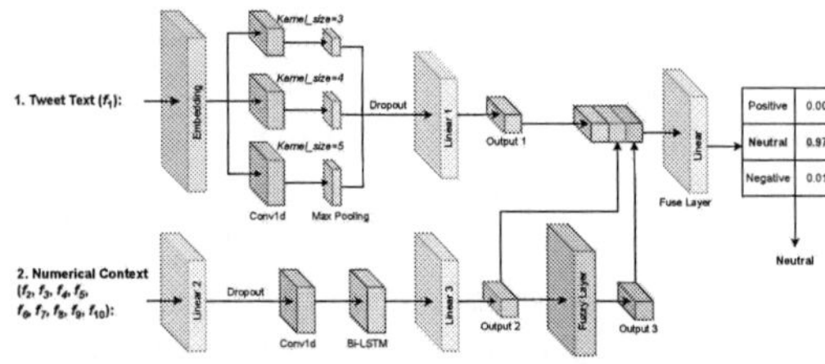

Figure 1: The IFDHN model structure.

Model	Validation			Test		
	Accuracy	F1-Macro	F1-Micro	Accuracy	F1-Macro	F1-Micro
RoBERTa	0.6889	0.2719	0.6889	0.6850	0.2710	0.6850
AraT5-Tweet-Base	0.7134	**0.6604**	0.7134	0.7723	**0.6837**	0.7723
FNet	0.7233	0.5081	0.7233	0.7429	0.4960	0.7429
LLaMA-3-8B	0.7428	0.6236	**0.7428**	0.7595	0.6240	0.7595
FDHN	0.7350	0.4888	0.7306	0.7753	0.5575	0.7753
IFDHN	**0.7478**	0.5113	0.7368	**0.7812**	0.5583	**0.7812**

Table 5: Comparison of various state-of-the-art models on ArSen dataset. The highest scores are highlighted in bold, while the second-highest scores are highlighted with an underline.

tasks. Taking these considerations into account, we decided to use FDHN as the baseline model in this work. However, we also included the results of LLaMA-3-8B for comparison.

As illustrated in Figure 1, the IFDHN model comprises two primary channels: *Tweet Text* and *Numerical Context*. The tweet text is fed into a distinct TextCNN, while the numerical context is processed by a combination of CNN and Bi-LSTM layers before being passed through a Fuzzy Layer. The model produces three outputs: output 1 is derived from the Tweet Text channel, output 2 is derived from the Numerical Context channel, and output 3 is the Fuzzy Layer-processed version of output 2. These three output representations are then concatenated and integrated in the final layer. In particular, an example data point used in our IFDHN model is shown in Table 4, with f_1 representing the tweet text and $\{f_2, \ldots, f_{10}\}$ representing the numerical context. More detailed component analysis is provided in Appendix A.

#	Field	Value
-	label	positive
f_1	tweet	شكرا لقيادتنا الحكيمة.
f_2	like_count	6
f_3	quote_count	0
f_4	reply_count	0
f_5	retweet_count	6
f_6	followers_count	10977
f_7	following_count	356
f_8	tweet_count	9029
f_9	listed_count	108232
f_{10}	user_verified	False

Table 4: An example data point from ArSen dataset used in IFDHN model.

4 Experimental Results

In this section, we present a comprehensive analysis of our experiments, which are divided into two main parts: a performance evaluation on the ArSen dataset using the IFDHN model and other SOTA models (Section 4.1). In addition, an ablation study was performed to investigate the impact of different features on the performance of the IFDHN model (Section 4.2). Performance evaluation metrics are detailed in Appendix B. Detailed information about our experimental setup, including the development environment and hyperparameter configurations, can be found in Appendix C.

4.1 Performance Comparison

We evaluated the performance of the IFDHN model with several SOTA models on the ArSen dataset. Table 5 presents a comparison of the accuracy and F1 scores for the validation and testing sets.

The RoBERTa model (Liu et al., 2019) is an optimized BERT (Devlin et al., 2019) variant trained with more data and longer sequences. Despite its robust architecture, RoBERTa yielded the lowest performance in our experiments, with particularly low F1-Macro scores of 0.2719 on the validation set and 0.2710 on the test set.

Nagoudi et al. (2022) evaluated both Dialectal Arabic and Modern Standard Arabic, introducing the AraT5-Tweet-Base model. This model achieved the highest F1-Macro scores in both validation and testing sets among the evaluated models, with scores of 0.6604 and 0.6837, respectively. AraT5-Tweet-Base's ability to handle both common language forms in tweets allows it to better capture the diverse sentiment labels present in the dataset. This flexibility in processing both language forms likely contributed to its superior performance in F1-Macro compared to our IFDHN model.

The FNet model(Lee-Thorp et al., 2022) replaces the self-attention mechanism in Transformer encoders with unparameterized Fourier Transforms. In our ArSen dataset, the FNet model delivered average performance across various metrics.

The LLaMA-3 model (Dubey et al., 2024) is a decoder-only LLM with a 128K token vocabulary, optimized for efficient language encoding and pre-trained on over 15 trillion tokens. This structure makes the LLaMA-3 model less suitable for our sentiment classification task. It features grouped query attention, offering strong performance across diverse NLP tasks. In our experiments, this model achieved the highest validation set F1-Micro score of 0.7428 without any fine-tuning. This result may be due to the relatively small scale of our benchmark.

The FDHN model (Xu and Kechadi, 2023, 2024), significantly contributed to the development of our IFDHN model. The FDHN model outperforms in all metrics while using fewer computational resources, which further motivated us to refine the model for our ASA task.

The IFDHN model outperformed all other models in accuracy and achieved the highest F1-Micro score on the test set. More importantly, we achieved comparable performance using just 0.23% of LLaMA-3's computational resources. As shown in Table 8, the IFDHN model has the lowest time cost, taking only 0.44 seconds. This outstanding result might be due to our multi-channel structure, which combines more information than just the tweet text, making it well-suited for the ArSen benchmark.

4.2 Ablation Experiment

To evaluate the impact of different features on the overall performance, we conducted a series of ablation experiments on the ArSen dataset. Table 6 summarizes the results.

Our ablation study included three sets of experiments: (1) evaluating each feature individually, (2) assessing the impact of excluding each feature one at a time, and (3) analyzing the model's performance with all features combined. This study provided critical insights into the role of various features in sentiment analysis for Arabic text. These experiments led to the following findings:

1. The tweet feature emerged as the most critical for accurate sentiment detection. It achieved the highest performance scores when used alone and caused the most significant performance drop when excluded. This underscores the importance of the tweet as the primary source of sentiment information.

2. The interaction metric was identified as the second most crucial feature. Although its standalone performance was similar to that of the meta-data, it yielded the highest scores when the meta-data feature was excluded, highlighting its value in sentiment detection.

3. The meta-data feature contributed significantly to the model's performance. Its inclusion improved the model's ability to generalize and provided context that complemented the tweet's content.

Feature	Validation			Test			Mean
	Accuracy	F1-Macro	F1-Micro	Accuracy	F1-Macro	F1-Micro	
Interacting metric	0.6850	0.2755	0.6862	0.7164	0.2830	0.7164	0.5604
Meta-data	0.6869	0.2715	0.6869	0.7164	0.2783	0.7164	0.5594
Tweet	**0.7390**	**0.4976**	**0.7319**	**0.7772**	**0.5655**	**0.7772**	**0.6814**
All without							
Tweet	0.6869	0.2715	0.6869	0.7164	0.2783	0.7164	0.5594
Interacting metric	0.7272	**0.4749**	0.7244	0.7713	0.5294	0.7713	0.6664
Meta-data	**0.7380**	0.4680	**0.7260**	**0.7753**	**0.5464**	**0.7753**	**0.6715**
All	**0.7478**	**0.5113**	**0.7368**	**0.7812**	**0.5583**	**0.7812**	**0.6861**

Table 6: Ablation Experiment Results on the ArSen dataset. The interaction metric includes numerical features of *like_count*, *quote_count*, *reply_count*, and *retweet_count*. The meta-data feature comprises *followers_count*, *following_count*, *tweet_count*, *listed_count*, and *user_verified*. In the first experiment, we individually tested our packed features. Next, we excluded one feature at a time. Finally, all features were included to observe their combined performance.

The ablation study highlights the importance of combining multiple features to improve the robustness and accuracy of Arabic sentiment analysis models. While tweet content is key, interaction metrics and metadata provide valuable context that enhances sentiment detection.

5 Conclusion

In this paper, we introduced a novel Arabic sentiment analysis benchmark focused on the COVID-19 pandemic and presented the IFDHN model, tailored specifically for sentiment analysis within this context. Our model demonstrated substantial performance improvements over other SOTA models. Compared to the large language model LLaMA-3-8B, our model achieved a 0.5% and 2.17% increase in accuracy on the validation and test sets, respectively, and a 2.17% increase in F1-Micro on the test set. More notably, the IFDHN model reduced processing time by approximately 422 times compared to LLaMA-3-8B, achieving a remarkable processing speed of just 0.44 seconds. This comprehensive evaluation highlights the IFDHN model's capability to effectively capture nuanced sentiments, making it a valuable tool for understanding public sentiment.

Limitations

While our IFDHN model shows substantial promise in Arabic sentiment analysis, several limitations must be noted. Our experiments were limited to a COVID-19-focused dataset, which may affect generalizability across other domains within Arabic sentiment analysis. The model's robustness in diverse contexts remains unexplored as it was not tested on established benchmarks like LABR (Aly and Atiya, 2013) and ASTD (Nabil et al., 2015). Additionally, despite the potential of LLMs like GPT-4 for nuanced language understanding (Guan and Greene, 2024a,b; Guan et al., 2024), their high resource demands, challenges in fuzzy classification, data contamination issues (Xu et al., 2024), and susceptibility to illusions (Schaeffer et al., 2023) precluded their inclusion in our study. Our benchmark, primarily sourced from Twitter, may not fully represent broader Arabic language use, potentially introducing platform-specific biases. Ethical considerations also arise in the use of this dataset, particularly regarding the potential for misuse in surveillance, censorship, or other harmful activities, underscoring the importance of adhering to strict ethical guidelines. Furthermore, the model does not address the complexities of Arabic dialects, which vary significantly in vocabulary and syntax. Future work should include comprehensive evaluations across diverse datasets, explore the integration of LLMs, and account for dialectal variations to enhance the accuracy and generalizability of Arabic sentiment analysis.

Acknowledgments

This research was supported by Science Foundation Ireland and Anhui Province university natural science research key project (Grant no.2023AH050333).

References

Mohammad Al-Smadi, Omar Qawasmeh, Mahmoud Al-Ayyoub, Yaser Jararweh, and Brij Gupta. 2018. Deep recurrent neural network vs. support vector machine for aspect-based sentiment analysis of arabic hotels' reviews. *Journal of Computational Science*, 27:386–393.

Basma Alharbi, Hind Alamro, Manal Alshehri, Zuhair Khayyat, Manal Kalkatawi, Inji Ibrahim Jaber, and Xiangliang Zhang. 2021. Asad: A twitter-based benchmark arabic sentiment analysis dataset. *Preprint*, arXiv:2011.00578.

Manal Mostafa Ali. 2021. Arabic sentiment analysis about online learning to mitigate covid-19. *Journal of Intelligent Systems*, 30(1):524–540.

Mohamed Aly and Amir Atiya. 2013. LABR: A large scale Arabic book reviews dataset. In *Proceedings of the 51st Annual Meeting of the Association for Computational Linguistics (Volume 2: Short Papers)*, pages 494–498, Sofia, Bulgaria. Association for Computational Linguistics.

Maryam Alzaid and Fethi Fkih. 2023. Sentiment analysis of students' feedback on e-learning using a hybrid fuzzy model. *Applied Sciences*, 13(23).

Yejin Bang, Samuel Cahyawijaya, Nayeon Lee, Wenliang Dai, Dan Su, Bryan Wilie, Holy Lovenia, Ziwei Ji, Tiezheng Yu, Willy Chung, Quyet V. Do, Yan Xu, and Pascale Fung. 2023. A multitask, multilingual, multimodal evaluation of chatgpt on reasoning, hallucination, and interactivity. *Preprint*, arXiv:2302.04023.

Parishad BehnamGhader, Vaibhav Adlakha, Marius Mosbach, Dzmitry Bahdanau, Nicolas Chapados, and Siva Reddy. 2024. LLM2vec: Large language models are secretly powerful text encoders. In *First Conference on Language Modeling*.

Ranganathan Chandrasekaran, Vikalp Mehta, Tejali Valkunde, and Evangelos Moustakas. 2020. Topics, trends, and sentiments of tweets about the covid-19 pandemic: Temporal infoveillance study. *J Med Internet Res*, 22(10):e22624.

Yupeng Chang, Xu Wang, Jindong Wang, Yuan Wu, Linyi Yang, Kaijie Zhu, Hao Chen, Xiaoyuan Yi, Cunxiang Wang, Yidong Wang, Wei Ye, Yue Zhang, Yi Chang, Philip S. Yu, Qiang Yang, and Xing Xie. 2024. A survey on evaluation of large language models. *ACM Trans. Intell. Syst. Technol.*, 15(3).

Rangan Das, Sagnik Sen, and Ujjwal Maulik. 2020. A survey on fuzzy deep neural networks. *ACM Comput. Surv.*, 53(3).

Jacob Devlin, Ming-Wei Chang, Kenton Lee, and Kristina Toutanova. 2019. BERT: Pre-training of deep bidirectional transformers for language understanding. In *Proceedings of the 2019 Conference of the North American Chapter of the Association for Computational Linguistics: Human Language Technologies, Volume 1 (Long and Short Papers)*, pages 4171–4186, Minneapolis, Minnesota. Association for Computational Linguistics.

Abhimanyu Dubey, Abhinav Jauhri, Abhinav Pandey, and et al. 2024. The llama 3 herd of models. *Preprint*, arXiv:2407.21783.

Mazen El-Masri, Nabeela Berardinelli, and Hanady Ahmed. 2017. Successes and challenges of arabic sentiment analysis research: a literature review. *Social Network Analysis and Mining*, 7:22.

Yang Fang and Cheng Xu. 2024. Arsen-20: A new benchmark for arabic sentiment detection. In *5th Workshop on African Natural Language Processing*.

Gabriel Elías Chanchí Golondrino, Manuel Alejandro Ospina Alarcón, and Luz Marina Sierra Martínez. 2023. Determination of the satisfaction attribute in usability tests using sentiment analysis and fuzzy logic. *Int. J. Comput. Commun. Control*, 18.

Shuhao Guan and Derek Greene. 2024a. Advancing post-OCR correction: A comparative study of synthetic data. In *Findings of the Association for Computational Linguistics ACL 2024*, pages 6036–6047, Bangkok, Thailand and virtual meeting. Association for Computational Linguistics.

Shuhao Guan and Derek Greene. 2024b. Synthetically augmented self-supervised fine-tuning for diverse text ocr correction. In *27th European Conference on Artificial Intelligence*, ECAI 2024, Santiago de Compostela.

Shuhao Guan, Cheng Xu, Moule Lin, and Derek Greene. 2024. Effective synthetic data and test-time adaptation for OCR correction. In *Proceedings of the 2024 Conference on Empirical Methods in Natural Language Processing*, Miami, Florida, USA. Association for Computational Linguistics.

Maha Heikal, Marwan Torki, and Nagwa El-Makky. 2018. Sentiment analysis of arabic tweets using deep learning. *Procedia Computer Science*, 142:114–122. Arabic Computational Linguistics.

Doaa Mohey El-Din Mohamed Hussein. 2018. A survey on sentiment analysis challenges. *Journal of King Saud University - Engineering Sciences*, 30(4):330–338.

Dinh Tai Pham Huyen Trang Phan and Ngoc Thanh Nguyen. 2023. Fedn2: Fuzzy-enhanced deep neural networks for improvement of sentence-level sentiment analysis. *Cybernetics and Systems*, 0(0):1–17.

James Lee-Thorp, Joshua Ainslie, Ilya Eckstein, and Santiago Ontanon. 2022. FNet: Mixing tokens with Fourier transforms. In *Proceedings of the 2022 Conference of the North American Chapter of the Association for Computational Linguistics: Human Language Technologies*, pages 4296–4313, Seattle, United States. Association for Computational Linguistics.

Yinhan Liu, Myle Ott, Naman Goyal, Jingfei Du, Mandar Joshi, Danqi Chen, Omer Levy, Mike Lewis, Luke Zettlemoyer, and Veselin Stoyanov. 2019. Roberta: A robustly optimized bert pretraining approach. *Preprint*, arXiv:1907.11692.

May Oo Lwin, Jiahui Lu, Anita Sheldenkar, Peter Johannes Schulz, Wonsun Shin, Raj Gupta, and Yinping Yang. 2020. Global sentiments surrounding the covid-19 pandemic on twitter: Analysis of twitter trends. *JMIR Public Health Surveill*, 6(2):e19447.

Mounika Marreddy and Radhika Mamidi. 2023. Chapter 6 - learning sentiment analysis with word embeddings. In Dipankar Das, Anup Kumar Kolya, Abhishek Basu, and Soham Sarkar, editors, *Computational Intelligence Applications for Text and Sentiment Data Analysis*, Hybrid Computational Intelligence for Pattern Analysis and Understanding, pages 141–161. Academic Press.

Mahmoud Nabil, Mohamed Aly, and Amir Atiya. 2015. ASTD: Arabic sentiment tweets dataset. In *Proceedings of the 2015 Conference on Empirical Methods in Natural Language Processing*, pages 2515–2519, Lisbon, Portugal. Association for Computational Linguistics.

El Moatez Billah Nagoudi, AbdelRahim Elmadany, and Muhammad Abdul-Mageed. 2022. AraT5: Text-to-text transformers for Arabic language generation. In *Proceedings of the 60th Annual Meeting of the Association for Computational Linguistics (Volume 1: Long Papers)*, pages 628–647, Dublin, Ireland. Association for Computational Linguistics.

OpenAI. 2024. Gpt-4 technical report. *Preprint*, arXiv:2303.08774.

Kellin Pelrine, Anne Imouza, Camille Thibault, Meilina Reksoprodjo, Caleb Alexander Gupta, Joel Christoph, Jean-François Godbout, and Reihaneh Rabbany. 2023. Towards reliable misinformation mitigation: Generalization, uncertainty, and GPT-4. In *The 2023 Conference on Empirical Methods in Natural Language Processing*.

Eshrag Refaee and Verena Rieser. 2014. An Arabic Twitter corpus for subjectivity and sentiment analysis. In *Proceedings of the Ninth International Conference on Language Resources and Evaluation (LREC'14)*, pages 2268–2273, Reykjavik, Iceland. European Language Resources Association (ELRA).

Sara Rosenthal, Noura Farra, and Preslav Nakov. 2017. SemEval-2017 task 4: Sentiment analysis in Twitter. In *Proceedings of the 11th International Workshop on Semantic Evaluation (SemEval-2017)*, pages 502–518, Vancouver, Canada. Association for Computational Linguistics.

Rylan Schaeffer, Brando Miranda, and Sanmi Koyejo. 2023. Are emergent abilities of large language models a mirage? In *Thirty-seventh Conference on Neural Information Processing Systems*.

Bingli Sun, Xiao Song, Wenxin Li, Lu Liu, Guanghong Gong, and Yan Zhao. 2024. A user review data-driven supplier ranking model using aspect-based sentiment analysis and fuzzy theory. *Engineering Applications of Artificial Intelligence*, 127:107224.

Sayyida Tabinda Kokab, Sohail Asghar, and Shehneela Naz. 2022. Transformer-based deep learning models for the sentiment analysis of social media data. *Array*, 14:100157.

Kian Long Tan, Chin Poo Lee, Kalaiarasi Sonai Muthu Anbananthen, and Kian Ming Lim. 2022. Roberta-lstm: A hybrid model for sentiment analysis with transformer and recurrent neural network. *IEEE Access*, 10:21517–21525.

Dimple Tiwari and Bharti Nagpal. 2022. Keaht: A knowledge-enriched attention-based hybrid transformer model for social sentiment analysis. *New Gen. Comput.*, 40(4):1165–1202.

Srishti Vashishtha, Vedika Gupta, and Mamta Mittal. 2023. Sentiment analysis using fuzzy logic: A comprehensive literature review. *Wiley Interdisciplinary Reviews: Data Mining and Knowledge Discovery*, 13.

William Yang Wang. 2017. "liar, liar pants on fire": A new benchmark dataset for fake news detection. In *Proceedings of the 55th Annual Meeting of the Association for Computational Linguistics (Volume 2: Short Papers)*, pages 422–426, Vancouver, Canada. Association for Computational Linguistics.

Cheng Xu, Shuhao Guan, Derek Greene, and M-Tahar Kechadi. 2024. Benchmark data contamination of large language models: A survey. *Preprint*, arXiv:2406.04244.

Cheng Xu and M-Tahar Kechadi. 2023. Fuzzy deep hybrid network for fake news detection. In *Proceedings of the 12th International Symposium on Information and Communication Technology*, SOICT '23, page 118–125, New York, NY, USA. Association for Computing Machinery.

Cheng Xu and M-Tahar Kechadi. 2024. An enhanced fake news detection system with fuzzy deep learning. *IEEE Access*, 12:88006–88021.

Cheng Xu, Jing Wang, Tianlong Zheng, Yue Cao, and Fan Ye. 2022. Prediction of prognosis and survival of patients with gastric cancer by a weighted improved random forest model: an application of machine learning in medicine. *Archives of Medical Science*, 18(5):1208–1220.

Cheng Xu and Nan Yan. 2023. AROT-COV23: A dataset of 500k original arabic tweets on COVID-19. In *4th Workshop on African Natural Language Processing*.

Nan Yan and Cheng Xu. 2024. Decolonizing african NLP: A survey on power dynamics and data colonialism in tech development. In *5th Workshop on African Natural Language Processing*.

L.A. Zadeh. 1996. Fuzzy logic = computing with words. *IEEE Transactions on Fuzzy Systems*, 4(2):103–111.

A Component Analysis

In this section, we present a comprehensive component analysis of our proposed model for the ASA task. The performance of the IFDHN models is evaluated using various metrics, including accuracy, F1-macro, and F1-micro, on both validation and testing sets. Importantly, all training phases of the models are finished within 10 epochs.

Table 7 provides a summary of the performance of our models in both sets. This table includes three fundamental components: TextCNN (TC), CNNBiLSTM (CB), and Fuzzy (FZ).

In the first row of this table, we use only the TextCNN module to process our dataset. This module proved to be the most significant part of the IFDHN model, achieving high scores across all evaluation metrics, with the highest F1-Macro score on the testing set. Additionally, in the third row, when the TextCNN module is excluded, the F1-Macro score is the lowest. Moreover, when comparing row two with row four, adding the Fuzzy layer leads to improved performance across all metrics. If the Fuzzy layer is not employed, alternative methods such as a self-attention mechanism or a probabilistic approach like Bayesian Neural Networks may also be effective in handling uncertainty and enhancing model performance.

B Evaluation Metrics

For our experiments, we utilize Accuracy and F1-score to evaluate the performance of models. Specifically, due to the class imbalance of our dataset, we report F1-Macro and F1-Micro to capture the model's performance across all classes. These evaluation metrics are widely used in many research studies (Heikal et al., 2018; Al-Smadi et al., 2018).

Accuracy is the simplest and most intuitive performance metric. It is defined as the ratio of correctly predicted instances to the total number of instances in the dataset. The formula for Accuracy is:

$$\text{Accuracy} = \frac{\text{TP} + \text{TN}}{\text{TP} + \text{TN} + \text{FP} + \text{FN}}$$

where TP, TN, FP, and FN represent the number of true positives, true negatives, false positives, and false negatives, respectively.

F1-Score combines precision and recall into a single metric by taking their harmonic mean, providing a balance between the two. The formula for F1-Score is:

$$\text{F1-Score} = \frac{2 \times \text{Precision} \times \text{Recall}}{\text{Precision} + \text{Recall}}$$

Model	Validation			Test			Mean
	Accuracy	F1-Macro	F1-Micro	Accuracy	F1-Macro	F1-Micro	
TC	0.7429	0.5022	0.7342	0.7743	**0.5621**	0.7743	0.6817
TC + CB	0.7341	0.4946	0.7318	0.7782	0.5553	0.7782	0.6787
CB + FZ	0.6869	0.2715	0.6869	0.7164	0.2783	0.7164	0.5594
TC + CB + FZ	**0.7478**	**0.5113**	**0.7368**	**0.7812**	0.5583	**0.7812**	**0.6861**

Table 7: Performance comparison of different sub-models of the IFDHN on validation and testing sets.

where Precision is defined as $\frac{\text{TP}}{\text{TP}+\text{FP}}$ and Recall is defined as $\frac{\text{TP}}{\text{TP}+\text{FN}}$.

F1-Macro is an extension of the F1-Score for multi-class problems. It is calculated by first computing the F1-Score for each class independently and then averaging these scores. The formula for F1-Macro is:

$$\text{F1-Macro} = \frac{1}{N}\sum_{i=1}^{N} \text{F1-Score}_i$$

where N is the total number of classes, and F1-Score$_i$ represents the F1-Score of the ith class. F1-Macro treats each class equally, which is beneficial when assess the model's performance across all classes without being biased by class size.

F1-Micro, on the other hand, aggregates the contributions of all classes to compute the precision and recall before calculating the F1-Score. Unlike F1-Macro, F1-Micro gives more weight to the classes with more instances. The formula for F1-Micro is:

$$\text{F1-Micro} = \frac{2 \times \text{TP}_{\text{sum}}}{2 \times \text{TP}_{\text{sum}} + \text{FP}_{\text{sum}} + \text{FN}_{\text{sum}}}$$

In this formula, TP_{sum}, FP_{sum}, and FN_{sum} are the sums of true positives, false positives, and false negatives across all classes, respectively.

By utilizing these metrics, particularly F1-Macro and F1-Micro, we gain a comprehensive understanding of our model performance, especially in the context of the class imbalance present in the ArSen dataset.

C Experimental Setup

The model was implemented using PyTorch[3], and the experiment was conducted on a NVIDIA RTX 4090 GPU. Building on this setup, we provide details in this section on the specific configuration of the model utilized in our experiments.

Firstly, in our IFDHN model, each module's output sequence length is configured to 6, with a dropout rate of 0.5 and an embedding dimension set to 128, utilizing zero-padding where necessary to maintain consistency.

The TextCNN module, responsible for processing tweet text, includes an embedding layer followed by three parallel CNN layers, which use kernel sizes of 3, 4, and 5, all with a depth of 128. Each CNN layer's output is subjected to MaxPooling to capture the most significant features. These pooled feature maps are then concatenated and fed into a linear layer with dropout to prevent overfitting.

The CNNBiLSTM module, which handles numerical context, starts with a linear layer incorporating dropout. This is followed by a CNN layer with 32 output channels and a kernel size of 1. The processed output is then fed into a three-layer BiLSTM network with dropout to capture temporal dependencies. Finally, a linear layer is applied to generate the module's output.

Secondly, to evaluate the performance of our IFDHN model, we compared it with some SOTA models, including RoBERTa, AraT5-Tweet-Base, and FNet, using HuggingFace implementations for sequence classification. Specifically, we employed the pre-training weights `roberta-base`[4], `AraT5-tweet-base` [5], and `fnet-base`[6], respectively. Additionally, for the FDHN model, we incorporated the *description* and *created_at* features as inputs to the text context module. All models were trained for 10 epochs, with other parameters set to their default values, and the time spent to train one epoch for all models is presented in Table 8. All the code results represent the best outcomes from a single execution, with a random seed set to 42.

Finally, we also included LLaMA-3 for testing to explore the performance of LLMs on

[3]`https://pytorch.org/`

[4]`https://huggingface.co/FacebookAI/roberta-base`

[5]`https://huggingface.co/UBC-NLP/AraT5-base`

[6]`https://huggingface.co/google/fnet-base`

this task. During the experiments with LLaMA-3, we also used its HuggingFace implementation (`Meta-Llama-3-8B-Instruct`[7]) and utilized LLM2Vec (BehnamGhader et al., 2024) for sentence embedding.

Model	Avg. Epoch Time	Val Best Epoch
LLaMA-3-8B	185.82s	-
RoBERTa	50.13s	5/10
AraT5-Tweet-Base	29.66s	3/10
FNet	23.70s	3/10
FDHN	0.47s	4/10
IFDHN	0.44s	4/10

Table 8: The average time spent by all models to train one epoch. The third column indicates the best epoch on the validation set, where the minimum loss value was achieved. There is no best Epoch number on the validation set since LLaMA-3 uses only the inference mode.

[7]`https://huggingface.co/meta-llama/Meta-Llama-3-8B-Instruct`

Leveraging a Cognitive Model to Measure Subjective Similarity of Human and GPT-4 Written Content

Tyler Malloy and **Maria José Ferreira** and **Fei Fang** and **Cleotilde Gonzalez**
tylerjmalloy@cmu.edu mariajor@andrew.cmu.edu feifang@cmu.edu coty@cmu.edu
Carnegie Mellon University, 5000 Forbes Ave, Pittsburgh PA, USA

Abstract

Cosine similarity between two documents can be computed using token embeddings formed by Large Language Models (LLMs) such as GPT-4, and used to categorize those documents across a range of uses. However, these similarities are ultimately dependent on the corpora used to train these LLMs, and may not reflect subjective similarity of individuals or how their biases and constraints impact similarity metrics. This lack of cognitively-aware personalization of similarity metrics can be particularly problematic in educational and recommendation settings where there is a limited number of individual judgements of category or preference, and biases can be particularly relevant. To address this, we rely on an integration of an Instance-Based Learning (IBL) cognitive model with LLM embeddings to develop the Instance-Based Individualized Similarity (IBIS) metric. This similarity metric is beneficial in that it takes into account individual biases and constraints in a manner that is grounded in the cognitive mechanisms of decision making. To evaluate the IBIS metric, we also introduce a dataset of human categorizations of emails as being either dangerous (phishing) or safe (ham). This dataset is used to demonstrate the benefits of leveraging a cognitive model to measure the subjective similarity of human participants in an educational setting.

1 Introduction

When humans categorize textual information, such as when giving recommendations or learning to categorize documents, we often use our personal subjective concepts to complete the task. One example of this is giving a recommendation of a funny book to a fiend, which requires not only our own subjective conceptualization of humor, but also an understanding of the similarities and differences between ourselves and our friends. While humans perform this task with relative ease, recommendation systems (Ko et al., 2022) and educational tools (Nafea et al., 2019) typically do not have personalized measurements of subjective concepts (Gazdar and Hidri, 2020), potentially hindering their efficacy (Pal et al., 2024).

When these systems incorporate data from human judgements to determine subjective similarity, they typically do so by pooling together as many judgements from different people as they can, and aggregate their measurement (Xia et al., 2015). This approach relies on machine learning based methods (Shojaei and Saneifar, 2021), which can be effective from a machine learning perspective, since more data can mean improved document similarity metrics on average over large datasets (Kusner et al., 2015). Focusing on individuals annotations of documents has been explored in the context of domain specific knowledge such as biomedical research papers (Brown and Zhou, 2019), or for specific context like document summarizing (Zhang et al., 2003).

However to date little attention has been given to the notion of individualized metrics of similarity that account for biases and constraints specifically, which are highly relevant for educational contexts (Chew and Cerbin, 2021). Related to the domain of this work in particular, recent work has demonstrated a broad range of human opinions and levels of trust associated with cybersecurity concepts such as Trusted Execution Environments (Carreira et al., 2024). This highlights the need for individualized metrics that take into account experience in training tasks such as the anti-phishing training dataset used in this work.

In this work, we propose a method for providing personalized metrics of subjective concepts that can determine the similarity between sets of text, with additional applications in selecting educational examples and providing natural language feedback. This is done by leveraging a cognitive model of human learning and decision making that can act as a digital twin to individuals, and predict their behav-

Proceedings of the 28th Conference on Computational Natural Language Learning, pages 517–527
November 15-16, 2024 ©2024 Association for Computational Linguistics

ior and opinions on a wider set of stimuli. We focus specifically on students categorizing emails as being safe (ham) or dangerous (phishing) in a training setting to help users identify and defend against phishing email attacks. Our proposed method for providing personalized similarity metrics of documents is compared to alternative methods using a dataset of a phishing education task experiment that we additionally present in this work.

The dataset of human annotations of emails as being either ham or phishing is described in (Malloy et al., 2024) and was made publicly available on OSF[1]. This dataset consists of human annotations of email documents that are either written by cybersecurity experts or a GPT-4 model, the emails shown to participants, and conversations between human participants and a GPT-4o model providing feedback to students. In total this dataset represents 39230 human judgements from 433 participants making decisions while observing a set from 1440 GPT-4 or human generated emails, as well as 20487 messages between human participants and the GPT-4o teacher model.

This type of learning task represents a serious challenge for traditional methods of adjusting document embedding similarity metrics to conform to human behavior, such as embedding pruning (Manrique et al., 2023) or embedding weighting (Onan, 2021). This is because these approaches typically rely on a large amount of annotations collected from many participants who are expected to have the same knowledge level throughout the annotation process. Instead, we are interested in measuring the subjective similarity of documents as participants learn the document annotation task in a training setting. To do this, we employ a cognitive model that can predict the learning trajectory of each individual participant as they learn to correctly annotate these documents.

2 Background: Cognitive Model

The cognitive model used in this work to predict the subjective similarity of human participants decisions on unseen emails relies on Instance Based Learning Theory (IBLT) (Gonzalez et al., 2003). One of the benefits of employing IBL models over alternatives like Reinforcement Learning is that they base their predictions on the full history of participant experience as well as the impact that limitations like memory size and decay can have on decision making.

IBL models have been applied onto predicting human behavior in dynamic decision making tasks, including binary choice tasks (Gonzalez and Dutt, 2011; Lejarraga et al., 2012), theory of mind applications (Nguyen and Gonzalez, 2022), and practical applications such as identifying phishing emails (Cranford et al., 2019; Malloy and Gonzalez, 2024), cyber defense (Cranford et al., 2020), and cyber attack decision-making (Aggarwal et al., 2022).

2.1 Activation

IBL models work by storing instances i in memory $\mathcal{M}$, composed of utility outcomes u_i and options k composed of features j in the set of features $\mathcal{F}$ of environmental decision alternatives. These options are observed in an order represented by the time step t, and the time step that an instance occurred in is given $\mathcal{T}(i)$. Option values are determined by selecting the action that maximizes the blended value $\mathcal{V}_k(t)$. In calculating this activation, the similarity between instances in memory and the current instance is represented by summing over all attributes the value S_{ij}, which is the similarity of attribute j of instance i to the current state. This gives the activation equation as:

$$A_i(t) = \ln\left(\sum_{t' \in \mathcal{T}_i(t)} (t-t')^{-d}\right) + \mu \sum_{j \in \mathcal{F}} \omega_j (S_{ij} - 1) + \sigma\xi \tag{1}$$

The parameters that are set either by modelers or set to default values are the decay parameter d; the mismatch penalty μ; the attribute weight of each j feature ω_j; and the noise parameter σ. The default values for these parameters are $(d, \mu, \omega_j, \sigma) = (0.5, 1, 1, 0.25)$. The value ξ is drawn from a normal distribution $\mathcal{N}(-1, 1)$ and multiplied by the noise parameter σ to add random noise to the activation.

2.2 Similarity Measure

The definition of the similarity measure S_{ij} is highly influential in the behavior of the IBL model, as it determines which instances from memory are drawn from to predict utility. In simple binary choice tasks without attributes (Gonzalez and Dutt, 2011; Lejarraga et al., 2012), the similarity metric can be defined as the equality function $S_{ij} = 1$ if $i == j$ else 0. In more complex domains such

[1] https://osf.io/wbg3r/

as the phishing email identification task used in this work, one approach is to use the embeddings of emails to compare the similarity of instances, and rely on the cosine similarity metric to compute the similarity of instances in memory (Malloy and Gonzalez, 2024). The model presented in this work relies on an initial baseline similarity metric, the standard cosine similarity, to then build more individual specific metrics of similarity.

2.3 Probability of Retrieval

The probability of retrieval represents the probability that a single instance in memory will be retrieved when estimating the value associated with an option. To calculate this probability of retrieval, IBL models apply a weighted soft-max function onto the memory instance activation values $A_i(t)$ giving the equation:

$$P_i(t) = \frac{\exp A_i(t)/\tau}{\sum_{i' \in \mathcal{M}_k} \exp A_{i'}(t)/\tau} \tag{2}$$

The parameter that is either set by modelers or set to its default value is the temperature parameter τ, which controls the uniformity of the probability distribution defined by this soft-max equation. The default value for this parameter is $\tau = \sigma\sqrt{2}$.

2.4 Blended Value

The blended value determines the ultimate action selected by the model and is calculated of an option k at time step t according to the utility outcomes u_i weighted by the probability of retrieval of that instance P_i and summing over all instances in memory $\mathcal{M}_k$ to give the equation:

$$V_k(t) = \sum_{i \in \mathcal{M}_k} P_i(t) u_i \tag{3}$$

These blended values are used to determine the action a_{t+1} selected by the model at the next time step.

$$a_{t+1} = \max_{k \in K} V_k(t) \tag{4}$$

In standard IBL models, this action can be used in simulations to allow the model to gain experience in a given task. In model tracing, which is used in the method proposed in this work, the memory of instances is made up of the past observations and decisions of the participant, with the action representing a prediction of their future behavior.

3 Phishing Email Categorization Dataset

The first component of this dataset is human behavioral experiment data from a study on human categorization of emails. This experiment compared human document annotation when categorizing emails as phishing (dangerous) or ham (safe). The conditions of this experiment varied depending on the email author (Human or GPT-4) and style (plain-text or GPT-4 stylized). There was also a comparison of the method of selecting emails to show to participants, either randomly selected, or chosen using an IBL model (IBL or Random). Finally, we compared the type of feedback given to participants between positive and negative point feedback and a natural language conversation with an GPT-4o chat-bot (Points or Written).

This experiment included 10 pre-training trials without feedback, 40 training trials with feedback, and 10 post-training trials without feedback. During all trials, participants made judgments of emails as phishing or ham and indicated their confidence in their judgment as well as which action out of 6 possibilities they would select after receiving the email. We recruited 433 participants online through the Amazon Mechanical Turk (AMT) platform. Participants (150 Female, 280 Male, 3 Non-binary) had an average age of 40.3 with a standard deviation of 11.02 years. Participants were compensated with a base payment of \$3-5 with the potential to earn up to a \$12-15 bonus payment depending on performance and the length of the experiment. This experiment was approved by the Carnegie Mellon University Institutional Review Board, and the study was pre-registered on OSF.

The second component of this dataset is the emails shown to participants, which were either written by human cybersecurity experts, a GPT-4 model working alone, or a combination of human and GPT-4 model work. 360 base emails written by human experts were used to form three additional versions of these base emails. These alternative versions included a 'human-written gpt4-styled' version that used the email body written by human experts, the 'gpt4-written and gpt4-styled' version that was fully rewritten by GPT-4, and the 'gpt4-written plaintext-styled' version that stripped the HTML and CSS styling applied by the GPT-4 model. These emails as well as the original prompts to generate them are included in dataset on OSF.

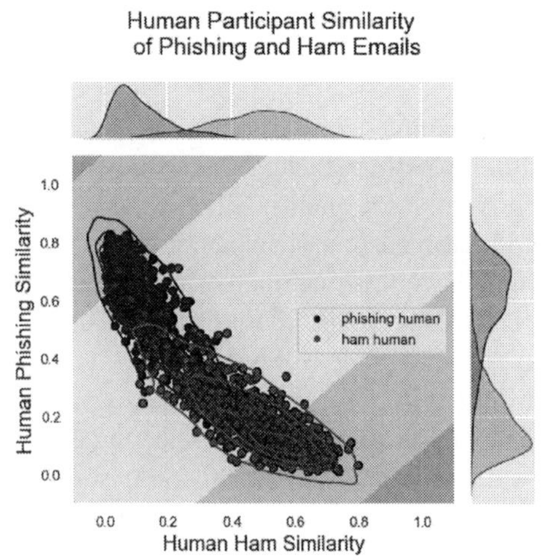

Figure 1: Human participant similarity measure for all 1440 phishing (blue) and ham (orange) emails. Shaded region is a logistic regression.

4 Methods of Measuring Similarity

4.1 Human Subjective Similarity

LLM embeddings have been suggested as a method of measuring human similarity judgements (Bhatia and Aka, 2022), while also capturing the wide range of individuals similarity measures. Additionally, comparisons of LLM behavior have also demonstrated human-like variability (Bhatia, 2024), suggesting these embeddings could be useful for capturing the variety of human similarity judgements. Cognitive models that rely on representations of information from GAI models have been shown to adequately account for the wide range of human behavior (Mitsopoulos et al., 2023).

However, for these methods to function properly there must be a connection between the way that similarity is measured in humans and GAI models. Previous applications in applying visual GAI models onto representing decision-making tasks in humans relied on the close connection to these model representations and human representations (Higgins et al., 2016, 2021). For this reason, we devised a metric of human subjective similarity that takes into account the confidence of document categorization as well as the time it takes participants to categorize documents.

To determine the human subjective similarity measure, we use the category of human participant annotations, their annotation confidence, and the speed of their annotation. For accuracy and confidence, a higher value in our human subjective similarity metric signifies that participants were more likely to categorize an emails as being a member of that group, and more confident in their categorization. For reaction time, a lower value indicates that the document is more immediately obviously a member of a group and thus has a higher similarity to other members of that group. The result is a value that is difficult for a standard similarity metric to account for, as the annotations made in this dataset occurred in a learning setting where earlier trials had less accuracy, which also impacted reaction time and confidence.

The reaction time and confidence weighted subjective similarity of an email x is given by multiplying the probability of a human participant categorizing that email as category c giving $cs(x|c) = p(c|x)r(c|x)c(c|x)$. where $p(c|x)$ is the probability of categorization, $r(c|x)$ is the reaction time normalized to between 0 and 1, and $c(c|x)$ is the confidence additionally normalized to between 0 and 1. The soft-max of this $cs(x|c)$ value is the resulting similarity metric, with the equation shown in the supplementary materials[2].

$$HS(x, x') = \frac{cs(x|c)cs(x'|c)}{\sum_{c' \in C} cs(x|c) \sum_{c' \in C} cs(x'|c')} \tag{5}$$

Figure 1 shows the average human similarity measures for each of the 1440 emails in the dataset. The human ham and human phishing similarities are calculated according to Equation 5 by averaging the accuracy, reaction time, and confidence across all participants in the dataset. It is also possible to calculate this subjective similarity for an individual only using the documents that subject categorized. We next compare similarity measures in their ability to capture individual human subjective similarity.

4.2 Semantic Similarity

One method of measuring the similarity of documents is to employ semantic information contained in documents and compare the similarities and differences between documents in terms of these semantic categories. This has been done in the past in applications such as topic modeling (Řehůřek and Sojka, 2010), document annotation (Pech et al., 2017), and calculating document similarity (Qurashi et al., 2020).

[2]https://osf.io/wbg3r/

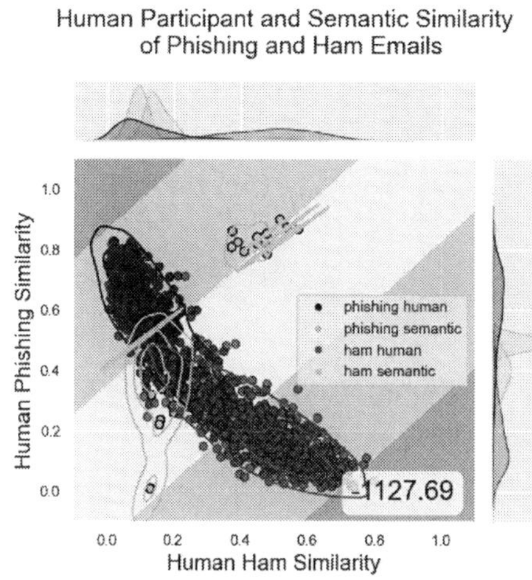

Figure 2: Semantic and human participant similarity for phishing (blue) and ham (orange) emails. Shaded region is a logistic regression. The Kernel Density Estimate log probability score between each distribution is shown on the bottom right, higher is better.

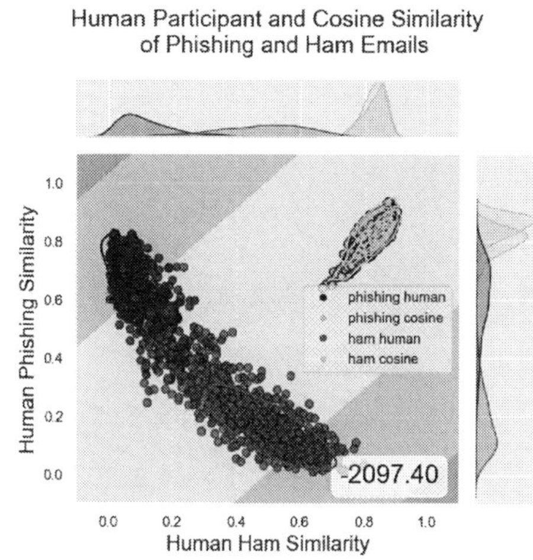

Figure 3: Cosine and human participant similarity for phishing (blue) and ham (orange) emails. Shaded region is a logistic regression. The Kernel Density Estimate log probability score between each distribution is shown on the bottom right, higher is better.

In this dataset, semantic similarity can be calculated using the categorizations of email features that were originally made by the cybersecurity experts who created the base email dataset. These features are Link Mismatch, Offer, Urgent, Subject Suspicious, Request Credentials, and Sender Mismatch. Figure 2 plots these semantic similarity measures for each of the 1440 emails in our dataset, and compares the distribution of these similarities to our human subjective similarity metric.

These semantic similarity metrics are close to human similarity for phishing emails (blue), but highly diverge from the similarity scores of ham emails (orange). This results in a low Kernel Density Estimate log probability score (-1127.69) between the two distributions compared to the semantic similarity metric. This metric compares the likelihood that the data-points in the human similarity metric distribution would have come from the semantic similarity distribution, summing all log probabilities. This low score is due to the fact that the majority of ham emails are very sparse for all of the six semantic categories previously mentioned.

4.3 Cosine Similarity

Cosine similarity is the most commonly used metric of similarity of word and document embeddings, with many applications from classification (Park et al., 2020), recommendation systems (Khatter et al., 2021), educational tutorial systems (Wu et al., 2023), question answering (Aithal et al., 2021), and more (Patil et al., 2023). However, there are limitations to using cosine similarity such as in documents with high-frequency words (Zhou et al., 2022), and the presence of false information (Borges et al., 2019), both of which are concerns for phishing email education.

The cosine similarity metric is calculated using an embedding of size 3072 formed by the 'text-embedding-3-large' model, accessed through the OpenAI API, these document embeddings are additionally included in our presented dataset. The cosine similarity of each email embedding is compared to the mean embedding of that category and shown in Figure 3, and compared to our metric of human subjective similarity. From this, we can see that on average the embeddings are calculated as being significantly more similar to each other compared to the subjective similarities of human participants. This results in a lower Kernel Density Estimate log probability score (-2097.40) between the two distributions compared to the semantic similarity metric.

4.4 Weighted Cosine Similarity

Distance weighted cosine similarity is a common method employed in utilizing embeddings (Li and Han, 2013), which has been applied onto measuring similarity of online instruction in educational settings (Lahitani et al., 2016), as well as several cy-

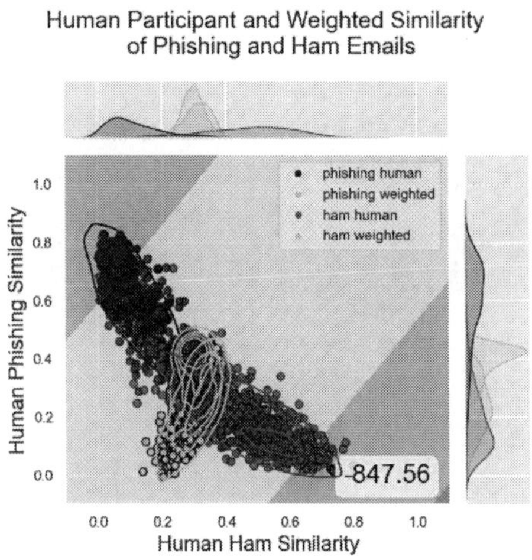

Figure 4: Cosine and human participant similarity for phishing (blue) and ham (orange) emails. Shaded region is a logistic regression. The Kernel Density Estimate log probability score between each distribution is shown on the bottom right, higher is better.

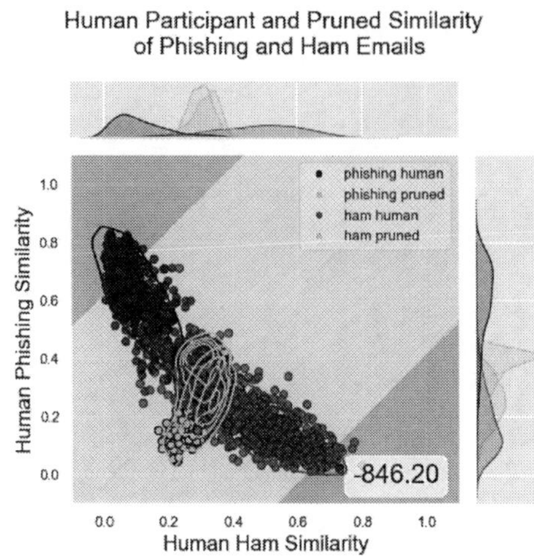

Figure 5: Pruned cosine and human participant similarity for phishing (blue) and ham (orange) emails. Shaded region is a logistic regression. The Kernel Density Estimate log probability score between each distribution is shown on the bottom right, higher is better.

bersecurity specific applications like ransomware detection (Moussaileb et al., 2021), and inside attacker detection (Khan et al., 2019). In this work, we employ weighted cosine similarities of embeddings formed from emails categorized as being either ham or phishing, and compare it to human subjective similarity judgements. This weighting is done by learning a weight transformation of size 3072, the same as the embedding size, which is applied onto the embedding prior to calculating the similarity. The results of this weighting are shown in Figure 4, which compares the average human participant subjective similarity and the weighted cosine similarity of email embeddings.

The KDE log probability score between weighted cosine similarities of phishing and ham emails compared to human subjective similarity has increased to -847.56 from the unweighted KDE score of -2097.40, surpassing the semantic similarity score at -1127.69. These improved similarity metrics indicate that weighting cosine similarity based on data from a large dataset of human participants can result in a metric that more accurately reflects the average of human subjects' subjective similarity metrics.

4.5 Pruning Document Embeddings

Another method of comparison documents is embedding pruning, where embeddings are reduced in size based on feedback from human categorizations to better account for their subjective similarity (Manrique et al., 2023). These approaches function by reducing the number of embedding values that are used in comparison, and are similar to the weighting method except with 0 or 1 values. We structured our embedding pruning method to select only the top 500 embedding values, representing just under 20% of the size of the embedding, as was done in (Manrique et al., 2023). These top predictive embedding values are retained, while all other values are masked to 0. After this, cosine similarity can be calculated with the standard approach, resulting in the similarity shown in Figure 6. Compared to the weighted cosine similarity method, the pruned cosine similarity has roughly the same KDE log probability score.

5 Ensemble Similarity

The final comparison method is based on using an ensemble of each of the previous similarity metrics, weighted to maximize the similarity to the average of the human subjective similarity metrics. This approach has been applied to document matching for patent documents (Yu et al., 2024), which requires the similarity of document embeddings be calculated to determine a match. This ensemble approach has the highest KDE log probability score of any individual method by itself, at a value of -812.23. Looking at the KDE distributions above and to the right of the scatter plot in 6 demonstrates

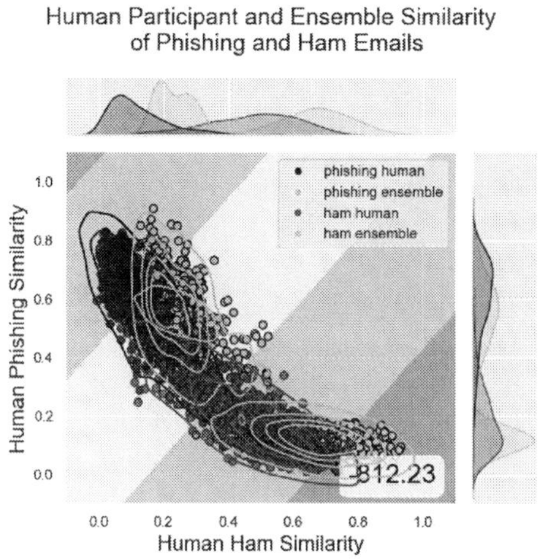

Figure 6: Ensemble and human participant similarity for phishing (blue) and ham (orange) emails. Shaded region is a logistic regression. The Kernel Density Estimate log probability score between each distribution is shown on the bottom right, higher is better.

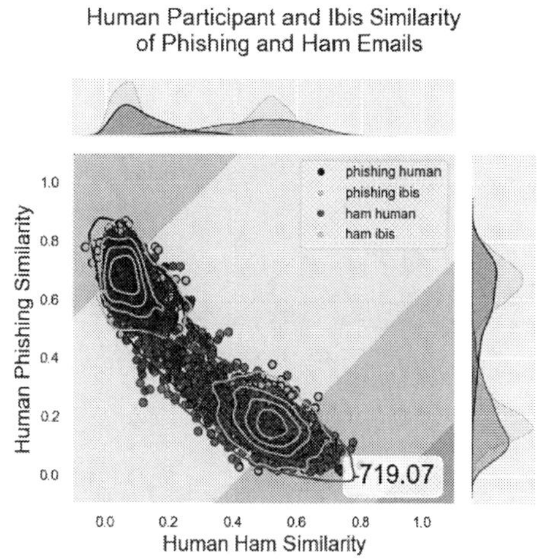

Figure 7: IBIS and human participant similarity for phishing (blue) and ham (orange) emails. Shaded region is a logistic regression. The Kernel Density Estimate log probability score between each distribution is shown on the bottom right, higher is better.

the high similarity of the ensemble similarity metric (light blue and light orange) and the human participant similarity metric (blue and orange). While this method is effective at resulting in a similarity metric that closely matches the average over all participants, it still does not fit as well to individual participants, as will be shown in our proposed model.

6 Instance-Based Individualized Similarity (IBIS)

To determine an individual participant's metric of similarity, we employ an IBL model that is serving as a digital twin of the participant. The result in an Instance-Based Individualized Similarity (IBIS) metric. The benefits of IBIS are in the ability to predict human judgements on unseen documents or feedback from recommendations, and enhance measurements of subjective similarity. Importantly, these predictions of human behavior are not merely relying on a separate machine learning based technique, but rather a cognitive model that is inspired by the human cognitive mechanisms underlying decision making and thus able to account for natural biases and constraints in humans.

Predictions of Instance-Bases Individual Similarity are done using an IBL model that is currently serving as a digital twin with the same experience as an individual participant. Using this we determine the value that the IBL model assigns to predicting a category c as $V_k(c|x)$, or the value the IBL model assigns to choosing option c as the category of document x. Then, we can divide this value by the same categorization value assigned to each alternative categorization of the same document. This results in the IBIS metric which can be calculated after each decision is made by a participant, pseudocode for the IBIS algorithm, The code-base for the IBIS method including all comparison methods, data, and scripts to generate similarity measures and figures is made available[3].

7 Case Study of IBIS: Individuals in Phishing Email Education Dataset

Previous comparisons of similarity metrics and human participant behavior compared the average of human performance. To highlight the benefits of the IBIS method, we replicate these calculations with one individual from the experiment. Here, the individual similarity of phishing and ham emails is based only on a single individuals categorization, confidence, and reaction time in their judgement. These graphs are shown for illustration in Figure 8, with the average accuracy of logistic regression of similarity metrics predicting individual participant similarity metrics reported in table 1.

The KDE score of the similarities for the pruned cosine method is -30.76, and for the ensemble method it is -27.82. Note that these scores are much

[3]github.com/TylerJamesMalloy/cognitive-similarity

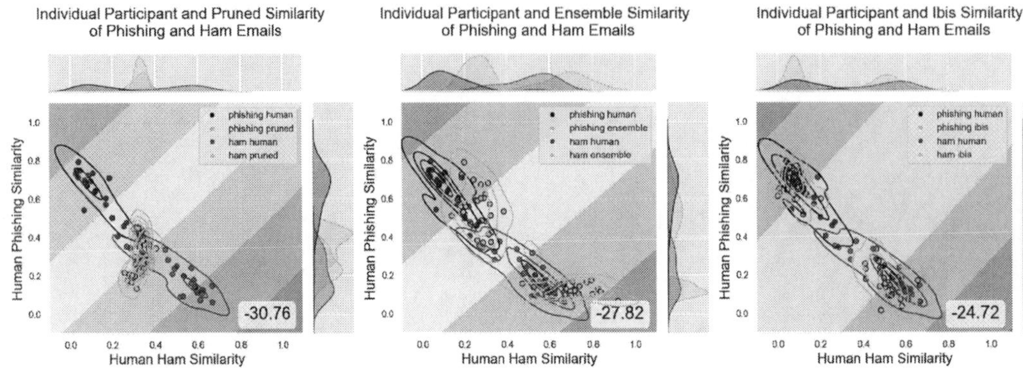

Figure 8: Top performing similarity metrics and individual participant similarity for phishing and ham emails. Shaded region is a logistic regression. The lower value is the individual KDE score

lower than the entire dataset scores since they are calculated using only the emails observed by the participant. Meanwhile, the IBIS metric gives a KDE score of -24.72. From this we can see that the IBIS method effectively learns the similarity measures of individual participants. These results are used for illustrative purposes, and the averages across all participants for regression accuracy, as well as the DKE score for individuals, is presented in Table 1.

An important aspect of individual similarity comparisons of the IBIS method is that it can compare emails that were not originally presented to an individual, meaning there are more embedding similarities used in the logistic regression and KDE score calculation. This comparison demonstrates the benefits of using a cognitively inspired method of modeling human participant decisions making that takes into account biases and cognitive constraints.

The results is a prediction of behavior that can accurately fill in the gaps of unseen elements of the dataset that have not been observed by a participant. This method more accurately predicts the subjective similarity of participants. Importantly, this is done while initially limiting the cognitive model to observing a single decision made by these participants, and increasing this data as the participant makes more decisions. This is important for the functioning of the IBL model as using too many instances in memory can slow compute performance.

The final comparison shown in the right most columns of Table 1 shows the percent accuracy in using the previously described logistic regressions, shown on all figure results, in predicting the categorization of participants based on the similarity metric applied onto the emails they observed. This regression has the potential to predict the annotations of individuals, similarly to the IBL model. Comparing these measures shows that the best performance comes from the IBIS metric when predicting participant annotations.

8 Discussion

Many applications of LLMs are interested in tailoring use cases to individuals, even when little information is known about that individual. While many approaches of individualization exist but have typically relied on advanced machine learning techniques. The method proposed in this work is relatively simple from a mathematical perspective, though there is a strength in its reliance on theories of cognition that underlie human learning and decision making. The result is a simple to understand and easy to implement method of calculating similarities of unseen documents using a cognitive model, which can augment datasets that contain only a small number of decisions.

The general method described here, of augmenting subjective similarity metrics with predicted decisions from a cognitive model, could be applied onto various other scenarios. This includes settings that leverage representations formed of visual information such as β-Variational Autoencoders (Higgins et al., 2016), which have been related to biological representation formation (Higgins et al., 2021). Overall, we believe that this method is useful for any application where the experience of end-users impacts future decisions.

For instance, in visual learning settings VAEs have been integrated with cognitive models to predict human utility learning of abstract visual in-

Similarity Metric	KDE Score Average Participants	KDE Score Individuals	Regression Accuracy
Semantic Similarity (Qurashi et al., 2020)	-1127.69	-37.69±1.19	0.46±0.11
Cosine Similarity (Park et al., 2020)	-2097.40	-47.26±2.27	0.52±0.10
Embedding Weighting (Onan, 2021)	-847.56	-29.28±2.32	0.86±0.14
Embedding Pruning (Manrique et al., 2023)	-846.20	-30.39±2.76	0.86±0.04
Ensemble Similarity (Yu et al., 2024)	-812.23	-28.64±3.28	0.89±0.12
IBIS (proposed)	**-719.07**	**-23.17**±**3.29**	**0.93**±**0.04**

Table 1: Comparison of the six previously described methods in their similarity to human behavior. Similarity to average participants is performed across the entire dataset of human judgements (see Figures 1-6). Similarity to individuals and regression accuracy are both done for each individual participant (see Figure 7). For all values higher is better. Reported values are means of all participants measured individually ± standard deviations.

formation (Malloy and Sims, 2024). Other integrations of Generative AI into cognitive models includes use of LLMs as a knowledge repositories within cognitive models (Kirk et al., 2023). In particular, ConceptNet (Speer et al., 2017) has previously been integrated into a cognitive model for question answering (Huet et al., 2021). Future research should investigate how additional uses of LLMs in integrations of cognitive models can aid in educational settings.

Overall, the results in this work demonstrate the usefulness of cognitive models in serving as digital twins to human participants. Leveraging these models and integrating their results into Large Language Model techniques has the potential to make measurements from these models more cognitively grounded. While there are existing methods of incorporating human behavior through the use of large datasets collected from many participants, these do not necessarily account for biases and constraints. The method proposed in this work takes these features of human learning and decision making into account in developing a similarity metric.

9 Limitations

The semantic similarity metric suffered from the sparsity of semantic categories in ham emails, additional annotations could raise the performance of this metric and can be explored in future work. However, this ensemble method was partially responsible for the high KDE score of the ensemble method, as it allowed for an integration of both semantic information and embedding similarity. Our IBIS method still outperformed the ensemble method suggesting that this ensemble alone does not address the issues of alternative methods.

One limitation inherent in IBL cognitive models is the time requirements to compare the current instance to all instances in memory. This may make the proposed model unsuitable for applications that rely on large datasets of individual behavior. However, methods in instance compression exist for IBL models (Nguyen et al., 2023). In this setting, we were able to predict individual participant's decisions fast enough that this was unnecessary.

The specific application we investigated is somewhat unique in that it is based on training human participants to make categorization judgements of textual information of one of two categories. Additionally, the task of annotating whether an email is phishing or ham relies heavily on a small number of features within the email. Namely, if an email contains a link that redirects to a nefarious website, or requests personal information, then it should be labelled as phishing. While students rely on many queues to make their judgements, the annotation is in reality simple. Future work in the area of learning subjective similarity metrics should expand into more complex domains.

10 Acknowledgement

This research was sponsored by the Army Research Office and accomplished under Australia-US MURI Grant Number W911NF-20-S-000, and the AI Research Institutes Program funded by the National Science Foundation under AI Institute for Societal Decision Making (AI-SDM), Award No. 2229881. Compute resources and GPT model credits were provided by the Microsoft Accelerate Foundation Models Research Program grant "Personalized Education with Foundation Models via Cognitive Modeling".

References

Palvi Aggarwal, Omkar Thakoor, Shahin Jabbari, Edward A Cranford, Christian Lebiere, Milind Tambe, and Cleotilde Gonzalez. 2022. Designing effective masking strategies for cyberdefense through human experimentation and cognitive models. *Computers & Security*, 117:102671.

Shivani G Aithal, Abishek B Rao, and Sanjay Singh. 2021. Automatic question-answer pairs generation and question similarity mechanism in question answering system. *Applied Intelligence*, pages 1–14.

Sudeep Bhatia. 2024. Exploring variability in risk taking with large language models. *Journal of Experimental Psychology: General*.

Sudeep Bhatia and Ada Aka. 2022. Cognitive modeling with representations from large-scale digital data. *Current Directions in Psychological Science*, 31(3):207–214.

Luís Borges, Bruno Martins, and Pável Calado. 2019. Combining similarity features and deep representation learning for stance detection in the context of checking fake news. *Journal of Data and Information Quality (JDIQ)*, 11(3):1–26.

Peter Brown and Yaoqi Zhou. 2019. Large expert-curated database for benchmarking document similarity detection in biomedical literature search. *Database*, 2019:baz085.

Carolina Carreira, McKenna McCall, and Lorrie Faith Cranor. 2024. How to explain trusted execution environments (tees)? In *USENIX Symposium on Usable Privacy and Security (SOUPS)*.

Stephen L Chew and William J Cerbin. 2021. The cognitive challenges of effective teaching. *The Journal of Economic Education*, 52(1):17–40.

Edward A Cranford, Cleotilde Gonzalez, Palvi Aggarwal, Sarah Cooney, Milind Tambe, and Christian Lebiere. 2020. Toward personalized deceptive signaling for cyber defense using cognitive models. *Topics in Cognitive Science*, 12(3):992–1011.

Edward A Cranford, Christian Lebiere, Prashanth Rajivan, Palvi Aggarwal, and Cleotilde Gonzalez. 2019. Modeling cognitive dynamics in end-user response to phishing emails. *Proceedings of the 17th ICCM*.

Achraf Gazdar and Lotfi Hidri. 2020. A new similarity measure for collaborative filtering based recommender systems. *Knowledge-Based Systems*, 188:105058.

Cleotilde Gonzalez and Varun Dutt. 2011. Instance-based learning: integrating sampling and repeated decisions from experience. *Psychological review*, 118(4):523.

Cleotilde Gonzalez, Javier F Lerch, and Christian Lebiere. 2003. Instance-based learning in dynamic decision making. *Cognitive Science*, 27(4):591–635.

Irina Higgins, Le Chang, Victoria Langston, Demis Hassabis, Christopher Summerfield, Doris Tsao, and Matthew Botvinick. 2021. Unsupervised deep learning identifies semantic disentanglement in single inferotemporal face patch neurons. *Nature communications*, 12(1):6456.

Irina Higgins, Loic Matthey, Arka Pal, Christopher Burgess, Xavier Glorot, Matthew Botvinick, Shakir Mohamed, and Alexander Lerchner. 2016. beta-vae: Learning basic visual concepts with a constrained variational framework. In *International conference on learning representations*, pages 1–6.

Armand Huet, Romain Pinquié, Philippe Véron, Antoine Mallet, and Frédéric Segonds. 2021. Cacda: A knowledge graph for a context-aware cognitive design assistant. *Computers in Industry*, 125:103377.

Ahmed Yar Khan, Rabia Latif, Seemab Latif, Shahzaib Tahir, Gohar Batool, and Tanzila Saba. 2019. Malicious insider attack detection in iots using data analytics. *IEEE Access*, 8:11743–11753.

Harsh Khatter, Nishtha Goel, Naina Gupta, and Muskan Gulati. 2021. Movie recommendation system using cosine similarity with sentiment analysis. In *2021 Third International Conference on Inventive Research in Computing Applications (ICIRCA)*, pages 597–603. IEEE.

James R Kirk, Robert E Wray, and John E Laird. 2023. Exploiting language models as a source of knowledge for cognitive agents. *arXiv preprint arXiv:2310.06846*.

Hyeyoung Ko, Suyeon Lee, Yoonseo Park, and Anna Choi. 2022. A survey of recommendation systems: recommendation models, techniques, and application fields. *Electronics*, 11(1):141.

Matt Kusner, Yu Sun, Nicholas Kolkin, and Kilian Weinberger. 2015. From word embeddings to document distances. In *International conference on machine learning*, pages 957–966. PMLR.

Alfirna Rizqi Lahitani, Adhistya Erna Permanasari, and Noor Akhmad Setiawan. 2016. Cosine similarity to determine similarity measure: Study case in online essay assessment. In *2016 4th International conference on cyber and IT service management*, pages 1–6. IEEE.

Tomás Lejarraga, Varun Dutt, and Cleotilde Gonzalez. 2012. Instance-based learning: A general model of repeated binary choice. *Journal of Behavioral Decision Making*, 25(2):143–153.

Baoli Li and Liping Han. 2013. Distance weighted cosine similarity measure for text classification. In *Intelligent Data Engineering and Automated Learning–IDEAL 2013: 14th International Conference, IDEAL 2013, Hefei, China, October 20-23, 2013. Proceedings 14*, pages 611–618. Springer.

Tyler Malloy, Maria Ferriera Jose, Fei Fang, and Cleotilde Gonzalez. 2024. Improving online anti-phishing training using cognitive large language models. *Under Review for Computers in Human Behavior.*

Tyler Malloy and Cleotilde Gonzalez. 2024. Applying generative artificial intelligence to cognitive models of decision making. *Frontiers in Psychology*, 15:1387948.

Tyler Malloy and Chris R Sims. 2024. Efficient visual representations for learning and decision making. *Psychological review.*

Natalia Flechas Manrique, Wanqian Bao, Aurelie Herbelot, and Uri Hasson. 2023. Enhancing interpretability using human similarity judgements to prune word embeddings. *arXiv preprint arXiv:2310.10262.*

Konstantinos Mitsopoulos, Rik Bose, Brodie Mather, Archna Bhatia, Kevin Gluck, Bonnie Dorr, Christian Lebiere, and Peter Pirolli. 2023. Psychologically-valid generative agents: A novel approach to agent-based modeling in social sciences. In *Proceedings of the 2023 AAAI Fall Symposium on Integrating Cognitive Architectures and Generative Models*, pages 1–6. AAAI Press.

Routa Moussaileb, Nora Cuppens, Jean-Louis Lanet, and Hélène Le Bouder. 2021. A survey on windows-based ransomware taxonomy and detection mechanisms. *ACM Computing Surveys (CSUR)*, 54(6):1–36.

Shaimaa M Nafea, François Siewe, and Ying He. 2019. A novel algorithm for course learning object recommendation based on student learning styles. In *2019 International Conference on Innovative Trends in Computer Engineering (ITCE)*, pages 192–201. IEEE.

Thuy Ngoc Nguyen and Cleotilde Gonzalez. 2022. Theory of mind from observation in cognitive models and humans. *Topics in Cognitive Science*, 14(4):665–686.

Thuy Ngoc Nguyen, Duy Nhat Phan, and Cleotilde Gonzalez. 2023. Speedyibl: A comprehensive, precise, and fast implementation of instance-based learning theory. *Behavior Research Methods*, 55(4):1734–1757.

Aytuğ Onan. 2021. Sentiment analysis on product reviews based on weighted word embeddings and deep neural networks. *Concurrency and computation: Practice and experience*, 33(23):e5909.

Saurabh Pal, Pijush Kanti Dutta Pramanik, and Prasenjit Choudhury. 2024. Aggregated relative similarity (ars): a novel similarity measure for improved personalised learning recommendation using hybrid filtering approach. *Multimedia Tools and Applications*, pages 1–48.

Kwangil Park, June Seok Hong, and Wooju Kim. 2020. A methodology combining cosine similarity with classifier for text classification. *Applied Artificial Intelligence*, 34(5):396–411.

Rajvardhan Patil, Sorio Boit, Venkat Gudivada, and Jagadeesh Nandigam. 2023. A survey of text representation and embedding techniques in nlp. *IEEE Access.*

Fernando Pech, Alicia Martinez, Hugo Estrada, and Yasmin Hernandez. 2017. Semantic annotation of unstructured documents using concepts similarity. *Scientific Programming*, 2017(1):7831897.

Abdul Wahab Qurashi, Violeta Holmes, and Anju P Johnson. 2020. Document processing: Methods for semantic text similarity analysis. In *2020 international conference on INnovations in Intelligent SysTems and Applications (INISTA)*, pages 1–6. IEEE.

Radim Řehůřek and Petr Sojka. 2010. Software Framework for Topic Modelling with Large Corpora. In *Proceedings of the LREC 2010 Workshop on New Challenges for NLP Frameworks*, pages 45–50, Valletta, Malta. ELRA.

Mansoore Shojaei and Hassan Saneifar. 2021. Mfsr: A novel multi-level fuzzy similarity measure for recommender systems. *Expert Systems with Applications*, 177:114969.

Robyn Speer, Joshua Chin, and Catherine Havasi. 2017. Conceptnet 5.5: An open multilingual graph of general knowledge. In *Proceedings of the AAAI conference on artificial intelligence*, volume 31, pages 1–6.

Xuansheng Wu, Xinyu He, Tianming Liu, Ninghao Liu, and Xiaoming Zhai. 2023. Matching exemplar as next sentence prediction (mensp): Zero-shot prompt learning for automatic scoring in science education. In *International conference on artificial intelligence in education*, pages 401–413. Springer.

Peipei Xia, Li Zhang, and Fanzhang Li. 2015. Learning similarity with cosine similarity ensemble. *Information sciences*, 307:39–52.

Liqiang Yu, Bo Liu, Qunwei Lin, Xinyu Zhao, and Chang Che. 2024. Semantic similarity matching for patent documents using ensemble bert-related model and novel text processing method. *arXiv preprint arXiv:2401.06782.*

Haiqin Zhang, Zheng Chen, Wei-ying Ma, and Qingsheng Cai. 2003. A study for document summarization based on personal annotation. In *Proceedings of the HLT-NAACL 03 Text Summarization Workshop*, pages 41–48.

Kaitlyn Zhou, Kawin Ethayarajh, Dallas Card, and Dan Jurafsky. 2022. Problems with cosine as a measure of embedding similarity for high frequency words. *arXiv preprint arXiv:2205.05092.*

Author Index